2007

Allan S. Wright & Dave Peel

MIDLAND
An imprint of
Ian Allan Publishing

Contents

Introduction and Acknowledgements	4
International Civil Aircraft Markings	6
Aircraft Type Designations & Abbreviations	10
British Civil Aircraft Registrations	13
Military to Civil Cross-Reference	293
Republic of Ireland Civil Registrations	299
Overseas Airliner Registrations	313
Radio Frequencies	402
Airline Flight Codes	403
BAPC Register	405
Future Allocations Logs	410
Future Allocation Groups	411
Overseas Airliners Registration Log	412
Addenda	414

This fifty-eighth edition published 2007

ISBN (10) 1 85780 250 0
ISBN (13) 978 1 85780 250 4

All rights reserved. No part of this book may be
reproduced or transmitted in any form or by any
means, electronic or mechanical, including photo-copying,
recording, or by any information storage and
retrieval system, without permission from
the Publisher in writing.

© Ian Allan Publishing Ltd 2007

Published by Midland Publishing

an imprint of Ian Allan Publishing Ltd,
Hersham, Surrey KT12 4RG.

Advertising: Dave Smith, Tel/Fax 01775 767184
6 Sunningdale Avenue, Spalding, Lincs, PE9 2PP, UK.

Printed in England by Ian Allan Printing Ltd,
Hersham, Surrey KT12 4RG

Visit the Ian Allan Publishing website at:
www.ianallanpublishing.com

Code: 0703/F

Front cover: Airbus A.380 prototype F-WWDD during its May 2006 visit
to London-Heathrow. *Richard Cooper*

*All photographs by Gerry Manning (GM) or Dave Peel (DP)
unless otherwise indicated.*

NOW YOU HAVE PURCHASED CIVIL AIRCRAFT MARKINGS WHY NOT EXPAND YOUR KNOWLEDGE WITH THE 'TAHS' RANGE OF SPECIALIST BOOKS FOR THE ENTHUSIAST, HISTORIAN OR SPOTTER?

If you plan to visit the shop and you belong to either LAAS International or Air Britain, bring your current LAAS International or Air Britain membership card with you, we offer a discount to LAAS International and Air Britain members of 10% on certain ranges of books and plastic model kits as well as membership prices on LAAS International and Air Britains range of publications. **NO CARD, NO DISCOUNT, PERSONAL SHOPPERS ONLY.**

EURO REG
A compendium of 43 different European Countries Current Aircraft Registers

This new addition to the range of publications produced by The Aviation Hobby Shop, contains 432 pages containing current civil aircraft registers from 43 different European countries. Euro Reg lists aircraft registration, type, constructors number, and last known previous identity, the information is current to early August 2006. Countries covered include:- **CS-** Portugal; **D-** Germany; **EC-** Spain; **EI-** Ireland; **EK-** Armenia; **ER-** Moldova; **ES-** Estonia; **EW-** Belarus; **F-** France; **HA-** Hungary; **HB-** Switzerland; **I-** Italy; **LN-** Norway; **LX-** Luxembourg; **LY-** Lithuania; **LZ-** Bulgaria; **OE-** Austria; **OH-** Finland; **OK-** Czech Republic; **OM-** Slovakia; **OO-** Belgium; **OY-** Denmark; **PH-** The Netherlands; **SE-** Sweden; **SP-** Poland; **SX-** Greece; **S5-** Slovenia; **TC-** Turkey; **TF-** Iceland; **T7-** San Marino; **T9-** Bosnia; **UR-** Ukraine; **YL-** Latvia; **YR-** Romania; **YU-** Serbia/Montenego; **ZA-** Albania; **Z3-** Macedonia; **3A-** Monaco; **4K-** Azerbaijan; **4L-** Georgia; **5B-** Cyprus; **9A-** Croatia; **9H-** Malta.

Contains 432 pages and is available in a handy A5 size and Square bound at price **£14.95**

JET AIRLINER PRODUCTION LIST - Volume 2

Published in July 2006 - Jet Airliner Production List - Volume 2 – has been completely revised and updated. Jet Airliner Production List Volume 2 gives full production and service histories of virtually every **JET AIRLINER** (not covered in Volume one) that has entered service since the start of the Jet age. Each aircraft is listed by manufacturer and type in construction number sequence. Each individual entry then lists line number (where applicable), sub-type, and first flight date where known. The entry then goes on to list every registration carried by the airframe, owners and delivery dates, leases, crash or withdrawal from service dates and any other relevant information. There is a complete cross reference of registration to c/n for every type covered. **Types covered in Volume 2 include:-** Airbus A.300, Airbus A.310, Airbus A.319/320/321, Airbus A.330/340, BAe 146, Canadair Regional Jet, Dornier 328 Jet, Douglas DC-8, Douglas DC-9, Douglas DC-10, Fokker F.28, Embraer Emb.135/145, Fokker 100, Lockheed 1011 Tri-Star, McDonnell-Douglas MD-11. **Jet Airliner Production List - Volume 2** - is available in a handy A5 size and is available in a choice of finish **[1]** comb bound lay-flat price **£18.95**; **[2]** Square bound with metal stitching and wrap around cover price **£18.95**; **[3]** Refill pages for those already have a loose-leaf binder price **£18.95**; **[4]** Loose-leaf Binder edition price **£22.95**.

AIRLINES 2007

Now in its 25th edition **AIRLINES** is now the established book for airline fleet listings in an easy to carry format. This publication lists airline fleets where aircraft from light twins to wide-bodies are operated. Each aircraft is listed with registration, type, constructors number, previous identity and line number (if applicable), fleet number and or name when applicable. **NEARLY 200 COUNTRIES; OVER 3,000 AIRLINES, OPERATORS & WATER TANKER FLEETS; OVER 33,000 REGISTRATIONS; NEARLY 6,000 ADDITIONS, CHANGES & AMENDMENTS SINCE LAST EDITION; CURRENT TO EARLY MARCH 2007; COLOUR COVER;** Available in a choice of finish:- **[1]** Comb bound lay-flat price **£11.95**; **[2]** Square bound with wrap around cover & metal stitching price **£11.95**; **[3]** Refill pages for those who already have a loose-leaf binder price **£11.95**; **[4]** Loose-leaf Binder edition price **£15.95**.

JET & PROPJET 2007
CORPORATE DIRECTORY

The 2007 edition of Jet & Propjet Corporate Directory is again the most comprehensive compilation of facts and information pertaining to business aircraft ever printed. More than 27,000 aircraft, now operating in the United States and 146 other nations, are now listed on the pages of this easy-to-follow guide. Represented in this new 530-plus page edition are over 300 different models and model derivatives built by more than 46 manufacturers. For easy access to information, a cross-reference index - by make, model, serial number and registration mark- is provided in the back of the book. Included again this year are aircraft which have been written off or otherwise withdrawn from service, piston-engine aircraft converted to turboprops, straight jets retrofitted to fanjets and military-operated business-type aircraft. Included are: Aircraft Registration marks; Models and variants; Owner identification; Aircraft manufacturers & Previous registration. **PRICE £11.95**

AIRLINES TO EUROPE 2007

Published in November 2006, Airlines to Europe 2007 has followed the format of previous editions. We have taken the main Airlines data base and stripped out any airlines or aircraft not likely to be seen in Europe. Airlines to Europe lists:- **1]** aircraft registration, **2]** Aircraft type, **3]** constructors number and line number if applicable, **4]** immediate previous identity, Colour cover. **PRICE £4.95**

TURBO PROP AIRLINER
PRODUCTION LIST

To be published in Spring 2007 this sixth edition of Turbo Prop Airliner Production List gives full production and service histories of **SELECTED WESTERN - BUILT TURBOPROP AIRLINER** to enter service since 1948. Each aircraft is listed by manufacturer and type in construction number sequence. Each individual entry then lists line number (where applicable), sub-type, and first flight date where known. The entry then goes on to list every registration carried by the airframe, owners and delivery dates, leases, crash or withdrawal from service dates and any other relevant information. There is a complete cross reference of registration to c/n for every type covered. Over 500 pages. **TYPES COVERED INCLUDE** – Aerospatiale/Aeritalia ATR.42/72; Avro (BAe) 748; Beech 99; Beech 1900; British Aerospace ATP; British Aerospace Jetstream 31; British Aerospace Jetstream 41; CASA/Nurtanio 212; CASA/ Nurtanio 235; Convair 580; deHavilland DHC-6 Twin Otter; deHavilland DHC-7; deHavilland DHC-8; Dornier/HAL 228; Dornier 328; Embraer Emb.110 Bandeirante; Embraer Emb.120 Brasilia; Fairchild/Swearingen Merlin/Metro; Fokker F.27; Fokker 50; Grumman G.159 Gulfstream; HAL 748; Lockheed 100 Hercules; Lockheed 188 Electra; NAMC YS-11; SAAB 340; SAAB 2000; Saunders ST-27; Shorts SC-7 Skyvan; Shorts 330; Shorts 360. **Turbo Prop Airliner Production List** – will be available in a handy A5 size and is available in a choice of finish **[1]** Comb bound lay-flat price **£18.95**; **[2]** Square bound - with heavy duty metal stitching at price **£18.95**; **[3]** Refill pages for those already have a loose-leaf binder price **£18.95**; **[4]** Loose-leaf Binder edition price **£22.95**.

JET AIRLINER PRODUCTION LIST - Volume 1 - BOEING

Published in mid February 2005 - **Jet Airliner Production List - Volume 1 - BOEING** has been completely revised and updated. Jet Airliner Production List gives full production and service histories of **EVERY BOEING - BUILT JET AIRLINER** that has entered service since the start of the Jet age. Each aircraft is listed by manufacturer and type in construction number sequence. Each individual entry then lists line number (where applicable), sub-type, and first flight date where known. The entry then goes on to list every registration carried by the airframe, owners and delivery dates, leases, crash or withdrawal from service dates and any other relevant information. There is a complete cross reference of registration to c/n for every type covered. **TYPES COVERED INCLUDE:- BOEING 707/720, BOEING 717, BOEING 727, BOEING 737, BOEING 737NG, BOEING 747, BOEING 757, BOEING 767, BOEING 777. Jet Airliner Production List - Volume 1 - BOEING** is available in a handy A5 size and is available in a choice of finish **[1]** comb bound lay-flat price **£14.95**; **2]** Square bound with metal stitching and wrap around cover price **£14.95**; **[3]** Refill pages for those already have a loose-leaf binder price **£14.95**; **[4]** Loose-leaf Binder edition price **£18.95**.

MILITARY TRANSPORT AIRCRAFT OF THE WORLD

Lists all known military transport aircraft serials, type, constructors numbers and previous ident. Also includes patrol aircraft derived from transport aircraft. Approx 100 pages, colour cover.**£5.95**

BAC ONE-ELEVEN

The eighth edition in the popular **Airlines & Airliners** series details the development and operational life of Britain's most successful commercial jet airliner, the BAC One-Eleven. Many fabulous colour schemes, ranging from all-time classics to brightly coloured and short-lived hybrid liveries, appear between the covers of this generously illustrated all-colour title. Featured operators include: Courtline Aviation, British United, British Caledonian, Germanair, Panair, Bavaria, Gulf Air, Merpati Nusantara, Air Siam, Aer Lingus, American Airlines, Braniff International, Mohawk, US Airways, Aloha Airlines, Lanica, Trans Brasil, Lacsa and Bahamas-air, not to mention a vast assortment of British Independent carriers and airline operators from Africa, Asia, Europe, Latin America, the Caribbean and Canada and the United States. Military and Executive operators are also taken into account. Also includes a production list detailing the service history and fate of every BAC One-Eleven produced. **PRICE £9.95**

VICKERS VISCOUNT 700 SERIES

Published in October 2002, the seventh edition in the popular Airlines & Airliners series details the development and operational life of the Vickers Viscount 700 Series. A comprehensive photographic record of the original Series 700 aircraft featuring approximately 100 all-colour Illustrations, including many rare and exclusive images from all corners of the globe. Operators of the Viscount 700 Series included: Air France, Air Inter, LAI/Alitalia, Aloha, United Airlines, Capital Airlines, Aer Lingus, Iranian Airlines, Trans Australia, Ansett-ANA, Indian Airlines, Iraqi Airways, Central African Airways, Icelandair, Turkish Airlines, BWIA, VASP, Trans Canada/Air Canada and BEA, not to mention a vast assortment of British Independent carriers and smaller airlines or private/military operators from Africa, Asia, Europe, Latin America, the Caribbean and Canada and the United States. Includes a production list detailing the service history and fate of every Viscount 700 produced. **Price £9.95**

VICKERS VIKING

The ninth edition in the popular **Airlines & Airliners** series details the development and operational life of a classic British built airliner – The Vickers Viking. Many fabulous colour schemes, ranging from all-time classics to brightly coloured and short-lived hybrid liveries, appear between the covers of this title. Many airline names from the past grace the photo pages of this title including BEA, Eagle, Cunard Eagle, Air Ferry, Invicta, Europe Aero Service, Airnautic, Lufthansa, Falcon Airways, Tradair, Channel Airways, Independent Air Transport, Blue Air, Balair, Misrair to name but a few, some in colour and some in black & white. Also includes a production list detailing the service history and fate of every Vickers Viking produced. The print run of this latest Airlines & Airlines has been limited to 1,500 copies. **Price £9.95**

We are just 10 minutes drive from Heathrow Airport, just off the M4/M25 motorways. Bus U3 operates between Heathrow Central and West Drayton BR station, two minutes walk from the shop. All major credit cards accepted. 24hr 'Ansaphone' service. Visit our website at www.tahs.com for the latest new book news.

The Aviation Hobby Shop

(Dept CAM07), 4 HORTON PARADE, HORTON ROAD, WEST DRAYTON, MIDDLESEX UB7 8EA
Tel: 01895 442123 Fax: 01895 421412

Introduction

The familiar 'G' prefixed four letter registration system was adopted in 1919 after a short-lived spell with serial numbers commencing at K-100. Until July 1928 the UK allocations were issued in the G-Exxx range but, as a result of further international agreements, this series ended at G-EBZZ, the replacement being G-Axxx. From this point registrations were issued in a reasonably orderly manner through to G-AZZZ, the position reached in July 1972. There were, however, two exceptions. In order to prevent possible confusion with signal codes, the G-AQxx sequence was omitted, while G-AUxx was reserved for Australian use originally. In recent years however, individual requests for a mark in the latter range have been granted by the Authorities.

Although the next logical sequence was started at G-Bxxx, it was not long before the strictly applied rules relating to aircraft registration began to be relaxed. Permission was readily given for personalised marks to be issued, incorporating virtually any four-letter combination, while re-registration also became a common feature – a practice almost unheard of in the past. In this book, where this has taken place at some time, all previous UK identities carried appear in parenthesis after the operator's/owner's name. For example, during its career Jetstream 31 G-PLAH has also carried the identities G-LOVA, G-OAKA, G-BUFM and G-LAKH.

Some aircraft have also been allowed to wear military markings without displaying their civil identity. In this case the serial number actually carried is shown in parenthesis after the type's name. For example Auster 6A G-ARRX flies in military colours as VF512, its genuine previous identity. As an aid to the identification of such machines, a conversion list is provided.

Other factors caused a sudden acceleration in the number of registrations allocated by the Civil Aviation Authority in the early 1980s. The first surge followed the discovery that it was possible to register plastic bags, and other items even less likely to fly, on payment of the standard fee. This erosion of the main register was checked in early 1982 by the issue of a special sequence for such devices commencing with G-FYAA. Powered hang-gliders provided the second glut of allocations as a result of the decision that these types should be officially registered. Although a few of the early examples penetrated the current in-sequence register, in due course all new applicants were given marks in special ranges, this time G-MBxx, G-MGxx, G-MJxx, G-MMxx, G-MNxx, G-MTxx, G-MVxx, G-MWxx, G-MYxx and G-MZxx. It took some time before all microlights displayed an official mark but gradually the registration was carried, the size and position depending on the dimensions of the component to which it was applied.

There was news of a further change in mid-1998 when the CAA announced that with immediate effect microlights would be issued with registrations in the normal sequence alongside aircraft in other classes. In addition, it meant that owners could also apply for a personalised identity upon payment of the then current fee of £170 from April 1999, a low price for those wishing to display their status symbol. These various changes played their part in exhausting the current G-Bxxx range after some 26 years, with G-BZxx coming into use before the end of 1999. As this batch approached completion the next series to be used began at G-CBxx instead of the anticipated G-CAxx. The reason for this step was to avoid the re-use of marks issued in Canada during the 1920s, although a few have appeared more recently as personalised UK registrations.

Another large increase in the number of aircraft registered will result from the EU-inspired changes in glider registration. After many years of self-regulation by the British Gliding Association, new gliders must now comply with EASA regulations and hence receive registrations in the main G-Cxxx sequence. The phasing-in of EASA registration for the existing glider fleet is likely to be a long and problematic process.

Throughout the UK section of the book, there are instances when the probable base of the aircraft has been included. This is positioned at the end of the owner/operator details preceded by an oblique stroke. It must of course be borne in mind that changes do take place and that no attempt has been made to record the residents at the many private strips. The base of airline equipment has been given as the company's headquarters airport, although frequently aircraft are outstationed for long periods.

Non-airworthy and preserved aircraft are shown with a star ★ after the type.

The three-letter codes used by airlines to prefix flight numbers are included for those carriers most likely to appear in or over the UK. Radio frequencies for the larger airfields/airports are also listed.

Acknowledgements

Once again thanks are extended to the Registration Department of the Civil Aviation Authority for its assistance and allowing access to its files. As always the comments and amendments flowing from Wal Gandy have proved of considerable value and thanks are also extended to all those who have contributed items for possible use and to Alan J. Wright and Nick Wright for their help and encouragement.

ASW & DP　　February 2007

AVIATIONRETAILDIRECT.COM
HEATHROW'S ONLY
100% AVIATION STORE
ORDER HOTLINE: 01895 231707

Aviation Retail Direct
10 Sutton Court Road
Hillingdon
Middlesex UB10 9HP

Opening times:
9am - 6pm Mon - Sat
Closed Sunday

Aviation Retail Direct
BAA Visitor Centre
Newall Road
Heathrow Airport

Opening times:
10am - 5pm
7 days a week

Aviation Retail Direct is Heathrow Airport's only professional aviation retail outlet specialising only in aircraft. We are proud not to have to diversify our attention to non-aviation related items, and have the best name in the business for customer care, attention to detail and personal service. We frequently have limited and rare model releases in our two retail branches, at the Heathrow Visitor Centre and in Hillingdon on the approaches to RAF Northolt in Middlesex.

Our website *www.aviationretaildirect.com* is updated daily with new products and releases, offering fair prices and an unrivalled selection of merchandise, and a fully secure ordering process. We offer a world-wide mail order service, and a wide range of products in-store.

We specialise in both Civil and Military aviation books, DVDs, models, souvenirs, and gift ideas, including ranges such as InFlight, Avion, Just Planes, World Air Routes, GeminiJets, Dragon Wings, Herpa, Sky Guardians, Corgi, Aeroclassics, Phoenix, Small World, Mach III Publishing, Ian Allan and many, many more!

Join the ARD Club for just £10 for a full year, and receive a mininum 10% discount on all products, and 25% on all Corgi 2007 releases! Contact us for more information and details on how to join.

Aviation Retail Direct, 10 Sutton Court Rd., Hillingdon, Middx. UB10 9HP Tel: 01895 231707 Fax: 01895 236707
Aviation Retail Direct, Heathrow Visitor Centre, Newall Rd., Heathrow Airport, 'Northside', Middx. UB3 5AP

International Civil Aircraft Markings

A2-	Botswana	LZ-	Bulgaria
A3-	Tonga	N-	United States of America
A4O-	Oman	OB-	Peru
A5-	Bhutan	OD-	Lebanon
A6-	United Arab Emirates	OE-	Austria
A7-	Qatar	OH-	Finland
A8-	Liberia	OK-	Czech Republic
A9C-	Bahrain	OM-	Slovakia
AP-	Pakistan	OO-	Belgium
B-	China/Taiwan/Hong Kong/Macao	OY-	Denmark
C-F/C-G	Canada	P-	Korea (North)
C2-	Nauru	P2-	Papua New Guinea
C3-	Andorra	P4-	Aruba
C5-	Gambia	PH-	Netherlands
C6-	Bahamas	PJ-	Netherlands Antilles
C9-	Mozambique	PK-	Indonesia and West Irian
CC-	Chile	PP-, PR-, PT-	Brazil
CN-	Morocco	PZ-	Surinam
CP-	Bolivia	RA-	Russia
CS-	Portugal	RDPL-	Laos
CU-	Cuba	RP-	Philippines
CX-	Uruguay	S2-	Bangladesh
D-	Germany	S5-	Slovenia
D2-	Angola	S7-	Seychelles
D4-	Cape Verde Islands	S9-	São Tomé
D6-	Comores Islands	SE-	Sweden
DQ-	Fiji	SP-	Poland
E3-	Eritrea	ST-	Sudan
EC-	Spain	SU-	Egypt
EI-	Republic of Ireland	SX-	Greece
EK-	Armenia	T2-	Tuvalu
EP-	Iran	T3-	Kiribati
ER-	Moldova	T7-	San Marino
ES-	Estonia	T8-	Palau
ET-	Ethiopia	T9-	Bosnia-Herzegovina
EW-	Belarus	TC-	Turkey
EX-	Kyrgyzstan	TF-	Iceland
EY-	Tajikistan	TG-	Guatemala
EZ-	Turkmenistan	TI-	Costa Rica
F-	France, inc Colonies and Protectorates	TJ-	Cameroon
G-	United Kingdom	TL-	Central African Republic
H4-	Solomon Islands	TN-	Republic of Congo (Brazzaville)
HA-	Hungary	TR-	Gabon
HB-	Switzerland and Liechtenstein	TS-	Tunisia
HC-	Ecuador	TT-	Tchad
HH-	Haiti	TU-	Ivory Coast
HI-	Dominican Republic	TY-	Benin
HK-	Colombia	TZ-	Mali
HL-	Korea (South)	UK-	Uzbekistan
HP-	Panama	UN-	Kazakhstan
HR-	Honduras	UR-	Ukraine
HS-	Thailand	V2-	Antigua
HV-	The Vatican	V3-	Belize
HZ-	Saudi Arabia	V4	St. Kitts & Nevis
I-	Italy	V5-	Namibia
J2-	Djibouti	V6	Micronesia
J3-	Grenada	V7-	Marshall Islands
J5-	Guinea Bissau	V8-	Brunei
J6-	St. Lucia	VH-	Australia
J7-	Dominica	VN-	Vietnam
J8-	St. Vincent	VP-B	Bermuda
JA-	Japan	VP-C	Cayman Islands
JU-	Mongolia	VP-F	Falkland Islands
JY-	Jordan	VP-G	Gibraltar
LN-	Norway	VP-L	British Virgin Islands
LV-	Argentina	VP-M	Montserrat
LX-	Luxembourg	VQ-T	Turks & Caicos Islands
LY-	Lithuania	VT-	India

COLLECTORS AIRCRAFT MODELS

"The World's No.1 supplier of aircraft models"
www.collectorsaircraft.com
Telephone: 0208 754 7281

Visit our world famous aircraft model showroom, located inside the Sheraton Skyline Hotel on the main A4 Bath Road, opposite Heathrow Airport.

An "Alladin's Cave", full of thousands of aircraft models for the collector, from all the leading manufacturers including Corgi Classics, Gemini Jets, Herpa Wings, Dragon Wings, Skyline Models, CDC Armour, Inflight Models, Witty Wings/Sky Guardians and many, many more.

Free parking for 1 hour - Regular BAA bus service to/from all Heathrow Terminals. Buses 111, 222, 81, 285, 105, H98, 90 and 140 all stop nearby - Ask for Harlington Corner

Open Monday - Saturday 9.00am to 6.00pm

Visit now and bring along the voucher below for a generous £10.00 discount when you spend £50.00 or more in the showroom.

---✂---

THIS VOUCHER WORTH
£10.00 OFF

(When you spend £50.00 or more at the Collectors Aircraft Models Showroom)

Original voucher must be presented - Photo copies not accepted.
Civil Aircraft Markings & Military Aircraft Markings offer
Expires December 31st 2007

Aviation Magazines from

AIRCRAFT ILLUSTRATED

A unique magazine for the modern aviation enthusiast, *Aircraft Illustrated* is unbeatable in its coverage of the complete aviation scene – civil, military, and historical.

Produced to the highest standards, each issue offers a heady mix of the finest action photographers and leading aviation authors in the business that puts readers literally 'in the cockpit' of the most exciting fast jets, airliners and warbirds.

Exclusives, full-length features, an extensive news section with aviation stories from around the world, the best airshow reports, interviews, comprehensive product reviews, competitions, plus special supplements and posters throughout the year – *Aircraft Illustrated* delivers it all in just one magazine.

COMBAT AIRCRAFT

Unrivalled in its coverage of the world of military aviation with a blend of modern and historic aircraft, *Combat Aircraft* delivers reports, briefings and special features on current military aircraft as well as warbirds from World War II and the Cold War years.

With strong emphasis on US subjects, *Combat Aircraft* is the only magazine to provide in-depth analysis of the US Air Force, US Navy, US Marine Corps and the US Army, plus cover all periods of military aviation in detail.

Packed with amazing action photographs, detailed artworks and a wealth of information, *Combat Aircraft* really is the world's best military aviation magazine.

For more information contact;

**Subscriptions Dept, Ian Allan Publishing Ltd,
Riverdene Business Park, Molesey Road
Hersham, Surrey, KT12 4RG**

Tel: 01932 266622 | Email: subs@ianallanpublishing.co.uk

Code	Country
XA-, XB-, XC-	Mexico
XT-	Burkina Faso
XU-	Cambodia
XY-	Myanmar
YA-	Afghanistan
YI-	Iraq
YJ-	Vanuatu
YK-	Syria
YL-	Latvia
YN-	Nicaragua
YR-	Romania
YS-	El Salvador
YU-	Serbia and Montenegro
YV-	Venezuela
Z-	Zimbabwe
Z3-	Macedonia
ZA-	Albania
ZK-	New Zealand
ZP-	Paraguay
ZS-	South Africa
3A-	Monaco
3B-	Mauritius
3C-	Equatorial Guinea
3D-	Swaziland
3X-	Guinea
4K-	Azerbaijan
4L-	Georgia
4R-	Sri Lanka
4X-	Israel
5A-	Libya
5B-	Cyprus
5H-	Tanzania
5N-	Nigeria
5R-	Malagasy Republic (Madagascar)
5T-	Mauritania
5U-	Niger
5V-	Togo
5W-	Western Samoa (Polynesia)
5X-	Uganda
5Y-	Kenya
6O-	Somalia
6V-	Senegal
6Y-	Jamaica
7O-	Yemen
7P-	Lesotho
7Q-	Malawi
7T-	Algeria
8P-	Barbados
8Q-	Maldives
8R-	Guyana
9A-	Croatia
9G-	Ghana
9H-	Malta
9J-	Zambia
9K-	Kuwait
9L-	Sierra Leone
9M-	Malaysia
9N-	Nepal
9Q-	Congo Kinshasa
9U-	Burundi
9V-	Singapore
9XR-	Rwanda
9Y-	Trinidad and Tobago

AVIATION BOOKS
NEW AND SECONDHAND
BOUGHT AND SOLD

THE AVIATION BOOKSHOP

**31/33 VALE ROAD
ROYAL TUNBRIDGE WELLS
KENT TN1 1BS**

Phone: 01892 539284

Email: *info@aviation-bookshop.com*
Website: *www.aviation-bookshop.com*

Shop opening hours Monday-Saturday 9.30-5.30

Aircraft Type Designations & Abbreviations

(for example PA-28 Piper Type 28)

A.	Beagle, Auster, Airbus
AAC	Army Air Corps
AA-	American Aviation, Grumman American
AB	Agusta-Bell
AESL	Aero Engine Services Ltd
AG	American General
An	Antonov
ANEC	Air Navigation & Engineering Co
ANG	Air National Guard
AS	Aérospatiale
A.S.	Airspeed
A.W.	Armstrong Whitworth
B.	Blackburn, Bristol, Boeing, Beagle
BA	British Airways
BAC	British Aircraft Company
BAC	British Aircraft Corporation
BAe	British Aerospace
BAPC	British Aviation Preservation Council
BAT	British Aerial Transport
B.K.	British Klemm
BN	Britten-Norman
Bo	Bolkow
Bü	Bücker
CAARP	Co-operatives des Ateliers Aéronautiques de la Région Parisienne
CAC	Commonwealth Aircraft Corporation
CAF	Canadian Air Force
CASA	Construcciones Aeronautics SA
CCF	Canadian Car & Foundry Co
CEA	Centre-Est Aviation
CH.	Chrislea
CHABA	Cambridge Hot-Air Ballooning Association
CLA.	Comper
CP.	Piel
CUAS	Cambridge University Air Squadron
Cycl	Cyclone
D.	Druine
DC-	Douglas Commercial
DH.	de Havilland
DHA.	de Havilland Australia
DHC.	de Havilland Canada
DR.	Jodel (Robin-built)
EE	English Electric
EAA	Experimental Aircraft Association
EMB	Embraer Empresa Brasileira de Aeronautica SA
EoN	Elliotts of Newbury
EP	Edgar Percival
ETPS	Empire Test Pilots School
F.	Fairchild, Fokker
F.A.A.	Fleet Air Arm
FFA	Flug und Fahrzeugwerke AG
FH	Fairchild-Hiller
FrAF	French Air Force
FRED	Flying Runabout Experimental Design
Fw	Focke-Wulf
G.	Grumman
GA	Gulfstream American
GAL.	General Aircraft
GC	Globe Aircraft
GECAS	General Electric Capital Aviation Services
GY	Gardan
H	Helio
HM.	Henri Mignet
HP.	Handley Page

No More Underlining

- ❑ Fed-up with the annual marking slog?
- ❑ Time to consider the alternatives?
- ❑ Require professionally supported logging software at an easily affordable price?
- ❑ Need a logging system that puts you in control and believes simplicity is the key?

If the answer to any of the above questions is YES then we invite you to take a check ride with our popular logging software **NMU Standard**. Just send your name and address and we will return you a fully functioning evaluation edition. If you choose to keep the software, you can register it for the modest sum of £19.95 inclusive and receive the UK civil register add-on for **FREE**.

Where to order:
Internet: www.nomoreunderlining.co.uk E-mail: cam2007@nomoreunderlining.co.uk

Logging software for the civil enthusiast

HPR.	Handley Page Reading	RAAF	Royal Australian Air Force
HR.	Robin	RAFGSA	Royal Air Force Gliding & Soaring Association
HS.	Hawker Siddeley	RCAF	Royal Canadian Air Force
ICA	Intreprinderea de Constructii Aeronau	RF	Fournier
IHM	International Helicopter Museum	R.N.	Royal Navy
I.I.I.	Iniziative Industriali Italiane	S.	Short, Sikorsky
IL	Ilyushin	SA,SE,SO	Sud-Aviation, Aérospatiale, Scottish Aviation
ILFC	International Lease Finance Corporation	SAAB	Svenska Aeroplan Aktieboleg
IMCO	Intermountain Manufacturing Co	SC	Short
IWM	Imperial War Museum	SCD	Side Cargo Door
JT	John Taylor	SNCAN	Société Nationale de Constructions Aéronautiques du Nord
KR	Rand-Robinson		
L.	Lockheed	SOCATA	Société de Construction d'Avions de Tourisme et d'Affaires
L.A.	Luton, Lake		
LET	Letecky Narodny Podnik	SpA	Societa per Azioni
LLP	Limited Liability Partnership	SPP	Strojirny Prvni Petiletky
L.V.G.	Luft-Verkehrs Gesellschaft	S.R.	Saunders-Roe, Stinson
M.	Miles, Mooney	SS	Special Shape
MBA	Micro Biplane Aviation	ST	SOCATA
MBB	Messerschmitt-Bölkow-Blohm	SW	Solar Wings
McD	McDonnell	T.	Tipsy
MDH	McDonnell Douglas Helicopters	TB	SOCATA
MH.	Max Holste	Tu	Tupolev
MHCA	Manhole Cover	UH.	United Helicopters (Hiller)
MJ	Jurca	UK	United Kingdom
MS.	Morane-Saulnier	USAF	United States Air Force
NA	North American	USAAC	United States Army Air Corps
NC	Nord	USN	United States Navy
NE	North East	V.	Vickers-Armstrongs
P.	Hunting (formerly Percival), Piaggio	VLM	Vlaamse Luchttransportmaatschappij
PA-	Piper	VS.	Vickers-Supermarine
PC.	Pilatus	WA	Wassmer
PZL	Panstwowe Zaklady Lotnicze	WAR	War Aircraft Replicas
QAC	Quickie Aircraft Co	WHE	W.H.Ekin
R.	Rockwell	WS	Westland
RAF	Rotary Air Force	Z.	Zlin

COME TO EAST MIDLANDS AIRPORT AND BIRMINGHAM INTERNATIONAL AIRPORT

For the very best in telescopes, binoculars, scanners, books and aircraft models

Telescopes by **Optocron - Acuter - Vanguard - Helios**
Binoculars by **Visionary - Blackfoot - Helios - Grossfeld**
Airband scanners by **Yupiteru - Yaesu - Icom - Uniden - GRE**

SPECIAL OFFER ON OLD COLOUR 1/200 MODELS

British Midland Boeing 737-500 and Airbus A321	**£10** for 2
British Airways Boeing 747-400, Boeing 757 and Boeing 777	**£15** for 3
Airworld A320, Peach Air Tristar, AB Airlines 737	**£15** for 3
Excellent quality Skyscan 777 Airband Radio	**£19.99**
Uniden UBC30XLT 200 Channel Scanner	**£59.99**

Everything sent post free

AIRTRANS LTD AVIATION GIFT CENTRE

MAIN TERMINAL, EAST MIDLANDS AIRPORT, DERBY DE74 2SA
TEL 01332 852915   FAX 01332 814125   EMAIL sales@airtrans.co.uk

AVIATION EXPERIENCE & GIFT CENTRE

SPECTATORS VIEWING AREA, 3rd FLOOR, BIRMINGHAM INTERNATIONAL AIRPORT B26 3QJ
TEL 0121 782 7901   FAX 0121 782 7902   EMAIL airtransbhx@btinternet.com

OPEN EVERY DAY

Whatever your interests, historic or modern, we have possibly the most extensive range for the aviation enthusiast.

Birmingham
47 Stephenson Street
Birmingham | B2 4DH
Tel: 0121 643 2496 | Fax: 0121 643 6855
Email: bcc@ianallanpublishing.co.uk

Cardiff
31 Royal Arcade
Cardiff | CF10 1AE
Tel: 029 2039 0615 | Fax: 029 2039 0621
Email: cardiff@ianallanpublishing.co.uk

London
45/46 Lower Marsh | Waterloo
London | SE1 7RG
Tel: 020 7401 2100 | Fax: 020 7401 2887
Email: waterloo@ianallanpublishing.co.uk

Manchester
5 Piccadilly Station Approach
Manchester | M1 2GH
Tel: 0161 237 9840 | Fax: 0161 237 9921
Email: manchester@ianallanpublishing.co.uk

Ian Allan BOOKSHOPS

- Books
- Magazines
- Diecast Models
- DVDs
- CD-ROMs

& much more...

Visit our website
www.ianallanpublishing.com

British Civil Aircraft Registrations

Reg	Type († False registration)	Owner or Operator	Notes
G-AAAH†	DH.60G Moth (replica) (BAPC 168) ★	Yorkshire Air Museum/Elvington	
G-AAAH	DH.60G Moth ★	Science Museum *Jason*/South Kensington	
G-AACA†	Avro 504K (BAPC 177) ★	Brooklands Museum of Aviation/Weybridge	
G-AACN	HP.39 Gugnunc ★	Science Museum/Wroughton	
G-AADR	DH.60GM Moth	E. V. Moffatt	
G-AAEG	DH.60G Gipsy Moth	I. B. Grace	
G-AAHI	DH.60G Moth	N. J. W. Reid	
G-AAHY	DH.60M Moth	D. J. Elliott	
G-AAIN	Parnall Elf II	The Shuttleworth Collection/Old Warden	
G-AAJT	DH.60G Moth	M. R. Paul	
G-AALY	DH.60G Moth	K. M. Fresson	
G-AAMX	DH.60GM Moth ★	RAF Museum/Hendon	
G-AAMY	DH.60GMW Moth	Totalsure Ltd	
G-AANG	Blériot XI	The Shuttleworth Collection/Old Warden	
G-AANH	Deperdussin Monoplane	The Shuttleworth Collection/Old Warden	
G-AANI	Blackburn Monoplane	The Shuttleworth Collection/Old Warden	
G-AANJ	L.V.G. C VI (7198/18)	Aerospace Museum/Cosford	
G-AANL	DH.60M Moth	A. L. Berry	
G-AANM	Bristol 96A F.2B (D7889) (BAPC166)	Aero Vintage Ltd/Duxford	
G-AANO	DH.60GMW Moth	A. W. & M. E. Jenkins	
G-AANV	DH.60G Moth	R. A. Seeley	
G-AAOK	Curtiss Wright Travel Air 12Q	Shipping & Airlines Ltd/Biggin Hill	
G-AAOR	DH.60G Moth	B. R. Cox & N. J. Stagg	
G-AAPZ	Desoutter I (mod.)	The Shuttleworth Collection/Old Warden	
G-AAUP	Klemm L.25-1A	J. I. Cooper	
G-AAWO	DH.60G Moth	N. J. W. Reid	
G-AAXK	Klemm L.25-1A ★	C. C. Russell-Vick (stored)	
G-AAYT	DH.60G Moth	P. Groves	
G-AAYX	Southern Martlet	The Shuttleworth Collection/Old Warden	
G-AAZG	DH.60G Moth	J. A. Pothecary & ptnrs	
G-AAZP	DH.80A Puss Moth	R. P. Williams	
G-ABAA	Avro 504K ★	Manchester Museum of Science & Industry	
G-ABAG	DH.60G Moth	A. & P. A. Wood	
G-ABBB	B.105A Bulldog IIA (K2227) ★	RAF Museum/Hendon	
G-ABDA	DH.60G Moth	R. A. Palmer	
G-ABDW	DH.80A Puss Moth (VH-UQB) ★	Museum of Flight/East Fortune	
G-ABDX	DH.60G Moth	M. D. Souch	
G-ABEV	DH.60G Moth	S. L. G. Darch	
G-ABLM	Cierva C.24 ★	De Havilland Heritage Museum/London Colney	
G-ABLS	DH.80A Puss Moth	R. A. Seeley	
G-ABMR	Hart 2 (J9941) ★	RAF Museum/Hendon	
G-ABNT	Civilian C.A.C.1 Coupe	Shipping & Airlines Ltd/Biggin Hill	
G-ABNX	Redwing 2	Redwing Syndicate/Redhill	
G-ABOI	Wheeler Slymph ★	Midland Air Museum/Coventry	
G-ABOX	Sopwith Pup (N5195)	C. M. D. & A. P. St. Cyrien/Middle Wallop	
G-ABSD	DHA.60G Moth	M. E. Vaisey	
G-ABTC	Comper CLA.7 Swift	P. Channon (stored)	
G-ABUL†	DH.82A Tiger Moth ★	F.A.A. Museum/Yeovilton (G-AOXG)	
G-ABUS	Comper CLA.7 Swift	R. C. F. Bailey	
G-ABVE	Arrow Active 2	Real Aircraft Co/Breighton	
G-ABWP	Spartan Arrow	R. E. Blain/Redhill	
G-ABXL	Granger Archaeopteryx ★	J. R. Granger	
G-ABYA	DH.60G Gipsy Moth	J. F. Moore & D. A. Hay/Biggin Hill	
G-ABZB	DH.60G-III Moth Major	G. M. Turner & N. Child	
G-ACBH	Blackburn B.2 ★	–/Redhill	
G-ACCB	DH.83 Fox Moth	E. A. Gautrey	
G-ACDA	DH.82A Tiger Moth	B. D. Hughes	
G-ACDC	DH.82A Tiger Moth	Tiger Club Ltd/Headcorn	
G-ACDI	DH.82A Tiger Moth	J. A. Pothecary/Shoreham	
G-ACEJ	DH.83 Fox Moth	Newbury Aeroplane Co	
G-ACET	DH.84 Dragon	M. D. Souch	
G-ACGT	Avro 594 Avian IIIA ★	Yorkshire Light Aircraft Ltd/Leeds	
G-ACGZ	DH.60G-III Moth Major	N. H. Lemon	
G-ACIT	DH.84 Dragon ★	Science Museum/Wroughton	
G-ACLL	DH.85 Leopard Moth	V. M & D. C. M. Stiles	
G-ACMA	DH.85 Leopard Moth	S. J. Filhol/Sherburn	
G-ACMD	DH.82A Tiger Moth	M. J. Bonnick	

13

G-ACMN – G-AEGV BRITISH CIVIL REGISTRATIONS

Notes	Reg	Type	Owner or Operator
	G-ACMN	DH.85 Leopard Moth	M. R. & K. E. Slack
	G-ACNS	DH.60G-III Moth Major	R. I. & D. Souch
	G-ACOJ	DH.85 Leopard Moth	Norman Aeroplane Trust/Rendcomb
	G-ACSP	DH.88 Comet ★	T. M., M. L., D. A. & P. M. Jones
	G-ACSS	DH.88 Comet ★	The Shuttleworth Collection *Grosvenor House*/Old Warden
	G-ACSS†	DH.88 Comet (replica) ★	G. Gayward (BAPC216)
	G-ACSS†	DH.88 Comet (replica) ★	The Galleria/Hatfield (BAPC257)
	G-ACTF	Comper CLA.7 Swift ★	The Shuttleworth Collection/Old Warden
	G-ACUS	DH.85 Leopard Moth	R. A. & V. A. Gammons
	G-ACUU	Cierva C.30A (HM580) ★	G. S. Baker/Duxford
	G-ACUX	S.16 Scion (VH-UUP) ★	Ulster Folk & Transport Museum
	G-ACVA	Kay Gyroplane ★	Museum of Flight/East Fortune
	G-ACWM	Cierva C.30A (AP506) ★	IHM/Weston-super-Mare
	G-ACWP	Cierva C.30A (AP507) ★	Science Museum/South Kensington
	G-ACXB	DH.60G-III Moth Major	D. F. Hodgkinson
	G-ACXE	B.K. L-25C Swallow	J. G. Wakeford
	G-ACYK	Spartan Cruiser III ★	Museum of Flight (front fuselage)/East Fortune
	G-ACZE	DH.89A Dragon Rapide	Wessex Aviation & Transport Ltd (G-AJGS)
	G-ADAH	DH.89A Dragon Rapide ★	Manchester Museum of Science & Industry *Pioneer*
	G-ADEV	Avro 504K (H5199)	The Shuttleworth Collection/Old Warden (G-ACNB)
	G-ADFV	Blackburn B-2 ★	D. Collings (stored)
	G-ADGP	M.2L Hawk Speed Six	R. A. Mills/White Waltham
	G-ADGT	DH.82A Tiger Moth (BB697)	Aviation Ventures Ltd/Sywell
	G-ADGV	DH.82A Tiger Moth	K. J. Whitehead (G-BACW)
	G-ADHD	DH.60G-III Moth Major	M. E. Vaisey
	G-ADIA	DH.82A Tiger Moth	S. J. Beaty
	G-ADJJ	DH.82A Tiger Moth	J. M. Preston
	G-ADKC	DH.87B Hornet Moth	A. J. Davy/White Waltham
	G-ADKK	DH.87B Hornet Moth	R. M. Lee
	G-ADKL	DH.87B Hornet Moth	P. R. & M. J. F. Gould
	G-ADKM	DH.87B Hornet Moth	L. V. Mayhead
	G-ADLY	DH.87B Hornet Moth	Totalsure Ltd
	G-ADMT	DH.87B Hornet Moth	S. & H. Roberts
	G-ADMW	M.2H Hawk Major (DG590) ★	RAF Museum Storage & Restoration Centre/RAF Stafford
	G-ADND	DH.87B Hornet Moth (W9385)	D. M. & S. M. Weston
	G-ADNE	DH.87B Hornet Moth	G-ADNE Group
	G-ADNL	M.5 Sparrowhawk ★	A. P. Pearson
	G-ADNZ	DH.82A Tiger Moth (DE673)	D. C. Wall
	G-ADOT	DH.87B Hornet Moth ★	De Havilland Heritage Museum/London Colney
	G-ADPC	DH.82A Tiger Moth	D. J. Marshall
	G-ADPJ	B.A.C. Drone ★	N. H. Ponsford/Brighton
	G-ADPS	B.A. Swallow 2	J. F. Hopkins
	G-ADRA	Pietenpol Air Camper	A. J. Mason
	G-ADRG†	Mignet HM.14 (replica) ★	Lower Stondon Transport Museum (BAPC77)
	G-ADRH	DH.87B Hornet Moth	R. G. Grocott/Switzerland
	G-ADRR	Aeronca C.3	S. J. Rudkin
	G-ADRX†	Mignet HM.14 (replica) ★	S. Copeland Aviation Group (BAPC231)
	G-ADRY†	Mignet HM.14 (replica) (BAPC29) ★	Brooklands Museum of Aviation/Weybridge
	G-ADUR	DH.87B Hornet Moth	W. A. Gerdes
	G-ADVU†	Mignet HM.14 (replica) ★	North East Aircraft Museum/Usworth (BAPC211)
	G-ADWJ	DH.82A Tiger Moth	C. Adams
	G-ADWO	DH.82A Tiger Moth (BB807) ★	Solent Sky, Southampton
	G-ADWT	M.2W Hawk Trainer	R. Earl & B. Morris
	G-ADXS	Mignet HM.14 ★	Thameside Aviation Museum/Shoreham
	G-ADXT	DH.82A Tiger Moth	J. R. Hanauer
	G-ADYS	Aeronca C.3	J. I. Cooper
	G-ADYV†	Mignet HM.14 (replica) ★	P. Ward (BAPC243)
	G-ADZW†	Mignet HM.14 (replica) ★	Solent Sky/Southampton (BAPC253)
	G-AEBB	Mignet HM.14 ★	The Shuttleworth Collection/Old Warden
	G-AEBJ	Blackburn B-2	BAe Systems (Operations) Ltd/Brough
	G-AEDB	B.A.C. Drone 2	R. E. Nerou & P. L. Kirk
	G-AEDU	DH.90 Dragonfly	Norman Aeroplane Trust/Rendcomb
	G-AEEG	M.3A Falcon Skysport	P. R. Holloway/Old Warden
	G-AEEH	Mignet HM.14 ★	Aerospace Museum/Cosford
	G-AEFG	Mignet HM.14 (BAPC75) ★	N. H. Ponsford/Brighton
	G-AEFT	Aeronca C.3	N. S. Chittenden
	G-AEGV	Mignet HM.14 ★	Midland Air Museum/Coventry

BRITISH CIVIL REGISTRATIONS

G-AEHM – G-AFZN

Reg	Type	Owner or Operator	Notes
G-AEHM	Mignet HM.14 ★	Science Museum/Wroughton	
G-AEJG	Mignet HM.14 (BAPC120) ★	South Yorkshire Aviation Museum/Doncaster	
G-AEKR	Mignet HM.14 (BAPC121) ★	Doncaster Museum & Art Gallery	
G-AEKV	Kronfeld Drone ★	Brooklands Museum of Aviation/Weybridge	
G-AEKW	M.12 Mohawk ★	RAF Museum	
G-AELO	DH.87B Hornet Moth	M. J. Miller	
G-AEML	DH.89 Dragon Rapide	Amanda Investments Ltd	
G-AENP	Hawker Hind (K5414) (BAPC78)	The Shuttleworth Collection/Old Warden	
G-AEOA	DH.80A Puss Moth	P. & A. Wood/Old Warden	
G-AEOF†	Mignet HM.14 (BAPC22) ★	Aviodrome/Lelystad, Netherlands	
G-AEOF	Rearwin 8500	Shipping & Airlines Ltd/Biggin Hill	
G-AEPH	Bristol F2B (D8096)	The Shuttleworth Collection/Old Warden	
G-AERV	M.11A Whitney Straight	R. A. Seeley	
G-AESB	Aeronca C.3	R. J. M. Turnbull	
G-AESE	DH.87B Hornet Moth	J. G. Green/Redhill	
G-AESZ	Chilton D.W.1	R. E. Nerou	
G-AETA	Caudron G.3 (3066) ★	RAF Museum/Hendon	
G-AEUJ	M.11A Whitney Straight	R. E. Mitchell	
G-AEVS	Aeronca 100	R. A. Fleming	
G-AEXD	Aeronca 100	Mrs M. A. & R. W. Mills	
G-AEXF	P6 Mew Gull	Real Aircraft Co/Breighton	
G-AEXT	Dart Kitten II	A. J. Hartfield	
G-AEXZ	Piper J-2 Cub	M. & J. R. Dowson/Leicester	
G-AEZF	S.16 Scion 2 ★	Acebell Aviation/Redhill	
G-AEZJ	P.10 Vega Gull	D. P. H. Hulme/Biggin Hill	
G-AFAP†	CASA C.352L ★	Aerospace Museum/Cosford	
G-AFAX	B. A. Eagle 2	Fundacion Infante de Orleans	
G-AFBS	M.14A Hawk Trainer 3 ★	G. D. Durbridge-Freeman/Duxford (G-AKKU)	
G-AFCL	B. A. Swallow 2	C. P. Bloxham	
G-AFDO	Piper J-3F-60 Cub	R. Wald	
G-AFDX	Hanriot HD.1 (HD-75) ★	RAF Museum/Hendon	
G-AFEL	Monocoupe 90A	M. Rieser	
G-AFFD	Percival Q-6 ★	B. D. Greenwood	
G-AFFH	Piper J-2 Cub	M. J. Honeychurch	
G-AFFI†	Mignet HM.14 (replica) (BAPC76) ★	Yorkshire Air Museum/Elvington	
G-AFGC	B. A. Swallow 2 ★	G. E. Arden (stored)	
G-AFGD	B. A. Swallow 2	A. T. Williams & ptnrs/Shobdon	
G-AFGE	B. A. Swallow 2	A. A. M. & C. W. N. Huke	
G-AFGH	Chilton D.W.1.	M. L. & G. L. Joseph	
G-AFGI	Chilton D.W.1.	J. E. & K. A. A. McDonald	
G-AFGM	Piper J-4A Cub Coupé	P. H. Wilkinson/Carlisle	
G-AFGZ	DH.82A Tiger Moth	M. R. Paul (G-AMHI)	
G-AFHA	Mosscraft MA.1. ★	C. V. Butler	
G-AFIN	Chrislea LC.1 Airguard (BAPC203) ★	N. Wright	
G-AFIR	Luton LA-4 Minor	A. J. Mason	
G-AFJA	Watkinson Dingbat ★	A. T. Christian	
G-AFJB	Foster-Wikner G.M.1. Wicko	J. Dible	
G-AFJR	Tipsy Trainer 1	M. E. Vaisey (stored)	
G-AFJU	M.17 Monarch	Museum of Flight/East Fortune	
G-AFJV	Mosscraft MA.2 ★	C. V. Butler	
G-AFNG	DH.94 Moth Minor	The Gullwing Trust	
G-AFNI	DH.94 Moth Minor	J. Jennings	
G-AFOB	DH.94 Moth Minor	K. Cantwell/Henlow	
G-AFOJ	DH.94 Moth Minor ★	De Havilland Heritage Museum/London Colney	
G-AFPN	DH.94 Moth Minor	J. W. & A. R. Davy/Redhill	
G-AFRZ	M.17 Monarch	R. E. Mitchell/Sleap (G-AIDE)	
G-AFSC	Tipsy Trainer 1	D. M. Forshaw	
G-AFSV	Chilton D.W.1A	R. E. Nerou	
G-AFSW	Chilton D.W.2 ★	R. I. Souch	
G-AFTA	Hawker Tomtit (K1786)	The Shuttleworth Collection/Old Warden	
G-AFTN	Taylorcraft Plus C2 ★	Leicestershire County Council Museums/Snibston	
G-AFUP	Luscombe 8A Silvaire	R. Dispain	
G-AFVE	DH.82A Tiger Moth (T7230)	Tigerfly/Booker	
G-AFWH	Piper J-4A Cub Coupé	C. W. Stearn & R. D. W. Norton	
G-AFWI	DH.82A Tiger Moth	E. Newbigin	
G-AFWT	Tipsy Trainer 1	N. Parkhouse	
G-AFYD	Luscombe 8F Silvaire	J. D. Iliffe	
G-AFYO	Stinson H.W.75	M. Lodge	
G-AFZA	Piper J-4A Cub Coupe	R. A. Benson	
G-AFZK	Luscombe 8A Silvaire	M. G. Byrnes	
G-AFZL	Porterfield CP50	P. G. Lucas & S. H. Sharpe/White Waltham	
G-AFZN	Luscombe 8A Silvaire	R. J. Griffin & J. L. Truscott	

G-AGAT – G-AHSS   BRITISH CIVIL REGISTRATIONS

Notes	Reg	Type	Owner or Operator
	G-AGAT	Piper J-3F-50 Cub	A. S. Bathgate
	G-AGBN	GAL.42 Cygnet 2 ★	Museum of Flight/East Fortune
	G-AGEG	DH.82A Tiger Moth	Norman Aeroplane Trust/Rendcomb
	G-AGFT	Avia FL.3 (8110)	K. Joynson & K. Cracknell
	G-AGHY	DH.82A Tiger Moth	P. Groves
	G-AGIV	Piper J-3C-65 Cub	C. D. Davidson
	G-AGJG	DH.89A Dragon Rapide	M. J. & D. J. T. Miller/Duxford
	G-AGLK	Auster 5D	C. R. Harris
	G-AGMI	Luscombe 8A Silvaire	Oscar Flying Group
	G-AGNJ	DH.82A Tiger Moth	B. P. Borsberry & ptnrs
	G-AGNV	Avro 685 York 1 (TS798) ★	Aerospace Museum/Cosford
	G-AGOH	Auster J/1 Autocrat ★	Newark Air Museum
	G-AGOS	R.S.4 Desford Trainer (VZ728) ★	Leicestershire County Council Museums
	G-AGPG	Avro 19 Srs 2 ★	Hooton Park Trust
	G-AGPK	DH.82A Tiger Moth	Aviation Ventures Ltd/Sywell
	G-AGRU	V.498 Viking 1A ★	Brooklands Museum of Aviation/Weybridge
	G-AGSH	DH.89A Dragon Rapide 6	Bournemouth Aviation Museum
	G-AGTM	DH.89A Dragon Rapide 6	Air Atlantique Ltd/Coventry
	G-AGTO	Auster J/1 Autocrat	M. J. Barnett & D. J. T. Miller/Duxford
	G-AGTT	Auster J/1 Autocrat	R. Farrer
	G-AGVG	Auster J/1 Autocrat (modified)	P. J. Benest
	G-AGVN	Auster J/1 Autocrat	P. McCloskey/Ireland
	G-AGVV	Piper J-3C-65 Cub	M. Molina-Ruano/Spain
	G-AGXN	Auster J/1N Alpha	Gentleman's Aerial Touring Carriage Group
	G-AGXT	Auster J/1N Alpha ★	Nene Valley Aircraft Museum
	G-AGXU	Auster J/1N Alpha	B. H. Austen
	G-AGXV	Auster J/1 Autocrat	B. S. Dowsett & I. M. Oliver
	G-AGYD	Auster J/1N Alpha	P. D. Hodson
	G-AGYH	Auster J/1N Alpha	I. M. Staves
	G-AGYK	Auster J/1 Autocrat	Autocrat Syndicate
	G-AGYL	Auster J/1 Autocrat ★	Military Vehicle Conservation Group
	G-AGYT	Auster J/1N Alpha	P. J. Barrett
	G-AGYU	DH.82A Tiger Moth (DE208)	P. L. Jones
	G-AGYY	Ryan ST3KR (27)	Dutch Nostalgic Wings/Holland
	G-AGZZ	DH.82A Tiger Moth	E. G. B. Mercer
	G-AHAG	DH.89A Rapide	S. G. Jones
	G-AHAL	Auster J/1N Alpha	Wickenby Aviation
	G-AHAM	Auster J/1 Autocrat	C. P. L. Jenkin
	G-AHAN	DH.82A Tiger Moth	Tiger Associates Ltd
	G-AHAP	Auster J/1 Autocrat	W. D. Hill
	G-AHAT	Auster J/1N Alpha ★	Dumfries & Galloway Aviation Museum
	G-AHAU	Auster J/1 Autocrat	Andreas Auster Group
	G-AHBL	DH.87B Hornet Moth	H. D. Labouchere
	G-AHBM	DH.87B Hornet Moth	P. A. & E. P. Gliddon
	G-AHCK	Auster J/1N Alpha	Skegness Air Taxi Service Ltd (stored)
	G-AHCL	Auster J/1N Alpha (modified)	Electronic Precision Ltd (G-OJVC)
	G-AHCN	Auster J/1N Alpha	C. L. Towell & E. Martinsen
	G-AHCR	Gould-Taylorcraft Plus D Special	D. E. H. Balmford & D. R. Shepherd/Dunkeswell
	G-AHEC	Luscombe 8A Silvaire	P. G. Baxter
	G-AHED	DH.89A Dragon Rapide (RL962) ★	RAF Museum Storage & Restoration Centre/RAF Stafford
	G-AHGD	DH.89A Dragon Rapide (Z7288)	S. G. Jones
	G-AHGW	Taylorcraft Plus D (LB375)	C. V. Butler
	G-AHGZ	Taylorcraft Plus D (LB367)	M. Pocock
	G-AHHH	Auster J/1 Autocrat	H. A. Jones
	G-AHHT	Auster J/1N Alpha	A. C. Barber & N. J. Hudson
	G-AHHU	Auster J/1N Alpha ★	L. A. Groves & I. R. F. Hammond
	G-AHIP	Piper J-3C-65 Cub	A. R. Mangham
	G-AHIZ	DH.82A Tiger Moth	C.F.G. Flying Ltd/Cambridge
	G-AHKX	Avro 19 Srs 2	The Shuttleworth Collection/Old Warden
	G-AHKY	Miles M.18 Series 2 ★	Museum of Flight/East Fortune
	G-AHLK	Auster 3	E. T. Brackenbury/Leicester
	G-AHLT	DH.82A Tiger Moth	M. P. Waring
	G-AHNR	Taylorcraft BC-12D	J. C. Holland
	G-AHOO	DH.82A Tiger Moth	J. T. & A. D. Milsom
	G-AHPZ	DH.82A Tiger Moth	N. J. Wareing
	G-AHRI	DH.104 Dove 1 ★	Newark Air Museum
	G-AHSA	Avro 621 Tutor (K3241)	The Shuttleworth Collection/Old Warden
	G-AHSD	Taylorcraft Plus D (LB323)	A. L. Hall-Carpenter
	G-AHSO	Auster J/1N Alpha	W. P. Miller
	G-AHSP	Auster J/1 Autocrat	R. M. Weeks
	G-AHSS	Auster J/1N Alpha	A. M. Roche

BRITISH CIVIL REGISTRATIONS

G-AHST – G-AJEM

Reg	Type	Owner or Operator	Notes
G-AHST	Auster J/1N Alpha	A. C. Frost	
G-AHTE	P.44 Proctor V	D. K. Tregilgas	
G-AHTW	A.S.40 Oxford (V3388) ★	Skyfame Collection/Duxford	
G-AHUF	DH.Tiger Moth	Dream Ventures Ltd	
G-AHUG	Taylorcraft Plus D	D. Nieman	
G-AHUI	M.38 Messenger 2A ★	The Aeroplane Collection/Hooton Park	
G-AHUJ	M.14A Hawk Trainer 3 (R1914) ★	Strathallan Aircraft Collection	
G-AHUN	Globe GC-1B Swift	R. J. Hamlett	
G-AHUV	DH.82A Tiger Moth	A. D. Gordon	
G-AHVU	DH.82A Tiger Moth (T6313)	J. B. Steel	
G-AHVV	DH.82A Tiger Moth	Ace Flight Training LLP	
G-AHWJ	Taylorcraft Plus D (LB294)	M. Pocock	
G-AHXE	Taylorcraft Plus D (LB312)	J. M. C. Pothecary	
G-AIBE	Fulmar II (N1854) ★	F.A.A. Museum/Yeovilton	
G-AIBH	Auster J/1N Alpha	M. J. Bonnick	
G-AIBM	Auster J/1 Autocrat	D. G. Greatrex	
G-AIBR	Auster J/1 Autocrat	P. R. Hodson	
G-AIBW	Auster J/1N Alpha	W. E. Bateson/Blackpool	
G-AIBX	Auster J/1 Autocrat	Wasp Flying Group	
G-AIBY	Auster J/1 Autocrat	D. Morris	
G-AICX	Luscombe 8A Silvaire	R. V. Smith	
G-AIDL	DH.89A Dragon Rapide 6	Atlantic Air Transport Ltd/Coventry	
G-AIDS	DH.82A Tiger Moth	K. D. Pogmore & T. Dann	
G-AIEK	M.38 Messenger 2A (RG333)	J. Buckingham	
G-AIFZ	Auster J/1N Alpha	M. D. Ansley	
G-AIGD	Auster V J/1 Autocrat	R. B. Webber	
G-AIGF	Auster J/1N Alpha	A. R. C. Mathie	
G-AIGT	Auster J/1N Alpha	R. R. Harris	
G-AIGU	Auster J/1N Alpha	N. K. Geddes	
G-AIIH	Piper J-3C-65 Cub	M. S. Pettit	
G-AIJI	Auster J/1N Alpha ★	C. J. Baker	
G-AIJM	Auster J/4	N. Huxtable	
G-AIJS	Auster J/4 ★	(stored)	
G-AIJT	Auster J/4 Srs 100	Aberdeen Auster Flying Group	
G-AIJZ	Auster J/1 Autocrat	A. A. Marshall (stored)	
G-AIKE	Auster 5	C. J. Baker	
G-AIPR	Auster J/4	M. A. & R. W. Mills/Popham	
G-AIPV	Auster J/1 Autocrat	W. P. Miller	
G-AIRC	Auster J/1 Autocrat	A. Noble/Perth	
G-AIRI	DH.82A Tiger Moth	E. R. Goodwin (stored)	
G-AIRK	DH.82A Tiger Moth	J. S. & P. R. Johnson	
G-AISA	Tipsy B Srs 1	A. A. M. Huke	
G-AISC	Tipsy B Srs 1	Wagtail Flying Group	
G-AISS	Piper J-3C-65 Cub	K. W. Wood & F. Watson/Insch	
G-AIST	VS.300 Spitfire 1A (AR213/PR-D)	Sheringham Aviation UK Ltd	
G-AISX	Piper J-3C-65 Cub	Cubfly/Booker	
G-AITB	A.S.10 Oxford (MP425) ★	RAF Museum/Hendon	
G-AIUA	M.14A Hawk Trainer 3 ★	D. S. Hunt	
G-AIUL	DH.89A Dragon Rapide 6	I. Jones/Chirk	
G-AIXA	Taylorcraft Plus D (LB264)★	RAF Museum/Hendon	
G-AIXJ	DH.82A Tiger Moth	D. Green/Goodwood	
G-AIXN	Benes-Mraz M.1C Sokol	A. J. Wood	
G-AIYG	SNCAN Stampe SV.4B	R. Lageirse & H. Ewaut//Belgium	
G-AIYR	DH.89A Dragon Rapide (HG691)	Spectrum Leisure Ltd/Duxford/Clacton	
G-AIYS	DH.85 Leopard Moth	R. A. & V. A. Gammons/Henlow	
G-AIZE	Fairchild F.24W Argus 2 (FS628) ★	Aerospace Museum/Cosford	
G-AIZG	VS.236 Walrus 1 (L2301) ★	F.A.A. Museum/Yeovilton	
G-AIZU	Auster J/1 Autocrat	C. J. & J. G. B. Morley	
G-AJAD	Piper J-3C-65 Cub	C. R. Shipley	
G-AJAE	Auster J/1N Alpha	Lichfield Auster Group	
G-AJAJ	Auster J/1N Alpha	R. B. Lawrence	
G-AJAM	Auster J/2 Arrow	D. A. Porter	
G-AJAP	Luscombe 8A Silvaire	M. Flint	
G-AJAS	Auster J/1N Alpha	C. J. Baker	
G-AJCP	D.31 Turbulent	B. R. Pearson	
G-AJDW	Auster J/1 Autocrat	D. R. Hunt	
G-AJEB	Auster J/1N Alpha ★	The Aeroplane Collection/Hooton Park	
G-AJEE	Auster J/1 Autocrat	P. Bate & A. C. Whitehead	
G-AJEH	Auster J/1N Alpha	J. T. Powell-Tuck	
G-AJEI	Auster J/1N Alpha	J. Siddall	
G-AJEM	Auster J/1 Autocrat	C. D. Wilkinson	

G-AJES – G-AKUH — BRITISH CIVIL REGISTRATIONS

Notes	Reg	Type	Owner or Operator
	G-AJES	Piper J-3C-65 Cub (330485:C-44)	G. W. Jarvis
	G-AJGJ	Auster 5 (RT486)	British Classic Aircraft Restoration Flying Group
	G-AJHJ	Auster 5 ★	(stored)
	G-AJHS	DH.82A Tiger Moth	Vliegend Museum/Netherlands
	G-AJIH	Auster J/1 Autocrat	D. G. Curran
	G-AJIS	Auster J/1N Alpha	Husthwaite Auster Group
	G-AJIT	Auster J/1 Kingsland Autocrat	A. J. Kay
	G-AJIU	Auster J/1 Autocrat	M. D. Greenhalgh/Netherthorpe
	G-AJIW	Auster J/1N Alpha	Truman Aviation Ltd/Tollerton
	G-AJJP	Fairey Jet Gyrodyne (XJ389) ★	Museum of Berkshire Aviation/Woodley
	G-AJJS	Cessna 120	Robhurst Flying Group
	G-AJJT	Cessna 120	J. S. Robson
	G-AJJU	Luscombe 8E Silvaire	S. C. Weston & R. J. Hopcraft/Enstone
	G-AJKB	Luscombe 8E Silvaire	A. F. Hall & S. P. Collins/Tibenham
	G-AJOC	M.38 Messenger 2A ★	Ulster Folk & Transport Museum
	G-AJOE	M.38 Messenger 2A	P. W. Bishop
	G-AJON	Aeronca 7AC Champion	A. Biggs & D. S. Moores
	G-AJOV†	Westland WS-51 Dragonfly ★	Aerospace Museum/Cosford
	G-AJOZ	Fairchild F.24W Argus 2 ★	Yorkshire Air Museum/Elvington
	G-AJPI	Fairchild F.24R-41a Argus 3 (314887)	K. A. Doornbos/Netherlands
	G-AJPZ	Auster J/1 Autocrat ★	(stored)/Bruntingthorpe
	G-AJRB	Auster J/1 Autocrat	P. D. Hamilton-Box
	G-AJRC	Auster J/1 Autocrat	M. Baker
	G-AJRE	Auster J/1 Autocrat (Lycoming)	Air Tech Spares
	G-AJRH	Auster J/1N Alpha ★	Charnwood Museum/Loughborough
	G-AJRS	M.14A Hawk Trainer 3 (P6382:C)	The Shuttleworth Collection/Old Warden
	G-AJTW	DH.82A Tiger Moth (N6965)	J. A. Barker/Tibenham
	G-AJUE	Auster J/1 Autocrat	P. H. B. Cole
	G-AJUL	Auster J/1N Alpha	M. J. Crees
	G-AJVE	DH.82A Tiger Moth	R. A. Gammons
	G-AJWB	M.38 Messenger 2A	P. W. Bishop
	G-AJXC	Auster 5	J. E. Graves
	G-AJXV	Auster 4 (NJ695)	B. A. Farries/Leicester
	G-AJXY	Auster 4	D. A. Hall
	G-AJYB	Auster J/1N Alpha	P. J. Shotbolt
	G-AKAT	M.14A Hawk Trainer 3 (T9738)	R. A. Fleming/Brighton
	G-AKAZ	Piper J-3C-65 Cub (57-H)	Frazerblades/Duxford
	G-AKBO	M.38 Messenger 2A	P. R. Holloway/Enstone
	G-AKDN	DHC.1A-1 Chipmunk	P. S. Derry/Canada
	G-AKDW	DH.89A Dragon Rapide ★	De Havilland Heritage Museum/London Colney
	G-AKEL	M.65 Gemini 1A ★	Ulster Folk & Transport Museum
	G-AKGE	M.65 Gemini 3C ★	Ulster Folk & Transport Museum
	G-AKHP	M.65 Gemini 1A	P. A. Brook/Shoreham
	G-AKHZ	M.65 Gemini 7 ★	The Aeroplane Collection/Hooton Park
	G-AKIB	Piper J-3C-90 Cub (480015:M-44)	M. C. Bennett
	G-AKIF	DH.89A Dragon Rapide	Airborne Taxi Services Ltd/Booker
	G-AKIN	M.38 Messenger 2A	Sywell Messenger Group
	G-AKIU	P.44 Proctor V	Air Atlantique Ltd/Coventry
	G-AKKB	M.65 Gemini 1A	J. Buckingham
	G-AKKH	M.65 Gemini 1A	J. S. Allison
	G-AKKR	M.14A Magister (T9707) ★	Museum of Army Flying/Middle Wallop
	G-AKKY	M.14A Hawk Trainer 3 (L6906) ★ (BAPC44)	Museum of Berkshire Aviation/Woodley
	G-AKLW	Short SA.6 Sealand 1 ★	Ulster Folk & Transport Museum
	G-AKOT	Auster 5 ★	C. J. Baker
	G-AKOW	Auster 5 (TJ569) ★	Museum of Army Flying/Middle Wallop
	G-AKPF	M.14A Hawk Trainer 3 (N3788)	P. R. Holloway/Old Warden
	G-AKRA	Piper J-3C-65 Cub	W. R. Savin
	G-AKRP	DH.89A Dragon Rapide 4	Eaglescott Dominie Group
	G-AKSY	Auster 5 (TJ534)	A. Brier/Brighton
	G-AKSZ	Auster 5C	P. W. Yates & R. G. Darbyshire
	G-AKTH	Piper J-3C-65 Cub	G. H. Harry & Viscount Goschen
	G-AKTI	Luscombe 8A Silvaire	M. W. Olliver
	G-AKTK	Aeronca 11AC Chief	Aeronca Tango Kilo Group
	G-AKTN	Luscombe 8A Silvaire	M. G. Rummey
	G-AKTO	Aeronca 7BCM Champion	D. C. Murray
	G-AKTP	PA-17 Vagabond	Golf Tango Papa Group
	G-AKTR	Aeronca 7AC Champion	C. Fielder
	G-AKTS	Cessna 120	M. Isterling
	G-AKTT	Luscombe 8A Silvaire	S. J. Charters
	G-AKUE	DH.82A Tiger Moth	D. F. Hodgkinson
	G-AKUH	Luscombe 8E Silvaire	E. J. Lloyd

BRITISH CIVIL REGISTRATIONS

G-AKLI – G-AMCM

Reg	Type	Owner or Operator	Notes
G-AKUI	Luscombe 8E Silvaire	D. A. Sims	
G-AKUJ	Luscombe 8E Silvaire	R. C. Green	
G-AKUK	Luscombe 8A Silvaire	O. R. Watts	
G-AKUL	Luscombe 8A Silvaire	E. A. Taylor	
G-AKUM	Luscombe 8F Silvaire	D. A. Young	
G-AKUN	Piper J-3F-65 Cub	W. R. Savin	
G-AKUO	Aeronca 11AC Chief	L. W. Richardson	
G-AKUP	Luscombe 8E Silvaire	D. A. Young	
G-AKUR	Cessna 140	J. Greenaway & C. A. Davies	
G-AKUW	Chrislea CH.3 Super Ace 2	J. & S. Rickett	
G-AKVF	Chrislea CH.3 Super Ace 2	B. Metters	
G-AKVM	Cessna 120	N. Wise & S. Walker	
G-AKVN	Aeronca 11AC Chief	P. A. Jackson	
G-AKVO	Taylorcraft BC-12D	M. Gibson	
G-AKVP	Luscombe 8A Silvaire	J. M. Edis	
G-AKVR	Chrislea CH.3 Skyjeep 4	R. B. Webber	
G-AKVZ	M.38 Messenger 4B	Shipping & Airlines Ltd/Biggin Hill	
G-AKWS	Auster 5A-160 (RT610)	The Interesting Aircraft Co	
G-AKWT	Auster 5 ★	C. Baker	
G-AKXP	Auster 5 (NJ633)	A. D. Pearce	
G-AKXS	DH.82A Tiger Moth	J. & G. J. Eagles	
G-AKZN	P.34A Proctor 3 (Z7197) ★	RAF Museum/Hendon	
G-ALAX	DH.89A Dragon Rapide ★	Durney Aeronautical Collection/Andover	
G-ALBJ	Auster 5	P. N. Elkington	
G-ALBK	Auster 5	V. L. Wesson	
G-ALBN	Bristol 173 (XF785) ★	RAF Museum Storage & Restoration Centre/Cardington	
G-ALCK	P.34A Proctor 3 (LZ766) ★	Skyfame Collection/Duxford	
G-ALCU	DH.104 Dove 2 ★	Midland Air Museum/Coventry	
G-ALDG	HP.81 Hermes 4 ★	Duxford Aviation Society (fuselage only)	
G-ALEH	PA-17 Vagabond	A. D. Pearce/White Waltham	
G-ALFA	Auster 5	S. P. Barrett	
G-ALFU	DH.104 Dove 6 ★	Duxford Aviation Society	
G-ALGA	PA-15 Vagabond	G. A. Brady	
G-ALGT	VS.379 Spitfire F.XIVH (RM689)	Rolls-Royce PLC	
G-ALIJ	PA-17 Vagabond	Popham Flying Group/Popham	
G-ALIW	DH.82A Tiger Moth	F. R. Curry	
G-ALJF	P.34A Proctor 3	J. F. Moore/Biggin Hill	
G-ALJL	DH.82A Tiger Moth	R. I. & D. Souch	
G-ALLF	Slingsby T.30A Prefect (ARK)	J. F. Hopkins & K. M. Fresson/Parham Park	
G-ALNA	DH.82A Tiger Moth	R. J. Doughton	
G-ALND	DH.82A Tiger Moth (N9191)	J. T. Powell-Tuck	
G-ALNV	Auster 5 ★	C. J. Baker (stored)	
G-ALOD	Cessna 140	J. R. Stainer	
G-ALRI	DH.82A Tiger Moth (T5672)	Mark Squared Ltd	
G-ALSP	Bristol 171 Sycamore (WV783) ★	RAF Museum/Hendon	
G-ALSS	Bristol 171 Sycamore (WA576) ★	Dumfries & Galloway Aviation Museum	
G-ALST	Bristol 171 Sycamore (WA577) ★	North East Aircraft Museum/Usworth	
G-ALSW	Bristol 171 Sycamore (WT933) ★	Newark Air Museum	
G-ALSX	Bristol 171 Sycamore (G-48-1) ★	IHM/Weston-super-Mare	
G-ALTO	Cessna 140	T. M. Jones & ptnrs	
G-ALTW	DH.82A Tiger Moth ★	A. Mangham (stored)	
G-ALUC	DH.82A Tiger Moth	D. R. & M. Wood	
G-ALVP	DH.82A Tiger Moth ★	V. & R. Wheele (stored)	
G-ALWB	DHC.1 Chipmunk 22A	D. M. Neville	
G-ALWF	V.701 Viscount ★	Duxford Aviation Society *RMA Sir John Franklin*/Duxford	
G-ALWS	DH.82A Tiger Moth	A. P. Benyon/Welshpool	
G-ALWW	DH.82A Tiger Moth	D. E. Findon	
G-ALXT	DH.89A Dragon Rapide ★	Science Museum/Wroughton	
G-ALXZ	Auster 5-150	G-ALXZ Syndicate	
G-ALYB	Auster 5 (RT520) ★	South Yorkshire Aviation Museum/Doncaster	
G-ALYG	Auster 5D	A. L. Young/Henstridge	
G-ALYW	DH.106 Comet 1 ★	RAF Exhibition Flight (fuselage converted to 'Nimrod')	
G-ALZE	BN-1F ★	M. R. Short/Solent Sky, Southampton	
G-ALZO	A.S.57 Ambassador ★	Duxford Aviation Society	
G-AMAW	Luton LA-4 Minor	A. J. E. Smith	
G-AMBB	DH.82A Tiger Moth	J. Eagles	
G-AMCK	DH.82A Tiger Moth	Aviation Ventures Ltd/Barton	
G-AMCM	DH.82A Tiger Moth	A. K. & J. I. Cooper	

19

G-AMDA – G-ANJD   BRITISH CIVIL REGISTRATIONS

Notes	Reg	Type	Owner or Operator
	G-AMDA	Avro 652A Anson 1 (N4877:MK-V) ★	Skyfame Collection/Duxford
	G-AMEN	PA-18 Super Cub 95	A. Lovejoy & W. Cook
	G-AMHF	DH.82A Tiger Moth	Wavendon Social Services Ltd
	G-AMHJ	Douglas C-47A Dakota 6 (KG651) ★	Assault Glider Association/Shawbury
	G-AMIU	DH.82A Tiger Moth	M. D. Souch
	G-AMIV	DH.82A Tiger Moth	K. F. Crumplin
	G-AMKU	Auster J/1B Aiglet	P. G. Lipman
	G-AMLZ	P.50 Prince 6E ★	Caernarfon Air World Museum
	G-AMMS	Auster J/5K Aiglet Trainer	R. B. Webber
	G-AMNN	DH.82A Tiger Moth	I. J. Perry
	G-AMOG	V.701 Viscount ★	Museum of Flight/East Fortune
	G-AMPG	PA-12 Super Cruiser	A. G. & S. M. Measey
	G-AMPI	SNCAN Stampe SV.4C	T. W. Harris
	G-AMPO	Douglas C-47B (FZ626/YS-DH) ★	(gate guardian)/RAF Lyneham
	G-AMPY	Douglas C-47B (KK116)	Atlantic Air Transport Ltd/Coventry
	G-AMPZ	Douglas C-47B ★	Air Service Berlin GmbH/Tempelhof
	G-AMRA	Douglas C-47B	Atlantic Air Transport Ltd/Coventry
	G-AMRF	Auster J/5F Aiglet Trainer	D. A. Hill
	G-AMRK	G.37 Gladiator I (423/427)	The Shuttleworth Collection/Old Warden
	G-AMSG	SIPA 903	S. W. Markham
	G-AMSN	Douglas C-47B ★	Aceball Aviation/Redhill
	G-AMSV	Douglas C-47B	The Mustang Restoration Co Ltd
	G-AMTA	Auster J/5F Aiglet Trainer	J. D. Manson
	G-AMTF	DH.82A Tiger Moth (T7842)	H. A. D. Monro
	G-AMTK	DH.82A Tiger Moth	S. W. McKay & M. E. Vaisey
	G-AMTM	Auster J/1 Autocrat	R. J. Stobo (G-AJUJ)
	G-AMTV	DH.82A Tiger Moth	Aviation Ventures Ltd
	G-AMUF	DHC.1 Chipmunk 21	Redhill Tailwheel Flying Club Ltd
	G-AMUI	Auster J/5F Aiglet Trainer	R. B. Webber
	G-AMVD	Auster 5 (TJ652)	M. Hammond
	G-AMVP	Tipsy Junior	A. R. Wershat
	G-AMVS	DH.82A Tiger Moth	J. T. Powell-Tuck
	G-AMXA	DH.106 Comet 2 (nose only) ★	(stored)
	G-AMYD	Auster J/5L Aiglet Trainer	S. Vince
	G-AMYI	BE.2c Replica	M. C. Boddington & S. Slater
	G-AMYJ	Douglas C-47B (KN353) ★	Yorkshire Air Museum/Elvington
	G-AMZI	Auster J/5F Aiglet Trainer	J. F. Moore/Biggin Hill
	G-AMZT	Auster J/5F Aiglet Trainer	D. Hyde & ptnrs/Cranfield
	G-AMZU	Auster J/5F Aiglet Trainer	J. A. Longworth & ptnrs
	G-ANAF	Douglas C-47B	Air Atlantique Ltd/Thales/Coventry
	G-ANAP	DH.104 Dove 6 ★	Brunel Technical College/Lulsgate
	G-ANCF	B.175 Britannia 308 ★	Bristol Aero Collection (stored)/Kemble
	G-ANCS	DH.82A Tiger Moth	C. E. Edwards & E. A. Higgins
	G-ANCX	DH.82A Tiger Moth	D. R. Wood/Biggin Hill
	G-ANDE	DH.82A Tiger Moth	Aviation Ventures Ltd (G-YVFS)
	G-ANDM	DH.82A Tiger Moth	N. J. Stagg
	G-ANEC	DH.82A Tiger Moth ★	(stored)
	G-ANEH	DH.82A Tiger Moth (N6797)	G. J. Wells/Goodwood
	G-ANEL	DH.82A Tiger Moth	Totalsure Ltd
	G-ANEM	DH.82A Tiger Moth	P. J. Benest
	G-ANEN	DH.82A Tiger Moth	A. J. D. Douglas-Hamilton
	G-ANEW	DH.82A Tiger Moth	A. L. Young
	G-ANEZ	DH.82A Tiger Moth	C. D. J. Bland/Sandown
	G-ANFC	DH.82A Tiger Moth	H. J. E. Pierce/Chirk
	G-ANFH	Westland WS-55 Whirlwind ★	IHM/Weston-super-Mare
	G-ANFI	DH.82A Tiger Moth (DE623)	G. P. Graham
	G-ANFL	DH.82A Tiger Moth	Felthorpe Tiger Group Ltd
	G-ANFM	DH.82A Tiger Moth	Reading Flying Group/White Waltham
	G-ANFP	DH.82A Tiger Moth	G. D. Horn
	G-ANFU	Auster 5 (NJ719) ★	North East Aircraft Museum/Usworth
	G-ANFV	DH.82A Tiger Moth (DF155)	R. A. L. Falconer
	G-ANGK	Cessna 140A	Conway Transport A/S /Denmark
	G-ANHK	DH.82A Tiger Moth	J. D. Iliffe
	G-ANHR	Auster 5	H. L. Swallow
	G-ANHS	Auster 4 (MT197)	Mike Tango Group
	G-ANHU	Auster 4	D. J. Baker (stored)
	G-ANHX	Auster 5D	D. J. Baker
	G-ANIE	Auster 5 (TW467)	R. T. Ingram
	G-ANIJ	Auster 5D (TJ672)	M. Pocock
	G-ANIS	Auster 5	J. Clarke-Cockburn
	G-ANJA	DH.82A Tiger Moth (N9389)	The Tiger Club (1990) Ltd
	G-ANJD	DH.82A Tiger Moth	I. Laws

BRITISH CIVIL REGISTRATIONS

G-ANKK – G-AOIR

Reg	Type	Owner or Operator	Notes
G-ANKK	DH.82A Tiger Moth (T5854)	Halfpenny Green Tiger Group	
G-ANKT	DH.82A Tiger Moth (K2585)	The Shuttleworth Collection/Old Warden	
G-ANKV	DH.82A Tiger Moth (T7793) ★	Westmead Business Group/Croydon Airport	
G-ANKZ	DH.82A Tiger Moth (N6466)	D. W. Graham	
G-ANLD	DH.82A Tiger Moth	K. Peters	
G-ANLS	DH.82A Tiger Moth	P. A. Gliddon	
G-ANLW	Westland WS-51/2 Widgeon ★	Norfolk & Suffolk Museum/Flixton	
G-ANMO	DH.82A Tiger Moth (K4259:71)	Aviation Ventures Ltd	
G-ANMY	DH.82A Tiger Moth (DE470)	Lotmead Flying Group	
G-ANNB	DH.82A Tiger Moth	G. C. Bates	
G-ANNE	DH.82A Tiger Moth	C. R. Hardiman	
G-ANNG	DH.82A Tiger Moth	P. F. Walter	
G-ANNI	DH.82A Tiger Moth (T6953)	C. E. Ponsford & ptnrs	
G-ANNK	DH.82A Tiger Moth	D. R. Wilcox	
G-ANOA	Hiller UH-12A ★	Redhill Technical College	
G-ANOH	DH.82A Tiger Moth	N. Parkhouse/White Waltham	
G-ANOK	SAAB S.91C Safir ★	A. F. Galt & Co (stored)	
G-ANOM	DH.82A Tiger Moth	T. G. I. Dark	
G-ANON	DH.82A Tiger Moth (T7909)	Hields Aviation/Sherburn	
G-ANOO	DH.82A Tiger Moth	R. K. Packman/Shoreham	
G-ANOV	DH.104 Dove 6 ★	Museum of Flight/East Fortune	
G-ANPE	DH.82A Tiger Moth	I. E. S. Huddleston/Clacton (G-IESH)	
G-ANPP	P.34A Proctor 3	C. P. A. & J. Jeffrey	
G-ANRF	DH.82A Tiger Moth	C. D. Cyster	
G-ANRM	DH.82A Tiger Moth (DF112)	Spectrum Leisure Ltd/Duxford/Clacton	
G-ANRN	DH.82A Tiger Moth	J. J. V. Elwes/Rush Green	
G-ANRP	Auster 5 (TW439)	I. C. Naylor	
G-ANRX	DH.82A Tiger Moth ★	De Havilland Heritage Museum/London Colney	
G-ANSM	DH.82A Tiger Moth	Northamptonshire School of Flying Ltd	
G-ANTE	DH.82A Tiger Moth (T6562)	Aviation Adventures Ltd	
G-ANTK	Avro 685 York ★	Duxford Aviation Society	
G-ANUO	DH.114 Heron 2D (G-AOXL) ★	Westmead Business Group/Croydon Airport	
G-ANUW	DH.104 Dove 6 ★	Jet Aviation Preservation Group	
G-ANWB	DHC.1 Chipmunk 21	G. Briggs/Blackpool	
G-ANWO	M.14A Hawk Trainer 3 ★	A. G. Dunkerley	
G-ANXB	DH.114 Heron 1B ★	Newark Air Museum	
G-ANXC	Auster J/5R Alpine	Alpine Group	
G-ANXR	P.31C Proctor 4 (RM221)	L. H. Oakins/Biggin Hill	
G-ANZT	Thruxton Jackaroo	D. J. Neville & P. A. Dear	
G-ANZU	DH.82A Tiger Moth	M. I. Lodge	
G-ANZZ	DH.82A Tiger Moth	J. I. B. Bennett & P. P. Amershi	
G-AOAA	DH.82A Tiger Moth	R. C. P. Brookhouse	
G-AOBG	Somers-Kendall SK 1	P. W. Bishop	
G-AOBH	DH.82A Tiger Moth (NL750)	P. Nutley/Thruxton	
G-AOBO	DH.82A Tiger Moth (N6473)	J. S. & S. V. Shaw	
G-AOBU	P.84 Jet Provost T.1 (XD693)	T. J. Manna/North Weald	
G-AOBX	DH.82A Tiger Moth	David Ross Flying Group	
G-AOCP	Auster 5 ★	C. J. Baker (stored)	
G-AOCR	Auster 5D (NJ673)	K. E. Ballington	
G-AOCU	Auster 5	S. J. Ball/Leicester	
G-AODA	Westland S-55 Srs 3 ★	IHM/Weston-super-Mare	
G-AODR	DH.82A Tiger Moth	G-AODR Group (G-ISIS)	
G-AODT	DH.82A Tiger Moth (R5250)	R. A. Harrowven	
G-AOEH	Aeronca 7AC Champion	A. Gregori	
G-AOEI	DH.82A Tiger Moth	C.F.G. Flying Ltd/Cambridge	
G-AOEL	DH.82A Tiger Moth ★	Museum of Flight/East Fortune	
G-AOES	DH.82A Tiger Moth	K. A. & A. J. Broomfield	
G-AOET	DH.82A Tiger Moth	Venom Jet Promotions Ltd/Bournemouth	
G-AOEX	Thruxton Jackaroo	A. T. Christian	
G-AOFE	DHC.1 Chipmunk 22A (WB702)	W. J. Quinn	
G-AOFJ	Auster J/1N Alpha	R. J. Bentley	
G-AOFS	Auster J/5L Aiglet Trainer	P. N. A. Whitehead	
G-AOGA	M.75 Aries ★	Irish Aviation Museum (stored)	
G-AOGE	P.34A Proctor 3 ★	N. I. Dalziel (stored)/Biggin Hill	
G-AOGI	DH.82A Tiger Moth	W. J. Taylor	
G-AOGR	DH.82A Tiger Moth (XL714)	R. J. S. G. Clark	
G-AOGV	Auster J/5R Alpine	R. E. Heading	
G-AOHY	DH.82A Tiger Moth (N6537)	R. H. & S. J. Cooper	
G-AOHZ	Auster J/5P Autocar	A. D. Hodgkinson	
G-AOIL	DH.82A Tiger Moth (XL716)	C. D. Davidson	
G-AOIM	DH.82A Tiger Moth	C. R. Hardiman	
G-AOIR	Thruxton Jackaroo	K. A. & A. J. Broomfield	

21

G-AOIS – G-APJZ — BRITISH CIVIL REGISTRATIONS

Notes	Reg	Type	Owner or Operator
	G-AOIS	DH.82A Tiger Moth (R5172)	J. K. Ellwood
	G-AOIY	Auster J/5G Autocar 160	R. A. Benson
	G-AOJH	DH.83C Fox Moth	Connect Properties Ltd/Kemble
	G-AOJJ	DH.82A Tiger Moth (DF128)	E. & K. M. Lay
	G-AOJK	DH.82A Tiger Moth	R. J. Willies
	G-AOJR	DHC.1 Chipmunk 22	G. J-H. Caubergs & N. Marien/Belgium
	G-AOJT	DH.106 Comet 1 (F-BGNX) ★	De Havilland Heritage Museum (fuselage only)
	G-AOKH	P40 Prentice 1	J. F. Moore/Biggin Hill
	G-AOKL	P40 Prentice 1 (VS610)	The Shuttleworth Collection/Old Warden
	G-AOKO	P40 Prentice 1	South Yorkshire Aviation Museum/Doncaster
	G-AOKZ	P40 Prentice 1 (VS623) ★	Midland Air Museum/Coventry
	G-AOLK	P40 Prentice 1	Hilton Aviation Ltd/Southend
	G-AOLU	P40 Prentice 1 (VS356)	N. J. Butler
	G-AORB	Cessna 170B	Eaglescott Parachute Centre
	G-AORG	DH.114 Heron 2	Duchess of Brittany (Jersey) Ltd
	G-AORW	DHC.1 Chipmunk 22A	Skylark Aviation Ltd
	G-AOSF	DHC.1 Chipmunk 22 (WB571:34)	T. S. Olsen/Germany
	G-AOSK	DHC.1 Chipmunk 22 (WB726)	L. J. Irvine
	G-AOSY	DHC.1 Chipmunk 22 (WB585:M)	WFG Chipmunk Group
	G-AOTD	DHC.1 Chipmunk 22 (WB588)	S. Piech
	G-AOTF	DHC.1 Chipmunk 23 (Lycoming)	Clevelands Gliding Club/Dishforth
	G-AOTI	DH.114 Heron 2D ★	De Havilland Heritage Museum/London Colney
	G-AOTK	D.53 Turbi	T. J. Adams
	G-AOTR	DHC.1 Chipmunk 22	Propshop Ltd
	G-AOTY	DHC.1 Chipmunk 22A (WG472)	A. A. Hodgson
	G-AOUJ	Fairey Ultra-Light ★	IHM/Weston-super-Mare
	G-AOUO	DHC.1 Chipmunk 22 (Lycoming)	Wrekin/Cosford
	G-AOUP	DHC.1 Chipmunk 22	A. R. Harding
	G-AOUR	DH.82A Tiger Moth ★	Ulster Folk & Transport Museum
	G-AOVF	B.175 Britannia 312F ★	Aerospace Museum/Cosford
	G-AOVS	B.175 Britannia 312F ★	Airport Fire Section/Luton
	G-AOVT	B.175 Britannia 312F ★	Duxford Aviation Society
	G-AOVW	Auster 5	B. Marriott/Cranwell
	G-AOXN	DH.82A Tiger Moth	S. L. G. Darch
	G-AOZH	DH.82A Tiger Moth (K2572)	M. H. Blois-Brooke
	G-AOZL	Auster J/5Q Alpine	R. M. Weeks/Stapleford
	G-AOZP	DHC.1 Chipmunk 22	S. J. Davies
	G-APAA	Auster J/5R Alpine ★	L. A. Groves (stored)
	G-APAF	Auster 5 (TW511)	J. J. J. Mostyn (G-CMAL)
	G-APAH	Auster 5	T. J. Goodwin
	G-APAJ	Thruxton Jackaroo	J. T. H. Page
	G-APAL	DH.82A Tiger Moth (N6847)	P. J. Shotbolt
	G-APAM	DH.82A Tiger Moth	R. P. Williams
	G-APAO	DH.82A Tiger Moth (R4922)	H. J. Maguire
	G-APAP	DH.82A Tiger Moth (R5136)	J. C. Wright
	G-APAS	DH.106 Comet 1XB ★	Aerospace Museum/Cosford
	G-APBE	Auster 5	R. B. Woods
	G-APBI	DH.82A Tiger Moth	C. J. Zeal
	G-APBO	D.53 Turbi	R. C. Hibberd
	G-APBW	Auster 5	C. R. W. Brown/France
	G-APCB	Auster J/5Q Alpine	A. A. Beswick
	G-APCC	DH.82A Tiger Moth	L. J. Rice/Henstridge
	G-APDB	DH.106 Comet 4 ★	Duxford Aviation Society
	G-APEP	V.953C Merchantman ★	Brooklands Museum of Aviation/Weybridge
	G-APFA	D.54 Turbi	F. J. Keitch
	G-APFG	Boeing 707-436 ★	Cabin water spray tests/Cardington
	G-APFJ	Boeing 707-436 ★	Museum of Flight/East Fortune
	G-APFU	DH.82A Tiger Moth	Leisure Assets Ltd
	G-APFV	PA-23-160 Apache	J. L. Thorogood (G-MOLY)
	G-APGL	DH.82A Tiger Moth	K. A. Broomfield
	G-APHV	Avro 19 Srs 2 (VM360) ★	Museum of Flight/East Fortune
	G-APIE	Tipsy Belfair B	D. Beale
	G-APIH	DH.82A Tiger Moth	K. Stewering
	G-APIK	Auster J/1N Alpha	J. H. Powell-Tuck
	G-APIM	V.806 Viscount ★	Brooklands Museum of Aviation/Weybridge
	G-APIT	P40 Prentice 1 (VR192) ★	WWII Aircraft Preservation Society/Lasham
	G-APIY	P40 Prentice 1 (VR249) ★	Newark Air Museum
	G-APIZ	D.31 Turbulent	G. M. Rundle
	G-APJB	P40 Prentice 1 (VR259)	Atlantic Air Transport Ltd/Coventry
	G-APJJ	Fairey Ultra-light ★	Midland Aircraft Preservation Society
	G-APJO	DH.82A Tiger Moth	D. R. & M. Wood
	G-APJZ	Auster J/1N Alpha	P. G. Lipman

BRITISH CIVIL REGISTRATIONS — G-APKM – G-ARAX

Reg	Type	Owner or Operator	Notes
G-APKM	Auster J/1N Alpha	D. E. A. Huggins (stored)	
G-APLG	Auster J/5L Aiglet Trainer ★	Solway Aviation Society	
G-APLO	DHC.1 Chipmunk 22A (WD379)	Lindholme Aircraft Ltd/Jersey	
G-APLU	DH.82A Tiger Moth	R. A. Bishop & M. E. Vaisey	
G-APMB	DH.106 Comet 4B ★	Gatwick Handling Ltd (ground trainer)	
G-APMH	Auster J/1U Workmaster	J. L. Thorogood	
G-APMX	DH.82A Tiger Moth	Foley Farm Flying Group	
G-APMY	PA-23 Apache 160 ★	South Yorkshire Aviation Museum/Doncaster	
G-APNJ	Cessna 310 ★	Chelsea College/Shoreham	
G-APNS	Garland-Bianchi Linnet	P. M. Busaidy	
G-APNT	Currie Wot	B. J. Dunford	
G-APNZ	D.31 Turbulent	J. Knight	
G-APOI	Saro Skeeter Srs 8	B. Chamberlain	
G-APPA	DHC.1 Chipmunk 22	D. M. Squires	
G-APPL	P.40 Prentice 1	S. J. Saggers/Biggin Hill	
G-APPM	DHC.1 Chipmunk 22 (WB711)	S. D. Wilch	
G-APPN	DH.82A Tiger Moth (T7328)	John Colours SRL/Spain	
G-APRL	AW.650 Argosy 101 ★	Midland Air Museum/Coventry	
G-APRR	Super Aero 45	R. E. Dagless	
G-APRS	SA Twin Pioneer Srs 3	Aviation Heritage Ltd/Coventry (G-BCWF)	
G-APRT	Taylor JT.1 Monoplane	R. A. Keech	
G-APSA	Douglas DC-6A	Atlantic Air Transport Ltd/Coventry	
G-APSR	Auster J/1U Workmaster	D. & K. Aero Services Ltd/Shobdon	
G-APTR	Auster J/1N Alpha	C. J. & D. J. Baker	
G-APTU	Auster 5	G-APTU Flying Group	
G-APTW	Westland WS-51/2 Widgeon ★	North East Aircraft Museum/Usworth	
G-APTY	Beech G.35 Bonanza	G. E. Brennand	
G-APTZ	D.31 Turbulent	The Tiger Club (1990) Ltd/Headcorn	
G-APUD	Bensen B.7M (modified) ★	Manchester Museum of Science & Industry	
G-APUE	L.40 Meta Sokol	S. E. & M. J. Aherne	
G-APUP	Sopwith Pup (replica) (N5182) ★	RAF Museum/Hendon	
G-APUR	PA-22 Tri-Pacer 160	S. T. A. Hutchinson	
G-APUW	Auster J/5V-160 Autocar	E. A. J. Hibbard	
G-APUY	D.31 Turbulent	C. Jones/Barton	
G-APUZ	PA-24 Comanche 250	Tatenhill Aviation	
G-APVF	Putzer Elster B (97+04)	A. & E. A. Wiseman	
G-APVG	Auster J/5L Aiglet Trainer	R. Farrer/Cranfield	
G-APVL	Saro P.531-2	R. E. Dagless	
G-APVN	D.31 Turbulent	R. Sherwin/Shoreham	
G-APVS	Cessna 170B	N. Simpson Stormin' Norman	
G-APVU	L.40 Meta Sokol	S. E. & M. J. Aherne	
G-APVZ	D.31 Turbulent	The Tiger Club (1990) Ltd	
G-APWA	HPR.7 Herald 101 ★	Museum of Berkshire Aviation/Woodley	
G-APWJ	HPR.7 Herald 201 ★	Duxford Aviation Society	
G-APWL	EoN AP.10 460 Srs 1A	D. G. Andrew	
G-APWN	Westland WS-55 Whirlwind 3 ★	Midland Air Museum/Coventry	
G-APWY	Piaggio P.166 ★	Science Museum/Wroughton	
G-APXJ	PA-24 Comanche 250	T. Wildsmith/Netherthorpe	
G-APXR	PA-22 Tri-Pacer 160	A. Troughton	
G-APXT	PA-22 Tri-Pacer 150 (modified)	A. E. Cuttler	
G-APXU	PA-22 Tri-Pacer 125 (modified)	The Scottish Aero Club Ltd/Perth	
G-APXW	EP9 Prospector (XM819) ★	Museum of Army Flying/Middle Wallop	
G-APXX	DHA.3 Drover 2 (VH-FDT) ★	WWII Aircraft Preservation Society/Lasham	
G-APXY	Cessna 150	Well Clinics Ltd	
G-APYB	Tipsy T.66 Nipper 3	B. O. Smith	
G-APYD	DH.106 Comet 4B ★	Science Museum/Wroughton	
G-APYG	DHC.1 Chipmunk 22	P. A. & J. M. Doyle	
G-APYI	PA-22 Tri-Pacer 135	B. T. & J. Cullen	
G-APYN	PA-22 Tri-Pacer 160	Fishburn Tripacer Group	
G-APYT	Champion 7FC Tri-Traveller	B. J. Anning	
G-APZJ	PA-18 Super Cub 150	Southern Sailplanes Ltd/Membury	
G-APZL	PA-22 Tri-Pacer 160	B. Robins	
G-APZX	Cessna 150 ★	(engine test-bed)/Biggin Hill	
G-APZX	PA-22 Tri-Pacer 150	Applied Signs Ltd	
G-ARAI	PA-22 Tri-Pacer 160	P. McCabe	
G-ARAM	PA-18 Super Cub 150	Skymax (Aviation) Ltd	
G-ARAN	PA-18 Super Cub 150	A. P. Docherty/Redhill	
G-ARAO	PA-18 Super Cub 95	R. G. Manton	
G-ARAS	Champion 7FC Tri-Traveller	Alpha Sierra Flying Group	
G-ARAT	Cessna 180C	S. D. Pryke & J. Graham	
G-ARAW	Cessna 182C Skylane	Ximango UK/Rufforth	
G-ARAX	PA-22 Tri-Pacer 150	J. W. Iliffe	

23

G-ARAZ – G-ARJT — BRITISH CIVIL REGISTRATIONS

Notes	Reg	Type	Owner or Operator
	G-ARAZ	DH.82A Tiger Moth (R4959:59)	D. A. Porter
	G-ARBE	DH.104 Dove 8	M. Whale & M. W. A. Lunn/Old Sarum
	G-ARBG	Tipsy T.66 Nipper 2	D. Shrimpton
	G-ARBO	PA-24 Comanche 250	Tatenhill Aviation Ltd
	G-ARBP	Tipsy T.66 Nipper 2	F. W. Kirk
	G-ARBS	PA-22 Tri-Pacer 160 (tailwheel)	S. D. Rowell
	G-ARBV	PA-22 Tri-Pacer 160	L. M. Williams
	G-ARBZ	D.31 Turbulent	G. Richards
	G-ARCF	PA-22 Tri-Pacer 150	M. J. Speakman
	G-ARCI	Cessna 310D ★	(stored)/Blackpool
	G-ARCS	Auster D6/180	E. A. Matty/Shobdon
	G-ARCT	PA-18 Super Cub 95	C. F. O'Neill
	G-ARCV	Cessna 175A	R. Francis & C. Campbell
	G-ARCW	PA-23 Apache 160	F. W. Ellis
	G-ARCX	A.W. Meteor 14 ★	Museum of Flight/East Fortune
	G-ARDB	PA-24 Comanche 250	P. Crook
	G-ARDD	CP.301C1 Emeraude	G-ARDD Group
	G-ARDE	DH.104 Dove 6 ★	T. E. Evans
	G-ARDJ	Auster D.6/180	RN Aviation (Leicester Airport) Ltd
	G-ARDO	Jodel D.112	W. R. Prescott
	G-ARDP	PA-22 Tri-Pacer 150	G. M. Jones
	G-ARDS	PA-22 Caribbean 150	N. P. McGowan
	G-ARDT	PA-22 Tri-Pacer 160	B. W. Haston
	G-ARDV	PA-22 Tri-Pacer 160	P. Heffron
	G-ARDY	Tipsy T.66 Nipper 2	D. House
	G-ARDZ	Jodel D.140A	M. J. Wright
	G-AREA	DH.104 Dove 8 ★	De Havilland Heritage Museum/London Colney
	G-AREF	PA-23 Aztec 250 ★	Southall College of Technology
	G-AREH	DH.82A Tiger Moth	C. D. Cyster & A. J. Hastings
	G-AREI	Auster 3 (MT438)	R. B. Webber
	G-AREL	PA-22 Caribbean 150	The Caribbean Flying Club
	G-AREO	PA-18 Super Cub 150	Vale of the White Horse Gliding Club
	G-ARET	PA-22 Tri-Pacer 160	I. S. Runnalls
	G-AREV	PA-22 Tri-Pacer 160	D. J. Ash/Barton
	G-AREX	Aeronca 15AC Sedan	R. J. M. Turnbull
	G-ARFB	PA-22 Caribbean 150	D. Shaw
	G-ARFD	PA-22 Tri-Pacer 160	J. R. Dunnett
	G-ARFG	Cessna 175A Skylark	Foxtrot Golf Group
	G-ARFI	Cessna 150A	A. R. Abrey
	G-ARFO	Cessna 150A	M. J. Whitwell
	G-ARFT	Jodel DR.1050	R. Shaw
	G-ARFV	Tipsy T.66 Nipper 2	T. J. Butler
	G-ARGB	Auster 6A ★	C. J. Baker (stored)
	G-ARGG	DHC.1 Chipmunk 22 (WD305)	D. Curtis
	G-ARGO	PA-22 Colt 108	D. R. Smith
	G-ARGV	PA-18 Super Cub 180	Wolds Gliding Club Ltd
	G-ARGY	PA-22 Tri-Pacer 160	D. H.& R. T. Tanner (G-JEST)
	G-ARGZ	D.31 Turbulent	The Tiger Club (1990) Ltd/Headcorn
	G-ARHB	Forney F-1A Aircoupe	K. J. Peacock & S. F. Turner/Earls Colne
	G-ARHC	Forney F-1A Aircoupe	A. P. Gardner/Elstree
	G-ARHI	PA-24 Comanche 180	D. D. Smith
	G-ARHL	PA-23 Aztec 250	C. J. Freeman/Headcorn
	G-ARHM	Auster 6A	R. C. P. Brookhouse
	G-ARHN	PA-22 Caribbean 150	I. S. Hodge & S. Haughton
	G-ARHP	PA-22 Tri-Pacer 160	Popham Flying Group
	G-ARHR	PA-22 Caribbean 150	A. R. Wyatt
	G-ARHT	PA-22 Caribbean 150 ★	Moston Technical College
	G-ARHW	DH.104 Dove 8	Pacelink Ltd
	G-ARHX	DH.104 Dove 8 ★	South Yorkshire Aviation Museum/Doncaster
	G-ARHZ	D.62 Condor	E. Shouler
	G-ARID	Cessna 172B	L. M. Edwards
	G-ARIF	Ord-Hume O-H.7 Minor Coupé ★	N. H. Ponsford (stored)
	G-ARIH	Auster 6A (TW591)	J. Wesson & R. Miller
	G-ARIK	PA-22 Caribbean 150	A. Taylor
	G-ARIL	PA-22 Caribbean 150	G-ARIL Group
	G-ARIM	D.31 Turbulent	R. M. White
	G-ARJB	DH.104 Dove 8	M. Whale & M. W. A. Lunn
	G-ARJE	PA-22 Colt 108	C. I. Fray
	G-ARJF	PA-22 Colt 108	Tandycel Co Ltd
	G-ARJH	PA-22 Colt 108	F. Vogels/France
	G-ARJR	PA-23 Apache 160G ★	Instructional airframe/Kidlington
	G-ARJS	PA-23 Apache 160G	Bencray Ltd/Blackpool
	G-ARJT	PA-23 Apache 160G	J. A. Cole

BRITISH CIVIL REGISTRATIONS

G-ARJU – G-ARUI

Reg	Type	Owner or Operator	Notes
G-ARJU	PA-23 Apache 160G	G. R. Manley	
G-ARJV	PA-23 Apache 160G	Metham Aviation Ltd/Blackbushe	
G-ARJW	PA-23 Apache 160G	(stored)/Bristol	
G-ARKG	Auster J/5G Autocar	S. J. Cooper	
G-ARKJ	Beech N35 Bonanza	P. D. & J. L. Jenkins	
G-ARKK	PA-22 Colt 108	R. D. Welfare	
G-ARKM	PA-22 Colt 108	D. Dytch & J. Moffatt	
G-ARKN	PA-22 Colt 108	R. Redfern	
G-ARKP	PA-22 Colt 108	J. P. A. Freeman/Headcorn	
G-ARKS	PA-22 Colt 108	R. A. Nesbitt-Dufort	
G-ARLB	PA-24 Comanche 250	D. Heater (G-BUTL)	
G-ARLG	Auster D.4/108	Auster D4 Group	
G-ARLK	PA-24 Comanche 250	I. Kazi	
G-ARLO	Beagle A.61 Terrier 1 ★	(stored)	
G-ARLP	Beagle A.61 Terrier 1	Gemini Flying Group	
G-ARLR	Beagle A.61 Terrier 2	M. Palfreman	
G-ARLU	Cessna 172B Skyhawk ★	Instructional airframe/Irish Air Corps	
G-ARLW	Cessna 172B Skyhawk ★	(spares source)/Barton	
G-ARLX	Jodel D.140B	J. S. & S. V. Shaw	
G-ARLZ	D.31A Turbulent	J. A. Thomas	
G-ARMC	DHC.1 Chipmunk 22A (WB703)	John Henderson Children's Trust	
G-ARMF	DHC.1 Chipmunk 22A (WZ868:H)	D. M. Squires/Wellesbourne	
G-ARMG	DHC.1 Chipmunk 22A	MG Group	
G-ARML	Cessna 175B Skylark	G. A. Copeland	
G-ARMN	Cessna 175B Skylark	B. R. Nash	
G-ARMO	Cessna 172B Skyhawk	I. M. Latiff	
G-ARMR	Cessna 172B Skyhawk	Sunsaver Ltd/Barton	
G-ARMZ	D.31 Turbulent	The Tiger Club (1990) Ltd	
G-ARNB	Auster J/5G Autocar	R. F. Tolhurst	
G-ARND	PA-22 Colt 108	C. D. Hardwick	
G-ARNE	PA-22 Colt 108	T. D. L. Bowden/Shipdham	
G-ARNG	PA-22 Colt 108	F. B. Rothera	
G-ARNH	PA-22 Colt 108 ★	Fenland Aircraft Preservation Society	
G-ARNJ	PA-22 Colt 108	R. A. Keech	
G-ARNK	PA-22 Colt 108 (tailwheel)	I. P. Burnett	
G-ARNL	PA-22 Colt 108	J. A. Dodsworth/White Waltham	
G-ARNO	Beagle A.61 Terrier 1 ★ (VX113)	–/Sywell	
G-ARNP	Beagle A.109 Airedale	S. W. & M. Isbister	
G-ARNY	Jodel D.117	D. P. Jenkins	
G-ARNZ	D.31 Turbulent	The Tiger Club (1990) Ltd/Headcorn	
G-AROA	Cessna 172B Skyhawk	D. E. Partridge	
G-AROC	Cessna 175B	A. J. Symes (G-OTOW)	
G-AROJ	Beagle A.109 Airedale ★	D. J. Shaw (stored)	
G-ARON	PA-22 Colt 108	The G ARON Flying Group	
G-AROO	Forney F-1A Aircoupe	W. J. McMeekan/Newtownards	
G-AROW	Jodel D.140B	A. R. Crome	
G-AROY	Boeing Stearman A75N.1	Abbey Security Services Ltd	
G-ARPH	HS.121 Trident 1C ★	Museum of Flight/East Fortune	
G-ARPK	HS.121 Trident 1C ★	Manchester Airport Authority	
G-ARPO	HS.121 Trident 1C ★	CAA Fire School/Teesside	
G-ARRD	Jodel DR.1050	D. J. Taylor & J. P. Brady	
G-ARRE	Jodel DR.1050	G. & R. Ward	
G-ARRI	Cessna 175B	R. D. Fowden	
G-ARRL	Auster J/1N Alpha	A. C. Ladd	
G-ARRM	Beagle B.206-X ★	Bristol Aero Collection (stored)	
G-ARRO	Beagle A.109 Airedale	M. & S. W. Isbister	
G-ARRS	CP301A Emeraude	J. P. Drake/Sturgate	
G-ARRT	Wallis WA-116-1	K. H. Wallis	
G-ARRU	D.31 Turbulent	D. G. Huck	
G-ARRX	Auster 6A (VF512)	J. E. D. Mackie	
G-ARRY	Jodel D.140B	Fictionview Ltd	
G-ARRZ	D.31 Turbulent	T. W. Harris	
G-ARSG	Roe Triplane Type IV (replica)	The Shuttleworth Collection/Old Warden	
G-ARSL	Beagle A.61 Terrier 1 (VF581)	D. J. Colclough	
G-ARSU	PA-22 Colt 108	D. P. Owen	
G-ARTH	PA-12 Super Cruiser	R. I. Souch & B. J. Dunford	
G-ARTJ	Bensen B.8M ★	Museum of Flight/East Fortune	
G-ARTL	DH.82A Tiger Moth (T7281)	F. G. Clacherty	
G-ARTT	MS.880B Rallye Club	R. N. Scott	
G-ARTZ	McCandless M.4 gyroplane	W. R. Partridge	
G-ARUG	Auster J/5G Autocar	D. P. H. Hulme/Biggin Hill	
G-ARUH	Jodel DR.1050	PFA Group/Denham	
G-ARUI	Beagle A.61 Terrier	T. W. J. Dann	

G-ARUL – G-ASGC — BRITISH CIVIL REGISTRATIONS

Notes	Reg	Type	Owner or Operator
	G-ARUL	LeVier Cosmic Wind	P. G. Kynsey/Headcorn
	G-ARUV	CP.301A Emeraude	P. O'Fee
	G-ARUY	Auster J/1N Alpha	D. Burnham
	G-ARUZ	Cessna 175C	Cardiff Skylark Group
	G-ARVM	V.1101 VC10 ★	Brooklands Museum of Aviation/Weybridge
	G-ARVO	PA-18 Super Cub 95	Northamptonshire School of Flying Ltd/Sywell
	G-ARVT	PA-28 Cherokee 160	Red Rose Aviation Ltd/Liverpool
	G-ARVU	PA-28 Cherokee 160	Barton Mudwing Ltd
	G-ARVV	PA-28 Cherokee 160	G. E. Hopkins/Shobdon
	G-ARVZ	D.62B Condor	A. A. M. Huke
	G-ARWB	DHC.1 Chipmunk 22 (WK611)	Thruxton Chipmunk Flying Club
	G-ARWH	Cessna 172C ★	(stored)
	G-ARWO	Cessna 172C	D. Bentley/Ireland
	G-ARWR	Cessna 172C	Devanha Flying Group/Insch
	G-ARWS	Cessna 175C	M. D. Fage
	G-ARXB	Beagle A.109 Airedale	S. W. & M. Isbister
	G-ARXD	Beagle A.109 Airedale	D. Howden
	G-ARXG	PA-24 Comanche 250	Fairoaks Comanche
	G-ARXH	Bell 47G	A. B. Searle
	G-ARXP	Luton LA-4 Minor	E. Evans
	G-ARXT	Jodel DR.1050	CJM Flying Group
	G-ARXU	Auster AOP.6A (VF526)	E. C. Tait & M. Pocock
	G-ARXW	MS.885 Super Rallye	M. J. Kirk
	G-ARYB	HS.125 Srs 1 ★	Midland Air Museum/Coventry
	G-ARYC	HS.125 Srs 1 ★	De Havilland Heritage Museum/London Colney
	G-ARYD	Auster AOP6 (WJ358) ★	Museum of Army Flying/Middle Wallop
	G-ARYF	PA-23 Aztec 250B	D. A. Hitchcockl
	G-ARYH	PA-22 Tri-Pacer 160	C. Watt
	G-ARYI	Cessna 172C	J. Rhodes
	G-ARYK	Cessna 172C	G. W. Goodban/Lydd
	G-ARYR	PA-28 Cherokee 180	G-ARYR Flying Group
	G-ARYS	Cessna 172C	Squires Gear & Engineering Ltd
	G-ARYV	PA-24 Comanche 250	D. C. Hanss
	G-ARYZ	Beagle A.109 Airedale	C. W. Tomkins
	G-ARZB	Wallis WA-116 Srs 1	K. H. Wallis
	G-ARZE	Cessna 172C ★	Parachute jump trainer/Cockerham
	G-ARZM	D.31 Turbulent ★	The Tiger Club (1990) Ltd/Headcorn
	G-ARZN	Beech N35 Bonanza	S. R. Cleary
	G-ARZS	Beagle A.109 Airedale	M. & S. W. Isbister
	G-ARZW	Currie Wot	B. R. Pearson/Eaglescott
	G-ASAA	Luton LA-4 Minor	M. J. Aubrey (stored)/Netherthorpe
	G-ASAI	Beagle A.109 Airedale	K. R. Howden
	G-ASAJ	Beagle A.61 Terrier 2 (WE569)	G-ASAJ Flying Group
	G-ASAL	SA Bulldog Srs 120/124	Pioneer Flying Co Ltd/Prestwick
	G-ASAM	D.31 Turbulent ★	The Tiger Club (1990) Ltd/Headcorn
	G-ASAT	MS.880B Rallye Club	M. Cutovic
	G-ASAU	MS.880B Rallye Club	M. S. Lonsdale
	G-ASAX	Beagle A.61 Terrier 2	P. G. Morris
	G-ASAZ	Hiller UH-12E4 (XS165)	Hields Aviation/Sherburn
	G-ASBA	Phoenix Currie Wot	J. C. Lister
	G-ASBH	Beagle A.109 Airedale	D. T. Smollett
	G-ASBY	Beagle A.109 Airedale	F. A. Forster
	G-ASCC	Beagle E3 Mk 11 (XP254)	P. T. Bolton
	G-ASCD	Beagle A.61 Terrier 2 (TJ704) ★	Yorkshire Air Museum/Elvington
	G-ASCM	Isaacs Fury II (K2050)	E. C. & P. King
	G-ASCU	PA-18A Super Cub 150	D. J. O'Mahony/Ireland
	G-ASCZ	CP.301A Emeraude	I. Denham-Brown
	G-ASDF	Edwards Gyrocopter ★	B. King
	G-ASDK	Beagle A.61 Terrier 2	J. Swallow (G-ARLM)
	G-ASDY	Wallis WA-116/F	K. H. Wallis
	G-ASEA	Luton LA-4A Minor	D. Underwood
	G-ASEB	Luton LA-4A Minor	S. R. P. Harper
	G-ASEO	PA-24 Comanche 250	M. Scott
	G-ASEP	PA-23 Apache 235	Arrowstate Ltd/Denham
	G-ASEU	D.62A Condor	W. M. Grant
	G-ASFA	Cessna 172D	D. Halfpenny
	G-ASFD	L-200A Morava	M. Emery
	G-ASFK	Auster J/5G Autocar	T. D. G. Lancaster
	G-ASFL	PA-28 Cherokee 180	J. Simpson & D. Kennedy
	G-ASFR	Bölkow Bö.208A1 Junior	S. T. Dauncey
	G-ASFX	D.31 Turbulent	E. F. Clapham & W. B. S. Dobie
	G-ASGC	V.1151 Super VC10 ★	Duxford Aviation Society

BRITISH CIVIL REGISTRATIONS

G-ASHD – G-ASSY

Reg	Type	Owner or Operator	Notes
G-ASHD	Brantly B.2A ★	IHM/Weston-super-Mare	
G-ASHH	PA-23 Aztec 250	C. Fordham & L. Barr	
G-ASHS	SNCAN Stampe SV.4C	D. G. Girling	
G-ASHT	D.31 Turbulent	C. W. N. Huke	
G-ASHU	PA-15 Vagabond (modified)	The Calybe Flying Group	
G-ASHV	PA-23 Aztec 250B	R. J. Ashley & G. O'Gorman	
G-ASHX	PA-28 Cherokee 180	Powertheme Ltd/Barton	
G-ASIB	Cessna F.172D	G-ASIB Flying Group	
G-ASII	PA-28 Cherokee 180	T. R. Hart & R. W. S. Matthews	
G-ASIJ	PA-28 Cherokee 180	G-ASIJ Group	
G-ASIL	PA-28 Cherokee 180	C. D. Powell	
G-ASIS	Jodel D.112	W. R. Prescott	
G-ASIT	Cessna 180	R. A. Seeley	
G-ASIY	PA-25 Pawnee 235	RAFGSA/Bicester	
G-ASJL	Beech H.35 Bonanza	A. J. Orchard	
G-ASJM	PA-30 Twin Comanche 160 ★	Via Nova Ltd	
G-ASJV	VS.361 Spitfire IX (MH434/PK-K)	Merlin Aviation Ltd/Duxford	
G-ASJY	Gardan GY-80 Horizon 160	No.6 Group Aviation Ltd	
G-ASKC	DH.98 Mosquito 35 (TA719) ★	Skyfame Collection/Duxford	
G-ASKK	HPR.7 Herald 211 ★	Norwich Aviation Museum	
G-ASKL	Jodel D.150	J. M. Graty	
G-ASKP	DH.82A Tiger Moth	Tiger Club (1990) Ltd/Headcorn	
G-ASKT	PA-28 Cherokee 180	T. J. Herbert	
G-ASLH	Cessna 182F	A. L. Brown & A. L. Butcher	
G-ASLL	Cessna 336 ★	(stored)/Bournemouth	
G-ASLR	Agusta-Bell 47J-2	N. M. G. Pearson	
G-ASLV	PA-28 Cherokee 235	Sackville Flying Group/Riseley	
G-ASLX	CP.301A Emeraude	J. J. Reilly	
G-ASMA	PA-30 Twin Comanche 160 C/R	K. Cooper	
G-ASME	Bensen B.8M	R. M. Harris	
G-ASMF	Beech D.95A Travel Air	M. J. A. Hornblower	
G-ASMJ	Cessna F.172E	Aeroscene Ltd	
G-ASML	Luton LA-4A Minor	R. W. Vince	
G-ASMM	D.31 Tubulent	W. J. Browning	
G-ASMO	PA-23 Apache 160G ★	Aviation Enterprises/Fairoaks	
G-ASMS	Cessna 150A	R. N. Ainsworth & M. A. Brown/Barton	
G-ASMT	Fairtravel Linnet 2	P. Harrison	
G-ASMW	Cessna 150D	C. Brown	
G-ASMY	PA-23 Apache 160 ★	R. D. Forster	
G-ASMZ	Beagle A.61 Terrier 2 (VF516)	B. Andrews	
G-ASNC	Beagle D.5/180 Husky	Peterborough & Spalding Gliding Club Ltd/Crowland	
G-ASNI	CP.1310-C3 Super Emeraude	D. Chapman	
G-ASNK	Cessna 205	Justgold Ltd	
G-ASNN	Cessna 182F ★	Parachute jump trainer/Tilstock	
G-ASNW	Cessna F.172E	G-ASNW Group	
G-ASNY	Campbell-Bensen B.8M gyroplane ★	R. Light & T. Smith	
G-ASOC	Auster 6A	M. J. Kirk	
G-ASOH	Beech 95-B55A Baron	GMD Group	
G-ASOI	Beagle A.61 Terrier 2	G.D.B. Delmege	
G-ASOK	Cessna F.172E	D. W. Disney	
G-ASOM	Beagle A.61 Terrier 2	D. Humphries (G-JETS)	
G-ASOX	Cessna 205A	S. M. C. Harvey	
G-ASPF	Jodel D.120	T. J. Bates	
G-ASPP	Bristol Boxkite (replica)	The Shuttleworth Collection/Old Warden	
G-ASPS	Piper J-3C-90 Cub	A. J. Chalkley/Blackbushe	
G-ASPV	DH.82A Tiger Moth	Z. J. Rockey	
G-ASRB	D.62B Condor	R. J. Bentley/Ireland	
G-ASRC	D.62C Condor	C. R. Isbell	
G-ASRI	PA-23 Aztec 250B ★	Graham Collins Associates Ltd	
G-ASRK	Beagle A.109 Airedale	Bio Pathica Ltd/Lydd	
G-ASRO	PA-30 Twin Comanche 160	D. W. Blake	
G-ASRT	Jodel 150	P. Turton	
G-ASRW	PA-28 Cherokee 180	G. N. Smith	
G-ASSF	Cessna 182G Skylane	J. D. Bingham	
G-ASSM	HS.125 Srs 1/522 ★	Science Museum/South Kensington	
G-ASSP	PA-30 Twin Comanche 160	P. H. Tavener	
G-ASSS	Cessna 172E	D. H. N. Squires & P. R. March/Filton	
G-ASST	Cessna 150D	F. R. H. Parker	
G-ASSU	CP.301A Emeraude	R. W. Millward (stored)/Redhill	
G-ASSV	Kensinger KF	C. I. Jefferson	
G-ASSW	PA-28 Cherokee 140	D. K. Roberts	
G-ASSY	D.31 Turbulent	V. E. Booth	

G-ASTA – G-ATCR — BRITISH CIVIL REGISTRATIONS

Notes	Reg	Type	Owner or Operator
	G-ASTA	D.31 Turbulent	P. A. Cooke
	G-ASTH	Mooney M.20C ★	E. L. Martin (stored)/Guernsey
	G-ASTI	Auster 6A	C. C. Burton
	G-ASTL	Fairey Firefly I (Z2033) ★	F.A. A. Museum/Yeovilton
	G-ASTP	Hiller UH-12C ★	IHM/Weston-super-Mare
	G-ASTV	Cessna 150D (tailwheel) ★	(stored)
	G-ASUB	Mooney M.20E Super 21	S. C. Coulbeck
	G-ASUD	PA-28 Cherokee 180	G-ASUD Group
	G-ASUE	Cessna 150D	D. Huckle
	G-ASUG	Beech E18S ★	Museum of Flight/East Fortune
	G-ASUI	Beagle A.61 Terrier 2	K. W. Chigwell & D. R. Lee
	G-ASUP	Cessna F.172E	GASUP Air/Cardiff
	G-ASUR	Dornier Do 28A-1	Sheffair Ltd
	G-ASUS	Jurca MJ.2B Tempete	R. Targonski/Coventry
	G-ASVG	CP.301B Emeraude	K. R. H. Wingate
	G-ASVM	Cessna F.172E	R. Seckington
	G-ASVN	Cessna U.206 Super Skywagon	British Skysports Parachute Centre
	G-ASVO	HPR.7 Herald 214 ★	Archive Visitor Centre/Shoreham (cockpit section)
	G-ASVP	PA-25 Pawnee 235	Aquila Gliding Club Ltd/Hinton-in-the-Hedges
	G-ASVZ	PA-28 Cherokee 140	J. S. Garvey
	G-ASWH	Luton LA-5A Major	J. T. Powell-Tuck
	G-ASWJ	Beagle 206 Srs 1 (8449M) ★	Brunel Technical College/Bristol
	G-ASWL	Cessna F.172F	Ensiform Aviation Ltd
	G-ASWN	Bensen B.8M	D. R. Shepherd
	G-ASWW	PA-30 Twin Comanche 160	R. Jenkins
	G-ASWX	PA-28 Cherokee 180	A. F. Dadds
	G-ASXD	Brantly B.2B	Lousada PLC
	G-ASXI	Tipsy T.66 Nipper 3	P. G. Blenkinsopp
	G-ASXJ	Luton LA-4A Minor	K. R. Snell
	G-ASXR	Cessna 210	A. Schofield
	G-ASXS	Jodel DR.1050	R. A. Hunter
	G-ASXU	Jodel D.120A	G-ASXU Group
	G-ASXX	Avro 683 Lancaster 7 (NX611) ★	Lincolnshire Aviation Heritage Centre/East Kirkby
	G-ASXY	Jodel D.117A	P. A. Davies & ptnrs/Cardiff
	G-ASXZ	Cessna 182G Skylane	Last Refuge Ltd
	G-ASYD	BAC One-Eleven 475 ★	Brooklands Museum of Aviation/Weybridge
	G-ASYG	Beagle A.61 Terrier 2 (VX927)	Terrane Auster Group
	G-ASYJ	Beech D.95A Travel Air	Crosby Aviation (Jersey) Ltd
	G-ASYN	Beagle A.61 Terrier 2 (frame) ★	(stored)/Bruntingthorpe
	G-ASYP	Cessna 150E	Henlow Flying Group
	G-ASYZ	Victa Airtourer 100	N. C. Grayson
	G-ASZB	Cessna 150E	R. J. Scott
	G-ASZD	Bölkow Bö.208A2 Junior	M. J. Ayers
	G-ASZE	Beagle A.61 Terrier 2	D. R. Ockleton
	G-ASZR	Fairtravel Linnet 2	R. Hodgson
	G-ASZS	Gardan GY-80 Horizon 160	ZS Group
	G-ASZU	Cessna 150E	S. L. Bassett & L. J. Baker
	G-ASZV	Tipsy T.66 Nipper 2	D. H. Greenwood
	G-ASZX	Beagle A.61 Terrier 1 (WJ368)	R. B. Webber
	G-ATAF	Cessna F.172F	Summit Media Ltd
	G-ATAG	Jodel DR.1050	T. M. Dawes-Gamble
	G-ATAS	PA-28 Cherokee 180	ATAS Group
	G-ATAT	Cessna 150E ★	(stored)/Bruntingthorpe
	G-ATAU	D.62B Condor	W. J. Forrest
	G-ATAV	D.62C Condor	V. A. Holliday
	G-ATBG	Nord 1002 (NJ+C11)	T. W. Harris/Little Snoring
	G-ATBH	Aero 145	P. D. Aberbach
	G-ATBI	Beech A.23 Musketeer	Three Musketeers Flying Group
	G-ATBJ	Sikorsky S-61N	British International
	G-ATBL	DH.60G Moth	J. M. Greenland
	G-ATBP	Fournier RF-3	D. McNicholl
	G-ATBS	D.31 Turbulent	J. A. Lear
	G-ATBU	Beagle A.61 Terrier 2	T. Jarvis
	G-ATBW	Tipsy T.66 Nipper 2	Stapleford Nipper Group
	G-ATBX	PA-20 Pacer 135	G. D. & P. M. Thomson
	G-ATBZ	Westland WS-58 Wessex 60 ★	IHM/Weston-super-Mare
	G-ATCC	Beagle A.109 Airedale	J. R. Bowden
	G-ATCD	Beagle D.5/180 Husky	T. C. O'Gorman
	G-ATCE	Cessna U.206	British Skysports Parachute Centre
	G-ATCJ	Luton LA-4A Minor	T. D. Boyle
	G-ATCL	Victa Airtourer 100	A. D. Goodall/Cardiff
	G-ATCR	Cessna 310 ★	ITD Aviation Ltd/Denham

BRITISH CIVIL REGISTRATIONS

G-ATCX – G-ATMM

Reg	Type	Owner or Operator	Notes
G-ATCX	Cessna 182 ★	R. Craft	
G-ATDA	PA-28 Cherokee 160	Portway Aviation Ltd/Shobdon	
G-ATDB	Nord 1101 Noralpha	J. W. Hardie	
G-ATDN	Beagle A.61 Terrier 2 (TW641)	S. J. Saggers/Biggin Hill	
G-ATDO	Bölkow Bö.208C1 Junior	P. Thompson/Crosland Moor	
G-ATEF	Cessna 150E	Swans Aviation/Blackbushe	
G-ATEM	PA-28 Cherokee 180	G. D. Wyles	
G-ATEP	EAA Biplane ★	E. L. Martin (stored)/Guernsey	
G-ATES	PA-32 Cherokee Six 260 ★	Parachute jump trainer/Stirling	
G-ATEV	Jodel DR.1050	J. C. Carter & J. L. Altrip	
G-ATEW	PA-30 Twin Comanche 160	Air Northumbria (Woolsington) Ltd	
G-ATEX	Victa Airtourer 100	Halton Victa Group	
G-ATEZ	PA-28 Cherokee 140	EFI Aviation Ltd	
G-ATFD	Jodel DR.1050	G-ATFD Group	
G-ATFF	PA-23 Aztec 250C	T. J. Wassell	
G-ATFG	Brantly B.2B ★	Museum of Flight/East Fortune	
G-ATFK	PA-30 Twin Comanche 160	D. J. Crinnon/White Waltham	
G-ATFM	Sikorsky S-61N	British International	
G-ATFR	PA-25 Pawnee 150	Borders (Milfield) Gliding Club Ltd	
G-ATFV	Agusta-Bell 47J-2A ★	Caernarfon Air World	
G-ATFW	Luton LA-4A Minor	P. A. Rose	
G-ATFY	Cessna F.172G	J. M. Vinall	
G-ATGE	Jodel DR.1050	H. A. McKnight	
G-ATGN	Thorn Coal Gas Balloon	British Balloon Museum/Newbury	
G-ATGO	Cessna F.172G	Poetpilot Ltd	
G-ATGP	Jodel DR.1050	Madley Flying Group/Shobdon	
G-ATGY	Gardan GY-80 Horizon	D. Cowen	
G-ATGZ	Griffiths GH-4 Gyroplane	R. W. J. Cripps	
G-ATHA	PA-23 Apache 235 ★	Brunel Technical College/Bristol	
G-ATHD	DHC.1 Chipmunk 22 (WP971)	Spartan Flying Group Ltd/Denham	
G-ATHF	Cessna 150F ★	Lincolnshire Aviation Heritage Centre/East Kirkby	
G-ATHK	Aeronca 7AC Champion	The Chase Flying Group	
G-ATHM	Wallis WA-116 Srs 1	Wallis Autogyros Ltd	
G-ATHN	Nord 1101 Noralpha ★	E. L. Martin (stored)/Guernsey	
G-ATHR	PA-28 Cherokee 180	Thomsonfly Ltd	
G-ATHT	Victa Airtourer 115	Cotswold Flying Group	
G-ATHU	Beagle A.61 Terrier 1	J. A. L. Irwin	
G-ATHV	Cessna 150F	Cessna Hotel Victor Group	
G-ATHZ	Cessna 150F	R. D. Forster	
G-ATIA	PA-24 Comanche 260	L. A. Brown	
G-ATIC	Jodel DR.1050	T. A. Major	
G-ATIE	Cessna 150F ★	Parachute jump trainer/Chetwynd	
G-ATIG	HPR.7 Herald 214 ★	Norwich Airport towing trainer	
G-ATIN	Jodel D.117	A. Ayre	
G-ATIR	AIA Stampe SV.4C	Austin Trueman Ltd	
G-ATIS	PA-28 Cherokee 160	M. J. Barton	
G-ATIZ	Jodel D.117	R. A. Smith	
G-ATJA	Jodel DR.1050	Bicester Flying Group	
G-ATJC	Victa Airtourer 100 (modfied)	Aviation West Ltd/Cumbernauld	
G-ATJG	PA-28 Cherokee 140	C. A. McGee & L. K. G. Manning	
G-ATJL	PA-24 Comanche 260	C. G. Sims t/a Juliet Lima Flying Group	
G-ATJM	Fokker Dr.1 (replica) (152/17)	R. Lamplough/North Weald	
G-ATJN	Jodel D.119	R. C. Smith	
G-ATJT	Gardan GY-80 Horizon 160	N. Huxtable	
G-ATJV	PA-32 Cherokee Six 260	Wingglider Ltd/Hibaldstow	
G-ATKF	Cessna 150F	P. Ashbridge	
G-ATKH	Luton LA-4A Minor	H. E. Jenner	
G-ATKI	Piper J-3C-65 Cub	KI Group	
G-ATKT	Cessna F.172G	KT Group	
G-ATKX	Jodel D.140C	Kilo Xray Syndicate	
G-ATLA	Cessna 182J Skylane	J. W. & J. T. Whicher	
G-ATLB	Jodel DR.1050/M1	Le Syndicate du Petit Oiseau/Breighton	
G-ATLC	PA-23 Aztec 250C ★	Alderney Air Charter Ltd (stored)	
G-ATLG	Hiller UH-12B	Bristow Helicopters Ltd	
G-ATLM	Cessna F.172G	Air Fotos Aviation Ltd/Newcastle	
G-ATLP	Bensen B.8M	R. F. G. Moyle	
G-ATLT	Cessna U.206A	Skydive UK Ltd	
G-ATLV	Jodel D.120	T. P. Hancock	
G-ATMC	Cessna F.150F	G. H. Farrah & D. Cunnane	
G-ATMH	Beagle D.5/180 Husky	Dorset Gliding Club Ltd	
G-ATMJ	HS.748 Srs 2A	PTB (Emerald) Pty Ltd/Blackpool	
G-ATML	Cessna F.150F	G. I. Smith	
G-ATMM	Cessna F.150F	R. Marshall	

G-ATMT – G-ATXD — BRITISH CIVIL REGISTRATIONS

Notes	Reg	Type	Owner or Operator
	G-ATMT	PA-30 Twin Comanche 160	Montagu-Smith & Co Ltd
	G-ATMW	PA-28 Cherokee 140	Bencray Ltd/Blackpool
	G-ATMY	Cessna 150F	AVB (UK) Ltd
	G-ATNB	PA-28 Cherokee 180	Ken Macdonald and Co
	G-ATNE	Cessna F.150F	A. D. Revill
	G-ATNK	Cessna F.150F	Pegasus Aviation Ltd
	G-ATNL	Cessna F.150F	D. F. Ranger
	G-ATNV	PA-24 Comanche 260	A. Heydn & K. Powell
	G-ATOA	PA-23 Apache 160G	Oscar Alpha Ltd/Stapleford
	G-ATOD	Cessna F.150F	D. Lugg
	G-ATOH	D.62B Condor	Three Spires Flying Group
	G-ATOI	PA-28 Cherokee 140	R. Ronaldson
	G-ATOJ	PA-28 Cherokee 140	A Flight Aviation Ltd
	G-ATOK	PA-28 Cherokee 140	ILC Flying Group
	G-ATOL	PA-28 Cherokee 140	L. J. Nation & G. Alford
	G-ATOM	PA-28 Cherokee 140	A. Flight Aviation Ltd
	G-ATON	PA-28 Cherokee 140	Stirling Flying Syndicate/Shobdon
	G-ATOO	PA-28 Cherokee 140	A. K. Komosa
	G-ATOP	PA-28 Cherokee 140	P. R. Coombs/Blackbushe
	G-ATOR	PA-28 Cherokee 140	Aligator Group
	G-ATOT	PA-28 Cherokee 180	Totair Ltd
	G-ATOU	Mooney M.20E Super 21	M20 Flying Group/Sherburn
	G-ATOY	PA-24 Comanche 260 ★	Museum of Flight/East Fortune
	G-ATOZ	Bensen B.8M	N. C. White
	G-ATPN	PA-28 Cherokee 140	M. F. Hatt & ptnrs/Southend
	G-ATPT	Cessna 182J Skylane	C. Beer t/a Papa Tango Group
	G-ATPV	JB.01 Minicab	J. K. Davies
	G-ATRA	LET L.13 Blanik (BXV)	Blanik Syndicate/Husbands Bosworth
	G-ATRB	LET L.13 Blanik (BXW)	Avon Soaring Centre/Bickmarsh
	G-ATRG	PA-18 Super Cub 150	Lasham Gliding Society Ltd
	G-ATRI	Bolkow Bö. 208C1 Junior	G. Johnson
	G-ATRK	Cessna F.150F	Armstrong Aviation
	G-ATRL	Cessna F.150F	A. A. W. Stevens
	G-ATRM	Cessna F.150F	J. Redfearn
	G-ATRO	PA-28 Cherokee 140	G. M. Malpass
	G-ATRR	PA-28 Cherokee 140	Keen Leasing (IOM) Ltd
	G-ATRW	PA-32 Cherokee Six 260	Pringle Brandon Architects
	G-ATRX	PA-32 Cherokee Six 260	A. M. Harrhy & ptnrs
	G-ATSI	Bölkow Bö.208C1 Junior	N. C. Ravine
	G-ATSL	Cessna F.172G	Alpha Aviation
	G-ATSR	Beech M.35 Bonanza	G-ATSR Group
	G-ATSX	Bölkow Bö.208C1 Junior	Little Bear Ltd
	G-ATSY	Wassmer Wa.41 Super Baladou IV	McLean Aviation
	G-ATSZ	PA-30 Twin Comanche 160B	Sierra Zulu Aviation Ltd
	G-ATTB	Wallis WA-116-1 (XR944)	D. A. Wallis
	G-ATTD	Cessna 182J	Atlantalia Eurobusiness SL
	G-ATTI	PA-28 Cherokee 140	G-ATTI Flying Group
	G-ATTK	PA-28 Cherokee 140	G-ATTK Flying Group/Southend
	G-ATTM	Jodel DR.250-160	R. W. Tomkinson
	G-ATTN	Piccard HA Balloon ★	Science Museum/South Kensington
	G-ATTR	Bölkow Bö.208C1 Junior	S. Luck
	G-ATTV	PA-28 Cherokee 140	D. B. & M. E. Meeks
	G-ATTX	PA-28 Cherokee 180	IPAC Aviation Ltd
	G-ATUB	PA-28 Cherokee 140	R. H. Partington & M. J. Porter
	G-ATUD	PA-28 Cherokee 140	J. J. Ferguson
	G-ATUF	Cessna F.150F	D. P. Williams
	G-ATUG	D.62B Condor	B. G. Ell
	G-ATUH	Tipsy T.66 Nipper 1	M. D. Barnard & C. Voelger
	G-ATUI	Bölkow Bö.208C1 Junior	M. J. Grundy
	G-ATUL	PA-28 Cherokee 180	Barry Fielding Aviation Ltd
	G-ATVF	DHC.1 Chipmunk 22	Four Counties Fling Club/Syerston
	G-ATVK	PA-28 Cherokee 140	Broadland Flyers Ltd
	G-ATVO	PA-28 Cherokee 140	G. R. Bright
	G-ATVP	Vickers FB.5 Gunbus replica (2345) ★	RAF Museum/Hendon
	G-ATVS	PA-28 Cherokee 180	T. A. Buckley
	G-ATVW	D.62B Condor	G. G. Roberts
	G-ATVX	Bölkow Bö.208C1 Junior	A. V. Hurley & ptnrs
	G-ATWA	Jodel DR.1050	One Twenty Group
	G-ATWB	Jodel D.117	Andrewsfield Whisky Bravo Group
	G-ATWJ	Cessna F.172F	J. P. A. Freeman/Headcorn
	G-ATWR	PA-30 Twin Comanche 160B	Lubair (Transport Services) Ltd/East Midlands
	G-ATXA	PA-22 Tri-Pacer 150	S. Hildrop
	G-ATXD	PA-30 Twin Comanche 160B	P. A. Brook

BRITISH CIVIL REGISTRATIONS

G-ATXJ – G-AVII

Reg	Type	Owner or Operator	Notes
G-ATXJ	HP.137 Jetstream 300 ★	Fire Service training airframe/Cardiff	
G-ATXM	PA-28 Cherokee 180	G-ATXM Flying Group	
G-ATXN	Mitchell-Proctor Kittiwake 1	R. G. Day/Biggin Hill	
G-ATXO	SIPA 903	D. F. Hurn	
G-ATXZ	Bölkow Bö.208C1 Junior	G-ATXZ Group	
G-ATYM	Cessna F.150G	A. J. Cooke	
G-ATYN	Cessna F.150G	J. S. Grant	
G-ATYS	PA-28 Cherokee 180	G-ATYS Flying Group	
G-ATZG	AFB2 gas balloon	S. Cameron	
G-ATZK	PA-28 Cherokee 180	G-ZK Group	
G-ATZM	Piper J-3C-90 Cub	N. D. Marshall	
G-ATZS	Wassmer Wa.41 Super Baladou IV	G-ATZS Flying Group	
G-ATZY	Cessna F.150G	Aircraft Engineers Ltd	
G-AVAK	MS.893A Rallye Commodore 180	W. K. Anderson (stored)/Perth	
G-AVAR	Cessna F.150G	J. A. Rees	
G-AVAW	D.62B Condor	Condor Aircraft Group	
G-AVAX	PA-28 Cherokee 180	J. J. Parkes	
G-AVBG	PA-28 Cherokee 180	M. C. Plomer-Roberts	
G-AVBH	PA-28 Cherokee 180	T. R. Smith (Agricultural Machinery) Ltd	
G-AVBS	PA-28 Cherokee 180	A. G. Arthur	
G-AVBT	PA-28 Cherokee 180	J. F. Mitchell	
G-AVCM	PA-24 Comanche 260	R. F. Smith/Stapleford	
G-AVCV	Cessna 182J Skylane	University of Manchester, School of Earth, Atmospheric and Environmental Sciences	
G-AVDA	Cessna 182K Skylane	F. W. Ellis	
G-AVDF	Beagle Pup 100 ★	Beagle Owners Club	
G-AVDG	Wallis WA-116 Srs 1	K. H. Wallis	
G-AVDS	Beech 65-B80 Queen Air ★	Airport Fire Service/Filton	
G-AVDT	Aeronca 7AC Champion	D. Cheney & G. Moore	
G-AVDV	PA-22 Tri-Pacer 150 (tailwheel)	S. C. Brooks/Slinfold	
G-AVDY	Luton LA-4A Minor	R. Targonski	
G-AVEB	Morane Saulnier MS.230Et2 (157)	T. McG. Leaver	
G-AVEC	Cessna F.172 ★	S. M. Furner	
G-AVEF	Jodel 150	Heavy Install Ltd	
G-AVEH	SIAI-Marchetti S.205	EH Aviation	
G-AVEM	Cessna F.150G	T. D. & J. A. Warren	
G-AVEN	Cessna F.150G	R. A. Lambert	
G-AVEO	Cessna F.150G	M. Howells (G-DENA)	
G-AVER	Cessna F.150G	LAC (Enterprises) Ltd/Barton	
G-AVEU	Wassmer Wa.41 Baladou IV	S. Roberts	
G-AVEX	D.62B Condor	C. A. Macleod	
G-AVEY	Currie Super Wot	B. J. Anning	
G-AVEZ	HPR.7 Herald 210 ★	Rescue trainer/Norwich	
G-AVFB	HS.121 Trident 2E ★	Duxford Aviation Society	
G-AVFE	HS.121 Trident 2E ★	Belfast Airport Authority	
G-AVFH	HS.121 Trident 2E ★	De Havilland Heritage Museum (fuselage only)/London Colney	
G-AVFM	HS.121 Trident 2E ★	Brunel Technical College/Bristol	
G-AVFP	PA-28 Cherokee 140	R. L. Howells/Barton	
G-AVFR	PA-28 Cherokee 140	R. R. Orr	
G-AVFU	PA-32 Cherokee Six 300	Trixstar Farms Ltd	
G-AVFX	PA-28 Cherokee 140	J. Watson	
G-AVFZ	PA-28 Cherokee 140	G-AVFZ Flying Group	
G-AVGA	PA-24 Comanche 260	G. McD. Moir	
G-AVGC	PA-28 Cherokee 140	S. R. Taylor	
G-AVGD	PA-28 Cherokee 140	T. Akeroyd	
G-AVGE	PA-28 Cherokee 140	A. J. Cutler	
G-AVGI	PA-28 Cherokee 140	GI Group/Barton	
G-AVGK	PA-28 Cherokee 180	M. A. Bush	
G-AVGU	Cessna F.150G	Coulson Flying Services Ltd	
G-AVGY	Cessna 182K Skylane	R. M. C. Sears	
G-AVGZ	Jodel DR.1050	D. C. Webb	
G-AVHH	Cessna F.172 ★	The Bristol & Wessex Aeroplane Club	
G-AVHL	Jodel DR.105A	P. J. McMahon	
G-AVHM	Cessna F.150G	W. D. Hill	
G-AVHT	Auster AOP.9 (WZ711)	Seething Jodel Group	
G-AVHY	Fournier RF.4D	I. G. K. Mitchell	
G-AVIA	Cessna F.150G	American Airplane Breakers	
G-AVIB	Cessna F.150G	Far North Aviation	
G-AVIC	Cessna F.172 ★	Leeside Flying Ltd	
G-AVID	Cessna 182K	Jaguar Aviation Ltd	
G-AVII	Agusta-Bell 206A JetRanger	Bristow Helicopters Ltd	

G-AVIL – G-AVRY | BRITISH CIVIL REGISTRATIONS

Notes	Reg	Type	Owner or Operator
	G-AVIL	Alon A.2 Aircoupe (VX147)	D. J. Hulks
	G-AVIN	MS.880B Rallye Club	B. Bunce
	G-AVIP	Brantly B.2B	Ilkeston Contractors
	G-AVIS	Cessna F.172 ★	J. P. A. Freeman
	G-AVIT	Cessna F.150G	P. Cottrell
	G-AVIZ	Scheibe SF.25A Motorfalke	Spilsby Gliding Trust
	G-AVJF	Cessna F.172H	J. A. & G. M. Rees
	G-AVJI	Cessna F.172H ★	Northbrook College/Shoreham
	G-AVJJ	PA-30 Twin Comanche 160B	A. H. Manser
	G-AVJK	Jodel DR.1050/M1	A. A. Robertson & D. S. Spillane
	G-AVJO	Fokker E.III (replica) (422/15)	Flying Aces Movie Aircraft Collection/ Compton Abbas
	G-AVJV	Wallis WA-117 Srs 1	K. H. Wallis (G-ATCV)
	G-AVJW	Wallis WA-118 Srs 2	K. H. Wallis (G-ATPW)
	G-AVKB	Brochet MB.50 Pipistrelle	W. B. Cooper
	G-AVKD	Fournier RF-4D	Lasham RF4 Group
	G-AVKE	Gadfly HDW.1 ★	IHM/Weston-super-Mare
	G-AVKG	Cessna F.172H	A. O. Heskett & S. F. Dowdall
	G-AVKI	Slingsby T.66 Nipper 3	J. M. Greenway
	G-AVKK	Slingsby T.66 Nipper 3	C. Watson
	G-AVKL	PA-30 Twin Comanche 160B	Northbrook College (Sussex)
	G-AVKN	Cessna 401	Law Leasing Ltd
	G-AVKP	Beagle A.109 Airedale	D. R. Williams
	G-AVKR	Bölkow Bö.208C1 Junior	C. H. Morris
	G-AVLB	PA-28 Cherokee 140	M. Wilson
	G-AVLC	PA-28 Cherokee 140	C. M. Tyers
	G-AVLE	PA-28 Cherokee 140	Video Security Services/Tollerton
	G-AVLF	PA-28 Cherokee 140	Woodbine Group
	G-AVLG	PA-28 Cherokee 140	C. H. R. Hewitt
	G-AVLI	PA-28 Cherokee 140	Lima India Group
	G-AVLJ	PA-28 Cherokee 140	Cherokee Aviation Holdings Jersey Ltd
	G-AVLM	Beagle B.121 Pup 3	T. M. & D. A. Jones/Egginton
	G-AVLN	Beagle B.121 Pup 2	Dogs Flying Group
	G-AVLO	Bölkow Bö.208C1 Junior	P. J. Swain
	G-AVLT	PA-28-140 Cherokee	C. Evans and Transcourt Ltd (G-KELC)
	G-AVLW	Fournier RF-4D	J. C. A. C. da Silva
	G-AVLY	Jodel D.120A	M. E. Wills & N. V. de Candole
	G-AVMA	Gardan GY-80 Horizon 180	Z. R. Hildick
	G-AVMB	D.62B Condor	L. J. Dray
	G-AVMD	Cessna 150G	Bagby Aviation Flying Group
	G-AVMF	Cessna F. 150G	J. F. Marsh
	G-AVMJ	BAC One-Eleven 510ED ★	European Aviation Ltd (cabin trainer)
	G-AVMK	BAC One-Eleven 510ED ★	Gravesend College (fuselage only)
	G-AVMO	BAC One-Eleven 510ED ★	Museum of Flight/East Fortune
	G-AVMU	BAC One-Eleven 510ED ★	Duxford Aviation Society
	G-AVNC	Cessna F.150G	J. Turner
	G-AVNE	Westland WS-58 Wessex Mk 60 Srs 1 ★	IHM/Weston-super-Mare
	G-AVNN	PA-28 Cherokee 180	G-AVNN Flying Group
	G-AVNO	PA-28 Cherokee 180	November Oscar Flying Group
	G-AVNS	PA-28 Cherokee 180	J. G. O'Brien
	G-AVNU	PA-28 Cherokee 180	D. Durrant
	G-AVNW	PA-28 Cherokee 180	Len Smith's (Aviation) Ltd
	G-AVNZ	Fournier RF-4D	C. D. Pidler
	G-AVOA	Jodel DR.1050	D. A. Willies/Cranwell
	G-AVOC	CEA Jodel DR.221	Alpha One Flying Group
	G-AVOH	D.62B Condor	Transcourt Ltd
	G-AVOM	CEA Jodel DR.221	Avon Flying Group
	G-AVOO	PA-18 Super Cub 150	Dublin Gliding Club Ltd
	G-AVOZ	PA-28 Cherokee 180	Oscar Zulu Flying Group
	G-AVPD	Jodel D.9 Bébé ★	S. W. McKay (stored)
	G-AVPI	Cessna F.172H	Air-Tech
	G-AVPJ	DH.82A Tiger Moth	C. C. Silk
	G-AVPM	Jodel D.117	J. C. Haynes/Breighton
	G-AVPN	HPR.7 Herald 213 ★	Yorkshire Air Museum/Elvington
	G-AVPO	Hindustan HAL-26 Pushpak	M. B. Johns
	G-AVPV	PA-18 Cherokee 180	K. A. Passmore
	G-AVPY	PA-25 Pawnee 235C	Southdown Gliding Club Ltd
	G-AVRK	PA-28 Cherokee 180	J. Gama & G. Leach
	G-AVRP	PA-28 Cherokee 140	M. Rhodes
	G-AVRS	Gardan GY-80 Horizon 180	N. M. Robbins
	G-AVRU	PA-28-Cherokee 180	Lanpro
	G-AVRW	Gardan GY-20 Minicab	Kestrel Flying Group/Tollerton
	G-AVRY	PA-28 Cherokee 180	Brigfast Ltd/Blackbushe

32

BRITISH CIVIL REGISTRATIONS
G-AVRZ – G-AWAX

Reg	Type	Owner or Operator	Notes
G-AVRZ	PA-28 Cherokee 180	Mantavia Group Ltd	
G-AVSA	PA-28 Cherokee 180	G-AVSA Flying Group/Barton	
G-AVSB	PA-28 Cherokee 180	D. L. Macdonald	
G-AVSC	PA-28 Cherokee 180	G-AVSC Syndicate	
G-AVSD	PA-28 Cherokee 180	C. B. D. Owen	
G-AVSE	PA-28 Cherokee 180	F. Glendon/Ireland	
G-AVSF	PA-28 Cherokee 180	Monday Club/Blackbushe	
G-AVSI	PA-28 Cherokee 140	G-AVSI Flying Group	
G-AVSP	PA-28 Cherokee 180	Airways Flight Training (Exeter) Ltd	
G-AVSR	Beagle D.5/180 Husky	G. R. Greenfield & S. D. J. Holwill	
G-AVSZ	Agusta-Bell 206B JetRanger	R. P. Harper	
G-AVTC	Slingsby Nipper T.66 RA.45 Srs 3	C. Baldwin	
G-AVTP	Cessna F.172H	Tango Papa Group/White Waltham	
G-AVTT	Ercoupe 415D	Wright's Farm Eggs Ltd/Andrewsfield	
G-AVTV	MS.893A Rallye Commodore	P. Storey	
G-AVUD	PA-30 Twin Comanche 160B	P. M. Fox	
G-AVUG	Cessna F.150H	Skyways Flying Group	
G-AVUH	Cessna F.150H	A. G. McLaren	
G-AVUS	PA-28 Cherokee 140	D. J. Hunter	
G-AVUT	PA-28 Cherokee 140	Bencray Ltd/Blackpool	
G-AVUU	PA-28 Cherokee 140	A. Jahanfar & ptnrs/Southend	
G-AVUZ	PA-32 Cherokee Six 300	Ceesix Ltd/Jersey	
G-AVVC	Cessna F.172H	Babs Flying Group	
G-AVVE	Cessna F.150H ★	R. Windley (stored)	
G-AVVJ	MS.893A Rallye Commodore	M. Powell	
G-AVVL	Cessna F.150H	A. L. Hather	
G-AVVO	Avro 652A Anson 19 (VL348) ★	Newark Air Museum	
G-AVWA	PA-28 Cherokee 140	SFG Ltd	
G-AVWD	PA-28 Cherokee 140	Evelyn Air	
G-AVWI	PA-28 Cherokee 140	L. M. Veitch	
G-AVWJ	PA-28 Cherokee 140	A. C. M. Harrhy	
G-AVWL	PA-28 Cherokee 140	S.H. & C.L. Maynard	
G-AVWM	PA-28 Cherokee 140	P. E. Preston & ptnrs/Southend	
G-AVWN	PA-28R Cherokee Arrow 180	Vawn Air Ltd/Jersey	
G-AVWO	PA-28R Cherokee Arrow 180	I. P. Scobell	
G-AVWR	PA-28R Cherokee Arrow 180	S. J. French & ptnrs/Dunkeswell	
G-AVWT	PA-28R Cherokee Arrow 180	Cloudbase Aviation Ltd/Barton	
G-AVWU	PA-28R Cherokee Arrow 180	A. M. Alam/Elstree	
G-AVWV	PA-28R Cherokee Arrow 180	Strathtay Flying Group	
G-AVWY	Fournier RF-4D	P. Turner	
G-AVXA	PA-25 Pawnee 235	S. Wales Gliding Club Ltd/Usk	
G-AVXD	Slingsby T.66 Nipper 3	Tayside Nipper Group	
G-AVXF	PA-28R Cherokee Arrow 180	G-AVXF Group	
G-AVXW	D.62B Condor	J. M. Alexander	
G-AVXY	Auster AOP.9	G. J. Siddall	
G-AVXZ	PA-28 Cherokee 140 ★	ATC Hayle (instructional airframe)	
G-AVYB	HS.121 Trident 1E-140 ★	SAS training airframe/Hereford	
G-AVYK	Beagle A.61 Terrier 3	R. Burgun	
G-AVYL	PA-28 Cherokee 180	G-AVYL Flying Group	
G-AVYM	PA-28 Cherokee 180	Carlisle Aviation (1985) Ltd/Crosby	
G-AVYR	PA-28 Cherokee 140	SAS Flying Group/Thruxton	
G-AVYS	PA-28R Cherokee Arrow 180	Musicbank Ltd	
G-AVYT	PA-28R Cherokee Arrow 180	J. R. Tindale	
G-AVYV	Jodel D.120	A. J. Sephton	
G-AVZB	Aero Z-37 Cmelak ★	Science Museum/Wroughton	
G-AVZI	Bölkow Bö.208C1 Junior	C. F. Rogers	
G-AVZM	Beagle B.121 Pup 1	ARAZ Group/Elstree	
G-AVZN	Beagle B.121 Pup 1	Shipdham Aviators Flying Group	
G-AVZO	Beagle B.121 Pup 1 ★	Thamesside Aviation Museum/East Tilbury	
G-AVZP	Beagle B.121 Pup 1	T. A. White/Bagby	
G-AVZR	PA-28 Cherokee 180	Lincoln Aero Club Ltd/Sturgate	
G-AVZU	Cessna F.150H	R. D. Forster	
G-AVZV	Cessna F.172H	E. L. King. & D. S. Lightbown/Crosland Moor	
G-AVZW	EAA Biplane Model P	R. G. Maidment & G. R. Edmundson/Goodwood	
G-AVZX	MS.880B Rallye Club	J. Nugent	
G-AWAA	MS.880B Rallye Club ★	P. A. Cairns (stored)/St. Just	
G-AWAC	Gardan GY-80 Horizon 180	P. B. Hodgson	
G-AWAJ	Beech 95-D55 Baron	Aflex Hose Ltd	
G-AWAT	D.62B Condor	Cumbernauld Flyers/Cumbernauld	
G-AWAU	Vickers FB.27A Vimy (replica) (F8614) ★	RAF Museum/Hendon	
G-AWAW	Cessna F.150F ★	Science Museum/South Kensington	
G-AWAX	Cessna 150D	J. Haunch	

G-AWAZ – G-AWLA BRITISH CIVIL REGISTRATIONS

Notes	Reg	Type	Owner or Operator
	G-AWAZ	PA-28R Cherokee Arrow 180	P. J. Manders t/a G-AWAZ Flying Group
	G-AWBA	PA-28R Cherokee Arrow 180	March Flying Group/Stapleford
	G-AWBB	PA-28R Cherokee Arrow 180	D. L. Claydon
	G-AWBC	PA-28R Cherokee Arrow 180	Anglo Aviation (UK) Ltd
	G-AWBE	PA-28 Cherokee 140	B. E. Boyle
	G-AWBG	PA-28 Cherokee 140	B. Patrick
	G-AWBH	PA-28 Cherokee 140	Mainstreet Aviation
	G-AWBJ	Fournier RF-4D	J. M. Adams
	G-AWBM	D.31 Turbulent	A. D. Pratt
	G-AWBN	PA-30 Twin Comanche 160B	Stourfield Investments Ltd/Jersey
	G-AWBS	PA-28 Cherokee 140	M. A. English & T. M. Brown
	G-AWBT	PA-30 Twin Comanche 160B ★	Instructional airframe/Cranfield
	G-AWBU	Morane-Saulnier N (replica) (MS824)	Flying Aces Movie Aircraft Collection/Compton Abbas
	G-AWBW	Cessna F.172H ★	Brunel Technical College/Bristol
	G-AWBX	Cessna F.150H	J. Meddings/Tatenhill
	G-AWCM	Cessna F.150H	R. Garbett
	G-AWCN	Cessna FR.172E	B. & C. Stobart-Hook
	G-AWCP	Cessna F.150H (tailwheel)	C. E. Mason/Shobdon
	G-AWDA	Slingsby T.66 Nipper 3	J. A. Cheeseborough
	G-AWDI	PA-23 Aztec 250C ★	Queens Head/Willington, Beds
	G-AWDO	D.31 Turbulent	R. N. Crosland
	G-AWDP	PA-28 Cherokee 180	B. H. & P. M. Illston/Shipdham
	G-AWDR	Cessna FR.172E	B. A. Wallace
	G-AWDU	Brantly B.2B	B. M. Freeman
	G-AWEF	SNCAN Stampe SV.4B	RAF Buchanan
	G-AWEI	D.62B Condor	A. M. Noble
	G-AWEK	Fournier RF-4D	P. Barrett
	G-AWEL	Fournier RF-4D	A. B. Clymo/Halfpenny Green
	G-AWEM	Fournier RF-4D	B. J. Griffin/Wickenby
	G-AWEP	Barritault JB-01 Minicab	A. Louth
	G-AWES	Cessna 150H	D. W. Vincent
	G-AWEV	PA-28 Cherokee 140	Norflight Ltd
	G-AWEX	PA-28 Cherokee 140	Sir W. G. Armstrong Whitworth Flying Group/Coventry
	G-AWEZ	PA-28R Cherokee Arrow 180	T. R. Leighton & ptnrs
	G-AWFB	PA-28R Cherokee Arrow 180	J. C. Luke/Filton
	G-AWFC	PA-28R Cherokee Arrow 180	B. J. Hines
	G-AWFD	PA-28R Cherokee Arrow 180	D. J. Hill
	G-AWFF	Cessna F.150H	S. Eustace
	G-AWFJ	PA-28R Cherokee Arrow 180	Parplon Ltd
	G-AWFN	D.62B Condor	P. B. Lowry
	G-AWFO	D.62B Condor	T. A. Major
	G-AWFP	D.62B Condor	Blackbushe Flying Club
	G-AWFT	Jodel D.9 Bébé	W. H. Cole
	G-AWFW	Jodel D.117	C. J. Rodwell
	G-AWFZ	Beech A23 Musketeer ★	Bob Crowe Aircraft Sales Ltd/Cranfield
	G-AWGA	Beagle A.109 Airedale ★	(stored)/Sevenoaks
	G-AWGD	Cessna F.172H	R. P. Vincent
	G-AWGJ	Cessna F.172H	J. & C. J. Freeman/Headcorn
	G-AWGK	Cessna F.150H	G. E. Allen
	G-AWGN	Fournier RF-4D	G-AWGN Group
	G-AWGZ	Taylor JT.1 Monoplane	R. L. Sambell
	G-AWHB	CASA 2-111D (6J+PR) ★	Aces High Ltd/North Weald
	G-AWHX	Rollason Beta B.2	S. G. Jones
	G-AWHY	Falconar F.11-3	Why Fly Group (G-BDPB)
	G-AWIF	Brookland Mosquito 2	C. A. Reeves/Gloucester
	G-AWII	VS.349 Spitfire VC (AR501)	The Shuttleworth Collection/Old Warden
	G-AWIP	Luton LA-4A Minor	J. Houghton
	G-AWIR	Midget Mustang	K. E. Sword/Leicester
	G-AWIT	PA-28 Cherokee 180	Cherry Orchard Aparthotel Ltd
	G-AWIV	Airmark TSR.3	F. R. Hutchings
	G-AWIW	SNCAN Stampe SV.4B	R. E. Mitchell/Sleap
	G-AWJE	Slingsby T.66 Nipper 3	K G. G. Howe/Barton
	G-AWJV	DH.98 Mosquito TT Mk 35 (TA634) ★	De Havilland Heritage Museum/London Colney
	G-AWJX	Zlin Z.526 Trener Master	P. A. Colman
	G-AWJY	Zlin Z.526 Trener Master	M. Gainza
	G-AWKD	PA-17 Vagabond	A. T. & M. R. Dowie/White Waltham
	G-AWKO	Beagle B.121 Pup 1	S. E. Ford
	G-AWKP	Jodel DR.253	G-AWKP Group
	G-AWKT	MS.880B Rallye Club	A. Ringland & P. Keating
	G-AWKX	Beech A65 Queen Air ★	(Instructional airframe)/Shoreham
	G-AWLA	Cessna F.150H	Bagby Aviation

BRITISH CIVIL REGISTRATIONS — G-AWLF – G-AWWE

Reg	Type	Owner or Operator	Notes
G-AWLF	Cessna F.172H	Gannet Aviation	
G-AWLG	SIPA 903	S. W. Markham	
G-AWLI	PA-22 Tri-Pacer 150	J. S. Lewery/Shoreham	
G-AWLO	Boeing Stearman E75	N. D. Pickard/Shoreham	
G-AWLP	Mooney M.20F	I. C. Lomax	
G-AWLR	Slingsby T.66 Nipper 3	T. D. Reid	
G-AWLS	Slingsby T.66 Nipper 3	G. A. Dunster & B. Gallagher	
G-AWLX	Auster 5 J/2 Arrow	W. J. Taylor	
G-AWLZ	Fournier RF-4D	Nympsfield RF-4 Group	
G-AWMD	Jodel D.11	G. P. Jewell	
G-AWMF	PA-18 Super Cub 150 (modified)	Booker Gliding Club Ltd	
G-AWMI	Glos-Airtourer 115	M. Furse/Cardiff/Wales	
G-AWMM	MS.893A Rallye Commodore 180	D. P. & S. White	
G-AWMN	Luton LA-4A Minor	B. J. Douglas	
G-AWMP	Cessna F.172H	R. J. D. Blois	
G-AWMR	D.31 Turbulent	M. J. Freeman	
G-AWMT	Cessna F.150H	Strategic Synergies Ltd	
G-AWMZ	Cessna F.172H ★	Parachute jump trainer/Cark	
G-AWNT	BN-2A Islander	Sterling Helicopters Ltd/Norwich	
G-AWOA	MS.880B Rallye Club	Britannia Flying Group	
G-AWOE	Aero Commander 680E	J. M. Houlder/Elstree	
G-AWOF	PA-15 Vagabond	C. M. Hicks/Barton	
G-AWOH	PA-17 Vagabond	A. Lovejoy & K. Downes	
G-AWOT	Cessna F.150H	M. J. Willoughby	
G-AWOU	Cessna 170B	S. Billington/Denham	
G-AWOX	Westland WS-58 Wessex 60 (150225) ★	Paintball Adventure West/Bristol	
G-AWPH	P.56 Provost T.1	J. A. D. Bradshaw	
G-AWPJ	Cessna F.150H	W. J. Greenfield	
G-AWPN	Shield Xyla	P. N. Stacey	
G-AWPS	PA-28 Cherokee 140	A. R. Matthews	
G-AWPU	Cessna F.150J	LAC (Enterprises) Ltd/Barton	
G-AWPW	PA-12 Super Cruiser	AK Leasing (Jersey) Ltd	
G-AWPY	Bensen B.8M	J. Jordan	
G-AWPZ	Andreasson BA-4B	J. M. Vening	
G-AWRK	Cessna F.150J	Systemroute Ltd/Shoreham	
G-AWRP	Cierva Rotorcraft ★	IHM/Weston-super-Mare	
G-AWRS	Avro 19 Srs. 2 (TX213) ★	North East Aircraft Museum/Usworth	
G-AWRY	P.56 Provost T.1 (XF836)	A. J. House	
G-AWSA	Avro 652A Anson 19 (VL349) ★	Norfolk & Suffolk Aviation Museum/Flixton	
G-AWSH	Zlin Z.526 Trener Master	Avia Special Ltd	
G-AWSL	PA-28 Cherokee 180D	Fascia Services Ltd/Southend	
G-AWSM	PA-28 Cherokee 235	Aviation Projects	
G-AWSN	D.62B Condor	M. K. A. Blyth	
G-AWSP	D.62B Condor	R. Q. & A. S. Bond/Wellesbourne	
G-AWSS	D.62A Condor	N. J. & D. Butler	
G-AWST	D.62B Condor	T. P. Lowe	
G-AWSV	Skeeter 12 (XM553)	Maj. M. Somerton-Rayner/Middle Wallop	
G-AWSW	Beagle D.5/180 Husky (XW635)	Windmill Aviation/Spanhoe	
G-AWTJ	Cessna F.150J	P. J. Jameson	
G-AWTL	PA-28 Cherokee 180D	I. R. Chaplin	
G-AWTS	Beech A.23 Musketeer	Cinque Ports Flying Group Ltd	
G-AWTV	Beech 19A Musketeer Sport	J. Whittaker	
G-AWTX	Cessna F.150J	R. D. Forster	
G-AWUB	Gardan GY-201 Minicab	R. A. Hand	
G-AWUE	Jodel DR.1050	K. W. Wood & F. M. Watson	
G-AWUG	Cessna F.150H	Aircraft Engineers Ltd	
G-AWUJ	Cessna F.150H	S. R. Hughes	
G-AWUL	Cessna F.150H	A. J. Baron	
G-AWUN	Cessna F.150H	E. C. Shimmin	
G-AWUO	Cessna F.150H	Uniform Oscar Flying Group	
G-AWUT	Cessna F.150J	B. F. Spafford	
G-AWUU	Cessna F.150J	G-AWUU Flying Group	
G-AWUX	Cessna F.172H	G-AWUX Group/St.Just	
G-AWUZ	Cessna F.172H	I. R. Judge	
G-AWVA	Cessna F.172H	Barton Air Ltd	
G-AWVB	Jodel D.117	H. Davies	
G-AWVC	Beagle B.121 Pup 1	J. J. West/Sturgate	
G-AWWE	Jodel DR.1050/M1	E. A. Taylor/Southend	
G-AWVF	P.56 Provost T.1 (XF877)	J. H. Powell-Tuck	
G-AWVG	AESL Airtourer T.2	C. J. Schofield	
G-AWVN	Aeronca 7AC Champion	Champ Flying Group	
G-AWVZ	Jodel D.112	D. C. Stokes	
G-AWWE	Beagle B.121 Pup 2	J. M. Randle/Coventry	

35

G-AWWI – G-AXIE | BRITISH CIVIL REGISTRATIONS

Notes	Reg	Type	Owner or Operator
	G-AWWI	Jodel D.117	W. J. Evans
	G-AWWM	Gardan GY-201 Minicab	P. J. Brayshaw
	G-AWWN	Jodel DR.1051	R. A. J. Hurst
	G-AWWP	Aerosport Woody Pusher III	M. S. Bird & R. D. Bird
	G-AWWU	Cessna FR.172F	Westward Airways (Lands End) Ltd
	G-AWXR	PA-28 Cherokee 180D	Aero Club de Portugal
	G-AWXS	PA-28 Cherokee 180D	J. A. Hardiman/Shobdon
	G-AWXY	MS.885 Super Rallye	K. Henderson/Hibaldstow
	G-AWXZ	SNCAN Stampe SV.4C	Bianchi Aviation Film Services Ltd
	G-AWYB	Cessna FR.172F	J. R. Sharpe/Southend
	G-AWYJ	Beagle B.121 Pup 2	H. C. Taylor
	G-AWYL	Jodel DR.253B	K. Gillham
	G-AWYO	Beagle B.121 Pup 1	B. R. C. Wild/Popham
	G-AWYX	MS.880B Rallye Club	M. J. Edwards/Henstridge
	G-AWYY	Slingsby T.57 Camel replica (B6401) ★	F.A.A. Museum/Yeovilton
	G-AWZI	HS.121 Trident 3B ★	A. Lee/FAST Museum (nose only)/Farnborough
	G-AWZJ	HS.121 Trident 3B ★	Dumfries & Galloway Museum
	G-AWZK	HS.121 Trident 3B ★	Trident Preservation Society/Manchester
	G-AWZM	HS.121 Trident 3B ★	Science Museum/Wroughton
	G-AWZP	HS.121 Trident 3B ★	Manchester Museum of Science & Industry (nose only)
	G-AWZX	HS.121 Trident 3B ★	BAA Airport Fire Services/Gatwick
	G-AXAB	PA-28 Cherokee 140	Bencray Ltd/Blackpool
	G-AXAN	DH.82A Tiger Moth (EM720)	Leading Edge Marketing Ltd
	G-AXAS	Wallis WA-116T	K. H. Wallis (G-AVDH)
	G-AXAT	Jodel D.117A	P. S. Wilkinson
	G-AXBF	Beagle D.5/180 Husky	J. H. Powell-Tuck
	G-AXBH	Cessna F.172H	D. F. Ranger
	G-AXBJ	Cessna F.172H	BJ Flying Group/Leicester
	G-AXBW	DH.82A Tiger Moth (T5879:RUC-W)	Hunter Wing Ltd/Bournemouth
	G-AXBZ	DH.82A Tiger Moth	W. J. de Jong Cleyndert
	G-AXCA	PA-28R Cherokee Arrow 200	W. H. Nelson
	G-AXCG	Jodel D.117	Charlie Golf Group/Andrewsfield
	G-AXCI	Bensen B.8M	N. Martin (stored)
	G-AXCM	MS.880B Rallye Club	D. C. Manifold
	G-AXCX	Beagle B.121 Pup 2	L. A. Pink
	G-AXCY	Jodel D.117A	R. S. Marom
	G-AXCZ	SNCAN Stampe SV.4C	J. Price
	G-AXDC	PA-23 Aztec 250D	N. J. Lilley
	G-AXDI	Cessna F.172H	M. F. & J. R. Leusby/Conington
	G-AXDK	Jodel DR.315	Delta Kilo Flying Group/Sywell
	G-AXDN	BAC-Sud Concorde 01 ★	Duxford Aviation Society
	G-AXDV	Beagle B.121 Pup 1	T. A. White/Bagby
	G-AXDW	Beagle B.121 Pup 1	Cranfield Delta Whisky Group
	G-AXDY	Falconar F-11	J. Nunn
	G-AXDZ	Cassutt Racer IIIM	A. Chadwick/Little Staughton
	G-AXEB	Cassutt Racer IIIM	G. E. Horder/Redhill
	G-AXED	PA-25 Pawnee 235	Wolds Gliding Club Ltd/Pocklington
	G-AXEH	B.125 Bulldog 1 ★	Museum of Flight/East Fortune
	G-AXEI	Ward Gnome ★	Real Aeroplane Club/Breighton
	G-AXEO	Scheibe SF.25B Falke	The Borders (Milfield) Gliding Club Ltd
	G-AXEV	Beagle B.121 Pup 2	D. S. Russell & D. G. Benson
	G-AXFG	Cessna 337D	County Garage (Cheltenham) Ltd
	G-AXFN	Jodel D.119	B. M. Jackson
	G-AXGE	MS.880B Rallye Club	R. P. Loxton
	G-AXGG	Cessna F.150J	A. J. Simpson & I. Coughlan
	G-AXGP	Piper J-3C-90 Cub	L. J. Brinkley
	G-AXGR	Luton LA-4A Minor	B. A. Schlussler
	G-AXGS	D.62B Condor	G-AXGS Condor Group
	G-AXGV	D.62B Condor	R. J. Wrixon
	G-AXGZ	D.62B Condor	A. J. Cooper
	G-AXHA	Cessna 337A	I. M. Latiff
	G-AXHC	SNCAN Stampe SV.4C	D. L. Webley
	G-AXHE	BN-2A Islander ★	Parachute jump trainer/Strathallan
	G-AXHO	Beagle B.121 Pup 2	L. W. Grundy/Stapleford
	G-AXHP	Piper J-3C-65 Cub (480636:A-58)	Witham (Specialist) Vehicles Ltd
	G-AXHR	Piper J-3C-65 Cub (329601:D-44)	K. B. Raven & E. Cundy
	G-AXHS	MS.880B Rallye Club	B. & A. Swales
	G-AXHT	MS.880B Rallye Club	P. M. Murray
	G-AXHV	Jodel D.117A	Derwent Flying Group/Hucknall
	G-AXIA	Beagle B.121 Pup 1	P. S. Shuttleworth
	G-AXIE	Beagle B.121 Pup 2	J. P. Thomas

BRITISH CIVIL REGISTRATIONS

G-AXIF – G-AXTP

Reg	Type	Owner or Operator	Notes
G-AXIF	Beagle B.121 Pup 2	J. R. Faulkner	
G-AXIG	Scottish Aviation B.125 Bulldog 104	A. A. A. Hamilton	
G-AXIO	PA-28 Cherokee 140B	T. Akeroyd	
G-AXIR	PA-28 Cherokee 140B	R. W. Howard	
G-AXIW	Scheibe SF.25B Falke	M. Pedley	
G-AXIX	Glos-Airtourer 150	J. C. Wood	
G-AXJB	Omega 84 balloon	Southern Balloon Group	
G-AXJH	Beagle B.121 Pup 2	The Henry Flying Group	
G-AXJI	Beagle B.121 Pup 2	J. J. Sanders	
G-AXJJ	Beagle B.121 Pup 2	M. L. Jones & ptnrs	
G-AXJO	Beagle B.121 Pup 2	J. A. D. Bradshaw	
G-AXJR	Scheibe SF.25B Falke	Falke Syndicate	
G-AXJV	PA-28 Cherokee 140B	British Disabled Flying Association	
G-AXJX	PA-28 Cherokee 140B	Patrolwatch Ltd/Sleap	
G-AXKH	Luton LA-4A Minor	M. E. Vaisey	
G-AXKJ	Jodel D.9	L. B. Roberts	
G-AXKO	Westland-Bell 47G-4A	M. Gallagher	
G-AXKS	Westland Bell 47G-4A ★	Museum of Army Flying/Middle Wallop	
G-AXKW	Westland-Bell 47G-4A	Eyre Spier Associates Ltd	
G-AXKX	Westland Bell 47G-4A	South Yorkshire Aviation Ltd	
G-AXLG	Cessna 310K	C. Koscso	
G-AXLI	Slingsby T.66 Nipper 3	D. & M. Shrimpton	
G-AXLS	Jodel DR.105A	Axle Flying Club	
G-AXLZ	PA-18 Super Cub 95	R. J. Quantrell	
G-AXMA	PA-24 Comanche 180	J. A. & S. M. Fletcher	
G-AXMD	Omega O-56 balloon ★	British Balloon Museum/Newbury	
G-AXMN	Auster J/5B Autocar	C. D. Wilkinson	
G-AXMT	Bücker Bü 133 Jungmeister	R. A. Fleming/Breighton	
G-AXMW	Beagle B.121 Pup 1	DJP Engineering (Knebworth) Ltd	
G-AXMX	Beagle B.121 Pup 2	Susan A. Jones/Cannes	
G-AXNJ	Wassmer Jodel D.120	Clive Flying Group/Sleap	
G-AXNM	Beagle B.121 Pup 1	J. K. Jensen	
G-AXNN	Beagle B.121 Pup 2	Gabrielle Aviation Ltd/Shoreham	
G-AXNP	Beagle B.121 Pup 2	J. W. Ellis & R. J. Hemmings	
G-AXNR	Beagle B.121 Pup 2	The November Romeo Group	
G-AXNS	Beagle B.121 Pup 2	Derwent Aero Group/Gamston	
G-AXNW	SNCAN Stampe SV.4C	C. S. Grace	
G-AXNX	Cessna 182M	H. A. Harper	
G-AXNZ	Pitts S.1C Special	C. D. Baglin	
G-AXOG	PA-E23 Aztec 250D	G. H. Nolan	
G-AXOH	MS.894 Rallye Minerva	T. A. D. Crook	
G-AXOJ	Beagle B.121 Pup 2	Pup Flying Group	
G-AXOR	PA-28 Cherokee 180D	Oscar Romeo Aviation Ltd	
G-AXOS	MS.894A Rallye Minerva	J D. Pasternak	
G-AXOT	MS.893 Rallye Commodore 180	P. Evans	
G-AXOZ	Beagle B.121 Pup 1	R. J. Ogborn/Liverpool	
G-AXPA	Beagle B.121 Pup 1	Papa-Alpha Group	
G-AXPB	Beagle B.121 Pup 1	M. J. K. Seary & R. T. Austin	
G-AXPC	Beagle B.121 Pup 2	T. A. White/Bagby	
G-AXPF	Cessna F.150K	D. R. Marks/Denham	
G-AXPG	Mignet HM.293	W. H. Cole (stored)	
G-AXPM	Beagle B.121 Pup 1	S. C. Stanton	
G-AXPN	Beagle B.121 Pup 2	A. Richardson	
G-AXPZ	Campbell Cricket	W. R. Partridge	
G-AXRC	Campbell Cricket	L. R. Morris	
G-AXRK	Practavia Pilot Sprite 115 ★	M. Oliver	
G-AXRP	SNCAN Stampe SV.4A	Skysport Engineering/Hatch (G-BLOL)	
G-AXRR	Auster AOP.9 (XR241)	R. B. Webber	
G-AXRT	Cessna FA.150K (tailwheel)	C. C. Walley	
G-AXSC	Beagle B.121 Pup 1	R. J. MacCarthy/Swansea	
G-AXSD	Beagle B.121 Pup 1	AURS Aviation Ltd	
G-AXSF	Nash Petrel	Nash Aircraft Ltd/Lasham	
G-AXSG	PA-28 Cherokee 180	The Tago Island Co Ltd	
G-AXSI	Cessna F.172H	R. Collins (G-SNIP)	
G-AXSM	Jodel DR.1051	T. R. G. Barnby & M. S. Regendanz	
G-AXSW	Cessna FA.150K	R. Mitchell	
G-AXSZ	PA-28 Cherokee 140B	White Wings Flying Group/White Waltham	
G-AXTA	PA-28 Cherokee 140B	G-AXTA Aircraft Group	
G-AXTC	PA-28 Cherokee 140B	G-AXTC Group	
G-AXTJ	PA-28 Cherokee 140B	K. Patel/Elstree	
G-AXTL	PA-28 Cherokee 140B	Pegasus Aviation (Midlands) Ltd	
G-AXTO	PA-24 Comanche 260	J. L. Wright	
G-AXTP	PA-28 Cherokee 180	M. Whyte/Ireland	

37

G-AXTX – G-AYFA — BRITISH CIVIL REGISTRATIONS

Notes	Reg	Type	Owner or Operator
	G-AXTX	Jodel D.112	C. Sawford
	G-AXUA	Beagle B.121 Pup 1	P. Wood
	G-AXUB	BN-2A Islander	Headcorn Parachute Club Ltd
	G-AXUC	PA-12 Super Cruiser	J. J. Bunton
	G-AXUF	Cessna FA.150K	W. B. Bateson/Blackpool
	G-AXUJ	Auster J/1 Autocrat	P. Gill (G-OSTA)
	G-AXUK	Jodel DR.1050	Downland Flying Group
	G-AXUM	HP.137 Jetstream 1 ★	Sodeteg Formation/France
	G-AXUW	Cessna FA.150K	Coventry Air Training School
	G-AXVB	Cessna F.172H	R. & J. Turner
	G-AXVK	Campbell Cricket	B. Jones
	G-AXVM	Campbell Cricket	D. M. Organ
	G-AXVN	McCandless M.4	W. R. Partridge
	G-AXWA	Auster AOP.9 (XN437)	C. M. Edwards
	G-AXWT	Jodel D.11	R. C. Owen
	G-AXWV	Jodel DR.253	R. Friedlander & D. C. Ray
	G-AXWZ	PA-28R Cherokee Arrow 200	P. Walkley
	G-AXXC	CP.301B Emeraude	Emy Group
	G-AXXV	DH.82A Tiger Moth (DE992)	C. N. Wookey
	G-AXXW	Jodel D.117	D. F. Chamberlain & M. A. Hughes
	G-AXYK	Taylor JT.1 Monoplane	G. D. Bailey
	G-AXYU	Jodel D.9 Bébé	P. Turton & H. C. Peake-Jones
	G-AXZD	PA-28 Cherokee 180E	G. M. Whitmore
	G-AXZF	PA-28 Cherokee 180E	E. P. C. & W. R. Rabson/Southampton
	G-AXZK	BN-2A-26 Islander	B-N Group Ltd
	G-AXZM	Slingsby T.66 Nipper 3	G. R. Harlow
	G-AXZO	Cessna 180	Bourne Park Flyers
	G-AXZP	PA-E23 Aztec 250D	D. M. Harbottle
	G-AXZT	Jodel D.117	P. Guest
	G-AXZU	Cessna 182N	British Skysports
	G-AYAB	PA-28 Cherokee 180E	J. R. Green
	G-AYAC	PA-28R Cherokee Arrow 200	Fersfield Flying Group
	G-AYAJ	Cameron O-84 balloon	E. T. Hall
	G-AYAL	Omega 56 balloon ★	British Balloon Museum/Newbury
	G-AYAN	Slingsby Motor Cadet III	D. C. Pattison
	G-AYAR	PA-28 Cherokee 180E	A. Jahanfar/Southend
	G-AYAT	PA-28 Cherokee 180E	G-AYAT Flying Group
	G-AYAW	PA-28 Cherokee 180E	G-AYAW Group
	G-AYBD	Cessna F.150K	Apollo Aviation Advisory Ltd/Shoreham
	G-AYBG	Scheibe SF.25B Falke	H. H. T. Wolf
	G-AYBO	PA-23 Aztec 250D	A. G. Gutknecht/Austria
	G-AYBP	Jodel D.112	G. J. Langston
	G-AYBR	Jodel D.112	I. S. Parker
	G-AYCC	Campbell Cricket	D. J. M. Charity
	G-AYCE	CP.301C Emeraude	S. D. Glover
	G-AYCF	Cessna FA.150K	E. J. Atkins/Popham
	G-AYCG	SNCAN Stampe SV.4C	N. Bignall/Booker
	G-AYCJ	Cessna TP.206D	White Knuckle Airways Ltd
	G-AYCK	AIA Stampe SV.4C	The Real Flying Co Ltd/Shoreham (G-BUNT)
	G-AYCN	Piper J-3C-65 Cub	W. R. & B. M. Young
	G-AYCO	CEA DR.360	Charlie Oscar Club
	G-AYCP	Jodel D.112	Charlie Papa Group
	G-AYCT	Cessna F.172H	P. A. & J. Rose
	G-AYDI	DH.82A Tiger Moth	R. B. Woods & ptnrs
	G-AYDR	SNCAN Stampe SV.4C	A. J. McLuskie
	G-AYDV	Coates SA.II-1 Swalesong	D. F. Coates
	G-AYDW	Beagle A.61 Terrier 2	A. S. Topen
	G-AYDX	Beagle A.61 Terrier 2	R. A. Kirby/Barton
	G-AYDY	Luton LA-4A Minor	J. Dible/Ireland
	G-AYDZ	Jodel DR.200	Zero One Group
	G-AYEB	Jodel D.112	P. Goring
	G-AYEC	CP.301A Emeraude	Redwing Flying Group
	G-AYEE	PA-28 Cherokee 180E	Demero Ltd & Transcourt Ltd
	G-AYEF	PA-28 Cherokee 180E	G-AYEF Group/Barton
	G-AYEG	Falconar F-9	A. L. Smith
	G-AYEH	Jodel DR.1050	John Scott Jodel Group
	G-AYEJ	Jodel DR.1050	J. M. Newbold
	G-AYEN	Piper J-3C-65 Cub	P. Warde & C. F. Morris
	G-AYET	MS.892A Rallye Commodore 150	A. T. R. Bingley
	G-AYEV	Jodel DR.1050	L. G. Evans/Headcorn
	G-AYEW	Jodel DR.1051	J. M. Gale & J. R. Hope
	G-AYFA	SA Twin Pioneer Srs 3 ★	Solway Aviation Society/Carlisle

BRITISH CIVIL REGISTRATIONS — G-AYFC – G-AYRG

Reg	Type	Owner or Operator	Notes
G-AYFC	D.62B Condor	A. R. Chadwick/Breighton	
G-AYFD	D.62B Condor	B. G. Manning	
G-AYFF	D.62B Condor	I. Macleod & A. W. Maycock	
G-AYFG	D.62C Condor	W. A. Braim	
G-AYFJ	MS.880B Rallye Club	Rallye FJ Group	
G-AYFP	Jodel D.140	J. J. L. Giradot	
G-AYFV	Crosby BA-4B	A. R. C. Mathie/Norwich	
G-AYGA	Jodel D.117	M. F. Sedgwick	
G-AYGB	Cessna 310Q ★	Instructional airframe/Perth	
G-AYGC	Cessna F.150K	Alpha Aviation Group/Barton	
G-AYGD	Jodel DR.1051	J. F. M. Barlett & J. P. Liber	
G-AYGE	SNCAN Stampe SV.4C	L. J. Proudfoot & ptnrs/Booker	
G-AYGG	Jodel D.120	J. M. Dean	
G-AYGX	Cessna FR.172G	Reims Rocket Group/Barton	
G-AYHA	AA-1 Yankee	S. J. Carr	
G-AYHX	Jodel D.117A	L. J. E. Goldfinch	
G-AYIA	Hughes 369HS ★	G. D. E. Bilton/Sywell	
G-AYIG	PA-28 Cherokee 140C	S. Empson	
G-AYII	PA-28R Cherokee Arrow 200	Double India Group/Exeter	
G-AYIJ	SNCAN Stampe SV.4B	T. C. Beadle/Headcorn	
G-AYIM	HS.748 Srs 2A	PTB (Emerald) Pty Ltd/Blackpool	
G-AYIT	DH.82A Tiger Moth	Ulster Tiger Group/Newtownards	
G-AYJA	Jodel DR.1050	G. Connell	
G-AYJB	SNCAN Stampe SV.4C	F. J. M. & J. P. Esson/Middle Wallop	
G-AYJD	Alpavia-Fournier RF-3	I. O. Bull	
G-AYJP	PA-28 Cherokee 140C	RAF Brize Norton Flying Club Ltd	
G-AYJR	PA-28 Cherokee 140C	Holdcroft Aviation Services Ltd	
G-AYJW	Cessna FR.172G	Sir W. G. Armstrong-Whitworth Flying Group	
G-AYJY	Isaacs Fury II	M. Austin	
G-AYKD	Jodel DR.1050	I. M. D. L. Weston	
G-AYKJ	Jodel D.117A	R. J. Hughes	
G-AYKK	Jodel D.117	J. M. Whitham	
G-AYKS	Leopoldoff L.7 Colibri	W. B. Cooper	
G-AYKT	Jodel D.117	D. I. Walker	
G-AYKW	PA-28 Cherokee 140C	S. P. Rooney & D. Griffiths	
G-AYKZ	SAI KZ-8	R. E. Mitchell/Cosford	
G-AYLA	Glos-Airtourer 115	D. S. P. Disney	
G-AYLC	Jodel DR.1051	E. W. B. Trollope	
G-AYLF	Jodel DR.1051 (modified)	Sicile Flying	
G-AYLL	Jodel DR.1050	C. Joly	
G-AYLP	AA-1 Yankee	D. Nairn	
G-AYLV	Jodel D.120	M. R. Henham	
G-AYLZ	SPP Super Aero 45 Srs 04	M. J. Cobb	
G-AYME	Fournier RF-5	R. D. Goodger & C. J. Norman	
G-AYMK	PA-28 Cherokee 140C	Piper Flying Group/Newcastle	
G-AYMO	PA-23 Aztec 250C	J. A. D. Richardson	
G-AYMP	Currie Wot	R. C. Hibberd	
G-AYMR	Lederlin 380L	P. J. Brayshaw	
G-AYMU	Jodel D.112	M. R. Baker	
G-AYMV	Western 20 balloon	R. G. Turnbull	
G-AYNA	Phoenix Currie Wot	J. James	
G-AYND	Cessna 310Q	Source Group Ltd/Bournemouth	
G-AYNF	PA-28 Cherokee 140C	BW Aviation Ltd	
G-AYNJ	PA-28 Cherokee 140C	R. H. Ribbons	
G-AYNN	Cessna 185B	Bencray Ltd/Blackpool	
G-AYNP	Westland WS-55 Whirlwind Srs 3 ★	IHM/Weston-super-Mare	
G-AYOW	Cessna 182N Skylane	D. W. & S. E. Suttill	
G-AYOY	Sikorsky S-61N Mk 2	British International	
G-AYOZ	Cessna FA.150L	S. A. Hughes	
G-AYPE	MBB Bö.209 Monsun	Papa Echo Ltd/Biggin Hill	
G-AYPG	Cessna F.177RG	D. P. McDermott	
G-AYPH	Cessna F.177RG	M. R. & K. E. Slack	
G-AYPJ	PA-28 Cherokee 180	R. B. Petrie	
G-AYPM	PA-18 Super Cub 95	R. Horner	
G-AYPO	PA-18 Super Cub 95	A. W. Knowles	
G-AYPR	PA-18 Super Cub 95	R. G. Manton	
G-AYPS	PA-18 Super Cub 95	R. J. Hamlett & ptnrs	
G-AYPT	PA-18 Super Cub 95	T. F. Lyddon & R. G. Brooks	
G-AYPU	PA-28R Cherokee Arrow 200	Monalto Investments Ltd	
G-AYPV	PA-28 Cherokee 140D	Ashley Gardner Flying Club Ltd	
G-AYPZ	Campbell Cricket	A. Melody	
G-AYRF	Cessna F.150L	D. T. A. Rees	
G-AYRG	Cessna F.172K	J. H. Mitchell	

G-AYRH – G-AZCN   BRITISH CIVIL REGISTRATIONS

Notes	Reg	Type	Owner or Operator
	G-AYRH	MS.892A Rallye Commodore 150	S. O'Ceallaigh & J. Barry
	G-AYRI	PA-28R Cherokee Arrow 200	A. E. Thompson & J. C. Houdret
	G-AYRM	PA-28 Cherokee 140D	M. J. Saggers/Biggin Hill
	G-AYRO	Cessna FA.150L Aerobat	Fat Boys Flying Club
	G-AYRS	Jodel D.120A	L. R. H. D'Eath
	G-AYRT	Cessna F.172K	P. E. Crees
	G-AYRU	BN-2A-6 Islander	Skydive Aircraft Ltd/Netheravon
	G-AYSB	PA-30 Twin Comanche 160C	N. J. Goff
	G-AYSD	Slingsby T.61A Falke	P. W. Hextall
	G-AYSH	Taylor JT.1 Monoplane	C. J. Lodge
	G-AYSX	Cessna F.177RG	A. P. R. Dean
	G-AYSY	Cessna F.177RG	S. A. Tuer
	G-AYTA	SOCATA MS.880B Rallye Club ★	Manchester Museum of Science & Industry
	G-AYTR	CP301A Emeraude	Croft Farm Flying Group
	G-AYTT	Phoenix PM-3 Duet	R. B. Webber & J. K. Houlgrave
	G-AYTV	MJ.2A Tempete	Shoestring Flying Group
	G-AYUA	Auster AOP.9 (XK416)	De Havilland Aviation Ltd/Swansea
	G-AYUB	CEA DR.253B	Rothwell Group
	G-AYUH	PA-28 Cherokee 180F	Broadland Flying Group Ltd
	G-AYUJ	Evans VP-1	T. N. Howard
	G-AYUM	Slingsby T.61A Falke	M. H. Simms
	G-AYUN	Slingsby T.61A Falke	G-AYUN Group
	G-AYUP	Slingsby T.61A Falke	P. R. Williams
	G-AYUR	Slingsby T.61A Falke	R. Hanningan & R. Lingard
	G-AYUS	Taylor JT.1 Monoplane	S. P. Collins
	G-AYUT	Jodel DR.1050	M. L. Robinson
	G-AYUV	Cessna F.172H	Justgold Ltd
	G-AYVO	Wallis WA-120 Srs 1	K. H. Wallis
	G-AYVP	Woody Pusher	J. R. Wraight
	G-AYVT	Brochet MB.84 ★	Dunelm Flying Group (stored)
	G-AYWA	Avro 19 Srs 2 ★	N. K. Geddes
	G-AYWD	Cessna 182N	Wild Dreams Group
	G-AYWE	PA-28 Cherokee 140	Intelcomm (UK) Ltd
	G-AYWH	Jodel D.117A	D. Kynaston/Cambridge
	G-AYWM	Glos-Airtourer Super 150	The Star Flying Group/Staverton
	G-AYWT	AIA Stampe SV.4C	R. A. Palmer
	G-AYXP	Jodel D.117A	G. N. Davies
	G-AYXS	SIAI-Marchetti S205-18R	P. J. Bloore & J. M. Biles
	G-AYXT	WS-55 Whirlwind Srs 2 (XK940:911) ★	IHM/Weston-super-Mare
	G-AYXU	Champion 7KCAB Citabria	Les Wallen Manufacturing Ltd
	G-AYYK	Slingsby T.61A Falke	Cornish Gliding & Flying Club Ltd/Perranporth
	G-AYYL	Slingsby T.61A Falke	C. Wood
	G-AYYO	Jodel DR.1050/M1	Bustard Flying Club Ltd
	G-AYYT	Jodel DR.1050/M1	Yankee Tango Group
	G-AYYU	Beech C23 Musketeer	G-AYYU Group
	G-AYYW	BN-2A-21 Islander	Secretary of State for Foreign & Commonwealth Affairs
	G-AYYX	MS.880B Ralle Club	J. G. MacDonald
	G-AYZE	PA-39 Twin Comanche 160 C/R	J. E. Palmer/Staverton
	G-AYZH	Taylor JT.2 Titch	T. D. Gardner/Wolverhampton
	G-AYZI	SNCAN Stampe SV.4C	D. M. & P. A. Fenton
	G-AYZJ	Westland WS-55 Whirlwind HAS.7 ★	Newark Air Museum (XM685)
	G-AYZK	Jodel DR.1050/M1	D. G. Hesketh
	G-AYZS	D.62B Condor	M. N. Thrush
	G-AYZU	Slingsby T.61A Falke	A. J. Harpley
	G-AYZW	Slingsby T.61A Falke	Y-ZW Group
	G-AZAB	PA-30 Twin Comanche 160B	Bickertons Aerodromes Ltd
	G-AZAJ	PA-28R Cherokee Arrow 200B	J. McHugh & P. Woulfe/Stapleford
	G-AZAW	Gardan GY-80 Horizon 160	J. W. Foley
	G-AZAZ	Bensen B.8M ★	F.A.A. Museum/Yeovilton
	G-AZBB	MBB Bö.209 Monsun 160FV	G. N. Richardson/Staverton
	G-AZBE	Glos-Airtourer Super 150	BE Flying Group/Staverton
	G-AZBI	Jodel 150	F. M. Ward
	G-AZBL	Jodel D.9 Bébé	J. Hill
	G-AZBN	Noorduyn AT-16 Harvard IIB (FT391)	Swaygate Ltd/Shoreham
	G-AZBU	Auster AOP9 (XR246)	Auster Nine Group
	G-AZBY	Westland WS-58 Wessex 60 Srs 1 ★	IHM/Weston-super-Mare
	G-AZBZ	Westland WS-58 Wessex 60 Srs 1 ★	IHM/Weston-super-Mare
	G-AZCB	SNCAN Stampe SV.4C	M. L. Martin
	G-AZCK	Beagle B.121 Pup 2	D. R. Newell
	G-AZCL	Beagle B.121 Pup 2	J. J. Watts & D. Fletcher
	G-AZCN	Beagle B.121 Pup 2	D. M. Callaghan & ptnrs

BRITISH CIVIL REGISTRATIONS

G-AZCP – G-AZLY

Reg	Type	Owner or Operator	Notes
G-AZCP	Beagle B.121 Pup 1	T. J. Watson/Elstree	
G-AZCT	Beagle B.121 Pup 1	J. Coleman	
G-AZCU	Beagle B.121 Pup 1	A. A. Harris/Shobdon	
G-AZCV	Beagle B.121 Pup 2	N. R. W. Long/Elstree	
G-AZCZ	Beagle B.121 Pup 2	L. & J. M. Northover/Cardiff-Wales	
G-AZDA	Beagle B.121 Pup 1	B. D. Deubelbeiss	
G-AZDD	MBB Bö.209 Monsun 150FF	Double Delta Flying Group/Elstree	
G-AZDE	PA-28R Cherokee Arrow 200B	C. Wilson	
G-AZDG	Beagle B.121 Pup 2	D. J. Sage & J. R. Heaps	
G-AZDJ	PA-32 Cherokee Six 300	K. J. Mansbridge & D. C. Gibbs	
G-AZDX	PA-28 Cherokee 180F	M. Cowan	
G-AZDY	DH.82A Tiger Moth	J. B. Mills	
G-AZEE	MS.880B Rallye Club	J. Shelton	
G-AZEF	Jodel D.120	D. Street	
G-AZEG	PA-28 Cherokee 140D	Ashley Gardner Flying Club Ltd	
G-AZET	S.A. Bulldog Srs. 100/101	P. S. Shuttleworth	
G-AZEU	Beagle B.121 Pup 2	G. M. Moir/Egginton	
G-AZEV	Beagle B.121 Pup 2	C. J. Partridge	
G-AZEW	Beagle B.121 Pup 2	Dukeries	
G-AZEY	Beagle B.121 Pup 2	M. E. Reynolds	
G-AZFA	Beagle B.121 Pup 2	J. Smith/Sandown	
G-AZFC	PA-28 Cherokee 140D	WLS Flying Group	
G-AZFF	Jodel D.112	J. Bolger/Ireland	
G-AZFI	PA-28R Cherokee Arrow 200B	G-AZFI Ltd/Sherburn	
G-AZFM	PA-28R Cherokee Arrow 200B	P. J. Jenness	
G-AZFR	Cessna 401B	Harding Wragg/Blackpool	
G-AZGA	Jodel D.120	A. F. Vizoso	
G-AZGE	SNCAN Stampe SV.4A	M. R. L. Astor/Booker	
G-AZGF	Beagle B.121 Pup 2	K. Singh/Barton	
G-AZGJ	MS.880B Rallye Club	P. Rose	
G-AZGL	MS.894A Rallye Minerva	The Cambridge Aero Club Ltd	
G-AZGY	CP.301B Emeraude	R. H. Braithwaite	
G-AZGZ	DH.82A Tiger Moth (NM181)	R. J. King	
G-AZHB	Robin HR.100/200B	P. Fenwick	
G-AZHC	Jodel D.112	Aerodel Flying Group/Netherthorpe	
G-AZHD	Slingsby T.61A Falke	R. J. Shallcrass	
G-AZHE	Slingsby T.61B Falke	M. R. Shelton/Tatenhill	
G-AZHH	SA 102.5 Cavalier	D. W. Buckle	
G-AZHI	Glos-Airtourer Super 150	Flying Grasshoppers Ltd	
G-AZHJ	SA Twin Pioneer Srs 3 ★	Air Atlantique Ltd/Coventry	
G-AZHK	Robin HR.100/200B	D. J. Sage (G-ILEG)	
G-AZHR	Piccard Ax6 balloon	C. Fisher	
G-AZHT	AESL Airtourer (modified)	Aviation West Ltd/Glasgow	
G-AZHU	Luton LA-4A Minor	W. Cawrey/Netherthorpe	
G-AZHX	S.A. Bulldog Srs. 100/101	R. D. Garretson	
G-AZIB	ST-10 Diplomate	W. B. Bateson/Blackpool	
G-AZID	Cessna FA.150L	Aerobat Ltd	
G-AZII	Jodel D.117A	J. S. Brayshaw	
G-AZIJ	Jodel DR.360	F. M. Carter	
G-AZIK	PA-34-200 Seneca II	Walkbury Aviation Ltd	
G-AZIL	Slingsby T.61A Falke	D. W. Savage/Portmoak	
G-AZIO	SNCAN Stampe SV.4C (Lycoming) ★	–/Booker	
G-AZIP	Cameron O-65 balloon	Dante Balloon Group	
G-AZJC	Fournier RF-5	W. St. G. V. Stoney/Italy	
G-AZJE	Ord-Hume JB-01 Minicab	J. B. Evans/Sandown	
G-AZJN	Robin DR.300/140	J. F. Wright	
G-AZJV	Cessna F.172L	G-AZJV Flying Group	
G-AZJY	Cessna FRA.150L	P. J. McCartney/Barton	
G-AZKC	MS.880B Rallye Club	L. J. Martin/Redhill	
G-AZKE	MS.880B Rallye Club	D. A. Thompson & J. D. Headlam/Germany	
G-AZKK	Cameron O-56 balloon	Gemini Balloon Group Gemini	
G-AZKO	Cessna F.337F	Willpower Garage Ltd	
G-AZKP	Jodel D.117	A. M. & J. L. Moar	
G-AZKR	PA-24 Comanche 180	J. Van Der Kwast	
G-AZKS	AA-1A Trainer	M. D. Henson	
G-AZKW	Cessna F.172L	J. C. C. Wright	
G-AZKZ	Cessna F.172L	R. D. & E. Forster/Swanton Morley	
G-AZLE	Boeing N2S-5 Kaydet (1102:102)	A. E. Paulson	
G-AZLF	Jodel D.120	M. S. C. Ball	
G-AZLH	Cessna F.150L	L. Papatheocharis & I. Buck	
G-AZLN	PA-28 Cherokee 180F	Liteflite Ltd/Kidlington	
G-AZLV	Cessna 172K	G-AZLV Flying Group	
G-AZLY	Cessna F.150L	S. Roberts	

G-AZMC – G-AZYD — BRITISH CIVIL REGISTRATIONS

Notes	Reg	Type	Owner or Operator
	G-AZMC	Slingsby T.61A Falke	G-AZMC Group
	G-AZMD	Slingsby T.61C Falke	R. A. Rice/Wellesbourne
	G-AZMJ	AA-5 Traveler	W. R. Partridge
	G-AZMN	Glos-Airtourer T.5	W. Crozier & I. Young
	G-AZMX	PA-28 Cherokee 140 ★	NE Wales Institute of Higher Education (Instructional airframe)/Flintshire
	G-AZMZ	MS.893A Rallye Commodore 150	D. R. Wilcox
	G-AZNK	SNCAN Stampe SV.4A	November Kilo Group
	G-AZNL	PA-28R Cherokee Arrow 200D	B. P. Liversidge
	G-AZNO	Cessna 182P	A. I. Bird
	G-AZOA	MBB Bö.209 Monsun 150FF	M. W. Hurst
	G-AZOB	MBB Bö.209 Monsun 150FF	G. N. Richardson/Staverton
	G-AZOE	Glos-Airtourer 115	G-AZOE 607 Group/Newcastle
	G-AZOF	Glos-Airtourer Super 150	Cirrus Flying Group/Denham
	G-AZOG	PA-28R Cherokee Arrow 200D	Southend Flying Club
	G-AZOL	PA-34-200 Seneca II	Stapleford Flying Club Ltd
	G-AZOS	Jurca MJ.5-H1 Sirocco	P. J. Tanulak
	G-AZOT	PA-34-200 Seneca II	M. Soojeri
	G-AZOU	Jodel DR.1050	Horsham Flying Group/Slinfold
	G-AZOZ	Cessna FRA.150L	Seawing Flying Club Ltd/Southend
	G-AZPA	PA-25 Pawnee 235	Black Mountains Gliding Club Ltd/Talgarth
	G-AZPC	Slingsby T.61C Falke	The Surrey Hills Gliding Club Ltd/Kenley
	G-AZPF	Fournier RF-5	R. Pye/Blackpool
	G-AZPH	Craft-Pitts S-1S Special ★	Science Museum/South Kensington
	G-AZPV	Luton LA-4A Minor	J. R. Faulkner
	G-AZRA	MBB Bö.209 Monsun 150FF	Alpha Flying Ltd/Denham
	G-AZRD	Cessna 401B	Romeo Delta Group
	G-AZRH	PA-28 Cherokee 140D	Trust Flying Group
	G-AZRK	Fournier RF-5	A. B. Clymo & J. F. Rogers
	G-AZRL	PA-18 Super Cub 95	B. J. Stead
	G-AZRM	Fournier RF-5	Romeo Mike Group
	G-AZRN	Cameron O-84 balloon	C. J. Desmet/Belgium
	G-AZRP	Glos-Airtourer 115	B. F. Strawford/Shobdon
	G-AZRS	PA-22 Tri-Pacer 150	R. H. Hulls
	G-AZSA	Cessna U.206F	Hinton Skydiving Centre Ltd
	G-AZSA	Stampe et Renard SV.4B	M. R. Dolman
	G-AZSC	Noorduyn AT-16 Harvard IIB (43:SC)	Goodwood Road Racing Co Ltd
	G-AZSF	PA-28R Cherokee Arrow 200D	Wellesbourne Aviation
	G-AZSW	Beagle B.121 Pup 1	G. Brinkley
	G-AZTA	MBB Bö.209 Monsun 150FF	A. J. Court
	G-AZTF	Cessna F.177RG	R. Burgun
	G-AZTK	Cessna F.172F	S. O'Ceallaigh
	G-AZTS	Cessna F.172L	C. E. Stringer
	G-AZTV	Stolp SA.500 Starlet	G. R. Rowland
	G-AZTW	Cessna F.177RG	I. M. Richmond
	G-AZUM	Cessna F.172L	Fowlmere Flyers
	G-AZUP	Cameron O-65 balloon	R. S. Bailey & A. B. Simpson
	G-AZUT	MS.893A Rallye Commodore 180	J. Palethorpe
	G-AZUV	Cameron O-65 balloon ★	British Balloon Museum/Newbury
	G-AZUY	Cessna E.310L	W. B. Bateson/Blackpool
	G-AZUZ	Cessna FRA.150L	D. J. Parker/Netherthorpe
	G-AZVA	MBB Bö.209 Monsun 150FF	C. Elder
	G-AZVB	MBB Bö.209 Monsun 150FF	E. & P. M. L. Cliffe
	G-AZVF	MS.894A Rallye Minerva	Minerva Flying Group
	G-AZVG	AA-5 Traveler	G-AZVG Group
	G-AZVH	MS.894A Rallye Minerva	P. L. Jubb
	G-AZVI	MS.892A Rallye Commodore	G. C. Jarvis
	G-AZVJ	PA-34-200 Seneca II	Andrews Professional Colour Laboratories Ltd/Lydd
	G-AZVL	Jodel D.119	S. P. Collins
	G-AZVP	Cessna F.177RG	C. R. Brown
	G-AZWB	PA-28 Cherokee 140	B. N. Rides & L. Connor
	G-AZWD	PA-28 Cherokee 140	M. Jeffries
	G-AZWF	SAN Jodel DR.1050	Cawdor Flying Group
	G-AZWS	PA-28R Cherokee Arrow 180	Arrow 88 Flying Group
	G-AZWT	Westland Lysander IIIA (V9367)	The Shuttleworth Collection/Old Warden
	G-AZWY	PA-24 Comanche 260	Keymer Son & Co Ltd/Biggin Hill
	G-AZXB	Cameron O-65 balloon	R. J. Mitchener & P. F. Smart
	G-AZXD	Cessna F.172L	R. J. R. Williams & D. Palmer
	G-AZXG	PA-23 Aztec 250D ★	Instructional airframe/Cranfield
	G-AZYA	Gardan GY-80 Horizon 160	R. G. Whyte
	G-AZYB	Bell 47H-1 ★	IHM/Weston-super-Mare
	G-AZYD	MS.893A Rallye Commodore	Staffordshire Gliding Club Ltd

BRITISH CIVIL REGISTRATIONS — G-AZYF – G-BAHE

Reg	Type	Owner or Operator	Notes
G-AZYF	PA-28-180 Cherokee D	AZYF Group	
G-AZYS	CP301C-1 Emeraude	C. G. Ferguson & D. Drew	
G-AZYU	PA-23 Aztec 250E	L. J. Martin/Biggin Hill	
G-AZYY	Slingsby T.61A Falke	J. A. Towers	
G-AZYZ	Wassmer Wa.51A Pacific	C. R. Buxton/France	
G-AZZH	Practavia Pilot Sprite	A. Moore	
G-AZZO	PA-28 Cherokee 140	R. J. Hind/Elstree	
G-AZZR	Cessna F.150L	A. J. Hobbs	
G-AZZS	PA-34-200 Seneca II	Robin Cook Aviation/Shoreham	
G-AZZT	PA-28 Cherokee 180 ★	Ground instruction airframe/Cranfield	
G-AZZV	Cessna F.172L	Zentelligence Ltd	
G-AZZZ	DH.82A Tiger Moth	S. W. McKay	
G-BAAD	Evans Super VP-1	Breighton VP-1 Group	
G-BAAF	Manning-Flanders MF1 (replica)	Aviation Film Services Ltd/Booker	
G-BAAI	MS.893A Rallye Commodore	R. D. Taylor/Thruxton	
G-BAAT	Cessna 182P	T. E. Earl	
G-BAAW	Jodel D.119	Alpha Whiskey Flying Group	
G-BABC	Cessna F.150L	G. R. Bright	
G-BABD	Cessna FRA.150L (modified)	Anglia Flight	
G-BABE	Taylor JT.2 Titch	M. Bonsall/Netherthorpe	
G-BABG	PA-28 Cherokee 180	Mendip Flying Group/Bristol	
G-BABH	Cessna F.150L	D. B. Ryder & Co Ltd	
G-BABK	PA-34-200 Seneca II	D. F. J. Flashman/Biggin Hill	
G-BACB	PA-34-200 Seneca II	Milbrooke Motors	
G-BACE	Fournier RF-5	G-BACE Fournier Group	
G-BACJ	Jodel D.120	Wearside Flying Association/Newcastle	
G-BACL	Jodel 150	M. L. Sargeant/Biggin Hill	
G-BACN	Cessna FRA.150L	F. Bundy	
G-BACO	Cessna FRA.150L	M. A. McLoughlin	
G-BACP	Cessna FRA.150L	M. Markwick	
G-BADC	Rollason Beta B.2A	D. H. Greenwood	
G-BADH	Slingsby T.61A Falke	A. P. Askwith	
G-BADJ	PA-E23 Aztec 250E	C. Papadakis	
G-BADM	D.62B Condor	D. J. Wilson	
G-BADV	Brochet MB50	W. B. Cooper	
G-BADW	Pitts S-2A Special	R. E. Mitchell/Cosford	
G-BAEB	Robin DR.400/160	R. Hatton	
G-BAEE	Jodel DR.1050/M1	R. Little	
G-BAEM	Robin DR.400/125	M. A. Webb/Booker	
G-BAEN	Robin DR.400/180	European Soaring Club Ltd	
G-BAEO	Cessna F.172M	L. W. Scattergood	
G-BAEP	Cessna FRA.150L (modified)	A. M. Lynn	
G-BAER	Cosmic Wind	R. S. Voice/Redhill	
G-BAET	Piper J-3C-65 Cub	C. J. Rees	
G-BAEU	Cessna F.150L	L. W. Scattergood	
G-BAEV	Cessna FRA.L150L	T. J. Richardson	
G-BAEW	Cessna F.172M ★	Westley Aircraft/Cranfield	
G-BAEY	Cessna F.172M	Skytrax Aviation Ltd	
G-BAEZ	Cessna FRA.150L	Donair Flying Club Ltd/East Midlands	
G-BAFA	AA-5 Traveler	C. F. Mackley/Stapleford	
G-BAFG	DH.82A Tiger Moth	Meinl Capital Markets Ltd	
G-BAFL	Cessna 182P	M. Langhammer	
G-BAFP	Robin DR.400/160	M. W. Bodger & M. H. Hoffmann	
G-BAFT	PA-18 Super Cub 150	T. J. Wilkinson/Riseley	
G-BAFU	PA-28 Cherokee 140	D. Matthews	
G-BAFV	PA-18 Super Cub 95	T. F. & S. J. Thorpe	
G-BAFW	PA-28 Cherokee 140	R. D. Masters	
G-BAFX	Robin DR.400/140	R. Foster	
G-BAGB	SIAI-Marchetti SF.260	British Midland Airways Ltd/East Midlands	
G-BAGC	Robin DR.400/140	W. P. Nutt	
G-BAGE	Cessna T.210L ★	Aeroplane Collection Ltd	
G-BAGF	Jodel D.92 Bébé	E. Evans	
G-BAGG	PA-32 Cherokee Six 300E	Channel Islands Aero Club (Jersey) Ltd	
G-BAGN	Cessna F.177RG	R. W. J. Andrews	
G-BAGR	Robin DR.400/140	J. D. Last	
G-BAGS	Robin DR.400/180 2+2	M. Whale & M. W. A. Lunn	
G-BAGT	Helio H.295 Courier	B. J. C. Woodall Ltd	
G-BAGV	Cessna U.206F	Scottish Parachute Club/Strathallan	
G-BAGX	PA-28 Cherokee 140	Golf X-Ray Group	
G-BAGY	Cameron O-84 balloon	P. G. Dunnington	
G-BAHD	Cessna 182P Skylane	Lambley Flying Group	
G-BAHE	PA-28 Cherokee 140	M. W. Kilvert & A. O. Jones	

43

G-BAHF – G-BAPL   BRITISH CIVIL REGISTRATIONS

Notes	Reg	Type	Owner or Operator
	G-BAHF	PA-28 Cherokee 140	BJ Services (Midlands) Ltd
	G-BAHH	Wallis WA-121	K. H. Wallis
	G-BAHI	Cessna F.150H	MJP Aviation & Sales
	G-BAHJ	PA-24 Comanche 250	K. Cooper
	G-BAHL	Robin DR.400/160	J. B. McVeighty
	G-BAHO	Beech C.23 Sundowner	C. K. Drake
	G-BAHP	Volmer VJ.22 Sportsman	Seaplane Group
	G-BAHS	PA-28R Cherokee Arrow 200-II	A. R. N. Morris
	G-BAHX	Cessna 182P	Dupost Group
	G-BAIG	PA-34-200-2 Seneca	Mid-Anglia School of Flying
	G-BAIH	PA-28R Cherokee Arrow 200-II	M. G. West
	G-BAII	Cessna FRA.150L	Cornwall Flying Club Ltd/Bodmin
	G-BAIK	Cessna F.150L	Wickenby Aviation
	G-BAIP	Cessna F.150L	G. & S. A. Jones
	G-BAIS	Cessna F.177RG	Cardinal Syndicate
	G-BAIW	Cessna F.172M	W. J. Greenfield/Humberside
	G-BAIX	Cessna F.172M	R. A. Nichols/Elstree
	G-BAIZ	Slingsby T.61A Falke	Falke Syndicate/Hinton-in-the-Hedges
	G-BAJA	Cessna F.177RG	D. W. Ward
	G-BAJB	Cessna F.177RG	LDJ Ltd
	G-BAJC	Evans VP-1	S. J. Greer
	G-BAJE	Cessna 177	Juliet Echo Group
	G-BAJN	AA-5 Traveler	J. M. Cuddy
	G-BAJO	AA-5 Traveler	Montgomery Aviation Ltd
	G-BAJR	PA-28 Cherokee 180	Belfast Flying Club Ltd
	G-BAJY	Robin DR.400/180	L. J. Murray
	G-BAJZ	Robin DR.400/125	Rochester Aviation Ltd
	G-BAKD	PA-34-200 Seneca II	Andrews Professional Colour Laboratories/Elstree
	G-BAKH	PA-28 Cherokee 140	Keen Leasing (IOM) Ltd
	G-BAKJ	PA-30 Twin Comanche 160B	G. D. Colover & ptnrs
	G-BAKK	Cessna F.172H ★	Parachute jump trainer/Hinton-in-the-Hedges
	G-BAKM	Robin DR.400/140	D. V. Pieri
	G-BAKN	SNCAN Stampe SV.4C	M. Holloway
	G-BAKR	Jodel D.117	R. W. Brown
	G-BAKV	PA-18 Super Cub 150	Western Air (Thruxton) Ltd & F. Taylor
	G-BAKW	Beagle B.121 Pup 2	H. Beavan
	G-BAKY	Slingsby T.61C Falke	Buckminster Gliding Club Ltd/Saltby
	G-BALF	Robin DR.400/140	G. & D. A. Wasey
	G-BALG	Robin DR.400/180	R. Jones
	G-BALH	Robin DR.400/140B	G-BALH Flying Group
	G-BALI	Robin DR.400 2+2	A. Brinkley
	G-BALJ	Robin DR.400/180	D. A. Bett & D. de Lacey-Rowe
	G-BALN	Cessna T.310Q	O'Brien Properties Ltd/Shoreham
	G-BALZ	Bell 212	Bristow Helicopters Ltd
	G-BAMB	Slingsby T.61C Falke	Flying Group G-BAMB
	G-BAMC	Cessna F.150L	K. Evans
	G-BAMJ	Cessna 182P	A. E. Kedros
	G-BAMK	Cameron D-96 airship ★	British Balloon Museum
	G-BAMM	PA-28 Cherokee 235	Group 235
	G-BAMR	PA-16 Clipper	H. Royce
	G-BAMS	Robin DR.400/160	G-BAMS Ltd/Headcorn
	G-BAMT	CEA DR400/160	S. G. Jones
	G-BAMU	Robin DR.400/160	The Alternative Flying Group
	G-BAMV	Robin DR.400/180	K. Jones & E. A. Anderson/Booker
	G-BAMY	PA-28R Cherokee Arrow 200-II	S. R. Pool
	G-BANA	Robin DR.221	G. T. Pryor
	G-BANB	Robin DR.400/180	D. R. L. Jones
	G-BANC	Gardan GY-201 Minicab	C. R. Shipley
	G-BANU	Wassmer Jodel D.120	W. M. & C. H. Kilner
	G-BANV	Phoenix Currie Wot	K. Knight
	G-BANW	CP.1330 Super Emeraude	P. S. Milner
	G-BANX	Cessna F.172M	Oakfleet 2000 Ltd
	G-BAOB	Cessna F.172M	S. O. Smith & R. H. Taylor/Andrewsfield
	G-BAOH	MS.880B Rallye Club	A. P. Swain
	G-BAOJ	MS.880B Rallye Club	R. E. Jones
	G-BAOM	MS.880B Rallye Club	P. J. D. Feehan
	G-BAOP	Cessna FRA.150L	R. D. Forster
	G-BAOS	Cessna F.172M	Wingtask 1995 Ltd
	G-BAOU	AA-5 Traveler	R. C. Mark
	G-BAPB	DHC.1 Chipmunk 22	G. V. Bunyan
	G-BAPI	Cessna FRA.150L	Marketing Management Services Ltd
	G-BAPJ	Cessna FRA.150L	M. D. Page/Manston
	G-BAPL	PA-23 Turbo Aztec 250E	Donington Aviation Ltd/East Midlands

BRITISH CIVIL REGISTRATIONS — G-BAPR – G-BBCC

Reg	Type	Owner or Operator	Notes
G-BAPR	Jodel D.11	J. B. Liber & J. F. M. Bartlett	
G-BAPS	Campbell Cougar ★	IHM/Weston-super-Mare	
G-BAPV	Robin DR.400/160	J. D. & M. Millne/Newcastle	
G-BAPW	PA-28R Cherokee Arrow 180	A.G. Bourne & M. W. Freeman	
G-BAPX	Robin DR.400/160	G-BAPX Group	
G-BAPY	Robin HR.100/210	G-BAPY Group	
G-BARC	Cessna FR.172J	Severn Valley Aviation Group	
G-BARF	Jodel D.112 Club	J. J. Penney	
G-BARG	Cessna E.310Q	IT Factor Ltd	
G-BARH	Beech C.23 Sundowner	G. Moorby & J. Hinchcliffe	
G-BARN	Taylor JT.2 Titch	R. G. W. Newton	
G-BARP	Bell 206B JetRanger 2	Western Power Distribution (South West) PLC	
G-BARS	DHC.1 Chipmunk 22 (1377)	J. Beattie/Yeovilton	
G-BARV	Cessna 310Q	Old England Watches Ltd/Elstree	
G-BARZ	Scheibe SF.28A Tandem Falke	K. Kiely	
G-BASH	AA-5 Traveler	BASH Flying Group	
G-BASJ	PA-28 Cherokee 180	Bristol Aero Club/Filton	
G-BASL	PA-28 Cherokee 140	Justgold Ltd	
G-BASM	PA-34-200 Seneca II	M. Gipps	
G-BASN	Beech C.23 Sundowner	O. M. O'Neill	
G-BASO	Lake LA-4 Amphibian	C. J. A. Macauley	
G-BASP	Beagle B.121 Pup 1	B. J. Coutts/Sywell	
G-BATC	MBB Bö.105D	Bond Air Services/Aberdeen	
G-BATJ	Jodel D.119	D. J. & K. S. Thomas	
G-BATN	PA-23 Aztec 250E	Marshall of Cambridge Ltd	
G-BATR	PA-34-200 Seneca II	Falcon Flying Services/Biggin Hill	
G-BATV	PA-28 Cherokee 180D	J. N. Rudsdale	
G-BATW	PA-28 Cherokee 140	C. D. Sainsbury	
G-BAUC	PA-25 Pawnee 235	Southdown Gliding Club Ltd/Parham Park	
G-BAUH	Jodel D.112	G. A. & D. Shepherd	
G-BAUZ	SNCAN NC.854S	W. A. Ashley & D. Horne	
G-BAVB	Cessna F.172M	T. S. Sheridan-McGinnitty	
G-BAVH	DHC.1 Chipmunk 22	Portsmouth Naval Gliding Club/Lee-on-Solent	
G-BAVL	PA-23 Aztec 250E	S. P. & A. V. Chillott	
G-BAVO	Boeing Stearman N2S (26)	(stored)	
G-BAVR	AA-5 Traveler	G. E. Murray	
G-BAWG	PA-28R Cherokee Arrow 200-II	Solent Air Ltd	
G-BAWK	PA-28 Cherokee 140	Northumbria Flying School Ltd	
G-BAWR	Robin HR.100/210	T. Taylor	
G-BAXE	Hughes 269A	Reethorpe Engineering Ltd	
G-BAXJ	PA-32 Cherokee Six 300B	UK Parachute Services/Stirling	
G-BAXK	Thunder Ax7-77 balloon ★	A. R. Snook	
G-DAXS	Bell 47G-5	RK Helicopters	
G-BAXU	Cessna F.150L	M. W. Sheppardson	
G-BAXV	Cessna F.150L	G. & S. A. Jones	
G-BAXY	Cessna F.172M	Eaglesoar Ltd	
G-BAXZ	PA-28 Cherokee 140	G-BAXZ (87) Syndicate	
G-BAYL	SNCAN Nord 1101 Norecrin ★	(stored)/Chirk	
G-BAYO	Cessna 150L	Messrs Rees of Poyston West	
G-BAYP	Cessna 150L	Yankee Papa Flying Group	
G-BAYR	Robin HR.100/210	P. D. Harries	
G-BAYV	SNCAN 1101 Noralpha (3+) ★	Macclesfield Historical Aviation Society/Barton	
G-BAZC	Robin DR.400/160	Southern Sailplanes Ltd/Membury	
G-BAZJ	HPR.7 Herald 209 ★	Guernsey Airport Fire Services	
G-BAZM	Jodel D.11	A. F. Simpson	
G-BAZS	Cessna F.150L	L. W. Scattergood	
G-BAZT	Cessna F.172M	Exeter Flying Club Ltd	
G-BBAW	Robin HR.100/210	J. R. Williams	
G-BBAX	Robin DR.400/140	G. J. Bissex & P. H. Garbutt	
G-BBAY	Robin DR.400/140	Rothwell Group	
G-BBBB	Taylor JT.1 Monoplane	P. J. Burgess	
G-BBBC	Cessna F.150L	W. J. Greenfield	
G-BBBI	AA-5 Traveler	Go Baby Aviation Group	
G-BBBK	PA-28-140 Cherokee	Comed Schedule Services Ltd	
G-BBBN	PA-28 Cherokee 180	Estuary Aviation Ltd	
G-BBBO	SIPA 903	G. E. Morris	
G-BBPP	PA-28 Cherokee 180	Big Red Kite Ltd (G-WACP)	
G-BBBW	FRED Srs 2	M. Palfreman	
G-BBBX	Cessna 310L	Atlantic Air Transport Ltd/Coventry	
G-BBBY	PA-28 Cherokee 140	W. R. & R. Davies	
G-BBCA	Bell 206B JetRanger 2	Heliflight (UK) Ltd/Wolverhampton	
G-BBCC	PA-23 Aztec 250D	Premier Flight Training Ltd	

G-BBCH – G-BBMH   BRITISH CIVIL REGISTRATIONS

Notes	Reg	Type	Owner or Operator
	G-BBCH	Robin DR.400/2+2	Oilburners (2006) Flying Association
	G-BBCI	Cessna 150H	A. M. & F. Alam
	G-BBCK	Cameron O-77 balloon	W. R. Teasdale
	G-BBCS	Robin DR.400/140	B. N. Stevens
	G-BBCY	Luton LA-4A Minor	T. D. Boyle & J. Angiolini
	G-BBCZ	AA-5 Traveler	No. 1 Investments Ltd
	G-BBDC	PA-28 Cherokee 140	G-BBDC Group
	G-BBDE	PA-28R Cherokee Arrow 200-II	R. L. Coleman & ptnrs
	G-BBDG	BAC-Aérospatiale Concorde 100 ★	BAE Systems (stored)/Filton
	G-BBDH	Cessna F.172M	J. D. Woodward
	G-BBDJ	Thunder Ax6-56 balloon	Balloon Preservation Flying Group
	G-BBDL	AA-5 Traveler	Delta Lima Flying Group
	G-BBDM	AA-5 Traveler	Jackeroo Aviation Group
	G-BBDO	PA-23 Turbo Aztec 250E	J. W. Anstee/Bristol
	G-BBDP	Robin DR.400/160	Robin Lance Aviation Associates Ltd
	G-BBDS	PA-31 Turbo Navajo	Fly (CI) Ltd (G-SKKB)
	G-BBDT	Cessna 150H	Delta Tango Group
	G-BBDV	SIPA S.903	W. McAndrew
	G-BBEA	Luton LA-4 Minor	M. Horner
	G-BBEB	PA-28R Cherokee Arrow 200-II	Anvils Flying Group
	G-BBEC	PA-28 Cherokee 180	A. A. Gardner
	G-BBED	MS.894A Rallye Minerva 220	Vista Products
	G-BBEF	PA-28 Cherokee 140	Liberty Group Assets Ltd
	G-BBEN	Bellanca 7GCBC Citabria	C. A. G. Schofield
	G-BBEV	PA-28-140 Cherokee D	Comed Schedule Services Ltd
	G-BBEX	Cessna 185A	Falcon Parachute Centre
	G-BBEY	PA-23 Aztec 250E	F. Walker
	G-BBFD	PA-28R Cherokee Arrow 200-II	C. H. Rose & A. R. Annable
	G-BBFL	Gardan GY-201 Minicab	R. Smith
	G-BBFV	PA-32 Cherokee Six 260	G-BBFV Syndicate
	G-BBGC	MS.893E Rallye 180GT	P. M. Nolan
	G-BBGI	Fuji FA.200-160	Tandycel Co Ltd
	G-BBGL	Baby Great Lakes	F. Ball
	G-BBGR	Cameron O-65 balloon	M. L. & L. P. Willoughby
	G-BBGZ	Cambridge HAB Association HAB	G. & R. A. Laslett & J. L. Hinton
	G-BBHF	PA-23 Aztec 250E	G. J. Williams/Sherburn
	G-BBHI	Cessna 177RG	T. G. W. Bunce
	G-BBHJ	Piper J-3C-65 Cub	R. V. Miller & J. Stanbridge
	G-BBHK	Noorduyn AT-16 Harvard IIB (212540:RF-40)	Sheringham Aviation UK Ltd
	G-BBHL	Sikorsky S-61N Mk II	Bristow Helicopters Ltd *Glamis*
	G-BBHY	PA-28 Cherokee 180	Air Operations Ltd/Guernsey
	G-BBIA	PA-28R Cherokee Arrow 200-II	G. H. Kilby/Stapleford
	G-BBIF	PA-23 Aztec 250E	D. M. Davies
	G-BBIH	Enstrom F-28A-UK	Stephenson Marine Co Ltd
	G-BBII	Fiat G-46-3B (4-97/MM52801)	G-BBII Ltd
	G-BBIL	PA-28 Cherokee 140	John West Consulting Ltd
	G-BBIO	Robin HR.100/210	R. P. Caley
	G-BBIX	PA-28 Cherokee 140	Sterling Aviation Ltd
	G-BBJB	Thunder Ax7-77 balloon	St. Crispin Balloon Group
	G-BBJI	Isaacs Spitfire (RN218)	R. F. Cresswell
	G-BBJU	Robin DR.400/140	J. C. Lister
	G-BBJV	Cessna F.177RG	3grcomm Ltd
	G-BBJX	Cessna F.150L	L. W. Scattergood
	G-BBJY	Cessna F.172M	Skytrax Aviation Ltd
	G-BBJZ	Cessna F.172M	J. K. & J. A. Green
	G-BBKA	Cessna F.150L	W. M. Wilson
	G-BBKB	Cessna F.150L	Justgold Ltd/Blackpool
	G-BBKE	Cessna F.150L	Xpedite (UK) Ltd
	G-BBKF	Cessna FRA.150L	D. W. Mickleburgh
	G-BBKG	Cessna FR.172J	R. Wright
	G-BBKI	Cessna F.172M	C. W. & S. A. Burman
	G-BBKL	CP301A Emeraude	Piel G-BBKL
	G-BBKX	PA-28 Cherokee 180	DRA Flying Club Ltd/Farnborough
	G-BBKY	Cessna F.150L	Telesonic Ltd/Barton
	G-BBKZ	Cessna 172M	KZ Flying Group/Exeter
	G-BBLH	Piper J-3C-65 Cub (31145:G-26)	Shipping & Airlines Ltd/Biggin Hill
	G-BBLL	Cameron O-84 balloon ★	British Balloon Museum/Newbury
	G-BBLM	SOCATA Rallye 100S	J. R. Rodgers
	G-BBLS	AA-5 Traveler	A. Grant
	G-BBLU	PA-34-200 Seneca II	R. H. R. Rue
	G-BBMB	Robin DR.400/180	Regent Flying Group
	G-BBMH	EAA. Sports Biplane Model P.1	G-BBMH Flying Group

46

BRITISH CIVIL REGISTRATIONS

G-BBMJ – G-BBXY

Reg	Type	Owner or Operator	Notes
G-BBMJ	PA-23 Aztec 250E	Nationwide Caravan Rental Services Ltd	
G-BBMN	DHC.1 Chipmunk 22	R. Steiner/Rush Green	
G-BBMO	DHC.1 Chipmunk 22 (WK514)	D. M. Squires/Wellesbourne	
G-BBMR	DHC.1 Chipmunk 22 (WB763:14)	P. J. Wood/Tollerton	
G-BBMT	DHC.1 Chipmunk 22	MT Group	
G-BBMV	DHC.1 Chipmunk 22 (WG348)	P. J. Reading	
G-BBMW	DHC.1 Chipmunk 22 (WK628)	G. Fielder & A. Wilson	
G-BBMX	DHC.1 Chipmunk 22	K. A. Doornbos/Netherlands	
G-BBMZ	DHC.1 Chipmunk 22	Wycombe Gliding School Syndicate/Booker	
G-BBNA	DHC.1 Chipmunk 22 (Lycoming)	Coventry Gliding Club Ltd/Husbands Bosworth	
G-BBNC	DHC.1 Chipmunk T.10 (WP790) ★	De Havilland Heritage Museum/London Colney	
G-BBND	DHC.1 Chipmunk 22 (WD286)	Bernoulli Syndicate	
G-BBNG	Bell 206B JetRanger 2	Helicopter Crop Spraying Ltd	
G-BBNH	PA-34-200 Seneca II	M. G. D. Baverstock & ptnrs/Bournemouth	
G-BBNI	PA-34-200 Seneca II	Noisy Moose Ltd	
G-BBNJ	Cessna F.150L	Sherburn Aero Club Ltd	
G-BBNO	PA-23 Aztec 250E ★	(stored)/Biggin Hill	
G-BBNT	PA-31-350 Navajo Chieftain	M. P. Goss	
G-BBNZ	Cessna F.172M	R. J. Nunn	
G-BBOA	Cessna F.172M	J. D & A. M. Black	
G-BBOC	Cameron O-77 balloon	J. A. B. Gray	
G-BBOD	Thunder O-45 balloon	B. R. & M. Boyle	
G-BBOH	Pitts S-1S Special	Venom Jet Promotions Ltd/Bournemouth	
G-BBOJ	PA-23 Aztec 250E ★	Instructional airframe/Cranfield	
G-BBOL	PA-18 Super Cub 150	N. Artt	
G-BBOO	Thunder Ax6-56 balloon	K. Meehan Tigerjack	
G-BBOR	Bell 206B JetRanger 2	M. J. Easey	
G-BBOX	Thunder Ax7-77 balloon	The British Balloon Museum and Library Ltd	
G-BBPN	Enstrom F-28A-UK	D. W. C. Holmes	
G-BBPO	Enstrom F-28A-UK	Henfield Lodge Aviation Ltd	
G-BBPP	PA-28 Cherokee 180	Big Red Kite Ltd (G-WACP)	
G-BBPS	Jodel D.117	A. Appleby/Redhill	
G-BBPX	PA-34-200 Seneca II	The G-BBPX Flying Group	
G-BBPY	PA-28 Cherokee 180	Sunsaver Ltd/Barton	
G-BBRA	PA-23 Aztec 250D	R. C. Lough/Elstree	
G-BBRB	DH.82A Tiger Moth (DF198)	R. Barham/Biggin Hill	
G-BBRC	Fuji FA.200-180	BBRC Ltd/Blackbushe	
G-BBRI	Bell 47G-5A	Alan Mann Helicopters Ltd/Fairoaks	
G-BBRN	Procter Kittiwake 1 (XW784/VL)	H. M. Price	
G-BBRV	DHC.1 Chipmunk 22 (WD347)	K. Rowell	
G-BBRX	SIAI-Marchetti S.205-18F	BBRX LLP	
G-BBSA	AA-5 Traveler	Usworth 84 Flying Associates Ltd	
G-BBSB	Beech C23 Sundowner	L. J. Welsh	
G-BBSM	PA-32 Cherokee Six 300E	G. C. Collings	
G-BBSS	DHC.1A Chipmunk 22	Coventry Gliding Club Ltd/Husbands Bosworth	
G-BBSW	Pietenpol Air Camper	J. K. S. Wills	
G-BBTB	Cessna FRA.150L	Global Engineering and Maintenance Ltd	
G-BBTG	Cessna F.172M	Triple X Flying Group/Biggin Hill	
G-BBTH	Cessna F.172M	Tayside Aviation Ltd	
G-BBTJ	PA-23 Aztec 250E	Cooper Aerial Surveys Ltd/Sandtoft	
G-BBTK	Cessna FRA.150L	Cleveland Flying School Ltd/Teesside	
G-BBTS	Beech V35B Bonanza	Eastern Air	
G-BBTU	ST-10 Diplomate	D. Hayden-Wright	
G-BBTY	Beech C23 Sundowner	A. W. Roderick & W. Price/Cardiff-Wales	
G-BBTZ	Cessna F.150L	Keen Leasing (IOM) Ltd	
G-BBUE	AA-5 Traveler	G. A. Chadfield & T. Shotton	
G-BBUF	AA-5 Traveler	S. & A. F. Williams	
G-BBUG	PA-16 Clipper	J. Dolan	
G-BBUJ	Cessna 421B	Coolflourish Ltd	
G-BBUT	Western O-65 balloon	R. G. Turnbull	
G-BBUU	Piper J-3C-65 Cub	C. Stokes	
G-BBVA	Sikorsky S-61N Mk 2	Bristow Helicopters Ltd	
G-BBVF	SA Twin Pioneer Srs 3 ★	Museum of Flight/East Fortune	
G-BBVG	PA-23 Aztec 250C ★	(stored)/Little Staughton	
G-BBVO	Isaacs Fury II (S1579)	R. W. Hinton	
G-BBWZ	AA-1B Trainer	A. C. Jacobs	
G-BBXB	Cessna FRA.150L	D. C. & M. Laycock	
G-BBXH	Cessna FR.172F	D. Ridley	
G-BBXK	PA-34-200 Seneca	Poyston Aviation	
G-BBXL	Cessna 310Q	Titan (Rak) Ltd	
G-BBXS	Piper J-3C-65 Cub	M. J. Butler/Langham (G-ALMA)	
G-BBXW	PA-28-151 Cherokee Warrior	Bristol Aero Club	
G-BBXY	Bellanca 7GCBC Citabria	R. R. L. Windus	

G-BBXZ – G-BCIH BRITISH CIVIL REGISTRATIONS

Notes	Reg	Type	Owner or Operator
	G-BBXZ	Evans VP-1	R. W. Burrows
	G-BBYB	PA-18 Super Cub 95	Tiger Club (1990) Ltd/Headcorn
	G-BBYH	Cessna 182P	Ramco (UK) Ltd
	G-BBYM	HP.137 Jetstream 200 ★	Aerospace Museum/Cosford (G-AYWR)
	G-BBYP	PA-28 Cherokee 140	E. Williams
	G-BBYS	Cessna 182P Skylane	I. M. Jones
	G-BBYU	Cameron O-56 balloon	British Balloon Museum
	G-BBZF	PA-28 Cherokee 140	East Coast Aviation
	G-BBZH	PA-28R Cherokee Arrow 200-II	ZH Flying Ltd/Exeter
	G-BBZN	Fuji FA.200-180	D. Kynaston & ptnrs
	G-BBZV	PA-28R Cherokee Arrow 200-II	P. B. Mellor/Kidlington
	G-BCAH	DHC.1 Chipmunk 22 (WG316)	A. W. Eldridge
	G-BCAP	Cameron O-56 balloon ★	Balloon Preservation Group/Lancing
	G-BCAR	Thunder Ax7-77 balloon ★	British Balloon Museum/Newbury
	G-BCAZ	PA-12 Super Cruiser	A. D. Williams
	G-BCBG	PA-23 Aztec 250E	M. J. L. Batt
	G-BCBH	Fairchild 24R-46A Argus III	Dreamticket Promotions Ltd
	G-BCBJ	PA-25 Pawnee 235	Deeside Gliding Club (Aberdeenshire) Ltd/Aboyne
	G-BCBL	Fairchild 24R-46A Argus III (HB751)	F. J. Cox
	G-BCBR	AJEP/Wittman W.8 Tailwind	D. P. Jones
	G-BCBX	Cessna F.150L	N. F. O'Neill
	G-BCBZ	Cessna 337C	J. Haden
	G-BCCC	Cessna F.150L	Triple Charlie Flying Group/Cranfield
	G-BCCD	Cessna F.172M	Austin Aviation Ltd
	G-BCCE	PA-23 Aztec 250E	Golf Charlie Echo Ltd/Shoreham
	G-BCCF	PA-28 Cherokee 180	Topcat Aviation Ltd/Manchester
	G-BCCG	Thunder Ax7-65 balloon	N. H. Ponsford
	G-BCCJ	AA-5 Traveler	T. Needham/Woodford
	G-BCCK	AA-5 Traveler	Prospect Air Ltd/Barton
	G-BCCR	CP301A Emeraude (modified)	J. H. & C. J. Waterman
	G-BCCX	DHC.1 Chipmunk 22 (Lycoming)	RAFGSA/Dishforth
	G-BCCY	Robin HR.200/100	Charlie Yankee Ltd/Filton
	G-BCDJ	PA-28 Cherokee 140	R. J. Whyham
	G-BCDK	Partenavia P.68B	Compass Air SRL
	G-BCDL	Cameron O-42 balloon	D. P. & Mrs B. O. Turner Chums
	G-BCDN	F.27 Friendship Mk 200 ★	Instructional airframe/Norwich
	G-BCDY	Cessna FRA.150L	R. L. Nunn & T. R. Edwards
	G-BCEA	Sikorsky S-61N Mk II	British International
	G-BCEB	Sikorsky S-61N Mk II	Veritair Ltd
	G-BCEE	AA-5 Traveler	P. J. Marchant
	G-BCEF	AA-5 Traveler	G-BCEF Group
	G-BCEN	BN-2A-26 Islander	Atlantic Air Transport Ltd/Coventry
	G-BCEP	AA-5 Traveler	R. J. Barber
	G-BCER	Gardan GY-201 Minicab	D. Beaumont/Sherburn
	G-BCEX	PA-23 Aztec 250E	DJ Aviation Ltd
	G-BCEY	DHC.1 Chipmunk 22 (WG465)	Gopher Flying Group
	G-BCEZ	Cameron O-84 balloon	Balloon Collection
	G-BCFD	West balloon ★	British Balloon Museum Hellfire/Newbury
	G-BCFF	Fuji FA-200-160	S. A. Cole
	G-BCFO	PA-18 Super Cub 150	Portsmouth Naval Gliding Club/Lee-on-Solent
	G-BCFR	Cessna FRA.150L	Bulldog Aviation Ltd & Motorhoods Colchester Ltd/Earls Colne
	G-BCFU	Thunder Ax6-56 balloon ★	British Balloon Museum/Newbury
	G-BCFW	SAAB 91D Safir	D. R. Williams
	G-BCFY	Luton LA-4A Minor	G. Capes
	G-BCGB	Bensen B.8	J. W. Birkett
	G-BCGC	DHC.1 Chipmunk 22 (WP903)	J. C. Wright
	G-BCGH	SNCAN NC.854S	Nord Flying Group
	G-BCGI	PA-28 Cherokee 140	T. Dodd
	G-BCGJ	PA-28 Cherokee 140	Demero Ltd & Transcourt Ltd
	G-BCGM	Jodel D.120	T. J. Roberts
	G-BCGN	PA-28 Cherokee 140	Golf November Ltd/Kidlington
	G-BCGS	PA-28R Cherokee Arrow 200	Arrow Aviation Group
	G-BCGW	Jodel D.11	G. H. & M. D. Chittenden
	G-BCHK	Cessna F.172H	D. Darby
	G-BCHL	DHC.1 Chipmunk 22A (WP788)	Shropshire Soaring Ltd/Sleap
	G-BCHM	Westland SA.341G Gazelle 1	MW Helicopters Ltd
	G-BCHP	CP.1310-C3 Super Emeraude	G. Hughes & A. G. Just (G-JOSI)
	G-BCHT	Schleicher ASK.16	Dunstable K16 Group
	G-BCHV	DHC.1 Chipmunk 22	K.I. Sutherland
	G-BCID	PA-34-200 Seneca II	Shenley Farms (Aviation) Ltd
	G-BCIH	DHC.1 Chipmunk 22 (WD363)	J. M. Hosey/Stansted

BRITISH CIVIL REGISTRATIONS

G-BCIJ – G-BCVC

Reg	Type	Owner or Operator	Notes
G-BCIJ	AA-5 Traveler	Arrow Association/Elstree	
G-BCIN	Thunder Ax7-77 balloon	R. A. Vale & ptnrs	
G-BCIR	PA-28-151 Warrior	R. W. Harris	
G-BCJM	PA-28 Cherokee 140	Topcat Aviation Ltd/Manchester	
G-BCJN	PA-28 Cherokee 140	Topcat Aviation Ltd/Manchester	
G-BCJO	PA-28R Cherokee Arrow 200	R. Ross	
G-BCJP	PA-28 Cherokee 140	Omletair Flying Group	
G-BCKN	DHC.1A Chipmunk 22 (Lycoming)	RAFGSA/Cranwell	
G-BCKS	Fuji FA.200-180AO	S. Hyland	
G-BCKT	Fuji FA.200-180	Kilo Tango Group	
G-BCKU	Cessna FRA.150L	Stapleford Flying Club Ltd	
G-BCKV	Cessna FRA.150L	Huck Air/Sheffield	
G-BCLC	Sikorsky S-61N	Bristow Helicopters/HM Coastguard	
G-BCLD	Sikorsky S-61N	Bristow Helicopters Ltd	
G-BCLI	AA-5 Traveler	W. D. Smith	
G-BCLL	PA-28 Cherokee 180	G-BCLL Group	
G-BCLS	Cessna 170B	N. Simpson	
G-BCLT	MS.894A Rallye Minerva 220	K. M. Bowen	
G-BCLU	Jodel D.117	S. J. Wynne	
G-BCLW	AA-1B Trainer	J. R. Faulkner	
G-BCMD	PA-18 Super Cub 95	P. Stephenson/Clacton	
G-BCMJ	Squarecraft Cavalier SA.102-5	N. F. Andrews	
G-BCMT	Isaacs Fury II	R.W. Burrows	
G-BCNC	Gardan GY-201 Minicab	J. R. Wraight	
G-BCNP	Cameron O-77 balloon	P. Spellward	
G-BCNX	Piper J-3C-65 Cub (540)	K. J. Lord	
G-BCNZ	Fuji FA.200-160	W. Dougan	
G-BCOB	Piper J-3C-65 Cub (329405:A-23)	J. W. Marjoram	
G-BCOI	DHC.1 Chipmunk 22 (WP970:12)	M. J. Diggins	
G-BCOJ	Cameron O-56 balloon	T. J. Knott & M. J. Webber	
G-BCOL	Cessna F.172M	November Charlie Flying Group	
G-BCOM	Piper J-3C-65 Cub	Dougal Flying Group/Shoreham	
G-BCOO	DHC.1 Chipmunk 22	T. G. Fielding & M. S. Morton/Blackpool	
G-BCOR	SOCATA Rallye 100ST	P. R. W. Goslin & I. M. Speight	
G-BCOU	DHC.1 Chipmunk 22 (WK522)	P. J. Loweth	
G-BCOY	DHC.1 Chipmunk 22	Coventry Gliding Club Ltd/Husbands Bosworth	
G-BCPD	Gardan GY-201 Minicab	P. R. Cozens	
G-BCPG	PA-28R Cherokee Arrow 200-II	Roses Flying Group/Liverpool	
G-BCPH	Piper J-3C-65 Cub (329934:B-72)	M. J. Janaway	
G-BCPJ	Piper J-3C-65 Cub	Piper Cub Group	
G-BCPK	Cessna F.172M	D. C. C. Handley/Cranfield	
G-BCPN	AA-5 Traveler	G. K. Todd	
G-BCPU	DHC.1 Chipmunk 22	P. Waller/Booker	
G-BCRB	Cessna F.172M	D. E. Lamb	
G-BCRE	Cameron O-77 balloon ★	Balloon Preservation Group/Lancing	
G-BCRH	Alaparma Baldo B.75 ★	A. L. Scadding (stored)	
G-BCRI	Cameron O-65 balloon	V. J. Thorne	
G-BCRK	SA.102.5 Cavalier	P. G. R. Brown	
G-BCRL	PA-28-151 Warrior	BCRL Ltd	
G-BCRP	PA-E23 Aztec 250E	Airlong Charter Ltd	
G-BCRR	AA-5B Tiger	Tiger Group	
G-BCRT	Cessna F.150M	Almat Flying Club Ltd	
G-BCRX	DHC.1 Chipmunk 22	Tuplin Ltd/Denham	
G-BCSA	DHC.1 Chipmunk 22 (Lycoming)	RAFGSA/Halton	
G-BCSL	DHC.1 Chipmunk 22	Chipmunk Flyers Ltd	
G-BCST	MS.893A Rallye Commodore 180	D. R. Wilcox	
G-BCSX	Thunder Ax7-77 balloon	C. Wolstenholm	
G-BCTF	PA-28-151 Warrior	The St. George Flying Club/Teesside	
G-BCTI	Schleicher ASK 16	Tango India Syndicate	
G-BCTK	Cessna FR.172J	R. T. Love	
G-BCTT	Evans VP-1	E. R. G. Ludlow	
G-BCUB	Piper J-3C-65 Cub	A. L. Brown	
G-BCUF	Cessna F.172M	Howell Plant Hire & Construction	
G-BCUH	Cessna F.150M	M. G. Montgomerie	
G-BCUJ	Cessna F.150M	j. Oleksyn & G. Astle	
G-BCUL	SOCATA Rallye 100ST	C. A. Ussher & Fountain Estates Ltd	
G-BCUO	SA Bulldog Srs 120/122	Cranfield University	
G-BCUS	SA Bulldog Srs 120/122	C. D. Hill	
G-BCUV	SA Bulldog Srs 120/122 (XX704)	Dolphin Property (Management) Ltd	
G-BCUW	Cessna F.177RG	S. J. Westley	
G-BCUY	Cessna FRA.150M	J. C. Carpenter	
G-BCVB	PA-17 Vagabond	A. T. Nowak/Popham	
G-BCVC	SOCATA Rallye 100ST	W. Haddow	

49

G-BCVE – G-BDIX — BRITISH CIVIL REGISTRATIONS

Notes	Reg	Type	Owner or Operator
	G-BCVE	Evans VP-2	D. Masterson & D. B. Winstanley/Barton
	G-BCVF	Practavia Pilot Sprite	D. G. Hammersley
	G-BCVG	Cessna FRA.150L	G-BCVG Flying Group
	G-BCVH	Cessna FRA.150L	M. A. James
	G-BCVJ	Cessna F.172M	Rothland Ltd
	G-BCVY	PA-34-200T Seneca II	Oxford Aviation Services Ltd/Kidlington
	G-BCWB	Cessna 182P	M. F. Oliver & A. J. Mew
	G-BCWH	Practavia Pilot Sprite	R. Tasker/Blackpool
	G-BCWK	Alpavia Fournier RF-3	T. J. Hartwell
	G-BCXB	SOCATA Rallye 100ST	A. Smails
	G-BCXE	Robin DR.400/2+2	Weald Air Services Ltd/Headcorn
	G-BCXJ	Piper L-4J Cub (480752:E-39)	W. Readman
	G-BCXN	DHC.1 Chipmunk 22 (WP800)	G. M. Turner/Halton
	G-BCYH	DAW Privateer Mk. 3	G-BCYH Group
	G-BCYK	Avro CF.100 Mk 4 Canuck (18393) ★	Imperial War Museum/Duxford
	G-BCYM	DHC.1 Chipmunk 22 (WK577)	G-BCYM Group/Kemble
	G-BCYR	Cessna F.172M	Highland Flying School Ltd
	G-BCZM	Cessna F.172M	Cornwall Flying Club Ltd/Bodmin
	G-BCZO	Cameron O-77 balloon	W. O. T. Holmes
	G-BDAD	Taylor JT.1 Monoplane	G-BDAD Group
	G-BDAG	Taylor JT.1 Monoplane	N. R. Osborne
	G-BDAH	Evans VP-1	G. H. J. Geurts
	G-BDAI	Cessna FRA.150M	D. F. Ranger
	G-BDAK	Rockwell Commander 112	M. C. Wilson
	G-BDAO	SIPA S.91	S. B. Churchill
	G-BDAP	AJEP Tailwind	J. Whiting
	G-BDAR	Evans VP-1	R. B. Valler
	G-BDAY	Thunder Ax5-42A balloon	T. M. Donnelly *Meconium*
	G-BDBD	Wittman W.8 Tailwind	Tailwindr Group
	G-BDBF	FRED Srs 2	G. E. & R. E. Collins
	G-BDBH	Bellanca 7GCBC Citabria	C. J. Gray
	G-BDBI	Cameron O-77 balloon	C. Jones
	G-BDBJ	Cessna 182P	H. C. Wilson
	G-BDBS	Short SD3-30 ★	Ulster Aviation Society
	G-BDBU	Cessna F.150M	Cumbernauld Flying School Ltd
	G-BDBV	Jodel D.11A	Seething Jodel Group
	G-BDBZ	Westland WS-55 Whirlwind (XJ398) ★	Aeroventure/Doncaster
	G-BDCD	Piper J-3C-85 Cub (480133:B-44)	Cubby Cub Group
	G-BDCI	CP.301A Emeraude	D. L. Sentance
	G-BDCL	AA-5 Traveler	J. Crowe
	G-BDCO	Beagle B.121 Pup 1	R. J. Page & M. N. Simms
	G-BDDD	DHC.1 Chipmunk 22	DRA Aero Club Ltd
	G-BDDF	Jodel D.120	J. V. Thompson
	G-BDDG	Jodel D.112	J. Pool & D. G. Palmer/Sturgate
	G-BDDS	PA-25 Pawnee 235	Vale of Neath Gliding Club/Rhigos
	G-BDDX	Whittaker MW2B Excalibur ★	Cornwall Aero Park/Helston
	G-BDDZ	CP.301A Emeraude	E. C. Mort
	G-BDEC	SOCATA Rallye 100ST	J. Fingleton
	G-BDEH	Jodel D.120A	EH Group
	G-BDEI	Jodel D.9 Bébé	The Noddy Group/Booker
	G-BDEU	DHC.1 Chipmunk 22 (WP808)	T. E. Earl
	G-BDEX	Cessna FRA.150M	R. A. Powell
	G-BDEY	Piper J-3C-65 Cub	Ducksworth Flying Club
	G-BDEZ	Piper J-3C-65 Cub	R. J. M. Turnbull
	G-BDFB	Currie Wot	J. Jennings
	G-BDFH	Auster AOP9 (XR240)	R. B. Webber
	G-BDFJ	Cessna F.150M	C. J. Hopewell
	G-BDFR	Fuji FA.200-160	M. S. Bird
	G-BDFU	Dragonfly MPA Mk 1 ★	Museum of Flight/East Fortune
	G-BDFW	Rockwell Commander 112	M. E. & E. G. Reynolds/Blackbushe
	G-BDFY	AA-5 Traveler	Grumman Group
	G-BDFZ	Cessna F.150M	L. W. Scattergood
	G-BDGB	Gardan GY-20 Minicab	D. G. Burden
	G-BDGH	Thunder Ax7-77 balloon	R. J. Mitchener & P. F. Smart
	G-BDGM	PA-28-151 Cherokee Warrior	J. H. Mitchell
	G-BDHK	Piper J-3C-65 Cub (329417)	Knight Flying Group
	G-BDIE	Rockwell Commander 112	R. J. Adams
	G-BDIG	Cessna 182P	Air Group 6/Sturgate
	G-BDIH	Jodel D.117	N. D. H. Stokes
	G-BDIJ	Sikorsky S-61N	Bristow Helicopters Ltd
	G-BDIN	SA Bulldog Srs 120/125 (408)	British Disabled Flying Association
	G-BDIX	DH.106 Comet 4C ★	Museum of Flight/East Fortune

BRITISH CIVIL REGISTRATIONS

G-BDJC – G-BDWO

Reg	Type	Owner or Operator	Notes
G-BDJC	AJEP W.8 Tailwind	R. Bertrand/Germany	
G-BDJD	Jodel D.112	J. E. Preston	
G-BDJG	Luton LA-4A Minor	Very Slow Flying Club	
G-BDJP	Piper J-3C-90 Cub	S. T. Gilbert	
G-BDJR	SNCAN Nord NC.858	R. F. M. Marson	
G-BDJV	BN-2A-21 Islander	Cormack (Aircraft Services) Ltd	
G-BDKC	Cessna A185F	Bridge of Tilt Co Ltd	
G-BDKD	Enstrom F-28A	P. J. Price	
G-BDKH	CP.301A Emeraude	G-BDKH Group	
G-BDKJ	K & S SA.102.5 Cavalier	D. A. Garner	
G-BDKM	SIPA 903	S. W. Markham	
G-BDKW	Rockwell Commander 112A	J. T. Klaschka	
G-BDLO	AA-5A Cheetah	S. & J. Dolan/Denham	
G-BDLT	Rockwell Commander 112	D. L. Churchward	
G-BDLY	K & S SA.102.5 Cavalier	P. R. Stevens/Southampton	
G-BDMM	Jodel D.11	P. N. Marshall	
G-BDMS	Piper J-3C-65 Cub (FR886)	A. T. H. Martin	
G-BDMW	Jodel DR.100A	Mike Whisky Group	
G-BDNC	Taylor JT.1 Monoplane	D. W. Mathie	
G-BDNG	Taylor JT.1 Monoplane	W. Long	
G-BDNO	Taylor JT.1 Monoplane	S. D. Glover	
G-BDNP	BN-2A Islander ★	Ground parachute trainer/Headcorn	
G-BDNT	Jodel D.92 Bébé	R. J. Stobo	
G-BDNU	Cessna F.172M	J. & K. G. McVicar	
G-BDNW	AA-1B Trainer	P. Mitchell	
G-BDNX	AA-1B Trainer	R. M. North	
G-BDOC	Sikorsky S-61N Mk II	Bristow Helicopters Ltd	
G-BDOD	Cessna F.150M	OD Group	
G-BDOE	Cessna FR.172J	D. Sansome	
G-BDOG	SA Bulldog Srs 200	D. C. Bonsall/Netherthorpe	
G-BDOL	Piper J-3C-65 Cub	L. R. Balthazor	
G-BDON	Thunder Ax7-77A balloon	M. J. Smith	
G-BDOT	BN-2A Mk.III-2 Trislander	Lyddair	
G-BDOW	Cessna FRA.150	Joystick Aviation Ltd	
G-BDPA	PA-28-151 Warrior	Aircraft Engineers Ltd	
G-BDPJ	PA-25 Pawnee 235B	RAFGSA/Bicester	
G-BDPK	Cameron O-56 balloon	K. J. & G. R. Ibbotson	
G-BDPN	BN-2A-21 Islander	Fly BN Ltd	
G-BDRD	Cessna FRA.150M	Aircraft Engineers Ltd	
G-BDRG	Taylor JT.2 Titch	D. R. Gray	
G-BDRJ	DHC.1 Chipmunk 22 (WP857)	WP857 Aircraft Trust	
G-BDRK	Cameron O-65 balloon	R. J. Mitchener & P. F. Smart	
G-BDSB	PA-28-181 Archer II	Testair Ltd/Blackbushe	
G-BDSE	Cameron O-77 balloon	British Airways Concorde	
G-BDSF	Cameron O-56 balloon	J. H. Greensides	
G-BDSH	PA-28 Cherokee 140 (modified)	The Wright Brothers Flying Group	
G-BDSK	Cameron O-65 balloon	Southern Balloon Group Carousel II	
G-BDSL	Cessna F.150M	M. Howells	
G-BDSM	Slingsby T.31B Cadet III	F. C. J. Wevers/Netherlands	
G-BDTB	Evans VP-1	P. F. Moffatt	
G-BDTL	Evans VP-1	A. K. Lang	
G-BDTO	BN-2A Mk III-2 Trislander	Aurigny Air Services Ltd (G-RBSI/G-OTSB)	
G-BDTU	Omega III gas balloon	R. G. Turnbull	
G-BDTV	Mooney M.20F	S. Redfearn	
G-BDTX	Cessna F.150M	F. W. Ellis	
G-BDUI	Cameron V-56 balloon	D. C. Johnson	
G-BDUL	Evans VP-1	C. K. Brown	
G-BDUM	Cessna F.150M	G-BDUM Group	
G-BDUN	PA-34-200T Seneca II	R. Paris	
G-BDUO	Cessna F.150M	D. W. Locke	
G-BDUX	Slingsby T.31B Cadet III	J. C. Anderson/Cranfield	
G-BDUY	Robin DR.400/140B	J. G. Anderson	
G-BDUZ	Cameron V-56 balloon	Zebedee Balloon Service	
G-BDVA	PA-17 Vagabond	I. M. Callier	
G-BDVB	PA-15 (PA-17) Vagabond	B. P Gardner	
G-BDVC	PA-17 Vagabond	A. R. Caveen	
G-BDVX	BN-2A-21 Islander	Fly BN Ltd	
G-BDWA	SOCATA Rallye 150ST	J. Thompson-Wilson	
G-BDWE	Flaglor Scooter	P. King	
G-BDWH	SOCATA Rallye 150ST	M. A. Jones	
G-BDWJ	SE-5A (replica) (F8010:Z)	D. W. Linney	
G-BDWM	Mustang scale replica (FB226)	D. C. Bonsall	
G-BDWO	Howes Ax6 balloon	R. B. & C. Howes	

G-BDWP – G-BELP — BRITISH CIVIL REGISTRATIONS

Notes	Reg	Type	Owner or Operator
	G-BDWP	PA-32R-300 Cherokee Lance	W. M. Brown/Coventry
	G-BDWX	Jodel D.120A	R. P. Rochester
	G-BDWY	PA-28-140 Cherokee E	A. A. Howard
	G-BDXE	Boeing 747-236B	European Aviation Ltd/Kemble
	G-BDXJ	Boeing 747-236B ★	Aces High Ltd/Dunsfold
	G-BDXX	SNCAN NC.858S	K. M. Davis
	G-BDYD	Rockwell Commander 114	J. R. Pybus
	G-BDYG	P.56 Provost T.1 (WV493) ★	Museum of Flight/East Fortune
	G-BDYH	Cameron V-56 balloon	B. J. Godding
	G-BDZA	Scheibe SF.25E Super Falke	Hereward Flying Group/Crowland
	G-BDZC	Cessna F.150M	A. M. Lynn/Sibson
	G-BDZD	Cessna F.172M	Zephyr Group
	G-BDZI	BN-21-21 Islander	Fly BN Ltd
	G-BDZU	Cessna 421C	Eagle Flying Group/East Midlands
	G-BEAB	Jodel DR.1051	R. C. Hibberd
	G-BEAC	PA-28 Cherokee 140	Clipwing Flying Group/Humberside
	G-BEAD	WG.13 Lynx ★	Instructional airframe/Middle Wallop
	G-BEAG	PA-34-200T Seneca II	Oxford Aviation Services Ltd/Kidlington
	G-BEAH	Auster J/2 Arrow	Bedwell Hey Flying Group
	G-BEBC	Westland WS-55 Whirlwind 3 (XP355) ★	Norwich Aviation Museum
	G-BEBE	AA-5A Cheetah	Bills Aviation Ltd
	G-BEBG	WSK-PZL SDZ-45A Ogar	The Ogar Syndicate
	G-BEBN	Cessna 177B	R. Turrell & P. Mason/Stapleford
	G-BEBS	Andreasson BA-4B	N. J. W. Reid
	G-BEBU	Rockwell Commander 112A	Aeros Engineering Ltd
	G-BEBZ	PA-28-151 Warrior	Airways Flight Training (Exeter) Ltd
	G-BECA	SOCATA Rallye 100ST	A. C. Stamp
	G-BECB	SOCATA Rallye 100ST	D. H. Tonkin
	G-BECF	Scheibe SF.25A Falke	North County Ltd
	G-BECK	Cameron V-56 balloon	M. E. White
	G-BECN	Piper J-3C-65 Cub (480480:E-44)	G. Denney/Earls Colne
	G-BECS	Thunder Ax6-56A balloon	A. Sieger/Germany
	G-BECT	CASA 1.131E Jungmann 2000 (A-57)	Alpha 57 Group
	G-BECW	CASA 1.131E Jungmann 2000 (A-10)	C. M. Rampton
	G-BECZ	CAARP CAP-10B	Aerobatic Associates Ltd
	G-BEDB	Nord 1203 Norecrin ★	B. F. G. Lister (stored)/Chirk
	G-BEDD	Jodel D.117A	Dubious Group
	G-BEDF	Boeing B-17G-105-VE (124485:DF-A)	B-17 Preservation Ltd/Duxford
	G-BEDG	Rockwell Commander 112	Hotels International Ltd
	G-BEDJ	Piper J-3C-65 Cub (44-80594)	R. Earl
	G-BEDP	BN-2A Mk.III-2 Trislander	Blue Island Air
	G-BEDV	V.668 Varsity T.1 (WJ945) ★	Duxford Aviation Society
	G-BEDW	BN-2A-21 Islander	Fly BN Ltd
	G-BEEE	Thunder Ax6-56A balloon ★	British Balloon Museum/Newbury
	G-BEEG	BN-2A-26 Islander	NW Parachute Centre Ltd/Cark
	G-BEEH	Cameron V-56 balloon	Sade Balloons Ltd
	G-BEER	Isaacs Fury II (K2075)	R. S. C. Andrews
	G-BEEU	PA-28 Cherokee 140F	E. & H. Merkado
	G-BEFA	PA-28-151 Warrior	Verran Freight
	G-BEFF	PA-28 Cherokee 140F	H. & E. Merkado
	G-BEFI	BN-2A-21 Islander	Fly BN Ltd
	G-BEGG	Scheibe SF.25E Super Falke	G-BEGG Flying Group
	G-BEHH	PA-32R Cherokee Lance 300	K. Swallow
	G-BEHU	PA-34-200T Seneca II	Pirin Aeronautical Ltd/Stapleford
	G-BEHV	Cessna F.172N	Edinburgh Air Centre Ltd
	G-BEIA	Cessna FRA.150M	C. J. Hopewell
	G-BEIF	Cameron O-65 balloon	C. Vening
	G-BEIG	Cessna F.150M	R. D. Forster & M. S. B. Thorp
	G-BEII	PA-25 Pawnee 235D	Burn Gliding Club Ltd
	G-BEIL	SOCATA Rallye 150T	The Rallye Flying Group
	G-BEIP	PA-28-181 Archer II	S. Pope
	G-BEIS	Evans VP-1	P. J. Hunt
	G-BEJD	Avro 748 Srs 1	PTB (Emerald) Pty Ltd *John Case*/Liverpool
	G-BEJK	Cameron S-31 balloon	Rango Balloon & Kite Co
	G-BEJV	PA-34-200T Seneca II	Oxford Aviation Services Ltd/Kidlington
	G-BEKL	Bede BD-4E-150	F. E.Tofield
	G-BEKM	Evans VP-1	G. J. McDill/Glenrothes
	G-BEKN	Cessna FRA.150M	A. L. Brown/Bourn
	G-BEKO	Cessna F.182Q	G. J. & F. J. Leese
	G-BEKR	Gardan GY-201 Minicab	M. Howells
	G-BELF	BN-2A-26 Islander	Cormack (Aircraft Services) Ltd
	G-BELP	PA-28-151 Warrior	Tatenhill Aviation Ltd

BRITISH CIVIL REGISTRATIONS — G-BELT – G-BEYO

Reg	Type	Owner or Operator	Notes
G-BELT	Cessna F.150J	A. kumar (G-AWUV)	
G-BEMB	Cessna F.172M	Stocklaunch Ltd	
G-BEMM	Slingsby T.31B Motor Cadet III	E. and P. McEvoy	
G-BEMU	Thunder Ax5-42 balloon	M. A. Hall	
G-BEMW	PA-28-181 Archer II	Touch & Go Ltd	
G-BEMY	Cessna FRA.150M	J. R. Power	
G-BEND	Cameron V-56 balloon	Dante Balloon Group	
G-BENJ	Rockwell Commander 112B	BENJ Flying Group	
G-BENK	Cessna F.172M	Graham Churchill Plant Ltd	
G-BENN	Cameron V-56 balloon	S. J. Hollingsworth & M. K. Bellamy	
G-BEOD	Cessna 180H	I. Addy	
G-BEOE	Cessna FRA.150M	W. J. Henderson	
G-BEOH	PA-28R-201T Turbo Arrow III	Gloucestershire Flying Club	
G-BEOI	PA-18 Super Cub 150	Southdown Gliding Club Ltd/Parham Park	
G-BEOK	Cessna F.150M	Oscar Kilo Flying Group	
G-BEOL	Short SC.7 Skyvan 3 variant 100	Invicta Aviation Ltd	
G-BEOX	Lockheed 414 Hudson IV (A16-199) ★	RAF Museum/Hendon	
G-BEOY	Cessna FRA.150L	R. W. Denny	
G-BEOZ	A.W.650 Argosy 101 ★	Aeropark/East Midlands	
G-BEPC	SNCAN Stampe SV.4C	Papa Charlie's Flying Circus Ltd	
G-BEPF	SNCAN Stampe SV.4A	C. C. Rollings & F. J. Hodson	
G-BEPS	Short SC.5 Belfast ★	(stored)/Southend	
G-BEPV	Fokker S.11-1 Instructor (174)	S. W. & M. Isbister & C. Tyers	
G-BEPY	Rockwell Commander 112B	PAM Aero Group	
G-BERA	SOCATA Rallye 150ST	B. Dolby	
G-BERC	SOCATA Rallye 150ST	Severn Valley Aero Group/Welshpool	
G-BERD	Thunder Ax6-56A balloon	P. M. Gaines	
G-BERI	Rockwell Commander 114	K. B. Harper/Blackbushe	
G-BERN	Saffrey S-330 balloon	B. Martin	
G-BERT	Cameron V-56 balloon	Southern Balloon Group Bert	
G-BERW	Rockwell Commander 114	Romeo Whisky Ltd	
G-BERY	AA-1B Trainer	R. H. J. Levi	
G-BETD	Robin HR.200/100	C. L. Wilsher	
G-BETE	Rollason B.2A Beta	T. M. Jones/Tatenhill	
G-BETF	Cameron 'Champion' SS balloon ★	British Balloon Museum/Newbury	
G-BETG	Cessna 180K Skywagon	J. A. Hart	
G-BETI	Pitts S-1D Special	On A Roll Aerobatics Group (G-PIII)	
G-BETL	PA-25 Pawnee 235D	Cambridge University Gliding Trust Ltd/ Gransden Lodge	
G-BETM	PA-25 Pawnee 235D	Yorkshire Gliding Club (Pty) Ltd/Sutton Bank	
G-BETW	Rand KR-2	S. C. Solley	
G-BEUA	PA-18 Super Cub 150	London Gliding Club (Pty) Ltd/Dunstable	
G-BEUD	Robin HR.100/285R	E. A. & L. M. C. Payton/Cranfield	
G-BEUI	Piper J-3C-65 Cub	P. K. Morley	
G-BEUM	Taylor JT.1 Monoplane	J. M. Burgess	
G-BEUP	Robin DR.400/180	Samuels Aviation/Biggin Hill	
G-BEUU	PA-18 Super Cub 95	F. Sharples/Sandown	
G-BEUX	Cessna F.172N	Multiflight Ltd/Leeds-Bradford	
G-BEUY	Cameron N-31 balloon	M. L. & L. P. Willoughby	
G-BEVA	SOCATA Rallye 150ST	The Rallye Group	
G-BEVB	SOCATA Rallye 150ST	G. G. Hammond	
G-BEVC	SOCATA Rallye 150ST	G-BEVC Ltd	
G-BEVG	PA-34-200T-2 Seneca	A. G. & J. Wintle	
G-BEVO	Sportavia-Pützer RF-5	W. E. R. Jenkins	
G-BEVP	Evans VP-2	G. Moscrop & R. C. Crowley	
G-BEVS	Taylor JT.1 Monoplane	D. Hunter	
G-BEVT	BN-2A Mk III-2 Trislander	Aurigny Air Services Ltd/Guernsey	
G-BEVW	SOCATA Rallye 150ST	P. G. A. Sumner	
G-BEWM	Sikorsky S-61N Mk II	Brintel Helicopters	
G-BEWN	DH.82A Tiger Moth	H. D. Labouchere	
G-BEWO	Zlin Z.326 Trener Master	P. A. Colman	
G-BEWR	Cessna F.172N	Cheshire Air Training Services Ltd/Liverpool	
G-BEWX	PA-28R-201 Arrow III	A. Vickers	
G-BEWY	Bell 206B JetRanger 3	Polo Aviation Ltd (G-CULL)	
G-BEXN	AA-1C Lynx	M. Holliday & D. C. Cooper	
G-BEXO	PA-23 Apache 160	Aviation Advisory Services Ltd	
G-BEXW	PA-28-181 Cherokee	J. O'Keeffe	
G-BEXZ	Cameron N-56 balloon	D. C. Eager & G. C. Clark	
G-BEYA	Enstrom 280C	Hovercam Ltd	
G-BEYB	Fairey Flycatcher (replica) (S1287) ★	F.A.A. Museum/Yeovilton	
G-BEYF	HPR.7 Herald 401 ★	Jet Heritage Museum/Bournemouth	
G-BEYL	PA-28 Cherokee 180	D. Gerrard & L. Phillips	
G-BEYO	PA-28 Cherokee 140	Eurocharter Aviation Ltd	

G-BEYT – G-BFHT — BRITISH CIVIL REGISTRATIONS

Notes	Reg	Type	Owner or Operator
	G-BEYT	PA-28 Cherokee 140	G. P & F. C. Coleman
	G-BEYV	Cessna T.210M	Castleridge Ltd
	G-BEYW	Taylor JT.1 Monoplane	R. A. Abrahams/Barton
	G-BEYZ	Jodel DR.1051/M1	M. L. Balding
	G-BEZC	AA-5 Traveler	C. M. O'Connell
	G-BEZE	Rutan Vari-Eze	S. K. Cockburn
	G-BEZF	AA-5 Traveler	G-BEZF Group
	G-BEZG	AA-5 Traveler	M. D. R. Harling
	G-BEZH	AA-5 Traveler	L. & S. M. Sims
	G-BEZI	AA-5 Traveler	G-BEZI Flying Group/Elstree
	G-BEZK	Cessna F.172H	S. Jones
	G-BEZL	PA-31-310 Turbo Navajo C	A. Jahanfar/Southend
	G-BEZO	Cessna F.172M	Staverton Flying School
	G-BEZP	PA-32 Cherokee Six 300D	T. P. McCormack & J. K. Zealley
	G-BEZR	Cessna F.172M	Kirmington Aviation Ltd
	G-BEZV	Cessna F.172M	Insch Flying Group
	G-BEZY	Rutan Vari-Eze	I. J. Pountney
	G-BEZZ	Jodel D.112	G-BEZZ Jodel Group/Barton
	G-BFAA	Gardan GY-80 Horizon 160	G. R. Williams
	G-BFAF	Aeronca 7BCM (7797)	D. C. W. Harper/Finmere
	G-BFAH	Phoenix Currie Wot	R. W. Clarke
	G-BFAI	Rockwell Commander 114	BFAI Flying Group
	G-BFAK	GEMS MS.892A Rallye Commodore 150	J. M. Hedges
	G-BFAP	SIAI-Marchetti S.205-20R	A. O. Broin
	G-BFAS	Evans VP-1	A. I. Sutherland
	G-BFAW	DHC.1 Chipmunk 22	R. V. Bowles/Husbands Bosworth
	G-BFAX	DHC.1 Chipmunk 22 (WG422)	N. Rushton
	G-BFBA	Jodel DR.100A	W. H. Sherlock
	G-BFBB	PA-23 Aztec 250E	D. Byrne
	G-BFBC	Taylor JT.1 Monoplane	G. Heins
	G-BFBE	Robin HR.200/100	A. C. Pearson
	G-BFBM	Saffery S.330 balloon	B. Martin
	G-BFBR	PA-28-161 Warrior II	John Wailing Ltd
	G-BFBU	Partenavia P68B	Geminair Services Ltd
	G-BFBY	Piper J-3C-65 Cub	U. Schuhmacher
	G-BFCT	Cessna Tu.206F	D. I. Schellingerhout
	G-BFDC	DHC.1 Chipmunk 22	N. F. O'Neill/Newtownards
	G-BFDE	Sopwith Tabloid (replica) (168) ★	RAF Museum/Hendon
	G-BFDF	SOCATA Rallye 235E	M. A. Wratten
	G-BFDI	PA-28-181 Archer II	Truman Aviation Ltd/Tollerton
	G-BFDK	PA-28-161 Warrior II	S. T. Gilbert
	G-BFDL	Piper J-3C-65 Cub (454537:J-04)	B. A. Nicholson
	G-BFDO	PA-28R-201T Turbo Arrow III	J. Blackburn & J. Driver
	G-BFDZ	Taylor JT.1 Monoplane	R. A. Collins
	G-BFEB	Jodel 150	Jodel Syndicate
	G-BFEF	Agusta-Bell 47G-3B1	M. P. Wilkinson
	G-BFEH	Jodel D.117A	J. A. Crabb
	G-BFEK	Cessna F.152	Staverton Flying School
	G-BFER	Bell 212	Bristow Helicopters Ltd
	G-BFEV	PA-25 Pawnee 235	Trent Valley Aerotowing Club Ltd/Kirton-in-Lindsey
	G-BFFB	Evans VP-2 ★	(stored)/Eaton Bray
	G-BFFC	Cessna F.152-II	Multiflight Ltd
	G-BFFE	Cessna F.152-II	A. J. Hastings/Edinburgh
	G-BFFJ	Sikorsky S-61N Mk II	Veritair Ltd *Tresco*/Penzance
	G-BFFP	PA-18 Super Cub 150 (modified)	East Sussex Gliding Club Ltd
	G-BFFT	Cameron V-56 balloon	R. I. M. Kerr & D. C. Boxall
	G-BFFW	Cessna F.152	Aircraft Engineers Ltd
	G-BFFY	Cessna F.150M	T. W. Oakley
	G-BFGD	Cessna F.172N-II	J. T. Armstrong
	G-BFGG	Cessna FRA.150M	J. M. Machin
	G-BFGH	Cessna F.337G	T. Perkins/Sherburn
	G-BFGK	Jodel D.117	B. F. J. Hope
	G-BFGL	Cessna FA.152	Multiflight Ltd
	G-BFGO	Fuji FA.200-160	R. J. Everett
	G-BFGS	MS.893E Rallye 180GT	Chiltern Flyers Ltd
	G-BFGX	Cessna FRA.150M	Aircraft Engineers Ltd
	G-BFGZ	Cessna FRA.150M	C. M. Barnes
	G-BFHH	DH.82A Tiger Moth	P. Harrison & M. J. Gambrell/Redhill
	G-BFHI	Piper J-3C-65 Cub	N. Glass & A. J. Richardson
	G-BFHP	Champion 7GCAA Citabria	Citabriation Group
	G-BFHR	Jodel DR.220/2+2	J. E. Sweetman
	G-BFHT	Cessna F.152-II	Westward Airways (Lands End) Ltd

BRITISH CIVIL REGISTRATIONS — G-BFHU – G-BFTX

Reg	Type	Owner or Operator	Notes
G-BFHU	Cessna F.152-II	D. J. Cooke & Co Ltd	
G-BFHV	Cessna F.152-II	Falcon Flying Services/Biggin Hill	
G-BFIB	PA-31 Turbo Navajo	Richard Hannon Ltd	
G-BFID	Taylor JT.2 Titch Mk III	R. W. Kilham	
G-BFIE	Cessna FRA.150M	J. P. A. Freeman	
G-BFIG	Cessna FR.172K XPII	Tenair Ltd/Barton	
G-BFIJ	AA-5A Cheetah	T. H. & M. G. Weetman	
G-BFIN	AA-5A Cheetah	Aircraft Engineers Ltd	
G-BFIP	Wallbro Monoplane 1909 (replica) ★	Norfolk & Suffolk Aviation Museum/Flixton	
G-BFIT	Thunder Ax6-56Z balloon	J. A. G. Tyson	
G-BFIU	Cessna FR.172K XP	The G-BFIU Flying Group	
G-BFIV	Cessna F.177RG	C. Fisher	
G-BFIX	Thunder Ax7-77A balloon	R. Owen	
G-BFIY	Cessna F.150M	R. J. Scott	
G-BFJJ	Evans VP-1	N. Clark	
G-BFJR	Cessna F.337G	Mannix Aviation Ltd/East Midlands	
G-BFJZ	Robin DR.400/140B	Weald Air Services Ltd/Headcorn	
G-BFKB	Cessna F.172N	Shropshire Flying Group	
G-BFKF	Cessna FA.152	Aerolease Ltd/Conington	
G-BFKH	Cessna F.152	TG Aviation Ltd/Manston	
G-BFKL	Cameron N-56 balloon	Merrythought Toys Ltd *Merrythought*	
G-BFLH	PA-34-200T Seneca II	Air Medical Ltd	
G-BFLI	PA-28R-201T Turbo Arrow III	J. K. Chudzicki	
G-BFLU	Cessna F.152	Atlantic Flight Training Ltd/Coventry	
G-BFLX	AA-5A Cheetah	A. M. Verdon	
G-BFLZ	Beech 95-A55 Baron	Caterite Food Service	
G-BFMF	Cassutt Racer IIIM	M. C. R. Sims	
G-BFMG	PA-28-161 Warrior II	Stardial Ltd	
G-BFMH	Cessna 177B	Aerofoil Aviation Ltd	
G-BFMK	Cessna FA.152	The Leicestershire Aero Club Ltd	
G-BFMR	PA-20 Pacer 125	J. Knight	
G-BFMX	Cessna F.172N	A2Z Wholesale Fashion Jewellery Ltd	
G-BFMZ	Payne Ax6 balloon	E. G. Woolnough	
G-BFNG	Jodel D.112	M. Cooke & P. H. Jeffcote	
G-BFNI	PA-28-161 Warrior II	Lion Services	
G-BFNK	PA-28-161 Warrior II	Oxford Aviation Services Ltd/Kidlington	
G BFNM	Globe GC-1B Swift	M. J. Butler	
G-BFOE	Cessna F.152	Redhill Air Services Ltd	
G-BFOF	Cessna F.152	Staverton Flying School	
G-BFOG	Cessna 150M	C. L. Day	
G-BFOJ	AA-1 Yankee	N. W. Thomas/Bournemouth	
G-BFOM	PA-31 Turbo Navajo C	Ashton Air Services Ltd	
G-BFOP	Jodel D.120	R. J. Wesley & G. D. Western	
G-BFOS	Thunder Ax6-56A balloon	N. T. Petty	
G-BFOU	Taylor JT.1 Monoplane	G. Bee	
G-BFOV	Cessna F.172N	D. J. Walker	
G-BFPA	Scheibe SF.25B Falke	R. Gibson & R. Hamilton	
G-BFPH	Cessna F.172K	Linc-Air Flying Group	
G-BFPM	Cessna F.172N	M. P. Wimsey & J. W. Cope	
G-BFPO	Rockwell Commander 112B	J. G. Hale Ltd	
G-BFPP	Bell 47J-2 Ranger	M. R. Masters	
G-BFPR	PA-25 Pawnee 235D	The Windrushers Gliding Club Ltd	
G-BFPS	PA-25 Pawnee 235D	Kent Gliding Club Ltd/Challock	
G-BFPZ	Cessna F.177RG Cardinal	D. M. Glinternick	
G-BFRD	Bowers Fly-Baby 1A	R. A. Phillips	
G-BFRI	Sikorsky S-61N	British International	
G-BFRR	Cessna FRA.150M	Romeo Romeo Flying Group/Tatenhill	
G-BFRS	Cessna F.172N	Poplar Aviation Ltd	
G-BFRV	Cessna FA.152	Solo Services Ltd	
G-BFRY	PA-25 Pawnee 260	Yorkshire Gliding Club (Pty) Ltd/Sutton Bank	
G-BFSA	Cessna F.182Q	Ensiform Aviation Ltd/Elstree	
G-BFSC	PA-25 Pawnee 235D	Essex Gliding Club Ltd/North Weald	
G-BFSD	PA-25 Pawnee 235D	Deeside Gliding Club (Aberdeenshire) Ltd/Aboyne	
G-BFSK	PA-23 Apache 160 ★	Sub-aqua instructional airframe/Croughton	
G-BFSR	Cessna F.150J	W. Ali	
G-BFSS	Cessna FR.172G	Albedale Farms Ltd	
G-BFSY	PA-28-181 Archer II	Downland Aviation	
G-BFTC	PA-28R-201T Turbo Arrow III	M. J. Milns/Sherburn	
G-BFTF	AA-5B Tiger	F. C. Burrow Ltd/Leeds	
G-BFTG	AA-5B Tiger	D. Hepburn & G. R. Montgomery	
G-BFTH	Cessna F.172N	J. Birkett	
G-BFTT	Cessna 421C	M. A. Ward	
G-BFTX	Cessna F.172N	Tri Society	

G-BFUB – G-BGGD

BRITISH CIVIL REGISTRATIONS

Notes	Reg	Type	Owner or Operator
	G-BFUB	PA-32RT-300 Lance II	Jolida Holdings Ltd
	G-BFUD	Scheibe SF.25E Super Falke	Lakes Libelle Syndicate/Walney Island
	G-BFUZ	Cameron V-77 balloon	Servowarm Balloon Syndicate
	G-BFVG	PA-28-181 Archer II	P. Anderson
	G-BFVH	DH.2 (replica) (5964)	M. J. Kirk
	G-BFVS	AA-5B Tiger	S. W. Biroth & T. Chapman/Denham
	G-BFVU	Cessna 150L	Aviation South West Ltd
	G-BFWB	PA-28-161 Warrior II	Mid-Anglia School of Flying
	G-BFWD	Currie Wot (C3009)	D. Silsbury & B. Proctor
	G-BFWE	PA-23 Aztec 250E	Air Navigation & Trading Co Ltd/Blackpool
	G-BFXF	Andreasson BA.4B	P. N. Birch
	G-BFXG	D.31 Turbulent	E. J. I. Musty & M. J. Whatley
	G-BFXK	PA-28 Cherokee 140	D. M. Wheeler
	G-BFXL	Albatros D.5a replica (D5397/17) ★	F.A.A. Museum/Yeovilton
	G-BFXR	Jodel D.112	M. R. Coreth
	G-BFXS	Rockwell Commander 114	Unipak (UK) Ltd
	G-BFXW	AA-5B Tiger	Campsol Ltd
	G-BFXX	AA-5B Tiger	W. R. Gibson
	G-BFYA	MBB Bö.105DB	Sterling Helicopters Ltd/Norwich
	G-BFYC	PA-32RT-300 Lance II	A. A. Barnes
	G-BFYE	Robin HR.100/285 ★	(stored)/Sywell
	G-BFYI	Westland-Bell 47G-3B1	K. P. Mayes
	G-BFYK	Cameron V-77 balloon	L. E. Jones
	G-BFYL	Evans VP-2	W. C. Brown
	G-BFYM	PA-28-161 Warrior II	Sheffield City Flying School Ltd/Sheffield
	G-BFYO	SPAD XIII (replica) (4513:1) ★	American Air Museum/Duxford
	G-BFZB	Piper J-3C-85 Cub (480723:E5-J)	M. S. Pettit
	G-BFZD	Cessna FR.182RG	R. B. Lewis & Co/Sleap
	G-BFZH	PA-28R Cherokee Arrow 200	Mason Aviation
	G-BFZM	Rockwell Commander 112TC	J. A. Hart & R. J. Lamplough
	G-BFZN	Cessna FA.152	Falcon Flying Services/Biggin Hill
	G-BFZO	AA-5A Cheetah	J. W. Cross & A. E. Kempson
	G-BFZT	Cessna FA.152	Herefordshire Aero Club Ltd/Shobdon
	G-BFZU	Cessna FA.152	C. R. Tilley
	G-BFZV	Cessna F.172M	Wessex Flying Group Ltd
	G-BGAA	Cessna 152 II	PJC Leasing Ltd
	G-BGAB	Cessna F.152 II	TG Aviation Ltd/Manston
	G-BGAE	Cessna F.152 II	Aerolease Ltd/Conington
	G-BGAF	Cessna FA.152	G-BGAF Group/Southend
	G-BGAG	Cessna F.172N	R. Clarke
	G-BGAJ	Cessna F.182Q II	Ground Airport Services Ltd/Guernsey
	G-BGAX	PA-28 Cherokee 140	G-BGAX Group
	G-BGAZ	Cameron V-77 balloon	C. J. Madigan & D. H. McGibbon
	G-BGBA	Robin R.2100A	Cotswold Aviation Services Ltd
	G-BGBE	Jodel DR.1050	J. A. & B. Mawby
	G-BGBF	D.31A Turbulent	Eaglescott Turbulent Group
	G-BGBG	PA-28-181 Archer II	Harlow Printing Ltd/Newcastle
	G-BGBI	Cessna F.150L	C. P. Tapp
	G-BGBK	PA-38-112 Tomahawk	Truman Aviation Ltd
	G-BGBN	PA-38-112 Tomahawk	Bonus Aviation Ltd/Cranfield
	G-BGBR	Cessna F.172N	Falcon Flying Services/Biggin Hill
	G-BGBW	PA-38-112 Tomahawk	Truman Aviation Ltd/Tollerton
	G-BGBZ	Rockwell Commander 114	R. S. Fenwick/Biggin Hill
	G-BGCG	Douglas C-47A ★	Datran Holdings Ltd (stored)
	G-BGCM	AA-5A Cheetah	G. & S. A. Jones
	G-BGCO	PA-44-180 Seminole	J. R. Henderson
	G-BGCY	Taylor JT.1 Monoplane	A. T. Lane
	G-BGEH	Monnett Sonerai II	D. & V. T. Hubbard
	G-BGEI	Baby Great Lakes	M. T. Taylor
	G-BGEW	SNCAN NC.854S	S. A. Francis
	G-BGFC	Evans VP-2	S. W. C. Hollins
	G-BGFF	FRED Srs 2	I. Daniels
	G-BGFG	AA-5A Cheetah	Foxtrot Gulf Group
	G-BGFH	Cessna F.182Q	Rayviation Ltd
	G-BGFI	AA-5A Cheetah	I. J. Hay & A. Nayyar/Biggin Hill
	G-BGFJ	Jodel D.9 Bébé	M. D. Mold
	G-BGFT	PA-34-200T Seneca II	Oxford Aviation Services Ltd/Kidlington
	G-BGFX	Cessna F.152	Redhill Air Services Ltd/Redhill
	G-BGGA	Bellanca 7GCBC Citabria	L. A. King
	G-BGGB	Bellanca 7GCBC Citabria	Citabria Syndicate
	G-BGGC	Bellanca 7GCBC Citabria	G-BGGC Flying Group
	G-BGGD	Bellanca 8GCBC Scout	Bristol & Gloucestershire Gliding Club/Nympsfield

BRITISH CIVIL REGISTRATIONS

G-BGGE – G-BGPL

Reg	Type	Owner or Operator	Notes
G-BGGE	PA-38-112 Tomahawk	Truman Aviation Ltd/Tollerton	
G-BGGI	PA-38-112 Tomahawk	Truman Aviation Ltd/Tollerton	
G-BGGL	PA-38-112 Tomahawk	Grunwick Processing Laboratories Ltd/Elstree	
G-BGGM	PA-38-112 Tomahawk	Grunwick Processing Laboratories Ltd/Elstree	
G-BGGN	PA-38-112 Tomahawk	Bell Aviation Ltd	
G-BGGO	Cessna F.152	East Midlands Flying School Ltd	
G-BGGP	Cessna F.152	East Midlands Flying School Ltd	
G-BGGU	Wallis WA-116/RR	K. H. Wallis	
G-BGGW	Wallis WA-112	K. H. Wallis	
G-BGGY	Agusta-Bell 206B Jet Ranger ★	Instructional airframe/Cranfield	
G-BGHF	Westland WG.30 ★	IHM/Weston-super-Mare	
G-BGHI	Cessna F.152	V. R. McCready	
G-BGHJ	Cessna F.172N	Air Plane Ltd	
G-BGHM	Robin R.1180T	H. Price	
G-BGHP	Beech 76 Duchess	Magneta Ltd/Exeter	
G-BGHS	Cameron N-31 balloon	W. R. Teasdale	
G-BGHT	Falconar F-12	C. R. Coates	
G-BGHU	NA T-6G Texan (115042:TA-042)	C. E. Bellhouse	
G-BGHV	Cameron V-77 balloon	E. Davies	
G-BGHY	Taylor JT.1 Monoplane	G. W. Hancox	
G-BGHZ	FRED Srs 2	A. J. Perry	
G-BGIB	Cessna 152 II	Redhill Air Services Ltd	
G-BGIG	PA-38-112 Tomahawk	Air Claire Ltd	
G-BGIO	Montgomerie-Bensen B.8MR	R. M. Savage	
G-BGIU	Cessna F.172H	A. G. Arthur	
G-BGIX	Helio H.295 Super Courier	C. M. Lee	
G-BGIY	Cessna F.172N	Air Claire Ltd	
G-BGJB	PA-44-180 Seminole	Ostend Air College/Belgium (G-ISFT)	
G-BGJU	Cameron V-65 Balloon	J. A. Folkes	
G-BGKC	SOCATA Rallye 110ST	J. H. Cranmer	
G-BGKJ	MBB Bö.105D ★	Instructional airframe/Bourn	
G-BGKO	Gardan GY-20 Minicab	M. N. King	
G-BGKS	PA-28-161 Warrior II	Mid America (UK) Ltd	
G-BGKT	Auster AOP.9 (XN441)	Kilo Tango Group	
G-BGKU	PA-28R-201 Arrow III	Aerolease Ltd	
G-BGKV	PA-28R-201 Arrow III	R. Haverson & A. K. Lake/Shipdham	
G-BGKY	PA-38-112 Tomahawk	APB Leasing Ltd	
G-BGKZ	Auster J/5F Aiglet Trainer	R. B. Webber	
G-BGLA	PA-38-112 Tomahawk	Norwich School of Flying	
G-BGLB	Bede BD-5B ★	Science Museum/Wroughton	
G-BGLF	Evans VP-1 Srs 2	B. A. Schlussler	
G-BGLG	Cessna 152	L. W. Scattergood	
G-BGLI	Cessna 152	Luton Flying Club	
G-BGLK	Monnett Sonerai 2L	J. Bradley	
G-BGLN	Cessna FA.152	Bournemouth Flying Club/Bournemouth	
G-BGLO	Cessna F.172N	J. R. Isabel/Southend	
G-BGLS	Oldfield FSuper Baby Lakes	J. F. Dowe	
G-BGLZ	Stits SA-3A Playboy	P. C. Sheard	
G-BGMJ	Gardan GY-201 Minicab	G-BGMJ Group	
G-BGMN	HS.748 Srs 2A	PTB (Emerald) Pty Ltd/Blackpool	
G-BGMO	HS.748 Srs 2A	PTB (Emerald) Pty Ltd/Blackpool	
G-BGMP	Cessna F.172G	R. W. Collings	
G-BGMR	Gardan GY-201 Minicab	Mike Romeo Flying Group	
G-BGMS	Taylor JT.2 Titch	M. A. J. Spice	
G-BGMT	SOCATA Rallye 235E	C. G. Wheeler	
G-BGMV	Scheibe SF.25B Falke	C. A. Bloom & A. P. Twort/Shoreham	
G-BGND	Cessna F.172N	A. J. M. Freeman	
G-BGNT	Cessna F.152	Aerolease Ltd/Conington	
G-BGNV	GA-7 Cougar	G. J. Bissex	
G-BGOD	Colt 77A balloon	C. Allen & M. D. Steuer	
G-BGOG	PA-28-161 Warrior II	W. D. Moore	
G-BGOI	Cameron O-56 balloon	M. J. Streat	
G-BGOJ	Cessna F.150L	D. J. Hockings (G-MABI)	
G-BGOL	PA-28R-201T Turbo Arrow III	R. G. Jackson	
G-BGON	GA-7 Cougar	Walsh Aviation	
G-BGOR	AT-6D Harvard III (14863)	P. Meyrick	
G-BGPA	Cessna 182Q	Hydestile Business Systems Ltd	
G-BGPB	CCF T-6J Texan (1747)	1959 Ltd	
G-BGPD	Piper J-3C-65 Cub (479744:M-49)	P. R. Whiteman	
G-BGPH	AA-5B Tiger	Shipping & Airlines Ltd/Biggin Hill	
G-BGPI	Plumb BGP-1	B. G. Plumb	
G-BGPJ	PA-28-161 Warrior II	W. Lancs Warrior Co Ltd/Woodvale	
G-BGPL	PA-28-161 Warrior II	Montash Properties Ltd	

57

G-BGPN – G-BHBE — BRITISH CIVIL REGISTRATIONS

Notes	Reg	Type	Owner or Operator
	G-BGPN	PA-18 Super Cub 150	D. McHugh
	G-BGPU	PA-28 Cherokee 140	Air Navigation & Trading Ltd/Blackpool
	G-BGRC	PA-28 Cherokee 140	Tecair Aviation Ltd & G. F. Haigh
	G-BGRE	Beech A200 Super King Air	Martin-Baker (Engineering) Ltd/Chalgrove
	G-BGRG	Beech 76 Duchess	Aviation Rentals/Bournemouth
	G-BGRH	Robin DR.400 2+2	C. R. Beard
	G-BGRI	Jodel DR.1051	B. J. L. P & W. J. A. L. de Saar
	G-BGRM	PA-38-112 Tomahawk	Classair/Biggin Hill
	G-BGRO	Cessna F.172M	Cammo Aviation
	G-BGRR	PA-38-112 Tomahawk	Goodair Leasing Ltd/Cardiff
	G-BGRS	Thunder Ax7-77Z balloon	P. M. Gaines
	G-BGRT	Steen Skybolt	O. Meier
	G-BGRX	PA-38-112 Tomahawk	Bonus Aviation Ltd
	G-BGSA	Morane MS.892E-150	P. C. Tonkin and Son
	G-BGSH	PA-38-112 Tomahawk	S. Padidar-Nazar
	G-BGSJ	Piper J-3C-65 Cub	A. J. Higgins
	G-BGSV	Cessna F.172N	Southwell Air Services Ltd
	G-BGSW	Beech F33 Debonair	C. Wood/Wellesbourne
	G-BGSY	GA-7 Cougar	Just Plane Trading Ltd
	G-BGTB	SOCATA TB10 Tobago ★	D. Pope (stored)
	G-BGTC	Auster AOP.9 (XP282)	Terranne Auster Group
	G-BGTF	PA-44-180 Seminole	NG Trustees & Nominees Ltd
	G-BGTG	PA-23 Aztec 250F	ASG Leasing Ltd/Guernsey
	G-BGTI	Piper J-3C-65 Cub	A. P. Broad
	G-BGTJ	PA-28 Cherokee 180	Serendipity Aviation/Staverton
	G-BGTT	Cessna 310R	Capital Trading (Aviation) Ltd/Exeter
	G-BGTX	Jodel D.117	Madley Flying Group/Shobdon
	G-BGUB	PA-32 Cherokee Six 300E	A. P. Diplock
	G-BGVB	Robin DR.315	P. J. Leggo
	G-BGVE	CP.1310-C3 Super Emeraude	H. T. Morris
	G-BGVH	Beech 76 Duchess	Velco Marketing
	G-BGVK	PA-28-161 Warrior II	R. S. Bristowe
	G-BGVN	PA-28RT-201 Arrow IV	C. Smith & S. Carrington
	G-BGVS	Cessna F.172M	Kirkwall Flying Club
	G-BGVV	AA-5A Cheetah	W. A. Davidson
	G-BGVY	AA-5B Tiger	R. J. C. Neal-Smith
	G-BGVZ	PA-28-181 Archer II	W. Walsh & S. R. Mitchell/Woodvale
	G-BGWC	Robin DR.400/180	M. A. Newman
	G-BGWH	PA-18 Super Cub 150	Spectrum Leisure Ltd (G-ARSR)
	G-BGWJ	Sikorsky S-61N	Bristow Helicopters Ltd
	G-BGWK	Sikorsky S-61N	Bristow Helicopters Ltd
	G-BGWM	PA-28-181 Archer II	Thames Valley Flying Club Ltd
	G-BGWN	PA-38-112 Tomahawk	R. T. Callow
	G-BGWO	Jodel D.112	G-BGWO Group/Sandtoft
	G-BGWR	Cessna U.206A	The Parachute Centre Ltd/Tilstock (G-DISC)
	G-BGWU	PA-38-112 Tomahawk	D. C. & M. Laycock
	G-BGWV	Aeronca 7AC Champion	RFC Flying Group/Popham
	G-BGWZ	Eclipse Super Eagle ★	F.A.A. Museum/Yeovilton
	G-BGXA	Piper J-3C-65 Cub (329471:F-44)	E. C. & P. King/Kemble
	G-BGXB	PA-38-112 Tomahawk	Signtest Ltd/Cardiff-Wales
	G-BGXC	SOCATA TB10 Tobago	D. H. Courtley
	G-BGXD	SOCATA TB10 Tobago	D. F. P. Finan
	G-BGXL	Bensen B.8MV	B. P. Triefus
	G-BGXO	PA-38-112 Tomahawk	Goodwood Terrena Ltd
	G-BGXR	Robin HR.200/100	J. R. Cross
	G-BGXS	PA-28-236 Dakota	G-BGXS Group
	G-BGXT	SOCATA TB10 Tobago	M. J. White & L. Chadwick
	G-BGYH	PA-28-161 Warrior II	Paper Space Ltd
	G-BGYN	PA-18 Super Cub 150	B. J. Dunford
	G-BGZF	PA-38-112 Tomahawk	Fly Me Ltd
	G-BGZZ	Thunder Ax6-56 balloon	J. M. Eaton & K. A. Willmore
	G-BHAA	Cessna 152 II	Herefordshire Aero Club Ltd/Shobdon
	G-BHAC	Cessna A.152	Herefordshire Aero Club Ltd/Shobdon
	G-BHAD	Cessna A.152	Shropshire Aero Club Ltd/Sleap
	G-BHAI	Cessna F.152	Cormack (Aircraft Services) Ltd
	G-BHAJ	Robin DR.400/160	Rowantask Ltd
	G-BHAR	Westland-Bell 47G-3B1	E. A. L. Sturmer
	G-BHAV	Cessna F.152	T. M. & M. L. Jones/Egginton
	G-BHAW	Cessna F.172N	A. Wright
	G-BHAX	Enstrom F-28C-UK-2	PVS (Barnsley) Ltd
	G-BHAY	PA-28RT-201 Arrow IV	Alpha Yankee Ltd
	G-BHBA	Campbell Cricket	S. N. McGovern
	G-BHBE	Westland-Bell 47G-3B1 (Soloy)	T. R. Smith (Agricultural Machinery) Ltd

BRITISH CIVIL REGISTRATIONS

G-BHBF – G-BHJU

Reg	Type	Owner or Operator	Notes
G-BHBF	Sikorsky S-76A	Bristow Helicopters Ltd	
G-BHBG	PA-32R Cherokee Lance 300	D. E. Gee	
G-BHBI	Mooney M.20J	G-BHBI Group	
G-BHBT	Marquart MA.5 Charger	R. G. & C. J. Maidment/Shoreham	
G-BHBZ	Partenavia P.68B	Geminair Services Ltd	
G-BHCC	Cessna 172M	D. Wood-Jenkins	
G-BHCE	Jodel D.112	D. G. Jones	
G-BHCM	Cessna F.172H	J. Dominic	
G-BHCP	Cessna F.152	Eastern Air Executive Ltd	
G-BHCZ	PA-38-112 Tomahawk	J. E. Abbott	
G-BHDD	V.668 Varsity T.1 (WL626:P) ★	Aeropark/East Midlands	
G-BHDE	SOCATA TB10 Tobago	Alpha-Alpha Ltd	
G-BHDK	Boeing B-29A-BN (461748:Y) ★	Imperial War Museum/Duxford	
G-BHDM	Cessna F.152 II	Big Red Kite Ltd	
G-BHDP	Cessna F.182Q II	Zone Travel Ltd/White Waltham	
G-BHDR	Cessna F.152 II	Heron-Air Ltd	
G-BHDS	Cessna F.152 II	Tayside Aviation Ltd/Dundee	
G-BHDU	Cessna F.152 II	Falcon Flying Services/Biggin Hill	
G-BHDV	Cameron V-77 balloon	P. Glydon	
G-BHDW	Cessna F.152 II	Aircraft Engineers Ltd	
G-BHDX	Cessna F.172N	GDX Ltd	
G-BHDZ	Cessna F.172N	Abbey Security Services Ltd	
G-BHEC	Cessna F.152 II	Stapleford Flying Club Ltd	
G-BHED	Cessna FA.152	TG Aviation Ltd/Manston	
G-BHEG	Jodel 150	D. M. Griffiths	
G-BHEK	CP.1315-C3 Super Emeraude	D. B. Winstanley/Barton	
G-BHEL	Jodel D.117	N. Wright & C. M. Kettlewell	
G-BHEM	Bensen B.8M	G. C. Kerr	
G-BHEN	Cessna FA.152	Leicestershire Aero Club Ltd	
G-BHEU	Thunder Ax7-65 balloon	D. G. Such	
G-BHEV	PA-28R Cherokee Arrow 200	7-Up Group	
G-BHEX	Colt 56A balloon	A. S. Dear & ptnrs	
G-BHEZ	Jodel 150	Air Yorkshire Group	
G-BHFC	Cessna F.152	Premier Flight Training Ltd	
G-BHFE	PA-44-180 Seminole	Grunwick Processing Laboratories Ltd	
G-BHFF	Jodel D.112	G. H. Gilmour-White	
G-BHFG	SNCAN Stampe SV.4C	A. D. R. Northeast & S. A. Cook	
G-BHFH	PA-34-200T Seneca II	Oxford Aviation Services Ltd/Kidlington	
G-BHFI	Cessna F.152	BAe (Warton) Flying Group/Blackpool	
G-BHFJ	PA-28RT-201T Turbo Arrow IV	J. K. Beauchamp	
G-BHFK	PA-28-151 Warrior	Ilkeston Car Sales Ltd	
G-BHFR	Eiri PIK-20E-1	J. T. Morgan	
G-BHGC	PA-18 Super Cub 150	Vectis Gliding Club Ltd	
G-BHGF	Cameron V-56 balloon	P. Smallward	
G-BHGJ	Jodel D.120	Q. M. B. Oswell	
G-BHGO	PA-32 Cherokee Six 260	S. A. Boyall	
G-BHGP	SOCATA TB10 Tobago	D. Suleyman	
G-BHGY	PA-28R Cherokee Arrow 200	Truman Aviation Ltd	
G-BHHB	Cameron V-77 balloon	R. Powell	
G-BHHE	Jodel DR.1051/M1	P. Bridges & P. C. Matthews	
G-BHHG	Cessna F.152 II	TG Aviation Ltd/Manston	
G-BHHH	Thunder Ax7-65 balloon	C. A. Hendley (Essex) Ltd	
G-BHHK	Cameron N-77 balloon	I. S. Bridge	
G-BHHN	Cameron V-77 balloon	Itchen Valley Balloon Group	
G-BHHX	Jodel D.112	G-BHHX Group	
G-BHIB	Cessna F.182Q	S. N. Chater & B. Payne	
G-BHIC	Cessna F.182Q	Oxford Aviation Services Ltd	
G-BHIG	Colt 31A Arm Chair SS balloon	P. A. Lindstrand/Sweden	
G-BHII	Cameron V-77 balloon	R. V. Brown	
G-BHIJ	Eiri PIK-20E-1 (898)	P. M. Yeoman	
G-BHIK	Adam RA-14 Loisirs	L. Lewis	
G-BHIN	Cessna F.152	Cristal Air Ltd	
G-BHIR	PA-28R Cherokee Arrow 200	Factorcore Ltd/Barton	
G-BHIS	Thunder Ax7-65 balloon	Hedgehoppers Balloon Group	
G-BHIT	SOCATA TB9 Tampico	C. J. P. Webster/Biggin Hill	
G-BHIY	Cessna F.150K	G. J. Ball	
G-BHJF	SOCATA TB10 Tobago	Flying Fox Group/Blackbushe	
G-BHJI	Mooney M.20J	Hearing Centre Aarhus/Denmark	
G-BHJK	Maule M5-235C Lunar Rocket	P. J. Kelsey	
G-BHJN	Fournier RF-4D	RF-4 Group	
G-BHJO	PA-28-161 Warrior II	Brackla Flying Group	
G-BHJS	Partenavia P.68B	J. J. Watts & D. Fletcher	
G-BHJU	Robin DR.400/2+2	J. Barlow & P. Crow	

59

G-BHKH – G-BHVB

BRITISH CIVIL REGISTRATIONS

Notes	Reg	Type	Owner or Operator
	G-BHKH	Cameron O-65 balloon	P. Donkin
	G-BHKJ	Cessna 421C	Totaljet Ltd
	G-BHKR	Colt 12A balloon ★	British Balloon Museum/Newbury
	G-BHKT	Jodel D.112	M. G. Davis
	G-BHLE	Robin DR.400/180	B. D. Greenwood
	G-BHLH	Robin DR.400/180	G-BHLH Group
	G-BHLJ	Saffery-Rigg S.200 balloon	I. A. Rigg
	G-BHLT	DH.82A Tiger Moth	Skymax (Aviation) Ltd
	G-BHLU	Fournier RF-3	G. Sabatino
	G-BHLW	Cessna 120	L. W. Scattergood
	G-BHLX	AA-5B Tiger	M. D. McPherson
	G-BHMA	SIPA 903	H. J. Taggart
	G-BHMG	Cessna FA.152	R. D. Smith
	G-BHMI	Cessna F.172N	GMI Aviation Ltd (G-WADE)
	G-BHMJ	Avenger T.200-2112 balloon	R. Light *Lord Anthony 1*
	G-BHMK	Avenger T.200-2112 balloon	P. Kinder *Lord Anthony 2*
	G-BHMR	Stinson 108-3	D. G. French/Sandown
	G-BHMT	Evans VP-1	P. E. J. Sturgeon
	G-BHMY	F.27 Friendship Mk.200 ★	Norwich Aviation Museum
	G-BHNC	Cameron O-65 balloon	D. & C. Bareford
	G-BHND	Cameron N-65 balloon	S. M. Wellband
	G-BHNK	Jodel D.120A	G-BHNK Flying Group
	G-BHNL	Jodel D.112	HNL Group
	G-BHNO	PA-28-181 Archer II	Airfluid Hydraulics & Pneumatics (Wolverhampton) Ltd
	G-BHNP	Eiri PIK-20E-1	D. A. Sutton/Riseley
	G-BHNV	Westlan-Bell 47G-3B1	Leyline Helicopters Ltd
	G-BHNX	Jodel D.117	A. J. Chalkley
	G-BHOA	Robin DR.400/160	Goudhurst Service Station Ltd
	G-BHOG	Sikorsky S-61N Mk.II	British International
	G-BHOH	Sikorsky S-61N Mk.II	Bristow Helicopters Ltd
	G-BHOJ	Colt 12A balloon	J. A. Folkes
	G-BHOL	Jodel DR.1050	S. P. Tilling
	G-BHOM	PA-18 Super Cub 95	Oscar Mike Flying Group
	G-BHOO	Thunder Ax7-65 balloon	D. Livesey & J. M. Purves
	G-BHOR	PA-28-161 Warrior II	Oscar Romeo Flying Group/Biggin Hill
	G-BHOT	Cameron V-65 balloon	Dante Balloon Group
	G-BHOZ	SOCATA TB9 Tampico	G-BHOZ Management Ltd/Kemble
	G-BHPK	Piper J-3C-65 Cub (238410:A-44)	L-4 Group
	G-BHPL	CASA 1.131E Jungmann 1000 (E3B-350:05-97) ★	A. Burroughes
	G-BHPS	Jodel D.120A	T. J. Price
	G-BHPY	Cessna 152 II	Transcourt Ltd
	G-BHPZ	Cessna 172N	O'Brien Properties Ltd/Redhill
	G-BHRB	Cessna F.152 II	LAC (Enterprises) Ltd/Barton
	G-BHRC	PA-28-161 Warrior II	Sherwood Flying Club Ltd/Tollerton
	G-BHRH	Cessna FA.150K	Merlin Flying Club Ltd/Hucknall
	G-BHRM	Cessna F.152	Tatenhill Aviation Ltd
	G-BHRN	Cessna F.152	Flight Academy Scotland Ltd
	G-BHRO	Rockwell Commander 112	R. A. Blackwell
	G-BHRP	PA-44-180 Seminole	M. S. Farmers
	G-BHRR	CP.301A Emeraude	T. W. Offen
	G-BHRW	Jodel DR.221	Dauphin Flying Club
	G-BHRY	Colt 56A balloon	A. S. Davidson
	G-BHSB	Cessna 172N	SB Aviation Ltd
	G-BHSD	Scheibe SF.25E Super Falke	Upwood Motorglider Group
	G-BHSE	Rockwell Commander 114	604 Sqdn Flying Group Ltd
	G-BHSN	Cameron N-56 balloon	I. Bentley
	G-BHSP	Thunder Ax7-77Z balloon	Out-Of-The-Blue
	G-BHSS	Pitts S-1C Special	C. W. Burkett
	G-BHSY	Jodel DR.1050	T. R. Allebone
	G-BHTA	PA-28-236 Dakota	Dakota Ltd
	G-BHTC	Jodel DR.1050/M1	G. Clark
	G-BHTG	Thunder Ax6-56 balloon	F. R. & Mrs S. H. MacDonald
	G-BHUB	Douglas C-47A (315509:W7-S) ★	Imperial War Museum/Duxford
	G-BHUE	Jodel DR.1050	M. J. Harris
	G-BHUG	Cessna 172N	FGT Aircraft Hire
	G-BHUI	Cessna 152	Galair International Ltd
	G-BHUJ	Cessna 172N	Uniform Juliet Group/Southend
	G-BHUM	DH.82A Tiger Moth	S. G. Towers
	G-BHUR	Thunder Ax3 balloon	B. F. G. Ribbans
	G-BHUU	PA-25 Pawnee 235	Booker Gliding Club Ltd
	G-BHVB	PA-28-161 Warrior II	P. J. Clarke

60

BRITISH CIVIL REGISTRATIONS
G-BHVC – G-BIDK

Reg	Type	Owner or Operator	Notes
G-BHVC	Cessna 172RG	K. O'Connor	
G-BHVF	Jodel 150A	J. D. Walton	
G-BHVP	Cessna 182Q	R. J. W. Wood	
G-BHVR	Cessna 172N	G-BHVR Group	
G-BHVV	Piper J-3C-65 Cub	C. A. Ward & C. A. Cash	
G-BHWA	Cessna F.152	Lincoln Enterprises Ltd/Wickenby	
G-BHWB	Cessna F.152	Lincoln Enterprises Ltd/Wickenby	
G-BHWH	Weedhopper JC-24A	G. A. Clephane	
G-BHWK	MS.880B Rallye Club	W. O. Wright & D.-J. Spencer	
G-BHWY	PA-28R Cherokee Arrow 200-II	Kilo Foxtrot Flying Group/Sandown	
G-BHWZ	PA-28-181 Archer II	M. A. Abbott	
G-BHXA	SA Bulldog Srs 120/1210	Air Plan Flight Equipment Ltd/Barton	
G-BHXD	Jodel D.120	D. A. Garner	
G-BHXK	PA-28 Cherokee 140	GXK Flying Group	
G-BHXS	Jodel D.120	Plymouth Jodel Group	
G-BHXY	Piper J-3C-65 Cub (44-79609:44-S)	F. W. Rogers/Aldergrove	
G-BHYA	Cessna R.182RG II	B. Davies	
G-BHYC	Cessna 172RG II	IB Aeroplanes Ltd	
G-BHYD	Cessna R.172K XP II	Sylmar Aviation Services Ltd	
G-BHYG	PA-34-200T Seneca II	Oxford Aviation Services Ltd/Kidlington	
G-BHYI	SNCAN Stampe SV.4A	C. V. Parkin & D. Hicklin	
G-BHYO	Cameron N-77 balloon	Adventure Balloon Co Ltd	
G-BHYP	Cessna F.172M	Avior Ltd/Biggin Hill	
G-BHYR	Cessna F.172M	G-BHYR Group	
G-BHYV	Evans VP-1	L. Chiappi/Blackpool	
G-BHYX	Cessna 152 II	Stapleford Flying Club Ltd	
G-BHZE	PA-28-181 Archer II	Zegruppe Ltd	
G-BHZH	Cessna F.152	Plymouth School of Flying Ltd	
G-BHZK	AA-5B Tiger	ZK Group/Elstree	
G-BHZO	AA-5A Cheetah	Scotia Safari Ltd/Prestwick	
G-BHZR	SA Bulldog Srs 120/1210	White Knuckle Air Ltd	
G-BHZS	SA Bulldog Srs 120/1210	Air Plan Flight Equipment Ltd/Hawarden	
G-BHZT	SA Bulldog Srs 120/1210	D. M. Curties	
G-BHZU	Piper J-3C-65 Cub	J. K. Tomkinson	
G-BHZV	Jodel D.120A	K. J. Scott	
G-BHZX	Thunder Ax7-65A balloon	R. J. & H. M. Beattie	
G-BIAC	SOCATA Rallye 235E	D. R. Watson & A. J. Haigh	
G-BIAH	Jodel D.112	T. K. Duffy	
G-BIAI	WMB.2 Windtracker balloon	I. Chadwick	
G-BIAP	PA-16 Clipper	P. J. Bish/White Waltham	
G-BIAR	Rigg Skyliner II balloon	I. A. Rigg	
G-BIAU	Sopwith Pup (replica) (N6452) ★	F.A.A. Museum/Yeovilton	
G-BIAX	Taylor JT.2 Titch	J. T. Everest	
G-BIAY	AA-5 Traveler	T. J. Kent & G. Frost	
G-BIBA	SOCATA TB9 Tampico	TB Aviation Ltd	
G-BIBB	Mooney M.20C	Lefay Engineering Ltd	
G-BIBG	Sikorsky S-76A II	Bristow Helicopters Ltd	
G-BIBJ	Enstrom 280C-UK-2	C. J. Swift	
G-BIBN	Cessna FA.150K	B. V. Mayo	
G-BIBO	Cameron V-65 balloon	I. Harris	
G-BIBS	Cameron P-20 balloon	Cameron Balloons Ltd	
G-BIBT	AA-5B Tiger	Horizon Aviation Ltd	
G-BIBW	Cessna F.172N	Drawflight Ltd	
G-BIBX	WMB.2 Windtracker balloon	I. A. Rigg	
G-BICD	Auster 5	T. R. Parsons	
G-BICE	NA AT-6C Harvard IIA (41-33275:CE)	C. M. L. Edwards	
G-BICG	Cessna F.152 II	Falcon Flying Services/Biggin Hill	
G-BICJ	Monnett Sonerai II	P. Daukas	
G-BICM	Colt 56A balloon	Avon Advertiser Balloon Club	
G-BICP	Robin DR.360	B. McVeighty	
G-BICR	Jodel D.120A	Beehive Flying Group/White Waltham	
G-BICS	Robin R.2100A	I. Young/Sandown	
G-BICU	Cameron V-56 balloon	Black Pearl Balloons	
G-BICW	PA-28-161 Warrior II	Charlie Whisky Flying Group	
G-BICX	Maule M5-235C Lunar Rocket	A. T. Jeans & J. F. Clarkson/Old Sarum	
G-BIDD	Evans VP-1	J. Hodgkinson	
G-BIDF	Cessna F.172P	C. J. Chaplin & N. J. C. Howard	
G-BIDG	Jodel 150A	D. R. Gray/Barton	
G-BIDH	Cessna 152 II	Hull Aero Club Ltd (G-DONA)	
G-BIDI	PA-28R-201 Arrow III	B. Webb	
G-BIDJ	PA-18A Super Cub 150	Flight Solutions Ltd	
G-BIDK	PA-18 Super Cub 150	J. & M. A. McCullough	

61

G-BIDO – G-BIMK   BRITISH CIVIL REGISTRATIONS

Notes	Reg	Type	Owner or Operator
	G-BIDO	CP.301A Emeraude	A. R. Plumb
	G-BIDU	Colt 14A balloon ★	British Balloon Museum/Newbury
	G-BIDW	Sopwith 1½ Strutter (replica) (A8226) ★	RAF Museum/Hendon
	G-BIDX	Jodel D.112	P. Turton & H. C. Peake-Jones
	G-BIEF	Cameron V-77 balloon	D. S. Bush
	G-BIEJ	Sikorsky S-76A	Bristow Helicopters Ltd
	G-BIEN	Jodel D.120A	C. Newton/France
	G-BIEO	Jodel D.112	Clipgate Flyers
	G-BIES	Maule M5-235C Lunar Rocket	William Proctor Farms
	G-BIET	Cameron O-77 balloon	G. M. Westley
	G-BIEY	PA-28-151 Warrior	Falcon Flying Services/Biggin Hill
	G-BIFA	Cessna 310R II	J. S. Lee
	G-BIFB	PA-28 Cherokee 150C	P. Coombs
	G-BIFO	Evans VP-1	R. Broadhead
	G-BIFY	Cessna F.150L	Bonus Aviation Ltd
	G-BIGJ	Cessna F.172M	Cirrus Aviation Ltd
	G-BIGK	Taylorcraft BC-12D	N. P. S. Ramsay
	G-BIGL	Cameron O-65 balloon	P. L. Mossman
	G-BIGP	Bensen B.8M	R. H. S. Cooper
	G-BIGR	Avenger T.200-2112 balloon	R. Light
	G-BIGZ	Scheibe SF.25B Falke	Big-Z Owners Group
	G-BIHD	Robin DR.400/160	A. J. Fieldman
	G-BIHF	SE-5A (replica) (F943)	S. H. O'Connell/White Waltham
	G-BIHI	Cessna 172M	Fenland Flying School
	G-BIHO	DHC.6 Twin Otter 310	Isles of Scilly Skybus Ltd/St. Just
	G-BIHP	Van Den Bemden gas balloon	J. J. Harris
	G-BIHT	PA-17 Vagabond	B. Carter
	G-BIHU	Saffrey S.200 balloon	B. L. King
	G-BIHW	Aeronca A65TAC Defender	T. J. Ingrouille
	G-BIHX	Bensen B.8M	P. P. Willmott
	G-BIIA	Fournier RF-3	J. D. Webb & J. D. Bally
	G-BIIB	Cessna F.172M	Civil Service Flying Club (Biggin Hill) Ltd
	G-BIID	PA-18 Super Cub 95	D. A. Lacey
	G-BIIE	Cessna F.172P	Sterling Helicopters Ltd
	G-BIIK	MS.883 Rallye 115	N. J. Garbett
	G-BIIP	BN-2B-27 Islander	Blue Island Air
	G-BIIT	PA-28-161 Warrior II	Highland Flying School Ltd
	G-BIIV	PA-28-181 Archer II	J. Thuret/France
	G-BIIZ	Great Lakes 2T-1A Sport Trainer	Circa 42 Ltd
	G-BIJB	PA-18 Super Cub 150	James Aero Ltd/Stapleford
	G-BIJD	Bölkow Bö.208C Junior	Sikh Sydicate
	G-BIJE	Piper J-3C-65 Cub	R. L. Hayward & A. G. Scott
	G-BIJS	Luton LA-4A Minor	I. J. Smith
	G-BIJU	CP-301A Emeraude	Eastern Taildraggers Flying Clug (G-BHTX)
	G-BIJV	Cessna F.152 II	Falcon Flying Services/Biggin Hill
	G-BIJW	Cessna F.152 II	Falcon Flying Services/Biggin Hill
	G-BIJX	Cessna F.152 II	Falcon Flying Services/Biggin Hill
	G-BIKC	Boeing 757-236F	DHL Air Ltd
	G-BIKE	PA-28R Cherokee Arrow 200	R. V. Webb
	G-BIKF	Boeing 757-236F	DHL Air Ltd
	G-BIKG	Boeing 757-236F	DHL Air Ltd
	G-BIKI	Boeing 757-236F	DHL Air Ltd
	G-BIKJ	Boeing 757-236F	DHL Air Ltd
	G-BIKK	Boeing 757-236F	DHL Air Ltd
	G-BIKM	Boeing 757-236F	DHL Air Ltd
	G-BIKN	Boeing 757-236F	DHL Air Ltd
	G-BIKO	Boeing 757-236F	DHL Air Ltd
	G-BIKP	Boeing 757-236F	DHL Air Ltd
	G-BIKS	Boeing 757-236F	DHL Air Ltd
	G-BIKU	Boeing 757-236F	DHL Air Ltd
	G-BIKV	Boeing 757-236F	DHL Air Ltd
	G-BIKZ	Boeing 757-236F	DHL Air Ltd
	G-BILB	WMB.2 Windtracker balloon	B. L. King
	G-BILE	Scruggs BL.2B balloon	P. D. Ridout
	G-BILG	Scruggs BL.2B balloon	P. D. Ridout
	G-BILI	Piper J-3C-65 Cub (454467:J-44)	G-BILI Flying Group
	G-BILJ	Cessna FA.152	D. G. Baverstock
	G-BILL	PA-25 Pawnee 235	Pawnee Aviation
	G-BILR	Cessna 152 II	Shropshire Aero Club Ltd/Sleap
	G-BILS	Cessna 152 II	Mona Flying Club
	G-BILU	Cessna 172RG	Full Sutton Flying Centre Ltd
	G-BILZ	Taylor JT.1 Monoplane	A. Petherbridge
	G-BIMK	Tiger T.200 Srs 1 balloon	M. K. Baron

BRITISH CIVIL REGISTRATIONS

G-BIMM – G-BIWB

Reg	Type	Owner or Operator	Notes
G-BIMM	PA-18 Super Cub 150	Spectrum Leisure Ltd/Clacton	
G-BIMN	Steen Skybolt	R. J. Thomas	
G-BIMO	SNCAN Stampe SV.4C (394)	R. A. Roberts	
G-BIMT	Cessna FA.152	Staverton Flying Services	
G-BIMU	Sikorsky S-61N	Bristow Helicopters Ltd	
G-BIMX	Rutan Vari-Eze	D. G. Crow/Biggin Hill	
G-BIMZ	Beech 76 Duchess	R. P. Smith	
G-BINL	Scruggs BL.2B balloon	P. D. Ridout	
G-BINM	Scruggs BL.2B balloon	P. D. Ridout	
G-BINR	Unicorn UE.1A balloon	Unicorn Group	
G-BINS	Unicorn UE.2A balloon	Unicorn Group	
G-BINT	Unicorn UE.1A balloon	D. E. Bint	
G-BINX	Scruggs BL.2B balloon	P. D. Ridout	
G-BINY	Oriental balloon	J. L. Morton	
G-BIOA	Hughes 369D	AH Helicopter Services Ltd	
G-BIOB	Cessna F.172P	Quick Flight Images LLP	
G-BIOC	Cessna F.150L	M. Taylor	
G-BIOI	Jodel DR.1051/M	R. Pidcock	
G-BIOJ	Rockwell Commander 112TCA	A. T. Dalby	
G-BIOK	Cessna F.152	A. D. H. Macdonald	
G-BIOM	Cessna F.152	J. B. P. E. Fernandes	
G-BIOU	Jodel D.117A	Jemalk Group	
G-BIOW	Slingsby T.67A	A. B. Slinger/Sherburn	
G-BIPA	AA-5B Tiger	Tri-Star Developments Ltd	
G-BIPH	Scruggs BL.2B balloon	C. M. Dewsnap	
G-BIPI	Everett gyroplane	C. A. Reeves	
G-BIPN	Fournier RF-3	J. C. R. Rogers & I. F. Fairhead	
G-BIPO	Mudry/CAARP CAP-20LS-200M	The CAP-20 Group/White Waltham	
G-BIPS	SOCATA Rallye 100ST	McAully Flying Group/Little Snoring	
G-BIPT	Jodel D.112	C. R. Davies	
G-BIPV	AA-5B Tiger	Databridge Services Ltd	
G-BIPW	Avenger T.200-2112 balloon	B. L. King	
G-BIPY	Montgomerie-Bensen B.8MR	P. A. Clare	
G-BIRD	Pitts S-1D Special	P. Metcalfe	
G-BIRE	Colt 56 Bottle SS balloon	M. J. Axtell	
G-BIRH	PA-18 Super Cub 135 (R-163)	Aquila Gliding Club Ltd	
G-BIRI	CASA 1.131E Jungmann 1000	D. Watt	
G-BIRL	Avenger T.200-2112 balloon	R. Light	
G-BIRP	Arena Mk 17 Skyship balloon	A. S. Viel	
G-BIRT	Robin R.1180TD	W. D'A. Hall/Booker	
G-BIRW	MS.505 Criquet (F+IS) ★	Museum of Flight/East Fortune	
G-BISG	FRED Srs 3	T. Littlefair	
G-BISH	Cameron V-65 balloon	P. J. Bish	
G-BISK	Rockwell Commander 112B ★	P. A. Warner	
G-BISL	Scruggs BL.2B balloon	P. D. Ridout	
G-BISM	Scruggs BL.2B balloon	P. D. Ridout	
G-BISS	Scruggs BL.2C balloon	P. D. Ridout	
G-BIST	Scruggs BL.2C balloon	P. D. Ridout	
G-BISX	Colt 56A balloon	C. D. Steel	
G-BISZ	Sikorsky S-76A	Bristow Helicopters Ltd	
G-BITA	PA-18 Super Cub 150	Intrepid Aviation Co/North Weald	
G-BITE	SOCATA TB10 Tobago	M. A. Smith/Fairoaks	
G-BITF	Cessna F.152 II	G-BITF Owners Group	
G-BITH	Cessna F.152 II	J. R. Hyde (G-TFSA)	
G-BITK	FRED Srs 2	D. J. Wood	
G-BITM	Cessna F.172P	Dreamtrade Ltd/Barton	
G-BITO	Jodel D.112D	A. Dunbar/Barton	
G-BITS	Drayton B-56 balloon	M. J. Betts	
G-BITY	FD.31T balloon	A. J. Bell	
G-BIUM	Cessna F.152	Sheffield Aero Club Ltd/Netherthorpe	
G-BIUP	SNCAN NC.854S	J. Greenaway & T. D. Cooper	
G-BIUU	PA-23 Aztec 250D ★	G. Cormack/Glasgow	
G-BIUV	HS.748 Srs 2A	PTB (Emerald) Pty Ltd *City of Liverpool*/Blackpool (G-AYYH)	
G-BIUW	PA-28-161 Warrior II	D. R. Staley/Sturgate	
G-BIUY	PA-28-181 Archer II	J. S. Devlin & Z. Islam	
G-BIVA	Robin R.2112	BIVA Group	
G-BIVB	Jodel D.112	N. M. Harwood	
G-BIVC	Jodel D.112	M. J. Barmby/Cardiff	
G-BIVF	CP.301C-3 Emeraude	R. J. Moore	
G-BIVK	Bensen B.8M	M. J. Atyeo	
G-BIVV	AA-5A Cheetah	Robert Afia Consulting Engineer	
G-BIWB	Scruggs RS.5000 balloon	P. D. Ridout	

G-BIWC – G-BJEF — BRITISH CIVIL REGISTRATIONS

Notes	Reg	Type	Owner or Operator
	G-BIWC	Scruggs RS.5000 balloon	P. D. Ridout
	G-BIWF	Warren balloon	P. D. Ridout
	G-BIWG	Zelenski Mk 2 balloon	P. D. Ridout
	G-BIWJ	Unicorn UE.1A balloon	B. L. King
	G-BIWK	Cameron V-65 balloon	I. R. Williams & R. G. Bickerdike
	G-BIWL	PA-32-301 Saratoga	Regularity Ltd
	G-BIWN	Jodel D.112	C. R. Coates
	G-BIWR	Mooney M.20F	A. C. Brink
	G-BIWU	Cameron V-65 balloon	W. Rousell & J. Tyrrell
	G-BIWW	AA-5 Traveler	S. J. Perkins & D. Dobson
	G-BIWY	Westland WG.30 ★	Instructional airframe/Yeovil
	G-BIXA	SOCATA TB9 Tampico	W. Maxwell
	G-BIXB	SOCATA TB9 Tampico	B. G. Adams
	G-BIXH	Cessna F.152	Northern Aviation Ltd
	G-BIXL	P-51D Mustang (472216:HO-M)	R. Lamplough/North Weald
	G-BIXN	Boeing Stearman A75N1 (FJ777)	V. S. E. Norman/Rendcomb
	G-BIXV	Bell 212	Bristow Helicopters Ltd
	G-BIXW	Colt 56B balloon	N. A. P. Bates
	G-BIXX	Pearson Srs 2 balloon	D. Pearson
	G-BIXZ	Grob G-109	D. L. Nind & I. Allum/Booker
	G-BIYI	Cameron V-65 balloon	Sarnia Balloon Group
	G-BIYJ	PA-18 Super Cub 95	S. Russell
	G-BIYK	Isaacs Fury II	S. M. Roberts
	G-BIYP	PA-20 Pacer 125	A. W. Hoy & S. W. M. Johnson
	G-BIYR	PA-18 Super Cub 150 (R-151)	Delta Foxtrot Flying Group
	G-BIYT	Colt 17A balloon	J. M. Francois/France
	G-BIYU	Fokker S.11.1 Instructor (E-15)	C. Briggs
	G-BIYW	Jodel D.112	Pollard/Balaam/Bye Flying Group
	G-BIYX	PA-28 Cherokee 140	W. B. Bateson/Blackpool
	G-BIYY	PA-18 Super Cub 95	A. E. & W. J. Taylor/Ingoldmells
	G-BIZE	SOCATA TB9 Tampico	C. Fordham
	G-BIZF	Cessna F.172P	R. S. Bentley/Bourn
	G-BIZG	Cessna F.152	M. A. Judge
	G-BIZI	Robin DR.400/120	Headcorn Flying School Ltd
	G-BIZK	Nord 3202 (78)	A. I. Milne/Swanton Morley
	G-BIZM	Nord 3202	Global Aviation Ltd/Humberside
	G-BIZO	PA-28R Cherokee Arrow 200	Lemas Air
	G-BIZR	SOCATA TB9 Tampico	Fenland Flying Group (G-BSEC)
	G-BIZU	Thunder Ax6-56Z balloon	M. J. Loades
	G-BIZV	PA-18 Super Cub 95 (18-2001)	R. W. Skelton
	G-BIZW	Champion 7GCBC Citabria	G. Read & Sons
	G-BIZY	Jodel D.112	Wayland Tunley & Associates/Cranfield
	G-BJAD	FRED Srs 2 ★	Newark (Nottinghamshire & Lincolnshire) Air Museum
	G-BJAE	Lavadoux Starck AS.80 ★	D. J. & S. A. E. Phillips/Coventry
	G-BJAF	Piper J-3C-65 Cub	P. J. Cottle
	G-BJAG	PA-28-181 Archer II	C. R. Chubb
	G-BJAJ	AA-5B Tiger	R. G. Seth-Smith & R. J. Jackson
	G-BJAL	CASA 1.131E Jungmann 1000	I. C. Underwood & S. B. J. Chandler/Breighton
	G-BJAO	Bensen B.8M	A. P. Lay
	G-BJAP	DH.82A Tiger Moth (K2587)	K. Knight
	G-BJAS	Rango NA.9 balloon	A. Lindsay
	G-BJAV	Gardan GY-80 Horizon 160	Alpha Victor Group
	G-BJAW	Cameron V-65 balloon	G. W. McCarthy
	G-BJAY	Piper J-3C-65 Cub	D. W. Finlay
	G-BJBK	PA-18 Super Cub 95	M. S. Bird/Old Sarum
	G-BJBM	Monnett Sonerai I	N. J. Cowley
	G-BJBO	Jodel DR.250/160	Wiltshire Flying Group
	G-BJBW	PA-28-161 Warrior II	152 Group
	G-BJBX	PA-28-161 Warrior II	Haimoss Ltd
	G-BJCA	PA-28-161 Warrior II	Plane Sailing (Southwest) Ltd
	G-BJCF	CP1310-C3 Super Emeraude	K. M. Hodson & C. G. H. Gurney
	G-BJCI	PA-18 Super Cub 150 (modified)	The Borders (Milfield) Gliding Club Ltd
	G-BJCW	PA-32R-301 Saratoga SP	Golf Charlie Whisky Ltd
	G-BJDE	Cessna F.172M	Cranfield Aircraft Partnership
	G-BJDF	MS.880B Rallye 100T	G-BJDF Group
	G-BJDJ	HS.125 Srs 700B	TAG Farnborough Engineering Ltd (G-RCDI)
	G-BJDK	European E.14 balloon	Aeroprint Tours
	G-BJDO	AA-5A Cheetah	Flying Services
	G-BJDW	Cessna F.172M	J. Rae
	G-BJEE	BN-2T Turbine Islander	Cormack (Aircraft Services) Ltd
	G-BJEF	BN-2T Turbine Islander	Cormack (Aircraft Services) Ltd

BRITISH CIVIL REGISTRATIONS

G-BJEI – G-BJVK

Reg	Type	Owner or Operator	Notes
G-BJEI	PA-18 Super Cub 95	H. J. Cox	
G-BJEJ	BN-2T Turbine Islander	Cormack (Aircraft Services) Ltd	
G-BJEL	SNCAN NC.854	C. A. James	
G-BJEV	Aeronca 11AC Chief (897)	R. F. Willcox	
G-BJEX	Bölkow Bö.208C Junior	G. D. H. Crawford/Thruxton	
G-BJFC	European E.8 balloon	P. D. Ridout	
G-BJFE	PA-18 Super Cub 95	P. H. Wilmot-Allistone	
G-BJFL	Sikorsky S-76A	Bristow Helicopters Ltd	
G-BJFM	Jodel D.120	J. V. George & P. A. Smith/Popham	
G-BJGK	Cameron V-77 balloon	M. E. Orchard	
G-BJGM	Unicorn UE.1A balloon	D. Eaves & P. D. Ridout	
G-BJGX	Sikorsky S-76A	Bristow Helicopters Ltd	
G-BJGY	Cessna F.172P	K. & S. Martin	
G-BJHB	Mooney M.20J	Zitair Flying Club Ltd/Redhill	
G-BJHK	EAA Acro Sport	M. R. Holden	
G-BJHV	Voisin Replica ★	Brooklands Museum of Aviation/Weybridge	
G-BJIA	Allport balloon	D. J. Allport	
G-BJIC	Dodo 1A balloon	P. D. Ridout	
G-BJID	Osprey 1B balloon	P. D. Ridout	
G-BJIG	Slingsby T.67A	A. D. Hodgkinson	
G-BJIV	PA-18 Super Cub 180	Yorkshire Gliding Club (Pty) Ltd/Sutton Bank	
G-BJKF	SOCATA TB9 Tampico	P. M. A. Croton	
G-BJKW	Wills Aera II	J. K. S. Wills	
G-BJKY	Cessna F.152	Air Charter & Travel Ltd/Ronaldsway	
G-BJLB	SNCAN NC.854S	M. J. Barnaby	
G-BJLC	Monnett Sonerai IIL	P. O. Yeo	
G-BJLX	Cremer balloon	P. W. May	
G-BJLY	Cremer balloon	P. Cannon	
G-BJML	Cessna 120	R. A. Smith	
G-BJMO	Taylor JT.1 Monoplane	R. C. Mark	
G-BJMR	Cessna 310R	J. McL. Robinson/Sherburn	
G-BJMW	Thunder Ax8-105 balloon	G. M. Westley	
G-BJMX	Jarre JR.3 balloon	P. D. Ridout	
G-BJMZ	European EA.8A balloon	P. D. Ridout	
G-BJNA	Arena Mk 117P balloon	P. D. Ridout	
G-BJND	Osprey Mk 1E balloon	A. Billington & D. Whitmore	
G-BJNF	Cessna F.152	D. M. & B. Cloke	
G-BJNG	Slingsby T.67AM	D. F. Hodgkinson	
G-BJNN	PA-38-112 Tomahawk	S. Padidar-Nazar	
G-BJNY	Aeronca 11CC Super Chief	P. I. & D. M. Morgans	
G-BJNZ	PA-23 Aztec 250F	Bonus Aviation Ltd/Cranfield (G-FANZ)	
G-BJOA	PA-28-181 Archer II	Tatenhill Aviation Ltd	
G-BJOB	Jodel D.140C	T. W. M. Beck & M. J. Smith	
G-BJOE	Jodel D.120A	Forth Flying Group	
G-BJOP	BN-2B-26 Islander	Loganair Ltd/BA Express	
G-BJOT	Jodel D.117	R. H. Ryle & ptnrs	
G-BJOV	Cessna F.150K	J. A. Boyd	
G-BJPI	Bede BD-5G	M. D. McQueen	
G-BJRA	Osprey Mk 4B balloon	E. Osborn	
G-BJRG	Osprey Mk 4B balloon	A. E. de Gruchy	
G-BJRH	Rango NA.36 balloon	N. H. Ponsford	
G-BJRP	Cremer balloon	M. D. Williams	
G-BJRR	Cremer balloon	M. D. Williams	
G-BJRV	Cremer balloon	M. D. Williams	
G-BJSS	Allport balloon	D. J. Allport	
G-BJST	CCF T-6J Harvard IV (KF729)	P. J. Tuplin & P. W. Portelli	
G-BJSV	PA-28-161 Warrior II	Airways Flight Training (Exeter) Ltd	
G-BJSW	Thunder Ax7-65 balloon	Sandicliffe Garage Ltd	
G-BJSZ	Piper J-3C-65 Cub	H. Gilbert	
G-BJTB	Cessna A.150M	V. D. Speck/Clacton	
G-BJTO	Piper J-3C-65 Cub	R. Horner	
G-BJTP	PA-18 Super Cub 95 (115302:TP)	J. T. Parkins	
G-BJTY	Osprey Mk 4B balloon	A. E. de Gruchy	
G-BJUB	BVS Special 01 balloon	P. G. Wild	
G-BJUC	Robinson R22HP	JD Gallagher Estate Agents Ltd	
G-BJUD	Robin DR.400/180R	Lasham Gliding Society Ltd	
G-BJUR	PA-38-112 Tomahawk	Truman Aviation Ltd/Tollerton	
G-BJUS	PA-38-112 Tomahawk	Panshanger School of Flying	
G-BJUV	Cameron V-20 balloon	P. Spellward	
G-BJVC	Evans VP-2	S. J. Greer & S. E. Clarke	
G-BJVH	Cessna F.182Q	R. J. de Courcy Cuming/Wellesbourne	
G-BJVJ	Cessna F.152	Henlow Flying Club	
G-BJVK	Grob G-109	B. Kimberley/Enstone	

G-BJVM – G-BKEU — BRITISH CIVIL REGISTRATIONS

Notes	Reg	Type	Owner or Operator
	G-BJVM	Cessna 172N	I. C. MacLennan
	G-BJVS	CP.1310-C3 Super Emeraude	BJVS Group
	G-BJVT	Cessna F.152	Northern Aviation Ltd
	G-BJVU	Thunder Ax6-56 Bolt SS balloon	G. V. Beckwith
	G-BJVV	Robin R.1180	P. Hawkins
	G-BJWH	Cessna F.152 II	Linkcrest Ltd/Elstree
	G-BJWI	Cessna F.172P	Bournemouth Flying Club
	G-BJWJ	Cameron V-65 balloon	R. G. Turnbull & S. G. Forse
	G-BJWO	BN-2A-26 Islander	Metachem Diagnostics Ltd (G-BAXC)
	G-BJWT	Wittman W.10 Tailwind	Tailwind Group
	G-BJWV	Colt 17A balloon	D. T. Meyes
	G-BJWW	Cessna F.172N	Air Charter & Travel Ltd/Blackpool
	G-BJWX	PA-18 Super Cub 95	G-BJWX Syndicate
	G-BJWY	S-55 Whirlwind HAR.21 (WV198) ★	Solway Aviation Museum/Carlisle
	G-BJWZ	PA-18 Super Cub 95	G-BJWZ Syndicate/Redhill
	G-BJXA	Slingsby T.67A	Chipmunk Flying Group
	G-BJXB	Slingsby T.67A	X-Ray Bravo Ltd/Barton
	G-BJXK	Fournier RF-5	RF5 Syndicate
	G-BJXP	Colt 56B balloon	H. J. Anderson
	G-BJXR	Auster AOP.9	I. Churm & J. Hanson
	G-BJXX	PA-23 Aztec 250E	V. Bojovic
	G-BJXZ	Cessna 172N	T. M. Jones/Egginton
	G-BJYD	Cessna F.152 II	N. J. James
	G-BJYF	Colt 56A balloon	H. Dos Santos
	G-BJYK	Jodel D.120A	T. Fox & D. A. Thorpe
	G-BJYN	PA-38-112 Tomahawk	Panshanger School of Flying Ltd (G-BJTE)
	G-BJZA	Cameron N-65 balloon	N. D. Hepworth
	G-BJZF	DH.82A Tiger Moth	M. I. Lodge
	G-BJZN	Slingsby T.67A	A. R. T. Marsland
	G-BJZR	Colt 42A balloon	Selfish Balloon Group
	G-BKAE	Jodel D.120	S. J. Harris
	G-BKAF	FRED Srs 2	J. Mc. D. Robinson
	G-BKAM	Slingsby T.67M Firefly160	R. C. B. Brookhouse
	G-BKAO	Jodel D.112	R. Broadhead
	G-BKAS	PA-38-112 Tomahawk	St. George Flying Club/Teesside
	G-BKAY	Rockwell Commander 114	D. L. Bunning
	G-BKAZ	Cessna 152	L. W. Scattergood/Sheffield
	G-BKBB	Hawker Fury Mk I (replica) (K1930)	Brandish Holdings Ltd/Old Warden
	G-BKBD	Thunder Ax3 balloon	M. J. Casson
	G-BKBF	MS.894A Rallye Minerva 220	K. A. Hale & L. C. Clark
	G-BKBN	SOCATA TB10 Tobago	F. L. Hunter
	G-BKBO	Colt 17A balloon	J. Armstrong & ptnrs
	G-BKBP	Bellanca 7GCBC Scout	M. G. & J. R. Jefferies
	G-BKBS	Bensen B8MV	L. Harrison
	G-BKBV	SOCATA TB10 Tobago	A. P. Orchard
	G-BKBW	SOCATA TB10 Tobago	Merlin Aviation
	G-BKCC	PA-28 Cherokee 180	DR Flying Club Ltd
	G-BKCE	Cessna F.172P II	The Leicestershire Aero Club Ltd/Leicester
	G-BKCI	Brügger MB.2 Colibri	M. R. Walters/Leicester
	G-BKCL	PA-30 Twin Comanche 160C	A. Burrows
	G-BKCN	Currie Wot	N. A. A. Podmore
	G-BKCR	SOCATA TB9 Tampico	P. A. Little
	G-BKCV	EAA Acro Sport II	M. J. Clark
	G-BKCW	Jodel D.120	Dundee Flying Group (G-BMYF)
	G-BKCX	Mudry/CAARP CAP-10B	G. P. Gorvett
	G-BKCY	PA-38-112 Tomahawk II ★	(stored)/Welshpool
	G-BKCZ	Jodel D.120A	I. K. Ratcliffe
	G-BKDC	Monnett Sonerai II	K. J. Towell
	G-BKDH	Robin DR.400/120	Dauphin Flying Group Ltd
	G-BKDI	Robin DR.400/120	Mistral Aviation Ltd/Fairoaks
	G-BKDJ	Robin DR.400/120	S. Pritchard & I. C. Colwell
	G-BKDK	Thunder Ax7-77Z balloon	A. J. Byrne
	G-BKDP	FRED Srs 3	M. Whittaker
	G-BKDR	Pitts S-1S Special	J. H. Milne & T. H. Bishop
	G-BKDS	Colt 14A Cloudhopper balloon	D. M. & K.R. Sandford
	G-BKDT	SE-5A (replica) (F943) ★	Yorkshire Air Museum/Elvington
	G-BKDX	Jodel DR.1050	G. J. Slater
	G-BKEK	PA-32 Cherokee Six 300	S. W. Turley
	G-BKEP	Cessna F.172M	R. M. Dalley
	G-BKER	SE-5A (replica) (F5447:N)	N. K. Geddes
	G-BKET	PA-18 Super Cub 95	H. M. MacKenzie
	G-BKEU	Taylor JT.1 Monoplane	A. J. Moore

BRITISH CIVIL REGISTRATIONS — G-BKEV – G-BKPZ

Reg	Type	Owner or Operator	Notes
G-BKEV	Cessna F.172M	Derby Arrows	
G-BKEW	Bell 206B JetRanger 3	N. R. Foster	
G-BKEY	FRED Srs 3	G. S. Taylor	
G-BKFC	Cessna F.152 II	Sulby Aerial	
G-BKFI	Evans VP-1	P. L. Naylor	
G-BKFK	Isaacs Fury II	G. G. C. Jones	
G-BKFL	Aerosport Scamp	J. Sherwood	
G-BKFM	QAC Quickie 1	G. E. Meakin	
G-BKFN	Bell 214ST	Bristow Helicopters Ltd	
G-BKFR	CP.301C Emeraude	Devonshire Flying Group	
G-BKFW	P.56 Provost T.1 (XF597)	Sylmar Aviation & Services Ltd	
G-BKFY	Beech C90 King Air	Blackbrooks LLP	
G-BKFZ	PA-28R Cherokee Arrow 200	Shacklewell Flying Group	
G-BKGA	MS.892E Rallye 150GT	C. J. Spradbery	
G-BKGB	Jodel D.120	B. A. Ridgway	
G-BKGC	Maule M.6-235	B. F. Walker	
G-BKGD	Westland WG.30 Srs.100 ★	IHM/Weston-super-Mare	
G-BKGL	Beech D.18S (1164:64)	A. T. J. Darrah/Duxford	
G-BKGM	Beech D.18S (HB275)	Skyblue Aviation Ltd	
G-BKGR	Cameron O-65 balloon	K. Kidner & L. E. More	
G-BKGT	SOCATA Rallye 110ST	Long Marston Flying Group	
G-BKGW	Cessna F.152-II	Leicestershire Aero Club Ltd	
G-BKHA	WS-55 Whirlwind HAR.10 (XJ763) ★	C. J. Evans	
G-BKHG	Piper J-3C-65 Cub (479766:D-63)	H. C. Cox	
G-BKHJ	Cessna 182P	Augur Films Ltd	
G-BKHW	Stoddard-Hamilton Glasair IIRG	D. Calabritto/Stapleford	
G-BKHY	Taylor JT.1 Monoplane	B. C. J. O'Neill	
G-BKHZ	Cessna F.172P	L. R. Leader	
G-BKIB	SOCATA TB9 Tampico	G. A. Vickers	
G-BKIC	Cameron V-77 balloon	C. A. Butler	
G-BKIF	Fournier RF-6B	Tiger Airways	
G-BKII	Cessna F.172L	Sealand Ap Ltd	
G-BKIJ	Cessna F.172M	V. Speck	
G-BKIK	Cameron DG-19 airship ★	Balloon Preservation Group/Lancing	
G-BKIR	Jodel D.117	R. Shaw & D. M. Hardaker/Sherburn	
G-BKIS	SOCATA TB10 Tobago	Wessex Flyers Group	
G-BKIT	SOCATA TB9 Tampico	Cavendish Aviation UK Ltd	
G-BKIY	Thunder Ax3 balloon ★	Balloon Preservation Group/Lancing	
G-BKIZ	Cameron V-31 balloon	A. P. S. Cox	
G-BKJB	PA-18 Super Cub 135	Haimoss Ltd/O. Sarum	
G-BKJF	MS.880B Rallye 100T	Journeyman Aviation Ltd	
G-BKJR	Hughes 269C	March Helicopters Ltd/Sywell	
G-BKJS	Jodel D.120A	B. F. Baldock & T. J. Nicholson	
G-BKJW	PA-23 Aztec 250E	Alan Williams Entertainments Ltd	
G-BKKN	Cessna 182R	R A. Marven/Elstree	
G-BKKO	Cessna 182R	E. L. King & D. S. Lightbown	
G-BKKZ	Pitts S-1D Special	G. M. Huffen	
G-BKLJ	Westland Scout AH.1 ★	N. R. Windley	
G-BKLO	Cessna F.172M	Stapleford Flying Club Ltd	
G-BKMA	Mooney M.20J Srs 201	Foxtrot Whisky Aviation	
G-BKMB	Mooney M.20J Srs 201	W. A. Cook & ptnrs	
G-BKMG	Handley Page O/400 (replica)	Paralyser Group	
G-BKMI	VS.359 Spitfire HF.VIIIc (MT928)	R. J. Lamplough/Filton	
G-BKMT	PA-32R-301 Saratoga SP	Severn Valley Aviation Group	
G-BKMX	Short SD3-60 Variant 100	BAC Leasing Ltd	
G-BKNI	Gardan GY-80 Horizon 160D	A. Hartigan & ptnrs/Fenland	
G-BKNO	Monnett Sonerai IIL	S. Hardy	
G-BKNP	Cameron V-77 balloon	E. K. K. & C. E. Odman	
G-BKNZ	CP.301A Emeraude	A. D. Heath	
G-BKOA	SOCATA MS.893E Rallye 180GT	P. Howick	
G-BKOB	Z.326 Trener Master	A. L. Rae	
G-BKOT	Wassmer Wa.81 Piranha	B. N. Rolfe	
G-BKOU	P.84 Jet Provost T.3 (XN637)	G-BKOU Group	
G-BKPA	Hoffmann H-36 Dimona	D. E. Puttock	
G-BKPB	Aerosport Scamp	B. R. Thompson	
G-BKPC	Cessna A.185F	Black Knights Parachute Centre	
G-BKPD	Viking Dragonfly	E. P Browne & G. J. Sargent	
G-BKPE	Jodel DR.250/160	J. S. & J. D. Lewer	
G-BKPN	Cameron N-77 balloon	R. H. Sanderson	
G-BKPS	AA-5B Tiger	A. E. T. Clarke	
G-BKPX	Jodel D.120A	D. M. Garrett & C. A. Jones	
G-BKPY	SAAB 91B/2 Safir (56321:U-AB) ★	Newark Air Museum	
G-BKPZ	Pitts S-1T Special	M. A. Frost	

G-BKRA – G-BLCH | BRITISH CIVIL REGISTRATIONS

Notes	Reg	Type	Owner or Operator
	G-BKRA	NA T-6G Texan (51-15227)	First Air Ltd
	G-BKRB	Cessna 172N	Saunders Caravans Ltd
	G-BKRF	PA-18 Super Cub 95	K. M. Bishop
	G-BKRH	Brügger MB.2 Colibri	M. R. Benwell
	G-BKRK	SNCAN Stampe SV.4C	Strathgadie Stampe Group
	G-BKRL	Chichester-Miles Leopard ★	(stored)/Cranfield
	G-BKRN	Beechcraft D.18S	A. A. Marshall & P. L. Turland/Bruntingthorpe
	G-BKRS	Cameron V-56 balloon	D. N. & L. J. Close
	G-BKRZ	Dragon G-77 balloon	J. R. Barber
	G-BKSB	Cessna T.310Q II	G. H. Smith & Son/Jersey
	G-BKSC	Saro Skeeter AOP.12 (XN351) ★	R. A. L. Falconer
	G-BKSD	Colt 56A balloon	M. J. Casson
	G-BKSE	QAC Quickie Q.1	M. D. Burns
	G-BKSP	Schleicher ASK.14	J. H. Bryson
	G-BKST	Rutan Vari-Eze	R. Towle
	G-BKSX	SNCAN Stampe SV.4C	C. A. Bailey & J. A. Carr
	G-BKTA	PA-18 Super Cub 95	M. J. Dyson
	G-BKTH	CCF Hawker Sea Hurricane IB (Z7015)	The Shuttleworth Collection/Duxford
	G-BKTM	PZL SZD-45A Ogar	J. T. Pajdak
	G-BKTR	Cameron V-77 balloon	C. M. Morley & C. Williamson
	G-BKTV	Cessna F.152	I. R. Chaplin
	G-BKTZ	Slingsby T.67M Firefly	P. R. Elvidge (G-SFTV)
	G-BKUE	SOCATA TB9 Tampico	Fife TB9ers
	G-BKUL	AS.355F1 Twin Squirrel	Premiair Aviation Services Ltd (G-FFHI/G-GWHH)
	G-BKUR	CP.301A Emeraude	R. Wells
	G-BKUU	Thunder Ax7-77-1 balloon	M. A. Mould
	G-BKVA	SOCATA Rallye 180T	Buckminster Gliding Club Ltd
	G-BKVB	SOCATA Rallye 110ST	A. & K. Bishop
	G-BKVC	SOCATA TB9 Tampico	D. M. Hook
	G-BKVF	FRED Srs 3	G. E. & R. E. Collins
	G-BKVG	Scheibe SF.25E Super Falke	G-BKVG Ltd
	G-BKVK	Auster AOP.9 (WZ662)	J. K. Houlgrave
	G-BKVL	Robin DR.400/160	Tatenhill Aviation Ltd
	G-BKVM	PA-18 Super Cub 150 (115684)	D. G. Caffrey
	G-BKVO	Pietenpol Air Camper	M. C. Hayes
	G-BKVP	Pitts S-1D Special	S. W. Doyle
	G-BKVS	Campbell Cricket (modified)	K. Hughes
	G-BKVT	PA-23 Aztec 250E	BKS Surveys Ltd (G-HARV)
	G-BKVW	Airtour 56 balloon	L. D. & H. Vaughan
	G-BKVX	Airtour 56 balloon	P. Aldridge
	G-BKVY	Airtour 31 balloon	M. Davies
	G-BKWD	Taylor JT.2 Titch	J. F. Sully
	G-BKWR	Cameron V-65 balloon	Window on the World Ltd
	G-BKWW	Cameron O-77 balloon	A. M. Marten
	G-BKWY	Cessna F.152	Northern Aviation Ltd
	G-BKXA	Robin R.2100	M. Wilson
	G-BKXD	SA.365N Dauphin 2	CHC Scotia Ltd
	G-BKXF	PA-28R Cherokee Arrow 200	P. L. Brunton/Caernarfon
	G-BKXM	Colt 17A balloon	R. G. Turnbull
	G-BKXN	ICA-Brasov IS-28M2A	Skyways Aviation Group
	G-BKXO	Rutan LongEz	M. G. Parsons
	G-BKXP	Auster AOP.6	B. J. Ellis
	G-BKXR	D.31A Turbulent	M. B. Hill
	G-BKZB	Cameron V-77 balloon	K. B. Chapple
	G-BKZE	AS.332L Super Puma	CHC Scotia Ltd
	G-BKZF	Cameron V-56 balloon	C. F. Sanger-Davies
	G-BKZG	AS.332L Super Puma	CHC Scotia Ltd
	G-BKZI	Bell 206B JetRanger 2	Dolphin Property (Management) Ltd
	G-BKZT	FRED Srs 2	U. Chakravorty
	G-BKZV	Bede BD-4A	G. I. J. Thomson
	G-BLAC	Cessna FA.152	D. C. C. Handley
	G-BLAF	Stolp SA.900 V-Star	P. R. Skeels
	G-BLAG	Pitts S-1D Special	I. S. Grosz
	G-BLAH	Thunder Ax7-77-1 balloon	T. M. Donnelly
	G-BLAI	Monnett Sonerai IIL	T. Simpon
	G-BLAM	Jodel DR.360	D. J. Durell
	G-BLAT	Jodel 150	G-BLAT Flying Group
	G-BLAX	Cessna FA.152	N. C. & M. L. Scanlan
	G-BLAY	Robin HR.100/200B	B. A. Mills
	G-BLCC	Thunder Ax7-77Z balloon	W. J. Treacy & P. Murphy/Ireland
	G-BLCG	SOCATA TB10 Tobago	Charlie Golf Flying Group/Shoreham (G-BHES)
	G-BLCH	Colt 65D balloon	Balloon Flights Club Ltd

BRITISH CIVIL REGISTRATIONS — G-BLCI – G-BLNJ

Reg	Type	Owner or Operator	Notes
G-BLCI	EAA Acro Sport	M. R. Holden	
G-BLCM	SOCATA TB9 Tampico	K. J. Steele & D. J. Hewitt	
G-BLCT	Jodel DR.220 2+2	R. S. Palmer & D. Scott	
G-BLCU	Scheibe SF.25B Falke	Charlie Uniform Syndicate	
G-BLCV	Hoffmann H-36 Dimona	R. & M. Weaver	
G-BLCW	Evans VP-1	M. Flint	
G-BLCY	Thunder Ax7-65Z balloon	C. M. George	
G-BLDB	Taylor JT.1 Monoplane	C. J. Bush	
G-BLDD	WAG-Aero CUBy AcroTrainer	A. F. Stafford	
G-BLDG	PA-25 Pawnee 260C	Ouse Gliding Club Ltd/Rufforth	
G-BLDK	Robinson R22	Flight Academy (Gyrocopters) Ltd	
G-BLDN	Rand-Robinson KR-2	P. R. Diffey	
G-BLDV	BN-2B-26 Islander	Loganair Ltd	
G-BLEB	Colt 69A balloon	I. R. M. Jacobs	
G-BLEP	Cameron V-65 balloon	D. Chapman	
G-BLES	Stolp SA.750 Acroduster Too	C. J. Kingswood	
G-BLET	Thunder Ax7-77-1 balloon	Servatruc Ltd	
G-BLEZ	SA.365N Dauphin 2	CHC Scotia Ltd/Aberdeen	
G-BLFI	PA-28-181 Archer II	Bonus Aviation Ltd	
G-BLFW	AA-5 Traveler	Grumman Club	
G-BLFY	Cameron V-77 balloon	A. N. F. Pertwee	
G-BLFZ	PA-31-310 Turbo Navajo C	London Executive Aviation Ltd	
G-BLGH	Robin DR.300/180R	Booker Gliding Club Ltd	
G-BLGS	SOCATA Rallye 180T	A. Waters	
G-BLGV	Bell 206B JetRanger 3	Heliflight (UK) Ltd	
G-BLHH	Jodel DR.315	S. J. Luck	
G-BLHI	Colt 17A balloon	J. A. Folkes	
G-BLHJ	Cessna F.172P	Flight Academy Scotland Ltd	
G-BLHK	Colt 105A balloon	Hale Hot-Air Balloon Club	
G-BLHM	PA-18 Super Cub 95	A. G. Edwards	
G-BLHN	Robin HR.100/285	K. A. & L. M. C. Payton	
G-BLHR	GA-7 Cougar	Affair Aircraft Leasing LLP	
G-BLHS	Bellanca 7ECA Citabria	Hotel Sierra Group	
G-BLHW	Varga 2150A Kachina	Kachina Hotel Whiskey Group	
G-BLID	DH.112 Venom FB.50 (J-1605) ★	P. G. Vallance Ltd/Charlwood	
G-BLIH	PA-18 Super Cub 135	I. R. F. Hammond	
G-BLIK	Wallis WA-116/F/S	K. H. Wallis	
G-BLIT	Thorp T-18 CW	A. P. Tyrwhitt-Drake	
G-BLIW	P.56 Provost T.51 (177)	A. D. M. & K. B. Edie	
G-BLIX	Saro Skeeter Mk 12 (XL809)	K. M. Scholes	
G-BLIY	MS.892A Rallye Commodore	A. J. Brasher	
G-BLJD	Glaser-Dirks DG.400	M. I. Gee	
G-BLJH	Cameron N-77 balloon ★	Balloon Preservation Group/Lancing	
G-BLJM	Beech 95-B55 Baron	A. Nitsche/Germany	
G-BLJO	Cessna F.152	Redhill School of Flying Ltd	
G-BLKA	DH.112 Venom FB.54 (WR410:N) ★	De Havilland Heritage Museum/London Colney	
G-BLKL	D.31 Turbulent	D. L. Ripley	
G-BLKM	Jodel DR.1051	Kilo Mike Group	
G-BLKY	Beech 95-58 Baron	R. A. Perrot/Guernsey	
G-BLKZ	Pilatus P2-05 (A-125)	Robert Hinton Design and Communications Ltd	
G-BLLA	Bensen B.8M	K. T. Donaghey	
G-BLLB	Bensen B.8M	D. H. Moss	
G-BLLD	Cameron O-77 balloon	G. Birchall	
G-BLLH	Jodel DR.220A 2+2	M. D. Hughes	
G-BLLN	PA-18 Super Cub 95	P. L. Pilch & C. G. Fisher	
G-BLLO	PA-18 Super Cub 95	D. G. Margetts	
G-BLLP	Slingsby T.67B	Air Navigation and Trading Co Ltd	
G-BLLR	Slingsby T.67B	R. L. Brinklow/Biggin Hill	
G-BLLS	Slingsby T.67B	Developing Assets (UK) Ltd	
G-BLLW	Colt 56B balloon	G. Fordyce & ptnrs	
G-BLLZ	Rutan LongEz	R. S. Stoddart-Stones	
G-BLMA	Zlin 326 Trener Master	G. P. Northcott/Redhill	
G-BLMC	Avro 698 Vulcan B.2A ★	Aeropark/East Midlands	
G-BLME	Robinson R22HP	Heli Air Ltd/Wellesbourne	
G-BLMG	Grob G.109B	Mike Golf Syndicate	
G-BLMI	PA-18 Super Cub 95	G-BLMI Flying Group	
G-BLMN	Rutan LongEz	G-BLMN Flying Group	
G-BLMP	PA-17 Vagabond	D. & M. Shrimpton.	
G-BLMR	PA-18 Super Cub 150	Limadelta Aviation Ltd	
G-BLMT	PA-18 Super Cub 135	I. S. Runnalls	
G-BLMW	T.66 Nipper 3	S. L. Millar	
G-BLMZ	Colt 105A balloon	M. D. Dickinson	
G-BLNJ	BN-2B-26 Islander	Hebridean Air Services Ltd/Cumbernauld	

G-BLNO – G-BLZJ · BRITISH CIVIL REGISTRATIONS

Notes	Reg	Type	Owner or Operator
	G-BLNO	FRED Srs 3	L. W. Smith
	G-BLOR	PA-30 Twin Comanche 160	R. L. C. Appleton
	G-BLOS	Cessna 185A (also flown with floats)	Orman (Carrolls Farm) Ltd
	G-BLOT	Colt Ax6-56B balloon	H. J. Anderson
	G-BLOV	Thunder Ax5-42 Srs 1 balloon	A. G. R. Calder
	G-BLPA	Piper J-3C-65 Cub	A. C. Frost
	G-BLPB	Turner TSW Hot Two Wot	I. R. Hannah
	G-BLPE	PA-18 Super Cub 95	A. A. Haig-Thomas
	G-BLPF	Cessna FR.172G	P. Kohl
	G-BLPG	Auster J/1N Alpha (16693:693)	Annic Marketing (G-AZIH)
	G-BLPH	Cessna FRA.150L	N. P. Lake
	G-BLPI	Slingsby T.67B	RAF Wyton Flying Group Ltd
	G-BLPM	AS.332L Super Puma	Bristow Helicopters Ltd
	G-BLPP	Cameron V-77 balloon	R. J. Gooch
	G-BLRA	BAe 146-100	BAE Systems (Operations) Ltd
	G-BLRC	PA-18 Super Cub 135	Supercub Group
	G-BLRF	Slingsby T.67C	R. C. Nicholls
	G-BLRG	Slingsby T.67B	R. L. Brinklow
	G-BLRL	CP.301C-1 Emeraude	J. A. & I. M. Macleod
	G-BLRM	Glaser-Dirks DG.400	J. A. & W. S. Y. Stephen
	G-BLSD	DH.112 Venom FB.54 (J-1758) ★	R. Lamplough/North Weald
	G-BLST	Cessna 421C	Cecil Aviation Ltd/Cambridge
	G-BLSX	Cameron O-105 balloon	B. J. Petteford
	G-BLTA	Thunder Ax7-77A	K. A. Schlussler
	G-BLTC	D.31A Turbulent	S. J. Butler
	G-BLTF	Robinson R22 Alpha	Brian Seedle Helicopters Ltd
	G-BLTK	Rockwell Commander 112TC	Commander TC Group
	G-BLTM	Robin HR.200/100	Barton Robin Group
	G-BLTN	Thunder Ax7-65 balloon	A. H. Symonds
	G-BLTR	Scheibe SF.25B Falke	V. Mallon/Germany
	G-BLTS	Rutan LongEz	R. W. Cutler
	G-BLTV	Slingsby T.67B	R. L. Brinklow
	G-BLTW	Slingsby T.67B	Cheshire Air Training Services Ltd/Liverpool
	G-BLTY	Westland WG.30 Srs 160	D. Brem-Wilson
	G-BLTZ	SOCATA TB10 Tobago	Martin Ltd/Biggin Hill
	G-BLUI	Thunder Ax7-65 balloon	S. Johnson
	G-BLUM	SA.365N Dauphin 2	CHC Scotia Ltd
	G-BLUN	SA.365N Dauphin 2	CHC Scotia Ltd
	G-BLUV	Grob G.109B	The 109 Flying Group/North Weald
	G-BLUX	Slingsby T.67M Firefly 200	R. L. Brinklow
	G-BLUZ	DH.82B Queen Bee (LF858)	The Bee Keepers Group
	G-BLVA	Airtour AH-56 balloon	A. Van Wyk
	G-BLVB	Airtour AH-56 balloon	R. W. Guild
	G-BLVI	Slingsby T.67M Firefly Mk II	Brooke Park Ltd
	G-BLVK	CAARP CAP-10B	E. K. Coventry/Earls Colne
	G-BLVL	PA-28-161 Warrior II	TG Aviation Ltd/Manston
	G-BLVS	Cessna 150M	R. Collier
	G-BLVW	Cessna F.172H	R. & D. Holloway Ltd
	G-BLWD	PA-34-200T Seneca 2	Bencray Ltd
	G-BLWF	Robin HR.100/210	Starguide Ltd
	G-BLWH	Fournier RF-6B-100	I. R. March
	G-BLWM	Bristol M.1C (replica) (C4994) ★	RAF Museum/Hendon
	G-BLWP	PA-38-112 Tomahawk	J. E. Rowley
	G-BLWT	Evans VP-1	J. S. Peplow
	G-BLWV	Cessna F.152	Redhill Flying Club
	G-BLWY	Robin R.2160D	K. D. Boardman
	G-BLXA	SOCATA TB20 Trinidad	Trinidad Flyers Ltd/Blackbushe
	G-BLXG	Colt 21A balloon	A. Walker
	G-BLXH	Fournier RF-3	J. E. Dallison
	G-BLXI	CP.1310-C3 Super Emeraude	R. Howard
	G-BLXO	Jodel 150	P. R. Powell
	G-BLXP	PA-28R Cherokee Arrow 200	M. B. Hamlett
	G-BLXR	AS.332L Super Puma	Bristow Helicopters Ltd
	G-BLYD	SOCATA TB20 Trinidad	Yankee Delta Corporation Ltd
	G-BLYE	SOCATA TB10 Tobago	Silverstar Aviation Ltd/Blackpool
	G-BLYK	PA-34-220T Seneca III	Fly (CI) Ltd
	G-BLYP	Robin 3000/120	Weald Air Services/Headcorn
	G-BLYT	Airtour AH-77 balloon	I. J. Taylor & R. C. Kincaid
	G-BLZA	Scheibe SF.25B Falke	Zulu Alpha Syndicate
	G-BLZE	Cessna F.152 II	Flairhire Ltd/Redhill (G-CSSC)
	G-BLZF	Thunder Ax7-77 balloon	H. M. Savage
	G-BLZH	Cessna F.152 II	Skytrek Aviation Services
	G-BLZJ	AS.332L Super Puma	Bristow Helicopters Ltd (G-PUMJ)

BRITISH CIVIL REGISTRATIONS

G-BLZN – G-BMJR

Reg	Type	Owner or Operator	Notes
G-BLZN	Bell 206B JetRanger	E. Miles	
G-BLZP	Cessna F.152	East Midlands Flying School Ltd	
G-BLZS	Cameron O-77 balloon	C. D. Steel	
G-BMAD	Cameron V-77 balloon	M. A. Stelling	
G-BMAL	Sikorsky S-76A	CHC Scotiia Ltd	
G-BMAO	Taylor JT.1 Monoplane	S. J. Alston	
G-BMAV	AS.350B Ecureuil	PLM Dollar Group Ltd	
G-BMAX	FRED Srs 2	D. A. Arkley	
G-BMAY	PA-18 Super Cub 135	R. W. Davies	
G-BMBB	Cessna F.150L	M. Bonsall	
G-BMBJ	Schempp-Hirth Janus CM	BJ Flying Group	
G-BMBS	Colt 105A balloon	H. G. Davies	
G-BMBW	Bensen B.8MR	M. E. Vahdat	
G-BMBZ	Scheibe SF.25E Super Falke	Cornish Gliding & Flying Club Ltd/Perranporth	
G-BMCC	Thunder Ax7-77 balloon	A. K. & C. M. Russell	
G-BMCD	Cameron V-65 balloon	R. Lillyman	
G-BMCG	Grob G.109B	Lagerholm Finnimport Ltd/Booker	
G-BMCI	Cessna F.172H	A. B. Davis/Edinburgh	
G-BMCN	Cessna F.152	Eastern Air Centre Ltd	
G-BMCS	PA-22 Tri-Pacer 135	P. R. Deacon	
G-BMCV	Cessna F.152	Leicestershire Aero Club Ltd	
G-BMCW	AS.332L Super Puma	Bristow Helicopters Ltd	
G-BMCX	AS.332L Super Puma	Bristow Helicopters Ltd	
G-BMDB	SE-5A (replica) (F235:B)	D. Biggs	
G-BMDC	PA-32-301 Saratoga	MacLaren Aviation/Newcastle	
G-BMDE	Pientenpol Air Camper	P. B. Childs	
G-BMDJ	Price Ax7-77S balloon	R. A. Benham	
G-BMDK	PA-34-220T Seneca III	Air Medical Fleet Ltd	
G-BMDP	Partenavia P.64B Oscar 200	S. T. G. Lloyd	
G-BMDS	Jodel D.120	R. T. Mosforth	
G-BMEA	PA-18 Super Cub 95	M. J. Butler	
G-BMEE	Cameron O-105 balloon	A. G. R. Calder/Los Angeles	
G-BMEG	SOCATA TB10 Tobago	P. Farmer	
G-BMEH	Jodel 150 Special Super Mascaret	R. J. & C. J. Lewis	
G-BMET	Taylor JT.1 Monoplane	M. K. A. Blyth	
G-BMEU	Isaacs Fury II	I. G. Harrison	
G-BMEX	Cessna A.150K	R. Barry	
G-BMFD	PA-23 Aztec 250F	Gold Air International Ltd (G-BGYY)	
G-BMFG	Dornier Do.27A-4	R. F. Warner	
G-BMFI	PZL SZD-45A Ogar	S. L. Morrey/Andreas, IoM	
G-BMFP	PA-28-161 Warrior II	Bravo-Mike-Fox-Papa Group/Blackbushe	
G-BMFU	Cameron N-90 balloon	J. J. Rudoni	
G-BMFY	Grob G.109B	P. J. Shoarer	
G-BMFZ	Cessna F.152 II	Cornwall Flying Club Ltd/Bodmin	
G-BMGB	PA-28R Cherokee Arrow 200	Malmesbury Specialist Cars	
G-BMGC	Fairey Swordfish Mk II (W5856)	F.A.A. Museum/Yeovilton	
G-BMGG	Cessna 152 II	Falcon Flying Services/Biggin Hill	
G-BMGR	Grob G.109B	G-BMGR Group	
G-BMHA	Rutan LongEz	S. F. Elvins	
G-BMHC	Cessna U.206F	British Skysports Parachute Centre	
G-BMHJ	Thunder Ax7-65 balloon	M. G. Robinson	
G-BMHL	Wittman W.8 Tailwind	O. M. Nash	
G-BMHS	Cessna F.172M	Tango X-Ray Flying Group	
G-BMHT	PA-28RT-201T Turbo Arrow	G. Lungley	
G-BMID	Jodel D.120	G-BMID Flying Group	
G-BMIG	Cessna 172N	BMIG Group	
G-BMIM	Rutan LongEz	R. M. Smith	
G-BMIO	Stoddard-Hamilton Glasair RG	P. Bint & L. McMahon	
G-BMIP	Jodel D.112	F. J. E. Brownsill	
G-BMIR	Westland Wasp HAS.1 (XT788) ★	Park Aviation Supply/Charlwood	
G-BMIS	Monnett Sonerai II	S. R. Edwards	
G-BMIV	PA-28R-201T Turbo Arrow III	Firmbeam Ltd	
G-BMIW	PA-28-181 Archer II	Oldbus Ltd	
G-BMIY	Oldfield Baby Great Lakes	J. B. Scott (G-NOME)	
G-BMJA	PA-32R-301 Saratoga SP	H. Merkado/Panshanger	
G-BMJC	Cessna 152 II	Northern Aviation Ltd	
G-BMJD	Cessna 152 II	Donair Flying Club Ltd/East Midlands	
G-BMJL	Rockwell Commander 114	D. J. & S. M. Hawkins	
G-BMJM	Evans VP-1	S. E. Clarke	
G-BMJN	Cameron O-65 balloon	P. M. Traviss	
G-BMJO	PA-34-220T Seneca III	Deep Cleavage Ltd	
G-BMJR	Cessna T.337H	John Roberts Services Ltd (G-NOVA)	

71

G-BMJX – G-BMTC BRITISH CIVIL REGISTRATIONS

Notes	Reg	Type	Owner or Operator
	G-BMJX	Wallis WA-116X	K. H. Wallis
	G-BMJY	Yakovlev C18M (07)	R. J. Lamplough/North Weald
	G-BMJZ	Cameron N-90 balloon	Bristol University Hot Air Ballooning Society
	G-BMKB	PA-18 Super Cub 135	Cubair Flight Training Ltd/Redhill
	G-BMKC	Piper J-3C-65 Cub (329854:R-44)	J. W. Salter
	G-BMKD	Beech C90A King Air	A. E. Bristow
	G-BMKF	Jodel DR.221	S. T. & L. A. Gilbert
	G-BMKG	PA-38-112 Tomahawk II	APB Leasing Ltd/Welshpool
	G-BMKI	Colt 21A balloon	A. C. Booth
	G-BMKJ	Cameron V-77 balloon	R. C. Thursby
	G-BMKK	PA-28R-200 Cherokee Arrow II	G-BMKK Ltd
	G-BMKP	Cameron V-77 balloon	R. Bayly
	G-BMKR	PA-28-161 Warrior II	Field Flying Group/Goodwood (G-BGKR)
	G-BMKW	Cameron V-77 balloon	M. H. Redman
	G-BMKY	Cameron O-65 balloon	A. R. Rich
	G-BMLB	Jodel D.120A	C. A. Croucher
	G-BMLC	Short SD3-60 Variant 100	BAC Leasing Ltd
	G-BMLJ	Cameron N-77 balloon	C. J. Dunkley
	G-BMLK	Grob G.109B	Brams Syndicate/Rufforth
	G-BMLL	Grob G.109B	G-BMLL Flying Group/Denham
	G-BMLM	Beech 95-58 Baron	Atlantic Bridge Aviation Ltd/Lydd
	G-BMLS	PA-28R-201 Arrow III	R. M. Shorter
	G-BMLT	Pietenpol Air Camper	W. E. R. Jenkins
	G-BMLW	Cameron O-77 balloon	M. L. & L. P Willoughby
	G-BMLX	Cessna F.150L	J. P. A. Freeman/Headcorn
	G-BMMF	FRED Srs 2	R. C. Thomas
	G-BMMI	Pazmany PL.4A	P. I. Morgans
	G-BMMK	Cessna 182P	G. G. Weston
	G-BMMM	Cessna 152 II	Luton Flight Training Ltd
	G-BMMP	Grob G.109B	G-BMMP Syndicate
	G-BMMV	ICA-Brasov IS-28M2A	J. F. Miles
	G-BMMW	Thunder Ax7-77 balloon	P. A. George
	G-BMMY	Thunder Ax7-77 balloon	S. W. Wade & S. E. Hadley
	G-BMNL	PA-28R Cherokee Arrow 200	Arrow Flying Group
	G-BMNV	SNCAN Stampe SV.4D	Wessex Aviation & Transport Ltd
	G-BMOE	PA-28R Cherokee Arrow 200	Piper Leasing Ltd
	G-BMOF	Cessna U206G	Wild Geese Skydiving Centre
	G-BMOG	Thunder Ax7-77 balloon	R. M. Boswell
	G-BMOH	Cameron N-77 balloon	P. J. Marshall & M. A. Clarke
	G-BMOI	Partenavia P68B	Simmette Ltd
	G-BMOK	ARV Super 2	R. E. Griffiths
	G-BMOL	PA-23 Aztec 250D	LDL Enterprises/Elstree (G-BBSR)
	G-BMOM	ICA-Brasov IS-28M2A	M. E. Todd
	G-BMOT	Bensen B.8M	Austin Trueman Ltd
	G-BMOV	Cameron O-105 balloon	C. Gillott
	G-BMPC	PA-28-181 Archer II	C. J. & R. J. Barnes
	G-BMPD	Cameron V-65 balloon	D. Triggs
	G-BMPL	Optica Industries OA.7 Optica	Aces High Ltd/North Weald
	G-BMPP	Cameron N-77 balloon	The Sarnia Balloon Group
	G-BMPR	PA-28R-201 Arrow III	T. J. Brammer & D. T. Colley
	G-BMPS	Strojnik S-2A	G. J. Green
	G-BMPY	DH.82A Tiger Moth	N. M. Eisenstein
	G-BMRA	Boeing 757-236F	DHL Air Ltd
	G-BMRB	Boeing 757-236F	DHL Air Ltd
	G-BMRC	Boeing 757-236F	DHL Air Ltd
	G-BMRD	Boeing 757-236F	DHL Air Ltd
	G-BMRE	Boeing 757-236F	DHL Air Ltd
	G-BMRF	Boeing 757-236F	DHL Air Ltd
	G-BMRH	Boeing 757-236F	DHL Air Ltd
	G-BMRJ	Boeing 757-236F	DHL Air Ltd
	G-BMSA	Stinson HW.75 Voyager	M. A. Thomas/Barton (G-BCUM)
	G-BMSB	VS.509 Spitfire IX (MJ627:9G-P)	M. S. Bayliss/Coventry (G-ASOZ)
	G-BMSC	Evans VP-2	L. G. Hunt
	G-BMSD	PA-28-181 Archer II	H. Merkado/Panshanger
	G-BMSE	Valentin Taifun 17E	A. J. Nurse
	G-BMSF	PA-38-112 Tornahawk	B. Catlow
	G-BMSG	SAAB 32A Lansen ★	J. E. Wilkie/Cranfield
	G-BMSL	FRED Srs 3	M. J. Veary
	G-BMSU	Cessna 152 II	G-BMSU Group
	G-BMTA	Cessna 152 II	J. McAuley
	G-BMTB	Cessna 152 II	Sky Leisure Aviation (Charters) Ltd
	G-BMTC	AS.355F1 Twin Squirrel	Cambridge & Essex Air Support Unit (G-SASU/G-BSSM/G-BKUK/G-EPOL)

BRITISH CIVIL REGISTRATIONS
G-BMTJ – G-BNCU

Reg	Type	Owner or Operator	Notes
G-BMTJ	Cessna 152 II	The Pilot Centre Ltd/Denham	
G-BMTN	Cameron O-77 balloon	Industrial Services (MH) Ltd	
G-BMTO	PA-38-112 Tomahawk	Falcon Flying Services/Biggin Hill	
G-BMTR	PA-28-161 Warrior II	Aeros Leasing Ltd	
G-BMTS	Cessna 172N	European Flyers/Blackbushe	
G-BMTU	Pitts S-1E Special	C. Lambropoulos	
G-BMTX	Cameron V-77 balloon	J. A. Langley	
G-BMUD	Cessna 182P	M. E. Taylor	
G-BMUG	Rutan LongEz	A. G. Sayers	
G-BMUJ	Colt Drachenfisch balloon	Virgin Airship & Balloon Co Ltd	
G-BMUO	Cessna A.152	Sky Leisure Aviation (Charters) Ltd	
G-BMUT	PA-34-200T Seneca II	G-DAD Air Ltd	
G-BMUU	Thunder Ax7-77 balloon	A. R. Hill	
G-BMUZ	PA-28-161 Warrior II	Northumbria Flying School Ltd	
G-BMVA	Scheibe SF.25B Falke	M. L. Jackson	
G-BMVB	Cessna F.152	M. P. Barnard	
G-BMVG	QAC Quickie Q.1	P. M. Wright	
G-BMVL	PA-38-112 Tomahawk	John Reynolds Racing Ltd	
G-BMVM	PA-38-112 Tomahawk	Brimpton Flying Group	
G-BMVS	Cameron 70 Benihana SS balloon	Benihana (UK) Ltd	
G-BMVT	Thunder Ax7-77A balloon	M. L. & L. P. Willoughby	
G-BMVU	Monnett Moni	R. M. Edworthy	
G-BMVW	Cameron O-65 balloon	S. P. Richards	
G-BMWA	Hughes 269C	D. G. Lewendon/France	
G-BMWE	ARV Super 2	R. J. N. Noble	
G-BMWF	ARV Super 2	G. E. Collard	
G-BMWM	ARV Super 2	G. B. Thomas	
G-BMWR	Rockwell Commander 112	M. & J. Edwards/Blackbushe	
G-BMWU	Cameron N-42 balloon ★	Balloon Preservation Group/Lancing	
G-BMWV	Putzer Elster B	Magpie Group	
G-BMXA	Cessna 152 II	I. R. Chaplin/Andrewsfield	
G-BMXB	Cessna 152 II	C. I. J. Young	
G-BMXC	Cessna 152 II	Devon and Somerset Flight Training Ltd	
G-BMXD	F.27 Friendship Mk 500	BAC Group Ltd	
G-BMXJ	Cessna F.150L	Arrow Aircraft Group	
G-BMXM	Colt 180A balloon	D. A. Michaud	
G-BMXX	Cessna 152 II	Evensport Ltd	
G-BMYC	SOCATA TB10 Tobago	E. A. Grady	
G-BMYD	Beech A36 Bonanza	Seabeam Partners Ltd	
G-BMYF	Bensen B.8M	G. Callaghan	
G-BMYG	Cessna FA.152	Greer Aviation Ltd/Prestwick	
G-BMYI	AA-5 Traveler	W. C. & S. C. Westran	
G-BMYJ	Cameron V-65 balloon	S. P. Harrowing	
G-BMYN	Colt 77A balloon	M. H. Read & J. E. Wetters	
G-BMYS	Thunder Ax7-77Z balloon	J. E. Weidema/Netherlands	
G-BMYU	Jodel D.120	N. P. Chitty	
G-BMZB	Cameron N-77 balloon	D. C. Eager	
G-BMZF	WSK-Mielec LiM-2 (MiG-15bis) (01420) ★	F.A.A. Museum/Yeovilton	
G-BMZN	Everett gyroplane	K. Ashford	
G-BMZP	Everett gyroplane	D. H. Kirton	
G-BMZS	Everett gyroplane	L. W. Cload	
G-BMZW	Bensen B.8MR	P. D. Widdicombe	
G-BMZX	Wolf W-11 Boredom Fighter	J. Nugent	
G-BNAG	Colt 105A balloon	R. W. Batchelor	
G-BNAI	Wolf W-II Boredom Fighter (146-11083)	C. M. Bunn	
G-BNAJ	Cessna 152 II	Galair Ltd/Biggin Hill	
G-BNAN	Cameron V-65 balloon	A. M. Lindsay	
G-BNAU	Cameron V-65 balloon	4-Flight Group	
G-BNAW	Cameron V-65 balloon	A. Walker	
G-BNBL	Thunder Ax7-77 balloon	F. W. Ewer	
G-BNBV	Thunder Ax7-77 balloon	J. M. Robinson	
G-BNBW	Thunder Ax7-77 balloon	I. S. & S. W. Watthews	
G-BNBY	Beech 95-B55A Baron	J. Butler/France (G-AXXR)	
G-BNCB	Cameron V-77 balloon	C. W. Brown	
G-BNCC	Thunder Ax7-77 balloon	C. J. Burnhope	
G-BNCJ	Cameron V-77 balloon	D. Johnson	
G-BNCL	WG.13 Lynx HAS.2 (XX469) ★	Lancashire Fire Brigade HQ/Lancaster	
G-BNCM	Cameron N-77 balloon	C. A. Stone	
G-BNCO	PA-38-112 Tomahawk	D. K. Walker	
G-BNCR	PA-28-161 Warrior II	Airways Aero Associations Ltd/Booker	
G-BNCS	Cessna 180	C. Elwell Transport Ltd	
G-BNCU	Thunder Ax7-77 balloon	W. De Bock	

G-BNCX – G-BNKP | BRITISH CIVIL REGISTRATIONS

Notes	Reg	Type	Owner or Operator
	G-BNCX	Hawker Hunter T.7 (XL621) ★	Brooklands Museum of Aviation/Weybridge
	G-BNCZ	Rutan LongEz	M. C. Davies
	G-BNDE	PA-38-112 Tomahawk	N. F. Duke
	G-BNDG	Wallis WA-201/R Srs1	K. H. Wallis
	G-BNDN	Cameron V-77 balloon	J. A. Smith
	G-BNDO	Cessna 152 II	Simair Ltd
	G-BNDP	Brügger MB.2 Colibri	J. P. Kynaston
	G-BNDR	SOCATA TB10 Tobago	Delta Fire Ltd
	G-BNDT	Brügger MB.2 Colibri	Colibri Flying Group/Waddington
	G-BNDV	Cameron N-77 balloon	R. E. Jones
	G-BNDW	DH.82A Tiger Moth	N. D. Welch
	G-BNED	PA-22 Tri-Pacer 135	P. Storey
	G-BNEE	PA-28R-201 Arrow III	Britannic Management Aviation
	G-BNEJ	PA-38-112 Tomahawk II	V. C. & S. G. Swindell
	G-BNEK	PA-38-112 Tomahawk II	APB Leasing Ltd/Welshpool
	G-BNEL	PA-28-161 Warrior II	S. C. Westran
	G-BNEN	PA-34-200T Seneca II	Jet Options Ltd
	G-BNEO	Cameron V-77 balloon	J. G. O'Connell
	G-BNES	Cameron V-77 balloon	G. Wells
	G-BNET	Cameron O-84 balloon	C. & A. I. Gibson
	G-BNEV	Viking Dragonfly	N. W. Eyre
	G-BNEX	Cameron O-120 balloon	The Balloon Club Ltd
	G-BNFG	Cameron O-77 balloon	Capital Balloon Club Ltd
	G-BNFI	Cessna 150J	A. Waters
	G-BNFM	Colt 21A balloon	M. E. Dworski/France
	G-BNFN	Cameron N-105 balloon	P. Glydon
	G-BNFO	Cameron V-77 balloon	4-Flight Group
	G-BNFP	Cameron O-84 balloon	M. Clarke
	G-BNFR	Cessna 152 II	A. Jahanfar
	G-BNFS	Cessna 152 II	P. J. Clarke
	G-BNFV	Robin DR.400/120	J. P. A. Freeman
	G-BNGE	Auster AOP.6 (TW536)	M. Pocock
	G-BNGJ	Cameron N-77 balloon	Lathams Ltd
	G-BNGN	Cameron N-77 balloon	N. Dykes
	G-BNGO	Thunder Ax7-77 balloon	J. S. Finlan
	G-BNGT	PA-28-181 Archer II	Edinburgh Flying Club Ltd
	G-BNGV	ARV Super 2	N. A. Onions
	G-BNGW	ARV Super 2	Southern Gas Turbines Ltd
	G-BNGY	ARV Super 2	S. C. Smith (G-BMWL)
	G-BNHB	ARV Super 2	C. J. Challener
	G-BNHG	PA-38-112 Tomahawk II	D. A. Whitmore
	G-BNHI	Cameron V-77 balloon	C. M. Duggan
	G-BNHJ	Cessna 152 II	The Pilot Centre Ltd/Denham
	G-BNHK	Cessna 152 II	Wayfarers Flying Group
	G-BNHN	Colt Ariel Bottle SS balloon ★	British Balloon Museum/Newbury
	G-BNHT	Fournier RF-3	G-BNHT Group
	G-BNID	Cessna 152 II	MK Aero Support Ltd
	G-BNII	Cameron N-90 balloon	Topless Balloon Group
	G-BNIK	Robin HR.200/120	G-BNIK Group
	G-BNIM	PA-38-112 Tomahawk	Air Claire Ltd
	G-BNIN	Cameron V-77 balloon	Cloud Nine Balloon Group
	G-BNIO	Luscombe 8A Silvaire	W. H. Bliss
	G-BNIP	Luscombe 8A Silvaire	D. E. Buckley
	G-BNIU	Cameron O-77 balloon	MC VH SA/Belgium
	G-BNIV	Cessna 152 II	Aerohire Ltd/Wolverhampton
	G-BNIW	Boeing Stearman PT-17	R. C. Goold
	G-BNJB	Cessna 152 II	Aerolease Ltd/Conington
	G-BNJC	Cessna 152 II	Stapleford Flying Club Ltd/Stapleford
	G-BNJD	Cessna 152 II	M. Howells
	G-BNJG	Cameron O-77 balloon	A. M. Figiel
	G-BNJH	Cessna 152 II	J. McAuley
	G-BNJL	Bensen B.8MR	S. Ram
	G-BNJO	QAC Quickie Q.2	J. D. McKay
	G-BNJR	PA-28RT-201T Turbo Arrow IV	D. Croker
	G-BNJT	PA-28-161 Warrior II	Hawarden Flying Group
	G-BNJX	Cameron N-90 balloon	Mars UK Ltd
	G-BNJZ	Cassutt Racer IIIM	J. Cull
	G-BNKC	Cessna 152 II	Herefordshire Aero Club Ltd/Shobdon
	G-BNKD	Cessna 172N	Barnes Olsen Aero Leasing Ltd
	G-BNKE	Cessna 172N	Kilo Echo Flying Group/Barton
	G-BNKH	PA-38-112 Tomahawk	Goodwood Terrena Ltd
	G-BNKI	Cessna 152 II	RAF Halton Aeroplane Club Ltd
	G-BNKP	Cessna 152 II	Spectrum Leisure Ltd/Clacton

BRITISH CIVIL REGISTRATIONS

G-BNKR – G-BNRA

Reg	Type	Owner or Operator	Notes
G-BNKR	Cessna 152 II	Keen Leasing (IOM) Ltd	
G-BNKS	Cessna 152 II	Shropshire Aero Club Ltd/Sleap	
G-BNKT	Cameron O-77 balloon	British Airways PLC	
G-BNKV	Cessna 152 II	S. C. Westran/Shoreham	
G-BNLA	Boeing 747-436	British Airways	
G-BNLB	Boeing 747-436	British Airways	
G-BNLC	Boeing 747-436	British Airways	
G-BNLD	Boeing 747-436	British Airways	
G-BNLE	Boeing 747-436	British Airways	
G-BNLF	Boeing 747-436	British Airways	
G-BNLG	Boeing 747-436	British Airways	
G-BNLH	Boeing 747-436	British Airways	
G-BNLI	Boeing 747-436	British Airways	
G-BNLJ	Boeing 747-436	British Airways	
G-BNLK	Boeing 747-436	British Airways FROM AMERICA JFK	
G-BNLL	Boeing 747-436	British Airways	
G-BNLM	Boeing 747-436	British Airways	
G-BNLN	Boeing 747-436	British Airways	
G-BNLO	Boeing 747-436	British Airways	
G-BNLP	Boeing 747-436	British Airways	
G-BNLR	Boeing 747-436	British Airways	
G-BNLS	Boeing 747-436	British Airways	
G-BNLT	Boeing 747-436	British Airways	
G-BNLU	Boeing 747-436	British Airways	
G-BNLV	Boeing 747-436	British Airways	
G-BNLW	Boeing 747-436	British Airways	
G-BNLX	Boeing 747-436	British Airways	
G-BNLY	Boeing 747-436	British Airways	
G-BNLZ	Boeing 747-436	British Airways	
G-BNMA	Cameron O-77 balloon	N. Woodham	
G-BNMB	PA-28-151 Warrior	Thomsonfly Ltd	
G-BNMC	Cessna 152 II	M. L. Jones/Egginton	
G-BNMD	Cessna 152 II	T. M. Jones/Egginton	
G-BNME	Cessna 152 II	Northamptonshire School of Flying Ltd/Sywell	
G-BNMF	Cessna 152 II	Central Aircraft Leasing Ltd	
G-BNMG	Cameron O-77 balloon	J. H. Turner	
G-BNMH	Pietenpol Air Camper	N. M. Hitchman	
G-BNMI	Colt Flying Fantasy SS balloon	Air 2 Air Ltd	
G-BNMK	Dornier Do.27A-1	G. Mackie	
G-BNML	Rand-Robinson KR-2	R. F. Cresswell	
G-BNMO	Cessna TR.182RG	Kenrye Developments Ltd	
G-BNMX	Thunder Ax7-77 balloon	S. A. D. Beard	
G-BNNA	Stolp SA.300 Starduster Too	Banana Group	
G-BNNE	Cameron N-77 balloon	J. A. Hibberd	
G-BNNG	Cessna T.337D	Somet Ltd (G-COLD)	
G-BNNO	PA-28-161 Warrior II	Tindon Engineering Ltd/Little Snoring	
G-BNNR	Cessna 152	Sussex Flying Club Ltd/Shoreham	
G-BNNS	PA-28-161 Warrior II	S. J. French	
G-BNNT	PA-28-151 Warrior	S. T. Gilbert & D. J. Kirkwood	
G-BNNU	PA-38-112 Tomahawk	Edinburgh Flying Club Ltd	
G-BNNX	PA-28R-201T Turbo Arrow III	J. G. Freeden	
G-BNNY	PA-28-161 Warrior II	Falcon Flying Services/Biggin Hill	
G-BNNZ	PA-28-161 Warrior II	Falcon Flying Services/Biggin Hill	
G-BNOB	Wittman W.8 Tailwind	M. Robson-Robinson	
G-BNOE	PA-28-161 Warrior II	Sherburn Aero Club Ltd	
G-BNOF	PA-28-161 Warrior II	Tayside Aviation Ltd/Dundee	
G-BNOH	PA-28-161 Warrior II	Sherburn Aero Club Ltd	
G-BNOI	PA-28-161 Warrior II	BAE Systems Flight Training Ltd	
G-BNOJ	PA-28-161 Warrior II	BAE Systems (Warton) Flying Club Ltd	
G-BNOM	PA-28-161 Warrior II	Air Navigation and Trading Co Ltd	
G-BNON	PA-28-161 Warrior II	Tayside Aviation Ltd/Dundee	
G-BNOP	PA-28-161 Warrior II	BAE Systems (Warton) Flying Club Ltd	
G-BNOU	PA-28-161 Warrior II	BAE Systems Flight Training Ltd	
G-BNOZ	Cessna 152 II	OZ Flying Group	
G-BNPE	Cameron N-77 balloon	Zebedee Balloon Service Ltd	
G-BNPF	Slingsby T.31M	S. Luck & ptnrs	
G-BNPH	P.66 Pembroke C.1 (WV740)	A. G. & G. A. G. Dixon	
G-BNPM	PA-38-112 Tomahawk	Papa Mike Aviation	
G-BNPO	PA-28-181 Archer II	Bonus Aviation Ltd	
G-BNPV	Bowers Fly-Baby 1B	J. G. Day & R. Gauld-Galliers	
G-BNPY	Cessna 152 II	Eastern Air Centre Ltd/Gamston	
G-BNPZ	Cessna 152 II	Tatenhill Aviation Ltd	
G-BNRA	SOCATA TB10 Tobago	Double D Airgroup	

75

BNRG – G-BNYD — BRITISH CIVIL REGISTRATIONS

Reg	Type	Owner or Operator
G-BNRG	PA-28-161 Warrior II	RAF Brize Norton Flying Club Ltd
G-BNRK	Cessna 152 II	Redhill Flying Club
G-BNRL	Cessna 152 II	Modi Aviation Ltd
G-BNRP	PA-28-181 Archer II	Bonua Aviation Ltd/Cranfield
G-BNRR	Cessna 172P	PHA Aviation Ltd
G-BNRX	PA-34-200T Seneca II	Truman Aviation Ltd/Tollerton
G-BNRY	Cessna 182Q	K. F. & S. J. Farey
G-BNSG	PA-28R-201 Arrow III	Stronghold Trust Ltd
G-BNSI	Cessna 152 II	Sky Leisure Aviation (Charters) Ltd
G-BNSL	PA-38-112 Tomahawk II	APB Leasing Ltd/Welshpool
G-BNSM	Cessna 152 II	Cornwall Flying Club Ltd/Bodmin
G-BNSN	Cessna 152 II	The Pilot Centre Ltd/Denham
G-BNSO	Slingsby T.67M Firefly Mk II	R. M. Rennoldson
G-BNSP	Slingsby T.67M Firefly Mk II	Slingsby Group
G-BNSR	Slingsby T.67M Firefly Mk II	Slingsby SR Group
G-BNST	Cessna 172N	CSG Bodyshop
G-BNSU	Cessna 152 II	Channel Aviation Ltd/Bourn
G-BNSV	Cessna 152 II	Channel Aviation Ltd/Bourn
G-BNSY	PA-28-161 Warrior II	BCT Aircraft Leasing Ltd
G-BNSZ	PA-28-161 Warrior II	Carill Aviation Ltd/Southampton
G-BNTC	PA-28RT-201T Turbo Arrow IV	Central Aircraft Leasing Ltd
G-BNTD	PA-28-161 Warrior II	A. M. & F. Alam/Elstree
G-BNTP	Cessna 172N	Westnet Ltd/Barton
G-BNTS	PA-28RT-201T Turbo Arrow IV	Nasaire Ltd/Liverpool
G-BNTT	Beech 76 Duchess	Plane Talking Ltd/Elstree
G-BNTW	Cameron V-77 balloon	P. Goss
G-BNTZ	Cameron N-77 balloon	Balloon Team
G-BNUC	Cameron O-77 balloon	T. J. Bucknall
G-BNUL	Cessna 152 II	Big Red Kite Ltd
G-BNUN	Beech 95-58PA Baron	British Midland Airways Ltd/East Midlands
G-BNUO	Beech 76 Duchess	G. A. F. Tilley
G-BNUS	Cessna 152 II	Stapleford Flying Club Ltd
G-BNUT	Cessna 152 Turbo	Stapleford Flying Club Ltd
G-BNUV	PA-23 Aztec 250F	L. J. Martin
G-BNUX	Hoffmann H-36 Dimona	Buckminster Dimona Syndicate/Saltby
G-BNUY	PA-38-112 Tomahawk II	D. J. Whitcombe
G-BNVB	AA-5A Cheetah	Grumman Group
G-BNVD	PA-38-112 Tomahawk	Flight Training Services
G-BNVE	PA-28-181 Archer II	Solent Flight Ltd
G-BNVT	PA-28R-201T Turbo Arrow III	Victor Tango Group
G-BNVZ	Beech 95-B55 Baron	A. Perez/Spain
G-BNWA	Boeing 767-336ER	British Airways HEATH ROW
G-BNWB	Boeing 767-336ER	British Airways
G-BNWC	Boeing 767-336ER	British Airways
G-BNWD	Boeing 767-336ER	British Airways
G-BNWH	Boeing 767-336ER	British Airways
G-BNWI	Boeing 767-336ER	British Airways
G-BNWM	Boeing 767-336ER	British Airways
G-BNWN	Boeing 767-336ER	British Airways
G-BNWO	Boeing 767-336ER	British Airways
G-BNWR	Boeing 767-336ER	British Airways
G-BNWS	Boeing 767-336ER	British Airways
G-BNWT	Boeing 767-336ER	British Airways
G-BNWU	Boeing 767-336ER	British Airways
G-BNWV	Boeing 767-336ER	British Airways
G-BNWW	Boeing 767-336ER	British Airways
G-BNWY	Boeing 767-336ER	British Airways
G-BNWX	Boeing 767-336ER	British Airways
G-BNWZ	Boeing 767-336ER	British Airways
G-BNXD	Cessna 172N	A. Jahanfar & I. R. Chaplin/Southend
G-BNXE	PA-28-161 Warrior II	M. S. Brown
G-BNXI	Robin DR.400/180R	London Gliding Club (Pty) Ltd/Dunstable
G-BNXK	Nott-Cameron ULD-3 balloon	J. R. P. Nott (G-BLJN)
G-BNXL	Glaser-Dirks DG.400	G-BNXL Syndicate
G-BNXM	PA-18 Super Cub 95	G-BNXM Group
G-BNXR	Cameron O-84 balloon	J. A. B. Gray
G-BNXT	PA-28-161 Warrior II	Falcon Flying Services/Manston
G-BNXU	PA-28-161 Warrior II	Friendly Warrior Group
G-BNXV	PA-38-112 Tomahawk	W. B. Bateson/Blackpool
G-BNXX	SOCATA TB20 Trinidad	D. M. Carr
G-BNXZ	Thunder Ax7-77 balloon	Hale Hot Air Balloon Group
G-BNYB	PA-28-201T Turbo Dakota	G-BNYB Ltd/Blackbushe
G-BNYD	Bell 206B JetRanger 3	Fast Helicopters Ltd

BRITISH CIVIL REGISTRATIONS — G-BNYK – G-BOFM

Reg	Type	Owner or Operator	Notes
G-BNYK	PA-38-112 Tomahawk	APB Leasing Ltd/Welshpool	
G-BNYL	Cessna 152 II	V. J. Freeman/Headcorn	
G-BNYM	Cessna 172N	Kestrel Syndicate	
G-BNYN	Cessna 152 II	Redhill Flying Club	
G-BNYO	Beech 76 Duchess	Multiflight Ltd	
G-BNYP	PA-28-181 Archer II	R. D. Cooper/Cranfield	
G-BNYS	Boeing 767-204ER	XL Airways UK Ltd	
G-BNYX	Denney Kitfox Mk 1	W. J. Husband	
G-BNYZ	SNCAN Stampe SV.4E	M. J. Parr	
G-BNZB	PA-28-161 Warrior II	Falcon Flying Services Ltd/Biggin Hill	
G-BNZC	DHC.1 Chipmunk 22 (18671:671)	The Shuttleworth Collection/Old Warden	
G-BNZK	Thunder Ax7-77 balloon	T. D. Marsden	
G-BNZL	Rotorway Scorpion 133	J. R. Wraight	
G-BNZM	Cessna T.210N	A. J. M. Freeman	
G-BNZN	Cameron N-56 balloon	Balloon Sports HB/Sweden	
G-BNZO	Rotorway Executive	C. O'Neill	
G-BNZR	FRED Srs 2	R. M. Waugh/Newtownards	
G-BNZV	PA-25 Pawnee 235	Aeroklub Alpski Letalski Center Lesce/Slovenia	
G-BNZZ	PA-28-161 Warrior II	Providence Aviation Ltd	
G-BOAA	BAC-Aérospatiale Concorde 102 ★	Museum Of Flight East Fortune (G-N94AA)	
G-BOAB	BAC-Aérospatiale Concorde 102 ★	Preserved at Heathrow (G-N94AB)	
G-BOAC	BAC-Aérospatiale Concorde 102 ★	Displayed in viewing area Manchester International (G-N81AC)	
G-BOAF	BAC-Aérospatiale Concorde 102 ★	Bristol Aero Collection/Filton (G-N94AF)	
G-BOAH	PA-28-161 Warrior II	Aircraft Engineers Ltd	
G-BOAI	Cessna 152 II	Aviation Spirit Ltd	
G-BOAL	Cameron V-65 balloon	N. H. Ponsford & A. M. Lindsay	
G-BOAM	Robinson R22 Beta	Plane Talking Ltd/Elstree	
G-BOAO	Thunder Ax7-77 balloon	D. V. Fowler	
G-BOAS	Air Command 503 Commander	R. Robinson	
G-BOAU	Cameron V-77 balloon	G. T. Barstow	
G-BOBA	PA-28R-201 Arrow III	Atlantic Flight Training Ltd	
G-BOBH	Airtour AH-77 balloon	J. & K. Francis	
G-BOBR	Cameron N-77 balloon	Trigger Concepts Ltd	
G-BOBT	Stolp SA.300 Starduster Too	G-BOBT Group	
G-BOBV	Cessna F.150M	Sheffield Aero Club Ltd/Netherthorpe	
G-BOBY	Monnett Sonerai II	R. G. Hallam (stored)/Sleap	
G-BOCG	PA-34-200T Seneca II	Oxford Aviation Services Ltd/Kidlington	
G-BOCI	Cessna 140A	J. B. Bonnell	
G-BOCK	Sopwith Triplane (replica) (N6290)	The Shuttleworth Collection/Old Warden	
G-BOCL	Slingsby T.67C	Richard Brinklow Aviation Ltd	
G-BOCM	Slingsby T.67C	Richard Brinklow Aviation Ltd	
G-BOCN	Robinson R22 Beta	Aga Property Development Ltd	
G-BODB	PA-28-161 Warrior II	Sherburn Aero Club Ltd	
G-BODC	PA-28-161 Warrior II	Sherburn Aero Club Ltd	
G-BODD	PA-28-161 Warrior II	L. W. Scattergood	
G-BODE	PA-28-161 Warrior II	Sherburn Aero Club Ltd	
G-BODI	Stoddard-Hamilton SH-3R Glasair III	S. Verhaaren	
G-BODM	PA-28 Cherokee 180	R. Emery	
G-BODO	Cessna 152	M. & D. C. Brooks	
G-BODP	PA-38-112 Tomahawk	B. Petrie	
G-BODR	PA-28-161 Warrior II	Airways Aero Associations Ltd/Booker	
G-BODS	PA-38-112 Tomahawk	Coulson Flying Services Ltd/Cranfield	
G-BODT	Jodel D.18	L. D. McPhillips	
G-BODU	Scheibe SF.25C Falke	Hertfordshire County Scout Council	
G-BODX	Beech 76 Duchess	Aviation Rentals/Bournemouth	
G-BODY	Cessna 310R	Atlantic Air Transport Ltd/Coventry	
G-BODZ	Robinson R22 Beta	Langley Aviation Ltd	
G-BOEE	PA-28-181 Archer II	T. B. Parmenter	
G-BOEH	Jodel DR.340	Piper Flyers Group	
G-BOEK	Cameron V-77 balloon	R. I. M. Kerr & ptnrs	
G-BOEN	Cessna 172M	C. Barlow	
G-BOER	PA-28-161 Warrior II	M. & W. Fraser-Urquhart	
G-BOET	PA-28RT-201 Arrow IV	B. C. Chambers (G-IBEC)	
G-BOEW	Robinson R22 Beta	Plane Talking Ltd/Elstree	
G-BOEZ	Robinson R22 Beta	Plane Talking Ltd/Elstree	
G-BOFC	Beech 76 Duchess	Magenta Ltd/Exeter	
G-BOFD	Cessna U.206G	D. M. Penny	
G-BOFE	PA-34-200T Seneca II	Alstons Upholstery Ltd	
G-BOFF	Cameron N-77 balloon	R. C. Corcoran	
G-BOFL	Cessna 152 II	GEM Rewinds Ltd/Coventry	
G-BOFM	Cessna 152 II	GEM Rewinds Ltd/Coventry	

G-BOFW – G-BOLS — BRITISH CIVIL REGISTRATIONS

Reg	Type	Owner or Operator
G-BOFW	Cessna A.150M	D. F. Donovan
G-BOFX	Cessna A.150M	N. F. O'Neill
G-BOFY	PA-28 Cherokee 140	BCT Aircraft Leasing Ltd
G-BOFZ	PA-28-161 Warrior II	R. W. Harris
G-BOGC	Cessna 152 II	E. Williams
G-BOGI	Robin DR.400/180	A. L. M. Shepherd
G-BOGK	ARV Super 2	M. K. Field
G-BOGM	PA-28RT-201T Turbo Arrow IV	RJP Aviation
G-BOGO	PA-32R-301T Saratoga SP	A. S. Doman/Biggin Hill
G-BOGP	Cameron V-77 balloon	Wealden Balloon Group
G-BOGV	Air Command 532 Elite	G. M. Hobman
G-BOGY	Cameron V-77 balloon	R. A. Preston
G-BOHA	PA-28-161 Warrior II	S. J. Gardiner
G-BOHD	Colt 77A balloon	D. B. Court
G-BOHF	Thunder Ax8-84 balloon	J. A. Harris
G-BOHG	Air Command 532 Elite	T. E. McDonald
G-BOHH	Cessna 172N	G-BOHH Group
G-BOHI	Cessna 152 II	V. D. Speck/Clacton
G-BOHJ	Cessna 152 II	Airlaunch/Old Buckenham
G-BOHL	Cameron A-120 balloon	J. M. Holmes
G-BOHM	PA-28 Cherokee 180	B. F. Keogh & R. A. Scott
G-BOHO	PA-28-161 Warrior II	Egressus Flying Group
G-BOHR	PA-28-151 Warrior	R. M. E. Garforth
G-BOHS	PA-38-112 Tomahawk	Falcon Flying Services/Biggin Hill
G-BOHT	PA-38-112 Tomahawk	St. George Flying Club/Teesside
G-BOHU	PA-38-112 Tomahawk	D. A. Whitmore
G-BOHV	Wittman W.8 Tailwind	R. A. Povall
G-BOHW	Van's RV-4	P. J. Robins
G-BOIA	Cessna 180K	R. E. Styles & ptnrs
G-BOIB	Wittman W.10 Tailwind	R. F. Bradshaw
G-BOIC	PA-28R-201T Turbo Arrow III	M. J. Pearson
G-BOID	Bellanca 7ECA Citabria	D. Mallinson
G-BOIG	PA-28-161 Warrior II	D. Vallence-Pell/Jersey
G-BOIJ	Thunder Ax7-77 balloon	K. Dodman
G-BOIK	Air Command 503 Commander	F. G. Shepherd
G-BOIL	Cessna 172N	Upperstack Ltd/Barton
G-BOIO	Cessna 152	Northumberland Aircraft Maintenance Ltd
G-BOIR	Cessna 152	Shropshire Aero Club Ltd/Sleap
G-BOIT	SOCATA TB10 Tobago	G-BOIT Flying Group
G-BOIV	Cessna 150M	India Victor Group
G-BOIX	Cessna 172N	JR Flying Ltd
G-BOIY	Cessna 172N	L. W. Scattergood
G-BOIZ	PA-34-200T Seneca II	S. F. Tebby & Son
G-BOJB	Cameron V-77 balloon	I. M. & S. D. Warner
G-BOJI	PA-28RT-201 Arrow IV	Arrow Two Group/Blackbushe
G-BOJK	PA-34-220T Seneca III	Redhill Flying Club (G-BRUF)
G-BOJM	PA-28-181 Archer II	R. P. Emms
G-BOJR	Cessna 172P	Exeter Flying Club Ltd
G-BOJS	Cessna 172P	B. A. Paul
G-BOJU	Cameron N-77 balloon	M. A. Scholes
G-BOJW	PA-28-161 Warrior II	Brewhamfield Farm Ltd
G-BOJZ	PA-28-161 Warrior II	Falcon Flying Services/Biggin Hill
G-BOKA	PA-28-201T Turbo Dakota	CBG Aviation Ltd/Biggin Hill
G-BOKB	PA-28-161 Warrior II	Apollo Aviation Advisory Ltd/Shoreham
G-BOKF	Air Command 532 Elite	J. K. Padden
G-BOKH	Whittaker MW7	G. J. Chater
G-BOKN	PA-28-161 Warrior II	BAE Systems Flight Training Ltd
G-BOKU	PA-28-161 Warrior II	BAE Systems Flight Training Ltd
G-BOKX	PA-28-161 Warrior II	Shenley Farms (Aviation) Ltd/Headcorn
G-BOKY	Cessna 152 II	D. F. F. & J. E. Poore
G-BOLB	Taylorcraft BC-12-65	A. D. Pearce
G-BOLC	Fournier RF-6B-100	J. D. Cohen/Dunkeswell
G-BOLD	PA-38-112 Tomahawk	G-BOLD Group/Eaglescott
G-BOLE	PA-38-112 Tomahawk	Double S Group
G-BOLF	PA-38-112 Tomahawk	P. W. Carlton
G-BOLG	Bellanca 7KCAB Citabria	B. R. Pearson/Eaglescott
G-BOLI	Cessna 172P	Boli Flying Club
G-BOLL	Lake LA-4 Skimmer	M. C. Holmes
G-BOLN	Colt 21A balloon	G. Everett
G-BOLO	Bell 206B JetRanger	Hargreaves Leasing Ltd
G-BOLP	Colt 21A balloon	J. E. Rose
G-BOLR	Colt 21A balloon	C. J. Sanger-Davies
G-BOLS	FRED Srs 2	I. F. Vaughan

BRITISH CIVIL REGISTRATIONS

G-BOLT – G-BOSR

Reg	Type	Owner or Operator	Notes
G-BOLT	Rockwell Commander 114	Harnett Air Services Ltd	
G-BOLU	Robin R.3000/120	Classair/Biggin Hill	
G-BOLV	Cessna 152 II	Synergy Aircraft Leasing Ltd	
G-BOLW	Cessna 152 II	A. Jahanfar	
G-BOLY	Cessna 172N	Simair Ltd	
G-BOLZ	Rand-Robinson KR-2	B. Normington	
G-BOMB	Cassutt Racer IIIM	R. S. Grace	
G-BOMN	Cessna 150F	Auburn Flying Group	
G-BOMO	PA-38-112 Tomahawk II	APB Leasing Ltd/Welshpool	
G-BOMP	PA-28-181 Archer II	D. Carter	
G-BOMS	Cessna 172N	Almat Flying Club Ltd & Penchant Ltd	
G-BOMU	PA-28-181 Archer II	J. Sawyer	
G-BOMY	PA-28-161 Warrior II	BOMY Group	
G-BOMZ	PA-38-112 Tomahawk	G-BOMZ Aviation/Booker	
G-BONC	PA-28RT-201 Arrow IV	Finglow Ltd	
G-BONG	Enstrom F-28A-UK	J. O. Beeson/Barton	
G-BONO	Cessna 172N	J. D. McCandless	
G-BONP	CFM Streak Shadow	R. Lawes	
G-BONR	Cessna 172N	D. I. Craik/Biggin Hill	
G-BONS	Cessna 172N	BONS Group/Elstree	
G-BONT	Slingsby T.67M Mk II	Babcock Defence Services	
G-BONU	Slingsby T.67B	R. L. Brinklow	
G-BONW	Cessna 152 II	Lincoln Aero Club Ltd/Sturgate	
G-BONY	Denney Kitfox Mk 1	G-BONY Group	
G-BONZ	Beech V35B Bonanza	P. M. Coulten	
G-BOOB	Cameron N-65 balloon	J. Rumming	
G-BOOC	PA-18 Super Cub 150	S. A. C. Whitcombe	
G-BOOD	Slingsby T.31M Motor Tutor	K. A. Hale	
G-BOOE	GA-7 Cougar	N. Gardner	
G-BOOF	PA-28-181 Archer II	H. Merkado/Panshanger	
G-BOOG	PA-28RT-201T Turbo Arrow IV	Simair Ltd	
G-BOOH	Jodel D.112	R. M. MacCormac	
G-BOOI	Cessna 152	Stapleford Flying Club Ltd	
G-BOOJ	Air Command 532 Elite II	Roger Savage Gyroplanes Ltd	
G-BOOL	Cessna 172N	Surrey & Kent Flying Club Ltd/Biggin Hill	
G-BOOW	Aerosport Scamp	D. A. Weldon/Ireland	
G-BOOX	Rutan LongEz	I. R. Wilde	
G-BOOZ	Cameron N-77 balloon	J. E. F. Kettlety	
G-BOPA	PA-28-181 Archer II	Flyco Ltd	
G-BOPB	Boeing 767-204ER	XL Airways UK Ltd	
G-BOPC	PA-28-161 Warrior II	Aeros Ltd	
G-BOPD	Bede BD-4	S. T. Dauncey	
G-BOPH	Cessna TR.182RG	Grandsam Investments Ltd	
G-BOPO	Brooklands OA.7 Optica	Aces High Ltd/North Weald	
G-BOPR	Brooklands OA.7 Optica	Aces High Ltd/North Weald	
G-BOPT	Grob G.115	LAC (Enterprises) Ltd/Barton	
G-BOPU	Grob G.115	LAC (Enterprises) Ltd/Barton	
G-BOPX	Cessna A.152	Aerohire Ltd/Wolverhampton	
G-BORB	Cameron V-77 balloon	M. H. Wolff	
G-BORD	Thunder Ax7-77 balloon	D. D. Owen	
G-BORE	Colt 77A balloon	Little Secret Hot-Air Balloon Group	
G-BORG	Campbell Cricket	G. Davison & H. Hayes	
G-BORH	PA-34-200T Seneca II	The Construction Workers Guild Ltd	
G-BORI	Cessna 152 II	Linkrest Ltd	
G-BORJ	Cessna 152 II	Silverstar Aviation Ltd/Blackpool	
G-BORK	PA-28-161 Warrior II	The Warrior Group (G-IIIC)	
G-BORL	PA-28-161 Warrior II	Westair Flying School Ltd/Blackpool	
G-BORM	HS.748 Srs 2B ★	Airport Fire Service/Exeter	
G-BORN	Cameron N-77 balloon	I. Chadwick	
G-BORO	Cessna 152 II	Tatenhill Aviation Ltd	
G-BORR	Thunder Ax8-90 balloon	W. J. Harris	
G-BORS	PA-28-181 Archer II	Pool Aviation (NW) Ltd	
G-BORT	Colt 77A balloon	J. Triquet/France	
G-BORW	Cessna 172P	Briter Aviation Ltd/Coventry	
G-BORY	Cessna 150L	Alexander Aviation	
G-BOSB	Thunder Ax7-77 balloon	M. Gallagher	
G-BOSD	PA-34-200T Seneca II	Bristol Flying Centre Ltd/Bristol	
G-BOSE	PA-28-181 Archer II	G-BOSE Group	
G-BOSJ	Nord 3400 (124)	A. I. Milne	
G-BOSM	Jodel DR.253B	A. G. Stevens	
G-BOSN	AS.355F1 Twin Squirrel	Helicopter Services/Booker	
G-BOSO	Cessna A.152	J. S. Develin & Z. Islam/Redhill	
G-BOSR	PA-28 Cherokee 140	Sierra Romeo Group	

G-BOSU – G-BOZS | BRITISH CIVIL REGISTRATIONS

Notes	Reg	Type	Owner or Operator
	G-BOSU	PA-28 Cherokee 140	G-BOSU Group
	G-BOTD	Cameron O-105 balloon	P. J. Beglan/France
	G-BOTF	PA-28-151 Warrior	G-BOTF Group/Southend
	G-BOTG	Cessna 152 II	Donington Aviation Ltd/East Midlands
	G-BOTH	Cessna 182Q	G-BOTH Group/Barton
	G-BOTI	PA-28-151 Warrior	Falcon Flying Services/Biggin Hill
	G-BOTK	Cameron O-105 balloon	N. Woodham
	G-BOTN	PA-28-161 Warrior II	Apollo Aviation Advisory
	G-BOTO	Bellanca 7ECA Citabria	G-BOTO Group
	G-BOTP	Cessna 150J	R. F. Finnis & C. P. Williams
	G-BOTU	Piper J-3C-65 Cub	T. L. Giles
	G-BOTV	PA-32RT-300 Lance II	Robin Lance Aviation Association Ltd
	G-BOTW	Cameron V-77 balloon	M. R. Jeynes
	G-BOUE	Cessna 172N	P. Gray & G. N. R. Bradley
	G-BOUF	Cessna 172N	B. P. & M. I. Sneap
	G-BOUJ	Cessna 150M	UJ Flying Group
	G-BOUK	PA-34-200T Seneca II	C. J. & R. J. Barnes
	G-BOUL	PA-34-200T Seneca II	Oxford Aviation Services Ltd/Kidlington
	G-BOUM	PA-34-200T Seneca II	Oxford Aviation Services Ltd/Kidlington
	G-BOUN	Rand-Robinson KR-2	P. J. Brookman
	G-BOUP	PA-28-161 Warrior II	Aeros Holdings Ltd
	G-BOUT	Colomban MC.12 Cri-Cri	C. K. Farley
	G-BOUV	Bensen B.8MR	L. R. Phillips
	G-BOUZ	Cessna 150G	Atlantic Bridge Aviation Ltd/Lydd
	G-BOVB	PA-15 Vagabond	J. R. Kimberley
	G-BOVC	Everett gyroplane	J. W. Highton
	G-BOVK	PA-28-161 Warrior II	Multiflight Ltd
	G-BOVT	Cessna 150M	C. J. Hopewell
	G-BOVU	Stoddard-Hamilton Glasair III	B. R. Chaplin
	G-BOVV	Cameron V-77 balloon	P. Glydon
	G-BOVW	Colt 69A balloon	V. Hyland
	G-BOVX	Hughes 269C	P. E. Tornberg
	G-BOWB	Cameron V-77 balloon	Zebedee Balloon Service Ltd
	G-BOWE	PA-34-200T Seneca II	Oxford Aviation Services Ltd/Kidlington
	G-BOWL	Cameron V-77 balloon	P. G. & G. R. Hall
	G-BOWM	Cameron V-56 balloon	C. G. Caldecott & G. Pitt
	G-BOWN	PA-12 Super Cruiser	T. L. Giles
	G-BOWO	Cessna R.182	D. A. H. Morris/Wolverhampton (G-BOTR)
	G-BOWP	Jodel D.120A	J. M. Pearson
	G-BOWU	Cameron O-84 balloon	St. Elmos Fire Syndicate
	G-BOWV	Cameron V-65 balloon	R. A. Harris
	G-BOWY	PA-28RT-201T Turbo Arrow IV	J. S. Develin & Z. Islam
	G-BOWZ	Bensen B.80V	W. M. Day
	G-BOXA	PA-28-161 Warrior II	Channel Islands Aero Club (Jersey) Ltd
	G-BOXB	PA-28-161 Warrior II	First Class Ltd
	G-BOXC	PA-28-161 Warrior II	Channel Islands Aero Club (Jersey) Ltd
	G-BOXG	Cameron O-77 balloon	R. A. Wicks
	G-BOXH	Pitts S-1S Special	R. Graham & E. Mason
	G-BOXJ	Piper J-3C-65 Cub	J. D. Tseliki/Shoreham
	G-BOXR	GA-7 Cougar	Plane Talking Ltd/Elstree
	G-BOXT	Hughes 269C	Goldenfly Ltd
	G-BOXU	AA-5B Tiger	Marcher Aviation Group/Welshpool
	G-BOXV	Pitts S-1S Special	C. Waddington
	G-BOXW	Cassutt Racer Srs IIIM	D. I. Johnson
	G-BOYB	Cessna A.152	Northamptonshire School of Flying Ltd/Sywell
	G-BOYC	Robinson R22 Beta	Yorkshire Helicopters/Leeds
	G-BOYF	Sikorsky S-76B	Darley Stud Management Co Ltd/Blackbushe
	G-BOYH	PA-28-151 Warrior	D. Wood-Jenkins & ptnrs
	G-BOYI	PA-28-161 Warrior II	G-BOYI Group/Welshpool
	G-BOYL	Cessna 152 II	Aerohire Ltd/Wolverhampton
	G-BOYM	Cameron O-84 balloon	M. P. Ryan
	G-BOYO	Cameron V-20 balloon	J. M. Willard
	G-BOYP	Cessna 172N	I. D. & D. Brierley
	G-BOYR	Cessna F.337G	Tri-Star Farms Ltd
	G-BOYS	Cameron N-77 balloon	Wye Valley Aviation Ltd
	G-BOYU	Cessna A.150L	Upperstack Ltd/Liverpool
	G-BOYV	PA-28R-201T Turbo Arrow III	Arrow Air Ltd
	G-BOYX	Robinson R22 Beta	R. Towle
	G-BOZI	PA-28-161 Warrior II	Aerolease Ltd/Conington
	G-BOZN	Cameron N-77 balloon	Calarel Developments Ltd
	G-BOZO	AA-5B Tiger	Caslon Ltd
	G-BOZR	Cessna 152 II	GEM Rewinds Ltd/Coventry
	G-BOZS	Pitts S-1C Special	T. A. S. Rayner

BRITISH CIVIL REGISTRATIONS

G-BOZU – G-BPGT

Reg	Type	Owner or Operator	Notes
G-BOZU	Sparrow Hawk Mk II	R. V. Phillimore	
G-BOZV	CEA DR.340 Major	C. J. Turner & S. D. Kent	
G-BOZW	Bensen B.8M	M. E. Wills	
G-BOZY	Cameron RTW-120 balloon	Magical Adventures Ltd	
G-BOZZ	AA-5B Tiger	Solent Tiger Group/Southampton	
G-BPAA	Acro Advanced	Acro Engines & Airframes Ltd	
G-BPAB	Cessna 150M	M. J. Diggins/Earls Colne	
G-BPAF	PA-28-161 Warrior II	RAF Brize Norton Flying Club Ltd	
G-BPAI	Bell 47G-3B-1 (modified)	LRC Leisure Ltd	
G-BPAJ	DH.82A Tiger Moth	P. A. Jackson (G-AOIX)	
G-BPAL	DHC.1 Chipmunk 22 (WG350)	K. F. & P. Tomsett (G-BCYE)	
G-BPAS	SOCATA TB20 Trinidad	Syndicate Clerical Services Ltd	
G-BPAV	FRED Srs 2	P. A. Valentine	
G-BPAW	Cessna 150M	G-BPAW Group	
G-BPAX	Cessna 150M	Dirty Dozen	
G-BPAY	PA-28-181 Archer II	D. A. C. Smith	
G-BPBB	Evans VP-2 (mod)	A. Bleese	
G-BPBG	Cessna 152 II	APB Leasing Ltd/Welshpool	
G-BPBI	Cessna 152 II	B. W. Wells & Burbage Farms Ltd	
G-BPBJ	Cessna 152 II	W. Shaw & P. G. Haines	
G-BPBK	Cessna 152 II	Atlantic Flight Training Ltd	
G-BPBM	PA-28-161 Warrior II	Halfpenny Green Flight Centre Ltd	
G-BPBO	PA-28RT-201T Turbo Arrow IV	Tile Holdings Ltd	
G-BPBP	Brügger MB.2 Colibri	D. A. Preston	
G-BPBV	Cameron V-77 balloon	S. J. Farrant	
G-BPBW	Cameron O-105 balloon	R. J. Mansfield	
G-BPBY	Cameron V-77 balloon	L. Hutley (G-BPCS)	
G-BPCA	BN-2B-26 Islander	Loganair Ltd (G-BLNX)	
G-BPCF	Piper J-3C-65 Cub	J. S. Evans	
G-BPCG	Colt AS-80 airship	N. Charbonnier/Italy	
G-BPCI	Cessna R.172K	S. Fyfe	
G-BPCK	PA-28-161 Warrior II	Compton Abbas Airfield Ltd	
G-BPCL	SA Bulldog Srs 120/128 (HKG-6)	Isohigh Ltd/Denham	
G-BPCM	Rotorway Executive	D. Rigby	
G-BPCR	Mooney M.20K	T. & R. Harris	
G-BPCV	Montgomerie-Bensen B.8MR	M. A. Hayward	
G-BPCX	PA-28-236 Dakota	Blue Yonder Aviation Ltd	
G-BPDE	Colt 56A balloon	J. E. Weidema/Netherlands	
G-BPDG	Cameron V-77 balloon	F. R. Battersby	
G-BPDJ	Chris Tena Mini Coupe	J. J. Morrissey/Popham	
G-BPDK	Sorrell SNS-7 Hyperbipe ★	A. J. Cable (stored)/Barton	
G-BPDM	CASA 1.131E Jungmann 2000 (781-32)	J. D. Haslam	
G-BPDT	PA-28-161 Warrior II	Channel Islands Aero Club (Jersey) Ltd	
G-BPDV	Pitts S-1S Special	J. Vize/Sywell	
G-BPEC	Boeing 757-236	British Airways	
G-BPED	Boeing 757-236	British Airways	
G-BPEE	Boeing 757-236	British Airways	
G-BPEI	Boeing 757-236	British Airways (G-BMRK)	
G-BPEJ	Boeing 757-236	British Airways (G-BMRL)	
G-BPEK	Boeing 757-236	British Airways (G-BMRM)	
G-BPEL	PA-28-151 Warrior	R. W. Harris & A. J. Jahanfar	
G-BPEM	Cessna 150K	R. G. Lindsey & R. Strong	
G-BPEO	Cessna 152 II	Cristal Air Ltd	
G-BPES	PA-38-112 Tomahawk II	Sherwood Flying Club Ltd/Tollerton	
G-BPEZ	Colt 77A balloon	J. W. Adkins	
G-BPFB	Colt 77A balloon	S. Ingram	
G-BPFC	Mooney M.20C	D. P. Wring	
G-BPFD	Jodel D.112	C. P. Whitwell	
G-BPFF	Cameron DP-70 airship	John Aimo Balloons SAS/Italy	
G-BPFH	PA-28-161 Warrior II	M. H. Kleiser	
G-BPFI	PA-28-181 Archer II	F. Teagle	
G-BPFL	Davis DA-2	B. W. Griffiths	
G-BPFM	Aeronca 7AC Champion	D. Boyce	
G-BPFN	Short SD3-60 Variant 100	Aurigny Air Services Ltd	
G-BPFZ	Cessna 152 II	Devon and Somerset Flight Training Ltd	
G-BPGC	Air Command 532 Elite	A. G. W. Davis	
G-BPGD	Cameron V-65 balloon	Gone With The Wind Ltd	
G-BPGE	Cessna U.206C	Scottish Parachute Club/Strathallan	
G-BPGF	Thunder Ax7-77 balloon	M. Schiavo	
G-BPGH	EAA Acro Sport II	G. M. Bradley	
G-BPGK	Aeronca 7AC Champion	D. A. Crompton & G. C. Holmes	
G-BPGT	Colt AS-80 Mk II airship	P. Porati/Italy	

G-BPGU – G-BPOA — BRITISH CIVIL REGISTRATIONS

Notes	Reg	Type	Owner or Operator
	G-BPGU	PA-28-181 Archer II	G. Underwood/Tollerton
	G-BPGV	Robinson R22 Beta	G. Gazza/Monaco
	G-BPGZ	Cessna 150G	J. B. Scott
	G-BPHB	PA-28-161 Warrior II	M. J. Wade
	G-BPHD	Cameron N-42 balloon	P. J. Marshall & M. A. Clarke
	G-BPHG	Robin DR.400/180	A. Hildreth
	G-BPHH	Cameron V-77 balloon	C. D. Aindow
	G-BPHI	PA-38-112 Tomahawk	J. S. Devlin & Z. Islam/Redhill
	G-BPHJ	Cameron V-77 balloon	C. W. Brown
	G-BPHK	Whittaker MW7	J. S. Shufflebottom
	G-BPHL	PA-28-161 Warrior II	J. D. Swales
	G-BPHO	Taylorcraft BC-12	B. J. Swanton
	G-BPHP	Taylorcraft BC-12-65	J. S. Jackson
	G-BPHR	DH.82A Tiger Moth (A17-48)	N. Parry
	G-BPHT	Cessna 152	I. A. Anderson
	G-BPHU	Thunder Ax7-77 balloon	R. P. Waite
	G-BPHW	Cessna 140	L. J. A. Bell
	G-BPHX	Cessna 140	M. McChesney
	G-BPHZ	MS.505 Criquet (DM+BK)	Aero Vintage Ltd
	G-BPID	PA-28-161 Warrior II	J. T. Nuttall
	G-BPIF	Bensen-Parsons 2-place gyroplane	B. J. L. P. & W. J. A. L. de Saar
	G-BPII	Denney Kitfox	G-BPII Group
	G-BPIJ	Brantly B.2B	Seething Brantly Group
	G-BPIK	PA-38-112 Tomahawk	Fly Me Ltd
	G-BPIL	Cessna 310B	A. L. Brown
	G-BPIN	Glaser-Dirks DG.400	J. N. Stevenson
	G-BPIO	Cessna F.152 II	I. D. McClelland
	G-BPIP	Slingsby T.31 Motor Cadet III	J. H. Beard
	G-BPIR	Scheibe SF.25E Super Falke	A. P. Askwith
	G-BPIT	Robinson R22 Beta	NA Air Ltd
	G-BPIU	PA-28-161 Warrior II	Golf India Uniform Group
	G-BPIV	B.149 Bolingbroke Mk IVT (R3821)	Blenheim (Duxford) Ltd
	G-BPIZ	AA-5B Tiger	D. A. Horsley
	G-BPJB	Schweizer 269C	Elborne Holdings Ltd/Portugal
	G-BPJD	SOCATA Rallye 110ST	L. P. Claydon
	G-BPJE	Cameron A-105 balloon	J. S. Eckersley
	G-BPJG	PA-18 Super Cub 150	M. W. Stein
	G-BPJH	PA-18 Super Cub 95	P. J. Heron
	G-BPJK	Colt 77A balloon	Saran UK Ltd
	G-BPJO	PA-28-161 Cadet	Aviation Rentals
	G-BPJP	PA-28-161 Cadet	Aviation Rentals/Bournemouth
	G-BPJR	PA-28-161 Cadet	Plane Talking Ltd
	G-BPJS	PA-28-161 Cadet	Abraxas Aviation Ltd
	G-BPJU	PA-28-161 Cadet	Aviation Rentals/Bournemouth
	G-BPJV	Taylorcraft F-21	TC Flying Group
	G-BPJW	Cessna A.150K	Heald Ltd
	G-BPJZ	Cameron O-160 balloon	M. L. Gabb
	G-BPKF	Grob G.115	Dorset Aviation Group
	G-BPKK	Denney Kitfox Mk 1	D. Moffat
	G-BPKM	PA-28-161 Warrior II	R. Cass
	G-BPKO	Cessna 140	M. G. Rummey
	G-BPKR	PA-28-151 Warrior	Aeros Leasing Ltd
	G-BPLH	Jodel DR.1051	C. K. Farley
	G-BPLM	AIA Stampe SV.4C	C. J. Jesson/Redhill
	G-BPLV	Cameron V-77 balloon	MC VH SA/Belgium
	G-BPLY	Christen Pitts S-2B Special	P. A. Greenhalgh
	G-BPLZ	Hughes 369HS	M. A. & R. J. Fawcett
	G-BPMB	Maule M5-235C Lunar Rocket	R. G. Marshall
	G-BPME	Cessna 152 II	A. Jahanfar
	G-BPMF	PA-28-151 Warrior	Mike Foxtrot Group
	G-BPML	Cessna 172M	N. A. Bilton
	G-BPMR	PA-28-161 Warrior II	Aeros Holdings Ltd
	G-BPMU	Nord 3202B	A. I. Milne (G-BIZJ)
	G-BPMW	QAC Quickie Q.2	P. M. Wright (G-OICI/G-OGKN)
	G-BPMX	ARV Super 2	C. R. James
	G-BPNA	Cessna 150L	Wolds Flyers Syndicate
	G-BPNI	Robinson R22 Beta	Heliflight (UK) Ltd
	G-BPNJ	HS.748 Srs 2A	Clewer Aviation Ltd
	G-BPNN	Montgomerie-Bensen B.8MR	M. E. Vahdat
	G-BPNO	Zlin Z.326 Trener Master	J. A. S. Bailey & S. T. Logan
	G-BPNT	BAe 146-300	Flightline Ltd
	G-BPNU	Thunder Ax7-77 balloon	M. J. Barnes
	G-BPOA	Gloster Meteor T.7 (WF877) ★	39 Restoration Group/North Weald

82

BRITISH CIVIL REGISTRATIONS

G-BPOB – G-BPVU

Reg	Type	Owner or Operator	Notes
G-BPOB	Sopwith Camel F.1 (replica) (B2458:R)	Flying Aces Movie Aircraft Collection/Compton Abbas	
G-BPOM	PA-28-161 Warrior II	POM Flying Group	
G-BPON	PA-34-200T Seneca II	Aeroshare Ltd/Staverton	
G-BPOO	Montgomerie-Bensen B.8MR	M. E. Vahdat	
G-BPOS	Cessna 150M	Brooke Park Ltd/Sheffield	
G-BPOT	PA-28-181 Archer II	Icarus Flyers Ltd	
G-BPOU	Luscombe 8A Silvaire	J. L. Grayer	
G-BPPA	Cameron O-65 balloon	Rix Petroleum Ltd	
G-BPPE	PA-38-112 Tomahawk	First Air Ltd	
G-BPPF	PA-38-112 Tomahawk	Bristol Strut Flying Group	
G-BPPJ	Cameron A-180 balloon	D. J. Farrar	
G-BPPK	PA-28-151 Warrior	Idfit Ltd	
G-BPPM	Beech B200 Super King Air	Gama Aviation Ltd/Fairoaks	
G-BPPO	Luscombe 8A Silvaire	M. G. Rummey	
G-BPPP	Cameron V-77 balloon	Sarnia Balloon Group	
G-BPPS	Mudry CAARP CAP-21	L. Van Vuuren	
G-BPPU	Air Command 532 Elite	J. Hough	
G-BPPY	Hughes 269B	M. D. Leeney	
G-BPPZ	Taylorcraft BC-12D	Kingsmuir Group	
G-BPRA	Aeronca 11AC Chief	P. L. Clements	
G-BPRC	Cameron 77 Elephant SS balloon	A. Schneider/Germany	
G-BPRD	Pitts S-1C Special	Parrot Aerobatic Group	
G-BPRI	AS.355F1 Twin Squirrel	MW Helicopters Ltd/Stapleford (G-TVPA)	
G-BPRJ	AS.355F1 Twin Squirrel	PLM Dollar Group Ltd/Inverness	
G-BPRL	AS.355F1 Twin Squirrel	MW Helicopters Ltd	
G-BPRM	Cessna F.172L	BJ Aviation Ltd (G-AZKG)	
G-BPRN	PA-28-161 Warrior II	Air Navigation & Trading Co Ltd/Blackpool	
G-BPRR	Rand-Robinson KR-2	P. E. Taylor	
G-BPRX	Aeronca 11AC Chief	M. G. Rumney	
G-BPRY	PA-28-161 Warrior II	White Wings Aviation	
G-BPSA	Luscombe 8A Silvaire	K. P Gorman/Staverton	
G-BPSH	Cameron V-77 balloon	P. G. Hossack	
G-BPSJ	Thunder Ax6-56 balloon	V. Hyland	
G-BPSK	Montgomerie-Bensen B.8M	P. T. Ambrozik	
G-BPSL	Cessna 177	K. S. Herbert	
G-BPSO	Cameron N-90 balloon	J. Oberprieler/Germany	
G-BPSR	Cameron V-77 balloon	K. J. A. Maxwell	
G-BPSS	Cameron A-120 balloon	Anglian Countryside Balloons Ltd	
G-BPTA	Stinson 108-2	M. L. Ryan	
G-BPTD	Cameron V-77 balloon	J. Lippett	
G-BPTE	PA-28-181 Archer II	J. S. Develin & Z. Islam	
G-BPTG	Rockwell Commander 112TC	L. G. Watteau	
G-BPTI	SOCATA TB20 Trinidad	N. Davis	
G-BPTL	Cessna 172N	J. Martinson	
G-BPTS	CASA 1.131E Jungmann 1000 (E3B-153:781-75)	Aerobatic Displays Ltd/Duxford	
G-BPTU	Cessna 152	A. M. Alam/Panshanger	
G-BPTV	Bensen B.8	C. Munro	
G-BPTX	Cameron O-120 balloon	Skybus Ballooning	
G-BPTZ	Robinson R22 Beta	Aero Maintenance Ltd	
G-BPUA	EAA Sport Biplane	M. D. Gorlov	
G-BPUB	Cameron V-31 balloon	M. T. Evans	
G-BPUE	Air Command 532 Elite	J. K. Padden	
G-BPUF	Thunder Ax6-56Z balloon	R. C. & M. A. Trimble (G-BHRL)	
G-BPUG	Air Command 532 Elite	T. A. Holmes	
G-BPUJ	Cameron N-90 balloon	D. Grimshaw	
G-BPUL	PA-18 Super Cub 150	C. D. Duthy-James	
G-BPUM	Cessna R.182RG	R. C. Chapman	
G-BPUP	Whittaker MW7	J. H. Beard	
G-BPUR	Piper J-3L-65 Cub ★	H. A. D. Monro	
G-BPUU	Cessna 140	D. R. Speight	
G-BPUW	Colt 90A balloon	Gefa-Flug GmbH/Germany	
G-BPVA	Cessna 172F	S. Lancashire Flyers Group/Barton	
G-BPVC	Cameron V-77 balloon	B. D. Pettitt	
G-BPVE	Bleriot IX (replica) (1) ★	Bianchi Aviation Film Services Ltd/Booker	
G-BPVH	Cub Aircraft J-3C-65 Prospector	D. E. Cooper-Maguire	
G-BPVI	PA-32R-301 Saratoga SP	M. T. Coppen/Booker	
G-BPVK	Varga 2150A Kachina	H. W. Hall	
G-BPVM	Cameron V-77 balloon	J. Dyer	
G-BPVN	PA-32R-301T Turbo Saratoga SP	R. Weston	
G-BPVO	Cassutt Racer IIIM	R. S. Grace	
G-BPVU	Thunder Ax7-77 balloon	B. J. Hammond	

G-BPVW – G-BRBT — BRITISH CIVIL REGISTRATIONS

Notes	Reg	Type	Owner or Operator
	G-BPVW	CASA 1.131E Jungmann 2000	C. & J-W. Labeij/Netherlands
	G-BPVX	Cassutt Racer IIIM	D. D. Milne
	G-BPVY	Cessna 172D	S. J. Davies & D. Toft
	G-BPVZ	Luscombe 8E Silvaire	W. E. Gillham & P. Ryman
	G-BPWB	Sikorsky S-61N	Bristow Helicopters Ltd/HM Coastguard
	G-BPWC	Cameron V-77 balloon	H. B. Roberts
	G-BPWD	Cessna 120	Peregrine Flying Group
	G-BPWE	PA-28-161 Warrior II	RPR Associates Ltd/Swansea
	G-BPWF	PA-28 Cherokee 140 ★	(Static display)/1244 Sqdn ATC/Swindon
	G-BPWG	Cessna 150M	A. B. Brock
	G-BPWI	Bell 206B JetRanger 3	Warren Aviation
	G-BPWK	Sportavia Fournier RF-5B	G-BPWK Flying Group/Usk
	G-BPWL	PA-25 Pawnee 235	Tecair Aviation Ltd/Shipdham
	G-BPWM	Cessna 150L	M. E. Creasey
	G-BPWN	Cessna 150L	Cardiff Academy of Aviation Ltd
	G-BPWP	Rutan LongEz (modified)	D. A. Field
	G-BPWR	Cessna R.172K	Messrs Rees
	G-BPWS	Cessna 172P	Chartstone Ltd
	G-BPXA	PA-28-181 Archer II	Cherokee Flying Group/Netherthorpe
	G-BPXB	Glaser-Dirks DG.400	G. C. Westgate & Ptnrs/Parham Park
	G-BPXE	Enstrom 280C Shark	A. Healy
	G-BPXF	Cameron V-65 balloon	D. Pascall
	G-BPXG	Colt 45A balloon	Zebedee Balloon Service Ltd
	G-BPXH	Colt 17A balloon	Sport Promotion SRL/Italy
	G-BPXJ	PA-28RT-201T Turbo Arrow IV	K. M. Hollamby/Biggin Hill
	G-BPXX	PA-34-200T Seneca II	Yorkshire Aviation Ltd
	G-BPXY	Aeronca 11AC Chief	P. L. Turner
	G-BPYJ	Wittman W.8 Tailwind	J. P. Mills and Y. Tutt
	G-BPYK	Thunder Ax7-77 balloon	A. R. Swinnerton
	G-BPYL	Hughes 369D	Morcorp (BVI) Ltd
	G-BPYN	Piper J-3C-65 Cub	The Aquila Group/White Waltham
	G-BPYO	PA-28-181 Archer II	Sherburn Aero Club Ltd
	G-BPYR	PA-31-310 Turbo Navajo	Synergy Aircraft Leasing Ltd (G-ECMA)
	G-BPYS	Cameron O-77 balloon	D. J. Goldsmith
	G-BPYT	Cameron V-77 balloon	M. H. Redman
	G-BPYV	Cameron V-77 balloon	R. J. Shortall
	G-BPYY	Cameron A-180 balloon	G. D. Fitzpatrick
	G-BPYZ	Thunder Ax7-77 balloon	J. E. Astall
	G-BPZA	Luscombe 8A Silvaire	M. J. Wright
	G-BPZB	Cessna 120	Cessna 120 Group
	G-BPZC	Luscombe 8A Silvaire	C. C. & J. M. Lovell
	G-BPZD	SNCAN NC.858S	Zula Delta Syndicate
	G-BPZE	Luscombe 8E Silvaire	WFG Luscombe Associates
	G-BPZK	Cameron O-120 balloon	D. L. Smith
	G-BPZM	PA-28RT-201 Arrow IV	Magenta Ltd (G-ROYW/G-CRTI)
	G-BPZP	Robin DR.400/180R	S. G. Jones
	G-BPZS	Colt 105A balloon	L. E. Giles
	G-BPZU	Scheibe SF.25C Falke	Southdown Gliding Club Ltd
	G-BPZY	Pitts S-1C Special	J. S. Mitchell
	G-BPZZ	Thunder Ax8-105 balloon	Capricorn Balloons Ltd
	G-BRAF	Supermarine 394 Spitfire FR.XVIIIe	The Fighter Collection/Duxford
	G-BRAK	Cessna 172N	The Burnett Group Ltd/Kemble
	G-BRAM	Mikoyan MiG-21PF (503) ★	FAST Museum/Farnborough
	G-BRAR	Aeronca 7AC Champion	R. B. Armitage
	G-BRAX	Payne Knight Twister 85B	R. Earl
	G-BRBA	PA-28-161 Warrior II	S. H. Pearce
	G-BRBB	PA-28-161 Warrior II	M. A. & A. J. Bell
	G-BRBC	NA T-6G Texan	A. P. Murphy
	G-BRBD	PA-28-151 Warrior	Compton Abbas Airfield Ltd
	G-BRBE	PA-28-161 Warrior II	Solo Services Ltd/Shoreham
	G-BRBG	PA-28 Cherokee 180	G-BRBG Group
	G-BRBH	Cessna 150H	J. Maffia & H. Merkado/Panshanger
	G-BRBI	Cessna 172N	Skyhawk Flying Group
	G-BRBJ	Cessna 172M	L. C. MacKnight
	G-BRBK	Robin DR.400/180	R. Kemp
	G-BRBL	Robin DR.400/180	C. A. Merren
	G-BRBM	Robin DR.400/180	R. W. Davies/Headcorn
	G-BRBN	Pitts S-1S Special	D. R. Evans
	G-BRBO	Cameron V-77 balloon	M. B. Murby
	G-BRBP	Cessna 152	Staverton Flying School
	G-BRBS	Bensen B.8M	K. T. MacFarlane
	G-BRBT	Trotter Ax3-20 balloon	R. M. Trotter

BRITISH CIVIL REGISTRATIONS — G-BRBV – G-BRIK

Reg	Type	Owner or Operator	Notes
G-BRBV	Piper J-4A Cub Coupe	B. Schonburg	
G-BRBW	PA-28 Cherokee 140	Air Navigation and Trading Co Ltd	
G-BRBX	PA-28-181 Archer II	Trent 199 Flying Group	
G-BRBY	Robinson R22 Beta	Abraxas Aviation Ltd	
G-BRCA	Jodel D.112	R. C. Jordan	
G-BRCE	Pitts S-1C Special	R. O. Rogers	
G-BRCF	Montgomerie-Bensen B.8MR	J. S. Walton	
G-BRCI	Pitts S-1C Special	G. L. A. Vandormael/Belgium	
G-BRCJ	Cameron H-20 balloon	M. E. White	
G-BRCM	Cessna 172L	S. G. E. Plessis & D. C. C. Handley	
G-BRCO	Cameron H-20 balloon	G. D. Jones	
G-BRCT	Denney Kitfox Mk 2	M. L. Roberts	
G-BRCV	Aeronca 7AC Champion	A. P. Amor	
G-BRCW	Aeronca 11AC Chief	R. B. McComish	
G-BRDB	Zenair CH.701 STOL	D. L. Bowtell	
G-BRDD	Avions Mudry CAP-10B	R. D. Dickson/Gamston	
G-BRDE	Thunder Ax7-77 balloon	D. J. Keys	
G-BRDF	PA-28-161 Warrior II	White Waltham Airfield Ltd	
G-BRDG	PA-28-161 Warrior II	Falcon Flying Services	
G-BRDJ	Luscombe 8A Silvaire	P. G. Stewart	
G-BRDM	PA-28-161 Warrior II	White Waltham Airfield Ltd	
G-BRDN	MS.880B Rallye Club	A. J. Gomes	
G-BRDO	Cessna 177B	Cardinal Aviation	
G-BRDT	Cameron DP-70 airship	Tim Balloon Promotion Airships Ltd	
G-BRDV	Viking Wood Products Spitfire Prototype replica (K5054) ★	Solent Sky, Southampton	
G-BRDW	PA-24 Comanche 180	I. P. Gibson/Southampton	
G-BREB	Piper J-3C-65 Cub	J. R. Wraight	
G-BREE	Whittaker MW7	D. A. Couchman	
G-BREH	Cameron V-65 balloon	S. E. & V. D. Hurst	
G-BREL	Cameron O-77 balloon	R. A. Patey	
G-BREP	PA-28RT-201 Arrow IV	Gary Key Aircraft Leasing	
G-BRER	Aeronca 7AC Champion	Rabbit Flight	
G-BREU	Montgomerie-Bensen B.8MR	J. S. Firth	
G-BREX	Cameron O-84 balloon	Ovolo Ltd	
G-BREY	Taylorcraft BC-12D	BREY Group	
G-BRFB	Rutan LongEz	R. Young	
G-BRFC	Percival P.57 Sea Prince T.Mk.1 (WP321)	A. & G. A. Gainsford-Dixon	
G-BRFE	Cameron V-77 balloon	Esmerelda Balloon Syndicate	
G-BRFF	Colt 90A balloon	Amber Valley Aviation	
G-BRFI	Aeronca 7DC Champion	A. C. Lines	
G-BRFJ	Aeronca 11AC Chief	J. M. Mooney	
G-BRFL	PA-38-112 Tomahawk	D. A. G. Day	
G-BRFM	PA-28-161 Warrior II	Atlantic Flight Training Ltd	
G-BRFO	Cameron V-77 balloon	Hedge Hoppers Balloon Group	
G-BRFW	Montgomerie-Bensen B.8 2-seat	A. J. Barker	
G-BRFX	Pazmany PL.4A	D. E. Hills	
G-BRGD	Cameron O-84 balloon	D. J. Phillips	
G-BRGE	Cameron N-90 balloon	Oakfield Farm Products Ltd	
G-BRGF	Luscombe 8E Silvaire	Luscombe Flying Group	
G-BRGG	Luscombe 8A Silvaire	M. A. Lamprell	
G-BRGI	PA-28 Cherokee 180	R. A. Buckfield	
G-BRGO	Air Command 532 Elite	A. McCredie	
G-BRGT	PA-32 Cherokee Six 260	P. Cowley	
G-BRGW	Gardan GY-201 Minicab	R. G. White	
G-BRHA	PA-32RT-300 Lance II	Lance G-BRHA Group	
G-BRHG	Colt 90A balloon	Bath University Students' Union	
G-BRHL	Montgomerie-Bensen B.8MR	T. M. Jones & B. Moore	
G-BRHO	PA-34-200 Seneca	D. A. Lewis/Luton	
G-BRHP	Aeronca O-58B Grasshopper (31923)	C. J. Willis/Italy	
G-BRHR	PA-38-112 Tomahawk	The Royal Artillery Aero Club Ltd	
G-BRHT	PA-38-112 Tomahawk	Ravenair Aircraft Ltd/Liverpool	
G-BRHW	DH.82A Tiger Moth	P. J. & A. J. Borsberry	
G-BRHX	Luscombe 8E Silvaire	J. Lakin	
G-BRHY	Luscombe 8E Silvaire	A. R. W. Taylor/Sleap	
G-BRIA	Cessna 310L	B. J. Tucker/Kemble	
G-BRIE	Cameron N-77 balloon	S. F. Redman	
G-BRIF	Boeing 767-204ER	Thomsonfly Ltd	
G-BRIG	Boeing 767-204ER	Thomsonfly Ltd	
G-BRIH	Taylorcraft BC-12D	IH Flying Group	
G-BRII	Zenair CH.600 Zodiac	A. C. Bowdrey	
G-BRIJ	Taylorcraft F-19	M. W. Olliver	
G-BRIK	T.66 Nipper 3	P. R. Bentley	

85

G-BRIL – G-BRPL   BRITISH CIVIL REGISTRATIONS

Notes	Reg	Type	Owner or Operator
	G-BRIL	Piper J-5A Cub Cruiser	P. L. Jobes & D. J. Bone
	G-BRIO	Turner Super T-40A	S. Bidwell
	G-BRIR	Cameron V-56 balloon	H. G. Davies & C. Dowd
	G-BRIV	SOCATA TB9 Tampico Club	S. J. Taft
	G-BRIY	Taylorcraft DF-65 (42-58678:IY)	S. R. Potts
	G-BRJA	Luscombe 8A Silvaire	A. D. Keen
	G-BRJB	Zenair CH.600 Zodiac	C. A. Hasell
	G-BRJC	Cessna 120	A. L. Hall-Carpenter
	G-BRJK	Luscombe 8A Silvaire	C. J. L. Peat & M. Richardson
	G-BRJL	PA-15 Vagabond	A. R. Williams
	G-BRJN	Pitts S-1C Special	W. Chapel
	G-BRJR	PA-38-112 Tomahawk	M. McGovern
	G-BRJT	Cessna 150H	Romeo Tango Group
	G-BRJV	PA-28-161 Cadet	Northumbria Flying School Ltd
	G-BRJW	Bellanca 7GCBC Citabria	Juliet Whiskey Flying Club
	G-BRJX	Rand-Robinson KR-2	J. R. Bell
	G-BRJY	Rand-Robinson KR-2	R. E. Taylor
	G-BRKC	Auster J/1 Autocrat	J. W. Conlon
	G-BRKH	PA-28-236 Dakota	A. P. H. Hay & C. C. Bennett
	G-BRKR	Cessna 182R	A. R. D. Brooker
	G-BRKW	Cameron V-77 balloon	T. J. Parker
	G-BRKX	Air Command 532 Elite	K. Davis
	G-BRKY	Viking Dragonfly Mk II	G. D. Price
	G-BRLB	Air Command 532 Elite	F. G. Shepherd
	G-BRLF	Campbell Cricket (replica)	J. L. G. McLane
	G-BRLG	PA-28RT-201T Turbo Arrow IV	P. Lodge & J. G. McVey
	G-BRLI	Piper J-5A Cub Cruiser	Little Bear Ltd
	G-BRLJ	Evans VP-2	R. L. Jones
	G-BRLL	Cameron A-105 balloon	Aerosaurus Balloons Ltd
	G-BRLO	PA-38-112 Tomahawk	St. George Flight Training/Teesside
	G-BRLP	PA-38-112 Tomahawk	P. D. Brooks
	G-BRLR	Cessna 150G	D. Carr & M. R. Muter
	G-BRLS	Thunder Ax7-77 balloon	E. C. Meek
	G-BRLT	Colt 77A balloon	D. Bareford
	G-BRLV	CCF Harvard IV (93542:LTA-542)	Extraviation Ltd/North Weald
	G-BRMA	WS-51 Dragonfly HR.5 (WG719) ★	IHM/Weston-super-Mare
	G-BRMB	B.192 Belvedere HC.1	IHM/Weston-super-Mare
	G-BRME	PA-28-181 Archer II	Keen Leasing Ltd
	G-BRMI	Cameron V-65 balloon	M. Davies
	G-BRMT	Cameron V-31 balloon	B. Reed
	G-BRMU	Cameron V-77 balloon	K. J. & G. R. Ibbotson
	G-BRMV	Cameron O-77 balloon	P. D. Griffiths
	G-BRMW	Whittaker MW7	G. S. Parsons
	G-BRNC	Cessna 150M	November Charlie Flying Group
	G-BRND	Cessna 152 II	T. M. & M. L. Jones/Egginton
	G-BRNE	Cessna 152 II	Redhill Air Services Ltd
	G-BRNK	Cessna 152 II	Sheffield Aero Club Ltd/Netherthorpe
	G-BRNN	Cessna 152 II	Sheffield Aero Club Ltd/Netherthorpe
	G-BRNT	Robin DR.400/180	C. E. Ponsford & ptnrs
	G-BRNU	Robin DR.400/180	November Uniform Travel Syndicate Ltd/Booker
	G-BRNV	PA-28-181 Archer II	B. S. Hobbs
	G-BRNW	Cameron V-77 balloon	N. Robertson & G. Smith
	G-BRNX	PA-22 Tri-Pacer 150	S. N. Askey
	G-BRNZ	PA-32 Cherokee Six 300B	Longfellow Flying Group
	G-BROB	Cameron V-77 balloon	J. W. Tomlinson
	G-BROE	Cameron N-65 balloon	A. I. Attwood
	G-BROG	Cameron V-65 balloon	R. Kunert
	G-BROH	Cameron O-90 balloon	P. A. Derbyshire
	G-BROI	CFM Streak Shadow Srs SA	A. Collinson
	G-BROJ	Colt 31A balloon	N. J. Langley
	G-BROO	Luscombe 8E Silvaire	P. R. Bush
	G-BROP	Vans RV-4	K. E. Armstrong
	G-BROR	Piper J-3C-65 Cub	White Hart Flying Group
	G-BROX	Robinson R22 Beta	TLC Handling Ltd
	G-BROY	Cameron V-77 balloon	T. G. S. Dixon
	G-BROZ	PA-18 Super Cub 150	P. G. Kynsey
	G-BRPE	Cessna 120	W. B. Bateson/Blackpool
	G-BRPF	Cessna 120	A. L. Hall-Carpenter
	G-BRPG	Cessna 120	I. C. Lomax
	G-BRPH	Cessna 120	J. A. Cook
	G-BRPJ	Cameron N-90 balloon	Cloud Nine Balloon Co
	G-BRPK	PA-28 Cherokee 140	G-BRPK Group
	G-BRPL	PA-28-140 Cherokee	Euroflight Ltd

BRITISH CIVIL REGISTRATIONS   G-BRPM – G-BRWD

Reg	Type	Owner or Operator	Notes
G-BRPM	T.66 Nipper 3	T. C. Horner	
G-BRPP	Brookland Hornet (modified)	B. J. L. P. & W. J. A. L. de Saar	
G-BRPR	Aeronca O-58B Grasshopper (31952)	C. S. Tolchard	
G-BRPS	Cessna 177B	R. C. Tebbett	
G-BRPT	Rans S.10 Sakota	A. R. Hawes	
G-BRPU	Beech 76 Duchess	Plane Talking Ltd/Elstree	
G-BRPV	Cessna 152	Eastern Air Executive Ltd	
G-BRPX	Taylorcraft BC-12D	The BRPX Group	
G-BRPY	PA-15 Vagabond	J. & V. Hobday/Barton	
G-BRPZ	Luscombe 8A Silvaire	G. L. Brown	
G-BRRB	Luscombe 8E Silvaire	J. Nicholls	
G-BRRD	Scheibe SF.25B Falke	G-BRRD Group	
G-BRRF	Cameron O-77 balloon	K. P. & G. J. Storey	
G-BRRG	Glaser-Dirks DG.500M	G-BRRG Syndicate	
G-BRRJ	PA-28RT-201T Turbo Arrow IV	M. Stower	
G-BRRK	Cessna 182Q	Werewolf Aviation Ltd	
G-BRRL	PA-18 Super Cub 95	Acebell G-BRRL Syndicate/Redhill	
G-BRRN	PA-28-161 Warrior II	G. Whitlow & I. C. Barlow	
G-BRRR	Cameron V-77 balloon	K. P. & G. J. Storey	
G-BRRU	Colt 90A balloon	Reach For The Sky Ltd	
G-BRRY	Robinson R22 Beta	Fast Helicopters Ltd	
G-BRSA	Cameron N-56 balloon	C. Wilkinson	
G-BRSD	Cameron V-77 balloon	T. J. & J.E. Porter	
G-BRSE	PA-28-161 Warrior II	Falcon Flying Services Ltd	
G-BRSF	VS.361 Spitfire HF.9c (RR232)	M. B. Phillips	
G-BRSJ	PA-38-112 Tomahawk II	APB Leasing Ltd/Welshpool	
G-BRSK	Boeing Stearman N2S-3 (1180)	M. Burpitt	
G-BRSL	Cameron N-56 balloon	S. Budd	
G-BRSN	Rand-Robinson KR-2	K. W. Darby	
G-BRSO	CFM Streak Shadow Srs SA	B. C. Norris	
G-BRSP	Air Command 532 Elite	G. M. Hobman	
G-BRSW	Luscombe 8A Silvaire	Bloody Mary Aviation/Fenland	
G-BRSX	PA-15 Vagabond	M. R. Holden	
G-BRSY	Hatz CB-1	C. Knight	
G-BRTD	Cessna 152 II	152 Group/Booker	
G-BRTJ	Cessna 150F	Avon Aviation Ltd	
G-BRTK	Boeing Stearman E.75 (217786)	Eastern Stearman Ltd/Rendcomb	
G-BRTL	Hughes 369E	Crewhall Ltd	
G-BRTP	Cessna 152 II	R. Lee	
G-BRTT	Schweizer 269C	Fairthorpe Ltd/Denham	
G-BRTV	Cameron O-77 balloon	R. J. Clements	
G-BRTW	Glaser-Dirks DG.400	I. J. Carruthers	
G-BRTX	PA-28-151 Warrior	Spectrum Flying Group	
G-BRTZ	Slingsby T.31 Motor Cadet III	R. R. Walters	
G-BRUB	PA-28-161 Warrior II	Flytrek Ltd/Bournemouth	
G-BRUD	PA-28-181 Archer II	Wilkins & Wilkins Special Auctions Ltd	
G-BRUG	Luscombe 8E Silvaire	K. Reeve & N. W. Barratt	
G-BRUH	Colt 105A balloon	D. C. Chipping/Portugal	
G-BRUI	PA-44-180 Seminole	F. Pilkington	
G-BRUJ	Boeing Stearman A.75N1 (6136:205)	R. M. Hughes	
G-BRUM	Cessna A.152	Central Aircraft Leasing Ltd	
G-BRUN	Cessna 120	O. C. Brun (G-BRDH)	
G-BRUO	Taylor JT.1 Monoplane	R. Hatton	
G-BRUV	Cameron V-77 balloon	T. W. & R. F. Benbrook	
G-BRUX	PA-44-180 Seminole	C. J. Thomas	
G-BRVB	Stolp SA.300 Starduster Too	G-VB Group	
G-BRVE	Beech D.17S	Patina Ltd	
G-BRVF	Colt 77A balloon	J. Adkins	
G-BRVG	NA SNJ-7 Texan (27)	D. Gilmour/Intrepid Aviation Co/Goodwood	
G-BRVI	Robinson R22 Beta	York Helicopters	
G-BRVJ	Slingsby T.31 Motor Cadet III	B. Outhwaite	
G-BRVL	Pitts S-1C Special	M. F. Pocock	
G-BRVN	Thunder Ax7-77 balloon	D. L. Beckwith	
G-BRVO	AS.350B Ecureuil	Rotorhire LLP	
G-BRVR	Barnett J4B-2 Rotorcraft	Ilkeston Contractors	
G-BRVS	Barnett J4B-2 Rotorcraft	Ilkeston Contractors	
G-BRVT	Pitts S-2B Special	R. Woollard	
G-BRVU	Colt 77A balloon	J. K. Woods	
G-BRVY	Thunder Ax8-90 balloon	G. E. Morris	
G-BRVZ	Jodel D.117	L. Holland	
G-BRWA	Aeronca 7AC Champion	D. D. Smith & J. R. Edwards	
G-BRWB	NA T-6G Texan (526)	R. Clifford/Duxford	
G-BRWD	Robinson R22 Beta	Air Charter Scotland (Holdings) Ltd	

G-BRWO – G-BSCO BRITISH CIVIL REGISTRATIONS

Notes	Reg	Type	Owner or Operator
	G-BRWO	PA-28 Cherokee 140	B. & C. Taylor
	G-BRWP	CFM Streak Shadow	R. Biffin
	G-BRWR	Aeronca 11AC Chief	A. W. Crutcher
	G-BRWT	Scheibe SF.25C Falke	Booker Gliding Club Ltd
	G-BRWU	Luton LA-4A Minor	R. B. Webber
	G-BRWV	Brügger MB.2 Colibri	M. P. Wakem/Barton
	G-BRWX	Cessna 172P	BCT Aircraft Leasing Ltd/Sheffield
	G-BRWZ	Cameron 90 Macaw SS balloon	Forbes Global Inc
	G-BRXA	Cameron O-120 balloon	R. J. Mansfield
	G-BRXB	Thunder Ax7-77 balloon	H. Peel
	G-BRXD	PA-28-181 Archer II	D. D. Stone
	G-BRXE	Taylorcraft BC-12D	B. T. Morgan & W. J. Durrad
	G-BRXF	Aeronca 11AC Chief	Aeronca Flying Group
	G-BRXG	Aeronca 7AC Champion	X-Ray Golf Flying Group
	G-BRXH	Cessna 120	BRXH Group
	G-BRXL	Aeronca 11AC Chief (42-78044)	P. L. Green
	G-BRXN	Montgomerie-Bensen B.8MR	C. M. Frerk
	G-BRXO	PA-34-200T Seneca II	Echo Charly SL
	G-BRXP	SNCAN Stampe SV.4C (modified)	T. Brown
	G-BRXS	Howard Special T Minus	A. Shuttleworth/Barton
	G-BRXV	Robinson R22 Beta	Heliflight (UK) Ltd
	G-BRXW	PA-24 Comanche 260	Oak Group
	G-BRXY	Pietenpol Air Camper	P. S. Ganczakowski
	G-BRYU	DHC.8-311 Dash Eight	British Airways Connect
	G-BRYV	DHC.8-311 Dash Eight	British Airways Connect
	G-BRYW	DHC.8-311 Dash Eight	British Airways Connect
	G-BRYX	DHC.8-311 Dash Eight	British Airways Connect
	G-BRYY	DHC.8-311 Dash Eight	British Airways Connect
	G-BRYZ	DHC.8-311 Dash Eight	British Airways Connect
	G-BRZA	Cameron O-77 balloon	L. & R. J. Mold
	G-BRZB	Cameron A-105 balloon	Headland Services Ltd
	G-BRZD	Hapi Cygnet SF-2A	C. I. Coghill
	G-BRZE	Thunder Ax7-77 balloon	G. V. Beckwith & F. Schoeder/Germany
	G-BRZG	Enstrom F-28A	L. Firbank
	G-BRZI	Cameron N-180 balloon	Eastern Balloon Rides
	G-BRZK	Stinson 108-2	Voyager G-BRZK Syndicate
	G-BRZL	Pitts S-1D Special	T. R. G. Barnby
	G-BRZS	Cessna 172P	YP Flying Group/Blackpool
	G-BRZT	Cameron V-77 balloon	B. Drawbridge
	G-BRZV	Colt Flying Apple SS balloon	Obst Vom Bodensee Marketing Gbr/Germany
	G-BRZW	Rans S.10 Sakota	D. L. Davies
	G-BRZX	Pitts S-1S Special	J. S. Dawson
	G-BRZZ	CFM Streak Shadow	Shetland Flying Group
	G-BSAI	Stoddard-Hamilton Glasair III	K. J. & P. J. Whitehead
	G-BSAJ	CASA 1.131E Jungmann 2000	P. G. Kynsey/Redhill
	G-BSAK	Colt 21A balloon	Black Pearl Balloons
	G-BSAS	Cameron V-65 balloon	J. R. Barber
	G-BSAV	Thunder Ax7-77 balloon	I. G. & C. A. Lloyd
	G-BSAW	PA-28-161 Warrior II	Carill Aviation Ltd/Southampton
	G-BSAZ	Denney Kitfox Mk 2	A. J. Lloyd & ptnrs
	G-BSBA	PA-28-161 Warrior II	Falcon Flying Services Ltd
	G-BSBG	CCF Harvard IV (20310:310)	A. P. St. John/Liverpool
	G-BSBH	Short SD3-30 ★	Ulster Aviation Society Museum (stored)
	G-BSBI	Cameron O-77 balloon	D. M. Billing
	G-BSBN	Thunder Ax7-77 balloon	B. Pawson
	G-BSBR	Cameron V-77 balloon	R. P. Wade
	G-BSBT	Piper J-3C-65 Cub	A. Ward
	G-BSBV	Rans S.10 Sakota	J. D. C. Henslow
	G-BSBW	Bell 206B JetRanger 3	D. T. Sharpe
	G-BSBX	Montgomerie-Bensen B.8MR	R. J. Roan & W. Toulmin
	G-BSBZ	Cessna 150M	DTG Aviation
	G-BSCA	Cameron N-90 balloon	J. Steiner
	G-BSCC	Colt 105A balloon	Capricorn Balloons Ltd
	G-BSCE	Robinson R22 Beta	H. Sugden
	G-BSCF	Thunder Ax7-77 balloon	V. P. Gardiner
	G-BSCG	Denney Kitfox Mk 2	P. Prescott
	G-BSCH	Denney Kitfox Mk 2	J. D. Cheeseman
	G-BSCI	Colt 77A balloon	J. L. & S. Wrigglesworth
	G-BSCK	Cameron H-24 balloon	J. D. Shapland
	G-BSCM	Denney Kitfox Mk 2	S. A. Hewitt
	G-BSCN	SOCATA TB20 Trinidad	B. W. Dye
	G-BSCO	Thunder Ax7-77 balloon	F. J. Whalley

BRITISH CIVIL REGISTRATIONS

G-BSCP – G-BSIG

Reg	Type	Owner or Operator	Notes
G-BSCP	Cessna 152 II	Moray Flying Club (1990) Ltd/Kinloss	
G-BSCS	PA-28-181 Archer II	Wingtask 1995 Ltd	
G-BSCV	PA-28-161 Warrior II	Southwood Flying Group/Earls Colne	
G-BSCW	Taylorcraft BC-65	S. Leach	
G-BSCX	Thunder Ax8-105 balloon	Balloon Flights Club Ltd	
G-BSCY	PA-28-151 Warrior	Take Flight Aviation Ltd	
G-BSCZ	Cessna 152 II	The RAF Halton Aeroplane Club Ltd	
G-BSDA	Taylorcraft BC-12D	D. G. Edwards	
G-BSDD	Denney Kitfox Mk 2	D. C. Crawley	
G-BSDH	Robin DR.400/180	R. L. Brucciani	
G-BSDI	Corben Junior Ace Model E	J. R. Ravenhill	
G-BSDJ	Piper J-4E Cub Coupe	W. J. Siertsema	
G-BSDK	Piper J-5A Cub Cruiser	J. E. Mead	
G-BSDL	SOCATA TB10 Tobago	Delta Lima Group/Sherburn	
G-BSDN	PA-34-200T Seneca II	McCormick Consulting Ltd	
G-BSDO	Cessna 152 II	J. Vickers//Humberside	
G-BSDP	Cessna 152 II	B. A. Paul	
G-BSDS	Boeing Stearman E75 (118)	A. Basso/Switzerland	
G-BSDV	Colt 31A balloon	S. J. Roake	
G-BSDW	Cessna 182P	Parker Diving Ltd	
G-BSDX	Cameron V-77 balloon	G. P. & S. J. Allen	
G-BSDZ	Enstrom 280FX	Avalon Group Ltd (G-ODSC)	
G-BSED	PA-22 Tri-Pacer 160 (modified)	Tayflite Ltd	
G-BSEE	Rans S.9	R. P. Hothersall	
G-BSEF	PA-28 Cherokee 180	I. D. Wakeling	
G-BSEG	Ken Brock KB-2 gyroplane	S. J. M. Ledingham	
G-BSEJ	Cessna 150M	D. J. Dimmer & B. Robins	
G-BSEK	Robinson R22	S. J. Strange	
G-BSEL	Slingsby T.61G Super Falke	D. G. Holley	
G-BSEP	Cessna 172	EPAviation	
G-BSER	PA-28 Cherokee 160	Yorkair Ltd	
G-BSEU	PA-28-181 Archer II	Euro Aviation 91 Ltd	
G-BSEV	Cameron O-77 balloon	P. B. Kenington	
G-BSEX	Cameron A-180 balloon	Heart of England Balloons	
G-BSEY	Beech A36 Bonanza	K. Phillips Ltd	
G-BSFA	Aero Designs Pulsar	P. F. Lorriman	
G-BSFB	CASA 1.131E Jungmann 2000 (S5-B06)	M. L. J. Goff	
G-BSFD	Piper J-3C-65 Cub	B. R. Emerson	
G-BSFE	PA-38-112 Tomahawk II	D. J. Campbell	
G-BSFF	Robin DR.400/180R	Lasham Gliding Society Ltd	
G-BSFP	Cessna 152T	The Pilot Centre Ltd	
G-BSFT	Cessna 152 II	Galair Ltd/Biggin Hill	
G-BSFV	Woods Woody Pusher	J. K. Cook	
G-BSFW	PA-15 Vagabond	J. R. Kimberley	
G-BSFX	Denney Kitfox Mk 2	H. Hedley-Lewis	
G-BSFY	Denney Kitfox Mk 2	C. I. Bates	
G-BSGB	Gaertner Ax4 Skyranger balloon	B. Gaertner	
G-BSGD	PA-28 Cherokee 180	R. J. Cleverley	
G-BSGF	Robinson R22 Beta	L. B. Clark	
G-BSGG	Denney Kitfox Mk 2	C. G. Richardson	
G-BSGH	Airtour AH-56B balloon	A. R. Hardwick	
G-BSGJ	Monnett Sonerai II	G. A. Brady	
G-BSGK	PA-34-200T Seneca II	Aeros Holdings Ltd	
G-BSGL	PA-28-161 Warrior II	Keywest Air Charter Ltd/Liverpool	
G-BSGP	Cameron N-65 balloon	T. D. Gibbs	
G-BSGS	Rans S.10 Sakota	M. R. Parr	
G-BSGT	Cessna T.210N	E. A. T. Brenninkmeyer	
G-BSHA	PA-34-200T Seneca II	Justgold Ltd/Blackpool	
G-BSHC	Colt 69A balloon	Magical Adventures Ltd	
G-BSHD	Colt 69A balloon	F. W. Ewer	
G-BSHH	Luscombe 8E Silvaire	S. L. Lewis	
G-BSHI	Luscombe 8F Silvaire	Calcott Garage Ltd	
G-BSHK	Denney Kitfox Mk 2	D. Doyle & C. Aherne	
G-BSHO	Cameron V-77 balloon	D. J. Duckworth & J. C. Stewart	
G-BSHP	PA-28-161 Warrior II	Aviation Rentals	
G-BSHR	Cessna F.172N	Deep Cleavage Ltd (G-BFGE)	
G-BSHT	Cameron V-77 balloon	ECM Construction Ltd	
G-BSHV	PA-18 Super Cub 135	G. T. Fisher	
G-BSHX	Enstrom F-28A	Stephenson Aviation Ltd/Goodwood	
G-BSHY	EAA Acro Sport I	R. J. Hodder	
G-BSIC	Cameron V-77 balloon	J. M. & A. Cornwall	
G-BSIF	Denney Kitfox Mk 2	R. J. Humphries	
G-BSIG	Colt 21A balloon	S. J. Humphreys	

G-BSIH – G-BSPA — BRITISH CIVIL REGISTRATIONS

Reg	Type	Owner or Operator
G-BSIH	Rutan LongEz	W. S. Allen
G-BSII	PA-34-200T Seneca II	N. H. N. Gardner
G-BSIJ	Cameron V-77 balloon	G. B. Davies
G-BSIK	Denney Kitfox	M. Bromage
G-BSIM	PA-28-181 Archer II	Halfpenny Green Flight Centre Ltd
G-BSIO	Cameron 80 Shed SS balloon	R. E. Jones
G-BSIU	Colt 90A balloon	S. Travaglia/Italy
G-BSIY	Schleicher ASK.14	P. W. Andrews
G-BSIZ	PA-28-181 Archer II	H. A. Barrs
G-BSJB	Bensen B.8	J. W. Limbrick
G-BSJU	Cessna 150M	A. C. Williamson
G-BSJX	PA-28-161 Warrior II	MK Aero Support Ltd
G-BSJZ	Cessna 150J	M. H. Campbell
G-BSKA	Cessna 150M	R. J. Cushing
G-BSKD	Cameron V-77 balloon	M. J. Gunston
G-BSKE	Cameron O-84 balloon	S. F. Redman
G-BSKG	Maule MX-7-180	J. R. Surbey
G-BSKI	Thunder Ax8-90 balloon	K. P. Barnes & L. A. Pibworth
G-BSKK	PA-38-112 Tomahawk	Falcon Flying Services/Biggin Hill
G-BSKL	PA-38-112 Tomahawk	Falcon Flying Services/Biggin Hill
G-BSKU	Cameron O-84 balloon	Alfred Bagnall & Sons (West) Ltd
G-BSKW	PA-28-181 Archer II	Shropshire Aero Club Ltd/Sleap
G-BSLA	Robin DR.400/180	A. B. McCoig/Biggin Hill
G-BSLH	CASA 1.131E Jungmann 2000	P. Warden/France
G-BSLI	Cameron V-77 balloon	R. C. Corcoran
G-BSLK	PA-28-161 Warrior II	R. A. Rose
G-BSLM	PA-28 Cherokee 160	R. Fulton
G-BSLT	PA-28-161 Warrior II	L. W. Scattergood
G-BSLU	PA-28 Cherokee 140	W. E. Lewis
G-BSLV	Enstrom 280FX	EVI (UK) Ltd
G-BSLW	Bellanca 7ECA Citabria	Shoreham Citabria Group
G-BSLX	WAR Focke-Wulf Fw 190 (replica) (4+)	Fw 190 Gruppe
G-BSMD	Nord 1101 Noralpha (+14)	J. W. Hardie
G-BSME	Bölkow Bö.208C1 Junior	D. J. Hampson
G-BSMG	Montgomerie-Bensen B.8M	A. C. Timperley
G-BSMK	Cameron O-84 balloon	G-BSMK Shareholders
G-BSML	Schweizer 269C	K. P. Foster & B. I. Winsor
G-BSMM	Colt 31A balloon	D. V. Fowler
G-BSMN	CFM Streak Shadow	P. J. Porter
G-BSMO	Denney Kitfox Mk 2	R. Brennan
G-BSMS	Cameron V-77 balloon	R. Ashford
G-BSMT	Rans S.10 Sakota	S. J. Kidd
G-BSMU	Rans S.6 Coyote II	A. Wright (G-MWJE)
G-BSMV	PA-17 Vagabond (modified)	A. Cheriton
G-BSMX	Bensen B.8MR	J. S. E. R. McGregor
G-BSND	Air Command 532 Elite	T. A. Holmes
G-BSNE	Luscombe 8E Silvaire	N. Reynolds & C. Watts
G-BSNF	Piper J-3C-65 Cub	D. A. Hammant
G-BSNG	Cessna 172N	A. J. & P. C. MacDonald/Edinburgh
G-BSNJ	Cameron N-90 balloon	D. P. H. Smith/France
G-BSNL	Bensen B.8MR	A. C. Breane
G-BSNN	Rans S.10 Sakota	M. Foulds
G-BSNP	PA-28-201T Turbo Arrow III	D. F. K. Singleton/Germany
G-BSNT	Luscombe 8A Silvaire	Luscombe Quartet
G-BSNU	Colt 105A balloon	Gone Ballooning
G-BSNX	PA-28-181 Archer II	Halfpenny Green Flight Centre Ltd
G-BSNY	Bensen B.8M	H. McCartney
G-BSNZ	Cameron O-105 balloon	J. Francis
G-BSOE	Luscombe 8A Silvaire	S. B. Marsden
G-BSOF	Colt 25A balloon	L. P. Hooper
G-BSOG	Cessna 172M	B. Chapman & A. R. Budden/Goodwood
G-BSOI	AS.332L Super Puma	CHC Scotia Ltd/Aberdeen
G-BSOJ	Thunder Ax7-77 balloon	R. J. S. Jones
G-BSOK	PA-28-161 Warrior II	Aeros Leasing Ltd/Gloucestershire
G-BSOM	Glaser-Dirks DG.400	G-BSOM Group/Tibenham
G-BSON	Green S.25 balloon	J. J. Green
G-BSOO	Cessna 172F	Double Oscar Flying Group
G-BSOR	CFM Streak Shadow Srs SA	A. Parr
G-BSOT	PA-38-112 Tomahawk II	APB Leasing Ltd/Welshpool
G-BSOU	PA-38-112 Tomahawk II	D. J. Campbell
G-BSOX	Luscombe 8AE Silvaire	P. S Lanary
G-BSOZ	PA-28-161 Warrior II	Grampian Airways Ltd
G-BSPA	QAC Quickie Q.2	G. V. McKirdy & B. K. Glover

BRITISH CIVIL REGISTRATIONS

G-BSPB – G-BSWC

Reg	Type	Owner or Operator	Notes
G-BSPB	Thunder Ax8-84 balloon	A. N. F. Pertwee	
G-BSPE	Cessna F.172P	T. W. Williamson	
G-BSPG	PA-34-200T Seneca II	Andrews Professional Colour Laboratories Ltd	
G-BSPI	PA-28-161 Warrior II	Transcourt Ltd	
G-BSPJ	Bensen B.8	D. Ross	
G-BSPK	Cessna 195A	A. G. & D. L. Bompas	
G-BSPL	CFM Streak Shadow Srs SA	G. L. Turner	
G-BSPM	PA-28-161 Warrior II	Aviation Rentals/White Waltham	
G-BSPN	PA-28R-201T Turbo Arrow III	V. E. H. Taylor	
G-BSPW	Avid Speed Wing	M. J. Sewell	
G-BSRD	Cameron N-105 balloon	A. Ockelmann	
G-BSRH	Pitts S-1C Special	C. D. Swift	
G-BSRI	Lancair 235	G. Lewis/Liverpool	
G-BSRK	ARV Super 2	D. M. Blair	
G-BSRL	Campbell Cricket Mk.4 gyroplane	I. Rosewall	
G-BSRP	Rotorway Executive	R. J. Baker	
G-BSRR	Cessna 182Q	C. M. Moore	
G-BSRT	Denney Kitfox Mk 2	A. J. Lloyd	
G-BSRX	CFM Streak Shadow	I. W. Southcott	
G-BSSA	Luscombe 8E Silvaire	Luscombe Flying Group/White Waltham	
G-BSSB	Cessna 150L	D. T. A. Rees	
G-BSSC	PA-28-161 Warrior II	G-BSSC Ltd	
G-BSSE	PA-28 Cherokee 140	D. Hoyle	
G-BSSF	Denney Kitfox Mk 2	A. M. Hemmings	
G-BSSI	Rans S.6 Coyote II	J. Currell (G-MWJA)	
G-BSSK	QAC Quickie Q.2	D. G. Greatrex	
G-BSSP	Robin DR.400/180R	Soaring (Oxford) Ltd	
G-BSST	BAC-Sud Concorde 002 ★	F.A.A. Museum/Yeovilton	
G-BSSV	CFM Streak Shadow	R. W. Payne	
G-BSSW	PA-28-161 Warrior II	D. J. Skidmore & E. F. Rowland	
G-BSSX	PA-28-161 Warrior II	Airways Aero Associations Ltd/Booker	
G-BSTC	Aeronca 11AC Chief	J. Armstrong & D. Lamb	
G-BSTE	AS.355F2 Twin Squirrel	Oscar Mayer Ltd	
G-BSTH	PA-25 Pawnee 235	Scottish Gliding Union Ltd/Portmoak	
G-BSTI	Piper J-3C-65 Cub	J. A. Scott	
G-BSTK	Thunder Ax8-90 balloon	M. Williams	
G-BSTL	Rand-Robinson KR-2	C. S. Hales & N. Brauns	
G-BSTM	Cessna 172L	G-BSTM Group/Cambridge	
G-BSTO	Cessna 152 II	Plymouth School of Flying Ltd	
G-BSTP	Cessna 152 II	FR Aviation Ltd/Bournemouth	
G-BSTR	AA-5 Traveler	B. D. Jones	
G-BSTT	Rans S.6 Coyote II	D. G. Palmer	
G-BSTV	PA-32 Cherokee Six 300	B. C. Hudson	
G-BSTX	Luscombe 8A Silvaire	G. R. Nicholson	
G-BSTY	Thunder Ax8-90 balloon	Shere Ballooning Group	
G-BSTZ	PA-28 Cherokee 140	Air Navigation & Trading Co Ltd/Blackpool	
G-BSUA	Rans S.6 Coyote II	A. J. Todd	
G-BSUB	Colt 77A balloon	J. M. Foster & M. P. Hill	
G-BSUD	Luscombe 8A Silvaire	I. G. Harrison/Egginton	
G-BSUE	Cessna U.206G II	J. Dyer & I. C. Austin & G. S. Chapman	
G-BSUF	PA-32RT-300 Lance II	S. A. Fell & J. Gibbs/Guernsey	
G-BSUK	Colt 77A balloon	A. J. Moore	
G-BSUO	Scheibe SF.25C Falke	Portmoak Falke Syndicate	
G-BSUT	Rans S.6-ESA Coyote II	N. J. Hancock & S. J. Mathison/Barton	
G-BSUU	Colt 180A balloon	British School of Ballooning	
G-BSUV	Cameron O-77 balloon	J. F. Trehern	
G-BSUW	PA-34-200T Seneca II	NPD Direct Ltd	
G-BSUX	Carlson Sparrow II	J. Stephenson	
G-BSUZ	Denney Kitfox Mk 3	P. C. Avery	
G-BSVB	PA-28-181 Archer II	K. A. Boost	
G-BSVE	Binder CP.301S Smaragd	Smaragd Flying Group	
G-BSVF	PA-28-161 Warrior II	Airways Aero Associations Ltd/Booker	
G-BSVG	PA-28-161 Warrior II	Airways Aero Associations Ltd/Booker	
G-BSVH	Piper J-3C-65 Cub	C. R. & K. A. Maher	
G-BSVI	PA-16 Clipper	Clipper Aviation	
G-BSVJ	Piper J-3C-65 Cub	V. S. E. Norman/Rendcomb	
G-BSVK	Denney Kitfox Mk 2	C. M. Looney	
G-BSVM	PA-28-161 Warrior II	EFG Flying Services/Biggin Hill	
G-BSVN	Thorp T-18	D. Prentice	
G-BSVR	Schweizer 269C	M. K. E. Askham	
G-BSVS	Robin DR.400/100	D. McK. Chalmers	
G-BSWB	Rans S.10 Sakota	F. A. Hewitt	
G-BSWC	Boeing Stearman E75 (112)	Richard Thwaites Aviation Ltd	

G-BSWF – G-BTCB — BRITISH CIVIL REGISTRATIONS

Notes	Reg	Type	Owner or Operator
	G-BSWF	PA-16 Clipper	T. M. Storey
	G-BSWG	PA-17 Vagabond	P. E. J. Sturgeon
	G-BSWH	Cessna 152 II	Airspeed Aviation Ltd
	G-BSWI	Rans S.10 Sakota	J. M. Mooney
	G-BSWL	Slingsby T.61F Venture T.2	K. Richards
	G-BSWM	Slingsby T.61F Venture T.2	Venture Gliding Group/Bellarena
	G-BSWR	BN-2T-26 Turbine Islander	Police Service of Northern Ireland
	G-BSWV	Cameron N-77 balloon	S. Charlish
	G-BSWX	Cameron V-90 balloon	B. J. Burrows
	G-BSWY	Cameron N-77 balloon	Nottingham Hot Air Balloon Club
	G-BSWZ	Cameron A-180 balloon	G. C. Ludlow
	G-BSXA	PA-28-161 Warrior II	Falcon Flying Services/Biggin Hill
	G-BSXB	PA-28-161 Warrior II	Aeroshow Ltd
	G-BSXC	PA-28-161 Warrior II	L. T. Halpin/Booker
	G-BSXD	Soko P-2 Kraguj (30146)	N. C. Stone
	G-BSXI	Mooney M.20E	A. N. Pain
	G-BSXM	Cameron V-77 balloon	C. A. Oxby
	G-BSXS	PA-28-181 Archer II	J. K. Milner
	G-BSXT	Piper J-5A Cub Cruiser	L. Jobes
	G-BSXX	Whittaker MW7	H. J. Stanley
	G-BSYA	Jodel D.18	K. Wright/Isle of Man
	G-BSYB	Cameron N-120 balloon	M. Buono/Italy
	G-BSYC	PA-32R-300 Lance	Gary Key Aircraft Leasing Ltd
	G-BSYD	Cameron A-180 balloon	R. H. Etherington
	G-BSYF	Luscombe 8A Silvaire	Atlantic Aviation
	G-BSYG	PA-12 Super Cruiser	Fat Cub Group
	G-BSYH	Luscombe 8A Silvaire	N. R. Osborne
	G-BSYI	AS.355F1 Twin Squirrel	Premiair Aviation Services Ltd
	G-BSYJ	Cameron N-77 balloon	Chubb Fire Ltd
	G-BSYO	Piper J-3C-90 Cub	C. R. Reynolds & J. D. Fuller (G-BSMJ/G-BRHE)
	G-BSYU	Robin DR.400/180	P. D. Smoothy
	G-BSYV	Cessna 150M	Fenland Flying School
	G-BSYW	Cessna 150M	D. R. Calo
	G-BSYY	PA-28-161 Warrior II	Aviation Rentals
	G-BSYZ	PA-28-161 Warrior II	Yankee Zulu Group
	G-BSZB	Stolp SA.300 Starduster Too	D. T. Gethin/Swansea
	G-BSZC	Beech C-45H (51-11701A:AF258)	Weston Ltd
	G-BSZD	Robin DR.400/180	M. Rowland
	G-BSZF	Jodel DR.250/160	J. B. Randle
	G-BSZG	Stolp SA.100 Starduster	D. F. Chapman
	G-BSZH	Thunder Ax7-77 balloon	P. K. Morris
	G-BSZI	Cessna 152 II	Eglinton Flying Club Ltd
	G-BSZJ	PA-28-181 Archer II	M. L. A. Pudney & R. D. Fuller
	G-BSZM	Montgomerie-Bensen B.8MR	A. McCredie
	G-BSZO	Cessna 152	A. Jahanfar & I. R. Chaplin/Southend
	G-BSZT	PA-28-161 Warrior II	Golf Charlie Echo Ltd
	G-BSZU	Cessna 150F	C. Partington
	G-BSZV	Cessna 150F	Kirmington Aviation Ltd
	G-BSZW	Cessna 152	Haimoss Ltd
	G-BTAG	Cameron O-77 balloon	R. A. Shapland
	G-BTAL	Cessna F.152 II	Thanet Flying Club/Manston
	G-BTAM	PA-28-181 Archer II	Tri-Star Farms Ltd
	G-BTAN	Thunder Ax7-65Z balloon	A. S. Newham
	G-BTAS	PA-38-112 Tomahawk	Ravenair Aircraft Ltd/Liverpool
	G-BTAT	Denney Kitfox Mk 2	M. Lawton
	G-BTAW	PA-28-161 Warrior II	A. J. Wiggins
	G-BTAZ	Evans VP-2	Norwich Aviation Museum
	G-BTBA	Robinson R22 Beta	Heliflight (UK) Ltd/Wolverhampton
	G-BTBB	Thunder Ax8-105 S2 balloon	G. J. Boulden
	G-BTBC	PA-28-161 Warrior II	Synergy Aircraft Leasing Ltd
	G-BTBF	Super Koala	E. A. Taylor (G-MWOZ)
	G-BTBG	Denney Kitfox Mk 2	R. Noble
	G-BTBH	Ryan ST3KR (854)	P. R. Holloway
	G-BTBI	WAR P-47 Thunderbolt (replica) (85)	M. W. Bodger
	G-BTBL	Montgomerie-Bensen B.8MR	AES Radionic Surveillance Systems
	G-BTBP	Cameron N-90 balloon	M. Catalani/Italy
	G-BTBU	PA-18 Super Cub 150	G-BTBU Syndicate
	G-BTBW	Cessna 120	M. J. Willies
	G-BTBX	Piper J-3C-65 Cub	Henlow Taildraggers
	G-BTBY	PA-17 Vagabond	G. J. Smith
	G-BTCA	PA-32R-300 Lance	Lance Group
	G-BTCB	Air Command 582 Sport	G. Scurrah

BRITISH CIVIL REGISTRATIONS

G-BTCC – G-BTHN

Reg	Type	Owner or Operator	Notes
G-BTCC	Grumman F6F-3 Hellcat (40467:19)	Patina Ltd/Duxford	
G-BTCD	P-51D-25-NA Mustang (44-13704:87-H)	Pelham Ltd/Duxford	
G-BTCE	Cessna 152	S. T. Gilbert	
G-BTCH	Luscombe 8E Silvaire	G-BTCH Flying Group/Popham	
G-BTCI	PA-17 Vagabond	T. R. Whittome	
G-BTCJ	Luscombe 8AE Silvaire	J. M. Lovell	
G-BTCM	Cameron N-90 balloon	G. Everett (G-BMPW)	
G-BTCR	Rans S.10 Sakota	B. J. Hewitt	
G-BTCS	Colt 90A balloon	R. C. Stone	
G-BTCZ	Cameron 84 Chateau SS balloon	Forbes Global Inc.	
G-BTDA	Slingsby T.61G Falke	Anglia Gliding Club/Wattisham	
G-BTDC	Denney Kitfox Mk 2	K. R. H. Wingate	
G-BTDD	CFM Streak Shadow	S. H. Merrony	
G-BTDE	Cessna C-165 Airmaster	I. H. Logan	
G-BTDF	Luscombe 8A Silvaire	Delta Foxtrot Group	
G-BTDN	Denney Kitfox Mk 2	Foxy Flyers Group	
G-BTDR	Aero Designs Pulsar	R. A. Blackwell	
G-BTDS	Colt 77A balloon	C. P. Witter Ltd	
G-BTDT	CASA 1.131E Jungmann 2000	T. A. Reed	
G-BTDV	PA-28-161 Warrior II	Central Aircraft Leasing Ltd/Wolverhampton	
G-BTDW	Cessna 152 II	J. A. Blenkharn/Carlisle	
G-BTDZ	CASA 1.131E Jungmann 2000	R. J. & M. Pickin	
G-BTEA	Cameron N-105 balloon	M. W. A. Shemilt	
G-BTEE	Cameron O-120 balloon	W. H. & J. P. Morgan	
G-BTEF	Pitts S-1 Special	C. Davidson	
G-BTEL	CFM Streak Shadow	J. E. Eatwell	
G-BTES	Cessna 150H	R. A. Forward	
G-BTET	Piper J-3C-65 Cub	K. Handley	
G-BTEU	SA.365N-2 Dauphin	CHC Scotia Ltd	
G-BTEW	Cessna 120	S. D. Pryke & L. M. Hamblyn	
G-BTEX	PA-28 Cherokee 140	McAully Flying Group Ltd/Little Snoring	
G-BTFA	Denney Kitfox Mk 2	K. R. Peek	
G-BTFC	Cessna F.152 II	Aircraft Engineers Ltd	
G-BTFE	Bensen-Parsons 2-seat gyroplane	J. R. Goldspink	
G-BTFF	Cessna T.310R II	United Sales Equipment Dealers Ltd	
G-BTFG	Boeing Stearman A75N1 (441)	TG Aviation Ltd/Manston	
G-BTFJ	PA-15 Vagabond	C. W. Thirtle	
G-BTFK	Taylorcraft BC-12D	A. O'Rourke	
G-BTFL	Aeronca 11AC Chief	BTFL Group	
G-BTFM	Cameron O-105 balloon	Edinburgh University Hot Air Balloon Club	
G-BTFO	PA-28-161 Warrior II	Flyfar Ltd	
G-BTFS	Cessna A.150M	P. A. James	
G-BTFT	Beech 58 Baron	Faslwing Air Charter Ltd	
G-BTFU	Cameron N-90 balloon	J. J. Rudoni & A. C. K. Rawson	
G-BTFV	Whittaker MW7	S. J. Luck	
G-BTFX	Bell 206B JetRanger 2	J. W. Moss	
G-BTGD	Rand-Robinson KR-2 (modified)	M. D. Gorlov	
G-BTGG	Rans S.10 Sakota	C. A. James	
G-BTGH	Cessna 152 II	P. J. Clarke	
G-BTGI	Rearwin 175 Skyranger	J. M. Fforde	
G-BTGJ	Smith DSA-1 Miniplane	G. J. Knowles	
G-BTGL	Light Aero Avid Flyer	I. Kazi	
G-BTGM	Aeronca 7AC Champion	G. P. Gregg/France	
G-BTGO	PA-28 Cherokee 140	Demero Ltd & Transcourt Ltd	
G-BTGP	Cessna 150M	Billins Air Service Ltd	
G-BTGR	Cessna 152 II	A. J. Gomes/Shoreham	
G-BTGS	Stolp SA.300 Starduster Too	G. N. Elliott & ptnrs (G-AYMA)	
G-BTGT	CFM Streak Shadow	G. J. Sargent (G-MWPY)	
G-BTGU	PA-34-220T Seneca III	Carill Aviation Ltd	
G-BTGV	PA-34-200T Seneca II	Oxford Aviation Services Ltd/Kidlington	
G-BTGW	Cessna 152 II	Stapleford Flying Club Ltd	
G-BTGX	Cessna 152 II	Stapleford Flying Club Ltd	
G-BTGY	PA-28-161 Warrior II	Stapleford Flying Club Ltd	
G-BTGZ	PA-28-181 Archer II	Allzones Ltd/Biggin Hill	
G-BTHA	Cessna 182P	Hotel Alpha Flying Group/Liverpool	
G-BTHE	Cessna 150L	Humberside Police Flying Club	
G-BTHF	Cameron V-90 balloon	N. J. & S. J. Langley	
G-BTHH	Jodel DR.100A	H. R. Leefe	
G-BTHI	Robinson R22 Beta	D. I. Pointon	
G-BTHJ	Evans VP-2	C. J. Moseley	
G-BTHK	Thunder Ax7-77 balloon	M. S.Trend	
G-BTHM	Thunder Ax8-105 balloon	J. K. Woods	
G-BTHN	Murphy Renegade 912	F. A. Purvis	

G-BTHP – G-BTOC | BRITISH CIVIL REGISTRATIONS

Notes	Reg	Type	Owner or Operator
	G-BTHP	Thorp T.211	M. Gardner
	G-BTHU	Light Aero Avid Flyer	R. C. Bowley
	G-BTHV	MBB Bö.105DBS/4	Bond Air Services/Aberdeen
	G-BTHW	Beech F33C Bonanza	Robin Lance Aviation Associates Ltd
	G-BTHX	Colt 105A balloon	Elmer Balloon Group
	G-BTHY	Bell 206B JetRanger 3	Suffolk Helicopters Ltd
	G-BTHZ	Cameron V-56 balloon	C. N. Marshall/Kenya
	G-BTID	PA-28-161 Warrior II	Plymouth School of Flying Ltd
	G-BTIE	SOCATA TB10 Tobago	Aviation Spirit Ltd
	G-BTIF	Denney Kitfox Mk 3	D. A. Murchie
	G-BTII	AA-5B Tiger	BTII Group
	G-BTIJ	Luscombe 8E Silvaire	S. J. Hornsby
	G-BTIK	Cessna 152 II	I. R. Chaplin/Andrewsfield
	G-BTIL	PA-38-112 Tomahawk	B. J. Pearson/Eaglescott
	G-BTIM	PA-28-161 Cadet	Aviation Rentals
	G-BTIO	SNCAN Stampe SV.4C	M. D. & C. F. Garratt
	G-BTIR	Denney Kitfox Mk 2	R. B. Wilson
	G-BTIU	SOCATA MS.882A Rallye Commodore 150	Cole Aviation Ltd
	G-BTIV	PA-28-161 Warrior II	Warrior Group/Eaglescott
	G-BTIZ	Cameron A-105 balloon	W. A. Board
	G-BTJA	Luscombe 8E Silvaire	M. W. Rudkin
	G-BTJB	Luscombe 8E Silvaire	M. Loxton
	G-BTJC	Luscombe 8F Silvaire	A. M. Noble
	G-BTJD	Thunder Ax8-90 S2 balloon	R. E. Vinten
	G-BTJF	Thunder Ax10-180 balloon	Airborne Adventures Ltd
	G-BTJH	Cameron O-77 balloon	H. Stringer
	G-BTJK	PA-38-112 Tomahawk	Ravenair Aircraft Ltd/Liverpool
	G-BTJL	PA-38-112 Tomahawk	J. S. Devlin & Z. Islam/Redhill
	G-BTJO	Thunder Ax9-140 balloon	G. P. Lane
	G-BTJS	Montgomerie-Bensen B.8MR	T. A. Holmes
	G-BTJU	Cameron V-90 balloon	C. W. Jones (Floorings) Ltd
	G-BTJX	Rans S.10 Sakota	T. Scarborough
	G-BTKA	Piper J-5A Cub Cruiser	J. M. Lister
	G-BTKB	Renegade Spirit 912	P. J. Calvert
	G-BTKC	BAe.146-200	Trident Aviation Leasing Services (Jersey) Ltd
	G-BTKD	Denney Kitfox Mk 4	N. Sansom & R. A. Hills
	G-BTKG	Light Aero Avid Flyer	Avid Group/Ireland
	G-BTKL	MBB Bö.105DB-4	Veritair Ltd
	G-BTKN	Cameron O-120 balloon	R. H. Etherington
	G-BTKP	CFM Streak Shadow	G. D. Martin
	G-BTKT	PA-28-161 Warrior II	Biggin Hill Flying Club Ltd
	G-BTKV	PA-22 Tri-Pacer 160	R. A. Moore
	G-BTKW	Cameron O-105 balloon	P. Spellward
	G-BTKX	PA-28-181 Archer II	D. J. Perkins
	G-BTKZ	Cameron V-77 balloon	S. P. Richards
	G-BTLB	Wassmer Wa.52 Europa	Popham Flying Group G-BTLB
	G-BTLG	PA-28R Cherokee Arrow 200	P. J. Moore
	G-BTLL	Pilatus P3-03 (A-806) ★	(stored)/Headcorn
	G-BTLM	PA-22 Tri-Pacer 160	F & H (Aircraft)
	G-BTLP	AA-1C Lynx	Partlease Ltd
	G-BTMA	Cessna 172N	East of England Flying Group Ltd
	G-BTMK	Cessna R.172K XPII	K. E. Halford
	G-BTMN	Thunder Ax9-120 S2 balloon	M. E. White
	G-BTMO	Colt 69A balloon	Thunder & Colt
	G-BTMP	Campbell Cricket	P. W. McLaughlin
	G-BTMR	Cessna 172M	Linley Aviation Ltd
	G-BTMS	Light Aero Avid Speedwing	J. Makonnen
	G-BTMT	Denney Kitfox Mk 1	L. G. Horne
	G-BTMV	Everett Srs 2 gyroplane	L. Armes
	G-BTMW	Zenair CH.701 STOL	L. Lewis
	G-BTMY	Cameron Train-80 SS balloon	Balloon Sports HB/Sweden
	G-BTNA	Robinson R22 Beta	N. J. Randall
	G-BTNC	AS.365N-2 Dauphin 2	CHC Scotia Ltd
	G-BTND	PA-38-112 Tomahawk	Ravenair Aircraft Ltd/Liverpool
	G-BTNE	PA-28-161 Warrior II	Fly Welle Ltd
	G-BTNH	PA-28-161 Warrior II	Falcon Flying Services Ltd/Biggin Hill (G-DENH)
	G-BTNO	Aeronca 7AC Champion	B. J. & B. G. Robe
	G-BTNR	Denney Kitfox Mk 3	High Notions Flying Group
	G-BTNT	PA-28-151 Warrior	Thomsonfly Ltd
	G-BTNV	PA-28-161 Warrior II	G. M. Bauer & A. W. Davies
	G-BTNW	Rans S.6-ESA Coyote II	R. H. Hughes
	G-BTOC	Robinson R22 Beta	D. I. Pointon

BRITISH CIVIL REGISTRATIONS

G-BTOG – G-BTUR

Reg	Type	Owner or Operator	Notes
G-BTOG	DH.82A Tiger Moth	P. T. Szluha	
G-BTOL	Denney Kitfox Mk 3	P. J. Gibbs	
G-BTON	PA-28 Cherokee 140	Group G-BTON	
G-BTOO	Pitts S-1C Special	G. H. Matthews	
G-BTOP	Cameron V-77 balloon	J. J. Winter	
G-BTOS	Cessna 140	J. L. Kaiser/France	
G-BTOT	PA-15 Vagabond	Vagabond Flying Group	
G-BTOU	Cameron O-120 balloon	J. J. Daly	
G-BTOW	SOCATA Rallye 180GT	Cambridge University Gliding Trust Ltd/ Gransden Lodge	
G-BTOZ	Thunder Ax9-120 S2 balloon	H. G. Davies	
G-BTPA	BAe ATP	Capital Bank Leasing 12 Ltd	
G-BTPC	BAe ATP	Capital Bank Leasing 1 Ltd	
G-BTPD	BAe ATP	Seaforth Maritime Ltd	
G-BTPE	BAe ATP	Capital Bank Leasing PLC	
G-BTPF	BAe ATP	Capital Bank Leasing 5 Ltd	
G-BTPG	BAe ATP	Capital Bank Leasing 5 Ltd	
G-BTPH	BAe ATP	Capital Bank Leasing 6 Ltd	
G-BTPJ	BAe ATP	Capital Bank Leasing 7 Ltd	
G-BTPL	BAe ATP	Trident Aviation Leasing Services (Jersey) Ltd	
G-BTPN	BAe ATP	Trident Aviation Leasing Services (Jersey) Ltd	
G-BTPT	Cameron N-77 balloon	H. J. Andrews	
G-BTPV	Colt 90A balloon	Balloon Preservation Group	
G-BTPX	Thunder Ax8-90 balloon	E. Cordall	
G-BTRB	Thunder Colt Mickey Mouse SS balloon	Benedikt Haggeney GmbH/Germany	
G-BTRC	Light Aero Avid Speedwing	Grangecote Ltd	
G-BTRF	Aero Designs Pulsar	C. Smith	
G-BTRG	Aeronca 65C Super Chief	A. Welburn	
G-BTRI	Aeronca 11CC Super Chief	P. A. Wensak	
G-BTRK	PA-28-161 Warrior II	Stapleford Flying Club Ltd	
G-BTRL	Cameron N-105 balloon	J. Lippett	
G-BTRN	Thunder Ax9-120 S2 balloon	A. R. Hardwick	
G-BTRO	Thunder Ax8-90 balloon	Capital Balloon Club Ltd	
G-BTRP	Hughes 369E	P. C. Shann	
G-BTRR	Thunder Ax7-77 balloon	P. J. Wentworth	
G-BTRS	PA-28-161 Warrior II	Airwise Flying Group/Barton	
G-BTRT	PA-28R Cherokee Arrow 200-II	Romeo Tango Group	
G-BTRU	Robin DR.400/180	R. H. Mackay	
G-BTRW	Slingsby T.61F Venture T.2	The Falke Syndicate	
G-BTRY	PA-28-161 Warrior II	Oxford Aviation Services Ltd/Kidlington	
G-BTRZ	Jodel D.18	A. P. Aspinall	
G-BTSB	Corben Baby Ace D	C. C. Ellis	
G-BTSJ	PA-28-161 Warrior II	Plymouth School of Flying Ltd	
G-BTSL	Cameron 70 Glass SS balloon	M. R. Humphrey & J. R. Clifton	
G-BTSM	Cessna 180A	C. Couston	
G-BTSN	Cessna 150G	J. N. Plange	
G-BTSP	Piper J-3C-65 Cub	J. A. Walshe & A. Corcoran	
G-BTSR	Aeronca 11AC Chief	R. D. & E. G. N. Morris	
G-BTSV	Denney Kitfox Mk 3	R. J. Folwell	
G-BTSW	Colt AS-80 Mk II airship	Gefa-Flug GmbH/Germany	
G-BTSX	Thunder Ax7-77 balloon	C. Moris-Gallimore/Portugal	
G-BTSY	EE Lightning F.6 (XR724) ★	Lightning Association	
G-BTSZ	Cessna 177A	W. J. Peachment	
G-BTTB	Cameron V-90 balloon	Royal Engineers Balloon Club	
G-BTTD	Montgomerie-Bensen B.8MR	A. J. P. Herculson	
G-BTTE	Cessna 150L	C. Wilson & W. B. Murray	
G-BTTL	Cameron V-90 balloon	A. J. Baird	
G-BTTO	BAe ATP	BAR Systems Inc (G-OEDE)	
G-BTTR	Aerotek Pitts S-2A Special	Yellowbird Adventures Ltd	
G-BTTS	Colt 77A balloon	Rutland Balloon Club	
G-BTTW	Thunder Ax7-77 balloon	J. Kenny	
G-BTTY	Denney Kitfox Mk 2	K. J. Fleming	
G-BTTZ	Slingsby T.61F Venture T.2	M. W. Olliver	
G-BTUA	Slingsby T.61F Venture T.2	Shenington Gliding Club	
G-BTUB	Yakovlev C.11	M. G. & J. R. Jefferies	
G-BTUC	EMB-312 Tucano ★	Ulster Aviation Heritage	
G-BTUG	SOCATA Rallye 180T	Herefordshire Gliding Club Ltd/Shobdon	
G-BTUH	Cameron N-65 balloon	B. J. Godding	
G-BTUJ	Thunder Ax9-120 balloon	ECM Construction Ltd	
G-BTUK	Aerotek Pitts S-2A Special	S. H. Elkington/Wickenby	
G-BTUL	Aerotek Pitts S-2A Special	J. M. Adams	
G-BTUM	Piper J-3C-65 Cub	G-BTUM Syndicate	
G-BTUR	PA-18 Super Cub 95 (modified)	N. T. Oakman	

95

G-BTUS – G-BUAT — BRITISH CIVIL REGISTRATIONS

Notes	Reg	Type	Owner or Operator
	G-BTUS	Whittaker MW7	C. T. Bailey
	G-BTUU	Cameron O-120 balloon	P. Dubois-Dauphin/France
	G-BTUV	Aeronca A65TAC Defender	M. B. Hamlett
	G-BTUW	PA-28-151 Warrior	T. S. Kemp
	G-BTUZ	American General AG-5B Tiger	Grocontinental Ltd/Tilstock
	G-BTVA	Thunder Ax7-77 balloon	C. M. Waters
	G-BTVB	Everett Srs 2 gyroplane	J. P. Whitter
	G-BTVC	Denney Kitfox Mk 2	M. J. Downes
	G-BTVE	Hawker Demon I (K8203)	Demon Displays Ltd
	G-BTVW	Cessna FA.337G	C. Keane
	G-BTVW	Cessna 152 II	Transcourt Ltd
	G-BTVX	Cessna 152 II	Eastern Air Centre Ltd/Gamston
	G-BTWB	Denney Kitfox Mk 3	J. E. Tootell (G-BTTM)
	G-BTWC	Slingsby T.61F Venture T.2	RAFGSA/Upavon
	G-BTWD	Slingsby T.61F Venture T.2	York Gliding Centre/Rufforth
	G-BTWE	Slingsby T.61F Venture T.2	RAFGSA/Upavon
	G-BTWF	DHC.1 Chipmunk 22 (WK549)	J. A. & V. G. Sims
	G-BTWI	EAA Acro Sport I	S. Alexander & W. M. Coffee
	G-BTWJ	Cameron V-77 balloon	R. G. Griffin & L. J. Dolan
	G-BTWL	WAG-Aero Acro Sport Trainer	I. M. Ashpole
	G-BTWM	Cameron V-77 balloon	R. C. Franklin
	G-BTWV	Cameron O-90 balloon	C. F. Sanger-Davies
	G-BTWX	SOCATA TB9 Tampico	Archer Two Ltd
	G-BTWY	Aero Designs Pulsar	R. Bishop
	G-BTWZ	Rans S.10 Sakota	P. C. Avery
	G-BTXB	Colt 77A balloon	A. Derbyshire
	G-BTXD	Rans S.6-ESA Coyote II	A. I. Sutherland
	G-BTXF	Cameron V-90 balloon	G. Thompson
	G-BTXG	BAe Jetstream 3102	Highland Airways Ltd/Inverness
	G-BTXH	Colt AS-56 airship	L. Kiefer/Germany
	G-BTXI	Noorduyn AT-16 Harvard IIB (FE695)	Patina Ltd/Duxford
	G-BTXK	Thunder Ax7-65 balloon	A. F. Selby
	G-BTXM	Colt 21A Cloudhopper balloon	
	G-BTXS	Cameron O-120 balloon	Southern Balloon Group
	G-BTXT	Maule MXT-7-180 Star Rocket	G-BTXT Group
	G-BTXW	Cameron V-77 balloon	P. C. Waterhouse
	G-BTXX	Bellanca 8KCAB Decathlon	Tatenhill Aviation Ltd
	G-BTXZ	Zenair CH.250	I. Parris & P. W. J. Bull
	G-BTYC	Cessna 150L	Polestar Aviation Ltd
	G-BTYE	Cameron A-180 balloon	K. J. A. Maxwell & D. S. Messmer
	G-BTYF	Thunder Ax10-180 S2 balloon	I. Bentley
	G-BTYH	Pottier P.80S	G. E. Livings
	G-BTYI	PA-28-181 Archer II	C. E. Wright
	G-BTYK	Cessna 310R	Revere Aviation Ltd
	G-BTYT	Cessna 152 II	Cristal Air Ltd/Shoreham
	G-BTYW	Cessna 120	R. Nisbet & A. R. Dix
	G-BTYY	Curtiss Robin C-2	R. R. L. Windus
	G-BTYZ	Colt 210A balloon	T. M. Donnelly
	G-BTZA	Beech F33A Bonanza	G-BTZA Group/Edinburgh
	G-BTZB	Yakovlev Yak-50 (10 yellow)	D. H. Boardman
	G-BTZD	Yakovlev Yak-1 (1342)	Historic Aircraft Collection Ltd
	G-BTZE	LET Yakovlev C.11	Bianchi Aviation Film Services Ltd/Booker
	G-BTZG	BAe ATP	Trident Aviation Leasing Services
	G-BTZK	BAe ATP	Trident Aviation Leasing Services
	G-BTZL	Oldfield Baby Lakes	M. R. Winter
	G-BTZO	SOCATA TB20 Trinidad	A. P. Howells
	G-BTZP	SOCATA TB9 Tampico	M. W. Orr
	G-BTZS	Colt 77A balloon	P. T. R. Ollivere
	G-BTZV	Cameron V-77 balloon	D. J. & H. M. Brown
	G-BTZX	Piper J-3C-65 Cub	ZX Cub Group
	G-BTZY	Colt 56A balloon	S. J. Wardle
	G-BTZZ	CFM Streak Shadow	D. R. Stennett
	G-BUAA	Corben Baby Ace D	C. J. Bragg
	G-BUAB	Aeronca 11AC Chief	J. Reed
	G-BUAC	Slingsby T.31 Motor Cadet III	D. A. Wilson & C. R. Partington
	G-BUAF	Cameron N-77 balloon	Zebedee Balloon Service Ltd
	G-BUAG	Jodel D.18	A. L. Silcox
	G-BUAI	Everett Srs 3 gyroplane	I. D. Bateson
	G-BUAJ	Cameron N-90 balloon	Kent Ballooning
	G-BUAM	Cameron V-77 balloon	N. Florence
	G-BUAO	Luscombe 8A Silvaire	K. E. Ballington
	G-BUAT	Thunder Ax9-120 balloon	J. Fenton

BRITISH CIVIL REGISTRATIONS — G-BUAV – G-BUGS

Reg	Type	Owner or Operator	Notes
G-BUAV	Cameron O-105 balloon	C. D. Monk	
G-BUAX	Rans S.10 Sakota	J. G. J. McDill	
G-BUBJ	BN-2B-20 Islander	G. Cormack	
G-BUBL	Thunder Ax8-105 balloon ★	British Balloon Museum/Newbury	
G-BUBN	BN-2B-26 Islander	Isles of Scilly Skybus Ltd/St. Just	
G-BUBS	Lindstrand LBL-77B balloon	B. J. Bower	
G-BUBT	Stoddard Hamilton Glasair IIS RG	R. P. Reeves	
G-BUBU	PA-34-220T Seneca III	Brinor (Holdings) Ltd	
G-BUBW	Robinson R22 Beta	Staske Construction Ltd	
G-BUBY	Thunder Ax8-105 S2 balloon	T. M. Donnelly	
G-BUCA	Cessna A.150K	BUCA Group	
G-BUCB	Cameron H-34 balloon	A. S. Jones	
G-BUCC	CASA 1.131E Jungmann 2000 (BU+CC)	P. L. Gaze (G-BUEM)	
G-BUCG	Schleicher ASW.20L (modified)	W. B. Andrews	
G-BUCH	Stinson V-77 Reliant	Gullwing Trading Ltd	
G-BUCI	Auster AOP.9 (XP242)	Historic Aircraft Flight Reserve Collection/Middle Wallop	
G-BUCK	CASA 1.131E Jungmann 1000 (BU+CK)	Jungmann Flying Group/White Waltham	
G-BUCM	Hawker Sea Fury FB.11	Patina Ltd/Duxford	
G-BUCO	Pietenpol Air Camper	A. James	
G-BUCS	Cessna 150F	Atlantic Bridge Aviation Ltd/Lydd	
G-BUCT	Cessna 150L	Aircraft Engineers Ltd	
G-BUDA	Slingsby T.61F Venture T.2	Cranwell Gliding Club	
G-BUDB	Slingsby T.61F Venture T.2	RAFGSA/Bicester	
G-BUDC	Slingsby T.61F Venture T.2 (ZA652)	T.61 Group	
G-BUDE	PA-22 Tri-Pacer 135 (tailwheel)	P. Robinson	
G-BUDF	Rand-Robinson KR-2	M. Stott	
G-BUDI	Aero Designs Pulsar	R. W. L. Oliver	
G-BUDK	Thunder Ax7-77 balloon	W. Evans	
G-BUDL	Auster 3 (NX534)	M. Pocock	
G-BUDN	Cameron 90 Shoe SS balloon	Magical Adventures Ltd	
G-BUDO	PZL-110 Koliber 150	A. S. Vine/Goodwood	
G-BUDR	Denney Kitfox Mk 3	N. J. P. Mayled	
G-BUDS	Rand-Robinson KR-2	D. W. Munday	
G-BUDT	Slingsby T.61F Venture T.2	G-BUDT Group	
G-BUDU	Cameron V-77 balloon	T. M. G. Amery	
G-BUDW	Brügger MB.2 Colibri	B. R. Whitehead (G-GODS)	
G-BUEC	Van's RV-6	A. H. Harper	
G-BUED	Slingsby T.61F Venture T.2	617 VGS Group	
G-BUEF	Cessna 152 II	Channel Aviation	
G-BUEG	Cessna 152 II	Plymouth School of Flying Ltd	
G-BUEI	Thunder Ax8-105 balloon	S. A. Adie	
G-BUEK	Slingsby T.61F Venture T.2	G-BUEK Group/Tibenham	
G-BUEN	VPM M-14 Scout	J. L. G. McLane	
G-BUEP	Maule MX-7-180	N. J. B. Bennett	
G-BUEV	Cameron O-77 balloon	K. C. Tanner	
G-BUEW	Rans S-6 Coyote II	J. D. Clabon (G-MWYE)	
G-BUEX	Schweizer 269C	Tout-Saints Hotels Ltd (G-HFLR)	
G-BUFA	Cameron R-77 gas balloon	Noble Adventures Ltd	
G-BUFC	Cameron R-77 gas balloon	Noble Adventures Ltd	
G-BUFE	Cameron R-77 gas balloon	Noble Adventures Ltd	
G-BUFG	Slingsby T.61F Venture T.2	Transcourt Ltd	
G-BUFH	PA-28-161 Warrior II	R. J. Gibson	
G-BUFI	Avro 146-RJ70	Trident Jet (Dublin) Ltd	
G-BUFJ	Cameron V-90 balloon	S. P. Richards	
G-BUFN	Slingsby T.61F Venture T.2	BUFN Group	
G-BUFR	Slingsby T.61F Venture T.2	East Sussex Gliding Club Ltd	
G-BUFT	Cameron O-120 balloon	D. Bron	
G-BUFV	Light Aero Avid Speedwing Mk.4	M. & B. Gribbin	
G-BUFW	AS.355F1 Twin Squirrel	RCR Aviation Ltd	
G-BUFY	PA-28-161 Warrior II	Bickertons Aerodromes Ltd/Denham	
G-BUGB	Stolp SA.750 Acroduster Too	R. M. Chaplin	
G-BUGD	Cameron V-77 balloon	Cameron Balloons Ltd	
G-BUGE	Bellanca 7GCAA Cltabria	V. Vaughan & N. O'Brien	
G-BUGG	Cessna 150F	C. P. J. Taylor & D. M. Forshaw/Panshanger	
G-BUGJ	Robin DR.400/180	W. M. Patterson	
G-BUGL	Slingsby T.61F Venture T.2	VMG Group	
G-BUGM	CFM Streak Shadow	The Shadow Group	
G-BUGO	Colt 56B balloon	Escuela de Aerostacion Mica/Spain	
G-BUGP	Cameron V-77 balloon	R. Churcher	
G-BUGS	Cameron V-77 balloon	S. J. Dymond	

G-BUGT – G-BULZ — BRITISH CIVIL REGISTRATIONS

Notes	Reg	Type	Owner or Operator
	G-BUGT	Slingsby T.61F Venture T.2	R. W. Hornsey/Rufforth
	G-BUGV	Slingsby T.61F Venture T.2	Oxfordshire Sportflying Ltd/Enstone
	G-BUGW	Slingsby T.61F Venture T.2	Transcourt Ltd
	G-BUGY	Cameron V-90 balloon	Dante Balloon Group
	G-BUGZ	Slingsby T.61F Venture T.2	Dishforth Flying Group
	G-BUHA	Slingsby T.61F Venture T.2 (ZA634:C)	K. E. Ballington
	G-BUHM	Cameron V-77 balloon	L. A. Watts
	G-BUHO	Cessna 140	W. B. Bateson/Blackpool
	G-BUHR	Slingsby T.61F Venture T.2	Connel Motor Glider Group
	G-BUHS	Stoddard-Hamilton Glasair SH TD-1	T. F. Horrocks
	G-BUHU	Cameron N-105 balloon	Unipart Balloon Club
	G-BUHZ	Cessna 120	Cessna 140 Group
	G-BUIE	Cameron N-90 balloon	B. Conway
	G-BUIF	PA-28-161 Warrior II	Northumbria Flying School Ltd
	G-BUIG	Campbell Cricket (replica)	J. A. English
	G-BUIH	Slingsby T.61F Venture T.2	Falcon Gliding Group
	G-BUIJ	PA-28-161 Warrior II	Tradecliff Ltd/Blackbushe
	G-BUIK	PA-28-161 Warrior II	Falcon Flying Services/Biggin Hill
	G-BUIL	CFM Streak Shadow	P. N. Bevan & L. M. Poor
	G-BUIN	Thunder Ax7-77 balloon	P. C. Johnson
	G-BUIP	Denney Kitfox Mk 2	Avcomm Developments Ltd
	G-BUIR	Light Aero Avid Speedwing Mk 4	E. Stinton
	G-BUIU	Cameron V-90 balloon	H. Micketeit/Germany
	G-BUIZ	Cameron N-90 balloon	Balloon Preservation Flying Group
	G-BUJA	Slingsby T.61F Venture T.2	Wrekin Gliding Club/Cosford
	G-BUJB	Slingsby T.61F Venture T.2	Falke Syndicate/Shobdon
	G-BUJE	Cessna 177B	FG93 Group
	G-BUJH	Colt 77B balloon	R. P. Cross & R. Stanley
	G-BUJI	Slingsby T.61F Venture T.2	Solent Venture Syndicate Ltd
	G-BUJJ	Avid Speedwing	R. A. Dawson
	G-BUJK	Montgomerie-Bensen B.8MR	P. C. W. Raine
	G-BUJL	Aero Designs Pulsar	J. J. Lynch
	G-BUJM	Cessna 120	Cessna 120 Flying Group/Yeoviilton
	G-BUJN	Cessna 172N	M. Djukic & J. Benfell
	G-BUJO	PA-28-161 Warrior II	Falcon Flying Services/Biggin Hill
	G-BUJP	PA-28-161 Warrior II	J. M. C. Manson
	G-BUJR	Cameron A-180 balloon	Dragon Balloon Co Ltd
	G-BUJV	Light Aero Avid Speedwing Mk 4	C. Thomas
	G-BUJW	Thunder Ax8-90 S2 balloon	G. J. Grimes
	G-BUJX	Slingsby T.61F Venture T.2	K. E. Ballington
	G-BUJY	DH.82A Tiger Moth	P. Winters
	G-BUJZ	Rotorway Executive 90 (modified)	M. P. Swoboda
	G-BUKB	Rans S.10 Sakota	M. K. Blatch
	G-BUKF	Denney Kitfox Mk 4	Kilo Foxtrot Group
	G-BUKH	D.31 Turbulent	R. B. Armitage
	G-BUKI	Thunder Ax7-77 balloon	Virgin Balloon Flights
	G-BUKJ	BAe ATP	Trident Aviation Leasing Services (Jersey) Ltd
	G-BUKK	Bücker Bü 133C Jungmeister (U-80)	E. J. F. McEntee/White Waltham
	G-BUKN	PA-15 Vagabond	M. A. Goddard
	G-BUKO	Cessna 120	S. Warrener
	G-BUKP	Denney Kitfox Mk 2	K. N. Cobb
	G-BUKR	MS.880B Rallye Club 100T	G-BUKR Flying Group
	G-BUKS	Colt 77B balloon	R. & M. Bairstow
	G-BUKT	Luscombe 8A Silvaire	R. J. F. Swain
	G-BUKU	Luscombe 8E Silvaire	Silvaire Flying Group
	G-BUKX	PA-28-161 Warrior II	LNP Ltd
	G-BUKZ	Evans VP-2	P. R. Farnell
	G-BULB	Thunder Ax7-77 balloon	G. B. Davies
	G-BULC	Light Aero Avid Flyer Mk 4	C. Nice
	G-BULD	Cameron N-105 balloon	R. J. Collins
	G-BULF	Colt 77A balloon	P. Goss & T. C. Davies
	G-BULG	Van's RV-4	G-BULG Group/Tibenham
	G-BULH	Cessna 172N Skyhawk II	Comed Schedule Services Ltd
	G-BULJ	CFM Streak Shadow	C. C. Brown
	G-BULK	Thunder Ax9-120 S2 balloon	Skybus Ballooning
	G-BULL	SA Bulldog Srs 120/128 (HKG-5)	Solo Leisure Ltd
	G-BULM	Aero Designs Pulsar	J. Bell
	G-BULN	Colt 210A balloon	H. G. Davies
	G-BULO	Luscombe 8A Silvaire	A. F. S. Caldecourt
	G-BULR	PA-28-140 Cherokee	G. R. Bright
	G-BULT	Campbell Cricket	A. T. Pocklington
	G-BULY	Light Aero Avid Flyer	P. A. Spurr
	G-BULZ	Denney Kitfox Mk 2	T. G. F. Trenchard

98

BRITISH CIVIL REGISTRATIONS   G-BUMP – G-BUTH

Reg	Type	Owner or Operator	Notes
G-BUMP	PA-28-181 Archer II	A. J. Keen	
G-BUNB	Slingsby T.61F Venture T.2	RAFGSA/Lee-on-Solent	
G-BUNC	PZL-104 Wilga 35	R. F. Goodman	
G-BUND	PA-28RT-201T Turbo Arrow IV	L. J. Martin	
G-BUNG	Cameron N-77 balloon	The Bungle Balloon Group	
G-BUNH	PA-28RT-201T Turbo Arrow IV	JH Sandham Aviation	
G-BUNJ	Squarecraft SA.102-5 Cavalier	J. A. Smith	
G-BUNM	Denney Kitfox Mk 3	P. N. Akass	
G-BUNO	Lancair 320	J. Softley	
G-BUNV	Thunder Ax7-77 balloon	R. M. Garnett & R. Stone	
G-BUNZ	Thunder Ax10-180 S2 balloon	M. A. Scholes	
G-BUOA	Whittaker MW6-S Fatboy Flyer	H. N. Graham	
G-BUOB	CFM Streak Shadow	W. J. Whyte	
G-BUOD	SE-5A (replica) (B595:W)	M. D. Waldron/Belgium	
G-BUOE	Cameron V-90 balloon	Dusters & Co	
G-BUOF	D.62B Condor	R. P. Loxton	
G-BUOI	PA-20 Pacer	Foley Farm Flying Group	
G-BUOJ	Cessna 172N	Falcon Flying Services Ltd/Biggin Hill	
G-BUOK	Rans S.6-ESA Coyote II	M. Morris	
G-BUOL	Denney Kitfox Mk 3	E. C. King	
G-BUON	Light Aero Avid Aerobat	S. R. Winder	
G-BUOR	CASA 1.131E Jungmann 2000	M. I. M. S. Voest/Netherlands	
G-BUOS	VS.394 Spitfire FR.XVIII (SM845:GZ-J)	Historic Flying Ltd	
G-BUOW	Aero Designs Pulsar XP	T. J. Hartwell	
G-BUOX	Cameron V-77 balloon	I. G. H. Woodmansey	
G-BUOZ	Thunder Ax10-180 balloon	Zebedee Balloon Service Ltd	
G-BUPA	Rutan LongEz	N. G. Henry	
G-BUPB	Stolp SA.300 Starduster Too	Starduster PB Group	
G-BUPC	Rollason Beta B.2	C. A. Rolph	
G-BUPF	Bensen B.8R	P. W. Hewitt-Dean	
G-BUPG	Cessna 180K	T. P. A. Norman/Rendcomb	
G-BUPH	Colt 25A balloon	BAB-Ballonwerbung GmbH/Germany	
G-BUPI	Cameron V-77 balloon	S. A. Masey (G-BUOC)	
G-BUPJ	Fournier RF-4D	M. R. Shelton	
G-BUPM	VPM M-16 Tandem Trainer	Roger Savage (Gyroplanes) Ltd	
G-BUPP	Cameron V-42 balloon	L. J. Schoeman	
G-BUPR	Jodel D.18	R. W. Burrows	
G-BUPU	Thunder Ax7-77 balloon	R. C. Barkworth & D. G. Maguire/USA	
G-BUPV	Great Lakes 2T-1A	R. J. Fray	
G-BUPW	Denney Kitfox Mk 3	Kitfox Group	
G-BURD	Cessna F.172N	Tayside Aviation Ltd	
G-BURE	Jodel D.9	L. J. Kingsford	
G-BURG	Colt 77A balloon	S. T. Humphreys	
G-BURH	Cessna 150E	C. A. Davis	
G-BURI	Enstrom F-28C	India Helicopters Group	
G-BURL	Colt 105A balloon	J. E. Rose	
G-BURN	Cameron O-120 balloon	Innovation Ballooning Ltd	
G-BURP	Rotorway Executive 90	N. K. Newman	
G-BURS	Sikorsky S-76A	Premiair Aviation Services Ltd (G-OHTL)	
G-BURT	PA-28-161 Warrior II	B. A. Paul	
G-BURU	BAe Jetstream 3202	Trident Aviation Leasing Services	
G-BURX	Cameron N-105 balloon	Balloon Preservation Flying Group (G-NPNP)	
G-BURZ	Hawker Nimrod II (K3661:362)	Historic Aircraft Collection Ltd	
G-BUSB	Airbus A.320-111	British Airways	
G-BUSC	Airbus A.320-111	British Airways	
G-BUSE	Airbus A.320-111	British Airways	
G-BUSF	Airbus A.320-111	British Airways	
G-BUSG	Airbus A.320-211	British Airways	
G-BUSH	Airbus A.320-211	British Airways	
G-BUSI	Airbus A.320-211	British Airways	
G-BUSJ	Airbus A.320-211	British Airways	
G-BUSK	Airbus A.320-211	British Airways	
G-BUSR	Aero Designs Pulsar	S. S. Bateman & R. A. Watts	
G-BUSS	Cameron 90 Bus SS balloon	Magical Adventures Ltd	
G-BUSV	Colt 105A balloon	M. N. J. Kirby	
G-BUSW	Rockwell Commander 114	J. M. J. Palmer	
G-BUSY	Thunder Ax6-56A balloon	M. E. Hooker	
G-BUTB	CFM Streak Shadow	S. Vestuti	
G-BUTD	Van's RV-6	N. W. Beadle	
G-BUTE	Anderson EA-1 Kingfisher	T. Crawford (G-BRCK)	
G-BUTF	Aeronca 11AC Chief	Fox Flying Group	
G-BUTG	Zenair CH.601HD	I. J. McNally	
G-BUTH	CEA DR.220 2+2	Phoenix Flying Group	

G-BUTJ – G-BUYO — BRITISH CIVIL REGISTRATIONS

Notes	Reg	Type	Owner or Operator
	G-BUTJ	Cameron O-77 balloon	R. J. Percival
	G-BUTK	Murphy Rebel	G. S. Claybourn
	G-BUTM	Rans S.6-116 Coyote II	G-BUTM Group
	G-BUTW	BAe Jetstream 3202	Trident Aviation Leasing Services
	G-BUTX	CASA 1.133C Jungmeister (ES.1-4)	A. J. E. Smith/Brighton
	G-BUTY	Brügger MB.2 Colibri	R. M. Lawday
	G-BUTZ	PA-28 Cherokee 180C	M. H. Canning (G-DARL)
	G-BUUA	Slingsby T.67M Firefly Mk II	Babcock Defence Services
	G-BUUB	Slingsby T.67M Firefly Mk II	Babcock Defence Services
	G-BUUC	Slingsby T.67M Firefly Mk II	Babcock Defence Services
	G-BUUD	Slingsby T.67M Firefly Mk II	N. J. Heard & S. J. Cowham
	G-BUUE	Slingsby T.67M Firefly Mk II	J. R. Bratty
	G-BUUF	Slingsby T.67M Firefly Mk II	Tiger Airways
	G-BUUI	Slingsby T.67M Firefly Mk II	Bustard Flying Club Ltd
	G-BUUJ	Slingsby T.67M Firefly Mk II	R. Manning
	G-BUUK	Slingsby T.67M Firefly Mk II	Babcock Defence Services
	G-BUUL	Slingsby T.67M Firefly Mk II	Witham (Specialist Vehicles) Ltd
	G-BUUM	PA-28RT-201 Arrow IV	Bluebird Flying Group
	G-BUUO	Cameron N-90 balloon	Gone Ballooning Group
	G-BUUP	BAe ATP	Trident Aviation Leasing Ltd (G-MANU)
	G-BUUT	Interavia 70TA balloon	Aero Vintage Ltd
	G-BUUU	Cameron Bottle SS balloon ★	British Balloon Museum/Newbury
	G-BUUX	PA-28 Cherokee 180D	Aero Group 78/Netherthorpe
	G-BUUZ	BAe Jetstream 3202	Trident Aviation Leasing Services
	G-BUVA	PA-22 Tri-Pacer 135	Oakesy VA Group
	G-BUVC	BAe Jetstream 3206	Eastern Airways
	G-BUVD	BAe Jetstream 3206	Eastern Airways
	G-BUVE	Colt 77B balloon	G. D. Philpot
	G-BUVL	Fisher Super Koala	A. D. Malcolm
	G-BUVM	CEA DR.250/160	G-BUVM Group
	G-BUVN	CASA 1.131E Jungmann 2000 (BI-005)	W. Van Egmond/Netherlands
	G-BUVO	Cessna F.182P	Romeo Mike Flying Group (G-WTFA)
	G-BUVR	Christen A.1 Husky	A. E. Poulson
	G-BUVS	Colt 77A balloon	J. R. Coney
	G-BUVT	Colt 77A balloon	N. A. Carr
	G-BUVW	Cameron N-90 balloon	P. Spellward
	G-BUVX	CFM Streak Shadow	T. J. Shaw
	G-BUVZ	Thunder Ax10-180 S2 balloon	A. Van Wyk
	G-BUWE	SE-5A (replica) (C9533:M)	Airpark Flight Centre Ltd/Coventry
	G-BUWF	Cameron N-105 balloon	R. E. Jones
	G-BUWH	Parsons 2-seat gyroplane	R. V. Brunskill
	G-BUWI	Lindstrand LBL-77A balloon	Capital Balloon Club Ltd
	G-BUWJ	Pitts S-1C Special	R. V. Barber
	G-BUWK	Rans S.6-116 Coyote II	R. Warriner
	G-BUWL	Piper J-4A	M. L. Ryan/Oakesy Park
	G-BUWR	CFM Streak Shadow	T. Harvey
	G-BUWS	Denney Kitfox Mk 2	J. E. Brewis
	G-BUWT	Rand-Robinson KR-2	C. M. Coombe
	G-BUWU	Cameron V-77 balloon	T. R. Dews
	G-BUXA	Colt 210A balloon	Balloon School International Ltd
	G-BUXC	CFM Streak Shadow	J. P. Mimnagh
	G-BUXD	Maule MXT-7-160	S. Baigent
	G-BUXI	Steen Skybolt	D. Tucker
	G-BUXJ	Slingsby T.61F Venture T.2	Venture Motor Glider Club/Halton
	G-BUXK	Pietenpol Air Camper	B. M. D. Nelson
	G-BUXL	Taylor JT.1 Monoplane	P. J. Hebdon
	G-BUXN	Beech C23 Sundowner	Private Pilots Syndicate
	G-BUXO	Pober P-9 Pixie	P-9 Flying Group
	G-BUXR	Cameron A-250 balloon	Celebration Balloon Flights
	G-BUXS	MBB Bö.105DBS/4	Bond Air Services (G-PASA/G-BGWP)
	G-BUXV	PA-22 Tri-Pacer 160 (tailwheel)	Romeo Delta Juliet Group
	G-BUXW	Thunder Ax8-90 S2 balloon	Nottingham Hot Air Balloon Club
	G-BUXX	PA-17 Vagabond	R. H. Hunt/Old Sarum
	G-BUXY	PA-25 Pawnee 235	Bath, Wilts & North Dorset Gliding Club Ltd/ Kingston Deverill
	G-BUYB	Aero Designs Pulsar	A. P. Fenn/Shobdon
	G-BUYC	Cameron 80 Concept balloon	R. P. Cross
	G-BUYD	Thunder Ax8-90 balloon	S. & P. McGuigan
	G-BUYF	Falcon XP	M. J. Hadland
	G-BUYJ	Lindstrand LBL-105A balloon	D. K. Fish & G. Fordyce
	G-BUYK	Denney Kitfox Mk 4	M. S. Shelton
	G-BUYL	RAF 2000GT gyroplane	Newtonair Gyroplanes Ltd
	G-BUYO	Colt 77A balloon	S. F. Burden/Netherlands

BRITISH CIVIL REGISTRATIONS G-BUYR – G-BVEN

Reg	Type	Owner or Operator	Notes
G-BUYR	Mooney M.20C	C. R. Weldon/Eire	
G-BUYS	Robin DR.400/180	G-BUYS Flying Group/Nuthampstead	
G-BUYU	Bowers Fly-Baby 1A	R. Metcalfe	
G-BUYY	PA-28 Cherokee 180	G-BUYY Group	
G-BUZA	Denney Kitfox Mk 3	A. O'Brien/Ireland	
G-BUZB	Aero Designs Pulsar XP	S. M. Lancashire	
G-BUZC	Everett Srs 3A gyroplane	M. P. L'Hermette	
G-BUZD	AS.332L Super Puma	CHC Scotia Ltd	
G-BUZE	Light Aero Avid Speedwing	D. P. Hirst	
G-BUZF	Colt 77B balloon	A. E. Austin	
G-BUZG	Zenair CH.601HD	P. G. Morris	
G-BUZH	Aero Designs Star-Lite SL-1	C. A. McDowall	
G-BUZK	Cameron V-77 balloon	J. T. Wilkinson	
G-BUZL	VPM M-16 Tandem Trainer	C. M. Jones	
G-BUZM	Light Aero Avid Flyer Mk 3	R. McLuckie & O. G. Jones	
G-BUZN	Cessna 172H	H. D. Jones/Barton	
G-BUZO	Pietenpol Air Camper	D. A. Jones	
G-BUZR	Lindstrand LBL-77A balloon	Lindstrand Technologies Ltd	
G-BUZS	Colt Flying Pig SS balloon	Banco Bilbao Vizcaya/Spain	
G-BUZT	Kolb Twinstar Mk 3	J. A. G. Robb	
G-BUZV	Ken Brock KB-2 gyroplane	K. Hughes	
G-BUZZ	Agusta-Bell 206B JetRanger 2	Rivermead Aviation Ltd	
G-BVAB	Zenair CH.601HDS	B. N. Rides	
G-BVAC	Zenair CH.601HD	A. G. Cozens	
G-BVAF	Piper J-3C-65 Cub	N. M. Hitchman/Leicester	
G-BVAG	Lindstrand LBL-90A balloon	The Whitchurch Aviation Training Syndicate	
G-BVAH	Denney Kitfox Mk.3	S. Allinson	
G-BVAI	PZL-110 Koliber 150	N. J. & R. F. Morgan	
G-BVAM	Evans VP-1	R. F. Selby	
G-BVAO	Colt 25A balloon	M. E. Dworski	
G-BVAW	Staaken Z-1 Flitzer (D-692)	L. R. Williams	
G-BVAX	Colt 77A balloon	P. H. Porter	
G-BVAY	Rutan Vari-Eze	D. A. Young	
G-BVAZ	Montgomerie-Bensen B.8MR	N. Steele	
G-BVBD	Sikorsky S-52-3	J. Windmill	
G-BVBF	PA-28-151 Warrior	R. K. Spence/Cardiff	
G-BVBR	Light Aero Avid Speedwing	P. D. Thomas	
G-BVBS	Cameron N-77 balloon	Heart of England Balloons	
G-BVBU	Cameron V-77 balloon	J. Manclark	
G-BVBV	Light Aero Avid Flyer	L. W. M. Summers	
G-BVCA	Cameron N-105 balloon	Unipart Balloon Club	
G-BVCC	Monnett Sonerai 2LT	J. Eggleston	
G-BVCG	Van's RV-6	P. C. J. Stone & K. Dennison	
G-BVCL	Rans S.6-116 Coyote II	R. J. Powell	
G-BVCM	Cessna 525 CitationJet	Kenmore Aviation Ltd & BLP 2003-19 Ltd	
G-BVCO	FRED Srs 2	I. W. Bremner	
G-BVCP	Piper CP.1 Metisse	B. M. Diggins	
G-BVCS	Aeronca 7BCM Champion	A. C. Lines	
G-BVCT	Denney Kitfox Mk 4	A. F. Reid	
G-BVCX	Sikorsky S76A (modified)	CHC Scotia Ltd	
G-BVCY	Cameron H-24 balloon	A. C. K. Rawson & J. J. Rudoni	
G-BVDB	Thunder Ax7-77 balloon	M. J. Smith & J. Towler (G-ORDY)	
G-BVDC	Van's RV-3	R. J. Hodder	
G-BVDD	Colt 69A balloon	R. M. Cambridge	
G-BVDH	PA-28RT-201 Arrow IV	Silverstar Aviation Ltd/Blackpool	
G-BVDI	Van's RV-4	J. Glen-Davis Gorman	
G-BVDJ	Campbell Cricket (replica)	S. Jennings	
G-BVDM	Cameron 60 Concept balloon	M. P Young	
G-BVDO	Lindstrand LBL-105A balloon	A. E. Still	
G-BVDP	Sequoia F.8L Falco	N. M. Turner	
G-BVDR	Cameron O-77 balloon	N. J. Logue	
G-BVDS	Lindstrand LBL-69A balloon	Lindstrand Hot-Air Balloons Ltd	
G-BVDT	CFM Streak Shadow	H. J. Bennet	
G-BVDW	Thunder Ax8-90 balloon	S. C. Vora	
G-BVDX	Cameron V-90 balloon	R. K. Scott	
G-BVDY	Cameron 60 Concept balloon	P. Baker/Ireland	
G-BVDZ	Taylorcraft BC-12D	P. N. W. England	
G-BVEA	Mosler Motors N.3 Pup	N. Lynch/Breighton (G-MWEA)	
G-BVEH	Jodel D.112	M. L. Copland	
G-BVEK	Cameron 80 Concept balloon	A. D. Malcolm	
G-BVEL	Evans VP-1 Srs.2	M. J. & S. J. Quinn	
G-BVEN	Cameron 80 Concept balloon	Hildon Associates	

G-BVEP – G-BVJZ | BRITISH CIVIL REGISTRATIONS

Notes	Reg	Type	Owner or Operator
	G-BVEP	Luscombe 8A Master	B. H. Austen
	G-BVER	DHC.2 Beaver 1 (XV268)	Seaflite Ltd/Duxford (G-BTDM)
	G-BVES	Cessna 340A	K. P. Gibbin & I. M. Worthington
	G-BVEU	Cameron O-105 balloon	G. J. Bell
	G-BVEV	PA-34-200 Seneca	R. W. Harris & ptnrs
	G-BVEW	Lindstrand LBL-150A balloon	A. Van Wyk
	G-BVEY	Denney Kitfox Mk 4-1200	J. H. H. Turner
	G-BVEZ	P.84 Jet Provost T.3A (XM479)	Newcastle Jet Provost Co Ltd
	G-BVFA	Rans S.10 Sakota	D. S. Wilkinson
	G-BVFB	Cameron N-31 balloon	R. Kunert
	G-BVFF	Cameron V-77 balloon	R. J. Kerr & G. P. Allen
	G-BVFM	Rans S.6-116 Coyote II	F. B. C. de Beer
	G-BVFO	Light Aero Avid Speedwing	M. S. Moat
	G-BVFP	Cameron V-90 balloon	D. E. & J. M. Hartland
	G-BVFR	CFM Streak Shadow	R. W. Chatterton
	G-BVFT	Maule M5-235C	Newnham Joint Flying Syndicate
	G-BVFU	Cameron 105 Sphere SS balloon	Stichting Phoenix/Netherlands
	G-BVFZ	Maule M5-180C Lunar Rocket	J. W. Macleod
	G-BVGA	Bell 206B JetRanger 3	Findon Air Services/Southend
	G-BVGB	Thunder Ax8-105 S2 balloon	M. E. Dunstan-Sewell
	G-BVGE	WS-55 Whirlwind HAR.10 (XJ729)	J. F. Kelly/Ireland
	G-BVGF	Shaw Europa	A. Graham & G. G. Beal
	G-BVGG	Lindstrand LBL-69A balloon	L. P. Hooper
	G-BVGH	Hawker Hunter T.7 (XL573)	Global Aviation Services Ltd/Humberside
	G-BVGI	Pereira Osprey II	A. A. Knight
	G-BVGJ	Cameron C-80 balloon	J. M. J. & V. F. Roberts
	G-BVGK	Lindstrand LBL Newspaper SS balloon	H. Holmqvist
	G-BVGO	Denney Kitfox Mk 4-1200	T. Marriott
	G-BVGP	Bücker Bü 133 Jungmeister (U-95)	M. V. Rijkse
	G-BVGS	Robinson R22 Beta	Polar Helicopters
	G-BVGT	Auster J/1 (modified)	K. D. & C. S. Rhodes
	G-BVGW	Luscombe 8A Silvaire	J. Smith
	G-BVGX	Thunder Ax8-90 S2 balloon	G-BVGX Group/New Zealand
	G-BVGY	Luscombe 8E Silvaire	M. C. Burlock
	G-BVGZ	Fokker Dr.1 (replica) (450/17) ★	R. A. Fleming
	G-BVHC	Grob G.115D-2 Heron	Tayside Aviation Ltd
	G-BVHD	Grob G.115D-2 Heron	Tayside Aviation Ltd
	G-BVHE	Grob G.115D-2 Heron	Tayside Aviation Ltd
	G-BVHF	Grob G.115D-2 Heron	Tayside Aviation Ltd
	G-BVHG	Grob G.115D-2 Heron	Tayside Aviation Ltd
	G-BVHI	Rans S.10 Sakota	J. D. Amos
	G-BVHJ	Cameron A-180 balloon	S. J. Boxall
	G-BVHK	Cameron V-77 balloon	A. R. Rich
	G-BVHL	Nicollier HN.700 Menestrel II	W. Goldsmith
	G-BVHM	PA-38-112 Tomahawk	A. J. Gomes (G-DCAN)
	G-BVHO	Cameron V-90 balloon	N. W. B. Bews
	G-BVHP	Colt 42A balloon	Huntair Ltd
	G-BVHR	Cameron V-90 balloon	G. P. Walton
	G-BVHS	Murphy Rebel	S. T. Raby
	G-BVHT	Light Aero Avid Speedwing Mk 4	L. H. B. S. Stephens
	G-BVHV	Cameron N-105 balloon	Wye Valley Aviation Ltd
	G-BVIA	Rand-Robinson KR-2	K. Atkinson
	G-BVIE	PA-18 Super Cub 95 (modified)	J. C. Best (G-CLIK/G-BLMB)
	G-BVIF	Montgomerie-Bensen B.8MR	R. M. & D. Mann
	G-BVIK	Maule MXT-7-180 Star Rocket	Graveley Flying Group
	G-BVIL	Maule MXT-7-180 Star Rocket	K. & S. C. Knight
	G-BVIN	Rans S.6-ESA Coyote II	P. C. Davis
	G-BVIR	Lindstrand LBL-69A balloon	Aerial Promotions Ltd
	G-BVIS	Brügger MB.2 Colibri	B. H. Shaw
	G-BVIT	Campbell Cricket	D. R. Owen
	G-BVIV	Light Aero Avid Speedwing	R. C. Holmes
	G-BVIW	PA-18-Super Cub 150	M. J. Medland
	G-BVIX	Lindstrand LBL-180A balloon	European Balloon Display Co Ltd
	G-BVIZ	Shaw Europa	The Europa Group
	G-BVJE	AS.350B1 Ecureuil	PLM Dollar Group Ltd
	G-BVJF	Montgomerie-Bensen B.8MR	D. M. F. Harvey
	G-BVJG	Cyclone AX3/K	T. D. Reid (G-MYOP)
	G-BVJK	Glaser-Dirks DG.800A	B. A. Eastwell & J. S. Forster
	G-BVJN	Shaw Europa	JN Europa Group
	G-BVJT	Cessna F.406	Nor Leasing
	G-BVJU	Evans VP-1	BVJU Flying Club & Associates
	G-BVJX	Marquart MA.5 Charger	E. Newsham
	G-BVJZ	PA-28-161 Warrior II	D. C. Farmer

BRITISH CIVIL REGISTRATIONS — G-BVKB – G-BVPR

Reg	Type	Owner or Operator	Notes
G-BVKB	Boeing 737-59D	bmi Baby	
G-BVKD	Boeing 737-59D	bmi Baby	
G-BVKF	Shaw Europa	T. R. Sinclair	
G-BVKG	Colt Flying Hot Dog SS balloon	Longbreak Ltd/USA	
G-BVKH	Thunder Ax8-90 balloon	L. Ashill	
G-BVKK	Slingsby T.61F Venture T.2	Buckminster Gliding Club Ltd	
G-BVKL	Cameron A-180 balloon	Dragon Balloon Co Ltd	
G-BVKM	Rutan Vari-Eze	J. P. G. Lindquist/Switzerland	
G-BVKR	Sikorsky S-76A	Bristow Helicopters Ltd	
G-BVKU	Slingsby T.61F Venture T.2	G-BVKU Syndicate	
G-BVKX	Colt 14A balloon	P. Baker	
G-BVKZ	Thunder Ax9-120 balloon	D. J. Head	
G-BVLD	Campbell Cricket (replica)	C. Berry	
G-BVLE	McCandless M.4 gyroplane	H. Walls	
G-BVLF	CFM Starstreak Shadow SS-D	R. W. Chatterton	
G-BVLG	AS.355F1 Twin Squirrel	PLM Dollar Group PLC	
G-BVLH	Shaw Europa	D. Barraclough	
G-BVLI	Cameron V-77 balloon	J. Lewis-Richardson/New Zealand	
G-BVLL	Lindstrand LBL-210A balloon	Pendle Balloon Company	
G-BVLN	Aero Designs Pulsar XP	D. A. Campbell	
G-BVLP	PA-38-112 Tomahawk	M. Housley	
G-BVLR	Van's RV-4	RV4 Group	
G-BVLT	Bellanca 7GCBC Citabria	M. A. N. Newall	
G-BVLU	D.31 Turbulent	C. D. Bancroft	
G-BVLV	Shaw Europa	Euro 39 Group	
G-BVLW	Light Aero Avid Flyer Mk 4	D. M. Johnstone/Shobdon	
G-BVLX	Slingsby T.61F Venture T.2	RAFGSA/Easterton	
G-BVLZ	Lindstrand LBL-120A balloon	Balloon Flights Club Ltd	
G-BVMA	Beech 200 Super King Air	Dragonfly Aviation Services LLP (G-VPLC)	
G-BVMC	Robinson R44 Astro	Tiger Helicopters Ltd	
G-BVMD	Luscombe 8E Silvaire	Luscombe Flyers	
G-BVMF	Cameron V-77 balloon	P. A. Meecham	
G-BVMH	WAG-Aero Sport Trainer (39624:D-39)	J. Mathews	
G-BVMI	PA-18 Super Cub 150	S. Sampson	
G-BVMJ	Cameron 95 Eagle SS balloon	R. D. Sargeant	
G-BVML	Lindstrand LBL-210A balloon	Ballooning Adventures Ltd	
G-BVMM	Robin HR.200/100	R. H. Ashforth	
G-BVMN	Ken Brock KB-2 gyroplane	S. A. Scally	
G-BVMP	BAe 146-200	Trident Jet (Jersey) Ltd	
G-BVMR	Cameron V-90 balloon	I. R. Comley	
G-BVMT	BAe 146-200	Trident Jet (Jersey) Ltd	
G-BVMU	Yakovlev Yak-52 (09 yellow)	Ascendances SPRL/Belgium	
G-BVNG	DH.60G-III Moth Major	P. & G. Groves	
G-BVNI	Taylor JT-2 Titch	T. V. Adamson/Rufforth	
G-BVNR	Cameron N-105 balloon	Liquigas SpA/Italy	
G-BVNS	PA-28-181 Archer II	Scottish Airways Flyers (Prestwick) Ltd	
G-BVNU	FLS Aerospace Sprint Club	C. F. Dukes	
G-BVNY	Rans S.7 Courier	D. M. Byers-Jones	
G-BVOA	PA-28-181 Archer II	Millen Aviation Services	
G-BVOB	F.27 Friendship Mk 500	BAC Group Ltd	
G-BVOC	Cameron V-90 balloon	H. W. R. Stewart	
G-BVOH	Campbell Cricket (replica)	A. Kitson	
G-BVOI	Rans S.6-116 Coyote II	W. G. Goodall	
G-BVOK	Yakovlev Yak-52 (55 grey)	Transair Aviation/Shoreham	
G-BVON	Lindstrand LBL-105A balloon	D. J. Farrar	
G-BVOO	Lindstrand LBL-105A balloon	T. G. Church	
G-BVOP	Cameron N-90 balloon	October Gold Ballooning Ltd	
G-BVOR	CFM Streak Shadow	J. M. Chandler	
G-BVOS	Shaw Europa	Durham Europa Group	
G-BVOU	HS.748 Srs 2A	PTB (Emerald) Pty Ltd/Blackpool	
G-BVOV	HS.748 Srs 2A	PTB (Emerald) Pty Ltd/Blackpool	
G-BVOW	Shaw Europa	H. P. Brooks	
G-BVOX	Taylorcraft F-22	R. K. Jordan	
G-BVOY	Rotorway Executive 90	Southern Helicopters Ltd	
G-BVOZ	Colt 56A balloon	British School of Ballooning	
G-BVPA	Thunder Ax8-105 S2 balloon	Firefly Balloon Promotions	
G-BVPD	CASA 1.131E Jungmann 2000	D. Bruton	
G-BVPK	Cameron O-90 balloon	D. V. Fowler	
G-BVPL	Zenair CH.601HD	D. A. Trueman	
G-BVPM	Evans VP-2 Coupé	P. Marigold	
G-BVPN	Piper J-3C-65 Cub	K. I. Munro (G-TAFY)	
G-BVPP	Folland Gnat T.1 (XR993)	Red Gnat Ltd/North Weald	
G-BVPR	Robinson R22 Beta	Helicentre Blackpool Ltd (G-KNIT)	

G-BVPS – G-BVXC — BRITISH CIVIL REGISTRATIONS

Notes	Reg	Type	Owner or Operator
	G-BVPS	Jodel D.112	P. J. Sharp
	G-BVPV	Lindstrand LBL-77B balloon	A. R. Greensides
	G-BVPW	Rans S.6-116 Coyote II	T. B. Woolley
	G-BVPX	Bensen B.8 (modified) Tyro Gyro	A. W. Harvey
	G-BVPY	CFM Streak Shadow	R. J. Mitchell
	G-BVRA	Shaw Europa	N. E. Stokes
	G-BVRH	Taylorcraft BL.65	M. J. Kirk
	G-BVRI	Thunder Ax6-56 balloon	S. Lyth
	G-BVRK	Rans S.6-ESA Coyote II	J. Secular (G-MYPK)
	G-BVRL	Lindstrand LBL-21A balloon	Exclusive Ballooning
	G-BVRR	Lindstrand LBL-77A balloon	M. Icam/France
	G-BVRU	Lindstrand LBL-105A balloon	R. P. Nash
	G-BVRV	Van's RV-4	A. Troughton
	G-BVRZ	PA-18 Super Cub 95	R. W. Davison
	G-BVSB	TEAM mini-MAX	D. G. Palmer
	G-BVSD	SE.3130 Alouette II (V-54)	M. J. Cuttell
	G-BVSF	Aero Designs Pulsar	S. N. & R. J. Freestone
	G-BVSN	Light Aero Avid Speedwing	T. J. Berry
	G-BVSO	Cameron A-120 balloon	Khos Ballooning
	G-BVSP	P.84 Jet Provost T.3A (XM370)	H. G. Hodges & Son Ltd
	G-BVSS	Jodel D.150	A. P. Burns
	G-BVST	Jodel D.150	A. Shipp/Breighton
	G-BVSX	TEAM mini-MAX 91	J. A. Clark
	G-BVSZ	Pitts S-1E (S) Special	H. J. Morton
	G-BVTA	Tri-R Kis	P. J. Webb
	G-BVTC	P.84 Jet Provost T.5A (XW333)	Global Aviation Ltd/Binbrook
	G-BVTD	CFM Streak Shadow	M. Walton
	G-BVTL	Colt 31A balloon	A. Lindsay
	G-BVTM	Cessna F.152 II	RAF Halton Aeroplane Club (G-WACS)
	G-BVTN	Cameron N-90 balloon	P. Zulehner/Austria
	G-BVTO	PA-28-151 Warrior	Falcon Flying Services/Biggin Hill (G-SEWL)
	G-BVTV	Rotorway Executive 90	Spencair Ltd
	G-BVTW	Aero Designs Pulsar	R. J. Panther
	G-BVTX	DHC.1 Chipmunk 22A (WP809)	TX Flying Group
	G-BVUA	Cameron O-105 balloon	D. C. Eager
	G-BVUC	Colt 56A balloon	J. F. Till
	G-BVUG	Betts TB.1 (Stampe SV.4C)	William Tomkins Ltd (G-BEUS)
	G-BVUH	Thunder Ax6-65B balloon	K. B. Chapple
	G-BVUI	Lindstrand LBL-25A balloon	J. W. Hole
	G-BVUJ	Ken Brock KB-2 gyroplane	R. J. Hutchinson
	G-BVUK	Cameron V-77 balloon	H. G. Griffiths & W. A. Steel
	G-BVUM	Rans S.6-116 Coyote II	M. A. Abbott
	G-BVUN	Van's RV-4	A. E. Kay
	G-BVUT	Evans VP-1 Srs. 2	M. J. Barnett
	G-BVUU	Cameron C-80 balloon	T. M. C. McCoy
	G-BVUV	Shaw Europa	R. J. Mills
	G-BVUZ	Cessna 120	N. O. Anderson
	G-BVVA	Yakovlev Yak-52	S. T. G. Lloyd
	G-BVVB	Carlson Sparrow II	L. M. McCullen
	G-BVVE	Jodel D.112	G. D. Gunby
	G-BVVG	Nanchang CJ-6A (68)	Nanchang Group
	G-BVVH	Shaw Europa	T. G. Hoult
	G-BVVI	Hawker Audax I (K5600)	Aero Vintage Ltd
	G-BVVK	DHC.6 Twin Otter 310	Loganair Ltd/British Airways
	G-BVVL	EAA Acro Sport II	G. A. Breen/Portugal
	G-BVVM	Zenair CH.601HD	D. Macdonald
	G-BVVN	Brügger MB.2 Colibri	T. C. Darters
	G-BVVP	Shaw Europa	I. Mansfield
	G-BVVR	Stits SA-3A Playboy	R. A. Chapman
	G-BVVS	Van's RV-4	E. G. & N. S. C. English
	G-BVVU	Lindstrand LBL Four SS balloon	Magical Adventures Ltd/USA
	G-BVVW	Yakovlev Yak-52	J. E. Blackman
	G-BVVZ	Corby CJ-1 Starlet	P. V. Flack
	G-BVWB	Thunder Ax8-90 S2 balloon	M. A. Stelling & K. C. Tanner
	G-BVWC	EE Canberra B.6 (WK163)	Classic Aviation Projects Ltd
	G-BVWI	Cameron 65 Light Bulb SS balloon	Balloon Preservation Flying Group
	G-BVWM	Shaw Europa	Europa Syndicate
	G-BVWW	Lindstrand LBL-90A balloon	Drawflight Ltd
	G-BVWY	Porterfield CP.65	R. L. Earl & B. Morris
	G-BVWZ	PA-32-301 Saratoga	The Saratoga (WZ) Group
	G-BVXA	Cameron N-105 balloon	R. E. Jones
	G-BVXB	Cameron V-77 balloon	J. A. Lawton
	G-BVXC	EE Canberra B.6 (WT333) ★	Classic Aviation Projects Ltd/Bruntingthorpe

BRITISH CIVIL REGISTRATIONS

G-BVXE – G-BWDO

Reg	Type	Owner or Operator	Notes
G-BVXE	Steen Skybolt	J. Buglass (G-LISA)	
G-BVXF	Cameron O-120 balloon	Off The Ground Balloon Co Ltd	
G-BVXJ	CASA 1.133 Jungmeister	A. C. Mercer	
G-BVXK	Yakovlev Yak-52 (26 grey)	E. Gavazzi	
G-BVXM	AS.350B Ecureuil	The Berkeley Leisure Group Ltd	
G-BVXR	DH.104 Devon C.2 (XA880)	M. Whale & M. W. A. Lunn	
G-BVXS	Taylorcraft BC-12D	D. Riley	
G-BVYF	PA-31-350 Navajo Chieftain	J. A. Rees & ptnrs (G-SAVE)	
G-BVYG	CEA DR.300/180	Ulster Gliding Club Ltd/Ballarena	
G-BVYK	TEAM mini-MAX	A. G. Ward	
G-BVYM	CEA DR.300/180	London Gliding Club (Pty) Ltd/Dunstable	
G-BVYO	Robin R.2160	D. J. S. McClean	
G-BVYP	PA-25 Pawnee 235B	Bidford Airfield Ltd	
G-BVYU	Cameron A-140 balloon	Balloon Flights Club Ltd	
G-BVYX	Light Aero Avid Speedwing Mk 4	M. E. Lloyd	
G-BVYY	Pietenpol Air Camper	Pietenpol G-BVYY Group	
G-BVYZ	Stemme S.10V	L. Gubbay	
G-BVZD	Tri-R Kis Cruiser	D. R. Morgan	
G-BVZE	Boeing 737-59D	bmi Baby	
G-BVZG	Boeing 737-5Q8	bmi Baby	
G-BVZH	Boeing 737-5Q8	bmi Baby	
G-BVZI	Boeing 737-5Q8	bmi Baby	
G-BVZJ	Rand-Robinson KR-2	P. D. Button	
G-BVZN	Cameron C-80 balloon	S. J. Clarke	
G-BVZO	Rans S.6-116 Coyote II	P. J. Brion	
G-BVZR	Zenair CH.601HD	R. A. Perkins	
G-BVZT	Lindstrand LBL-90A balloon	S. J. Hollingsworth & M. K. Bellamy	
G-BVZV	Rans S.6-116 Coyote II	A. R. White	
G-BVZX	Cameron H-34 balloon	Chianti Balloon Club/Italy	
G-BVZZ	DHC.1 Chipmunk 22 (WP795)	Portsmouth Naval Gliding Club/Lee-on-Solent	
G-BWAA	Cameron N-133 balloon	Bailey Balloons	
G-BWAB	Jodel D.14	W. A. Braim	
G-BWAC	Waco YKS-7	D. N. Peters	
G-BWAD	RAF 2000GT gyroplane	Newtonair Gyroplanes Ltd	
G-BWAF	Hawker Hunter F.6A (XG160:U) ★	Bournemouth Aviation Museum/Bournemouth	
G-BWAG	Cameron O-120 balloon	P. M. Skinner	
G-BWAH	Montgomerie-Bensen B.8MR	J. B. Allan	
G-BWAI	CFM Streak Shadow	C. M. James	
G-BWAJ	Cameron V-77 balloon	R. S. & S. H. Ham	
G-BWAK	Robinson R22 Beta	Caudwell Communications Ltd	
G-BWAN	Cameron N-77 balloon	Balloon Preservation Flying Group	
G-BWAO	Cameron C-80 balloon	M. D. Freeston & S. Mitchell	
G-BWAP	FRED Srs 3	G. A. Shepherd	
G-BWAR	Denney Kitfox Mk 3	I. Wightman	
G-BWAT	Pietenpol Air Camper	P. W. Aitchison/Enstone	
G-BWAU	Cameron V-90 balloon	K. M. & A. M. F. Hall	
G-BWAV	Schweizer 269C	Helihire	
G-BWAW	Lindstrand LBL-77A balloon	D. Bareford	
G-BWBA	Cameron V-65 balloon	Dante Balloon Group	
G-BWBB	Lindstrand LBL-14A balloon	Oxford Promotions (UK) Ltd	
G-BWBE	Colt Flying Ice Cream Cone SS balloon	Benedikt Haggeney GmbH/Germany	
G-BWBF	Colt Flying Ice Cream Cone SS balloon	Benedikt Haggeney GmbH/Germany	
G-BWBI	Taylorcraft F-22A	P. J. Wallace	
G-BWBJ	Colt 21A balloon	U. Schneider/Germany	
G-BWBT	Lindstrand LBL-90A balloon	British Telecommunications PLC	
G-BWBY	Schleicher ASH.26E	J. S. Ward	
G-BWBZ	ARV K1 Super 2	J. A. Straw (G-BMWG)	
G-BWCA	CFM Streak Shadow	I. C. Pearson	
G-BWCC	Van Den Bemden Gas balloon	Piccard Balloon Group	
G-BWCG	Lindstrand LBL-42A balloon	Oxford Promotions (UK) Ltd	
G-BWCK	Everett Srs 2 gyroplane	A. C. S. M. Hart	
G-BWCO	Dornier Do.28D-2	Wingglider Ltd/Hibaldstow	
G-BWCS	P.84 Jet Provost T.5 (XW293:Z)	R. E. Todd/Sandtoft	
G-BWCT	Tipsy T.66 Nipper 1	J. S. Hemmings & C. R. Steer	
G-BWCV	Shaw Europa	G. C. McKirdy	
G-BWCY	Murphy Rebel	S. Burrow	
G-BWDA	ATR-72-202	Aurigny Air Services Ltd	
G-BWDB	ATR-72-202	Aurigny Air Services Ltd	
G-BWDF	PZL-104 Wilga 35A	Sky Banners Ltd	
G-BWDH	Cameron N-105 balloon	Bridges Van Hire Ltd	
G-BWDM	Lindstrand LBL-120A balloon	A. N. F. Pertwee	
G-BWDO	Sikorsky S-76B	Trustair Ltd	

G-BWDP – G-BWIR   BRITISH CIVIL REGISTRATIONS

Notes	Reg	Type	Owner or Operator
	G-BWDP	Shaw Europa	S. Attubato
	G-BWDR	P.84 Jet Provost T.3A (XM376)	Global Aviation Ltd
	G-BWDS	P.84 Jet Provost T.3A (XM424)	S. T. G. Lloyd
	G-BWDT	PA-34-220T Seneca II	H. R. Chambers/Biggin Hill (G-BKHS)
	G-BWDU	Cameron V-90 balloon	D. M. Roberts
	G-BWDV	Schweizer 269C	Helicopter One Ltd
	G-BWDX	Shaw Europa	J. Robson
	G-BWDZ	Sky 105-24 balloon	D. J. Constant
	G-BWEA	Lindstrand LBL-120A balloon	S. R. Seager
	G-BWEB	P.84 Jet Provost T.3A (XW422:3)	S. Patrick/North Weald
	G-BWEC	Cassutt-Colson Variant	N. R. Thomason & M. P. J. Hill
	G-BWEE	Cameron V-42 balloon	A. J. Davey/Germany
	G-BWEF	SNCAN Stampe SV.4C	Acebell BWEF Syndicate (G-BOVL)
	G-BWEG	Shaw Europa	R. J. Marsh
	G-BWEM	VS.358 Seafire L.IIIC (RX168)	C. J. Warrilow & S. W. Atkins
	G-BWEN	Macair Merlin GT	D. A. Hill
	G-BWEU	Cessna F.152 II	Affair Aircraft Leasing LLP
	G-BWEV	Cessna 152 II	MK Aero Support Ltd
	G-BWEW	Cameron N-105 balloon	Unipart Balloon Club
	G-BWEY	Bensen B.8	F. G. Shepherd
	G-BWEZ	Piper J-3C-65 Cub (436021)	J. G. McTaggart
	G-BWFG	Robin HR.200/120B	Atlantic Air Transport Ltd/Coventry
	G-BWFH	Shaw Europa	B. L. Wratten
	G-BWFI	HOAC Katana DV.20	Air Aqua Ltd
	G-BWFJ	Evans VP-1	P. A. West
	G-BWFK	Lindstrand LBL-77A balloon	Balloon Preservation Flying Group
	G-BWFM	Yakovlev Yak-50	Fox Mike Group
	G-BWFN	Hapi Cygnet SF-2A	G-BWFN Group
	G-BWFO	Colomban MC.15 Cri-Cri	K. D. & C. S. Rhodes
	G-BWFP	Yakovlev Yak-52	M. C. Lee/Manchester
	G-BWFR	Hawker Hunter F.58 (J-4031)	Classic Aviation Ltd/Scampton
	G-BWFT	Hawker Hunter T.8M (XL602)	Global Aviation Services Ltd
	G-BWFV	HOAC Katana DV.20	Walsh Aviation/Cranfield
	G-BWFX	Shaw Europa	A. D. Stewart
	G-BWFZ	Murphy Rebel	S. Beresford (G-SAVS)
	G-BWGA	Lindstrand LBL-105A balloon	I. Chadwick
	G-BWGF	P.84 Jet Provost T.5A (XW325)	Specialscope Jet Provost Group/Woodford
	G-BWGG	MH.1521C-1 Broussard	M. J. Burnett & R. B. Maalouf/France
	G-BWGJ	Chilton DW.1A	T. J. Harrison
	G-BWGK	Hawker Hunter GA.11 (XE689)	B. R. Pearson & GA11 Group/Exeter
	G-BWGL	Hawker Hunter T.8C (XJ615)	Elvington Events Ltd
	G-BWGM	Hawker Hunter T.8C (XE665)	The Admirals Barge/Exeter
	G-BWGN	Hawker Hunter T.8C (WT722)	T8C Group
	G-BWGO	Slingsby T.67M Firefly 200	R. Gray
	G-BWGP	Cameron C-80 balloon	D. J. Groombridge
	G-BWGS	BAC.145 Jet Provost T.5A (XW310)	G-BWGS Ltd/North Weald
	G-BWGT	P.84 Jet Provost T.4	R. E. Todd/Sandtoft
	G-BWGU	Cessna 150F	Goodair Leasing Ltd
	G-BWGX	Cameron N-42 balloon	Newbury Building Society
	G-BWGY	HOAC Katana DV.20	Stars Fly Ltd/Elstree
	G-BWHA	Hawker Hurricane IIB (Z5252)	Historic Flying Ltd/Duxford
	G-BWHC	Cameron N-77 balloon	Travelsphere Ltd
	G-BWHD	Lindstrand LBL-31A balloon	Army Air Corps Balloon Club
	G-BWHF	PA-31-325 Navajo	Awyr Cymru Cyf/Welshpool
	G-BWHG	Cameron N-65 balloon	M. Stefanini & F. B. Alaou
	G-BWHI	DHC.1 Chipmunk 22A (WK624)	N. E. M. Clare
	G-BWHK	Rans S.6-116 Coyote II	D. A. Buttress
	G-BWHM	Sky 140-24 balloon	C. J. S. Limon
	G-BWHP	CASA 1.131E Jungmann (S4+A07)	J. F. Hopkins
	G-BWHR	Tipsy Nipper T.66 Srs 1	L. R. Marnef
	G-BWHS	RAF 2000 gyroplane	J. M. Cox
	G-BWHU	Westland Scout AH.1 (XR595)	N. J. F. Boston
	G-BWHV	Denney Kitfox Mk 2	A. C. Dove
	G-BWHY	Robinson R22	P. Boal
	G-BWIA	Rans S.10 Sakota	L. H. & M. Van Cleeff
	G-BWIB	SA Bulldog Srs 120/122 (XX514)	B. I. Robertson
	G-BWID	D.31 Turbulent	A. M. Turney
	G-BWII	Cessna 150G	J. D. G. Hicks (G-BSKB)
	G-BWIJ	Shaw Europa	R. Lloyd
	G-BWIK	DH.82A Tiger Moth (NL985)	B. J. Ellis
	G-BWIL	Rans S.10 Sakota	P. C. Avery (G-WIEN)
	G-BWIP	Cameron N-90 balloon	S. H. Fell
	G-BWIR	Dornier 328-100	Scot Airways Ltd

106

BRITISH CIVIL REGISTRATIONS

G-BWIV – G-BWOH

Reg	Type	Owner or Operator	Notes
G-BWIV	Shaw Europa	T. G. Ledbury	
G-BWIW	Sky 180-24 balloon	J. A. Cooper	
G-BWIX	Sky 120-24 balloon	J. M. Percival	
G-BWIZ	QAC Quickie Tri-Q 200	M. C. Davies	
G-BWJB	Thunder Ax8-105 balloon	Justerini & Brooks Ltd	
G-BWJG	Mooney M.20J	S. Nahum	
G-BWJH	Shaw Europa	T. P. Cripps	
G-BWJI	Cameron V-90 balloon	Calarel Developments Ltd	
G-BWJM	Bristol M.1C (replica) (C4918)	The Shuttleworth Collection/Old Warden	
G-BWJN	Montgomerie-Bensen B.8	G. C. Kerr	
G-BWJR	Sky 120-24 balloon	W. J. Brogan	
G-BWJW	Westland Scout AH.Mk.1 (XV130)	S. Dadak & G. Sobell	
G-BWJY	DHC.1 Chipmunk 22 (WG469)	K. J. Thompson	
G-BWKD	Cameron O-120 balloon	L. J. & M. Schoeman	
G-BWKE	Cameron AS-105GD airship	W. Arnold/Germany	
G-BWKF	Cameron N-105 balloon	R. M. M. Botti/Italy	
G-BWKG	Shaw Europa	E. H. Keppert/Austria	
G-BWKJ	Rans S.7 Courier	Three Point Aviation	
G-BWKK	Auster A.O.P.9 (XP279)	C. A. Davis & D. R. White	
G-BWKR	Sky 90-24 balloon	B. Drawbridge	
G-BWKT	Stephens Akro Laser	P. D. Begley	
G-BWKU	Cameron A-250 balloon	British School of Ballooning	
G-BWKV	Cameron V-77 balloon	Poppies (UK) Ltd	
G-BWKW	Thunder Ax8-90 balloon	Venice Simplon Orient Express Ltd	
G-BWKX	Cameron A-250 balloon	Hot Airlines/Thailand	
G-BWKZ	Lindstrand LBL-77A balloon	J. H. Dobson	
G-BWLA	Lindstrand LBL-69A balloon	Balloon Preservation Flying Group	
G-BWLD	Cameron O-120 balloon	D. Pedri & ptnrs/Italy	
G-BWLF	Cessna 404	Simmons Aerofilms Ltd (G-BNXS)	
G-BWLJ	Taylorcraft DCO-65	C. Evans	
G-BWLL	Murphy Rebel	F. W. Parker	
G-BWLM	Sky 65-24 balloon	W. J. Brogan	
G-BWLN	Cameron O-84 balloon	Reggiana Riduttori SRL/Italy	
G-BWLP	HOAC Katana DV.20	Flight Academy Scotland Ltd	
G-BWLR	MH.1521M Broussard (185)	Chicory Crops Ltd	
G-BWLS	HOAC Katana DV.20-100	Shadow Aviation/Elstree	
G-BWLY	Rotorway Executive 90	P. W. & I. P. Bewley	
G-BWLZ	Wombat gyroplane	M. R. Harrisson	
G-BWMA	Colt 105A balloon	L. Lacroix/France	
G-BWMB	Jodel D.119	C. Hughes	
G-BWMC	Cessna 182P	Eggesford Eagles Flying Group	
G-BWMF	Gloster Meteor T.7 (WA591)	Meteor Flight (Yatesbury)	
G-BWMH	Lindstrand LBL-77B balloon	J. W. Hole	
G-BWMI	PA-28RT-201T Turbo Arrow IV	O. Cowley	
G-BWMJ	Nieuport 17/2B (replica) (N1977:8)	R. Gauld-Galliers & L. J. Day/Popham	
G-BWMK	DH.82A Tiger Moth (T8191)	APB Leasing Ltd/Welshpool	
G-BWML	Cameron A-275 balloon	A. J. Street	
G-BWMN	Rans S.7 Courier	G. J. Knee	
G-BWMO	Oldfield Baby Lakes	D. Maddocks (G-CIII)	
G-BWMS	DH.82A Tiger Moth	Foundation Early Birds/Netherlands	
G-BWMU	Cameron 105 Monster Truck SS balloon	Magical Adventures Ltd/Canada	
G-BWMV	Colt AS-105 Mk II airship	D. Stuber/Germany	
G-BWMX	DHC.1 Chipmunk 22 (WG407:67)	407th Flying Group	
G-BWMY	Cameron Bradford & Bingley SS balloon	Magical Adventures Ltd/USA	
G-BWNB	Cessna 152 II	Galair International Ltd	
G-BWNC	Cessna 152 II	Galair International Ltd	
G-BWND	Cessna 152 II	Galair International Ltd & G. Davies	
G-BWNI	PA-24 Comanche 180	W. A. Stewart	
G-BWNJ	Hughes 269C	L. R. Fenwick	
G-BWNK	D,H,C,1 Chipmunk 22 (WD390)	B. Whitworth	
G-BWNM	PA-28R Cherokee Arrow 180	M. & R. C. Ramnial	
G-BWNO	Cameron O-90 balloon	T. Knight	
G-BWNP	Cameron 90 Club SS balloon	C. J. Davies & P. Spellward	
G-BWNS	Cameron O-90 balloon	Smithair Ltd	
G-BWNT	DHC.1 Chipmunk 22 (WP901)	P. G. D. Bell & A. Stafford	
G-BWNU	PA-38-112 Tomahawk	Kemble Aero Club Ltd	
G-BWNY	Aeromot AMT-200 Super Ximango	A. E. Mayhew	
G-BWNZ	Agusta A109C	Anglo Beef Processors Ltd	
G-BWOA	Sky 105-24 balloon	Akhter Group PLC	
G-BWOB	Luscombe 8F Silvaire	P. J. Tanulak & H. T. Law	
G-BWOD	Yakovlev Yak-52 (139 yellow)	Insurefast Ltd/Sywell	
G-BWOF	P.84 Jet Provost T.5	Techair London Ltd	
G-BWOH	PA-28-161 Cadet	Abraxas Aviation Ltd	

G-BWOI – G-BWUV
BRITISH CIVIL REGISTRATIONS

Notes	Reg	Type	Owner or Operator
	G-BWOI	PA-28-161 Cadet	Aviation Rentals
	G-BWOJ	PA-28-161 Cadet	Aviation Rentals
	G-BWON	Shaw Europa	H. J. Fish
	G-BWOR	PA-18 Super Cub 135	C. D. Baird
	G-BWOT	P.84 Jet Provost T.3A (XN459)	Red Pelicans Ltd/North Weald
	G-BWOU	Hawker Hunter F.58A (XF303)	Classic Aviation Ltd
	G-BWOV	Enstrom F-28A	P. A. Goss
	G-BWOW	Cameron N-105 balloon	Skybus Ballooning
	G-BWOX	DHC.1 Chipmunk 22 (WP844)	J. St. Clair-Quentin
	G-BWOY	Sky 31-24 balloon	C. Wolstenholme
	G-BWOZ	CFM Streak Shadow SA	J. A. Lord
	G-BWPB	Cameron V-77 balloon	Fair Weather Friends Ballooning Co
	G-BWPC	Cameron V-77 balloon	H. Vaughan
	G-BWPE	Murphy Renegade Spirit UK	J. Hatswell/France
	G-BWPF	Sky 120-24 balloon	Zebedee Balloon Service Ltd
	G-BWPH	PA-28-181 Archer II	E. & H. Merkado
	G-BWPJ	Steen Skybolt	D. Houghton
	G-BWPP	Sky 105-24 balloon	The Sarnia Balloon Group
	G-BWPS	CFM Streak Shadow SA	P. J. Mogg
	G-BWPT	Cameron N-90 balloon	G. Everett
	G-BWPX	BN-2T-4S Defender 4000	Britten-Norman Aircraft Ltd
	G-BWPZ	Cameron N-105 balloon	D. M. Moffat
	G-BWRA	Sopwith LC-1T Triplane (replica) (N500)	S. M. Truscott & J. M. Hoblyn (G-PENY)
	G-BWRC	Light Aero Avid Speedwing	M. J. E. Walsh
	G-BWRM	Colt 105A balloon	N. Charbonnier/Italy
	G-BWRO	Shaw Europa	G-BWRO Group
	G-BWRR	Cessna 182Q	D. Ridley
	G-BWRS	SNCAN Stampe SV.4C	G. P. J. M. Valvekens/Belgium
	G-BWRT	Cameron 60 Concept balloon	W. R. Teasdale
	G-BWRY	Cameron N-105 balloon	G. Aimo/Italy
	G-BWRZ	Lindstrand LBL-105A balloon	D. J. Palmer
	G-BWSB	Lindstrand LBL-105A balloon	R. Calvert-Fisher
	G-BWSC	PA-38-112 Tomahawk II	J. Hornby
	G-BWSD	Campbell Cricket	R. F. G. Moyle
	G-BWSG	P.84 Jet Provost T.5 (XW324/K)	R. M. Kay
	G-BWSH	P.84 Jet Provost T.3A (XN498)	Global Aviation Ltd/Binbrook
	G-BWSI	K & S SA.102.5 Cavalier	B. W. Shaw
	G-BWSJ	Denney Kitfox Mk 3	J. M. Miller
	G-BWSL	Sky 77-24 balloon	D. Baggley
	G-BWSN	Denney Kitfox Mk 3	M. J. Laundy
	G-BWSO	Cameron 90 Apple SS balloon	Flying Pictures Ltd
	G-BWSP	Cameron 80 Carrots SS balloon	Flying Pictures Ltd
	G-BWST	Sky 200-24 balloon	S. A. Townley
	G-BWSU	Cameron N-105 balloon	A. M. Marten
	G-BWSV	Yakovlev Yak-52	M. W. Fitch
	G-BWSZ	Montgomerie-Bensen B.8MR	D. Cawkwell
	G-BWTA	HOAC Katana DV.20	Plane Talking Ltd
	G-BWTB	Lindstrand LBL-105A balloon	Servatruc Ltd
	G-BWTC	Zlin Z.242L	P. Shaw
	G-BWTD	Zlin Z.242L	Oxford Aviation Services Ltd/Kidlington
	G-BWTE	Cameron O-140 balloon	R. J. & A. J. Mansfield
	G-BWTG	DHC.1 Chipmunk 22 (WB671:910)	Chipmunk 4 Ever/Netherlands
	G-BWTH	Robinson R22 Beta	Helicopter Services
	G-BWTJ	Cameron V-77 balloon	A. J. Montgomery
	G-BWTK	RAF 2000 GTX-SE gyroplane	M. Love
	G-BWTN	Lindstrand LBL-90A balloon	Clarks Drainage Ltd
	G-BWTO	DHC.1 Chipmunk 22 (WP984)	Skycraft Services Ltd
	G-BWTR	Slingsby T.61F Venture T.2	P. R. Williams
	G-BWTW	Mooney M.20C	A. P. Daines
	G-BWUA	Campbell Cricket	N. J. Orchard
	G-BWUB	PA-18S Super Cub 135	Caledonian Seaplanes Ltd/Cumbernauld
	G-BWUE	Hispano HA.1112M1L	Spitfire Ltd/Duxford (G-AWHK)
	G-BWUH	PA-28-181 Archer III	G-BWUH Flying Group/Cambridge
	G-BWUJ	Rotorway Executive 162F	Southern Helicopters Ltd
	G-BWUK	Sky 160-24 balloon	Cameron Flights Southern Ltd
	G-BWUL	Noorduyn AT-16 Harvard IIB	M. Scaglia/Italy
	G-BWUM	Sky 105-24 balloon	P. Stern & F. Kirchberger/Germany
	G-BWUN	DHC.1 Chipmunk 22 (WD310)	T. Henderson
	G-BWUP	Shaw Europa	G. W. Grant
	G-BWUS	Sky 65-24 balloon	N. A. P. Bates
	G-BWUT	DHC.1 Chipmunk 22 (WZ879)	Aero Vintage Ltd
	G-BWUU	Cameron N-90 balloon	Bailey Balloons Ltd
	G-BWUV	DHC.1 Chipmunk 22A (WK640)	P. Ray

BRITISH CIVIL REGISTRATIONS — G-BWUZ – G-BWZG

Reg	Type	Owner or Operator	Notes
G-BWUZ	Campbell Cricket (replica)	K. A. Touhey	
G-BWVB	Pietenpol Air Camper	D. Platt	
G-BWVC	Jodel D.18	R. W. J. Cripps	
G-BWVH	Robinson R44 Astro	Heli Air Ltd	
G-BWVI	Stern ST.80	I. M. Godfrey-Davies	
G-BWVM	Colt AA-1050 balloon	B. B. Baxter Ltd	
G-BWVN	Whittaker MW7	L. C. Coyne	
G-BWVP	Sky 16-24 balloon	JK (England) Ltd	
G-BWVR	Yakovlev Yak-52 (52 yellow)	I. Parkinson	
G-BWVS	Shaw Europa	D. R. Bishop	
G-BWVT	DHA.82A Tiger Moth	R. Jewitt	
G-BWVU	Cameron O-90 balloon	J. Atkinson	
G-BWVV	Jodel D.18	D. S. Howarth	
G-BWVY	DHC.1 Chipmunk 22 (WP896)	P. W. Portelli	
G-BWVZ	DHC.1 Chipmunk 22A (WK590)	D. Campion/Belgium	
G-BWWA	Ultravia Pelican Club GS	J. S. Aplin	
G-BWWB	Shaw Europa	S. M. O'Reilly	
G-BWWC	DH.104 Dove 7 (XM223)	Air Atlantique Ltd/Coventry	
G-BWWE	Lindstrand LBL-90A balloon	B. J. Newman	
G-BWWF	Cessna 185A	S. M. C. Harvey	
G-BWWG	SOCATA Rallye 235E	J. J. Frew	
G-BWWI	AS.332L Super Puma	Bristow Helicopters Ltd	
G-BWWK	Hawker Nimrod I (S1581)	Patina Ltd/Duxford	
G-BWWL	Colt Flying Egg SS balloon	Magical Adventures Ltd/USA	
G-BWWN	Isaacs Fury II (K8303:D)	F. J. Ball	
G-BWWP	Rans S.6-116 Coyote II	P. Lewis	
G-BWWT	Dornier 328-100	Scot Airways Ltd	
G-BWWU	PA-22 Tri-Pacer 150	K. M. Bowen	
G-BWWW	BAe Jetstream 3102	British Aerospace PLC/Warton	
G-BWWX	Yakovlev Yak-50	J. L. Pfundt/Netherlands	
G-BWWY	Lindstrand LBL-105A balloon	M. J. Smith	
G-BWWZ	Denney Kitfox Mk 3	A. I. Eskander	
G-BWXA	Slingsby T.67M Firefly 260	Babcock Defence Services/Barkston Heath	
G-BWXB	Slingsby T.67M Firefly 260	Babcock Defence Services/Barkston Heath	
G-BWXC	Slingsby T.67M Firefly 260	Babcock Defence Services/Barkston Heath	
G-BWXD	Slingsby T.67M Firefly 260	Babcock Defence Services/Barkston Heath	
G-BWXE	Slingsby T.67M Firefly 260	Babcock Defence Services/Barkston Heath	
G-BWXF	Slingsby T.67M Firefly 260	Babcock Defence Services/Barkston Heath	
G-BWXG	Slingsby T.67M Firefly 260	Babcock Defence Services/Barkston Heath	
G-BWXH	Slingsby T.67M Firefly 260	Babcock Defence Services/Barkston Heath	
G-BWXI	Slingsby T.67M Firefly 260	Babcock Defence Services/Barkston Heath	
G-BWXJ	Slingsby T.67M Firefly 260	Babcock Defence Services/Barkston Heath	
G-BWXK	Slingsby T.67M Firefly 260	Babcock Defence Services/Barkston Heath	
G-BWXL	Slingsby T.67M Firefly 260	Babcock Defence Services/Barkston Heath	
G-BWXM	Slingsby T.67M Firefly 260	Babcock Defence Services/Barkston Heath	
G-BWXN	Slingsby T.67M Firefly 260	Babcock Defence Services/Barkston Heath	
G-BWXO	Slingsby T.67M Firefly 260	Babcock Defence Services/Barkston Heath	
G-BWXP	Slingsby T.67M Firefly 260	D. S. McGregor	
G-BWXR	Slingsby T.67M Firefly 260	Babcock Defence Services/Barkston Heath	
G-BWXS	Slingsby T.67M Firefly 260	Babcock Defence Services/Barkston Heath	
G-BWXT	Slingsby T.67M Firefly 260	Babcock Defence Services/Barkston Heath	
G-BWXU	Slingsby T.67M Firefly 260	Babcock Defence Services/Barkston Heath	
G-BWXV	Slingsby T.67M Firefly 260	Babcock Defence Services/Barkston Heath	
G-BWXW	Slingsby T.67M Firefly 260	Babcock Defence Services/Barkston Heath	
G-BWXX	Slingsby T.67M Firefly 260	Babcock Defence Services/Barkston Heath	
G-BWXY	Slingsby T.67M Firefly 260	Babcock Defence Services/Barkston Heath	
G-BWXZ	Slingsby T.67M Firefly 260	Babcock Defence Services/Barkston Heath	
G-BWYB	PA-28 Cherokee 160	I. M. Latiff	
G-BWYD	Shaw Europa	F. H. Mycroft	
G-BWYE	Cessna 310R II	ACS Contracts Ltd	
G-BWYG	Cessna 310R II	Kissair Aviation	
G-BWYH	Cessna 310R II	Aircraft Engineers Ltd	
G-BWYI	Denney Kitfox Mk3	J. Adamson	
G-BWYK	Yakovlev Yak-50	Foley Farm Flying Group	
G-BWYM	HOAC Katana DV.20	Plane Talking Ltd/Elstree	
G-BWYN	Cameron O-77 balloon	W. H. Morgan (G-ODER)	
G-BWYO	Sequoia F.8L Falco	N. G. Abbott & J. Copeland	
G-BWYP	Sky 56-24 balloon	Sky High Leisure	
G-BWYR	Rans S.6-116 Coyote II	E. A. Pearson	
G-BWYS	Cameron O-120 balloon	Aire Valley Balloons	
G-BWYU	Sky 120-24 balloon	D. J. Tofton	
G-BWZA	Shaw Europa	T. G. Cowlishaw	
G-BWZG	Robin R.2160	Sherburn Aero Club Ltd	

G-BWZJ – G-BXEB BRITISH CIVIL REGISTRATIONS

Notes	Reg	Type	Owner or Operator
	G-BWZJ	Cameron A-250 balloon	Balloon Club of Great Britain
	G-BWZK	Cameron A-210 balloon	Balloon Club of Great Britain
	G-BWZU	Lindstrand LBL-90B balloon	K. D. Pierce
	G-BWZX	AS.332L Super Puma	Bristow Helicopters Ltd
	G-BWZY	Hughes 269A	Reeve Newfields Ltd (G-FSDT)
	G-BXAB	PA-28-161 Warrior II	TG Aviation Ltd (G-BTGK)
	G-BXAC	RAF 2000 GTX-SE gyroplane	J. A. Robinson
	G-BXAD	Thunder Ax11-225 S2 balloon	M. W. White
	G-BXAF	Pitts S-1D Special	N. J. Watson
	G-BXAH	CP.301A Emeraude	A. P. Goodwin
	G-BXAJ	Lindstrand LBL-14A balloon	Oscair Project AB/Sweden
	G-BXAK	Yakovlev Yak-52 (44 black)	D. P. Holland
	G-BXAL	Cameron 90 Bertie Bassett SS balloon	Trebor Bassett Ltd
	G-BXAM	Cameron N-90 balloon	Trebor Bassett Ltd
	G-BXAN	Scheibe SF-25C Falke	C. Falke Syndicate/Winthorpe
	G-BXAO	Avtech Jabiru SK	P. J. Thompson
	G-BXAR	Avro RJ100	British Airways Connect
	G-BXAS	Avro RJ100	British Airways Connect
	G-BXAU	Pitts S-1 Special	P. Tomlinson
	G-BXAV	Yakovlev Yak-52	RA 293 Group Ltd
	G-BXAX	Cameron N-77 balloon ★	Balloon Preservation Group
	G-BXAY	Bell 206B JetRanger 3	Viewdart Ltd
	G-BXBA	Cameron A-210 balloon	Reach For The Sky Ltd
	G-BXBB	PA-20 Pacer 150	M. E. R. Coghlan
	G-BXBC	EA.1 Kingfisher amphibian	S. Bichan
	G-BXBG	Cameron A-275 balloon	M. L. Gabb
	G-BXBI	P.84 Jet Provost T.3A (XN510:40)	Global Aviation Ltd/Binbrook
	G-BXBK	Avions Mudry CAP-10B	S. Skipworth
	G-BXBL	Lindstrand LBL-240A balloon	Firefly Balloon Promotions
	G-BXBM	Cameron O-105 balloon	Bristol University Hot Air Ballooning Society
	G-BXBP	Denney Kitfox	G. S. Adams
	G-BXBR	Cameron A-120 balloon	M. G. Barlow
	G-BXBU	Avions Mudry CAP-10B	J. F. Cosgrave & H. R. Pearson
	G-BXBY	Cameron A-105 balloon	S. P. Watkins
	G-BXBZ	PZL-104 Wilga 80	Bravo Zulu Group
	G-BXCA	Hapi Cygnet SF-2A	G. E. Collard
	G-BXCC	PA-28-201T Turbo Dakota	Greer Aviation Ltd
	G-BXCD	TEAM mini-MAX 91A	R. Davies
	G-BXCG	Jodel DR.250/160	CG Group
	G-BXCH	Shaw Europa	D. M. Stevens/Enstone
	G-BXCJ	Campbell Cricket (replica)	F. Knowles
	G-BXCL	Montgomerie-Bensen B.8MR	M. L. L. Temple
	G-BXCM	Lindstrand LBL-150A balloon	Aerosaurus Balloons Ltd
	G-BXCN	Sky 105-24 balloon	Nottingham Hot-Air Balloon Club
	G-BXCO	Colt 120A balloon	T. G. Church
	G-BXCP	DHC.1 Chipmunk 22 (WP859)	Propshop Ltd/Duxford
	G-BXCT	DHC.1 Chipmunk 22 (WB697)	Wickenby Aviation
	G-BXCU	Rans S.6-116 Coyote II	R. S. Gent
	G-BXCV	DHC.1 Chipmunk 22 (WP929)	Ocean Flight Holdings Ltd/Hong Kong
	G-BXCW	Denney Kitfox Mk 3	M. J. Blanchard
	G-BXDA	DHC.1 Chipmunk 22 (WP860)	S. R. Cleary & D. Mowat
	G-BXDB	Cessna U.206F	D. A. Howard (G-BMNZ)
	G-BXDD	RAF 2000GTX-SE gyroplane	A. Wane
	G-BXDE	RAF 2000GTX-SE gyroplane	A. McRedie
	G-BXDF	Beech 95-B55 Baron	Chesh-Air Ltd
	G-BXDG	DHC.1 Chipmunk 22 (WK630)	Felthorpe Flying Group
	G-BXDH	DHC.1 Chipmunk 22 (WD331)	Victory Workware Ltd
	G-BXDI	DHC.1 Chipmunk 22 (WD373)	Propshop Ltd/Duxford
	G-BXDM	DHC.1 Chipmunk 22 (WP840)	RAF Halton Aeroplane Club Ltd
	G-BXDN	DHC.1 Chipmunk 22 (WK609)	W. D. Lowe & L. A. Edwards
	G-BXDO	Rutan Cozy	D. G. Foreman/Lydd
	G-BXDP	DHC.1 Chupmunk 22 (WK642)	T. A. McBennett & J. Kelly
	G-BXDR	Lindstrand LBL-77A balloon	British Telecommunications PLC
	G-BXDS	Bell 206B JetRanger 3	Sterling Helicopters Ltd (G-OVBJ)
	G-BXDT	Robin HR.200/120B	Multiflight Ltd/Leeds-Bradford
	G-BXDU	Aero Designs Pulsar	M. P. Board
	G-BXDV	Sky 105-24 balloon	Loughborough Students Union Hot Air Balloon Club
	G-BXDY	Shaw Europa	D. G. & S. Watts
	G-BXDZ	Lindstrand LBL-105A balloon	D. J. & A. D. Sutcliffe
	G-BXEA	RAF 2000 GTX-SE gyroplane	R. Firth
	G-BXEB	RAF 2000 GTX-SE gyroplane	Penny Hydraulics Ltd

BRITISH CIVIL REGISTRATIONS

G-BXEC – G-BXJM

Reg	Type	Owner or Operator	Notes
G-BXEC	DHC.1 Chipmunk 22 (WK633)	D. S. Hunt/Redhill	
G-BXEJ	VPM M-16 Tandem Trainer	AES Radionic Surveillance Systems	
G-BXEN	Cameron N-105 balloon	G. Aimo/Italy	
G-BXES	P66 Pembroke C.1 (XL954)	Atlantic Air Transport Ltd/Coventry	
G-BXET	PA-38-112 Tomahawk II	Highland Flying School Ltd	
G-BXEX	PA-28-181 Archer II	R. Mayle	
G-BXEY	Colt AS-105GD airship	D. Mayer/Germany	
G-BXEZ	Cessna 182P	Forhawk Ltd	
G-BXFB	Pitts S-1 Special	O. P Sparrow	
G-BXFC	Jodel D.18	B. S. Godbold	
G-BXFD	Enstrom 280C	Buckland Newton Hire Ltd	
G-BXFE	Avions Mudry CAP-10B	Avion Aerobatic Ltd	
G-BXFG	Shaw Europa	A. Rawicz-Szczerbo	
G-BXFI	Hawker Hunter T.7 (WV372)	Fox-One Ltd/Bournemouth	
G-BXFK	CFM Streak Shadow	S. J. M. French & T. I. Gorrell	
G-BXFN	Colt 77A balloon	Blue Sky Ballooning Ltd	
G-BXFU	BAC.167 Strikemaster 83	Global Aviation Ltd/Binbrook	
G-BXFV	BAC.167 Strikemaster 83	Global Aviation Ltd/Binbrook	
G-BXFY	Cameron 90 Bierkrug SS balloon	M. J. Coulter	
G-BXGA	AS.350B2 Ecureuil	PLM Dollar Group Ltd/Inverness	
G-BXGC	Cameron N-105 balloon	Cliveden Ltd	
G-BXGD	Sky 90-24 balloon	Servo & Electronic Sales Ltd	
G-BXGG	Shaw Europa	C. J. H. & P. A. J. Richardson	
G-BXGH	Diamond Katana DA20-A1	Cumbernauld Flying School Ltd	
G-BXGL	DHC.1 Chipmunk 22	Airways Aero Associations Ltd/Booker	
G-BXGM	DHC.1 Chipmunk 22 (WP928:D)	Chipmunk G-BXGM Group	
G-BXGO	DHC.1 Chipmunk 22 (WB654:U)	Trees Group/Booker	
G-BXGP	DHC.1 Chipmunk 22 (WZ882)	Eaglescott Chipmunk Group	
G-BXGS	RAF 2000 gyroplane	C. R. Gordon	
G-BXGT	I.I.I. Sky Arrow 650T	D. & B. D. C. Barnard & J. S. C. Goodale	
G-BXGV	Cessna 172R	Skyhawk Group	
G-BXGW	Robin HR.200/120B	Multiflight Ltd/Leeds-Bradford	
G-BXGX	DHC.1 Chipmunk 22 (WK586:V)	Interflight (Air Charter) Ltd	
G-BXGY	Cameron V-65 balloon	Dante Balloon Group	
G-BXGZ	Stemme S.10V	D. Tucker & K. Lloyd	
G-BXHA	DHC.1 Chipmunk 22 (WP925)	F. A. de Munck & C. S. Huijers/Netherlands	
G-BXHD	Beech 76 Duchess	Plane Talking Ltd/Elstree	
G-BXHE	Lindstrand LBL-105A balloon	L. H. Ellis	
G-BXHF	DHC.1 Chipmunk 22 (WP930:J)	Hotel Fox Syndicate/Redhill	
G-BXHH	AA-5A Cheetah	Oaklands Flying/Biggin Hill	
G-BXHJ	Hapi Cygnet SF-2A	I. J. Smith	
G-BXHL	Sky 77-24 balloon	R. K. Gyselynck	
G-BXHN	Lindstrand Pop Can SS balloon	Ornithological Desires Balloon Group	
G-BXHO	Lindstrand Telewest Sphere SS balloon	Magical Adventures Ltd	
G-BXHR	Stemme S.10V	J. H. Rutherford	
G-BXHT	Bushby-Long Midget Mustang	P. P. Chapman	
G-BXHU	Campbell Cricket Mk 6	P. J. Began	
G-BXHY	Shaw Europa	Jupiter Flying Group	
G-BXIA	DHC.1 Chipmunk 22 (WB615)	Dales Aviation/Blackpool	
G-BXIC	Cameron A-275 balloon	Aerosaurus Balloons LLP	
G-BXID	Yakovlev Yak-52	E. S. Ewen	
G-BXIE	Colt 77B balloon	R. M. Horn	
G-BXIF	PA-28-161 Warrior II	Piper Flight Ltd	
G-BXIG	Zenair CH.701 STOL	A. J. Perry	
G-BXIH	Sky 200-24 balloon	Kent Ballooning	
G-BXII	Shaw Europa	D. A. McFadyean	
G-BXIJ	Shaw Europa	R. James	
G-BXIM	DHC.1 Chipmunk 22 (WK512)	A. B. Ashcroft & P. R. Joshua	
G-BXIO	Jodel DR.1050M	D. N. K. & M. A. Symon	
G-BXIT	Zebedee V-31 balloon	Zebedee Balloon Service Ltd	
G-BXIW	Sky 105-24 balloon	Idea Balloon SAS/Italy	
G-BXIX	VPM M-16 Tandem Trainer	D. Beevers	
G-BXIY	Blake Bluetit (BAPC37)	J. Bryant	
G-BXIZ	Lindstrand LBL-31A balloon	Balloon Preservation Flying Group	
G-BXJA	Cessna 402B	Lydford Farley Ltd	
G-BXJB	Yakovlev Yak-52	A. M. Playford & ptnrs	
G-BXJC	Cameron A-210 balloon	British School of Ballooning	
G-BXJD	PA-28 Cherokee 180C	M. A. Powell	
G-BXJG	Lindstrand LBL-105B balloon	C. E. Wood	
G-BXJH	Cameron N-42 balloon	B. Conway	
G-BXJI	Tri-R Kis	R. M. Wakeford	
G-BXJJ	PA-28-161 Cadet	Aviation Rentals/Bournmouth (G-GFCC)	
G-BXJM	Cessna 152	I. R. Chaplin	

111

G-BXJO – G-BXPP — BRITISH CIVIL REGISTRATIONS

Notes	Reg	Type	Owner or Operator
	G-BXJO	Cameron O-90 balloon	Dragon Balloon Co Ltd
	G-BXJP	Cameron C-80 balloon	AR. Cobaleno Pasta Fresca SRL/Italy
	G-BXJS	Schempp-Hirth Janus CM	Janus Syndicate
	G-BXJT	Sky 90-24 balloon	J. G. O'Connell
	G-BXJV	Diamond Katana DA20-A1	M. Dorrian
	G-BXJW	Diamond Katana DA20-A1	Enniskillen Flying School Ltd
	G-BXJY	Van's RV-6	D. J. Sharland
	G-BXJZ	Cameron C-60 balloon	R. S. Mohr
	G-BXKA	Airbus A.320-214	Thomas Cook Airlines Ltd
	G-BXKB	Airbus A.320-214	Thomas Cook Airlines Ltd
	G-BXKC	Airbus A.320-214	Thomas Cook Airlines Ltd
	G-BXKD	Airbus A.320-214	Thomas Cook Airlines Ltd
	G-BXKF	Hawker Hunter T.7(XL577/V)	R. F. Harvey
	G-BXKH	Colt 90 Sparkasse Box SS balloon	Westfalisch-Lippischer Sparkasse und Giroverband/Germany
	G-BXKL	Bell 206B JetRanger 3	Swattons Aviation Ltd
	G-BXKM	RAF 2000 GTX-SE gyroplane	J. R. Huggins
	G-BXKO	Sky 65-24 balloon	J-M. Reck/France
	G-BXKU	Colt AS-120 Mk II airship	D. C. Chipping/Portugal
	G-BXKW	Slingsby T.67M Firefly 200	N. A. Watling
	G-BXKX	Auster V	J. A. Clark
	G-BXLC	Sky 120-24 balloon	Dragon Balloon Co Ltd
	G-BXLF	Lindstrand LBL-90A balloon	W. Rousell & J. Tyrrell
	G-BXLG	Cameron C-80 balloon	S. M. Anthony
	G-BXLK	Shaw Europa	R. G. Fairall
	G-BXLN	Fournier RF-4D	P. W. Cooper
	G-BXLO	P84 Jet Provost T.4 (XR673/L)	S. J. Davies & S. Eagle
	G-BXLP	Sky 90-24 balloon	G. B. Lescott
	G-BXLR	PZL-110 Koliber 160A	Sligo Koliber Group
	G-BXLS	PZL-110 Koliber 160A	D. C. Bayes
	G-BXLT	SOCATA TB200 Tobago XL	R. M. Shears/Blackbushe
	G-BXLW	Enstrom F-28F	I. Martin
	G-BXLY	PA-28-151 Warrior	Multiflight Ltd (G-WATZ)
	G-BXMF	Cassutt Racer IIIM	P. R. Fabish
	G-BXMG	RAF 2000 GTX gyroplane	J. S. Wright
	G-BXMH	Beech 76 Duchess	Plane Talking Ltd/Elstree
	G-BXML	Mooney M.20A	G. Kay
	G-BXMM	Cameron A-180 balloon	B. Conway
	G-BXMV	Scheibe SF.25C Falke 1700	Falcon Flying Group/Shrivenham
	G-BXMX	Currie Wot	M. J. Hayman
	G-BXMY	Hughes 269C	Oxford Aviation Services Ltd/Kidlington
	G-BXMZ	Diamond Katana DA20-A1	Flight Academy Scotland Ltd
	G-BXNA	Light Aero Avid Flyer	G. Haynes
	G-BXNC	Shaw Europa	J. K. Cantwell
	G-BXNG	Beech 58 Baron	Bonanza Flying Club Ltd
	G-BXNN	DHC.1 Chipmunk 22 (WP983:B)	J. N. Robinson
	G-BXNS	Bell 206B JetRanger 3	Sterling Helicopters Ltd/Norwich
	G-BXNT	Bell 206B JetRanger 3	Sterling Helicopters Ltd/Norwich
	G-BXNV	Colt AS-105GD airship	The Sleeping Society/Belgium
	G-BXNX	Lindstrand LBL-210A balloon	Balloon School (International) Ltd
	G-BXOA	Robinson R22 Beta	MG Group Ltd
	G-BXOC	Evans VP-2	H. J. & E. M. Cox
	G-BXOF	Diamond Katana DA20-A1	Cumbernauld Flying School Ltd
	G-BXOI	Cessna 172R	E. J. Watts
	G-BXOJ	PA-28-161 Warrior III	P. Foster
	G-BXOM	Isaacs Spitfire	J. H. Betton
	G-BXON	Auster AOP.9	C. J. & D. J. Baker
	G-BXOR	Robin HR.200/120B	Multiflight Ltd
	G-BXOS	Cameron A-200 balloon	Airborne Balloon Management
	G-BXOT	Cameron C-70 balloon	Dante Balloon Group
	G-BXOU	CEA DR.360	S. H. & J. A. Lofthouse/Blackpool
	G-BXOW	Colt 105A balloon	M. E. White
	G-BXOX	AA-5A Cheetah	R. L. Carter & P. J. Large
	G-BXOY	QAC Quickie Q.235	C. C. Clapham
	G-BXOZ	PA-28-181 Archer II	Spritetone Ltd
	G-BXPC	Diamond Katana DA20-A1	Cubair Flight Training Ltd/Redhill
	G-BXPD	Diamond Katana DA20-A1	Cubair Flight Training Ltd/Redhill
	G-BXPE	Diamond Katana DA20-A1	Brinkley Aircraft Services Ltd
	G-BXPI	Van's RV-4	Cavendish Aviation Ltd
	G-BXPK	Cameron A-250 balloon	Alba Ballooning Ltd
	G-BXPL	PA-28 Cherokee 140	C. R. Guggenheim
	G-BXPM	Beech 58 Baron	Foyle Flyers Ltd
	G-BXPP	Sky 90-24 balloon	S. J. Farrant

BRITISH CIVIL REGISTRATIONS

G-BXPR – G-BXVL

Reg	Type	Owner or Operator	Notes
G-BXPR	Colt 110 Can SS balloon	FRB Fleishwarenfabrik Rostock-Bramow/Germany	
G-BXPT	Ultramagic H-77 balloon	G. D. O. Bartram/Andorra	
G-BXPY	Robinson R44	G. De Angelis	
G-BXRA	Avions Mudry CAP-10B	B. H. D. H. Frere	
G-BXRB	Avions Mudry CAP-10B	T. T. Duhig	
G-BXRC	Avions Mudry CAP-10B	Group Alpha/Sibson	
G-BXRD	Enstrom 280FX	R. P. Bateman	
G-BXRF	CP.1310-C3 Super Emeraude	D. T. Gethin	
G-BXRG	PA-28-181 Archer II	Alderney Flying Training Ltd	
G-BXRH	Cessna 185A	R. E. M. Holmes	
G-BXRM	Cameron A-210 balloon	Dragon Balloon Co Ltd	
G-BXRO	Cessna U.206G	M. Penny	
G-BXRP	Schweizer 269C	Exmouth Developments Ltd	
G-BXRR	Westland Scout AH.1	BN Helicopters Ltd/Bembridge	
G-BXRS	Westland Scout AH.1	B-N Group Ltd/Bembridge	
G-BXRT	Robin DR.400-180	R. A. Ford	
G-BXRV	Van's RV-4	Cleeve Flying Grouip	
G-BXRY	Bell 206B JetRanger	Corbett Holdings Ltd	
G-BXRZ	Rans S.6-116 Coyote II	J. R. Pearce	
G-BXSC	Cameron C-80 balloon	S. J. Coates	
G-BXSD	Cessna 172R	R. Paston	
G-BXSE	Cessna 172R	MK Aero Support Ltd/Andrewsfield	
G-BXSG	Robinson R22 Beta II	Rivermead Aviation Ltd	
G-BXSH	Glaser-Dirks DG.800B	R. O'Conor	
G-BXSI	Avtech Jabiru SK	Leath Ltd	
G-BXSJ	Cameron C-80 balloon	British School of Ballooning	
G-BXSP	Grob G.109B	Deeside Grob Group	
G-BXSR	Cessna F172N	S. A. Parkes	
G-BXST	PA-25 Pawnee 235C	The Northumbria Gliding Club Ltd	
G-BXSU	TEAM mini-MAX 91A	M. R. Overall (G-MYGL)	
G-BXSV	SNCAN Stampe SV.4C	B. A. Bower	
G-BXSX	Cameron V-77 balloon	D. R. Medcalf	
G-BXSY	Robinson R22 Beta II	N. M. G. Pearson	
G-BXTB	Cessna 152	Haimoss Ltd	
G-BXTD	Shaw Europa	P. R. Anderson	
G-BXTE	Cameron A-275 balloon	Global Ballooning Ltd	
G-BXTF	Cameron N-105 balloon	Flying Pictures Ltd	
G-BXTG	Cameron N-42 balloon	P. M. Watkins & S. M. M. Carden	
G-BXTH	Westland Gazelle HT.1 (XW866)	Flightline Ltd/Southend	
G-BXTI	Pitts S-1S Special	A. B. Treherne-Pollock	
G-BXTJ	Cameron N-77 balloon	Chubb Fire Ltd Chubb	
G-BXTL	Schweizer 269C-1	Oxford Aviation Services Ltd/Kidlington	
G-BXTN	ATR-72-202	Aurigny Air Services Ltd	
G-BXTO	Hindustan HAL-6 Pushpak	S. Slater	
G-BXTP	Diamond Katana DA20-A1	Brinkley Aircraft Services Ltd	
G-BXTS	Diamond Katana DA20-A1	I. M. Armitage	
G-BXTT	AA-5B Tiger	G-BXTT Group	
G-BXTV	Bug helicopter	B. R. Cope	
G-BXTW	PA-28-181 Archer III	Davison Plant Hire	
G-BXTY	PA-28-161 Cadet	Bournemouth Flying Club	
G-BXTZ	PA-28-161 Cadet	Bournemouth Flying Club	
G-BXUA	Campbell Cricket Mk.5	R. N. Bodley	
G-BXUC	Robinson R22 Beta	Rivermead Aviation Ltd/Switzerland	
G-BXUE	Sky 240-24 balloon	Scotair Balloons	
G-BXUF	Agusta-Bell 206B JetRanger 3	SJ Contracting Services Ltd	
G-BXUG	Lindstrand Baby Bel SS balloon	Balloon Preservation Flying Group	
G-BXUH	Lindstrand LBL-31A balloon	Balloon Preservation Flying Groupt	
G-BXUI	Glaser-Dirks DG.800B	J. Le Coyte	
G-BXUM	Shaw Europa	D. Bosomworth	
G-BXUS	Sky 65-24 balloon	PSH Skypower Ltd	
G-BXUU	Cameron V-65 balloon	M. D. Freeston & S. Mitchell	
G-BXUW	Cameron Colt 90A balloon	Zycomm Electronics Ltd	
G-BXUX	Brandli Cherry BX-2	M. F. Fountain	
G-BXUY	Cessna 310Q	Massair Ltd	
G-BXVA	SOCATA TB200 Tobago XL	H. R. Palser/Cardiff-Wales	
G-BXVB	Cessna 152 II	PJC (Leasing) Ltd	
G-BXVD	CFM Streak Shadow SA	R. C. Osler	
G-BXVE	Lindstrand LBL-330A balloon	Adventure Balloon Co Ltd	
G-BXVG	Sky 77-24 balloon	M. Wolf	
G-BXVI	VX.361 Spitfire LF.XVIe (RW386:NG-D)	Historic Flying Ltd	
G-BXVJ	Cameron O-120 balloon	Aerosaurus Balloons Ltd (G-IMAX)	
G-BXVK	Robin HR.200/120B	Northamptonshire School of Flying Ltd/Sywell	
G-BXVL	Sky 180-24 balloon	A. W. Talbott	

G-BXVM – G-BYAD — BRITISH CIVIL REGISTRATIONS

Notes	Reg	Type	Owner or Operator
	G-BXVM	Van's RV-6A	J. C. Lomax
	G-BXVO	Van's RV-6A	P. J. Hynes & M. E. Holden
	G-BXVP	Sky 31-24 balloon	T. Dudman
	G-BXVR	Sky 90-24 balloon	P. Hegarty
	G-BXVS	Brügger MB.2 Colibri	G. T. Snoddon
	G-BXVT	Cameron O-77 balloon	R. P. Wade
	G-BXVU	PA-28-161 Warrior II	London Ashford Airport Ltd
	G-BXVV	Cameron V-90 balloon	Floating Sensations Ltd
	G-BXVW	Colt Piggy Bank SS balloon	G. Binder/Germany
	G-BXVX	Rutan Cozy	G. E. Murray
	G-BXVY	Cessna 152	Stapleford Flying Club Ltd
	G-BXVZ	WSK-PZL Mielec TS-11 Iskra	J.Ziubrzynski
	G-BXWA	Beech 76 Duchess	Plymouth School of Flying Ltd
	G-BXWB	Robin HR.100/200B	W. A. Brunwin
	G-BXWC	Cessna 152	PJC (Leasing) Ltd/Stapleford
	G-BXWG	Sky 120-24 balloon	M. E. White
	G-BXWH	Denney Kitfox Mk.4-1200	B. J. Finch
	G-BXWK	Rans S.6-ESA Coyote II	R. J. Teal
	G-BXWL	Sky 90-24 balloon	D. J. Baggley
	G-BXWO	PA-28-181 Archer II	J. S. Develin & Z. Islam
	G-BXWP	PA-32 Cherokee Six 300	Alliance Aviation/Barton
	G-BXWR	CFM Streak Shadow	M. A. Hayward (G-MZMI)
	G-BXWT	Van's RV-6	R. C. Owen
	G-BXWU	FLS Aerospace Sprint 160	Eurojet Aircraft Leasing 3 Ltd
	G-BXWV	FLS Aerospace Sprint 160	Eurojet Aircraft Leasing 3 Ltd
	G-BXWX	Sky 25-16 balloon	Zebedee Balloon Service Ltd
	G-BXXC	Scheibe SF.25C Falke 1700	K. E. Ballington
	G-BXXD	Cessna 172R	Oxford Aviation Services Ltd/Kidlington
	G-BXXG	Cameron N-105 balloon	Allen Owen Ltd
	G-BXXH	Hatz CB-1	R. D. Shingler
	G-BXXI	Grob G.109B	M. N. Martin
	G-BXXJ	Colt Flying Yacht SS balloon	Magical Adventures Ltd/USA
	G-BXXK	Cessna FR.172N	I. R. Chaplin/Andrewsfield
	G-BXXL	Cameron N-105 balloon	Flying Pictures Ltd
	G-BXXN	Robinson R22 Beta	Helicopter Services/Booker
	G-BXXO	Lindstrand LBL-90B balloon	K. Temple
	G-BXXP	Sky 77-24 balloon	C. J. James
	G-BXXR	Lovegrove AV-8 gyroplane	P. C. Lovegrove
	G-BXXS	Sky 105-24 balloon	Flying Pictures Ltd
	G-BXXT	Beech 76 Duchess	Pridenote Ltd
	G-BXXU	Colt 31A balloon	Sade Balloons Ltd
	G-BXXW	Enstrom F-28F	Eastern Atlantic Helicopters Ltd (G-SCOX)
	G-BXYC	Schweizer 269C	Sycamore Aviation
	G-BXYD	Eurocopter EC 120B	Aero Maintenance Ltd
	G-BXYE	CP.301-C1 Emeraude	D. T. Gethin
	G-BXYF	Colt AS-105 GD airship	LN Flying Ltd
	G-BXYG	Cessna 310D	Equitus SARL/France
	G-BXYH	Cameron N-105 balloon	N. J. Langley
	G-BXYI	Cameron H-34 balloon	D. J. Groombridge
	G-BXYJ	Jodel DR.1050	G-BXYJ Group
	G-BXYK	Robinson R22 Beta	D. N. Whittlestone
	G-BXYM	PA-28 Cherokee 235	Redfly Aviation Ltd/Shoreham
	G-BXYO	PA-28RT-201 Arrow IV	Airways Flight Training (Exeter) Ltd
	G-BXYP	PA-28RT-201 Arrow IV	G. I. Cooper
	G-BXYR	PA-28RT-201 Arrow IV	A. Dayani
	G-BXYT	PA-28RT-201 Arrow IV	Checkflight Ltd
	G-BXYX	Van's RV-6A	A. G. Palmer
	G-BXZA	PA-38-112 Tomahawk	P. D. Brooks/Inverness
	G-BXZB	Nanchang CJ-6A (2632019)	Wingglider Ltd/Hibaldstow
	G-BXZF	Lindstrand LBL-90A balloon	R. G. Carrell
	G-BXZI	Lindstrand LBL-90A balloon	J. A. Viner
	G-BXZK	MDH MD-900 Explorer	Dorset Police Air Support Unit
	G-BXZM	Cessna 182S	AB Integro Aviation Ltd
	G-BXZO	Pietenpol Air Camper	P. J. Cooke
	G-BXZS	Sikorsky S-76A (modified)	Bristow Helicopters Ltd
	G-BXZT	MS.880B Rallye Club	Limerick Flying Club (Coonagh) Ltd
	G-BXZU	Micro Aviation Bantam B.22-S	M. E. Whapham & R. W. Hollamby
	G-BXZY	CFM Streak Shadow Srs DD	Cloudbase Aviation Services Ltd
	G-BXZZ	Sky 160-24 balloon	Skybus Ballooning
	G-BYAA	Boeing 767-204ER	Thomsonfly Ltd
	G-BYAB	Boeing 767-204ER	Thomsonfly Ltd
	G-BYAD	Boeing 757-204ER	Thomsonfly Ltd

BRITISH CIVIL REGISTRATIONS

G-BYAE – G-BYEC

Reg	Type	Owner or Operator	Notes
G-BYAE	Boeing 757-204ER	Thomsonfly Ltd	
G-BYAF	Boeing 757-204ER	Thomsonfly Ltd	
G-BYAH	Boeing 757-204ER	Thomsonfly Ltd	
G-BYAI	Boeing 757-204ER	Thomsonfly Ltd	
G-BYAJ	Boeing 757-204ER	Thomsonfly Ltd	
G-BYAK	Boeing 757-28AER	Thomsonfly Ltd	
G-BYAL	Boeing 757-28AER	Thomsonfly Ltd	
G-BYAN	Boeing 757-204ER	Thomsonfly Ltd	
G-BYAO	Boeing 757-204ER	Thomsonfly Ltd	
G-BYAP	Boeing 757-204ER	Thomsonfly Ltd	
G-BYAR	Boeing 757-204ER	Thomsonfly Ltd	
G-BYAS	Boeing 757-204ER	Thomsonfly Ltd	
G-BYAT	Boeing 757-204ER	Thomsonfly Ltd	
G-BYAU	Boeing 757-204ER	Thomsonfly Ltd	
G-BYAV	Taylor JT.1 Monoplane	J. S. Marten-Hale	
G-BYAW	Boeing 757-204ER	Thomsonfly Ltd	
G-BYAX	Boeing 757-204ER	Thomsonfly Ltd	
G-BYAY	Boeing 757-204ER	Thomsonfly Ltd	
G-BYAZ	CFM Streak Shadow	A. G. Wright	
G-BYBA	Agusta-Bell 206B JetRanger 3	D. L. & S. M. Dennett (G-BHXV/G-OWJM)	
G-BYBC	Agusta-Bell 206B JetRanger 2	Sky Charter UK Ltd (G-BTWW)	
G-BYBD	Cessna F.172H	D. G. Bell & J. Cartmell (G-OBHX/G-AWMU)	
G-BYBE	Jodel D.120A	P. G. Wiggett & O. Downes	
G-BYBF	Robin R.2160i	D. J. R. Lloyd-Evans	
G-BYBH	PA-34-200T Seneca II	Goldspear (UK) Ltd	
G-BYBI	Bell 206B JetRanger 3	Winkburn Air Ltd	
G-BYBJ	Medway Hybred 44XLR	M. Gardner	
G-BYBK	Murphy Rebel	M. J. Whiteman-Heywood	
G-BYBL	Gardan GY-80 Horizon 160D	R. H. W. Beath	
G-BYBM	Avtech Jabiru SK	P. J. Hatton	
G-BYBN	Cameron N-77 balloon	M. G. & R. D. Howard	
G-BYBO	Medway Hybred 44XLR Eclipser	D. R. Purslow	
G-BYBP	Cessna A.185F	G. M. S. Scott	
G-BYBR	Rans S.6-116 Coyote II	J. B. Robinson/Blackpool	
G-BYBS	Sky 80-16 balloon	G. W. Mortimore	
G-BYBU	Renegade Spirit UK	L. C. Cook	
G-BYBV	Mainair Rapier	M. W. Robson	
G-BYBW	TEAM mini-MAX	D. W. Pearce	
G-BYBX	Slingsby T.67M Firefly 260	Slingsby Aviation Ltd	
G-RYRY	Thorp T.18C Tiger	L. J. Joyce	
G-BYBZ	Jabiru SK	N. P. D. Smith	
G-BYCA	PA-28 Cherokee 140D	A. Reay	
G-BYCB	Sky 21-16 balloon	S. J. Colin	
G-BYCD	Cessna 140 (modified)	G. P. James	
G-BYCE	Robinson R44	Jim Davies Civil Engineering Ltd	
G-BYCF	Robinson R22 Beta II	R. F. McLachlan	
G-BYCJ	CFM Shadow Srs DD	J. Kennedy	
G-BYCL	Raj Hamsa X'Air Jabiru (1)	D. O'Keefe & ptnrs	
G-BYCM	Rans S.6-ES Coyote II	E. W. McMullan	
G-BYCN	Rans S.6-ES Coyote II	T. J. Croskery	
G-BYCP	Beech B200 Super King Air	London Executive Aviation Ltd	
G-BYCS	Jodel DR.1051	M. C. Bennett	
G-BYCT	Aero L-29 Delfin	Propeller BVBA/Belgium	
G-BYCU	Robinson R22 Beta	Tiger Helicopters Ltd (G-OCGJ)	
G-BYCV	Meridian Maverick 430	P. Shackleton	
G-BYCW	Mainair Blade 912	P. C. Watson	
G-BYCX	Westland Wasp HAS.1	BN Helicopters Ltd/Bembridge	
G-BYCY	I.I.I. Sky Arrow 650T	K. A. Daniels	
G-BYCZ	Avtech Jabiru SK	R. Scroby	
G-BYDB	Grob G.115B	J. B. Baker	
G-BYDE	VS.361 Spitfire LF. IX (PT879)	P. A. Teichman	
G-BYDF	Sikorsky S-76A	Brecqhou Development Ltd	
G-BYDG	Beech C24R Sierra	Professional Flight Simulation Ltd/Bournemouth	
G-BYDJ	Colt 120A balloon	D. K. Hempleman-Adams	
G-BYDK	SNCAN Stampe SV.4C	Bianchi Aviation Film Services Ltd/Booker	
G-BYDL	Hawker Hurricane IIB (Z5207)	R. A. Roberts	
G-BYDT	Cameron N-90 balloon	N. J. Langley	
G-BYDU	Cameron Cart SS balloon	N. J. Langley	
G-BYDV	Van's RV-6	B. F. Hill	
G-BYDY	Beech 58 Baron	J. F. Britten	
G-BYDZ	Pegasus Quantum 15-912	P. Newson	
G-BYEA	Cessna 172P	Flacon Flying Services Ltd	
G-BYEC	Glaser-Dirks DG.800B	P. R. Redshaw	

G-BYEE – G-BYIT | BRITISH CIVIL REGISTRATIONS

Notes	Reg	Type	Owner or Operator
	G-BYEE	Mooney M.20K	Double Echo Flying Group
	G-BYEH	CEA Jodel DR.250	Nicholson Decommissioning Ltd
	G-BYEJ	Scheibe SF-28A Tandem Falke	D. Shrimpton
	G-BYEK	Stoddard Hamilton Glastar	G. M. New
	G-BYEL	Van's RV-6	D. Millar
	G-BYEM	Cessna R.182 RG	Wycombe Air Centre Ltd/Booker
	G-BYEO	Zenair CH.601HDS	Cloudbase Flying Group
	G-BYEP	Lindstrand LBL-90B balloon	R. C. Barkworth & D. G. Maguire
	G-BYER	Cameron C-80 balloon	J. M. Langley
	G-BYES	Cessna 172P	Redhill Air Services Ltd
	G-BYET	Cessna 172P	Redhill Air Services Ltd
	G-BYEW	Pegasus Quantum 15-912	D. Martin
	G-BYEX	Sky 120-24 balloon	Ballongflyg Upp & Ner AB/Sweden
	G-BYEY	Lindstrand LBL-21 Silver Dream balloon	Oscair Project Ltd/Sweden
	G-BYEZ	Dyn' Aero MCR-01	J. P. Davies
	G-BYFA	Cessna F.152 II	A. J. Gomes (G-WACA)
	G-BYFC	Avtech Jabiru SK	I. P. Fisher
	G-BYFD	Grob G.115A	Kane Group/Ireland (G-BSGE)
	G-BYFE	Pegasus Quantum 15-912	G-BYFE Syndicate
	G-BYFF	Pegasus Quantum 15-912	Kemble Flying Club
	G-BYFG	Shaw Europa XS	P. R. Brodie
	G-BYFI	CFM Starstreak Shadow SA	D. G. Cook
	G-BYFJ	Cameron N-105 balloon	R. J. Mercer
	G-BYFL	Diamond HK.36 TTS	Seahawk Gliding Club/Culdrose
	G-BYFM	Jodel DR.1050M-1 (replica)	A. J. Roxburgh
	G-BYFR	PA-32R-301 Saratoga II HP	Buckleton Ltd
	G-BYFT	Pietenpol Air Camper	M. W. Elliott
	G-BYFU	Lindstrand LBL-105B balloon	Balloons Lindstrand France
	G-BYFV	TEAM mini-MAX 91	W. E. Gillham
	G-BYFX	Colt 77A balloon	Flying Pictures Ltd
	G-BYFY	Avions Mudry CAP-10B	R. N. Crosland
	G-BYGA	Boeing 747-436	British Airways
	G-BYGB	Boeing 747-436	British Airways
	G-BYGC	Boeing 747-436	British Airways
	G-BYGD	Boeing 747-436	British Airways
	G-BYGE	Boeing 747-436	British Airways
	G-BYGF	Boeing 747-436	British Airways
	G-BYGG	Boeing 747-436	British Airways
	G-BYHC	Cameron Z-90 balloon	S. M. Sherwin
	G-BYHE	Robinson R22 Beta	Kent Aviation Ltd
	G-BYHG	Dornier 328-100	Scot Airways Ltd
	G-BYHH	PA-28-161 Warrior III	Stapleford Flying Club Ltd
	G-BYHI	PA-28-161 Warrior III	Haimoss Ltd
	G-BYHJ	PA-28R-201 Arrow	Bournemouth Flying Club
	G-BYHK	PA-28-181 Archer III	T-Air Services
	G-BYHL	DHC.1 Chipmunk 22 (WG308)	M. R. & I. D. Higgins
	G-BYHM	BAe 125 Srs 800B	Bookajet Operations Ltd
	G-BYHN	Mainair Blade 912	R. Stone
	G-BYHO	Mainair Blade 912	K. Bailey
	G-BYHP	CEA DR.253B	The G-BYHP Group
	G-BYHR	Pegasus Quantum 15-912	I. D. Chantler
	G-BYHS	Mainair Blade 912	T. J. Widdison
	G-BYHT	Robin DR.400/180R	Deeside Robin Group
	G-BYHU	Cameron N-105 balloon	ABC Flights Ltd
	G-BYHV	Raj Hamsa X'Air 582	J. S. Mason
	G-BYHX	Cameron A-250 balloon	Balloon School (International) Ltd
	G-BYHY	Cameron V-77 balloon	P. Spellward
	G-BYIA	Avtech Jabiru SK	Teesside Aviators Group
	G-BYIB	Rans S.6-ES Coyote II	W. Anderson
	G-BYIC	Cessna U.206G	Wild Geese Parachute Club
	G-BYID	Rans S.6-ES Coyote II	J. A. E. Bowen
	G-BYIE	Robinson R22 Beta	Jepar Rotorcraft
	G-BYII	TEAM mini-MAX	J. Edwards
	G-BYIJ	CASA 1.131E Jungmann 2000	P. R. Teager & R. N. Crosland
	G-BYIK	Shaw Europa	P. M. Davis
	G-BYIL	Cameron N-105 balloon	Oakfield Farm Products Ltd
	G-BYIM	Avtech Jabiru UL	S. D. Miller
	G-BYIN	RAF 2000 gyroplane	J. R. Legge
	G-BYIO	Colt 105A balloon	N. Charbonnier/Italy
	G-BYIP	Aerotek Pitts S-2A Special	D. P. Heather-Hayes
	G-BYIR	Aerotek Pitts S-1S Special	Hampshire Aeroplane Co Ltd/St Just
	G-BYIS	Pegasus Quantum 15-912	L. M. Tidman
	G-BYIT	Robin DR.400/500	D. Quirke

116

BRITISH CIVIL REGISTRATIONS

G-BYIU – G-BYMI

Reg	Type	Owner or Operator	Notes
G-BYIU	Cameron V-90 balloon	H. Micketeit/Germany	
G-BYIV	Cameron PM-80 balloon	A. Schneider/Germany	
G-BYIX	Cameron PM-80 balloon	A. Schneider/Germany	
G-BYIY	Lindstrand LBL-105B balloon	J. H. Dobson	
G-BYIZ	Pegasus Quantum 15-912	J. D. Gray	
G-BYJB	Mainair Blade 912	M. Atkinson	
G-BYJC	Cameron N-90 balloon	A. G. Merry	
G-BYJD	Avtech Jabiru UL	M. W. Knights	
G-BYJE	TEAM Mini-MAX 91	A. M. Witt	
G-BYJF	Thorpe T.211	AD Aviation Ltd/Barton	
G-BYJG	Lindstrand LBL-77A balloon	Lindstrand Hot-Air Balloons Ltd	
G-BYJH	Grob G.109B	A. J. Buchanan	
G-BYJI	Shaw Europa	P. S. Jones (G-ODTI)	
G-BYJJ	Cameron C-80 balloon	Proximm Franchising SRL/Italy	
G-BYJK	Pegasus Quantum 15-912	B. S. Smy	
G-BYJL	Aero Designs Pulsar	F. A. H. Ashmead	
G-BYJM	Cyclone AX2000	Caunton AX2000 Syndicate	
G-BYJN	Lindstrand LBL-105A balloon	B. Meeson	
G-BYJO	Rans S.6-ES Coyote II	G. Ferguson	
G-BYJP	Aerotek Pitts S-1S Special	Eaglescott Pitts Group	
G-BYJR	Lindstrand LBL-77B balloon	C. D. Duthy-James	
G-BYJS	SOCATA TB20 Trinidad	Juliet Sierra Group	
G-BYJT	Zenair CH.601HD	J. D. T. Tannock	
G-BYJU	Raj Hamsa X'Air 582	G. P. Morling	
G-BYJW	Cameron 105 Sphere SS balloon	Forbes Global Inc.	
G-BYJX	Cameron C-70 balloon	B. Perona	
G-BYJZ	Lindstrand LBL-105A balloon	M. A. Webb	
G-BYKA	Lindstrand LBL-69A balloon	Aerial Promotions Ltd	
G-BYKB	Rockwell Commander 114	A. Walton	
G-BYKC	Mainair Blade 912	G. J. Wharmby	
G-BYKD	Mainair Blade 912	D. C. Boyle	
G-BYKF	Enstrom F-28F	Battle Helicopters Ltd	
G-BYKG	Pietenpol Air Camper	K. B. Hodge	
G-BYKI	Cameron N-105 balloon	J. A. Leahy/Ireland	
G-BYKJ	Westland Scout AH.1	Austen Associates	
G-BYKK	Robinson R44	Heli Air Ltd	
G-BYKL	PA-28-181 Archer II	Transport Command Ltd	
G-BYKN	PA-28-161 Warrior II	Oxford Aviation Services Ltd/Kidlington	
G-BYKO	PA-28-161 Warrior II	Oxford Aviation Services Ltd/Kidlington	
G-BYKP	PA-28R-201T Turbo Arrow IV	D. W. Knox & D. L. Grimes	
G-BYKR	PA-28-161 Warrior II	Oxford Aviation Services Ltd/Kidlington	
G-RYKS	Leopoldoff L-6 Colibri	I. M. Callier	
G-BYKT	Pegasus Quantum 15-912	D. A. Bannister & N. J. Howarth	
G-BYKU	BFC Challenger II	K. W. Seedhouse	
G-BYKW	Lindstrand LBL-77B balloon	P-J. Fuseau/France	
G-BYKX	Cameron N-90 balloon	G. Davis	
G-BYKZ	Sky 140-24 balloon	D. J. Head	
G-BYLC	Pegasus Quantum 15-912	A. R. Graham	
G-BYLD	Pietenpol Air Camper	S. Bryan	
G-BYLF	Zenair CH.601HDS	G. Waters	
G-BYLH	Robin HR.200/120B	Multiflight Ltd	
G-BYLI	Nova Vertex 22 hang glider	M. Hay	
G-BYLJ	Letov LK-2M Sluka	W. J. McCarroll	
G-BYLL	Sequoia F.8L Falco	N. J. Langrick/Breighton	
G-BYLN	Raj Hamsa X'Air 582	R. Gillespie & S. P. McGirr	
G-BYLO	T.66 Nipper Srs 1	M. J. A. Trudgill	
G-BYLP	Rand-Robinson KR-2	C. S. Hales	
G-BYLR	Cessna 404	Hardy Aviation (NT) Pty.Ltd	
G-BYLS	Bede BD-4	G. H. Bayliss/Shobdon	
G-BYLT	Raj Hamsa X'Air 582	T. W. Phipps & B. G. Simons	
G-BYLV	Thunder Ax8-105 S2 balloon	Wind Line SRL/Italy	
G-BYLW	Lindstrand LBL-77A balloon	Associazione Gran Premio Italiano	
G-BYLX	Lindstrand LBL-105A balloon	Italiana Aeronavi/Italy	
G-BYLY	Cameron V-77 balloon (1)	R. Bayly/Italy (G-ULIA)	
G-BYLZ	Rutan Cozy	E. R. Allen	
G-BYMB	Diamond Katana DA20-C1	Enstone Flying Club	
G-BYMC	PA-38-112 Tomahawk II	Central Aircraft Leasing Ltd	
G-BYMD	PA-38-112 Tomahawk II	Surrey & Kent Flying Club Ltd/Biggin Hill	
G-BYME	Gardan GY-80 Horizon 180	Air Venturas Ltd	
G-BYMF	Pegasus Quantum 15-912	G. R. Stockdale	
G-BYMG	Cameron A-210 balloon	Cloud Nine Balloon Co	
G-BYMH	Cessna 152	PJC (Leasing) Ltd/Stapleford	
G-BYMI	Pegasus Quantum 15	N. C. Grayson	

G-BYMJ – G-BYRH   BRITISH CIVIL REGISTRATIONS

Reg	Type	Owner or Operator
G-BYMJ	Cessna 152	PJC (Leasing) Ltd/Stapleford
G-BYMK	Dornier 328-100	Scot Airways Ltd
G-BYML	Dornier 328-100	Scot Airways Ltd
G-BYMN	Rans S.6-ESA Coyote II	R. L. Barker
G-BYMO	Campbell Cricket	P. G. Rawson
G-BYMP	Campbell Cricket Mk 1	J. J. Fitzgerald
G-BYMR	Raj Hamsa X'Air R100(3)	W. Drury
G-BYMT	Pegasus Quantum 15-912	C. M. Mackinnon
G-BYMU	Rans S.6-ES Coyote II	I. R. Russell & S. Palmer
G-BYMV	Rans S.6-ES Coyote II	G. A. Squires
G-BYMW	Boland 52-12 balloon	C. Jones
G-BYMX	Cameron A-105 balloon	H. Reis/Germany
G-BYMY	Cameron N-90 balloon	A. Cakss
G-BYNA	Cessna F.172H	Heliview Ltd/Blackbushe (G-AWTH)
G-BYND	Pegasus Quantum 15	D. G. Baker
G-BYNE	Pilatus PC-6/B2-H4 Turbo Porter	D. M. Penny
G-BYNF	NA-64 Yale I (3349)	R. S. Van Dijk/Duxford
G-BYNH	Rotorway Executive 162F	R. C. MacKenzie
G-BYNI	Rotorway Exec 90	M. Bunn
G-BYNJ	Cameron N-77 balloon	A. Giovanni/Italy
G-BYNK	Robin HR.200/160	Penguin Flight Group
G-BYNM	Mainair Blade 912	J. P. Hanlon & A. C. McAllister
G-BYNN	Cameron V-90 balloon	M. K. Grigson
G-BYNO	Pegasus Quantum 15-912	R. J. Newsham & G. J. Slater
G-BYNP	Rans S.6-ES Coyote II	R. J. Lines
G-BYNR	Avtech Jabiru UL	M. P. Maughan
G-BYNS	Avtech Jabiru SK	D. K. Lawry
G-BYNT	Raj Hamsa X'Air 582 (1)	A. Evans
G-BYNU	Cameron Thunder Ax7-77 balloon	P. M. Gaines
G-BYNV	Sky 105-24 balloon	Par Rovelli Construzioni SRL/Italy
G-BYNW	Cameron H-34 balloon	I. M. Ashpole
G-BYNX	Cameron RX-105 balloon	Cameron Balloons Ltd
G-BYNY	Beech 76 Duchess	Magenta Ltd/Exeter
G-BYOB	Slingsby T.67M Firefly 260	Stapleford Flying Club Ltd
G-BYOD	Slingsby T.67C	TDR Aviation Ltd
G-BYOG	Pegasus Quantum 15-912	M. D. Hinge
G-BYOH	Raj Hamsa X'Air 582 (1)	P. H. J. Kent
G-BYOI	Sky 80-16 balloon	I. S. & S. W. Watthews
G-BYOJ	Raj Hamsa X'Air 582 (1)	H. M. Owen
G-BYOK	Cameron V-90 balloon	D. S. Wilson
G-BYOM	Sikorsky S-76C (modified)	Starspeed Ltd/Blackbushe (G-IJCB)
G-BYON	Mainair Blade	P. G. Mallon
G-BYOO	CFM Streak Shadow	G. R. Eastwood
G-BYOR	Raj Hamsa X'Air 582 (1)	B. Bisley
G-BYOS	Mainair Blade 912	M. B. Sears
G-BYOT	Rans S.6-ES Coyote II	H. F. Blakeman
G-BYOU	Rans S.6-ES Coyote II	P. G. Bright & P. L. Parker
G-BYOV	Pegasus Quantum 15-912	Microlight Hire Ltd
G-BYOW	Mainair Blade	M. Forsyth
G-BYOX	Cameron Z-90 balloon	D. G. Such
G-BYOZ	Mainair Rapier	M. Morgan
G-BYPA	AS.355F2 Twin Squirrel	P. & J. Carter (G-NWPI)
G-BYPB	Pegasus Quantum 15-912	S. Graham
G-BYPD	Cameron A-105 balloon	Headland Hotel Ltd
G-BYPE	Gardan GY-80 Horizon 160D	H. I. Smith & P. R. Hendry-Smith
G-BYPF	Thruster T.600N	Canary Syndicate
G-BYPG	Thruster T.600N	G-BYPG Syndicate
G-BYPH	Thruster T.600N	D. M. Canham
G-BYPJ	Pegasus Quantum 15-912	M. E. Oakman
G-BYPL	Pegasus Quantum 15-912	I. T. Carlse
G-BYPM	Shaw Europa XS	P. Mileham
G-BYPN	MS.880B Rallye Club	R. & T. C. Edwards
G-BYPO	Raj Hamsa X'Air 582 (1)	D. W. Willis
G-BYPP	Medway Rebel SS	J. L. Gowens
G-BYPR	Zenair CH.601HD Zodiac	Zodiac Flying Group
G-BYPT	Rans S.6-ES Coyote II	M. A. Sims
G-BYPU	PA-32R-301 Saratoga SP	AM Blatch Electrical Contractors Ltd
G-BYPW	Raj Hamsa X'Air 583 (3)	A. D. Worrall & B. J. Ellis
G-BYPY	Ryan ST3KR (001)	T. Curtis-Taylor
G-BYPZ	Rans S.6-116 Super 6	R. A. Blackbourne
G-BYRC	Westland WS-58 Wessex HC.2 (XT671)	D. Brem-Wilson
G-BYRG	Rans S.6-ES Coyote II	S. J. Macmillan
G-BYRH	Medway Hybred 44XLR	G. R. Puffett

BRITISH CIVIL REGISTRATIONS

G-BYRJ – G-BYVB

Reg	Type	Owner or Operator	Notes
G-BYRJ	Pegasus Quantum 15-912	A. L. Brown	
G-BYRK	Cameron V-42 balloon	R. Kunert	
G-BYRO	Mainair Blade	P. W. F. Coleman	
G-BYRP	Mainair Blade 912	J. T. & A. C. Swannick	
G-BYRR	Mainair Blade 912	G. R. Sharples	
G-BYRS	Rans S.6-ES Coyote II	A. E. Turner	
G-BYRU	Pegasus Quantum 15-912	Sarum QTM 912 Group	
G-BYRV	Raj Hamsa X'Air 582 (1)	D. R. Darby	
G-BYRX	Westland Scout AH.1 (XT634)	Historic Helicopters Ltd	
G-BYRY	Slingsby T.67M Firefly 200	T. R. Pearson	
G-BYRZ	Lindstrand LBL-77M balloon	Challenge Transatlantique/France	
G-BYSA	Shaw Europa XS	B. Allsop	
G-BYSE	Agusta-Bell 206B JetRanger 2	Alspath Properties Ltd (G-BFND)	
G-BYSF	Avtech Jabiru UL	M. W. Sayers	
G-BYSG	Robin HR.200/120B	Modi Aviation Ltd	
G-BYSI	WSK-PZL Koliber 160A	J. & D. F. Evans	
G-BYSJ	DHC.1 Chipmunk 22 (WB569:R)	C. H. Green/Kemble	
G-BYSK	Cameron A-275 balloon	Balloon School (International) Ltd	
G-BYSM	Cameron A-210 balloon	Balloon School (International) Ltd	
G-BYSN	Rans S.6-ES Coyote II	A. L. & A. R. Roberts	
G-BYSP	PA-28-181 Archer II	Central Aircraft Leasing Ltd	
G-BYSR	Pegasus Quantum 15-912	A. C. Stuart/Canada	
G-BYSS	Medway Rebel SS	D. W. Allen	
G-BYSV	Cameron N-120 balloon	S. Simmington	
G-BYSW	Enstrom 280FX	D. A. Marks	
G-BYSX	Pegasus Quantum 15-912	RAF Microlight Flying Association (SX)	
G-BYSY	Raj Hamsa X'Air 582 (1)	J. M. Davidson	
G-BYTA	Kolb Twinstar Mk 3 (modified)	L. C. Stockman	
G-BYTB	SOCATA TB20 Trinidad	Mogato Ltd	
G-BYTC	Pegasus Quantum 15-912	R. J. Marriott	
G-BYTE	Robinson R22 Beta	Patriot Aviation Ltd/Cranfield	
G-BYTG	Glaser-Dirks DG.400	P. R. Williams	
G-BYTH	Airbus A320-231	MyTravel Airways Ltd	
G-BYTI	PA-24 Comanche 250	M. Carruthers & G. Auchterlonie	
G-BYTJ	Cameron C-80 balloon	M. White	
G-BYTK	Avtech Jabiru UL	P. J. Reilly	
G-BYTL	Mainair Blade 912	P. B. Spencer	
G-BYTM	Dyn' Aero MCR-01	I. Lang	
G-BYTN	DH.82A Tiger Moth (N6720:VX)	B. D. Hughes	
G-BYTR	Raj Hamsa X'Air 582 (1)	R. Dunn	
G-BYTS	Montgomerie-Bensen B.8MR gyroplane	M. G. Mee	
G-BYTT	Raj Hamsa X'Air 582 (1)	B. P. Nugent/Ireland	
G-BYTU	Mainair Blade 912	K. Roberts	
G-BYTV	Avtech Jabiru UK	A. D. Tomlins	
G-BYTW	Cameron O-90 balloon	Sade Balloons Ltd	
G-BYTZ	Raj Hamsa X'Air 582 (1)	R. Armstrong	
G-BYUA	Grob G.115E Tutor	VT Aerospace Ltd/Wyton	
G-BYUB	Grob G.115E Tutor	VT Aerospace Ltd/Cranwell	
G-BYUC	Grob G.115E Tutor	VT Aerospace Ltd/Cranwell	
G-BYUD	Grob G.115E Tutor	VT Aerospace Ltd/Glasgow	
G-BYUE	Grob G.115E Tutor	VT Aerospace Ltd/Cranwell	
G-BYUF	Grob G.115E Tutor	VT Aerospace Ltd/Cosford	
G-BYUG	Grob G.115E Tutor	VT Aerospace Ltd/Glasgow	
G-BYUH	Grob G.115E Tutor	VT Aerospace Ltd/Colerne	
G-BYUI	Grob G.115E Tutor	VT Aerospace Ltd/Woodvale	
G-BYUJ	Grob G.115E Tutor	VT Aerospace Ltd/Boscombe Down	
G-BYUK	Grob G.115E Tutor	VT Aerospace Ltd/Cosford	
G-BYUL	Grob G.115E Tutor	VT Aersoapce Ltd/Boscombe Down	
G-BYUM	Grob G.115E Tutor	VT Aerospace Ltd/Boscombe Down	
G-BYUN	Grob G.115E Tutor	VT Aerospace Ltd/St Athan	
G-BYUO	Grob G.115E Tutor	VT Aerospace Ltd/Wyton	
G-BYUP	Grob G.115E Tutor	VT Aerospace Ltd/Leuchars	
G-BYUR	Grob G.115E Tutor	VT Aerospace Ltd/Glasgow	
G-BYUS	Grob G.115E Tutor	VT Aerospace Ltd/Wyton	
G-BYUT	Grob G.115E Tutor	VT Aerospace Ltd/St Athan	
G-BYUU	Grob G.115E Tutor	VT Aerospace Ltd/Leuchars	
G-BYUV	Grob G.115E Tutor	VT Aerospace Ltd/Benson	
G-BYUW	Grob G.115E Tutor	VT Aerospace Ltd/Leuchars	
G-BYUX	Grob G.115E Tutor	VT Aerospace Ltd/Woodvale	
G-BYUY	Grob.G.115E Tutor	VT Aerospace Ltd/Leuchars	
G-BYUZ	Grob G.115E Tutor	VT Aerospace Ltd/Woodvale	
G-BYVA	Grob G.115E Tutor	VT Aerospace Ltd/Cranwell	
G-BYVB	Grob G.115E Tutor	VT Aerospace Ltd/Leuchars	

G-BYVC – G-BYYA BRITISH CIVIL REGISTRATIONS

Notes	Reg	Type	Owner or Operator
	G-BYVC	Grob G.115E Tutor	VT Aerospace Ltd/Wyton
	G-BYVD	Grob G.115E Tutor	VT Aerospace Ltd/Wyton
	G-BYVE	Grob G.115E Tutor	VT Aerospace Ltd/Wyton
	G-BYVF	Grob G.115E Tutor	VT Aerospace Ltd/Yeovilton
	G-BYVG	Grob G.115E Tutor	VT Aerospace Ltd/Church Fenton
	G-BYVH	Grob G.115E Tutor	VT Aerospace Ltd/Leuchars
	G-BYVI	Grob G.115E Tutor	VT Aerospace Ltd/Wyton
	G-BYVJ	Grob G.115E Tutor	VT Aerospace Ltd/Church Fenton
	G-BYVK	Grob G.115E Tutor	VT Aerospace Ltd/Yeovilton
	G-BYVL	Grob G.115E Tutor	VT Aerospace Ltd/Benson
	G-BYVM	Grob G.115E Tutor	VT Aerospace Ltd/Glasgow
	G-BYVN	Grob G.115E Tutor	VT Aerospace Ltd/Yeovilton
	G-BYVO	Grob G.115E Tutor	VT Aerospace Ltd/Wyton
	G-BYVP	Grob G.115E Tutor	VT Aerospace Ltd/Cranwell
	G-BYVR	Grob G.115E Tutor	VT Aerospace Ltd/Cranwell
	G-BYVS	Grob G.115E Tutor	VT Aerospace Ltd/Cranwell
	G-BYVT	Grob G.115E Tutor	VT Aerospace Ltd/Wyton
	G-BYVU	Grob G.115E Tutor	VT Aerospace Ltd/Benson
	G-BYVV	Grob G.115E Tutor	VT Aerospace Ltd/Leeming
	G-BYVW	Grob G.115E Tutor	VT Aerospace Ltd/St Athan
	G-BYVX	Grob G.115E Tutor	VT Aerospace Ltd/Church Fenton
	G-BYVY	Grob G.115E Tutor	VT Aerospace Ltd/Cosford
	G-BYVZ	Grob G.115E Tutor	VT Aerospace Ltd/Church Fenton
	G-BYWA	Grob G.115E Tutor	VT Aerospace Ltd/Benson
	G-BYWB	Grob G.115E Tutor	VT Aerospace Ltd/Cranwell
	G-BYWC	Grob G.115E Tutor	VT Aerospace Ltd/Colerne
	G-BYWD	Grob G.115E Tutor	VT Aerospace Ltd/Woodvale
	G-BYWE	Grob G.115E Tutor	VT Aerospace Ltd/Colerne
	G-BYWF	Grob G.115E Tutor	VT Aerospace Ltd/Cranwell
	G-BYWG	Grob G.115E Tutor	VT Aerospace Ltd/Cranwell
	G-BYWH	Grob G.115E Tutor	VT Aerospace Ltd/Leeming
	G-BYWI	Grob G.115E Tutor	VT Aerospace Ltd/Wyton
	G-BYWJ	Grob G.115E Tutor	VT Aerospace Ltd/Woodvale
	G-BYWK	Grob G.115E Tutor	VT Aerospace Ltd/Colerne
	G-BYWL	Grob G.115E Tutor	VT Aerospace Ltd/Cranwell
	G-BYWM	Grob G.115E Tutor	VT Aerospace Ltd/Yeovilton
	G-BYWN	Grob G.115E Tutor	VT Aerospace Ltd/Woodvale
	G-BYWO	Grob G.115E Tutor	VT Aerospace Ltd/Church Fenton
	G-BYWP	Grob G.115E Tutor	VT Aerospace Ltd/Church Fenton
	G-BYWR	Grob G.115E Tutor	VT Aerospace Ltd/Wyton
	G-BYWS	Grob G.115E Tutor	VT Aerospace Ltd/Church Fenton
	G-BYWT	Grob G.115E Tutor	VT Aerospace Ltd/Leeming
	G-BYWU	Grob G.115E Tutor	VT Aerospace Ltd/Wyton
	G-BYWV	Grob G.115E Tutor	VT Aerospace Ltd/Church Fenton
	G-BYWW	Grob G.115E Tutor	VT Aerospace Ltd/Cranwell
	G-BYWX	Grob G.115E Tutor	VT Aerospace Ltd/Colerne
	G-BYWY	Grob G.115E Tutor	VT Aerospace Ltd/Cranwell
	G-BYWZ	Grob G.115E Tutor	VT Aerospace Ltd/Cranwell
	G-BYXA	Grob G.115E Tutor	VT Aerospace Ltd/Cosford
	G-BYXB	Grob G.115E Tutor	VT Aerospace Ltd/Boscombe Down
	G-BYXC	Grob G.115E Tutor	VT Aerospace Ltd/Benson
	G-BYXD	Grob G.115E Tutor	VT Aerospace Ltd/Boscombe Down
	G-BYXE	Grob G.115E Tutor	VT Aerospace Ltd/Church Fenton
	G-BYXF	Grob G.115E Tutor	VT Aerospace Ltd/Cosford
	G-BYXG	Grob G.115E Tutor	VT Aerospace Ltd/Wyton
	G-BYXH	Grob G.115E Tutor	VT Aerospace Ltd/Colerne
	G-BYXI	Grob G.115E Tutor	VT Aerospace Ltd/Woodvale
	G-BYXJ	Grob G.115E Tutor	VT Aerospace Ltd/Boscombe Down
	G-BYXK	Grob G.115E Tutor	VT Aerospace Ltd/Yeovilton
	G-BYXL	Grob G.115E Tutor	VT Aerospace Ltd/Cosford
	G-BYXM	Grob G.115E Tutor	VT Aerospace Ltd/Boscombe Down
	G-BYXN	Grob G.115E Tutor	VT Aerospace Ltd/Cranwell
	G-BYXO	Grob G.115E Tutor	VT Aerospace Ltd/Cosford
	G-BYXP	Grob G.115E Tutor	VT Aerospace Ltd/Wyton
	G-BYXR	Grob G.115E Tutor	VT Aerospace Ltd/Benson
	G-BYXS	Grob G.115E Tutor	VT Aerospace Ltd/Yeovilton
	G-BYXT	Grob G.115E Tutor	VT Aerospace Ltd/Wyton
	G-BYXV	Medway Eclipser	K. A. Christie
	G-BYXW	Medway Eclipser	G. A. Hazell
	G-BYXX	Grob G.115E Tutor	VT Aerospace Ltd
	G-BYXY	Grob G.115E Tutor	VT Aerospace Ltd/Wyton
	G-BYXZ	Grob G.115E Tutor	VT Aerospace Ltd/Cranwell
	G-BYYA	Grob G.115E Tutor	VT Aerospace Ltd/Leeming

BRITISH CIVIL REGISTRATIONS

G-BYYB – G-BZBX

Reg	Type	Owner or Operator	Notes
G-BYYB	Grob G.115E Tutor	VT Aerospace Ltd/Cranwell	
G-BYYC	Hapi Cygnet SF-2A	G. H. Smith	
G-BYYD	Cameron A-250 balloon	C. & J. M. Bailey	
G-BYYE	Lindstrand LBL-77A balloon	D. J. Cook	
G-BYYG	Slingsby T.67C	S. E. Marples & B. Dixon	
G-BYYL	Avtech Jabiru UL 450	K. C. Lye	
G-BYYM	Raj Hamsa X'Air 582 (1)	P. C. Bishop	
G-BYYN	Pegasus Quantum 15-912	S. E. Robinson & A. Dixon	
G-BYYO	PA-28R -201 Arrow III	Stapleford Flying Club Ltd	
G-BYYP	Pegasus Quantum 15	D. A. Linsey-Bloom	
G-BYYR	Raj Hamsa X'Air 582 (4)	T. D. Bawden	
G-BYYT	Avtech Jabiru UL 450	A. C. Cale and A. J. Young.	
G-BYYX	TEAM mini-MAX 91	J. Batchelor	
G-BYYY	Pegasus Quantum 15-912	Redlands Airfield	
G-BYYZ	Staaken Z-21A Flitzer	T. White	
G-BYZA	AS.355F2 Twin Squirrel	MMAir Ltd	
G-BYZB	Mainair Blade	A. M. Thornley	
G-BYZD	Kis Cruiser	M. G. Thatcher	
G-BYZF	Raj Hamsa X'Air 582 (1)	R. P. Davies	
G-BYZG	Cameron A-275 balloon	Horizon Ballooning Ltd	
G-BYZJ	Boeing 737-3Q8	bmi Baby (G-COLE)	
G-BYZL	Cameron GP-65 balloon	P. Thibo	
G-BYZM	PA-28-161 Warrior II	Central Aircraft Leasing Ltd/Wolverhampton	
G-BYZO	Rans S.6-ES Coyote II	B. E. J. Badger & J. E. Storer	
G-BYZP	Robinson R22 Beta	Propwash Investments Ltd	
G-BYZR	I.I.I. Sky Arrow 650TC	G-BYZR Group	
G-BYZS	Avtech Jabiru UL-450	N. Fielding	
G-BYZT	Nova Vertex 26	M. Hay	
G-BYZU	Pegasus Quantum 15	N. I. Clifton	
G-BYZV	Sky 90-24 balloon	P. Farmer	
G-BYZW	Raj Hamsa X'Air 582 (2)	H. C. Lowther	
G-BYZX	Cameron R-90 balloon	D. K. Hempleman-Adams	
G-BYZY	Pietenpol Aircamper	D. M. Hanchett	
G-BYZZ	Robinson R22 Beta II	Astra Helicopters Ltd	
G-BZAA	Mainair Blade	G. P. Spittles	
G-BZAB	Mainair Rapier	R. H. Stockton	
G-BZAD	Cessna 152	Cristal Air Ltd	
G-BZAE	Cessna 152	Horizon Aviation Ltd	
G-BZAF	Raj Hamsa X'Air 582 (1)	Y. A. Evans	
G-BZAG	Lindstrand LBL-105A balloon	A. M. Figiel	
G-BZAI	Pegasus Quantum 15	D. Rhodes	
G-BZAK	Raj Hamsa X'Air 582 (1)	R. J. Ripley	
G-BZAL	Mainair Blade 912	K. Worthington	
G-BZAM	Europa	D. U. Corbett/Shobdon	
G-BZAO	Rans S.12XL	M. L. Robinson	
G-BZAP	Avtech Jabiru UL-450	I. J. Grindley & D. R. Griffiths	
G-BZAR	Denney Kitfox 4-1200 Speedster	C. E. Brookes (G-LEZJ)	
G-BZAS	Isaacs Fury II (K5673)	Bournemouth Aviation Museum	
G-BZAT	Avro RJ100	British Airways Connect	
G-BZAU	Avro RJ100	British Airways Connect	
G-BZAV	Avro RJ100	British Airways Connect	
G-BZAW	Avro RJ100	British Airways Connect	
G-BZAX	Avro RJ100	British Airways Connect	
G-BZAY	Avro RJ100	British Airways Connect	
G-BZAZ	Avro RJ100	British Airways Connect	
G-BZBC	Rans S.6-ES Coyote II	A. J. Baldwin	
G-BZBE	Cameron A-210 balloon	Dragon Balloon Co Ltd	
G-BZBF	Cessna 172M	L. W. Scattergood	
G-BZBH	Thunder Ax6-65 balloon	P. J. Hebdon & A. C. Fraser	
G-BZBI	Cameron V-77 balloon	C. & A. I. Gibson	
G-BZBJ	Lindstrand LBL-77A balloon	P. T. R. Ollivere	
G-BZBL	Lindstrand LBL-120A balloon	East Coast Balloons Ltd	
G-BZBM	Cameron A-315 balloon	Listers of Coventry (Motors) Ltd	
G-BZBN	Thunder Ax9-120 balloon	K. Willie	
G-BZBO	Stoddard-Hamilton Glasair III	M. B. Hamlett/France	
G-BZBP	Raj Hamsa X'Air 582 (1)	D. P. Sudworth	
G-BZBR	Pegasus Quantum 15-912	E. Lewis	
G-BZBS	PA-28-161 Warrior iii	Aviation Rentals	
G-BZBT	Cameron H-34 Hopper balloon	British Telecommunications PLC	
G-BZBU	Robinson R22	I. C. Macdonald	
G-BZBW	Rotorway Executive 162F	Southern Helicopters Ltd	
G-BZBX	Rans S.6-ES Coyote II	P. E. De-Ville & M. W. Shepherd	

G-BZBZ – G-BZGL — BRITISH CIVIL REGISTRATIONS

Notes	Reg	Type	Owner or Operator
	G-BZBZ	Jodel D.9	S. Marom
	G-BZDA	PA-28-161 Warrior III	Aviation Rentals
	G-BZDB	Thruster T.600T	M. R. Jones
	G-BZDC	Mainair Blade	E. J. Wells & P. J. Smith
	G-BZDD	Mainair Blade 912	Barton Blade Group
	G-BZDE	Lindstrand LBL-210A balloon	Toucan Travel Ltd
	G-BZDF	CFM Streak Shadow SA	W. M. Moylan
	G-BZDH	PA-28R Cherokee Arrow 200-II	I. R. Chaplin
	G-BZDI	Aero L-39C Albatros	C. C. Butt
	G-BZDJ	Cameron Z-105 balloon	BWS Security Systems Ltd
	G-BZDK	Raj Hamsa X'Air 582 (4)	B. Park
	G-BZDL	Pegasus Quantum 15-912	D. M. Merritt-Colman/Spain
	G-BZDM	Stoddard-Hamilton Glastar	F. G. Miskelly
	G-BZDN	Cameron N-105 balloon	I. R. Warrington & H. W. R. Stewart
	G-BZDP	SA Bulldog Srs 120/121 (XX551:E)	R. M. Raikes
	G-BZDR	Tri-R Kis	D. P. Williams
	G-BZDS	Pegasus Quantum 15-912	P. K. Dale
	G-BZDT	Maule MXT-7-180	Strongcrew Ltd
	G-BZDU	DHC.1 Chipmunk 22	M. R. Clark
	G-BZDV	Westland Gazelle HT.2	AJR Developments Ltd
	G-BZDX	Cameron Colt 90 Sugarbox SS balloon	Stratos Ballooning GmbH & Co KG/Germany
	G-BZDY	Cameron Colt 90 Sugarbox SS balloon	Stratos Ballooning GmbH & Co KG/Germany
	G-BZDZ	Avtech Jabiru SP	R. M. Whiteside
	G-BZEA	Cessna A.152	Sky Leisure Aviation (Charters) Ltd
	G-BZEB	Cessna 152	Sky Leisure Aviation (Charters) Ltd
	G-BZEC	Cessna 152	Sky Leisure Aviation (Charters) Ltd
	G-BZED	Pegasus Quantum 15-912	D. Crozier
	G-BZEE	Agusta-Bell 206B JetRanger 2	Yateley Helicopters Ltd (G-OJCB)
	G-BZEG	Mainair Blade	R. P. Cookson
	G-BZEH	PA-28 Cherokee 235B	A. D. Wood
	G-BZEJ	Raj Hamsa X'Air 582 (7)	X'Air Flying Group
	G-BZEK	Cameron C-70 balloon	Ballooning 50 Degrees Nord/Luxembourg
	G-BZEL	Mainair Blade 912	M. W. Bush
	G-BZEM	Glaser-Dirks DG.800G	I. M. Stromberg
	G-BZEN	Avtech Jabiru UL-450	B. W. Stockil
	G-BZEP	SA Bulldog Srs 120/121 (XX561:7)	A. J. Amato/Biggin Hill
	G-BZER	Raj Hamsa X'Air R100 (1)	N. P. Lloyd & H. Lloyd-Jones
	G-BZES	Rotorway Executive 90	Southern Helicopters Ltd (G-LUFF)
	G-BZET	Robin HR.200/120B	Modi Aviation Ltd
	G-BZEU	Raj Hamsa X'Air 582 (2)	M. J. Saywell
	G-BZEV	Semicopter 1 gyroplane	M. E. Vahdat
	G-BZEW	Rans S.6-ES Coyote II	M. J. Wooldridge
	G-BZEX	Raj Hamsa X'Air R.200 (2)	J. M. McCullough & R. T. Henry
	G-BZEY	Cameron N-90 balloon	Northants Auto Parts and Service Ltd
	G-BZEZ	CFM Streak Shadow	G. J. Pearce
	G-BZFB	Robin R.2112A	T. F. Wells
	G-BZFC	Pegasus Quantum 15-912	G. Addison
	G-BZFD	Cameron N-90 balloon	David Hataway Holdings Ltd
	G-BZFF	Raj Hamsa X'Air 582 (2)	L. H. S. Stephens
	G-BZFG	Sky 105 balloon	Virgin Airship & Balloon Co Ltd
	G-BZFH	Pegasus Quantum 15-912	Kent Scout Microlights
	G-BZFI	Avtech Jabiru UL	Group Family
	G-BZFK	TEAM mini-MAX	I. Macleod
	G-BZFN	SA Bulldog Srs 120/121 (XX667:16)	Risk Logical Ltd/Isle of Man
	G-BZFO	Mainair Blade 912	D. G. Bowden
	G-BZFP	DHC.6 Twin Otter 310	Loganair Ltd/British Airways
	G-BZFR	Extra EA.300/L	Powerhunt Ltd/Biggin Hill
	G-BZFS	Mainair Blade 912	S. R. McKiernan
	G-BZFT	Murphy Rebel	N. A. Evans
	G-BZFU	Lindstrand LBL HS-110 HA Airship	Lindstrand Hot Air Balloons Ltd
	G-BZFV	Zenair CH.601UL	M. E. Caton
	G-BZGA	DHC.1 Chipmunk 22 (WK585)	The Real Flying Co Ltd/Duxford
	G-BZGB	DHC.1 Chipmunk 22 (WZ872:E)	Silverstar Aviation Ltd/Blackpool
	G-BZGC	AS.355F1 Twin Squirrel	McAlpine Helicopters Ltd/Kidlington (G-CCAO/ G-SETA/ G-NEAS/G-CMMM/G-BNBJ)
	G-BZGD	PA-18 Super Cub 150	Proline Aviation
	G-BZGF	Rans S.6-ES Coyote II	D. F. Castle
	G-BZGG	SE-3130B Alouette II	J. T. Meall (G-POSE)
	G-BZGH	Cessna F.172N	Golf Hotel Group
	G-BZGI	Ultramagic M-145 balloon	European Balloon Co Ltd
	G-BZGJ	Thunder Ax10-180 S2 balloon	Merlin Balloons
	G-BZGK	NA OV-10B Bronco (99+32)	Aircraft Restoration Co Ltd/Duxford
	G-BZGL	NA OV-10B Bronco (99+26)	Aircraft Restoration Co Ltd/Duxford

BRITISH CIVIL REGISTRATIONS

G-BZGM – G-BZJZ

Reg	Type	Owner or Operator	Notes
G-BZGM	Mainair Blade 912	D. Young	
G-BZGN	Raj Hamsa X'Air 582 (2)	C. S. Warr & P. A. Pilkington	
G-BZGO	Robinson R44	P. Durkin	
G-BZGP	Thruster T.600N 460	M. L. Smith/Popham	
G-BZGR	Rans S.6-ES Coyote II	J. M. Benton	
G-BZGS	Mainair Blade 912	R. J. Coppin	
G-BZGT	Avtech Jabiru UL-450	Hytec Applications Ltd	
G-BZGU	Raj Hamsa X'Air 582 (4)	W. Bracken/Ireland	
G-BZGV	Lindstrand LBL-77A balloon	J. H. Dryden	
G-BZGW	Mainair Blade	C. S. M. Hallam	
G-BZGX	Raj Hamsa X'Air 582 (6)	A. Crowe	
G-BZGY	Dyn'Aéro CR.100	D. Hayes & T. Sullivan	
G-BZGZ	Pegasus Quantum 15-912	D. W. Beech	
G-BZHA	Boeing 767-336ER	British Airways	
G-BZHB	Boeing 767-336ER	British Airways	
G-BZHC	Boeing 767-336ER	British Airways	
G-BZHE	Cessna 152	Simair Ltd	
G-BZHF	Cessna 152	Modi Aviation Ltd	
G-BZHG	Tecnam P92 Echo	R. W. F. Boarder	
G-BZHI	Enstrom F-28A-UK	Tindon Engineering Ltd (G-BPOZ)	
G-BZHJ	Raj Hamsa X'Air 582 (7)	T. Harrison-Smith	
G-BZHK	PA-28-181 Archer III	J. Middlemass	
G-BZHL	Noorduyn AT-16 Harvard IIB	R. H. Cooper & S. Swallow	
G-BZHN	Pegasus Quantum 15-912	Eaglescott Microlights	
G-BZHO	Pegasus Quantum 15	R. L. Williams	
G-BZHP	Quad City Challenger II	G. Cousins	
G-BZHR	Avtech Jabiru UL-450	G. W. Rowbotham	
G-BZHS	Shaw Europa	P. Waugh	
G-BZHT	PA-18A Super Cub 150	Lakes Gliding Club/Walney	
G-BZHU	Wag-Aero CUBy Sport Trainer	D. M. Lewington	
G-BZHV	PA-28-181 Archer III	M. J. Hill/Bournemouth	
G-BZHW	PA-28-181 Archer III	Delta Kilo Services LLP	
G-BZHX	Thunder Ax11-250 S2 balloon	T. H. Wilson	
G-BZHY	Mainair Blade 912	D. A. Valentine	
G-BZIA	Raj Hamsa X'Air 700 (1)	J. L. Pritchett	
G-BZIC	Lindstrand LBL Sun SS balloon	Ballongaventyr 1 Sakne AB/Sweden	
G-BZID	Montgomerie-Bensen B.8MR	A. Gault	
G-BZIG	Thruster T.600N	Ultra Air Ltd	
G-BZIH	Lindstrand LBL-31A balloon	Skyart Balloons	
G-BZII	Extra EA.300/1	R. J. Verrall	
G-BZIJ	Robin DR.400/500	Rob Airways Ltd	
G-BZIK	Cameron A-250 balloon	Breckland Balloons Ltd	
G BZIL	Colt 120A balloon	Champagne Flights	
G-BZIM	Pegasus Quantum 15-912	A. & S. Cuthbertson	
G-BZIO	PA-28-161 Warrior III	Aviation Rentals/Bournemouth	
G-BZIP	Montgomerie-Bensen B.8MR	S. J. Boxall	
G-BZIS	Raj Hamsa X'Air 582 (2)	M. J. Badham	
G-BZIT	Beech 95-B55 Baron	Propellorhead Aviation Ltd	
G-BZIV	Avtech Jabiru UL	V. R. Leggott	
G-BZIW	Pegasus Quantum 15-912	J. M. Hodgson	
G-BZIX	Cameron N-90 balloon	Sport Promotion SRL/Italy	
G-BZIY	Raj Hamsa X'Air 582 (2)	A. L. A. Gill	
G-BZIZ	Ultramagic H-31 balloon	G. D. O. Bartram	
G-BZJA	Cameron 90 Fire SS balloon	Chubb Fire Ltd	
G-BZJB	Aerostar Yakovlev Yak-52	Matristar Ltd	
G-BZJC	Thruster T.600N	M. H. Moulai	
G-BZJD	Thruster T.600T	P. G. Valentine/France	
G-BZJF	Pegasus Quantum 15	R. S. McMaster	
G-BZJG	Cameron A-400 balloon	Cameron Balloons Ltd	
G-BZJH	Cameron Z-90 balloon	Cameron Balloons Ltd	
G-BZJI	Nova X-Large 37 paraplane	M. Hay	
G-BZJJ	Robinson R22 Beta	M. J. Burgess	
G-BZJL	Mainair Blade 912S	D. N. Powell	
G-BZJM	VPM M-16 Tandem Trainer	J. Musil	
G-BZJN	Mainair Blade 912	L. Campbell & M. A. Haughey	
G-BZJO	Pegasus Quantum 15	J. D. Doran	
G-BZJP	Zenair CH.701UL	J. A. Ware	
G-BZJS	Taylor JT.2 Titch	R. W. Clarke	
G-BZJU	Cameron A-200 balloon	Leeds Castle Enterprises Ltd	
G-BZJV	CASA 1-131E Jungmann 1000	J. A. Sykes	
G-BZJW	Cessna 150F	P. Ligertwood	
G-BZJX	Ultramagic N-250 balloon	Hot Air Balloons Ltd	
G-BZJZ	Pegasus Quantum 15	S. Baker	

G-BZKC – G-BZNT | BRITISH CIVIL REGISTRATIONS

Notes	Reg	Type	Owner or Operator
	G-BZKC	Raj Hamsa X'Air 582 (2)	P. J. Cheney
	G-BZKD	Stolp Starduster Too	P. & C. Edmunds
	G-BZKE	Lindstrand LBL-77B balloon	R. M. Cambridge
	G-BZKF	Rans S.6-ES Coyote II	J. T. Spencer
	G-BZKG	Extreme/Silex	R. M. Hardy
	G-BZKH	Flylight Airsports Doodle Bug/Target	B. Tempest
	G-BZKI	Flylight Airsports Doodle Bug/Target	S. Bond
	G-BZKJ	Flylight Airsports Doodle Bug/Target	Flylight Airsports Ltd/Sywell
	G-BZKK	Cameron V-56 balloon	P. J. Green & C. Bosley Gemini II
	G-BZKL	PA-28R-201 Arrow III	I. R. Chaplin/Andrewsfield
	G-BZKN	Campbell Cricket Mk 4	C. G. Ponsford
	G-BZKO	Rans S.6-ES Coyote II	S. G. Beeson
	G-BZKR	Cameron 90 Sugarbox SS balloon	Stratos Ballooning GmbH & Co KG
	G-BZKS	Ercoupe 415CD	A. H. Harper
	G-BZKT	Pegasus Quantum 15	G. Cousins
	G-BZKU	Cameron Z-105 balloon	N. A. Fishlock
	G-BZKV	Cameron Sky 90-24 balloon	Omega Selction Services Ltd
	G-BZKW	Ultramagic M-27 balloon	T. G. Church
	G-BZKX	Cameron V-90 balloon	Cameron Balloons Ltd
	G-BZKY	Focke Wulf Fw.189A-1	M. T. Pearce-Ware
	G-BZLA	Aérospatiale SA.341G Gazelle 1	P. J. Brown
	G-BZLB	SA Bulldog Srs 120/121	L. Bax
	G-BZLC	WSK-PZL Koliber 160A	G. F. Smith
	G-BZLE	Rans S.6-ES Coyote II	J. C. Rose
	G-BZLF	CFM Shadow Srs CD	D. W. Stacey
	G-BZLG	Robin HR.200/120B	M. C. Turner
	G-BZLH	PA-28-161 Warrior II	Aviation Rentals
	G-BZLI	SOCATA TB21 Trinidad TC	K. B. Hallam
	G-BZLK	Slingsby T.31M Motor Tutor	I. P. Manley
	G-BZLL	Pegasus Quantum 15-912	Caunton Graphites Syndicate
	G-BZLP	Robinson R44	Rotorways Helicopters
	G-BZLS	Cameron Sky 77-24 balloon	D. W. Young
	G-BZLT	Raj Hamsa X'Air 582 (1)	G. Millar
	G-BZLU	Lindstrand LBL-90A balloon	A. E. Lusty
	G-BZLV	Avtech Jabiru UL-450	G. Dalton
	G-BZLX	Pegasus Quantum 15-912	D. McCabe
	G-BZLY	Grob G.109B	A. Baker
	G-BZLZ	Pegasus Quantum 15-912	A. S. Martin
	G-BZMB	PA-28R-201 Arrow III	Thurrock Arrow Group
	G-BZMC	Avtech Jabiru UL	D. G. Harkness
	G-BZMD	SA Bulldog Srs 120/121 (XX554)	C. Hunter
	G-BZME	SA Bulldog Srs 120/121 (XX698:9)	B. Whitworth/Breighton
	G-BZMF	Rutan LongEz	R. A. Gardiner
	G-BZMG	Robinson R44	Total Digital Solutions Ltd
	G-BZMH	SA Bulldog Srs 120/121 (XX692:A)	M. E. J. Hingley & Co Ltd
	G-BZMI	Pegasus Quantum 15-912	P. J. Barton
	G-BZMJ	Rans S.6-ES Coyote II	S. B. Walsh
	G-BZML	SA Bulldog Srs 120/121 (XX693:07)	I. D. Anderson
	G-BZMM	Robin DR.400/180R	N. A. C. Norman
	G-BZMO	Robinson R22 Beta	Heli Charter Ltd
	G-BZMR	Raj Hamsa X'Air 582 (2)	M. Grime
	G-BZMS	Mainair Blade	Beccles Buzzards
	G-BZMT	PA-28-161 Warrior III	Aviation Rentals
	G-BZMV	Cameron 80 Concept balloon	Latteria Soresinese Soc. Coop SRL/Italy
	G-BZMW	Pegasus Quantum 15-912	G. C. Kemp
	G-BZMY	SPP Yakovlev Yak C-11	Griffin Aviation Ltd
	G-BZMZ	CFM Streak Shadow	J. F. F. Fouche
	G-BZNB	Pegasus Quantum 15	T. J. Drew
	G-BZNC	Pegasus Quantum 15-912	D. E. Wall
	G-BZND	Sopwith Pup (replica) (N5199)	M. A. Goddard
	G-BZNE	Beech B300 Super King Air	Skyhopper LLP
	G-BZNF	Colt 120A balloon	N. Charbonnier/Italy
	G-BZNG	Raj Hamsa X'Air 700 (1)	J. Walshe
	G-BZNH	Rans S.6-ES Coyote II	L. J. Field
	G-BZNI	Bell 206B JetRanger 2	Dorset Country Homes Ltd (G-ODIG/G-NEEP)
	G-BZNJ	Rans S.6-ES Coyote Ii	J. G. McMinn
	G-BZNK	Morane Saulnier MS.315-D2	R. H. Cooper & S. Swallow
	G-BZNM	Pegasus Quantum 15	M. Tomlinson
	G-BZNN	Beech 76 Duchess	Aviation Rentals/Bournemouth
	G-BZNO	Ercoupe 415C	D. K. Tregilgas
	G-BZNP	Thruster T.600N	J. D. Gibbons
	G-BZNS	Mainair Blade	A. G. Laycock
	G-BZNT	Aero L-29 Delfin	E. Harper

BRITISH CIVIL REGISTRATIONS   G-BZNU – G-BZSL

Reg	Type	Owner or Operator	Notes
G-BZNU	Cameron A-300 balloon	Balloon School (International) Ltd	
G-BZNV	Lindstrand LBL-31A balloon	G. R. Down	
G-BZNW	Isaacs Fury II (K2048)	J. E. D. Rogerson	
G-BZNX	SOCATA MS.880B Rallye Club	R. K. Stewart	
G-BZNY	Shaw Europa XS	W. J. Harrison	
G-BZNZ	Lindstrand LBL Cake SS balloon	Oxford Promotions (UK) Ltd	
G-BZOB	Slepcev Storch (6G-ED)	R. G. Fairall	
G-BZOD	Pegasus Quantum 15-912	S. M. Wilson	
G-BZOE	Pegasus Quantum 15	B. N. Thresher	
G-BZOF	Montgomerie-Bensen B.8MR gyroplane	S. J. M. Ledingham	
G-BZOG	Dornier 328-100	Scot Airways Ltd	
G-BZOI	Nicollier HN.700 Menestrel II	S. J. McCollum	
G-BZOL	Robin R.3000/140	S. D. Baker	
G-BZOM	Rotorway Executive 162F	J. A. Jackson	
G-BZON	SA Bulldog Srs 120/121 (XX528:D)	D. J. Critchley	
G-BZOO	Pegasus Quantum 15-912	I. M. Gibson	
G-BZOP	Robinson R44	Caudwell Holdings Ltd	
G-BZOR	TEAM mini-MAX 91	A. Watt	
G-BZOU	Pegasus Quantum 15-912	P. V. Stevens	
G-BZOV	Pegasus Quantum 15-912	D. Turner	
G-BZOW	Whittaker MW7	G. W. Peacock	
G-BZOX	Cameron Colt 90B balloon	D. J. Head	
G-BZOY	Beech 76 Duchess	Aviation Rentals	
G-BZOZ	Van's RV-6	V. Edmondson	
G-BZPA	Mainair Blade 912S	J. McGoldrick	
G-BZPB	Hawker Hunter GA.11 (WB188 duck-egg green)	B. R. Pearson	
G-BZPC	Hawker Hunter GA.11 (WB188 red)	B. R. Pearson	
G-BZPD	Cameron V-65 balloon	P. Spellward	
G-BZPE	Lindstrand LBL-310 balloon	Aerosaurus Balloons Ltd	
G-BZPF	Scheibe SF.24B Motorspatz 1	J. S. Gorrett	
G-BZPG	Beech C24R Sierra 200	Plane Talking Ltd	
G-BZPH	Van's RV-4	G-BZPH RV-4 Group	
G-BZPI	SOCATA TB20 Trinidad	K. M. Brennan	
G-BZPJ	Beech 76 Duchess	Aviation Rentals	
G-BZPK	Cameron C-80 balloon	Horizon Ballooning Ltd	
G-BZPL	Robinson R44	M. K. Shaw	
G-BZPM	Cessna 172S	Pooler-LMT Ltd	
G-BZPN	Mainair Blade 912S	S. Wing	
G-BZPP	Westland Wasp HAS.1 (XT793:456)	C. J. Marsden	
G-BZPR	Ultramagic N-210 balloon	European Balloon Display Co Ltd	
G-BZPS	SA Bulldog Srs 120/121 (XX658:07)	D. M. Squires	
G-BZPT	Ultramagic N-210 balloon	European Balloon Display Co Ltd	
G-BZPV	Lindstrand LBL-90B balloon	D. P. Hopkins	
G-BZPW	Cameron V-77 balloon	J. Vonka	
G-BZPX	Ultramagic S-105 balloon	Scotair Balloons	
G-BZPY	Ultramagic H-31 balloon	Scotair Balloons	
G-BZPZ	Mainair Blade	K. Lynn	
G-BZRA	Rans S.6-ES Coyote II	K. J. Warburton	
G-BZRB	Mainair Blade	J-B. Weber	
G-BZRG	Hunt Wing	W. G. Reynolds	
G-BZRJ	Pegasus Quantum 15-912	G-BZRJ Group	
G-BZRO	PA-30 Twin Comanche C	Comanche Hire Ltd	
G-BZRP	Pegasus Quantum 15-912	RAF Microlight Flying Association (RP)	
G-BZRR	Pegasus Quantum 15-912	F. G. Green & T. Hudson	
G-BZRS	Eurocopter EC 135T2	Bond Air Services Ltd	
G-BZRT	Beech 76 Duchess	Aviation Rentals/Bournemouth	
G-BZRU	Cameron V-90 balloon	Dragon Balloon Group	
G-BZRV	Van's RV-6	N. M. Hitchman	
G-BZRW	Mainair Blade 912S	S. E. Kearney	
G-BZRX	Ultramagic M-105 balloon	Specialist Recruitment Group PLC	
G-BZRY	Rans S.6-ES Coyote II	A. G. Smith	
G-BZRZ	Thunder Ax11-250 S2 balloon	A. C. K. Rawson & J. J. Rudoni	
G-BZSA	Pegasus Quantum 15	D. W. Melville	
G-BZSB	Pitts S-1S Special	A. D. Ingold	
G-BZSC	Sopwith Camel F.1 (replica)	The Shuttleworth Collection/Old Warden	
G-BZSD	PA-46-350P Malibu Mirage	Thistle Aircraft Leasing Ltd	
G-BZSE	Hawker Hunter T.8B (WV322:Y)	Towerdrive Ltd/Kemble	
G-BZSF	Hawker Hunter T.8B (XF995:K)	Towerdrive Ltd/Kemble	
G-BZSG	Pegasus Quantum 15-912	S. Andrews	
G-BZSH	Ultramagic H-77 balloon	P. M. G. Vale	
G-BZSI	Pegasus Quantum 15	M. O. O'Brien	
G-BZSL	Sky 25-16 balloon	A. E. Austin	

G-BZSM – G-BZWH — BRITISH CIVIL REGISTRATIONS

Notes	Reg	Type	Owner or Operator
	G-BZSM	Pegasus Quantum 15	J. Walker & A. J. Johnson
	G-BZSO	Ultramagic M-77C balloon	C. C. Duppa-Miller
	G-BZSP	Stemme S.10	A. Flewelling & L. Bleaken
	G-BZSS	Pegasus Quantum 15-912	T. R. Marsh
	G-BZST	Avtech Jabiru UL	G. Hammond
	G-BZSU	Cameron A-315 balloon	Ballooning Network Ltd
	G-BZSV	Barracuda	M. J. Aherne
	G-BZSX	Pegasus Quantum 15-912	G. L. Hall
	G-BZSY	SNCAN Stampe SV.4A	G. J. N. Valvekens/Belgium
	G-BZSZ	Avtech Jabiru UL-450	M. P. Gurr & D. R. Burridge
	G-BZTA	Robinson R44	Jarretts Motors Ltd
	G-BZTC	TEAM mini-MAX 91	G. G. Clayton
	G-BZTD	Thruster T.600T 450 JAB	B. O. & B. C. McCartan
	G-BZTF	Yakovlev Yak-52	KY Flying Group
	G-BZTG	PA-34-220T Seneca V	Mainstreet Aviation Ltd
	G-BZTH	Shaw Europa	T. J. Houlihan
	G-BZTI	Shaw Europa XS	W. Hoolachan
	G-BZTJ	CASA Bü 133C Jungmeister	R. A. Seeley
	G-BZTK	Cameron V-90 balloon	E. Appollodorus
	G-BZTL	Cameron Colt Flying Ice Cream Cone SS balloon	Stratos Ballooning GmbH & Co KG/Germany
	G-BZTM	Mainair Blade	D. C. Clark
	G-BZTN	Shaw Europa XS	S. A. Smith & M. K. McGreavey
	G-BZTR	Mainair Blade	A. Raithby & N. McCusker
	G-BZTS	Cameron 90 Bertie Bassett SS balloon	Trebor Bassett Ltd
	G-BZTT	Cameron A-275 balloon	Cameron Flights Southern Ltd
	G-BZTV	Mainair Blade 912S	D. J. Cook
	G-BZTW	Hunt Wing Avon 582 (1)	T. S. Walker
	G-BZTX	Mainair Blade 912	K. A. Ingham
	G-BZTY	Avtech Jabiru UL	R. P. Lewis
	G-BZUB	Mainair Blade	S. E. Kearney
	G-BZUC	Pegasus Quantum 15-912	G. Breen/Portugal
	G-BZUD	Lindstrand LBL-105A balloon	A. Nimmo
	G-BZUE	Pegasus Quantum 15	M. P. & R. A. Wells
	G-BZUF	Mainair Rapier	C. A. Denver
	G-BZUG	RL.7A XP Sherwood Ranger	J. G. Boxall
	G-BZUH	Rans S.6-ES Coyote II	J. D. Sinclair-Day
	G-BZUI	Pegasus Quantum 15-912	A. P. Slade
	G-BZUK	Lindstrand LBL-31A balloon	G. R. J. Luckett/USA
	G-BZUL	Avtech Jabiru UL	P. Hawkins
	G-BZUN	Mainair Blade 912	A. D. Jones
	G-BZUO	Cameron A-340HL balloon	Anglian Countryside Balloons Ltd
	G-BZUP	Raj Hamsa X'Air 582 (5)	A. A. A. Lappin
	G-BZUU	Cameron C-90 balloon	D. C. Ball & C. F. Pooley
	G-BZUV	Cameron H-24 balloon	J. N. Race
	G-BZUX	Pegasus Quantum 15	K. M. MacRae & ptnrs
	G-BZUY	Van's RV-6	R. D. Masters
	G-BZUZ	Hunt Avon-Blade R.100 (1)	C. Hershaw
	G-BZVA	Zenair CH.701UL	M. W. Taylor
	G-BZVB	Cessna FR.172H	K. G. Worcester (G-BLMX)
	G-BZVC	Mickleburgh L107	D. R. Mickleburgh
	G-BZVD	Cameron Colt 105 Forklift SS balloon	Stratos Ballooning GmbH & Co KG/Germany
	G-BZVE	Cameron N-133 balloon	I. M. Ashpole
	G-BZVG	Eurocopter AS.350B3 Ecureuil	Windrush Aviation Ltd
	G-BZVH	Raj Hamsa X'Air 582(1)	M. Smullen
	G-BZVI	Nova Vertex 24 hang glider	M. Hay
	G-BZVJ	Pegasus Quantum 15	T. Mc.Mahon
	G-BZVK	Raj Hamsa X'Air 582 (2)	A. P. & J. M. Cadd
	G-BZVM	Rans S.6-ES Coyote II	N. N. Ducker
	G-BZVN	Van's RV-6	J. A. Booth
	G-BZVO	Cessna TR.182 RG	Swiftair Ltd
	G-BZVR	Raj Hamsa X'Air 582 (8)	Hummingbird Club
	G-BZVS	CASA 1-131E Jungmann 2000	W. R. M. Beesley
	G-BZVT	I.I.I. Sky Arrow 650T	D. J. Goldsmith
	G-BZVU	Cameron Z-105 balloon	The Mall Balloon Team Ltd
	G-BZVV	Pegasus Quantum 15-912	M. M. P. Evans
	G-BZVW	Ilyushin IL-2 Stormovik	S. Swallow & R. H. Cooper/Sandtoft
	G-BZVX	Ilyushin IL-2 Stormovik	S. Swallow & R. H. Cooper/Sandtoft
	G-BZWB	Mainair Blade 912	L. Parker
	G-BZWC	Raj Hamsa X'Air Falcon 912 (1)	C. McAfee
	G-BZWF	Colt AS-120 airship	MA Flying Ltd
	G-BZWG	PA-28 Cherokee 140	E. & H. Merkado
	G-BZWH	Cessna 152	J. & H. Aviation Services Ltd

126

BRITISH CIVIL REGISTRATIONS
G-BZWI – G-CBAL

Reg	Type	Owner or Operator	Notes
G-BZWI	Medway Eclipser	R. A. Keene	
G-BZWJ	CFM Streak Shadow	T. A. Morgan	
G-BZWK	Avtech Jabiru SK	G. M. R. Abrey	
G-BZWM	Pegasus XL-Q	D. T. Evans	
G-BZWN	Van's RV-8	A. J. Symms & R. D. Harper	
G-BZWS	Pegasus Quantum 15-912	G-BZWS Syndicate	
G-BZWT	Technam P92-EM Echo	R. F. Cooper	
G-BZWU	Pegasus Quantum 15-912	J. Needham	
G-BZWV	Steen Skybolt	P. D. & K. Begley	
G-BZWX	Whittaker MW5D Sorcerer	G. E. Richardson	
G-BZWY	CFM Streak Shadow SA	B. Cartwright	
G-BZWZ	Van's RV-6	J. Shanley	
G-BZXA	Raj Hamsa X'Air V2 (1)	D. W. Mullin	
G-BZXB	Van's RV-6	B. J. King-Smith & D. J. Akerman	
G-BZXC	SA Bulldog Srs 120/121 (XX612:A, 03)	A. R. Oliver	
G-BZXD	Rotorway Executive 162F	P. G. King	
G-BZXE	DHC.1 Chipmunk 22	K. Moore	
G-BZXF	Cameron A-210 balloon	S. Whatley & ptnrs	
G-BZXG	Dyn' Aero MCR-01	J. L. Ker	
G-BZXI	Nova Philou 26 hang glider	M. Hay	
G-BZXJ	Schweizer 269-1	Helicentre Liverpool Ltd/Liverpool	
G-BZXK	Robin HR.200/120B	Helicopter One Ltd	
G-BZXL	Whittaker MW5D Sorcerer	R. Hatton	
G-BZXM	Mainair Blade 912	M. E. Fowler	
G-BZXN	Avtech Jabiru UL-450	J. Armstrong	
G-BZXP	Kiss 400-582 (1)	A. Fairbrother	
G-BZXR	Cameron N-90 balloon	H. J. Andrews	
G-BZXS	SA Bulldog Srs 120/121 (XX631:W)	K. J. Thompson	
G-BZXT	Mainair Blade 912	Barton 912 Flyers	
G-BZXV	Pegasus Quantum 15-912	P. I. Oliver	
G-BZXW	VPM M-16 Tandem Trainer	S. J. Tyler (G-NANA)	
G-BZXX	Pegasus Quantum 15-912	G-BZXX Group	
G-BZXY	Robinson R44	Helicopter Services Ltd	
G-BZXZ	SA Bulldog Srs 120/121 (XX629:V)	J. A. D. Richardson	
G-BZYA	Rans S.6-ES Coyote II	M. R. Osbourn	
G-BZYD	Westland Gazelle AH.1	Aerocars Ltd	
G-BZYE	Robinson R22 Beta	Plane Talking Ltd/Elstree	
G-BZYG	Glaser-Dirks DG.500MB	R. C. Bromwich	
G-BZYI	Nova Phocus 123 hang glider	M. Hay	
G-BZYK	Avtech Jabiru UL	Cloudbase Aviation G-BZYK/Redhill	
G-BZYL	Rans S.6-ES Coyote II	C. B. Heslop	
G-BZYM	Raj Hamsa X'Air 700 (1A)	D. R. Sutton	
G-BZYN	Pegasus Quantum 15-912	J. Cannon	
G-BZYO	Colt 210A balloon	P. M. Forster	
G-BZYR	Cameron N-31 balloon	C. J. Sanger-Davies	
G-BZYS	Micro Aviation Bantam B.22-S	D. L. Howell	
G-BZYT	Interavia 80TA	J. King	
G-BZYU	Whittaker MW6 Merlin	K. J. Cole	
G-BZYV	Snowbird Mk.V 582 (1)	S. Jones	
G-BZYW	Cameron N-90 balloon	Bailey Balloons	
G-BZYX	Raj Hamsa X'Air 700 (1A)	A. M. Sutton	
G-BZYY	Cameron N-90 balloon	Mason Zimbler Ltd	
G-BZZD	Cessna F.172M	R. H. M. Richardson-Bunbury (G-BDPF)	
G-CAHA	PA-34-200T Seneca II	Aeros Holdings Ltd	
G-CAIN	CFM Shadow Srs CD	G. D. Haimes (G-MTKU)	
G-CALL	PA-23 Aztec 250F	J. D. Moon	
G-CAMB	AS.355F2 Twin Squirrel	Tiger Helicopters Ltd	
G-CAMM	Hawker Cygnet (replica)	D. M. Cashmore	
G-CAMP	Cameron N-105 balloon	Hong Kong Balloon & Airship Club	
G-CAMR	BFC Challenger II	P. R. A. Walker	
G-CAPI	Mudry/CAARP CAP-10B	PI Group (G-BEXR)	
G-CAPX	Avions Mudry CAP-10B	H. J. Pessall	
G-CARS†	Pitts S-2A Special (replica)★	Toyota Ltd	
G-CBAB	SA Bulldog Srs 120/121 (XX543:F)	Propshop Ltd/Duxford	
G-CBAD	Mainair Blade 912	P. Lister	
G-CBAE	BAe 146-200	BAE Systems (Operations) Ltd	
G-CBAF	Lancair 320	L. H. & M. van Cleeff	
G-CBAH	Raj Hamsa X'Air 133 (1)	D. N. B. Hearn	
G-CBAI	Flight Design CT2K	Newtownards Microlight Group	
G-CBAK	Robinson R44	CEL Electrical Logistics Ltd	
G-CBAL	PA-28-161 Warrior II	Thomsonfly Ltd	

G-CBAN – G-CBEG — BRITISH CIVIL REGISTRATIONS

Notes	Reg	Type	Owner or Operator
	G-CBAN	SA Bulldog Srs 120/121 (XX668:1)	C. Hilliker
	G-CBAP	Zenair CH.601UL	A. G. Marsh
	G-CBAR	Stoddard-Hamilton Glastar	C. M. Barnes
	G-CBAS	Rans S.6-ES Coyote II	S. R. Green
	G-CBAT	Cameron Z-90 balloon	British Telecommunications PLC
	G-CBAU	Rand-Robinson KR-2	B. Normington
	G-CBAV	Raj Hamsa X'Air V.2 (1)	D. W. Stamp & G. J. Lampitt
	G-CBAW	Cameron A-300 balloon	D. K. Hempleman-Adams
	G-CBAX	Tecnam P92-EM Echo	R. P. Reeves
	G-CBAZ	Rans S.6-ES Coyote II	J. G. J. McDill
	G-CBBA	Robin DR.400/180	H. P. K. Ferdinand/North Weald
	G-CBBB	Pegasus Quantum 15-912	I. A. Macadam
	G-CBBC	SA Bulldog Srs 120/121 (XX515:4)	Bulldog Support Ltd
	G-CBBF	Beech 76 Duchess	Liddell Aircraft Ltd
	G-CBBG	Mainair Blade	S. L. Cogger
	G-CBBH	Raj Hamsa X'Air V2 (2)	R. D. Parkinson
	G-CBBK	Robinson R22	R. J. Everett
	G-CBBL	SA Bulldog Srs 120/121 (XX550:Z)	I. R. Bates
	G-CBBM	MXP-740 Savannah J (1)	C. E. Passmore
	G-CBBN	Pegasus Quantum 15-912	G-CBBN Group
	G-CBBO	Whittaker MW5D Sorcerer	P. J. Gripton
	G-CBBP	Pegasus Quantum 15-912	P. F. Warren
	G-CBBR	SA Bulldog Srs 120/121 (XX625:01, N)	G. V. Crowe & D. L. Thompson
	G-CBBS	SA Bulldog Srs 120/121 (XX694:E)	European Light Aviation Ltd
	G-CBBT	SA Bulldog Srs 120/121 (XX695:3)	Newcastle Bulldog Group Ltd
	G-CBBU	SA Bulldog Srs 120/121 (XX711:X)	Newcastle Bulldog Group Ltd
	G-CBBV	Westland Gazelle HT.3 (XZ940:O)	C3 Consulting
	G-CBBW	SA Bulldog Srs 120/121 (XX619:T)	S. E. Robottom-Scott
	G-CBBX	Lindstrand LBL-69A balloon	J. L. F. Garcia
	G-CBBZ	Pegasus Quantum 15-912	N. Groome
	G-CBCA	PA-32R-301T Saratoga IITC	W. P. J. Davison/Monaco
	G-CBCB	SA Bulldog Srs 120/121 (XX537:C)	The General Aviation Trading Co Ltd
	G-CBCD	Pegasus Quantum 15	I. A. Lumley
	G-CBCF	Pegasus Quantum 15-912	G-CBCF Group
	G-CBCH	Zenair CH.701UL	L. G. Millen
	G-CBCI	Raj Hamsa X'Air 582 (2)	C. P. Lincoln
	G-CBCJ	RAF 2000 GTX-SE gyroplane	J. P. Comerford
	G-CBCK	Tipsy T.66 Nipper Srs 3	N. M. Bloom (G-TEDZ)
	G-CBCL	Stoddard-Hamilton Glastar	M. I. Weaver
	G-CBCM	Raj Hamsa X'Air 700 (1A)	G. Firth
	G-CBCN	Schweizer 269C-1	Helicentre Liverpool Ltd
	G-CBCP	Van's RV-6A	G-CBCP Group
	G-CBCR	SA Bulldog Srs 120/121 (XX702:II)	D. Wells
	G-CBCV	SA Bulldog Srs 120/121 (XX699:F)	C. A. Patter
	G-CBCX	Pegasus Quantum 15	D. V. Lawrence
	G-CBCY	Beech C24R Sierra Super	Plane Talking Ltd
	G-CBCZ	CFM Streak Shadow SLA	J. O'Malley-Kane
	G-CBDC	Thruster T.600N 450-JAB	David Clarke Microlight Aircraft
	G-CBDD	Mainair Blade	R. D. Smith
	G-CBDG	Zenair CH.601HD	R. E. Lasnier
	G-CBDH	Flight Design CT2K	K. Tuck
	G-CBDI	Denney Kitfox Mk.2	J. G. D. Barbour
	G-CBDJ	Flight Design CT2K	P. J. Walker
	G-CBDK	SA Bulldog Srs 120/121 (XX611:7)	J. N. Randle
	G-CBDL	Mainair Blade	D. Lightwood
	G-CBDM	Tecnam P92-EM Echo	J. J. Cozens
	G-CBDN	Mainair Blade	T. Peckham
	G-CBDO	Raj Hamsa X'Air 582(1)	A. Campbell
	G-CBDP	Mainair Blade 912	D. S. Parker
	G-CBDS	SA Bulldog Srs 120/121 (XX707:4)	J. R. Parry
	G-CBDT	Zenair CH.601HD	D. G. Watt
	G-CBDU	Quad City Challenger II	Hiscox Cases Ltd
	G-CBDV	Raj Hamsa X'Air 582	T. S. Davis
	G-CBDW	Raj Hamsa X'Air Jabiru (1)	A. A. Passmore
	G-CBDX	Pegasus Quantum 15	P. Sinkler
	G-CBDY	Raj Hamsa X'Air V.2 (2)	P. M. Stoney
	G-CBDZ	Pegasus Quantum 15-912	J. J. Brutnell
	G-CBEB	Kiss 400-582 (1)	M. Harris
	G-CBEC	Cameron Z-105 balloon	A. L. Ballarino/Italy
	G-CBED	Cameron Z-90 balloon	John Aimo Balloons SAS/Italy
	G-CBEE	PA-28R Cherokee Arrow 200	IHV Aviation Ltd
	G-CBEF	SA Bulldog Srs 120/121 (XX621:H)	J. A. Ingram
	G-CBEG	Robinson R44	MGB Trading Ltd

BRITISH CIVIL REGISTRATIONS — G-CBEH – G-CBHX

Reg	Type	Owner or Operator	Notes
G-CBEH	SA Bulldog Srs 120/121 (XX521:H)	J. E. Lewis	
G-CBEI	PA-22 Colt 108	D. Sharp	
G-CBEJ	Colt 120A balloon	J. A. Gray	
G-CBEK	SA Bulldog Srs 120/121 (XX700:17)	S. Landregan	
G-CBEL	Hawker Iraqi Fury FB.11	J. A. D. Bradshaw	
G-CBEM	Mainair Blade	M. Earp	
G-CBEN	Pegasus Quantum 15-912	S. Clarke	
G-CBEO	BAe Jetstream 3206	Trident Aviation Leasing Services Ltd	
G-CBES	Shaw Europa XS	M. R. Hexley	
G-CBET	Mainair Blade 912S	D. F. Kenny	
G-CBEU	Pegasus Quantum 15-912	C. Lee	
G-CBEV	Pegasus Quantum 15-912	G-CBEV Group	
G-CBEW	Flight Design CT2K	Shy Talk Group	
G-CBEX	Flight Design CT2K	A. G. Quinn	
G-CBEY	Cameron C-80 balloon	D. V. Fowler	
G-CBEZ	Robin DR.400/180	K. V. Field	
G-CBFA	Diamond DA40 Star	Lyrastar Ltd	
G-CBFE	Raj Hamsa X'Air V.2 (1)	M. L. Powell	
G-CBFF	Cameron O-120 balloon	T. M. C. McCoy	
G-CBFH	Thunder Ax8-105 S2 balloon	D. V. Fowler & A. N. F. Pertwee	
G-CBFJ	Robinson R44	Safedem Ltd	
G-CBFK	Murphy Rebel	P. J. Gibbs	
G-CBFM	SOCATA TB21 Trinidad	Exec Flight Ltd	
G-CBFN	Robin DR.100/200B	Foxtrot November Group	
G-CBFO	Cessna 172S	Transcourt Ltd	
G-CBFP	SA Bulldog Srs 120/121 (XX636:Y)	D. J. Scott	
G-CBFT	Raj Hamsa X'Air 582 (5)	L. Reilly	
G-CBFU	SA Bulldog Srs 120/121 (XX628:9)	J. R. & S. J. Huggins	
G-CBFV	Ikarus C.42	A. W. Leadley	
G-CBFW	Bensen B.8	I. McLean	
G-CBFX	Rans S.6-ES Coyote II	J. R. Lowman	
G-CBFY	Cameron Z-250 balloon	M. L. Gabb	
G-CBFZ	Avtech Jabiru SPL-450	A. H. King	
G-CBGA	PZL-110 Koliber 160A	STG Fabrications Ltd	
G-CBGB	Zenair CH.601UL	J. F. Woodham	
G-CBGC	SOCATA TB10 Tobago	Tobago Aviation Ltd	
G-CBGD	Zenair CH.701UL	I. S. Walsh	
G-CBGE	Tecnam P92-EM Echo	I. D. Rutherford	
G-CBGG	Pegasus Quantum 15	T. E. Davies	
G-CBGH	Teverson Bisport	R. C. Teverson	
G-CBGI	CFM Streak Shadow	M. W. W. Clotworthy	
G-CBGJ	Aeroprakt A.22 Foxbat	M. J. Whiteman-Haywood	
G-CBGL	MH.1521M Broussard	A. I. Milne	
G-CBGN	Van's RV-4	G. A. Nash	
G-CBGO	Murphy Maverick 430	C. R. Ellis & E. A. Wrathall	
G-CBGP	Ikarus C.42 FB UK	C. F. Welby	
G-CBGR	Avtech Jabiru UL-450	R. G. Kirkland	
G-CBGS	Cyclone AX2000	S. M. Newton	
G-CBGU	Thruster T.600N 450-JAB	B. R. Cardosi	
G-CBGV	Thruster T.600N 450-JAB	G. V. Rodgers & P. J. Whitmore	
G-CBGW	Thruster T.600N 450-JAB	M. C. Arnold & A. R. Pluck	
G-CBGX	SA Bulldog Srs 120/121 (XX622:B)	Henfield Lodge Aviation Ltd	
G-CBGZ	Westland Gazelle HT.2 (ZB646:59/CU)	D. Weatherhead Ltd	
G-CBHA	SOCATA TB10 Tobago	Oscar Romeo Aviation Ltd	
G-CBHB	Raj Hamsa X'Air 582 (5)	R. A. J. Graham	
G-CBHC	RAF 2000 GTX-SE gyroplane	A. J. Thomas	
G-CBHD	Cameron Z-160 balloon	Ballooning 50 Degrees Nord/Luxembourg	
G-CBHG	Mainair Blade 912S	B. S. Hope	
G-CBHI	Shaw Europa XS	B. Price	
G-CBHJ	Mainair Blade 912	B. C. Jones	
G-CBHK	Pegasus Quantum 15 (HKS)	B. Dossett	
G-CBHL	AS.350B2 Ecureuil	C. S. McRae	
G-CBHM	Mainair Blade 912	W. T. Milburn	
G-CBHN	Pegasus Quantum 15-912	G. G. Cook	
G-CBHO	Gloster Gladiator II (N5719)	Retro Track & Air (UK) Ltd	
G-CBHP	Corby CJ-1 Starlet	D. H. Barker	
G-CBHR	Lazer Z200	G-CBHR Flying Group	
G-CBHT	Dassault Falcon 900EX	TAG Aviation (UK) Ltd (G-GPWH)	
G-CBHU	RL.5A Sherwood Ranger	M. J. Gooch	
G-CBHV	Raj Hamsa X'Air 582 (5)	S. Soar	
G-CBHW	Cameron Z-105 balloon	Bristol Chamber of Commerce, Industry & Shipping	
G-CBHX	Cameron V-77 balloon	N. A. Apsey	

G-CBHY – G-CBLH BRITISH CIVIL REGISTRATIONS

Notes	Reg	Type	Owner or Operator
	G-CBHY	Pegasus Quantum 15-912	M. W. Abbott
	G-CBHZ	RAF 2000 GTX-SE gyroplane	M. P. Donnelly
	G-CBIB	Flight Design CT2K	J. A. Moss
	G-CBIC	Raj Hamsa X'Air V2 (2)	J. T. Blackburn & D. R. Sutton
	G-CBID	SA Bulldog Srs 120/121)XX549:6)	D. A. Steven
	G-CBIE	Flight Design CT2K	R. K. Jenkins
	G-CBIF	Avtech Jabiru SPL-450	J. A. Iszard
	G-CBIG	Mainair Blade 912	I. Johnson
	G-CBIH	Cameron Z-31 balloon	Cameron Balloons Ltd
	G-CBII	Raj Hamsa X'Air 582 (2)	G. H. Speakman
	G-CBIJ	Ikarus C.42 FB UK Cyclone	M. W. Hanley
	G-CBIK	Rotorway Executive 162F	J. Hodson
	G-CBIL	Cessna 182K	E. Bannister & J. R. C. Spooner/East Midlands (G-BFZZ)
	G-CBIM	Lindstrand LBL-90A balloon	R. K. Parsons
	G-CBIN	TEAM mini-MAX 91	K. J. Walton
	G-CBIO	Thruster T.600N 450-JAB	CJW Holdings Ltd t/a Fairway Flying Services
	G-CBIP	Thruster T.600N 450-JAB	K. D. Mitchell
	G-CBIR	Thruster T.600N 450-JAB	E. G. White
	G-CBIS	Raj Hamsa X'Air 582 (2)	P. T. W. T. Derges
	G-CBIT	RAF 2000 GTX-SE gyroplane	Terrafirma Services Ltd
	G-CBIU	Cameron 95 Flame SS balloon	PSH Skypower Ltd
	G-CBIV	Skyranger 912 (1)	K. Brown
	G-CBIW	Lindstrand LBL-310A balloon	C. E. Wood
	G-CBIX	Zenair CH.601UL	R. A. & B. M. Roberts
	G-CBIY	Aerotechnik EV-97 Eurostar	M. G. Titmus
	G-CBIZ	Pegasus Quantum 15-912	M. P. Duckett
	G-CBJA	Kiss 400-582 (1)	M. S. R. Burak
	G-CBJD	Stoddard-Hamilton Glastar	K. F. Farey
	G-CBJE	RAF 2000 GTX-SE gyroplane	V. G. Freke
	G-CBJG	DHC.1 Chipmunk 20	C. J. Rees
	G-CBJH	Aeroprakt A.22 Foxbat	H. Smith
	G-CBJJ	SA Bulldog Srs 120/121 (XX525)	G. V. Crowe & D. L. Thompson
	G-CBJK	SA Bulldog Srs 120/121 (XX713:2)	G. V. Crowe & D. L. Thompson
	G-CBJL	Kiss 400-582 (1)	R. E. Morris
	G-CBJM	Avtech Jabiru SP-470	A. T. Moyce
	G-CBJN	RAF 2000 GTX-SE gyroplane	R. Hall
	G-CBJO	Pegasus Quantum 15-912	P. A. Martland
	G-CBJP	Zenair CH.601UL	R. E. Peirse
	G-CBJR	Aerotechnik EV-97 Eurostar	R. B. Skinner
	G-CBJS	Cameron C-60 balloon	N. Ivison
	G-CBJT	Mainair Blade	M. B. Smith
	G-CBJU	Van's RV-7A	T. W. Waltham
	G-CBJV	Rotorway Executive 162F	R. J. Green
	G-CBJW	Ikarus C.42 Cyclone FB UK	P. Harper & P. J. Morton
	G-CBJX	Raj Hamsa X'Air Falcon J22	M. A. Bastian
	G-CBJZ	Westland Gazelle HT.3	K. G. Theurer/Germany
	G-CBKA	Westland Gazelle HT.3 (XZ937:Y)	MW Helicopters Ltd/Stapleford
	G-CBKB	Bücker Bü 181C Bestmann	W. R. & G. D. Snadden
	G-CBKC	Westland Gazelle HT.3	T. E. Westley
	G-CBKD	Westland Gazelle HT.2	Flying Scout Ltd
	G-CBKE	Kiss 400-582 (1)	R. J. Howell
	G-CBKF	Easy Raider J2.2 (1)	R. R. Armstrong
	G-CBKG	Thruster T.600N 450 JAB	A. S. Mitchell
	G-CBKI	Cameron Z-90 balloon	Wheatfields Park Ltd
	G-CBKJ	Cameron Z-90 balloon	Invista (UK) Holdings Ltd
	G-CBKK	Ultramagic S-130 balloon	Airbourne Adventures Ltd
	G-CBKL	Raj Hamsa X'Air 582 (1)	Caithness X-Air Group
	G-CBKM	Mainair Blade 912	N. Purdy
	G-CBKN	Mainair Blade 912	D. S. Clews
	G-CBKO	Mainair Blade 912S	P. W. Jordan
	G-CBKR	PA-28-161 Warrior III	Devon and Somerset Flight Training Ltd
	G-CBKS	Kiss 400-582 (1)	S. Kilpin
	G-CBKU	Ikarus C.42 Cyclone FB UK	C. Blackburn
	G-CBKV	Cameron Z-77 balloon	J. F. Till
	G-CBKW	Pegasus Quantum 15-912	W. G. Coulter
	G-CBKY	Avtech Jabiru SP-470	P. R. Sistern
	G-CBLA	Aero Designs Pulsar XP	J. P. Kynaston
	G-CBLB	Technam P.92-EM Echo	F. G. Walker
	G-CBLD	Mainair Blade 912S	N. E. King
	G-CBLE	Robin R.2120U	Cardiff Academy of Aviation Ltd/Cardiff
	G-CBLF	Raj Hamsa X'Air 582 (11)	E. G. Bishop
	G-CBLH	Raj Hamsa X'Air 582 (11)	S. Rance

BRITISH CIVIL REGISTRATIONS

G-CBLJ – G-CBPG

Reg	Type	Owner or Operator	Notes
G-CBLJ	Aerostar Yakovlev Yak-52	A. R. Richards	
G-CBLK	Hawker Hind	Aero Vintage Ltd	
G-CBLL	Pegasus Quantum 15-912	P. R. Jones	
G-CBLM	Mainair Blade 912	P. A. Flaherty	
G-CBLN	Cameron Z-31 balloon	L. P. Hooper	
G-CBLO	Lindstrand LBL-42A balloon	N. K. & R. H. Calvert	
G-CBLP	Raj Hamsa X'Air Falcon	A. C. Parsons	
G-CBLS	Fiat CR.42	Fighter Collection Ltd/Duxford	
G-CBLT	Mainair Blade 912	C. D. Hayle	
G-CBLU	Cameron C-90 balloon	A. G. Martin	
G-CBLV	Flight Design CT2K	A. R. Pickering	
G-CBLW	Raj Hamsa X'Air Falcon V2 (1)	R. G. Halliwell	
G-CBLX	Kiss 400-582 (1)	J. P. Doswell	
G-CBLY	Grob G.109B	G-CBLY Syndicate	
G-CBLZ	Rutan LongEz	S. K. Cockburn	
G-CBMA	Raj Hamsa X'Air 582 (10)	B. L. Crick	
G-CBMB	Cyclone Ax2000	York Microlight Centre Ltd/Rufforth	
G-CBMC	Cameron Z-105 balloon	First Flight	
G-CBMD	IDA Bacau Yakovlev Yak-52 (10 yellow)	R. J. Hunter	
G-CBME	Cessna F.172M	Skytrax Aviation Ltd	
G-CBMI	Yakovlev Yak-52	D. P. Holland	
G-CBMJ	RAF 2000 GTX-SE gyroplane	C. D. Upsall	
G-CBMK	Cameron Z-120 balloon	G. Davies	
G-CBML	DHC.6 Twin Otter 310	Isles of Scilly Skybus Ltd	
G-CBMM	Mainair Blade 912	L. E. Donaldson	
G-CBMO	PA-28 Cherokee 180	C. Woodliffe	
G-CBMP	Cessna R.182	Orman (Carrolls Farm) Ltd	
G-CBMR	Medway Eclipser	A. Bradfield	
G-CBMS	Medway Eclipser	R. R. Bagge	
G-CBMT	Robin DR.400/180	A. C. Williamson	
G-CBMU	Whittaker MW6-S Fat Boy Flyer	F. J. Brown	
G-CBMV	Pegasus Quantum 15	B. Hamilton	
G-CBMW	Zenair CH.701 UL	C. Long	
G-CBMX	Kiss 400-582 (1)	D. L. Turner	
G-CBMZ	Aerotechnik EV-97 Eurostar	J. C. O'Donnell	
G-CBNA	Flight Design CT2K	D. M. Wood	
G-CBNB	Eurocopter EC 120B	Arenberg Consultadoria E Servicos LDA/Madeira	
G-CBNC	Mainair Blade 912	A. C. Rowlands	
G-CBNF	Rans S.7 Courier	M. Rockliff	
G-CBNG	Robin R.2112	Solway Flyers Ltd/Carlisle	
G-CBNI	Lindstrand LBL-180A balloon	Cancer Research UK	
G-CBNJ	Raj Hamsa X'Air 912 (1)	M. G. Lynes	
G-CBNL	Dyn'Aéro MCR-01 Club	D. H. Wilson	
G-CBNM	NA P-51D Mustang (463864:HL-W)	Patina Ltd/Duxford	
G-CBNO	CFM Streak Shadow	D. J. Goldsmith	
G-CBNT	Pegasus Quantum 15-912	B. H. Goldsmith	
G-CBNU	VS.361 Spitfire LF.IX	M. Aldridge	
G-CBNV	Rans S.6-ES Coyote II	F. H. Cook	
G-CBNW	Cameron N-105 balloon	Bailey Balloons	
G-CBNX	Mongomerie-Bensen B.8MR	K. Ashford	
G-CBNY	Kiss 400-582 (1)	R. Redman	
G-CBNZ	TEAM hi-MAX 1700R	A. P. S. John	
G-CBOA	Auster B.8 Agricola Srs 1	C. J. Baker	
G-CBOC	Raj Hamsa X'Air 582 (5)	A. J. McAleer	
G-CBOE	Hawker Hurricane IIB	P. J. Tuplin & P. W. Portelli	
G-CBOF	Shaw Europa XS	I. W. Ligertwood	
G-CBOG	Mainair Blade 912S	J. S. Little	
G-CBOK	Rans S.6-ES Coyote II	S. A. Clarehughr	
G-CBOM	Mainair Blade 912	G. Suckling	
G-CBOO	Mainair Blade 912S	R. G. Mason	
G-CBOP	Avtech Jabiru UL-450	D. W. Batchelor	
G-CBOR	Cessna F.172N	P. Seville	
G-CBOS	Rans S.6-ES Coyote II	R. Skene	
G-CBOT	Robinson R44	Aviation Rentals	
G-CBOU	Bensen-Parsons 2-place gyroplane	R. Collin & M.S.Sparkes	
G-CBOV	Mainair Blade	H. D. Lynch	
G-CBOW	Cameron Z-120 balloon	Associated Technologies Ltd	
G-CBOY	Pegasus Quantum 15-912	T. G. Jackson	
G-CBOZ	IDA Bacau Yakovlev Yak-52	T. M. Knight	
G-CBPC	Sportavia-Putzer RF-5B Sperber	Lee RF-5B Group	
G-CBPD	Ikarus C.42 Cyclone FB UK	Waxwing Group	
G-CBPE	SOCATA TB10 Tobago	A. F. Welch	
G-CBPG	Balloon Works Firefly 7 balloon	Balloon Preservation Flying Group	

131

G-CBPH – G-CBUI — BRITISH CIVIL REGISTRATIONS

Notes	Reg	Type	Owner or Operator
	G-CBPH	Lindstrand LBL-105A balloon	I. Vastano/Italy
	G-CBPI	PA-28R-201 Arrow III	Benair Aviation Ltd
	G-CBPK	Rand-Robinson KR-2	R. J. McGoldrick
	G-CBPL	TEAM mini-MAX 93	K. M. Moores
	G-CBPM	Yakovlev Yak-50 (50 black)	P. W. Ansell
	G-CBPN	Thruster T.600N 450 Jabiru	J. S. Webb
	G-CBPP	Avtech Jabiru UL-450	C. J. Cullen
	G-CBPR	Avtech Jabiru UL-450	F. B. Hall
	G-CBPU	Raj Hamsa X'Air R100 (2)	X'Air Group
	G-CBPV	Zenair CH.601UL	R. D. Barnard
	G-CBPW	Lindstrand LBL-105A balloon	Flying Pictures Ltd
	G-CBPY	Yakovlev Yak-52	Lyttondale Associate
	G-CBPZ	Ultramagic N-300 balloon	Kent Ballooning
	G-CBRB	Ultramagic S-105 balloon	I. S. Bridge
	G-CBRC	Jodel D.18	B. W. Shaw
	G-CBRD	Jodel D.18	J. D. Haslam
	G-CBRE	Mainair Blade 912	R. J. Davey
	G-CBRF	Ikarus C.42 FB100 VLA	T. W. Gale
	G-CBRG	Cessna 560XL Citation Excel	Queensway Aviation Ltd
	G-CBRH	IDA Yakovlev Yak-52	B. M. Gwynnett
	G-CBRJ	Mainair Blade 912S	R. W. Janion
	G-CBRK	Ultramagic M-77 balloon	R. T. Revel
	G-CBRL	IDA Bacau Yakovlev Yak-52	P. S. Mirams
	G-CBRM	Mainair Blade	M. H. Levy
	G-CBRO	Robinson R44	R. D. Jordan
	G-CBRP	IDA Bacau Yakovlev Yak-52	R. J. Pinnock
	G-CBRR	Aerotechnik EV-97 Eurostar	G-CBRR Group
	G-CBRT	Murphy Elite	T. W. Baylie
	G-CBRU	IDA Bacau Yakovlev Yak-52 (42 white)	G. M. Smith & J. A. Pasquale
	G-CBRV	Cameron C-90 balloon	C. J. Teall
	G-CBRW	Aerostar Yakovlev Yak-52 (50 grey)	M. A. Gainza
	G-CBRX	Zenair CH.601UL Zodiac	J. B. Marshall
	G-CBRY	Pegasus Quik	Cyclone Airsports
	G-CBRZ	Kiss 400-582(1)	J. J. Ryan/Ireland
	G-CBSD	Westland Gazelle HT.2 (XW854:46)	Mexsky Ltd
	G-CBSF	Westland Gazelle HT.2	Falcon Aviation Ltd
	G-CBSH	Westland Gazelle HT.3 (XX406:P)	Alltask Ltd
	G-CBSI	Westland Gazelle HT.3 (XZ934:U)	P. S. Unwin
	G-CBSK	Westland Gazelle HT.3 (ZB627:A)	Falcon Flying Group
	G-CBSL	IDA Bacau Yakovlev Yak-52 (67 red)	N. & A. D. Barton
	G-CBSM	Mainair Blade 912	Mainair Sports Ltd
	G-CBSN	Aerostar Yakovlev Yak-52 (48 grey)	S. Attree
	G-CBSO	PA-28-181 Archer II	Archer One Ltd
	G-CBSP	Pegasus Quantum 15-912	D. S. Carstairs
	G-CBSR	Yakovlev Yak-52	L. Olivier
	G-CBSS	IDA Bacau Yakovlev Yak-52	E. J. F. Verhellen/Belgium
	G-CBSU	Avtech Jabiru UL	P. K. Sutton
	G-CBSV	Montgomerie-Bensen B.8MR	J. A. McGill
	G-CBSX	Kiss 400-582 (1)	G. A. G. Parnell
	G-CBSZ	Mainair Blade 912S	D. M. Newton
	G-CBTB	I.I.I. Sky Arrow 650TS	D. A. & J. A. S. T. Hood
	G-CBTD	Pegasus Quantum 15-912	D. Baillie
	G-CBTE	Mainair Blade 912|S	K. J. Miles
	G-CBTG	Ikarus C.42 FB UK Cyclone	Ikarus Group
	G-CBTK	Raj Hamsa X'Air 582 (5)	W. E. Richards
	G-CBTL	Monnett Moni	G. Dawes
	G-CBTM	Mainair Blade	D. A. A. Hewitt
	G-CBTN	PA-31 Navajo C	Durban Aviation Services Ltd
	G-CBTO	Rans S.6-ES Coyote II	C. G. Deeley
	G-CBTR	Lindstrand LBL-120A balloon	R. H. Etherington
	G-CBTS	Gloster Gamecock (replica)	Retro Track & Air (UK) Ltd
	G-CBTT	PA-28-181 Archer II	Citicourt Aviation Ltd (G-BFMM)
	G-CBTW	Mainair Blade 912	D. Hyatt
	G-CBTX	Denney Kitfox Mk.2	G. I. Doake
	G-CBTZ	Pegasus Quantum 15-912	P. M. Connelly
	G-CBUA	Extra EA.230	R. Howarth
	G-CBUC	Raj Hamsa X'Air 582 (5)	M. N. Watson
	G-CBUD	Pegasus Quantum 15-912	G. N. S. Farrant
	G-CBUE	Ultramagic N-250 balloon	Elinore French Ltd
	G-CBUF	Flight Design CT2K	B. G. Cox
	G-CBUG	Technam P.92-EM Echo	R. C. Mincik
	G-CBUH	Westland Scout AH.1	C. J. Marsden
	G-CBUI	Westland Wasp HAS.1 (XT420:606)	BN Helicopters Ltd/Bembridge

BRITISH CIVIL REGISTRATIONS

G-CBUJ – G-CBXZ

Reg	Type	Owner or Operator	Notes
G-CBUJ	Raj Hamsa X'Air 582 (10)	G-CBUJ Flying Group	
G-CBUK	Van's RV-6A	P. G. Greenslade	
G-CBUN	Barker Charade	D. R. Wilkinson & T. Coldwell	
G-CBUO	Cameron O-90 balloon	W. J. Treacy & P. M. Smith	
G-CBUP	VPM M-16 Tandem Trainer	J. S. Firth	
G-CBUR	Zenair CH.601UL	N. A. Jack	
G-CBUS	Pegasus Quantum 15	J. Liddiard	
G-CBUU	Pegasus Quantum 15-912	I. D. Town	
G-CBUW	Cameron Z-133 balloon	Balloon School (International) Ltd	
G-CBUX	Cyclone AX2000	J. C. Kitchen	
G-CBUY	Rans S.6-ES Coyote II	K. R. Crawley	
G-CBUZ	Pegasus Quantum 15	D. G. Seymour	
G-CBVA	Thruster T.600N 450	D. J. Clingan	
G-CBVB	Robin R.2120U	Cardiff Academy of Aviation Ltd/Cardiff	
G-CBVC	Raj Hamsa X'Air 582 (5)	M. J. Male	
G-CBVD	Cameron C-60 balloon	Phoenix Balloons Ltd	
G-CBVE	Raj Hamsa X'Air Falcon 912 (1)	P. K. Bennett	
G-CBVF	Murphy Maverick	J. Hopkinson	
G-CBVG	Mainair Blade 912S	A. M. Buchanan	
G-CBVH	Lindstrand LBL-120A balloon	Line Packaging & Display Ltd	
G-CBVI	Robinson R44	Happy Chopper Ltd	
G-CBVK	Schroeder Fire Balloons G balloon	S. Travaglia	
G-CBVL	Robinson R22 Beta II	Heli Air Ltd/Wellesbourne	
G-CBVM	Aerotechnik EV-97 Eurostar	R. J. Butler	
G-CBVN	Pegasus Quik	C. Kearney	
G-CBVO	Raj Hamsa X'Air 582 (5)	G. J. Burley	
G-CBVR	Skyranger 912 (2)	S. H. Lunney	
G-CBVS	Skyranger 912 (2)	S. C. Cornock	
G-CBVT	IDA Yakovlev Yak-52	Lancair Espana SL/Spain	
G-CBVU	PA-28R Cherokee Arrow 200-II	E. W. Guess (Holdings) Ltd	
G-CBVV	Cameron N-120 balloon	John Aimo Balloons SAS/Italy	
G-CBVX	Cessna 182P	P. & A. de Weerdt	
G-CBVY	Ikarus C.42 Cyclone FB UK	M. J. Hendra & Gossage	
G-CBVZ	Flight Design CT2K	A. N. D. Arthur	
G-CBWA	Flight Design CT2K	Charlie Tango Group	
G-CBWB	PA-34-200T Seneca II	Fairoaks Airport Ltd	
G-CBWD	PA-28-161 Warrior III	Fleetwash Ltd	
G-CBWE	Aerotechnik EV-97 Eurostar	J. & C. W. Hood	
G-CBWG	Aerotechnik EV-97A Eurostar	Southside Flyers	
G-CBWI	Thruster T. 600N 450	T. Lee	
G-CBWJ	Thruster T. 600N 450	T. Harrison-Smith	
G-CBWK	Ultramagic H-77 balloon	H. C. Peel	
G-CBWM	Mainair Blade 912	C. Middleton	
G-CBWN	Campbell Cricket Mk.6	P. G. Rawson	
G-CBWO	Rotorway Executive 162F	Handyvalue Ltd	
G-CBWP	Shaw Europa	T. W. Greaves	
G-CBWS	Whittaker MW6 Merlin	D. W. McCormack	
G-CBWU	Rotorway Executive 162F	Usk Valley Trout Farm	
G-CBWV	Falconar F-12A Cruiser	A. Ackland	
G-CBWW	Skyranger 912 (2)	R. L. & S. H. Tosswill	
G-CBWX	Slingsby T.67M-260	Slingsby Aviation Ltd/Kirkbymoorside	
G-CBWY	Raj Hamsa X'Air 582 (6)	G. C. Linley	
G-CBWZ	Robinson R22 Beta	Plane Talking Ltd/Elstree	
G-CBXA	Raj Hamsa X'Air 582 (5)	A. J. Sharratt	
G-CBXB	Lindstrand LBL-150A balloon	M. A. Webb	
G-CBXC	Ikarus C.42 Cyclone FB UK	B. J. Mould	
G-CBXD	Bell 206L-3 LongRanger 3	Whirlybird Charters Ltd & Automotive and General Supply Co Ltd	
G-CBXE	Easy Raider J2.2 (2)	A. Appleby	
G-CBXF	Easy Raider J2.2 (2)	F. Colman	
G-CBXG	Thruster T.600N 450	Newtownards Microlight Group	
G-CBXH	Thruster T.600N 450	M. L. Smith	
G-CBXJ	Cessna 172S	A. Reay	
G-CBXK	Robinson R22 Mariner	Aero Maintenance Ltd	
G-CBXM	Mainair Blade	B. A. Coombe	
G-CBXN	Robinson R22 Beta II	N. M. G. Pearson	
G-CBXR	Raj Hamsa X-Air Falcon 582 (1)	A. R. Rhodes	
G-CBXS	Skyranger J2.2 (1)	C. J. Erith	
G-CBXT	Westland Gazelle HT.3 (XW898:G)	C. D. Evans & R. Paskey	
G-CBXU	TEAM mini-MAX 91A	C. D. Hatcher	
G-CBXV	Mainair Blade	C. Turner	
G-CBXW	Shaw Europa XS	R. G. Fairall	
G-CBXZ	Rans S.6-ES Coyote II	D. Tole	

G-CBYB – G-CCBL — BRITISH CIVIL REGISTRATIONS

Notes	Reg	Type	Owner or Operator
	G-CBYB	Rotorway Executive 162F	Clark Contracting
	G-CBYC	Cameron Z-275 balloon	First Flight
	G-CBYD	Rans S.6-ES Coyote II	R. Burland
	G-CBYE	Pegasus Quik	C. E. Morris
	G-CBYF	Mainair Blade	C. P. Lemon
	G-CBYH	Aeroprakt A.22 Foxbat	G. C. Moore
	G-CBYI	Pegasus Quantum 15-503	J. M. Hardy
	G-CBYJ	Steen Skybolt	F. G. Morris
	G-CBYM	Mainair Blade	A. Clarke
	G-CBYN	Shaw Europa XS	A. B. Milne
	G-CBYO	Pegasus Quik	C. J. Roper & P. F. Mayo
	G-CBYP	Whittaker MW6-S Fat Boy Flyer	R. J. Grainger
	G-CBYS	Lindstrand LBL-21 balloon France	J. J. C. Bernardin
	G-CBYT	Thruster T.600N 450	B. E. Smith
	G-CBYU	PA-28-161 Warrior II	Stapleford Flying Club Ltd
	G-CBYV	Pegasus Quantum 15-912	A. R. Wright
	G-CBYW	Hatz CB-1	T. A. Hinton
	G-CBYX	Bell 206B JetRanger 3	RCR Aviation Ltd
	G-CBYY	Robinson R44	Helicopter Training & Hire Ltd
	G-CBYZ	Tecnam P92-EM Echo-Super	B. Weaver
	G-CBZA	Mainair Blade	R. K. Johnson
	G-CBZB	Mainair Blade	A. Bennion
	G-CBZD	Mainair Blade	G. F. Jones
	G-CBZE	Robinson R44	Alps (Scotland) Ltd
	G-CBZF	Robinson R22 Beta	Suffolk Helicopters Ltd
	G-CBZG	Rans S.6-ES Coyote II	A. D. Thelwall
	G-CBZH	Pegasus Quik	M. Bond
	G-CBZI	Rotorway Executive 162F	T. D. Stock
	G-CBZJ	Lindstrand LBL-25A balloon	Pegasus Ballooning
	G-CBZK	Robin DR.400/180	R. A. Fleming
	G-CBZL	Westland Gazelle HT.3	Armstrong Aviation Ltd
	G-CBZM	Avtech Jabiru SPL-450	M. E. Ledward
	G-CBZN	Rans S.6-ES Coyote II	A. James
	G-CBZP	Hawker Fury 1 (K5674)	Historic Aircraft Collection
	G-CBZR	PA-28R-201 Arrow III	S. J. Skilton
	G-CBZS	Aurora	J. Lynden
	G-CBZT	Pegasus Quik	N. Hartley
	G-CBZU	Lindstrand LBL-180A balloon	Great Escape Ballooning Ltd
	G-CBZV	Ultramagic S-130 balloon	J. D. Griffiths
	G-CBZW	Zenair CH.701UL	T. M. Siles
	G-CBZX	Dyn' Aero MCR-01 ULC	A. C. N. Freeman & M. P. Wilson
	G-CBZY	Flight Airsports Doodle Bug	A. I. Calderhead-Lea
	G-CBZZ	Cameron Z-275 balloon	A. C. K. Rawson & J. J. Rudoni
	G-CCAB	Mainair Blade	A. J. Morris
	G-CCAC	Aerotech EV-97 Eurostar	J. S. Holden
	G-CCAD	Mainair Pegasus Quik	E. G. Cartwright
	G-CCAE	Avtech Jabiru UL-450	M. P. & R. A. Wells
	G-CCAF	Skyranger 912 (1)	D. W. & M. L. Squire
	G-CCAG	Mainair Blade 912	W. Cope
	G-CCAH	Magni M16C Tandem Trainer	Magni Gyro Ltd
	G-CCAK	Zenair CN.601HD	A. Kimmond
	G-CCAL	Technam P92-EM Echo	D. Cassidy
	G-CCAM	Mainair Blade	M. D. Peacock
	G-CCAN	Cessna 182P	D. J. Hunter
	G-CCAP	Robinson R22 Beta II	HJS Helicopters Ltd
	G-CCAR	Cameron N-77 balloon	D. P. Turner
	G-CCAS	Pegasus Quik	C. M. Addison
	G-CCAT	AA-55A Cheetah	A. Ohringer (G-OAJH/G-KILT/G-BJFA)
	G-CCAU	Eurocopter EC 135T1	West Mercia Constabulary
	G-CCAV	PA-28-181 Archer II	Archer II Ltd
	G-CCAW	Mainair Blade 912	C. A. Woodhouse
	G-CCAY	Cameron Z-42 balloon	P. Stern
	G-CCAZ	Mainair Pegasus Quik	P. S. Martin
	G-CCBA	Skyranger R.100	Fourstrokes Group
	G-CCBB	Cameron N-90 balloon	S. C. A. & L. D. Craze
	G-CCBC	Thruster T.600N 450	M. L. Smith
	G-CCBF	Maule M.5-235C	R. Windley (G-NHVH)
	G-CCBG	Skyranger V.2 + (1)	C. A. Hardy
	G-CCBH	PA-28 Cherokee 236	J. R. Hunt & S. M. Packer
	G-CCBJ	Skyranger 912 (2)	M. A. Russell
	G-CCBK	Aerotechnik EV-97 Eurostar	B. S. Waycott
	G-CCBL	Agusta-Bell 206B JetRanger 3	S. W. Adamson-Haulage

BRITISH CIVIL REGISTRATIONS

G-CCBM – G-CCEW

Reg	Type	Owner or Operator	Notes
G-CCBM	Aerotechnik EV-97 Eurostar	W. Graves	
G-CCBN	Scale Replica SE-5A	V. C. Lockwood	
G-CCBP	Lindstrand LBL-60X balloon	Lindstrand Hot-Air Balloons Ltd	
G-CCBR	Jodel D.120	A. Dunne & M. Munnelly	
G-CCBT	Cameron Z-90 balloon	I. J. Sharpe	
G-CCBU	Raj Hamsa X'Air 582 (9)	J. S. Rakker	
G-CCBV	Cameron Z-225 balloon	Compagnie Aéronautique du Grand-Duché de Luxembourg	
G-CCBW	Sherwood Ranger	P. H. Wiltshire	
G-CCBX	Raj Hamsa X'Air 133 (2)	A. D'Amico	
G-CCBY	Avtech Jabiru UL-450	D. M. Goodman	
G-CCBZ	Aero Designs Pulsar	J. M. Keane	
G-CCCA	VS.509 Spitfire Tr.IX (161)	Historic Flying Ltd/Duxford (G-BHRH/G-TRIX)	
G-CCCB	Thruster T.600N 450	J. Williams	
G-CCCD	Mainair Pegasus Quantum 15	R. N. Gamble	
G-CCCE	Aeroprakt A.22 Foxbat	C. V. Ellingworth	
G-CCCF	Thruster T.600N 450	Thruster Group 2004	
G-CCCG	Mainair Pegasus Quik	C. J. Haste	
G-CCCI	Medway Eclipse R	V. Grayson	
G-CCCJ	Nicollier HN.700 Menestrel II	G. A. Rodmell	
G-CCCK	Skyranger 912 (2)	P. L. Braniff	
G-CCCM	Skyranger 912 (2)	I. A Forrest & C. K. Richardson	
G-CCCN	Robin R.3000/160	R. W. Denny	
G-CCCO	Aerotechnik EV-97 Eurostar	Connel Flying Club Eurostar Group	
G-CCCP	IDA Yakovlev Yak-52	A. H. Soper	
G-CCCR	Skyranger 912 (2)	D. M. Robbins	
G-CCCT	Ikarus C.42 FB UK Cyclone	J. Kilpatrick	
G-CCCU	Thruster T.600N 450	A. F. Cashin	
G-CCCV	Raj Hamsa X'Air Falcon 133 (1)	A. J. Fraley	
G-CCCW	Pereira Osprey 2	D. J. Southward	
G-CCCY	Skyranger 912 (2)	A. Watson	
G-CCDB	Mainair Pegasus Quik	C. J. Van Dyke	
G-CCDC	Rans S.6-ES Coyote II	A. S. Luketa	
G-CCDD	Mainair Pegasus Quik	M. P. Hadden & M. H. Rollins	
G-CCDE	Robinson R22 Beta II	J. K. and M. Houldcroft and Sons	
G-CCDF	Mainair Pegasus Quik	R. P. McGann	
G-CCDG	Skyranger 912 (1)	T. H. Filmer	
G-CCDH	Skyranger 912 (2)	P. & V. C. Reynolds	
G-CCDJ	Raj Hamsa X'Air Falcon 582 (2)	J. M. Spitz	
G-CCDK	Pegasus Quantum 15-912	S. Brock	
G-CCDL	Raj Hamsa X'Air Falcon 582 (2)	G. M. Brown	
G-CCDM	Mainair Blade	P. R. G. Morley	
G-CCDN	PA-28-181 Archer III	J. D. Scott	
G-CCDO	Mainair Pegasus Quik	J. L. Guy	
G-CCDP	Raj Hamsa X'Air R.100 (3)	J. A. McKie	
G-CCDR	Raj Hamsa X'Air Falcon Jabiru	P. D. Sibbons	
G-CCDS	Nicollier HN.700 Menestrel II	B. W. Gowland	
G-CCDU	Tecnam P92-EM Echo	M. J. Barrett	
G-CCDV	Thruster T.600N 450	D. J. Whysall	
G-CCDW	Skyranger 582 (1)	Debts R Us Family Group	
G-CCDX	Aerotechnik EV-97 Eurostar	J. M. Swash	
G-CCDY	Skyranger 912 (2)	N. H. Copperthwaite	
G-CCDZ	Pegasus Quantum 15-912	K. D. Baldwin	
G-CCEA	Mainair Pegasus Quik	G. D. Ritchie	
G-CCEB	Thruster T.600N 450	Thruster Air Services Ltd	
G-CCEC	Evans VP-1	C. R. Harrison (G-ROSE)	
G-CCED	Zenair CH.601UL	R. P Reynolds	
G-CCEE	PA-15 Vagabond	I. M. Callier (G-VAGA)	
G-CCEF	Shaw Europa	C. P Garner	
G-CCEG	Rans S.6-ES Coyote II	W. F. Whitfield	
G-CCEH	Skyranger 912 (2)	ZC Owners	
G-CCEI	Evans VP-2	I. P. Manley & J. Pearce (G-BJZB)	
G-CCEJ	Aerotechnik EV-97 Eurostar	C. R. Ashley	
G-CCEK	Kiss 400-582 (1)	G. S. Sage	
G-CCEL	Avtech Jabiru UL	R. Ryper	
G-CCEM	Aerotechnik EV-97 Eurostar	G. K. Kenealy/Barton	
G-CCEN	Cameron Z-120 balloon	R. Hunt	
G-CCEO	Thunder Ax10-180 S2 balloon	P. Heitzeneder/Austria	
G-CCEP	Raj Hamsa X'Air Falcon Jabiru	K. Angel	
G-CCES	Raj Hamsa X'Air 2706	G. V. McCloskey	
G-CCET	Nova Vertex 28 hang glider	M. Hay	
G-CCEU	RAF 2000 GTX-SE gyroplane	N. G. Dovaston	
G-CCEW	Mainair Pegasus Quik	N. F. Mackenzie	

G-CCEY – G-CCIF — BRITISH CIVIL REGISTRATIONS

Notes	Reg	Type	Owner or Operator
	G-CCEY	Raj Hamsa X'582 (11)	P. F. F. Spedding
	G-CCEZ	Easy Raider J2.2	S. A. Chambers
	G-CCFA	Kiss 400-582 (1)	N. Hewitt
	G-CCFB	Mainair Pegasus Quik	W. T. Davis
	G-CCFC	Robinson R44 II	M. Entwistle
	G-CCFD	Quad City Challenger II	W. Oswald
	G-CCFE	Tipsy Nipper T.66 Srs 2	F. Hambly
	G-CCFF	Lindstrand LBL-150A balloon	Airborne Adventures Ltd
	G-CCFG	Dyn'Aéro MCR-01 Club	GFG Group
	G-CCFI	PA-32 Cherokee Six 260	McManus Truck & Trailer Spares Ltd
	G-CCFJ	Kolb Twinstar Mk.3	D. Travers
	G-CCFK	Shaw Europa	C. R. Knapton
	G-CCFL	Mainair Pegasus Quik	S. A. Noble
	G-CCFM	Mainair Blade 912	J. Owen
	G-CCFN	Cameron N-105 balloon	ABC Flights Ltd
	G-CCFO	Pitts S-1S Special	R. J. Anderson
	G-CCFP	Diamond DA40D Star	Diamond Aircraft UK Ltd/Gamston
	G-CCFR	Diamond DA40D Star	B. Wronski
	G-CCFS	Diamond DA40D Star	Principle Aircraft
	G-CCFT	Mainair Pegasus Quantum 15-912	D. Tasker
	G-CCFU	Diamond DA40D Star	Egnatia Aviation Ltd/Greece
	G-CCFV	Lindstrand LBL-77A balloon	Alton Aviation Ltd
	G-CCFW	WAR Focke-Wulf Fw.190	D. B. Conway
	G-CCFX	EAA Acrosport 2	C. D. Ward
	G-CCFY	Rotorway Executive 162F	Southern Helicopters Ltd
	G-CCFZ	Ikarus C.42 FB UK	B. W. Drake
	G-CCGB	TEAM mini-MAX	A. D, Pentland
	G-CCGC	Mainair Pegasus Quik	R. W. Street
	G-CCGE	Robinson R22 Beta	Heli Aitch Be Ltd
	G-CCGF	Robinson R22 Beta	A. Tallis
	G-CCGG	Jabiru Aircraft Jabiru J400	G. E. Hall
	G-CCGH	Supermarine Aircraft Spitfire Mk.26	K. D. Pearce
	G-CCGI	Mainair Pegasus Quik	M. C. Kerr
	G-CCGK	Mainair Blade	G. Kerr
	G-CCGL	SOCATA TB20 Trinidad	Pembroke Motor Services Ltd
	G-CCGM	Kiss 450-582 (1)	A. I. Lea
	G-CCGO	Medway Microlights AV8R	Medway Microlights
	G-CCGP	Bristol Type 200	R. L. Holman
	G-CCGR	Raj Hamsa X'Air 133 (1)	C. M. Wilkes
	G-CCGS	Dornier 328-100	Scot Airways Ltd
	G-CCGT	Cameron Z-425 balloon	A. A. Brown
	G-CCGU	Van's RV-9A	B. J. Main & ptnrs
	G-CCGV	Lindstrand LBL-150A balloon	High On Adventure Balloons Ltd
	G-CCGW	Shaw Europa	G. C. Smith
	G-CCGY	Cameron Z-105 balloon	Cameron Balloons Ltd
	G-CCGZ	Cameron Z-250 balloon	Ballooning Adventures Ltd
	G-CCHA	Diamond DA40D Star	Diamond Aircraft UK Ltd/Gamston
	G-CCHB	Diamond DA40D Star	Diamond Aircraft UK Ltd/Gamston
	G-CCHC	Diamond DA40D Star	Diamond Aircraft UK Ltd/Gamston
	G-CCHD	Diamond DA40D Star	Diamond Aircraft UK Ltd/Gamston
	G-CCHE	Diamond DA40D Star	Diamond Aircraft UK Ltd/Gamston
	G-CCHF	Diamond DA40D Star	Cabair College of Air Training Ltd
	G-CCHG	Diamond DA40D Star	Plane Talking Ltd
	G-CCHH	Pegasus Quik	D. J. Cornelius
	G-CCHI	Mainair Pegasus Quik	M. R. Starling
	G-CCHJ	Kiss 400-582 (1)	H. C. Jones
	G-CCHK	Diamond DA40D Star	Plane Talking Ltd
	G-CCHL	PA-28-181 Archer iii	Archer Three Ltd
	G-CCHM	Kiss 450	M. J. Jessup
	G-CCHN	Corby CJ.1 Starlet	D. C. Mayle
	G-CCHO	Mainair Pegasus Quik	M. Allan
	G-CCHP	Cameron Z-31 balloon	M. H. Redman
	G-CCHR	Easy Raider 583 (1)	R. B. M. Etherington
	G-CCHS	Raj Hamsa X'Air 582	I. Lonsdale
	G-CCHT	Cessna 152	J. S. Devlin & Z. Islam
	G-CCHV	Mainair Rapier	A. Butterworth
	G-CCHW	Cameron Z-77 balloon	A. Murphy
	G-CCHX	Scheibe SF.25C Falke	Lasham Gliding SocietyLtd
	G-CCHY	Bücker Bü 131 Jungmann (A+12)	M. V. Rijkse
	G-CCIC	Thruster T.600N 450	M. L. Smith
	G-CCID	Jabiru Aircraft Jabiru J400	J. Bailey
	G-CCIE	Colt 31A balloon	T. M. Donnelly
	G-CCIF	Mainair Blade	D. J. Kennedy

BRITISH CIVIL REGISTRATIONS   G-CCIG – G-CCME

Reg	Type	Owner or Operator	Notes
G-CCIG	Aero Designs Pulsar	P. Maguire	
G-CCIH	Mainair Pegasus Quantum 15	R. Bennett	
G-CCII	ICP Savannah Jabiru (3)	J. R. Livett & D. Chaloner	
G-CCIJ	PA-28R Cherokee Arrow 180	I. R. Chaplin/Andrewsfield	
G-CCIK	Skyranger 912 (2)	J. J. Bodnarec	
G-CCIO	Skyranger 912 (2)	B. Berry	
G-CCIR	Van's RV-8	G. Johnson	
G-CCIS	Scheibe SF.28A Tandem Falke	P. T. Ross	
G-CCIT	Zenair CH.701UL	I. M. Sinclair	
G-CCIU	Cameron N-105 balloon	Bianchi Aviation Film Services Ltd	
G-CCIV	Mainair Pegasus Quik	F. Omaraie-Hamdanie	
G-CCIW	Raj Hamsa X'Air 582 (2)	J. A. Brown	
G-CCIY	Skyranger 912 (2)	L. F. Tanner	
G-CCIZ	PZL-Koliber 160A	Horizon Aviation Ltd	
G-CCJA	Skyranger 912 (2)	C. Day	
G-CCJB	Zenair CH.701 STOL	E. G. Brown	
G-CCJD	Mainair Pegasus Quantum 15	P. Clark	
G-CCJF	Cameron C-90 balloon	Balloon School International Ltd	
G-CCJG	Cameron A-200 balloon	Aire Valley Balloons	
G-CCJH	Lindstrand LBL-90A balloon	J. R. Hoare	
G-CCJI	Van's RV-6	Charlie Charlie Flying Group	
G-CCJJ	Medway Pirana	Medway Microlights	
G-CCJK	Aerostar Yakovlev Yak-52	R. K. Howell	
G-CCJL	Super Marine Aircraft Spitfire XXVI	M. W. Hanley & P. M. Whitaker	
G-CCJM	Mainair Pegasus Quik	P. Crosby	
G-CCJN	Rans S.6ES Coyote II	M. G. A. Wood	
G-CCJO	ICP-740 Savannah Jabiru 4	R. & I. Fletcher	
G-CCJS	Flying K Enterprises Easy Raider	K. Wright	
G-CCJT	Skyranger 912 (2)	J. W. Taylor	
G-CCJU	ICP MXP-740 Savannah Jabiru (4)	K. R. Wootton & A. Colverson	
G-CCJV	Aeroprakt A.22 Foxbat	Foxbat UK015 Syndicate	
G-CCJW	Skyranger 912 (2)	J. R. Walter	
G-CCJX	Shaw Europa XS	J. S. Baranski	
G-CCJY	Cameron Z-42 balloon	D. J. Griffin	
G-CCKF	Skyranger 912 (2)	T. P. M. Turnbull	
G-CCKG	Skyranger 912 (2)	J. Hannibal	
G-CCKH	Diamond DA40D Star	Diamond Aircraft UK Ltd/Gamston	
G-CCKI	Diamond DA40D Star	S. C. Horwood	
G-CCKJ	Raj Hamsa X'Air 582 (5)	S. Thompson & J. N. Roberts	
G-CCKL	Aerotechnik EV-97 Eurostar	J. D. Thomson	
G-CCKM	Mainair Pegasus Quik	C. I. Poole	
G-CCKN	Nicollier HN.700 Menestrel II	C. R. Partington	
G-CCKO	Mainair Pegasus Quik	M. J. Mawle & ptnrs	
G-CCKP	Robin DR.400/120	Duxford Flying Group	
G-CCKR	Pietenpol Air Camper	T. J. Wilson	
G-CCKS	Hughes 369E	JLC Aviation Ltd	
G-CCKT	Hapi Cygnet SF-2	P. W. Abraham	
G-CCKU	Canadian Home Rotors Safari	J. C. Collingwood	
G-CCKV	Isaacs Fury II	S. T. G. Ingram	
G-CCKW	PA-18 Super Cub 135	G. T. Fisher (G-GDAM)	
G-CCKX	Lindstrand LBL-210A balloon	Alba Ballooning Ltd	
G-CCKY	Lindstrand LBL-240A balloon	Cameron Flights Southern Ltd	
G-CCKZ	Customcraft A-25 balloon	A. Van Wyk	
G-CCLB	Diamond DA40D	The Millen Corporation	
G-CCLC	Diamond DA40D	Diamond Aircraft UK Ltd/Gamston	
G-CCLE	Aerotechnik EV-97 Eurostar	W. S. Long	
G-CCLF	Best Off Skyranger 912 (2)	N. J. Sutherland	
G-CCLG	Lindstrand LBL-105A balloon	M. A. Derbyshire	
G-CCLH	Rans S.6-ES Coyote II	K. R. Browne	
G-CCLJ	PA-28 Cherokee Cruiser 140	A. M. George	
G-CCLL	Zenair CH.601XL Zodiac	L. Lewis	
G-CCLM	Mainair Pegasus Quik	P. M. Ryder & D. J. Shippen	
G-CCLO	Ultramagic H-77 balloon	J. P. Moore	
G-CCLP	ICP MXP-740 Savannah	S. Woolmington	
G-CCLR	Schleicher Ash 26E	M. T. Burton & S. Edwards	
G-CCLS	Comco Ikarus C.42 FB UK	SLS Computing Services Ltd	
G-CCLU	Best Off Skyranger 912	M. Hurn	
G-CCLV	Diamond DA40D Star	Diamond Aircraft UK Ltd/Gamston	
G-CCLW	Diamond DA40D Star	Diamond Aircraft UK Ltd/Gamston	
G-CCLX	Mainair Pegasus Quik	S. D. Pain	
G-CCMC	Jabiru Aircraft Jabiru UL 450	J. Johnston	
G-CCMD	Mainair Pegasus Quik	J. T. McCormack	
G-CCME	Mainair Pegasus Quik	A. Bloomfield & A. Underwood	

G-CCMF – G-CCPT   BRITISH CIVIL REGISTRATIONS

Notes	Reg	Type	Owner or Operator
	G-CCMF	Diamond DA40D Star	Plane Talking Ltd
	G-CCMH	M.2H Hawk Major	J. A. Pothecary
	G-CCMI	SA Bulldog Srs 120/121 (XX513:10)	H. R. M. Tyrrell (G-KKKK)
	G-CCMJ	Easy Raider J2.2 (1)	G. F. Clews
	G-CCMK	Raj Hamsa X'Air Falcon	G. Taylor
	G-CCML	Mainair Pegasus Quik	M. T. Beattie
	G-CCMM	Dyn'Aéro MCR-01 ULC Banbi	J. D. Harris
	G-CCMN	Cameron C-90 balloon	A.E. Austin
	G-CCMO	Aerotechnik EV-97A Eurostar	E. M. Woods
	G-CCMP	Aerotechnik EV-97A Eurostar	W. K. Wilkie
	G-CCMR	Robinson R22 Beta	G. F. Smith
	G-CCMS	Mainair Pegasus Quik	A. J. Roche
	G-CCMT	Thruster T.600N 450	S. P. McCaffrey
	G-CCMU	Rotorway Executive 162F	D. J. Fravigar & J. Smith
	G-CCMW	CFM Shadow Srs.DD	M. Wilkinson
	G-CCMX	Skyranger 912 (2)	K. J. Cole
	G-CCMZ	Best Off Skyranger 912 (2)	D. D. Appleford
	G-CCNA	Jodel DR.100A (Replica)	W. R. Davis-Smith & R. Everitt
	G-CCNB	Rans S.6ES Coyote II	M. S. Lawrence
	G-CCNC	Cameron Z-275 balloon	D. Ling
	G-CCND	Van's RV-9A	K. S. Woodard
	G-CCNE	Mainair Pegasus Quantum 15	P. R. Hanman
	G-CCNF	Raj Hamsa X'Air 582 Falcon 133	M. F. Eddington
	G-CCNG	Flight Design CT2K	David Goode Sculpture Ltd
	G-CCNH	Rans S.6ES Coyote II	Coyote Group
	G-CCNJ	Skyranger 912 (2)	J. D. Buchanan
	G-CCNM	Mainair Pegasus Quik	G. T. Snoddon
	G.CCNN	Cameron Z-90 balloon	J. H. Turner
	G-CCNP	Flight Design CT2K	n. a. tHOMAS
	G-CCNR	Skyranger 912 (2)	S. N. J. Huxtable
	G-CCNS	Skyranger 912 (2)	G. G. Rowley & M. Liptrot
	G-CCNT	Ikarus C.42 FB80	Sunfun Group
	G-CCNU	Skyranger J2.2 (1)	P. D. Priestley
	G-CCNV	Cameron Z-210 balloon	J. A. Cooper
	G-CCNW	Mainair Pegasus Quantum Lite	J. Childs
	G-CCNX	CAB CAP-10B	Arc Input Ltd
	G-CCNY	Robinson R44	C. M. Evans & J. W. Blaylock
	G-CCNZ	Raj Hamsa X'Air 133 (1)	P. C. Bishop
	G-CCOB	Aero C.104 Jungmann	W. Tomkins Ltd
	G-CCOC	Mainair Pegasus Quantum 15	F. E. J. Moore
	G-CCOF	Rans S.6-ESA Coyote II	A. J. Wright & M. Govan
	G-CCOG	Mainair Pegasus Quik	A. O. Sutherland
	G-CCOH	Raj Hamsa X'Air Falcon 133(1)	M. O. Roach
	G-CCOI	Lindstrand LBL-90A balloon	D. J. Groombridge
	G-CCOK	Mainair Pegasus Quik	E. McCallum
	G-CCOM	Westland Lysander IIIA (V9312)	Propshop Ltd
	G-CCOO	Raj Hamsa X'Air 133	A. Hipkin
	G-CCOP	Ultramagic M-105 balloon	Firefly Balloon Team
	G-CCOR	Sequoia F.8L Falco	D. J. Thoma
	G-CCOS	Cameron Z-350 balloon	M. L. Gabb
	G-CCOT	Cameron Z-105 balloon	Airborne Adventures Ltd
	G-CCOU	Mainair Pegasus Quik	R. M. Cornwell
	G-CCOV	Shaw Europa XS	G.N. Drake
	G-CCOW	Mainair Pegasus Quik	G. P. Couttie
	G-CCOX	Piper J-3C-65 Cub	R.P. Marks
	G-CCOY	NA AT-6D Harvard II	Classic Aero Services Ltd/Bruntingthorpe
	G-CCOZ	Monnett Sonerai II	P. R. Cozens
	G-CCPA	Kiss 400-582(1)	C.P. Astridge
	G-CCPC	Mainair Pegasus Quik	P. M. Coppola
	G-CCPD	Campbell Cricket Mk.4	N.C. Smith
	G-CCPE	Steen Skybolt	C. Moore
	G-CCPF	Skyranger 912 (2)	R.K. Willcox & ptnrs
	G-CCPG	Mainair Pegasus Quik	M. A. Rhodes
	G-CCPH	EV-97 TeamEurostar UK	A. H. Woolley
	G-CCPJ	Aerotechnik EV-97 TeamEurostar UK	S. R. Winter
	G-CCPK	Murphy Rebel	B. A. Bridgewater & D. Webb
	G-CCPL	Skyranger 912 (2)	G-CCPL Group
	G-CCPM	Mainair Blade 912	T.D. Thompson
	G-CCPN	Dyn'Aéro MCR-01 Club	P. H. Nelson
	G-CCPO	Cameron N-77 balloon	A. C. Booth & M. J. Woodcock (G-MITS)
	G-CCPP	Cameron 70 Concept balloon	Sarnia Balloon Group
	G-CCPS	Ikarus C.42 FB100 VLA	H. Cullens
	G-CCPT	Cameron Z-90 balloon	Blue Sky Ballooning Ltd

BRITISH CIVIL REGISTRATIONS
G-CCPV – G-CCUJ

Reg	Type	Owner or Operator	Notes
G-CCPV	Jabiru J400	J. R. Lawrence	
G-CCPW	BAe Jetstream 3102	Keen Leasing (IOM) Ltd/Manx2	
G-CCPX	Diamond DA400 Star	R. T. Dickinson	
G-CCPY	Hughes 369D	London Air Ltd	
G-CCPZ	Cameron Z-225 balloon	Horizon Ballooning Ltd	
G-CCRA	Glaser-Dirks DG-800B	R. Arkle	
G-CCRB	Kolb Twinstar Mk.3 (modified)	R. W. Burge	
G-CCRC	Cessna Tu.206G	D. M. Penny	
G-CCRD	Robinson R44 II	Heli Air Ltd/Wellesbourne	
G-CCRF	Mainair Pegasus Quantum 15	R. D. Ballard	
G-CCRG	Ultramagic M-77 balloon	Aerial Promotions Ltd	
G-CCRH	Cameron Z-315 balloon	Ballooning Network Ltd	
G-CCRI	Raj Hamsa X'Air 582 (5)	M. Law	
G-CCRJ	Shaw Europa	J. F. Cliff	
G-CCRK	Luscombe 8A Silvaire	J. R. Kimberley	
G-CCRN	Thruster T.600N 450	G. Bennett & C. E. Daniels	
G-CCRR	Skyranger 912 (1)	F. Omaraie-Hamdanie	
G-CCRS	Lindstrand LBL-210A balloon	Aerosaurus Ballooning Ltd	
G-CCRT	Mainair Pegasus Quantum 15	C. R. Whitton	
G-CCRV	Skyranger 912 (2)	M. R. Mosley	
G-CCRW	Mainair Pegasus Quik	S. O. Hutchinson	
G-CCRX	Jabiru UL-450	M. Everest	
G-CCSA	Cameron Z-350 balloon	Ballooning Network Ltd	
G-CCSD	Mainair Pegasus Quik	S. E. Dancaster	
G-CCSF	Mainair Pegasus Quik	J. S. Walton	
G-CCSG	Cameron Z-275 balloon	M. L. Gabb	
G-CCSH	Mainair Pegasus Quik	C. M. Sperring	
G-CCSI	Cameron Z-42 balloon	IKEA Ltd	
G-CCSJ	Cameron A-275 balloon	Dragon Balloon Co Ltd	
G-CCSK	Zenair CH.701	Thomas & Thomas Surveyors Ltd	
G-CCSL	Mainair Pegasus Quik	A. J. Harper	
G-CCSM	Lindstrand LBL-105A balloon	M. A. Webb	
G-CCSN	Cessna U.206G	K. Brady	
G-CCSO	Raj Hamsa X'Air Falcon	D. Thorpe & K. N. Rigley	
G-CCSP	Cameron N-77 balloon	Ballongforeningen Oscair I Goteberg/Sweden	
G-CCSR	Aerotechnik EV-97A Eurostar	Sierra Romeo Group	
G-CCSS	Lindstrand LBL-90A balloon	British Telecom	
G-CCST	PA-32R-301 Saratoga	G. R. Balls	
G-CCSU	IDA Bacau Yakovlev Yak-52	S. Ullrich/Germany	
G-CCSV	ICP MXP-740 Savannah Jabiru	R. D. Wood	
G-CCSW	Nott PA balloon	J. R. P.Nott	
G-CCSX	Skyranger 912	T. Jackson	
G-CCSY	Mainair Pegasus Quik	T. P. Richardson	
G-CCTA	Zenair CH.601UL Zodiac	R. E. Gray & G. T. Harris	
G-CCTC	Mainair Pegasus Quik	D. G. Emery & M. R. Smith	
G-CCTD	Mainair Pegasus Quik	R. N. S. Taylor	
G-CCTE	Dyn'Aéro MCR-01 Banbi	J. M. Keane	
G-CCTF	Aerotek Pitts S-2A Special	M. S. Hill	
G-CCTG	Van's RV-3B	M. & I. G. Glenn	
G-CCTH	Aerotechnik EV-97 TeamEurostar UK	Fly UK Ltd	
G-CCTI	Aerotechnik EV-97 Teameurostar	Flylight Airsports Ltd	
G-CCTK	Glaser-Dirks DG-800B	G. W. English	
G-CCTL	Robinson R44 II	Aerocorp Ltd	
G-CCTM	Mainair Blade	J. N. Hanso	
G-CCTN	Ultramagic T-180 balloon	A. Derbyshire	
G-CCTO	Aerotechnik EV-97 Eurostar	A. J. Bolton	
G-CCTP	Aerotechnik EV-97 Eurostar	P. E. Rose	
G-CCTR	Skyranger 912	A. H. Trapp	
G-CCTS	Cameron Z-120 balloon	F. R. Hart	
G-CCTT	Cessna 172S	A. Reay	
G-CCTU	Mainair Pegasus Quik	B. J. Syson	
G-CCTV	Rans S.6ESA Coyote II	P. D. Lucas	
G-CCTW	Cessna 152	R. J. Dempsey	
G-CCTX	Rans S.8ES Coyote II	D. A. Tibbals	
G-CCTZ	Mainair Pegasus Quik 912S	S. Baker	
G-CCUA	Mainair Pegasus Quik	H. M. Manning	
G-CCUB	Piper J-3C-65 Cub	Cormack (Aircraft Services) Ltd	
G-CCUD	Skyranger J.2	A. D. Haughey	
G-CCUE	Ultramagic T-180 balloon	Espiritu Balloon Flights Ltd	
G-CCUF	Skyranger 912(2)	R. E. Parker	
G-CCUH	RAF 2000 GTX-SE gyroplane	J. H. Haverhals	
G-CCUI	Dyn'Aéro MCR-01 Banbi	J. T. Morgan	
G-CCUJ	Cameron C-90 balloon	Rudgleigh Inn	

139

G-CCUK – G-CCXO | BRITISH CIVIL REGISTRATIONS

Notes	Reg	Type	Owner or Operator
	G-CCUK	Agusta A109-II	Castle Air Charters Ltd
	G-CCUL	Shaw Europa XS	Europa 6
	G-CCUN	Hughes 369D	Heliogistics Ltd
	G-CCUO	Hughes 369D	London Air Ltd
	G-CCUP	Wessex 60 Mk.2 (XR502:Z)	D. Brem-Wilson & J. Buswell
	G-CCUR	Mainair Pegasus Quantum 15-912	P. S. & N. Bewley
	G-CCUS	Diamond DA.40D Star	The Millen Corporation
	G-CCUT	Aerotechnik EV-97 Eurostar	Doctor and the Medics
	G-CCUU	Shiraz gyroplane	M. E. Vahdat-Hagh
	G-CCUV	PA-25-260 Pawnee C	D. B. Almey
	G-CCUY	Shaw Europa	N. Evans
	G-CCUZ	Thruster T.600N 450	Fly 365 Ltd
	G-CCVA	Aerotechnik EV-97 Eurostar	D. A. Palmer
	G-CCVB	Mainair Pegasus Quik	L. Chesworth
	G-CCVD	Cameron Z-105 balloon	Associazione Sportiva/Italy
	G-CCVE	Raj Hamsa X'Air Jabiru	G. J. Slate
	G-CCVF	Lindstrand LBL-105 balloon	Alan Patterson Design
	G-CCVG	Schweizer 269C-1	Radcliffe Engineering Services Ltd
	G-CCVH	Curtiss H-75A-1 (82:8)	The Fighter Collection/Duxford
	G-CCVI	Zenair CH.701 SP	C. R. Hoveman
	G-CCVJ	Raj Hamsa X'Air Falcon 133	A. Davis
	G-CCVK	Aerotechnik EV-97 TeamEurostar UK	Kent Eurostar Group
	G-CCVL	Zenair CH.601XL Zodiac	A. Y.-T. Leungr & G. Constantine
	G-CCVM	Van's RV-7A	J. G. Small
	G-CCVN	Jabiru SP-470	J. C. Collingwood
	G-CCVO	Bell 206B JetRanger 3	London Heli-Charters Ltd
	G-CCVP	Beech 58	Richard Nash Cars Ltd
	G-CCVR	Skyranger 912(2)	M. J. Batchelor
	G-CCVS	Van's RV-6A	J. Edgeworth (G-CCVC)
	G-CCVT	Zenair CH.601UL Zodiac	P. Millar
	G-CCVU	Robinson R22 Beta II	Helieagle Ltd
	G-CCVW	Nicollier HN.700 Menestrel II	B. F. Enock
	G-CCVX	Mainair Tri Flyer 330	J. A. Shufflebotham
	G-CCVY	Robinson R22 Beta	S. Klinge
	G-CCVZ	Cameron O-120 balloon	T. M. C. McCoy
	G-CCWA	PA-28-181 Archer III	T. P. Gooley
	G-CCWB	Aero L-39ZA Albatros	Freespirit Charters Ltd
	G-CCWC	Skyranger 912	Carlisle Skyrangers
	G-CCWD	Robinson R44	J. Henderson
	G-CCWE	Lindstrand LBL-330A balloon	Adventure Balloons Ltd
	G-CCWF	Raj Hamsa X'Air 133	N. G. Middletown
	G-CCWG	Whittaker MW6 Merlin	D. E. Williams
	G-CCWH	Dyn'Aéro MCR-01 Bambi	M. G. Rasch
	G-CCWI	Robinson R44 II	Saxon Logistics Ltd
	G-CCWJ	Robinson R44 II	Saxon Logistics Ltd
	G-CCWK	AS.355F2 Twin Squirrel	D. J. & L. Mulryan
	G-CCWL	Mainair Blade	W. D. Joyner
	G-CCWM	Robin DR.400/180	M. R. Clark
	G-CCWN	Mainair Pegasus Quantum 15-912	T. H. Ferguson
	G-CCWO	Mainair Pegasus Quantum 15-912	P. K. Dean
	G-CCWP	Aerotechnik EV-97 TeamEurostar UK	T. R. Murfet
	G-CCWR	Mainair Pegasus Quik	J. A. Robinson
	G-CCWT	Balóny Kubíček BB20GP balloon	H. C. J. & S. A. G. Williams
	G-CCWU	Skyranger 912	D. M. Lane
	G-CCWV	Mainair Pegasus Quik	W. J. Dawson
	G-CCWW	Mainair Pegasus Quantum 15-912	Double Whisky Syndicate
	G-CCWY	Pilatus PC-12/45	Harpin Ltd
	G-CCWZ	Raj Hamsa X'Air Falcon 133	M. A. Evans
	G-CCXA	Boeing Stearman A75N-1 Kaydet (669)	Skymax (Aviation) Ltd
	G-CCXB	Boeing Stearman B75N-3 Kaydet (699)	Skymax (Aviation) Ltd
	G-CCXC	Avion Mudry CAP-10B	Skymax (Aviation) Ltd
	G-CCXD	Lindstrand LBL-105B balloon	J. H. Dobson
	G-CCXE	Cameron Z-120 balloon	H-J. Haas-Wittmuess/Germany
	G-CCXF	Cameron Z-90 balloon	R. G. March & T. J. Maycock
	G-CCXG	SE-5A (replica) (C5430)	C. Morris
	G-CCXH	Skyranger J2.2	N. Jones
	G-CCXI	Thorpe T.211	J. Gilro
	G-CCXJ	Cessna 340A	Kilo Aviation Ltd
	G-CCXK	Pitts S-1S Special	P. G. Bond
	G-CCXL	Skyranger 912(1)	F. W. McCann
	G-CCXM	Skyranger 912(1)	C. J. Finnigan
	G-CCXN	Skyranger 912(1)	C. I. Chegwen
	G-CCXO	Corgy CJ-1 Starlet	I. W. L. Aikman

BRITISH CIVIL REGISTRATIONS

G-CCXP – G-CDAY

Reg	Type	Owner or Operator	Notes
G-CCXP	ICP Savannah Jabiru	B. J. Harper & T. D. Bale	
G-CCXS	Montgomerie-Bensen B.8MR	S. A. Sharp	
G-CCXR	Mainair Pegasus Blade	M. Fowler	
G-CCXT	Mainair Pegasus Quik	C. Turner	
G-CCXU	Diamond DA40D Star	R. J. & L. Hole	
G-CCXV	Thruster T.600N 450	W. G. Dunn	
G-CCXW	Thruster T.600N 450	J. Walsh	
G-CCXX	AG-5B Tiger	Osprey Flying Group	
G-CCXZ	Mainair Pegasus Quik	K. J. Sene/Barton	
G-CCYA	Jabiru J430	D. J. Royce	
G-CCYB	Escapade 912(1)	B. E. & S. M. Renehan	
G-CCYC	Robinson R44 II	Derg Developments Ltd/Ireland	
G-CCYE	Mainair Pegasus Quik	J. Lane	
G-CCYF	Aerophile 5500 tethered gas balloon	High Point Balloons Ltd	
G-CCYG	Robinson R44	Moorland Windows	
G-CCYH	Embraer RJ145EP	bmi regional	
G-CCYI	Cameron O-105 balloon	Media Balloons Ltd	
G-CCYJ	Mainair Pegasus Quik	J. Ellis	
G-CCYK	Cessna 180	K. V. McKinnon	
G-CCYL	MainairPegasus Quantum 15	M. j. L. Morris	
G-CCYM	Skyranger 912	K. A. O'Neill	
G-CCYN	Cameron C-80 balloon	D. R. Firkins	
G-CCYO	Christen Eagle II	J. R. Pearce	
G-CCYP	Colt 56A balloon	L. P. Hooper	
G-CCYR	Ikarus C.42 FB80	M. L. Smith	
G-CCYS	Cessna F.182Q	S. Dyson	
G-CCYT	Robinson R44 II	Bell Commercials	
G-CCYU	Ultramagic S-90 balloon	A. R. Craze	
G-CCYX	Bell 412	RCR Aviation Ltd	
G-CCYY	PA-28-161 Warrior II	Flightcontrol Ltd	
G-CCYZ	Dornier EKW C3605	William Tomkins Ltd	
G-CCZA	SOCATA MS.894A Rallye Minerva 220	J. Greenwood.	
G-CCZB	Mainair Pegasus Quantum 15	J. Hartley	
G-CCZD	Van's RV-7	D. Powell	
G-CCZG	Robinson R44 II	Westinbrook Ltd	
G-CCZH	Robinson R44	Newtown Aviation Ltd/Ireland	
G-CCZI	Cameron A-275 balloon	Balloon School (International) Ltd	
G-CCZJ	Raj Hamsa X' Air Falcon 582	A. B. Gridley	
G-CCZK	Zenair CH.601 UL Zodiac	R. J. Hopkins	
G-CCZL	Ikarus C.42 FB 80	I. D. Stokes	
G-CCZM	Skyranger 912S	D. Woodward	
G-CCZN	Rans S.6-ES Coyote II	J. P. & D. J. Kennedy	
G-CCZO	Mainair Pegasus Quik	S. B. Williams	
G-CCZP	Super Marine Aircraft Spitfire 26 (JF343:JW-P)	J. W. E. Pearson	
G-CCZR	Medway Raven Eclipse R	R. A. Keene	
G-CCZS	Raj Hamsa X'Air Falcon 582	P. J. Sheehy	
G-CCZT	Van's RV-9A	N. A. Henderson	
G-CCZU	Diamond DA40D Star	Diamond Finance Services GmbH	
G-CCZV	PA-28-151 Warrior	P. D. P. Deal	
G-CCZW	Mainair Pegasus Blade	C. J. Wright	
G-CCZX	Robin DR.400/180	M. Conrad	
G-CCZY	Van's RV-9A	Mona RV-9 Group	
G-CCZZ	Aerotechnik EV-97 Eurostar	B. M Starck & J. P. Aitken	
G-CDAA	Mainair Pegasus Quantum 15-912	I. A. Macadam	
G-CDAB	Stoddard-Hamilton Glasair 115RG	W. L. Hitchins	
G-GDAC	Aerotechnik EV-97 TeamEurostar	Fly CB Ltd	
G-CDAD	Lindstrand LBL-25A balloon	G. J. Madelin	
G-CDAE	Van's RV-6A	K. J. Fleming	
G-CDAF	Bell 412	RCR Aviation Ltd	
G-CDAG	Mainair Blade	D. K. May	
G-CDAI	Robin DR.400/140B	Cole Aviation Ltd	
G-CDAK	Zenair CH.601 UK Zodiac	K. Kerr	
G-CDAL	Zenair CH.601UL Zodiac	S. P. Read & M. H. Wise	
G-CDAM	Sky 77-24 balloon	M. Morris & P. A. Davies	
G-CDAO	Mainair Pegasus Quantum 15 -912	J. C. Duncan	
G-CDAP	Aerotechnik EV-97 TeamEurostar UK	R. Clark	
G-CDAR	Mainair Pegasus Quik	A. R. Pitcher	
G-CDAT	ICP MXP-740 Savannah Jabiru	R. Simpson	
G-CDAW	Robinson R22 Beta	Airtask Group PLC	
G-CDAX	Mainair Pegasus Quik	M. Winship	
G-CDAY	Skyranger 912	D. A. Perkins	

G-CDAZ – G-CDEL — BRITISH CIVIL REGISTRATIONS

Notes	Reg	Type	Owner or Operator
	G-CDAZ	Aerotechnik EV-97 Eurostar	M. C. J. Ludlow
	G-CDBA	Skyranger 912(S)	P. J. Brennan/Barton
	G-CDBB	Mainair Pegasus Quik	A. H. Mackinnon & J. P. Witcher
	G-CDBC	Aviation Enterprises Magnum	Aviation Enterprises Ltd
	G-CDBD	Jabiru J400	S. Derwin
	G-CDBE	Montgomerie-Bensen B.8M	P. Harwood
	G-CDBF	Robinson R22 Beta	Wisky Charter Ltd
	G-CDBG	Robinson R22 Beta	CC Helicopters Ltd
	G-CDBK	Rotorway Executive 162F	NF Auto Development
	G-CDBM	Robin DR.400/180	C. M. Simmonds
	G-CDBO	Skyranger 912	A. C. Turnbull
	G-CDBR	Stolp SA.300 Starduster Too	R. J. Warren
	G-CDBS	MBB Bö.105DBS-4	Bond Air Services Ltd
	G-CDBU	Ikarus C.42 FB100	S. E. Meehan
	G-CDBV	Skyranger 912S	K. Hall
	G-CDBX	Shaw Europa XS	R. Marston
	G-CDBY	Dyn'Aero MCR-01 ULC	R. Germany
	G-CDBZ	Thruster T.600N 450	J. A. Lynch
	G-CDCA	Robinson R44 II	L. Behan & Sons Ltd
	G-CDCB	Robinson R44 II	Microwave Sales and Services Ltd
	G-CDCC	Aerotechnik EV-97A Eurostar	R. E. & & N. G. Nicholson
	G-CDCD	Van's RVF-9A	RV9ers
	G-CDCE	Avions Mudry CAP-10B	The Tiger Club (1990) Ltd
	G-CDCF	Mainair Pegasus Quik	T. J. Gayton-Polley
	G-CDCG	Ikarus C.42 FB UK	N. E. Ashton & R. H. J. Jenkins
	G-CDCH	Skyranger 912	K. Laud
	G-CDCI	Pegasus Quik	S. G. Murray
	G-CDCK	Mainair Pegasus Quik	S. G. Ward
	G-CDCM	Ikarus C.42 FB UK	S. T. Allen
	G-CDCO	Ikarus C.42 FB UK	G. G. Bevis
	G-CDCP	Avtech Jabiru J400	M. W. T. Wilson
	G-CDCR	Savannah Jabiru(1)	T. Davidson
	G-CDCS	PA-12 Super Cruiser	D. Todorovic
	G-CDCT	Aerotechnik EV-97 TeamEurostar UK	J. Lynch
	G-CDCU	Mainair Pegasus Blade	N. A. Farrow
	G-CDCV	Robinson R44 II	Central Chiswick Developments Ltd
	G-CDCW	Escapade 912 (1)	P. Nicholls
	G-CDCX	Citation 750	Pendley Farm Ltd
	G-CDCY	Mainair Pegasus Quantum 15	H. Kearns/Ireland
	G-CDDA	SOCATA TB20 Trinidad	Oxford Aviation Services Ltd
	G-CDDB	Grob/Schempp-Hirth CS-11	K. D. Barber/France
	G-CDDC	Cameron A-275 balloon	Airborne Balloon Management Ltd
	G-CDDD	Robinson R22 Beta	TDR Aviation Ltd
	G-CDDE	WSK PZL-110 Koliber 160A	Horizon Aviation Ltd
	G-CDDF	Mainair Pegasus Quantum 15-912	B. C. Blackburn
	G-CDDG	PA-26-161 Warrior II	A. Oxenham
	G-CDDH	Raj Hamsa X'Air Falcon	B. & L. Stanbridge
	G-CDDI	Thruster T.600N 450	R. Nayak
	G-CDDK	Cessna 172M	M. H. & P. R. Kavern
	G-CDDL	Cameron Z-350 balloon	Balloon School (International) Ltd
	G-CDDM	Lindstrand LBL 90A balloon	S. P. Harrowing
	G-CDDN	Lindstrand LBL 90A balloon	Flying Enterprises
	G-CDDO	Raj Hamsa X'Air 133	R. N. Tarrant, L. Robinson, B. J. Reynolds & N. McAllister
	G-CDDP	Lazer Z.230	A. Smith
	G-CDDR	Skyranger 582(1)	R. J. Milward
	G-CDDS	Zenair CH.601HD	S. Foreman
	G-CDDT	SOCATA TB20 Trinidad	Oxford Aviation Services Ltd/Kidlington
	G-CDDU	Skyranger 912(2)	R. C. Reynolds
	G-CDDV	Cameron Z-250 balloon	High Adventure
	G-CDDW	Aeroprakt A.22 Foxbat	M. Raflewski
	G-CDDX	Thruster T.600N 450	P. A. G. Harper
	G-CDDY	Van's RV-8	The AV8ors
	G-CDEA	SAAB 2000	Air Kilroe Ltd
	G-CDEB	SAAB 2000	Eastern Airways
	G-CDEC	Pagasus Quik	S. Bradie & A. Huyton
	G-CDED	Robinson R22 Beta	Ad Bly Aircraft Leasing Ltd
	G-CDEF	PA-28-161 Cadet	Western Air (Thruxton) Ltd
	G-CDEG	Boeing 737-8BK	Flyglobespan.com
	G-CDEH	ICP MXP-740 Savannah	A. J. Webb
	G-CDEJ	Diamond DA40D Star	Diamond Aircraft UK Ltd/Gamston
	G-CDEK	Diamond DA40D Star	ADR Aviation
	G-CDEL	Diamond DA40D Star	Diamond Aircraft UK Ltd/Gamston

BRITISH CIVIL REGISTRATIONS   G-CDEM – G-CDIA

Reg	Type	Owner or Operator	Notes
G-CDEM	Raj Hamsa X' Air 133	R. J. Froud	
G-CDEN	Mainair Pegasus Quantum 15 912	J. D. J. Spragg	
G-CDEO	PA-28 Cherokee 180	G. G. Hammond	
G-CDEP	Aerotechnik EV-97 TeamEurostar	Echo Papa Group	
G-CDER	PA-28-161 Warrior II	Cinque Ports Aviation Ltd	
G-CDET	Culver LCA Cadet	H. B. Fox/Booker	
G-CDEU	Lindstrand LBL-90B balloon	P. J. Marshall & N. Florence	
G-CDEV	Escapade 912 (1)	M. B. Devenport	
G-CDEW	Pegasus Quik	K. M. Sullivan	
G-CDEX	Shaw Europa	J. M. Carter	
G-CDEZ	Robinson R44 II	Heli Air Ltd	
G-CDFA	Kolb Twinstar Mk3 Extra	M. H. Moulai	
G-CDFC	Ultramagic S-160 balloon	Over The Rainbow Balloon Flights Ltd	
G-CDFD	Scheibe SF.25C Falke	T. M. Holloway	
G-CDFE	IAV Bacau Yakovlev YAK-52	D. R. Farley	
G-CDFF	ATR-42-300	Aurigny Air Services Ltd/Guernsey (G-BVEF)	
G-CDFG	Mainair Pegasus Quik	D. Gabbott	
G-CDFI	Colt 31A balloon	A. M. Holly	
G-CDFJ	Skyranger 912	Heskin Flyers Group	
G-CDFK	Jabiru SPL-450	H. J. Bradley	
G-CDFL	Zenair CH.601UL	Caunton Zodiac Group	
G-CDFM	Raj Hamsa X'Air 582 (5)	W. A. Keel-Stocker	
G-CDFN	Thunder Ax7-77 balloon	E. Rullo	
G-CDFO	Pegasus Quik	C. J. Gordon	
G-CDFP	Skyranger 912 (2)	J. M. Gammidge	
G-CDFR	Mainair Pegasus Quantum 15	C. J. E. Hartshorne, J. Madhvani & L. M. Pickles	
G-CDFS	Embraer EMB-135ER	City Airline	
G-CDFU	Rans S.6-ES	P. W. Taylor	
G-CDFW	Sheffy Gyroplane	P. C. Lovegrove	
G-CDFY	Beech B.200 Super King Air	BAE Systems Marine Ltd	
G-CDGA	Taylor JT.1 Monoplane	R. M. Larimore	
G-CDGB	Rans S.6-116 Coyote	S. Penoyre	
G-CDGC	Pegasus Quik	A. T. K. Crozier	
G-CDGD	Pegasus Quik	I. D. & V. A. Milne	
G-CDGE	Edge XT912-IIIB	G. J. Crago	
G-CDGF	Ultramagic S-105 balloon	D. & K. Bareford	
G-CDGG	Dyn'Aéro MCR-01 Club	N. Rollins	
G-CDGH	Rans S.6-ES Coyote	K. T. Vinning	
G-CDGI	Thruster T600N 450	R. L. J. Goodridge	
G-CDGJ	American Champion 7ECA Citabria	T. A. Mann	
G-CDGN	Cameron C-90 balloon	M. C. Gibbons	
G-CDGO	Pegasus Quik	J. C. Townsend	
G-CDGP	Zenair CH 601XL	T. J. Bax	
G-CDGR	Zenair CH 701UL	M. Morris	
G-CDGS	AG-5B Tiger	Premier Flying Group/Ireland	
G-CDGT	Montgomerie-Parsons Two Place g/p	A. A. Craig	
G-CDGU	VS.300 Spitfire I (X4276)	A. J. E. Smith/Breighton	
G-CDGW	PA-28-181 Archer III	Stamp Aviation Ltd	
G-CDGX	Pegasus Quantum 15-912	S. R. Green	
G-CDGY	VS.349 Spitfire Mk VC	Aero Vintage Ltd	
G-CDHA	Skyranger 912S(1)	K. J. Gay	
G-CDHB	BVAC. 167 Strikemaster Mk.80A (1130)	S. J. Davies	
G-CDHC	Slingsby T67C	N. J. Morgan	
G-CDHD	Balóny Kubíček BB-22 balloon	R. C. Franklin	
G-CDHE	Skyranger 912(2)	Barton Syndicate	
G-CDHF	PA-30 Twin Comanche B	Reid International (Guernsey) Ltd	
G-CDHG	Mainair Pegasus Quik	T. W. Pelan	
G-CDHH	Robinson R44 II	Abwood Homes/Ireland	
G-CDHI	P-51D-25-NA Mustang (472773:QP-M)	A. J. E. & A. E. Smith (G-SUSY)	
G-CDHJ	Lindstrand LBL-90B balloon	Lindstrand Hot Air Balloons Ltd	
G-CDHK	Lindstrand LBL-330A balloon	Richard Nash Cars Ltd	
G-CDHL	Lindstrand LBL-330A balloon	Richard Nash Cars Ltd	
G-CDHM	Pegasus Quantum 15	M. K. Morgan	
G-CDHN	Lindstrand LBL-317A balloon	Aerosaurus Balloons Ltd	
G-CDHO	Raj Hamsa X'Air 133 (1)	J. D. Aitchison	
G-CDHP	Lindstrand LBL-150A balloon	Floating Sensations Ltd (G-OHRH)	
G-CDHR	Ikarus C.42 FB80	M. L. Smith	
G-CDHS	Cameron N-90 balloon	Cameron Balloons Luxembourg	
G-CDHU	Skyranger 912 (2)	S. J. Smith	
G-CDHX	Aeroprakt A.22 Foxbat	N. E. Stokes & B. N. Searle	
G-CDHY	Cameron Z-90 balloon	D. M. Roberts	
G-CDHZ	Nicollier HN.700 Menestrel II	G. E. Whittaker	
G-CDIA	Thruster T.600N 450	R. S. O'Carroll	

G-CDIB – G-CDLP — BRITISH CIVIL REGISTRATIONS

Notes	Reg	Type	Owner or Operator
	G-CDIB	Cameron Z-350Z balloon	Ballooning Network Ltd
	G-CDIF	Mudry CAP-10B	J. D. Gordon
	G-CDIG	Aerotechnik EV-97 Eurostar	J. Cunliffe & A. Costello
	G-CDIH	Cameron Z-275 balloon	Bailey Balloons Ltd
	G-CDIJ	Skyranger 912 (2)	E. B. Toulson
	G-CDIK	Cameron Z-120 balloon	Cameron Balloons Ltd
	G-CDIL	Pegasus Quantum 15-912	G. W. Hillidge
	G-CDIM	Robin DR.400/180	L. R. Marks
	G-CDIO	Cameron Z-90 balloon	P. Oggioni
	G-CDIP	Skyranger 912S(1)	M. S. McCrudden
	G-CDIR	Mainair Pegasus Quantum 15-912	Somerset Microlights
	G-CDIS	Cessna 150F	S. P. Fox
	G-CDIT	Cameron Z-105 balloon	Bailey Balloons Ltd
	G-CDIU	Skyranger 912S(1)	C. P. Dawes & J. English
	G-CDIV	Lindstrand LBL-90A balloon	The Packhouse Ltd
	G-CDIW	Lindstrand LBL-35A balloon	G. J. Bell
	G-CDIX	Ikarus C.42 FB.100	Assured Quality Catering Management Services Ltd
	G-CDIY	Aerotechnik EV-97A Eurostar	E. J. & M. P. Hill
	G-CDIZ	Escapade 912(1)	E. G. Bishop & E. N. Dunn
	G-CDJC	Skyranger 912 (2)	J. L. A. Campell
	G-CDJD	ICP MXP-740 Savannah Jabiru (1)	D. W. Mullin
	G-CDJE	Thruster T.600N 450	K. R. Ford
	G-CDJF	Flight Design CT2K	P. A. James
	G-CDJG	Zenair 601UL Zodiac	J. Garcia
	G-CDJI	Ultramagic M-120 balloon	The Ballooning Business Ltd
	G-CDJJ	IAV Yakovlev Yak-52	J. J. Miles
	G-CDJK	Ikarus C.42 FB 80	Cornish Aviation Ltd
	G-CDJL	Avtech Jabiru J400	T. R. Sinclair & T. Clyde
	G-CDJM	Zenair CH.601XL	T. J. Adams-Lewis
	G-CDJN	RAF 2000 GTX-SE gyroplane	D. J. North
	G-CDJO	DH.82A Tiger Moth	D. Dal Bon
	G-CDJP	Skyranger 912(2)	J. S. Potts
	G-CDJR	Aerotechnik EV-97 TeamEurostar	W. J. Gale & Son
	G-CDJT	Aérospatiale SA.341G Gazelle 1	MW Helicopters Ltd
	G-CDJU	CASA 1.131E Jungmann Srs.1000	B. Roemer/Ireland
	G-CDJV	Beech A.36 Bonanza	Atlantic Bridge Aviation Ltd/Lydd
	G-CDJW	Van's RV-7	D. J. Williams
	G-CDJX	Cameron N-56 balloon	Cameron Balloons Ltd
	G-CDJY	Cameron C-80 balloon	British Airways Connect
	G-CDJZ	Robinson R44 II	JTS Aviation Ltd
	G-CDKA	SAAB 2000	Eastern Airways
	G-CDKB	SAAB 2000	Eastern Airways
	G-CDKC	Raj Hamsa X'Air 582 (3)	F. G. Walker
	G-CDKD	Boeing 737-683	Flyglobespan.com
	G-CDKE	Rans S6-ES Coyote II	J. E. Holloway
	G-CDKF	Escapade 912 (1)	P. J. Little
	G-CDKH	Skyranger 912S (1)	R. J. Gilbert
	G-CDKI	Skyranger 912S (1)	J. M. Hucker
	G-CDKJ	Silence Twister	European Land Solutions Ltd
	G-CDKK	Mainair Pegasus Quik	S. C. Reeve
	G-CDKL	Escapade 912 (2)	D. Harker
	G-CDKM	Pegasus Quik	P. Barrow
	G-CDKN	ICP MXP-740 Savannah Jabiru (4)	F. McGuigan
	G-CDKO	ICP MXP-740 Savannah Jabiru (4)	C. Jones & B. Hunter
	G-CDKP	Avtech Jabiru UL-D Calypso	Rochester Microlights Ltd
	G-CDKR	Diamond DA42 Twin Star	Principle Aircraft
	G-CDKT	Boeing 737-383	Flyglobespan.com
	G-CDKU	Robinson R44	Blackberry Aviation
	G-CDKX	Skyranger J.2 .2 (1)	M. S. Ashby
	G-CDKY	Robinson R44	Bernard Hunter Ltd
	G-CDKZ	Thunder Ax10-160 S2 balloon	D. J. Head
	G-CDLA	Mainair Pegasus Quik	C. R. Stevens
	G-CDLB	Cameron Z-120 balloon	Interbrew UK Ltd
	G-CDLC	CASA 1.131E Jungmann 2000	R. D. & M. Loder
	G-CDLD	Mainair Pegasus Quik 912S	W. Williams
	G-CDLE	Escapade 912 (1)	R. A. J. Paddock
	G-CDLG	Skyranger 912 (2)	D. J. Saunders
	G-CDLI	Airco DH.9 (E8894)	Aero Vintage Ltd
	G-CDLJ	Mainair Pegasus Quik	M. L. Johnston
	G-CDLK	Skyranger 912S	L. E. Cowling
	G-CDLL	Dyn'Aéro MCR-01 ULC	D. Cassidy
	G-CDLP	AS.355F1 Twin Squirrel 2	Valley Helicopter Services Ltd (G-GRID)

BRITISH CIVIL REGISTRATIONS

G-CDLR – G-CDPE

Reg	Type	Owner or Operator	Notes
G-CDLR	ICP MXP / 740 Savannah Jabiru (4)	R. Locke	
G-CDLS	Jabiru Aircrraft Jabiru J400	G. M. Geary	
G-CDLT	Raytheon Hawker 800XP	Gama Aviation Ltd	
G-CDLV	Lindstrand LBL-105A balloon	Smartfusion SV Ltd	
G-CDLW	Zenair ZH.601UL Zodiac	W. A. Stphen	
G-CDLX	Robinson R44	Tony Kelly Car Sales Ltd	
G-CDLY	Cirrus SR20	Partside Aviation Ltd	
G-CDLZ	Mainair Pegasus Quantum 15-912	L. C. Brown	
G-CDMA	PA-28-151 Warrior	A. Cabre	
G-CDMC	Cameron Z-105 balloon	First Flight	
G-CDMD	Robin DR.400/500	P. R. Liddle	
G-CDME	Van's RV-7	M. W. Elliott	
G-CDMF	Van's RV-9A	S. Shanley	
G-CDMG	Robinson R22 Beta	Heli Aitch Be Ltd	
G-CDMH	Cessna P.210N	J. G. Hinley	
G-CDMI	Robinson R44 II	Casey Enterprises/Ireland	
G-CDMJ	Mainair Pegasus Quik 912S	J. Rodgers/Barton	
G-CDMK	Montgomerie-Bensen B8MR	P. Rentell	
G-CDML	Mainair Pegasus Quik	P. Ritchie	
G-CDMM	Cessna 172P Skyhawk	Cristal Air Ltd	
G-CDMN	Van's RV-9	G. J. Smith	
G-CDMO	Cameron S Can-100 balloon	A. Schneider/Germany	
G-CDMP	Best Off Skyranger 912(1)	J. A. Charlton	
G-CDMS	Ikarus C,42 FB 80	M. L. Smith	
G-CDMT	Zenair CH.601XL Zodiac	L. Hogan	
G-CDMU	Mainair Pegasus Quik	A. M. Burrows & T. M. Bolton	
G-CDMV	Best Off Skyranger 912S(1)	D. O'Keeffe & ptnrs	
G-CDMX	PA-28-161 Warrior II	FlyUK.com Ltd	
G-CDMY	PA-28-161 Warrior II	J. S. Develin & Z. Islam	
G-CDMZ	Mainair Pegasus Quik	G. Edwards	
G-CDNA	Grob G.109A	J. R. Chapman	
G-CDNB	Avro 146-RJ70	Trident Jet (Dublin) Ltd	
G-CDNC	Avro 146-RJ70	Trident Jet (Dublin) Ltd	
G-CDND	GA-7 Cougar	C. J. Chaplin	
G-CDNE	Best Off Skyranger 912S(1)	G. S. Gee-Carter	
G-CDNF	Aero Design Pulsar 3	D. Ringer	
G-CDNG	Aerotechnik EV-97 TeamEurostar UK	G. E. Hillyer-Jones	
G-CDNH	Mainair Pegasus Quik	C. D. Andrews	
G-CDNI	Aerotechnik EV-97 TeamEurostar UK	Fly CB Ltd	
G-CDNJ	Colomban MC-15 Cri Cri	N. J. Johnson	
G-CDNK	Learjet 45	Gold Air International Ltd	
G-CDNM	Aerotechnik EV-97 TeamEurostar UK	J. Quaife	
G-CDNO	Westland Gazelle AH.1 (XX432)	Falcon Aviation Ltd	
G-CDNP	Aerotechnik EV-97 TeamEurostar UK	Eaglescott Eurostar Group	
G-CDNR	Ikarus C.42 FB1000	R. S. O'Carroll	
G-CDNS	Westland Gazelle AH.1 (XZ321)	Falcon Aviation Ltd	
G-CDNT	Zenair CH.601XL Zodiac	W. McCormack	
G-CDNU	Ultralair AX3-16	M. R. Corrick	
G-CDNW	Ikarus C.42 FB UK	W. Gabbott	
G-CDNY	Jabiru SP-470	G. Lucey	
G-CDNZ	Ultramagic M-120 balloon	R. H. Etherington/Italy	
G-CDOA	EV-97 TeamEurostar UK	A. Halsall	
G-CDOB	Cameron C-90 balloon	P. Burrows	
G-CDOC	Mainair Quik GT450	P. J. Clegg	
G-CDOD	Aviat A-1B Husky	K. Anspach	
G-CDOG	Lindstrand LBL-Dog SS balloon	ABC Flights Ltd	
G-CDOI	Cameron Z-90 balloon	Cameron Balloons Ltd	
G-CDOJ	Schweizer 269C-1	Sterling Helicopters Ltd	
G-CDOK	Ikarus C.42 FB 100	B. S. Keene	
G-CDOM	Mainair Pegasus Quik	G-CDOM Flying Group	
G-CDON	PA-28-161 Warrior II	East Midlands Flying School Ltd	
G-CDOO	Mainair Pegasus Quantum 15-912	O. C. Harding	
G-CDOP	Mainair Pegasus Quik	A. W. Hay & G. R. Craig	
G-CDOR	Mainair Blade	F. Wilkinson	
G-CDOT	Ikarus C.42 FB 100	A. C. Anderson	
G-CDOV	Skyranger 912(2)	B. Richardson	
G-CDOW	Mainair Pegasus Quik	D. H. Marsh	
G-CDOY	Robin DR.400/180R	Lasham Gliding Society Ltd	
G-CDOZ	EV-97 TeamEurostar UK	J. P. McCall	
G-CDPA	Alpi Pioneer 300	A. R. Lloyd	
G-CDPB	Skyranger 982(1)	N. S. Bishop	
G-CDPD	Mainair Pegasus Quik	P. C. Davis	
G-CDPE	Skyranger 912(2)	P. A. Mercer	

G-CDPF – G-CDTH | BRITISH CIVIL REGISTRATIONS

Notes	Reg	Type	Owner or Operator
	G-CDPF	BAe146-300A	Casco Aero Ltd
	G-CDPG	Crofton Auster J1-A	P. & T. Groves
	G-CDPH	Tiger Cub RL5A LW Sherwood Ranger ST	K. F. Crumplin
	G-CDPI	Zenair CH.601UL Zodiac	M. J. Kaye
	G-CDPJ	Van's RV-8	P. Johnson
	G-CDPL	EV-97 TeamEurostar UK	C. I. D. H Garrison
	G-CDPM	Jurca Spitfire	J. E. D. Rogerson
	G-CDPN	Ultramagic S-105	Horizon Ballooning Ltd
	G-CDPO	Aerochute Dual	G. Martin
	G-CDPP	Ikarus C42 FB UK	H. M. Owen
	G-CDPR	PA-18 Super Cub 95	J. P. Hibble/Guernsey
	G-CDPS	Raj Hamsa X'Air 133	P. R. Smith
	G-CDPT	Boeing 767-319ER	Flyglobespan.com
	G-CDPV	PA-34-200T Seneca II	G. G. L. James
	G-CDPW	Mainair Pegasus Quantum 15-912	T. P. R. Wright
	G-CDPX	Schleicher ASH-25M	P. Pozerskis
	G-CDPY	Shaw Europa	A. Burrill
	G-CDPZ	Flight Design CT2K	M. E. Henwick
	G-CDRA	Boeing 737-683	Flyglobespan.com
	G-CDRB	Boeing 737-683	Fjyglobespan.com
	G-CDRC	Cessna 182Q Skylane	R. S. Hill and Sons
	G-CDRD	AirBorne XT912-B Edge/Streak III-B	G. C. Ellis
	G-CDRE	Robinson R44	Tercoy Helicopters Ltd
	G-CDRF	Cameron Z-90 balloon	Chalmers Ballong Corps
	G-CDRG	Mainair Pegasus Quik	R. J. Gabriel
	G-CDRH	Thruster T.600N	Carlisle Thruster Group/Carlisle
	G-CDRI	Cameron O-105 balloon	Snapdragon Balloon Group
	G-CDRJ	Tanarg/Ixess 15 912S(1)	J. H. Hayday
	G-CDRK	Avro RJ100	Trident Jet (Dublin) Ltd
	G-CDRM	Van's RV-7A	R. A. Morris
	G-CDRN	Cameron Z-225 balloon	Balloon School (International) Ltd
	G-CDRO	Ikarus C42 F880	M. L. Smith
	G-CDRP	Ikarus C42 FB80	D. S. Parker
	G-CDRR	Mainair Pegasus Quantum 15-912	Light Flight Ltd
	G-CDRS	Rotorway Executive 162F	R. C. Swann
	G-CDRT	Mainair Pegasus Quik	R. Tetlow
	G-CDRU	CASA 1.131E Jungmann 2000	P. Cunniff/White Waltham
	G-CDRV	Van's RV-9A	R. J. Woodford
	G-CDRW	Mainair Pegasus Quik	P and M Aviation Ltd
	G-CDRX	Cameron Z-225 balloon	Balloon School (International) Ltd
	G-CDRY	Ikarus C42 FB100 VLA	R. J. Mitchell
	G-CDRZ	Balóny Kubíček BB22 balloon	Club Amatori Del Volo In Montgolfiera
	G-CDSA	Mainair Pegasus Quik	P. J. Shergold
	G-CDSB	Alpi Pioneer 200	T. A. & P. M. Pugh
	G-CDSC	Scheibe SF.25C Rotax-Falke	Devon & Somerset Motorglider Group
	G-CDSD	Alpi Pioneer 200	Pioneer Aviation UK Ltd
	G-CDSF	Diamond DA40D Star	Spirit Communications (UK) Ltd
	G-CDSG	Sud SA316B Alouette III	G. Snook
	G-CDSH	ICP MXP-740 Savannah Jabiru(5)	J. P. Bell
	G-CDSI	Jabiru J400	G. H. Gilmour-White
	G-CDSJ	Sud SA316B Alouette III	S.Atherton
	G-CDSK	Reality Escapade Jabiru(3)	R. H. Sear
	G-CDSL	Cessna 182R	A. G. Craig
	G-CDSM	Mainair Pegasus Quik	A. M. Dalgetty
	G-CDSN	Raj Hamsa X'Air Jabiru(3)	G. W. Cole
	G-CDSO	Thruster T.600N	S. J. Reynolds
	G-CDSR	Learjet 45	Gold Air International Ltd
	G-CDSS	Mainair Pegasus Quik	P. A. Bass
	G-CDST	Ultramagic N-250 balloon	Sky High Leisure
	G-CDSU	Robinson R22	M. Horrell
	G-CDSV	AS.332L Super Puma	CHC Helicopters International Inc
	G-CDSW	Ikarus C.42 FB UK	P. J. Barton
	G-CDSX	EE Canberra T.Mk.4 (VN799)	Aviation Heritage Ltd
	G-CDSY	Robinson R44	E. Meegan
	G-CDSZ	Diamond DA42 Twin Star	Aviation Services Ltd
	G-CDTA	EV-97 TeamEurostar UK	R. D. Stein
	G-CDTB	Mainair Pegasus Quantum 15-912	D. W. Corbett
	G-CDTC	Mainair Pegasus Quantum 15-912	C. W. J. Davis
	G-CDTD	AS350B2 Ecureuil	London Helicopter Centres Ltd
	G-CDTE	Tecnam P2002-JF	Tecnam General Aviation Ltd
	G-CDTF	Whittaker MW5-D Sorcerer	R. J. Smyth
	G-CDTG	Diamond DA42 Twin Star	Twinstar Ltd
	G-CDTH	Schempp-Hirth Nimbus 4DM	M. A. V. Gatehouse

BRITISH CIVIL REGISTRATIONS

G-CDTI – G-CDXB

Reg	Type	Owner or Operator	Notes
G-CDTI	Messerschmitt Bf.109E (4034)	Rare Aero Ltd	
G-CDTJ	Just/Reality Escapade Jabiru	D. Little	
G-CDTK	Schweizer 269C-1	Caserwright Ltd	
G-CDTL	Avtech Jabiru J-400	M. I. Sistern	
G-CDTM	VS.384 Seafire Mk.XVII	T. J. Manna	
G-CDTN	A.S.332L Super Puma	CHC Helicopters International Inc	
G-CDTO	P & M Quik GT450	J. R. Houston	
G-CDTP	Skyranger 912S (1)	J. R. S. Heaton	
G-CDTR	P & M Quik GT450	Sunfun Group	
G-CDTT	Savannah Jabiru(4)	M. P. Middleton	
G-CDTU	EV-97 TeamEurostar UK	D. R. Stevens	
G-CDTV	Tecnam P2002 EA Sierra	M. Rudd	
G-CDTW	Schweizer 269C-1	Armstrong Aviation Ltd	
G-CDTX	Cessna F.152	J. S. Develin & Z. Islam	
G-CDTY	Savannah Jabiru (5)	J. N. Anyan	
G-CDTZ	Aeroprakt A.22 Foxbat	P. C. Piggott & M. E. Hughes	
G-CDUE	Robinson R44	Scotia Helicopters Ltd	
G-CDUH	P & M Quik GT450	R. W. Thornborough	
G-CDUI	Avro RJ100	Trident Jet (Dublin) Ltd	
G-CDUJ	Lindstrand LBL 31A balloon	J. M. Frazer	
G-CDUK	Ikarus C.42 FB UK	D. M. Lane	
G-CDUL	Skyranger 912S (2)	T. W. Thiele & C. D. Hogbourne	
G-CDUS	Skyranger 912S (1)	W. P. Byrne	
G-CDUT	Jabiru J400	T. W. & A. Pullin.	
G-CDUU	P & M Quik GT450	Caunton Charlie Delta Group	
G-CDUV	Savannah Jabiru(5)	D. M. Blackman	
G-CDUW	Aeronca C3	N. K. Geddes	
G-CDUX	PA-32 Cherokee Six 300	D. J. Mason	
G-CDUY	Thunder & Colt 77A balloon	De-Hippo Balloon Group	
G-CDVA	Skyranger 912 (2)	Skyview Systems Ltd	
G-CDVD	Aerotechnik EV-97 Eurostar	G. R. Pritchard	
G-CDVF	Rans S.6-ES Coyote II	G. P. Jones	
G-CDVG	Pegasus Quik	M. Overend	
G-CDVH	Pegasus Quantum 15	M. J. Hyde	
G-CDVI	Ikarus C42 FB80	M. L. Smith	
G-CDVJ	Montgomerie-Bensen B8MR	D. J. Martin	
G-CDVK	Savannah Jabiru (5)	M. Peters	
G-CDVL	Alpi Pioneer 300	A. N. Pascoe	
G-CDVN	P & M Quik GT450	R. E. J. Pattenden	
G-CDVO	Pegasus Quik	S. D. J. Harvey	
G-CDVP	Aerotechnik EV-97 Eurostar	S. R. Pike	
G-CDVR	P & M Quik GT450	A. V. Cosser	
G-CDVS	Europa XS	J. F. Lawn	
G-CDVT	Van's RV-6	P. J. Wood	
G-CDVU	Aerotechnik EV-97 TeamEurostar	D. J. Dick	
G-CDVV	SA Bulldog Srs. 120/121 (XX626:02, W)	D. M. Squires	
G-CDVX	Republic TP-47G-10-GU Thunderbolt	Patina Ltd/Duxford	
G-CDVZ	P & M Quik GT450	A. K. Burden	
G-CDWA	Balóny Kubíček BB37 balloon	Fly In Balloons SRL	
G-CDWB	Skyranger 912(2)	V. R. Morris	
G-CDWD	Cameron Z-105 balloon	Bristol University Ballooning Society	
G-CDWE	Nord NC.856 Norvigie	R. H. & S. J. Cooper	
G-CDWF	DHC.1 Chipmunk 22	K. B. Owen	
G-CDWG	Dyn'Aéro MCR-01 Club	S. E. Gribble	
G-CDWI	Ikarus C42 FB80	P. Chamberlayne	
G-CDWJ	Flight Design CTSW	B. W. T. Rood	
G-CDWK	Robinson R44	Aston Helicopters Ltd	
G-CDWL	Raj Hamsa X'Air 582 (5)	C. Lenaghan	
G-CDWM	Skyranger 912S (1)	W. H. McMinn	
G-CDWN	Ultramagic N-210 balloon	S. R. Seager	
G-CDWO	P & M Quik GT450	M. D. Harris	
G-CDWP	P & M Quik GT450	S. M. Hall	
G-CDWR	P & M Quik GT450	D. P. Creedy	
G-CDWS	P & M Quik GT450	H. N. Barrott	
G-CDWT	Flight Design CTSW	R. Scammell	
G-CDWU	Zenair CH.601UL Zodiac	A. D. Worrall	
G-CDWV	Lindstrand LBL House SS balloon	LSB Public Relations Ltd	
G-CDWW	P & M Quik GT450	J. H. Bradbury	
G-CDWX	Lindstrand LBL 77A balloon	LSB Public Relations Ltd	
G-CDWY	Agusta A109S Grand	Sports World International Ltd	
G-CDWZ	P & M Quik GT450	B. J. Holloway	
G-CDXA	Robinson R44 Raven	J and D Graham	
G-CDXB	Robinson R44 Raven	HJS Helicopters Ltd	

G-CDXD – G-CEAU | BRITISH CIVIL REGISTRATIONS

Notes	Reg	Type	Owner or Operator
	G-CDXD	Medway SLA100 Executive	Medway Microlights
	G-CDXE	Westland Gazelle AH.Mk.1	S. Atherton
	G-CDXF	Lindstrand LBL 31A balloon	Roman Trading Ltd
	G-CDXG	P & M Pegasus Quantum 15-912	E. H. Gatehouse
	G-CDXH	Avro RJ100	Trident Jet Leasing (Ireland) Ltd
	G-CDXI	Cessna 182P	R. D. Masters
	G-CDXJ	Jabiru J400	J. C. Collingwood
	G-CDXK	Diamond DA42 Twin Star	A. M. Healy
	G-CDXL	Flight Design CTSW	A. K. Paterson
	G-CDXM	Pegasus Quik	Mainair Microlight Centre Ltd
	G-CDXN	P & M Quik GT450	Microflight Aviation Ltd
	G-CDXO	Zenair CH.601UL Zodiac	R. O. Lewthwaite
	G-CDXP	Aerotechnik EV-97 Eurostar	R. J. Crockett
	G-CDXR	Replica Fokker DR.1	J. G. Day
	G-CDXS	Aerotechnik EV-97 Eurostar	R. T. P. Harris
	G-CDXT	Van's RV-9	T. M. Storey
	G-CDXU	Chilton DW.1A	R. W. Burrows
	G-CDXV	Campbell Cricket Mk.6A	W. G. Spencer
	G-CDXW	Cameron Orange 120 SS balloon	A. Biasioli
	G-CDXX	Robinson R44 Raven II	Emsway Developments Ltd
	G-CDXY	Skystar Kitfox Mk.7	D. E. Steade
	G-CDYA	Gippsland GA-8 Airvan	P. Marsden
	G-CDYB	Rans S.6-ES Coyote II	D. Sykes & J. M. Hardstaff
	G-CDYC	PA-28RT-201 Arrow IV	Arrowflight Ltd
	G-CDYD	Ikarus C42 FB80	C42 Group
	G-CDYF	Rotorsport UK MT-03	A. J. P Herculson
	G-CDYG	Cameron Z-105 balloon	A. Service Di Tartaglini Emanuela
	G-CDYH	BAe Jetstream 4102	Eastern Airways
	G-CDYI	BAe Jetstream 4102	Eastern Airways
	G-CDYJ	Skyranger 912(1)	D. S. Taylor
	G-CDYK	Avro RJ85	BAE Systems (Funding One) Ltd
	G-CDYL	Lindstrand LBL-77A balloon	J. H. Dobson
	G-CDYM	Murphy Maverick 430	G. T. Leedham
	G-CDYN	Extra EA.300/L	A. Caramella
	G-CDYO	Ikarus C42 FB80	B. Goodridge
	G-CDYP	Aerotechnik EV-97 TeamEurostar UK	R. V. Buxton & R. Cranborne
	G-CDYS	Bell 206B-3 JetRanger III	Cardy Construction Ltd (G-BOTM)
	G-CDYT	Ikarus C42 FB80	J. W. D. Blythe
	G-CDYU	Zenair CH.701UL	M. Henderson
	G-CDYW	Schweizer 269C-1	Caseright Ltd
	G-CDYX	Lindstrand LBL-77B balloon	H. M. Savage
	G-CDYY	Alpi Pioneer 300	B. Williams
	G-CDYZ	Van's RV-7	G. A. Martin & W. D. Garlick
	G-CDZA	Alpi Pioneer 300	C. A. Young
	G-CDZB	Zenair CH.601UL Zodiac	L. J. Dutch
	G-CDZD	Van's RV-9A	R. T. Clegg
	G-CDZG	Ikarus C42-FB80	Mainair Microlight School Ltd
	G-CDZH	Boeing 737-804	Thomsonfly
	G-CDZI	Boeing 737-804	Thomsonfly
	G-CDZJ	Tecnam P92-JS	Tecnam General Aviation Ltd
	G-CDZK	Tecnam P92-JS	Tecnam General Aviation Ltd
	G-CDZL	Boeing 737-804	Thomsonfly (G-BYNC)
	G-CDZM	Boeing 737-804	Thomsonfly (G-BYNB)
	G-CDZO	Lindstrand LBL-60X balloon	R. D. Parry
	G-CDZR	Nicollier HN.700 Menestrel II	T. M. Williams
	G-CDZS	Kolb Twinstar Mk.3 Extra	P. W. Heywood
	G-CDZT	Beech B200 Super King Air	BAE Systems Ltd
	G-CDZU	ICP MXP-740 Savannah Jabiru (5)	P. J. Cheney
	G-CDZW	Cameron N-105 balloon	P. Lesser
	G-CDZY	Medway SLA 80 Executive	Medway Microlights
	G-CDZZ	Rotorsport UK MT-03	S. J. Boxall
	G-CEAE	Boeing 737-229	European Skybus Ltd
	G-CEAF	Boeing 737-229	European Skybus Ltd
	G-CEAG	Boeing 737-229	European Aviation Ltd/Bournemouth
	G-CEAH	Boeing 737-229	European Aviation Ltd/Bournemouth
	G-CEAK	Ikarus C42 FB80	Barton Heritage Flying Group/Barton
	G-CEAM	Aerotechnik EV-97 TeamEurostar UK	Flylight Airsports Ltd
	G-CEAN	Ikarus C42 FB80	Airbourne Aviation Ltd
	G-CEAO	Jurca MJ.5 Sirocco	P. S. Watts
	G-CEAR	Alpi Pioneer 300	A. Parker
	G-CEAT	Zenair CH.601HDS Zodiac	T. B. Smith
	G-CEAU	Robinson R44	Mullahead Property Co Ltd

BRITISH CIVIL REGISTRATIONS

G-CEAV – G-CEEC

Reg	Type	Owner or Operator	Notes
G-CEAV	Ultramagic M-105 balloon	G. Everett	
G-CEAW	Schweizer 269C-1	Aerocorp Ltd	
G-CEAX	Ultramagic S-130 balloon	Anglian Countryside Balloons Ltd	
G-CEAY	Ultramagic H-42 balloon	J. D. A. Shields	
G-CEBA	Zenair CH.601XL Zodiac	I. J. M. Donnelly	
G-CEBC	ICP MXP-740 Savannah Jabiru (5)	E. W. Chapman	
G-CEBD	P & M Quik GT450	E. J. Douglas	
G-CEBE	Schweizer 269C-1	Caseright Ltd	
G-CEBF	Aerotechnik EV-97A Eurostar	M. Lang	
G-CEBG	Balóny Kubíček BB26 balloon	P. M. Smith	
G-CEBH	Tanarg/Ixess 15 912S (1)	D. A. Chamberlain	
G-CEBI	Kolb Twinstar Mk.3	R. W. Livingstone	
G-CEBK	PA-31-350 Navajo Chieftain	Skydrift Ltd	
G-CEBL	Balóny Kubíček BB20GP balloon	Associazione Sportiva Aerostatica Lombada/Italy	
G-CEBM	P & M Quik GT450	P and M Aviation Ltd	
G-CEBN	Avro RJ100	Trident Jet Leasing (Ireland) Ltd	
G-CEBO	Ultramagic M-65C balloon	R. D. Howard	
G-CEBP	EV-97 TeamEurostar UK	T. R. Southall	
G-CEBR	BAe 146-200	Bae Systems (Operations) Ltd	
G-CEBS	Avro RJ85	BAe Systems (Funding One) Ltd	
G-CEBT	P & M Quik GT450	A. J. Riddell	
G-CEBU	Avro RJ85	BAe Systems (Funding One) Ltd	
G-CEBV	Europa XS	S. Vestuti	
G-CEBW	P-51D Mustang	Classic (UW) Ltd	
G-CEBY	Tanarg/Ixess 15 912S (2)	P. S. Bewley	
G-CEBZ	Zenair CH.601UL Zodiac	I. M. Ross & A Watt	
G-CECA	P & M Quik GT450	A. Weatherall	
G-CECB	ELA Aviacion ELA 07S	A. D. Gordon	
G-CECC	Ikarus C42 FB80	G-CECC Group	
G-CECD	Cameron C-90 balloon	Exclusive Holdings	
G-CECE	Jabiru UL-D	ST Aviation Ltd	
G-CECF	Just/Reality Escapade Jabiru (3)	T. F. Francis	
G-CECG	Jabiru UL-D	R. K. Watson	
G-CECH	Jodel D.150	J. Simpson & D. Kennedy	
G-CECI	Pilatus PC-6/B2-H4 Turbo Porter	D. M. Penny	
G-CECJ	Aeromot AMT-200S Super Ximango	C. J. & S. C. Partridge	
G-CECK	ICP MXP-740 Savannah Jabiru (5)	K. W. Eskins	
G-CECL	Ikarus C42 FB80	C. Lee	
G-CECM	P & M Quik GT450	C. S. Mackenzie	
G-CECO	Hughes 269C	P. A. Leverton	
G-CECP	Best Off Skyranger 912(2)	D. C. Davies	
G-CECR	Bilsam Sky Cruiser	J. C. Collingwood	
G-CECS	Lindstrand LBL-105A balloon	Beam Global Distribution (UK) Ltd	
G-CECT	Eurocopter EC 135T2	McAlpine Helicopters Ltd	
G-CECU	Boeing 767-222	UK International Airlines Ltd	
G-CECV	Van's RV-7	D. M. Stevens	
G-CECW	Robinson R44 II	VHE Construction Ltd	
G-CECX	Robinson R44	Dolphin Property (Management) Ltd	
G-CECY	EV-97 Eurostar	M. R. M. Welch	
G-CECZ	Zenair CH.601XL Zodiac	G. M. Johnson	
G-CEDA	Cameron Z-105 balloon	N. Charbonnier	
G-CEDB	Just/Reality Escapade Jabiru (3)	D. Bedford	
G-CEDC	Ikarus C42 FB100	P. D. Ashley	
G-CEDD	PA-28RT-201 Arrow IV	R. Hammond	
G-CEDE	Flight Design CTSW	F. Williams & J. A. R. Hartley	
G-CEDF	Cameron N-105 balloon	Bailey Balloons Ltd	
G-CEDG	Robinson R44	Heli-Air Ltd	
G-CEDI	Best Off Skyranger 912(2)	P. B. Davey	
G-CEDJ	Aero Designs Pulsar XP	R. R. Walters	
G-CEDL	TEAM Minimax 91	J. W. Taylor	
G-CEDM	Flight Design CTSW	S. A. Fair	
G-CEDN	Pegasus Quik	N. J. Hargreaves	
G-CEDO	Raj Hamsa X'Air Falcon 133(1)	J. Lane & A. P. Lambert	
G-CEDP	ELA Aviacion ELA 07R	Roger Savage (Penrith) Ltd	
G-CEDR	Ikarus C42 FB80	R. S. O'Carroll	
G-CEDT	Tanarg/Ixess 15 912S(1)	R. A. Taylor	
G-CEDV	Evektor EV-97 TeamEurostar UK	M. L. Smith	
G-CEDW	TEAM Minimax 91	A. T. Peatman	
G-CEDX	Evektor EV-97 TeamEurostar UK	M. W. Houghton	
G-CEDZ	Best Off Skyranger 912(2)	J. E. Walendowski	
G-CEEA	ELA Aviacion ELA 07R	S. J. Tyler	
G-CEEB	Cameron C-80 balloon	Cameron Balloons Ltd	
G-CEEC	Raj Hamsa X'Air Hawk	G. A. J. Salter	

G-CEED – G-CEHX — BRITISH CIVIL REGISTRATIONS

Reg	Type	Owner or Operator
G-CEED	ICP MXP-740 Savannah Jabiru(5)	A. U. I. Hudson
G-CEEE	Robinson R44	Caswell Environmental Services Ltd
G-CEEF	ELA 07R	G. Millward
G-CEEG	Alpi Pioneer 300	D. McCormack
G-CEEI	P & M Quik GT450	R. A. Hill
G-CEEJ	Rans S-7S Courier	J. G. J. McDill
G-CEEK	Cameron Z-105 balloon	PSH Skypower Ltd
G-CEEL	Ultramagic S-90 balloon	Impresa San Paolo SRL
G-CEEM	P & M Quik GT450	T. Griffiths
G-CEEN	PA-28-161 Cadet	Plane Talking Ltd/Elstree
G-CEEO	Flight Design CTSW	E. McCallum
G-CEEP	Van's RV-9A	W. H. Greenwood
G-CEER	ELA 07R	M. Johnston
G-CEES	Cameron C-90 balloon	P. C. May
G-CEEV	PA-28-161 Warrior III	Plane Talking Ltd
G-CEEW	Ikarus C42 FB100	Autocom Products Ltd
G-CEEX	ICP MXP-740 Savannah Jabiru(5)	Savannah Flying Group
G-CEEY	PA-28-161 Warrior III	Plane Talking Ltd
G-CEEZ	PA-28-161 Warrior III	Plane Talking Ltd
G-CEFA	Ikarus C42 FB UK	J. Little
G-CEFB	Ultramagic H-31 balloon	P. Dickinson
G-CEFC	Super Marine Spitfire 26	D. R. Bishop
G-CEFF	Boeing 747-422	Blue Sky Three Ltd
G-CEFG	Boeing 767-319ER	Flyglobespan.com
G-CEFH	ELA 07S	M. L. L. Temple
G-CEFI	BAe Jetstream 4101	Trident Turboprop (Dublin) Ltd
G-CEFJ	Sonex	M. H. Moulai
G-CEFK	Evektor EV-97 TeamEurostar UK	P. Morgan
G-CEFL	Avro RJ85	BAE Systems (Funding One) Ltd
G-CEFM	Cessna 152	Cristal Air Ltd
G-CEFN	Avro RJ85	BAE Systems (Funding One) Ltd
G-CEFP	Jabiru J430	G. Hammond
G-CEFR	Robinson R44	Beechview Aviation Ltd
G-CEFS	Cameron C-100 balloon	Gone with the wind Ltd
G-CEFT	Whittaker MW5-D Sorcerer	W. Bruce
G-CEFV	Cessna 182T Skylane	G. H. Smith and Son
G-CEFW	Avro RJ100	Trident Jet (Dublin) Ltd
G-CEFX	Diamond DA42 Twin Star	Diamond Aircraft UK Ltd
G-CEFY	ICP MXP-740 Savannah Jabiru(4)	P. Openshaw & B. Hartley
G-CEFZ	Evektor EV-97 TeamEurostar UK	Robo Flying Group
G-CEGC	Cameron Z-105 balloon	First Flight
G-CEGF	Eurocopter EC 135T2	McAlpine Helicopters Ltd
G-CEGG	Lindstrand LBL-25A Cloudhopper balloon	C. G. Dobson
G-CEGH	Van's RV-9A	M. E. Creasey
G-CEGI	Van's RV-8	W. H. Greenwood
G-CEGJ	P & M Quik GT450	Flylight Airsports Ltd
G-CEGK	ICP MXP-740 Savannah VG Jabiru(1)	Sandtoft Ultralights Partnership
G-CEGL	Ikarus C42 FB100	Aerosport Ltd
G-CEGO	Evektor EV-97A Eurostar	N. J. Keeling, R. F. McLachlan & J. A. Charlton
G-CEGP	Beech 200 Super King Air	Cega Aviation Ltd (G-BXMA)
G-CEGR	Beech 200 Super King Air	Henfield Lodge Aviation Ltd
G-CEGS	PA-28-161 Warrior II	Aviation Rentals
G-CEGT	P & M Quik GT450	J. Plenderleith
G-CEGU	PA-28-151 Warrior	Aviation Rentals
G-CEGV	P & M Quik GT450	Sunfun Group
G-CEGW	P & M Quik GT450	P. Barrow
G-CEGY	ELA 07R	A. Buchanan
G-CEGZ	Ikarus C42 FB80	Ikarus Flying Group
G-CEHC	P & M Quik GT450	G. H. Sharwood-Smith
G-CEHD	Best Off Skyranger 912(2)	A. A. Howland
G-CEHG	Ikarus C42 FB100	G. E. Cole
G-CEHH	Edge XT912-B/Streak III-B	J. Madhvani & K. Bolton
G-CEHI	P & M Quik GT450	A. Costello
G-CEHK	Robinson R44 II	Heli Air Ltd
G-CEHL	EV-97 TeamEurostar UK	B. P. Connally
G-CEHM	Rotorsport UK MT-03	K. O. Maurer
G-CEHN	Rotorsport UK MT-03	P. A. Harwood
G-CEHR	Auster AOP.9	J. Cooke & R. B. Webber
G-CEHT	Rand KR-2	P. P. Geoghegan
G-CEHU	Cameron Z-105 balloon	Cameron Balloons Ltd
G-CEHV	Ikarus C42 FB80	Mainair Microlight School Ltd
G-CEHW	P & M Quik GT450	P and M Aviation Ltd
G-CEHX	Lindstrand LBL-9A balloon	P. Baker

BRITISH CIVIL REGISTRATIONS — G-CEHZ – G-CHAS

Reg	Type	Owner or Operator	Notes
G-CEHZ	Edge XT912-B/Streak III-B	Fly NI Ltd	
G-CEIA	Rotorsport UK MT-03	M. P Chetwynd-Talbot	
G-CEID	Van's RV-7	A. Moyce	
G-CEIE	Flight Design CTSW	D. K. Ross	
G-CEIG	Van's RV-7	W. K. Wilkie	
G-CEIL	Bassett Escapade 912(2)	D. E. Bassett	
G-CEIN	Cameron Z-105 balloon	Cameron Balloons Ltd	
G-CEIO	BN-2T-4S Islander	Britten-Norman Aircraft Ltd	
G-CEIP	BN-2T-4S Islander	Britten-Norman Aircraft Ltd	
G-CEIR	BN-2T-4S Islander	Britten-Norman Aircraft Ltd	
G-CEIS	Jodel DR.1050	M. Hales	
G-CEIT	Van's RV-7	S. S. Gould	
G-CEIV	Tanarg/Ixess 15 912S(2)	Focus Property Services Ltd	
G-CEIW	Europa	R. Scanlan	
G-CEJA	Cameron V-77 balloon	L. & C. Gray (G-BTOF)	
G-CEJB	PA-46-500TP Malibu	The Van Meeuwen Flying Company Ltd	
G-CEJC	Cameron N-77 balloon	Zebedee Balloon Service Ltd	
G-CEJE	Wittman W.10 Tailwind	R. A. Povall	
G-CEJH	ELA 07S	M. C. Woodhouse	
G-CEJJ	P & M Quik GT450	I. M. Bracegirdle	
G-CEJS	Agusta A.109E Power	Castle Air Charters Ltd	
G-CEJW	Ikarus C42 FB80	M. I. Deeley	
G-CEKJ	Evektor EV-97A Eurostar	C. W. J. Vershoyle-Greene	
G-CEKW	Jabiru J430	J. G. Culley	
G-CELA	Boeing 737-377	Jet 2	
G-CELB	Boeing 737-377	Jet 2	
G-CELC	Boeing 737-377	Jet 2 (G-OBMA)	
G-CELD	Boeing 737-377	Jet 2 (G-OBMB)	
G-CELE	Boeing 737-377	Jet 2 (G-MONN)	
G-CELF	Boeing 737-377	Jet 2	
G-CELG	Boeing 737-377	Jet 2	
G-CELH	Boeing 737-330	Jet 2	
G-CELI	Boeing 737-330	Jet 2	
G-CELJ	Boeing 737-330	Jet 2	
G-CELK	Boeing 737-330	Jet 2	
G-CELO	Boeing 737-33AQC	Jet 2	
G-CELP	Boeing 737-330QC	Jet 2	
G-CELR	Boeing 737-330QC	Jet 2	
G-CELS	Boeing 737-377	Jet 2	
G-CELU	Boeing 737-377	Jet 2	
G-CELV	Boeing 737-377	Jet 2	
G-CELW	Boeing 737-377	Jet 2	
G-CELX	Boeing 737-377	Jet 2	
G-CELY	Boeing 737-377	Jet 2	
G-CELZ	Boeing 737-377	Jet 2	
G-CEPT	SOCATA TB20 Trinidad	P. J. Caiger (G-BTEK)	
G-CERI	Shaw Europa XS	S. J. M. Shepherd	
G-CERT	Mooney M.20K	J. A. Nisbet	
G-CEXP	HPR.7 Herald 209 ★	Towing and rescue trainer/Gatwick	
G-CEYE	PA-32R-300 Cherokee Lance	Fleetlands Flying Association Ltd	
G-CFAA	Avro RJ100	British Airways Connect	
G-CFBI	Colt 56A balloon	G. A. Fisher	
G-CFME	SOCATA TB10 Tobago	Charles Funke Associates Ltd	
G-CFOG	Ikarus C42 FB UK	P. D. Coppin	
G-CFRY	Zenair CH 601UL	C. K. Fry	
G-CFSA	PA-44-180 Seminole	Northern Aviation Ltd (G-CCDA)	
G-CFTJ	Aerotechnik EV-97A Eurostar	C. B. Flood	
G-CFWR	Skyranger 912 (2)	R. W. Clarke	
G-CFWW	Schleicher ASH 25E	FWW Syndicate	
G-CGDJ	PA-28-161 Warrior II	C. G. D. Jones (G-ETDA)	
G-CGHM	PA-28 Cherokee 140	A. Reay	
G-CGOD	Cameron N-77 balloon	G. P. Lane	
G-CGRI	Agusta A109S Grand	C. G. Roach	
G-CHAD	Aeroprakt A.22 Foxbat	C. J. Rossiter	
G-CHAH	Shaw Europa	T. Higgins	
G-CHAM	Cameron 90 Pot SS balloon	High Exposure Balloons	
G-CHAN	Robinson R22 Beta	Artall Air LLP	
G-CHAP	Robinson R44	Brierley Lifting Tackle Co Ltd	
G-CHAR	Grob G.109B	RAFGSA/Bicester	
G-CHAS	PA-28-181 Archer II	C. H. Elliott	

G-CHAV – G-CIVX   BRITISH CIVIL REGISTRATIONS

Notes	Reg	Type	Owner or Operator
	G-CHAV	Shaw Europa	R. P. Robinson
	G-CHCD	Sikorsky S-76A (modified)	CHC Scotia Ltd (G-CBJB)
	G-CHCF	AS.332L-2 Super Puma	CHC Scotia Ltd
	G-CHCG	AS.332L-2 Super Puma	CHC Scotia Ltd
	G-CHCH	AS.332L-2 Super Puma	CHC Scotia Ltd
	G-CHCI	AS.332L-2 Super Puma	CHC Scotia Ltd
	G-CHCK	Sikorsky S-92A	CHC Scotia Ltd
	G-CHCP	Agusta AB.139	CHC Scotia Ltd
	G-CHCT	Agusta AB.139	CHC Scotia Ltd
	G-CHEB	Shaw Europa	P. Whittingham
	G-CHEL	Colt 77B balloon	Chelsea Financial Services PLC
	G-CHEM	PA-34-200T Seneca II	London Executive Aviation Ltd
	G-CHER	PA-38-112 Tomahawk II	Aerohire Ltd/Wolverhampton (G-BVBL)
	G-CHET	Shaw Europa	H. H. R. Lagache
	G-CHEY	PA-31T2 Cheyenne IIXL	Air Medical Fleet Ltd
	G-CHEZ	BN-2B-20 Islander	Cheshire Police Authority/Liverpool (G-BSAG)
	G-CHGL	Bell 206B JetRanger II	Engineaward Ltd (G-BPNG/G-ORTC)
	G-CHIK	Cessna F.152	Stapleford Flying Club Ltd (G-BHAZ)
	G-CHIP	PA-28-181 Archer II	C. M. Hough/Fairoaks
	G-CHIS	Robinson R22 Beta	P. J. & J. L. Myatt
	G-CHIX	Robin DR.400/500	P. A. & R. Stephens
	G-CHKL	Cameron 120 Kookaburra SS balloon	Eagle Ltd/Australia
	G-CHKN	Kiss 400-582 (1)	D. A. Edwards
	G-CHLL	Lindstrand LBL-90A balloon	ABC Flights Ltd
	G-CHMP	Bellanca 7ACA Champ	I. J. Langley
	G-CHOK	Cameron V-77 balloon	A. J. Moore
	G-CHOP	Westland-Bell 47G-3B1	Classic Rotors Ltd
	G-CHOX	Shaw Europa XS	Chocs Away Ltd
	G-CHPR	Robinson R-28B	Meadow Helicopters Ltd
	G-CHPY	DHC.1 Chipmunk 22 (WB652:V)	Devonair Executive Business Travel Ltd
	G-CHSU	Eurocopter EC 135T1	Thames Valley Police Authority Chiltern Air Support Unit/Benson
	G-CHTA	AA-5A Cheetah	T. Hale (G-BFRC)
	G-CHTG	Rotorway Executive 90	G. Cooper (G-BVAJ)
	G-CHUG	Shaw Europa	C. M. Washington
	G-CHUK	Cameron O-77 balloon	R. Ashford
	G-CHUM	Robinson R44	Vitapage Ltd
	G-CHYL	Robinson R22 Beta	C. M. Gough-Cooper
	G-CHZN	Robinson R22 Beta	Cloudbase Ltd (G-GHZM/G-FENI)
	G-CIAO	I.I.I. Sky Arrow 1450-L	G. Arscott
	G-CIAS	BN-2B-21 Islander	Channel Island Air Search Ltd (G-BKJM)
	G-CIBO	Cessna 180K	CIBO Ops Ltd
	G-CICI	Cameron R-15 balloon	Noble Adventures Ltd
	G-CIDD	Bellanca 7ECA Citabria	A. & P. West
	G-CIEL	Cessna 560XL Citation Excel	Enerway Ltd
	G-CIFR	PA-28-181 Archer II	Shropshire Aero Club Ltd/Sleap
	G-CIGY	Westland-Bell 47G-3B1	Heli-Highland Ltd (G-BGXP)
	G-CITR	Cameron Z-105 balloon	Flying Pictures Ltd
	G-CITY	PA-31-350 Navajo Chieftain	Woodgate Aviation (IOM) Ltd
	G-CIVA	Boeing 747-436	British Airways
	G-CIVB	Boeing 747-436	British Airways
	G-CIVC	Boeing 747-436	British Airways
	G-CIVD	Boeing 747-436	British Airways
	G-CIVE	Boeing 747-436	British Airways
	G-CIVF	Boeing 747-436	British Airways
	G-CIVG	Boeing 747-436	British Airways
	G-CIVH	Boeing 747-436	British Airways
	G-CIVI	Boeing 747-436	British Airways
	G-CIVJ	Boeing 747-436	British Airways
	G-CIVK	Boeing 747-436	British Airways
	G-CIVL	Boeing 747-436	British Airways
	G-CIVM	Boeing 747-436	British Airways
	G-CIVN	Boeing 747-436	British Airways
	G-CIVO	Boeing 747-436	British Airways
	G-CIVP	Boeing 747-436	British Airways
	G-CIVR	Boeing 747-436	British Airways
	G-CIVS	Boeing 747-436	British Airways
	G-CIVT	Boeing 747-436	British Airways
	G-CIVU	Boeing 747-436	British Airways
	G-CIVV	Boeing 747-436	British Airways
	G-CIVW	Boeing 747-436	British Airways
	G-CIVX	Boeing 747-436	British Airways

BRITISH CIVIL REGISTRATIONS

G-CIVY – G-CKKV

Reg	Type	Owner or Operator	Notes
G-CIVY	Boeing 747-436	British Airways	
G-CIVZ	Boeing 747-436	British Airways	
G-CJAB	Dornier 328-300 JET	Corporate Jet Services Ltd	
G-CJAD	Cessna 525 CitationJet	Davis Aircraft Operations	
G-CJAG	Raytheon 390 Premier 1	Corporate Jet Services Ltd	
G-CJAH	Raytheon 390 Premier 1	Corporate Jet Services Ltd	
G-CJAY	Mainair Pegasus Quik	Jaye Airsports	
G-CJBC	PA-28 Cherokee 180	J. B. Cave/Halfpenny Green	
G-CJCI	Pilatus P2-06 (CC+43)	Pilatus P2 Flying Group	
G-CJUD	Denney Kitfox Mk 3	AV8 Air	
G-CKCK	Enstrom 280FX	GTS Engineering (Coventry) Ltd	
G-CKEM	Robinson R44	True Course Helicopter Ltd	
G-CKEY	PA-28-161 Warrior II	G. Key	
G-CKFY	Schleicher ASK.21	Cambridge Gliding Club	
G-CKGA	Schempp-Hirth Ventus 2cxT	D. R. Campbell	
G-CKGB	Schempp-Hirth Ventus 2cxT	D. R. Irving	
G-CKGC	Schempp-Hirth Ventus 2cxT	C. A. Marren	
G-CKGD	Schempp-Hirth Ventus 2cxT	C. Morris	
G-CKGF	Schempp-Hirth Duo Discus T	Duo 233 Group	
G-CKGH	Grob G.102 Club Astir II	M. W. Talbot & M. Butters	
G-CKGK	Schleicher ASK-21	RAF Gliding & Soaring Association	
G-CKGL	Schempp-Hirth Ventus 2cT	Bidford Airfield Ltd	
G-CKGN	Schleicher ASW-28	M. Jerman	
G-CKGT	Schempp-Hirth Standard Cirrus 75-VTC	Del Moro Raffaelo	
G-CKGU	Schleicher ASW-19B	D. M. Ruttle	
G-CKGV	Schleicher ASW-20	A. H. Reynolds	
G-CKGX	Schleicher ASK-21	Coventry Gliding Club Ltd	
G-CKGY	Scheibe Bergfalke IV	B. R. Pearson	
G-CKHA	PZL SZD-51-1 Junior	Devon & Somerset Gliding Club Ltd	
G-CKHB	Rolladen-Schneider LS3	P. A. Dunthorne	
G-CKHC	DG Flugzeugbau DG.505	P. A. G. & P. L Holland	
G-CKHD	Schleicher ASW-27B	N. D Tillett	
G-CKHE	AB Sportine Aviacija LAK-17A	N. J. Gough	
G-CKHF	Schleicher ASW-20	C. H. Brown	
G-CKHG	Schleicher ASW-27B	R. A. F. King	
G-CKHH	Schleicher ASK-13	Lincolnshire Gliding Club Ltd	
G-CKHK	Schempp-Hirth Duo Discus T	Duo Discus Syndicate	
G-CKHM	Centrair 101A Pegase 90	A. Bland	
G-CKHN	PZL SZD-51-1 Junior	The Nene Valley Gliding Club Ltd	
G-CKHP	Rolladen-Schneider LS8-18	A. D. May	
G-CKHR	PZL-Bielsko SZD-51-1 Junior	Wolds Gliding Club Ltd	
G-CKHS	Rolladen-Schneider LS7-WL	G. F. Coles & E. W. Russell	
G-CKHT	Schempp-Hirth Standard Cirrus	M. Holden	
G-CKHX	Schleicher ASW-28-18E	M. C. Foreman & P. J. O'Connell	
G-CKJA	Schleicher ASW-28-18	J. M. Fryer & S. M. C. Barker	
G-CKJB	Schempp-Hirth Ventus bT	J. D. Sorrell	
G-CKJC	Schempp-Hirth Nimbus 3T	A. C. Wright	
G-CKJE	DG Flugzeugbau LS8-18	M. D. Wells	
G-CKJF	Schempp-Hirth Standard Cirrus	G-CKJF Group	
G-CKJG	Schempp-Hirth Cirrus VTC	S. J. Wright	
G-CKJH	Glaser-Dirks DG.303	Yorkshire Gliding Club	
G-CKJJ	DG Flugzeugbau DG-505 Elan Orion	Ulster Gliding Club Ltd	
G-CKJL	Scleicher ASK-13	Lincolnshire Gliding Club Ltd	
G-CKJM	Schempp-Hirth Ventus cT	J. Ferguson	
G-CKJN	Schleicher ASW-20	R. Logan	
G-CKJP	Schleicher ASK-21	T. M. Holloway	
G-CKJS	Schleicher ASW-28-18E	J. R. Warren & A. Hegner	
G-CKJV	Schleicher ASW-28-18E	A. C. Price	
G-CKJZ	Schempp-Hirth Discus bT	G-CKJZ Group	
G-CKKB	Centrair 101A Pegase	D. M. Rushton	
G-CKKC	DG Flugzeugbau DG-300 Elan Acro	Charlie Kilo Kilo Charlie Syndicate	
G-CKKD	Schleicher ASW-28-18E	A. Palmer	
G-CKKE	Schempp-Hirth Duo Discus T	T. Moyes & M. Powell-Brett	
G-CKKF	Schempp-Hirth Ventus 2cT	A. R. MacGregor	
G-CKKH	Schleicher ASW-27B	A. L. Green	
G-CKKK	AB Sportine Aviacija LAK-17A	C. J. Nicolas	
G-CKKM	Schleicher ASW-28-18	R. F. Thirkell	
G-CKKN	Schempp-Hirth Duo Discus	M. Jordy	
G-CKKP	Schleicher ASK-21	Bowland Forest Gliding Club Ltd	
G-CKKR	Schleicher ASK-13	Aquila Gliding Club Ltd	
G-CKKV	DG Flugzeugbau DG-1000S	Lasham Gliding Society Ltd	

G-CKKX – G-CLOS | BRITISH CIVIL REGISTRATIONS

Notes	Reg	Type	Owner or Operator
	G-CKKX	Rolladen-Schneider LS4-A	B. W. Svenson
	G-CKKY	Schempp-Hirth Duo Discus T	P. D. Duffin
	G-CKLA	Schleicher ASK-13	Booker Gliding Club Ltd
	G-CKLB	Schleicher ASW-27B	S. J. Ridlington & C. Curtis
	G-CKLC	Glasflugel H206 Hornet	P. R. Thomas
	G-CKLD	Schempp-Hirth Discus 2cT	J. P. Galloway
	G-CKLF	Schempp-Hirth Janus	T. J. Edmunds
	G-CKLG	Rolladen-Schneider LS4	P. M. Scheiwiller, P. S. Graham & J. P. Heath
	G-CKLN	Rolladen-Schneider LS4-A	K. E. Jenkinson
	G-CKLP	Scleicher ASW-28-18	J. T. Birch
	G-CKLR	Pezetel SZD-55-1	Zulu Five Gliding Group (G-CKLM)
	G-CKLS	Rolladen-Schneider LS4	Wolds Gliding Club Ltd
	G-CKLT	Schempp-Hirth Nimbus 3/24.5	G. N. Thomas
	G-CKLV	Schempp-Hirth Discus 2cT	J. Iglehart
	G-CKLW	Schleicher ASK-21	Yorkshire Gliding Club
	G-CKLY	DG Flugzeugbau DG-1000T	G-CKLY Group
	G-CKMA	DG Flugzeugbau LS8-st	G. Rizk
	G-CKMC	Grob G.102	L. J. Gregoire
	G-CKMD	Schempp-Hirth Standard Cirrus	C. I. Roberts
	G-CKME	DG Flugzeugbau LS8-st	D. Bradley
	G-CKMF	Centrair 101A Pegase	D. L. M. Jamin
	G-CKMG	Glaser-Dirks DG-101G Elan	A. W. Roberts
	G-CKMI	Schleicher K8C	V. Mallon
	G-CKMJ	Schleicher Ka 6CR	V. Mallon
	G-CKML	Schempp-Hirth Duo Discus T	KML Group
	G-CKMM	Schleicher ASW-28-18E	R. G. Munro
	G-CKMO	Rolladen-Schneider LS7-WL	G. E. M. Turpin
	G-CKMP	AB Sportine Aviacija LAK-17A	J. L. McIver
	G-CKMR	Letov LF-107 Lunak	W. Seitz
	G-CKMT	Grob G103C	The Borders (Milfield) Gliding Club Ltd
	G-CKMV	Rolladen-Schneider LS3-17	F. Roles
	G-CKMW	Schleicher ASK-21	RAF Gliding & Soaring Association
	G-CKMY	Schleicher ASW-20L	C. M. Davey
	G-CKMZ	Schleicher ASW-28-18	J. R. Martindale
	G-CKNB	Schempp-Hirth Standard Cirrus	D. Kershaw & A. Booker
	G-CKNC	Caproni Calif A21S	J. J. & M. E. Pritchard
	G-CKND	DG Flugzeugbau DG-1000T	KND Group
	G-CKNE	Schempp-Hirth Standard Cirrus 75-VTC	G. D. E. Macdonald
	G-CKNF	DG Flugzeugbau DG-1000T	Six November Fox
	G-CKNG	Schleicher ASW-28-18E	M. P. Brockinhton
	G-CKNJ	Schempp-Hirth Duo Discus T	Duo D11 Flying Group
	G-CKNK	Glaser-Dirks DG.500	Cotswold Gliding Club
	G-CKNL	Schleicher ASK-21	Buckminster Gliding Club Ltd
	G-CKNM	Scleicher ASK-18	I. L. Pattingale
	G-CKNN	Slingsby T.21B Sedbergh	R. Wassermann
	G-CKNO	Schempp-Hirth Ventus 2cxT	C. McEwen
	G-CKNR	Schempp-Hirth Ventus 2cxT	R. J. Nicholls
	G-CKNS	Rolladen-Schneider LS4-A	I. R. Willows
	G-CKNV	Schleicher ASW-28-18E	D. G. Brain
	G-CKOD	Schempp-Hirth Discus BT	A. L. Harris & M. W. Talbot
	G-CKOH	DG Flugzeugbau DG-1000T	Lasham Gliding Society Ltd
	G-CKOI	AB Sportine Aviacija LAK-17AT	C. G. Corbett
	G-CKOJ	Schempp-Hirth Duo Discus	M. R. Dawson
	G-CKOR	Glaser-Dirks DG-300 Elan	C. D. Prescott & J. A. Sparrow
	G-CLAC	PA-28-161 Warrior II	M. A. Steadman/Blackbushe
	G-CLAS	Short SD3-60 Variant 100	BAC Group Ltd (G-BLED)
	G-CLAV	Shaw Europa	G. Laverty
	G-CLAX	Jurca MJ.5 Sirocco F2/39	G. D. Claxton (G-AWKB)
	G-CLAY	Bell 206B JetRanger 3	Claygate Distribution Ltd (G-DENN)
	G-CLCG	Beech 200 Super King Air	Powersense Ltd
	G-CLEA	PA-28-161 Warrior II	R. J. Harrison & A. R. Carpenter
	G-CLEE	Rans S.6-ES Coyote II	R. Holt
	G-CLEM	Bölkow Bö.208A2 Junior	Bolkow Group (G-ASWE)
	G-CLEO	Zenair CH.601HD	K. M. Bowen
	G-CLFC	Mainair Blade	G. N. Cliffe & G. Marshall
	G-CLHD	BAe 146-200	Flightline Ltd (G-DEBF)
	G-CLIC	Cameron A-105 balloon	R. S. Mohr
	G-CLIF	Ikarus C.42 FB UK	C. Sims
	G-CLKE	Robinson R44	Clarke Business (G-HREH)
	G-CLOE	Sky 90-24 balloon	J. Skinner
	G-CLOP	PA-32-301T Turbo Saratoga	G. F. A. Craig
	G-CLOS	PA-34-200 Seneca II	S. H. Kirkby

BRITISH CIVIL REGISTRATIONS

G-CLOW – G-CPTM

Reg	Type	Owner or Operator	Notes
G-CLOW	Beech 200 Super King Air	Clowes (Estates) Ltd	
G-CLRK	Sky 77-24 balloon	William Clark & Son (Parkgate) Ltd	
G-CLUB	Cessna FRA.150N	D. C. C. Handley	
G-CLUE	PA-34-200T Seneca II	J. P. Spencer Ltd	
G-CLUX	Cessna F.172N	J. & K. Aviation	
G-CMBS	MDH MD-900 Explorer	Cambridgeshire Constabulary	
G-CMED	SOCATA TB9 Tampico	Enstone Flying Club	
G-CMGC	PA-25 Pawnee 235	Midland Gliding Club Ltd/Long Mynd (G-BFEX)	
G-CMOR	Skyranger 912(2)	P. Moore	
G-CMOS	Cessna T.303 Crusader	C. J. Moss	
G-CMSN	Robinson R22 Beta	S. Meadows (G-MGEE//G-RUMP)	
G-CMXX	Robinson R44 II	Northern Excavators Ltd	
G-CNAB	Avtech Jabiru UL	W. A. Brighouse	
G-CNCN	Rockwell Commander 112CA	R. A. & P. Symonds	
G-COAI	Cranfield A.1	Cranfield University (G-BCIT)	
G-COCO	Cessna F.172M	P. C. Sheard & R. C. Larder	
G-CODE	Bell 206B JetRanger 3	T. C. Smith	
G-CODY	Kolb Twinstar Mk.3 Extra	J. W. Codd	
G-COIN	Bell 206B JetRanger 2	S. Pool & ptnrs	
G-COLA	Beech F33C Bonanza	J. R. C. Spooner & P. M. Scarratt (G-BUAZ)	
G-COLH	PA-28 Cherokee 140	Full Sutton Flying Centre Ltd (G-AVRT)	
G-COLL	Enstrom 280C-UK-2 Shark	M. G. Roberts	
G-COLR	Colt 69A balloon ★	British School of Ballooning/Lancing	
G-COLS	Van's RV-7A	C. Terry	
G-COMB	PA-30 Twin Comanche 160B	J. T. Bateson/Ronaldsway (G-AVBL)	
G-COMP	Cameron N-90 balloon	Computacenter Ltd	
G-CONB	Robin DR.400/180	M. D. Souster (G-BUPX)	
G-CONC	Cameron N-90 balloon	British Airways	
G-CONL	SOCATA TB10 Tobago	J. M. Huntington	
G-CONR	Champion 7GCBC Scout	N. O'Brien	
G-CONV	Convair CV-440-54 ★	Reynard Nursery/Carluke	
G-COOK	Cameron N-77 balloon	IAZ (International) Ltd	
G-COOT	Taylor Coot A	P. M. Napp	
G-COPS	Piper J-3C-65 Cub	R. W. Sproat	
G-COPZ	Van's RV-7	R. S. Horan	
G-CORA	Shaw Europa XS	A. P. Gardner (G-ILUM)	
G-CORB	SOCATA TB20 Trinidad	G. D. Corbin	
G-CORD	Slingsby T.66 Nipper 3	A. V. Lamprell (G-AVTB)	
G-CORN	Bell 206B JetRanger 3	John A.Wells Ltd (G-BHTR)	
G-CORP	BAe ATP	Trident Aviation (G-BTNK)	
G-COSY	Lindstrand LBL-56A balloon	D. D. Owen	
G-COTT	Cameron 60 Cottage SS balloon	Dragon Balloon Co Ltd	
G-COUP	Ercoupe 415C	S. M. Gerrard	
G-COVA	PA-26-161 Warrior III	Coventry (Civil) Aviation Ltd (G-CDCL)	
G-COVB	PA-28-161 Warrior III	Coventry (Civil) Aviation Ltd	
G-COVD	Robin R.21601	Coventry Flying School Ltd (G-BYOF)	
G-COVE	Avtech Jabiru UL	A. A. Rowson	
G-COXS	Aeroprakt A.22 Foxbat	S. Cox	
G-COXY	Kiss 400-582 (1)	B. G. Cox	
G-COZI	Rutan Cozy III	R. Machin	
G-CPCD	CEA DR.221	P. J. Taylor	
G-CPDA	DH.106 Comet 4C (XS235) ★	C. Walton Ltd/Bruntingthorpe	
G-CPEL	Boeing 757-236	British Airways (G-BRJE)	
G-CPEM	Boeing 757-236	British Airways	
G-CPEN	Boeing 757-236	British Airways	
G-CPEO	Boeing 757-236	British Airways	
G-CPEP	Boeing 757-2Y0	First Choice Airways Ltd	
G-CPER	Boeing 757-236	British Airways	
G-CPES	Boeing 757-236	British Airways	
G-CPET	Boeing 757-236	British Airways	
G-CPEU	Boeing 757-236	First Choice Airways Ltd	
G-CPEV	Boeing 757-236	First Choice Airways Ltd	
G-CPFC	Cessna F.152 II	Willowair Flying Club (1996) Ltd/Southend	
G-CPMK	DHC.1 Chipmunk 22 (WZ847)	P. A. Walley	
G-CPMS	SOCATA TB20 Trinidad	Charlotte Park Management Services Ltd	
G-CPOL	AS.355F1 Twin Squirrel	MW Helicopters Ltd/Stapleford	
G-CPSF	Cameron N-90 balloon	S. A. Simington & J. D. Rigden (G-OISK)	
G-CPSH	Eurocopter EC 135T1	Thames Valley Police Authority/Booker	
G-CPTM	PA-28-151 Warrior	T. J. & C. Mackay (G-BTOE)	

155

G-CPTS – G-CUBY — BRITISH CIVIL REGISTRATIONS

Notes	Reg	Type	Owner or Operator
	G-CPTS	Agusta-Bell 206B JetRanger 2	A. R. B. Aspinall
	G-CPXC	Avions Mudry CAP-10C	J. M. Wicks
	G-CRAB	Skyranger 912 (1)	R. A. Weller
	G-CRAY	Robinson R22 Beta	Moorland Windows
	G-CRBV	Balóny Kubíček BB26 balloon	Blue Sky Ballooning Ltd
	G-CRDY	Agusta-Bell 206A JetRanger	Cardy Construction Ltd (G-WHAZ)
	G-CRES	Denney Kitfox Mk 3	K. Handley
	G-CREY	SeaRey	P. J. Gallagher
	G-CRIB	Robinson R44	Cribarth Helicopters (G-JJWL)
	G-CRIC	Colomban MC.15 Cri-Cri	R. S. Stoddart-Stones
	G-CRIK	Colomban MC.15 Cri-Cri	A.R. Robinson
	G-CRIL	Rockwell Commander 112B	Rockwell Aviation Group/Cardiff
	G-CRIS	Taylor JT.1 Monoplane	C. R. Steer
	G-CRLH	Bell 206B JetRanger 3	R. L. Hartshorn (G-RJTT)
	G-CROB	Shaw Europa XS T-G	R. G. Hallam
	G-CROL	Maule MXT-7-180	N. G. P. Evans
	G-CROW	Robinson R44	Longmoore Ltd
	G-CROY	Shaw Europa	M. T. Austin
	G-CRPH	Airbus A.320-231	MyTravel Airways
	G-CRUM	Westland Scout AH.1 (XV137)	G-CRUM Group
	G-CRUZ	Cessna T.303	Bank Farm Ltd
	G-CSAV	Thruster T.600N 450	P. R. Mowbray
	G-CSBM	Cessna F.150M	Transcourt Ltd
	G-CSBD	PA-28-236 Dakota	S. B. & S-J. Dunnett (G-CSBO)
	G-CSCS	Cessna F.172N	C.Sullivan/Stapleford
	G-CSDJ	Avtech Jabiru UL	D. W. Johnston & ptnrs
	G-CSFC	Cessna 150L	Foxtrot Charlie Flying Group
	G-CSFD	Ultramagic M-90 balloon	L. A. Watts
	G-CSFT	PA-23 Aztec 250D ★	Aces High Ltd/North Weald (G-AYKU)
	G-CSGT	PA-28-161 Warrior II	M. J. Wade (G-BPHB)
	G-CSIX	PA-32 Cherokee Six 300	A. J. Hodge
	G-CSMK	Aerotechnik EV-97 Eurostar	R. Frey
	G-CSNA	Cessna 421C	Blue Swan Aviation Ltd
	G-CSSE	Cessna 172S Skyhawk	Creative Software Solutions (Europe) Ltd
	G-CSUE	ICP MXP-740 Savannah Jabiru (5)	J. R. Stratton
	G-CSWH	PA-28R Cherokee Arrow 180	J. F. Gould
	G-CSWL	Bell 206L-1 Long Ranger 2	Milford Garage Ltd (G-VOLK/G-GBAY/G-SIRI)
	G-CSZM	Zenair CH.601XL Zodiac	C. Budd
	G-CTAA	Schempp-Hirth Janus	AA Group
	G-CTAV	Aerotechnik EV-97 Eurostar	P. Simpson
	G-CTCD	Diamond DA42 Twin Star	CTC Aviation Group PLC
	G-CTCE	Diamond DA42 Twin Star	CTC Aviation Group PLC
	G-CTCF	Diamond DA42 Twin Star	CTC Aviation Group PLC
	G-CTCG	Diamond DA42 Twin Star	I. Annenskiy
	G-CTCL	SOCATA TB10 Tobago	Gift Aviation Ltd (G-BSIV)
	G-CTDH	Flight Design CT2K	A. S. Evans
	G-CTEC	Stoddard-Hamilton Glastar	B. N. C. Mogg
	G-CTEL	Cameron N-90 balloon	M. R. Noyce
	G-CTFF	Cessna T.206H	Rajair Ltd
	G-CTGR	Cameron N-77 balloon	T. G. Read (G-CCDI)
	G-CTIO	SOCATA TB20 Trinidad	I. R. Hunt
	G-CTIX	VS.509 Spitfire T.IX (PT462)	A. A. Hodgson
	G-CTKL	Noorduyn AT-16 Harvard IIB (54137)	M. R. Simpson
	G-CTOY	Denney Kitfox Mk 3	B. McNeilly
	G-CTPW	Bell 206B JetRanger 3	Aviation Rentals
	G-CTRL	Robinson R22 Beta	Central Helicopters Ltd
	G-CTSW	Flight Design CTSW	P and M Aviation Ltd
	G-CTUG	PA-25 Pawnee 235	The Borders (Milfield) Gliding Club Ltd
	G-CTWW	PA-34-200T Seneca II	Centreline Air Charter Ltd (G-ROYZ/G-GALE)
	G-CTZO	SOCATA TB20 Trinidad GT	M. R. Munn
	G-CUBB	PA-18 Super Cub 180	Bidford Gliding Ltd
	G-CUBE	Skyranger 912 (2)	T.R. Villa
	G-CUBI	PA-18 Super Cub 125	G. T. Fisher
	G-CUBJ	PA-18 Super Cub 150 (18-5395:CDG)	P. B. Rice
	G-CUBN	PA-18 Super Cub 150	N. J. R. Minchin
	G-CUBP	PA-18 Super Cub 150	D. W. Berger
	G-CUBS	Piper J-3C-65 Cub	Sunbeam Aviation (G-BHPT)
	G-CUBW	WAG-Aero Acro Trainer	B. G. Plumb & ptnrs
	G-CUBY	Piper J-3C-65 Cub	C. A. Bloom (G-BTZW)

BRITISH CIVIL REGISTRATIONS

G-CUCU – G-DAKK

Reg	Type	Owner or Operator	Notes
G-CUCU	Colt 180A balloon	S. R. Seage	
G-CUIK	QAC Quickie Q.200	C. S. Rayner	
G-CUPS	IAV Bacau Yakolev YAK-52	Fenland Flying School	
G-CURR	Cessna 172R II	JS Aviation Ltd (G-BXOH)	
G-CURV	Avid Speedwing	K. S. Kelso	
G-CUTE	Dyn'Aéro MCR-01	E. G. Shimmin	
G-CUTY	Shaw Europa	D. J. & M. Watson	
G-CVAL	Ikarus C42 FB100	J. I. Greenshields	
G-CVBF	Cameron A-210 balloon	Virgin Balloon Flights Ltd	
G-CVCV	Rotorway Executive 162F	Hartland Electronics Ltd	
G-CVII	Dan Rihn DR.107 One Design	One Design Group	
G-CVIP	Bell 206B JetRanger	Sloane Helicopters Ltd/Skywell	
G-CVIX	DH.110 Sea Vixen D.3 ('Red Bull')	Drilling Systems Ltd	
G-CVLH	PA-32-200T Seneca II	Atlantic Aviation Ltd	
G-CVMI	PA-18 Super Cub 150	T. P. Spurge	
G-CVPM	VPM M-16 Tandem Trainer	C. S. Teuber/Germany	
G-CVST	Jodel D.140	A. Shipp	
G-CWAG	Sequoia F. 8L Falco	D. R. Austin	
G-CWAL	Raj Hamsa X'Air 133	C. Walsh	
G-CWBM	Phoenix Currie Wot	B. V. Mayo (G-BTVP)	
G-CWFA	PA-38-112 Tomahawk	K. R. W. Scull & J. Watkins (G-BTGC)	
G-CWFB	PA-38-112 Tomahawk	P. M. Moyle (G-OAAL)	
G-CWFC	PA-38-112 Tomahawk ★	Cardiff-Wales Flying Club Ltd (G-BRTA)	
G-CWFD	PA-38-112 Tomahawk	I. A. Qureshi (G-BSVY)	
G-CWIC	Mainair Pegasus Quik	G-CWIC Group/Barton	
G-CWIK	Mainair Pegasus Quik	L. Kirk	
G-CWIZ	AS.350B Ecureuil	PLM Dollar Group Ltd (G-DJEM/G-ZBAC/G-SEBI/G-BMCU)	
G-CWMC	P & M Quik GT450	A. R. Hughes	
G-CWMT	Dyn'Aéro MCR-01 Bambi	J. Jones	
G-CWOT	Currie Wot	D. Doyle & H. Duggan	
G-CWTD	Aeroprakt A.22 Foxbat	J. V. Harris	
G-CWVY	Mainair Pegasus Quik	K. L. Chorley	
G-CXCX	Cameron N-90 balloon	Cathay Pacific Airways (London) Ltd	
G-CXDZ	Cassutt Speed Two	J. A. H. Chadwick	
G-CXHK	Cameron N-77 balloon	Cathay Pacific Airways (London) Ltd	
G-CXIP	Thruster T.600N	India Papa Syndicate	
G-CYLL	Sequoia F.8L Falco	N. J. Langrick & A. J. Newall	
G-CYLS	Cessna T.303	Gledhill Water Storage Ltd/Blackpool (G-BKXI)	
G-CYMA	GA-7 Cougar	Cyma Petroleum (UK) Ltd/Elstree (G-BKOM)	
G-CYRA	Kolb Twinstar Mk. 3 (Modified)	S. J. Fox (G-MYRA)	
G-CYRS	Bell 206L Long Ranger	Sky Charter UK Ltd	
G-CZAC	Zenair CH.601XL	D. Pitt	
G-CZAG	Sky 90-24 balloon	S. McCarthy	
G-CZAW	CZAW Sportcruiser	Sprite Aviation Services Ltd	
G-CZBE	CFM Streak Shadow	M. I. M. Smith (G-MZBE)	
G-CZCZ	Avions Mudry CAP-10B	M. Farmer	
G-CZMI	Skyranger 912 (2)	L. M. Bassett	
G-CZNE	BN-2B-20 Islander	Skyhopper LLP (G-BWZF)	
G-DAAH	PA-28RT-201T Turbo Arrow IV	R. Peplow/Halfpenny Green	
G-DAAM	Robinson R22 Beta	J. N. Plange	
G-DAAT	Eurocopter EC 135T2	Bond Air Services Ltd	
G-DAAZ	PA-28RT-201T Turbo Arrow IV	Calais Ltd	
G-DABS	Robinson R22 Beta II	Foxtrot Golf Helicopters Ltd	
G-DACA	P57 Sea Prince T.1 (WF118) ★	P. G. Vallance Ltd/Charlwood	
G-DACC	Cessna 401B	Niglon Ltd/Birmingham (G-AYOU)	
G-DACF	Cessna 152 II	T. M. & M. L. Jones/Egginton (G-BURY)	
G-DACN	Agusta A109S Grand	Errigal Aviation Ltd	
G-DADG	PA-18-150 Super Cub	F. J. Cox	
G-DAEX	Dassault Falcon 900EX	Triair (Bermuda) Ltd	
G-DAFY	Beech 58 Baron	P. R. Earp	
G-DAGJ	Zenair CH.601HD Zodiac	D. A. G. Johnson	
G-DAIR	Luscombe 8A Silvaire	D. F. Soul (G-BURK)	
G-DAIV	Ultramagic H-77 balloon	D. Harrison-Morris	
G-DAJB	Boeing 757-2T7	Monarch Airlines Ltd/Luton	
G-DAJC	Boeing 757-31K	MyTravel Airways	
G-DAKK	Douglas C-47A	General Technics Ltd	

G-DAKM – G-DEFY

BRITISH CIVIL REGISTRATIONS

Notes	Reg	Type	Owner or Operator
	G-DAKM	Diamond DA40D Star	K. MacDonald
	G-DAKO	PA-28-236 Dakota	Methods Application Ltd
	G-DAMY	Shaw Europa	U. A. Schliessler & R. J. Kelly
	G-DANA	Jodel DR.200 (replica)	Cheshire Eagles (G-DAST)
	G-DAND	SOCATA TB10 Tobago	Portway Aviation Ltd
	G-DANT	Rockwell Commander 114	D. P. Tierney
	G-DANY	Avtech Jabiru UL	D. A. Crosbie
	G-DANZ	AS.355N Twin Squirrel	Melesey Ltd
	G-DAPH	Cessna 180K	M. R. L. Astor
	G-DARA	PA-34-220T Seneca III	SYS (Scaffolding Contractors) Ltd
	G-DARK	CFM Shadow Srs DD	R. W. Hussey
	G-DASH	Rockwell Commander 112	D. & M. Nelson (G-BDAJ)
	G-DASS	Ikarus C.42 FB100	DAS Services
	G-DATG	Cessna F.182P	Oxford Aeroplane Co Ltd/Kidlington
	G-DATH	Aerotechnik EV-97 Eurostar	D. N. E. D'Ath
	G-DAUF	AS.365N2	Gama Leasing Ltd
	G-DAVD	Cessna FR.172K	D. M. Driver & S. Copeland
	G-DAVE	Jodel D.112	Temple Flying Group
	G-DAVG	Robinson R44 II	AG Aviation Ltd (G-WOWW)
	G-DAVO	AA-5B Tiger	Douglas Head Consulting Ltd/Elstree (G-GAGA/G-BGPG/G-BGRW)
	G-DAVS	AB Sportine Aviacija LAK-17AT	G-DAVS Syndicate
	G-DAVV	Robinson R44 Raven II	D. A. Gold
	G-DAWG	SA Bulldog Srs 120/121 (XX522:06)	R. H. Goldstone/Barton
	G-DAWZ	Glasflugel 304 CZ-17	D. A. Whitley
	G-DAYS	Shaw Europa	D. J. Bowie
	G-DAYZ	Pietenpol Air Camper	J. G. Cronk
	G-DAZY	PA-34-200T Seneca	Centreline Air Charter Ltd
	G-DAZZ	Van's RV-8	Wishanger RV8
	G-DBAT	Lindstrand LBL-56A balloon	G. J. Bell
	G-DBCA	Airbus A.319-131	bmi british midland
	G-DBCB	Airbus A.319-131	bmi british midland
	G-DBCC	Airbus A.319-131	bmi british midland
	G-DBCD	Airbus A.319-131	bmi british midland
	G-DBCE	Airbus A.319-131	bmi british midland
	G-DBCF	Airbus A.319-131	bmi british midland
	G-DBCG	Airbus A.319-131	bmi british midland
	G-DBCH	Airbus A.319-131	bmi british midland
	G-DBCI	Airbus A.319-131	bmi british midland
	G-DBCJ	Airbus A.319-131	bmi british midland
	G-DBDB	VPM M-16 Tandem Trainer	D. R. Bolsover (G-IROW)
	G-DBLA	Boeing 767-35EER	First Choice Airways Ltd
	G-DBOY	Agusta A109C	Maison Air Ltd
	G-DBUG	Robinson R44	Dio (Aviation) Ltd (G-OBHI)
	G-DBYE	Mooney M.20M	P. Farmer
	G-DCEA	PA-34-200T Seneca II	Barnes Olsen Aero Leasing Ltd
	G-DCKK	Cessna F.172N	J. Maffia/Panshanger
	G-DCMI	Mainair Pegasus Quik	S. J. E. Smith
	G-DCON	Robinson R44	D. Connolly/Ireland
	G-DCPA	MBB BK.117C-1C	Devon & Cornwall Constabulary (G-LFBA)
	G-DCSE	Robinson R44	An Agency Called England Ltd
	G-DCSG	Robinson R44	Enable International Ltd (G-TRYG)
	G-DCTA	BAe 125 Srs 800B	Direct Air Executive Ltd/Oxford (G-OSPG/G-ETOM/G-BVFC/G-TPHK/G-FDSL)
	G-DCXL	Jodel D.140C	A. C. D. Norris/France
	G-DDAY	PA-28R-201T Turbo Arrow III	G-DDAY Group/Tatenhill (G-BPDO)
	G-DDBD	Shaw Europa XS	B. Davies
	G-DDIG	Rockwell Commander 114	D. H. Munro (G-CCDT)
GLIDER	G-DDJF	Schempp-Hirth Duo Discus T	R. J. H. Fack
	G-DDMV	NA T-6G Texan (493209)	C. Dabin
	G-DDOG	SA Bulldog Srs 120/121 (XX524:04)	Deltaero Ltd
	G-DEAN	Solar Wings Pegasus XL-Q	Y. G. Richardson (G-MVJV)
	G-DEBR	Shaw Europa	A. J. Calvert & C. T. Smallwood
	G-DEBT	Pioneer 300	N. J. T. Tonks
	G-DECK	Cessna T.210N	R. J. Howard
	G-DECO	Dyn'Aéro MCR-01 Club	G-DECO Flying Group
	G-DEER	Robinson R22 Beta II	S. R. Baber
	G-DEFM	BAe 146-200	Flightline Ltd (G-DEBM)
	G-DEFY	Robinson R22 Beta	P. M. M. P. Silveira/Portugal

BRITISH CIVIL REGISTRATIONS
G-DEKA – G-DIRK

Reg	Type	Owner or Operator	Notes
G-DEKA	Cameron Z-90 balloon	Sport Promotion SRL	
G-DELF	Aero L-29A Delfin	B. R. Green/Manston	
G-DEMH	Cessna F.172M (modified)	M. Hammond (G-BFLO)	
G-DEMM	AS.350B2 Ecureuil	Abbeyflight Ltd	
G-DENB	Cessna F.150G	N. Yosof (G-ATZZ)	
G-DENC	Cessna F.150G	M. Dovey (G-AVAP)	
G-DEND	Cessna F.150M	R. N. Tate (G-WAFC/G-BDFI)	
G-DENE	PA-28 Cherokee 140	D. V. Magee (G-ATOS)	
G-DENI	PA-32 Cherokee Six 300	A. Bendkowski (G-BAIA)	
G-DENS	Binder CP.301S Smaragd	Garston Smaragd Group	
G-DENZ	PA-44-180 Seminole	Horizon Ballooning Ltd (G-INDE/G-BHNM)	
G-DERB	Robinson R22 Beta	S. Thompson (G-BPYH)	
G-DERI	PA-46-500TP Malibu Meridian	Intesa Leasing SPA/Italy (G-PCAR)	
G-DERK	PA-46-500TP Malibu Meridian	D. Priestley	
G-DERV	Cameron Truck SS balloon	J. M. Percival	
G-DEST	Mooney M.20J	Allegro Aviation Ltd	
G-DEUX	AS.355F Ecureuil 2	Elmridge Ltd	
G-DEVL	Eurocopter EC 120B	Swift Frame Ltd	
G-DEVS	PA-28 Cherokee 180	180 Group/Blackbushe (G-BGVJ)	
G-DEXP	ARV Super 2	W. G. McKinnon	
G-DEXT	Robinson R44 II	Heli Air Ltd	
G-DFKI	Westland Gazelle HT.2	Foremans Aviation Ltd (G-BZOT)	
G-DFLY	PA-38-112 Tomahawk	Ravenair Aircraft Ltd/Liverpool	
G-DFOX	AS.355F1 Twin Squirrel	Venturi Capital Ltd (G-NAAS/G-BPRG/G-NWPA)	
G-DFUN	Van's RV-6	G-DFUN Flying Group	
G-DGCL	Glaser-Dirks DG.800B	C. J. Lowrie	
G-DGET	Canadair CL-600-2B16 Challenger	TAG Aviation (UK) Ltd	
G-DGHD	Robinson R44 II	Advanced Diesel Engineering Ltf	
G-DGHI	Dyn'Aéro MCR-01 Club	D. G. Hall	
G-DGIK	DG Flugzeugbau DG.1000S	R. P. Davis	
G-DGIV	Glaser-Dirks DG.800B	R. Parkin	
G-DGOD	Robinson R22 Beta	Astra Helicopters Ltd	
G-DGWW	Rand-Robinson KR-2	W. Wilson/Liverpool	
G-DHAH	Aeronca 7AC Champion	G. D. Horn (G-JTYE)	
G-DHCC	DHC.1 Chipmunk 22 (WG321:G)	Eureka Aviation BVBA/Belgium	
G-DHCZ	DHC.2 Beaver 1	Propshop Ltd (G-BUCJ)	
G-DHDV	DH.104 Dove 8 (VP981)	Air Atlantique Ltd/Coventry	
G-DHJH	Airbus A.321-211	MyTravel Airways	
G-DHJZ	Airbus A.320-214	MyTravel Airways	
G-DHLB	Cameron N-90 balloon	B. A. Bower	
G-DHLI	Colt 90 World SS balloon	Balloon Preservation Flying Group	
G-DHPM	OGMA DHC.1 Chipmunk 20 (1365)	P. Meyrick	
G-DHSS	DH.112 Venom FB.50 (WR360:K)	D. J. L. Wood/Bournemouth	
G-DHTM	DH.82A Tiger Moth (replica)	E. G. Waite-Roberts	
G-DHTT	DH.112 Venom FB.50 (WR421)	Source Classic Jet Flight (G-BMOC)	
G-DHUU	DH.112 Venom FB.50 (WR410)	Source Classic Jet Flight (G-BMOD)	
G-DHVM	DH.112 Venom FB.50 (WR470)	Air Atlantique Ltd/Coventry (G-GONE)	
G-DHVV	DH.115 Vampire T.55 (XE897)	Source Classic Jet Flight	
G-DHWW	DH.115 Vampire T.55 (XG775)	Source Classic Jet Flight	
G-DHXX	DH.100 Vampire FB.6 (VT871)	Source Classic Jet Flight	
G-DHZF	DH.82A Tiger Moth (N9192)	C. A.Parker & M. R. Johnson/Sywell (G-BSTJ)	
G-DHZZ	DH.115 Vampire T.55 (WZ589)	K. Aarkvisla	
G-DIAL	Cameron N-90 balloon	A. J. Street	
G-DIAM	Diamond DA40D Star	Direct Line Connections Ltd	
G-DIAT	PA-28 Cherokee 140	Bristol Flying Centre Ltd (G-BCGK)	
G-DICK	Thunder Ax6-56Z balloon	R. D. Sargeant	
G-DIDY	Thruster T600T 450	D. R. Sims	
G-DIGI	PA-32 Cherokee Six 300	D. Stokes	
G-DIKY	Murphy Rebel	R. J. P. Herivel	
G-DIMB	Boeing 767-31KER	Monarch Airlines Ltd	
G-DIME	Rockwell Commander 114	H. B. Richardson	
G-DINA	AA-5B Tiger	Portway Aviation Ltd/Shobdon	
G-DING	Colt 77A balloon	G. J. Bell	
G-DINK	Lindstrand Bulb SS balloon	Dinkelacker-Schwaben Brau AG/Germany	
G-DINO	Pegasus Quantum 15	R. A. Watering (G-MGMT)	
G-DINT	B.156 Beaufighter IF (X7688)	T. E. Moore	
G-DIPI	Cameron 80 Tub SS balloon	C. G. Dobson	
G-DIPM	PA-46-350P Malibu Mirage	Intesa Leasing SPA/Italy	
G-DIRK	Glaser-Dirks DG.400	G-DIRK Syndicate	

G-DISA – G-DOFY — BRITISH CIVIL REGISTRATIONS

Notes	Reg	Type	Owner or Operator
	G-DISA	SA Bulldog Srs 120/125	British Disabled Flying Association
	G-DISK	PA-24 Comanche 250	A. Johnston (G-APZG)
	G-DISO	Jodel 150	P. F. Craven
	G-DIWY	PA-32 Cherokee Six 300	IFS Chemicals Ltd
	G-DIXY	PA-28-181 Archer III	M. G. Bird/Fowlmere
	G-DIZI	Escapade 912 (1)	N. Baumber
	G-DIZO	Jodel D.120A	D. Aldersea/Breighton (G-EMKM)
	G-DIZY	PA-28R-201T Turbo Arrow III	Calverton Flying Club Ltd/Cranfield
	G-DIZZ	Hughes 369HE	R. H. Kirke/Portugal
	G-DJAE	Cessna 500 Citation	Billion-Air Ltd (G-JEAN)
	G-DJAY	Avtech Jabiru UL-450	D. J. Pearce
	G-DJCR	Varga 2150A Kachina	D. J. C. Robertson (G-BLWG)
	G-DJET	Diamond DA42 Twin Star	Papa Bravo Ltd
	G-DJJA	PA-28-181 Archer II	Choice Aircraft/Fowlmere
	G-DJMM	Cessna 172S	M. Manston
	G-DJNH	Denney Kitfox Mk 3	D. J. N. Hall
	G-DJST	Ixess 912(1)	D. J. Stimpson
	G-DKDP	Grob G.109	D. W. & J. E. Page
	G-DKEY	PA-28-161 Warrior II	Gary Key Aircraft Leasing
	G-DKGF	Viking Dragonfly ★	(stored)/Enstone
	G-DKMK	Robinson R44 II	Clear Sky Views Ltd/Ireland
	G-DLCB	Shaw Europa	K. Richards
	G-DLCH	Boeing 737-8Q8	Flyglobespan.com
	G-DLDL	Robinson R22 Beta	Airtask Group PLC/Stapleford
	G-DLEE	SOCATA TB9 Tampico Club	D. A. Lee (G-BPGX)
	G-DLOM	SOCATA TB20 Trinidad	J. N. A. Adderley/Guernsey
	G-DLTR	PA-28 Cherokee 180E	BCT Aircraft Leasing Ltd (G-AYAV)
	G-DMAC	Avtech Jabiru UL	C. J. Pratt
	G-DMAH	SOCATA TB20 Trinidad	R. C. & C. G. Bell
	G-DMCA	Douglas DC-10-30 ★	Forward fuselage/Manchester Airport Viewing Park
	G-DMCD	Robinson R22 Beta	Heli Air Ltd/Wellesbourne (G-OOLI)
	G-DMCS	PA-28R Cherokee Arrow 200-II	Arrow Associates (G-CPAC)
	G-DMCT	Flight Design CT2K	B. Zajac
	G-DMND	Diamond DA42 Twin Star	MC Air Ltd
	G-DMRS	Robinson R44 II	Nottinghamshire Helicopters (2004) Ltd
	G-DMSS	Westland Gazelle HT.3 (XW858:C)	Woods of York Ltd
	G-DMWW	CFM Shadow Srs DD	Microlight Sport Aviation Ltd
	G-DNCS	PA-28R-201T Turbo Arrow III	BC Arrow Ltd
	G-DNGA	Balóny Kubíček BB.20	G. J. Bell
	G-DNGR	Colt 31A balloon	G. J. Bell
	G-DNHI	Agusta A109A	DNH Helicopters Ltd
	G-DNKS	Ikarus C42 FB80	D. N. K. & M. A. Symon
	G-DNOP	PA-46-350P Malibu Mirage	Campbell Aviation Ltd
	G-DOCA	Boeing 737-436	British Airways
	G-DOCB	Boeing 737-436	British Airways
	G-DOCE	Boeing 737-436	British Airways
	G-DOCF	Boeing 737-436	British Airways
	G-DOCG	Boeing 737-436	British Airways
	G-DOCH	Boeing 737-436	British Airways
	G-DOCL	Boeing 737-436	British Airways
	G-DOCN	Boeing 737-436	British Airways
	G-DOCO	Boeing 737-436	British Airways
	G-DOCS	Boeing 737-436	British Airways
	G-DOCT	Boeing 737-436	British Airways
	G-DOCU	Boeing 737-436	British Airways
	G-DOCV	Boeing 737-436	British Airways
	G-DOCW	Boeing 737-436	British Airways
	G-DOCX	Boeing 737-436	British Airways
	G-DOCY	Boeing 737-436	British Airways (G-BVBY)
	G-DOCZ	Boeing 737-436	British Airways (G-BVBZ)
	G-DODB	Robinson R22 Beta	M. Gallagher
	G-DODD	Cessna F.172P-II	K. Watts/Denham
	G-DODG	Aerotechnik EV-97A Eurostar	K. L. Clarke & R. Barton
	G-DODR	Robinson R22 Beta	Exmoor Helicopters Ltd
	G-DOEA	AA-5A Cheetah	Fairway Flying Services (G-RJMI)
	G-DOFY	Bell 206B JetRanger 3	Cinnamond Ltd

BRITISH CIVIL REGISTRATIONS — G-DOGE – G-DUOT

Reg	Type	Owner or Operator	Notes
G-DOGE	SA Bulldog Srs 100/101	W. P. Cooper (G-AZHX)	
G-DOGG	SA Bulldog Srs 120/121 (XX638)	P. Sengupta	
G-DOGZ	Horizon 1	J. E. D. Rogerson	
G-DOIN	Skyranger 912	C. D. & L. J. Church	
G-DOIT	AS.350B1 Ecureuil	C. C. Blakey	
G-DOLY	Cessna T.303	KW Aviation Ltd (G-BJZK)	
G-DOME	PA-28-161 Warrior III	Haimoss Ltd	
G-DOMS	Aerotechnik EV-97A Eurostar	D. J. Cross	
G-DONI	AA-5B Tiger	W. P. Moritz (G-BLLT)	
G-DONS	PA-28RT-201T Turbo Arrow IV	C. E. Griffiths/Blackbushe	
G-DONT	Xenair CH.601XL Zodiac	N. C. & A. C. J. Butcher	
G-DOOM	Cameron Z-105 balloon	Test Flight	
G-DOOZ	AS.355F2 Twin Squirrel	Patriot Aviation Ltd (G-BNSX)	
G-DORA	Focke-Wulf Fw 190-D9	G. R. Lacey	
G-DORN	EKW C-3605	R. G. Gray	
G-DORS	Eurocopter EC 135T2+	Premier Fund Leasing	
G-DOTT	CFM Streak Shadow	R. J. Bell	
G-DOVE	Cessna 182Q	Carel Investments Ltd	
G-DOVE†	D. H. 104 Devon C.2 ★	E. Surrey College/Gatton Point, Redhill (G-KOOL)	
G-DOWN	Colt 31A balloon	M. Williams	
G-DOZI	Ikarus C.42 FB100	D. A. Izod	
G-DPHN	SA.365N1 Dauphin 2	Atlantic Air Ltd	
G-DPPF	Augusta A.109E Power	Dyfed-Powys Police Authority	
G-DPYE	Robin DR400/500	Pye Consulting Group Ltd	
G-DRAG	Cessna 152 (tailwheel)	L. A. Maynard & M. E. Scouller (G-REME/G-BRNF)	
G-DRAM	Cessna FR.172F (floatplane)	Clyde River Rats	
G-DRAW	Colt 77A balloon	A. G. Odell	
G-DRAY	Taylor JT.1 Monoplane	L. J. Dray	
G-DRBG	Cessna 172M	Henlow Flying Club Ltd (G-MUIL)	
G-DREX	Cameron 110 Saturn SS balloon	LRC Products Ltd	
G-DRFC	ATR-42-300	Atlantic Air Transport Ltd/Coventry	
G-DRGN	Cameron N-105 balloon	W. I. Hooker & C. Parker	
G-DRGS	Cessna 182S	Walter Scott & Partners Ltd	
G-DRID	Cessna FR.172J	D. T. J. Hoskins & ptnrs	
G-DRIV	Robinson R44 II	C. Reynard	
G-DRMM	Shaw Europa	T. J. Harrison	
G-DRNT	Sikorsky S-76A	CHC Scotia Ltd	
G-DROP	Cessna U.206C	K. Brady/Sibson (G-UKNO/G-BAMN)	
G-DRSV	CEA DR.315 (modified)	R. S. Voice	
G-DRYI	Cameron N-77 balloon	C. A. Butter	
G-DRYS	Cameron N-90 balloon	C. A. Butter	
G-DRZF	CEA DR.360	P. K. Kaufeler	
G-DSFT	PA-28R Cherokee Arrow 200-II	J. Jones (G-LFSE/G-BAXT)	
G-DSGC	PA-25 Pawnee 235C	Devon & Somerset Gliding Club Ltd	
G-DSID	PA-34-220T Seneca III	Atsi Aviation Ltd	
G-DSKI	Aerotechnik EV-97 Eurostar	D. R. Skill	
G-DSLL	Pegasus Quantum 15-912	R. G. Jeffery	
G-DSPI	Robinson R44	Catscan Ltd (G-DPSI)	
G-DSPK	Cameron Z-140	Bailey Balloons Ltd	
G-DSPZ	Robinson R44 II	Focal Point Communications Ltd	
G-DTFF	Cessna T.182T Turbo Skylane	Rajair Ltd	
G-DTOY	Ikarus C.42.FB100	C. W. Laske	
G-DTUG	Wag-Aero Super Sport	D. A. Bullock	
G-DTWO	Schempp-Hirth Discus 2A	O. Walters	
G-DUAL	Cirrus SR22	J. P. & T. M. Jones	
G-DUBI	Lindstrans LBL-120A balloon	A. Nimmo	
G-DUDE	Van's RV-8	W. M. Hodgkins	
G-DUDZ	Robin DR.400/180	D. H. Pattison (G-BXNK)	
G-DUGE	Ikarus C.42 FB UK	D. Stevenson	
G-DUGI	Lindstrand LBL-90A balloon	D. J. Cook	
G-DUKK	Extra EA.300/L	R. A. & K. M. Roberts	
G-DUKY	Robinson R44	English Braids Ltd	
G-DUMP	Customcraft A-25 balloon	P. C. Bailey	
G-DUOA	Bombardier CL-600-2C10	Maersk Aircraft A/S (stored)/Denmark	
G-DUOC	Bombardier CL-600-2C10	Maersk Aircraft A/S (stored)/Denmark	
G-DUOD	Bombardier CL-600-2C10	Maersk Aircraft A/S (stored)/Denmark	
G-DUOT	Schempp-Hirth Duo Discus T	G-DUOT Group	

G-DUOX – G-EDES — BRITISH CIVIL REGISTRATIONS

Notes	Reg	Type	Owner or Operator
	G-DUOX	Schempp-Hirth Duo Discus	British Gliding Association Ltd
	G-DURO	Shaw Europa	D. J. Sagar
	G-DURX	Thunder 77A balloon	V. Trimble
	G-DUSK	DH.115 Vampire T.11 (XE856)	R. M. A. Robinson & R. Horsfield
	G-DUST	Stolp SA.300 Starduster Too	N. M. Robinson
	G-DUVL	Cessna F.172N	G-DUVL Flying Group
	G-DVBF	Lindstrand LBL-210A balloon	Virgin Balloon Flights
	G-DVON	DH.104 Devon C.2 (VP955)	C. L. Thatcher
	G-DWCE	Robinson R44 II	Heli Air Ltd
	G-DWEL	SIPA 903	B. L. Procter (G-ASXC)
	G-DWIA	Chilton D.W.1A	D. Elliott
	G-DWIB	Chilton D.W.1B (replica)	J. Jennings
	G-DWJM	Cessna 550 Citation II	MP Aviation LLP (G-BJIR)
	G-DWMS	Avtech Jabiru UL-450	D. H. S. Williams
	G-DWPF	Tecnam P.92-EM Echo	G-DWPF Group
	G-DWPH	Ultramagic M-77 balloon	Ultramagic UK
	G-DXCC	Ultramagic M-77 balloon	A. Murphy
	G-DYCE	Robinson R44 II	G. Walters (Leasing) Ltd
	G-DYKE	Dyke JD.2 Delta	M. S. Bird
	G-DYNA	Dynamic WT9 UK	Yeoman Light Aircraft Co Ltd
	G-DYNE	Cessna 414	J and G Aviation/Tollerton
	G-DYNG	Colt 105A balloon	M. J. Gunston (G-HSHS)
	G-EAGA	Sopwith Dove (replica)	A. Wood/Old Warden
	G-EAOU†	Vickers Vimy (replica)(NX71MY)	Greenco (UK) Ltd
	G-EASD	Avro 504L	G. M. New
	G-EASQ†	Bristol Babe (replica) (BAPC87) ★	Bristol Aero Collection (stored)/Kemble
	G-EAVX	Sopwith Pup (B1807)	K. A. M. Baker
	G-EBED†	Vickers 60 Viking (replica) (BAPC114) ★	Brooklands Museum of Aviation/Weybridge
	G-EBHX	DH.53 Humming Bird	The Shuttleworth Collection/Old Warden
	G-EBIA	RAF SE-5A (F904)	The Shuttleworth Collection/Old Warden
	G-EBIB	RAF SE-5A ★	Science Museum/South Kensington
	G-EBIC	RAF SE-5A (F938) ★	RAF Museum/Hendon
	G-EBIR	DH.51	The Shuttleworth Collection/Old Warden
	G-EBJE	Avro 504K (E449) ★	RAF Museum/Hendon
	G-EBJG	Parnall Pixie IIIH	Midland Aircraft Preservation Society
	G-EBJI	Hawker Cygnet (replica)	C. J. Essex
	G-EBJO	ANEC IIH	The Shuttleworth Collection/Old Warden
	G-EBKY	Sopwith Pup (9917)	The Shuttleworth Collection/Old Warden
	G-EBLV	DH.60 Cirrus Moth	British Aerospace PLC/Woodford
	G-EBMB	Hawker Cygnet I ★	RAF Museum/Cosford
	G-EBNV	English Electric Wren	The Shuttleworth Collection/Old Warden
	G-EBQP	DH.53 Humming Bird (J7326) ★	Russavia Collection/London Colney
	G-EBWD	DH.60X Hermes Moth	The Shuttleworth Collection/Old Warden
	G-EBZM	Avro 594 Avian IIIA ★	Manchester Museum of Science & Industry
	G-EBZN	DH.60X Moth	J. Hodgkinson (G-UAAP)
	G-ECAN	DH.84 Dragon	Norman Aircraft Trust/Chilbolton
	G-ECBH	Cessna F.150K	ECBH Flying Group
	G-ECDX	DH.71 Tiger Moth (replica)	M. D. Souch
	G-ECGC	Cessna F.172N-II	Cranfield Aviation Leasing Ltd/Cranfield
	G-ECGO	Bölkow Bö.208C1 Junior	A Flight Aviation Ltd
	G-ECIL	Robinson R44 II	C. Ashe
	G-ECJI	Dassault Falcon 10	Fleet International Avn. and Maritime Finance Ltd
	G-ECJM	PA-28R-201T Turbo Arrow III	Regishire Ltd (G-FESL/G-BNRN)
	G-ECLI	Schweizer 269C	Central Communications Group
	G-ECON	Cessna 172M	Aviation Rentals (G-JONE)
	G-ECOX	Grega GN.1 Air Camper	H. C. Cox
	G-ECUB	PA-18 Super Cub 150	E. Hopper (G-CBFI)
	G-ECVB	Pietenpol Air Camper	K. S. Matcham
	G-EDAV	SA Bulldog Srs 120/121 (XX534:B)	Historic Helicopters Ltd
	G-EDCJ	Cessna 525 CitationJet	Air Charter Scotland (Holdings) Ltd/Prestwick
	G-EDCK	Cessna 525 CitationJet	Air Charter Scotland (Holdings) Ltd/Prestwick
	G-EDCS	Raytheon 400A	Mountain Aviation Ltd
	G-EDEE	Comco Ikarus C.42 FB100	Microavionics
	G-EDEN	SOCATA TB10 Tobago	Group Eden
	G-EDES	Robinson R44 II	A. D. Russell

BRITISH CIVIL REGISTRATIONS — G-EDFS – G-EGUR

Reg	Type	Owner or Operator	Notes
G-EDFS	Pietenpol Air Camper	D. F. Slaughter	
G-EDGA	PA-28-161 Warrior II	The RAF Halton Aeroplane Club Ltd	
G-EDGE	Jodel 150	A. D. Edge	
G-EDGI	PA-28-161 Warrior II	R. A. Forster	
G-EDLY	Airborne Edge 912/Streak IIIB	M. & P. L. Eardley	
G-EDMC	Pegasus Quantum 15-912	M. W. Riley	
G-EDNA	PA-38-112 Tomahawk	Top Cat Aviation Ltd	
G-EDRE	Lindstrand LBL 90A balloon	Edren Homes Ltd	
G-EDRV	Van's RV-6A	E. A. Yates	
G-EDTO	Cessna FR.172F	N. G. Hopkinson	
G-EDVL	PA-28R Cherokee Arrow 200-II	J. S. Devlin & Z. Islam (G-BXIN)	
G-EECO	Lindstrand LBL-25A balloon	P. A. & A. J. A. Bubb	
G-EEEK	Extra EA.300/200	A. R. Willis	
G-EEGL	Christen Eagle II	M. P. Swoboda	
G-EEGU	PA-28-161 Warrior II	B. C. Barber	
G-EEJE	PA-31 Navajo B	Geeje Ltd	
G-EEKY	PA-28 Cherokee 140B	Gauntlet Holdings	
G-EELS	Cessna 208B Caravan 1	Glass Eels Ltd	
G-EENA	PA-32R-301 Saratoga SP	Gamit Ltd	
G-EENI	Shaw Europa	M. P. Grimshaw	
G-EENY	GA-7 Cougar	Jade Air PLC	
G-EERH	Ruschmeyer R.90-230RG	D. Sadler	
G-EERV	Van's RV-6	C. B. Stirling (G-NESI)	
G-EESA	Shaw Europa	C. Deith (G-HIIL)	
G-EETG	Cessna 172Q Cutlass	Tango Golf Flying Group	
G-EEUP	SNCAN Stampe SV.4C	A. M. Wajih	
G-EEWZ	Mainair Pegasus Quik	M. J. Hawkins	
G-EEYE	Mainair Blade 912	B. J. Egerton	
G-EEZA	Robinson R44 II	Teleology Ltd	
G-EEZR	Robinson R44	Veee Helicopters Ltd	
G-EEZS	Cessna 182P	W. B. Bateson	
G-EEZZ	Zenair CH.601XL Zodiac	B. Fraser	
G-EFAM	Cessna 182S Skylane	G-EFAM Flying Group	
G-EFBP	Cessna FR.172K	A. Webster	
G-EFFI	Rotorway Executive 162F	P. D. Annison	
G-EFGH	Robinson R22 Beta	Foxtrot Golf Helicopters Ltd (G-ROGG)	
G-EFIR	PA-28-181 Archer II	Leicestershire Aero Club Ltd	
G-EFOF	Robinson R22 Beta	NT Burton Aviation	
G-EFRY	Light Aero Avid Aerobat	J. M. Rawles	
G-EFSM	Slingsby T.67M Firefly 260	The Cambridge Aero Club Ltd (G-BPLK)	
G-EFTE	Bölkow Bö.207	L. J. & A. A. Rice	
G-EFTF	AS.350B Ecureuil	T. J. French (G-CWIZ/G-DJEM/G-ZBAC/G-SEBI/G-BMCU)	
G-EGAG	SOCATA TB20 Trinidad	D. & E. Booth	
G-EGAL	Christen Eagle II	Eagle Partners	
G-EGAN	Enstrom F-28A-UK	P. J. Egan (G-BAHU/G-SERA)	
G-EGBS	Van's RV-9A	Shobdon RV-9A Group	
G-EGEE	Cessna 310Q	R. C. Devine	
G-EGEG	Cessna 172R	C. D. Lever	
G-EGEL	Christen Eagle II	G-EGEL Flying Group	
G-EGGI	Ikarus C.42FB UK	A. G. & G. J. Higgins	
G-EGGS	Robin DR.400/180	R. Foot	
G-EGGY	Robinson R22 Beta	R. S. & A. G. Higgins (G-CCGD)	
G-EGHB	Ercoupe 415D	P. G. Vallance	
G-EGHH	Hawker Hunter F.58 (J-4083)	Heritage Aviation Developments Ltd	
G-EGJA	SOCATA TB20 Trinidad	D. A. Williamson/Alderney	
G-EGLE	Christen Eagle II	M. Buckland t/a Eagle Group	
G-EGLG	PA-31 Turbo Navajo C	H. Merkado (G-OATC/G-OJPW/G-BGCC)	
G-EGLL	PA-28-161 Warrior II	Airways Aero Associations Ltd (G-BLEJ)	
G-EGLS	PA-28-181 Archer III	Haimoss Ltd	
G-EGLT	Cessna 310R	Capital Trading (Aviation) Ltd (G-BHTV)	
G-EGNA	Diamond DA42 Twin Star	Egnatia Aviation Ltd	
G-EGNR	PA-38-112 Tomahawk	R. Bestek	
G-EGPG	PA-18-135 Super Cub	G. Cormack (G-BWUC)	
G-EGTB	PA-28-161 Warrior II	Airways Aero Association Ltd (G-BPWA)	
G-EGTC	Robinson R44	Beds Heli Services Ltd (G-CCNK)	
G-EGTR	PA-28-161 Cadet	Stars Fly Italia/Elstree (G-BRSI)	
G-EGUL	Christen Eagle II	S. Shutt (G-FRYS)	
G-EGUR	Jodel D.140B	S. H. Williams	

G-EHBJ – G-EMBG — BRITISH CIVIL REGISTRATIONS

Notes	Reg	Type	Owner or Operator
	G-EHBJ	CASA 1.131E Jungmann 2000	E. P. Howard
	G-EHDS	CASA 1.131E Jungmann 2000	C. W. N. & A. A. M. Huke (G-DUDS)
	G-EHGF	PA-28-181 Archer II	Pegasus Flying Group/Barton
	G-EHIC	Jodel D.140B	M. Tolson & D. W. Smith
	G-EHLX	PA-28-181 Archer II	ASG Leasing Ltd/Guernsey
	G-EHMF	Isaacs Fury II	M. A. Farrelly
	G-EHMJ	Beech S35 Bonanza	A. L. Burton & A. J. Daley
	G-EHMM	Robin DR.400/180R	Booker Gliding Club Ltd
	G-EHMS	MD Helicopters MD-900	Virgin HEMS (London) Ltd
	G-EHUP	Aérospatiale SA.341G Gazelle 1	MW Helicopters Ltd
	G-EHXP	Rockwell Commander 112A	A. L. Stewart
	G-EIBM	Robinson R22 Beta	MMM and P Helicopters (G-BUCL)
	G-EIII	Extra EA.300	D. Dobson (G-HIII)
	G-EIKY	Shaw Europa	J. D. Milbank
	G-EIRE	Cessna T.182T	J. Byrne
	G-EISO	SOCATA MS.892A Rallye Commodore 150	EISO Group
	G-EITE	Luscombe 8F Silvaire	S. R. H. Martin
	G-EIWT	Cessna FR.182RG	P. P. D. Howard-Johnston/Edinburgh
	G-EIZO	Eurocopter EC 120B	R. M. Bailey
	G-EJAR	Airbus A.319-111	EasyJet Airline Co Ltd/Luton
	G-EJEL	Cessna 550 Citation II	A. J. & E. A. Elliott
	G-EJGO	Z.226HE Trener	S. K. T. & C. M. Neofytou
	G-EJJB	Airbus A.319-111	EasyJet Airline Co Ltd/Luton
	G-EJMG	Cessna F.150H	P. R. Booth
	G-EJOC	AS.350B Ecureuil	Leisure & Retail Helicopters (G-GEDS/G-HMAN/G-SKIM/G-BIVP)
	G-EJRS	PA-28-161 Cadet	Caspian Air Services Ltd
	G-EJTC	Robinson R44	N. Parkhouse
	G-EKIM	Alpi Pioneer 300	M. Langmead & M. Elliott
	G-EKIR	PA-28-262 Cadet	Aeros Leasing Ltd
	G-EKKC	Cessna FR.172G	L. B. W. & F. Hancock
	G-EKKL	PA-28-161 Warrior II	Apollo Aviation Advisory Ltd/Shoreham
	G-EKKO	Robinson R44	W. A. Hawkeswood
	G-EKMN	Zlin Z.242L	Aeroshow Ltd
	G-EKOS	Cessna FR.182 RG	S. Charlton
	G-EKWS	Cessna 550 Citation Bravo	Aircraft Leasing Overseas Ltd
	G-EKYD	Robinson R44 II	EK Aviation Ltd
	G-ELAM	PA-30 Twin Comanche 160B	Hangar 39 Ltd (G-BAWU/G-BAWV)
	G-ELDR	PA-32 Cherokee Six 260	Elder Aviation Ltd
	G-ELEE	Cameron Z-105 balloon	D. Eliot
	G-ELEN	Robin DR.400/180	N. R. & E. Foster
	G-ELIS	PA-34-200T Seneca II	Bristol Flying Centre Ltd (G-BOPV)
	G-ELIT	Bell 206L LongRanger	Henfield Lodge Aviation Ltd
	G-ELIZ	Denney Kitfox Mk 2	A. J. Ellis
	G-ELKA	Christen Eagle II	J. T. Matthews
	G-ELKS	Avid Speedwing Mk 4	H. S. Elkins
	G-ELLA	PA-32R-301 Saratoga IIHP	C. C. W. Hart
	G-ELLE	Cameron N-90 balloon	N. D. Eliot
	G-ELLI	Bell 206B JetRanger 3	Italian Clothes Ltd
	G-ELMH	NA AT-6D Harvard III (42-84555:EP-H)	M. Hammond
	G-ELMO	Robinson R44 II	Locumlink Associates Ltd/Ireland
	G-ELNX	Canadair CL-600-2B19 Regional Jet	Citelynx Travel Ltd
	G-ELSE	Diamond DA42 Twin Star	R. Swann
	G-ELSI	Tanarg/Ixess 15 912S(1)	D. Daniel
	G-ELTE	Agusta A109A II	Henfield Lodge Aviation Ltd (G-BWZI)
	G-ELUN	Robin DR.400/180R	Cotswold DR.400 Syndicate
	G-ELUT	PA-28R Cherokee Arrow 200-II	Green Arrow Europe Ltd
	G-ELZN	PA-28-161 Warrior II	Northamptonshire School of Flying Ltd/Sywell
	G-ELZY	PA-28-161 Warrior II	Goodwood Road Racing School Ltd
	G-EMAA	Eurocopter EC 135T2	Bond Air Services Ltd
	G-EMAS	Eurocopter EC 135T1	East Midlands Air Support Unit
	G-EMAX	PA-31-350 Navajo Chieftain	Atlantic Bridge Aviation Ltd
	G-EMBC	Embraer RJ145EU	British Airways Connect
	G-EMBD	Embraer RJ145EU	British Airways Connect
	G-EMBE	Embraer RJ145EU	British Airways Connect
	G-EMBF	Embraer RJ145EU	British Airways Connect
	G-EMBG	Embraer RJ145EU	British Airways Connect

BRITISH CIVIL REGISTRATIONS — G-EMBH – G-EPAR

Reg	Type	Owner or Operator	Notes
G-EMBH	Embraer RJ145EU	British Airways Connect	
G-EMBI	Embraer RJ145EU	British Airways Connect	
G-EMBJ	Embraer RJ145EU	British Airways Connect	
G-EMBK	Embraer RJ145EU	British Airways Connect	
G-EMBL	Embraer RJ145EU	British Airways Connect	
G-EMBM	Embraer RJ145EU	British Airways Connect	
G-EMBN	Embraer RJ145EU	British Airways Connect	
G-EMBO	Embraer RJ145EU	British Airways Connect	
G-EMBP	Embraer RJ145EU	British Airways Connect	
G-EMBS	Embraer RJ145EU	British Airways Connect	
G-EMBT	Embraer RJ145EU	British Airways Connect	
G-EMBU	Embraer RJ145EU	British Airways Connect	
G-EMBV	Embraer RJ145EU	British Airways Connect	
G-EMBW	Embraer RJ145EU	British Airways Connect	
G-EMBX	Embraer RJ145EU	British Airways Connect	
G-EMBY	Embraer RJ145EU	British Airways Connect	
G-EMCA	Commander Aircraft 114B	Merlin Mail Order Ltd	
G-EMDM	Diamond DA40-P9 Star	D. J. Munson	
G-EMER	PA-34-200 Seneca II	Haimoss Ltd/Old Sarum	
G-EMHB	Agusta A109E Power	East Midlands Helicopters	
G-EMHH	AS.355F2 Twin Squirrel	Hancocks Holdings Ltd (G-BYKH)	
G-EMHK	MBB Bö.209 Monsun 150FV	T. A. Crone (G-BLRD)	
G-EMID	Eurocopter EC 135P2	McAlpine Helicopters Ltd	
G-EMIN	Shaw Europa	S. A. Lamb	
G-EMJA	CASA 1.131E Jungmann 2000	N. J. Radford	
G-EMLE	Aerotechnik EV-97 Eurostar	A. R. White	
G-EMLY	Pegasus Quantum 15	S. J. Reid	
G-EMMI	Robinson R44 II	Hub Of The Wheel Ltd	
G-EMMS	PA-38-112 Tomahawk	Ravenair Aircraft Ltd/Liverpool	
G-EMMY	Rutan Vari-Eze	M. J. Tooze	
G-EMSB	PA-22-160 Tri-Pacer	M. S. Bird (G-ARHU)	
G-EMSI	Shaw Europa	P. W. L. Thomas	
G-EMSL	PA-28-161 Warrior II	Environmental Maintenance Services Ltd (G-TSFT/G-BLDJ)	
G-EMSY	DH.82A Tiger Moth	G-EMSY Group (G-ASPZ)	
G-ENCE	Partenavia P68B	Bicton Aviation (G-OROY/G-BFSU)	
G-ENEE	CFM Streak Shadow SA	T. Green	
G-ENES	Bell 206B JetRanger III	Autogen Bioclear UK Ltd	
G-ENGL	PA-28-140 Cherokee	M. A. English	
G-ENGO	Steen Skybolt	R. G. Fulton	
G-ENHP	Enstrom 480B	H. J. Pelham	
G-ENIE	Tipsy T.66 Nipper 3	R. W. Chatterton & R. A. Durance	
G-ENII	Cessna F.172M	J. Howley	
G-ENNI	Robin R.3000/180	P. F. Taylor	
G-ENNK	Cessna 172S	Holden Group Ltd	
G-ENNY	Cameron V-77 balloon	J. H. Dobson	
G-ENOA	Cessna F.172F	M. K. Acors (G-ASZW)	
G-ENRE	Avtech Jabiru UL	J. C. Harris	
G-ENRI	Lindstrand LBL-105A balloon	P. G. Hall	
G-ENRM	Cessna 182L	P. Murray	
G-ENRY	Cameron N-105 balloon	P. G. & G. R. Hall	
G-ENTS	Van's RV-9A	L. G. Johnson	
G-ENTT	Cessna F.152 II	C. & A. R. Hyett (G-BHHI)	
G-ENTW	Cessna F.152 II	Firecrest Aviation Ltd, R. Spencer & C. Castledine (G-BFLK)	
G-ENVY	Mainair Blade 912	P. Millership	
G-ENYA	Robinson R44 II	GT Investigations (International) Ltd/Ireland	
G-ENZO	Cameron Z-105 balloon	Garelli VI SPA	
G-EODE	PA-46-350P Malibu Mirage	Betterbox Aviation Ltd (G-BYLM)	
G-EOFF	Taylor JT.2 Titch	A. Sharp	
G-EOFS	Shaw Europa	G. T. Leedham	
G-EOFW	Pegasus Quantum 15-912	G-EOFW Microlight Group	
G-EOHL	Cessna 182L	G. B. Dale & M. C. Terris	
G-EOIN	Zenair CH.701UL	D. G. Palmer	
G-EOLD	PA-28-161 Warrior II	Goodwood Road Racing Co Ltd	
G-EOLX	Cessna 172N	Westward Airways (Lands End) Ltd	
G-EOMA	Airbus A.330-243	Monarch Airlines Ltd	
G-EORG	PA-38-112 Tomahawk	P. Sharpe	
G-EORJ	Shaw Europa	P. E. George	
G-EPAR	Robinson R22 Beta II	Jepar Rotorcraft	

G-EPDI – G-EUOI

BRITISH CIVIL REGISTRATIONS

Notes	Reg	Type	Owner or Operator
	G-EPDI	Cameron N-77 balloon	R. Moss
	G-EPED	PA-31-350 Navajo Chieftain	Pedley Furniture International Ltd (G-BMCJ)
	G-EPIC	Jabiru UL-450	T. Chadwick
	G-EPOC	Jabiru UL-450	S. Cope
	G-EPOX	Aero Designs Pulsar XP	M. J. Whatley
	G-EPPO	Robinson R44	North West Service SRL/Italy (G-JBBS)
	G-EPTR	PA-28R Cherokee Arrow 200-II	Tayflite Ltd
	G-ERBL	Robinson R22 Beta II	G. V. Maloney
	G-ERCO	Ercoupe 415D	A. R. & M. V. Tapp
	G-ERDA	Staaken Z-21A Flitzer	J. Cresswell
	G-ERDS	DH.82A Tiger Moth	W. A. Gerdes
	G-ERFS	PA-28-161 Warrior II	S. Harrison
	G-ERIC	Rockwell Commander 112TC	Atomchoice Ltd
	G-ERIK	Cameron N-77 balloon	T. M. Donnelly
	G-ERIS	Hughes 369D	R. J. Howard (G-PJMD/G-BMJV)
	G-ERIW	Staaken Z-21 Flitzer	R. I. Wasey
	G-ERJA	Embraer RJ145EP	British Airways Connect
	G-ERJB	Embraer RJ145EP	British Airways Connect
	G-ERJC	Embraer RJ145EP	British Airways Connect
	G-ERJD	Embraer RJ145EP	British Airways Connect
	G-ERJE	Embraer RJ145EP	British Airways Connect
	G-ERJF	Embraer RJ145EP	British Airways Connect
	G-ERJG	Embraer RJ145EP	British Airways Connect
	G-ERMO	ARV Super 2	T. Pond (G-BMWK)
	G-ERMS	Thunder Ax3 balloon	B. R. & M. Boyle
	G-ERNI	PA-28-181 Archer II	The G-ERNI Flying Group (G-OSSY)
	G-EROL	Westland SA.341G Gazelle 1	The Coin Group Ltd (G-NONA/G-FDAV/G-RIFA/G-ORGE/G-BBHU)
	G-EROM	Robinson R22 Beta	Airtask Group PLC/Stapleford
	G-EROS	Cameron H-34 balloon	Evening Standard Co Ltd
	G-ERRY	AA-5B Tiger	Haniel Aviation Ltd (G-BFMJ)
	G-ERTE	Skyranger 912S (1)	A. P. Trumper
	G-ERTI	Staaken Z-21A Flitzer	B. S. Carpenter
	G-ESCA	Escapade Jabiru (1)	W. R. Davis-Smith
	G-ESCC	Escapade 912	G. & S. Simons
	G-ESCP	Escapade Jabiru (1)	R. G. Hughes
	G-ESEX	Eurocopter EC 135T2	Essex Police Authority
	G-ESFT	PA-28-161 Warrior II	Falcon Flying Services Ltd (G-ENNA)
	G-ESKA	Escapade 912	J. H. Beard
	G-ESKY	PA-23 Aztec 250D	C. J. Williams (G-BBNN)
	G-ESLH	Agusta A109E Power	Caledonian Heritable Ltd
	G-ESME	Cessna R.182 II (15211)	G. C. Cherrington (G-BNOX)
	G-ESSL	Cessna 182R Skylane II	Euro Seaplane Services Ltd
	G-ESSY	Robinson R44	EW Guess (Holdings) Ltd
	G-ESTA	Cessna 550 Citation II	Executive Aviation Services Ltd (G-GAUL)
	G-ESTR	Van's RV-6	R. M. Johnson
	G-ESUS	Rotorway Executive 162F	J. Tickner
	G-ETAT	Cessna 172S Skyhawk	ADR Aviation
	G-ETBY	PA-32 Cherokee Six 260	G-ETBY Group (G-AWCY)
	G-ETCW	Stoddard-Hamilton Glastar	P. G. Hayward
	G-ETDC	Cessna 172P	The Moray Flying Club
	G-ETHI	IDABacau Yakovlev Yak-52	J. S. Thrush
	G-ETHY	Cessna 208	N. A. Moore
	G-ETIM	Eurocopter EC 120B	Agricultural Machinery Ltdl
	G-ETIN	Robinson R22 Beta	D. I. Pointon
	G-ETIV	Robin DR.400/180	J. MacGilvray
	G-ETME	Nord 1002 Pingouin (KG+EM)	108 Flying Group
	G-ETNT	Robinson R44	Heli Air Ltd/Wellesbourne
	G-ETOU	Agusta A.109S Grand	Helimand Ltd
	G-ETPS	Hawker Hunter FGA.9 (XE601)	Skyblue Aviation Ltd
	G-EUOA	Airbus A.319-131	British Airways
	G-EUOB	Airbus A.319-131	British Airways
	G-EUOC	Airbus A.319-131	British Airways
	G-EUOD	Airbus A.319-131	British Airways
	G-EUOE	Airbus A.319-131	British Airways
	G-EUOF	Airbus A.319-131	British Airways
	G-EUOG	Airbus A.319-131	British Airways
	G-EUOH	Airbus A.319-131	British Airways
	G-EUOI	Airbus A.319-131	British Airways

BRITISH CIVIL REGISTRATIONS
G-EUOJ – G-EWBC

Reg	Type	Owner or Operator	Notes
G-EUOJ	Airbus A.319-131	British Airways	
G-EUOK	Airbus A.319-131	British Airways	
G-EUOL	Airbus A.319-131	British Airways	
G-EUPA	Airbus A.319-131	British Airways	
G-EUPB	Airbus A.319-131	British Airways	
G-EUPC	Airbus A.319-131	British Airways	
G-EUPD	Airbus A.319-131	British Airways	
G-EUPE	Airbus A.319-131	British Airways	
G-EUPF	Airbus A.319-131	British Airways	
G-EUPG	Airbus A.319-131	British Airways	
G-EUPH	Airbus A.319-131	British Airways	HEATHROW
G-EUPJ	Airbus A.319-131	British Airways	HEATHROW
G-EUPK	Airbus A.319-131	British Airways	
G-EUPL	Airbus A.319-131	British Airways	
G-EUPM	Airbus A.319-131	British Airways	
G-EUPN	Airbus A.319-131	British Airways	
G-EUPO	Airbus A.319-131	British Airways	
G-EUPP	Airbus A.319-131	British Airways	
G-EUPR	Airbus A.319-131	British Airways	
G-EUPS	Airbus A.319-131	British Airways	
G-EUPT	Airbus A.319-131	British Airways	
G-EUPU	Airbus A.319-131	British Airways	
G-EUPV	Airbus A.319-131	British Airways	
G-EUPW	Airbus A.319-131	British Airways	
G-EUPX	Airbus A.319-131	British Airways	
G-EUPY	Airbus A.319-131	British Airways	
G-EUPZ	Airbus A.319-131	British Airways	
G-EURX	Shaw Europa XS	C. C. Napier	
G-EUSO	Robin DR.400/140 Major	Weald Air Services Ltd	
G-EUUA	Airbus A.320-232	British Airways	
G-EUUB	Airbus A.320-232	British Airways	
G-EUUC	Airbus A.320-232	British Airways	
G-EUUD	Airbus A.320-232	British Airways	
G-EUUE	Airbus A.320-232	British Airways	
G-EUUF	Airbus A.320-232	British Airways	
G-EUUG	Airbus A.320-232	British Airways	
G-EUUH	Airbus A.320-232	British Airways	
G-EUUI	Airbus A.320-232	British Airways	
G-EUUJ	Airbus A.320-232	British Airways	
G-EUUK	Airbus A.320-232	British Airways	HEATHROW
G-EUUL	Airbus A.320-232	British Airways	
G-EUUM	Airbus A.320-232	British Airways	
G-EUUN	Airbus A.320-232	British Airways	
G-EUUO	Airbus A.320-232	British Airways	
G-EUUP	Airbus A.320-232	British Airways	
G-EUUR	Airbus A.320-232	British Airways	
G-EUUS	Airbus A.320-232	British Airways	
G-EUUT	Airbus A.320-232	British Airways	
G-EUUU	Airbus A.320-232	British Airways	
G-EUXC	Airbus A.321-231	British Airways	
G-EUXD	Airbus A.321-231	British Airways	
G-EUXE	Airbus A.321-231	British Airways	
G-EUXF	Airbus A.321-231	British Airways	
G-EUXG	Airbus A.321-231	British Airways	
G-EUXH	Airbus A.321-231	British Airways	
G-EUXI	Airbus A.321-231	British Airways	
G-EUXJ	Airbus A.321-231	British Airways	
G-EUXK	Airbus A.321-231	British Airways	HEATHROW
G-EUXL	Airbus A.321-231	British Airways	
G-EVBF	Cameron Z-350 balloon	Virgin Balloon Flights	
G-EVET	Cameron 80 Concept balloon	L. O. & H. Vaughan	
G-EVEY	Thruster T.600N 450-JAB	K. J. Crompton	
G-EVIE	PA-28-181 Warrior II	L. Richardson (G-ZULU)	
G-EVLE	Rearwin 8125 Cloudster	M. C. Hiscock (G-BVLK)	
G-EVLN	Gulfstream 4	Metropix Ltd	
G-EVPI	Evans VP-1 Srs 2	C. P. Martyr	
G-EVRO	Aerotechnik EV-97 Eurostar	Movie-Go	
G-EVTO	PA-28-161 Warrior II	Redhill Air Services Ltd/Redhill	
G-EWAN	Prostar PT-2C	C. G. Shaw	
G-EWAW	Bell 206B-3 JetRanger 3	D. Seymour (G-DORB)	
G-EWBC	Avtec Jabiru SK	E. W. B. Comber	

G-EWES – G-EZEF

BRITISH CIVIL REGISTRATIONS

Notes	Reg	Type	Owner or Operator
	G-EWES	Pioneer 300	R. Y. Kendal & D. A. Ions
	G-EWHT	Robinson R-2112	Ewan Ltd
	G-EWIZ	Pitts S-2E Special	P. A. Soper
	G-EWME	PA-28 Cherokee 235	C. J. Mewis & E. S. Ewen
	G-EWRT	Eurocopter EC 135T2	William Ewart Properties Ltd
	G-EXAM	PA-28RT-201T Turbo Arrow IV	Zwetsloot
	G-EXEA	Extra EA.300/L	P. J. Lawton
	G-EXEC	PA-34-200 Seneca	Sky Air Travel Ltd
	G-EXES	Shaw Europa XS	D. Barraclough
	G-EXEX	Cessna 404	Atlantic Air Transport Ltd/Coventry
	G-EXIT	MS.893E Rallye 180GT	G-EXIT Group
	G-EXLL	Zenair CH.601	B. McFadden
	G-EXON	PA-28-161 Cadet	Plane Talking Ltd/Elstree (G-EGLD)
	G-EXPD	Stemme S.10-VT	Global Gliding Expeditions
	G-EXPL	Champion 7GCBC Citabria	E. J. F. McEntee
	G-EXTR	Extra EA.260	S. J. Carver
	G-EXXO	PA-28-161 Cadet	Aviation Rentals/Elstree (G-CBXP)
	G-EYAK	Yakovlev Yak-50 (50 yellow)	P. N. A. Whitehead
	G-EYAS	Denney Kitfox Mk 2	R. W. Line
	G-EYCO	Robin DR.400/180	Cherokee G-AVYL Flying Group Ltd
	G-EYES	Cessna 402C	Atlantic Air Transport Ltd/Coventry (G-BLCE)
	G-EYNL	MBB Bö.105DBS/5	Sterling Helicopters Ltd
	G-EYOR	Van's RV-6	S. I. Fraser
	G-EYRE	Bell 206L-1 LongRanger	Lightgaze Ltd (G-STVI)
	G-EZAA	Airbus A.319-111	easyJet Airline Co Ltd/Luton
	G-EZAB	Airbus A.319-111	easyJet Airline Co Ltd/Luton
	G-EZAC	Airbus A.319-111	easyJet Airline Co Ltd/Luton
	G-EZAD	Airbus A.319-111	easyJet Airline Co Ltd/Luton
	G-EZAE	Airbus A.319-111	easyJet Airline Co Ltd/Luton
	G-EZAF	Airbus A.319-111	easyJet Airline Co Ltd/Luton
	G-EZAG	Airbus A.319-111	easyJet Airline Co Ltd/Luton
	G-EZAH	Airbus A.319-111	easyJet Airline Co Ltd/Luton
	G-EZAI	Airbus A.319-111	easyJet Airline Co Ltd/Luton
	G-EZAJ	Airbus A.319-111	easyJet Airline Co Ltd/Luton
	G-EZAK	Airbus A.319-111	easyJet Airline Co Ltd/Luton
	G-EZAL	Airbus A.319-111	easyJet Airline Co Ltd/Luton
	G-EZAM	Airbus A.319-111	easyJet Airline Co Ltd/Luton (G-CCKA)
	G-EZAN	Airbus A.319-111	easyJet Airline Co Ltd/Luton
	G-EZAO	Airbus A.319-111	easyJet Airline Co Ltd/Luton
	G-EZAP	Airbus A.319-111	easyJet Airline Co Ltd/Luton
	G-EZAR	Pegasus Quik	I. B. Smith & P. Thompson
	G-EZAS	Airbus A.319-111	easyJet Airline Co Ltd/Luton
	G-EZAT	Airbus A.319-111	easyJet Airline Co Ltd/Luton
	G-EZAU	Airbus A.319-111	easyJet Airline Co Ltd/Luton
	G-EZAV	Airbus A.319-111	easyJet Airline Co Ltd/Luton
	G-EZAW	Airbus A.319-111	easyJet Airline Co Ltd/Luton
	G-EZAX	Airbus A.319-111	easyJet Airline Co Ltd/Luton
	G-EZAY	Airbus A.319-111	easyJet Airline Co Ltd/Luton
	G-EZAZ	Airbus A.319-111	easyJet Airline Co Ltd/Luton
	G-EZBA	Airbus A.319-111	easyJet Airline Co Ltd/Luton
	G-EZBB	Airbus A.319-111	easyJet Airline Co Ltd/Luton
	G-EZBC	Airbus A.319-111	easyJet Airline Co Ltd/Luton
	G-EZBD	Airbus A.319-111	easyJet Airline Co Ltd/Luton
	G-EZBE	Airbus A.319-111	easyJet Airline Co Ltd/Luton
	G-EZBF	Airbus A.319-111	easyJet Airline Co Ltd/Luton
	G-EZBG	Airbus A.319-111	easyJet Airline Co Ltd/Luton
	G-EZBH	Airbus A.319-111	easyJet Airline Co Ltd/Luton
	G-EZBI	Airbus A.319-111	easyJet Airline Co Ltd/Luton
	G-EZBJ	Airbus A.319-111	easyJet Airline Co Ltd/Luton
	G-EZBK	Airbus A.319-111	easyJet Airline Co Ltd/Luton
	G-EZBL	Airbus A.319-111	easyJet Airline Co Ltd/Luton
	G-EZBM	Airbus A.319-111	easyJet Airline Co Ltd/Luton
	G-EZBN	Airbus A.319-111	easyJet Airline Co Ltd/Luton
	G-EZCL	Airbus A.319-111	easyJet Airline Co Ltd/Luton
	G-EZDC	Airbus A.319-111	easyJet Airline Co Ltd/Luton (G-CCKB)
	G-EZDG	Rutan Vari-Eze	D. M. Gale (G-EZOS)
	G-EZEA	Airbus A.319-111	easyJet Airline Co Ltd/Luton
	G-EZEB	Airbus A.319-111	easyJet Airline Co Ltd/Luton
	G-EZEC	Airbus A.319-111	easyJet Airline Co Ltd/Luton
	G-EZED	Airbus A.319-111	easyJet Airline Co Ltd/Luton
	G-EZEF	Airbus A.319-111	easyJet Airline Co Ltd/Luton

BRITISH CIVIL REGISTRATIONS — G-EZEG – G-EZPG

Reg	Type	Owner or Operator	Notes
G-EZEG	Airbus A.319-111	easyJet Airline Co Ltd/Luton	
G-EZEJ	Airbus A.319-111	easyJet Airline Co Ltd/Luton	
G-EZEK	Airbus A.319-111	easyJet Airline Co Ltd/Luton	
G-EZEL	Westland SA.341G Gazelle 1	W. R. Pitcher (G-BAZL)	
G-EZEO	Airbus A.319-111	easyJet Airline Co Ltd/Luton	
G-EZEP	Airbus A.319-111	easyJet Airline Co Ltd/Luton	
G-EZER	Cameron N-34 balloon	D. P. Tuck	
G-EZES	Airbus A.319-111	easyJet Airline Co Ltd/Luton	
G-EZET	Airbus A.319-111	easyJet Airline Co Ltd/Luton	
G-EZEU	Airbus A.319-111	easyJet Airline Co Ltd/Luton	
G-EZEV	Airbus A.319-111	easyJet Airline Co Ltd/Luton	
G-EZEW	Airbus A.319-111	easyJet Airline Co Ltd/Luton	
G-EZEZ	Airbus A.319-111	easyJet Airline Co Ltd/Luton	
G-EZIA	Airbus A.319-111	easyJet Airline Co Ltd/Luton	
G-EZIC	Airbus A.319-111	easyJet Airline Co Ltd/Luton	
G-EZID	Airbus A.319-111	easyJet Airline Co Ltd/Luton	
G-EZIE	Airbus A.319-111	easyJet Airline Co Ltd/Luton	
G-EZIF	Airbus A.319-111	easyJet Airline Co Ltd/Luton	
G-EZIG	Airbus A.319-111	easyJet Airline Co Ltd/Luton	
G-EZIH	Airbus A.319-111	easyJet Airline Co Ltd/Luton	
G-EZII	Airbus A.319-111	easyJet Airline Co Ltd/Luton	
G-EZIJ	Airbus A.319-111	easyJet Airline Co Ltd/Luton	
G-EZIK	Airbus A.319-111	easyJet Airline Co Ltd/Luton	
G-EZIL	Airbus A.319-111	easyJet Airline Co Ltd/Luton	
G-EZIM	Airbus A.319-111	easyJet Airline Co Ltd/Luton	
G-EZIN	Airbus A.319-111	easyJet Airline Co Ltd/Luton	
G-EZIO	Airbus A.319-111	easyJet Airline Co Ltd/Luton	
G-EZIP	Airbus A.319-111	easyJet Airline Co Ltd/Luton	
G-EZIR	Airbus A.319-111	easyJet Airline Co Ltd/Luton	
G-EZIS	Airbus A.319-111	easyJet Airline Co Ltd/Luton	
G-EZIT	Airbus A.319-111	easyJet Airline Co Ltd/Luton	
G-EZIU	Airbus A.319-111	easyJet Airline Co Ltd/Luton	
G-EZIV	Airbus A.319-111	easyJet Airline Co Ltd/Luton	
G-EZIW	Airbus A.319-111	easyJet Airline Co Ltd/Luton	
G-EZIX	Airbus A.319-111	easyJet Airline Co Ltd/Luton	
G-EZIY	Airbus A.319-111	easyJet Airline Co Ltd/Luton	
G-EZIZ	Airbus A.319-111	easyJet Airline Co Ltd/Luton	
G-EZJA	Boeing 737-73V	easyJet Airline Co Ltd/Luton	
G-EZJB	Boeing 737-73V	easyJet Airline Co Ltd/Luton	
G-EZJC	Boeing 737-73V	easyJet Airline Co Ltd/Luton	
G-EZJF	Boeing 737-73V	easyJet Airline Co Ltd/Luton	
G-EZJG	Boeing 737-73V	easyJet Airline Co Ltd/Luton	
G-EZJH	Boeing 737-73V	easyJet Airline Co Ltd/Luton	
G-EZJI	Boeing 737-73V	easyJet Airline Co Ltd/Luton	
G-EZJJ	Boeing 737-73V	easyJet Airline Co Ltd/Luton	
G-EZJK	Boeing 737-73V	easyJet Airline Co Ltd/Luton	
G-EZJL	Boeing 737-73V	easyJet Airline Co Ltd/Luton	
G-EZJM	Boeing 737-73V	easyJet Airline Co Ltd/Luton	
G-EZJN	Boeing 737-73V	easyJet Airline Co Ltd/Luton	
G-EZJO	Boeing 737-73V	easyJet Airline Co Ltd/Luton	
G-EZJP	Boeing 737-73V	easyJet Airline Co Ltd/Luton	
G-EZJR	Boeing 737-73V	easyJet Airline Co Ltd/Luton	
G-EZJS	Boeing 737-73V	easyJet Airline Co Ltd/Luton	
G-EZJT	Boeing 737-73V	easyJet Airline Co Ltd/Luton	
G-EZJU	Boeing 737-73V	easyJet Ailrine Co Ltd/Luton	
G-EZJV	Boeing 737-73V	easyJet Airline Co Ltd/Luton	
G-EZJW	Boeing 737-73V	easyJet Airline Co Ltd/Luton	
G-EZJX	Boeing 737-73V	easyJet Airline Co Ltd/Luton	
G-EZJY	Boeing 737-73V	easyJet Airline Co Ltd/Luton	
G-EZJZ	Boeing 737-73V	easyJet Airline Co Ltd/Luton	
G-EZKA	Boeing 737-73V	easyJet Airline Co Ltd/Luton	
G-EZKB	Boeing 737-73V	easyJet Airline Co Ltd/Luton	
G-EZKC	Boeing 737-73V	easyJet Airline Co Ltd/Luton	
G-EZKD	Boeing 737-73V	easyJet Airline Co Ltd/Luton	
G-EZKE	Boeing 737-73V	easyJet Airline Co Ltd/Luton	
G-EZKF	Boeing 737-73V	easyJet Airline Co Ltd/Luton	
G-EZKG	Boeing 737-73V	easyJet Airline Co Ltd/Luton	
G-EZMH	Airbus A.319-111	easyJet Airline Co Ltd/Luton (G-CCKD)	
G-EZMS	Airbus A.319-111	easyJet Airline Co Ltd/Luton	
G-EZNC	Airbus A.319-111	easyJet Airline Co Ltd/Luton (G-CCKC)	
G-EZNM	Airbus A.319-111	easyJet Airline Co Ltd/Luton	
G-EZPG	Airbus A.319-111	easyJet Airline Co Ltd/Luton	

G-EZPZ – G-FEFE — BRITISH CIVIL REGISTRATIONS

Notes	Reg	Type	Owner or Operator
	G-EZPZ	American Champion 8KCAB Super Decathlon	Decathlon Aviation Ltd
	G-EZSM	Airbus A.319-111	easyJet Airline Co Ltd/Luton (G-CCKE)
	G-EZUB	Zenair CH.601HD Zodiac	R. A. C. Stephens
	G-EZVS	Colt 77B balloon	A. J. Lovell
	G-EZXO	Colt 56A balloon	A. J. Lovell
	G-EZYU	PA-34-200 Seneca II	B. V. Goodman (G-BCDB)
	G-EZZA	Shaw Europa XS	J. C. R. Davey
	G-EZZY	Evektor EV-97 Eurostar	G. & P. M. G. Verity
	G-FABB	Cameron V-77 balloon	P. Trumper
	G-FABI	Robinson R44	Professional Helicopter Services Ltd
	G-FABM	Beech 95-B55 Baron	F. B. Miles J. E. Balmer & P. E. T. Price (G-JOND/G-BMVC)
	G-FABS	Thunder Ax9-120 S2 balloon	R. C. Corrall
	G-FACE	Cessna 172S	Oxford Aviation Services Ltd/Kidlington
	G-FAIR	SOCATA TB10 Tobago	Fairwings Ltd
	G-FAKE	Robinson R44 II	Arden Ridge Developments Ltd
	G-FALC	Aeromere F.8L Falco	D. M. Burbridge (G-AROT)
	G-FALO	Sequoia F.8L Falco	M. J. & S. E. Aherne
	G-FAME	Starstreak Shadow SA-II	T. J. Palmer
	G-FAMH	Zenair CH.701	G. T. Neale
	G-FANC	Fairchild 24R-46 Argus III	A. T. Fines
	G-FANL	Cessna FR.172K XP-II	J. A. Rees
	G-FANY	Bell 206L-1 Long Ranger	Eagle Helicopters (G-CCUG)
	G-FARE	Robinson R44 II	Toriamos Ltd/Ireland
	G-FARL	Pitts S-1E Special	F. L. McGee
	G-FARM	SOCATA Rallye 235GT	Bristol Cars Ltd
	G-FARO	Aero Designs Star-Lite SL.1	M. K. Faro
	G-FARR	Jodel 150	G. H. Farr
	G-FARY	QAC Quickie Tri-Q	F. Sayyah
	G-FATB	Rockwell Commander 114B	James D. Pearce & Co
	G-FAUX	Cessna 182S	R. S. Faux
	G-FAVC	DH.80A Puss Moth	Liddell Aircraft Ltd
	G-FBAT	Aeroprakt A.22 Foxbat	J. Jordan
	G-FBEA	Embraer ERJ190-200LR	Flybe.com
	G-FBEB	Embraer ERJ190-200LR	Flybe.com
	G-FBFI	Canadair CL.601-3R	TAG Aviation (UK) Ltd
	G-FBII	Ikarus C.42 FB100	F. Beeson
	G-FBMW	Cameron N-90 balloon	K-J. Schwer/Germany
	G-FBPI	ANEC IV Missel Thrush	R. Trickett
	G-FBRN	PA-28-181 Archer II	Herefordshire Aero Club Ltd/Shobdon
	G-FBWH	PA-28R Cherokee Arrow 180	F. A. Short
	G-FCAB	Diamond DA42 Twin Star	Halfpenny Green Flight Centre Ltd
	G-FCDB	Cessna 550 Citation Bravo	Eurojet Aviation Ltd
	G-FCED	PA-31T2 Cheyenne IIXL	Air Medical Fleet Ltd/Kidlington
	G-FCKD	Eurocopter EC 120B	Pacific Helicopters Ltd
	G-FCLA	Boeing 757-28A	Thomas Cook Airlines
	G-FCLB	Boeing 757-28A	Thomas Cook Airlines
	G-FCLC	Boeing 757-38A	Thomas Cook Airlines
	G-FCLD	Boeing 757-25F	Thomas Cook Airlines
	G-FCLE	Boeing 757-28A	Thomas Cook Airlines
	G-FCLF	Boeing 757-28A	Thomas Cook Airlines
	G-FCLG	Boeing 757-28A	Thomas Coor Airlines
	G-FCLH	Boeing 757-28A	Thomas Cook Airlines
	G-FCLI	Boeing 757-28A	Thomas Cook Airlines
	G-FCLJ	Boeing 757-2Y0	Thomas Cook Airlines
	G-FCLK	Boeing 757-2Y0	Thomas Cook Airlines
	G-FCSP	Robin DR.400/180	FCS Photochemicals
	G-FCUK	Pitts S-1C Special	M. O'Hearne
	G-FDPS	Aviat Pitts S-2C Special	Flights and Dreams Ltd
	G-FDZA	Boeing 737-8K5	Thomsonfly Ltd
	G-FEAB	PA-28-181 Archer III	Feabrex Ltd
	G-FEBE	Cessna 340A	Just Plane Trading Ltd
	G-FEBY	Robinson R22 Beta	Astra Helicopters Ltd
	G-FEDA	Eurocopter EC 120B	CI Motors Ltd
	G-FEES	Eurocopter EC 135T2	Cairnsilver Ltd
	G-FEET	Mainair Pegasus Quik	A. N. Wilkinson
	G-FEFE	Scheibe SF.25B Falke	D. G. Roberts

BRITISH CIVIL REGISTRATIONS — G-FELL – G-FLEX

Reg	Type	Owner or Operator	Notes
G-FELL	Shaw Europa	R. A. Blackwell	
G-FELT	Cameron N-77 balloon	Allan Industries Ltd	
G-FERN	Mainair Blade 912	M. H. Moulai	
G-FEWG	Fuji FA.200-160	Caseright Ltd (G-BBNV)	
G-FEZZ	Bell 206B JetRanger II	R. J. Myram	
G-FFAB	Cameron N-105 balloon	B. J. Hammond	
G-FFAF	Cessna F.150L	M. Howells	
G-FFEN	Cessna F.150M	Golf Foxtrot Foxtrot Echo November Group	
G-FFFT	Lindstrand LBL-31A balloon	W. Rousell & J. Tyrrell	
G-FFIT	Pegasus Quik	K. A. Armstrong	
G-FFOX	Hawker Hunter T.7B	Delta Engineering Aviation Ltd/Kemble	
G-FFRA	Dassault Falcon 20DC	FR Aviation Ltd/Bournemouth	
G-FFRI	AS.355F1 Twin Squirrel	Sterling Helicopters Ltd (G-GLOW/G-PAPA/G-CNET/G-MCAH)	
G-FFTI	SOCATA TB20 Trinidad	R. Lenk	
G-FFTT	Lindstrand LBL Newspaper SS balloon	City of London Balloon Group Ltd	
G-FFUN	Pegasus Quantum 15	P. R. Mailer (G-MYMD)	
G-FFWD	Cessna 310R	T. S. Courtman (G-TVKE/G-EURO)	
G-FGID	Vought FG-1D Corsair (KD345:130-A)	Patina Ltd/Duxford	
G-FGSK	Cameron 120 Beer Crate SS balloon	Ballon-Sport und Luftwerbung Dresden GmbH/Germany	
G-FHAS	Scheibe SF.25E Super Falke	Burn Gliding Club Ltd	
G-FIAT	PA-28 Cherokee 140	Demero Ltd & Transcourt Ltd (G-BBYW)	
G-FIBS	AS.350BA Ecureuil	Pristheath Ltd	
G-FIFE	Cessna FA.152	Tayside Aviation Ltd/Dundee (G-BFYN)	
G-FIFI	SOCATA TB20 Trinidad	F. A. Saker (G-BMWS)	
G-FIFT	Ikarus C.42 FB 100	A. R. Jones	
G-FIGA	Cessna 152	Central Aircraft Leasing Ltd	
G-FIGB	Cessna 152	Aerohire Ltd/Wolverhampton	
G-FIGP	Boeing 737-2E7	European Skybus Ltd (G-BMDF)	
G-FIII	Extra EA.300/L	G. G. Feriman (G-RGEE)	
G-FIJJ	Cessna F.177RG	D. R. Vale (G-AZFP)	
G-FIJR	Lockheed L.188PF Electra	Atlantic Airlines Ltd/Coventry	
G-FIJV	Lockheed L.188CF Electra	Atlantic Airlines Ltd/Coventry	
G-FILE	PA-34-200T Seneca	A. J. Warren	
G-FILL	PA-31-310 Navajo	P. V. Naylor-Leyland	
G-FINA	Cessna F.150L	A. G. Freeman (G-BIFT)	
G-FIND	Cessna F.406	Atlantic Airlines Ltd/Coventry	
G-FINK	BAe 125-1000B	B. T. Fink	
G-FINZ	I.I.I Sky Arrow 650T	A. G. Counsell	
G-FIRM	Cessna 550 Citation Bravo	Marshall of Cambridge Aerospace Ltd	
G-FIRS	Robinson R22 Beta II	Multiflight Ltd	
G-FIRZ	Murphy Renegade Spirit UK	P. J. Houtman	
G-FISH	Cessna 310R-II	ACS Contracts Ltd	
G-FITZ	Cessna 335	J. R. Naylor & D. Hughes (G-RIND)	
G-FIXX	Van's RV-7	Hambilton Engineering Ltd	
G-FIZU	Lockheed L.188CF Electra	Atlantic Airlines Ltd/Coventry	
G-FIZY	Shaw Europa XS	G. N. Holland (G-DDSC)	
G-FIZZ	PA-28-161 Warrior II	Tecair Aviation Ltd	
G-FJEA	Boeing 757-23AER	Flyjet Ltd (G-LCRC/G-IEAB)	
G-FJEB	Boeing 757-23A	Flyjet Ltd (G-OOOJ)	
G-FJET	Cessna 550 Citation II	London Executive Aviation Ltd (G-DCFR/G-WYLX/G-JETD)	
G-FJMS	Partenavia P.68B	J. B. Randle (G-SVHA)	
G-FJTH	Aeroprakt A.22 Foxbat	F. J. T. Hancock	
G-FKNH	PA-15 Vagabond	M. J. Mothershaw/Liverpool	
G-FLAG	Colt 77A balloon	B. A. Williams	
G-FLAK	Beech 95-E55 Baron	D. Clarke/Swanton Morley	
G-FLAV	PA-28-161 Warrior II	The Crew Flying Group/Tollerton	
G-FLBI	Robinson R44 II	Heli Air Ltd	
G-FLCA	Fleet Model 80 Canuck	E. C. Taylor	
G-FLCT	Hallam Fleche	R. G. Hallam	
G-FLDG	Skyranger 912	A. J. Gay	
G-FLEA	SOCATA TB10 Tobago	TB Group	
G-FLEW	Lindstrand LBL-90A balloon	A. Nimmo	
G-FLEX	Mainair Pegasus Quik	H. D. Colliver	

G-FLGT – G-FOXL | BRITISH CIVIL REGISTRATIONS

Notes	Reg	Type	Owner or Operator
	G-FLGT	Lindstrand LBL-105A balloon	Ballongaventyr I. Skane AB/Sweden
	G-FLIK	Pitts S-1S Special	R. P. Millinship/Leicester
	G-FLIP	Cessna FA.152	Cloud 9 Aviation (Leasing) Ltd (G-BOES)
	G-FLIT	Rotorway Executive 162F	R. S. Snell
	G-FLIZ	Staaken Z-21 Flitzer	M. A. Wood
	G-FLKE	Scheibe SF.25C Falke	RAF Gliding & Soaring Association
	G-FLKS	Scheibe SF.25C Falke	London Gliding Club Propietary Ltd
	G-FLOA	Cameron O-120 balloon	Floating Sensations Ltd
	G-FLOP	Cessna 152	Cloud 9 Aviation (Leasing) Ltd
	G-FLOR	Shaw Europa	A. F. C. van Eldik
	G-FLOW	Cessna 172N	M. P. Dolan
	G-FLOX	Shaw Europa	DPT Group
	G-FLPI	Rockwell Commander 112	H. J. Freeman
	G-FLSH	Yakovlev Yak-52	Flash Air Ltd
	G-FLTA	BAe 146-200	Flightline Ltd
	G-FLTC	BAe 146-300	Flightline Ltd (G-JEBH/G-BVTO/G-NJID)
	G-FLTD	BAe 146-200A	Flightline Ltd/Manchester (G-BMFM)
	G-FLTG	Cameron A-140 balloon	Floating Sensations Ltd
	G-FLTZ	Beech 58 Baron	Flightline Ltd/Southend (G-PSVS)
	G-FLUX	PA-28-181 Archer III	TEC Air Hire Ltd
	G-FLYA	Mooney M.20J	BRF Aviation Ltd
	G-FLYB	Ikarus C.42 FB100	G-FLYB Group
	G-FLYC	Ikarus C.42 FB100	Solent Flight Ltd
	G-FLYE	Cameron A-210 balloon	Exclusive Ballooning
	G-FLYF	Mainair Blade 912	Cool Water Direct Ltd
	G-FLYG	Slingsby T.67C	G. Laden
	G-FLYH	Robinson R22 Beta	Cyclone Helicopters (G-BXMR)
	G-FLYI	PA-34-200 Seneca II	Willowair Flying Club/Southend (G-BHVO)
	G-FLYP	Beagle B.206 Srs 2	Key Publishing Ltd/Cranfield (G-AVHO)
	G-FLYS	Robinson R44	Newmarket Plant Hire Ltd
	G-FLYT	Shaw Europa	K. F. & R. Richardson
	G-FLYY	BAC.167 Strikemaster 80A	B. T. Barber
	G-FLZR	Staaken Z-21 Flitzer	J. F. Govan
	G-FMAH	Fokker 100	Gazelle Ltd
	G-FMAM	PA-28-151 Warrior (modified)	Lima Tango Flying Group (G-BBXV)
	G-FMGG	Maule M5-235C Lunar Rocket	S. Bierbaum (G-RAGG)
	G-FMKA	Diamond HK.36TC Super Dimona	G. P. Davis
	G-FMSG	Cessna FA.150K	G. Owen/Gamston (G-POTS/G-AYUY)
	G-FNEY	Cessna F.177RG	F. Ney
	G-FNLD	Cessna 172N	Papa Hotel Flying Group
	G-FNLY	Cessna F.172M	Skytrax Aviation Ltd (G-WACX/G-BAEX)
	G-FNPT	PA-28-161 Warrior III	Fleetwash Ltd
	G-FOFO	Robinson R44 II	Towers Aviation
	G-FOGG	Cameron N-90 balloon	J. P. E. Money-Kyrle
	G-FOGI	Shaw Europa XS	B. Fogg
	G-FOGY	Robinson R22 Beta	Dragonfly Aviation
	G-FOKK	Fokker DR1 (replica)	P. R. Holloway
	G-FOLD	Light Aero Avid Speedwing	B. W. & G. Evans
	G-FOLI	Robinson R22 Beta II	G. M. Duckworth
	G-FOLY	Aerotek Pitts S-2A Modified	D. G. Gilmour
	G-FONZ	Best Off Skyranger 912 (12)	G-FONZ Sky Ranger Group
	G-FOPP	Lancair 320	Airsport (UK) Ltd
	G-FORC	SNCAN Stampe SV.4C	C. C. Rollings & F. J. Hodson
	G-FORD	SNCAN Stampe SV.4C	P. H. Meeson
	G-FORM	Learjet 45	Broomco 3598 Ltd
	G-FORR	PA-28-181 Archer III	Buchanan Partnership
	G-FORZ	Pitts S-1S Special	N. W. Parkinson
	G-FOSY	MS.880B Rallye Club	A. G. Foster (G-AXAK)
	G-FOWL	Colt 90A balloon	The Packhouse Ltd
	G-FOWS	Cameron N-105 balloon	F. R. Hart
	G-FOXA	PA-28-161 Cadet	Leicestershire Aero Club Ltd
	G-FOXB	Aeroprakt A.22 Foxbat	G. D. McCullough
	G-FOXC	Denney Kitfox Mk 3	G. Hawkins
	G-FOXD	Denney Kitfox Mk 2	P. P. Trangmar
	G-FOXE	Denney Kitfox Mk 2	K. M. Pinkar
	G-FOXF	Denney Kitfox Mk 4	M. S. Goodwin
	G-FOXG	Denney Kitfox Mk 2	J. U. McKercher
	G-FOXI	Denney Kitfox	B. Johns
	G-FOXL	Zenair CH.601XL Zodiac	M. J. Lloyd
	G-FOXM	Bell 206B JetRanger 2	Tyringham Charter & Group Services (G-STAK/G-BNIS)

BRITISH CIVIL REGISTRATIONS

G-FOXS – G-FXII

Reg	Type	Owner or Operator	Notes
G-FOXS	Denney Kitfox Mk 2	S. P. Watkins & C. C. Rea	
G-FOXX	Denney Kitfox	M. N. & R. J. King	
G-FOXZ	Denney Kitfox	S. C. Goozee	
G-FOZZ	Beech A36 Bonanza	Go To Air Ltd	
G-FPIG	PA-28-151 Warrior	G. F. Strain (G-BSSR)	
G-FPLA	Beech 200 Super King Air	Cobham Leasing Ltd	
G-FPLB	Beech 200 Super King Air	Cobham Leasing Ltd	
G-FPLD	Beech 200 Super King Air	FR Aviation Ltd/Bournemouth	
G-FPLE	Beech 200 Super King Air	Cobham Leasing Ltd	
G-FPSA	PA-28-161 Warrior II	Deep Cleavage Ltd (G-RSFT/G-WARI)	
G-FRAD	Dassault Falcon 20E	Cobham Leasing Ltd (G-BCYF)	
G-FRAF	Dassault Falcon 20E	FR Aviation Ltd/Bournemouth	
G-FRAG	PA-32 Cherokee Six 300E	T. A. Houghton	
G-FRAH	Dassault Falcon 20DC	FR Aviation Ltd/Bournemouth	
G-FRAI	Dassault Falcon 20E	FR Aviation Ltd/Bournemouth	
G-FRAJ	Dassault Falcon 20E	FR Aviation Ltd/Bournemouth	
G-FRAK	Dassault Falcon 20DC	FR Aviation Ltd/Bournemouth	
G-FRAL	Dassault Falcon 20DC	FR Aviation Ltd/Bournemouth	
G-FRAN	Piper J-3C-90 Cub (480321:H-44)	Essex L-4 Group (G-BIXY)	
G-FRAO	Dassault Falcon 20DC	FR Aviation Ltd/Bournemouth	
G-FRAP	Dassault Falcon 20DC	FR Aviation Ltd/Bournemouth	
G-FRAR	Dassault Falcon 20DC	FR Aviation Ltd/Bournemouth	
G-FRAS	Dassault Falcon 20C	FR Aviation Ltd/Bournemouth	
G-FRAT	Dassault Falcon 20C	FR Aviation Ltd/Bournemouth	
G-FRAU	Dassault Falcon 20C	FR Aviation Ltd/Bournemouth	
G-FRAW	Dassault Falcon 20ECM	FR Aviation Ltd/Bournemouth	
G-FRAY	Cassutt IIIM (modified)	C. I. Fray	
G-FRBA	Dassault Falcon 20C	FR Aviation Ltd/Bournemouth	
G-FRCE	Folland Gnat T.1 (XS104)	Airborne Innovations Ltd	
G-FRGN	PA-28-236 Dakota	P. J. Vacher	
G-FRIL	Lindstrand LBL-105A balloon	S. Travaglia	
G-FRJB	Britten Sheriff SA-1 ★	Aeropark/East Midlands	
G-FRNK	Skyranger 912(2)	F. Tumelty	
G-FROH	AS.350B2 Ecureuil	PLM Dollar Group Ltd	
G-FROM	Ikarus C.42 FB100	Fly Buy Ultralights Ltd	
G-FRYI	Beech 200 Super King Air	London Executive Aviation Ltd/London City (G-OAVX/G-IBCA/G-BMCA)	
G-FRYL	Beech 390 Premier 1	Gregg Air/Kidlington	
G-FSEU	Beech 200 Super King Air	Air Mercia Ltd	
G-FSHA	Denney Kitfox Mk 2	P. P. Trangman	
G-FTAX	Cessna 421C	Gold Air International Ltd (G BFFM)	
G-FTIL	Robin DR.400/180R	RAF Wyton Flying Club Ltd	
G-FTIM	Robin DR.400/100	Madley Flying Group	
G-FTIN	Robin DR.400/100	G. D. Clark & M. J. D. Theobold/Blackpool	
G-FTSE	BN-2A Mk.III-2 Trislander	Aurigny Air Services Ltd/Guernsey (G-BEPI)	
G-FTSL	Canadair CL.600-2B16 604	Farglobe transport Services Ltd	
G-FTUO	Van's RV-4	R. S. Jordan	
G-FUEL	Robin DR.400/180	R. Darch/Compton Abbas	
G-FUKM	Westland Gazelle AH.1	Falcon Aviation Ltd	
G-FULL	PA-28R Cherokee Arrow 200-II	Stapleford Flying Club Ltd (G-HWAY/G-JULI)	
G-FULM	Sikorsky S-76C	Air Harrods Ltd	
G-FUND	Thunder Ax7-65Z balloon	G. Everett	
G-FUNK	Yakovlev Yak-50	Redstar Aero Services Ltd	
G-FUNN	Plumb BGP-1	J. D. Anson/France	
G-FUNY	Robinson R44	Concept Group International Ltd	
G-FURI	Isaacs Fury II	S. M. Johnston	
G-FUSE	Cameron N-105 balloon	LE Electrical Ltd	
G-FUZY	Cameron N-77 balloon	Allan Industries Ltd	
G-FUZZ	PA-18 Super Cub 95	G. W. Cline	
G-FVEL	Cameron Z-90 balloon	Fort Vale Engineering Ltd	
G-FVRY	Colt 105A balloon	R. Thompson	
G-FWAY	Lindstrand LBL-90A balloon	Fairway Furniture Ltd	
G-FWPW	PA-28-236 Dakota	P. A. & F. C. Winters	
G-FXBT	Aeroprakt A.22 Foxbat	R. H. Jago	
G-FXII	VS.366 Spitfire F.XII (EN224)	P. R. Arnold	

173

G-FYAN – G-GBTA — BRITISH CIVIL REGISTRATIONS

Notes	Reg	Type	Owner or Operator
	G-FYAN	Williams Westwind MLB	M. D. Williams
	G-FYAO	Williams Westwind MLB	M. D. Williams
	G-FYAU	Williams Westwind Mk 2 MLB	M. D. Williams
	G-FYAV	Osprey Mk 4E2 MLB	C. D. Egan & C. Stiles
	G-FYBX	Portswood Mk XVI MLB	I. Chadwick
	G-FYCL	Osprey Mk 4G MLB	P. J. Rogers
	G-FYCV	Osprey Mk 4D MLB	M. Thomson
	G-FYCZ	Osprey Mk 4D2 MLB	P. Middleton
	G-FYDF	Osprey Mk 4DV	K. A. Jones
	G-FYDI	Williams Westwind Two MLB	M. D. Williams
	G-FYDN	European 8C MLB	P. D. Ridout
	G-FYDO	Osprey Mk 4D MLB	N. L. Scallan
	G-FYDP	Williams Westwind Three MLB	M. D. Williams
	G-FYDS	Osprey Mk 4D MLB	N. L. Scallan
	G-FYEK	Unicorn UE.1C MLB	D. & D. Eaves
	G-FYEO	Eagle Mk 1 MLB	M. E. Scallan
	G-FYEV	Osprey Mk 1C MLB	M. E. Scallan
	G-FYEZ	Firefly Mk 1 MLB	M. E. & N. L. Scallan
	G-FYFI	European E.84DS MLB	M. Stelling
	G-FYFJ	Williams Westland 2 MLB	M. D. Williams
	G-FYFN	Osprey Saturn 2 MLB	J. & M. Woods
	G-FYFW	Rango NA-55 MLB	Rango Kite & Balloon Co
	G-FYFY	Rango NA-55RC MLB	A. M. Lindsay
	G-FYGC	Rango NA-42B MLB	L. J. Wardle
	G-FYGI	Rango NA-55RC MLB	Advertair Ltd
	G-FYGJ	Airspeed 300 MLB	N. Wells
	G-FYGM	Saffrey/Smith Princess MLB	A. Smith
	G-FZZA	General Avia F22-A	APB Leasing Ltd/Welshpool
	G-FZZI	Cameron H-34 balloon	Magical Adventures Ltd
	G-GACA	P.57 Sea Prince T.1 (WP308:572CU) ★	P. G. Vallance Ltd/Charlwood
	G-GACB	Robinson R44 II	A. C. Barker
	G-GAFA	PA-34-200T Seneca II	Oxford Aviation Services Ltd
	G-GAFT	PA-44-180 Seminole	Atlantic Flight Training Ltd
	G-GAII	Hawker Hunter GA.11 (XE685)	A. G. Fowles
	G-GAJB	AA-5B Tiger	G. A. J. Bowles (G-BHZN)
	G-GALA	PA-28 Cherokee 180E	Flyteam Aviation Ltd/Elstree (G-AYAP)
	G-GALB	PA-28-161 Warrior II	LB Aviation Ltd
	G-GALL	PA-38-112 Tomahawk	M. Lowe & K. Hazelwood (G-BTEV)
	G-GALX	Dassault Falcon 900 EX	Charter Air Ltd
	G-GAME	Cessna T.303	P. Heffron
	G-GAND	Agusta-Bell 206B Jet Ranger	The Henderson Group (G-AWMK)
	G-GANE	Sequoia F.8L Falco	S. J. Gane
	G-GAOH	Robin DR.400 / 2 +2.	L. J. Millbank
	G-GAOM	Robin DR.400 / 2+2	Exeter Aviation Ltd
	G-GASC	Hughes 369HS	A. C. Richardson (G-WELD/G-FROG)
	G-GASP	PA-28-181 Archer II	G-GASP Flying Group
	G-GASS	Thunder Ax7-77 balloon	Servowarm Balloon Syndicate
	G-GATE	Robinson R44 II	J. W. Gate
	G-GATT	Robinson R44 II	N. R. Gatt
	G-GAWA	Cessna 140	C140 Group (G-BRSM)
	G-GAZA	Aérospatiale SA.341G Gazelle 1	The Auster Aircraft Co Ltd (G-RALE/G-SFTG)
	G-GAZI	Aérospatiale SA.341G Gazelle 1	MW Helicopters Ltd (G-BKLU)
	G-GAZZ	Aérospatiale SA.341G Gazelle 1	Stratton Motor Co (Norfolk) Ltd
	G-GBAB	PA-28-161 Warrior II	B. A. Mills
	G-GBAO	Robin R.1180TD	J. Kay-Mova
	G-GBEE	Mainair Pegasus Quik	L. G. Whitet
	G-GBFF	Cessna F.172N	Aviation Rentals
	G-GBFR	Cessna F.177RG	Airspeed Aviation Ltd
	G-GBGA	Scheibe SF.25C Falke	British Gliding Association Ltd
	G-GBGB	Ultramagic M.105	Universal Car Services Ltd
	G-GBHI	SOCATA TB10 Tobago	Robert Purvis Plant Hire Ltd
	G-GBJP	Mainair Pegasus Quantum 15	R. G. Mulford
	G-GBJS	Robin HR200/100S Club	B. A. Mills
	G-GBLP	Cessna F.172M	Aviate Scotland Ltd/Edinburgh (G-GWEN)
	G-GBLR	Cessna F.150L	Almat Flying Club Ltd
	G-GBMR	Beech B200 Super King Air	M and R Aviation LLP
	G-GBRB	PA-28 Cherokee 180C	Border Air Training Ltd
	G-GBRU	Bell 206B JetRanger 3	Merlin Estate Management Ltd (G-CDGV)
	G-GBSL	Beech 76 Duchess	M. H. Cundsy (G-BGVG)
	G-GBTA	Boeing 737-436	British Airways (G-BVHA)

174

BRITISH CIVIL REGISTRATIONS — G-GBTB – G-GFTB

Reg	Type	Owner or Operator	Notes
G-GBTB	Boeing 737-436	British Airways (G-BVHB)	
G-GBTL	Cessna 172S	Bohana Technology Ltd	
G-GBUE	Robin DR.400/120A	G-GBUE Group (G-BPXD)	
G-GBUN	Cessna 182T	G. M. Bunn	
G-GBVX	Robin DR400/120A	M. Patterson	
G-GBXF	Robin HR200/120	B. A. Mills	
G-GBXS	Shaw Europa XS	P. G. Wood	
G-GCAC	Shaw Europa XS T-G	J. L. Gunn	
G-GCAT	PA-28 Cherokee 140B	Group Cat (G-BFRH)	
G-GCBC	American Champion 7GCBC	B. A. & L. A. Mills	
G-GCCL	Beech 76 Duchess	Aerolease Ltd	
G-GCEA	Pegasus Quik	J. D. Ash	
G-GCKI	Mooney M.20K	B. Barr	
G-GCUF	Robin DR400/160	S. T. Bates	
G-GCYC	Cessna F.182Q	G-GCYC Ltd/Barton	
G-GDAV	Robinson R44 II	K. G. Ward	
G-GDER	Robin R.1180TD	Berkshire Aviation Services Ltd	
G-GDKR	Robin DR400/140B	L. J. Milbank	
G-GDMW	Beech 76 Duchess	Apollo Aviation Advisory Ltd	
G-GDOG	PA-28R Cherokee Arrow 200-II	The Mutley Crew Group (G-BDXW)	
G-GDOV	Robinson R44	D. B. Hamilton	
G-GDSG	Agusta A109E Power	Pendley Aviation LLP	
G-GDRV	Van's RV-6	J. R. S. Heaton & R. Feather	
G-GDTL	Airbus A.320-231	MyTravel Airways	
G-GDTU	Avions Mudry CAP-10B	Sherburn Aero Club Ltd	
G-GEDY	Dassault Falcon 2000	Victoria Aviation Ltd	
G-GEEP	Robin R.1180TD	The Aiglon Flying Group	
G-GEES	Cameron N-77	N. A. Carr	
G-GEEZ	Cameron N-77 balloon	Charnwood Forest Turf Accountants Ltd	
G-GEHL	Cessna 172S	Ebryl Ltd	
G-GEHP	PA-28RT-201 Arrow IV	Aeros Leasing Ltd	
G-GEMM	Cirrus SR20	R. J. & B. Howard	
G-GEMS	Thunder Ax8-90 S2 balloon	B. Sevenich & ptnrs/Germany	
G-GENI	Robinson R44 II	G-GENI LLP	
G-GENN	GA-7 Cougar	Plane Talking Ltd/Elstree (G-BNAB/G-BGYP)	
G-GEOF	Pereira Osprey 2	G. Crossley	
G-GEOS	Diamond HK.36 TTC-ECO Super Dimona	University Court (School of Geosciences) of the University of Edinburgh	
G-GERT	Van's RV-7	Barnstormers	
G-GERY	Stoddard-Hamilton Glastar	S. G. Brown	
G-GEST	Robinson R44	Gest Air Ltd	
G-GFCA	PA-28-161 Cadet	Aeros Leasing Ltd	
G-GFCB	PA-28-161 Cadet	AM & T Aviation Ltd/Bristol	
G-GFCD	PA-34-220T Seneca III	Stonehurst Aviation Ltd (G-KIDS)	
G-GFEA	Cessna 172S	Allan Jefferies (G-CEDY)	
G-GFEY	PA-34-200T Seneca II	Mann Air Ltd	
G-GFFA	Boeing 737-59D	British Airways (G-BVZF)	
G-GFFB	Boeing 737-505	British Airways	
G-GFFD	Boeing 737-59D	British Airways (G-OBMY)	
G-GFFE	Boeing 737-528	British Airways	
G-GFFF	Boeing 737-53A	British Airways (G-OBMZ)	
G-GFFG	Boeing 737-505	British Airways	
G-GFFH	Boeing 737-5H6	British Airways	
G-GFFI	Boeing 737-528	British Airways	
G-GFFJ	Boeing 737-5H6	British Airways	
G-GFIA	Cessna 152	Aircraft Grouping Ltd	
G-GFIB	Cessna F.152	Aircraft Grouping Ltd (G-BPIO)	
G-GFKY	Zenair CH.250	R. G. Kelsall	
G-GFLY	Cessna F.150L	Leagate Ltd	
G-GFMT	Cessna 172S	G-GFMT Flying Group	
G-GFNO	Robin ATL	D. J. Watson	
G-GFOX	Aeroprakt A.22 Foxbat	I. A. Love & G. F. Elvis	
G-GFPA	PA-28-181 Archer III	Allan Jefferies	
G-GFRD	Robin ATL L	Gloster Aero Group	
G-GFRO	Robin ATL	B. F. Walker	
G-GFSA	Cessna 172R Skyhawk	Aircraft Grouping Ltd	
G-GFTA	PA-28-161 Warrior III	One Zero Three Ltd	
G-GFTB	PA-28-161 Warrior III	One Zero Three Ltd	

G-GGGG – G-GOLF   BRITISH CIVIL REGISTRATIONS

Notes	Reg	Type	Owner or Operator
	G-GGGG	Thunder Ax7-77A balloon	T. A. Gilmour
	G-GGHZ	Robin ATL	P. L. Bowman
	G-GGJK	Robin DR.400/140B	Headcorn Jodelers
	G-GGLE	PA-22 Colt 108 (tailwheel)	P. Mather
	G-GGNG	Robinson R44	Burton Helicopters Ltd
	G-GGOW	Colt 77A balloon	G. Everett
	G-GGRR	SA Bulldog Srs 120/121 (XX614:V)	M. Litherland (G-CBAM)
	G-GGTT	Agusta-Bell 47G-4A	Phoenix Aviation Refinishers Ltd
	G-GHDC	Robinson R44 II	Heli Air Ltd
	G-GHEE	Aerotechnik EV-97 Eurostar	C. J. Ball
	G-GHIA	Cameron N-120 balloon	J. A. Marshall
	G-GHIN	Thunder Ax7-77 balloon	N. T. Parry
	G-GHKX	PA-28-161 Warrior II	Aviation Rentals
	G-GHOW	Cessna F.182Q	G. How
	G-GHPG	Cesna 550 Citation 2	MCP Aviation (Charter) Ltd
	G-GHRW	PA-28RT-201 Arrow IV	Bonus Aviation Ltd (G-ONAB/G-BHAK)
	G-GHSI	PA-44-180T Turbo Seminole	M. G. Roberts
	G-GHZJ	SOCATA TB9 Tampico	M. Haller
	G-GIDY	Shaw Europa XS	Gidy Group
	G-GIGI	MS.893A Rallye Commodore	D. J. Moore (G-AYVX)
	G-GILI	Robinson R44	Twylight Management Ltd
	G-GILT	Cessna 421C	Skymaster Air Services (G-BMZC)
	G-GIRY	AG-5B Tiger	Romeo Yankee Flying Group
	G-GIWT	Shaw Europa XS	A. Twigg
	G-GJCD	Robinson R22 Beta	J. C. Lane
	G-GJKK	Mooney M.20K	Pergola Ltd
	G-GKAT	Enstrom 280C	D. Cummaford
	G-GKFC	RL-5A LW Sherwood Ranger	T. R. Janaway (G-MYZI)
	G-GKKI	Avions Mudry CAP 231EX	Acro Laser Company Ltd
	G-GLAD	Gloster G.37 Gladiator II (N5903:H)	Patina Ltd/Duxford
	G-GLAW	Cameron N-90 balloon	R. A. Vale
	G-GLED	Cessna 150M	Firecrest Aviation Ltd/Booker
	G-GLHI	Skyranger 912	S. F. Winter
	G-GLIB	Robinson R44	Helisport UK Ltd
	G-GLID	Schleicher ASW-28-18E	R. A. Bateson & P. N. Marriott
	G-GLST	Great Lakes Sport Trainer	D. A. Graham
	G-GLSU	Bücker Bü 181B-1 Bestmann	P. R. Holloway
	G-GLTT	PA-31-350 Navajo Chieftain	Airtime Aviation Ltd
	G-GLUC	Van's RV-6	Speedfreak Ltd
	G-GLUE	Cameron N-65 balloon	L. J. M. Muir & G. D. Hallett
	G-GLUG	PA-31-350 Navajo Chieftain	Champagne-Air Ltd/Newcastle (G-BLOE/G-NITE)
	G-GMAA	Learjet 45	Gama Aviation Ltd
	G-GMAB	BAe 125 Srs 1000A	Gama Aviation Ltd (G-BUWX)
	G-GMAC	Gulfstream G-IVSP	Gama Aviation Ltd
	G-GMAX	SNCAN Stampe SV.4C	Glidegold Ltd (G-BXNW)
	G-GMKD	Robin HR200/120B	B. A. Mills
	G-GMPB	BN-2T-4S Defender 4000	Greater Manchester Police Authority (G-BWPU)
	G-GMPS	MDH MD-902 Explorer	Greater Manchester Police Authority
	G-GMSI	SOCATA TB9 Tampico	M. L. Rhodes
	G-GNAA	MDH MD-900	Police Aviation Services Ltd
	G-GNJW	Ikarus C.42	I. R. Westrope
	G-GNMG	Cessna U.206F	P. Marsden
	G-GNRV	Van's RV-9A	N. K. Beavins
	G-GNTB	SAAB SF.340A	Loganair Ltd
	G-GNTF	SAAB SF.340A	Loganair Ltd
	G-GNTZ	BAe 146-200	British Airways Connect (G-CLHB)
	G-GOAC	PA-34-200T Seneca II	Oxford Aviation Ltd
	G-GOBD	PA-32R-301 Saratoga IIHP	B. J. De'Ath (G-OARW)
	G-GOBT	Colt 77A balloon	British Telecom PLC
	G-GOCX	Cameron N-90 balloon	R. D. Parry/Hong Kong
	G-GOGB	Lindstrand LBL ,90A	J. Dyer (G-CDFX)
	G-GOGS	PA-34-200T Seneca II	A. Semple
	G-GOGW	Cameron N-90 balloon	S. E. Carroll
	G-GOJP	PA-46-350P Malibu Mirage	Plato Management Ltd (G-CREW)
	G-GOLF	SOCATA TB10 Tobago	Golf Golf Group

BRITISH CIVIL REGISTRATIONS — G-GOMO – G-GWIZ

Reg	Type	Owner or Operator	Notes
G-GOMO	Learjet 45	Gold Air International Ltd (G-OLDF/G-JRJR)	
G-GOOD	SOCATA TB20 Trinidad	T. M. Sloane & M. P. Bowcock	
G-GORE	CFM Streak Shadow	M. S. Clinton	
G-GOSL	Robin DR.400/180	R. M. Gosling (G-BSDG)	
G-GOSS	Jodel DR.221	Avon Flying Group	
G-GOTC	GA-7 Cougar	WakeliteLtd	
G-GOTH	PA-28-161 Warrior III	Goose Aviation Syndicate	
G-GOTF	Cessna 208B Grand Caravan	Trailfinders (Services) Ltd	
G-GOTO	PA-32R-301T Turbo Saratoga II	J. A. Varndell	
G-GOUP	Robinson R22 Beta	Heli Air Ltd (G-DIRE)	
G-GPAG	Van's RV-6	P. A. Green	
G-GPAS	Avtech Jabiru UL-450	G. D. Allen	
G-GPEG	Sky 90-24 balloon	N. T. Parry	
G-GPFI	Boeing 737-229	European Skybus Ltd	
G-GPMW	PA-28RT-201T Turbo Arrow IV	Calverton Flying Group Ltd	
G-GPPN	Cameron TR-70 balloon	P. Lesser	
G-GPSF	Jabiru J430	P. S. Furlow	
G-GPST	Phillips ST.1 Speedtwin	Speedtwin Developments Ltd	
G-GREY	PA-46-350P Malibu Mirage	S. T. Day & S. C. Askham	
G-GRIN	Van's RV-6	A. Phillips	
G-GRMN	Aerospool Dynamic WT9 UK	Yeoman Light Aircraft Co Ltd	
G-GRND	Agusta A109S	DFS Trading Ltd	
G-GROE	Grob G.115A	H. & E. Merkado	
G-GROL	Maule MXT-7-180	D. C. Croll & ptnrs	
G-GROW	Cameron N-77 balloon	Derbyshire Building Society	
G-GRPA	Ikarus C.42 FB100	G. R Page	
G-GRRC	PA-28-161 Warrior II	Goodwood Road Racing Co Ltd (G-BXJX)	
G-GGRH	Robinson R44	Heli Air Ltd	
G-GRRR	SA Bulldog Srs 120/122	Horizons Europe Ltd (G-BXGU)	
G-GRWL	Lilliput Type 4 balloon	A. E. & D. E. Thomas	
G-GRWW	Robinson R44 II	G. R. Williams (G-HEEL)	
G-GRYZ	Beech F33A Bonanza	J. Kawadri & M. Kaveh	
G-GSCV	Ikarus C.42 FB UK	G. Sipson	
G-GSIL	Eurocopter AS.355N Ecureuil 2	Silcoge-Sociedade Constructora De Obras Gerais SA/Portugal (G-RANI/G-CCIN)	
G-GSJH	Bell 206B JetRanger 3	T. J. Morris Ltd (G-PENT/G-IIRB)	
G-GSPG	Hughes 369HS	S. Giddings Aviation	
G-GSPN	Boeing 737-31S	Flyglobespan.com	
G-GSPY	Robinson R44 II	Alphatec (UK) Ltd	
G-GSSA	Boeing 747-47UF	Global Supply Systems Ltd	
G-GSSB	Boeing 747-47UF	Global Supply Systems Ltd	
G-GSSC	Boeing 747-47UF	Global Supply Systems Ltd	
G-GSSO	Gulfstream GV-SP	TAG Aviation (UK) Ltd	
G-GSYJ	Diamond DA42 Twin Star	Crosby Aviation (Jersey) Ltd	
G-GTAX	PA-31-350 Navajo Chieftain	Hadagain Investments Ltd (G-OIAS)	
G-GTFC	P & M Quik	W. Lofts	
G-GTGT	P & M Quik GT.450	G. C. Weighell	
G-GTHM	PA-38-112 Tomahawk	A. B. King & T. P. Powley	
G-GTJD	P & M Quik GT450	Robert McKellar Aviation	
G-GTJM	Eurocopter EC 120B Colibri	T. J. Morris Ltd	
G-GTSO	P & M Quik GT450	J. R. North	
G-GTTP	P & M Quik GT450	T. A. H. Pollock	
G-GUAY	Enstrom 480	Heliway Aviation	
G-GUCK	Beech C23 Sundowner 180	J. T. Francis (G-BPYG)	
G-GUFO	Cameron 80 Saucer SS balloon	Magical Adventures Ltd (G-BOUB)	
G-GULF	Lindstrand LBL-105A balloon	M. A. Webb	
G-GULP	I.I.I. Sky Arrow 650T	S. Marriott	
G-GUMS	Cessna 182P	L. W. Scattergood (G-CBMN)	
G-GUNS	Cameron V-77 balloon	J. Pithois	
G-GURN	PA-31 Navajo C	Neric Ltd (G-BHGA)	
G-GURU	PA-28-161 Warrior II	Fly Guru LLP	
G-GUSS	PA-28-151 Warrior	M. J. Cleaver & J. M. Newman (G-BJRY)	
G-GUST	Agusta-Bell 206B JetRanger 2	DNH Helicopters Ltd (G-CBHH/G-AYBE)	
G-GUYS	PA-34-200T Seneca	Jowett Homes Ltd (G-BMWT)	
G-GVPI	Evans VP-1	G. Martin	
G-GWIZ	Colt Clown SS balloon	Magical Adventures Ltd	

177

G-GWYN – G-HCSL — BRITISH CIVIL REGISTRATIONS

Notes	Reg	Type	Owner or Operator
	G-GWYN	Cessna F.172M	Magic Carpet Flying Co
	G-GYAK	Yakovlev Yak-50	M. W. Levy & M. V. Rijske
	G-GYAT	Gardan GY-80 Horizon 180	Rochester GYAT Flying Group Club
	G-GYAV	Cessna 172N	Southport & Merseyside Aero Club (1979) Ltd/Liverpool
	G-GYBO	Gardan GY-80 Horizon 160	A. L. Fogg
	G-GYMM	PA-28R Cherokee Arrow 200	MRR Aviation Ltd (G-AYWW)
	G-GYRO	Campbell Cricket	J. W. Pavitt
	G-GYTO	PA-28-161 Warrior III	Wellesbourne Aviation
	G-GZDO	Cessna 172N	Cambridge Hall Aviation
	G-GZLE	Aérospatiale SA.341G Gazelle 1	R. G. Fairall (G-PYOB//G-IYOB/GWELA/G-G-SFTD/G-RIFC)
	G-GZRP	P-42-720 Cheyenne IIIA	Air Medical Fleet Ltd
	G-HAAM	Dassault Falcon 900	TAG Aviation (UK) Ltd
	G-HABT	Supermarine Aircraft Spitfire Mk.26	B. Trumble
	G-HACE	Van's RV-6A	D. C. McElroy
	G-HACK	PA-18 Super Cub 150	Intrepid Aviation Co/North Weald
	G-HADA	Enstrom 480	W. B. Steele
	G-HAEC	CAC-18 Mustang 23 (472218:WZ-I)	R. W. Davies/Duxford
	G-HAFG	Cessna 340A	Haller & Sons (Dereham) Ltd
	G-HAFT	Diamond DA42 Twin Star	Atlantic Flight Training Ltd
	G-HAIB	Aviat A-1B Husky	H. Brockmueller
	G-HAIG	Rutan LongEz	C. Docherty
	G-HAIR	Robin DR.400/180	P. R. Holloway & S. P. Copson
	G-HAJJ	Glaser-Dirks DG.400	W. G. Upton & J. G. Kosak
	G-HALC	PA-28R Cherokee Arrow 200	Halcyon Aviation Ltd
	G-HALJ	Cessna 140	H. A. Lloyd-Jennings
	G-HALL	PA-22 Tri-Pacer 160	F. P. Hall (G-ARAH)
	G-HALP	SOCATA TB10 Tobago	D. H. Halpern (stored)/Elstree
	G-HALT	Mainair Pegasus Quik	J. A. Horn
	G-HAMI	Fuji FA.200-180	K. G. Cameron, M. P. Antoniak and Renzacci (UK) PLC (G-OISF/G-BAPT)
	G-HAMM	Yakovlev Yak-50	A. D. Hammond/North Weald
	G-HAMP	Bellanca 7ACA Champ	K. MacDonald
	G-HAMR	PA-28-161 Warrior II	Electric Scribe 2000 Ltd
	G-HAMS	Pegasus Quik	P. C. D. Hamilton
	G-HAMY	Van's RV-6	P. W. Armstrong
	G-HANA	Westland WS-58 Wessex HC.2	R. A. Fidler
	G-HANG	Diamond DA42 Twin Star	Atlantic Flight Training Ltd
	G-HANS	Robin DR.400 2+2	J. S. Russell
	G-HANY	Agusta-Bell 206B JetRanger 3	Eastern Atlantic Helicopters Ltd (G-ESAL/G-BHXW/G-JEKP)
	G-HAPI	Lindstrand LBL-105A balloon	Adventure Balloons Ltd
	G-HAPR	B.171 Sycamore HR.14 (XG547:S-T) ★	IHM/Weston-super-Mare
	G-HAPY	DHC.1 Chipmunk 22A (WP803)	Astrojet Ltd
	G-HARD	Dyn'Aéro MCR-01 ULC	M. A. Claydon
	G-HARE	Cameron N-77 balloon	D. H. Sheryn & C. A. Buck
	G-HARI	Raj Hamsa X'Air V2 (2)	S. T. Welsh
	G-HARK	Canadair CL.600-2B16	Corbridge Ltd
	G-HARN	PA-28-181 Archer II	K. Saxton (G-DENK/G-BXRJ)
	G-HARR	Robinson R22 Beta	Unique Helicopters Ltd
	G-HART	Cessna 152 (tailwheel)	Atlantic Air Transport Ltd/Coventry (G-BPBF)
	G-HARY	Alon A-2 Aircoupe	M. B. Willis (G-ATWP)
	G-HASO	Diamond DA40D Star	Plane Talking Ltd (G-CCLZ)
	G-HATF	Thorp T-18CW	A. T. Fraser
	G-HATZ	Hatz CB-1	S. P. Rollason
	G-HAUL	Westland WG.30 Srs 300 ★	IHM/Weston-super-Mare
	G-HAUS	Hughes 369HM	Pulford Aviation/Sywell (G-KBOT/G-RAMM)
	G-HAZE	Thunder Ax8-90 balloon	T. G. Church
	G-HBBC	DH.104 Dove 8	BBC Air Ltd (G-ALFM)
	G-HBBH	Ikarus C42 FB100	B. R. W. Hay
	G-HBEK	Agusta A109C	Bek Helicopters (G-RNLD/G-DATE)
	G-HBMW	Robinson R22	Northumbria Helicopters Ltd (G-BOFA)
	G-HBOS	Scheibe SF-25C Rotax-Falke	Coventry Gliding Club Ltd
	G-HBUG	Cameron N-90 balloon	R. T. & H. Revel (G-BRCN)
	G-HCBI	Schweizer 269C-1	Oxford Aviation Services Ltd/Kidlington
	G-HCSA	Cessna 525A CJ2	Hangar 8 Ltd
	G-HCSL	PA-34-220T Seneca III	Fly (CI) Ltd

BRITISH CIVIL REGISTRATIONS — G-HDAE – G-HMBJ

Reg	Type	Owner or Operator	Notes
G-HDAE	DHC.1 Chipmunk 22	Airborne Classics Ltd	
G-HDEW	PA-32R-301 Saratoga SP	G. R. Williams (G-BRGZ)	
G-HDTV	Agusta A109A-II	Castle Air Charters Ltd (G-BXWD)	
G-HDIX	Enstrom 280FX	Clovetree Ltd	
G-HEBE	Bell 206B JetRanger 3	M and E Building and Civil Engineering Contractors Ltd	
G-HECB	Fuji FA.200-160	H. E. W. E. Bailey (G-BBZO)	
G-HEDI	Cessna 182T Skylane	Carpe D Aviation Ltd (G-CEDU)	
G-HELA	SOCATA TB10 Tobago	Group TB.10	
G-HELE	Bell 206B JetRanger 3	B. E. E. Smith (G-OJFR)	
G-HELN	Piper PA-28-95	Helen Group	
G-HELV	DH.115 Vampire T.55 (XJ771)	Aviation Heritage Ltd/Coventry	
G-HEMS	SA.365N Dauphin 2	PLM Dollar Group Ltd	
G-HENT	SOCATA Rallye 110ST	R. J. Patton	
G-HENY	Cameron V-77 balloon	R. S. D'Alton	
G-HERB	PA-28R-201 Arrow III	Consort Aviation Ltd	
G-HERC	Cessna 172S	Cambridge Aero Club Ltd	
G-HERD	Lindstrand LBL-77B balloon	S. W. Herd	
G-HERM	ATR-72-201	Atlantic Air Transport Ltd	
G-HEVN	SOCATA TB200 Tobago XL	I. K. Maclean	
G-HEWI	Piper J-3C-90 Cub	Denham Grasshopper Group (G-BLEN)	
G-HEWS	Hughes 369D ★	Spares' use/Sywell	
G-HEXE	Colr 17A balloon	A. Dunnington	
G-HEYY	Cameron 72 Bear SS balloon	Magical Adventures Ltd	
G-HFBM	Curtiss Robin C-2	D. M. Forshaw	
G-HFCA	Cessna A.150L	T. H. Scott	
G-HFCB	Cessna F.150L	G-HFCB Group (G-AZVR)	
G-HFCI	Cessna F.150L	D. Bishop	
G-HFCL	Cessna F.152	Modi Aviation Ltd (G-BGLR)	
G-HFCT	Cessna F.152	Stapleford Flying Club Ltd	
G-HGAS	Cameron N-77 balloon	N. J. Tovey	
G-HGPI	SOCATA TB20 Trinidad	M. J. Jackson/Bournemouth	
G-HGRB	Robinson R44	Hangar 8 Ltd (G-BZIN)	
G-HHAA	HS. Buccaneer S.2B (XX885)	Hawker Hunter Aviation Ltd/Scampton	
G-HHAB	Hawker Hunter F.58	Hawker Hunter Aviation Ltd	
G-HHAC	Hawker Hunter F.58 (J-4021)	Hawker Hunter Aviation Ltd/Scampton (G-BWIU)	
G-HHAF	Hawker Hunter F.58 (J-4081)	Hawker Hunter Aviation Ltd (G-BWKB)	
G-HHAV	MS.894A Rallye Minerva	AV Flying Group (G-AYDG)	
G-HHOG	Robinson R44 II	Longmint Group Ltd	
G-HIBM	Cameron N-145 balloon	Alba Ballooning Ltd	
G-HIEL	Robinson R22 Beta	Hields Aviation/Sherburn	
G-HIJK	Cessna 421C	Caernarfon Airworld Ltd (G-OSAL)	
G-HIJN	Ikarus C.42 FB100	J. R. North	
G-HILO	Rockwell Commander 114	F. H. Parkes	
G-HILS	Cessna F.172H	Lowdon Aviation Group/Blackbushe (G-AWCH)	
G-HILT	SOCATA TB10 Tobago	S. R. O'Brien	
G-HILZ	Van's RV-8	A. G. & E. A. Hill	
G-HIND	Maule MT-7-235	M. A. Ashmole	
G-HINZ	Avtec Jabiru SK	B. Faupel	
G-HIPE	Sorrell SNS-7 Hiperbipe	B. G. Ell	
G-HIPO	Robinson R22 Beta	SI Plan Electronics (Research) Ltd (G-BTGB)	
G-HIRE	GA-7 Cougar	London Aerial Tours Ltd/Biggin Hill (G-BGSZ)	
G-HISS	Aerotek Pitts S-2A Special	L. V. Adams & J. Maffia/Panshanger (G-BLVU)	
G-HITM	Raj Hamsa X'Air 582 (1)	G-HITM Flying Group	
G-HIUP	Cameron A-250 balloon	Bridges Van Hire Ltd	
G-HIVA	Cessna 337A	G. J. Banfield (G-BAES)	
G-HIVE	Cessna F.150M	M. P. Lynn/Sibson (G-BCXT)	
G-HIYA	Best Off Skyranger 912(2)	R. D. & C. M. Parkinson	
G-HIZZ	Robinson R22 Beta – II	Flyfare (G-CNDY/G-BXEW)	
G-HJSM	Schempp-Hirth Nimbus 4DM	60 Group (G-ROAM)	
G-HJSS	AIA Stampe SV.4C (modified)	H. J. Smith (G-AZNF)	
G-HKHM	Hughes 369B	Heli Air Ltd/Wellesbourne	
G-HLCF	Starstreak Shadow SA-II	G. J. Chater	
G-HMBJ	Rockwell Commander 114B	Bravo Juliet Aviation Ltd	

G-HMED – G-HSDW | BRITISH CIVIL REGISTRATIONS

Notes	Reg	Type	Owner or Operator
	G-HMED	PA-28-161 Warrior III	Eglinton Flying Club Ltd
	G-HMEI	Dassault Falcon 900	Executive Jet Group Ltd
	G-HMEV	Dassault Falcon 900	Maughold Ltd
	G-HMJB	PA-34-220T Seneca III	Cross Atlantic Ventures Ltd
	G-HMMV	Cessna 525 CitationJet	EBJ Sales Ltd
	G-HMPF	Robinson R44	Mightycraft Ltd
	G-HMPH	Bell 206B JetRanger 2	Bubnell Ltd (G-BBUY)
	G-HMPT	Agusta-Bell 206B JetRanger 2	Helicopter Express Ltd
	G-HMSS	Bell 206B JetRanger 2	Kilrush Aviation Services
	G-HNGE	Ikarus C42 FB100	Haimoss Ltd
	G-HNJC	Dassault Falcon 900EX	Newjetco (Europe) Ltd
	G-HNTR	Hawker Hunter T.7 (XL571:V) ★	Yorkshire Air Museum/Elvington
	G-HOBO	Denney Kitfox Mk 4	J. P. Donovan
	G-HOCK	PA-28 Cherokee 180	G-HOCK Flying Club (G-AVSH)
	G-HOFC	Shaw Europa	W. R. Mills
	G-HOFM	Cameron N-56 balloon	Magical Adventures Ltd
	G-HOGS	Cameron 90 Pig SS balloon	Magical Adventures Ltd
	G-HOHO	Colt Santa Claus SS balloon	Oxford Promotions (UK) Ltd/USA
	G-HOLY	ST.10 Diplomate	M. K. Barsham
	G-HOLZ	Agusta-Bell 206B JetRanger II	Skylink UK Ltd/Gamston (G-CDBT)
	G-HOME	Colt 77A balloon	Anglia Balloon School Tardis
	G-HONG	Slingsby T.67M Firefly 200	Jewel Aviation Ltd
	G-HONI	Robinson R22 Beta	Patriot Aviation Ltd/Cranfield (G-SEGO)
	G-HONK	Cameron O-105 balloon	T. G. S. Dixon
	G-HONY	Lilliput Type 1 Srs A balloon	A. E. & D. E. Thomas
	G-HOOD	SOCATA TB20 Trinidad GT	M. J. Hoodless
	G-HOOV	Cameron N-56 balloon	H. R. Evans
	G-HOPA	Lindstrand LBL-35A balloon	S. F. Burden/Netherlands
	G-HOPE	Beech F33A Bonanza	Hope Aviation
	G-HOPI	Cameron N-42 balloon	Ballonwerbung Hamburg GmbH/Germany
	G-HOPR	Lindstrand LBL-25A balloon	K. C. Tanner
	G-HOPY	Van's RV-6A	R. C. Hopkinson
	G-HORN	Cameron V-77 balloon	S. Herd
	G-HOSS	Beech F33A	T. D. Broadhurst
	G-HOTI	Colt 77A balloon	R. Ollier
	G-HOTT	Cameron O-120 balloon	D. L. Smith
	G-HOTZ	Colt 77B balloon	C. J. & S. M. Davies
	G-HOUS	Colt 31A balloon	The British Balloon Museum and Library
	G-HOWE	Thunder Ax7-77 balloon	M. F. Howe
	G-HOWL	RAF 2000 GTX-SE gyroplane	C. J. Watkinson
	G-HOXN	Van's RV-9	XRay November Flying Club
	G-HPAD	Bell 206B JetRanger 2	Helipad Ltd (G-CITZ/G-BRTB)
	G-HPOL	MDH MD-902 Explorer	Humberside Police Authority
	G-HPSB	Rockwell Commander 114B	International Employment Services Ltd/Guernsey
	G-HPSE	Rockwell Commander 114B	Commander High Performance School Europe Ltd/Guernsey
	G-HPSF	Rockwell Commander 114B	Three Foxtrot Group/Guernsey
	G-HPSL	Rockwell Commander 114B	Hallard (Guernsey) Ltd
	G-HPUX	Hawker Hunter T.7 (XL587)	Hawker Hunter Aviation Ltd/Scampton
	G-HRAK	AS.350B. Ecureuil	R. A. Kingston
	G-HRBS	Robinson R22 Beta	Insight Human Resource and Management Consultancy Ltd
	G-HRCC	Robin HR200/100	P. S. Wilson
	G-HRDS	Gulfstream GV-SP(550)	Fayair (Jersey) Ltd
	G-HRHE	Robinson R22 Beta	Mandarin Aviation Ltd (G-BTWP)
	G-HRHI	Beagle B.206 Srs 1 Basset (XS770)	M. D. Lewis
	G-HRHS	Robinson R44	Stratus Aviation Ltd/Hong Kong
	G-HRIO	Robin HR.100/120	C. D. B. Cope/Isle of Man
	G-HRLI	Hawker Hurricane 1 (V7497)	Hawker Restorations Ltd
	G-HRLK	SAAB 91D/2 Safir	Sylmar Aviation & Services Ltd (G-BRZY)
	G-HRLM	Brügger MB.2 Colibri	D. G. Reid
	G-HRLO	Hawker Hurricane Mk. X	Hawker Restorations Ltd
	G-HRNT	Cessna 182S	Dingle Star Ltd
	G-HROI	Rockwell Commander RC.112	Intereuropean Aviation Ltd
	G-HRPN	Robinson R44	Spirit Communications (UK) Ltd/Gamston
	G-HRVD	CCF Harvard IV	Anglia Flight (G-BSBC)
	G-HRYZ	PA-28-180 Cherokee Archer	Lees Avionics Ltd (G-WACR/G-BCZF)
	G-HSDW	Bell 206B JetRanger 2	Greatsearch Ltd

180

BRITISH CIVIL REGISTRATIONS

G-HSKI – G-ICAB

Reg	Type	Owner or Operator	Notes
G-HSKI	Aviat A-1B	C. J. R. Flint	
G-HSLA	Robinson R22 Beta	D. I. Pointon (G-BRTI)	
G-HSOO	Hughes 369HE	Edwards Aviation (G-BFYJ)	
G-HSTH	Lindstrand LBL. HS-110 balloon	Balloonsport Helmut Seitz/Germany	
G-HTAX	PA-31-350 Navajo Chieftain	Hadagain Investments Ltd	
G-HTEL	Robinson R44	Forestdale Hotels Ltd	
G-HTRL	PA-34-220T Seneca III	Air Medical Fleet Ltd (G-BXXY)	
G-HUBB	Partenavia P.68B	G-HUBB Ltd	
G-HUCH	Cameron 80 Carrots SS balloon	Magical Adventures Ltd (G-BYPS)	
G-HUEW	Shaw Europa XS	C, R. Wright	
G-HUEY	Bell UH-1H	Argonauts Holdings Ltd	
G-HUFF	Cessna 182P	A. E. G. Cousins	
G-HUGO	Colt 240A balloon	P. G. Hall	
G-HUGS	Robinson R22 Beta	C. G. P. Holden (G-BYHD)	
G-HUKA	MDH Hughes 369E	B. P. Stein (G-OSOO)	
G-HULK	Skyranger 912(2)	L. C. Stockman	
G-HULL	Cessna F.150M	Hull Aero Club Ltd	
G-HUMH	Van's RV-9A	H. A. Daines	
G-HUNI	Bellanca 7GCBC Scout	T. I. M. Paul	
G-HUPW	Hawker Hurricane 1 (R4118:UP-W)	Minmere Farm Partnership	
G-HURI	CCF Hawker Hurricane XIIA	Historic Aircraft Collection Ltd/Duxford (Z5140/HA-C)	
G-HURN	Robinson R22 Beta	Sloane Helicopters Ltd	
G-HURR	Hawker Hurricane XIIB (BE417)	Spitfire Ltd/Duxford	
G-HUSK	Aviat A-1B	P. H. Yarrow & A. T. Duke	
G-HUTT	Denney Kitfox Mk 2	P. J. Gibbs	
G-HUTY	Van's RV-7	S. A. Hutt	
G-HVAN	RL-5A LW Sherwood Ranger	H. T. H. van Neck	
G-HVBF	Lindstrand LBL-210A balloon	Virgin Balloon Flights	
G-HVIP	Hawker Hunter T.68	K. G. Theurer/Germany	
G-HVRD	PA-31-350 Navajo Chieftain	T. Khalil (G-BEZU)	
G-HVRZ	Eurocopter EC 120B	EDM Helicopters Ltd	
G-HWAA	Eurocopter EC 135T2	Bond Air Services Ltd	
G-HXTD	Robin DR.400/180	Richmond Aviation Ltd	
G-HYAK	IDA Bacau Yakovlev Yak-52	Goodridge (UK) Ltd	
G-HYLT	PA-32R-301 Saratoga SP	G. G. L. James	
G-HYST	Enstrom 280FX	S. Patten/Barton	
G-IAGD	Robinson R22 Beta	E. Warren & ptnrs/Ireland (G-DRAI)	
G-IAJS	Ikarus C.42 FB UK	A. J. Slater	
G-IANB	Glaser-Dirks DG-800B	I. S. Bullous	
G-IANC	SOCATA TB10 Tobago	I. Corbin (G-BIAK)	
G-IANH	SOCATA TB10 Tobago	XD Flight Management Ltd	
G-IANI	Shaw Europa XS T-G	I. F. Rickard & I. A. Watson	
G-IANJ	Cessna F.150K	Messrs Rees of Poyston West (G-AXVW)	
G-IANN	Kolb Twinstar Mk 3	I. Newman	
G-IANV	Diamond DA42 Twin Star	Spirit Communications (UK) Ltd	
G-IANW	AS.350B3 Ecureuil	Milford Aviation Services Ltd	
G-IARC	Stoddard-Hamilton Glastar	A. A. Craig	
G-IASL	Beech 60 Duke	Applied Sweepers Ltd (G-SING)	
G-IATU	Cessna 182P	R. J. Bird (G-BIRS)	
G-IBAZ	Ikarus C.42 FB100	B. R. Underwood	
G-IBBC	Cameron 105 Sphere SS balloon	Balloon Preservation Group	
G-IBBS	Shaw Europa	R. H. Gibbs	
G-IBED	Robinson R22A	Brian Seedle Helicopters Blackpool (G-BMHN)	
G-IBET	Cameron 70 Can SS balloon	M. R. Humphrey & J. R. Clifton	
G-IBFC	BFC Challenger II	K. N. Dickinson	
G-IBFP	VPM .M.16 Tandem Trainer	B. F. Pearson	
G-IBFW	PA-28R-201 Arrow III	B. Walker & Co (Dursley) Ltd	
G-IBHH	Hughes 269C	Biggin Hill Helicopters (G-BSCD)	
G-IBIG	Bell 206B JetRanger 3	Big Heli-Charter Ltd (G-BORV)	
G-IBLU	Cameron Z-90 balloon	John Aimo Balloons SAS/Italy	
G-IBMS	Robinson R44	Beoley Mill Software Ltd	
G-IBZS	Cessna 182S	D. C. Shepherd	
G-ICAB	Robinson R44	Northumbria Helicopters Ltd	

G-ICAS – G-IIIT BRITISH CIVIL REGISTRATIONS

Notes	Reg	Type	Owner or Operator
	G-ICAS	Pitts S-2B Special	J. C. Smith
	G-ICBM	Stoddard-Hamilton Glasair III Turbine	G. V. Walters & D. N. Brown
	G-ICCL	Robinson R22 Beta	Torfield Aviation Ltd (G-ORZZ)
	G-ICES	Thunder Ax6-56 balloon	British Balloon Museum & Library Ltd
	G-ICKY	Lindstrand LBL-77A balloon	M. J. Green
	G-ICMT	Evektor EV-97 Eurostar	C. M. Theakstone
	G-ICOI	Lindstrand LBL-105A balloon	F. Schroeder/Germany
	G-ICOM	Cessna F.172M	C. G. Elesmore (G-BFXI)
	G-ICON	Rutan LongEz	S. J. & M. A. Carradice
	G-ICRS	Ikarus C.42 FB UK Cyclone	Ikarus Flying Group Ltd
	G-ICSG	AS.355F1 Twin Squirrel	Stratton Motor Co (Norfolk) Ltd (G-PAMI/G-BUSA)
	G-ICWT	Pegasus Quantum 15-912	C. W. Taylor
	G-IDAB	Cessna 550 Citation Bravo	Errigal Aviation Ltd
	G-IDAY	Skyfox CA-25N Gazelle	G. G. Johnstone
	G-IDDI	Cameron N-77 balloon	PSH Skypower Ltd
	G-IDII	Dan Rihn DR.107 One Design	C. Darlow
	G-IDOL	Evektor EV-97 Eurostar	T. D. Baker, J. J. Lynch & C. Moore
	G-IDPH	PA-28-181 Archer III	D. Holland
	G-IDSL	Flight Design CT2K	W. D. Dewey
	G-IDUP	Enstrom 280C Shark	Antique Buildings Ltd (G-BRZF)
	G-IDWR	Hughes 369HS	Copley Electrical Contractors (G-AXEJ)
	G-IEIO	PA-34-200T Seneca II	Jade Air PLC
	G-IEJH	Jodel 150A	A. Turner & D. Worth/Crowfield (G-BPAM)
	G-IEYE	Robin DR.400/180	G. Wood
	G-IFAB	Cessna F.182Q	Manda Construction Ltd
	G-IFBP	AS.350B2 Ecureuil	Frank Bird Aviation
	G-IFFR	PA-32 Cherokee Six 300	D. J. D. Ritchie & ptnrs (G-BWVO)
	G-IFIF	Cameron TR-60 balloon	Cameron Balloons Ltd
	G-IFIT	PA-31-350 Navajo Chieftain	Dart Group PLC/Bournemouth (G-NABI/G-MARG)
	G-IFLE	Aerotechnik EV-97 TeamEurostar UK	Euravia Glight
	G-IFLI	AA-5A Cheetah	I-Fly Group Ltd
	G-IFLP	PA-34-200T Seneca II	Tayflite Ltd/Perth
	G-IFTE	HS.125 Srs 700B	Albion Aviation Management Ltd (G-BFVI)
	G-IFTS	Robinson R44	G. P. Jones
	G-IGEL	Cameron N-90 balloon	Computacenter Ltd
	G-IGGL	SOCATA TB10 Tobago	G-IGGL Flying Group/White Waltham (G-BYDC)
	G-IGHH	Enstrom 480	Axecroft Ltd
	G-IGII	Shaw Europa	C. D. Peacock
	G-IGLA	Colt 240A balloon	Heart of England Balloons
	G-IGLE	Cameron V-90 balloon	A. A. Laing
	G-IGLZ	Champion 8KCAB	Woodgate Aviation (IOM) Ltd
	G-IGNL	Robinson R44	Fly Freedom Ltd
	G-IGPW	Eurocopter EC 120B	Helihopper Ltd (G-CBRI)
	G-IGTE	SIAI Marchetti F.260	D. Fletcher & J. J. Watts
	G-IHOP	Cameron Z-31 balloon	N. W. Roberts
	G-IHOT	Aerotechnik EV-97 Eurostar UK	S. Sebastian
	G-IIAC	Aeronca 11AC Chief	G. R. Moore (G-BTPY)
	G-IIAN	Aero Designs Pulsar	I. G. Harrison
	G-IICI	Aviat Pitts S-2C Special	D. G. Cowden
	G-IICX	Schempp-Hirth Ventus 2cxT	Southern Sailplanes
	G-IIDI	Extra EA.300/L	Power Aerobatics Ltd (G-XTRS)
	G-IIDY	Aerotek Pitts S-2B Special	The S-2B Group (G-BPVP
	G-IIEI	Extra EA.300/S	Aerobatic Displays Ltd
	G-IIEX	Extra EA.300/L	Extreme Aerobatics Ltd/Kemble
	G-IIFR	Robinson R22 Beta II	Wrightson Aviation & Engineering
	G-IIGI	Van's RV-4	IIGI Flying Club
	G-IIID	Dan Rihn DR.107 One Design	D. A. Kean
	G-IIIE	Aerotek Pitts S-2B Special	D. Dobson
	G-IIIG	Boeing Stearman A75N1	F. & S. Vormezeele/Belgium (G-BSDR)
	G-IIII	Aerotek Pitts S-2B Special	Four Eyes Aerobatics Ltd/Barton
	G-IIIL	Pitts S-1T Special	Empyreal Airways Ltd
	G-IIIM	Stolp SA.100 Starduster	H. Mackintosh
	G-IIIO	Schempp-Hirth Ventus 2CM	S. J. Clark
	G-IIIR	Pitts S-1S Special	R. O. Rogers
	G-IIIS	Sukhoi Su-26M2	Airtime Aerobatics Ltd
	G-IIIT	Aerotek Pitts S-2A Special	Aerobatic Displays Ltd

BRITISH CIVIL REGISTRATIONS   G-IIIV – G-INGA

Reg	Type	Owner or Operator	Notes
G-IIIV	Pitts Super Stinker 11-260	S. D. Barnard	
G-IIIX	Pitts S-1S Special	D. S. T. Eggleton (G-LBAT/G-UCCI/G-BIYN)	
G-IIIZ	Sukhoi Su-26M	P. M. M. Bonhommy	
G-IIMI	Extra EA.300/L	Firebird Aerobatics Ltd/Denham	
G-IIMT	Bushby-Long Midget Mustang	J. J. Cooke (G-BDGA)	
G-IINI	Van's RV-9A	G. J. Burlington	
G-IIPT	Robinson R22 Beta	Milford Aviation (G-FUSI)	
G-IIRG	Stoddard-Hamilton Glasair IIS RG	A. C. Lang	
G-IIUI	Extra EA.300/S	M. G. & J. R. Jefferies & C. Scrope (G-CCBD)	
G-IIVI	CAP-232	Skylane Aviation Ltd	
G-IIXI	Extra EA.300/L	S. G. Jones & Pelham Ltd	
G-IIXX	Parsons 2-seat gyroplane	J. M. Montgomerie	
G-IIYK	Yakovlev Yak-50	D. A. Hammant	
G-IIZI	Extra EA.300	S. G. Jones & Power Aerobatics Ltd	
G-IJAC	Light Aero Avid Speedwing Mk 4	I. J. A. Charlton	
G-IJAG	Cessna 182T Skylane	AG Group	
G-IJBB	Enstrom 480	Toure International Ltd (G-LIVA/G-PBTT)	
G-IJMC	VPM M-16 Tandem Trainer	D. C. Fairbrass (G-POSA/G-BVJM)	
G-IJMI	Extra EA.300/L	Aerobatiques LLP	
G-IJQE	PA-28RT-201T Turbo Arrow IV	J. H. Bailey	
G-IJYS	BAe Jetstream 3102	Eastern Airways (G-BTZT)	
G-IKAP	Cessna T.303	T. M. Beresford	
G-IKAT	Diamond DA20-C1	S. J. Phillips	
G-IKBP	PA-28-161 Warrior II	K. B. Page	
G-IKEA	Cameron 120 Ikea SS balloon	IKEA Ltd	
G-IKES	Stoddard-Hamilton GlaStar	M. Stow	
G-IKEV	Jabiru UL-450	K. J. Bream	
G-IKON	Van's RV-4	S. Sampson	
G-IKOS	Cessna 550 Citation Bravo	Medox Enterprises Ltd	
G-IKRK	Shaw Europa	K. R. Kesterton	
G-IKRS	Ikarus C.42 FK UK Cyclone	J. E. Lockwood	
G-IKUS	Ikarus C.42 FB UK Cyclone	C. I. Law	
G-ILDA	VS.361 Spitfire HF.IX	P. W. Portelli (G-BXHZ)	
G-ILEE	Colt 56A balloon	G. I. Lindsay	
G-ILES	Cameron O-90 balloon	G. N. Lantos	
G-ILET	Robinson R44 II	Lear Group Ltd	
G-ILLE	Boeing Stearman A75L3 (379)	M. Minkler	
G-ILLG	Robinson R44 II	C. B. Ellis	
G-ILLY	PA-28-181 Archer II	R. A. & G. M. Spiers	
G-ILMD	Pilatus PC-12/45	N. J. Vetch	
G-ILRS	Ikarus C.42 FB UK Cyclone	Knitsley Mill Leisure Ltd	
G-ILSE	Corby CJ-1 Starlet	S. Stride	
G-ILTS	PA-32 Cherokee Six 300	Foremans Aviation Ltd (G-CVOK)	
G-IMAC	Canadair CL-600-2A12 Challenger	Gama Aviation Ltd	
G-IMAB	Europa XS	T. J. Price	
G-IMAG	Colt 77A balloon ★	Balloon Preservation Group	
G-IMAN	Colt 31A balloon	Benedikt Haggeney GmbH/Germany	
G-IMBI	QAC Quickie 1	J. D. King (G-BWIT)	
G-IMBY	Pietenpol AirCamper	P. F. Bockh	
G-IMCD	Van's RV-7	I. G. McDowell	
G-IMEA	Beech 200 Super King Air	M. Magrabi (G-OWAX)	
G-IMEC	PA-31 Navajo C	Airtime Aviation France Ltd (G-BFOM)	
G-IMGL	Beech 200 Super King Air	Errigal Aviation Ltd	
G-IMIC	IDA Bacau Yakovlev Yak-52	C Vogelgesang & R. Hockey	
G-IMLI	Cessna 310Q	Oakwood Leisure Ltd (G-AZYK)	
G-IMME	Zenair CH.701 STOL	M. Spearman	
G-IMNY	Escapade 912	D. S. Bremner	
G-IMOK	Hoffmann HK-36R Super Dimona	A. L. Garfield	
G-IMPX	Rockwell Commander 112B	J. C. Stewart	
G-IMPY	Light Aero Avid Flyer C	T. R. C. Griffin	
G-IMUP	Tanarg/Ixess 15 912S (1)	P. D. Hill	
G-INAV	Aviation Composites Mercury	I. Shaw	
G-INCA	Glaser-Dirks DG.400	K. D. Hook	
G-INCE	Skyranger 912(2)	N.P. Sleigh	
G-INDC	Cessna T.303	J-Ross Developments Ltd	
G-INDX	Robinson R44	Kinetic Computers Ltd	
G-INDY	Robinson R44	Lincoln Aviation	
G-INGA	Thunder Ax8-84 balloon	M. L. J. Ritchie	

183

G-INGE – G-ITWB — BRITISH CIVIL REGISTRATIONS

Notes	Reg	Type	Owner or Operator
	G-INGE	Thruster T.600N	Thruster 1 Group
	G-INIT	SOCATA TB9 Tampico	P. R. Shakeshaft
	G-INJA	Ikarus C42 FB 100VLA	J. W. G. Andrews
	G-INKY	Robinson R22 Beta	Saltire Helicopters Ltd (G-UDAY)
	G-INNI	Jodel D.112	V. E. Murphy
	G-INNY	SE-5A (replica) (F5459:Y)	M. J. Speakman
	G-INOW	Monnett Moni	W. C. Brown
	G-INSR	Cameron N-90 balloon	The Smith and Pinching Group Ltd & P. Phillips
	G-INTO	Pilatus PC-12/45	Pilatus PC-12 Centre UK Ltd
	G-INTS	Van's RV-4	N. J. F. Campbell
	G-IOCO	Beech 58 Baron	Arenberg Consultadoria E Servicos Lda/Madeira
	G-IOFR	Lindstrand LBL-105A balloon	RAF Halton Hot Air Balloon Club
	G-IOIA	I.I.I. Sky Arrow 650T	P.J. Lynch, P.G. Ward, N.J.C. Ray
	G-IOOI	Robin DR.400/160	N. B. Mason
	G-IOOX	Learjet 45	Hundred Percent Aviation Ltd
	G-IOPT	Cessna 182P	Indy Oscar Group
	G-IORG	Robinson R22 Beta	Beds Heli Services Ltd (G-ZAND)
	G-IOSI	Jodel DR.1051	Sicile Flying Group
	G-IOSO	Jodel DR.1050	A. E. Jackson
	G-IOWA	FBN BN-2A-27 Islander	Isle of Wight Aviation Ltd (G-BCWO)
	G-IOWE	Shaw Europa XS	P. A. Lowe
	G-IPAL	Cessna 550 Citation Bravo	Pacific Aviation Ltd
	G-IPAT	Jabiru SP	G. Fleck
	G-IPAX	Cessna 560XL Citation Excel	Pacific Aviation Ltd
	G-IPFM	Mongomerie-Bensen B.8MR	I. P. F. Meikeljohn (G-BZJR)
	G-IPKA	Alpi Pioneer 300	I. P. King
	G-IPSI	Grob G.109B	D. G. Margetts (G-BMLO)
	G-IPSY	Rutan Vari-Eze	R. A. Fairclough/Biggin Hill
	G-IPUP	Beagle B.121 Pup 2	R. G. Hayes
	G-IRAF	RAF 2000 GTX-SE gyroplane	P. Robichaud
	G-IRAL	Thruster T600N 450	J. Giraldez
	G-IRIS	AA-5B Tiger	C. Nichol (G-BIXU)
	G-IRJX	Avro RJX-100 ★	Manchester Heritage Museum
	G-IRKB	PA-28R-201 Arrow III	R. K. Brierley
	G-IRLY	Colt 90A balloon	C. E. R. Smart
	G-IRLZ	Lindstrand LBL-60X balloon	A. M. Holly
	G-IRON	Shaw Europa XS	T. M. Clark
	G-IRPC	Cessna 182Q	R. Warner (G-BSKM)
	G-IRTH	Lindstrand LBL-150A balloon	A. M. Holly (G-BZTO)
	G-IRYC	Schweizer 269-1	GC Heating
	G-ISAX	PA-28-181 Archer III	M. S. Kontowtt
	G-ISCA	PA-28RT-201 Arrow IV	D. J. & P. Pay
	G-ISDB	PA-28-161 Warrior II	Action Air Services Ltd (G-BWET)
	G-ISDN	Boeing Stearman A75N1	D. R. L. Jones
	G-ISEH	Cessna 182R	C. M. White & R. MacFarlane (G-BIWS)
	G-ISEL	Best Off Skyranger 912 (2)	P. A. Robertson
	G-ISEW	P & M Quik GT450	J. R. Moore
	G-ISFC	PA-31-310 Turbo Navajo B	T. M. Latiff (G-BNEF)
	G-ISHA	PA-28-161 Warrior III	Clever Clogs (Middleton) Ltd
	G-ISHK	Cessna 172S	Matchpage Ltd
	G-ISKA	WSK-PZL Mielec TS-11 Iskra (1018)	P. C. Harper
	G-ISLB	BAe Jetstream 3201	Blue Island Air
	G-ISLC	BAe Jetstream 3202	Blue Island Air
	G-ISLD	BAe Jetstream 3202	Blue Island Air
	G-ISMO	Robinson R22 Beta	Moy Motorsport Ltd
	G-ISPH	Bell 206B JetRanger 2	Blades Aviation (UK) LLP (G-OPJM)
	G-ISSV	Eurocopter EC 155B1	Bristow Helicopters Ltd/Norwich
	G-ISSW	Eurocopter EC 155B1	Bristow Helicopters Ltd/Norwich
	G-ISSY	Eurocopter EC 120B	D. R. Williams (G-CBCG)
	G-ISTT	Thunder Ax8-84 balloon	RAF Halton Hot Air Balloon Club
	G-ITIH	Mystere Falcon 50	Tag Aviation (UK) Ltd
	G-ITII	Aerotech Pitts S-2A Special	Aerobatic Displays Ltd/Booker
	G-ITOI	Cameron N-90 balloon	Flying Pictures Ltd
	G-ITON	Maule MX-7-235	J. R. S. Heaton
	G-ITTI	Pitts S-1S Special	S. C. Hipwell
	G-ITUG	PA-28 Cherokee 180	S. I. Tugwell (G-AVNR)
	G-ITVM	Lindstrand LBL-105A balloon	N. C. Lindsay
	G-ITWB	DHC.1 Chipmunk 22	I. T. Whitaker-Bethe

BRITISH CIVIL REGISTRATIONS

G-IUAN – G-JANI

Reg	Type	Owner or Operator	Notes
G-IUAN	Cessna 525 CitationJet	R. F. Celada SPA/Italy	
G-IUII	Aerostar Yakovlev Yak-52	W. Hanekom	
G-IVAC	Airtour AH-77B balloon	T. D. Gibbs	
G-IVAL	CAB CAP-10B	I. Valentine	
G-IVAN	Shaw TwinEze	A. M. Aldridge	
G-IVAR	Yakovlev Yak-50	A. H. Soper	
G-IVAS	Bell 206B JetRanger 3	G. N. Ratcliffe (G-ONTB/G-MCPI)	
G-IVDM	Schempp Hirth Nimbus 4DM	G. W. Lynch	
G-IVEL	Fournier RF-4D	V. S. E. Norman/Rendcomb (G-AVNY)	
G-IVEN	Robinson R44 II	OKR Group/Ireland	
G-IVER	Shaw Europa XS	I. Phillips	
G-IVET	Shaw Europa	K. J. Fraser	
G-IVII	Vqn's RV-7	M. A. N. Newall	
G-IVIV	Robinson R44	Heletrain Ltd	
G-IVOR	Aeronca 11AC Chief	South Western Aeronca Group	
G-IVYS	Parsons 2-seat gyroplane	R. M. Harris	
G-IWDB	Hawker 800XP	Markoss Aviation Ltd	
G-IWON	Cameron V-90 balloon	D. P. P. Jenkinson (G-BTCV)	
G-IWRB	Agusta A109A-II	Fuel The Jet LLP (G-VIPT)	
G-IWRC	Eurocopter EC 135T2	McAlpine Helicopters Ltd/Kidlington	
G-IXES	Air Creation Ixess 912	G. J. Little	
G-IXII	Christen Eagle II	Eagle Flying Group (G-BPZI)	
G-IXIX	I.I.I. Sky Arrow 650T	M. A. Newman	
G-IYAK	Yakovlev C-11	G. G. L. James	
G-IYCO	Robin DR.400/500	Timgee Holdings Ltd	
G-IZII	Marganski Swift S-1	G. C. Westgate	
G-IZIT	Rans S.6-116 Coyote II	A. J. Best & M. Watson	
G-IZOD	Avtech Jabiru UL	N. J. Stillwell	
G-IZZI	Cessna T.182T	T. J. & P. S. Nicholson	
G-IZZS	Cessna 172S	Walkbury Aviation Ltd	
G-IZZY	Cesna 172R	M. J. Parsons (G-BXSF)	
G-IZZZ	Champion 8KCAB	A.M. Read	
G-JAAB	Avtech Jabiru UL	E. Fogarty	
G-JABB	Avtech Jabiru UL	D. J. Abbott	
G-JABE	Jabiru Aircraft Jabiru UL-D	Alan Developments Ltd (G-CDZX)	
G-JABI	Jabiru Aircraft Jabiru J400	R. A. Shaw Aviation Ltd	
G-JABJ	Jabiru Aircraft Jabiru J400	Hamsard 2668 Ltd	
G-JABO	WAR Focke-Wulf Fw.190A-3	S. P. Taylor (replica)	
G-JABS	Avtech Jabiru UL-450	Jabiru Flying Group	
G-JABU	Jabiru J430	R. J. Chapman	
G-JABY	Avtech Jabiru UL	J. T. Grant	
G-JABZ	Jabiru UL-450	A. C. Barnes	
G-JACA	PA-28-161 Warrior II	Channel Islands Aero Club (Jersey) Ltd	
G-JACB	PA-28-181 Archer III	Channel Islands Aero Club (Jersey) Ltd (G-PNNI)	
G-JACC	PA-28-181 Archer III	Magnum Holdings Ltd (G-GIFT/G-IMVA)	
G-JACK	Cessna 421C	JCT 600 Ltd	
G-JACO	Avtech Jabiru UL	C. D. Matthews/Ireland	
G-JACS	PA-28-181 Archer III	Vector Air Ltd	
G-JADJ	PA-28-181 Archer III	Cumulus Aircraft Rentals Ltd	
G-JAEE	Van's RV-6A	J. A. E. Edser	
G-JAES	Bell 206B JetRanger 3	Heli Charter Wales (G-STOX/G-BNIR)	
G-JAGS	Cessna FRA.150L	RAF Marham Aero Club (G-BAUY)	
G-JAIR	Mainair Blade	A. J. Varga	
G-JAJB	AA-5A Cheetah	J. Bradley	
G-JAJK	PA-31-350 Navajo Chieftain	Keen Leasing (IOM) Ltd (G-OLDB/G-DIXI)	
G-JAJP	Avtech Jabiru UL	J. W. E. Pearson & J. Anderson	
G-JAKF	Robinson R44 Raven II	J. Froggatt Ltd	
G-JAKI	Mooney M.20R	J. M. Moss & D. M. Abrahamson	
G-JAKS	PA-28 Cherokee 160	K. Harper (G-ARVS)	
G-JAMA	Schweizer 269C-1	JWL Helicopters Ltd	
G-JAME	Zenair CH 601UL	S. Hoyle (G-CDFZ)	
G-JAMP	PA-28-151 Warrior	Lapwing Flying Group Ltd/White Waltham (G-BRJU)	
G-JAMY	Shaw Europa XS	J. P. Sharp	
G-JANA	PA-28-181 Archer II	Croaker Aviation/Stapleford	
G-JANB	Colt Flying Bottle SS balloon	Justerini & Brooks Ltd	
G-JANI	Robinson R44	JT Helicopters Ltd	

G-JANN – G-JECF — BRITISH CIVIL REGISTRATIONS

Notes	Reg	Type	Owner or Operator
	G-JANN	PA-34-220T Seneca III	MBC Aviation Ltd/Headcorn
	G-JANO	PA-28RT-201 Arrow IV	Blackpool Aviators Ltd
	G-JANS	Cessna FR.172J	I. G. Aizlewood/Luton
	G-JANT	PA-28-181 Archer II	Janair Aviation Ltd
	G-JARA	Robinson R22 Beta	Northumbria Helicopters Ltd
	G-JASE	PA-28-161 Warrior II	Mid-Anglia School of Flying
	G-JAST	Mooney M.20J -201	S. J. Tillotson
	G-JATD	Robinson R22 Beta	Sycamore Ltd (G-HUMF)
	G-JAVO	PA-28-161 Warrior II	Victor Oscar Ltd/Wellesbourne (G-BSXW)
	G-JAWC	Pegasus Quantum 15-912	M. H. Husey
	G-JAWZ	Pitts S-1S Special	A. R. Harding
	G-JAXS	Avtech Jabiru UL	J. P. Pullin
	G-JAYI	Auster J/1 Autocrat	Aviation Heritage Ltd
	G-JAYS	Skyranger 912S(1)	J. Williams
	G-JAZZ	AA-5A Cheetah	A. J. Radford
	G-JBAS	Neico Lancair 200	B. A. Slater
	G-JBBZ	AS.350B3 Ecureuil	Powersense Ltd
	G-JBDB	Agusta-Bell 206B JetRanger	Dicksons Van World Ltd (G-OOPS/G-BNRD)
	G-JBDH	Robin DR.400/180	W. A. Clark
	G-JBEK	Agusta A109C	Bek Helicopters
	G-JBEN	Mainair Blade 912	G. J. Bentley
	G-JBHH	Bell 206B JetRanger 2	Biggin Hill Helicopters (G-BBFB/G-CJHI/G-CORC/G-SCOO)
	G-JBII	Robinson R22 Beta	Longmint Group Ltd (G-BXLA)
	G-JBIS	Cessna 550 Citation II	247 Jet Ltd
	G-JBIZ	Cessna 550 Citation II	247 Jet Ltd
	G-JBJB	Colt 69A balloon	Justerini & Brooks Ltd
	G-JBKA	Robinson R44	Bon Accord Glass Ltd
	G-JBMC	SOCATA TB10 Tobago	J. McCloskey
	G-JBRN	Cessna 182S	Parallel Flooring Accessories Ltd (G-RITZ)
	G-JBSP	Avtech Jabiru SP-470	C. R. James
	G-JBTR	Van's RV-8A	R. A. Ellis
	G-JBUZ	Robin DR400/180R Remorqueur	G-JBUZ Syndicate
	G-JCAP	Robinson R22 Beta	Italian Clothes Ltd
	G-JCAR	PA-46-350P Malibu Mirage	Aquarelle Investments Ltd
	G-JCAS	PA-28-181 Archer II	Charlie Alpha Ltd
	G-JCBA	Sikorsky S-76B	J. C. Bamford Excavators Ltd/East Midlands
	G-JCBC	Gulfstream GV-SP(550)	J. C. Bamford Excavators Ltd
	G-JCBJ	Sikorsky S-76C	J. C. Bamford Excavators Ltd/East Midlands
	G-JCBX	Dassault Falcon 900EX	J. C. Bamford Excavators Ltd/East Midlands
	G-JCIT	Cessna 208B Grand Caravan	Fly CI Ltd
	G-JCKT	Stemme S.10VT	J. C. Taylor
	G-JCMW	Rand-Robinson KR-2	M. Wildish & J. Cook
	G-JCUB	PA-18 Super Cub 135	N. Cummins & S. Bennett
	G-JDBC	PA-34-200T Seneca II	Bowdon Aviation Ltd (G-BDEF)
	G-JDEE	SOCATA TB20 Trinidad	M. J. Wright & ptnrs (G-BKLA)
	G-JDEL	Jodel 150	K. F. & R. Richardson (G-JDLI)
	G-JDIX	Mooney M.20B	A. L. Hall-Carpenter (G-ARTB)
	G-JDJM	PA-28 Cherokee 140	Hare Flying Group (G-HSJM/G-AYIF)
	G-JEAJ	BAe 146-200	MCC Leasing (No.24) Ltd (G-OLCA)
	G-JEAK	BAe 146-200	Flybe.com (G-OLCB)
	G-JEAM	BAe 146-300	Flybe.com/Air France (G-BTJT)
	G-JEAO	BAe 146-100	Trident Aviation Leasing Services Ltd (G-UKPC/G-BKXZ) (stored)
	G-JEAS	BAe 146-200	Flybe.com (G-OLHB/G-BSRV/G-OSUN)
	G-JEAU	BAe 146-100	Flybe.com/Air France (G-BVUW)
	G-JEAV	BAe 146-200	BAE Systems (Operations) Ltd/Warton
	G-JEAW	BAe 146-200	Flybe.com.
	G-JEAY	BAe-146-200	Flybe.com
	G-JEBA	BAe 146-300	Flybe.com (G-BSYR)
	G-JEBB	BAe 146-300	Flybe.com/Air France
	G-JEBC	BAe 146-300	Flybe.com
	G-JEBD	BAe 146-300	Flybe.com
	G-JEBE	BAe 146-300	Flybe.com
	G-JEBF	BAe 146-300	Flybe.com (G-BTUY/G-NJIC)
	G-JEBG	BAe 146-300	Flybe.com (G-BVCE/G-NJIE)
	G-JEBV	Avro RJ100	Trident Jet Leasing (Ireland) Ltd (G-CDCN)
	G-JECE	DHC.8Q-402 Dash Eight	Flybe.com
	G-JECF	DHC.8Q-402 Dash Eight	Flybe.com

BRITISH CIVIL REGISTRATIONS

G-JECG – G-JGSI

Reg	Type	Owner or Operator	Notes
G-JECG	DHC.8Q-402 Dash Eight	Flybe.com	
G-JECH	DHC.8Q-402 Dash Eight	Flybe.com	
G-JECI	DHC.8Q-402 Dash Eight	Flybe.com	
G-JECJ	DHC.8Q-402 Dash Eight	Flybe.com	
G-JECK	DHC.8Q-402 Dash Eight	Flybe.com	
G-JECL	DHC.8Q-402 Dash Eight	Flybe.com	
G-JECM	DHC.8Q-402 Dash Eight	Flybe.com	
G-JECN	DHC.8Q-402 Dash Eight	Flybe.com	
G-JECO	DHC.8Q-402 Dash Eight	Flybe.com	
G-JECP	DHC.8Q-402 Dash Eight	Flybe.com	
G-JECR	DHC.8Q-402 Dash Eight	Flybe.com	
G-JECS	DHC.8Q-402 Dash Eight	Flybe.com	
G-JECT	DHC.8Q-402 Dash Eight	Flybe.com	
G-JECU	DHC.8Q-402 Dash Eight	Flybe.com	
G-JEDH	Robin DR.400/180	J. B. Hoolahan/Biggin Hill	
G-JEDI	DHC.8Q-402 Dash Eight	Flybe.com	
G-JEDJ	DHC.8Q-402 Dash Eight	Flybe.com	
G-JEDK	DHC.8Q-402 Dash Eight	Flybe.com	
G-JEDL	DHC.8Q-402 Dash Eight	Flybe.com	
G-JEDM	DHC.8Q-402 Dash Eight	Flybe.com	
G-JEDN	DHC.8Q-402 Dash Eight	Flybe.com	
G-JEDO	DHC.8Q-402 Dash Eight	Flybe.com	
G-JEDP	DHC.8Q-402 Dash Eight	Flybe com	
G-JEDR	DHC.8Q-402 Dash Eight	Flybe com	
G-JEDS	Andreasson BA-4B	S. B. Jedburgh (G-BEBT)	
G-JEDT	DHC.8Q-402 Dash Eight	Flybe com	
G-JEDU	DHC.8Q-402 Dash Eight	Flybe com	
G-JEDV	DHC.8Q-402 Dash Eight	Flybe.com	
G-JEDW	DHC.8Q-402 Dash Eight	Flybe.com	
G-JEEP	Evektor EV-97 Eurostar	P. A. Brigstock (G-CBNK)	
G-JEET	Cessna FA.152	Willowair Flying Club (1996) Ltd/Southend (G-BHMF)	
G-JEFA	Robinson R44	Simlot Ltd	
G-JEJE	RAF 2000 GTX-SE gyroplane	J. W. Erswell	
G-JEMA	BAe ATP	PTB (Emerald) Pty Ltd/Blackpool	
G-JEMB	BAe ATP	PTB (Emerald) Pty Ltd/Coventry	
G-JEMC	BAe ATP	PTB (Emerald) Pty Ltd/Blackpool	
G-JEMD	BAe ATP	PTB (Emerald) Pty Ltd/Blackpool	
G-JEME	BAe ATP	PTB (Emerald) Pty Ltd	
G-JEMH	AS.355F2 Twin Squirrel	PJM Helicopters LLP (G-CDFV)	
G-JEMX	Short SD3-60 Variant 100	BAC Leasing Ltd (G-SSWX/G-BNDL)	
G-JEMY	Lindstrand LBL-90A balloon	J. A. Lawton	
G-JENA	Mooney M.20K	P. Leverkuehn/Biggin Hill	
G-JENI	Cessna R.182	R. A. Bentley	
G-JENN	AA-5B Tiger	Shadow Aviation Ltd/Elstree	
G-JENO	Lindstrand LBL-105A balloon	S. F. Redman	
G-JERO	Shaw Europa XS	B. Robshaw & P. Jenkinson	
G-JERS	Robinson R22 Beta	Sloane Helicopters Ltd/Sywell	
G-JESA	Southdown Raven X (modified)	A. E. James (G-MNLB)	
G-JESG	Robinson R44	D. A. Gold	
G-JESI	AS.350B Ecureuil	Staske Construction Ltd (G-JOSS/G-WILX/ G-RAHM/G-UNIC/G-COLN/G-BHIV)	
G-JESS	PA-28R-201T Turbo Arrow III	R. E. Trawicki (G-REIS)	
G-JETC	Cessna 550 Citation II	SJL Aviation LLP (G-JCFR)	
G-JETF	Dassault Falcon 2000EX	TAG Aviation (UK) Ltd	
G-JETH	Hawker Sea Hawk FGA.6 (XE489) ★	P. G. Vallance Ltd/Charlwood	
G-JETI	BAe 125 Srs 800B	Ford Motor Co Ltd/Stansted	
G-JETJ	Cessna 550 Citation II	G-JETJ Ltd (G-EJET/G-DJBE)	
G-JETM	Gloster Meteor T.7 (VZ638) ★	P. G. Vallance Ltd/Charlwood	
G-JETO	Cessna 550 Citation II	Jet Options Ltd (G-RVHT)	
G-JETU	AS.355F2 Twin Squirrel	Marlborough Aviation Ltd	
G-JETX	Bell 206B JetRanger 3	AGL Helicopters	
G-JETZ	Hughes 369E	John Matchett Ltd	
G-JEZZ	Skyranger 582	J. W. Barwick & P. J. Harris	
G-JFMK	Zenair CH.701SP	J. D. Pearson	
G-JFRV	Van's RV-7A	J. H. Fisher	
G-JFWI	Cessna F.172N	Staryear Ltd	
G-JGBI	Bell 206L-4 LongRanger	Dorbcrest Homes Ltd	
G-JGMN	CASA 1.131E Jungmann 2000	P. D. Scandrett/Staverton	
G-JGSI	Pegasus Quantum 15-912	R. Leigh	

G-JHAC – G-JOJO — BRITISH CIVIL REGISTRATIONS

Notes	Reg	Type	Owner or Operator
	G-JHAC	Cessna FRA.150L	J. H. A. Clarke (G-BACM)
	G-JHEW	Robinson R22 Beta	Burbage Farms Ltd
	G-JHKP	Shaw Europa XS	J. D. Heykoop
	G-JHNY	Cameron A.210 balloon	Floarting Sensations Ltd
	G-JHYS	Shaw Europa	S. M. Dawson
	G-JIFI	Schempp-Hirth Duo Discus T	D. K. McCarthy
	G-JIII	Stolp SA.300 Starduster Too	VTIO Co/Cumbernauld
	G-JILL	Rockwell Commander 112TCA	D. Carlton
	G-JILS	Van's RV-8	M. R. Tingle
	G-JILY	Robinson R44	D. B. Heaney
	G-JIMB	Beagle B.121 Pup 1	K. D. H. Gray & P. G. Fowler (G-AWWF)
	G-JIMH	Cessna F.152 II	I. R. Chaplin (G-SHAH)
	G-JIMM	Shaw Europa XS	J. Riley
	G-JIMZ	Van's RV-4	J.W.Hale
	G-JIVE	MDH Hughes 369E	Sleekform Ltd (G-DRAR)
	G-JJAB	Jabiru J400	Propitious Aviation Ltd
	G-JJAN	PA-28-181 Archer II	Redhill Flying Club
	G-JJDC	Aviat A-18 Husky	Technoforce Ltd
	G-JJEN	PA-28-181 Archer III	J. E. Jenkins
	G-JJMX	Dassault Falcon 900EX	J-Max Air Services
	G-JJPJ	Cessna F.172N	P. S. Jegachandran (G-BHKG)
	G-JJSI	BAe 125 Srs 800B	Gama Aviation Ltd (G-OMGG)
	G-JJWL	Robinson R44	Willbeth Ltd
	G-JKAY	Robinson R44	Jamiroquai Ltd
	G-JKMF	Diamond DA40D Star	ADR Aviation
	G-JKMG	Diamond DA40D Star	Diamond Aircraft UK Ltd/Gamston
	G-JKMH	Diamond DA42 Twin Star	ADR Aviation
	G-JKMJ	Diamond DA42 Twin Star	Medox Enterprises Ltd
	G-JLAT	Aerotechnik EV-97 Eurostar	J. Latimer/Barton
	G-JLCA	PA-34-200T Seneca II	C. A. S. Atha (G-BOKE)
	G-JLEE	Agusta-Bell 206B JetRanger 3	J. S. Lee (G-JOKE/G-CSKY/G-TALY)
	G-JLHS	Beech A36 Bonanza	I. G. Meredith
	G-JLIN	PA-28-161 Cadet	Westmorland Aviation Ltd
	G-JLLT	Aerotechnik EV-97 Eurostar	J. Latimer
	G-JLMW	Cameron V-77 balloon	J. L. McK. Watkins
	G-JLRW	Beech 76 Duchess	Airways Flight Training
	G-JMAA	Boeing 757-3CQ	Thomas Cook Airlines
	G-JMAB	Boeing 757-3CQ	Thomas Cook Airlines
	G-JMAC	BAe Jetstream 4100 ★	Jetstream Club, Liverpool Marriott Hotel South, Speke (G-JAMD/G-JXLI)
	G-JMAN	Mainair Blade 912S	J. Manuel
	G-JMAX	Hawker 800XP	J-Max Air Services
	G-JMCD	Boeing 757-25F	Thomas Cook Airlines
	G-JMCE	Boeing 757-25F	Thomas Cook Airlines
	G-JMCF	Boeing 757-28A	Thomas Cook Airlines
	G-JMCG	Boeing 757-2G5	Thomas Cook Airlines
	G-JMDI	Schweizer 269C	J. J. Potter (G-FLAT)
	G-JMDW	Cessna 550 Citation II	Phoenix Air Ltd
	G-JMJR	Cameron Z-90	J. M. Reck/France
	G-JMKE	Cessna 172S	115CR (146) Ltd
	G-JMON	Agusta A109A-II	Jermon Ltd (G-RFDS/G-BOLA)
	G-JMTS	Robin DR.400/180	P. A. Mansbridge
	G-JMTT	PA-28R-201T Turbo Arrow III	TT Group (G-BMHM)
	G-JMXA	Agusta A109E Power	J-Max Air Services
	G-JNAS	AA-5A Cheetah	C. J. Williams
	G-JNET	Robinson R22 Beta	R. L. Hartshorn
	G-JNNB	Colt 90A balloon	N. A. P. Godfrey
	G-JOAL	Beech B200 Super King Air	South Coast Air Charter LLP
	G-JOBA	P & M Quik GT450	A. R. Oliver
	G-JODI	Agusta A109A-II	Foxdale Consulting Ltd/Isle of Man (G-BVCJ/G-CLRL/G-EJCB)
	G-JODL	Jodel D.1050/M	D. Silsbury
	G-JOEM	Airbus A.320-231	MyTravel Airways (G-OUZO)
	G-JOEY	BN-2A Mk III-2 Trislander	Aurigny Air Services/Guernsey (G-BDGG)
	G-JOIE	American Champion 7GCAA Citabria	N. Baumber
	G-JOJO	Cameron A-210 balloon	A. C. Rawson & J. J. Rudoni

BRITISH CIVIL REGISTRATIONS

G-JOLY – G-JWBI

Reg	Type	Owner or Operator	Notes
G-JOLY	Cessna 120	B. V. Meade	
G-JONB	Robinson R22 Beta	J. Bignall	
G-JONG	Rotorway Executive 162F	J. V. George	
G-JONH	Robinson R22 Beta	Productivity Computer Solutions Ltd	
G-JONI	Cessna FA.152	P. J. Gerrard & M. Cunliffe (G-BFTU)	
G-JONO	Colt 77A balloon	The Sandcliffe Motor Group	
G-JONY	Cyclone AX2000 HKS	K. R. Matheson	
G-JONZ	Cessna 172P	Truman Aviation Ltd/Tollerton	
G-JOOL	Mainair Blade 912	J. R. Gibson	
G-JOON	Cessna 182D	Go Skydive Group	
G-JOPT	Cessna 560 Citation V	Jet Options Ltd	
G-JOSH	Cameron N-105 balloon	M. White	
G-JOST	Shaw Europa	A. V. Orchard & J. A. Austin	
G-JOYD	Robinson R22 Beta	RH Property Services Ltd (G-SIMN)	
G-JOYT	PA-28-181 Archer II	John K. Cathcart Ltd (G-BOVO)	
G-JOYZ	PA-28-181 Archer III	S. W. & J. E. Taylor	
G-JPAL	AS.355N Twin Squirrel	JPM Ltd	
G-JPAT	Robin HR.200/100	L. Giraidier & A. J. McCulloch (G-BDJN)	
G-JPJR	Robinson R44	Anglian Helicopters Ltd	
G-JPMA	Avtech Jabiru UL	J. P. Metcalfe	
G-JPOT	PA-32R-301 Saratoga SP	P.J.Wolstencroft (G-BIYM)	
G-JPRO	P.84 Jet Provost T.5A (XW433)	Edwalton Aviation Ltd	
G-JPSX	Dassault Falcon 900EX Easy	Sorven Aviation Ltd	
G-JPTT	Enstrom 480	P. G. Lawrence (G-PPAH)	
G-JPTV	P.84 Jet Provost T.5A (XW354)	S. J. Davies	
G-JPVA	P.84 Jet Provost T.5A (XW289)	T. J. Manna/North Weald (G-BVXT)	
G-JPWM	Skyranger 912 (2)	R. S. Waters & M. Pittock	
G-JRED	Robinson R44	J. Reddington Ltd	
G-JREE	Maule MX-7-180	J. M. P. Ree	
G-JRKD	Jodel D.18	R. K. Davies	
G-JRME	Jodel D.140E	J. E. & L. L. Rex	
G-JRSL	Agusta A109E Power	Perment Ltd	
G-JSAK	Robinson R22 Beta II	Tukair Aircraft Charter	
G-JSAR	AS.332L-2 Super Puma	Bristow Helicopters Ltd	
G-JSAT	BN-2T Turbine Islander	Rhine Army Parachute Association/Germany (G-BVFK)	
G-JSON	Cameron N-105 balloon	Up and Away Ballooning Ltd	
G-JSPC	BN-2T Turbine Islander	Rhine Army Parachute Association/ Germany (G-BUBG)	
G-JSPL	Avtech Jabiru SPL-450	J. A. Lord	
G-JSRV	Van's RV-6	J. Stringer	
G-JSSD	HP.137 Jetstream 3001 ★	Museum of Flight/East Fortune	
G-JTCA	PA-23 Aztec 250E	J. D. Tighe/Sturgate (G-BBCU)	
G-JTEM	Van's RV-7	J. C. Bacon	
G-JTNC	Cessna 500 Citation	Eurojet Aviation Ltd (G-OEJA/G-BWFL)	
G-JTPC	Aeromot AMT-200 Super Ximango	G-JTPC Falcon 3 Group	
G-JTWO	Piper J-2 Cub	C. C. Silk (G-BPZR)	
G-JUDD	Avtech Jabiru UL-450H	C. Judd	
G-JUDE	Robin DR.400/180	Bravo India Flying Group Ltd/Liverpool	
G-JUDI	AT-6D Harvard III (FX301)	A. A. Hodgson	
G-JUDY	AA-5A Cheetah	Gray Hooper Holt LLP	
G-JUGE	Aerotechnik EV-97 TeamEurostar UK	L. J. Appleby	
G-JUIN	Cessna 303	M. J. & J. M. Newman/Denham	
G-JULE	P & M Quik GT450	J. A. Gilchrist	
G-JULL	Stemme S.10VT	J. P. C. Fuchs	
G-JULU	Cameron V-90 balloon	N. J. Appleton	
G-JULZ	Shaw Europa	M. Parkin	
G-JUNG	CASA 1.131E Jungmann 1000 (E3B-143)	K. H. Wilson/White Waltham	
G-JUPP	PA-32RT-300 Lance II	Jupp Air Ltd (G-BNJF)	
G-JURA	BAe Jetstream 3102	Highland Airways Ltd/Inverness	
G-JURE	SOCATA TB10 Tobago	G-JURE Flying Group	
G-JURG	Rockwell Commander 114A	N. A. Southern	
G-JUST	Beech F33A Bonanza	Budge It Aviation Ltd/Elstree	
G-JVBF	Lindstrand LBL-210A balloon	Virgin Balloon Flights	
G-JVBP	Aerotechnik EV-97 Team Eurostar UK	B. J. Partridge & J. A. Valentine	
G-JWBI	Agusta-Bell 206B JetRanger 2	J. W. Bonser (G-RODS/G-NOEL/G-BCWN)	

G-JWCM – G-KEMC — BRITISH CIVIL REGISTRATIONS

Reg	Type	Owner or Operator
G-JWCM	SA Bulldog Srs 120/1210	M. L. J. Goff (G-BHXB)
G-JWDB	Ikarus C.42 FB80	J. W. D. Blythe
G-JWDS	Cessna F.150G	G. Sayer (G-AVNB)
G-JWEB	Robinson R44	Mastercraft Helicopter Hire Ltd
G-JWFT	Robinson R22 Beta	J. P. O'Brien
G-JWIV	Jodel DR.1051	C. M. Fitton
G-JWJW	CASA 1-131E Jungmann Srs.2000	J. W. & J. T. Whicher
G-JWXS	Shaw Europa XS T-G	J. Wishart
G-JXTA	BAe Jetstream 3102	Jetstream Executive Travel Ltd
G-JXTC	BAe Jetstream 3108	Jetstream Executive Travel Ltd (G-LOGT/G-BSFH)
G-JYAK	Yakovlev Yak-50 (93 white outline)	J. W. Stow/North Weald
G-JYRO	Rotorsport UK MT-03	A. Richards
G-KAAT	MDH MD-902 Explorer	Police Aviation Services Ltd (G-PASS)
G-KAEW	Fairey Gannet AEW.3 (XL500:CU) ★	T. J. Manna/North Weald
G-KAFE	Cameron N-65 balloon	J. R. Rivers-Scott
G-KAFT	Diamond DA40D Star	Atlantic Flight Training Ltd
G-KAIR	PA-28-181 Archer II	Keen Leasing (IOM) Ltd
G-KALS	Bombardier BD-100-1A10	MCP Continental Ltd
G-KAMM	Hawker Hurricane XIIA (5429)	Alpine Deer Group Ltd/New Zealand
G-KAMP	PA-18 Super Cub 135	J. R. G. Furnell
G-KANZ	Westland Wasp HAS.1	T. J. Manna
G-KAOM	Scheibe SF.25C Falke	Falke G-KAOM Syndicate
G-KAOS	Van's RV-7	A. E. N. Nicholas, D. F. McGarvey
G-KAPW	P.56 Provost T.1 (XF603)	The Shuttleworth Collection/Old Warden
G-KARA	Brügger MB.2 Colibri	C. L. Hill (G-BMUI)
G-KARI	Fuji FA.200-160	C. P. Rowley
G-KARK	Dyn'Aéro MCR-01 Club	R. Bailes-Brown
G-KART	PA-28-161 Warrior II	N. Clark
G-KASX	VS.384 Seafire Mk.XVII	T. J. Manna (G-BRMG)
G-KATE	Westland WG.30 Srs 100 ★	(stored)/Yeovil
G-KATI	Rans S.7 Courier	N. Rawlinson
G-KATS	PA-28 Cherokee 140	G-KATS Group (G-BIRC)
G-KATT	Cessna 152 II	Central Aircraft Leasing Ltd (G-BMTK)
G-KATZ	Flight Design CT2K	A. N. D. Arthur
G-KAWA	Denney Kitfox Mk 2	C. J. Bellworthy
G-KAXF	Hawker Hunter F.6A (XF515)	Kennet Aviation/North Weald
G-KAXT	Westland Wasp HAS.1 (XT787)	Kennet Aviation/North Weald
G-KAYH	Extra EA.300/L	Integrated Management Practices Ltd/Netherlands
G-KAYI	Cameron Z-90 balloon	Snow Business International Ltd
G-KAZA	Sikorsky S-76C	Bristow Helicopters Ltd
G-KAZB	Sikorsky S-76C	Bristow Helicopters Ltd
G-KAZI	Mainair Pegasus Quantum 15-912	Edren Homes Ltd
G-KBKB	Thunder Ax8-90 S2 balloon	G. Boulden
G-KBPI	PA-28-161 Warrior II	Goodwood Aerodrome & Motor Circuit Ltd (G-BFSZ)
G-KCHG	Schempp-Hirth Ventus Ct	D. S. Jones
G-KCIG	Sportavia RF-5B	Deeside Fournier Group
G-KCIN	PA-28-161 Cadet	G. Conrad (G-CDOX)
G-KDCC	Shaw Europa XS	K. A. C. Dodd
G-KDCD	Thruster T600N	K. J. Draper (G-MZNW)
G-KDET	PA-28-161 Cadet	Rapidspin Ltd/Biggin Hill
G-KDEY	Scheibe SF.25E Super Falke	Falke Syndicate
G-KDIX	Jodel D.9 Bébé	P. M. Bowden/Barton
G-KDMA	Cessna 560 Citation V	Gamston Aviation Ltd
G-KDOG	SA Bulldog Srs 120/121 (XX624:E)	Gamit Ltd
G-KEAM	Schleicher ASH 26E	D. T. Reilly
G-KEEF	Commander Aircraft 112A	K. D. Pearse
G-KEEN	Stolp SA.300 Starduster Too	Sharp Aerobatics Ltd/Netherlands
G-KEES	PA-28 Cherokee 180	C. N. Ellerbrook
G-KEJY	Aerotechnik EV-97 TeamEurostar UK	Kemble Eurostar 1
G-KELI	Robinson R44 Raven II	Kellys Sales and Service Donegal Ltd
G-KELL	Van's RV-6	R. G. Stephens/Ireland
G-KELS	Van's RV-7	J. D. Kelsall
G-KELV	Diamond DA42 Twin Star	K. K. Freeman (G-CTCH)
G-KELZ	Van's RV-8	J. D. Kelsall (G-DJRV)
G-KEMC	Grob G.109	Norfolk Gliding Club Ltd

BRITISH CIVIL REGISTRATIONS — G-KEMI – G-KNYT

Reg	Type	Owner or Operator	Notes
G-KEMI	PA-28-181 Archer III	K. B. Kempster	
G-KEMY	Cessna 182T	Allen Aircraft Rental Ltd	
G-KENB	Air Command 503 Commander	K. Brogden	
G-KENG	Rotorsport UK MT-03	K. A. Graham	
G-KENI	Rotorway Executive	A. J. Wheatley	
G-KENM	Luscombe 8EF Silvaire	M. G. Waters	
G-KENW	Robin DR400/500	K. J. White	
G-KENZ	Rutan Vari-Eze	K. M. McConnel l (G-BNUI)	
G-KEPE	Schempp-Hirth Nimbus 3DT	Nimbus Syndicate	
G-KEPP	Rans S.6-ES Coyote II	W. Goldsmith	
G-KESS	Glaser-Dirks DG-400	N. H. T. Cottrell & T. Flude	
G-KEST	Steen Skybolt	G-KEST Syndicate	
G-KETH	Agusta-Bell 206B JetRanger 2	DAC Leasing Ltd	
G-KEVB	PA-28-181 Archer III	Palmair Ltd	
G-KEVI	Jabiru J400	K. A. Allen	
G-KEWT	Ultramagic M.90 balloon	Kew Technik Ltd	
G-KEYS	PA-23 Aztec 250F	R. E. Myson	
G-KEYY	Cameron N-77 balloon	B. N. Trowbridge (G-BORZ)	
G-KFAN	Scheibe SF.25B Falke	R. G. & J. A. Boyes	
G-KFOX	Denney Kitfox	I. R. Lawrence	
G-KFRA	PA-32 Cherokee Six 300	West India Flying Group (G-BGII)	
G-KFZI	KFZ-1 Tigerfalck	L. R. Williams	
G-KGAO	Scheibe SF.25C Falke 1700	Falke 2000 Group	
G-KGED	Campbell Cricket Mk.4	K. G. Edwards	
G-KHCC	Schempp-Hirth Ventus Bt	J. L. G. McLane	
G-KHOM	Aeromot AMT-200 Super Ximango	Bowland Ximango Group	
G-KHOP	Zenair CH.601HDS Zodiac	K. Hopkins	
G-KHRE	MS.893E Rallye 150SV	D. M. Gale & K. F. Crumplin	
G-KICK	Pegasus Quantum 15-912	G. van der Gaag	
G-KIDD	Jabiru J430	R. L. Lidd (G-CEBB)	
G-KIII	Extra EA.300/L	Extra 200 Ltd	
G-KIMA	Zenair CH.601XL Zodiac	K. Martindale	
G-KIMB	Robin DR.340/140	R. M. Kimbell	
G-KIMK	Partenavia P.68B	M. Konstantinovic (G-BCPO)	
G-KIMM	Shaw Europa XS	P. A. D. Clarke	
G-KIMY	Robin DR.400/140B	S. G. Jones	
G-KINE	AA-5A Cheetah	Plane Talking Ltd	
G-KIPP	Thruster T.600 450	T. K. Duffy	
G-KIRB	Europa XS	European Flight Training News Ltd (G-OIZI)	
G-KIRC	Pietenpol Air Camper	M. Kirk (G-BSVZ)	
G-KIRK	Piper J-3C-65 Cub	M. Kirk	
G-KISS	Rand-Robinson KR-2	E. A. Rooney	
G-KITE	PA-28-181 Archer II	R. I. Sharpe	
G-KITF	Denney Kitfox	B. J. Lyford	
G-KITH	Alpi Pioneer 300	K. G. Atkinson	
G-KITI	Pitts S-2E Special	B. R. Cornes	
G-KITS	Shaw Europa	J. R. Evernden	
G-KITT	Curtiss P-40M Kittyhawk (49)	P. A. Teichman	
G-KITY	Denney Kitfox Mk 2	Kitfox KFM Group/Tollerton	
G-KIZZ	Kiss 450-582	J. C. A. Page	
G-KKCW	Flight Design CT2K	K. C. Wigley & Co Ltd	
G-KKER	Avtech Jabiru UL-450	W. K. Evans	
G-KKES	SOCATA TB20 Trinidad	Knightsgate Ltd (G-BTLH)	
G-KLAS	Robinson R44	Executive Hotels Ltd	
G-KMRV	Van-s RV-9A	G. K. Mutch	
G-KNAP	PA-28-161 Warrior II	Keen Leasing (IoM) Ltd (G-BIUX)	
G-KNEE	Ultramagic M-77C balloon	M. A. Green	
G-KNEK	Grob G.109B	Syndicate 109	
G-KNIB	Robinson R22 Beta II	C. G. Knibb	
G-KNIX	Cameron Z-315 balloon	A. M. Holly	
G-KNOB	Lindstrand LBL-180A balloon	Wye Valley Aviation Ltd	
G-KNOT	P.84 Jet Provost T.3A (XN629)	R. S. Partridge-Hicks (G-BVEG)	
G-KNOW	PA-32 Cherokee Six 300	B. R. & G. E. Mullady	
G-KNOX	Robinson R22 Beta	T. A. Knox Shopfitters Ltd	
G-KNYT	Robinson R44	Aircol	

G-KOBH – G-LAIR   BRITISH CIVIL REGISTRATIONS

Notes	Reg	Type	Owner or Operator
	G-KOBH	Schempp-Hirth Discus bT	C. F. M. Smith & K. Neave
	G-KODA	Cameron O-77 balloon	K. Stamurs
	G-KOFM	Glaser-Dirks DG.600/18M	A. Mossman
	G-KOHF	Schleicher ASK.14	J. Houlihan
	G-KOKL	Hoffmann H-36 Dimona	R. Smith & R. Stembrowicz
	G-KOLB	Kolb Twinstar Mk 3A	J. L. Moar
	G-KOLI	WSK PZL-110 Koliber 150	J. R. Powell
	G-KONG	Slingsby T.67M Firefly 200	R. C. Morton
	G-KOOL	DH.104 Devon C.2 (G-DOVE)	D. S. Hunt
	G-KORN	Cameron 70 Berentzen SS balloon	Balloon Preservation Flying Group
	G-KOTA	PA-28-236 Dakota	JF Packaging
	G-KOYY	Schempp-Hirth Nimbus 4T	R. Kalin
	G-KPAO	Robinson R44	Avonair Ltd (G-SSSS)
	G-KPTT	SOCATA TB20 Trinidad	IAE Ltd
	G-KRES	Stoddard-Hamilton Glasair IIS RG	A. D. Murray
	G-KRII	Rand-Robinson KR-2	M. R. Cleveley
	G-KRMA	Cessna 425 Corsair	Speedstar Holdings Ltd
	G-KRNW	Eurocopter EC 135T2	Bond Air Services Ltd/Aberdeen
	G-KSIR	Stoddard-Hamilton Glasair IIS RG	K. M. Bowen
	G-KSKS	Cameron N-105 balloon	A. M. Holly
	G-KSKY	Sky 77-24 balloon	J. W. Dale
	G-KSPB	Robinson R44 II	Heli2
	G-KSVB	PA-24 Comanche 260	S. Juggler (G-ENIU/G-AVJU)
	G-KTEE	Cameron V-77 balloon	D. C. & N. P. Bull
	G-KTKT	Sky 260-24 balloon	T. M. Donnelly
	G-KTOL	Robinson R44	JNK 2000 (G-DCOM)
	G-KTTY	Denney Kitfox Model 3	S. D. Morris (G-LESJ)
	G-KTWO	Cessna 182T	S. J. G. Mole
	G-KUBB	SOCATA TB20 Trinidad GT	Offshore Marine Consultants Ltd
	G-KUIK	Mainair Pegasus Quik	G. R. Hall & P. R. Brooker
	G-KUKI	Robinson R22 Beta	R. D. Masters (G-BTNB)
	G-KULA	Best Off Skyranger 912ULS	C.R. Mason
	G-KUPP	Flight Design CTSW	S. Munday
	G-KUTU	Quickie Q.2	R. Nash & J. Parkinson
	G-KUUI	J-3C-65 Cub	V. S. E. Norman
	G-KVBF	Cameron A-340HL balloon	Virgin Balloon Flights
	G-KVIP	Beech 200 Super King Air	Capital Aviation Ltd (G-CBFS/G-PLAT)
	G-KWAK	Scheibe SF.25C	Mendip Gliding Club Ltd
	G-KWAX	Cessna 182E	D. Shaw
	G-KWIC	Mainair Pegasus Quik	T. Southall
	G-KWIK	Partenavia P.68B	ACD Cidra BV/Belgium
	G-KWIN	Dassault Falcon 2000EX	Quinn Aviation Ltd
	G-KWKI	QAC Quickie Q.200	B. M. Jackson
	G-KWLI	Cessna 421C	Langley Aviation Ltd (G-DARR/G-BNEZ)
	G-KYAK	Yakovlev Yak C-11	M. Gainza
	G-KYLE	Thruster T600N 450	W. D. Kyle
	G-KYTE	Piper PA-28-161 Warrior II	G. Whitlow (G-BRRN)
	G-LABS	Shaw Europa	C. T. H. Pattinson
	G-LACA	PA-28-161 Warrior II	LAC (Enterprises) Ltd/Barton
	G-LACB	PA-28-161 Warrior II	LAC (Enterprises) Ltd/Barton
	G-LACC	Cameron C-90 balloon	Directorate Army Aviation
	G-LACD	PA-28-181 Archer III	Central Aircraft Leasing Ltd (G-BYBG)
	G-LACE	Shaw Europa	J. H. Phillingham
	G-LACI	Cessna 172S Skyhawk	L. Endresz
	G-LACR	Denney Kitfox	C. M. Rose
	G-LADD	Enstrom 480	Combi-Lift Ltd
	G-LADI	PA-30 Twin Comanche 160	S. H. Eastwood (G-ASOO)
	G-LADS	Rockwell Commander 114	D. F. Soul
	G-LADZ	Enstrom 480	Falcon Helicopters Ltd
	G-LAFT	Diamond DA40D Star	Atlantic Flight Training Ltd
	G-LAGR	Cameron N-90 balloon	J. R. Clifton
	G-LAID	Robinson R44	Helitech Charter Ltd
	G-LAIN	Robinson R22 Beta	Patriot Aviation Ltd/Cranfield
	G-LAIR	Stoddard-Hamilton Glasair IIS FT	A. I.O'Broin & S. T. Raby

192

BRITISH CIVIL REGISTRATIONS

G-LAJT – G-LENF

Reg	Type	Owner or Operator	Notes
G-LAJT	Beech D.17S	G. W. Lynch	
G-LAKE	Lake LA-250 Renegade	P. J. McGoldrick	
G-LAKI	Jodel DR.1050	V. Panteli (G-JWBB)	
G-LAMA	SA.315B Lama	PLM Dollar Group Ltd	
G-LAMM	Shaw Europa	S. A. Lamb	
G-LAMP	Cameron 110 Lampbulb SS balloon	LE Electrical Ltd	
G-LAMS	Cessna F.152 II	Horizon Aviation Ltd	
G-LANC	Avro 683 Lancaster X (KB889) ★	Imperial War Museum/Duxford	
G-LAND	Robinson R22 Beta	Heli Air Ltd/Wellesbourne	
G-LANE	Cessna F.172N	G. C. Bantin	
G-LAOK	Yakovlev Yak-52 (62 white)	I. F. Vaughan	
G-LAOL	PA-28RT-201 Arrow IV	Goodwood Road Racing Co Ltd	
G-LAOR	Hawker 800XP	Select Plant Hire Co Ltd	
G-LAPN	Light Aero Avid Aerobat	I. A. P. Harper	
G-LARA	Robin DR.400/180	K. D. & C. A. Brackwell	
G-LARE	PA-39 Twin Comanche 160 C/R	Glareways (Neasden) Ltd	
G-LARK	Helton Lark 95	J. Fox	
G-LARR	AS.350B3 Squirrel	McAlpine Helicopters Ltd	
G-LARS	Dyn'Aéro MCR-01 Banbi	L. A. Oyno	
G-LARY	Robinson R44 II	L. Behan & Sons Ltd/Ireland (G-CCRZ)	
G-LASN	Skyranger J2.2	L. C. F. Lasne	
G-LASR	Stoddard-Hamilton Glasair II	G. Lewis	
G-LASS	Rutan Vari-Eze	J. Mellor	
G-LASU	Eurocopter EC 135T2	Lancashire Constabulary Air Support Unit	
G-LAVE	Cessna 172R	M. L. Roland (G-BYEV)	
G-LAXY	Everett Gyroplane Srs.3	E. J. Barton	
G-LAZA	Lazer Z.200	D. G. Jenkins	
G-LAZL	PA-28-161 Warrior II	P. and J. Awdry and Son	
G-LAZR	Cameron O-77 balloon	Laser Holdings (UK) Ltd	
G-LAZY	Lindstrand Armchair SS balloon	The Air Chair Co Ltd/USA	
G-LAZZ	Stoddard-Hamilton Glastar	A. N. Evans	
G-LBDC	Bell 206B JetRanger III	Fresh Direct Espana Ltd	
G-LBLI	Lindstrand LBL-105A balloon	Lindstrand Balloons Ltd	
G-LBMM	PA-28-161 Warrior II	Flexi-Soft Ltd	
G-LBRC	PA-28RT-201 Arrow IV	D. J. V. Morgan	
G-LBUK	Lindstrand LBL-77A balloon	Lindstrand Balloons Ltd	
G-LBUZ	Aerotechnick EV-97A Eurostar	D. P. Tassart	
G-LCGL	Comper CLA.7 Swift (replica)	J. M. Greenland	
G-LCOC	BN-2A Mk III Trislander	Blue Island Air	
G-LCOK	Colt 69A balloon	Hot-Air Balloon Co Ltd (G-BLWI)	
G-LCPL	AS.365N-2 Dauphin 2	Charterstyle Ltd	
G-LCYA	Dassault 900EX	London City Airport Jet Centre Ltd	
G-LDAH	Skyranger 912 (2)	P. D. Brookes & L. Dickinson	
G-LDFM	Cessna 560XL Citation Excel	Granard Ltd	
G-LDWS	Jodel D.150	D. H. Wilson Spratt (G-BKSS)	
G-LEAF	Cessna F.406	Atlantic Air Transport Ltd/Coventry	
G-LEAH	Pioneer 300	J. C. Ferguson	
G-LEAM	PA-28-236 Dakota	G-LEAM Group (G-BHLS)	
G-LEAP	BN-2T Turbine Islander	Skydive Aircraft Ltd/Netheravon (G-BLND)	
G-LEAS	Sky 90-24 balloon	C. I. Humphrey	
G-LEAU	Cameron N-31 balloon	P. L. Mossman	
G-LEBE	Shaw Europa	P. Atkinson	
G-LECA	AS.355F1 Twin Squirrel	Western Power Distribution (South West) PLC (G-BNBK)	
G-LEDR	Westland Gazelle HT.2	P. J. Whitaker (G-CBSB)	
G-LEED	Denney Kitfox Mk 2	S. J. Walker	
G-LEEE	Avtech Jabiru UL-450	J. P. Mimnagh & L. E. G. Fekete	
G-LEEH	Ultramagic M-90 balloon	Sport Promotion SRL/Italy	
G-LEEN	Aero Designs Pulsar XP	R. B. Hemsworth (G-BZMP/G-DESI)	
G-LEES	Glaser-Dirks DG.400 (800)	J. Bradley	
G-LEEZ	Bell 206L-1 LongRanger 2	Pennine Helicopters Ltd (G-BPCT)	
G-LEGG	Cessna F.182Q	P. J. Clegg/Barton (G-GOOS)	
G-LEGO	Cameron O-77 balloon	P. M. Traviss	
G-LEIC	Cessna FA.152	Leicestershire Aero Club Ltd	
G-LEKT	Robin DR400/180 Regent	P. & J. P. Bromley and T. D. Allan	
G-LELE	Lindstrand LBL-31A balloon	L. E. Electrical Ltd	
G-LEMO	Cessna U206G Stationair G Floatplane	Garden House Properties Ltd	
G-LENA	IDA Bacau Yakovlev Yak-52	Yak-52 Ltd	
G-LENF	Mainair Blade 912S	G. D. Fuller	

G-LENI – G-LINN | BRITISH CIVIL REGISTRATIONS

Notes	Reg	Type	Owner or Operator
	G-LENI	AS.355F1 Twin Squirrel	Grid Aviation Ltd (G-ZFDB/G-BLEV)
	G-LENN	Cameron V-56 balloon	M. Jesper/Germany
	G-LENS	Thunder Ax7-77Z balloon	R. S. Breakwell
	G-LENX	Cessna 172N	M. W, Glencross (G-BMVJ)
	G-LENY	PA-34-220T Seneca III	Air Medical Fleet Ltd
	G-LEOD	Pietenpol Aircamper	I. D. McCleod
	G-LEOS	Robin DR.400/120	R. J. O. Walker
	G-LESZ	Denney Kitfox Mk 5	D. A. Lord
	G-LEVI	Aeronca 7AC Champion	G-LEVI Group
	G-LEVO	Robinson R44 II	Leavesley Aviation Ltd
	G-LEXI	Cameron N-77 balloon	T. Gilbert
	G-LEXX	Van's RV-8	A. A. Wordsworth
	G-LEZE	Rutan LongEz	K. G. M. Loyal & ptnrs
	G-LEZZ	Stoddard-Hamilton Glastar	L. A. James (G-BYCR)
	G-LFIX	VS.509 Spitfire T.IX (ML407)	C. S. Grace
	G-LFLY	Flight Design CTSW	I. A. Gaetan
	G-LFSA	PA-38-112 Tomahawk	Liverpool Flying School Ltd (G-BSFC)
	G-LFSB	PA-38-112 Tomahawk	Cambrian Flying Club Ltd (G-BLYC)
	G-LFSC	PA-28 Cherokee 140	P. A. Harvie (G-BGTR)
	G-LFSD	PA-38-112 Tomahawk II	Liverpool Flying School Ltd (G-BNPT)
	G-LFSG	PA-28 Cherokee 180E	Liverpool Flying School Ltd (G-AYAA)
	G-LFSH	PA-38-112 Tomahawk	Liverpool Flying School Ltd (G-BOZM)
	G-LFSI	PA-28 Cherokee 140	M. J. Green (G-AYKV)
	G-LFSJ	PA-28-161 Warrior II	Cloud 9 Aviation (Leasing) Ltd (G-BPHE)
	G-LFSK	PA-28-161 Warrior II	Cloud 9 Aviation (Leasing) Ltd
	G-LFSM	PA-38-112 Tomahawk	Liverpool Flying School Ltd (G-BWNR)
	G-LFSN	PA-38-112 Tomahawk	Liverpool Flying School Ltd (G-BNYV)
	G-LFVB	VS.349 Spitfire LF.Vb (EP120)	Patina Ltd/Duxford
	G-LFVC	VS.349 Spitfire LF.Vc (JG891:T-B)	Historic Flying Ltd/Duxford
	G-LGAR	Learjet 60	TAG Aviation (UK) Ltd
	G-LGCA	Robin DR.400/180R	London Gliding Club Proprietary Ltd
	G-LGCB	Robin DR.400/180R	London Gliding Club Proprietary Ltd
	G-LGEZ	Rutan Long-EZ	P. C. Elliott
	G-LGKO	Canadair CL-600-2816 Challenger	TAG Aviation (UK) Ltd
	G-LGLG	Cameron Z-210 balloon	Flying Circus SRL/Spain
	G-LGNA	SAAB SF.340B	Loganair Ltd/BA
	G-LGNB	SAAB SF.340B	Loganair Ltd/BA
	G-LGNC	SAAB SF.340B	Loganair Ltd/BA
	G-LGND	SAAB SF.340B	Loganair Ltd/BA (G-GNTH)
	G-LGNE	SAAB SF.340B	Loganair Ltd/BA (G-GNTI)
	G-LGNF	SAAB SF.340B	Loganair Ltd/BA (G-GNTJ)
	G-LGNG	SAAB SF.340B	Loganair Ltd/BA
	G-LGNH	SAAB SF.340B	Loganair Ltd/BA
	G-LGNI	SAAB SF.340B	Loganair Ltd/BA
	G-LGNJ	SAAB SF.340B	Loganair Ltd/BA
	G-LGNK	SAAB SF.340B	Loganir Ltd/BA
	G-LGTE	Boeing 737-3Y0	British Airways
	G-LGTF	Boeing 737-382	British Airways
	G-LGTG	Boeing 737-3Q8	British Airways
	G-LGTH	Boeing 737-3Y0	British Airways (G-BNGL)
	G-LGTI	Boeing 737-3Y0	British Airways (G-BNGM)
	G-LHCA	Robinson R22 Beta	Rotorcraft Ltd/Redhill
	G-LHCB	Robinson R22 Beta	London Helicopter Centres Ltd (G-SIVX)
	G-LHCC	Eurocopter EC 120B Colibri	Devris Ltd
	G-LHEL	AS.355F2 Twin Squirrel	Lloyd Helicopters Europe Ltd
	G-LIBB	Cameron V-77 balloon	R. J. Mercer
	G-LIBS	Hughes 369HS	R. J. H. Strong
	G-LICK	Cessna 172N II	Sky Back Ltd (G-BNTR)
	G-LIDA	Hoffmann H36 Dimona	Bidford Airfield Ltd
	G-LIDE	PA-31-350 Navajo Chieftain	Keen Leasing (IOM) Ltd
	G-LIFE	Thunder Ax6-56Z balloon	Lakeside Lodge Golf Centre
	G-LILA	Bell 206L-1 LongRanger 2	Lothian Helicopters Ltd (G-NEUF/G-BVVV)
	G-LILP	Shaw Europa XS	G. L. Jennings
	G-LILY	Bell 206B JetRanger 3	T. S. Brown (G-NTBI)
	G-LIMO	Bell 206L-1 LongRanger	Heliplayer Ltd
	G-LIMP	Cameron C-80 balloon	T. & B. Chamberlain
	G-LINC	Hughes 369HS	Wavendon Social Housing Ltd
	G-LINE	AS.355N Twin Squirrel	National Grid PLC
	G-LINN	Shaw Europa XS	T. Pond

BRITISH CIVIL REGISTRATIONS — G-LINX – G-LOWS

Reg	Type	Owner or Operator	Notes
G-LINX	Schweizer 269C-1	Heli-Lynx Ltd	
G-LIOA	Lockheed 10A Electra★ (NC5171N)	Science Museum/South Kensington	
G-LION	PA-18 Super Cub 135 (R-167)	JG Jones Haulage Ltd	
G-LIOT	Cameron O-77 balloon	N. D. Eliot	
G-LIPE	Robinson R22 Beta	Highland Helicopter Leasing Ltd (G-BTXJ)	
G-LIPS	Cameron 90 Lips SS balloon	Reach For The Sky Ltd (G-BZBV)	
G-LISO	SIAI Marchetti SM.1019	Castiglioni Daliso/Italy	
G-LITE	Rockwell Commander 112A	I. Hopwood	
G-LITZ	Pitts S-1E Special	R. P. Millinship	
G-LIVH	Piper J-3C-65 Cub (330238:A-24)	M. D. Cowburn/Barton	
G-LIZA	Cessna 340A II	Tayflight Ltd (G-BMDM)	
G-LIVS	Schleicher ASH-26E	P. O. Sturley	
G-LIZI	PA-28 Cherokee 160	G-LIZI Group (G-ARRP)	
G-LIZY	Westland Lysander III (V9673) ★	G. A. Warner/Duxford	
G-LIZZ	PA-E23 Aztec 250E	T. J. Nathan (G-BBWM)	
G-LJCC	Murphy Rebel	P. H. Hyde	
G-LJRM	Sikorsky S-76C	Ballymore Management Services Ltd/Ireland	
G-LKET	Cameron 100 Kindernet Dog SS balloon	G. R. J. Luckett	
G-LKTB	PA-28-181 Archer III	Top Cat Aviation Ltd	
G-LLAN	Grob G.109B	J. D. Scott	
G-LLEW	Aeromot AMT-200S Super Ximango	Echo Whiskey Ximango Syndicate	
G-LLMC	Cessna T.310Q II	Bravo Aviation Ltd (G-BKSB)	
G-LLMW	Diamond DA42 Twin Star	Diamond Aircraft UK Ltd/Gamston	
G-LLOY	Alpi Pioneer 300	A. R. Lloyd	
G-LMAX	Sequoia F.8L Falco	J. Maxwell	
G-LMCG	Robinson R44 II	Glendale Helicopter Services Ltd	
G-LMLV	Dyn'Aéro MCR-01	L. & M. La Vecchia	
G-LNAA	MDH MD-902 Explorer	Police Aviation Services Ltd	WADDINGTON
G-LNDS	Robinson R44	MC Air Ltd/Wellesbourne	
G-LNTY	AS.355F1 Twin Squirrel	Helix Aviation Ltd (G-ECOS/G-DORL/G-BPVB)	
G-LNYS	Cessna F.177RG	Heliview Ltd (G-BDCM)	
G-LOAD	Dan Rihn DR.107 One Design	M. J. Clark	
G-LOAN	Cameron N-77 balloon	P. Lawman	
G-LOBO	Cameron O-120 balloon	Solo Aerostatics	
G-LOCH	Piper J-3C-90 Cub	J. M. Greenland	
G-LOCO	Robinson R44 Raven II	TJS Self Drive (G-TEMM)	
G-LOFB	Lockheed L.188CF Electra	Atlantic Airlines Ltd/Coventry	
G-LOFC	Lockheed L.188CF Electra	Atlantic Airlines Ltd/Coventry	
G-LOFD	Lockheed L.188CF Electra	Atlantic Airlines Ltd/Coventry	
G-LOFE	Lockheed L.188CF Electra	Atlantic Airlines Ltd/Coventry	
G-LOFF	Lockheed L.188CF Electra	Atlantic Airlines Ltd/Coventry	
G-LOFM	Maule MX-7-180A	Atlantic Air Transport Ltd/Coventry	
G-LOFT	Cessna 500 Citation I	Atlantic Air Transport Ltd/Coventry	
G-LOGO	Hughes 369E	Eastern Atlantic Helicopters Ltd (G-BWLC)	
G-LOIS	Avtech Jabiru UL	D. W. Newman	
G-LOKI	Ultramagic M-77C balloon	L. J. M. Muir & G. D. Hallett	
G-LOKM	WSK-PZL Koliber 160A	PZL International Aviation Marketing & Sales PLC/North Weald (G-BYSH)	
G-LOLA	Beech A36 Bonanza	J. H. & L. F. Strutt	
G-LOLL	Cameron V-77 balloon	R. K. McCulloch	
G-LONE	Bell 206L-1 LongRanger	Sky Charter UK Ltd (G-CDAJ)	
G-LOOP	Pitts S-1C Special	D. Shutter	
G-LOOT	EMB-110P1 Bandeirante	(stored)/Southend (G-BNOC)	
G-LORC	PA-28-161 Cadet	Sherburn Aero Club Ltd	
G-LORD	PA-34-200T Seneca II	Carill Aviation Ltd & R. P. Thomas	
G-LORN	Avions Mudry CAP-10B	J. D. Gailey	
G-LORR	PA-28-181 Archer III	S. J. Sylvester	
G-LORT	Light Aero Avid Speedwing 4	P.Mitchell	
G-LORY	Thunder Ax4-31Z balloon	A. J. Moore	
G-LOSI	Cameron Z-105 balloon	Aeropubblicita Vicenza SRL/Italy	
G-LOSM	Gloster Meteor NF.11 (WM167)	Aviation Heritage Ltd/Coventry	
G-LOST	Denney Kitfox Mk 3	J. H. S. Booth	
G-LOSY	Aerotechnik EV-97 Eurostar	J. A. Shufflebotham	
G-LOTA	Robinson R44	Rahtol Ltd	
G-LOTI	Bleriot XI (replica) ★	Brooklands Museum Trust Ltd	
G-LOVB	BAe Jetstream 3102	Ocean Sky (UK) Ltd (G-BLCB)	
G-LOWS	Sky 77-24 balloon	A. J. Byrne & D. J. Bellinger	

195

G-LOYA – G-LYAK — BRITISH CIVIL REGISTRATIONS

Notes	Reg	Type	Owner or Operator
	G-LOYA	Cessna FR.172J	K. A. D. Mitchell (G-BLVT)
	G-LOYD	Aérospatiale SA.341G Gazelle 1	I. G. Lloyd (G-SFTC)
	G-LPAD	Lindstrand LBL-105A balloon	Line Packaging & Display Ltd
	G-LRBW	Lindstrand HS-110 airship	Croymark Ltd
	G-LRGE	Lindstrand LBL-330A balloon	Adventure Balloons Ltd
	G-LPGI	Cameron A-210 balloon	A. Derbyshire
	G-LRSN	Robinson R44	Larsen Manufacturing Ltd
	G-LSAA	Boeing 757-236	Jet 2 (G-BNSF)
	G-LSAB	Boeing 757-27B	Jet 2 (G-OAHF)
	G-LSAC	Boeing 757-23A	Jet 2
	G-LSAD	Boeing 757-236	Jet 2 (G-OOOS/G-BRJD)
	G-LSAE	Boeing 757-27B	Jet 2
	G-LSAG	Boeing 757-21B	Jet 2
	G-LSAH	Boeing 757-21B	Jet 2
	G-LSAI	Boeing 757-21B	Jet 2
	G-LSAJ	Boeing 757-225	Jet 2
	G-LSCM	Cessna 172S	G. A. Luscombe
	G-LSFI	AA-5A Cheetah	G-LSFI Group (G-BGSK)
	G-LSFT	PA-28-161 Warrior II	Biggin Hill Flying Club Ltd (G-BXTX)
	G-LSGM	Rolladen-Schneider LS3-17	M. W. Bewley
	G-LSHI	Colt 77A balloon	J. H. Dobson
	G-LSKY	Mainair Pegasus Quik	I. A. Gaetan
	G-LSMI	Cessna F.152	Falcon Flying Services/Biggin Hill
	G-LSPA	Agusta-Bell 206B JetRanger 2	LKL LLP (G-INVU/G-XXII/G-GGCC/G-BEHG)
	G-LSTR	Stoddard-Hamilton Glastar	R. Y. Kendal
	G-LSWL	Robinson R22 Beta	GLS Wales Ltd
	G-LTFB	PA-28 Cherokee 140	C. W. J. Cunningham (G-AVLU)
	G-LTFC	PA-28 Cherokee 140B	The Bristol and Wessex Aeroplane Club/Lulsgate (G-AXTI)
	G-LTRF	Sportavia Fournier RF-7	Skyview Systems Ltd (G-EHAP)
	G-LTSB	Cameron LTSB-90 balloon	ABC Flights Ltd
	G-LUBE	Cameron N-77 balloon	A. C. K. Rawson
	G-LUBY	Jabiru J430	K. Luby
	G-LUCK	Cessna F.150M	Cranfield Aviation Training School Ltd/Cranfield
	G-LUDM	Van's RV-8	D. F. Sargant
	G-LUED	Aero Designs Pulsar	J. C. Anderson
	G-LUFT	Pützer Elster C	A. & E. A. Wiseman (G-BOPY)
	G-LUKE	Rutan LongEz	R. A. Pearson
	G-LUKI	Robinson R44	A. and D. Douglas (G-BZLN)
	G-LUKY	Robinson R44	Hack Aviation
	G-LULA	Cameron C-90 balloon	S. D. Davis
	G-LULU	Grob G.109	A. P. Bowden
	G-LUMB	Best Off Skyranger 912(2)	S. Allcock
	G-LUNA	PA-32RT-300T Turbo Lance II	Lance Aviation Ltd
	G-LUND	Cessna 340 II	Prospect Developments (Northern) Ltd (G-LAST/G-UNDY/G-BBNR)
	G-LUNE	Mainair Pegasus Quik	D. Muir
	G-LUSC	Luscombe 8E Silvaire	M. Fowler
	G-LUSH	PA-28-151 Warrior	Willowair Flying Club (1996) Ltd
	G-LUSI	Luscombe 8F Silvaire	J. P. Hunt & D. M. Robinson
	G-LUST	Luscombe 8E Silvaire	M. Griffiths
	G-LUVY	AS.355F1 Twin Squirrel	DNH Helicopters Ltd
	G-LUXE	BAe 146-301	BAE Systems (Operations) Ltd (G-SSSH)
	G-LUXY	Cessna 551	Mitre Aviation Ltd
	G-LVBF	Lindstrand LBL-330A balloon	Virgin Balloon Flights
	G-LVES	Cessna 182S	R. W. & A. M. Glaves (G-ELIE)
	G-LVLV	Canadair CL.604 Challenger	Gama Aviation Ltd
	G-LVPL	Edge XT912 B/Streak III/B	C. D. Connor
	G-LWAY	Robinson R44	Glenkerrin Aviation Ltd
	G-LWNG	Aero Designs Pulsar	C. Moffat (G-OMKF)
	G-LWUK	Robinson R44	Wyberton Developments Ltd
	G-LXRS	Bombardier BD-700 Global Express	Profed Partners LLP
	G-LXUS	Alpi Pioneer 300	W. C. Walters
	G-LYAK	IDA Bacau Yakovlev Yak-52	Lee52 Ltd

BRITISH CIVIL REGISTRATIONS

G-LYDA – G-MAMH

Reg	Type	Owner or Operator	Notes
G-LYDA	Hoffmann H-36 Dimona	G-LYDA Flying Group/Booker	
G-LYDB	PA-31-350 Chieftain	Atlantic Bridge Aviation Ltd	
G-LYDC	PA-31-350 Navajo Chieftain	Atlantic Bridge Aviation Ltd	
G-LYDF	PA-31-350 Navajo Chieftain	Atlantic Bridge Aviation Ltd	
G-LYDR	Schempp-Hirth Discus 2cT	A. Firmin	
G-LYFA	IDABacau Yakovlev Yak-52	Fox Alpha Group	
G-LYNC	Robinson R22 Beta II	Traffic Management Services Ltd	
G-LYND	PA-25 Pawnee 235	York Gliding Centre Ltd/Rufforth (G-ASFX/G-BSFZ)	
G-LYNE	Aerotechnik EV-97 Eurostar	G. Evans	
G-LYNK	CFM Shadow Srs DD	I. Fernihough	
G-LYNX	Westland WG.13 Lynx (ZB500)	IHM/Weston-super-Mare	
G-LYPG	Avtech Jabiru UL	A. J. Geary	
G-LYTB	P & M Quik GT450	B. Light	
G-LYTE	Thunder Ax7-77 balloon	G. M. Bulmer	
G-LZZY	PA-28RT-201T Turbo Arrow IV	A. C. Gradidge (G-BMHZ)	
G-MAAN	Shaw Europa XS	P. S. Mann	
G-MAAV	AS.350B3 Squirrel	Silver Line Aviation LLP	
G-MAAX	Bell 206L-1 LongRanger 2	Lothian Helicopters Ltd (G-EYLE/G-OCRP/G-BWCU)	
G-MABE	Cessna F.150L	A. C. Saunders/Shobdon (G-BLJP)	
G-MABH	Fokker 100	Gazelle Ltd	
G-MABR	BAe 146-100	British Airways Connect (G-DEBN)	
G-MACA	Robinson R22 Beta	Helicentre Blackpool Ltd	
G-MACE	Hughes 369E	Chardstock House Ltd	
G-MACH	SIAI-Marchetti SF.260	Cheyne Motors Ltd/Old Sarum	
G-MACK	PA-28R Cherokee Arrow 200-II	M. D. Hinge	
G-MAFA	Cessna F.406	Directflight Ltd (G-DFLT)	
G-MAFB	Cessna F.406	Directflight Ltd	
G-MAFE	Dornier 228-202K	FR Aviation Ltd/Bournemouth (G-OALF/G-MLDO)	
G-MAFF	BN-2T Turbine Islander	FR Aviation Ltd/Bournemouth (G-BJEO)	
G-MAFI	Dornier 228-202K	FR Aviation Ltd/Bournemouth	
G-MAGC	Cameron Grand Illusion SS balloon	Magical Adventures Ltd	
G-MAGG	Pitts S-1SE Special	O. T. Elmer	
G-MAGL	Sky 77-24 balloon	RCM SRL/Luxembourg	
G-MAGZ	Robin DR.400/500	T. J. Thomas	
G-MAIE	PA-32RT-301T Turbo Saratoga II TC	B. R. Sennett	
G-MAIK	PA-34-220T Seneca V	Modern Air (UK) Ltd	
G-MAIN	Mainair Blade 912	D. P. Pryke	
G-MAIR	PA-34-200T Seneca II	A. J Warren	
G-MAJA	BAe Jetstream 4102	Eastern Airways	
G-MAJB	BAe Jetstream 4102	Eastern Airways (G-BVKT)	
G-MAJC	BAe Jetstream 4102	Eastern Airways (G-LOGJ)	
G-MAJD	BAe Jetstream 4102	Eastern Airways (G-WAWR)	
G-MAJE	BAe Jetstream 4102	Eastern Airways (G-LOGK)	
G-MAJF	BAe Jetstream 4102	Eastern Airways (G-WAWL)	
G-MAJG	BAe Jetstream 4102	Eastern Airways (G-LOGL)	
G-MAJH	BAe Jetstream 4102	Eastern Airways (G-WAYR)	
G-MAJI	BAe Jetstream 4102	Eastern Airways (G-WAND)	
G-MAJJ	BAe Jetstream 4102	Eastern Airways (G-WAFT)	
G-MAJK	BAe Jetstream 4102	Eastern Airways	
G-MAJL	BAe Jetstream 4102	Eastern Airways	
G-MAJM	BAe Jetstream 4102	Eastern Airways	
G-MAJN	BAe Jetstream 4102	Eastern Airways	
G-MAJP	BAe Jetstream 4101	Eastern Airways	
G-MAJO	BAe Jetstream 4102	Eastern Airways (Europe) Ltd (G-BVZC)	
G-MAJR	DHC.1 Chipmunk 22 (WP805)	Chipmunk Shareholders	
G-MAJS	Airbus A.300B4-605R	Monarch Airlines Ltd/Luton	
G-MAJT	BAe Jetstream 4101	Eastern Airways	
G-MAJU	BAe Jetstream 4102	Eastern Airways	
G-MAJV	BAe Jetstream 4102	Eastern Airways	
G-MAJW	BAe Jetstream 4102	Eastern Airways	
G-MAJX	BAe Jetstream 4102	Eastern Airways	
G-MAJY	BAe Jetstream 4102	Eastern Airways	
G-MAJZ	BAe Jetstream 4102	Eastern Airways	
G-MALA	PA-28-181 Archer II	M. & D. Aviation (G-BIIU)	
G-MALC	AA-5 Traveler	B. P. Hogan (G-BCPM)	
G-MALS	Mooney M.20K-231	M. A. Cummings	
G-MALT	Colt Flying Hop SS balloon	P. J. Stapley	
G-MAMC	Rotorway Executive 90	J. R. Carmichael	
G-MAMH	Fokker 100	Gazelle Ltd/Norwich	

G-MAMO – G-MBIA BRITISH CIVIL REGISTRATIONS

Notes	Reg	Type	Owner or Operator
	G-MAMO	Cameron V-77 balloon	The Marble Mosaic Co Ltd
	G-MANE	BAe ATP	British Airways Connect (G-LOGB)
	G-MANF	BAe ATP	British Airways Connect (G-LOGA)
	G-MANG	BAe ATP	Trident Aviation Leasing Services (Jersey) Ltd (G-LOGD/G-OLCD)
	G-MANH	BAe ATP	Trident Aviation Leasing Services (Jersey) Ltd (G-LOGC/G-OLCC)
	G-MANL	BAe ATP	WestLB AG (G-ERIN/G-BMYK)
	G-MANM	BAe ATP	Trident Aviation Leasing Services (Jersey) Ltd (G-OATP/G-BZWW)
	G-MANN	Aérospatiale SA.341G Gazelle 1	N. E. R. Brunt (G-BKLW)
	G-MANO	BAe ATP	BAE Systems (Operations) Ltd (G-UIET)
	G-MANS	BAe 146-200	British Airways Connect (G-CLHC/G-CHSR)
	G-MANW	Tri-R Kis	M. T. Manwaring
	G-MANX	FRED Srs 2	S. Styles
	G-MAPL	Robinson R44	M. G. Mazzocchi (G-BZPV)
	G-MAPP	Cessna 402B	Simmons Aerofilms Ltd
	G-MAPR	Beech A36 Bonanza	Moderandum Ltd
	G-MARA	Airbus A.321-231	Monarch Airlines Ltd/Luton
	G-MARE	Schweizer 269C	The Earl of Caledon
	G-MARO	Skyranger J2.2 (2)	C. P. Whitford
	G-MARX	Van's RV-4	M. W. Albery
	G-MARZ	Thruster T.600N 450	S. P. Warburton
	G-MASC	Jodel 150A	K. F. & R. Richardson
	G-MASF	PA-28-181 Archer II	Mid-Anglia School of Flying
	G-MASH	Westland-Bell 47G-4A	Kinetic Avionics Ltd (G-AXKU)
	G-MASI	P & M Quik GT450	M. A. Sweet
	G-MASS	Cessna 152 II	MK Aero Support Ltd (G-BSHN)
	G-MASZ	Masquito M.58	Masquito Aircraft NV/Belgium
	G-MATE	Moravan Zlin Z.50LX	S. A. W. Becker
	G-MATS	Colt GA-42 airship	P. A. Lindstrand
	G-MATT	Robin R.2160	V. P. O'Brien (G-BKRC)
	G-MATX	Pilatus PC-12/45	Air Matrix Ltd
	G-MATY	Robinson R22 Beta	MT Aviation
	G-MATZ	PA-28 Cherokee 140	Midland Air Training School/Coventry (G-BASI)
	G-MAUK	Colt 77A balloon	B. Meeson
	G-MAUS	Shaw Europa XS	A. P. Ringrose
	G-MAVI	Robinson R22 Beta	Northumbria Helicopters Ltd
	G-MAXG	Pitts S-1S Special	Jenks Air Ltd/RAF Halton
	G-MAXI	PA-34-200T Seneca II	Draycott Seneca Syndicate Ltd
	G-MAXR	Ultramagic S-90 balloon	M. J. Axtell
	G-MAXS	Mainair Pegasus Quik 912S	S. P. Maxwell
	G-MAXV	Van's RV-4	R. S. Partridge-Hicks
	G-MAYB	Robinson R44	Highmark Aviation Ltd
	G-MAYE	Bell 407	M. Maye
	G-MAYO	PA-28-161 Warrior II	Air Navigation and Trading Company Ltd/Blackpool (G-BFBG)
	G-MAZY†	DH.82A Tiger Moth ★	Newark Air Museum
	G-MBAA	Hiway Skytrike Mk 2	M. J. Aubrey
	G-MBAB	Hovey Whing-Ding II	M. J. Aubrey
	G-MBAD	Weedhopper JC-24A	M. Stott
	G-MBAF	R. J. Swift 3	C. G. Wrzesien
	G-MBAW	Pterodactyl Ptraveller	J. C. K. Scardifield
	G-MBBB	Skycraft Scout 2	A. J. & B. Chalkley
	G-MBBM	Eipper Quicksilver MX	J. Brown
	G-MBCJ	Mainair Sports Tri-Flyer	R. A. Smith
	G-MBCK	Eipper Quicksilver MX	P. Rowbotham
	G-MBCL	Sky-Trike/Typhoon	P. J. Callis
	G-MBCU	American Aerolights Eagle	J. L. May
	G-MBCX	Airwave Nimrod 165	M. Maylor
	G-MBDG	Eurowing Goldwing	B. Fussell
	G-MBDM	Southdown Sigma Trike	A. R. Prentice
	G-MBET	MEA Mistral Trainer	B. H. Stephens
	G-MBEU	Hiway Demon T.250	R. C. Smith
	G-MBFK	Hiway Demon	D. W. Stamp
	G-MBGF	Twamley Trike	T. B. Woolley
	G-MBGS	Rotec Rally 2B	P. C. Bell
	G-MBGX	Southdown Lightning	T. Knight
	G-MBHE	American Aerolights Eagle	R. J. Osborne
	G-MBHK	Flexiform Skytrike	K. T. Vinning
	G-MBHZ	Pterodactyl Ptraveller	J. C. K. Scardifield
	G-MBIA	Flexiform Sealander Skytrike	I. P. Cook

BRITISH CIVIL REGISTRATIONS — G-MBIO – G-MEDS

Reg	Type	Owner or Operator	Notes
G-MBIO	American Eagle 215B	S. Montandon	
G-MBIT	Hiway Demon Skytrike	K. S. Hodgson	
G-MBIY	Ultrasports Tripacer	J. W. Burton	
G-MBIZ	Mainair Tri-Flyer	D. M. A. Templeman/E. F. C. Clapham/ S. P. Slade/W. B. S. Dobie	
G-MBJF	Hiway Skytrike Mk II	C. H. Bestwick	
G-MBJG	Airwave Nimrod	D. H. George	
G-MBJK	American Aerolights Eagle	B. W. Olley	
G-MBJL	Airwave Nimrod	A. G. Lowe	
G-MBJM	Striplin Lone Ranger	C. K. Brown	
G-MBKY	American Aerolight Eagle	M. J. Aubrey	
G-MBKZ	Hiway Skytrike	S. I. Harding	
G-MBLU	Southdown Lightning L.195	C. R. Franklin	
G-MBMG	Rotec Rally 2B	J. R. Pyper	
G-MBOF	Pakes Jackdaw	L. G. Pakes	
G-MBOH	Microlight Engineering Mistral	N. A. Bell	
G-MBPG	Hunt Skytrike	S. D. Thorpe	
G-MBPJ	Moto-Delta	J. B. Jackson	
G-MBPX	Eurowing Goldwing	A. R. Channon	
G-MBPY	Ultrasports Tripacer 330	D. Hawkes & C. Poundes	
G-MBRB	Electraflyer Eagle 1	R. C. Bott	
G-MBRD	American Aerolights Eagle	R. J. Osborne	
G-MBRH	Ultraflight Mirage Mk II	R. W. F. Boarder	
G-MBRS	American Aerolights Eagle	L. K. Fowler	
G-MBST	Mainair Gemini Sprint	G. J. Bowen	
G-MBSX	Ultraflight Mirage II	C. J. Draper	
G-MBTF	Mainair Tri-Flyer Skytrike	D. E. J. McVicker	
G-MBTH	Whittaker MW4	L. Greenfield & M. W. J. Whittaker	
G-MBTJ	Solar Wings Microlight	H. A. Comber	
G-MBTW	Raven Vector 600	W. A. Fuller	
G-MBUZ	Wheeler Scout Mk II	A. C. Thorne	
G-MBWG	Huntair Pathfinder	T. Mahmood	
G-MBYI	Ultraflight Lazair	C. M. Mackinnon	
G-MBYL	Huntair Pathfinder	S. Porter	
G-MBYM	Eipper Quicksilver MX	M. P. Harper & L. L. Perry	
G-MBZH	Eurowing Goldwing	J. Spavins	
G-MBZO	Tri-Pacer 330	A. N. Burrows	
G-MBZV	American Aerolights Eagle	M. J. Aubrey	
G-MCAI	Robinson R44 II	M. C. Allen	
G-MCAP	Cameron C-80 balloon	L. D. Thurgar	
G-MCCF	Thruster T.600N	C. C. F. Fuller	
G-MCCY	IDA Bacau Yakolev Yak-52	D. P. McCoy/Ireland	
G-MCEL	Pegasus Quantum 15-912	F. Hodgson	
G-MCJL	Pegasus Quantum 15-912	M. C. J. Ludlow	
G-MCMC	SOCATA TBM-700	SogestaoAdministraca Gerencia SA	
G-MCMS	Aero Designs Pulsar	B. R. Hunter	
G-MCOW	Lindstrand LBL-77A balloon	S. & S. Villiers	
G-MCOX	Fuji FA.200-180AO	W. Surrey Engineering (Shepperton) Ltd	
G-MCOY	Flight Design CT2K	Pegasus Flight Training (Cotswolds)	
G-MCPI	Bell 206B JetRanger 3	Castle Air Charters Ltd (G-ONTB)	
G-MCXV	Colomban MC.15 Cri-Cri	H. A. Leek	
G-MDAC	PA-28-181 Archer II	Alpha Charlie Flying Group	
G-MDAY	Cessna 170B	M. Day	
G-MDBC	Pegasus Quantum 15-912	D. B. Caiden	
G-MDBD	Airbus A.330-243	MyTravel Airways	
G-MDCA	PA-34-220 Seneca V	Eagle Power Ltd (G-OGOG/G-TILL)	
G-MDDT	Robinson R44 II	MT Helicopters Ltd	
G-MDJN	Beech 95-B55 Baron	D. J. Nock (G-SUZI/G-BAXR)	
G-MDKD	Robinson R22 Beta	Blue Sky Helicopters	
G-MDPI	Agusta A109A-II	Langfast Ltd (G-PERI/G-EXEK/G-SLNE/G-EEVS/G-OTSL)	
G-MEAH	PA-28R Cherokee Arrow 200-II	I. R. Chaplin (G-BSNM)	
G-MEDE	Airbus A.320-232	BMed – British Mediterranean Airways	
G-MEDF	Airbus A.321-231	BMed – British Mediterranean Airways	
G-MEDG	Airbus A.321-231	BMed – British Mediterranean Airways	
G-MEDH	Airbus A.320-232	BMed – British Mediterranean Airways	
G-MEDJ	Airbus A.321-232	BMed – British Mediterranean Airways	
G-MEDK	Airbus A.320-232	BMed – British Mediterranean Airways	
G-MEDL	Airbus A.321-231	BMed – British Mediterranean Airways	
G-MEDM	Airbus A.321-231	BMed – British Mediterranean Airways	
G-MEDS	Agusta A109E Power	Sloane Helicopters Ltd	

G-MEEK – G-MHRV — BRITISH CIVIL REGISTRATIONS

Notes	Reg	Type	Owner or Operator
	G-MEEK	Enstrom 480	Rocket Rentals Ltd
	G-MEET	Learjet 40	TAG Aviation (UK) Ltd
	G-MEGA	PA-28R-201T Turbo Arrow III	A. W. Bean
	G-MEGG	Shaw Europa XS	M. E. Mavers
	G-MEGN	Beech B200 Super King Air	Dragonfly Aviation Services LLP
	G-MELT	Cessna F.172H	Falcon Aviation Ltd (G-AWTI)
	G-MELV	SOCATA Rallye 235E	J. W. Busby (G-BIND)
	G-MEME	PA-28R-201 Arrow III	Henry J. Clare Ltd
	G-MEOW	CFM Streak Shadow	G. J. Moor
	G-MEPU	Rotorsport UK MT-03	M. C. Elliott
	G-MERC	Colt 56A balloon	A. F. & C. D. Selby
	G-MERE	Lindstrand LBL-77A balloon	R. D. Baker
	G-MERF	Grob G.115A	G-MERF Group
	G-MERL	PA-28RT-201 Arrow IV	M. Giles/Cardiff-Wales
	G-METH	Cameron C-90 balloon	A. & D. Methley
	G-MEUP	Cameron A-120 balloon	Innovation Ballooning Ltd
	G-MFAC	Cessna F.172H	Ravenair Aircraft Ltd (G-AVGZ)
	G-MFEF	Cessna FR.172J	M. & E. N. Ford
	G-MFHI	Shaw Europa	Hi Fliers
	G-MFHT	Robinson R22 Beta II	MFH Ltd
	G-MFLI	Cameron V-90 balloon	J. M. Percival
	G-MFLY	Mainair Rapier	J. J. Tierney
	G-MFMF	Bell 206B JetRanger 3	Western Power Distribution (South West) PLC (G-BJNJ)
	G-MFMM	Scheibe SF.25C Falke	J. E. Selman
	G-MGAA	BFC Challenger II	J. C. Craddock & R. J. Speight
	G-MGAG	Aviasud Mistral	M. Raj
	G-MGAN	Robinson R44	E. J. R. Canvin
	G-MGCA	Jabiru Aircraft Jabiru UL	K. D. Pearce
	G-MGCB	Pegasus XL-Q	M. G. Gomez
	G-MGCK	Whittaker MW6 Merlin	M. W. J. Whittaker & L. R. Orriss
	G-MGDL	Pegasus Quantum 15	M. J. Buchanan
	G-MGEC	Rans S.6-ESD-XL Coyote II	G. Clipston
	G-MGEF	Pegasus Quantum 15	G. D. Castell
	G-MGFK	Pegasus Quantum 15	F. A. A. Kay
	G-MGGG	Pegasus Quantum 15	R. A. Beauchamp
	G-MGGT	CFM Streak Shadow SAM	D. R. Stansfield
	G-MGGV	Pegasus Quantum 15-912	S. M. Green
	G-MGMC	Pegasus Quantum 15	G. J. Slater
	G-MGMM	PA-18 Super Cub 150	M. J. Martin
	G-MGND	Rans S.6-ESD Coyote IIXL	P. Vallis
	G-MGOD	Medway Raven	A. Wherrett/N. R. Andrew/D. J. Millward
	G-MGOO	Renegade Spirit UK Ltd	P. J. Dale
	G-MGPA	Ikarus C42 FB100	P. D. Ashley
	G-MGPD	Pegasus XL-R	H. T. Mounfield
	G-MGPH	CFM Streak Shadow	V. C. Readhead (G-RSPH)
	G-MGRH	Quad City Challenger II	M. R. Brumby
	G-MGTG	Pegasus Quantum 15	R. B. Milton (G-MZIO)
	G-MGTR	Hunt Wing	A. C. Ryall
	G-MGTV	Thruster T.600N 450	R. Bingham & P. A. Durrans
	G-MGTW	CFM Shadow Srs DD	G. T. Webster
	G-MGUN	Cyclone AX2000	I. Lonsdale
	G-MGUY	CFM Shadow Srs BD	Shadow Flight Centre Ltd
	G-MGWH	Thruster T300	J. J. Hill
	G-MGWI	Robinson R44	Ed Murray and Sons Ltd (G-BZEF)
	G-MGYB	Embraer RJ135BJ	Haughey Air
	G-MHCB	Enstrom 280C	Springbank Aviation Ltd
	G-MHCD	Enstrom 280C-UK	S. J. Ellis (G-SHGG)
	G-MHCE	Enstrom F-28A	Wyke CommercialServices (G-BBHD)
	G-MHCF	Enstrom 280C-UK	HKC Helicopter Services (G-GSML/G-BNNV)
	G-MHCG	Enstrom 280C-UK	G. L. Pritchard (G-HAYN/G-BPOX)
	G-MHCI	Enstrom 280C	Charlie India Helicopters Ltd/Barton
	G-MHCJ	Enstrom F-28C-UK	Paradise Helicopters (G-CTRN)
	G-MHCK	Enstrom 280FX	D. Shakespeare (G-BXXB)
	G-MHCL	Enstrom 280C	J. A. Newton
	G-MHCM	Enstrom 280FX	Kingswood Bank LLP (G-IBWF/G-ZZWW/G-BSIE)
	G-MHGS	Stoddard-Hamilton Glastar	M. Henderson
	G-MHJK	Diamond DA42 Twin Star	Diamond Aircraft UK Ltd
	G-MHMR	Pegasus Quantum 15-912	L. Zivanovic
	G-MHRV	Van's RV-6A	M. R. Harris

BRITISH CIVIL REGISTRATIONS

G-MICH – G-MJFX

Reg	Type	Owner or Operator	Notes
G-MICH	Robinson R22 Beta	Tiger Helicopters Ltd/Shobdon (G-BNKY)	
G-MICI	Cessna 182S	Steve Parrish Racing (G-WARF)	
G-MICK	Cessna F.172N	G-MICK Flying Group	
G-MICY	Everett Srs 1 gyroplane	D. M. Hughes	
G-MIDC	Airbus A.321-231	bmi british midland	
G-MIDD	PA-28 Cherokee 140	Midland Air Training School/Coventry (G-BBDD)	
G-MIDG	Midget Mustang	C. E. Bellhouse	
G-MIDJ	Airbus A.321-231	bmi british midland	
G-MIDK	Airbus A.321-231	bmi british midland	
G-MIDL	Airbus A.321-231	bmi british midland	
G-MIDM	Airbus A.321-231	bmi british midland	
G-MIDO	Airbus A.320-232	bmi british midland	
G-MIDP	Airbus A.320-232	bmi british midland	
G-MIDR	Airbus A.320-232	bmi british midland	
G-MIDS	Airbus A.320-232	bmi british midland	
G-MIDT	Airbus A.320-232	bmi british midland	
G-MIDU	Airbus A.320-232	bmi british midland	
G-MIDV	Airbus A.320-232	bmi british midland	
G-MIDW	Airbus A.320-232	bmi british midland	
G-MIDX	Airbus A.320-232	bmi british midland	
G-MIDY	Airbus A.320-232	bmi british midland	
G-MIDZ	Airbus A.320-232	bmi british midland	
G-MIFF	Robin DR.400/180	G. E. Snushall	
G-MIGG	WSK-Mielec LiM-5 (1211) ★	D. Miles (G-BWUF)	
G-MIII	Extra EA.300/L	Angels High Ltd	
G-MIKE	Brookland Hornet	M. H. J. Goldring	
G-MIKI	Rans S.6-ESA Coyote II	S. P. Slade	
G-MIKS	Robinson R44	Direct Timber Ltd	
G-MILA	Cessna F.172N	P. J. Miller	
G-MILD	Scheibe SF.25C Falke	The Borders (Milfield) Gliding Club Ltd	
G-MILE	Cameron N-77 balloon	Miles Air Ltd	
G-MILI	Bell 206B JetRanger 3	Milford Aviation	
G-MILN	Cessna 182Q	Meon Hill Farms (Stockbridge) Ltd	
G-MILY	AA-5A Cheetah	Plane Talking Ltd/Elstree (G-BFXY)	
G-MIMA	BAe 146-200	Cityjet Ltd (G-CNMF)/Ireland	
G-MIME	Shaw Europa	N. W. Charles	
G-MIND	Cessna 404	Atlantic Air Transport Ltd/Coventry (G-SKKC/G-OHUB)	
G-MINN	Lindstrand LBL-90A balloon	S. M. & D. Johnson	
G-MINS	Nicollier HN.700 Menestrel II	R. Fenion	
G-MINT	Pitts S-1S Special	T. G. Sanderson/Tollerton	
G-MIOO	M.100 Student ★	Museum of Berkshire Aviation/Woodley (G-APLK)	
G-MIRA	Jabiru SP-340	C. P. L. Helson/Belgium (G-LUMA)	
G-MISH	Cessna 182R	Graham Churchill Plant Ltd (G-RFAB/G-BIXT)	
G-MITE	Raj Hamsa X'Air Falcon	T. Jestico	
G-MITS	Cameron N-77 balloon	G. B. Davies	
G-MITZ	Cameron N-77 balloon	Colt Car Co Ltd	
G-MIWS	Cessna 310R II	Wilcott Sport and Construction Ltd (G-ODNP)	
G-MJAE	American Aerolights Eagle	T. B. Woolley	
G-MJAJ	Eurowing Goldwing	M. J. Aubrey	
G-MJAM	Eipper Quicksilver MX	J. C. Larkin	
G-MJAN	Hiway Skytrike	G. M. Sutcliffe	
G-MJAY	Eurowing Goldwing	M. Anthony	
G-MJAZ	Aerodyne Vector 610	B. Fussell	
G-MJBK	Swallow B	M. A. Newbould	
G-MJBL	American Aerolights Eagle	B. W. Olley	
G-MJBS	Ultralight Stormbuggy	G. I. Sargeant	
G-MJBV	American Aerolights Eagle	A. W. Johnson	
G-MJBZ	Huntair Pathfinder	J. C. Rose	
G-MJCE	Ultrasports Tripacer	L. I. Bateup	
G-MJCU	Tarjani	J. K. Ewing	
G-MJDE	Huntair Pathfinder	P. Rayson	
G-MJDJ	Hiway Skytrike Demon	A. J. Cowan	
G-MJDP	Eurowing Goldwing	B. L. R. J. Keeping	
G-MJDR	Hiway Demon Skytrike	D. R. Redmile	
G-MJDW	Eipper Quicksilver MX	J. A. Brumpton	
G-MJEE	Mainair Triflyer Trike	M. F. Eddington	
G-MJEO	American Aerolights Eagle	A. M. Shaw	
G-MJER	Flexiform Striker	D. S. Simpson	
G-MJFB	Flexiform Striker	B. Tetley	
G-MJFM	Huntair Pathfinder	R. Gillespie & S. P. Girr	
G-MJFX	Skyhook TR-1	M. R. Dean	

G-MJFZ – G-MKAS **BRITISH CIVIL REGISTRATIONS**

Notes	Reg	Type	Owner or Operator
	G-MJFZ	Hiway Sky-Trike	A. W. Lowrie
	G-MJHC	Ultrasports Tripacer 330	E. J. Allen
	G-MJHR	Southdown Lightning	B. R. Barnes
	G-MJHV	Hiway Demon 250	A. G. Griffiths
	G-MJIA	Flexiform Striker	D. G. Ellis
	G-MJIC	Ultrasports Puma 330	J. Curran
	G-MJIF	Mainair Triflyer	R. J. Payne
	G-MJIR	Eipper Quicksilver MX	H. Feeney
	G-MJJA	Huntair Pathfinder	J. M. Watkins & R. D. Bateman
	G-MJKB	Striplin Skyranger	A. P. Booth
	G-MJKF	Hiway Demon	S. D. Hill
	G-MJKO	Goldmarque 250 Skytrike	M. J. Barry
	G-MJKX	Ultralight Skyrider Phantom	A. P. Love
	G-MJMR	Solar Wings Typhoon	J. C. S. Jones
	G-MJMS	Hiway Skytrike	D. E. Peace
	G-MJNM	American Aerolights Double Eagle	A. W. Johnson
	G-MJNO	American Aerolights Double Eagle	R. S. Martin
	G-MJNU	Skyhook Cutlass	R. W. Taylor
	G-MJNY	Skyhook Sabre Trike	P. Ratcliffe
	G-MJOC	Huntair Pathfinder	A. J. Glynn
	G-MJOE	Eurowing Goldwing	R. J. Osborne
	G-MJPA	Rotec Rally 2B	R. Boyd
	G-MJPE	Hiway Demon Skytrike	E. G. Astin
	G-MJPV	Eipper Quicksilver MX	F. W. Ellis
	G-MJRL	Eurowing Goldwing	M. Daniels
	G-MJRO	Eurowing Goldwing	H. P. Welch
	G-MJRR	Striplin Skyranger Srs 1	J. R. Reece
	G-MJRS	Eurowing Goldwing	R. M. Newlands
	G-MJRU	MBA Tiger Cub 440	D. J. Short
	G-MJSE	Skyrider Airsports Phantom	K. H. A. Negal
	G-MJSF	Skyrider Airsports Phantom	B. J. Towers
	G-MJSL	Dragon 200	M. J. Aubrey
	G-MJSO	Hiway Skytrike	D. C. Read
	G-MJSP	Romain Tiger Cub 440	A. R. Sunley
	G-MJST	Pterodactyl Ptraveller	B. W. Olley
	G-MJSY	Eurowing Goldwing	A. J. Rex
	G-MJSZ	DH Wasp	J. J. Hill
	G-MJTC	Ultrasports Tri-Pacer	V. C. Readhead
	G-MJTE	Skyrider Phantom	L. Zivanovic
	G-MJTM	Aerostructure Pipistrelle 2B	A. M. Sirant
	G-MJTP	Flexiform Striker	P. Milton
	G-MJTR	Southdown Puma DS Mk 1	T. Abro & A. G. Rodenburg
	G-MJTX	Skyrider Airsports Phantom	P. D. Coppin
	G-MJTZ	Skyrider Airsports Phantom	B. J. Towers
	G-MJUC	MBA Tiger Cub 440	P. C. Avery
	G-MJUR	Skyrider Aviation Phantom	M. J. Whiteman-Haywood
	G-MJUU	Eurowing Goldwing	E. F. Clapham
	G-MJUW	MBA Tiger Cub 440	D. G. Palmer
	G-MJUX	Skyrider Airsports Phantom	P. J. Glover
	G-MJVE	Hybred Skytrike	T. A. Clark
	G-MJVF	CFM Shadow	J. A. Cook
	G-MJVN	Ultrasports Puma 440	R. McGookin
	G-MJVP	Eipper Quicksilver MX II	G. J. Ward
	G-MJVU	Eipper Quicksilver MX II	F. J. Griffith
	G-MJVX	Skyrider Phantom	J. R. Harris
	G-MJVY	Dragon Srs 150	J. C. Craddock
	G-MJWB	Eurowing Goldwing	D. G. Palmer
	G-MJWF	Tiger Cub 440	R. A. & T. Maycock
	G-MJWK	Huntair Pathfinder	Kemble Flying Club
	G-MJWZ	Ultrasports Panther XL	A. L. Davies
	G-MJXY	Hiway Demon Skytrike	H. C. Lowther
	G-MJYD	MBA Tiger Cub 440	R. A. Budd
	G-MJYP	Mainair Triflyer 440	M. S. Whitehouse
	G-MJYV	Mainair Triflyer 2 Seat	H. L. Phillips
	G-MJYW	Wasp Gryphon III	P. D. Lawrence
	G-MJYX	Mainair Triflyer	K. A. Wright
	G-MJZE	MBA Tiger Cub 440	Fishburn Flying Tigers
	G-MJZK	Southdown Puma Sprint 440	R. J. Osborne
	G-MJZU	Flexiform Striker	C. G. Chambers
	G-MKAA	Boeing 747-2S4F	MK Airlines Ltd
	G-MKAK	Colt 77A balloon	M. Kendrick
	G-MKAS	PA-28 Cherokee 140	MK Aero Support Ltd (G-BKVR)

BRITISH CIVIL REGISTRATIONS — G-MKIA – G-MMKM

Reg	Type	Owner or Operator	Notes
G-MKIA	VS.300 Spitfire 1 (P9374)	Spitfire Partners LLC/Italy	
G-MKSS	HS.125 Srs 700B	Markoss Aviation Ltd	
G-MKVB	VS.349 Spitfire LF.VB (BM597)	Historic Aircraft Collection/Duxford	
G-MKVI	DH. Vampire FB.6 (WL505)	C. T. Topen	
G-MKXI	VS.365 Spitfire PR.XI (PL624:R)	P. A. Teichman	
G-MLAL	Jabiru J400	M. A. Scudder	
G-MLAS	Cessna 182E ★	Parachute jump trainer/St. Merryn	
G-MLFF	PA-23 Aztec 250E	W. C. Cullinane (G-WEBB/G-BJBU)	
G-MLGL	Colt 21A balloon	P. Baker	
G-MLHI	Maule MX-7-180 Star Rocket	Maulehigh (G-BTMJ)	
G-MLJL	Airbus A.330-243	MyTravel Airways	
G-MLLA	SOCATA T.8200 Tobago XL	C. E. Millar	
G-MLLE	CEA DR.200A-B	A. D. Evans	
G-MLSN	Hughes 369E	Molson Holdings Ltd (G-HMAC)	
G-MLTY	AS.365N-2 Dauphin 2	Crosby Enterprises Ltd	
G-MLWI	Thunder Ax7-77 balloon	M. L. & L. P. Willoughby	
G-MMAC	Dragon Srs.200	J. F. Ashton & J. P. Kirwan	
G-MMAE	Dragon Srs 150	P. J. Sheehy & K. S. Matcham	
G-MMAG	MBA Tiger Cub 440	M. J. Aubrey	
G-MMAI	Dragon Srs 2	G. S. Richardson	
G-MMAR	Southdown Puma Sprint	A. R. & J. Fawkes	
G-MMAZ	Southdown Puma Sprint	A. R. Smith	
G-MMBL	Southdown Puma	B. J. Farrell	
G-MMBN	Eurowing Goldwing	E. H. Jenkins	
G-MMBT	MBA Tiger Cub 440	B. Chamberlain	
G-MMBU	Eipper Quicksilver MX II	D. A. Norwood	
G-MMBV	Huntair Pathfinder	P. J. Bishop	
G-MMBY	Solar Wings Panther XL	P. Huddleston & R. M. Sheppard	
G-MMBZ	Solar Wings Typhoon P	S. C. Mann	
G-MMCI	Southdown Puma Sprint	D. M. Parsons	
G-MMCN	Hiway Skytrike	P. J. Ramsey	
G-MMCV	Solar Wings Typhoon III	G. Addison	
G-MMCX	MBA Super Tiger Cub 440	D. Harkin	
G-MMCZ	Flexiform Striker	T. D. Adamson	
G-MMDF	Southdown Lightning II	J. C. Haigh	
G-MMDK	Flexiform Striker	P. E. Blyth	
G-MMDN	Flexiform Striker	M. G. Griffiths	
G-MMDP	Southdown Sprint	G. V. Cowle	
G-MMDR	Huntair Pathfinder II	C. Dolling	
G-MMEK	Medway Hybred 44XL	M. G. J. Bridges	
G-MMFD	Flexiform Striker	M. E. & W. L. Chapman	
G-MMFE	Flexiform Striker	W. Camm	
G-MMFG	Flexiform Striker	M. G. Dean & M. J. Hadland	
G-MMFS	MBA Tiger Cub 440	G. S. Taylor	
G-MMFV	Flexiform Striker	R. A. Walton	
G-MMFY	Flexiform Dual Striker	K. R. M. Adair & S. R. Browne	
G-MMGF	MBA Tiger Cub 440	J. G. Boxall	
G-MMGL	MBA Tiger Cub 440	H. E. Dunning	
G-MMGS	Solar Wings Panther XL	R. J. Hood	
G-MMGT	Solar Wings Typhoon	H. Cook	
G-MMGU	Flexiform Sealander	A. D. Cranfield	
G-MMGV	Whittaker MW5 Sorcerer	M. W. J. Whittaker & G. N. Haffey	
G-MMHE	Gemini Sprint	N. L. Zaman	
G-MMHK	Hiway Super Scorpion	S. Davison	
G-MMHL	Hiway Super Scorpion	E. J. Blyth	
G-MMHN	MBA Tiger Cub 440	M. J. Aubrey	
G-MMHS	SMD Viper	C. J. Meadows	
G-MMIE	MBA Tiger Cub 440	B. M. Olliver	
G-MMIW	Southdown Puma Sprint	J. Ryland	
G-MMIX	MBA Tiger Cub 440	N. J. McKain	
G-MMJD	Southdown Puma Sprint	C. A. Sargent	
G-MMJF	Ultrasports Panther Dual 440	K. J. Hoare	
G-MMJG	Mainair Tri-Flyer 440	A. Strang	
G-MMJT	Southdown Puma Sprint	D. C. de la Haye	
G-MMJV	MBA Tiger Cub 440	D. G. Palmer	
G-MMJX	Teman Mono-Fly	M. Ingleton	
G-MMKA	Ultrasports Panther Dual	R. S. Wood	
G-MMKE	Birdman Chinook WT-11	D. M. Jackson	
G-MMKG	Solar Wings Typhoon XL	G. P. Lane	
G-MMKL	Mainair Gemini/Flash	D. W. Cox	
G-MMKM	Flexiform Dual Striker	S. W. Hutchinson	

G-MMKP – G-MMXW   BRITISH CIVIL REGISTRATIONS

Notes	Reg	Type	Owner or Operator
	G-MMKP	MBA Tiger Cub 440	J. W. Beaty
	G-MMKR	Southdown Lightning DS	C. R. Madden
	G-MMKV	Southdown Puma Sprint	A. L. Flude
	G-MMKX	Skyrider Phantom 330	G. J. Lampitt
	G-MMLE	Eurowing Goldwing SP	A. D. Bales
	G-MMLH	Hiway Demon	D. J. Lukey & P. M. Hendry
	G-MMMG	Eipper Quicksilver MXL	J. G. Campbell
	G-MMMH	Hadland Willow	M. J. Hadland
	G-MMML	Dragon 150	R. G. Huntley
	G-MMMN	Ultrasports Panther Dual 440	C. Downton
	G-MMNB	Eipper Quicksilver MX	M. J. Lindop
	G-MMNC	Eipper Quicksilver MX	W. S. Toulmin
	G-MMNH	Dragon 150	T. J. Barlow
	G-MMNN	Buzzard	E. W. Sherry
	G-MMNS	Mitchell U-2 Super Wing	C. Lawson & J. C. Lister
	G-MMNT	Flexiform Striker	C. R. Thorne
	G-MMOB	Southdown Sprint	D. Woolcock
	G-MMOH	Solar Wings Typhoon XL	T. H. Scott
	G-MMOK	Solar Wings Panther XL	R. F. & A. J. Foster
	G-MMOW	Mainair Gemini/Flash	D. P. Quaintrell
	G-MMPG	Southdown Puma	T. J. Hector
	G-MMPH	Southdown Puma Sprint	J. Siddle
	G-MMPL	Flexiform Dual Striker	P. D. Lawrence
	G-MMPO	Mainair Gemini/Flash	M.A Feber
	G-MMPU	Ultrasports Tripacer 250	J. T. Halford
	G-MMPZ	Teman Mono-Fly	P. B. Kylo
	G-MMRH	Highway Skytrike	A. M. Sirant
	G-MMRL	Solar Wings Panther XL	R. J. Hood
	G-MMRN	Southdown Puma Sprint	D. C. Read
	G-MMRP	Mainair Gemini	J. C. S. Jones
	G-MMRW	Flexiform Dual Striker	M. D. Hinge
	G-MMSA	Ultrasports Panther XL	T. W. Thiele & G. Savage
	G-MMSG	Solar Wings Panther XL-S	R. W. McKee
	G-MMSH	Solar Wings Panther XL	I. J. Drake
	G-MMSO	Mainair Tri-Flyer 440	K. A. Maughan
	G-MMSP	Mainair Gemini/Flash	J. Whiteford
	G-MMTA	Ultrasports Panther XL	P. A. McMahon
	G-MMTC	Ultrasports Panther Dual	T. L. Moses
	G-MMTD	Mainair Tri-Flyer 330	W. E. Teare
	G-MMTG	Mainair Gemini Sprint	J. C. F. Dalton
	G-MMTJ	Southdown Puma Sprint	P. J. Kirwan
	G-MMTL	Mainair Gemini	K. Birkett
	G-MMTR	Ultrasports Panther	P. M. Kelsey
	G-MMTS	Solar Wings Panther XL	A. E. James
	G-MMTV	American Aerolights Eagle Seaplane	L. K. Fowler
	G-MMTX	Mainair Gemini 440	A. Worthington
	G-MMTY	Fisher FP.202U	B. E. Maggs
	G-MMTZ	Eurowing Goldwing	R. B. D. Baker
	G-MMUA	Southdown Puma Sprint	M. R. Crowhurst
	G-MMUH	Mainair Tri-Flyer	J. P. Nicklin
	G-MMUM	MBA Tiger Cub 440	Coulson Flying Services Ltd
	G-MMUO	Mainair Gemini/Flash	D. R. Howells & B. D. Bastin
	G-MMUV	Southdown Puma Sprint	D. C. Read
	G-MMUW	Mainair Gemini/Flash	J. C. K. Scardifield
	G-MMUX	Gemini Sprint	M. D. Howe
	G-MMVA	Southdown Puma Sprint	C. E. Tomkins
	G-MMVH	Southdown Raven	G. W. & K. M. Carwardine
	G-MMVI	Southdown Puma Sprint	G. R. Williams
	G-MMVS	Skyhook Pixie	B. W. Olley
	G-MMVX	Southdown Puma Sprint	M. P. Jones
	G-MMVZ	Southdown Puma Sprint	P. Whelan/Ireland
	G-MMWA	Mainair Gemini/Flash	N. Roberts
	G-MMWC	Eipper Quicksilver MXII	M. Holmes & J. S. Harris
	G-MMWG	Greenslade Mono-Trike	C. R. Green
	G-MMWL	Eurowing Goldwing	A.D Bales
	G-MMWS	Mainair Tri-Flyer	P. H. Risdale
	G-MMWX	Southdown Puma Sprint	B. E. Wagenhauser
	G-MMXD	Mainair Gemini/Flash	W. A. Bibby
	G-MMXJ	Mainair Gemini/Flash	R. Meredith-Hardy
	G-MMXO	Southdown Puma Sprint	D. J. Tasker
	G-MMXU	Mainair Gemini/Flash	T. J. Franklin
	G-MMXV	Mainair Gemini/Flash	D. Rowland
	G-MMXW	Mainair Gemini/Sprint	A. Hodgson

BRITISH CIVIL REGISTRATIONS

G-MMYA – G-MNFM

Reg	Type	Owner or Operator	Notes
G-MMYA	Solar Wings Pegasus XL	R. G. Mason	
G-MMYF	Southdown Puma Sprint	M. Campbell	
G-MMYL	Cyclone 70	E. W. P. Van Zeller	
G-MMYN	Ultrasports Panther XL	H. J. Long	
G-MMYO	Southdown Puma Sprint	P. R. Whitehouse	
G-MMYT	Southdown Puma Sprint	J. K. Divall	
G-MMYU	Southdown Puma Sprint	M. V. Harris	
G-MMYV	Webb Trike	S. B. Herbert	
G-MMYY	Southdown Puma Sprint	D. J. Whittle	
G-MMZA	Mainair Gemini/Flash	G. T. Johnston	
G-MMZD	Mainair Gemini/Flash	P. L. Dowd	
G-MMZF	Mainair Gemini/Flash	J. Tait	
G-MMZG	Ultrasports Panther XL-S	R. C. Bailey	
G-MMZI	Medway 130SX	J. Messenger	
G-MMZK	Mainair Gemini/Flash	G. Jones & B. Lee	
G-MMZM	Mainair Gemini/Flash	H. Brown	
G-MMZN	Mainair Gemini/Flash	W. K. Dulas	
G-MMZV	Mainair Gemini/Flash	R. Till	
G-MMZW	Southdown Puma Sprint	M. G. Ashbee	
G-MNAC	Mainair Gemini/Flash	I. E. S. Cole	
G-MNAE	Mainair Gemini/Flash	G. C. luddington	
G-MNAI	Ultrasports Panther XL-S	R. G. Cameron	
G-MNAV	Southdown Puma Sprint	G. P. Morling	
G-MNAW	Solar Wings Pegasus XL-R	D. J. Harber	
G-MNAX	Solar Wings Pegasus XL-R	B. J. Phillips	
G-MNAY	Ultrasports Panther XL-S	A. Seaton	
G-MNAZ	Solar Wings Pegasus XL-R	R. W. houldsworth	
G-MNBA	Solar Wings Pegasus XL-R	A. J. Todd	
G-MNBB	Solar Wings Pegasus XL-R	R. Piper	
G-MNBC	Solar Wings Pegasus XL-R	N. Kelly	
G-MNBD	Mainair Gemini/Flash	P. Woodcock	
G-MNBE	Southdown Puma Sprint	D. Newton	
G-MNBF	Mainair Gemini/Flash	P. Mokryk & S. King	
G-MNBG	Mainair Gemini/Flash	T. Barnett	
G-MNBI	Solar Wings Panther XL-S	M. O'Connell	
G-MNBM	Southdown Puma Sprint	I. H. Gates	
G-MNBN	Mainair Gemini/Flash	I. Bond	
G-MNBP	Mainair Gemini/Flash	G. A. Harper	
G-MNBS	Mainair Gemini/Flash	P. A. Comins	
G-MNBT	Mainair Gemini/Flash	P. Robshaw	
G-MNBV	Mainair Gemini/Flash	J. Walshe	
G-MNCA	Hiway Demon 175	M. A. Sirant	
G-MNCF	Mainair Gemini/Flash	S. R. Bell	
G-MNCG	Mainair Gemini/Flash	J. E. F. Fletcher	
G-MNCI	Southdown Puma Sprint	R. M. Waite & N. Hewitt	
G-MNCJ	Mainair Gemini/Flash	R. S. McLeister	
G-MNCM	CFM Shadow Srs B	K. G. D. Macrae	
G-MNCO	Eipper Quicksilver MXII	S. Lawton	
G-MNCP	Southdown Puma Sprint	D. M. Lane & S. Baker	
G-MNCS	Skyrider Airsports Phantom	S. P. Allen	
G-MNCV	Medway Hybred 44XL	D. M. Mickleburgh	
G-MNDC	Mainair Gemini/Flash	M. Medlock	
G-MNDD	Mainair Scorcher Solo	L. Hurman	
G-MNDE	Medway Half Pint	C. D. Wills	
G-MNDF	Mainair Gemini/Flash	W. G. Nicol	
G-MNDO	Mainair Flash	R. H. Cooke	
G-MNDU	Midland Sirocco 377GB	M. A. Collins	
G-MNDY	Southdown Puma Sprint	A. M. Coupland	
G-MNEF	Mainair Gemini/Flash	P. G. Richards	
G-MNEG	Mainair Gemini/Flash	A. Sexton/Ireland	
G-MNEH	Mainair Gemini/Flash	I. Rawson	
G-MNEI	Medway Hybred 440	L. G. Thompson	
G-MNEK	Medway Half Pint	M. I. Dougall	
G-MNER	CFM Shadow Srs B	F. C. Claydon	
G-MNET	Mainair Gemini/Flash	I. P. Stubbins	
G-MNEV	Mainair Gemini/Flash	M. Gardiner	
G-MNEY	Mainair Gemini/Flash	D. A. Spiers	
G-MNFB	Southdown Puma Sprint	C. Lawrence	
G-MNFF	Mainair Gemini/Flash	C. H. Spencer & R. P. Cook	
G-MNFG	Southdown Puma Sprint	A. C. Hing	
G-MNFL	AMF Chevvron	P. W. Wright	
G-MNFM	Mainair Gemini/Flash	P. M. Fidell	

G-MNFN – G-MNLY

Notes	Reg	Type	Owner or Operator
	G-MNFN	Mainair Gemini/Flash	J. R. Martin
	G-MNFP	Mainair Gemini/Flash	P. Howarth & S. Farnsworth
	G-MNGD	Tri-Pacer/Typhoon	E. K. Perchard
	G-MNGG	Solar Wings Pegasus XL-R	I. D. Mallinson
	G-MNGK	Mainair Gemini/Flash	J. Pulford
	G-MNGM	Mainair Gemini/Flash	D. R. Beale & J. E. Caffull
	G-MNGT	Mainair Gemini/Flash	J. W. Biegus
	G-MNGU	Mainair Gemini/Flash	G. Macpherson-Irvine
	G-MNGW	Mainair Gemini/Flash	F. R. Stephens
	G-MNGX	Southdown Puma Sprint	A. J. Morris
	G-MNHD	Solar Wings Pegasus XL-R	P. D. Stiles
	G-MNHE	Solar Wings Pegasus XL-R	D. Stevens
	G-MNHF	Solar Wings Pegasus XL-R	J. E. Cox
	G-MNHH	Solar Wings Panther XL-S	F. J. Williams
	G-MNHI	Solar Wings Pegasus XL-R	R. W. Matthews
	G-MNHJ	Solar Wings Pegasus XL-R	S. J. Wood
	G-MNHK	Solar Wings Pegasus XL-R	K. Buckley
	G-MNHL	Solar Wings Pegasus XL-R	The Microlight School (Lichfield) Ltd
	G-MNHM	Solar Wings Pegasus XL-R	A. C. Bell
	G-MNHN	Solar Wings Pegasus XL-R	Northwest Microlights Ltd
	G-MNHR	Solar Wings Pegasus XL-R	B. D. Jackson
	G-MNHS	Solar Wings Pegasus XL-R	M. D. Packer
	G-MNHT	Solar Wings Pegasus XL-R	J. W. Coventry
	G-MNHZ	Mainair Gemini/Flash	I. O. S. Ross
	G-MNIA	Mainair Gemini/Flash	A. E. Dix
	G-MNID	Mainair Gemini/Flash	G. Nicholls
	G-MNIE	Mainair Gemini/Flash	G. M. Hewer
	G-MNIF	Mainair Gemini/Flash	M. Devlin
	G-MNIG	Mainair Gemini/Flash	A. B. Woods
	G-MNIH	Mainair Gemini/Flash	S. I. Laurance
	G-MNII	Mainair Gemini/Flash	R. F. Finnis
	G-MNIK	Pegasus Photon	J. Grotrian
	G-MNIL	Southdown Puma Sprint	A. Bishop
	G-MNIM	Maxair Hummer	K. Wood
	G-MNIS	CFM Shadow Srs B	R. W. Payne
	G-MNIT	Aerial Arts 130SX	M. J. Edmett
	G-MNIU	Solar Wings Pegasus Photon	S. Ferguson
	G-MNIZ	Mainair Gemini/Flash	A. G. Power
	G-MNJB	Southdown Raven	W. Flood
	G-MNJD	Southdown Puma Sprint	M. L. Smith
	G-MNJF	Dragon 150	B. W. Langley
	G-MNJG	Gemini Sprint MS	T. J. Gayton-Polley
	G-MNJH	Solar Wings Pegasus Flash	C. P. Course
	G-MNJJ	Solar Wings Pegasus Flash	P. A. Shelley
	G-MNJL	Solar Wings Pegasus Flash	S. D. Thomas
	G-MNJN	Solar Wings Pegasus Flash	D. Thorn
	G-MNJO	Solar Wings Pegasus Flash	S. Clarke
	G-MNJR	Solar Wings Pegasus Flash	M. G. Ashbee
	G-MNJS	Southdown Puma Sprint	E. A. Frost
	G-MNJT	Southdown Raven	P. A. Harris
	G-MNJU	Mainair Gemini/Flash	J. P. Wilmans
	G-MNJX	Medway Hybred 44XL	H. A. Stewart
	G-MNKB	Solar Wings Pegasus Photon	M. E. Gilbert
	G-MNKC	Solar Wings Pegasus Photon	C. Murphy
	G-MNKD	Solar Wings Pegasus Photon	D. Glasper
	G-MNKE	Solar Wings Pegasus Photon	M. J. Olsen
	G-MNKG	Solar Wings Pegasus Photon	T. W. Thompson
	G-MNKK	Solar Wings Pegasus Photon	M. E. Gilbert
	G-MNKM	MBA Tiger Cub 440	A. R. Sunley
	G-MNKO	Solar Wings Pegasus Flash	J. H. Treadwell
	G-MNKP	Solar Wings Pegasus Flash	I. N. Miller
	G-MNKR	Solar Wings Pegasus Flash	A. Young
	G-MNKU	Southdown Puma Sprint	S. P. O'Hannrachain
	G-MNKV	Solar Wings Pegasus Flash	K. S. G. Lindfield
	G-MNKW	Solar Wings Pegasus Flash	S. P. Halford
	G-MNKX	Solar Wings Pegasus Flash	P. Samal
	G-MNKZ	Southdown Raven	G. B. Gratton
	G-MNLH	Romain Cobra Biplane	J. W. E. Romain
	G-MNLI	Mainair Gemini/Flash	P. M. Fessi
	G-MNLM	Southdown Raven	A. P. White
	G-MNLN	Southdown Raven	A. S. Windley
	G-MNLT	Southdown Raven	J. L. Stachini
	G-MNLY	Mainair Gemini/Flash	P. D. Parry

BRITISH CIVIL REGISTRATIONS   G-MNLZ – G-MNUU

Reg	Type	Owner or Operator	Notes
G-MNLZ	Southdown Raven	R. Downham	
G-MNMC	Mainair Gemini Sprint	G. A. Davidson	
G-MNMD	Southdown Raven	P. G. Overall	
G-MNMG	Mainair Gemini/Flash	N. A. M. Beyer-Kay	
G-MNMI	Mainair Gemini/Flash	A. D. Bales	
G-MNMK	Solar Wings Pegasus XL-R	A. F. Smallacombe	
G-MNML	Southdown Puma Sprint	R. C. Carr	
G-MNMM	Aerotech MW5 Sorcerer	S. F. N. Warnell	
G-MNMN	Medway Hybred 44XLR	D. S. Blofeld	
G-MNMU	Southdown Raven	M. J. Curley	
G-MNMV	Mainair Gemini/Flash	S. Staig	
G-MNMW	Aerotech MW6 Merlin	E. F. Clapham	
G-MNMY	Cyclone 70	N. R. Beale	
G-MNNA	Southdown Raven	D. & G. D. Palfrey	
G-MNNB	Southdown Raven	J. F. Horn	
G-MNNC	Southdown Raven	S. A. Sacker	
G-MNNF	Mainair Gemini/Flash	W. J. Gunn	
G-MNNG	Solar Wings Photon	K. B. Woods	
G-MNNI	Mainair Gemini/Flash	J. C. Miller	
G-MNNJ	Mainair Gemini/Flash II	H. D. Lynch	
G-MNNL	Mainair Gemini/Flash	D. Wilson	
G-MNNM	Mainair Scorcher Solo	L. L. Perry & S. R. Leeper	
G-MNNO	Southdown Raven	M. J. Robbins	
G-MNNR	Mainair Gemini/Flash	W. A. B. Hill	
G-MNNS	Eurowing Goldwing	J. S. R. Moodie	
G-MNNY	Solar Wings Pegasus Flash	C. W. Payne	
G-MNNZ	Solar Wings Pegasus Flash	R. D. A. Henderson	
G-MNPA	Solar Wings Pegasus Flash	N. T. Murphy	
G-MNPC	Mainair Gemini/Flash	M. S. McGimpsey	
G-MNPV	Mainair Scorcher Solo	M. L. Walsh	
G-MNPY	Mainair Scorcher Solo	R. N. O. Kingsbury	
G-MNPZ	Mainair Scorcher Solo	S. Stevens	
G-MNRD	Ultraflight Lazair IIIE	Sywell Lazair Group	
G-MNRE	Mainair Scorcher Solo	A. P. Pearce	
G-MNRI	Hornet Dual Trainer	R. H. Goll	
G-MNRK	Hornet Dual Trainer	M. A. H. Milne	
G-MNRM	Hornet Dual Trainer	I. C. Cannan	
G-MNRP	Southdown Raven	C. Moore	
G-MNRS	Southdown Raven	M. C. Newman	
G-MNRT	Midland Ultralights Sirocco	R. F. Hinton	
G-MNRW	Mainair Gemini/Flash II	D. Buckthorpe	
G-MNRX	Mainair Gemini/Flash II	R. Downham	
G-MNRZ	Mainair Scorcher Solo	Mainair Microlight Centre Ltd/Barton	
G-MNSA	Mainair Gemini/Flash	W. F. G. Panayiotiou	
G-MNSD	Solar Wings Typhoon S4	A. Strydom	
G-MNSH	Solar Wings Pegasus Flash II	D. Lee	
G-MNSI	Mainair Gemini/Flash II	J-P. Trouillard	
G-MNSJ	Mainair Gemini/Flash	G. J. Cadden	
G-MNSL	Southdown Raven X	P. B. Robinson	
G-MNSX	Southdown Raven X	S. F. Chave	
G-MNSY	Southdown Raven X	L. A. Hosegood	
G-MNTC	Southdown Raven X	D. S. Bancarlari	
G-MNTD	Aerial Arts Chaser 110SX	B. Richardson	
G-MNTE	Southdown Raven X	E. Foster	
G-MNTI	Mainair Gemini/Flash	R. T. Strathie	
G-MNTK	CFM Shadow Srs B	A. B. Potts	
G-MNTM	Southdown Raven X	D. M. Garland	
G-MNTN	Southdown Raven X	J. Hall	
G-MNTP	CFM Shadow Srs B	E. G. White	
G-MNTT	Medway Half Pint	P. J. Burrow	
G-MNTU	Mainair Gemini/Flash II	G.S. Brewer	
G-MNTV	Mainair Gemini/Flash II	A.M. Sirant	
G-MNTY	Southdown Raven X	S. Phillips	
G-MNTZ	Mainair Gemini/Flash II	D. E. Milner	
G-MNUA	Mainair Gemini/Flash II	P. Hughes & S. Beggan	
G-MNUD	Solar Wings Pegasus Flash II	P. G. H. Milbank	
G-MNUE	Solar Wings Pegasus Flash II	C. A. Keeble	
G-MNUF	Mainair Gemini/Flash II	C, Hannaby	
G-MNUG	Mainair Gemini/Flash II	A. S. Nader	
G-MNUI	Skyhook Cutlass Dual	M. Holling	
G-MNUO	Mainair Gemini/Flash II	P. S. Taylor	
G-MNUR	Mainair Gemini/Flash II	J. C. Greves	
G-MNUU	Southdown Raven X	P. N. Jackson	

G-MNUX – G-MOHS **BRITISH CIVIL REGISTRATIONS**

Notes	Reg	Type	Owner or Operator
	G-MNUX	Solar Wings Pegasus XL-R	A. M. Smith
	G-MNVB	Solar Wings Pegasus XL-R	M. J. Melvin
	G-MNVC	Solar Wings Pegasus XL-R	M. N. C. Ward
	G-MNVE	Solar Wings Pegasus XL-R	M. P. Aris
	G-MNVG	Solar Wings Pegasus Flash II	D. J. Ward
	G-MNVH	Solar Wings Pegasus Flash II	J. A. Clarke & C. Hall
	G-MNVI	CFM Shadow Srs B	D. R. C. Pugh
	G-MNVJ	CFM Shadow Srs CD	V. C. Readhead
	G-MNVK	CFM Shadow Srs B	M. Cheetham
	G-MNVN	Southdown Raven X	R. J. Styles
	G-MNVO	Hovey Whing-Ding II	C. Wilson
	G-MNVT	Mainair Gemini/Flash II	ACB Hydraulics
	G-MNVV	Mainair Gemini/Flash II	T. Wilbor
	G-MNVW	Mainair Gemini/Flash II	J. C. Munro-Hunt
	G-MNVZ	Solar Wings Pegasus Photon	J. J. Russ
	G-MNWD	Mainair Gemini/Flash	M. B. Rutherford
	G-MNWG	Southdown Raven X	D. Murray
	G-MNWI	Mainair Gemini/Flash II	G. Shaw
	G-MNWL	Aerial Arts 130SX	E. H. Snook
	G-MNWU	Solar Wings Pegasus Flash II	S. P. Wass
	G-MNWV	Solar Wings Pegasus Flash II	Pegasus Group
	G-MNWW	Solar Wings Pegasus XL-R	Chiltern Flyers Aero Tow Group
	G-MNWY	CFM Shadown Srs B	N. E. Gormley
	G-MNWZ	Mainair Gemini/Flash II	W. T. Hume
	G-MNXB	Solar Wings Photon	G. W. Carwardine
	G-MNXE	Southdown Raven X	A. E. Silvey
	G-MNXF	Southdown Raven X	D. E. Gwenin
	G-MNXG	Southdown Raven X	E. M. & M. A. Williams
	G-MNXI	Southdown Raven X	P. K. Morley
	G-MNXO	Medway Hybred 44XLR	D. L. Turner
	G-MNXP	Pegasus Flash II	I. K. Priestley
	G-MNXS	Mainair Gemini/Flash II	F. T. Rawlins
	G-MNXU	Mainair Gemini/Flash II	J. M. Hucker
	G-MNXX	CFM Shadow Srs BD	P. J. Mogg
	G-MNXZ	Whittaker MW5 Sorcerer	A. J. Glynn
	G-MNYA	Solar Wings Pegasus Flash II	C. Trollope
	G-MNYC	Solar Wings Pegasus XL-R	A. N. Papworth
	G-MNYD	Aerial Arts 110SX Chaser	B. Richardson
	G-MNYE	Aerial Arts 110SX Chaser	R. J. Ripley
	G-MNYF	Aerial Arts 110SX Chaser	B. Richardson
	G-MNYG	Southdown Raven	K. Clifford
	G-MNYJ	Mainair Gemini/Flash II	G. B. Jones
	G-MNYK	Mainair Gemini/Flash II	J. J. Ryan
	G-MNYL	Southdown Raven X	A. D. F. Clifford
	G-MNYM	Southdown Raven X	R. L. Davis
	G-MNYP	Southdown Raven X	A. G. Davies
	G-MNYU	Pegasus XL-R	G. L. Turner
	G-MNYW	Solar Wings Pegasus XL-R	M. P. Waldock
	G-MNYX	Solar Wings Pegasus XL-R	P. Mayes & J. P. Widdowson
	G-MNYZ	SW Pegasus Flash	A. C. Bartolozzi
	G-MNZB	Mainair Gemini/Flash II	P. A. Ryder
	G-MNZC	Mainair Gemini/Flash II	C. J. Whittaker
	G-MNZD	Mainair Gemini/Flash II	N. D. Carter
	G-MNZF	Mainair Gemini/Flash II	P. C. Askew
	G-MNZJ	CFM Shadow Srs BD	T. E. P. Eves
	G-MNZK	Solar Wings Pegasus XL-R	P. J. Appleby
	G-MNZP	CFM Shadow Srs B	J. G. Wakeford
	G-MNZR	CFM Shadown Srs BD	P. J. Watson
	G-MNZS	Aerial Arts 130SX	N. R. Beale
	G-MNZU	Eurowing Goldwing	P. D. Coppin & P. R. Millen
	G-MNZW	Southdown Raven X	T. A. Willcox
	G-MNZX	Southdown Raven X	B. F. Hole
	G-MNZZ	CFM Shadow Srs B	Shadow Aviation Ltd
	G-MOAC	Beech F33A Bonanza	R. M. Camrass
	G-MOAN	Aeromot AMT-200S Super Ximango	A. J. Leigh
	G-MODE	Eurocopter EC 120B	P. A. Cripps
	G-MOFB	Cameron O-120 balloon	D. M. Moffat
	G-MOFF	Cameron O-77 balloon	D. M. Moffat
	G-MOFZ	Cameron O-90 balloon	D. M. Moffat
	G-MOGI	AA-5A Cheetah	MOGI Flying Group (G-BFMU)
	G-MOGY	Robinson R22 Beta	Northumbria Helicopters Ltd
	G-MOHS	PA-31-350 Navajo Chieftain	Sky Air Travel Ltd (G-BWOC)

BRITISH CIVIL REGISTRATIONS
G-MOKE – G-MSFT

Reg	Type	Owner or Operator	Notes
G-MOKE	Cameron V-77 balloon	D. D. Owen/Luxembourg	
G-MOLE	Taylor JT.2 Titch	R. Calverley	
G-MOLI	Cameron A-250 balloon	Wickers Air Balloon Co	
G-MOLL	PA-32-301T Turbo Saratoga	M. S. Bennett	
G-MOMA	Thruster T.600N 450	Turley Farms Ltd (G-CCIB)	
G-MOMO	Agusta A109E Power Elite	Air Harrods Ltd/Stansted	
G-MONB	Boeing 757-2T7	Monarch Airlines Ltd/Luton	
G-MONC	Boeing 757-2T7	Monarch Airlines Ltd/Luton	
G-MOND	Boeing 757-2T7	Monarch Airlines Ltd/Luton	
G-MONE	Boeing 757-2T7	Monarch Airlines Ltd/Luton	
G-MONI	Monnett Moni	R. M. Edworthy	
G-MONJ	Boeing 757-2T7	Monarch Airlines Ltd/Luton	
G-MONK	Boeing 757-2T7	Monarch Airlines Ltd/Luton	
G-MONR	Airbus A.300-605R	Monarch Airlines Ltd/Luton	
G-MONS	Airbus A.300-605R	Monarch Airlines Ltd/Luton	
G-MONX	Airbus A.320-212	Monarch Airlines Ltd/Luton	
G-MOOO	Learjet 40	LPC Aviation Ltd	
G-MOOR	SOCATA TB10 Tobago	P. D. Kirkham (G-MILK)	
G-MOOS	P.56 Provost T.1 (XF690)	T. J. Manna/Cranfield (G-BGKA)	
G-MOSS	Beech 95-D55 Baron	S. C. Tysoe (G-AWAD)	
G-MOSY	Cameron O-84 balloon	P. L. Mossman	
G-MOTA	Bell 206B JetRanger 3	J. W. Sandle	
G-MOTH	DH.82A Tiger Moth (K2567)	P. T. Szluha	
G-MOTI	Robin DR.400/500	Tango India Flying Group	
G-MOTO	PA-24 Comanche 180	L. T. & S. Evans/Sandown (G-EDHE/G-ASFH)	
G-MOTR	Enstrom 280C Shark	Motor Provider Ltd (G-BGWS)	
G-MOUL	Maule M6-235	M. Klinge	
G-MOUN	Beech B200 Super King Air	Real Aero Club de Valencia	
G-MOUR	HS. Gnat T.1 (XR991)	Yellowjack Group/Kemble	
G-MOUT	Cessna 182T	C. Mountain	
G-MOVE	PA-60-601P Aerostar	Flight Consultancy Services	
G-MOVI	PA-32R-301 Saratoga SP	G-BOON Ltd (G-MARI)	
G-MOWG	Aeroprakt A22-L Foxbat	J. Smith	
G-MOZZ	Avions Mudry CAP-10B	N. Skipworth & J. R. W. Luxton	
G-MPAA	PA-28-181 Archer III	MPFC Ltd	
G-MPAC	Ultravia Pelican PL	J. H. Leigh t/a The Clipgate Flying Grp	
G-MPBH	Cessna FA.152	The Moray Flying Club (1996) Ltd (G-FLIC/G-BILV)	
G-MPBI	Cessna 310R	M. P. Bolshaw	
G-MPCD	Airbus A.320-212	Monarch Airlines Ltd	
G-MPRL	Cessna 210M	Myriad Public Relations Ltd	
G-MPSA	Eurocopter MBB BK-117C-2	McAlpine Helicopters Ltd	
G-MPSB	Eurocopter MBB BK-117C-2	McAlpine Helicopters Ltd	
G-MPSC	Eurocopter MBB BK-117C-2	McAlpine Helicopters Ltd	
G-MPWI	Robin HR.100/210	P. G. Clarkson & S. King	
G-MPWT	PA-34-220T Seneca III	R. L. Burt	
G-MRAF	Aeroprakt A22 Foxbat	M. Raflewski	
G-MRAJ	Hughes 369E	A. Jardine	
G-MRAM	Mignet HM.1000 Balerit	R. A. Marven	
G-MRED	Christavia Mk 1	E. Hewett	
G-MRJJ	Mainair Pegasus Quik	J.H. Sparks	
G-MRJK	Airbus A.320-214	Monarch Airlines Ltd/Luton	
G-MRKI	Extra EA.200/300	Extra 200 Ltd	
G-MRKS	Robinson R44	TJD Trade Ltd (G-RAYC)	
G-MRKT	Lindstrand LBL-90A balloon	Marketplace Public Relations (London) Ltd	
G-MRLL	NA P-51D Mustang (414419)	M. Hammond	
G-MRLN	Sky 240-24 balloon	Merlin Balloons	
G-MRMJ	Eurocopter AS.365N3 Dauphin 2	Whirligig Ltd	
G-MRMR	PA-31-350 Navajo Chieftain	MRMR (Flight Services) (G-WROX/G-BNZI)	
G-MROC	Pegasus Quantum 15-912	M. Convine	
G-MROD	Van's RV-7A	M. Rhodes	
G-MROY	Ikarus C.42	D. M. Jobbins & K. R. Rowland	
G-MRRR	Hughes 369E	Estate Air Ltd	
G-MRSN	Robinson R22 Beta	Yorkshire Helicopters Ltd	
G-MRST	PA-28 RT-201 Arrow IV	Calverton Flying Group Ltd	
G-MRTN	SOCATA TB10 Tobago	P. A Gange & M. S. Colebrook (G-BHET)	
G-MRTY	Cameron N-77 balloon	R. A. Vale & ptnrs	
G-MRVL	Van's RV-7	L. W. Taylor	
G-MSAL	MS.733 Alcyon (143)	M. Isbister t/a Alcyon Flying Group	
G-MSFC	PA-38-112 Tomahawk	Sherwood Flying Club Ltd/Tollerton	
G-MSFT	PA-28-161 Warrior II	Western Air (Thruxton) Ltd (G-MUMS)	

G-MSIX – G-MTEU   BRITISH CIVIL REGISTRATIONS

Notes	Reg	Type	Owner or Operator
	G-MSIX	Glaser-Dirks DG.800B	G-MSIX Group
	G-MSKY	Ikarus C.42	G-MSKY Group
	G-MSOO	Revolution Mini 500 helicopter	R. H. Ryan
	G-MSPT	Eurocopter EC 135T2	M Sport Ltd
	G-MSPY	Pegasus Quantum 15-912	J. Madhvani & R. K. Green
	G-MSTC	AA-5A Cheetah	Association of Manx Pilots/Isle of Man (G-BIJT)
	G-MSTG	NA P-51D Mustang (414419:LH-F)	M. Hammond
	G-MSTR	Cameron 110 Monster SS Baloon	ABC Flights Ltd (G-OJOB)
	G-MTAA	Solar Wings Pegasus XL-R	M. Skrinar
	G-MTAB	Mainair Gemini/Flash II	C. Thompson & J. Todd
	G-MTAC	Mainair Gemini/Flash II	R. Massey
	G-MTAE	Mainair Gemini/Flash II	C. E. Hannigan
	G-MTAF	Mainair Gemini/Flash II	P. A. Long
	G-MTAG	Mainair Gemini/Flash II	M. J. Cowie & J. P. Hardy
	G-MTAH	Mainair Gemini/Flash II	G. F. Atkinson
	G-MTAI	Solar Wings Pegasus XL-R	S. T. Elkington
	G-MTAJ	Solar Wings Pegasus XL-R	M. F. Jakeman
	G-MTAL	Solar Wings Photon	R. P. Wilkinson
	G-MTAO	Solar Wings Pegasus XL-R	S. P. Disney
	G-MTAP	Southdown Raven X	M. C. Newman
	G-MTAR	Mainair Gemini/Flash II	J. B. Woolley
	G-MTAS	Whittaker MW5 Sorcerer	R. L. Nyman
	G-MTAV	Solar Wings Pegasus XL-R	C. L. Harris & S. Fairweather
	G-MTAW	Solar Wings Pegasus XL-R	M. G. Ralph
	G-MTAX	Solar Wings Pegasus XL-R	G. Hawes
	G-MTAY	Solar Wings Pegasus XL-R	S. A. McLatchie
	G-MTAZ	Solar Wings Pegasus XL-R	T. L. Moses
	G-MTBB	Southdown Raven X	A. Miller
	G-MTBD	Mainair Gemini/Flash II	T. D. Holder
	G-MTBE	CFM Shadow Srs BD	S. K. Brown
	G-MTBH	Mainair Gemini/Flash II	P. & T. Sludds
	G-MTBJ	Mainair Gemini/Flash II	P. J. & R. M. Perry
	G-MTBK	Southdown Raven X	G. Davies
	G-MTBL	Solar Wings Pegasus XL-R	R. N. Whiting
	G-MTBN	Southdown Raven X	A. J. & S. E. Crosby-Jones
	G-MTBO	Southdown Raven X	J. Liversuch
	G-MTBP	Aerotech MW5 Sorcerer	G. Bennett
	G-MTBR	Aerotech MW5 Sorcerer	R. Poulter
	G-MTBS	Aerotech MW5 Sorcerer	T. B. Fowler
	G-MTBV	Solar Wings Pegasus XL-R	T. H. Scott
	G-MTBX	Mainair Gemini/Flash II	B. D. Hanscomb
	G-MTBY	Mainair Gemini/Flash II	D. Pearson
	G-MTBZ	Southdown Raven X	K. W. E. Brunnenkant
	G-MTCA	CFM Shadow Srs B	J. R. L. Murray
	G-MTCE	Mainair Gemini/Flash II	H. Shaw
	G-MTCK	SW Pegasus Flash	A. R. Cook
	G-MTCM	Southdown Raven X	J. C. Rose
	G-MTCN	Solar Wings Pegasus XL-R	S. R. Hughes
	G-MTCO	Solar Wings Pegasus XL-R	R. Johnson
	G-MTCP	Aerial Arts Chaser 110SX	B. Richardson
	G-MTCR	Solar Wings Pegasus XL-R	P. A. Gibbs
	G-MTCT	CFM Shadow Srs BD	R. Lawes
	G-MTCU	Mainair Gemini/Flash II	T. J. Philip
	G-MTDD	Aerial Arts Chaser 110SX	B. Richardson
	G-MTDE	American Aerolights 110SX	M. N. Hudson
	G-MTDF	Mainair Gemini/Flash II	P. G. Barnes
	G-MTDG	Solar Wings Pegasus XL-R	E. W. Laidlaw
	G-MTDI	Solar Wings Pegasus XL-R	D. Allan
	G-MTDK	Aerotech MW5 Sorcerer	C. C. Wright
	G-MTDO	Eipper Quicksilver MXII	D. L. Ham
	G-MTDR	Mainair Gemini/Flash II	A. L. S. Routledge & G. Bullock
	G-MTDU	CFM Shadow Srs BD	P. G. Hutchins
	G-MTDW	Mainair Gemini/Flash II	S. R. Leeper
	G-MTDY	Mainair Gemini/Flash II	S. Penoyre
	G-MTEC	Solar Wings Pegasus XL-R	R. W. Glover
	G-MTEE	Solar Wings Pegasus XL-R	M. Worthington
	G-MTEI	Mainair Gemini/Flash II	J. J. Littler
	G-MTEJ	Mainair Gemini/Flash II	M. Atkinson
	G-MTEK	Mainair Gemini/Flash II	G. M. Wrigley & M. O'Hearne
	G-MTES	Solar Wings Pegasus XL-R	N. P. Read
	G-MTET	Solar Wings Pegasus XL-R	K. Gilsenan
	G-MTEU	Solar Wings Pegasus XL-R	B. Harris

BRITISH CIVIL REGISTRATIONS
G-MTEW – G-MTJT

Reg	Type	Owner or Operator	Notes
G-MTEW	Solar Wings Pegasus XL-R	P. J. & R. W. Holley	
G-MTEX	Solar Wings Pegasus XL-R	C. M. & K. M. Bradford	
G-MTEY	Mainair Gemini/Flash II	A. Wells	
G-MTFA	Pegasus XL-R	S. Hindle	
G-MTFB	Solar Wings Pegasus XL-R	S. J. M. Morling	
G-MTFC	Medway Hybred 44XLR	J. K. Masters	
G-MTFG	AMF Chevvron 232	R. Gardner	
G-MTFI	Mainair Gemini/Flash II	L. Parker	
G-MTFM	Solar Wings Pegasus XL-R	P. R. G. Morley	
G-MTFN	Aerotech MW5 Sorcerer	S. M. King	
G-MTFP	Solar Wings Pegasus XL-R	C. Rickards	
G-MTFR	Solar Wings Pegasus XL-R	S. Ballantyne	
G-MTFT	Solar Wings Pegasus XL-R	A. T. Smith	
G-MTFU	CFM Shadow Srs CD	J. Anderson	
G-MTFZ	CFM Shadow Srs BD	R. P. Stoner	
G-MTGA	Mainair Gemini/Flash	B. S. Ogden	
G-MTGB	Thruster TST Mk 1	M. J. Aubrey	
G-MTGC	Thruster TST Mk 1	P. Smith & B. Foster	
G-MTGD	Thruster TST Mk 1	W. J. Lister	
G-MTGE	Thruster TST Mk 1	G. W. R. Swift	
G-MTGF	Thruster TST Mk 1	B. Swindon	
G-MTGH	Mainair Gemini/Flash IIA	J. R. Gillies	
G-MTGJ	Solar Wings Pegasus XL-R	M. S. Taylor	
G-MTGK	Solar Wings Pegasus XL-R	I. A. Smith	
G-MTGL	Solar Wings Pegasus XL-R	R. & P. J. Openshaw	
G-MTGM	Solar Wings Pegasus XL-R	TGM Sybdicate	
G-MTGO	Mainair Gemini/Flash	P. Jephcott	
G-MTGR	Thruster TST Mk 1	M. R. Grunwell	
G-MTGS	Thruster TST Mk 1	R. J. Nelson	
G-MTGT	Thruster TST Mk 1	A. W. Paterson & P. McVay	
G-MTGU	Thruster TST Mk 1	J. Jordan	
G-MTGV	CFM Shadow Srs BD	V. R. Riley	
G-MTGW	CFM Shadow Srs BD	A. D. Grix	
G-MTGX	Hornet Dual Trainer	M. A. Pantling	
G-MTHB	Aerotech MW5B Sorcerer	K.H.A. Negal	
G-MTHG	Solar Wings Pegasus XL-R	H. E. Paterson	
G-MTHH	Solar Wings Pegasus XL-R	J. Palmer	
G-MTHI	Solar Wings Pegasus XL-R	Thames Valley Aerosports Ltd	
G-MTHJ	Solar Wings Pegasus XL-R	M. R. Harrison	
G-MTHN	Solar Wings Pegasus XL-R	M. T. Seal	
G-MTHT	CFM Shadow Srs BD	S. H. Leahy	
G-MTHV	CFM Shadow Srs BD	K. R. Bircher	
G-MTHW	Mainair Gemini/Flash II	M. P. Dickens	
G-MTHZ	Mainair Gemini/Flash IIA	A. I. Kinnear	
G-MTIA	Mainair Gemini/Flash IIA	G. W. Jennings	
G-MTIB	Mainair Gemini/Flash IIA	K. P. Hayes	
G-MTIE	Solar Wings Pegasus XL-R	P. Wibberley	
G-MTIH	Solar Wings Pegasus XL-R	K. N. Rabey	
G-MTIJ	Solar Wings Pegasus XL-R	M. J. F. Gilbody	
G-MTIK	Southdown Raven X	G. A. Oldershaw	
G-MTIL	Mainair Gemini/Flash IIA	P. G. Nolan	
G-MTIM	Mainair Gemini/Flash IIA	T. M. Swan	
G-MTIN	Mainair Gemini/Flash IIA	S. J. Firth	
G-MTIO	Solar Wings Pegasus XL-R	M. Smith	
G-MTIP	Solar Wings Pegasus XL-R	M. P. Williams	
G-MTIR	Solar Wings Pegasus XL-R	G. Teasdale	
G-MTIS	Solar Wings Pegasus XL-R	N. P. Power	
G-MTIU	Solar Wings Pegasus XL-R	D. E. Pedder	
G-MTIV	Solar Wings Pegasus XL-R	P. J. Culverhouse	
G-MTIW	Solar Wings Pegasus XL-R	G. S. Francis	
G-MTIX	Solar Wings Pegasus XL-R	S. Pickering	
G-MTIY	Solar Wings Pegasus XL-R	P. J. Tanner	
G-MTIZ	Solar Wings Pegasus XL-R	S. L. Blount	
G-MTJA	Mainair Gemini/Flash IIA	A. McJannett-Smith & A. J. Holland	
G-MTJB	Mainair Gemini/Flash IIA	B. Skidmore	
G-MTJC	Mainair Gemini/Flash IIA	T. A. Dockrell	
G-MTJD	Mainair Gemini/Flash IIA	I. M. Armitage	
G-MTJE	Mainair Gemini/Flash IIA	I. O. S. Ross	
G-MTJG	Medway Hybred 44XLR	M. A. Trodden	
G-MTJH	SW Pegasus Flash	C. G. Ludgate	
G-MTJL	Mainair Gemini/Flash IIA	J. Murphy	
G-MTJS	Solar Wings Pegasus XL-Q	R. J. H. Hayward	
G-MTJT	Mainair Gemini/Flash IIA	D. T. A. Rees	

G-MTJV – G-MTOO

Notes	Reg	Type	Owner or Operator
	G-MTJV	Mainair Gemini/Flash IIA	T. A. Dobbins
	G-MTJW	Mainair Gemini/Flash IIA	J. F. Ashton
	G-MTJX	Hornet Dual Trainer/Raven	J. P. Kirwan
	G-MTJZ	Mainair Gemini/Flash IIA	J. G. & J. A. Hamnett
	G-MTKA	Thruster TST Mk 1	C. M. Bradford & D. C. Marsh
	G-MTKB	Thruster TST Mk 1	M. Hanna
	G-MTKD	Thruster TST Mk 1	E. Spain/Ireland
	G-MTKE	Thruster TST Mk 1	M. R. Jones
	G-MTKG	Solar Wings Pegasus XL-R	D. J. Wilkinson & D. H. May
	G-MTKH	Solar Wings Pegasus XL-R	K. Brooker
	G-MTKI	Solar Wings Pegasus XL-R	M. Wady
	G-MTKN	Mainair Gemini/Flash IIA	A. J. Altori
	G-MTKR	CFM Shadow Srs BD	D. P. Eichhorn
	G-MTKW	Mainair Gemini/Flash IIA	J. H. McIvor
	G-MTKX	Mainair Gemini/Flash IIA	G. E. Jones
	G-MTKZ	Mainair Gemini/Flash IIA	I. S. McNeill & W. J. F. McLean
	G-MTLB	Mainair Gemini/Flash IIA	B. L. Crouch
	G-MTLC	Mainair Gemini/Flash IIA	R. J. Alston
	G-MTLG	Solar Wings Pegasus XL-R	G. J. Simoni
	G-MTLI	Solar Wings Pegasus XL-R	M. McKay
	G-MTLJ	Solar Wings Pegasus XL-R	A. Brumby
	G-MTLL	Mainair Gemini/Flash IIA	M. S. Lawrence
	G-MTLM	Thruster TST Mk 1	R.J. Nelson
	G-MTLN	Thruster TST Mk 1	P. J. Fahie
	G-MTLT	Solar Wings Pegasus XL-R	K. M. Mayling
	G-MTLV	Solar Wings Pegasus XL-R	R. W. Keene
	G-MTLX	Medway Hybred 44XLR	D. A. Coupland
	G-MTLY	Solar Wings Pegasus XL-R	I. Johnston
	G-MTLZ	Whittaker MW5 Sorceror	M. J. Davenport
	G-MTMA	Mainair Gemini/Flash IIA	S. J. Farr
	G-MTMC	Mainair Gemini/Flash IIA	A. R. Johnson
	G-MTME	Solar Wings Pegasus XL-R	P. C. J. Coidan
	G-MTMF	Solar Wings Pegasus XL-R	J. T. M. Smith
	G-MTMG	Solar Wings Pegasus XL-R	C. W. & P. E. F. Suckling
	G-MTMI	Solar Wings Pegasus XL-R	J. Hunter
	G-MTML	Mainair Gemini/Flash IIA	J. F. Ashton
	G-MTMO	Raven X	H. Tuvey
	G-MTMP	Hornet Dual Trainer/Raven	P. G. Owen
	G-MTMR	Hornet Dual Trainer/Raven	D. J. Smith
	G-MTMT	Mainair Gemini/Flash IIA	C. Pickvance
	G-MTMV	Mainair Gemini/Flash IIA	G. J. Small
	G-MTMW	Mainair Gemini/Flash IIA	F. Lees
	G-MTMX	CFM Shadow Srs BD	D. R. White
	G-MTMY	CFM Shadow Srs BD	A. J. Harpley
	G-MTNC	Mainair Gemini/Flash IIA	D. J. Kelly & M. Titmus
	G-MTND	Medway Hybred 44XLR	Butty Boys Flying Group
	G-MTNE	Medway Hybred 44XLR	A. G. Rodenburg
	G-MTNF	Medway Hybred 44XLR	P. A. Bedford
	G-MTNG	Mainair Gemini/Flash IIA	A. N. Bellis
	G-MTNH	Mainair Gemini/Flash IIA	J. R. Smart
	G-MTNI	Mainair Gemini/Flash IIA	D. Gatland
	G-MTNJ	Mainair Gemini/Flash IIA	S. F. Kennedy
	G-MTNK	Weedhopper JC-24B	S. R. Davis
	G-MTNL	Mainair Gemini/Flash IIA	R. A. Matthews
	G-MTNM	Mainair Gemini/Flash IIA	C. J. Janson
	G-MTNO	Solar Wings Pegasus XL-Q	A. F. Batchelor
	G-MTNP	Solar Wings Pegasus XL-Q	G. G. Roberts
	G-MTNR	Thruster TST Mk 1	A. M. Sirant
	G-MTNT	Thruster TST Mk 1	M. J. Clifford
	G-MTNU	Thruster TST Mk 1	T. H. Brearley
	G-MTNV	Thruster TST Mk 1	J. B. Russell
	G-MTNY	Mainair Gemini/Flash IIA	R. .C. Granger
	G-MTOA	Solar Wings Pegasus XL-R	R. A. Bird
	G-MTOB	Solar Wings Pegasus XL-R	P. S. Lemm
	G-MTOD	Solar Wings Pegasus XL-R	T. A. Gordon
	G-MTOE	Solar Wings Pegasus XL-R	K. J. Bright
	G-MTOF	Solar Wings Pegasus XL-R	J. C. Ettridge
	G-MTOG	Solar Wings Pegasus XL-R	J. M. McLay
	G-MTOH	Solar Wings Pegasus XL-R	H. Cook
	G-MTOJ	Solar Wings Pegasus XL-R	S. Jelley
	G-MTOK	Solar Wings Pegasus XL-R	W. S. Davis
	G-MTON	Solar Wings Pegasus XL-R	D. J. Willett
	G-MTOO	Solar Wings Pegasus XL-R	G. W. Bulmer

BRITISH CIVIL REGISTRATIONS — G-MTOP – G-MTUL

Reg	Type	Owner or Operator	Notes
G-MTOP	Solar Wings Pegasus XL-R	J. Pooler	
G-MTOR	Solar Wings Pegasus XL-R	W. F. G. Panayiotiou	
G-MTOS	Solar Wings Pegasus XL-R	C. McKay	
G-MTOT	Solar Wings Pegasus XL-R	A. J. Lloyd	
G-MTOU	Solar Wings Pegasus XL-R	D. T. Smith	
G-MTOY	Solar Wings Pegasus XL-R	G-MTOY Group	
G-MTOZ	Solar Wings Pegasus XL-R	M. A. Furber	
G-MTPA	Mainair Gemini/Flash IIA	C. Janes	
G-MTPB	Mainair Gemini/Flash IIA	M. J. Jones	
G-MTPC	Raven X	G. W. Carwardine	
G-MTPE	Solar Wings Pegasus XL-R	J. Bassett	
G-MTPF	Solar Wings Pegasus XL-R	P. M. Watts & A. S. Mitchel	
G-MTPG	Solar Wings Pegasus XL-R	J. Sullivan	
G-MTPI	Solar Wings Pegasus XL-R	R. J. Bullock	
G-MTPJ	Solar Wings Pegasus XL-R	D. Lockwood	
G-MTPK	Solar Wings Pegasus XL-R	S. H. James	
G-MTPL	Solar Wings Pegasus XL-R	C. J. Jones	
G-MTPM	Solar Wings Pegasus XL-R	D. K. Seal	
G-MTPP	Solar Wings Pegasus XL-R	P. Molyneux	
G-MTPR	Solar Wings Pegasus XL-R	T. Kenny	
G-MTPS	Solar Wings Pegasus XL-Q	G. Tyler	
G-MTPT	Thruster TST Mk 1	Chilbolton Thruster Group	
G-MTPU	Thruster TST Mk 1	K. J. Foxall	
G-MTPW	Thruster TST Mk 1	K. Hawthorne	
G-MTPX	Thruster TST Mk 1	T. Snook	
G-MTPY	Thruster TST Mk 1	C. M. Bradford	
G-MTRA	Mainair Gemini/Flash IIA	E. N. Alms	
G-MTRC	Midlands Ultralights Sirocco 377G	D. Thorpe	
G-MTRL	Hornet Dual Trainer	J. McAlpine	
G-MTRM	Solar Wings Pegasus XL-R	R.O. Kibble	
G-MTRO	Solar Wings Pegasus XL-R	H. Lloyd-Hughes	
G-MTRS	Solar Wings Pegasus XL-R	J. J. R. Tickle	
G-MTRT	Raven X	G. S. Stokes	
G-MTRV	Solar Wings Pegasus XL-Q	J. C. Field	
G-MTRW	Raven X	P. K. J. Chun	
G-MTRX	Whittaker MW5 Sorceror	W. Turner	
G-MTRZ	Mainair Gemini/Flash IIA	D. F. G. Barlow	
G-MTSC	Mainair Gemini/Flash IIA	K. Wilson	
G-MTSG	CFM Shadow Srs BD	C. A. Purvis	
G-MTSH	Thruster TST Mk 1	R. R. Orr	
G-MTSJ	Thruster TST Mk 1	Sierra Juliet Group	
G-MTSK	Thruster TST Mk 1	J. S. Pyke	
G-MTSM	Thruster TST Mk 1	D. J. Flower	
G-MTSN	Solar Wings Pegasus XL-R	G. P. Lane	
G-MTSP	Solar Wings Pegasus XL-R	R. J. Nelson	
G-MTSR	Solar Wings Pegasus XL-R	J. Norman	
G-MTSS	Solar Wings Pegasus XL-R	R. J. Turner	
G-MTSY	Solar Wings Pegasus XL-R	N. F. Waldron	
G-MTSZ	Solar Wings Pegasus XL-R	J. R. Appleton	
G-MTTA	Solar Wings Pegasus XL-R	J. J. McMennum	
G-MTTB	Solar Wings Pegasus XL-R	P. J. Soukup	
G-MTTD	Pegasus XL-Q	J. P. Dilley	
G-MTTE	Solar Wings Pegasus XL-R	M. C. Mawson	
G-MTTF	Aerotech MW6 Merlin	P. Cotton	
G-MTTH	CFM Shadow Srs BD	A. Y-T. Leung & G. F. Hill	
G-MTTI	Mainair Gemini/Flash IIA	S. P. Maher	
G-MTTM	Mainair Gemini/Flash IIA	M. Anderson	
G-MTTN	Ultralight Flight Phantom	T. M. Weaver	
G-MTTP	Mainair Gemini/Flash IIA	A. Ormson	
G-MTTR	Mainair Gemini/Flash IIA	A. Westoby	
G-MTTU	Solar Wings Pegasus XL-R	A. Friend	
G-MTTW	Mainair Gemini/Flash IIA	A. F. Glover	
G-MTTX	Pegasus XL-Q	B. Richardson	
G-MTTY	Solar Wings Pegasus XL-Q	G. A. Tegg	
G-MTTZ	Solar Wings Pegasus XL-Q	J. Haskett	
G-MTUA	Solar Wings Pegasus XL-R	M. D. Reardon	
G-MTUB	Thruster TST Mk 1	M. Curtin	
G-MTUC	Thruster TST Mk 1	E. J. Girling	
G-MTUD	Thruster TST Mk 1	T. Driffield	
G-MTUF	Thruster TST Mk 1	P. Stark	
G-MTUI	Solar Wings Pegasus XL-R	R. Green	
G-MTUK	Solar Wings Pegasus XL-R	G. L. Hall	
G-MTUL	Solar Wings Pegasus XL-R	P. J. Armitage	

G-MTUN – G-MTZF | BRITISH CIVIL REGISTRATIONS

Notes	Reg	Type	Owner or Operator
	G-MTUN	Solar Wings Pegasus XL-Q	M. J. O'Connor
	G-MTUP	Solar Wings Pegasus XL-Q	G. Davies
	G-MTUR	Solar Wings Pegasus XL-Q	G. Ball
	G-MTUS	Solar Wings Pegasus XL-Q	A. I. McPherson
	G-MTUT	Solar Wings Pegasus XL-Q	F. A. Dimmock
	G-MTUU	Mainair Gemini/Flash IIA	M. Harris
	G-MTUV	Mainair Gemini/Flash IIA	J. F. Bolton
	G-MTUX	Medway Hybred 44XLR	P. A. R. Wilson
	G-MTUY	Solar Wings Pegasus XL-Q	H. C. Lowther
	G-MTVB	Solar Wings Pegasus XL-R	J. Williams
	G-MTVG	Mainair Gemini/Flash IIA	R. Wiseman
	G-MTVH	Mainair Gemini/Flash IIA	C. Royle
	G-MTVI	Mainair Gemini/Flash IIA	R. A. McDowell
	G-MTVJ	Mainair Gemini/Flash IIA	D. W. Buck
	G-MTVK	Solar Wings Pegasus XL-R	J. D. Macnamara
	G-MTVL	Solar Wings Pegasus XL-R	P. A. Bibby
	G-MTVM	Solar Wings Pegasus XL-R	M. D. Howard
	G-MTVN	Solar Wings Pegasus XL-R	A. I. Crighton
	G-MTVO	Solar Wings Pegasus XL-R	D. A. Payne
	G-MTVP	Thruster TST Mk 1	J. M. Evans
	G-MTVR	Thruster TST Mk 1	J. A. Hindley
	G-MTVS	Thruster TST Mk 1	J. G. McMinn
	G-MTVT	Thruster TST Mk 1	A. T. Farmer & M. L. Welch
	G-MTVV	Thruster TST Mk 1	C. Jones
	G-MTVX	Solar Wings Pegasus XL-Q	D. A. Foster
	G-MTWB	Solar Wings Pegasus XL-R	R. W. T. Gibbs
	G-MTWC	Solar Wings Pegasus XL-R	E. K. Perchard
	G-MTWD	Solar Wings Pegasus XL-R	J. C. Rawlings
	G-MTWF	Mainair Gemini/Flash IIA	W. Porter
	G-MTWG	Mainair Gemini/Flash IIA	N. Mackenzie & P. S. Bunting
	G-MTWH	CFM Shadow Srs BD	A. A. Ross
	G-MTWK	CFM Shadow Srs BD	B. E. Trinder & J. P. Batty
	G-MTWL	CFM Shadow Srs BD	J. M. Gray
	G-MTWR	Mainair Gemini/Flash IIA	J. B. Hodson
	G-MTWS	Mainair Gemini/Flash IIA	K. W. Roberts
	G-MTWX	Mainair Gemini/Flash IIA	M. Rushworth
	G-MTWZ	Thruster TST Mk 1	T. A. Colman
	G-MTXA	Thruster TST Mk 1	J. Upex
	G-MTXB	Thruster TST Mk 1	J. J. Hill
	G-MTXD	Thruster TST Mk 1	D. J. Flower
	G-MTXE	Hornet Dual Trainer	F. J. Marton
	G-MTXI	Solar Wings Pegasus XL-Q	S. A. Mallett
	G-MTXJ	Solar Wings Pegasus XL-Q	J. E. Wright
	G-MTXL	Noble Hardman Snowbird Mk IV	P. J. Collins
	G-MTXM	Mainair Gemini/Flash IIA	W. Archibald
	G-MTXO	Whittaker MW6	S. J. Whyatt
	G-MTXP	Mainair Gemini/Flash IIA	G. S. Duerden
	G-MTXR	CFM Shadow Srs BD	S. A. O'Neill
	G-MTXS	Mainair Gemini/Flash IIA	J. Kennedy
	G-MTXU	Snowbird Mk.IV	J. A. Rees
	G-MTXZ	Mainair Gemini/Flash IIA	P. Cave
	G-MTYA	Solar Wings Pegasus XL-Q	R. J. Nixon
	G-MTYC	Solar Wings Pegasus XL-Q	C. I. D. H. Garrison
	G-MTYD	Solar Wings Pegasus XL-Q	R. S. Colebrook
	G-MTYE	Solar Wings Pegasus XL-Q	A. J. Cook
	G-MTYF	Solar Wings Pegasus XL-Q	M. Quarterman
	G-MTYH	Solar Wings Pegasus XL-Q	P. R. Hanman
	G-MTYI	Solar Wings Pegasus XL-Q	The Microlight School (Lichfield) Ltd
	G-MTYL	Solar Wings Pegasus XL-Q	E. T. H. Cox
	G-MTYP	Solar Wings Pegasus XL-Q	J. Gray
	G-MTYR	Solar Wings Pegasus XL-Q	M. E. Grafton
	G-MTYS	Solar Wings Pegasus XL-Q	R. G. Wall
	G-MTYU	Solar Wings Pegasus XL-Q	S. East
	G-MTYV	Southdown Raven X	S. R. Jones
	G-MTYW	Raven X	R. Solomons
	G-MTYX	Raven X	C. Rean
	G-MTYY	Solar Wings Pegasus XL-R	L. A. Hosegood
	G-MTZA	Thruster TST Mk 1	J. F. Gallagher
	G-MTZB	Thruster TST Mk 1	L. J & J. L Eden
	G-MTZC	Thruster TST Mk 1	R. W. Marshall
	G-MTZD	Thruster TST Mk 1	A. Spence
	G-MTZE	Thruster TST Mk 1	B. S. P. Finch
	G-MTZF	Thruster TST Mk 1	D. C. Marsh

BRITISH CIVIL REGISTRATIONS — G-MTZG – G-MVCE

Reg	Type	Owner or Operator	Notes
G-MTZG	Mainair Gemini/Flash IIA	P. J. Bent	
G-MTZH	Mainair Gemini/Flash IIA	D. C. Hughes	
G-MTZJ	Solar Wings Pegasus XL-R	C. Gogarty	
G-MTZK	Solar Wings Pegasus XL-R	G. F. Jones	
G-MTZL	Mainair Gemini/Flash IIA	N. S. Brayn	
G-MTZM	Mainair Gemini/Flash IIA	K. L. Smith	
G-MTZO	Mainair Gemini/Flash IIA	R. C. Hinds	
G-MTZP	Solar Wings Pegasus XL-Q	M. J. Newman	
G-MTZR	Solar Wings Pegasus XL-Q	P. J. Hatchett	
G-MTZS	Solar Wings Pegasus XL-Q	P. A. Darling	
G-MTZV	Mainair Gemini/Flash IIA	G. J. Donnellon/Barton	
G-MTZW	Mainair Gemini/Flash IIA	J. E. Rourke	
G-MTZX	Mainair Gemini/Flash IIA	J. C. Thompson & R. G. Cuckow	
G-MTZY	Mainair Gemini/Flash IIA	C. N. Thornton	
G-MTZZ	Mainair Gemini/Flash IIA	P. J. Litchfield	
G-MUCK	Lindstrand LBL 77A	C. J. Wootton	
G-MUIR	Cameron V-65 balloon	L. C. M. Muir	
G-MULT	Beech 76 Duchess	Folada Aero & Technical Services Ltd	
G-MUMM	Colt 180A balloon	D. K. Hempleman-Davis	
G-MUMY	Vans RV-4	S. D. Howes	
G-MUNI	Mooney M.20J	M. W. Fane	
G-MURG	Van's RV-6	E.C. Murgatroyd	
G-MURP	AS.350 Ecureuil	M. Murphy	
G-MURR	Whittaker MW6 Merlin	D. Murray	
G-MUSH	Robinson R44 II	Heli Air Ltd/Wellesbourne	
G-MUSO	Rutan LongEz	C. J. Tadjeran/Sweden	
G-MUTD	Learjet 45	Woodlands Air LLP	
G-MUTE	Colt 31A balloon	Redmalt Ltd	
G-MUTZ	Avtech Jabiru J400	N. C. Dean	
G-MVAA	Mainair Gemini/Flash IIA	R. M. Wigman	
G-MVAB	Mainair Gemini/Flash IIA	B. Hindley	
G-MVAC	CFM Shadow Srs BD	C. A. S. Powell	
G-MVAD	Mainair Gemini/Flash IIA	N. D. Fox & C. J. Hemmingway	
G-MVAF	Southdown Puma Sprint	J. F. Horn	
G-MVAG	Thruster TST Mk 1	P. Higgins/Ireland	
G-MVAH	Thruster TST Mk 1	M. W. H. Henton	
G-MVAI	Thruster TST Mk 1	A. M. R. Wasse	
G-MVAJ	Thruster TST Mk 1	A. T. Harvey	
G-MVAK	Thruster TST Mk 1	L. A. Hosegood	
G-MVAL	Thruster TST Mk 1	G. C. Brooke	
G-MVAM	CFM Shadow Srs BD	C. P. Barber	
G-MVAN	CFM Shadow Srs BD	I. Brewster	
G-MVAO	Mainair Gemini/Flash IIA	S. W. Grainger	
G-MVAP	Mainair Gemini/Flash IIA	R. J. Miller	
G-MVAR	Solar Wings Pegasus XL-R	A. J. Thomas	
G-MVAT	Solar Wings Pegasus XL-R	R. Hickman	
G-MVAV	Solar Wings Pegasus XL-R	D. J. Utting	
G-MVAW	Solar Wings Pegasus XL-Q	G. Sharman	
G-MVAX	Solar Wings Pegasus XL-Q	P. M. Golden	
G-MVAY	Solar Wings Pegasus XL-Q	V. O. Morris	
G-MVBB	CFM Shadow Srs BD	R. Garrod	
G-MVBC	Aerial Arts Tri-Flyer 130SX	D. Beer	
G-MVBD	Mainair Gemini/Flash IIA	J. Batchelor	
G-MVBE	Mainair Scorcher	G. Roberts	
G-MVBF	Mainair Gemini/Flash IIA	D. P. Stacey	
G-MVBG	Mainair Gemini/Flash IIA	M. P. Edwards	
G-MVBI	Mainair Gemini/Flash IIA	P. Thomas	
G-MVBK	Mainair Gemini/Flash IIA	B. R. McLoughlin	
G-MVBL	Mainair Gemini/Flash IIA	P. M. Wright	
G-MVBM	Mainair Gemini/Flash IIA	A. J. Graham	
G-MVBN	Mainair Gemini/Flash IIA	M. Frankcom	
G-MVBO	Mainair Gemini/Flash IIA	J. A. Brown	
G-MVBP	Thruster TST Mk 1	K. J. Crompton	
G-MVBT	Thruster TST Mk 1	TST Group Flying	
G-MVBY	Solar Wings Pegasus XL-R	M. Doyle/Ireland	
G-MVBZ	Solar Wings Pegasus XL-R	A. G. Butler	
G-MVCA	Solar Wings Pegasus XL-R	R. Walker	
G-MVCB	Solar Wings Pegasus XL-R	G. T. Clipstone	
G-MVCC	CFM Shadow Srs BD	S. J. Payne	
G-MVCD	Medway Hybred 44XLR	J. Thompson	
G-MVCE	Mainair Gemini/Flash IIA	N. Ford	

G-MVCF – G-MVGE BRITISH CIVIL REGISTRATIONS

Notes	Reg	Type	Owner or Operator
	G-MVCF	Mainair Gemini/Flash IIA	J. S. Harris
	G-MVCI	Noble Hardman Snowbird Mk IV	W. L. Chapman
	G-MVCJ	Noble Hardman Snowbird Mk IV	C. W. Buxton
	G-MVCL	Solar Wings Pegasus XL-Q	T. E. Robinson
	G-MVCM	Solar Wings Pegasus XL-Q	P. J. Croney
	G-MVCN	Solar Wings Pegasus XL-Q	S. R. S. Evans
	G-MVCP	Solar Wings Pegasus XL-Q	J. R. Fulcher
	G-MVCR	Solar Wings Pegasus XL-Q	P. Hoeft
	G-MVCS	Solar Wings Pegasus XL-Q	J. J. Sparrow
	G-MVCT	Solar Wings Pegasus XL-Q	G. S. Lampitt
	G-MVCV	Solar Wings Pegasus XL-Q	P. J. Walker
	G-MVCW	CFM Shadow Srs BD	P. K. Appleton
	G-MVCY	Mainair Gemini/Flash IIA	A. M. Smith
	G-MVCZ	Mainair Gemini/Flash IIA	B. Hall
	G-MVDA	Mainair Gemini/Flash IIA	C. Tweedley
	G-MVDD	Thruster TST Mk 1	D. J. Love
	G-MVDE	Thruster TST Mk 1	R. H. Davis
	G-MVDF	Thruster TST Mk 1	G-MVDF Syndicate
	G-MVDG	Thruster TST Mk 1	A. B., D. G. & P. M. Smith
	G-MVDH	Thruster TST Mk 1	P. E. Terrell
	G-MVDJ	Medway Hybred 44XLR	W. D. Hutchins
	G-MVDK	Aerial Arts Chaser S	S. Adams
	G-MVDL	Aerial Arts Chaser S	J. R. Hall
	G-MVDT	Mainair Gemini/Flash IIA	D. C. Stephens
	G-MVDV	Solar Wings Pegasus XL-R	D. Ewing
	G-MVDW	Solar Wings Pegasus XL-R	R. P. Brown
	G-MVDX	Solar Wings Pegasus XL-R	C. Kett
	G-MVDY	Solar Wings Pegasus XL-R	C. G. Murphy
	G-MVDZ	Aerial Arts Chaser S	A. K. Pickering
	G-MVEC	Solar Wings Pegasus XL-R	J. A. Jarvis
	G-MVED	Solar Wings Pegasus XL-R	P. A. Sleightholme
	G-MVEE	Medway Hybred 44XLR	D. S. L. Evans
	G-MVEF	Solar Wings Pegasus XL-R	A. W. Leadley
	G-MVEG	Solar Wings Pegasus XL-R	P. J. Tranmer
	G-MVEH	Mainair Gemini/Flash IIA	K. Bailey
	G-MVEI	CFM Shadow Srs BD	R. H. Faux
	G-MVEJ	Mainair Gemini/Flash IIA	P. G. Richards
	G-MVEK	Mainair Gemini/Flash IIA	R. M. Rea
	G-MVEL	Mainair Gemini/Flash IIA	M. R. Starling
	G-MVEN	CFM Shadow Srs BD	N. J. Mepham
	G-MVEO	Mainair Gemini/Flash IIA	K. Donaldson
	G-MVER	Mainair Gemini/Flash IIA	J. R. Davis
	G-MVES	Mainair Gemini/Flash IIA	J. Helm
	G-MVET	Mainair Gemini/Flash IIA	T. Bailey
	G-MVEV	Mainair Gemini/Flash IIA	C. Allen
	G-MVEX	Solar Wings Pegasus XL-Q	D. Maher
	G-MVEZ	Solar Wings Pegasus XL-Q	P. W. Millar
	G-MVFA	Solar Wings Pegasus XL-Q	A. Johnson
	G-MVFB	Solar Wings Pegasus XL-Q	M. O. Bloy
	G-MVFC	Solar Wings Pegasus XL-Q	D. R. Joint
	G-MVFD	Solar Wings Pegasus XL-Q	C. D. Humphries
	G-MVFE	Solar Wings Pegasus XL-Q	S. J. Weeks
	G-MVFF	Solar Wings Pegasus XL-Q	A. Makepiece
	G-MVFH	CFM Shadow Srs BD	G-MVFH Group
	G-MVFJ	Thruster TST Mk 1	B. E. Reneham
	G-MVFK	Thruster TST Mk 1	C. A Gray
	G-MVFL	Thruster TST Mk 1	E. J. Wallington
	G-MVFM	Thruster TST Mk 1	G. J. Boyer
	G-MVFN	Thruster TST Mk 1	A. G. Ward
	G-MVFO	Thruster TST Mk 1	S. R. James Humberstone & A. L. Higgins
	G-MVFP	Solar Wings Pegasus XL-R	Shropshire Tow Group
	G-MVFS	Solar Wings Pegasus XL-R	A. Cordes
	G-MVFT	Solar Wings Pegasus XL-R	S. J. Walley
	G-MVFV	Solar Wings Pegasus XL-R	L. R. M. Grigg
	G-MVFW	Solar Wings Pegasus XL-R	S. F. Chaplin
	G-MVFX	Thruster TST Mk 1	A. M. Dalgetty
	G-MVFY	Solar Wings Pegasus XL-R	T. D. Bawden
	G-MVFZ	Solar Wings Pegasus XL-R	R. K. Johnson
	G-MVGA	Aerial Arts Chaser S	N. R. Beale
	G-MVGB	Medway Hybred 44XLR	R. Graham
	G-MVGC	AMF Chevvron 2-32	W. Fletcher
	G-MVGD	AMF Chevvron 2-32	T. R. James
	G-MVGE	AMF Chevvron 2-32	V. H. Hallam

BRITISH CIVIL REGISTRATIONS

G-MVGF – G-MVKL

Reg	Type	Owner or Operator	Notes
G-MVGF	Aerial Arts Chaser S	P. J. Higgins	
G-MVGG	Aerial Arts Chaser S	S. P. Clifton	
G-MVGH	Aerial Arts Chaser S	J. E. Borrill & J. Rochead	
G-MVGM	Mainair Gemini/Flash IIA	W. G. Colyer	
G-MVGN	Solar Wings Pegasus XL-R	M. J. Smith	
G-MVGO	Solar Wings Pegasus XL-R	J. B. Peacock	
G-MVGP	Solar Wings Pegasus XL-R	J. P. Cox	
G-MVGU	Solar Wings Pegasus XL-Q	T. D. Turner	
G-MVGW	Solar Wings Pegasus XL-Q	G-MVGW Group/Portugal	
G-MVGY	Medway Hybred 44XL	G. M. Griffiths	
G-MVGZ	Ultraflight Lazair IIIE	D. M. Broom	
G-MVHA	Aerial Arts Chaser S	R. Meredith-Hardy	
G-MVHB	Powerchute Raider	A. E. Askew	
G-MVHC	Powerchute Raider	G. Martin	
G-MVHD	CFM Shadow Srs BD	D. Raybould	
G-MVHE	Mainair Gemini/Flash IIA	B. J. Thomas	
G-MVHF	Mainair Gemini/Flash IIA	M. G. Nicholson	
G-MVHG	Mainair Gemini/Flash II	C. A. J. Elder	
G-MVHH	Mainair Gemini/Flash IIA	A. M. Lynch	
G-MVHI	Thruster TST Mk 1	L. Hurman	
G-MVHJ	Thruster TST Mk 1	S. P. Macdonald	
G-MVHK	Thruster TST Mk 1	D. J. Gordon	
G-MVHL	Thruster TST Mk 1	G. Jones	
G-MVHP	Solar Wings Pegasus XL-Q	J. B. Gasson	
G-MVHR	Solar Wings Pegasus XL-Q	J. M. Hucker	
G-MVHS	Solar Wings Pegasus XL-Q	C. L. Lebeter	
G-MVHW	Solar Wings Pegasus XL-Q	Ultralight Training Ltd	
G-MVHY	Solar Wings Pegasus XL-Q	R. P. Paine	
G-MVHZ	Hornet Dual Trainer	J. M. Addison	
G-MVIB	Mainair Gemini/Flash IIA	LSA Systems	
G-MVIE	Aerial Arts Chaser S	T. M. Stiles	
G-MVIF	Medway Raven X	J. R. Harrison	
G-MVIG	CFM Shadow Srs B	M. P. & P. A. G. Harper	
G-MVIH	Mainair Gemini/Flash IIA	T. M. Gilesnan	
G-MVIL	Noble Hardman Snowbird Mk IV	Marine Power (Scotland) Ltd	
G-MVIM	Noble Hardman Snowbird Mk IV	W. G. Goodall	
G-MVIN	Noble Hardman Snowbird Mk.IV	C. P. Dawes	
G-MVIO	Noble Hardman Snowbird Mk IV	Mobility Advice Line	
G-MVIP	AMF Chevvron 232	P. C. Avery	
G-MVIR	Thruster TST Mk 1	T. D. B. Gardner	
G-MVIT	Thruster TST Mk 1	A. C. Bell	
G-MVIU	Thruster TST Mk 1	E. Bentley	
G-MVIV	Thruster TST Mk 1	G. Rainey	
G-MVIX	Mainair Gemini/Flash IIA	R. S. T. Macewen	
G-MVIY	Mainair Gemini/Flash IIA	J. J. Valentine	
G-MVIZ	Mainair Gemini/Flash IIA	P. R. Hutty	
G-MVJA	Mainair Gemini/Flash IIA	J. R. Harrison	
G-MVJC	Mainair Gemini/Flash IIA	B. Temple	
G-MVJD	Solar Wings Pegasus XL-R	B. L. Prime	
G-MVJE	Mainair Gemini/Flash IIA	S. D. Morris	
G-MVJF	Aerial Arts Chaser S	V. S. Rudham	
G-MVJG	Aerial Arts Chaser S	T. H. Scott	
G-MVJH	Aerial Arts Chaser S	M. V. Rompaey	
G-MVJI	Aerial Arts Chaser S	T. Beckham	
G-MVJJ	Aerial Arts Chaser S	C. W. Potts	
G-MVJK	Aerial Arts Chaser S	K. J. Samuels	
G-MVJL	Mainair Gemini/Flash IIA	F. Huxley	
G-MVJM	Microflight Spectrum	S. E. Mathews	
G-MVJN	Solar Wings Pegasus XL-Q	R. A. Paintain	
G-MVJO	Solar Wings Pegasus XL-Q	P. Robinson	
G-MVJP	Solar Wings Pegasus XL-Q	S. H. Bakowski	
G-MVJR	Solar Wings Pegasus XL-Q	C. A. Reynolds	
G-MVJS	Solar Wings Pegasus XL-Q	S. D. Morley	
G-MVJT	Solar Wings Pegasus XL-Q	L. A. Hosegood	
G-MVJU	Solar Wings Pegasus XL-Q	J. C. Longmore	
G-MVJW	Solar Wings Pegasus XL-Q	D. W. Stamp	
G-MVKB	Medway Hybred 44XLR	J. Newby	
G-MVKC	Mainair Gemini/Flash IIA	R. L. Bladon	
G-MVKF	Solar Wings Pegasus XL-R	B. Shaw	
G-MVKH	Solar Wings Pegasus XL-R	K. M. Elson	
G-MVKJ	Solar Wings Pegasus XL-R	G. V. Warner	
G-MVKK	Solar Wings Pegasus XL-R	G. P. Burns	
G-MVKL	Solar Wings Pegasus XL-R	J. Powell-Tuck	

G-MVKM – G-MVOX BRITISH CIVIL REGISTRATIONS

Notes	Reg	Type	Owner or Operator
	G-MVKM	Solar Wings Pegasus XL-R	A. E. Dobson
	G-MVKN	Solar Wings Pegasus XL-Q	R. A. & C. A. Allen
	G-MVKO	Solar Wings Pegasus XL-Q	A. M. Latham
	G-MVKP	Solar Wings Pegasus XL-Q	P. Mokryk & S. King
	G-MVKS	Solar Wings Pegasus XL-Q	K. S. Wright
	G-MVKT	Solar Wings Pegasus XL-Q	N. C. Williams
	G-MVKU	Solar Wings Pegasus XL-Q	J. R. F. Shepherd
	G-MVKV	Solar Wings Pegasus XL-Q	D. R. Stansfield
	G-MVKW	Solar Wings Pegasus XL-Q	A. T. Scott
	G-MVKZ	Aerial Arts Chaser S	T. J. Barley
	G-MVLA	Aerial Arts Chaser S	T. Birch
	G-MVLB	Aerial Arts Chaser S	R. P. Wilkinson
	G-MVLC	Aerial Arts Chaser S	B. R. Barnes
	G-MVLD	Aerial Arts Chaser S	D. Porteous
	G-MVLE	Aerial Arts Chaser S	R. G. hooker
	G-MVLF	Aerial Arts Chaser S	I. B. Smith
	G-MVLG	Aerial Arts Chaser S	A. Strang
	G-MVLJ	CFM Shadow Srs B	R. S. Cochrane
	G-MVLL	Mainair Gemini/Flash IIA	M. I. Deeley
	G-MVLP	CFM Shadow Srs BD	D. Bridgland & D. T. Moran
	G-MVLR	Mainair Gemini/Flash IIA	P. A. Louis
	G-MVLS	Aerial Arts Chaser S	T. C. Brown
	G-MVLT	Aerial Arts Chaser S	B. D. Searle
	G-MVLW	Aerial Arts Chaser S	E. W. P. Van Zeller
	G-MVLX	Solar Wings Pegasus XL-Q	J. F. Smith
	G-MVLY	Solar Wings Pegasus XL-Q	I. B. Osborn
	G-MVMA	Solar Wings Pegasus XL-Q	G. C. Winter-Goodwin
	G-MVMC	Solar Wings Pegasus XL-Q	P. Smith & I. W. Barlow
	G-MVMG	Thruster TST Mk 1	A. D. McCaldin
	G-MVMI	Thruster TST Mk 1	G. J. Johnson
	G-MVMK	Medway Hybred 44XLR	D. J. Lewis
	G-MVML	Aerial Arts Chaser S	G. C. Luddington
	G-MVMM	Aerial Arts Chaser S	D. Margereson
	G-MVMO	Mainair Gemini/Flash IIA	K. Austwick
	G-MVMR	Mainair Gemini/Flash IIA	P. W. Ramage
	G-MVMT	Mainair Gemini/Flash IIA	R. F. Sanders
	G-MVMU	Mainair Gemini/Flash IIA	P. A. Brunt
	G-MVMV	Aerotech MW5 (K) Sorcerer	M. J. A. New & A. Clift
	G-MVMW	Mainair Gemini/Flash IIA	K. Downes & B. Nock
	G-MVMX	Mainair Gemini/Flash IIA	N. M. Corr
	G-MVMY	Mainair Gemini/Flash IIA	N. G. Leteney
	G-MVMZ	Mainair Gemini/Flash IIA	S. Richards
	G-MVNA	Powerchute Raider	J. McGoldrick
	G-MVNB	Powerchute Raider	P. J. Fahie
	G-MVNC	Powerchute Raider	W. R. Hanley
	G-MVNK	Powerchute Raider	J. Lockyer
	G-MVNL	Powerchute Raider	S. Penoyre
	G-MVNM	Gemini/Flash IIA	C. D. Phillips
	G-MVNO	Aerotech MW5 (K) Sorcerer	R. L. Wadley
	G-MVNP	Aerotech MW5 (K) Sorcerer	A. M. Edwards
	G-MVNR	Aerotech MW5 (K) Sorcerer	E. I. Rowlands-Jones
	G-MVNS	Aerotech MW5 (K) Sorcerer	A. M. Sirant
	G-MVNT	Whittaker MW5 (K) Sorcerer	P. E. Blyth
	G-MVNU	Aerotech MW5 Sorcerer	J. C. Rose
	G-MVNW	Mainair Gemini/Flash IIA	R. J. Boydell
	G-MVNX	Mainair Gemini/Flash IIA	I. Sidebotham/Barton
	G-MVNY	Mainair Gemini/Flash IIA	M. K. Buckalns
	G-MVNZ	Mainair Gemini/Flash IIA	J. Howarth
	G-MVOB	Mainair Gemini/Flash IIA	G. L. Logan
	G-MVOD	Aerial Arts Chaser 110SX	N. R. Beale
	G-MVOF	Mainair Gemini/Flash IIA	P. J. Nolan
	G-MVOH	CFM Shadow Srs B	D. I. Farmer
	G-MVOJ	Noble Hardman Snowbird Mk IV	C. D. Beetham
	G-MVOL	Noble Hardman Snowbird Mk IV	Swansea Snowbird Flyers
	G-MVON	Mainair Gemini/Flash IIA	W. R. Astbury
	G-MVOO	AMF Chevvron 2-32	M. K. Field
	G-MVOP	Aerial Arts Chaser S	D. Thorpe
	G-MVOR	Mainair Gemini/Flash IIA	P. T. & R. M. Jenkins
	G-MVOT	Thruster TST Mk.1	B. L. R. J. Keeping
	G-MVOU	Thruster TST Mk.1	D. W. Tewson
	G-MVOV	Thruster TST Mk.1	G-MVOV Group
	G-MVOW	Thruster TST Mk 1	B. J. Merret & J. Short
	G-MVOX	Thruster TST Mk 1	J. E. Davies

BRITISH CIVIL REGISTRATIONS

G-MVOY – G-MVUL

Reg	Type	Owner or Operator	Notes
G-MVOY	Thruster TST Mk 1	C. Jones	
G-MVPA	Mainair Gemini/Flash IIA	J. E. Milburn	
G-MVPB	Mainair Gemini/Flash IIA	O. Carter	
G-MVPC	Mainair Gemini/Flash IIA	N. C. Marciano	
G-MVPD	Mainair Gemini/Flash IIA	P. Thelwel	
G-MVPE	Mainair Gemini/Flash IIA	M. D. Jealous & M. Goodrick	
G-MVPF	Medway Hybred 44XLR	G. H. Crick	
G-MVPH	Whittaker MW6 Merlin	A. K. Mascord	
G-MVPI	Mainair Gemini/Flash IIA	R. J. Bowden	
G-MVPJ	Rans S.5 Coyote	J. E. D. Rogerson	
G-MVPK	CFM Shadow Srs B	P. Sarfas	
G-MVPL	Medway Hybred 44XLR	J. N. J. Roberts	
G-MVPM	Whittaker MW6 Merlin	K. W. Curry	
G-MVPN	Whittaker MW6 Merlin	A. M. Field	
G-MVPR	Solar Wings Pegasus XL-Q	R. S. Swift	
G-MVPS	Solar Wings Pegasus XL-Q	B. R. Chamberlain	
G-MVPX	Solar Wings Pegasus XL-Q	N. D. Leak	
G-MVPY	Solar Wings Pegasus XL-Q	G. H. Dawson	
G-MVRA	Mainair Gemini/Flash IIA	J. C. Bond	
G-MVRB	Mainair Gemini/Flash	G. Callaghan/Northern Ireland	
G-MVRC	Mainair Gemini/Flash IIA	M. O'Connell	
G-MVRD	Mainair Gemini/Flash IIA	A. R. Helm	
G-MVRF	Rotec Rally 2B	A. I. Edwards	
G-MVRG	Aerial Arts Chaser S	J. P. Kynaston	
G-MVRH	Solar Wings Pegasus XL-Q	K. Farr	
G-MVRI	Solar Wings Pegasus XL-Q	P. Martin	
G-MVRJ	Solar Wings Pegasus XL-Q	J. Goldsmith-Ryan	
G-MVRL	Aerial Arts Chaser S	C. N. Beale	
G-MVRM	Mainair Gemini/Flash IIA	J. S. Stevenson	
G-MVRO	CFM Shadow Srs CD	K. H. Creed	
G-MVRP	CFM Shadow Srs BD	B. Barrass	
G-MVRR	CFM Shadow Srs BD	S. Fairweather & S. P. Christian	
G-MVRT	CFM Shadow Srs BD	B. J. Palfreyman	
G-MVRU	Solar Wings Pegasus XL-Q	P. Copping	
G-MVRV	Powerchute Kestrel	G. M. Fletcher	
G-MVRW	Solar Wings Pegasus XL-Q	M. A. Baldwin	
G-MVRX	Solar Wings Pegasus XL-Q	M. Everest	
G-MVRY	Medway Hybred 44XLR	K. Dodman	
G-MVRZ	Medway Hybred 44XLR	I. Oswald	
G-MVSB	Solar Wings Pegasus XL-Q	D. Forde & M. Jennings	
G-MVSD	Solar Wings Pegasus XL-Q	D. C. Maxwell-Grice	
G-MVSE	Solar Wings Pegasus XL-Q	L. B. Richardson	
G-MVSG	Aerial Arts Chaser S	M. Roberts	
G-MVSI	Medway Hybred 44XLR	R. J. Matthews	
G-MVSJ	Aviasud Mistral 532	P. R. Hall & J. D. Hewitson	
G-MVSM	Midland Ultralights Sirocco	C. G. Benham	
G-MVSN	Mainair Gemini/Flash IIA	D. W. Watson	
G-MVSP	Mainair Gemini/Flash IIA	D. R. Buchanan	
G-MVST	Mainair Gemini/Flash IIA	D. Curtis	
G-MVSV	Mainair Gemini/Flash IIA	P. Shelton	
G-MVSW	Solar Wings Pegasus XL-Q	G. F. Ryland	
G-MVSX	Solar Wings Pegasus XL-Q	A. R. Law	
G-MVSY	Solar Wings Pegasus XL-Q	G. P. Turnball	
G-MVSZ	Solar Wings Pegasus XL-Q	G. P. Jones	
G-MVTA	Solar Wings Pegasus XL-Q	P. Hanby	
G-MVTC	Mainair Gemini/Flash IIA	R. A. Neal	
G-MVTD	Whittaker MW6 Merlin	G. J. Green	
G-MVTF	Aerial Arts Chaser S	P. Mundy	
G-MVTI	Solar Wings Pegasus XL-Q	D. Burdett	
G-MVTJ	Solar Wings Pegasus XL-Q	A. J. Gibbins	
G-MVTK	Solar Wings Pegasus XL-Q	I. P. Sissons	
G-MVTL	Aerial Arts Chaser S	N. D. Meer	
G-MVTM	Aerial Arts Chaser S	G. L. Davies	
G-MVUA	Mainair Gemini/Flash IIA	E. W. Hughes	
G-MVUB	Thruster T.300	S. Silk	
G-MVUC	Medway Hybred 44XLR	B. Pounder	
G-MVUD	Medway Hybred 44XLR	T. W. Nelson	
G-MVUF	Solar Wings Pegasus XL-Q	D. Friel	
G-MVUG	Solar Wings Pegasus XL-Q	I. J. Morgan	
G-MVUI	Solar Wings Pegasus XL-Q	J. K. Edgecombe	
G-MVUJ	Solar Wings Pegasus XL-Q	J. H. Cooper	
G-MVUK	Solar Wings Pegasus XL-Q	D. Greenslade	
G-MVUL	Solar Wings Pegasus XL-Q	D. Hamilton-Brown	

G-MVUM – G-MVZZ **BRITISH CIVIL REGISTRATIONS**

Notes	Reg	Type	Owner or Operator
	G-MVUM	Solar Wings Pegasus XL-Q	M. A. Howson
	G-MVUO	AMF Chevvron 2-32	P. Rawlinson
	G-MVUP	Aviasud Mistral	B. W. & C. J. Foulds
	G-MVUR	Hornet ZA	M. J. Moulton
	G-MVUS	Aerial Arts Chaser S	H. Poyzer
	G-MVUU	Hornet ZA	K. W. Warn
	G-MVVH	Medway Hybred 44XLR	M. S. Henson
	G-MVVI	Medway Hybred 44XLR	T. R. Villa
	G-MVVK	Solar Wings Pegasus XL-R	A. J. Weir
	G-MVVN	Solar Wings Pegasus XL-Q	J. R. Butler
	G-MVVO	Solar Wings Pegasus XL-Q	A. L. Scarlett
	G-MVVP	Solar Wings Pegasus XL-Q	A. E. Ciantar
	G-MVVR	Medway Hybred 44XLR	H. J. Long
	G-MVVT	CFM Shadow Srs BD	W. G. Nicol
	G-MVVU	Aerial Arts Chaser S	J. T. Davies
	G-MVVV	AMF Chevvron 2-32	P. R. Turton
	G-MVVZ	Powerchute Raider	J. H. Cadman
	G-MVWJ	Powerchute Raider	N. J. Doubek
	G-MVWN	Thruster T.300	Whisky November Group
	G-MVWR	Thruster T.300	A. Allen
	G-MVWS	Thruster T.300	R. J. Hunphries
	G-MVWW	Medway Hybred 44XLR	H. Tuvey
	G-MVWW	Aviasud Mistral	P. S. Balmer & B. H. D. Minto
	G-MVWZ	Aviasud Mistral	Chilbolton Mistral Group
	G-MVXA	Brewster I MW6	I. Brewster
	G-MVXB	Mainair Gemini/Flash IIA	S. P. Elliot
	G-MVXC	Mainair Gemini/Flash IIA	D. Wood
	G-MVXD	Medway Hybred 44XLR	P. R. Millen
	G-MVXE	Medway Hybred 44XLR	A. M. Brittle
	G-MVXI	Medway Hybred 44XLR	T. de Landro
	G-MVXJ	Medway Hybred 44XLR	P. J. Wilks
	G-MVXL	Thruster TST Mk 1	A. J. Smith
	G-MVXM	Medway Hybred 44XLR	P. J. Short
	G-MVXN	Aviasud Mistral	N. C. & A. C. J. Butcher
	G-MVXR	Mainair Gemini/Flash IIA	D. M. Bayne
	G-MVXS	Mainair Gemini/Flash IIA	J. W. Wood
	G-MVXV	Aviasud Mistral	Mistral G-MVXW Group
	G-MVXW	Rans S.4 Coyote	J. Kilpatrick/Ireland
	G-MVXX	AMF Chevvron 232	C. K. Brown
	G-MVYC	Solar Wings Pegasus XL-Q	P. E. L. Street
	G-MVYD	Solar Wings Pegasus XL-Q	T. M. Wakeley
	G-MVYE	Thruster TST Mk 1	G. Elwes
	G-MVYK	Hornet R-ZA	P. Asbridge
	G-MVYL	Hornet R-ZA	J. L. Thomas
	G-MVYN	Hornet R-ZA	W. M. Studley
	G-MVYP	Medway Hybred 44XLR	S. I. Laurence
	G-MVYR	Medway Hybred 44XLR	K. J. Clarke
	G-MVYS	Mainair Gemini/Flash IIA	B. Hall
	G-MVYT	Noble Hardman Snowbird Mk IV	D. T. A. Rees
	G-MVYU	Noble Hardman Snowbird Mk IV	B. Foster & P. Meah
	G-MVYV	Noble Hardman Snowbird Mk IV	D. W. Hayden
	G-MVYW	Noble Hardman Snowbird Mk IV	T. J. Harrison
	G-MVYX	Noble Hardman Snowbird Mk IV	R. McBlain
	G-MVYY	Aerial Arts Chaser S508	C. J. Gordon & R. H. Bird
	G-MVYZ	CFM Shadow Srs BD	C. Day
	G-MVZA	Thruster T.300	C. C. Belcher
	G-MVZC	Thruster T.300	R. A. Knight
	G-MVZD	Thruster T.300	G-MVZD Syndicate
	G-MVZG	Thruster T.300	R. Lewis-Evans
	G-MVZI	Thruster T.300	R. R. R. Whittern
	G-MVZJ	Solar Wings Pegasus XL-Q	P. Mansfield
	G-MVZK	Challenger II	G-MVZK Group
	G-MVZL	Solar Wings Pegasus XL-Q	P. R. Dobson
	G-MVZM	Aerial Arts Chaser S	J. L. Parker
	G-MVZO	Medway Hybred 44XLR	A. G. Woodward
	G-MVZP	Murphy Renegade Spirit UK	H. M. Doyle
	G-MVZS	Mainair Gemini/Flash IIA	R. L. Beese
	G-MVZT	Solar Wings Pegasus XL-Q	C. J. Meadows
	G-MVZU	Solar Wings Pegasus XL-Q	M. G. McMurray
	G-MVZV	Solar Wings Pegasus XL-Q	C. R. Cawley
	G-MVZW	Hornet R-ZA	K. W. Warn
	G-MVZX	Renegade Spirit UK	G. Holmes
	G-MVZZ	AMF Chevvron 232	D. Patrick

BRITISH CIVIL REGISTRATIONS   G-MWAB – G-MWFI

Reg	Type	Owner or Operator	Notes
G-MWAB	Mainair Gemini/Flash IIA	J. E. Buckley	
G-MWAC	Solar Wings Pegasus XL-Q	H. Lloyd-Hughes	
G-MWAD	Solar Wings Pegasus XL-Q	J. K.Evans	
G-MWAE	CFM Shadow Srs BD	D. J. Adams	
G-MWAF	Solar Wings Pegasus XL-R	J. P. Bonner	
G-MWAG	Solar Wings Pegasus XL-R	X. Norman	
G-MWAJ	Renegade Spirit UK	M. Mailey	
G-MWAL	Solar Wings Pegasus XL-Q	A. W. Hill	
G-MWAN	Thruster T.300	E. J. Girling	
G-MWAP	Thruster T.300	A. G. Spurway & S. F. Chave	
G-MWAR	Thruster T.300	B. Cassidy	
G-MWAT	Solar Wings Pegasus XL-Q	D. G. Seymour	
G-MWAV	Solar Wings Pegasus XL-R	I. J. Rawlingson	
G-MWAW	Whittaker MW6 Merlin	G. Hawes	
G-MWBI	Medway Hybred 44XLR	G. E. Coates	
G-MWBJ	Medway Sprint	C. C. Strong	
G-MWBK	Solar Wings Pegasus XL-Q	P. J. Harrison	
G-MWBL	Solar Wings Pegasus XL-Q	J. A. Valentine	
G-MWBO	Rans S.4 Coyote	E. W. Laidlaw and B. M. Tibenham	
G-MWBP	Hornet RS-ZA	S. Brader	
G-MWBR	Hornet RS-ZA	I. A. Clark	
G-MWBS	Hornet RS-ZA	P. D. Jaques	
G-MWBW	Hornet RS-ZA	C. G. Bentley	
G-MWBY	Hornet RS-ZA	G. P. Austin	
G-MWCB	Solar Wings Pegasus XL-Q	M. Foreman	
G-MWCC	Solar Wings Pegasus XL-R	L. Robinson	
G-MWCE	Mainair Gemini/Flash IIA	B. A. Tooze	
G-MWCF	Solar Wings Pegasus XL-R	R. McKie	
G-MWCG	Microflight Spectrum	M. W. Shepherd	
G-MWCH	Rans S.6 Coyote	G-MWCH Group	
G-MWCI	Powerchute Kestrel	E. G. Bray	
G-MWCK	Powerchute Kestrel	A. E. Askew	
G-MWCM	Powerchute Kestrel	G. E. Lockyer	
G-MWCN	Powerchute Kestrel	J. D. McKibben	
G-MWCO	Powerchute Kestrel	G. Martin	
G-MWCR	Southdown Puma Sprint	S. R. Hall	
G-MWCS	Powerchute Kestrel	R. S. McFadyen	
G-MWCU	Solar Wings Pegasus XL-R	T. P. Noonan	
G-MWCW	Mainair Gemini/Flash IIA	M. L. Harbourne	
G-MWCY	Medway Hybred 44XLR	J. K. Masters	
G-MWCZ	Medway Hybred 44XLR	A. Titcombe	
G-MWDB	CFM Shadow Srs BD	M. D. Meade	
G-MWDC	Solar Wings Pegasus XL-R	A. N. Edwards	
G-MWDD	Solar Wings Pegasus XL-Q	G. Cross	
G-MWDE	Hornet RS-ZA	H. G. Reid	
G-MWDI	Hornet RS-ZA	R. J. Perrin	
G-MWDJ	Mainair Gemini/Flash IIA	M. Gardiner	
G-MWDK	Solar Wings Pegasus XL-R	T. Wicks	
G-MWDL	Solar Wings Pegasus XL-R	S. R. Isaac	
G-MWDM	Renegade Spirit UK	E. J. J. Pels/France	
G-MWDN	CFM Shadow Srs BD	A. A. Duffas	
G-MWDP	Thruster TST Mk 1	J. Walker	
G-MWDS	Thruster T.300	A. R. Elliott	
G-MWDZ	Eipper Quicksilver MXL II	R. G. Cook	
G-MWEE	Solar Wings Pegasus XL-Q	R. J. Sharp	
G-MWEF	Solar Wings Pegasus XL-Q	N. R. Williams	
G-MWEG	Solar Wings Pegasus XL-Q	S. P. Michlig	
G-MWEH	Solar Wings Pegasus XL-Q	K. A. Davidson	
G-MWEK	Whittaker MW5 Sorcerer	D. W. & M. L. Squire	
G-MWEL	Mainair Gemini/Flash IIA	S. E. Bettley	
G-MWEN	CFM Shadow Srs BD	C. Dawn	
G-MWEO	Whittaker MW5 Sorcerer	J. Morton	
G-MWEP	Rans S.4 Coyote	E. J. Wallington	
G-MWER	Solar Wings Pegasus XL-Q	S. V. Stojanovic	
G-MWES	Rans S.4 Coyote	G. Scott	
G-MWEY	Hornet RS-ZA	J. Kidd	
G-MWEZ	CFM Shadow Srs CD	G-MWEZ Group	
G-MWFB	CFM Shadow Srs BD	K. W. E. Brunnenkant	
G-MWFC	TEAM mini-MAX (G-BTXC)	M. Bradley	
G-MWFD	TEAM mini-MAX	J. T. Blackburn	
G-MWFF	Rans S.4 Coyote	J. S. Sweetingham	
G-MWFG	Powerchute Kestrel	R. I. Simpson	
G-MWFI	Powerchute Kestrel	R. R. O'Neill	

G-MWFL – G-MWKE   BRITISH CIVIL REGISTRATIONS

Notes	Reg	Type	Owner or Operator
	G-MWFL	Powerchute Kestrel	A. Vincent
	G-MWFS	Solar Wings Pegasus XL-Q	C. P. Hughes
	G-MWFT	MBA Tiger Cub 440	J. R. Ravenhill
	G-MWFU	Quad City Challenger II UK	M. Ellis
	G-MWFV	Quad City Challenger II UK	P. Bowers
	G-MWFW	Rans S.4 Coyote	M. P. Hallam
	G-MWFX	Quad City Challenger II UK	I. M. Walton
	G-MWFY	Quad City Challenger II UK	C. C. B. Soden
	G-MWFZ	Quad City Challenger II UK	A. Slade
	G-MWGA	Rans S.5 Coyote	J. Bolton
	G-MWGC	Medway Hybred 44XLR	C. Spalding
	G-MWGG	Mainair Gemini/Flash IIA	D. Lopez
	G-MWGI	Whittaker MW5 (K) Sorcerer	B. Barrass
	G-MWGJ	Whittaker MW5 (K) Sorcerer	I. Pearson
	G-MWGK	Whittaker MW5 (K) Sorcerer	R. M. Thomas
	G-MWGL	Solar Wings Pegasus XL-Q	G. D. Haimes & A. R. Campbell
	G-MWGM	Solar Wings Pegasus XL-Q	G. C. Christopher
	G-MWGN	Rans S.4 Coyote II	V. Hallam
	G-MWGO	Aerial Arts Chaser 110SX	B. Nicolson
	G-MWGR	Solar Wings Pegasus XL-Q	A. Maskell
	G-MWGU	Powerchute Kestrel	M. Pandolfino
	G-MWGV	Powerchute Kestrel	G. Martin
	G-MWGW	Powerchute Kestrel	S. P. Tomlinson
	G-MWGZ	Powerchute Kestrel	J. L. Lynch
	G-MWHC	Solar Wings Pegasus XL-Q	P. J. Lowery
	G-MWHF	Solar Wings Pegasus XL-Q	N. J. Troke
	G-MWHG	Solar Wings Pegasus XL-Q	I. A. Lumley
	G-MWHH	TEAM mini-MAX	B. F. Crick
	G-MWHI	Mainair Gemini/Flash	P. Harwood
	G-MWHL	Solar Wings Pegasus XL-Q	S. J. Reader
	G-MWHM	Whittaker MW6 Merlin	G. H. Davies
	G-MWHO	Mainair Gemini/Flash IIA	B. Epps
	G-MWHP	Rans S.6-ESD Coyote	J. F. Bickerstaffe
	G-MWHR	Mainair Gemini/Flash IIA	B. Brazier
	G-MWHT	Solar Wings Pegasus Quasar	E. H. Gatehouse
	G-MWHU	Solar Wings Pegasus Quasar	S. J. Park & A. F. Frost
	G-MWHX	Solar Wings Pegasus XL-Q	N. P. Kelly
	G-MWIA	Mainair Gemini/Flash IIA	M. Raj
	G-MWIB	Aviasud Mistral	N. W. Finn-Kelcey
	G-MWIC	Whittaker MW5 Sorcerer	A. M. Witt
	G-MWIE	Solar Wings Pegasus XL-Q	R. Mercer
	G-MWIF	Rans S.6-ESD Coyote II	J. Parks
	G-MWIG	Mainair Gemini/Flash IIA	A. P. Purbrick
	G-MWIH	Mainair Gemini/Flash IIA	J. P. Norton
	G-MWIL	Medway Hybred 44XLR	P. J. Bosworth
	G-MWIM	Solar Wings Pegasus Quasar	P. J. Bates & T. S. Smith
	G-MWIO	Rans S.4 Coyote	S. R Davies & G. J. Simoni
	G-MWIP	Whittaker MW6 Merlin	B. J. Merret & D. Beer
	G-MWIR	Solar Wings Pegasus XL-Q	C. E. Dagless
	G-MWIS	Solar Wings Pegasus XL-Q	C. J. Hunt
	G-MWIU	Pegasus Quasar TC	N. P. Chitty
	G-MWIV	Mainair Gemini/Flash IIA	J. & P. Calvert
	G-MWIW	Solar Wings Pegasus Quasar	T. Yates
	G-MWIX	Solar Wings Pegasus Quasar	T. D. Neal
	G-MWIY	Solar Wings Pegasus Quasar	N. S. Payne
	G-MWIZ	CFM Shadow Srs BD	T. P. Ryan
	G-MWJF	CFM Shadow Srs BD	S. N. White
	G-MWJG	Solar Wings Pegasus XL-R	M. J. Piggott
	G-MWJH	Solar Wings Pegasus XL-Q	S. W. Walker
	G-MWJI	Solar Wings Pegasus Quasar	L. Luscombe
	G-MWJJ	Solar Wings Pegasus Quasar	R. Langham
	G-MWJK	Solar Wings Pegasus Quasar	M. Richardson
	G-MWJN	Solar Wings Pegasus XL-Q	J. C. Corrall
	G-MWJP	Medway Hybred 44XLR	C. D. Simmons
	G-MWJR	Medway Hybred 44XLR	T. G. Almond
	G-MWJS	Solar Wings Pegasus Quasar	R. J. Milward
	G-MWJT	Solar Wings Pegasus Quasar	N. D. Townend
	G-MWJV	Solar Wings Pegasus Quasar	E. L. Pillinger
	G-MWJW	Whittaker MW5 Sorcerer	S. Badby
	G-MWJX	Medway Puma Sprint	K. Wales
	G-MWJY	Mainair Gemini/Flash IIA	M. D. Walton
	G-MWKA	Renegade Spirit UK	Downlands Flying Group
	G-MWKE	Hornet R-ZA	D. R. Stapleton

BRITISH CIVIL REGISTRATIONS   G-MWKO – G-MWOP

Reg	Type	Owner or Operator	Notes
G-MWKO	Solar Wings Pegasus XL-Q	P. M. Golden	
G-MWKP	Solar Wings Pegasus XL-Q	J. D. Otter	
G-MWKX	Microflight Spectrum	C. R. Ions	
G-MWKY	Solar Wings Pegasus XL-Q	I. D. Edwards	
G-MWKZ	Solar Wings Pegasus XL-Q	T. G. Burston & I. A. Fox-Mills	
G-MWLA	Rans S.4 Coyote	D. C. Lees	
G-MWLB	Medway Hybred 44XLR	M. W. Harmer	
G-MWLD	CFM Shadow Srs BD	R. H. Cooke	
G-MWLE	Solar Wings Pegasus XL-R	D. Stevenson	
G-MWLG	Solar Wings Pegasus XL-R	C. Cohen	
G-MWLH	Solar Wings Pegasus Quasar	B. Chapman	
G-MWLJ	Solar Wings Pegasus Quasar	M. J. Olsen	
G-MWLK	Solar Wings Pegasus Quasar	D. J. Shippen	
G-MWLL	Solar Wings Pegasus XL-Q	A. J. Bacon	
G-MWLM	Solar Wings Pegasus XL-Q	A. A. Judge	
G-MWLN	Whittaker MW6-S Fatboy Flyer	S. J. Field	
G-MWLO	Whittaker MW6 Merlin	G-MWLO Flying Group	
G-MWLP	Mainair Gemini/Flash IIA	C. Moultrie & C. Poziemski	
G-MWLS	Medway Hybred 44XLR	M. A. Oliver	
G-MWLU	Solar Wings Pegasus XL-R	T. P. G. Ward	
G-MWLW	TEAM mini-MAX	L. G. Horne	
G-MWLX	Mainair Gemini/Flash IIA	S. D. Buchanan	
G-MWLZ	Rans S.4 Coyote	B. O. McCartan	
G-MWMB	Powerchute Kestrel	D. J. Whysall	
G-MWMC	Powerchute Kestrel	Talgarreg Flying Club	
G-MWMD	Powerchute Kestrel	D. J. Jackson	
G-MWMF	Powerchute Kestrel	P. J. Blundell	
G-MWMG	Powerchute Kestrel	M. D. Walton	
G-MWMH	Powerchute Kestrel	E. W. Potts	
G-MWMI	SolarWings Pegasus Quasar	A. R. Winton	
G-MWMJ	SolarWings Pegasus Quasar	A. J. Thomas	
G-MWMK	SolarWings Pegasus Quasar TC	P. Adams	
G-MWML	SolarWings Pegasus Quasar	S. C. Key	
G-MWMM	Mainair Gemini/Flash IIA	R. H. Church	
G-MWMN	Solar Wings Pegasus XL-Q	P. A. Arnold & N. A. Rathbone	
G-MWMO	Solar Wings Pegasus XL-Q	D. S. F. McNair	
G-MWMP	Solar Wings Pegasus XL-Q	M. P. Darke	
G-MWMR	Solar Wings Pegasus XL-R	M. I. Stone	
G-MWMT	Mainair Gemini/Flash IIA	R. Findlay	
G-MWMU	CFM Shadow Srs C	A. J. Thomas	
G-MWMV	Solar Wings Pegasus XL-R	M. A. Oakley	
G-MWMW	Renegade Spirit UK	H. Feeney	
G-MWMX	Mainair Gemini/Flash IIA	P. G. Hughes/Ireland	
G-MWMY	Mainair Gemini/Flash IIA	P .J. Harrison	
G-MWMZ	Solar Wings Pegasus XL-Q	P. M. Scrivener	
G-MWNA	Solar Wings Pegasus XL-Q	S. N. Robson	
G-MWNB	Solar Wings Pegasus XL-Q	P. F. J. Rogers	
G-MWNC	Solar Wings Pegasus XL-Q	G-MWNC Group	
G-MWND	Tiger Cub Developments RL.5A	D. A. Pike	
G-MWNE	Mainair Gemini/Flash IIA	T. C. Edwards	
G-MWNF	Renegade Spirit UK	D. J. White	
G-MWNG	Solar Wings Pegasus XL-Q	H. C. TRhomson	
G-MWNK	Solar Wings Pegasus Quasar	G. S. Lynn	
G-MWNL	Solar Wings Pegasus Quasar	P. Richardson	
G-MWNO	AMF Chevvron 232	I. K. Hogg	
G-MWNP	AMF Chevvron 232	M. K. Field	
G-MWNR	Renegade Spirit UK	RJR Flying Group	
G-MWNS	Mainair Gemini/Flash IIA	J. G. Hilliard	
G-MWNT	Mainair Gemini/Flash IIA	November Tango Group	
G-MWNU	Mainair Gemini/Flash IIA	C. C. Muir	
G-MWNV	Powerchute Kestrel	K. N. Byrne	
G-MWNX	Powerchute Kestrel	J. H. Greenroyd	
G-MWOC	Powerchute Kestrel	D. M. F. Harvey	
G-MWOD	Powerchute Kestre	T. Morgan	
G-MWOE	Powerchute Kestrel	E. G. Woolnough	
G-MWOF	Microflight Spectrum	P. Williams & M. E. Caton	
G-MWOH	Solar Wings Pegasus XL-R	J. D. Buchanan	
G-MWOI	Solar Wings Pegasus XL-R	B. T. Geoghegan	
G-MWOJ	Mainair Gemini/Flash IIA	C. J. Pryce	
G-MWOK	Mainair Gemini/Flash IIA	J. C. Miller	
G-MWON	CFM Shadow Srs CD	R. E. M. Gibson-Bevan	
G-MWOO	Renegade Spirit UK	R. C. Wood	
G-MWOP	Solar Wings Pegasus Quasar	A. Baynes	

G-MWOR – G-MWTL — BRITISH CIVIL REGISTRATIONS

Notes	Reg	Type	Owner or Operator
	G-MWOR	Solar Wings Pegasus XL-Q	M. J. Saich
	G-MWOV	Whittaker MW6 Merlin	I. R. Hodgson
	G-MWOY	Solar Wings Pegasus XL-Q	S. P. Griffin
	G-MWPB	Mainair Gemini/Flash IIA	J. Fenton
	G-MWPC	Mainair Gemini/Flash IIA	M. Johnson
	G-MWPD	Mainair Gemini/Flash IIA	P. Gazinski
	G-MWPE	Solar Wings Pegasus XL-Q	E. C. R. Hudson
	G-MWPF	Mainair Gemini/Flash IIA	L. H. Black
	G-MWPG	Microflight Spectrum	D. Payn
	G-MWPH	Microflight Spectrum	S. Rickett & M. J. Deacon
	G-MWPJ	Solar Wings Pegasus XL-Q	D. S. Parker
	G-MWPK	Solar Wings Pegasus XL-Q	M. Harris
	G-MWPN	CFM Shadow Srs CD	W. R. H. Thomas
	G-MWPO	Mainair Gemini/Flash IIA	C. G. Adams
	G-MWPP	CFM Streak Shadow	A. J. Burton (G-BTEM)
	G-MWPR	Whittaker MW6 Merlin	S. F. N. Warnell
	G-MWPS	Renegade Spirit UK	M. D. Stewart
	G-MWPU	Solar Wings Pegasus Quasar TC	T. A. Jennings
	G-MWPX	Solar Wings Pegasus XL-R	R. J. Wheeler
	G-MWPZ	Renegade Spirit UK	J. levers
	G-MWRB	Mainair Gemini/Flash IIA	R. Campbell-Moore
	G-MWRC	Mainair Gemini/Flash IIA	D. R. Talbot
	G-MWRD	Mainair Gemini/Flash IIA	S. J. P. Gibbs
	G-MWRE	Mainair Gemini/Flash IIA	A. D. Dias
	G-MWRF	Mainair Gemini/Flash IIA	N. Hay
	G-MWRG	Mainair Gemini/Flash IIA	F. J. Clarehugh
	G-MWRH	Mainair Gemini/Flash IIA	E. G. Astin
	G-MWRJ	Mainair Gemini/Flash IIA	R. J. Lindley
	G-MWRL	CFM Shadow Srs.CD	R. A. & C. A. Allen
	G-MWRM	Medway Hybred 44XLR	M. A. Jones
	G-MWRN	Solar Wings Pegasus XL-R	D. T. Mackenzie
	G-MWRP	Solar Wings Pegasus XL-R	A. R. Hughes
	G-MWRR	Mainair Gemini/Flash IIA	J. Clark
	G-MWRS	Ultravia Super Pelican	T. B. Woolley
	G-MWRT	Solar Wings Pegasus XL-R	G. L. Gunnell
	G-MWRU	Solar Wings Pegasus XL-R	S. W. Kettell
	G-MWRV	Solar Wings Pegasus XL-R	M. S. Adams
	G-MWRW	Solar Wings Pegasus XL-Q	L. B. Hughes
	G-MWRX	Solar Wings Pegasus XL-Q	W. Parkes
	G-MWRY	CFM Shadow Srs CD	A. W. Hodder
	G-MWRZ	AMF Chevvron 232	P. V. Prowse
	G-MWSA	TEAM mini-MAX	P. Smith
	G-MWSB	Mainair Gemini/Flash IIA	P. J. Bosworth
	G-MWSC	Rans S.6-ESD Coyote II	C. J. Meadows
	G-MWSD	Solar Wings Pegasus XL-Q	A. M. Harley
	G-MWSE	Solar Wings Pegasus XL-R	Ultralight Training Ltd
	G-MWSF	Solar Wings Pegasus XL-R	N. A. & F. W. Milne
	G-MWSH	Solar Wings Pegasus Quasar TC	J. P. Beeley
	G-MWSI	Solar Wings Pegasus Quasar TC	J. A. Ganderton
	G-MWSJ	Solar Wings Pegasus XL-Q	R. A. Barrett
	G-MWSK	Solar Wings Pegasus XL-Q	J. Doogan
	G-MWSL	Mainair Gemini/Flash IIA	C. W. Frost
	G-MWSM	Mainair Gemini/Flash IIA	R. M. Wall
	G-MWSO	Solar Wings Pegasus XL-R	M. A. Clayton
	G-MWSP	Solar Wings Pegasus XL-R	R. Wilkinson
	G-MWSR	Solar Wings Pegasus XL-R	G. P. J. Davies
	G-MWSS	Medway Hybred 44XLR	F. S. Ogden
	G-MWST	Medway Hybred 44XLR	A. Ferguson
	G-MWSU	Medway Hybred 44XLR	T. De Landro
	G-MWSW	Whittaker MW6 Merlin	S. F. N. Warnell
	G-MWSX	Whittaker MW5 Sorcerer	A. T. Armstrong
	G-MWSY	Whittaker MW5 Sorcerer	J. E. Holloway
	G-MWSZ	CFM Shadow Srs CD	D. R. Drewett & P. A. Da Silva Turner
	G-MWTB	Solar Wings Pegasus XL-Q	G. S. Highley
	G-MWTC	Solar Wings Pegasus XL-Q	M. M. Chittenden
	G-MWTD	Microflight Spectrum	J. V. Harris
	G-MWTE	Microflight Spectrum	T. H. Evans
	G-MWTG	Mainair Gemini/Flash IIA	M. R. Smith
	G-MWTH	Mainair Gemini/Flash IIA	A. Strang
	G-MWTI	Solar Wings Pegasus XL-Q	O. G. Johns
	G-MWTJ	CFM Shadow Srs CD	T. D. Wolstenholme
	G-MWTK	Solar Wings Pegasus XL-R	G. Munro
	G-MWTL	Solar Wings Pegasus XL-R	B. Lindsay

BRITISH CIVIL REGISTRATIONS — G-MWTN – G-MWXX

Reg	Type	Owner or Operator	Notes
G-MWTN	CFM Shadow Srs CD	M. J. Broom	
G-MWTO	Mainair Gemini/Flash IIA	J. Greenhalgh	
G-MWTP	CFM Shadow Srs CD	R. E. M. Gibson-Bevan	
G-MWTR	Mainair Gemini/Flash IIA	J. E. Lipinski	
G-MWTT	Rans S.6-ESD Coyote II	L. E. Duffin	
G-MWTU	Solar Wings Pegasus XL-R	S. Woods	
G-MWTY	Mainair Gemini/Flash IIA	A. McGing & J. C. Townsend	
G-MWTZ	Mainair Gemini/Flash IIA	C. W. R. Felce	
G-MWUA	CFM Shadow Srs CD	Cloudbase Aviation G-MWUA	
G-MWUB	Solar Wings Pegasus XL-R	T. R. L. Bayley	
G-MWUC	Solar Wings Pegasus XL-R	M. A. Hicks	
G-MWUD	Solar Wings Pegasus XL-R	M. J. Taggart	
G-MWUH	Renegade Spirit UK	A. I. Grant	
G-MWUI	AMF Chevvron 2-32C	N. D. A. Graham	
G-MWUK	Rans S.6-ESD Coyote II	S. J. C. Pollock	
G-MWUL	Rans S.6-ESD Coyote II	C. P. Whitford	
G-MWUN	Rans S.6-ESD Coyote II	C. N. Nairn	
G-MWUO	Solar Wings Pegasus XL-Q	A. P. Slade	
G-MWUR	Solar Wings Pegasus XL-R	Nottingham Aerotow Club	
G-MWUS	Solar Wings Pegasus XL-R	H. R. Loxton	
G-MWUU	Solar Wings Pegasus XL-R	B. R. Underwood	
G-MWUV	Solar Wings Pegasus XL-R	C. D. Baines	
G-MWUW	Solar Wings Pegasus XL-R	Ultraflight Microlights Ltd	
G-MWUX	Solar Wings Pegasus XL-Q	B. D. Attwell	
G-MWUY	Solar Wings Pegasus XL-Q	M. J. Sharp	
G-MWUZ	Solar Wings Pegasus XL-Q	S. R. Nanson	
G-MWVA	Solar Wings Pegasus XL-Q	P. J. Hopkins	
G-MWVE	Solar Wings Pegasus XL-R	W. A. Keel-Stocker	
G-MWVF	Solar Wings Pegasus XL-R	J. B. Wright	
G-MWVG	CFM Shadow Srs CD	Shadow Aviation Ltd	
G-MWVH	CFM Shadow Srs CD	M. McKenzie	
G-MWVK	Mainair Mercury	S. B. Walters	
G-MWVL	Rans S.6-ESD Coyote II	A. J. T., O. D. & A. Lewis	
G-MWVM	Solar Wings Pegasus Quasar II	A. A. Edmonds & J. D. Jones	
G-MWVN	Mainair Gemini/Flash IIA	J. McCafferty	
G-MWVO	Mainair Gemini/Flash IIA	P. Webb	
G-MWVP	Renegade Spirit UK	P. D. Mickleburgh	
G-MWVR	Mainair Gemini/Flash IIA	G. Cartwright	
G-MWVS	Mainair Gemini/Flash IIA	S. J. J. Griffiths	
G-MWVT	Mainair Gemini/Flash IIA	C. Osiejuk & J. Barlow	
G-MWVY	Mainair Gemini/Flash IIA	J. D. Hinton	
G-MWVZ	Mainair Gemini/Flash IIA	S. J. Taft	
G-MWWB	Mainair Gemini/Flash IIA	W. P. Seward	
G-MWWC	Mainair Gemini/Flash IIA	D. & A. Margereson	
G-MWWD	Renegade Spirit	J. & A. Oswald	
G-MWWE	TEAM mini-MAX	J. Entwistle	
G-MWWG	Solar Wings Pegasus XL-Q	A. W. Guerri	
G-MWWH	Solar Wings Pegasus XL-Q	A. J. Alexander	
G-MWWI	Mainair Gemini/Flash IIA	M. A. S. Nesbitt	
G-MWWJ	Mainair Gemini/Flash IIA	I. M. Ferdinand & A. F. Glover	
G-MWWK	Mainair Gemini/Flash IIA	J. C. Boyd	
G-MWWL	Rans S.6-ESD Coyote II	J. C. Field	
G-MWWN	Mainair Gemini/Flash IIA	F. Watts	
G-MWWP	Rans S.4 Coyote	R. P. Cross	
G-MWWR	Microflight Spectrum	K. A. Wright	
G-MWWS	Thruster T.300	D. P. Wring	
G-MWWV	Solar Wings Pegasus XL-Q	R. W. Livingstone	
G-MWWZ	Cyclone Chaser S	J. F. Willoughby	
G-MWXA	Mainair Gemini/Flash IIA	M. Briongos	
G-MWXB	Mainair Gemini/Flash IIA	N. W. Barnett	
G-MWXC	Mainair Gemini/Flash IIA	G. Dufton-Kelly	
G-MWXF	Mainair Mercury	P. E. Jackson	
G-MWXG	Solar Wings Pegasus Quasar IITC	J. E. Moseley	
G-MWXH	Solar Wings Pegasus Quasar IITC	R. P. Wilkinson	
G-MWXJ	Mainair Mercury	P. J. Taylor	
G-MWXK	Mainair Mercury	M. P. Wilkinson	
G-MWXL	Mainair Gemini/Flash IIA	S. N. Catchpole	
G-MWXP	Solar Wings Pegasus XL-Q	A. P. Attfield	
G-MWXR	Solar Wings Pegasus XL-Q	G. W. Craig	
G-MWXU	Mainair Gemini/Flash IIA	C. M. Mackinnon	
G-MWXV	Mainair Gemini/Flash IIA	A. W. Lowrie	
G-MWXW	Cyclone Chaser S	K. C. Dodd	
G-MWXX	Cyclone Chaser S 447	P. I. Frost	

G-MWXY – G-MYBM — BRITISH CIVIL REGISTRATIONS

Notes	Reg	Type	Owner or Operator
	G-MWXY	Cyclone Chaser S 447	C. A. Benjamin
	G-MWXZ	Cyclone Chaser S 508	D. L. Hadley
	G-MWYA	Mainair Gemini/Flash IIA	R. F. Hunt
	G-MWYB	Solar Wings Pegasus XL-Q	Wilts Microlight Centre
	G-MWYC	Solar Wings Pegasus XL-Q	M. A. Collins
	G-MWYD	CFM Shadow Srs C	D. W. Hermiston-Hooper
	G-MWYE	Rans S.6-ESD Coyote II	G. A. M. Moffat
	G-MWYG	Mainair Gemini/Flash IIA	P. G. Fox
	G-MWYH	Mainair Gemini/Flash IIA	R. S. Sanby
	G-MWYI	Solar Wings Pegasus Quasar II	T. S. Chadfield
	G-MWYJ	Solar Wings Pegasus Quasar IITC	J. W. Edwards
	G-MWYL	Mainair Gemini/Flash IIA	A. J. Hinks
	G-MWYM	Cyclone Chaser S 1000	C. J. Meadows
	G-MWYN	Rans S.6-ESD Coyote	W. R. Tull
	G-MWYS	CGS Hawk 1 Arrow	Civilair
	G-MWYT	Mainair Gemini/Flash IIA	M. A. Hodgson
	G-MWYU	Solar Wings Pegasus XL-Q	N. Hammerton
	G-MWYV	Mainair Gemini/Flash IIA	J. N. Whitworth
	G-MWYY	Mainair Gemini/Flash IIA	R. D. Allard
	G-MWYZ	Solar Wings Pegasus XL-Q	A. Boston
	G-MWZA	Mainair Mercury	A. J. Malham
	G-MWZB	AMF Chevvron 2-32C	C. M. Lewis & M. J. Wilson
	G-MWZC	Mainair Gemini/Flash IIA	R. B. Huyshe
	G-MWZD	Solar Wings Pegasus Quasar IITC	J. R. Burton
	G-MWZE	Solar Wings Pegasus Quasar IITC	H. Lorimer
	G-MWZF	Solar Wings Pegasus Quasar IITC	R. G. T. Corney
	G-MWZG	Mainair Gemini/Flash IIA	C. J. O'Sullivan/Ireland
	G-MWZI	Solar Wings Pegasus XL-R	K. J. Slater
	G-MWZJ	Solar Wings Pegasus XL-R	P. Kitchen
	G-MWZL	Mainair Gemini/Flash IIA	D. Renton
	G-MWZM	TEAM mini-MAX 91	C. Leighton-THomas
	G-MWZN	Mainair Gemini/Flash IIA	D. F. Greatbanks
	G-MWZO	Solar Wings Pegasus Quasar IITC	A. Robinson
	G-MWZP	Solar Wings Pegasus Quasar IITC	C. M. Lewis
	G-MWZR	Solar Wings Pegasus Quasar IITC	R. Veart
	G-MWZS	Solar Wings Pegasus Quasar IITC	G. Bennett
	G-MWZT	Solar Wings Pegasus XL-R	J. R. Lowman
	G-MWZU	Solar Wings Pegasus XL-R	A. D. Winebloom
	G-MWZV	Solar Wings Pegasus XL-R	D. J. Newby
	G-MWZW	Solar Wings Pegasus XL-R	S. N. Pryor
	G-MWZY	Solar Wings Pegasus XL-R	S. J. Barkworth
	G-MWZZ	Solar Wings Pegasus XL-R	The Microlight School (Lichfield) Ltd
	G-MXVI	VS.361 Spitfire LF.XVIe (TE184:D)	P. M. Andrews
	G-MYAB	Solar Wings Pegasus XL-R	A. N. F. Stewart
	G-MYAC	Solar Wings Pegasus XL-Q	M. A. Garner
	G-MYAE	Solar Wings Pegasus XL-Q	K. J. Legg
	G-MYAF	Solar Wings Pegasus XL-Q	N. D. Pitt
	G-MYAG	Quad City Challenger II	R. Shewan
	G-MYAH	Whittaker MW5 Sorcerer	K. R. Emery
	G-MYAI	Mainair Mercury	J. Ellerton
	G-MYAJ	Rans S.6-ESD Coyote II	P. J. Fahie
	G-MYAK	Solar Wings Pegasus Quasar IITC	I. E. Brunning
	G-MYAM	Renegade Spirit UK	S. R. Groves
	G-MYAN	Whittaker MW5 (K) Sorcerer	A. F. Reid
	G-MYAO	Mainair Gemini/Flash IIA	J. H. Livingstone
	G-MYAR	Thruster T.300	H. G. Denton
	G-MYAS	Mainair Gemini/Flash IIA	A. N. Duncanson
	G-MYAT	TEAM mini-MAX	A. D. Bales
	G-MYAU	Mainair Gemini/Flash IIA	P. P. Allen
	G-MYAY	Microflight Spectrum	P. F. Craggs
	G-MYAZ	Renegade Spirit UK	R. Smith
	G-MYBA	Rans S.6-ESD Coyote II	Climsland Climber Society
	G-MYBB	Maxair Drifter	M. Ingleton
	G-MYBC	CFM Shadow Srs CD	M. E. Gilbert
	G-MYBD	SolarWings Pegasus Quaser IITC	A. Gunn
	G-MYBE	Solar Wings Pegasus Quaser IITC	D. Lumsdon
	G-MYBF	Solar Wings Pegasus XL-Q	K. H. Pead
	G-MYBI	Rans S.6-ESD Coyote II	N. C. Tambiah
	G-MYBJ	Mainair Gemini/Flash IIA	G. C. Bowers
	G-MYBL	CFM Shadow Srs C	A. A. Castleton & D. N. Owens
	G-MYBM	TEAM mini-MAX	B. Hunter

BRITISH CIVIL REGISTRATIONS   G-MYBN – G-MYFN

Reg	Type	Owner or Operator	Notes
G-MYBN	Hiway Demon 175	B. R. Lamming	
G-MYBO	Solar Wings Pegasus XL-R	D. Gledhill	
G-MYBP	Solar Wings Pegasus XL-R	S. H. Williams	
G-MYBR	Solar Wings Pegasus XL-Q	M. J. Larbey & G. T. Hunt	
G-MYBS	Solar Wings Pegasus XL-Q	T. Smith	
G-MYBT	Solar Wings Pegasus Quasar IITC	G. A. Rainbow-Ockwell	
G-MYBU	Cyclone Chaser S 447	R. L. Arscott	
G-MYBV	Solar Wings Pegasus XL-Q	P. M. Langdon	
G-MYBW	Solar Wings Pegasus XL-Q	J. S. Chapman	
G-MYBY	Solar Wings Pegasus XL-Q	I. D. A. Spanton	
G-MYBZ	Solar Wings Pegasus XL-Q	A. J. Blackwell	
G-MYCA	Whittaker MW6 Merlin	R. A. L-V. Harris	
G-MYCB	Cyclone Chaser S 447	P. Sykes	
G-MYCE	Solar Wings Pegasus Quasar IITC	S. W. Barker	
G-MYCJ	Mainair Mercury	J. Agnew	
G-MYCK	Mainair Gemini/Flash IIA	J. P Hanlon & A. C. McAllister	
G-MYCL	Mainair Mercury	P. B. Cole	
G-MYCM	CFM Shadow Srs CD	T. Jones	
G-MYCN	Mainair Mercury	P. Lowham	
G-MYCO	Renegade Spirit UK	S. Desormes	
G-MYCP	Whittaker MW6 Merlin	A. C. Jones	
G-MYCR	Mainair Gemini/Flash IIA	A. P. King	
G-MYCS	Mainair Gemini/Flash IIA	Husthwaite Alpha Group	
G-MYCT	TEAM mini-MAX	D. D. Rayment	
G-MYCV	Mainair Mercury	G. Zuchowski	
G-MYCX	Powerchute Kestrel	S. J. Pugh-Jones	
G-MYCY	Powerchute Kestrel	D. R. M. Powell	
G-MYCZ	Powerchute Kestrel	R. R. O'Neill	
G-MYDA	Powerchute Kestrel	K. J. Greatrix	
G-MYDC	Mainair Mercury	G. K. Thornton	
G-MYDD	CFM Shadow Srs CD	C. H. Gem/Spain	
G-MYDE	CFM Shadow Srs CD	D. N. L. Howell	
G-MYDF	TEAM mini-MAX	A. M. Hughes	
G-MYDI	Solar Wings Pegasus XL-R	M. D. Howard	
G-MYDJ	Solar Wings Pegasus XL-R	Cambridgeshire Aerotow Club	
G-MYDK	Rans S.6-ESD Coyote II	R. W. Thompson	
G-MYDM	Whittaker MW6-S Fatboy Flyer	K. Gregan	
G-MYDN	Quad City Challenger II	T. C. Hooks	
G-MYDO	Rans S.5 Coyote	B. J. Benton	
G-MYDP	Kolb Twinstar Mk 3	Norberts Flying Group	
G-MYDR	Thruster Tn.300	H. G. Soper	
G-MYDS	Quad City Challenger II	L. R. Graham	
G-MYDT	Thruster T.300	C. R. Bunce	
G-MYDU	Thruster T.300	S. Collins	
G-MYDV	Thruster T.300	M. Griffiths	
G-MYDW	Whittaker MW6 Merlin	A. Chidlow	
G-MYDX	Rans S.6-ESD Coyote II	R. J. Goodburn	
G-MYDZ	Mignet HM.1000 Balerit	D. S. Simpson	
G-MYEA	Solar Wings Pegasus XL-Q	A. M. Taylor	
G-MYEC	Solar Wings Pegasus XL-Q	J. I. King	
G-MYED	Solar Wings Pegasus XL-R	P. K. Dale	
G-MYEF	Whittaker MW6 Merlin	R. D. Thomasson	
G-MYEG	Solar Wings Pegasus XL-R	I. D. Nuttall	
G-MYEH	Solar Wings Pegasus XL-R	G-MYEH Flying Group	
G-MYEI	Cyclone Chaser S447	G. Charles-Jones	
G-MYEJ	Cyclone Chaser S447	K. J. Underwood	
G-MYEK	Solar Wings Pegasus Quasar IITC	M. N. Dando	
G-MYEM	Solar Wings Pegasus Quasar IITC	D. J. Moore	
G-MYEN	Solar Wings Pegasus Quasar IITC	J. C. Higham	
G-MYEO	Solar Wings Pegasus Quasar IITC	A. G. Curtis	
G-MYEP	CFM Shadow Srs CD	J. S. Seddon-Harvey	
G-MYER	Cyclone AX3/503	T. F. Horrocks	
G-MYES	Rans S.6-ESD Coyote II	Dairy House Flyers	
G-MYET	Whittaker MW6 Merlin	G. Campbell	
G-MYEU	Mainair Gemini/Flash IIA	C. Parry	
G-MYEV	Whittaker MW6 Merlin	M. J. Batchelor	
G-MYEX	Powerchute Kestrel	R. J. Watkin	
G-MYFH	Quad City Challenger II	P. S. Fossy	
G-MYFI	Cyclone AX3/503	A. F. Cashin	
G-MYFK	Solar Wings Pegasus Quasar IITC	R. L. Harris	
G-MYFL	Solar Wings Pegasus Quasar IITC	S. B. Wilkes	
G-MYFM	Renegade Spirit UK	A. C. Cale	
G-MYFN	Rans S.5 Coyote	P. Doran	

G-MYFO – G-MYKB | BRITISH CIVIL REGISTRATIONS

Notes	Reg	Type	Owner or Operator
	G-MYFO	Cyclone Chaser S	D. M. Broom
	G-MYFP	Mainair Gemini/Flash IIA	R. Nicklin
	G-MYFR	Mainair Gemini/Flash IIA	P. G. Bright
	G-MYFS	Pegasus XL-R	B. J. Palfreyman
	G-MYFT	Mainair Scorcher	T. Williams
	G-MYFU	Mainair Gemini/Flash IIA	J. Payne
	G-MYFV	Cyclone AX3/503	J. K. Sargent
	G-MYFW	Cyclone AX3/503	Microlight School (Lichfield) Ltd
	G-MYFX	Solar Wings Pegasus XL-Q	J. R. Bluett
	G-MYFY	Cyclone AX3/503	T. A. Simpson
	G-MYFZ	Cyclone AX3/503	G. Gates
	G-MYGD	Cyclone AX3/503	AX3 Cavaliers
	G-MYGE	Whittaker MW6 Merlin	M. D. & S. M. North
	G-MYGF	TEAM mini-MAX	R. D. Barnard
	G-MYGH	Rans S.6ESD Coyote II	J. R. Mosey
	G-MYGJ	Mainair Mercury	J. R. Harnett
	G-MYGK	Cyclone Chaser S 508	P. C. Collins
	G-MYGM	Quad City Challenger II	G. J. Williams & J. White
	G-MYGN	AMF Chevvron 2-32C	A. C. Barber
	G-MYGO	CFM Shadow Srs CD	A. C. St. H. Mason
	G-MYGP	Rans S.6-ESD Coyote II	D. J. Millin
	G-MYGR	Rans S.6-ESD Coyote II	M. E. Parker
	G-MYGT	Solar Wings Pegasus XL-R	Condors Aerotow Syndicate
	G-MYGU	Solar Wings Pegasus XL-R	D. R. Western
	G-MYGV	Solar Wings Pegasus XL-R	J. A. Crofts & G. M. Birkett
	G-MYGZ	Mainair Gemini/Flash IIA	P. M. Reddington
	G-MYHF	Mainair Gemini/Flash IIA	P. J. Bloor
	G-MYHG	Cyclone AX/503	N. P. Thomson & C. Alsop
	G-MYHH	Cyclone AX/503	M. L. Smith
	G-MYHI	Rans S.6-ESD Coyote II	D. S. Berry
	G-MYHK	Rans S.6-ESD Coyote II	M. R. Williamson
	G-MYHL	Mainair Gemini/Flash IIA	B. J. Riley
	G-MYHM	Cyclone AX3/503	A. J. Bergman
	G-MYHN	Mainair Gemini/Flash IIA	T. J. Widdison
	G-MYHP	Rans S.6-ESD Coyote II	K. E. Gair & J. G. E. Lane
	G-MYHR	Cyclone AX3/503	D. A. Archer
	G-MYHS	Powerchute Kestrel	R. R. O'Neill
	G-MYIA	Quad City Challenger II	I. J. Arkieson
	G-MYIE	Whittaker MW6 Merlin	A. M. Morris
	G-MYIF	CFM Shadow Srs CD	P. J. Edwards
	G-MYIH	Mainair Gemini/Flash IIA	A. N. Huddart
	G-MYII	TEAM mini-MAX	P. A. Gasson
	G-MYIJ	Cyclone AX3/503	Ultralight Training Ltd
	G-MYIK	Kolb Twinstar Mk 3	T. R. Janeway
	G-MYIL	Cyclone Chaser S 508	R. A. Rawes
	G-MYIN	Solar Wings Pegasus Quasar IITC	W. P. Hughes
	G-MYIO	Solar Wings Pegasus Quasar IITC	E. Foster & J. H. Peet
	G-MYIP	CFM Shadow Srs CD	G. J. Chapman
	G-MYIR	Rans S.6-ESD Coyote II	P. Vergette
	G-MYIS	Rans S.6-ESD Coyote II	I. S. Everett & M. Stott
	G-MYIT	Cyclone Chaser S 508	R. Barringer
	G-MYIU	Cyclone AX3/503	G. R. Hill
	G-MYIV	Mainair Gemini/Flash IIA	P. S. Nicholls
	G-MYIX	Quad City Challenger II	A. Studley
	G-MYIY	Mainair Gemini/Flash IIA	I. C. Macbeth
	G-MYIZ	TEAM mini-MAX 2	S. E. Richardson
	G-MYJC	Mainair Gemini/Flash IIA	R. G. Hearsey
	G-MYJD	Rans S.6-ESD Coyote II	D. R. Coller
	G-MYJF	Thruster T.300	P. F. McConville
	G-MYJG	Thruster Super T.300	M. R. Wyatt
	G-MYJJ	Solar Wings Pegasus Quasar IITC	D. Murray
	G-MYJK	Solar Wings Pegasus Quasar IITC	T. H. Parr
	G-MYJM	Mainair Gemini/Flash IIA	S. McMaster
	G-MYJO	Cyclone Chaser S 508	S. Brader
	G-MYJR	Mainair Mercury	D. Dreux
	G-MYJS	Solar Wings Pegasus Quasar IITC	P. R. Saunders
	G-MYJT	Solar Wings Pegasus Quasar IITC	H. A. Duthie
	G-MYJU	Solar Wings Pegasus Quasar IITC	P. G. Penhaligan
	G-MYJW	Cyclone Chaser S 508	A. R. Mikolajczyk
	G-MYJY	Rans S.6-ESD Coyote II	F. N. Pearson
	G-MYJZ	Whittaker MW5D Sorcerer	My Jazz Group
	G-MYKA	Cyclone AX3/503	R. Nicklin
	G-MYKB	Kolb Twinstar Mk 3	T. Antell

BRITISH CIVIL REGISTRATIONS

G-MYKC – G-MYNR

Reg	Type	Owner or Operator	Notes
G-MYKC	Mainair Gemini/Flash IIA	R. Bricknell	
G-MYKD	Cyclone Chaser S 447	J. B. Allan	
G-MYKE	CFM Shadow Srs BD	MKH Engineering	
G-MYKF	Cyclone AX3/503	M. A. Collins	
G-MYKG	Mainair Gemini/Flash IIA	B. D. Walker	
G-MYKH	Mainair Gemini/Flash IIA	G. F. Atkinson	
G-MYKJ	TEAM mini-MAX	T. de Breffe Gardner	
G-MYKL	Medway Raven	A. Williams	
G-MYKN	Rans S.6-ESD Coyote II	G. C. Alderson	
G-MYKO	Whittaker MW6-S Fat Boy Flyer	K. R. Challis & C. S. Andersson	
G-MYKP	Solar Wings Pegasus Quasar IITC	R. F. Dye & G. S. B. Airth	
G-MYKR	Solar Wings Pegasus Quasar IITC	C. Stallard	
G-MYKS	Solar Wings Pegasus Quasar IITC	D. J. Oskis	
G-MYKT	Cyclone AX3/503	J. D. Sanger & J. E. Seager	
G-MYKV	Mainair Gemini/Flash IIA	P. J. Gulliver	
G-MYKX	Mainair Mercury	B. W. Hunter	
G-MYKY	Mainair Mercury	R. P. Jewitt	
G-MYKZ	TEAM mini-MAX	C. Libby (G-BVAV)	
G-MYLB	TEAM mini-MAX	J. G. Burns	
G-MYLC	Solar Wings Pegasus Quantum 15	J. Urwin	
G-MYLD	Rans S.6-ESD Coyote II	B. Cartwright	
G-MYLE	Solar Wings Pegasus Quantum 15	S. E. Powell	
G-MYLF	Rans S.6-ESD Coyote II	A. J. Spencer	
G-MYLG	Mainair Gemini/Flash IIA	N. J. Axworthy & C. Dunning	
G-MYLH	Solar Wings Pegasus Quantum 15	J. W. Atkin	
G-MYLI	Solar Wings Pegasus Quantum 15	A. M. Keyte	
G-MYLK	Solar Wings Pegasus Quantum 15	G-MYLK Group	
G-MYLL	Solar Wings Pegasus Quantum 15	S. Hayes	
G-MYLM	Solar Wings Pegasus Quasar IITC	P. A. Ashton	
G-MYLN	Kolb Twinstar Mk 3	J. F. Joyes	
G-MYLO	Rans S.6-ESD Coyote II	P. Bowers	
G-MYLP	Kolb Twinstar Mk 3	R. Thompson (G-BVCR)	
G-MYLR	Mainair Gemini/Flash IIA	I. J. Cleland & M. D. Calder	
G-MYLS	Mainair Mercury	D. Burnell-Higgs	
G-MYLT	Mainair Blade	T. D. Hall	
G-MYLV	CFM Shadow Srs CD	Aviation for Paraplegics and Tetraplegics Trust	
G-MYLW	Rans S.6-ESD Coyote II	M. J. Phillips	
G-MYLX	Medway Raven	T. M. Knight	
G-MYLY	Medway Raven	C. R. Smith	
G-MYLZ	Solar Wings Pegasus Quantum 15	W. G. McPherson	
G-MYMB	Solar Wings Pegasus Quantum 15	C. A. Green	
G-MYMC	Solar Wings Pegasus Quantum 15	D. Murray	
G-MYME	Cyclone AX3/503	S. Bradie	
G-MYMH	Rans S.6-ESD Coyote II	A. R. Cattell	
G-MYMJ	Medway Raven	N. Brigginshaw	
G-MYMK	Mainair Gemini/Flash IIA	A. Britton	
G-MYML	Mainair Mercury	D. J. Dalley	
G-MYMM	Ultraflight Fun 18S	W. H. Greenwood	
G-MYMN	Whittaker MW6 Merlin	K. J. Cole	
G-MYMO	Mainair Gemini/Flash IIA	S. P. Moores	
G-MYMP	Rans S.6-ESD Coyote II	R. L. Flowerday (G-CHAZ)	
G-MYMR	Rans S.6-ESD Coyote II	R. J. Bentley	
G-MYMS	Rans S.6-ESD Coyote II	M. R. Johnson & P. G. Briscoe	
G-MYMV	Mainair Gemini/Flash IIA	A. J. Evans	
G-MYMW	Cyclone AX3/503	L. J. Perring	
G-MYMX	Solar Wings Pegasus Quantum 15	A. R. Watt	
G-MYMY	Cyclone Chaser S 508	D. L. Hadley	
G-MYMZ	Cyclone AX3/503	Microlight School (Lichfield) Ltd	
G-MYNA	CFM Shadow Srs C	R. W. Frost	
G-MYNB	Solar Wings Pegasus Quantum 15	S. D. Powell & R. Maude	
G-MYNC	Mainair Mercury	N. L. Northend	
G-MYND	Mainair Gemini/Flash IIA	S. Wild	
G-MYNE	Rans S.6-ESD Coyote II	J. L. Smoker	
G-MYNF	Mainair Mercury	W. Gray	
G-MYNH	Rans S.6-ESD Coyote II	E. F. & V. M. Clapham	
G-MYNI	TEAM mini-MAX	J. M. Burgess	
G-MYNJ	Mainair Mercury	S. M. Buchan	
G-MYNK	Solar Wings Pegasus Quantum 15	M. J. Tarrant	
G-MYNL	Solar Wings Pegasus Quantum 15	C. Hodgkiss	
G-MYNN	Solar Wings Pegasus Quantum 15	G. E. & K. D. MacCuish	
G-MYNO	Solar Wings Pegasus Quantum 15	A. J. Hodson	
G-MYNP	Solar Wings Pegasus Quantum 15	RAF Microlight Flying Association (NP)	
G-MYNR	Solar Wings Pegasus Quantum 15	A. S. Wason	

G-MYNS – G-MYSI — BRITISH CIVIL REGISTRATIONS

Notes	Reg	Type	Owner or Operator
	G-MYNS	Solar Wings Pegasus Quantum 15	F. J. McVey
	G-MYNT	Solar Wings Pegasus Quantum 15	C. D. Arnold
	G-MYNV	Solar Wings Pegasus Quantum 15	J. Goldsmith-Ryan
	G-MYNX	CFM Streak Shadow Srs S-A1	M. D. & T. J. Palmer
	G-MYNY	Kolb Twinstar Mk 3	B. Alexander
	G-MYNZ	Solar Wings Pegasus Quantum 15	P. W. Rogers
	G-MYOA	Rans S.6-ESD Coyote II	R. W. Trenholm t/a Orcas Syndicate
	G-MYOB	Mainair Mercury	P. J. Higgins
	G-MYOF	Mainair Mercury	G. Bonnar
	G-MYOG	Kolb Twinstar Mk 3	A. P. De Legh
	G-MYOH	CFM Shadow Srs CD	D. R. Sutton
	G-MYOI	Rans S.6-ESD Coyote II	R. M. Moulton
	G-MYOL	Air Creation Fun 18S GTBIS	S. N. Bond
	G-MYOM	Mainair Gemini/Flash IIA	M. A. Haughey
	G-MYON	CFM Shadow Srs CD	D. W. & S. E. Suttill
	G-MYOO	Kolb Twinstar Mk 3	P. D. Coppin
	G-MYOR	Kolb Twinstar Mk 3	J. J. Littler
	G-MYOS	CFM Shadow Srs CD	C. A. & E. J. Bowles
	G-MYOT	Rans S.6-ESD Coyote II	D. E. Wilson
	G-MYOU	Solar Wings Pegasus Quantum 15	M. Botten & O. Kent
	G-MYOV	Mainair Mercury	P. Newton
	G-MYOW	Mainair Gemini/Flash IIA	A. J. A. Fowler
	G-MYOX	Mainair Mercury	K. Driver
	G-MYOY	Cyclone AX3/503	M. R. Smith
	G-MYOZ	Quad City Challenger II UK	A. R. Thomson
	G-MYPA	Rans S.6-ESD Coyote II	R. S. McLeister
	G-MYPC	Kolb Twinstar Mk 3	J. Young & S. Hussain
	G-MYPD	Mainair Mercury	R. D. McManus
	G-MYPE	Mainair Gemini/Flash IIA	R. Cant
	G-MYPG	Solar Wings Pegasus XL-Q	R. D. Howie
	G-MYPH	Solar Wings Pegasus Quantum 15	P. M. J. White
	G-MYPI	Solar Wings Pegasus Quantum 15	P. L. Jarvis
	G-MYPJ	Rans S.6-ESD Coyote II	K. A. Eden
	G-MYPL	CFM Shadow Srs CD	G. I. Madden
	G-MYPM	Cyclone AX3/503	Microflight (Ireland) Ltd
	G-MYPN	Solar Wings Pegasus Quantum 15	P. J. S. Albon
	G-MYPP	Whittaker MW6-S Fat Boy Flyer	G. Everett & D. Smith
	G-MYPR	Cyclone AX3/503	W. R. Hibberd
	G-MYPS	Whittaker MW6 Merlin	I. S. Bishop
	G-MYPT	CFM Shadow Srs CD	M. G. & S. A. Collins
	G-MYPV	Mainair Mercury	B. Donnan
	G-MYPW	Mainair Gemini/Flash IIA	R. E. Parker
	G-MYPX	Solar Wings Pegasus Quantum 15	M. Aylett & P. J. Callis
	G-MYPY	Solar Wings Pegasus Quantum 15	C. J. Johnson
	G-MYPZ	Quad City Challenger II	E. G. Astin
	G-MYRB	Whittaker MW5 Sorcerer	P. J. Careless
	G-MYRC	Mainair Blade	J. F. Murphy
	G-MYRD	Mainair Blade	W. J. Walker
	G-MYRE	Cyclone Chaser S	A. W. Lowrie
	G-MYRF	Solar Wings Pegasus Quantum 15	A. O. Sutherland
	G-MYRG	TEAM mini-MAX	V. Grayson
	G-MYRH	Quad City Challenger II	C. M. Gray
	G-MYRJ	BFC Challenger II	C. G. Trow
	G-MYRK	Renegade Spirit UK	D. J. Newton
	G-MYRL	TEAM mini-MAX	J. N. Hanson
	G-MYRM	Solar Wings Pegasus Quantum 15	G. Turner
	G-MYRN	Solar Wings Pegasus Quantum 15	G. Ferries
	G-MYRO	Cyclone AX3/503	R. I. Simpson
	G-MYRP	Letov LK-2M Sluka	R. M. C. Hunter
	G-MYRR	Letov LK-2M Sluka	B. C. McCartan
	G-MYRS	Solar Wings Pegasus Quantum 15	R. M. Summers
	G-MYRT	Solar Wings Pegasus Quantum 15	M. C. Taylor
	G-MYRU	Cyclone AX3/503	W. A. Emmerson
	G-MYRV	Cyclone AX3/503	M. Gardiner
	G-MYRW	Mainair Mercury	G. C. Hobson
	G-MYRY	Solar Wings Pegasus Quantum 15	G. M. Cruise-Smith
	G-MYRZ	Solar Wings Pegasus Quantum 15	G. D. Black
	G-MYSA	Cyclone Chaser S 508	P. Nicholls
	G-MYSB	Solar Wings Pegasus Quantum 15	P. H. Woodward
	G-MYSC	Solar Wings Pegasus Quantum 15	K. R. White
	G-MYSD	BFC Challlenger II	C. E. Bell
	G-MYSG	Mainair Mercury	M. Donnelly
	G-MYSI	HM14/93	A. R. D. Seaman

BRITISH CIVIL REGISTRATIONS

G-MYSJ – G-MYWC

Reg	Type	Owner or Operator	Notes
G-MYSJ	Mainair Gemini/Flash IIA	A. Warnock	
G-MYSK	TEAM mini-MAX	A. D. Bolshaw	
G-MYSL	Aviasud Mistral	N. W. Cawley	
G-MYSM	CFM Shadow Srs CD	L. W. Stevens	
G-MYSO	Cyclone AX3/50	N. J. Stoneman & S. Mather	
G-MYSP	Rans S.6-ESD Coyote II	A. J. Alexander, B. Knight & K. G. Diamond	
G-MYSR	Solar Wings Pegasus Quatum 15	W. G. Craig	
G-MYSU	Rans S.6-ESD Coyote II	K. W. Allan	
G-MYSV	Aerial Arts Chaser	R. J. Sims & I. G. Reason	
G-MYSW	Solar Wings Pegasus Quantum 1	C. Lamb & P.J. Cragg	
G-MYSX	Solar Wings Pegasus Quantum 1	J. L. Treves	
G-MYSY	Solar Wings Pegasus Quantum 15	Premier Aviation (UK) Ltd	
G-MYSZ	Mainair Mercury	R. G. McCron	
G-MYTB	Mainair Mercur	P. J. Higgins	
G-MYTC	Solar Wings Pegasus XL-Q	M. J. Edmett	
G-MYTD	Mainair Blade	M. P Law & B. E. Warburton	
G-MYTE	Rans S.6-ESD Coyote II	N. D. Austin	
G-MYTG	Mainair Blade	O. P Farrell	
G-MYTH	CFM Shadow Srs CD	H. A. Leek	
G-MYTI	Solar Wings Pegasus Quantum 15	J. Madhvani	
G-MYTJ	Solar Wings Pegasus Quantum 15	K. Laud	
G-MYTK	Mainair Mercury	D. A. Holroyd	
G-MYTL	Mainair Blade	S. Ostrowski	
G-MYTM	Cyclone AX3/503	J. P. Gardiner	
G-MYTN	Solar Wings Pegasus Quantum 15	M. Hoggett & M. F. Ambrose	
G-MYTO	Quad City Challenger II	R. W. Sage	
G-MYTP	Arrowflight Hawk II	R. J. Turner	
G-MYTT	Quad City Challenger II	J. Bolton	
G-MYTU	Mainair Blade	C. J. Barker	
G-MYTV	Hunt Avon Skytrike	M. Carson	
G-MYTX	Mainair Mercury	R. Steel	
G-MYTY	CFM Streak Shadow Srs M	K. H. A. Negal	
G-MYTZ	Air Creation Fun 18S GTBIS	A. Davis	
G-MYUA	Air Creation Fun 18S GTBIS	J. Leden	
G-MYUB	Mainair Mercury	T. A. Ross	
G-MYUC	Mainair Blade	A. D. Clayton	
G-MYUD	Mainair Mercury	P. W. Margetson	
G-MYUE	Mainair Mercury	D. W. Power	
G-MYUF	Renegade Spirit	F. Overall	
G-MYUH	Solar Wings Pegasus XL-Q	K. S. Daniels	
G-MYUI	Cyclone AX3/503	R. & M. Bailey	
G-MYUK	Mainair Mercury	S. Lear	
G-MYUN	Mainair Blade	G. A. Barratt	
G-MYUO	Solar Wings Pegasus Quantum 15	G. R. I. Tyler	
G-MYUP	Letov LK-2M Sluka	S. Burchfield	
G-MYUR	Hunt Wing	T. C. Saltmarsh	
G-MYUS	CFM Shadow Srs CD	Aviation for Paraplegics and Tetraplegics Trust	
G-MYUU	Pegasus Quantum 15	J. A. Slocombe	
G-MYUV	Pegasus Quantum 15	D. W. Wilson	
G-MYUW	Mainair Mercury	G. C. Hobson	
G-MYUZ	Rans S.6-ESD Coyote II	J. E. Gattrell & A. R. Trace	
G-MYVA	Kolb Twinstar Mk 3	E. Bayliss	
G-MYVB	Mainair Blade	P. J. Lomax & J. A. Robinson	
G-MYVC	Pegasus Quantum 15	R. Howes & O. Lloyd	
G-MYVE	Mainair Blade	S. Cooke	
G-MYVG	Letov LK-2M Sluka	S. Burchfield	
G-MYVH	Mainair Mercury	S. E. Wilks	
G-MYVI	Air Creation Fun 18S GTBIS	Northampton Aerotow Club	
G-MYVJ	Pegasus Quantum 15	A. I. McPherson & P. W. Davidson	
G-MYVK	Pegasus Quantum 15	J. Hammond	
G-MYVL	Mainair Mercury	P. J. Judge	
G-MYVM	Pegasus Quantum 15	T. P. Hunt	
G-MYVN	Cyclone AX3/503	F. Watt	
G-MYVO	Mainair Blade	S. S. Raines	
G-MYVP	Rans S.6-ESD Coyote II	P. J. Reeves	
G-MYVR	Pegasus Quantum 15	J. M. Webster	
G-MYVS	Mainair Mercury	P. S. Flynn	
G-MYVT	Letov LK-2M Sluka	J. P. Gardiner	
G-MYVV	Medway Hybred 44XLR	S. Perity	
G-MYVY	Mainair Blade	S. Farrow	
G-MYVZ	Mainair Blade	R. Llewellyn	
G-MYWA	Mainair Mercury	R. A. Atkinson	
G-MYWC	Hunt Wing	M. A. Coffin	

G-MYWD – G-MYZF

BRITISH CIVIL REGISTRATIONS

Notes	Reg	Type	Owner or Operator
	G-MYWD	Thruster T.600	M. D. Kirby
	G-MYWE	Thruster T.600	W. A. Stephenson
	G-MYWF	CFM Shadow Srs CD	M. A. Newman
	G-MYWG	Pegasus Quantum 15	S. L. Greene
	G-MYWH	Hunt Wing/Experience	G. N. Hatchett
	G-MYWI	Pegasus Quantum 15	J. R. Fulcher
	G-MYWJ	Pegasus Quantum 15	L. M. Sams & I. Clarkson
	G-MYWK	Pegasus Quantum 15	G. Hanna
	G-MYWL	Pegasus Quantum 15	E. Smith
	G-MYWM	CFM Shadow Srs CD	N. J. McKinley
	G-MYWN	Cyclone Chaser S 508	N. R. Beale
	G-MYWO	Pegasus Quantum 15	S. Gill & D. Hume
	G-MYWP	Kolb Twinstar Mk 3	P. R. Day
	G-MYWR	Pegasus Quantum 15	R. Horton
	G-MYWS	Cyclone Chaser S 447	M. H. Broadbent
	G-MYWT	Pegasus Quantum 1	A. G. Ransom
	G-MYWU	Pegasus Quantum 15	J. R. Buttle
	G-MYWV	Rans S.4 Coyote	I. D. Daniels
	G-MYWW	Pegasus Quantum 15	C. W. Bailie
	G-MYWX	Pegasus Quantum 15	D. J. Revell
	G-MYWY	Pegasus Quantum 15	A. Czajka
	G-MYWZ	Thruster TST Mk 1	W. H. J. Knowles
	G-MYXA	TEAM mini-MAX 91	H. L. S. Stephens
	G-MYXB	Rans S.6-ESD Coyote II	V. G. J. Davies & D. A. Hall
	G-MYXC	Quad City Challenger II	K. N. Dickinson
	G-MYXD	Pegasus Quasar IITC	A. Cochrane
	G-MYXE	Pegasus Quantum 15	W. Bowen
	G-MYXF	Air Creation Fun GT503	T. A. Morgan
	G-MYXH	Cyclone AX3/503	K. G. Underwood
	G-MYXI	Aries 1	H. Cook
	G-MYXJ	Mainair Blade	L. Seddon
	G-MYXK	Quad City Challenger II	V. Vaughan
	G-MYXL	Mignet HM.1000 Baleri	R. W. Hollamby
	G-MYXM	Mainair Blade	S. C. Hodgson
	G-MYXN	Mainair Blade	M. R. Sands
	G-MYXO	Letov LK-2M Sluka	G. W. Allport
	G-MYXP	Rans S.6-ESD Coyote II	R. S. Amor
	G-MYXR	Renegade Spirit UK	S. Hooker
	G-MYXS	Kolb Twinstar Mk 3	D. Robertson
	G-MYXT	Pegasus Quantum 15	P. G. Hill
	G-MYXU	Thruster T.300	D. W. Wilson
	G-MYXV	Quad City Challenger II	M. L. Sumner
	G-MYXW	Pegasus Quantum 15	D. T. Abbott
	G-MYXX	Pegasus Quantum 15	J. H. Arnold
	G-MYXY	CFM Shadow Srs CD	K. R. Payne
	G-MYXZ	Pegasus Quantum 15	J. Ayre
	G-MYYA	Mainair Blade	D. E. Bassett
	G-MYYB	Pegasus Quantum 15	A. L. Johnson
	G-MYYC	Pegasus Quantum 15	G. F. Atkinson
	G-MYYD	Cyclone Chaser S 447	K. A. Armstrong
	G-MYYE	Huntwing Avon 462	N. S. Payne
	G-MYYF	Quad City Challenger II	J. G. & J. A. Smith
	G-MYYG	Mainair Blade	A. Corson
	G-MYYH	Mainair Blade	C. Nicholson
	G-MYYI	Pegasus Quantum 15	M. R. Rowlands
	G-MYYJ	Hunt Wing	R. M. Jarvis
	G-MYYK	Pegasus Quantum 15	J. D. & N. G. Philp
	G-MYYL	Cyclone AX3/503	D. Bedborough
	G-MYYN	Pegasus Quantum 15	J. Darby
	G-MYYP	AMF Chevvron 2-45CS	I. D. Smith
	G-MYYR	TEAM mini-MAX 91	K. Stevens
	G-MYYS	TEAM mini-MAX	J. R. Hopkinson
	G-MYYU	Mainair Mercury	J. T. & A. C. Swannick
	G-MYYV	Rans S.6-ESD Coyote IIXL	M. B. Buttle
	G-MYYW	Mainair Blade	M. D. Kirby
	G-MYYX	Pegasus Quantum 15	I. H. Calder
	G-MYYY	Mainair Blade	E. D. Lockie/Barton
	G-MYYZ	Medway Raven X	J. W. Leaper
	G-MYZA	Whittaker MW6 Merlin	D. C. Davies
	G-MYZB	Pegasus Quantum 15	W. Russell
	G-MYZC	Cyclone AX3/503	P. E. Owen
	G-MYZE	TEAM mini-MAX	R. B. McKenzie
	G-MYZF	Cyclone AX3/503	Microflight (Ireland) Ltd

BRITISH CIVIL REGISTRATIONS G-MYZG – G-MZCV

Reg	Type	Owner or Operator	Notes
G-MYZG	Cyclone AX3/503	D. R. Western & J. F. Northey	
G-MYZJ	Pegasus Quantum 1	P. Millar	
G-MYZK	Pegasus Quantum 15	J. D. G. Welch	
G-MYZL	Pegasus Quantum 15	T. J. Gayton-Polley	
G-MYZM	Pegasus Quantum 15	D. Hope	
G-MYZN	Whittaker MW6-S Fatboy Flyer	M. K. Shaw	
G-MYZO	Medway Raven X	M. C. Arnold	
G-MYZP	CFM Shadow Srs DD	R. M. Davies & P. I. Hodgson	
G-MYZR	Rans S.6-ESD Coyote II	S. E. J. McLaughlin	
G-MYZV	Rans S.6-ESD Coyote II	B. W. Savory	
G-MYZY	Pegasus Quantum 15	N. C. O. Watney	
G-MZAA	Mainair Blade	P. R. Proost	
G-MZAB	Mainair Blade	A. Meadley	
G-MZAC	Quad City Challenger II	M. N. Calhaem	
G-MZAE	Mainair Blade	D. J. Guild & M. R. Revelle	
G-MZAF	Mainair Blade	M. J. Naylor/Barton	
G-MZAG	Mainair Blade	P. W. Brewer & D. R. G. Cornwell	
G-MZAH	Rans S.6-ESD Coyote II	C. J. Collett	
G-MZAJ	Mainair Blade	M. P. Daley	
G-MZAM	Mainair Blade	B. M. Marsh & P. David	
G-MZAN	Pegasus Quantum 15	P. M. Leahy	
G-MZAP	Mainair Blade	K. D. Adams	
G-MZAR	Mainair Blade	C. Bayliss	
G-MZAS	Mainair Blade	T. Carter	
G-MZAT	Mainair Blade	K. Horrobin	
G-MZAU	Mainair Blade	A. F. Glover	
G-MZAV	Mainair Blade	B. B. Boniface	
G-MZAW	Pegasus Quantum 15	C. A. Mackenzie	
G-MZAY	Mainair Blade	E. J. Carass	
G-MZAZ	Mainair Blade	T. Porter & D. Whiteley	
G-MZBA	Mainair Blade 912	S. Stone	
G-MZBB	Pegasus Quantum 15	T. Campbell	
G-MZBC	Pegasus Quantum 15	B. M. Quinn	
G-MZBD	Rans S.6-ESD Coyote II	T. Ali & C. Brant	
G-MZBF	Letov LK-2M Sluka	V. Simpson	
G-MZBG	Hodder MW6-A	E. I. Rowlands-Jons & M. W. Kilvert	
G-MZBH	Rans S.6-ESD Coyote II	D. Sutherland	
G-MZBI	Pegasus Quantum 15	I. W. Barlow A. L. Bagnall & A. B. Sev	
G-MZBK	Letov LK-2M Sluka	A. N. Buchan	
G-MZBL	Mainair Blade	C. J. Rubery	
G-MZBM	Pegasus Quantum 15	J. Strachan	
G-MZBN	CFM Shadow Srs B	Cloudbase Aviation G-MZBN	
G-MZBO	Pegasus Quantum 15	K. C. Beattie	
G-MZBR	Southdown Raven	D. M. Lane	
G-MZBS	CFM Shadow Srs D	S. K. Ryan	
G-MZBT	Pegasus Quantum 15	A. P Whitmarsh	
G-MZBU	Rans S.6-ESD Coyote II	R. S. Marriott & C. Clark	
G-MZBV	Rans S.6-ESD Coyote II	C. L. Barham & R. I. Cannan	
G-MZBW	Quad City Challenger II UK	R. T. L. Chaloner	
G-MZBX	Whittaker MW6-S Fatboy Flye	A. A. Comper	
G-MZBY	Pegasus Quantum 15	L. G. Wray	
G-MZBZ	Quad City Challenger II UK	T. R. Gregory	
G-MZCA	Rans S.6-ESD Coyote II	G. R. Inston	
G-MZCB	Cyclone Chaser S 447	G. P. Hodgson	
G-MZCC	Mainair Blade 912	K. S. Rissmann	
G-MZCD	Mainair Blade	T. J. Mellor	
G-MZCE	Mainair Blade	C. T. Halliday	
G-MZCF	Mainair Blade	C. Hannanby	
G-MZCG	Mainair Blade	J. F. Bennett	
G-MZCH	Whittaker MW6-S Fatboy Flyer	J. T. Moore	
G-MZCI	Pegasus Quantum 15	P. H. Risdale	
G-MZCJ	Pegasus Quantum 15	F. E. Hall	
G-MZCK	AMF Chevvron 2-32C	T. K. Lane	
G-MZCM	Pegasus Quantum 15	S. G. McLachlan	
G-MZCN	Mainair Blade	P. C. Williams	
G-MZCO	Mainair Mercury	E. Rush	
G-MZCP	Solar Wings Pegasus XL-Q	C. Hamblin	
G-MZCR	Pegasus Quantum 15	J. E. P. Stubberfield	
G-MZCS	TEAM mini-MAX	D. T. J. Stanley	
G-MZCT	CFM Shadow Srs CD	W. G. Gill	
G-MZCU	Mainair Blade	C. E. Pearce	
G-MZCV	Pegasus Quantum 15	B. S. Toole	

G-MZCW – G-MZGD — BRITISH CIVIL REGISTRATIONS

Notes	Reg	Type	Owner or Operator
	G-MZCW	Pegasus Quantum 15	K. L. Baldwin
	G-MZCX	Hunt Wing	Huntwing Group
	G-MZCY	Pegasus Quantum 15	J. R. Appleton & G. A. Davidson
	G-MZDA	Rans S.6-ESD Coyote IIXL	C. W. Lombard
	G-MZDB	Pegasus Quantum 15	Scottish Aerotow Club
	G-MZDC	Pegasus Quantum 15	M. T. Jones
	G-MZDD	Pegasus Quantum 15	C. D. Reves
	G-MZDE	Pegasus Quantum 15	R. G. Hedley
	G-MZDF	Mainair Blade	M. Liptrot
	G-MZDG	Rans S.6-ESD Coyote IIXL	J. M. Coffin
	G-MZDH	Pegasus Quantum 15	J. H. Bradbury
	G-MZDJ	Medway Raven X	R. Bryan & S. Digby
	G-MZDK	Mainair Blade	B. L. Cook
	G-MZDL	Whittaker MW6-S Fatboy Flyer	S. M. Pink
	G-MZDM	Rans S.6-ESD Coyote II	M. E. Nicholas
	G-MZDN	Pegasus Quantum 15	P. G. Ford
	G-MZDP	AMF Chevvron 2-32	F. Overall
	G-MZDR	Rans S.6-ESD Coyote IIXL	J. D. Gibbons
	G-MZDS	Cyclone AX3/503	M. P. James & T. H. Mitchell
	G-MZDT	Mainair Blade	T. J. Williams
	G-MZDU	Pegasus Quantum 15	G. Breen/Portugal
	G-MZDV	Pegasus Quantum 15	M. P. Wilkinson
	G-MZDX	Letov LK-2M Sluka	J. L. Barker
	G-MZDY	Pegasus Quantum 15	R. Bailey
	G-MZDZ	Hunt Wing	E. W. Laidlaw
	G-MZEA	Quad City Challenger II UK	G. S. Cridland
	G-MZEB	Mainair Blade	G. Todd
	G-MZEC	Pegasus Quantum 15	A. B. Godber
	G-MZED	Mainair Blade	C. W. Potts
	G-MZEE	Pegasus Quantum 15	M. Hassan
	G-MZEG	Mainair Blade	R. & A. Soltysik
	G-MZEH	Pegasus Quantum 15	P. S. Hall
	G-MZEJ	Mainair Blade	P. G. Thomas
	G-MZEK	Mainair Mercury	G. Crane
	G-MZEL	Cyclone AX3/503	T. I. Ball
	G-MZEM	Pegasus Quantum 15	D. E. J. McVicker
	G-MZEN	Rans S.6-ESD Coyote II	S. Longstaff & S. A. Clayton
	G-MZEO	Rans S.6-ESD Coyote IIXL	R. W. Lenthall
	G-MZEP	Mainair Rapier	B. O'Conner
	G-MZER	Cyclone AX2000	J. H. Keep
	G-MZES	Letov LK-2N Sluka	J. L. Self
	G-MZEU	Rans S.6-ESD Coyote IIXL	N. Grugan
	G-MZEV	Mainair Rapier	W. T. Gardner
	G-MZEW	Mainair Blade	S. J. Meehan
	G-MZEX	Pegasus Quantum 15	B. Woolley & G. Redfern
	G-MZEY	Micro Bantam B.22	K. T. Bettington & D. Harris
	G-MZEZ	Pegasus Quantum 15	M. G. Evans
	G-MZFA	Cyclone AX2000	R. S. McMaster
	G-MZFB	Mainair Blade	A. J. Plant
	G-MZFC	Letov LK-2M Sluka	P. W. Maddocks
	G-MZFD	Mainair Rapier	R. J. Allerton
	G-MZFE	Hunt Wing	G. J. Latham
	G-MZFF	Hunt Wing	B. J. Adamson
	G-MZFG	Pegasus Quantum 15	A. M. Prentice
	G-MZFH	AMF Chevvron 2-32C	P. J. Tyler
	G-MZFI	Iolaire	H. Lorimer
	G-MZFK	Whittaker MW6 Merlin	G-MZFL Flying Group
	G-MZFL	Rans S.6-ESD Coyote IIXL	H. Adams
	G-MZFM	Pegasus Quantum 15	G. A. Ratcliffe
	G-MZFN	Rans S.ESD Coyote IIXL	C. J. & W. R. Wallbank
	G-MZFO	Thruster T.600N	J. Berry/Barton
	G-MZFR	Thruster T.600N	Blue Bird Syndicate
	G-MZFS	Mainair Blade	K. E. Ashworth
	G-MZFT	Pegasus Quantum 15	C. R. Cawley
	G-MZFU	Thruster T.600N	G. J. Slater
	G-MZFV	Pegasus Quantum 15	B. Cook
	G-MZFX	Cyclone AX2000	Flylight Airsports Ltd
	G-MZFY	Rans S.6-ESD Coyote IIXL	L. G. Tserkezos
	G-MZFZ	Mainair Blade	D. C. Keeble
	G-MZGA	Cyclone AX2000	T. K. Duffy
	G-MZGB	Cyclone AX2000	P. Hegarty
	G-MZGC	Cyclone AX2000	C. E. Walls
	G-MZGD	Rans S.6 Coyote II	M. J. Olsen

234

BRITISH CIVIL REGISTRATIONS

G-MZGF – G-MZJL

Reg	Type	Owner or Operator	Notes
G-MZGF	Letov LK-2M Sluka	G. Lombardi	
G-MZGG	Pegasus Quantum 15	R. W. Partington	
G-MZGH	Hunt Wing/Avon 462	J. H. Cole	
G-MZGI	Mainair Blade 912	H. M. Roberts	
G-MZGJ	Kolb Twinstar Mk 1	S. J. Pugh-Jones	
G-MZGK	Pegasus Quantum 15	A. J. Wells	
G-MZGL	Mainair Rapier	V. J. Noonan	
G-MZGM	Cyclone AX2000	W. G. Dunn	
G-MZGN	Pegasus Quantum 15	B. J. Youngs	
G-MZGO	Pegasus Quantum 15	S. F. G. Allen	
G-MZGP	Cyclone AX2000	Buchan Light Aeroplane Club	
G-MZGR	TEAM mini-MAX	K. G. Seeley	
G-MZGS	CFM Shadow Srs BD	P. Bayliss	
G-MZGT	RH78 Tiger Light	P. J. Fahie	
G-MZGU	Arrowflight Hawk II (UK)	J. N. Holden	
G-MZGV	Pegasus Quantum 15	G-MZGV Syndicate	
G-MZGW	Mainair Blade	R. Almond	
G-MZGX	Thruster T.600N	G. E. Norton	
G-MZGY	Thruster T.600N	D. G. Bone	
G-MZGZ	Thruster T.600N	Golf Zulu Group	
G-MZHA	Thruster T.600N	R. V. Buxton	
G-MZHB	Mainair Blade	A. Szczepanek	
G-MZHC	Thruster T.600N	P. Higgins	
G-MZHD	Thruster T.600N	B. E. Foster	
G-MZHE	Thruster T.600N	R. Bellew	
G-MZHF	Thruster T.600N	R. Benner & K. Harmston	
G-MZHG	Whittaker MW6-T	R. Hatton	
G-MZHI	Pegasus Quantum 15	F. R. Macdonald	
G-MZHJ	Mainair Rapier	D. J. King	
G-MZHK	Pegasus Quantum 15	O. Goodwin	
G-MZHL	Mainair Rapier	K. Mallin	
G-MZHM	Team Himax 1700R	M. H. McKeown	
G-MZHN	Pegasus Quantum 15	C. P. Dean	
G-MZHO	Quad City Challenger II	J. Pavelin	
G-MZHP	Pegasus Quantum 15	A. J. Fell	
G-MZHR	Cyclone AX2000	C. P. Dawes & J. Leden	
G-MZHS	Thruster T.600T	D. Mahajan	
G-MZHT	Whittaker MW6 Merlin	G. J. Chadwick	
G-MZHU	Thruster T.600T	E. Lewis	
G-MZHV	Thruster T.600T	Hotel Victor Group	
G-MZHW	Thruster T.600N	K. H. Smalley	
G-MZHY	Thruster T.600N	G. Jones	
G-MZIA	Team Himax 1700R	I. J. Arkieson	
G-MZIB	Pegasus Quantum 15	S. Murphy	
G-MZIC	Pegasus Quantum 15	Swansea Airports Services	
G-MZID	Whittaker MW6 Merlin	C. P. F. Sheppard	
G-MZIE	Pegasus Quantum 15	Flylight Airsports Ltd	
G-MZIF	Pegasus Quantum 15	J. V. Clewer	
G-MZII	TEAM MiniMax 88	M. J. Kirk	
G-MZIJ	Pegasus Quantum 15	D. L. Wright	
G-MZIK	Pegasus Quantum 15	L. A. Read	
G-MZIL	Mainair Rapier	G. S. Highley	
G-MZIM	Mainair Rapier	M. J. McKegney	
G-MZIR	Mainair Blade	S. W. Tallamy	
G-MZIS	Mainair Blade	M. K. Richings	
G-MZIT	Mainair Blade 912	P. M. Horn	
G-MZIU	Pegasus Quantum 15	S. Timperley	
G-MZIV	Cyclone AX2000	C. J. Tomlin	
G-MZIW	Mainair Blade	N. E. J. Hayes	
G-MZIX	Mignet HM.1000 Balerit	P. E. H. Scott	
G-MZIY	Rans S.6-ESD Coyote II	P. A. Bell/Barton	
G-MZIZ	Renegade Spirit UK (G-MWGP)	R. B. Hawkins	
G-MZJA	Mainair Blade	R. C. McArthur	
G-MZJB	Aviasud Mistral	J. M. Whitham	
G-MZJD	Mainair Blade	P. Barker	
G-MZJE	Mainair Rapier	J. E. Davies	
G-MZJF	Cyclone AX2000	P. W. Hastings	
G-MZJG	Pegasus Quantum 15	P. D. Myer	
G-MZJH	Pegasus Quantum 15	D. W. Ormond	
G-MZJI	Rans S.6-ESD Coyote II	M. A. Newbould & C. Topp	
G-MZJJ	Maverick	R. J. Collins	
G-MZJK	Mainair Blade	P. G. Angus	
G-MZJL	Cyclone AX2000	M. H. Owen	

G-MZJM – G-MZMT — BRITISH CIVIL REGISTRATIONS

Notes	Reg	Type	Owner or Operator
	G-MZJM	Rans S.6-ESD Coyote IIXL	K. A. Hastie
	G-MZJN	Pegasus Quantum 15	J. Nelson
	G-MZJO	Pegasus Quantum 15	D. J. Cook
	G-MZJP	Whittaker MW6-S Fatboy Flyer	C. A. J. Funnell & D. J. Burton
	G-MZJR	Cyclone AX2000	N. A. Martin
	G-MZJS	Meridian Maverick	P. C. E. Roberts
	G-MZJT	Pegasus Quantum 15	M. A. McClelland
	G-MZJV	Mainair Blade 912	M. A. Roberts
	G-MZJW	Pegasus Quantum 15	W. H. J. Knowles
	G-MZJX	Mainair Blade	A. D. Taylor
	G-MZJY	Pegasus Quantum 15	M. F. Turff
	G-MZJZ	Mainair Blade	P. McParlin
	G-MZKA	Pegasus Quantum 15	A. S. R. McSherry
	G-MZKC	Cyclone AX2000	Broad Farm Flyers
	G-MZKD	Pegasus Quantum 15	S. B. Brady
	G-MZKE	Rans S.6-ESD Coyote IIXL	I. Findlay
	G-MZKF	Pegasus Quantum 15	T. A. Howe
	G-MZKG	Mainair Blade	N. S. Rigby
	G-MZKH	CFM Shadow Srs DD	S. P. H. Calvert
	G-MZKI	Mainair Rapier	D. L. Aspinall
	G-MZKJ	Mainair Blade	L. G. M. Maddick
	G-MZKK	Mainair Blade 912	D. I. Lee
	G-MZKL	Pegasus Quantum 15	G. Williams
	G-MZKM	Mainair Blade 912	G. F. J. Field
	G-MZKN	Mainair Rapier	J. McAloney
	G-MZKR	Thruster T.600N	R. J. Arnett
	G-MZKS	Thruster T.600N	P. J. Hepburn
	G-MZKT	Thruster T.600N	M. J. O'Connor
	G-MZKU	Thruster T.600N	A. S. Day
	G-MZKV	Mainair Blade 912	J. D. Harriman
	G-MZKW	Quad City Challenger II	K. W. Warn
	G-MZKX	Pegasus Quantum 15	D. B. Jones
	G-MZKY	Pegasus Quantum 15	P. S. Constable
	G-MZKZ	Mainair Blade	R. P. Wolstenholme
	G-MZLA	Pegasus Quantum 15	G-MZLA Quantum Syndicate
	G-MZLC	Mainair Blade 912	N. J. Rummery
	G-MZLD	Pegasus Quantum 15	D. C. Dewey
	G-MZLE	Maverick (G-BXSZ)	J. S. Hill
	G-MZLF	Pegasus Quantum 15	S. Seymour
	G-MZLG	Rans S.6-ESD Coyote IIXL	G-MZLG Group
	G-MZLH	Pegasus Quantum 15	G. J. Howley
	G-MZLI	Mignet HM.1000 Balerit	A. G. Barr
	G-MZLJ	Pegasus Quantum 15	J. H. Bradbury
	G-MZLL	Rans S.6-ESD Coyote II	J. A. Willats & G. W. Champion
	G-MZLM	Cyclone AX2000	P. E. Hadley
	G-MZLN	Pegasus Quantum 15	C. J. Kew
	G-MZLP	CFM Shadow Srs O	C. S. Robinson
	G-MZLR	Solar Wings Pegasus XL-Q	I. W. Barlow & L. M. Courtney
	G-MZLS	Cyclone AX2000	A. C. A. Hayes
	G-MZLT	Pegasus Quantum 15	M. H. Colin
	G-MZLU	Cyclone AX2000	E. Pashley
	G-MZLV	Pegasus Quantum 15	A. Armsby
	G-MZLW	Pegasus Quantum 15	R. W. R. Crevel & G. Cuncliffe
	G-MZLX	Micro Bantam B.22-5	D. L. Howell
	G-MZLY	Letov LK-2M Sluka	W. McCarthy
	G-MZLZ	Mainair Blade 912	S. R. Winter
	G-MZMA	Solar Wings Pegasus Quasar IITC	S. Dixon
	G-MZMB	Mainair Blade	J. T. Hearle
	G-MZMC	Pegasus Quantum 15	J. J. Baker
	G-MZMD	Mainair Blade 912	T. Gate
	G-MZME	Medway Eclipser	T. Bowles
	G-MZMF	Pegasus Quantum 15	A. J. Tranter
	G-MZMG	Pegasus Quantum 15	I. Abraham
	G-MZMH	Pegasus Quantum 15	M. Hurtubise
	G-MZMJ	Mainair Blade	T. F. R. Calladine
	G-MZMK	Chevvron 2-32C	K. D. Calvert
	G-MZML	Mainair Blade 912	G. Fearon
	G-MZMM	Mainair Blade 912	J. Lynch
	G-MZMN	Pegasus Quantum 912	L. A. Hosegood
	G-MZMO	TEAM mini-MAX 91	I. M. Ross
	G-MZMP	Mainair Blade	A. Munro
	G-MZMS	Rans S.6-ESD Coyote II	D. G. Mathews
	G-MZMT	Pegasus Quantum 15	B. J. Kitson

BRITISH CIVIL REGISTRATIONS

G-MZMU – G-NACP

Reg	Type	Owner or Operator	Notes
G-MZMU	Rans S.6-ESD Coyote II	J. P. Lamb & J. Willcox	
G-MZMV	Mainair Blade	J. Mayer	
G-MZMW	Mignet HM.1000 Balerit	M. E. Whapham	
G-MZMX	Cyclone AX2000	L. A. Lacy	
G-MZMY	Mainair Blade	C. J. Millership	
G-MZMZ	Mainair Blade	W. A. Stacey	
G-MZNA	Quad City Challenger II UK	S. Hennessy	
G-MZNB	Pegasus Quantum 15	F. Gorse	
G-MZNC	Mainair Blade 912	A. Costello	
G-MZND	Mainair Rapier	D. W. Stamp	
G-MZNE	Whittaker MW6-S Fatboy Flyer	M. B. Horan	
G-MZNG	Pegasus Quantum 15	S. B. Wilkes	
G-MZNH	CFM Shadow Srs DD	Cloudbase Aviation	
G-MZNI	Mainair Blade 912	A. Joyce	
G-MZNJ	Mainair Blade	G. E. Cole	
G-MZNL	Mainair Blade 912	M. A. Williams	
G-MZNM	TEAM mini-MAX	P. Stark	
G-MZNN	TEAM mini-MAX	D. M. Dronsfield	
G-MZNO	Mainair Blade	R. C. Colclough	
G-MZNP	Pegasus Quantum 15	S. Smith	
G-MZNR	Pegasus Quantum 15	E. S. Wills	
G-MZNS	Pegasus Quantum 15	M. J. Robbins	
G-MZNT	Pegasus Quantum 15-912	R. V. Barber	
G-MZNU	Mainair Rapier	G. G. Wilson & R. Winstanley	
G-MZNV	Rans S.6-ESD Coyote II	A. P. Thomas	
G-MZNX	Thruster T.600N	B. S. Beacroft	
G-MZNY	Thruster T.600N	L. O. Partington & G. Price/Barton	
G-MZNZ	Letov LK-2M Sluka	B. F. Crick	
G-MZOC	Mainair Blade	R. A. Carr	
G-MZOD	Pegasus Quantum 15	J. W. Mann	
G-MZOE	Cyclone AX2000	York Microlight Centre Ltd	
G-MZOF	Mainair Blade	R. M. Ellis	
G-MZOG	Pegasus Quantum 15-912	H. Cooke	
G-MZOH	Whittaker MW5D Sorcerer	M. Field	
G-MZOI	Letov LK-2M Sluka	B. S. P. Finch	
G-MZOJ	Pegasus Quantum 15	A. C. Lane	
G-MZOK	Whittaker MW6 Merlin	G-MZOK Syndicate	
G-MZOM	CFM Shadow Srs DD	Side Stick Syndicate	
G-MZON	Mainair Rapier	C. King	
G-MZOP	Mainair Blade 912	M. Gardiner	
G-MZOR	Mainair Blade 912	D. L. Foxley	
G-MZOS	Pegasus Quantum 15-912	R. J. Field	
G-MZOT	Letov LK-2M Sluka	A. M. Brumpton	
G-MZOV	Pegasus Quantum 15	Pegasus XL Group	
G-MZOW	Pegasus Quantum 15-912	J. C. Kitchen	
G-MZOX	Letov LK-2M Sluka	C. M. James	
G-MZOY	TEAM Mini-MAX 91	P. R. & S. E. Whitehouse	
G MZOZ	Rans S.6-ESD Coyote IIXL	S. G. & D. C. Emmons	
G-MZPB	Mignet HM.1000 Balerit	N. H. Frost	
G-MZPD	Pegasus Quantum 15	P. M. Dewhurst	
G-MZPH	Mainair Blade	J. D. Hoyland	
G-MZPJ	TEAM mini-MAX	P. R. Jenson	
G-MZPW	Pegasus Quantum 15	D. R. Griffiths	
G-MZRC	Pegasus Quantum 15	M Hopkins	
G-MZRH	Pegasus Quantum 15	R. J. Ware	
G-MZRM	Pegasus Quantum 15	D. Morrison	
G-MZRS	CFM Shadow Srs CD	P. C. Hancox	
G-MZSC	Pegasus Quantum 15-912	C. J. Meadows	
G-MZSD	Mainair Blade 912	M. D. Vearncombe	
G-MZSM	Mainair Blade	R. R. Anderson	
G-MZTA	Mignet HM.1000 Balerit	Sky Light Group	
G-MZTS	Aerial Arts Chaser S	D. G. Ellis (G-MVDM)	
G-MZUB	Rans S.6-ESD Coyote IIXL	B. O. Dowsett	
G-MZZT	Kolb Twinstar Mk 3	D. E. Martin	
G-MZZY	Mainair Blade 912	A. Mucznik	
G-NAAA	MBB Bö.105DBS/4	Bond Air Services/Aberdeen (G-BUTN/G-AZTI)	
G-NAAB	MBB Bö.105DBS/4	Bond Air Services/Aberdeen	
G-NACA	Norman NAC-2 Freelance 180	B. E. Norman	
G-NACI	Norman NAC-1 Srs 100	L. J. Martin & D. G. French (G-AXFB)	
G-NACL	Norman NAC-6 Fieldmaster	EPA Aircraft Co Ltd (G-BNEG)	
G-NACO	Norman NAC-6 Fieldmaster	EPA Aircraft Co Ltd	
G-NACP	Norman NAC-6 Fieldmaster	EPA Aircraft Co Ltd	

G-NADS – G-NIKE | BRITISH CIVIL REGISTRATIONS

Notes	Reg	Type	Owner or Operator
	G-NADS	TEAM mini-MAX 91	S. Stockill
	G-NANI	Robinson R44 II	MOS Gmbh
	G-NAPO	Pegasus Quantum 15-912	A. J. Varga
	G-NAPP	Van's RV-7	R. J. Napp
	G-NARG	Tanarg/Ixess 15 912S (1)	K. Kirby
	G-NARO	Cassutt Racer	D. A. Wirdnam (G-BTXR)
	G-NATT	Rockwell Commander 114A	Northgleam Ltd
	G-NATX	Cameron O-65 balloon	A. G. E. Faulkner
	G-NATY	HS. Gnat T.1 (XR537) ★	Drilling Systems Ltd
	G-NBDD	Robin DR.400/180	J. N. Binks & I. H. Taylor
	G-NBSI	Cameron N-77 balloon	Nottingham Hot-Air Balloon Club
	G-NCFC	PA-38-112 Tomahawk II	J. D. Yorke(G-BNOA)
	G-NCFE	PA-38-112 Tomahawk	R. M. Browes (G-BKMK)
	G-NCUB	Piper J-3C-65 Cub	B. A. Mills (G-BGXV)
	G-NDAA	MBB Bö.105DBS-4	Bond Air Services Ltd (G-WMAA/G-PASB/G-BDMC)
	G-NDGC	Grob G.109	J. E. Bedford & M. Mathieson
	G-NDOL	Shaw Europa	S. Longstaff
	G-NDOT	Thruster T.600N	P. C. Bailey
	G-NDPA	Ikarus C42 FB UK	D. L. Thomas (G-OOMW)
	G-NEAL	PA-32 Cherokee Six 260	VSD Group (G-BFPY)
	G-NEAT	Shaw Europa	M. Burton
	G-NEAU	Eurocopter EC 135T2	Northumbria Police Authority
	G-NEEL	Rotorway Executive 90	I. C. Bedford
	G-NEEN	MDH MD 500N	Otus Associates Ltd (G-NOTR)
	G-NEGG	Acrosport 2	D. K. Keays & R.S. Goodwin
	G-NEGS	Thunder Ax7-77 balloon	M. Rowlands
	G-NEIL	Thunder Ax3 balloon	N. A. Robertson
	G-NELI	PA-28R Cherokee Arrow 180	A. Jahanfar
	G-NELY	MDH MD.600N	Ottoman Empire Ltd
	G-NEMO	Raj Hamsa X'Air Jabiru	D. G. Smith
	G-NEON	PA-32 Cherokee Six 300B	S. C. A. Lever
	G-NEPB	Cameron N-77 balloon	The Post Office
	G-NERC	PA-31-350 Navajo Chieftain	Natural Environment Research Council/Coventry (G-BBXX)
	G-NESA	Shaw Europa XS	K. G. & V. E. Summerhill
	G-NESE	Tecnam P2002-JF	N. & S. Easton
	G-NEST	Christen Eagle II	P. R. Cox
	G-NESV	Eurocopter EC 135T1	Northumbria Police Authority
	G-NESW	PA-34-220T Seneca III	G. C. U. Guida
	G-NESY	PA-18 Super Cub 95	V. Fisher
	G-NETB	Cirrus SR22	IDS Aircraft Ltd
	G-NETR	AS.355F1 Twin Squirrel	PLM Dollar Group Ltd (G-JARV/G-OGHL)
	G-NETY	PA-18 Super Cub 150	N. B. Mason
	G-NEWR	PA-31-350 Navajo Chieftain	Eastern Air Executive Ltd/Sturgate
	G-NEWS	Bell 206B JetRanger 3	Lanthwaite Aviation
	G-NEWT	Beech 35 Bonanza	J. S. Allison (G-APVW)
	G-NEWZ	Bell 206B JetRanger 3	Guay Tulliemet Aviation Ltd
	G-NFLA	BAe Jetstream 3102	Cranfield University (G-BRGN/G-BLHC)
	G-NFLC	HP.137 Jetstream 1H (G-AXUI) ★	Instructional airframe/Perth
	G-NFNF	Robin DR.400/180	N. French
	G-NGRM	Spezio DAL.1 Tuholer	S. H. Crook
	G-NHRH	PA-28 Cherokee 140	J. E. & I. Parkinson
	G-NHRJ	Shaw Europa XS	D. A. Lowe
	G-NICC	Aerotechnik EV-97 Team Eurostar UK	Pickup & Son Property Maintenance Ltd
	G-NICI	Robinson R44	David Fishwick Helicopters Ltd
	G-NIDG	Aerotechnik EV-97 Eurostar	Skydrive Ltd
	G-NIEN	Van's RV-9A	G. R. Pybus
	G-NIFE	SNCAN Stampe SV.4A (156)	Tiger Airways
	G-NIGC	Avtech Jabiru UL-450	N. Creeney
	G-NIGE	Luscombe 8E Silvaire	Garden Party Ltd (G-BSHG)
	G-NIGL	Shaw Europa	N. M. Graham
	G-NIGS	Thunder Ax7-65 balloon	S. D. Annett
	G-NIJM	PA-28R Cherokee Arrow 180	A. P. Thorne
	G-NIKE	PA-28-181 Archer II	Key Properties Ltd/White Waltham

238

BRITISH CIVIL REGISTRATIONS — G-NIKK – G-NSUK

Reg	Type	Owner or Operator	Notes
G-NIKK	Diamond Katana DA20-C1	Cubair Flight Training Ltd	
G-NIKO	Airbus A.321-211	MyTravel Airways	
G-NIMA	Balóny Kubíček BB30Z balloon	C. Williamson	
G-NINA	PA-28-161 Warrior II	A. P. Gorrod (G-BEUC)	
G-NINB	PA-28 Cherokee 180G	P. A. Layzell	
G-NINC	PA-28 Cherokee 180G	P. A. Layzell	
G-NINE	Murphy Renegade 912	R. F. Bond	
G-NIOG	Robinson R44 II	Farm Aviation Ltd	
G-NIOS	PA-32R-301 Saratoga SP	Plant Aviation	
G-NIPA	Slingsby T.66 Nipper 3	R. J. O. Walker (G-AWDD)	
G-NIPP	Slingsby T.66 Nipper 3	R. J. Porter (G-AVKJ)	
G-NIPR	Slingsby T.66 Nipper 3	P. A. Gibbs (G-AVXC)	
G-NIPY	Hughes 369HS	Jet Aviation (Northwest) Ltd	
G-NITA	PA-28 Cherokee 180	T. Clifford (G-AVVG)	
G-NIVA	Eurocopter EC 155B1	Lanthwaite Aviation Ltd	
G-NJAG	Cessna 207	G. H. Nolan Ltd	
G-NJBA	Rotorway Executive 162F	British Waterproofing Ltd	
G-NJIM	PA-32R-301T Turbo Saratoga	J. L. Rivers	
G-NJPW	P & M Quik GT450	N. J. P. West	
G-NJSH	Robinson R22 Beta	A. J. Hawes	
G-NJSP	Jabiru J430	N. J. S. Pitman	
G-NJTC	Aeroprakt A22-L Foxbat	B. Jackson & T. F. Casey	
G-NLEE	Cessna 182Q	G. Hall (G-TLTD)	
G-NLYB	Cameron N-105 balloon	P. H. E. Van Overwalle/Belgium	
G-NMAK	Airbus A.319-115	Twinjet Aircraft Sales Ltd	
G-NMBG	Jabiru J400	D. K. Shead	
G-NMEN	AS.355N Ecureuil 2	NM Developments	
G-NMID	Eurocopter EC 135T2	Derbyshire Constabulary	
G-NMOS	Cameron C-80 balloon	C. J. Thomas & M. C. East	
G-NNAC	PA-18 Super Cub 135	PAW Flying Services Ltd	
G-NOBI	Spezio HES-1 Tuholer Sport	M. G. Parsons	
G-NOCK	Cessna FR.182RG II	F. J. Whidbourne (G-BGTK)	
G-NODE	AA-5B Tiger	Strategic Telecom Networks Ltd	
G-NODY	American General AG-5B Tiger	Abraxas Aviation Ltd	
G-NOIR	Bell 222	Arlington Property Developments (2003) (G-OJLC/G-OSEB/G-BNDA)	
G-NOIZ	Yakovlev Yak-55M	S. C. Cattlin	
G-NOMO	Cameron O-31 balloon	Tim Balloon Promotion Airships Ltd	
G-NONE	Dyn'Aéro MCR-01 ULC	J. Fisher	
G-NONI	AA-5 Traveler	November India Group (G-BBDA)	
G-NOOK	Mainair Blade 912S	P. M. Knight	
G-NOOR	Commander 114B	As-Al Ltd	
G-NORA	Ikarus C.42 FB UK	N. A. Rathbone	
G-NORB	Saturne S110K hang glider	R. N. Pearce	
G-NORD	SNCAN NC.854	W. J. McCollum	
G-NORT	Robinson R22 Beta	Plane Talking Ltd	
G-NOSE	Cessna 402B	Atlantic Air Transport Ltd/Coventry (G-MPCU)	
G-NOSY	Robinson R44	Hields Aviation (G-LATK/G-BVMK)	
G-NOTE	PA-28-181 Archer III	J. Beach	
G-NOTS	Skyranger 912S(1)	P. M. Dewhurst	
G-NOTT	Nott ULD-2 balloon	J. R. P. Nott	
G-NOTY	Westland Scout AH.1	R. P. Coplestone	
G-NOWW	Mainair Blade 912	C. Bodill	
G-NPKJ	Van's RV-6	H. M. Darlington	
G-NPPL	Comco Ikarus C.42 FB.100	Papa Lima Group	
G-NROY	PA-32RT-300 Lance II	B. Nedjati-Gilani (G-LYNN/G-BGNY)	
G-NRRA	SIAI-Marchetti SF.260 ★	G. Boot	
G-NRSC	PA-23 Aztec 250E	Geminair Services Ltd (G-BSFL)	
G-NRYL	Mooney M.20R	C. D. Wood	
G-NSBB	Ikarus C.42 FB-100 VLA	B. Bayes & N. E. Sams	
G-NSEW	Robinson R44	Captive Audience (UK) Ltd	
G-NSOF	Robin HR.200/120B	Northamptonshire School of Flying Ltd/Sywell	
G-NSTG	Cessna F.150F	Westair Flying Services Ltd/Blackpool (G-ATNI)	
G-NSUK	PA-34-220T Seneca V	Genus PLC	

G-NTWK – G-OASP — BRITISH CIVIL REGISTRATIONS

Notes	Reg	Type	Owner or Operator
	G-NTWK	AS.355F2 Twin Squirrel	PLM Dollar Group (G-FTWO/G-OJOR/G-BMUS)
	G-NUDE	Robinson R44	The Last Great Journey Ltd (G-NSYT)
	G-NUKA	PA-28-181 Archer II	N. Ibrahim
	G-NULA	Flight Design CT2K	G-NULA Flying Group
	G-NUTA	Christen Eagle II	Blue Eagle Group
	G-NUTS	Cameron Mr Peanut 35SS balloon	Bristol Balloons
	G-NUTT	Mainair Pegasus Quik	G. P. Nutter
	G-NUTY	AS.350B Ecureuil	J. A. Ruck (G-BXKT)
	G-NVBF	Lindstrand LBL-210A balloon	Virgin Balloon Flights
	G-NVSA	DHC.8-311 Dash Eight	British Airways Connect
	G-NVSB	DHC.8-311 Dash Eight	British Airways Connect
	G-NWAA	Eurocopter EC 135T2	Bond Air Services Ltd
	G-NWAR	Agusta A109S Grand	N. D. Warr
	G-NWPR	Cameron N-77 balloon	D. B. Court
	G-NWPS	Eurocopter EC 135T1	North-West Police Authority
	G-NXUS	Nexus Mustang	G. W. Miller
	G-NYLE	Robinson R44 II	Heli Air Ltd
	G-NYMF	PA-25 Pawnee 235D	Bristol Gliding Club Pty Ltd/Nympsfield
	G-NYZS	Cessna 182G	P. Ragg (G-ASRR)
	G-NZGL	Cameron O-105 balloon	R. A. Vale & ptnrs
	G-NZSS	Boeing Stearman N2S-5 (343251:27)	Anglian Aircraft Co Ltd
	G-OAAA	PA-28-161 Warrior II	Halfpenny Green Flight Centre Ltd
	G-OABB	Jodel D.150	K. Manley
	G-OABC	Colt 69A balloon	P. A. C. Stuart-Kregor
	G-OABO	Enstrom F-28A	D. P. Johnson (G-BAIB)
	G-OABR	AG-5B Tiger	Vulcan House Management UK Ltd
	G-OACA	PA-44-180 Seminole	Plane Talking Ltd/Elstree (G-GSFT)
	G-OACE	Valentin Taifun 17E	D. R. Piercy
	G-OACF	Robin DR.400/180	A. C. Fletcher
	G-OACG	PA-34-200T Seneca II	Cega Aviation Ltd (G-BUNR)
	G-OACI	MS.893E Rallye 180GT	A. M. Quayle (G-DOOR)
	G-OACP	OGMA DHC.1 Chipmunk 20	Aeroclub de Portugal
	G-OADY	Beech 76 Duchess	Multiflight Ltd
	G-OAER	Lindstrand LBL-105A balloon	T. M. Donnelly
	G-OAFT	Cessna 152 II	Evensport Ltd (G-BNKM)
	G-OAGI	FLS Aerospace Sprint 160	Eurojet Aircraft Leasing 3 Ltd (G-FLSI)
	G-OAHC	Beech F33C Bonanza	V. D. Speck/Clacton (G-BTTF)
	G-OAJB	Cyclone AX2000	G. K. R. Linney (G-MZFJ)
	G-OAJC	Robinson R44	Sloane Helicopters Ltd
	G-OAJL	Ikarus C.42 FB100	T. Collins
	G-OAJS	PA-39 Twin Comanche 160 C/R	Go-AJS Ltd (G-BCIO)
	G-OAKR	Cessna 172S	A. K. Robson
	G-OAKW	Cessna 206B Grand Caravan	A. K. Webb
	G-OALD	SOCATA TB20 Trinidad	Gold Aviation/Biggin Hill
	G-OALH	Tecnam P92-EM Echo	L. Hill
	G-OAMF	Pegasus Quantum 15-912	C. J. Kew
	G-OAMG	Bell 206B JetRanger 3	Alan Mann Helicopters Ltd/Fairoaks
	G-OAMI	Bell 206B JetRanger 2	Techno Solutions Ltd (G-BAUN)
	G-OAML	Cameron AML-105 balloon	Stratton Motor Co (Norfolk) Ltd
	G-OAMP	Cessna F.177RG	S. McCaughey (G-AYPF)
	G-OANI	PA-28-161 Warrior II	J. F. Mitchell
	G-OANN	Zenair CH.601HDS	I. J. M. Donnelly
	G-OAPE	Cessna T.303	C. Twiston-Davies & P. L. Drew
	G-OAPR	Brantly B.2B	Helicopter International Magazine
	G-OAPW	Glaser-Dirks DG.400	D. Bonucchi
	G-OARA	PA-28R-201 Arrow III	Airsure
	G-OARC	PA-28RT-201 Arrow IV	Plane Talking Ltd (G-BMVE)
	G-OARG	Cameron C-80 balloon	G. & R. Madelin
	G-OARI	PA-28R-201 Arrow III	Plane Talking Ltd/Elstree
	G-OARO	PA-28R-201 Arrow III	Plane Talking Ltd/Elstree
	G-OART	PA-23 Aztec 250D	A. N. J. & S. L. Palmer (G-AXKD)
	G-OARU	PA-28R-201 Arrow III	Maximum Lift Ltd
	G-OARV	ARV Super 2	N. R. Beale
	G-OASH	Robinson R22 Beta	J. C. Lane
	G-OASJ	Thruster T.600N 450	A. S. Johnson
	G-OASP	AS.355F2 Twin Squirrel	Helicopter Services Ltd

240

BRITISH CIVIL REGISTRATIONS

G-OASW – G-OCCD

Reg	Type	Owner or Operator	Notes
G-OASW	Schleicher ASW-27B	M. P. W. Mee	
G-OATE	Mainair Pegasus Quantum 15-912	S. J. Goate	
G-OATV	Cameron V-77 balloon	W. G. Andrews	
G-OAVA	Robinson R22 Beta	J. G. M. McDiarmid	
G-OAVB	Boeing 757-23A	Astraeus Ltd/Gatwick (G-OOOI)	
G-OAWD	AS.350B Ecureuil	Helicopter Ltd (G-IIPM/G-GWIL)	
G-OAWS	Colt 77A balloon	E. A. & H. A. Evans	
G-OBAK	PA-28R-201T Turbo Arrow III	DP Group Aviation	
G-OBAL	Mooney M.20J	Thomsonfly Ltd	
G-OBAM	Bell 206B JetRanger 3	Cherwell Tobacco Ltd	
G-OBAN	Jodel D.140B	S. R. Cameron (G-ATSU)	
G-OBAX	Thruster T.600N 450-JAB	J. Northage & M. E. Hutchinson	
G-OBAZ	Best Off Skyranger 912(2)	B. J. Marsh	
G-OBBC	Colt 90A balloon	R. A. & M. A. Riley	
G-OBBO	Cessna 182S	F. Friedenberg	
G-OBBY	Robinson R44	Holdsmart Ltd	
G-OBCC	Cessna 560	MP Aviation LLP	
G-OBDA	Diamond Katana DA20-A1	Oscar Papa Ltd	
G-OBDM	Shaw Europa XS	B. D. McHugh	
G-OBDN	PA-28-161 Warrior II	R. M. Bennett	
G-OBEE	Boeing Stearman A75N-1 (3397:174)	P. G. Smith	
G-OBEI	SOCATA TB200 Tobago XL	Rapido Aviation Ltd/Ireland	
G-OBEK	Agusta A109C	P. W. Beck/Manchester (G-CDDJ)	
G-OBEN	Cessna 152 II	Airbase Aircraft Ltd (G-NALI/G-BHVM)	
G-OBET	Sky 77-24 balloon	P. M. Watkins & S. M. Carden	
G-OBEV	Shaw Europa	M. B. & N. I. Hill	
G-OBFC	PA-28-161 Warrior II	Bournemouth Flying Club	
G-OBFE	Sky 120-24 balloon	H. Schmidt	
G-OBFS	PA-28-161 Warrior III	Plane Talking Ltd/Elstree	
G-OBGC	SOCATA TB20 Trinidad	Bidford Airfield Ltd	
G-OBHD	Short SD3-60 Variant 100	BAC Leasing Ltd (G-BNDK)	
G-OBIB	Colt 120A balloon	M. W. A. Shemilt	
G-OBIL	Robinson R22 Beta	Aerolease Ltd	
G-OBIO	Robinson R22 Beta	Heli Air Ltd	
G-OBJB	Lindstrand LBL-90A balloon	B. J. Bower	
G-OBJH	Colt 77A balloon	Hayrick Ltd	
G-OBJP	Pegasus Quantum 15-912	S. J. Baker	
G-OBJT	Shaw Europa	B. J. Tarmar (G-MUZO)	
G-OBLC	Beech 76 Duchess	Pridenote Ltd	
G-OBLU	Cameron H-34 balloon	John Aimo Balloons SAS/Italy	
G-OBMI	Mainair Blade	P. Clark	
G-OBMP	Boeing 737-3Q8	bmi Baby	
G-OBMS	Cessna F.172N	D. Beverley & ptnrs	
G-OBMW	AA-5 Traveler	Fretcourt Ltd (G-BDFV)	
G-OBNA	PA-34-220T Seneca V	Palmair Ltd	
G-OBNC	BN-2B-20 Islander	Britten-Norman Aircraft Ltd	
G-OBNW	PA-31-350 Navajo Chieftain	British North West Airlines (G-BFDA)	
G-OBRA	Cameron Z-315 balloon	A. M. Holly	
G-OBRY	Cameron N-180 balloon	A. C. K. Rawson & J. J. Rudoni	
G-OBSM	Robinson R44 Raven	Flight Solutions Ltd (G-CDSE)	
G-OBTS	Cameron C-80 balloon	C. F. Cushion	
G-OBUN	Cameron A-250 balloon	A. C. K. Rawson & J. J. Roudoni	
G-OBUU	Replica Comper CLA Swift	J. A. Pothecary	
G-OBUY	Colt 69A balloon	Balloon Preservation Flying Group	
G-OBWR	BAe ATP	Trident Aviation Leasing Services Ltd (G-BUWP)	
G-OBYB	Boeing 767-304ER	Thomsonfly Ltd	
G-OBYD	Boeing 767-304ER	Thomsonfly Ltd	
G-OBYE	Boeing 767-304ER	Thomsonfly Ltd	
G-OBYF	Boeing 767-304ER	Thomsonfly Ltd	
G-OBYG	Boeing 767-3Q8ER	Thomsonfly Ltd	
G-OBYH	Boeing 767-304ER	Thomsonfly Ltd	
G-OBYI	Boeing 767-304ER	Thomsonfly Ltd	
G-OBYJ	Boeing 767-304ER	Thomsonfly Ltd	
G-OBYT	Agusta-Bell 206A JetRanger	R. J. Everett (G-BNRC)	
G-OCAD	Sequoia F.8L Falco	Falco Flying Group	
G-OCAM	AA-5A Cheetah	I. H. Seach-Allen (G-BLHO)	
G-OCAR	Colt 77A balloon	S. C. J. Derham	
G-OCBI	Schweizer 269C-1	JWL Helicopters Ltd	
G-OCBS	Lindstrand LBL-210A balloon	G. Binder	
G-OCBT	IDA Bacau Yakovlev Yak-52	Cambridge Business Travel	
G-OCCD	Diamond DA40D Star	Chalrey Ltd	

G-OCCE – G-ODSK — BRITISH CIVIL REGISTRATIONS

Notes	Reg	Type	Owner or Operator
	G-OCCE	Diamond DA40D Star	Plane Talking Ltd/Elstree
	G-OCCF	Diamond DA40D Star	Plane Talking Ltd/Elstree
	G-OCCG	Diamond DA40D Star	Plane Talking Ltd/Elstree
	G-OCCH	Diamond DA40D Star	Plane Talking Ltd/Elstree
	G-OCCK	Diamond DA40D Star	Diamond Aircraft UK Ltd
	G-OCCL	Diamond DA40D Star	Plane Talking Ltd/Elstree
	G-OCCM	Diamond DA40D Star	Plane Talking Ltd/Elstree
	G-OCCN	Diamond DA40D Star	Diamond Aircraft UK Ltd
	G-OCCO	Diamond DA40D Star	Diamond Aircraft UK Ltd
	G-OCCP	Diamond DA40D Star	Diamond Aircraft UK Ltd
	G-OCCR	Diamond DA40D Star	Diamond Aircraft UK Ltd
	G-OCCS	Diamond DA40D Star	Diamond Aircraft UK Ltd
	G-OCCT	Diamond DA40D Star	Diamond Aircraft UK Ltd
	G-OCCU	Diamond DA40D Star	Diamond Aircraft UK Ltd
	G-OCCW	Diamond DA42 Twin Star	Plane Talking Ltd/Elstree
	G-OCCX	Diamond DA42 Twin Star	Plane Talking Ltd/Elstree
	G-OCCY	Diamond DA42 Twin Star	Venturi Capital Ltd
	G-OCCZ	Diamond DA42 Twin Star	Venturi Capital Ltd
	G-OCDP	Flight Design CTSW	M. A. Beadman
	G-OCDW	Jabiru UL	K. R. Haskell & N. Quintin
	G-OCFC	Robin R.2160	Cornwall Flying Club Ltd/Bodmin
	G-OCFD	Bell 206B JetRanger 3	Cranfield Helicopters Ltd (G-WGAL/G-OICS)
	G-OCFM	PA-34-200 Seneca II	Stapleford Flying Club Ltd (G-ELBC/G-BANS)
	G-OCHM	Robinson R44	Westleigh Developments Ltd
	G-OCIT	Cessna 208B	Fly CI Ltd/Jersey
	G-OCJK	Schweizer 269C	P. Crawley
	G-OCMM	Agusta A109A II	Meade Hall LLP (G-BXCB/G-ISEB/G-IADT/G-HBCA)
	G-OCMT	EV-97 TeamEurostar UK	P. Crowhurst
	G-OCON	Robinson R44	Conwell Contracts (UK) Ltd
	G-OCOV	Robinson R22 Beta	Flight Training Ltd
	G-OCPC	Cessna FA.152	Westward Airways (Lands End) Ltd/St. Just
	G-OCRI	Colomban MC.15 Cri-Cri	M. J. J. Dunning
	G-OCSC	Canadair CL.600-2B16	Ocean Sky (UK) Ltd
	G-OCSD	Canadair CL.600-2B16	Ocean Sky (UK) Ltd
	G-OCST	Agusta-Bell 206B JetRanger 3	Lift West Ltd (G-BMKM)
	G-OCTI	PA-32 Cherokee Six 260	D. G. Williams (G-BGZX)
	G-OCTU	PA-28-161 Cadet	Aviation Rentals
	G-OCUB	Piper J-3C-90 Cub	C. A. Foss & P. A. Brook/Shoreham
	G-ODAC	Cessna F.152 II	T. M. Jones/Egginton (G-BITG)
	G-ODAD	Colt 77A balloon	K. Meehan
	G-ODAF	Lindstrand LBL-105A balloon	T. J. Horne
	G-ODAK	PA-28-236 Dakota	Airways Aero Associations Ltd/Booker
	G-ODAT	Aero L-29 Delfin	Graniteweb Ltd
	G-ODAV	Aerotechnik EV-97 Eurostar	B. R. Davies
	G-ODAY	Cameron N-56 balloon	British Balloon Museum & Library
	G-ODBN	Lindstrand LBL Flowers SS balloon	Magical Adventures Ltd
	G-ODCS	Robinson R22 Beta II	Heli Air Ltd/Wellesbourne
	G-ODDS	Aerotek Pitts S-2A	A. C. Cassidy
	G-ODDY	Lindstrand LBL-105A balloon	P. & T. Huckle
	G-ODEB	Cameron A-250 balloon	A. Derbyshire
	G-ODEL	Falconar F-11-3	G. F. Brummell
	G-ODEN	PA-28-161 Cadet	Aviation Rentals/Elstree
	G-ODGS	Avtech Jabiru UL-450	D. G. Salt
	G-ODHB	Robinson R44	D. H. Brown
	G-ODHL	Cameron N-77 balloon	DHL International (UK) Ltd
	G-ODIN	Avions Mudry CAP-10B	T. W. Harris
	G-ODJB	Robinson R22 Beta	N. T. Burton
	G-ODJD	Raj Hamsa X'Air 582 (7)	M. Bastin
	G-ODJF	Lindstrand LBL-90B balloon	D. J. Farrar
	G-ODJG	Shaw Europa	D. J. Goldsmith
	G-ODJH	Mooney M.20C	R. M. Schweitzer/Netherlands (G-BMLH)
	G-ODLY	Cessna 310J	B. Chalabi (G-TUBY/G-ASZZ)
	G-ODMC	AS.350B1 Squirrel	D. M. Coombs/Denham (G-BPVF)
	G-ODMG	AS.350B2 Squirrel	D. McGarrity
	G-ODNH	Schweizer 269C-1	Oxford Aviation Services Ltd/Kidlington
	G-ODOC	Robinson R44	Gas & Air Ltd
	G-ODOG	PA-28R Cherokee Arrow 200-II	Advanced Investments Ltd (G-BAAR)
	G-ODOT	Robinson R22 Beta II	Ribbands Explosives
	G-ODPJ	VPM M-16 Tandem Trainer	K. J. Robinson & S. Palmer (G-BVWX)
	G-ODRD	PA-32R-301T Saratoga II	Interceptor Properties Ltd
	G-ODRY	EV-97 TeamEurostar UK	C. Prince & P. Maddox
	G-ODSK	Boeing 737-37Q	bmi Baby

BRITISH CIVIL REGISTRATIONS — G-ODTW – G-OGOH

Reg	Type	Owner or Operator	Notes
G-ODTW	Shaw Europa	D. T. Walters	
G-ODUD	PA-28-181 Archer II	G-ODUD Aviation Ltd (G-IBBO)	
G-ODVB	CFM Shadow Srs DD	R. J. Slatter (G-MGDB)	
G-OEAC	Mooney M.20J	S. Lovatt	
G-OEAT	Robinson R22 Beta	C. Y. O. Seeds Ltd (G-RACH)	
G-OEBJ	Cessna 525 CitationJet	European Business Jets Syndicate GNS LLP	
G-OECM	Commander 114B	ECM (Vehicle Delivery Service) Ltd	
G-OEDB	PA-38-112 Tomahawk	B. W. Gomez (G-BGGJ)	
G-OEDP	Cameron N-77 balloon	M. J. Betts	
G-OEGG	Cameron Egg-65 SS balloon	Calorie Watch Balloon Team	
G-OEGL	Christen Eagle II	The Eagle Flight Syndicate/Shoreham	
G-OEJC	Robinson R44	A. J. Cain	
G-OELD	Pegasus Quantum 15-912	R. P. Butler	
G-OELZ	Wassmer Wa.52 Europa	E. A. Wiseman	
G-OEMT	MBB BK-117 C-1	Sterling Helicopters Ltd	
G-OERR	Lindstrand LBL-60A balloon	P. C. Gooch	
G-OERS	Cessna 172N	E. R. Stevens (G-SSRS)	
G-OERX	Cameron O-65 balloon	R. Roehsler/Austria	
G-OESY	Easy Raider J2.2 (1)	G. C. Long	
G-OETI	Bell 206B JetRanger 3	Elec-Track Installations Ltd (G-RMIE/G-BPIE)	
G-OETV	PA-31-350 Navajo Chieftain	Skydrift Ltd	
G-OEVA	PA-32-260 Cherokee Six	M. G. Cookson (G-FLJA/G-AVTJ)	
G-OEWD	Raytheon 390 Premier 1	Bookajet Aircraft Management Ltd	
G-OEYE	Rans S.10 Sakota	I. M. J. Mitchell	
G-OEZI	Easy Raider J.2	M. A. Claydon	
G-OEZY	Shaw Europa	A. W. Wakefield	
G-OFAA	Cameron Z-105 balloon	D. J. Constant	
G-OFAS	Robinson R22 Beta	Fast Helicopters Ltd	
G-OFBJ	Thunder Ax7-77 balloon	N. D. Hicks	
G-OFBU	Ikarus C.42 FB UK	Old Sarum C42 Group	
G-OFCM	Cessna F.172L	F. C. M. Aviation Ltd)/Guernsey (G-AZUN)	
G-OFER	PA-18 Super Cub 150	M. S. W. Meagher/Edgehill	
G-OFFA	Pietenpol Air Camper	OFFA Group	
G-OFFO	Extra EA.300/L	2 Excel Aviation Ltd	
G-OFIL	Robinson R44	North Helicopters	
G-OFIT	SOCATA TB10 Tobago	GFI Aviation Group (G-BRIU)	
G-OFLI	Colt 105A balloon	Virgin Airship & Balloon Co Ltd	
G-OFLT	EMB-110P1 Bandeirante ★	Rescue trainer/Aveley, Essex (G-MOBL/G-BGCS)	
G-OFLY	Cessna 210M	A. P. Mothew/Stapleford	
G-OFOA	BAe 146-100	Formula One Administration Ltd/Biggin Hill (G-BKMN/G-ODAN)	
G-OFOM	BAe 146-100	Formula One Management Ltd/Biggin Hill (G-BSLP/G-BRLM)	
G-OFOX	Denney Kitfox	P. R. Skeels	
G-OFRB	Everett gyroplane	C. Gilholm	
G-OFRY	Cessna 152	Devon and Somerset Flight Training Ltd	
G-OFST	Bell 206L Long Ranger III	Ground Effect Ltd (G-BXIB)	
G-OFTI	PA-28 Cherokee 140	G. S. A. Spencer (G-BRKU)	
G-OGAN	Shaw Europa	J. R. Malpass	
G-OGAR	PZL SZD-45A Ogar	P. Rasmussen t/a Perranporth Ogar Flying Group	
G-OGAS	Westland WG.30 Srs 100 ★	(stored)/Yeovil (G-BKNW)	
G-OGAY	Balóny Kubíček BB26 balloon	J. W. Soukup	
G-OGAZ	Aérospatiale SA.341G Gazelle 1	Killochries Fold (G-OCJR/G-BRGS)	
G-OGBD	Boeing 737-3L9	bmi Baby	
G-OGBE	Boeing 737-3L9	bmi Baby	
G-OGCA	PA-28-161 Warrior II	Cardiff-Wales Aviation Services Ltd	
G-OGCE	Bell 206L Long Ranger III	General Cabins and Engineering	
G-OGEM	PA-28-181 Archer II	GEM Rewinds Ltd	
G-OGEO	Aérospatiale SA.341G Gazelle 1	MW Helicopters Ltd (G-BXJK)	
G-OGES	Enstrom 280FX Shark	Eastern Atlantic Helicopters Ltd (G-CBYL)	
G-OGET	PA-39 Twin Comanche	D.L. Lewendon (G-AYXY)	
G-OGGS	Thunder Ax8-84 balloon	G. Gamble & Sons (Quorn) Ltd	
G-OGGY	Aviat A.1B	Chris Irvine Aviation Ltd	
G-OGIL	Short SD3-30 Variant 100 ★	North East Aircraft Museum/Usworth (G-BITV)	
G-OGJM	Cameron C-80 balloon	G. F. Madelin	
G-OGJP	Commander 114B	MJ Church Plant Ltd	
G-OGJS	Puffer Cozy	G. J. Stamper	
G-OGKB	Sequoia Falco F8L	G. K. Brothwood	
G-OGOA	AS.350B Ecureuil	Lomas Brothers Ltd (G-PLMD/G-NIAL)	
G-OGOH	Robinson R22 Beta II	E. K. Richardson (G-IPDM/G-OMSG)	

243

G-OGOS – G-OJMR   BRITISH CIVIL REGISTRATIONS

Notes	Reg	Type	Owner or Operator
	G-OGOS	Everett gyroplane	N. A. Seymour
	G-OGSA	Avtech Jabiru UL 450	M. M. Danek
	G-OGSS	Lindstrand LBL-120A balloon	R. Klarer/Germany
	G-OGTS	Air Command 532 Elite	GTS Engineering (Coventry) Ltd
	G-OHAC	Cessna F.182Q	The RAF Halton Aeroplane Club
	G-OHAL	Pietenpol Air Camper	H. C. Danby
	G-OHCP	AS.355F1 Twin Squirrel	AJJ Developments Ltd (G-BTVS/G-STVE/G-TOFF/G-BKJX)
	G-OHDC	Colt Film Cassette SS balloon ★	Balloon Preservation Group
	G-OHGC	Scheibe SF.25C Falke	Heron Gliding Club
	G-OHHI	Bell 206L-1 LongRanger	Bradmore Helicopters (G-BWYJ)
	G-OHIG	EMB-110P1 Bandeirante ★	Air Salvage International/Alton (G-OPPP)
	G-OHIO	Dyn'Aéro MCR-01	J. M. Keane
	G-OHKS	Pegasus Quantum 15-912	York Microlight Centre Ltd
	G-OHLI	Robinson R44 II	NCS Partnership
	G-OHMS	AS.355F1 Twin Squirrel	Western Power Distribution (South West) PLC
	G-OHOV	Rotorway Executive 162F	M. G. Bird
	G-OHSA	Cameron N-77 balloon	D. N. & L. J. Close
	G-OHSL	Robinson R22 Beta	Tiger Helicopters Ltd (G-BPNF)
	G-OHVA	Mainair Blade 912	M. C. Metatidj
	G-OHVR	Robinson R44 II	NMC Developments Ltd (G-STOT)
	G-OHWV	Raj Hamsa X'Air 582 (5)	H. W. Vasey
	G-OHYE	Thruster T.600N 450	G-OHYE Group (G-CCRO)
	G-OIBM	Rockwell Commander 114	E. J. Percival (G-BLVZ)
	G-OIBO	PA-28 Cherokee 180	Thomsonfly Ltd (G-AVAZ)
	G-OICO	Lindstrand LBL-42A balloon	B. Esposito
	G-OIDW	Cessna F.150G	A. Naish
	G-OIFM	Cameron 90 Dude SS balloon	Magical Adventures Ltd
	G-OIHC	PA-32R-301 Saratoga IIHP	N. J. Lipczynski (G-PUSK)
	G-OIIO	Robinson R22 Beta	Whizzard Helicopters (G-ULAB)
	G-OIMC	Cessna 152 II	East Midlands Flying School Ltd
	G-OING	AA-5A Cheetah ★	Abraxas Aviation Ltd/Denham (G-BFPD)
	G-OINK	Piper J-3C-65 Cub	A. R. Harding (G-BILD/G-KERK)
	G-OINV	BAe 146-300	British Airways Connect
	G-OIOZ	Thunder Ax9-120 S2 balloon	M. G. Barlow
	G-OISO	Cessna FRA.150L	L. A. Mills & B. A. Mills (G-BBJW)
	G-OITV	Enstrom 280C-UK-2	C. W. Brierley Jones (G-HRVY/G-DUGY/G-BEEL)
	G-OJAB	Avtech Jabiru SK	S. D. Athalye & J. Berger
	G-OJAC	Mooney M.20J	Hornet Engineering Ltd
	G-OJAE	Hughes 269C	D. P. Wring
	G-OJAG	Cessna 172S	Wycombe Air Centre Ltd
	G-OJAN	Robinson R22 Beta	Heliflight (UK) Ltd (G-SANS/G-BUHX)
	G-OJAS	Auster J/1U Workmaster	D. S. Hunt
	G-OJAV	BN-2A Mk III-2 Trislander	Lyddair Ltd/Lydd (G-BDOS)
	G-OJAZ	Robinson R44	GS Hughes Ltd
	G-OJBB	Enstrom 280FX	Pendragon (Design & Build) Ltd
	G-OJBM	Cameron N-90 balloon	P. Spinlove
	G-OJBS	Cameron N-105A balloon	Up & Away Ballooning Ltd
	G-OJBW	Lindstrand LBL J & B Bottle SS balloon	N. A. P. Godfrey
	G-OJCW	PA-32RT-300 Lance II	P. G. Dobson
	G-OJDA	EAA Acrosport II	D. B. Almey
	G-OJDC	Thunder Ax7-77 balloon	A. Heginbottom
	G-OJDS	Ikarus C.42 FB 80	J. D. Smith
	G-OJEG	Airbus A.321-231	Monarch Airlines Ltd/Luton
	G-OJEH	PA-28-181 Archer II	P. C. & M. A. Greenaway
	G-OJEN	Cameron V-77 balloon	G. Holtam
	G-OJGT	Maule M.5-235C	J. G. Townsend
	G-OJHB	Colt Flying Ice Cream Cone SS balloon	Benedikt Haggeney GmbH/Germany
	G-OJHL	Shaw Europa	J. H. Lace
	G-OJIB	Boeing 757-23A	Astraeus Ltd/Gatwick (G-OOOG)
	G-OJIL	PA-31-350 Navajo Chieftain	Redhill Aviation Ltd
	G-OJIM	PA-28R-201T Turbo Arrow III	Piper Arrow Group
	G-OJJB	Mooney M.20K	G. Italiano/Italy
	G-OJJF	D.31 Turbulent	J. J. Ferguson
	G-OJKM	Rans S.7 Courier	M. Jackson
	G-OJLH	TEAM mini-MAX 91	J. L. Hamer (G-MYAW)
	G-OJMB	Airbus A.330-243	Thomas Cook Airlines
	G-OJMC	Airbus A.330-243	Thomas Cook Airlines
	G-OJMF	Enstrom 280FX	JMF Ltd (G-DDOD)
	G-OJMR	Airbus A.300B4-605R	Monarch Airlines Ltd/Luton

244

BRITISH CIVIL REGISTRATIONS — G-OJMS – G-OMAT

Reg	Type	Owner or Operator	Notes
G-OJMS	Cameron Z-90 balloon	Joinerysoft Ltd	
G-OJMW	Cessna 550 Citation Bravo	Horizon Air Charter LLP (G-ORDB)	
G-OJNB	Linsdstrand LBL-21A balloon	N. A. P. Godfrey	
G-OJOD	Jodel D.18	D. Hawkes & C. Poundes	
G-OJON	Taylor JT.2 Titch	A. Donald	
G-OJPS	Bell 206B JetRanger 2	Just Plain Sense Ltd (G-UEST/G-ROYB/G-BLWU)	
G-OJRH	Robinson R44	Holgate Construction Ltd	
G-OJRM	Cessna T.182T	Colne Airways Ltd	
G-OJSA	BAe Jetstream 3102	JS Airlines Ltd (G-BTYG)	
G-OJSF	PA-23 Aztec 250F	Comed Aviation Ltd/Blackpool (G-SFHR/G-BHSO)	
G-OJSH	Thruster T.600N 450 JAB	November Whiskey Flying Club	
G-OJTA	Stemme S.10V	OJT Associates	
G-OJVA	Van's RV-6	J. A. Village	
G-OJVH	Cessna F.150H	A. W. Cairns (G-AWJZ)	
G-OJVL	Van's RV-6	S. E. Tomlinson	
G-OJWS	PA-28-161 Warrior II	P. J. Ward	
G-OKAG	PA-28R Cherokee Arrow 180	B. R. Green	
G-OKBT	Colt 25A Mk II balloon	British Telecommunications PLC	
G-OKCC	Cameron N-90 balloon	D. J. Head	
G-OKCP	Lindstrand LBL Battery SS balloon	M. J. Coulter (G-MAXX)	
G-OKED	Cessna 150L	L. J. Pluck	
G-OKEM	Mainair Pegasus Quik	G. R. F. Daniel	
G-OKEN	PA-28R-201T Turbo Arrow III	W. B. Bateson/Blackpool	
G-OKER	Van's RV-7	R. M. Johnson	
G-OKEV	Shaw Europa	K. R. Pilcher	
G-OKEY	Robinson R22 Beta	Heli-Wales Ltd	
G-OKIM	Best Off Sykyranger 912 (2)	K. P. Taylor	
G-OKIS	Tri-R Kis	M. R. Cleveley	
G-OKMA	Tri-R Kis	K. Miller	
G-OKPW	Tri-R Kis	K. P. Wordsworth	
G-OKYA	Cameron V-77 balloon	R. J. Pearce	
G-OKYM	PA-28 Cherokee 140	Hi-Fliers Aviation Ltd (G-AVLS)	
G-OLAU	Robinson R22 Beta	MPW Aviation Ltd	
G-OLAW	Lindstrand LBL-25A balloon	George Law Plant	
G-OLCP	AS.355N Twin Squirrel	Charterstyle Ltd (G-CLIP)	
G-OLDD	BAe 125 Srs 800B	Gold Air International Ltd	
G-OLDG	Cessna T.182T	Gold Air International Ltd (G-CBTJ)	
G-OLDH	Aérospatiale SA.341G Gazelle 1	Gold Air International Ltd (G-UTZY/G-BKLV)	
G-OLDK	Learjet 45	Gold Air International Ltd	
G-OLDM	Pegasus Quantum 15-912	A. P. Watkins	
G-OLDN	Bell 206L LongRanger	Sky Charter UK Ltd (G-TBCA/G-BFAL)	
G-OLDP	Mainair Pegasus Quik	M. J. Wilson & G. Lace	
G-OLDT	Learjet 45	Gold Air International Ltd	
G-OLDW	Learjet 45XR	Gold Air International Ltd	
G-OLDX	Cessna 182T	Gold Air International Ltd (G-IBZT)	
G-OLEE	Cessna F.152	Redhill Air Services Ltd	
G-OLEM	Jodel D.18	G. E. Roe (G-BSBP)	
G-OLEO	Thunder Ax10-210 S2 balloon	P. J. Waller	
G-OLEZ	Piper J-3C-65 Cub	L. Powell (G-BSAX)	
G-OLFA	AS.350B3 Ecureuil	Heliaviation Ltd	
G-OLFB	Pegasus Quantum 15-912	A. J. Boyd	
G-OLFC	PA-38-112 Tomahawk	M. W. Glencross (G-BGZG)	
G-OLFO	Robinson R44	Crinstown Aviation Ltd	
G-OLFT	Rockwell Commander 114	D. A. Tubby (G-WJMN)	
G-OLGA	CFM Starstreak Shadow SA-II	N. F. Smith	
G-OLJT	Mainair Gemini/Flash IIA	A. Wraith (G-MTKY)	
G-OLLI	Cameron O-31 SS balloon	N. A. Robertson	
G-OLLS	Cessna U.206H Floatplane	Loch Lomond Seaplanes Ltd	
G-OLMA	Partenavia P.68B	C. M. Evans (G-BGBT)	
G-OLNT	SA.365N1 Dauphin 2	LNT Aviation Ltd (G-POAV/G-BOPI)	
G-OLOW	Robinson R44	Hields Aviation	
G-OLRT	Robinson R22 Beta	The Henderson Group	
G-OLSF	PA-28-161 Cadet	Bournemouth Flying Club (G-OTYJ)	
G-OLTT	Pilatus PC-12/45	H. Nathanson	
G-OMAF	Dornier 228-200	FR Aviation Ltd/Bournemouth	
G-OMAG	Cessna 182B	M. L. B. Warriner & J.Thorhill	
G-OMAL	Thruster T.600N 450	M. Howland	
G-OMAP	Rockwell Commander 685	Cooper Aerial Surveys Ltd/Sandtoft	
G-OMAT	PA-28 Cherokee 140	Midland Air Training School/Coventry (G-JIMY/G-AYUG)	

G-OMAX – G-OOAH — BRITISH CIVIL REGISTRATIONS

Reg	Type	Owner or Operator
G-OMAX	Brantly B.2B	P. D. Benmax (G-AVJN)
G-OMCC	AS.350B Ecureuil	Michael Car Centres Ltd (G-JTCM/G-HLEN/G-LOLY)
G-OMCD	Robinson R44 II	McDiarmid Partnership
G-OMDB	Van's V-6A	D. A. Roseblade
G-OMDD	Thunder Ax8-90 S2 balloon	M. D. Dickinson
G-OMDG	Hoffmann H-36 Dimona	P. Turner/Halesland
G-OMDH	Hughes 369E	Stilgate Ltd/Booker
G-OMDR	Agusta-Bell 206B JetRanger 3	Atlas Helicopters Ltd (G-HRAY/G-VANG/G-BIZA)
G-OMEL	Robinson R44	Helitrain Ltd (G-BVPB)
G-OMEN	Cameron Z-90 balloon	MRC Howard Ltd
G-OMEX	Zenair CH.701 UL	S. J. Perry
G-OMEZ	Zenair CH.601HDS	C. J. Gow
G-OMFG	Cameron A-120 balloon	M. F. Glue
G-OMGH	Robinson R44 II	Universal Energy Ltd
G-OMGI	Beech B200 Super King Air	MGI Aviation Ltd
G-OMHC	PA-28RT-201 Arrow IV	Tatenhill Aviation Ltd
G-OMHD	EE Canberra PR.Mk.9 (XH134)	Midair SA
G-OMHI	Mills MH-1	J. P. Mills
G-OMHP	Avtech Jabiru UL	M. H. Player
G-OMIA	MS.893A Rallye Commodore 180	P. W. Portelli
G-OMIK	Shaw Europa	M. J. Clews
G-OMIW	Pegasus Quik	M. I. Woodward
G-OMJC	Beech 390 Premier 1	Manhattan Jet Charter/Blackbushe
G-OMJT	Rutan LongEz	M. J. Timmons
G-OMKA	Robinson R44 II	Heli Air Ltd
G-OMLC	EAA Acrosport 2	M. A. C. Chapman
G-OMLS	Bell 206B JetRanger 2	M. L. Scott
G-OMMG	Robinson R22 Beta	Preston Associates Ltd (G-BPYX)
G-OMMM	Colt 90A balloon	V. Trimble
G-OMNI	PA-28R Cherokee Arrow 200D	Cotswold Aviation Services Ltd (G-BAWA)
G-OMOL	Maule MX-7-180C	Highland Seaplanes Ltd
G-OMPW	Mainair Pegasus Quik	MPW Decorators Ltd
G-OMRB	Cameron V-77 balloon	I. J. Jevons
G-OMRH	Cessna 550 Citation Bravo	McAir Services LLP
G-OMSS	Skyranger 912(2)	J. T. James
G-OMST	PA-28-161 Warrior III	Mid-Sussex Timber Co Ltd (G-BZUA)
G-OMUM	Rockwell Commander 114	C. E. Campbell
G-OMWE	Zenair CH.601HD	G. Cockburn (G-BVXU)
G-OMYT	Airbus A.330-243	MyTravel Airways (G-MOJO)
G-ONAF	Naval Aircraft Factory N3N-3 (4406:12)	N3N-3 Group
G-ONAL	Beech 200 Super King Air	Northern Aviation Ltd (G-HAMA)
G-ONAV	PA-31-310 Turbo Navajo C	Panther Aviation Ltd (G-IGAR)
G-ONCB	Lindstrand LBL-31A balloon	R. J. Mole
G-ONCL	Colt 77A balloon	T. J. Gouder
G-ONCS	Slingsby T.66 Nipper 3	Ardleigh Flying Group (G-AZBA)
G-ONEP	Robinson R44 II	Neptune Property Developments Ltd
G-ONER	Van's RV-8	S. L. Morris
G-ONES	Slingsby T.67M Firefly 200	E. P. Lambert
G-ONET	PA-28 Cherokee 180E	Hatfield Flying Club/Elstree (G-AYAU)
G-ONFL	Meridian Maverick	M. J. Whiteman-Haywood (G-MYUJ)
G-ONGA	Robinson R44 II	Mash Enterprises Ltd
G-ONGC	Robin DR.400/180R	Norfolk Gliding Club Ltd/Tibenham
G-ONHH	Forney F-1A Aircoupe	R. D. I. Tarry (G-ARHA)
G-ONIG	Murphy Elite	N. S. Smith
G-ONIX	Cameron C-80 balloon	D. J. Griffin
G-ONJC	Embraer EMB-135BJ	Newjetco (Europe) Ltd
G-ONKA	Aeronca K	N. J. R. Minchin
G-ONMT	Robinson R22 Beta II	Redcourt Enterprises Ltd
G-ONON	RAF 2000 GTX-SE gyroplane	M. P. Lhermette
G-ONPA	PA-31-350 Navajo Chieftain	Mann Air Ltd
G-ONSF	PA-28R-201 Arrow III	Northamptonshire School of Flying Ltd (G-EMAK)
G-ONSO	Pitts S-1C Special	A. P. S. Maynard (G-BRRS)
G-ONTV	Agusta-Bell 206B JetRanger 3	Castle Air Charters Ltd
G-ONUN	Van's RV-6A	R. E. Nunn
G-ONUP	Enstrom F-28C-UK	S. Brophy (G-MHCA/G-SHWW/G-SMUJ/G-BHTF)
G-ONYX	Bell 206B JetRanger 3	N. C. Wheelwright (G-BXPN)
G-ONZO	Cameron N-77 balloon	K. Temple
G-OOAE	Airbus A.321-211	First Choice Airways Ltd (G-UNIF)
G-OOAF	Airbus A.321-211	First Choice Airways Ltd (G-UNID/G-UKLO)
G-OOAH	Airbus A.321-211	First Choice Airways Ltd

BRITISH CIVIL REGISTRATIONS
G-OOAN – G-OPFR

Reg	Type	Owner or Operator	Notes
G-OOAN	Boeing 767-39HER	First Choice Airways Ltd (G-UKLH)	
G-OOAP	Airbus A.320-214	First Choice Airways Ltd	
G-OOAR	Airbus A.320-214	First Choice Airways Ltd	
G-OOAU	Airbus A.320-214	First Choice Airways Ltd	
G-OOAV	Airbus A.321-211	First Choice Airways Ltd	
G-OOAW	Airbus A.320-214	First Choice Airways Ltd	
G-OOAX	Airbus A.320-214	First Choice Airways Ltd	
G-OOBA	Boeing 757-26N	First Choice Airways Ltd	
G-OOBC	Boeing 757-28A	First Choice Airways Ltd	
G-OOBD	Boeing 757-28A	First Choice Airways Ltd	
G-OOBE	Boeing 757-28A	First Choice Airways Ltd	
G-OOBF	Boeing 757-28A	First Choice Airways Ltd	
G-OOBG	Boeing 757-236	First Choice Airways Ltd	
G-OOBH	Boeing 757-236	First Choice Airways Ltd	
G-OOBI	Boeing 757-2B7	First Choice Airways Ltd	
G-OOBJ	Boeing 757-2B7	First Choice Airways Ltd	
G-OOBK	Boeing 767-324ER	First Choice Airways Ltd	
G-OOBL	Boeing 767-324ER	First Choice Airways Ltd	
G-OOBM	Boeing 767-324ER	First Choice Airways Ltd	
G-OOCS	Hughes 369E	K. S. Williams (G-OTDB/G-BXUR)	
G-OODE	SNCAN Stampe SV.4C (modified)	A. R. Radford (G-AZNN)	
G-OODI	Pitts S-1D Special	R. M. Buchan (G-BBBU)	
G-OODM	Cessna 525A Citation CJ2	Hangar 8 Ltd	
G-OODW	PA-28-181 Archer II	Goodwood Terrena Ltd	
G-OOER	Lindstrand LBL-25A balloon	Airborne Adventures Ltd	
G-OOFE	Thruster T.600N 450	Rochester Microlights Ltd	
G-OOFT	PA-28-161 Warrior III	Plane Talking Ltd	
G-OOGA	GA-7 Cougar	B. Robinson	
G-OOGI	GA-7 Cougar	Plane Talking Ltd (G-PLAS/G-BGHL)	
G-OOGL	Hughes 369E	Eastern Atlantic Helicopters Ltd	
G-OOGO	GA-7 Cougar	A. McIntyre	
G-OOGS	GA-7 Cougar	Cloud 9 Aviation (Leasing) Ltd (G-BGJW)	
G-OOIO	AS.350B3 Ecureuil	Hovering Ltd	
G-OOJC	Bensen B.8MR	J. R. Cooper	
G-OOJP	Commander 114B	R. J. Rother	
G-OOLE	Cessna 172M	P. S. Eccersley (G-BOSI)	
G-OOLL	Tanarg/Ixess 15 912S(1)	J. W. McCarthy	
G-OOMF	PA-18-150 Super Cub	R. C. & C. G. Bell	
G-OONA	Robinson R44 Clipper II	Stein and Lester Ltd	
G-OONE	Mooney M.20J	Go One Aviation Ltd	
G-OONI	Thunder Ax7-77 balloon	Fivedata Ltd	
G-OONK	Cirrus SR22	Heathfield Rentals Ltd	
G-OONY	PA-28-161 Warrior II	D. A. Field	
G-OOOB	Boeing 757-28A	Astraeus Ltd/Gatwick	
G-OOOK	Boeing 757-236	First Choice Airways Ltd	
G-OOON	PA-34-220T Seneca III	Goon Aviation Ltd	
G-OOOX	Boeing 757-2Y0	First Choice Airways Ltd	
G-OOOZ	Boeing 757-236	First Choice Airways Ltd (G-BUDZ)	
G-OORV	Van's RV-6	T. I. Williams	
G-OOSE	Rutan Vari-Eze	B. O. Smith & J. A. Towers	
G-OOSH	Zenair CH.601UL Zodiac	D. J. Paget	
G-OOSI	Cessna 404	Cooper Aerial Surveys Ltd	
G-OOSY	DH.82A Tiger Moth	Flying Tigers	
G-OOTB	SOCATA TB20 Trinidad	A. T. Paton	
G-OOTC	PA-28R-201T Turbo Arrow III	D. G. & C. M. King (G-CLIV)	
G-OOTT	Eurocopter AS.350B3 Ecureuil	Liberties UK Ltd	
G-OOTW	Cameron Z-275 balloon	Airborne Balloon Management Ltd	
G-OOUT	Colt Flying Shuttlecock SS balloon	Shiplake Investments Ltd	
G-OOXP	Aero Designs Pulsar XP	T. D. Baker	
G-OPAG	PA-34-200 Seneca II	A. H. Lavender/Biggin Hill (G-BNGB)	
G-OPAM	Cessna F.152 II (tailwheel)	PJC Leasing Ltd (G-BFZS)	
G-OPAT	Beech 76 Duchess	R. D. J. Axford (G-BHAO)	
G-OPAZ	Pazmany PL.2	K. Morris	
G-OPCG	Cessna 182T	P. L. Nolan	
G-OPCS	Hughes 369E	Productivity Computer Solutions Ltd	
G-OPDS	Denney Kitfox Mk 4	P. Madden	
G-OPEJ	TEAM Minimax 91A	J. E. Butler	
G-OPEN	Bell 206B	Gazelle Aviation LLP	
G-OPEP	PA-28RT-201T Turbo Arrow IV	Sam Aviation/Cranfield	
G-OPET	PA-28-181 Archer II	Cambrian Flying Group Ltd	
G-OPFA	Pioneer 300	S. Eddison & R. Minett	
G-OPFR	Diamond DA42 Twin Star	P. F. Rothwell	

G-OPFT – G-ORZA — BRITISH CIVIL REGISTRATIONS

Notes	Reg	Type	Owner or Operator
	G-OPFT	Cessna 172R Skyhawk	Northern Aviation Ltd
	G-OPFW	HS.748 Srs 2A	PTB (Emerald) Pty Ltd/Blackpool (G-BMFT)
	G-OPHT	Schleicher ASH-26E	P. Turner
	G-OPIC	Cessna FRA.150L	M. T. Hodgson (G-BGNZ)
	G-OPIK	Eiri PIK-20E	A. J. McWilliam/Newtownards
	G-OPIT	CFM Streak Shadow Srs SA	I. Sinnett
	G-OPJB	Boeing 757-23A	Astraeus Ltd/Gatwick
	G-OPJC	Cessna 152 II	PJC Leasing Ltd/Stapleford
	G-OPJD	PA-28RT-201T Turbo Arrow IV	J. M. McMillan
	G-OPJH	D.62B Condor	P. J. Hall (G-AVDW)
	G-OPJK	Shaw Europa	P. J. Kember
	G-OPJS	Pietenpol Air Camper	P. J. Shenton
	G-OPKF	Cameron 90 Bowler SS balloon	D. K. Fish
	G-OPLC	DH.104 Dove 8	W. G. T. Pritchard (G-BLRB)
	G-OPME	PA-23 Aztec 250D	Portway Aviation Ltd (G-ODIR/G-AZGB)
	G-OPMT	Lindstrand LBL-105A balloon	K. R. Karlstrom
	G-OPNH	Stoddard-Hamilton Glasair IIRG	J. L. Mangelschots/Belgium (G-CINY)
	G-OPPL	AA-5A Cheetah	Plane Talking Ltd/Elstree (G-BGNN)
	G-OPRC	Shaw Europa XS	M. J. Ashby-Arnold
	G-OPSF	PA-38-112 Tomahawk	Panshanger School of Flying (G-BGZI)
	G-OPSL	PA-32R-301 Saratoga SP	P. R. Tomkins (G-IMPW)
	G-OPSS	Cirrus SR20	Public Sector Software Ltd
	G-OPST	Cessna 182R	Lota Ltd/Shoreham
	G-OPTF	Robinson R44 II	Heli Air Ltd/Wellesbourne
	G-OPTI	PA-28-161 Warrior II	A. K. Hulme/Andrewsfield
	G-OPUB	Slingsby T.67M Firefly 160	P. M. Barker (G-DLTA/G-SFTX)
	G-OPUP	Beagle B.121 Pup 2	F. A. Zubiel (G-AXEU)
	G-OPUS	Avtech Jabiru SK	G. J. Baldock
	G-OPVM	Van's RV-9A	P. Mather
	G-OPWK	AA-5A Cheetah	W. J. Howe (G-OAEL)
	G-OPWS	Mooney M.20K	A. R. Mills
	G-OPYE	Cessna 172S	Far North Aviation/Wick
	G-ORAC	Cameron 110 Van SS balloon	A. G. Kennedy
	G-ORAE	Van's RV-7	R. W. Eaton
	G-ORAF	CFM Streak Shadow	A. P. Hunn
	G-ORAL	HS.748 Srs 2A	PTB (Emerald) Pty Ltd/Blackpool (G-BPDA/G-GLAS)
	G-ORAR	PA-28-181 Archer III	P. N. & S. M. Thornton
	G-ORAS	Clutton FRED Srs 2	A. I. Sutherland
	G-ORAY	Cessna F.182Q II	Yorkshire Estates Ltd/Isle of Man (G-BHDN)
	G-ORBK	Robinson R44 II	GTC (UK) Ltd (G-CCNO)
	G-ORBS	Mainair Blade	J. W. Dodson
	G-ORCA	Van's RV-4	M. R. H. Wishart
	G-ORCP	HS.748 Srs 2A	PTB (Emerald) Pty Ltd/Blackpool
	G-ORCW	Schempp-Hirth Ventus 2cT	R. C. Wilson
	G-ORDB	Cessna 550 Citation Bravo	Equipe Air Ltd/Gamston
	G-ORDH	AS.355N Twin Squirrel	Harpin Ltd
	G-ORDS	Thruster T.600N 450	Thruster Air Services Ltd
	G-ORED	BN-2T Turbine Islander	Fly BN Ltd (G-BJYW)
	G-OREV	Revolution Mini 500 helicopter	R. H. Everett
	G-ORGY	Cameron Z-210 balloon	Cameron Flights Southern Ltd
	G-ORHE	Cessna 500 Citation	Eassda Ireland Ltd (G-BOGA/G-OBEL)
	G-ORIG	Glaser-Dirks DG.800A	I. Godfrey
	G-ORIX	ARV K1 Super 2	T. M. Lyons (G-BUXH/G-BNVK)
	G-ORJA	Beech B.200 Super King Air	Airwest Ltd
	G-ORJW	Laverda F.8L Falco Srs 4	Viking BV/Netherlands
	G-ORMA	AS.355F1 Twin Squirrel	MW Helicopters Ltd (G-SITE/G-BPHC)
	G-ORMB	Robinson R22 Beta	Scotia Helicopters Ltd
	G-ORMG	Cessna 172R II	J. R. T. Royle
	G-ORMW	Ikarus C.42 FB100	Swallow Ikarus Group 2
	G-OROB	Robinson R22 Beta	Corniche Helicopters (G-TBFC)
	G-OROD	PA-18 Super Cub 150	B. W. Faulkner
	G-OROS	Ikarus C.42 FB80	R. I. Simpson
	G-ORPC	Shaw Europa XS	P. W. Churms
	G-ORPR	Cameron O-77 balloon	S. R. Vining
	G-ORTH	Beech E90 King Air	P. A. & C. J. Crowther
	G-ORUG	Thruster T.600N 450	Lincoln Enterprises Ltd
	G-ORVB	McCulloch J-2	R. V. Bowles (G-BLGI/G-BKKL)
	G-ORVG	Van's RV-6	RV Group
	G-ORVR	Partenavia P.68B	Ravenair Aircraft Ltd/Liverpool (G-BFBD)
	G-ORZA	Diamond DA42 Twin Star	M. J. Hill (G-FCAC)

BRITISH CIVIL REGISTRATIONS
G-OSAT – G-OTOY

Reg	Type	Owner or Operator	Notes
G-OSAT	Cameron Z-105 balloon	Lotus Balloons Ltd	
G-OSAW	QAC Quickie Q.2	S. A. Wilson (G-BVYT)	
G-OSCC	PA-32 Cherokee Six 300	BG & G Airlines Ltd (G-BGFD)	
G-OSCH	Cessna 421C	Northern Aviation Ltd (G-SALI)	
G-OSCO	TEAM mini-MAX 91	M. A. Perry	
G-OSDI	Beech 95-58 Baron	A. W. Eldridge & J. A. Heard (G-BHFY)	
G-OSEA	BN-2B-26 Islander	W. T. Johnson & Sons (Huddersfield) Ltd (G-BKOL)	
G-OSEE	Robinson R22 Beta	Aero-Charter Ltd	
G-OSEP	Mainair Blade 912	J. D. Smith	
G-OSFA	Diamond HK.36TC Super Dimona	Oxfordshire Sportflying Ltd	
G-OSFS	Cessan F.177RG	Staverton Flying School	
G-OSGB	PA-31-350 Navajo Chieftain	Aerial Support Services Ltd (G-YSKY)	
G-OSHL	Robinson R22 Beta	Sloane Helicopters Ltd/Sywell	
G-OSIC	Pitts S-1C Special	J. A. Dodd (G-BUAW)	
G-OSII	Cessna 172N	K. J. Abrams (G-BIVY)	
G-OSIS	Pitts S-1S Special	C. Butler	
G-OSIT	Pitts S-1T Special	P. J. Tomlinson	
G-OSIX	PA-32 Cherokee Six 260	J. T. Le Bon (G-AZMO)	
G-OSJF	PA-23-250 Aztec F	S. J. Fawley (G-SFHR/G-BHSO)	
G-OSJL	Robinson R44 II	Heli Air Ltd	
G-OSJN	Shaw Europa XS	S. J. Nash	
G-OSKP	Enstrom 480	C. C. Butt	
G-OSKR	Skyranger 912 (2)	Skyranger UK Ltd	
G-OSKY	Cessna 172M	Skyhawk Leasing Ltd/Wellesbourne	
G-OSLD	Shaw Europa XS	Opus Software Ltd	
G-OSLO	Schweizer 269C	A. H. Helicopter Services Ltd	
G-OSMD	Bell 206B JetRanger 2	Stuart Aviation Ltd (G-LTEK/G-BMIB)	
G-OSMS	Robinson R22 Beta	Heliflight (UK) Ltd (G-BXYW)	
G-OSND	Cessna FRA.150M	Wilkins & Wilkins Special Auctions Ltd (G-BDOU)	
G-OSOE	HS.748 Srs 2A	PTB (Emerald) Pty Ltd/Blackpool (G-AYYG)	
G-OSPD	Aerotechnik EV-97 TeamEurostar UK	V. C. Garwood	
G-OSPK	Cessna 172S	Kenward Orthopaedic Ltd	
G-OSPS	PA-18 Super Cub 95	J. P. Orrissey	
G-OSPY	Cirrus SR20	Sandawn Ltd	
G-OSSA	Cessna Tu.206B	Skydive St.Andrews Ltd	
G-OSSF	AA-5A Cheetah	The Burnett Group Ltd (G-MELD/G-BHCB)	
G-OSSI	Robinson R44 II	Goss Air Ltd	
G-OSST	Colt 77A balloon	British Airways PLC	
G-OSTC	AA-5A Cheetah	5th Generation Designs Ltd	
G-OSTL	Ikarus C.42 FB 100	S. T. Ling	
G-OSTU	AA-5A Cheetah	The Burnett Group Ltd (G-BGCL)	
G-OSTY	Cessna F.150G	R. F. Newman (G-AVCU)	
G-OSUP	Lindstrand LBL-90A balloon	British Airways Balloon Club	
G-OSUS	Mooney M.20K	J. B. King/Goodwood	
G-OSUT	Scheibe SF-25C Rotax-Falke	Yorkshire Gliding Club (Pty.) Ltd	
G-OSZA	Aerotek Pitts S-2A	P. J. Heilbron	
G-OSZB	Christen Pitts S-2B Special	P. M. Ambrose (G-OGEE)	
G-OTAL	ARV Super 2	N. R. Beale (G-BNGZ)	
G-OTAM	Cessna 172M	G. V. White	
G-OTAN	PA-18 Super Cub 135 (54-2445)	S. D. Turner	
G-OTBA	HS.748 Srs 2A	PTB (Emerald) Pty Ltd/Blackpool	
G-OTBY	PA-32 Cherokee Six 300	M. J. Willing	
G-OTCH	CFM Streak Shadow	H. E. Gotch	
G-OTCV	Skyranger 912S (1)	T. C. Viner	
G-OTCZ	Schempp-Hirth Ventus 2cT	D. H. Conway t/a CZ Group	
G-OTDA	Boeing 737-31S	Flyglobespan.com	
G-OTDI	Diamond DA40D Star	Atrium Ltd	
G-OTEL	Thunder Ax8-90 balloon	D. N. Belton	
G-OTFL	Eurocopter EC 120B	Tyrone Fabrication Ltd (G-IBRI)	
G-OTFT	PA-38-112 Tomahawk	P. Tribble (G-BNKW)	
G-OTGA	PA-28R-201 Arrow III	TG Aviation Ltd	
G-OTHE	Enstrom 280C-UK Shark	G. E. Heritage (G-OPJT/G-BKCO)	
G-OTIB	Robin DR.400/180R	Norfolk Gliding Club Ltd/Tibenham	
G-OTIG	AA-5B Tiger	D. H. Green/Elstree (G-PENN)	
G-OTIM	Bensen B.8MV	T. J. Deane	
G-OTJB	Robinson R44	D. N. & J. Farrell	
G-OTJH	Pegasus Quantum 15-912	L. R. Gartside	
G-OTNA	Robinson R44 Raven II	Abel Developments Ltd	
G-OTOE	Aeronca 7AC Champion	J. M. Gale (G-BRWW)	
G-OTOO	Stolp SA.300 Starduster Too	I. M. Castle	
G-OTOY	Robinson R22 Beta	Tickstop Ltd (G-BPEW)	

G-OTRV – G-OXTC   BRITISH CIVIL REGISTRATIONS

Notes	Reg	Type	Owner or Operator
	G-OTRV	Van's RV-6	W. R. C. Williams-Wynne
	G-OTSP	AS.355F1 Twin Squirrel	Saxonair Ltd (G-XPOL/G-BPRF)
	G-OTTI	Cameron 34 Otti SS balloon	Ballonwerbung Hamburg GmbH/Germany
	G-OTTO	Cameron 82 Katalog SS balloon	Ballonwerbung Hamburg GmbH/Germany
	G-OTUG	PA-18 Super Cub 150	B. F. Walker
	G-OTUI	SOCATA TB20 Trinidad	D. J. Taylor & J. T. Flint (G-KKDL/G-BSHU)
	G-OTUN	Aerotechnik EV-97 Eurostar	E. O. Otun
	G-OTUP	Lindstrand LBL-180A balloon	Westcountry Ballooning Ltd
	G-OTVI	Robinson R44 II	Hields Aviation
	G-OTVR	PA-34-220T Seneca V	Bladerunner Aviation Ltd
	G-OTWO	Rutan Defiant	B. Wronski
	G-OTYE	Aerotechnik EV-97 Eurostar	A. B. Godber & J. Tye
	G-OTYP	PA-28 Cherokee 180	I. R. Chaplin
	G-OUCH	Cameron N-105 balloon	Flying Pictures Ltd
	G-OUHI	Shaw Europa XS	Airplan Flight Equipment Ltd
	G-OUIK	Mainair Pegasus Quik	M. C. Shortman
	G-OUMC	Lindstrand LBL-105A balloon	Executive Ballooning
	G-OURO	Shaw Europa	M. Crunden
	G-OUVI	Cameron O-105 balloon	Bristol University Hot Air Ballooning Society
	G-OVAA	Colt Jumbo SS balloon	Virgin Airship & Balloon Co Ltd
	G-OVAG	Tipsy Nipper T.66 Srs 1	L. D. Johnston
	G-OVAL	Ikarus C.42 FB100	N. G. Tomes
	G-OVAX	Colt AS-80 Mk II airship	Fly In Balloons SRL
	G-OVBF	Cameron A-250 balloon	Virgin Balloon Flights
	G-OVBL	Lindstrand LBL-150A balloon	R. J. Henderson
	G-OVET	Cameron O-56 balloon	R. Gorman
	G-OVFM	Cessna 120	A. P. Bacon & A. Sutherland
	G-OVFR	Cessna F.172N	Cumulus Aircraft Rentals Ltd
	G-OVIA	Lindstrand LBL-105A balloon	N. C. Lindsey
	G-OVIC	Cameron A-250 balloon	M. E. White/Ireland
	G-OVID	Light Aero Avid Flyer	G. G. Ansell
	G-OVII	Van's RV-7	T. J. Richardson
	G-OVIN	Rockwell Commander 112TC	G-OVIN Aviation Ltd
	G-OVLA	Ikarus C.42 FB	Webb Plant Sales
	G-OVMC	Cessna F.152 II	Samm Ventures Ltd
	G-OVNE	Cessna 401A ★	Norwich Aviation Museum
	G-OVNR	Robinson R22 Beta	Helicopter Training & Hire Ltd
	G-OVOL	Skyranger 912S(1)	A. S. Docherty
	G-OVON	PA-18-95 Super Cub	V. F. A. Stanley
	G-OWAC	Cessna F.152	Aviation South West Ltd (G-BHEB)
	G-OWAK	Cessna F.152	Falcon Flying Services (G-BHEA)
	G-OWAL	PA-34-220T Seneca III	R. G. & W. Allison
	G-OWAP	PA-28-161 Cherokee Warrior II	Airways Aero Association Ltd (G-BXNH)
	G-OWAR	PA-28-161 Warrior II	Bickertons Aerodromes Ltd
	G-OWAZ	Pitts S-1C Special	P. E. S. Latham (G-BRPI)
	G-OWCS	Cessna 182J	P. Ragg
	G-OWEL	Colt 105A balloon	S. R. Seager
	G-OWEN	K & S Jungster	R. C. Owen
	G-OWET	Thurston TSC-1A2 Teal	D. Nieman
	G-OWFS	Cessna A.152	Westair Flying Services Ltd (G-DESY/G-BNJE)
	G-OWGC	Slingsby T.61F Venture T.2	Wolds Gliding Club Ltd/Pocklington
	G-OWLC	PA-31 Turbo Navajo	Channel Airways Ltd (G-AYFZ)
	G-OWMC	Thruster T.600N	Wilts Microlight Centre
	G-OWND	Robinson R44 Astro	W. N. Dore
	G-OWOW	Cessna 152 II	Plane Talking Ltd (G-BMSZ)
	G-OWRC	Cessna F.152 II	Unimat SA/France
	G-OWRD	Agusta A109C	MW Helicopters Ltd (G-USTC/G-LAXO)
	G-OWRT	Cessna 182G	Blackpool & Flyde Aero Club Ltd (G-ASUL)
	G-OWWW	Shaw Europa	Whisky Group
	G-OWYE	Lindstrand LBL-240A balloon	Wye Valley Aviation Ltd
	G-OWYN	Aviamilano F.14 Nibbio	R. Nash
	G-OXBC	Cameron A-140 balloon	J. E. Rose
	G-OXBY	Cameron N-90 balloon	C. A. Oxby
	G-OXKB	Cameron 110 Sports Car SS balloon	D. M. Moffat
	G-OXLB	Boeing 737-81Q	XL Airways UK Ltd
	G-OXLC	Boeing 737-8BK	XL Airways UK Ltd
	G-OXLS	Cessna 560XL Citation XLS	Go XLS Ltd
	G-OXOM	PA-28-161 Cadet	Aviation Rentals/Elstree (G-BRSG)
	G-OXTC	PA-23 Aztec 250D	Falcon Flying Services/Biggin Hill (G-AZOD)

250

BRITISH CIVIL REGISTRATIONS

G-OXVI – G-PCCC

Reg	Type	Owner or Operator	Notes
G-OXVI	VS.361 Spitfire LF.XVIe (TD248:CR-S)	Spitfire Ltd	
G-OYAK	Yakovlev C-11 (9 white)	A. H. Soper/Earls Colne	
G-OYES	Mainair Blade 912	B. McAdam & A. Hatton	
G-OYST	Agusta-Bell 206B JetRanger 2	Adroit Services Corporation (G-JIMW/G-UNIK/G-TPPH/G-BCYP)	
G-OYTE	Rans S.6ES Coyote II	I. M. Vass	
G-OZAR	Enstrom 480	Benham Helicopters Ltd (G-BWFF)	
G-OZBB	Airbus A.320-212	Monarch Airlines Ltd/Luton	
G-OZBE	Airbus A.321-231	Monarch Airlines Ltd/Luton	
G-OZBF	Airbus A.321-231	Monarch Airlines Ltd/Luton	
G-OZBG	Airbus A.321-231	Monarch Airlines Ltd/Luton	
G-OZBH	Airbus A.321-231	Monarch Airlines Ltd/Luton	
G-OZBI	Airbus A.321-231	Monarch Airlines Ltd/Luton	
G-OZBJ	Airbus A.320-212	Monarch Airlines Ltd/Luton (G-MONZ)	
G-OZBK	Airbus A.320-214	Monarch Airlines Ltd/Luton	
G-OZBL	Airbus A.321-231	Monarch Airlines Ltd/Luton (G-MIDE)	
G-OZEE	Light Aero Avid Speedwing Mk 4	G. D. Bailey	
G-OZEF	Shaw Europa XS	Z. M. Ahmad	
G-OZIE	Jabiru J400	S. A. Bowkett	
G-OZOI	Cessna R.182	J. R. G. & F. L. G. Fleming (G-ROBK)	
G-OZOO	Cessna 172N	BCT Aircraft Leasing Ltd (G-BWEI)	
G-OZRH	BAe 146-200	Flightline Ltd	
G-OZZI	Jabiru SK	A. H. Godfrey	
G-OZZY	Robinson R22 Beta	G. T. Kozlowski (G-PWEL)	
G-PACE	Robin R.1180T	P. S. Kenyon	
G-PACL	Robinson R22 Beta	R. Wharam	
G-PACT	PA-28-181 Archer III	Burscombe Consulting Ltd	
G-PADD	AA-5A Cheetah	Caseright Ltd (G-ESTE/G-GHNC)	
G-PADE	Escapade Jabiru(3)	C. L. G. Innocent	
G-PADI	Cameron V-77 balloon	R. F. Penney	
G-PAGS	Aérospatiale SA.341G Gazelle 1	P. A. G. Seers (G-OAFY/G-SFTH/G-BLAP)	
G-PAIZ	PA-12 Super Cruiser	B. R. Pearson/Eaglescott	
G-PALS	Enstrom 280C-UK-2 Shark	Cast Designer	
G-PARG	Pitts S-1C Special	M. Kotsageridis	
G-PARI	Cessna 172RG Cutlass	Applied Signs Ltd/Tatenhill	
G-PART	Partenavia P68B	Ravenair Aircraft Ltd/Liverpool	
G-PASG	MBB Bö.105DBS/4	Police Aviation Services Ltd/Staverton (G-MHSL)	
G-PASH	AS.355F1 Twin Squirrel	Diamond Aviation Ltd	
G-PASN	Enstrom F-28F	Passion 4 Health International Ltd (G-BSHZ)	
G-PASV	BN-2B-21 Islander	Police Aviation Services Ltd/Teesside (G-BKJH)	
G-PASX	MBB Bö.105DBS/4	Police Aviation Services Ltd/Shoreham	
G-PATF	Shaw Europa	E. P. Farrell	
G-PATG	Cameron O-90 balloon	Bath University Students Union	
G-PATI	Cessna F.172M	Nigel Kenny Aviation Ltd (G-WACZ/G-BCUK)	
G-PATN	SOCATA TB10 Tobago	G-PATN Owners Group (G-LUAR)	
G-PATO	Zenair CH.601UL Zodiac	D. L. Walker	
G-PATP	Lindstrand LBL-77A balloon	P. Pruchnickyj	
G-PATS	Shaw Europa	G-PATS Flying Group	
G-PATX	Lindstrand LBL-90A balloon	P. A. Bubb	
G-PATZ	Shaw Europa	H. P. H. Griffin	
G-PAVL	Robin R.3000/120	S. Baker	
G-PAWL	PA-28 Cherokee 140	G-PAWL Group/Barton (G-AWEU)	
G-PAWN	PA-25 Pawnee 260C	A. P. Meredith/Lasham (G-BEHS)	
G-PAWS	AA-5A Cheetah	M. J. Patrick	
G-PAXX	PA-20 Pacer 135 (modified)	D. W. Grace	
G-PAYD	Robin DR.400/180	A. Head	
G-PAZY	Pazmany PL.4A	M. Richardson (G-BLAJ)	
G-PBEE	Robinson R44	P. Barnard	
G-PBEK	Agusta A109A	Blue Skies (Guernsey) Ltd (G-BXIV)	
G-PBEL	CFM Shadow Srs DD	S. J. Joseph	
G-PBRL	Robinson R22	Barley Mo Ltd	
G-PBUS	Avtech Jabiru SK	J. F. Heath	
G-PBYA	Consolidated PBY-5A Catalina (433915)	Catalina Aircraft Ltd	
G-PBYY	Enstrom 280FX	Hogan Holdings Ltd (G-BXKV)	
G-PCAF	Pietenpol Air Camper	C. C. & F. M. Barley	
G-PCAM	BN-2A Mk.III-2 Trislander	Aurigny Air Services Ltd (G-BEPH)	
G-PCAT	SOCATA TB10 Tobago	Lortell Ltd (G-BHER)	
G-PCCC	Alpi Pioneer 300	F. Paolini	

G-PCDP – G-PHYS — BRITISH CIVIL REGISTRATIONS

Notes	Reg	Type	Owner or Operator
	G-PCDP	Zlin Z.526F Trener Master	J. Mann
	G-PCOP	Beech B200 Super King Air	Albert Batlett and Sons (Airdrie) Ltd
	G-PDGE	Eurocopter EC 120B	A. J. Wicklow
	G-PDGG	Aeromere F.8L Falco Srs 3	P. D. G. Grist
	G-PDGN	SA.365N Dauphin 2	PLM Dollar Group Ltd (G-TRAF/G-BLDR)
	G-PDGR	AS.350B-2 Ecureil	PLM Dollar Group Ltd (G-RICC/G-BTXA)
	G-PDHJ	Cessna T.182R	P. G. Vallance Ltd
	G-PDOC	PA-44-180 Seminole	Medicare/Newcastle (G-PVAF)
	G-PDOG	Cessna O-1E Bird Dog	J. D. Needham
	G-PDSI	Cessna 172N	DA Flying Group
	G-PEAK	Agusta-Bell 206B JetRanger 2	Techanimation (G-BLJE)
	G-PECK	PA-32-300 Cherokee Six D	H. Peck (G-ETAV/G-MCAR/G-LADA/G-AYWK)
	G-PEGA	Pegasus Quantum 15-912	B. A. Showell
	G-PEGE	Skyranger 912	A. N. Hughes
	G-PEGG	Colt 90A balloon	Ballon Vole Association/France
	G-PEGI	PA-34-200T Seneca II	Tayflite Ltd
	G-PEGY	Shaw Europa	M. T. Dawson
	G-PEJM	PA-28-181 Archer III	D. A. Earle
	G-PEKT	SOCATA TB20 Trinidad	A. J. Dales
	G-PELS	Agusta-Bell 206A JetRanger	M. P. May (G-DNCN)
	G-PEPA	Cessna 206H	R. D. Lygo (G-MGMG)
	G-PEPS	Robinson R44	J. M. Pepper (G-LFBW/G-ODES)
	G-PEPL	MDH MD.600N	Blue Anchor Leisure Ltd
	G-PERC	Cameron N-90 balloon	P. A. Foot & I. R. Warrington
	G-PERE	Robinson R22 Beta	Central Helicopters Ltd
	G-PERR	Cameron 60 Bottle SS balloon ★	British Balloon Museum/Newbury
	G-PERZ	Bell 206B JetRanger 3	C. P. Lockyer
	G-PEST	Hawker Tempest II (MW401)	Tempest Two Ltd
	G-PETH	PA-24 Comanche 260C	S. H. Petherbridge
	G-PETR	PA-28 Cherokee 140	A. A. Gardner (G-BCJL)
	G-PETS	Diamond DA42 Twin Star	Airways Aircraft Leasing Ltd
	G-PFAA	EAA Biplane Model P	R. J. Marshall
	G-PFAD	Wittman W.8 Tailwind	M. R. Stamp
	G-PFAF	FRED Srs 2	M. S. Perkins
	G-PFAG	Evans VP-1	D. Pope
	G-PFAH	Evans VP-1	J. A. Scott
	G-PFAL	FRED Srs 2	J. McD. Robinson/Bann Foot
	G-PFAO	Evans VP-1	P. W. Price
	G-PFAP	Currie Wot/SE-5A (C1904:Z)	J. H. Seed
	G-PFAR	Isaacs Fury II (K2059)	G. Edwards
	G-PFAT	Monnett Sonerai II	H. B. Carter
	G-PFAW	Evans VP-1	R. F. Shingler
	G-PFCI	PA-34-220T Seneca IV	Offshore Nautical Cl Ltd
	G-PFCL	Cessna 172S	Critical Simulations Ltd
	G-PFFN	Beech 200 Super King Air	The Puffin Club Ltd
	G-PFML	Robinson R44	M. J. Magowan
	G-PFSL	Cessna F.152	P. A. Simon
	G-PGAC	cMCR-01	D. T. S. Walsh & G. A. Coatesworth
	G-PGFG	Tecnam P92-EM Echo	P. G. Fitzgerald
	G-PGGY	Robinson R44	Linic Consultants Ltd
	G-PGHM	Air Creation Kiss 450	P. G. H. Millbank
	G-PGSA	Thruster T.600N	A. J. A. Hitchcock
	G-PGSI	Robin R.2160	M. A. Spencer
	G-PGUY	Sky 70-16 balloon	Black Sheep Balloons (G-BXZJ)
	G-PHAA	Cessna F.150M	PHA Aviation (G-BCPE)
	G-PHIL	Brookland Hornet	A. J. Philpotts
	G-PHLB	RAF 2000GTX-SE gyroplane	P. R. Bell
	G-PHLY	Cessna FRA150L	M. Bonsall
	G-PHML	AG-5B Tiger	R. K. Hyatt
	G-PHOR	Cessna FRA.150L Aerobat	M. Bonsall (G-BACC)
	G-PHSI	Colt 90A balloon	P. H. Strickland
	G-PHTG	SOCATA TB10 Tobago	A. J. Baggarley
	G-PHTO	Beech 390 Premier 1	Bookajet Aircraft Management Ltd
	G-PHUN	Cessna FRA.150L Aerobat	M. Bonsall (G-BAIN)
	G-PHXS	Shaw Europa XS	P. Handford
	G-PHYL	Denney Kitfox Mk 4	J. Dunn
	G-PHYS	Jabiru SP-470	P. C. Knight

BRITISH CIVIL REGISTRATIONS

G-PIAF – G-PNIX

Reg	Type	Owner or Operator	Notes
G-PIAF	Thunder Ax7-65 balloon	L. Battersley	
G-PIDG	Robinson R44	P. J. Rogers	
G-PIEL	CP.301A Emeraude	P. R. Thorne (G-BARY)	
G-PIES	Thunder Ax7-77Z balloon	S. J. Hollingsworth & M. K. Bellamy	
G-PIET	Pietenpol Air Camper	N. D. Marshall	
G-PIGG	Lindstrand LBL Pig SS balloon	I. Heidenreich/Germany	
G-PIGI	Aerotechnik EV-97 Eurostar	Pigs Might Fly Group	
G-PIGS	SOCATA Rallye 150ST	Boonhill Flying Group (G-BDWB)	
G-PIGY	Short SC.7 Skyvan Srs 3A Variant 100	Invicta Aviation Ltd	
G-PIIX	Cessna P.210N	Kedala Aviation Ltd (G-KATH)	
G-PIKE	Robinson R22 Mariner	Sloane Helicopters Ltd/Sywell	
G-PIKK	PA-28 Cherokee 140	Coventry Aviators Flying Group (G-AVLA)	
G-PILE	Rotorway Executive 90	J. B. Russell	
G-PILL	Light Aero Avid Flyer Mk 4	D. R. Meston	
G-PIMM	Ultramagic M-77 balloon	G. Everett	
G-PINC	Cameron Z-90 balloon	M. Cowling	
G-PING	AA-5A Cheetah	P. J. Kirkpatrick (G-OCWC/G-WULL)	
G-PINT	Cameron 65 Barrel SS balloon	D. K. Fish	
G-PINX	Lindstrand Pink Panther SS balloon	Magical Adventures Ltd/USA	
G-PION	Alpi Pioneer 300	C. D. King t/a G-PION Group	
G-PIPI	Mainair Pegasus Quik	R. D. Kay	
G-PIPR	PA-18 Super Cub 95	D. S. Sweet (G-BCDC)	
G-PIPS	Van's RV-4	F. W. Hardiman	
G-PIPY	Cameron 105 Pipe SS balloon	Cameron Balloons Ltd	
G-PIRO	Cameron TR-70 balloon	A. C. Booth	
G-PITS	Pitts S-2AE Special	P. N. A. & S. N. Whithead	
G-PITZ	Pitts S-2A Special	J. A. Coutts	
G-PIXE	Colt 31A balloon	N. D. Eliot	
G-PIXI	Pegasus Quantum 15-912	K. J. Rexter	
G-PIXL	Robinson R44 II	Flying TV Ltd	
G-PIXS	Cessna 336	Atlantic Bridge Aviation Ltd/Lydd	
G-PIXX	Robinson R44 II	Flying TV Ltd	
G-PIXY	Supermarine Aircraft Spitfire Mk.26	R. Collenette	
G-PIZZ	Lindstrand LBL-105A balloon	HD Bargain SRL/Italy	
G-PJLO	Boeing 767-35EER	First Choice Airways Ltd	
G-PJMT	Lancair 320	V. Hatton & P. Gilroy	
G-PJNZ	Commander 114B	P. D. Jackson	
G-PJSY	Van's RV-6	P. J. York	
G-PJTM	Cessna FR.172K II	Jane Air (G-BFIF)	
G-PKPK	Schweizer 269C	C. H. Dobson	
G-PKRG	Cessna 560XL Citation XLS	Parkridge (Aviation) Ltd	
G-PLAC	PA-31-350 Navajo Chieftain	Y. Leyson (G-OLDA/G-BNDS)	
G-PLAD	Kolb Twinstar Mk 3 Extra	P. J. Ladd	
G-PLAH	BAe Jetstream 3102	Jetstream Executive Travel Ltd (G-LOVA/G-OAKA/G-BUFM/G-LAKH)	
G-PLAJ	BAe Jetstream 3102	Jetstream Executive Travel Ltd	
G-PLAL	Eurocopter EC 135T2	Pure Leisure Air Ltd	
G-PLAN	Cessna F.150L	G-PLAN Flying Group/Barton	
G-PLAY	Robin R.2112	A. M. and G. F. Granger t/a Alpha Flying Group	
G-PLAZ	Rockwell Commander 112	I. Hunt (G-RDCI/G-BFWG)	
G-PLBI	Cessna 172S	G. Greenall	
G-PLEE	Cessna 182Q	Peterlee Parachute Centre	
G-PLIV	Pazmany PL.4A	B. P. North	
G-PLMB	AS.350B Ecureuil	PLM Dollar Group Ltd (G-BMMB)	
G-PLMH	AS.350B2 Ecureuil	PLM Dollar Group Ltd	
G-PLMI	SA.365C-1 Dauphin	PLM Dollar Group Ltd	
G-PLOD	Tecnam P92-EM Echo	C. M. Jupp & S. P. Pearson	
G-PLOW	Hughes 269B	Sulby Aerial Surveys (G-AVUM)	
G-PLPC	Schweizer Hughes 269C	Power Lines, Pipes & Cables Ltd (G-JMAT)	
G-PLPM	Shaw Europa XS	P. L. P Mansfield	
G-PLSA	Aero Designs Pulsar XP	Air Ads Ltd (G-NEVS)	
G-PLXI	BAe ATP/Jetstream 61	BAe (Operations) Ltd/Woodford (G-MATP)	
G-PMAM	Cameron V-65 balloon	P. A. Meecham	
G-PMAX	PA-31-350 Navajo Chieftain	Liberty Group Assets Ltd (G-GRAM/G-BRHF)	
G-PMNF	VS.361 Spitfire HF.IX (TA805:FX-M)	P. R. Monk	
G-PNEU	Colt 110 Bibendum SS balloon	Balloon Preservation Group	
G-PNGC	Schleicher ASK-21	Portsmouth Naval Gliding Club	
G-PNIX	Cessna FRA.150L	Dukeries Aviation (G-BBEO)	

253

G-POCO – G-PUFF — BRITISH CIVIL REGISTRATIONS

Notes	Reg	Type	Owner or Operator
	G-POCO	Cessna 152	K. M. Watts
	G-POGO	Flight Design CT2K	L. I. Bailey
	G-POLL	Skyranger 912 (1)	D. L. Pollitt
	G-POLY	Cameron N-77 balloon	Empty Wallets Balloon Group
	G-POND	Oldfield Baby Lakes	U. Reichert/Germany
	G-POOH	Piper J-3C-65 Cub	P. & H. Robinson
	G-POOL	ARV Super 2	P. A. Dawson (G-BNHA)
	G-POOP	Dyn'Aéro MCR-01	Eurodata Computer Supplies
	G-POPA	Beech A36 Bonanza	C. J. O'Sullivan
	G-POPE	Eiri PIK-20E-1	J. C. Mills
	G-POPI	SOCATA TB10 Tobago	I. S. Hacon & C. J. Earle (G-BKEN)
	G-POPP	Colt 105A balloon	R. Ashford
	G-POPS	PA-34-220T Seneca III	Alpine Ltd
	G-POPW	Cessna 182S	Cider Press Investment Co Ltd
	G-PORK	AA-5B Tiger	C. M. M. Grange & D. Thomas (G-BFHS)
	G-PORT	Bell 206B JetRanger 3	J. Poole
	G-POSH	Colt 56A balloon	B. K. Rippon (G-BMPT)
	G-POWL	Cessna 182R	Powell Print Ltd
	G-POZA	Escapade Jabiru (1)	M. R. Jones
	G-PPLC	Cessna 560 Citation V	Sterling Aviation
	G-PPLG	Rotorsport UK MT-03	J. E. Butler
	G-PPLL	Van's RV-7A	P. G. Leonard
	G-PPPP	Denney Kitfox Mk 3	R. Powers
	G-PPTS	Robinson R44	J. & L. Prowse
	G-PRAG	Brügger MB.2 Colibri	Colibri Flying Group
	G-PRAH	Flight Design CT2K	P. R. A. Hammond
	G-PREI	Raytheon 390 Premier 1	Craft Air SA/Luxembourg
	G-PRET	Robinson R44	J. A. Wilson
	G-PREY	Pereira Osprey II	N. S. Dalrymple (G-BEPB)
	G-PREZ	Robin DR.400/500	Regent Group
	G-PRII	Hawker Hunter PR.11 (WT723:866VL)	Stick & Rudder Aviation Ltd/Belgium
	G-PRIM	PA-38-112 Tomahawk	Braddock Ltd
	G-PRKR	Canadair CL600-2B16 Challenger 604	TAG Aviation (UK) Ltd
	G-PRLY	Avtech Jabiru SK	N. C. Cowell (G-BYKY)
	G-PRNT	Cameron V-90 balloon	Shaun Bradley Project Services Ltd
	G-PROB	AS.350B2 Ecureuil	Irvine Aviation Ltd (G-PROD)
	G-PROF	Lindstrand LBL-90A balloon	S. J. Wardle
	G-PROG	Robinson R44 Raven II	Multiflight Ltd
	G-PROM	AS.350B Ecureuil	General Cabins & Engineering Ltd (G-MAGY/G-BIYC)
	G-PROS	Van's RV-7A	S. A. Jarrett
	G-PROV	P.84 Jet Provost T.52A (T.4)	Provost Group
	G-PROW	Aerotechnik EV-97 Eurostar	G. M. Prowling
	G-PRSI	Pegasus Quantum 15-912	J. C. Kitchen
	G-PRTT	Cameron N-31 balloon	J. M. Albury
	G-PRXI	VS.365 Spitfire PR.XI (PL983)	Propshop Ltd/Duxford
	G-PSAX	Lindstrand LBL-77B balloon	P. A. Sachs
	G-PSGC	PA-25 Pawnee 260C (modified)	Peterborough & Spalding Gliding Club Ltd (G-BDDT)
	G-PSHR	Agusta-Bell 206B JetRanger III	Helix Aviation Ltd (G-HSLB)
	G-PSKY	Skyranger 912S(1)	Skyranger Flying Group G-PSKY
	G-PSNI	Eurocopter EC 135T2	Police Service of Northern Ireland
	G-PSON	Colt Cylinder One SS balloon	Balloon Preservation Flying Group
	G-PSRT	PA-28-151 Warrior	P. A. S. Dyke (G-BSGN)
	G-PSST	Hunter F.58A	Heritage Aviation Developments Ltd/Bournemouth
	G-PSUE	CFM Shadow Srs CD	D. A. Crosbie (G-MYAA)
	G-PSUK	Thruster T.600N 450	A. J. Dunlop
	G-PTAG	Shaw Europa	R. C. Harrison
	G-PTAR	Best Off Skyranger 912S(1)	A. C. Aiken
	G-PTDP	Bücker Bü133C Jungmeister	T. J. Reeve (G-AEZX)
	G-PTRE	SOCATA TB20 Trinidad	Trantshore Ltd (G-BNKU)
	G-PTTS	Aerotek Pitts S-2A	D. C. Avery
	G-PTWB	Cessna T.303	F. Kratky (G-BYNG)
	G-PTWO	Pilatus P2-05 (U-110)	R. G. Meredith
	G-PTYE	Shaw Europa	Hitech International
	G-PUDL	PA-18 Super Cub 150	R. A. Roberts
	G-PUDS	Shaw Europa	P. H. Mountain
	G-PUFF	Thunder Ax7-77A balloon	Intervarsity Balloon Club

254

BRITISH CIVIL REGISTRATIONS — G-PUFN – G-RAGE

Reg	Type	Owner or Operator	Notes
G-PUFN	Cessna 340A	G. R. Case	
G-PUGS	Cessna 182H	N. C. & M. F. Shaw	
G-PUKA	Jabiru Aircraft Jabiru J400	D. P Harris	
G-PUMA	AS.332L Super Puma	CHC Scotia Ltd	
G-PUMB	AS.332L Super Puma	CHC Scotia Ltd	
G-PUMD	AS.332L Super Puma	CHC Scotia Ltd	
G-PUME	AS.332L Super Puma	CHC Scotia Ltd	
G-PUMH	AS.332L Super Puma	Bristow Helicopters Ltd	
G-PUMI	AS.332L Super Puma	Bristow Helicopters Ltd	
G-PUML	AS.332L Super Puma	CHC Scotia Ltd	
G-PUMN	AS.332L Super Puma	CHC Scotia Ltd	
G-PUMO	AS.332L-2 Super Puma	CHC Scotia Ltd	
G-PUMS	AS.332L-2 Super Puma	CHC Scotia Ltd	
G-PUNK	Thunder Ax8-105 balloon	S. C. Kinsey	
G-PUPP	Beagle B.121 Pup 2	M. D. O'Brien (G-BASD)	
G-PUPY	Shaw Europa XS	P. G. Johnson	
G-PURL	PA-32R-301 Saratoga II	I. Blamire	
G-PURR	AA-5A Cheetah	Nabco Retail Display (G-BJDN)	
G-PURS	Rotorway Executive	J. E. Houseman	
G-PUSH	Rutan LongEz	E. G. Peterson	
G-PUSI	Cessna T.303	Crusader Craft	
G-PUSS	Cameron N-77 balloon	L. D. Thurgar	
G-PUSY	RL-5A LW Sherwood Ranger	S. C. Briggs(G-MZNF)	
G-PUTT	Cameron 76 Golf SS balloon	Lakeside Lodge Golf Centre	
G-PVBF	Lindstrand LBL-260S balloon	Virgin Balloon Flights	
G-PVCV	Robin DR400/140	Exavia Ltd	
G-PVET	DHC.1 Chipmunk 22 (WB565)	Connect Properties Ltd	
G-PVIP	Cessna 421C	Passion 4 Health International Ltd (G-RLMC)	
G-PVML	Robin DR400/140B	Weald Air Services Ltd	
G-PVPC	Pilatus PC-12/45	GE Capital Corporation (Leasing) Ltd	
G-PVST	Thruster T.600N 450	R. H. Bradwell	
G-PWBE	DH.82A Tiger Moth	P. W. Beales	
G-PWIT	Bell 206L-1 LongRanger	A. R. King (G-DWMI)	
G-PWUL	Van's RV-6	P. C. Woolley	
G-PYNE	Thruster T.600N 450	R. Dereham	
G-PYPE	Van's RV-7	R. & L. Pyper	
G-PYRO	Cameron N-65 balloon	A. C. Booth	
G-PZAZ	PA-31-350 Navajo Chieftain	Air Medical Fleet Ltd (G-VTAX/G-UTAX)	
G-PZIZ	PA-31-350 Navajo Chieftain	Air Medical Fleet Ltd (G-CAFZ/G-BPPT)	
G-RABA	Cessna FR.172H	Air Ads Ltd	
G-RABS	Alpi Pioneer 300	J. Mullen	
G-RACA	P.57 Sea Prince T.1 (571/CU) ★	(stored)/Long Marston	
G-RACI	Beech C90 King Air (modified)	Errigal Aviation Ltd (G-SHAM)	
G-RACO	PA-28R Cherokee Arrow 200-II	Graco Group Ltd/Barton	
G-RACR	Ultramagic M-65C balloon	R. A. Vale	
G-RACY	Cessna 182S	N. J. Fuller	
G-RADA	Soko P-2 Kraguj (30140)	Flight Consultancy Services	
G-RADI	PA-28-161 Archer II	M. Ruter	
G-RADR	Douglas AD-4NA Skyraider (126922:402)	T. J. Manna/North Weald (G-RAID)	
G-RAEM	Rutan LongEz	G. F. H. Singleton	
G-RAES	Boeing 777-236	British Airways	
G-RAFA	Grob G.115	RAF College Flying Club Ltd/Cranwell	
G-RAFB	Grob G.115	RAF College Flying Club Ltd/Cranwell	
G-RAFC	Robin R.2112	RAF Charlie Group	
G-RAFE	Thunder Ax7-77 balloon	Giraffe Balloon Syndicate	
G-RAFG	Slingsby T.67C Firefly	Arrow Flying Ltd	
G-RAFH	Thruster T.600N 450	RAF Microlight Flying Association (FH)	
G-RAFI	P.84 Jet Provost T.4 (XP672:03)	R. J. Everett/North Weald	
G-RAFO	Beech B.200 Super King Air	Serco Ltd/Cranwell	
G-RAFP	Beech B.200 Super King Air	Serco Ltd/Cranwell	
G-RAFR	Skyranger J2.2(1)	RAF Microlight Flying Association (FR)	
G-RAFS	Thruster T.600N 450	RAF Microlight Flying Association (FS)	
G-RAFT	Rutan LongEz	B. Wronsk	
G-RAFV	Avid Speedwing	A. F. Vizoso (G-MOTT)	
G-RAFW	Mooney M.20E	Vinola (Knitwear) Manufacturing Co Ltd (G-ATHW)	
G-RAFZ	RAF 2000 GTX-SE	John Pavitt (Engineers) Ltd	
G-RAGE	Wilson Cassutt IIIM	R. S. Grace (G-BEUN)	

G-RAGS – G-REAL   BRITISH CIVIL REGISTRATIONS

Notes	Reg	Type	Owner or Operator
	G-RAGS	Pietenpol Air Camper	R. F. Billington
	G-RAGT	PA-32-301FT Cherokee Six	Oxhill Aviation
	G-RAIG	SA Bulldog Srs 100/101	Power Aerobatics Ltd
	G-RAIL	Colt 105A balloon	Ballooning World Ltd
	G-RAIN	Maule M5-235C Lunar Rocket	P. J. Sweeting
	G-RAIX	CCF AT-16 Harvard 4 (KF584)	M. R. Paul (G-BIWX)
	G-RAJA	Raj Hamsa X'Air 582 (2)	M. S. Ling
	G-RALA	Robinson R44 Clipper II	Rala Aviation Ltd
	G-RALD	Robinson R22HP	Heli Air Ltd (G-CHIL)
	G-RAMA	Cameron C-70 balloon	Poppies (UK) Ltd
	G-RAMI	Bell 206B JetRanger 3	Yorkshire Helicopters/Leeds
	G-RAMP	Piper J-3C-65 Cub	R. N. Whittall
	G-RAMS	PA-32R-301 Saratoga SP	Air Tobago Ltd/Netherthorpe
	G-RAMY	Bell 206B JetRanger 2	Lincair Ltd
	G-RANS	Rans S.10 Sakota	J. D. Weller
	G-RAPH	Cameron O-77 balloon	L. P. Hooper
	G-RAPI	Lindstrand LBL-105A balloon	Rapido Balloons
	G-RAPP	Cameron H-34 balloon	Cameron Balloons Ltd
	G-RARB	Cessna 172N	Richlyn Aviation Ltd (G-BOII)
	G-RARE	Thunder Ax5-42 SS balloon ★	Balloon Preservation Group
	G-RASA	Diamond DA42 Twin Star	C. D. Hill
	G-RASC	Evans VP-2	E. Phillips
	G-RASH	Grob G.109E	G-RASH Syndicate
	G-RATA	Robinson R22 Beta	Itervolo Ltd
	G-RATC	Van's RV-4	A. F. Ratcliffe
	G-RATE	AA-5A Cheetah	B. P. Robinson (G-BIFF)
	G-RATH	Rotorway Executive 162F	M. S. Cole
	G-RATI	Cessna F.172M	The Howells Group PLC (G-PATI/G-WACZ/G-BCUK)
	G-RATV	PA-28RT-201T Turbo Arrow IV	Redapple Ltd (G-WILS)
	G-RATZ	Shaw Europa	W. Goldsmith
	G-RAVE	Southdown Raven X	M. J. Robbins (G-MNZV)
	G-RAVN	Robinson R44	Heli Air Ltd/Wellesbourne
	G-RAWS	Rotorway Executive 162F	Raw Sports Ltd
	G-RAYA	Denney Kitfox Mk 4	L. A. James
	G-RAYE	PA-32 Cherokee Six 260	A. P. Adshead (G-ATTY)
	G-RAYH	Zenair CH.701UL	R. Horner
	G-RAYO	Lindstrand LBL-90A balloon	R. Owen
	G-RAYS	Zenair CH.250	M. J. Malbon
	G-RAZY	PA-28-181 Archer II	R. W. Cooper (G-REXS)
	G-RAZZ	Maule MX-7-180	C. S. Baird
	G-RBBB	Shaw Europa	T. J. Hartwell
	G-RBCI	BN-2A Mk.III-2 Trislander	Aurigny Air Services Ltd (G-BDWV)
	G-RBJW	Shaw Europa XS	J. Worthington & R. J. Bull
	G-RBMV	Cameron O-31 balloon	P. D. Griffiths
	G-RBOS	Colt AS-105 airship ★	Science Museum/Wroughton
	G-RBOW	Thunder Ax-7-65 balloon	R. S. McDonald
	G-RBSN	Ikarus C.42 FB80	P. B. & M. Robinson
	G-RCED	Rockwell Commander 114	D. G. Welch
	G-RCEJ	BAe 125 Srs 800B	Albion Aviation Management Ltd (G-GEIL)
	G-RCHY	Aerotechnik EV-97 Eurostar	N. McKenzie
	G-RCKT	Harmon Rocket II	K. E. Armstrong
	G-RCMC	Murphy Renegade 912	R. C. M. Collisson
	G-RCMF	Cameron V-77 balloon	J. M. Percival
	G-RCML	Sky 77-24 balloon	R. C. M. Sarl/Luxembourg
	G-RCNB	Eurocopter EC 120B	Furbs Pension Fund
	G-RCOM	Bell 206L-3 LongRanger 3	3GRComm Ltd
	G-RCST	Jabiru J430	G. R. Cotterell
	G-RDBS	Cessna 550 Citation II	Albion Aviation Management Ltd (G-JETA)
	G-RDCO	Avtech Jabiru J400	RDCO (International) LLP
	G-RDDT	Schempp-Hirth Duo Discus T	R. Witter
	G-RDEL	Robinson R44	Jara Aviation
	G-RDHS	Shaw Europa XS	R. D. H. Spencer
	G-RDMV	Hawker 800XP	Clearwater Aviation Ltd
	G-RDNS	Rans S.6-S Super Coyote	P. G. Cowling & J. S. Crofts
	G-RDWD	Robinson R44 Raven	Redwood Properties Ltd/Ireland (G-EUGN)
	G-READ	Colt 77A balloon	J. Keena
	G-REAH	PA-32R-301 Saratoga SP	M. Q. Tolbod & S. J. Rogers (G-CELL)
	G-REAL	AS.350B2 Ecureuil	Imagine Leisure Ltd (G-DRHL)

256

BRITISH CIVIL REGISTRATIONS

G-REAN – G-RIDL

Reg	Type	Owner or Operator	Notes
G-REAN	Enstrom 480B	Janabeck Investments Ltd	
G-REAP	Pitts S-1S Special	R. Dixon	
G-REAR	Lindstrand LBL-69X balloon	A. M. Holly	
G-REAS	Van's RV-6A	T. J. Smith	
G-REBA	RAF 2000 GTX-SE gyroplane	D. J. Pearce	
G-REBB	Murphy Rebel	M. Stow	
G-REBL	Hughes 269B	Farmax Ltd	
G-RECK	PA-28 Cherokee 140B	R. J. Grantham & D. Boatswain (G-AXJW)	
G-RECO	Jurca MJ-5L Sirocco	J. D. Tseliki	
G-RECS	PA-38-112 Tomahawk	S. H. & C. L. Maynard	
G-REDB	Cessna 310Q	Red Baron Haulage Ltd (G-BBIC)	
G-REDC	Pegasus Quantum 15-912	R. F. Richardson	
G-REDD	Cessna 310R II	G. Wightman (G-BMGT)	
G-REDI	Robinson R44	Redeye.com Ltd	
G-REDJ	Eurocopter AS.332L-2 Super Puma	International Aviation Leasing Ltd	
G-REDK	Eurocopter AS.332L-2 Super Puma	International Aviation Leasing Ltd	
G-REDL	Eurocopter AS.332L-2 Super Puma	International Aviation Leasing Ltd	
G-REDM	Eurocopter AS.332L-2 Super Puma	International Aviation Leasing Ltd	
G-REDN	Eurocopter AS.332L-2 Super Puma	International Aviation Leasing Ltd	
G-REDO	Eurocopter AS.332L-2 Super Puma	International Aviation Leasing Ltd	
G-REDP	Eurocopter AS.332L-2 Super Puma	International Aviation Leasing Ltd	
G-REDS	Cessna 560XL Citation Excel	Bridge Aviation Ltd	
G-REDX	Experimental Aviation Berkut	G. V. Waters	
G-REDY	Robinson R22 Beta	Plane Talking Ltd/Elstree (G-CBXO)	
G-REDZ	Thruster T.600N 450	S. L. & W. J. Smith	
G-REEC	Sequoia F.8L Falco	J. D. Tseliki	
G-REED	Mainair Blade 912S	D. Jessop	
G-REEF	Mainair Blade 912S	G. Mowll	
G-REEM	AS.355F1 Twin Squirrel	Heliking Ltd (G-EMAN/G-WEKR/G-CHLA)	
G-REEN	Cessna 340	R. D. Cornish (G-AZYR)	
G-REES	Jodel D.140C	G-REES Flying Group	
G-REET	Grumman American AA-5B Tiger	Tiger AA-5B Ltd (G-BFBP)	
G-REGE	Robinson R44	Rege Aviation LLP	
G-REGI	Cyclone Chaser S508	G. S. Stokes (G-MYZW)	
G-REJP	Europa XS	A. Milner	
G-REKO	Pegasus Quasar IITC	M. Sims (G-MWWA)	
G-RENO	SOCATA TB10 Tobago	Lamond Ltd	
G-REPH	Pegasus Quantum 15-912	R. S. Partridge-Hicks	
G-RESG	Dyn'Aéro MCR-01 Club	R. E. S. Greenwood	
G-REST	Beech P35 Bonanza	C. R. Taylor (G-ASFJ)	
G-RETA	CASA 1.131 Jungmann 2000	Richard Shuttleworth Trustees (G-BGZC)	
G-REUB	Embraer RJ135BJ Legacy	London Executive Aviation Ltd	
G-REVO	Skyranger 912(2)	M. J. Burns	
G-REYS	Canadair CL600-2B16 Challenger 604	TAG Aviation	
G-RFIO	Aeromot AMT-200 Super Ximango	M. D. Evans	
G-RFOX	Denney Kitfox Mk 3	L. G. G. Faulkner & R. Nicklin	
G-RFSB	Sportavia RF-5B	G-RFSB Group	
G-RFUN	Robinson R44	PTA Developments Ltd	
G-RGAP	Cessna 172S	Certrain Ltd	
G-RGEN	Cessna T.337D	Legoprint SpA/Italy (G-EDOT/G-BJIY)	
G-RGNT	Robinson R44 II	Regent Aviation (G-DMCG)	
G-RGUS	Fairchild 24A-46A Argus III (44-83184)	P. J. & J. L. Bryan	
G-RHAM	Skyranger 582(1)	G. Eden	
G-RHCB	Schweizer 269C-1	Helicopter One Ltd	
G-RHHT	PA-32RT-300 Lance II	M. R. Boutel	
G-RHOP	BN-2A Mk III-2 Trislander	Blue Island Air (G-BEFP/G-WEAC)	
G-RHUM	ATR-42-300	Atlantic Air Transport Ltd	
G-RHYM	PA-31-310 Turbo Navajo B	ATC Trading Ltd (G-BJLO)	
G-RHYS	Rotorway Executive 90	A. K. Voase	
G-RIAT	Robinson R22 Beta	HJS Helicopters Ltd	
G-RIBA	P & M Quik GT450	R. J. Murphy	
G-RIBZ	Enstrom 480B	Premiair Aviation Group Ltd	
G-RICK	Beech 95-B55 Baron	James Jack Lifting Services Ltd (G-BAAG)	
G-RICO	AG-5B Tiger	I. J. Ward	
G-RICS	Shaw Europa	The Flying Property Doctor	
G-RIDD	Robinson R22 Beta	KTwo Ltd	
G-RIDE	Stephens Akro	R. Mitchell/Coventry	
G-RIDG	Van's RV-7	B. A. Ridgway	
G-RIDL	Robinson R22 Beta	Corserve International Ltd	

G-RIEF – G-RMAX — BRITISH CIVIL REGISTRATIONS

Notes	Reg	Type	Owner or Operator
	G-RIEF	DG Flugzeugbau DG-1000T	J. T. Hitchcock
	G-RIET	Hoffmann H.36 Dimona	Dimona Gliding Group
	G-RIFB	Hughes 269C	J. McHugh & Son (Civil Engineering Contractors) Ltd
	G-RIFN	Avion Mudry CAP-10B	D. E. Starkey & R. A. J. Spurrell
	G-RIGB	Thunder Ax7-77 balloon	N. J. Bettin
	G-RIGH	PA-32R-301 Saratoga IIHP	Right Aviation Ltd
	G-RIGS	PA-60 Aerostar 601P	G. G. Caravatti & P. G. Penati/Italy
	G-RIHN	Dan Rihn DR.107 One Design	J. P. Brown
	G-RIIN	WSK PZL-104MN Wilga 2000	E. A. M. Austin
	G-RIKI	Mainair Blade 912	R. Cook
	G-RIKS	Shaw Europa XS	R. Morris
	G-RIKY	Mainair Pegasus Quik	R. J. Cook
	G-RILA	Flight Design CTSW	P. Mahony
	G-RIMB	Lindstrand LBL-105A balloon	D. Grimshaw
	G-RIME	Lindstrand LBL-25A balloon	Poppies (UK) Ltd
	G-RIMM	Westland Wasp HAS.1 (XT435:430)	M. P. Grimshaw & T. Martin
	G-RING	SA Bulldog Srs.100/101	C. S. Beevers/North Weald (G-AZMR)
	G-RINN	Mainair Blade	J. P. Lang
	G-RINO	Thunder Ax7-77 balloon	D. J. Head
	G-RINS	Rans S.6-ESD Coyote II	D. Watt
	G-RINT	CFM Streak Shadow	D. Grint
	G-RIPS	Cameron 110 Parachutist SS balloon ★	Balloon Preservation Group
	G-RISE	Cameron V-77 balloon	D. L. Smith
	G-RISH	Rotorway Exeecutive 162F	C. S. Rische
	G-RISK	Hughes 369E	Wavendon Social Housing Ltd
	G-RIST	Cessna 310R II	F. B. Spriggs (G-DATS)
	G-RISY	Van's RV-7A	A. J. A. Weal
	G-RITT	Pegasus Quik	R. Stalker
	G-RIVE	Jodel D.153	P. Fines
	G-RIVR	Thruster T.600N	Thruster Air Services Ltd
	G-RIVT	Van's RV-6	N. Reddish
	G-RIXA	Schempp-Hirth Discus 2	J. G. Arnold
	G-RIXS	Shaw Europa XS	R. Iddon
	G-RIXY	Cameron Z-77 balloon	Rix Petroleum Ltd
	G-RIZE	Cameron O-90 balloon	S. F. Burden/Netherlands
	G-RIZI	Cameron N-90 balloon	R. Wiles
	G-RIZZ	PA-28-161 Warrior II	Northamptonshire School of Flying Ltd/Sywell
	G-RJAH	Boeing Stearman A75N1	R. J. Horne
	G-RJAM	Sequoia F.8C Falco	R. J. Marks
	G-RJCP	Rockwell Commander 114B	Heltor Ltd
	G-RJMS	PA-28R-201 Arrow III	M. G. Hill
	G-RJWW	Maule M5-235C Lunar Rocket	PAW Flying Services Ltd (G-BRWG)
	G-RJWX	Shaw Europa XS	J. R. Jones
	G-RJXA	Embraer RJ145EP	bmi regional
	G-RJXB	Embraer RJ145EP	bmi regional
	G-RJXC	Embraer RJ145EP	bmi regional
	G-RJXD	Embraer RJ145EP	bmi regional
	G-RJXE	Embraer RJ145EP	bmi regional
	G-RJXF	Embraer RJ145EP	bmi regional
	G-RJXG	Embraer RJ145EP	bmi regional
	G-RJXH	Embraer RJ145EP	bmi regional
	G-RJXI	Embraer RJ145EP	bmi regional
	G-RJXJ	Embraer RJ135LR	bmi regional
	G-RJXK	Embraer RJ135LR	bmi regional
	G-RJXL	Embraer RJ135LR	bmi regional
	G-RJXM	Embraer RJ145MP	bmi regional
	G-RJXN	Embraer RJ145MP	bmi regional
	G-RJXO	Embraer RJ145MP	bmi regional
	G-RKEL	Agusta-Bell 206B JetRanger 3	Nunkeeling Ltd
	G-RKET	Taylor JT.2 Titch	P. A. Dunkley (G-BIBK)
	G-RLFI	Cessna FA.152	Tayside Aviation Ltd/Aberdeen (G-DFTS)
	G-RLGG	Embraer RJ135BJ Legacy	Rangemile Ltd
	G-RLMW	Tecnam P2002-EA Sierra	J. S. Melville & R. O'Malley-White
	G-RLON	BN-2A Mk III-2 Trislander	Aurigny Air Services Ltd/Guernsey (G-ITEX/G-OCTA/G-BCXW)
	G-RMAC	Shaw Europa	P. J. Lawless
	G-RMAN	Aero Designs Pulsar	M. B. Redman
	G-RMAX	Cameron C-80 balloon	M. Quinn & D. Curtain

BRITISH CIVIL REGISTRATIONS

G-RMBM – G-RPAF

Reg	Type	Owner or Operator	Notes
G-RMBM	Robinson R44 Raven II	Bramble Developments	
G-RMHE	Aerospool Dynamic WT9 UK	Yeoman Light Aircraft Co Ltd	
G-RMIT	Van's RV-4	J. P. Kloos	
G-RMMT	Europa XS	N. Schmitt	
G-RMPY	Aerotechnik EV-97 Eurostar	N. R. Beale	
G-RMUG	Cameron 90 Mug SS balloon	Nestle UK Ltd	
G-RNAC	IDA Bacau Yakovlev Yak-52	RNAEC Ltd	
G-RNAS	DH.104 Sea Devon C.20 (XK896) ★	Airport Fire Service/Filton	
G-RNBW	Bell 206B JetRanger 2	Rainbow Helicopters Ltd	
G-RNCH	PA-28-181 Archer II	Caspian Air Services Ltd	
G-RNDD	Robin DR.400/500	Sterna Aviation Ltd	
G-RNGO	Robinson R22 Beta II	Janabeck Investments Ltd	
G-RNIE	Cameron 70 Ball SS balloon	N. J. Bland	
G-RNLI	VS.236 Walrus I (W2718) ★	Solent Sky Ltd	
G-RNRM	Cessna A.185F	Skydive St. Andrews Ltd	
G-RNRS	SA Bulldog Srs.100/101	Power Aerobatics Ltd (G-AZIT)	
G-ROBD	Shaw Europa	R. D. Davies	
G-ROBN	Robin R.1180T	N. D. Anderson	
G-ROBT	Hawker Hurricane I (P2902:DX-X)	R. A. Roberts	
G-ROBY	Colt 17A balloon	Virgin Airship & Balloon Co Ltd	
G-ROCH	Cessna T.303	R. S. Bentley	
G-ROCK	Thunder Ax7-77 balloon	M. A. Green	
G-ROCR	Schweizer 269C	C. J. Williams	
G-RODC	Steen Skybolt	J. W. Teesdale & S. Yelland	
G-RODD	Cessna 310R II	R. J. Herbert Engineering Ltd (G-TEDD/G-MADI)	
G-RODG	Avtech Jabiru UL	S. Jackson	
G-RODI	Isaacs Fury (K3731)	C. J. Riley	
G-ROGE	Robinson R44 II	Phil Rogerson Ltd	
G-ROGY	Cameron 60 Concept balloon	S. A. Laing	
G-ROKT	Cessna FR.172E	Sylmar Aviation & Services Ltd	
G-ROLF	PA-32R-301 Saratoga SP	P. F. Larkins	
G-ROLL	Pitts S-2A Special	Aerial & Aerobatic Services	
G-ROLY	Cessna F.172N	R. G. Froggatt (G-BHIH)	
G-ROME	I.I.I. Sky Arrow 650TC	Sky Arrow (Kits) UK Ltd	
G-ROMP	Extra 230H	J. S. Allison	
G-ROMW	Cyclone AX2000	K. V. Falvey	
G-RONA	Shaw Europa	C. M. Noakes	
G-ROND	Short SD3-60 Variant 100	BAC Leasing Ltd (G-OLAH/G-BPCO/G-RMSS/G-BKKU)	
G-RONG	PA-28R Cherokee Arrow 200-II	E. Tang	
G-RONI	Cameron V-77 balloon	R. E. Simpson	
G-RONS	Robin DR.400/180	R. & K. Baker	
G-RONW	FRED Srs 2	V. Magee	
G-ROOK	Cessna F.172P	Rolim Ltd	
G-ROOV	Shaw Europa XS	P. W. Hawkins & K. Siggery	
G-RORI	Folland Gnat T.1 (01)	Swept Wing Ltd	
G-RORY	Piaggio FWP.149D	M. Edwards (G-TOWN)	
G-ROSI	Thunder Ax7-77 balloon	J. E. Rose	
G-ROSS	Practavia Pilot Sprite	A. D. Janaway	
G-ROTF	Robinson R22	Rotorflight Ltd	
G-ROTI	Luscombe 8A Silvaire	A. L. Chapman & R. Ludgate	
G-ROTR	Brantly B.2B	P. G. R. Brown	
G-ROTS	CFM Streak Shadow Srs SA	A. G. Vallis & C. J. Kendal	
G-ROUP	Cessna F.172M	Perranporth Flying School Ltd (G-BDPH)	
G-ROUS	PA-34-200T Seneca II	Oxford Aviation Services Ltd/Kidlington	
G-ROUT	Robinson R22 Beta	Preston Associates Ltd	
G-ROVE	PA-18 Super Cub 135	S. J. Gaveston	
G-ROVY	Robinson R22 Beta	Plane Talking Ltd/Elstree	
G-ROWE	Cessna F.182P	D. Rowe/Liverpool	
G-ROWI	Shaw Europa XS	R. M. Carson	
G-ROWL	AA-5B Tiger	T. A. Timms	
G-ROWN	Beech 200 Super King Air	Valentia Air Ltd (G-BHLC)	
G-ROWR	Robinson R44	R. A. Oldworth	
G-ROWS	PA-28-151 Warrior	S. Goodchild	
G-ROXY	Skystar Kitfox Mk.7	P. N. Akass	
G-ROYC	Avtech Jabiru UL450	M. Daleki	
G-ROZI	Robinson R44	Rotormotive Ltd	
G-ROZY	Cameron R.36 balloon	J. W. Soukup	
G-ROZZ	Ikarus C.42 FB 80	A. J. Blackwell	
G-RPAF	Europa XS	R. P. Frost	

G-RPBM – G-RVET — BRITISH CIVIL REGISTRATIONS

Notes	Reg	Type	Owner or Operator
	G-RPBM	Cameron Z-210 balloon	First Flight
	G-RPCC	Europa XS	R. P. Churchill-Coleman
	G-RPEZ	Rutan LongEz	D. G. Foreman
	G-RPRV	Van's RV-9A	G. R. Pybus
	G-RRCU	CEA DR.221B Dauphin	Merlin Flying Club Ltd
	G-RRFC	SOCATA TB20 Trinidad GT	C. A. Hawkins
	G-RRGN	VS.390 Spitfire PR.XIX (PS853)	Rolls-Royce PLC/Filton (G-MXIX)
	G-RROB	Robinson R44 II	Something Different Charters LLP
	G-RROD	PA-30 Twin Comanche 160B	R. P. Coplestone (G-SHAW)
	G-RROW	Lindstrand LBL-105A balloon	Lindstrand Hot Air Balloons Ltd
	G-RRSR	Piper J-3C-65 Cub (480173:57-H)	R. W. Roberts
	G-RRVX	Van's RV-10	R. E. Garforth
	G-RSAF	BAC.167 Strikemaster 80A	M. A. Petrie & J. E. Rowley
	G-RSKR	PA-28-161 Warrior II	Transport Command Ltd (G-BOJY)
	G-RSKY	Skyranger 912(2)	C. G. Benham
	G-RSSF	Denney Kitfox Mk 2	R. W. Somerville
	G-RSUK	Rotorsport UK MT-03	Rotorsort UK Ltd
	G-RSVP	Robinson R22 Beta	Plane Talking Ltd/Elstree
	G-RSWO	Cessna 172R	AC Management Associates Ltd
	G-RSWW	Robinson R22 Beta	Woodstock Enterprises
	G-RTBI	Thunder Ax6-56 balloon	P. J. Waller
	G-RTMS	Rans S.6 ES Coyote II	C. J. Arthur
	G-RTMY	Ikarus C.42 FB 100	Mike Yankee Group
	G-RTRT	PZL-104MA Wilga 2000	PZL International Aviation Marketing and Sales PLC
	G-RTUG	Robin DR.400/180	Windrushers Robin Syndicate
	G-RTWO	Robinson R44 II	Stanley Air Ltd
	G-RTWW	Robinson R44	Rotorvation
	G-RUBB	AA-5B Tiger	D. E. Gee/Blackbushe
	G-RUBI	Thunder Ax7-77 balloon	Warren & Johnson
	G-RUBN	Embraer RJ135BJ Legacy	Seafire Intertrade Ltd
	G-RUBY	PA-28-RT-201T Turbo Arrow IV	Arrow Aircraft Group (G-BROU)
	G-RUDD	Cameron V-65 balloon	N. A. Apsey
	G-RUES	Robin HR.100/210	R. H. R. Rue
	G-RUFF	Mainair Blade 912	M. Chambers & A. Scott
	G-RUFS	Avtech Jabiru UL	S. Richens
	G-RUGS	Campbell Cricket Mk 4 gyroplane	J. L. G. McLane
	G-RUIA	Cessna F.172N	Knockin Flying Club Ltd
	G-RULE	Robinson R44 Raven II	Wiksy Charter Ltd
	G-RUMI	Noble Harman Snowbird Mk.IV	G. Crossley (G-MVOI)
	G-RUMM	Grumman F8F-2P Bearcat (121714:201B)	Patina Ltd/Duxford
	G-RUMN	AA-1A Trainer	M. T. Manwaring
	G-RUMT	Grumman F7F-3P Tigercat (80425:WT-4)	Patina Ltd/Duxford
	G-RUMW	Grumman FM-2 Wildcat (JV579:F)	Patina Ltd/Duxford
	G-RUNT	Cassutt Racer IIIM	R. S. Grace
	G-RUSA	Pegasus Quantum 15-912	A. D. Stewart
	G-RUSI	SOCATA TB9 Tampico	Aviation Sales and Leasing Ltd
	G-RUSL	Van's RV-6A	G. R. Russell
	G-RUSO	Robinson R22 Beta	R. M. Barnes-Gorell
	G-RUSS	Cessna 172N ★	Leisure Lease (stored)/Southend
	G-RUVI	Zenair CH.601UL	P. G. Depper
	G-RUVY	Van's RV-9A	R. D. Taylor
	G-RUZZ	Robinson R44 II	Russell Harrison PLC
	G-RVAB	Van's RV-7	I. M. Belmore & A. T. Banks
	G-RVAC	Van's RV-7	A. F. S. & B. Caldecourt
	G-RVAL	Van's RV-8	R. N. York
	G-RVAN	Van's RV-6	D. Broom
	G-RVAW	Van's RV-6	High Flatts RV Group
	G-RVBA	Van's RV-8A	D. P. Richard
	G-RVBC	Van's RV-6A	B. J. Clifford
	G-RVBF	Cameron A-340 balloon	Virgin Balloon Flights
	G-RVCE	Van's RV-6A	M. D. Barnard & C. Voelger
	G-RVCG	Van's RV-6A	G. C. Calder
	G-RVCL	Van's RV-6	C. T. Lamb
	G-RVDG	Van's RV-9A	D. M. Gill
	G-RVDJ	Van's RV-6	J. D. Jewitt
	G-RVDP	Van's RV-4	D. H. Pattison
	G-RVDR	Van's RV-6A	P. R. Redfern
	G-RVEE	Van's RV-6	J. C. A. Wheeler
	G-RVET	Van's RV-6	D. R. Coleman

BRITISH CIVIL REGISTRATIONS

G-RVGA – G-SABA

Reg	Type	Owner or Operator	Notes
G-RVGA	Van's RV-6A	D. P. Dawson	
G-RVIA	Van's RV-6A	K. R. Emery	
G-RVIB	Van's RV-6	K. Martin & P. Gorman	
G-RVIC	Van's RV-6A	I. T. Corse	
G-RVII	Van's RV-7	P. H. C. Hall	
G-RVIN	Van's RV-6	R. G. Jines	
G-RVIO	Van's RV-10	R. C. Hopkinson	
G-RVIS	Van's RV-8	I. V. Sharman	
G-RVIT	Van's RV-6	P. J. Shotbolt	
G-RVIV	Van's RV-4	G. S. Scott	
G-RVIX	Van's RV-9A	R. E. Garforth	
G-RVJM	Van's RV-6	M. D. Challoner	
G-RVJO	Van's RV-9A	J. E. Singleton	
G-RVJP	Van's RV-9A	R. M. Palmer	
G-RVJW	Van's RV-4	J. M. Williams	
G-RVMB	Van's RV-9A	M. James & R. W. Littledale	
G-RVMC	Van's RV-7	M. R. McNeil	
G-RVMJ	Van's RV-4	M. J. de Ruiter	
G-RVMT	Van's RV-6	R. I. Warman	
G-RVMZ	Van's RV-8	M. W. Zipfel	
G-RVNH	Van's RV-9A	N. R. Haines	
G-RVPH	Van's RV-8	J. C. P. Herbert	
G-RVPL	Van's RV-8	A. P. Lawton	
G-RVPM	Van's RV-4	P. J. McMahon (G-RVDS)	
G-RVPW	Van's RV-6A	P. Waldron	
G-RVRA	PA-28 Cherokee 140	Mona Flying Club (G-OWVA)	
G-RVRB	PA-34-200T Seneca II	Ravenair Aircraft Ltd/Liverpool (G-BTAJ)	
G-RVRC	PA-23 Aztec 250E	West-Tec Ltd/Liverpool (G-BNPD)	
G-RVRD	PA-23 Aztec 250E	Ravenair Aircraft Ltd/Liverpool (G-BRAV/G-BBCM)	
G-RVRE	Partenavia P68B	Ravenair Aircraft Ltd/Liverpool	
G-RVRF	PA-38-112 Tomahawk	Ravenair Aircraft Ltd/Liverpool (G-BGEL)	
G-RVRG	PA-38-112 Tomahawk	Ravenair Aircraft Ltd/Liverpool (G-BHAF)	
G-RVRI	Cessna 172H Skyhawk	Ravenair Aircraft Ltd/Liverpool (G-CCCC)	
G-RVRJ	PA-E23 Aztec 250E	Ravenair Aircraft Ltd/Liverpool (G-BBGB)	
G-RVRK	PA-38-112 Tomahawk	Ravenair Aircraft Ltd/Liverpool (G-BGZW)	
G-RVRL	PA-38-112 Tomahawk	Ravenair Aircraft Ltd/Liverpool (G-BGZW/G-BGBY)	
G-RVRM	PA-38-112 Tomahawk	Ravenair Aircraft Ltd/Liverpool (G-BGEK)	
G-RVRN	PA-28-161 Warrior II	Ravenair Aircraft Ltd/Liverpool (G-BPID)	
G-RVRO	PA-38-112 Tomahawk II	Ravenair Aircraft Ltd/Liverpool (G-BOUD)	
G-RVRP	Van's RV-7	R. C. Parris	
G-RVRT	PA-28-140 Cherokee C	Ravenair Aircraft Ltd/Liverpool (G-AYKX)	
G-RVRV	Van's RV-4	P. Jenkins	
G-RVRW	PA-23 Aztec 250E	Ravenair Aircraft Ltd/Liverpool (G-BAVZ)	
G-RVSA	Van's RV-6A	W. H. Knott	
G-RVSD	Van's RV-9A	S. W. Damarell	
G-RVSG	Van's RV-9A	S. Gerrish	
G-RVSH	Van's RV-6A	S. J. D. Hall	
G-RVSX	Van's RV-6	R. L. & V. A. West	
G-RVUK	Van's RV-7	R. J. Fray	
G-RVVI	Van's RV-6	J. E. Alsford & J. N. Parr	
G-RWAY	Rotorway Executive 162F	A. G. Rackstraw (G-URCH)	
G-RWEW	Robinson R44	Northern Heli Charters	
G-RWHC	Cameron A-180 balloon	Wickers World Hot Air Balloon Co	
G-RWIN	Rearwin 175	A. B. Bourne & N. D. Battye	
G-RWLY	Shaw Europa XS	C. R. Arcle	
G-RWMW	Zenair CH.601XL Zodiac	R. W. H. Watson & M. Whyte (G-DROO)	
G-RWRW	Ultramagic M-77 balloon	Flying Pictures Ltd	
G-RWSS	Denney Kitfox Mk 2	R. W. Somerville	
G-RWWW	WS-55 Whirlwind HCC.12 (XR486) ★	IHM/Weston-super-Mare	
G-RXUK	Lindstrand LBL-105A balloon	P. A. Hames	
G-RXVH	Cessna 182T	Standard Aviation Ltd (G-CDID)	
G-RYAL	Avtech Jabiru UL	A. C. Ryall	
G-RYPH	Mainair Blade 912	I. A. Cunningham	
G-RYZZ	Robinson R44 II	Rivermead Aviation Ltd	
G-SAAA	Flight Design CTSW	Sunfun Group	
G-SAAB	Rockwell Commander 112TC	J. B. Barbour (G-BEFS)	
G-SAAM	Cessna T.182R	Sound Power Ltd (G-TAGL)	
G-SAAW	Boeing 737-8Q8	Globespan. com	
G-SABA	PA-28R-201T Turbo Arrow III	C. A. Burton (G-BFEN)	

G-SABB – G-SCII — BRITISH CIVIL REGISTRATIONS

Notes	Reg	Type	Owner or Operator
	G-SABB	Eurocopter EC 135T1	Bond Air Services Ltd
	G-SABR	NA F-86A Sabre (8178:FU-178)	Golden Apple Operations Ltd/Bournemouth
	G-SACB	Cessna F.152 II	P. Wilson (G-BFRB)
	G-SACD	Cessna F.172H	Northbrook College (Sussex)/Shoreham (G-AVCD)
	G-SACH	Stoddard-Hamilton Glastar	R. S. Holt
	G-SACI	PA-28-161 Warrior II	PJC (Leasing) Ltd
	G-SACK	Robin R.2160	Sherburn Aero Club Ltd
	G-SACO	PA-28-161 Warrior II	Stapleford Flying Club Ltd
	G-SACR	PA-28-161 Cadet	Sherburn Aero Club Ltd
	G-SACS	PA-28-161 Cadet	Sherburn Aero Club Ltd
	G-SACT	PA-28-161 Cadet	Sherburn Aero Club Ltd
	G-SAFE	Cameron N-77 balloon	P. J. Waller
	G-SAFI	CP.1320 Super Emeraude	C. S. Carleton-Smith
	G-SAFR	SAAB 91D Safir	Sylmar Aviation & Services Ltd
	G-SAGA	Grob G.109B	G-GROB Ltd/Booker
	G-SAGE	Luscombe 8A Silvaire	C. Howell (G-AKTL)
	G-SAHI	Trago Mills SAH-1	M. J. A. Trudgill
	G-SAIG	Robinson R44 II	Torfield Aviation Ltd
	G-SAIR	Cessna 421C	Air Support Aviation Services Ltd (G-OBCA)
	G-SAIX	Cameron N-77 balloon	C. Walther & ptnrs
	G-SAJA	Schempp-Hirth Discus 2	J. G. Arnold
	G-SALA	PA-32 Cherokee Six 300E	Stonebold Ltd
	G-SALE	Cameron Z-90 balloon	R. D. Baker
	G-SALL	Cessna F.150L (Tailwheel)	D. & P. A. Hailey
	G-SAMG	Grob G.109B	RAFGSA/Bicester
	G-SAMJ	Partenavia P.68B	Ravenair Aircraft Ltd/Liverpool
	G-SAMM	Cessna 340A	Calverton Flying Group Ltd
	G-SAMP	Agusta A109E Power	Hagondale Ltd
	G-SAMY	Shaw Europa	K. R. Tallent
	G-SAMZ	Cessna 150D	S. Bradshaw & P. Shankar (G-ASSO)
	G-SAPM	SOCATA TB20 Trinidad	Trinidair Ltd (G-EWFN)
	G-SARA	PA-28-181 Archer II	Apollo Aviation Advisory Ltd
	G-SARH	PA-28-161 Warrior II	Sussex Flying Club Ltd/Shoreham
	G-SARK	BAC.167 Strikemaster Mk 84 (311)	Tubetime Ltd
	G-SARM	Ikarus C.42 FB100	G-SARM group
	G-SARO	Saro Skeeter Mk 12 (XL812)	B. Chamberlain
	G-SARV	Van's RV-4	Hinton Flying Group
	G-SASA	Eurocopter EC 135T1	Bond Air Services Ltd
	G-SASB	Eurocopter EC 135T2	Bond Air Services Ltd
	G-SASC	Beech B200C Super King Air	Gama Aviation Ltd
	G-SASD	Beech B200C Super King Air	Gama Aviation Ltd
	G-SASH	MDH MD.900 Explorer	Yorkshire Air Ambulance Ltd
	G-SASK	PA-31P Pressurised Navajo	Middle East Business Club Ltd (G-BFAM)
	G-SATL	Cameron 105 Sphere SS balloon	Ballonwerbung Hamburg GmbH/Germany
	G-SATN	PA-25-260 Pawnee C	RAF Gliding and Soaring Association
	G-SAUF	Colt 90A balloon	K. H. Medau
	G-SAUK	Rans S6-ES	M. D. Tulloch
	G-SAWI	PA-32RT-300T Turbo Lance II	S. T. Day
	G-SAXC	Cameron N-105 balloon	Altitude Balloon Co Ltd (G-SAXO)
	G-SAXN	Beech 200 Super King Air	Saxonair Ltd (G-OMNH)
	G-SAYS	RAF 2000 GTX-SE gyroplane	Aziz Corporation Ltd
	G-SAZY	Avtech Jabiru J400	J. E. Howe
	G-SAZZ	CP.328 Super Emeraude	D. J. Long
	G-SBAE	Cessna F.172P	Warton Flying Club/Blackpool
	G-SBAR	Robinson R22 Beta	H. Weston
	G-SBHH	Schweizer 269C	Biggin Hill Helicopters Ltd (G-XALP)
	G-SBIZ	Cameron Z-90 balloon	Snow Business International Ltd
	G-SBKR	SOCATA TB10 Tobago	S. C. M. Bagley
	G-SBLT	Steen Skybolt	Skybolt Group
	G-SBMM	PA-28R Cherokee Arrow 180	K. S. Kalsi (G-BBEL)
	G-SBMO	Robin R.2160I	D. Henderson & ptnrs
	G-SBRA	Robinson R44 II	Airpoint Aviation Ltd/Ireland
	G-SBUS	BN-2A-26 Islander	Isles of Scilly Skybus Ltd/St. Just (G-BMMH)
	G-SBUT	Robinson R22 Beta	Heli Air Ltd (G-BXMT)
	G-SCAN	Vinten-Wallis WA-116/100	K. H. Wallis
	G-SCBI	SOCATA TB20 Trinidad	Ace Services
	G-SCFO	Cameron O-77 balloon	M. K. Grigson
	G-SCHI	AS.350B2 Ecureuil	Patriot Aviation Ltd
	G-SCHO	Robinson R22 Beta	J. H. Scholefield
	G-SCII	Agusta A109C	C and M Coldstores (G-JONA)

262

BRITISH CIVIL REGISTRATIONS G-SCIP – G-SHAR

Reg	Type	Owner or Operator	Notes
G-SCIP	SOCATA TB20 Trinidad GT	The Studio People Ltd	
G-SCLX	FLS Aerospace Sprint 160	Aces High Ltd/North Weald (G-PLYM)	
G-SCOI	Agusta A109E Power	Trustair Ltd (G-HPWH/G-HWPH)	
G-SCOL	Gippsland GA-8 Airvan	Sunderland Parachute Centre Ltd	
G-SCPD	Escapade 912 (1)	R. W. L. Breckell	
G-SCPL	PA-28 Cherokee 140	Aeros Leasing Ltd (G-BPVL)	
G-SCTA	Westland Scout AH.1	G. R. Harrison	
G-SCUB	PA-18 Super Cub 135 (542447)	M. E. Needham	
G-SCUD	Montgomerie-Bensen B.8MR	D. Taylor	
G-SCUL	Rutan Cozy	K. R. W. Scull	
G-SDCI	Bell 206B JetRanger 2	S. D. Coomes (G-GHCL/G-SHVV)	
G-SDEV	DH. 104 Sea Devon C.20 (XK895)	Aviation Heritage Ltd	
G-SDFM	Aerotechnik EV-97 Eurostar	G-SDFM Eurostar Group	
G-SDLW	Cameron O-105 balloon	S. P. Watkins	
G-SDOB	Tecnam P2002-EA Sierra	G. E. Collard & S. P. S. Dornan	
G-SDOI	Aeroprakt A.22 Foxbat	S. A. Owen	
G-SDOZ	Tecnam P92-EA Echo Super	S. P. S. Dornan	
G-SEAI	Cessna U.206G (amphibian)	K. O'Conner	
G-SEDO	Cameron N-105 balloon	Flying Pictures Ltd	
G-SEED	Piper J-3C-65 Cub	J. H. Seed	
G-SEEE	Pegasus Quik GT450	S. J. E. Smith	
G-SEEK	Cessna T.210N	A. Hopper	
G-SEFI	Robinson R44 II	Kermann Avionics Sales Ltd	
G-SEGA	Cameron 90 Sonic SS balloon	Balloon Preservation Flying Group	
G-SEJW	PA-28-161 Warrior II	Keen Leasing Ltd	
G-SELC	Diamond DA42 Twin Star	Stapleford Flying Club Ltd	
G-SELF	Shaw Europa	N. D. Crisp & ptnrs	
G-SELL	Robin DR.400/180	J. A. Warters	
G-SELX	BN-2T Islander	Fly BN Ltd (G-BJEC)	
G-SELY	Agusta-Bell 206B JetRanger 3	CT-Rental Ltd	
G-SEMI	PA-44-180 Seminole	M. Djukic & J. Benfell (G-DENW)	
G-SENA	Rutan LongEz	G. Bennett	
G-SEND	Colt 90A balloon	Air du Vent/France	
G-SENE	PA-34-200T Seneca II	R. Clarke	
G-SENX	PA-34-200T Seneca II	First Air Ltd (G-DARE/G-WOTS/G-SEVL)	
G-SEPA	AS.355N Twin Squirrel	Metropolitan Police (G-METD/G-BUJF)	
G-SEPB	AS.355N Twin Squirrel	Metropolitan Police (G-BVSE)	
G-SEPC	AS.355N Twin Squirrel	Metropolitan Police (G-BWGV)	
G-SEPT	Cameron N-105 balloon	P. Gooch	
G-SERC	Beech B300 Super King Air	Bridgtown Plant Ltd	
G-SERL	SOCATA TB10 Tobago	R. J. Searle/Rochester (G-LANA)	
G-SERV	Cameron N-105 balloon	PSH Skypower Ltd	
G-SETI	Cameron Sky 80-16 balloon	R. P. Allan	
G-SEVA	SE-5A (replica) (F141:G)	I. D. Gregory	
G-SEVE	Cessna 172N	MK Aero Support Ltd	
G-SEVN	Van's RV-7	N. Reddish	
G-SEWP	AS.355F2 Twin Squirrel	Veritair Ltd (G-OFIN/G-DANS/G-BTNM)	
G-SEXE	Scheibe SF.25C Falke	Repulor Ltd	
G-SEXX	PA-28-161 Warrior II	Weald Air Services Ltd	
G-SEXY	AA-1 Yankee ★	Jetstream Club, Liverpool Marriott Hotel South, Speke (G-AYLM)	
G-SFCJ	Cessna 525 CitationJet	Sureflight Aviation Ltd	
G-SFLY	Diamond DA40 Star	L. & N. P. L. Turner	
G-SFOX	Rotorway Executive 90	Magpie Technology Ltd (G-BUAH)	
G-SFPA	Cessna F.406	Scottish Fisheries Protection Agency	
G-SFPB	Cessna F.406	Scottish Fisheries Protection Agency	
G-SFRY	Thunder Ax7-77 balloon	M. Rowlands	
G-SFSL	Cameron Z-105 balloon	Somerfield Staff Lottery Fund	
G-SFTZ	Slingsby T.67M Firefly 160	Western Air (Thruxton) Ltd	
G-SGAS	Colt 77A balloon	A. Derbyshire	
G-SGEC	Beech B.200 Super King Air	Keypoint Aviation LLP	
G-SGEN	Ikarus C.42 FB 80	G. A. Arturi	
G-SGSE	PA-28-181 Archer II	U. Patel (G-BOJX)	
G-SHAA	Enstrom 280-UK	ELT Radio Telephones	
G-SHAF	Robinson R44 II	Tresillian Leisure Ltd	
G-SHAN	Robinson R44 II	Helitech Charter Ltd	
G-SHAR	Cessna 182T Skylane	S. Harding	

G-SHAY – G-SKPH | BRITISH CIVIL REGISTRATIONS

Reg	Type	Owner or Operator
G-SHAY	PA-28R-201T Turbo Arrow III	Alpha Yankee Flying Group (G-BFDG/G-JEFS)
G-SHCB	Schweizer 269C-1	Oxford Aviation Services Ltd/Kidlington
G-SHED	PA-28-181 Archer II	G-SHED Flying Group (G-BRAU)
G-SHEZ	Mainair Pegasus Quik	C. Surman
G-SHIM	CFM Streak Shadow	K. R. Anderson
G-SHIP	PA-23 Aztec 250F ★	Midland Air Museum/Coventry
G-SHOG	Colomban MC.15 Cri-Cri	C. R. Thompson (G-PFAB)
G-SHOW	MS.733 Alycon	Vintage Aircraft Team/Cranfield
G-SHPP	Hughes TH-55A	Helirouge Ltd
G-SHRK	Enstrom 280C-UK	Flighthire Ltd/Belgium (G-BGMX)
G-SHRT	Robinson R44 II	Overby Ltd
G-SHSH	Shaw Europa	S. G. Hayman & J. Price
G-SHSP	Cessna 172S	Shropshire Aero Club Ltd/Sleap
G-SHUF	Mainair Blade	R. G. Bradley
G-SHUG	PA-28R-201T Turbo Arrow III	G-SHUG Ltd
G-SHUU	Enstrom 280C-UK-2	D. Ellis (G-OMCP/G-KENY/G-BJFG)
G-SHUV	Aerosport Woody Pusher	J. R. Wraigh
G-SHWK	Cessna 172S	Cambridge Aero Club Ltd
G-SIAI	SIAI-Marchetti SF.260W	D. Gage
G-SIAL	Hawker Hunter F.58 (J-4090)	Old Flying Machine Club/Scampton
G-SIAM	Cameron V-90 balloon	J. A. W. Dyer (G-BXBS)
G-SICA	BN-2B-20 Islander	Britten-Norman Aircraft Ltd (G-SLAP)
G-SICB	BN-2B-20 Islander	Shetlands Islands Council (G-NESU/G-BTVN)
G-SIGN	PA-39 Twin Comanche 160 C/R	D. Buttle/Blackbushe
G-SIIB	Pitts S-2B Special	M. Zikes (G-BUVY)
G-SIID	Sukhoi Su-26M2	Technoforce Ltd
G-SIIE	Christen Pitts S-2B Special	Aviat Aircraft (UK) Ltd (G-SKYD)
G-SIII	Extra EA.300	Fun Flight Ltd
G-SIIS	Pitts S-1S Special	I. H. Searson (G-RIPE)
G-SIJJ	North American P-51D-NA Mustang (472035)	P. A. Teichman
G-SIJW	SA Bulldog Srs 120/121 (XX630:5)	M. Miles
G-SILS	Pietenpol Skyscout	D. Silsbury
G-SILY	Pegasus Quantum 15	J. I. Smith
G-SIMI	Cameron A-315 balloon	Balloon Safaris
G-SIMM	Ikarus C.42 FB 100 VLA	D. Simmons
G-SIMP	Avtech Jabiru SP	E. Bentley
G-SIMS	Robinson R22 Beta	Heli-One
G-SIMY	PA-32-300 Cherokee Six	I. Simpson (G-OCPF/G-BOCH)
G-SIPA	SIPA 903	A. C. Leak & J. H. Dilland (G-BGBM)
G-SIRA	Embraer EMB-135BJ Legacy	Amsair Aircraft Ltd
G-SIRS	Cessna 560XL Citation Excel	London Executive Aviation Ltd
G-SISU	P & M Quik GT450	Executive and Business Aviation Support Ltd
G-SITA	Pegasus Quantum 15-912	A. D. Curtin
G-SIVJ	Westland Gazelle HT.2	Skytrace (UK) Ltd (G-CBSG)
G-SIVN	MDH MD.500N	Cumbrian Seafoods Ltd
G-SIVR	MDH MD.900 Explorer	Mandarin Aviation Ltd
G-SIVW	Lake LA-250 Renegade	C. J. Siva-Jothy
G-SIXC	Douglas DC-6A	Atlantic Air Transport Ltd/Coventry
G-SIXD	PA-32 Cherokee Six 300D	M. B. Paine & I. Gordon
G-SIXS	Whittaker MW6S Fat Boy Flyer	P. E. Young
G-SIXX	Colt 77A balloon	M. Dear & M. Taylor
G-SIXY	Van's RV-6	C. J. Hall & C. R. P. Hamlett
G-SIZZ	Jabiru J400	K. J. Betteley
G-SJCH	BN-2T-4S Defender 4000	Hampshire Police Authority (G-BWPK)
G-SJDI	Robinson R44	Helicopter Support Ltd
G-SJEN	Ikarus C.42 FB 80	C. M. Mackinnon
G-SJET	Boeing 767-216ER	Flyjet Ltd (G-FJEC)
G-SJKR	Lindstrand LBL-90A balloon	S. J. Roake
G-SJMC	Boeing 767-31K	MyTravel Airways
G-SKAN	Cessna F.172M	Bustard Flying Club Ltd (G-BFKT)
G-SKCI	Rutan Vari-Eze	S. K. Cockburn
G-SKEW	Mudry CAP-232	J. H. Askew
G-SKIE	Steen Skybolt	P. G. Kavanagh
G-SKII	Augusta-Bell 206B JetRanger 3	K. P. Toner (Developments)
G-SKKY	Cessna 172S Skyhawk	Skyquest Ltd
G-SKNT	Aerotek S-2A	T. G. Lloyd (G-PEAL)
G-SKOT	Cameron V-42 balloon	S. A. Laing
G-SKPG	Best Off Skyranger 912 (2)	P. Gibbs
G-SKPH	Yakovlev Yak-50	R. S. Partridge-Hicks & I. C. Austin (G-BWWH)

BRITISH CIVIL REGISTRATIONS — G-SKRA – G-SOPH

Reg	Type	Owner or Operator	Notes
G-SKRA	Best Off Skyranger 912S (1)	P. A. Banks	
G-SKRG	Best Off Skyranger 912 (2)	R. W. Goddin	
G-SKYC	Slingsby T.67M Firefly	T. W. Cassells (G-BLDP)	
G-SKYE	Cessna TU.206G	RAF Sport Parachute Association	
G-SKYF	SOCATA TB10 Tobago	W. L. McNeil	
G-SKYK	Cameron A-275 balloon	Cameron Flights Southern Ltd	
G-SKYL	Cessna 182S	Skylane Aviation Ltd/Sherburn	
G-SKYM	Cessna F.337E	Bencray Ltd (G-AYHW) (stored)/Blackpool	
G-SKYN	AS.355F1 Twin Squirrel	Arena Aviation Ltd (G-OGRK/G-BWZC/G-MODZ)	
G-SKYO	Slingsby T.67M-200	R. H. Evelyn	
G-SKYR	Cameron A-180 balloon	Cameron Flights Southern Ltd	
G-SKYT	I.I.I. Sky Arrow 650TC	W. M. Bell & S. J. Brooks	
G-SKYU	Cameron A-210 balloon	Cameron Flights Southern Ltd	
G-SKYV	PA-28RT-201T Turbo Arrow IV	A. Wright (G-BNZG)	
G-SKYW	AS355F1	Skywalker Aviation Ltd (G-BTIS/G-TALI)	
G-SKYX	Cameron A-210 balloon	Cameron Flights Southern Ltd	
G-SKYY	Cameron A-275 balloon	Cameron Flights Southern Ltd	
G-SLCE	Cameron C-80 balloon	A. M. Holly	
G-SLCT	Diamond DA42 Twin Star	Stapleford Flying Club Ltd	
G-SLEA	Mudry/CAARP CAP-10B	M. J. M. Jenkins	
G-SLII	Cameron O-90 balloon	R. B. & A. M. Harris	
G-SLIP	Easy Raider	D. R. Squires	
G-SLMG	Diamond HK.36 TTC Super Dimona	G-SLMG Syndicate	
G-SLNW	Robinson R22 Beta	Heli-4 Charter LLP (G-LNIC)	
G-SLOK	Robinson R44 II	Heli-4 Charter LLP	
G-SLTN	SOCATA TB20 Trinidad	Oceana Air Ltd	
G-SLYN	PA-28-161 Warrior II	Haimoss Ltd	
G-SMAC	MDH MD 500N Notar	MAC Helicopters LLP	
G-SMAN	Airbus A.330-243	Monarch Airlines Ltd	
G-SMAS	BAC.167 Strikemaster 80A (1104)	M. A. Petrie	
G-SMBM	Pegasus Quantum 15-912	N. Charles & P. A. Henretty	
G-SMDH	Shaw Europa XS	S. W. Pitt	
G-SMDJ	AS.350B2 Ecureuil	Denis Ferranti Hoverknights Ltd	
G-SMIG	Cameron O-65 balloon	R. D. Parry	
G-SMJJ	Cessna 414A	Gull Air Ltd/Guernsey	
G-SMKM	Cirrus SR20	K. Mallet	
G-SMRS	Cessna 172F	M. R. Sarling	
G-SMRT	Lindstrand LBL-260A balloon	M. E. White	
G-SMTC	Colt Flying Hut SS balloon	Shiplake Investments Ltd/Switzerland	
G-SMTH	PA-28 Cherokee 140	R. W. Harris & A. Jahanfar (G-AYJS)	
G-SMTJ	Airbus A.321-211	MyTravel Airways	
G-SNAK	Lindstrand LBL-105A balloon	Ballooning Adventures Ltd	
G-SNAP	Cameron V-77 balloon	C. J. S. Limon	
G-SNEV	CFM Streak Shadow SA	J. D. Reed	
G-SNIF	Cameron A-300 balloon	A. C. K. Rowson & Sudoni	
G-SNOG	Kiss 400-582 (1)	B. H. Ashman	
G-SNOP	Shaw Europa	Bob Crowe Aircraft Sales Ltd (G-DESL/G-WWWG)	
G-SNOW	Cameron V-77 balloon	M. J. Ball	
G-SNOZ	Shaw Europa	M. P. Wiseman (G-DONZ)	
G-SNUZ	PA-28-161 Warrior II	JCOA Ltd (G-PSFT/G-BPDS)	
G-SOAF	BAC.167 Strikemaster Mk. 82A (425)	M. A. Petrie & J.E. Rowley	
G-SOAR	Eiri PIK-20E	R. I. Huttlestone	
G-SOAY	Cessna T.303	Wrekin Construction Co Ltd	
G-SOBI	PA-28-181 Archer II	Northern Aviation Ltd	
G-SOCK	Mainair Pegasus Quik	J. F. Shaw & K. R. McCartney	
G-SOCT	Yakovlev Yak-50 (AR-B)	C. R. Turton	
G-SOEI	HS.748 Srs 2A	PTB (Emerald) Pty Ltd/Blackpool	
G-SOFT	Thunder Ax7-77 balloon	A. J. Bowen	
G-SOHO	Diamond DA40D Star	Soho Aviation Ltd	
G-SOKO	Soko P-2 Kraguj (30149)	R. P. Cross (G-BRXK)	
G-SOLA	Aero Designs Star-Lite SL.1	G. P. Thomas	
G-SOLH	Bell 47G-5	SOL Helicopters Ltd (G-AZMB)	
G-SONA	SOCATA TB10 Tobago	G-SONA Group (G-BIBI)	
G-SOOC	Hughes 369HS	R.J.H. Strong (G-BRRX)	
G-SOOM	Glaser-Dirks DG-500M	G. W. Kirton	
G-SOOS	Colt 21A balloon	P. J. Stapley	
G-SOOT	PA-28 Cherokee 180	J. A. Bridger/Exeter (G-AVNM)	
G-SOOZ	Rans S.6-ES Coyote II	A. Batters	
G-SOPH	Skyranger 912(2)	G. E. Reynolds	

G-SOPP – G-STRH BRITISH CIVIL REGISTRATIONS

Notes	Reg	Type	Owner or Operator
	G-SOPP	Enstrom 280FX	F. J. Sopp (G-OSAB)
	G-SORT	Cameron N-90 balloon	A. Brown
	G-SOUL	Cessna 310R	Atlantic Air Transport Ltd/Coventry
	G-SOVA	Cessna 550 Citation II	Sovereign Air Ltd
	G-SOVB	Learjet 45	Sovereign Air Ltd (G-OLDJ)
	G-SPAM	Avid Aerobat (modified)	Full Sutton Flying Centre Ltd
	G-SPAT	Aero AT-3 R100	S2T Aero Ltd
	G-SPDR	DH.115 Sea Vampire T.22 (N6-766)	M. J. Cobb/Bournemouth
	G-SPEE	Robinson R22 Beta	Verve Systems Ltd (G-BPJC)
	G-SPEL	Sky 220-24 balloon	Pendle Balloon Co
	G-SPEY	Agusta-Bell 206B JetRanger 3	Castle Air Charters Ltd (G-BIGO)
	G-SPFX	Rutan Cozy	B. D. Tutty
	G-SPHU	Eurocopter EC 135T2	Bond Air Services Ltd
	G-SPIN	Pitts S-2A Special	S. D. Judd
	G-SPIT	VS.379 Spitfire FR.XIV (MV268)	Patina Ltd/Duxford (G-BGHB)
	G-SPOG	Jodel DR.1050	J. Cook & J. Pool (G-AXVS)
	G-SPOR	Beech B200 Super King Air	Select Plant Hire Company Ltd/Southend
	G-SPUR	Cessna 550 Citation II	London Executive Aviation Ltd
	G-SPYS	Robinson R44 II	SKB Partners LLP
	G-SRAW	Alpi Pioneer 300	M. Clare & A. R. Lloyd
	G-SRII	Easy Raider 503	Sierra Romeo India India Group
	G-SROE	Westland Scout AH.1 (XP907)	Bolenda Engineering Ltd
	G-SRVA	Cirrus SR20	Aero GB Ltd
	G-SRVO	Cameron N-90 balloon	Servo & Electronic Sales Ltd
	G-SRWN	PA-28-161 Warrior II	S. Smith (G-MAND/G-BRKT)
	G-SRYY	Shaw Europa XS	S. R. Young
	G-SRZO	Cirrus SR20	D. A. Clarkson
	G-SSCL	MDH Hughes 369E	Shaun Stevens Contractors Ltd
	G-SSEA	ATR-42-300	Air Wales Ltd
	G-SSEX	Rotorway Executive 162F	M. Middleby
	G-SSIX	Rans S.6-116 Coyote II	R. I. Kelly
	G-SSJP	Robinson R44 II	Global Helicopters Ltd
	G-SSKY	BN-2B-26 Islander	Isles of Scilly Skybus Ltd (G-BSWT)
	G-SSLF	Lindstrand LBL-210A balloon	Exclusive Ballooning
	G-SSSC	Sikorsky S-76C	CHC Scotia Ltd
	G-SSSD	Sikorsky S-76C	CHC Scotia Ltd
	G-SSSE	Sikorsky S-76C	CHC Scotia Ltd
	G-SSTI	Cameron N-105 balloon	British Airways
	G-SSWE	Short SD3-60 Variant 100	BAC Leasing Ltd
	G-SSWM	Short SD3-60 Variant 100	BAC Leasing Ltd (G-OAAS/G-BLIL)
	G-SSWO	Short SD3-60 Variant 100	BAC Leasing Ltd (G-BKMY)
	G-SSWR	Short SD3-60 Variant 100	BAC Leasing Ltd (G-BLWJ)
	G-SSWV	Sportavia Fournier RF-5B	N. Fisher & Arhey
	G-SSXX	Eurocopter EC 135T2	Bond Air Services Ltd (G-SSSX)
	G-STAA	Robinson R44	Walker Plant Services Ltd (G-HALE)
	G-STAF	Van's RV-7A	A. F. Stafford
	G-STAV	Cameron O-84 balloon	F. Horsfall
	G-STAY	Cessna FR.172K	G. A. Owston
	G-STCH	Fiesler Fi 156A-1 Storch	G. R. Lacey
	G-STDL	Phillips ST.2 Speedtwin	Speedtwin Developments Ltd (G-DPST)
	G-STEA	PA-28R Cherokee Arrow 200	J. P. Walsh
	G-STEM	Stemme S.10V	G-STEM Group
	G-STEN	Stemme S.10 (4)	G-STEN Syndicate
	G-STEP	Schweizer 269C	M. Johnson
	G-STER	Bell 206B JetRanger 3	Maintopic Ltd
	G-STEV	Jodel DR.221	S. W. Talbot/Long Marston
	G-STIG	Focke Wulf Fw-44J Steiglitz	P. R. Holloway
	G-STMP	SNCAN Stampe SV.4A	A. C. Thorne
	G-STNS	Agusta A109A-II	Heliflight (UK) Ltd
	G-STOK	Colt 77B balloon	A. C. Booth
	G-STON	AS355N Ecureuil 2	Narragansett LLP
	G-STOO	Stolp Starduster Too	K. F. Crumplin
	G-STOP	Robinson R44 Raven II	Cartis Ltd & ptnrs/Ireland
	G-STOW	Cameron 90 Wine Box SS balloon	Flying Enterprises
	G-STPH	Robinson R44	S. Harron
	G-STPI	Cameron A-210 balloon	The Ballooning Business Ltd
	G-STRF	Boeing 737-76N	Astraeus Ltd/Gatwick
	G-STRG	Cyclone AX2000	Pegasus Flight Training (Cotswolds)/Kemble
	G-STRH	Boeing 737-36N	Astraeus Ltd/Gatwick

BRITISH CIVIL REGISTRATIONS

G-STRI – G-TAFI

Reg	Type	Owner or Operator	Notes
G-STRI	Boeing 737-33A	Astraeus Ltd/Gatwick	
G-STRJ	Boeing 737-33A	Astraeus Ltd/Gatwick	
G-STRK	CFM Streak Shadow Srs SA	E. J. Hadley/Switzerland	
G-STRL	AS.355N Twin Squirrel	Harrier Enterprises Ltd	
G-STRM	Cameron N-90 balloon	A. Brown	
G-STUA	Aerotek Pitts S-2A Special (modified)	G-STUA Group	
G-STUB	Christen Pitts S-2B Special	P. T. Borchert	
G-STUE	Europa	S. Philp	
G-STUY	Robinson R44 II	S. Mayers	
G-STWO	ARV Super 2	P. M. Paul	
G-STYL	Pitts S-1S Special	C. R. Hampson	
G-SUCH	Cameron V-77 balloon	D. G. Such (G-BIGD)	
G-SUCK	Cameron Z-105 balloon	ABC Flights Ltd	
G-SUCT	Robinson R22	C. R. Turton	
G-SUEB	PA-28-181 Archer III	Saxon Logistics Ltd	
G-SUEC	PA-32-301XTC Saratoga	H. L. Chan	
G-SUED	Thunder Ax8-90 balloon	E. C. Lubbock & S. A. Kidd (G-PINE)	
G-SUEW	Airbus A.320-214	MyTravel Airways	
G-SUEY	Bell 206L-1 Long Ranger	Aerospeed Ltd	
G-SUEZ	Agusta-Bell 206B JetRanger 2	Aerospeed Ltd	
G-SUFF	Eurocopter EC 135T1	Suffolk Constabulary Air Support Unit	
G-SUKI	PA-38-112 Tomahawk	Ravenair Aircraft Ltd/Liverpool (G-BPNV)	
G-SUMX	Robinson R22 Beta	Total Digital Solutions Ltd	
G-SUMZ	Robinson R44 II	Frankham Bros Ltd	
G-SUNN	Robinson R44	C. Wilkins	
G-SUPA	PA-18 Super Cub 150	Supa Group	
G-SURG	PA-30 Twin Comanche 160B	A. R. Taylor/Kidlington (G-VIST/G-AVHG)	
G-SURY	Eurocopter EC 135T2	Surrey Police Authority	
G-SUSE	Shaw Europa XS	P. R. Tunney	
G-SUSI	Cameron V-77 balloon	J. H. Dryden	
G-SUSX	MDH MD-902 Explorer	Sussex Police Authority	
G-SUTD	Jabiru UL-D	A. E. Broughton	
G-SUTN	I.I.I. Sky Arrow 650TC	D. J. Goldsmith	
G-SUZN	PA-28-161 Warrior II	The St. George Flying Club/Teesside	
G-SUZY	Taylor JT.1 Monoplane	N. Gregson	
G-SVDG	Jabiru SK	R. Tellegen	
G-SVEA	PA-28-161 Warrior II	E-C. V. Dunning	
G-SVET	Yakovlev Yak-50	Yak 52 Ltd	
G-SVIP	Cessna 421B Golden Eagle II	T. Stone-Brown (G-BNYJ)	
G-SVIV	SNCAN Stampe SV.4C	R. Taylor	
G-SVPN	PA-32R-301T Turbo Saratoga	Caspian Air Services Ltd	
G-SVSB	Cessna 680 Citation Sovereign	Ferron Trading Ltd	
G-SWEE	Beech 95-B55 Baron	Mirage Aircraft Leasing Ltd (G-AZDK)	
G-SWEL	Hughes 369HS	M. A. Crook & A. E. Wright (G-RBUT)	
G-SWIF	VS.541 Swift F.7 (XF114) ★	Solent Sky, Southampton	
G-SWLL	Aero AT-3 R100	Sywell Aerodrome Ltd	
G-SWON	Pitts S-1S Special	S. L. Goldspink	
G-SWOT	Currie Wot (C3011:S)	D. A. Porter	
G-SWPR	Cameron N-56 balloon	A. Brown	
G-SWWM	Westland Gazelle HT.Mk.2	M. S. Beaton	
G-SYDE	PA-32R-301T Turbo Saratoga	Sherborne Aviation Ltd	
G-SYEL	Aero AT-3 R100	Sywell Aerodrome Ltd/Sywell	
G-SYFW	Focke-Wulf Fw.190 replica (2+1)	R. P. Cross	
G-SYLJ	Embraer RJ135BJ	TAG Aviation (UK) Ltd	
G-SYPA	AS.355F2 Twin Squirrel	British International (G-BPRE)	
G-SYPS	MDH MD.900 Explorer	South Yorkshire Police Authority	
G-SYUT	Tanarg/Ixess 15 912S (1)	L. Cottle	
G-SYWL	Aero AT-3 R100	Sywell Aerodrome Ltd	
G-TAAA	Cirrus SR20 GTS	TAA UK Ltd	
G-TAAB	Cirrus SR22	TAA UK Ltd	
G-TAAC	Cirrus SR20	Caseright Ltd	
G-TABI	Cirrus SR20	N. Carter	
G-TABS	EMB-110P1 Bandeirante	Skydrift Ltd (G-PBAC)	
G-TACK	Grob G.109B	A. P. Mayne	
G-TADC	Aeroprakt A.22 Foxbat	R. J. Sharp	
G-TAFC	Maule M7-2358 Super Rocket	The Amphibious Flying Club Ltd	
G-TAFF	CASA 1.131E Jungmann 1000	A. J. E. Smith/Breighton (G-BFNE)	
G-TAFI	Bücker Bü 133C Jungmeister	R. P. Lamplough	

G-TAGG – G-TCTC BRITISH CIVIL REGISTRATIONS

Notes	Reg	Type	Owner or Operator
	G-TAGG	Eurocopter EC 135T2	Taggart Homes Ltd
	G-TAGH	Beech B200 Super King Air	Taggart Aviation Ltd
	G-TAGR	Europa	P. C. Avery
	G-TAGT	Robinson R22	Taggart Aviation Ltd
	G-TAIL	Cessna 150J	L. I. D. Denham-Brown
	G-TAIR	PA-34-200T Seneca II	Nigel Kenny Aviation Ltd
	G-TAIT	Cessna 172R	Centenary Flying Group Ltd (G-DREY)
	G-TAJF	Lindstrand LBL-77A balloon	T. A. J. Fowles
	G-TAKE	AS.355F1 Twin Squirrel	Arena Aviation Ltd (G-OITN)
	G-TAMA	Schweizer 269D	Total Air Management Services Ltd
	G-TAMB	Schweizer 269D	Total Air Management Services Ltd
	G-TAMC	Schweizer 269D	Total Air Management Services Ltd
	G-TAMD	Schweizer 269D	Total Air Management Services Ltd
	G-TAME	Schweizer 269D	Total Air Management Services Ltd
	G-TAMR	Cessna 172S	Apem Ltd
	G-TAMS	Beech A23-24 Musketeer Super	Aerograde Ltd
	G-TAMY	Cessna 421B	Charniere Ltd
	G-TANA	Tanarg/Ixess 15 912S(2)	A. P. Marks
	G-TAND	Robinson R44	Southwest Helicharter Ltd
	G-TANI	GA-7 Cougar	S. Spier/Elstree (G-VJAI/G-OCAB/G-BICF)
	G-TANJ	Raj Hamsa X'Air 582(5)	R. Thorman
	G-TANK	Cameron N-90 balloon	C. A. Oxby
	G-TANS	SOCATA TB20 Trinidad	Tettenhall Leisure
	G-TANY	EAA Acrosport 2	P. J. Tanulak
	G-TAPE	PA-23 Aztec 250D	D. J. Hare (G-AWVW)
	G-TAPS	PA-28RT-201T Turbo Arrow IV	P. G. Doble
	G-TARG	Tanarg/Ixess 15 912S (2)	P. M. Dewhurst
	G-TARN	Pietenpol Air Camper	P. J. Heilbron
	G-TART	PA-28-236 Dakota	Prescot Planes Ltd
	G-TASH	Cessna 172N (modified)	A. Ashpitel
	G-TASK	Cessna 404	Bravo Aviation Ltd
	G-TATS	AS.350BA Ecureuil	T. J. Hoare
	G-TATT	Gardan GY-20 Minicab	Tatt's Group
	G-TAXI	PA-23 Aztec 250E	M. Roberts
	G-TAYC	Gulfstream G450	TAG Aviation (UK) Ltd
	G-TAYI	Grob G.115	K. P. Widdowson & K. Hackshall (G-DODO)
	G-TAYS	Cessna F.152 II	Tayside Aviation Ltd/Aberdeen (G-LFCA)
	G-TAZZ	Dan Rihn DR.107 One Design	C. J. Gow
	G-TBAE	BAe 146-200	BAE Systems (Corporate Travel Ltd) (G-HWPB/G-BSRU/G-OSKI/G-JEAR)
	G-TBAG	Murphy Renegade II	M. R. Tetley
	G-TBAH	Bell 206B JetRanger 2	RB Helicopters (G-OMJB)
	G-TBBC	Pegasus Quantum 15-912	J. Horn
	G-TBEA	Cessna 525A Citation CJ2	Hangar 8 Ltd
	G-TBGL	Agusta A109A-II	Bulford Holdings Ltd (G-VJCB/G-BOUA)
	G-TBGT	SOCATA TB10 Tobago GT	P. G. Sherry & A. J. Simmonds/Liverpool
	G-TBHH	AS355F2 Twin Squirrel	Biggin Hill Helicopters (G-HOOT/G-SCOW/G-POON/G-MCAL)
	G-TBIC	BAe 146-200	Flightline Ltd
	G-TBIO	SOCATA TB10 Togago	Delta Bird Aviation Ltd
	G-TBJP	Mainair Pegasus Quik	S. M. Neil
	G-TBLB	P & M Quik GT450	B. L. Benson
	G-TBLY	Eurocopter EC 120B	AD Bly Aircraft Leasing Ltd
	G-TBMW	Murphy Renegade Spirit	S. J. & M. J. Spavins (G-MYIG)
	G-TBOK	SOCATA TB10 Tobago	TB10 Ltd
	G-TBSV	SOCATA TB20 Trinidad GT	Condron Concrete Ltd
	G-TBTB	Robinson R44	ARB Helicopters (G-CDUN)
	G-TBTN	SOCATA TB10 Tobago	Airways International Ltd (G-BKIA)
	G-TBXX	SOCATA TB20 Trinidad	Aeroplane Ltd
	G-TBZI	SOCATA TB21 Trinidad TC	PMM Management Ltd
	G-TBZO	SOCATA TB20 Trinidad	R. P. Lewis & D. L. Clarke
	G-TCAN	Colt 69A balloon	H. C. J. Williams
	G-TCAP	BAe 125 Srs 800B	BAE Systems Ltd
	G-TCAS	Cameron Z-275 balloon	The Ballooning Business Ltd
	G-TCBA	Boeing 757-28A	Thomas Cook Airlines UK Ltd (G-OOOY)
	G-TCEE	Hughes 369HS	Tony Castro Aircraft Interiors Ltd (G-AZVM)
	G-TCMM	Agusta-Bell 206B-3 Jet Ranger 3	Westair Aviation Ltd (G-JMVB/G-OIML)
	G-TCNM	Tecnam P92-EA Echo	F. G. Walker
	G-TCNY	Mainair Pegasus Quik	T. Butler
	G-TCOM	PA-30 Twin Comanche 160B	Commair Ltd
	G-TCTC	PA-28RT-200 Arrow IV	T. Haigh

BRITISH CIVIL REGISTRATIONS — G-TCUB – G-THOE

Reg	Type	Owner or Operator	Notes
G-TCUB	Piper J-3C-65 Cub	C. Kirk	
G-TCXA	Airbus A.330-243	Thomas Cook Airlines UK Ltd	
G-TDFS	Callair A.9A	P. Stephenson/Gamston (G-AVZA)	
G-TDOG	SA Bulldog Srs 120/121 (XX538:O)	G. S. Taylor	
G-TDRA	Cessna 172S Skyhawk	TDR Aviation Ltd	
G-TDVB	Dyn' Aero MCR-01ULC	D. V. Brunt	
G-TDYN	Aerospool Dynamic WT9 UK	Yeoman Light Aircraft Co Ltd	
G-TEAS	Tanarg/Ixess 15 912S (2)	G. C. Teasdale	
G-TEBZ	PA-28R-201 Arrow III	S. F. Tebby & Son	
G-TECC	Aeronca 7AC Champion	N. J. Orchard-Armitage	
G-TECH	Rockwell Commander 114	P. A. Reed & S. Rae/Elstree (G-BEDH)	
G-TECK	Cameron V-77 balloon	M. W. A. Shemilt	
G-TECM	Tecnam P92-EM Echo	N. G. H. Staunton	
G-TECO	Tecnam P92-EM Echo	A. N. Buchan	
G-TECS	Tecnam P2002-EA Sierra	D. A. Lawrence	
G-TECZ	Tecnam P92-E	Tecnam UK Ltd	
G-TEDB	Cessna F.150L	E. L. Bamford (G-AZLZ)	
G-TEDF	Cameron N-90 balloon	Fort Vale Engineering Ltd	
G-TEDI	Best Off Skyranger J2.2(1)	K. Lorenzen	
G-TEDS	SOCATA TB10 Tobago	G-TEDS Group Aviation (G-BHCO)	
G-TEDW	Kiss 450-582 (2)	F. P. Welsh	
G-TEDY	Evans VP-1	N. K. Marston (G-BHGN)	
G-TEFC	PA-28 Cherokee 140	Foxtrot Charlie Flyers	
G-TEHL	CFM Streak Shadow Srs M	J. Anderson (G-MYJE)	
G-TELY	Agusta A109A-II	Castle Air Charters Ltd	
G-TEMB	Tecnam P2000-EA Sierra	M. B. Hill	
G-TEMP	PA-28 Cherokee 180	G-TEMP Group (G-AYBK)	
G-TEMT	Hawker Tempest II (MW763)	Tempest Two Ltd/Gamston	
G-TENG	Extra EA.300/L	10G Aerobatics Ltd	
G-TENS	DV.20 Katana	D. C.Wellard	
G-TENT	Auster J/1N Alpha	R. Callaway-Lewis (G-AKJU)	
G-TERN	Shaw Europa	J. Smith	
G-TERR	Mainair Pegasus Quik	T. R. Thomas	
G-TERY	PA-28-181 Archer II	J. R. Bratherton (G-BOXZ)	
G-TESI	Tecnam P2002 EA Sierra	P. J. Mitchell	
G-TEST	PA-34-200 Seneca	Stapleford Flying Club Ltd (G-BLCD)	
G-TETI	Cameron N-90 balloon	Teti SPA/Italy	
G-TEWS	PA-28 Cherokee 140	P. M. Ireland (G-KEAN/G-AWTM)	
G-TEXN	North American T-6G Texan (3072:72)	Thunderprop Ltd (G-BHTH)	
G-TEXS	Van's RV-6	W. H. Greenwood	
G-TEXT	Robinson R44 II	Sunken Ltd/Ireland	
G-TFCI	Cessna FA-152	Tayside Aviation Ltd/Dundee	
G-TFIN	PA-32RT-300T Turbo Lance II	M. D. Parker	
G-TFIX	Mainair Pegasus Quantum 15-912	T. G. Jones	
G-TFLY	Air Creation Kiss 450-582 (1)	A. J. Ladell	
G-TFOG	Best Off Skyranger 912 (2)	T. J. Fogg	
G-TFOX	Denney Kitfox Mk.2	G. W. Bold	
G-TFRB	Air Command 532 Elite	F. R. Blennerhassett	
G-TFUN	Valentin Taifun 17E	North West Taifun Group	
G-TFYN	PA-32RT-300 Lance II	R. C. Poolman	
G-TGER	AA-5B Tiger	Photonic Science Ltd/Biggin Hill (G-BFZP)	
G-TGGR	Eurocopter EC 120B	E. P. & R. S. Sadler	
G-TGRA	Agusta A109A	Tiger Helicopters Ltd/Shobdon	
G-TGRD	Robinson R22 Beta II	Tiger Helicopters Ltd/Shobdon (G-OPTS)	
G-TGRE	Robinson R22A	Tiger Helicopters Ltd/Shobdon (G-SOLD)	
G-TGRS	Robinson R22 Beta	Tiger Helicopters Ltd/Shobdon (G-DELL)	
G-TGRZ	Bell 206B JetRanger 3	Tiger Helicopters Ltd/Shobdon (G-BXZX)	
G-THAT	Raj Hamsa X'Air Falcon 912 (1)	A. N. Green	
G-THEL	Robinson R44	Kapital Aviation Ltd (G-OCCB/G-STMM)	
G-THEO	TEAM mini-MAX 91	C. Fletcher	
G-THIN	Cessna FR.172G	I. C. A. Ussher (G-BXYY)	
G-THLA	Robinson R22 Beta	Thurston Helicopters Ltd	
G-THMB	Van's RV-9A	C. H. P. Bell	
G-THOA	Boeing 737-5L9	Thomsonfly Ltd (G-MSKA)	
G-THOB	Boeing 737-5L9	Thomsonfly Ltd (G-MSKB)	
G-THOC	Boeing 737-59D	Thomsonfly Ltd (G-BVKA)	
G-THOD	Boeing 737-59D	Thomsonfly Ltd (G-BVKC)	
G-THOE	Boeing 737-3Q8	Thomsonfly Ltd (G-BZZH)	

G-THOF – G-TMWC — BRITISH CIVIL REGISTRATIONS

Notes	Reg	Type	Owner or Operator
	G-THOF	Boeing 737-3Q8	Thomsonfly Ltd (G-BZZI)
	G-THOG	Boeing 737-31S	Thomsonfly Ltd
	G-THOH	Boeing 737-31S	Thomsonfly Ltd
	G-THOI	Boeing 737-36Q	Thomsonfly Ltd (G-OFRA)
	G-THOJ	Boeing 737-36Q	Thomsonfly Ltd (G-ODUS)
	G-THOK	Boeing 737-36Q	Thomsonfly Ltd (G-IGOB)
	G-THOL	Boeing 737-36N	Thomsonfly Ltd (G-IGOK)
	G-THOM	Thunder Ax-6-56 balloon	T. H. Wilson
	G-THON	Boeing 737-36N	Thomsonfly Ltd (G-IGOL)
	G-THOO	Boeing 737-33V	Thomsonfly Ltd (G-EZYK)
	G-THOS	Thunder Ax7-77 balloon	C. E. A. Breton
	G-THOT	Avtech Jabiru SK	S. G. Holton
	G-THRE	Cessna 182S	C. Malet
	G-THSL	PA-28R-201 Arrow III	D. M. Markscheffe
	G-THZL	SOCATA TB20 Trinidad	Thistle Aviation Ltd
	G-TICH	Taylor JT.2 Titch	R. Davitt
	G-TIDS	Jodel 150	M. R. Parker
	G-TIGA	DH.82A Tiger Moth	D. E. Leatherland/Tollerton (G-AOEG)
	G-TIGB	AS.332L Super Puma	Bristow Helicopters Ltd (G-BJXC)
	G-TIGC	AS.332L Super Puma	Bristow Helicopters Ltd (G-BJYH)
	G-TIGE	AS.332L Super Puma	Bristow Helicopters Ltd (G-BJYJ)
	G-TIGF	AS.332L Super Puma	Bristow Helicopters Ltd
	G-TIGG	AS.332L Super Puma	Bristow Helicopters Ltd
	G-TIGJ	AS.332L Super Puma	Bristow Helicopters Ltd
	G-TIGO	AS.332L Super Puma	Bristow Helicopters Ltd
	G-TIGS	AS.332L Super Puma	Bristow Helicopters Ltd
	G-TIGT	AS.332L Super Puma	Bristow Helicopters Ltd
	G-TIGV	AS.332L Super Puma	Bristow Helicopters Ltd
	G-TIII	Aerotek Pitts S-2A Special	D. G. Cowden (G-BGSE)
	G-TILE	Robinson R22 Beta	Fenland Helicopters Ltd
	G-TILI	Bell 206B JetRanger 2	CIM Helicopters
	G-TIMB	Rutan Vari-Eze	P. G. Kavanagh (G-BKXJ)
	G-TIMC	Robinson R44	T. Clark Aviation LLP (G-CDUR)
	G-TIMK	PA-28-181 Archer II	T. Baker
	G-TIML	Cessna 172S Skyhawk	Tim Leacock Aircraft Sales Ltd
	G-TIMM	Folland Gnat T.1 (XM693)	T. J. Manna/Cranfield
	G-TIMP	Aeronca 7BCM Champion	R. B. Valler
	G-TIMS	Falconar F-12A	T. Sheridan
	G-TIMY	Gardan GY-80 Horizon 160	R. G. Whyte
	G-TINA	SOCATA TB10 Tobago	A. Lister
	G-TING	Cameron O-120 balloon	Floating Sensations Ltd
	G-TINK	Robinson R22 Beta	Helicentre Liverpool Ltd
	G-TINS	Cameron N-90 balloon	J. R. Clifton
	G-TINT	Aerotechnik EV-97 Team Eurostar UK	I. A. Cunningham
	G-TINY	Z.526F Trener Master	D. Evans
	G-TIPS	Tipsy T.66 Nipper Srs 3	R. F. L. Cuypers/Belgium
	G-TIVS	Rans S.6-ES Coyote II	D. Kay
	G-TIVV	Aerotechnik EV-97 Team Eurostar UK	I. Shulver
	G-TJAL	Jabiru SPL-430	D. W. Cross
	G-TJAV	Mainair Pegasus Quik	B. Robertson
	G-TJAY	PA-22 Tri-Pacer 135	D. D. Saint
	G-TKAY	Shaw Europa	A. M. Kay
	G-TKGR	Lindstrand LBL Racing Car SS balloon	Brown & Williams Tobacco Corporation (Export) Ltd/USA
	G-TKIS	Tri-R Kis	T. J. Bone
	G-TKNT	Agusta A109A II	Clifford Kent Ltd
	G-TKPZ	Cessna 310R	Aircraft Engineers Ltd (G-BRAH)
	G-TLDK	PA-22 Tri-Pacer 150	A. M. Thomson
	G-TLEL	American Blimp Corp A.60+ airship	Lightship Europe Ltd
	G-TLET	PA-28-161 Cadet	ADR Aviation (G-GFCF/G-RHBH)
	G-TMCB	Best Off Skyranger 912 (2)	A. H. McBreen
	G-TMCC	Cameron N-90 balloon	Prudential Assurance Co Ltd
	G-TMKI	P56 Provost T.1 (WW453)	B. L. Robinson
	G-TMOL	SOCATA TB20 Trinidad	West Wales Airport Ltd
	G-TMRA	Short SD3-60 Variant 100	BAC Express Airlines Ltd (G-SSWC/G-BMHX)
	G-TMRB	Short SD3-60 Variant 100	BAC Express Airlines Ltd (G-SSWB/G-BMLE)
	G-TMRO	Short SD3-60 Variant 100	BAC Group Ltd (G-OBLK/G-BNDI)
	G-TMWC	Agusta A109E Power	A. Murtagh

BRITISH CIVIL REGISTRATIONS — G-TNRG – G-TROY

Reg	Type	Owner or Operator	Notes
G-TNRG	Tanarg/Ixess 15 912S(2)	C. M. Saysell	
G-TNTN	Thunder Ax6-56 balloon	H. M. Savage & J. F. Trehern	
G-TOAD	Jodel D.140B	J. H. Stevens	
G-TOAK	SOCATA TB20 Trinidad	Phoenix Group	
G-TOBA	SOCATA TB10 Tobago	E. Downing	
G-TOBI	Cessna F.172K	The Toby Flying Group (G-AYVB)	
G-TODD	ICA IS-28M2A	C. I. Roberts & C. D. King/Shobdon	
G-TODE	Ruschmeyer R.90-230RG	A. I. D. Rich	
G-TOFT	Colt 90A balloon	C. S. Perceval	
G-TOGO	Van's RV-6	I. R. Thomas	
G-TOHS	Cameron V-31 balloon	J. P. Moore	
G-TOIL	Enstrom 480B	Toughers Oil Distributors Ltd/Ireland	
G-TOLL	PA-28R-201 Arrow III	Plymouth School of Flying Ltd	
G-TOLY	Robinson R22 Beta	Helicopter Services Ltd (G-NSHR)	
G-TOMC	NA AT-6D Harvard III	A. A. Marshall/Bruntingthorpe	
G-TOMJ	Flight Design CT2K	P. T. Knight	
G-TOMM	Robinson R22 Beta	EBG (Helicopters) Ltd	
G-TOMS	PA-38-112 Tomahawk	G-TOMS Group	
G-TOMZ	Denney Kitfox Mk.2	E. B. Atalay	
G-TONN	Mainair Pegasus Quik	P. C. Bishop	
G-TONS	Slingsby T.67M-200	D. I. Stanbridge	
G-TOOL	Thunder Ax8-105 balloon	D. V. Howard	
G-TOOT	Dyn'Aéro MCR-01	S. W. Hosking	
G-TOPC	AS.355F1 Twin Squirrel	Bridge Street Nominees Ltd	
G-TOPK	Shaw Europa XS	P. J. Kember	
G-TOPO	PA-23-250 Turbo Aztec	Keen Leasing (IOM) Ltd (G-BGWW)	
G-TOPS	AS.355F1 Twin Squirrel	Sterling Helicopters (G-BPRH)	
G-TOPZ	Aérospatiale SA.342J Gazelle	Top Yachts Ltd	
G-TORC	PA-28R Cherokee Arrow 200	Haimoss Ltd	
G-TORE	P84 Jet Provost T.3A ★	Instructional airframe/City University, Islington	
G-TORK	Cameron Z-105 balloon	M. E. Dunstan-Sewell	
G-TORS	Robinson R22 Beta	IW Aviation Ltd	
G-TOSH	Robinson R22 Beta	JT Helicopters Ltd	
G-TOTN	Cessna 210M	K. Bettoney (G-BVZM)	
G-TOTO	Cessna F.177RG	Horizon Flyers Ltd (G-OADE/G-AZKH)	
G-TOUR	Robin R.2112	Mardenair Ltd	
G-TOWS	PA-25 Pawnee 260	Lasham Gliding Society Ltd	
G-TOYA	Boeing 737-3Q8	bmi Baby (G-BZZE)	
G-TOYB	Boeing 737-3Q8	bmi Baby (G-BZZF)	
G-TOYC	Boeing 737-3Q8	bmi Baby (G-BZZG)	
G-TOYD	Boeing 737-33V	bmi Baby (G-EZYT)	
G-TOYE	Boeing 737-33A	bmi Baby	
G-TOYF	Boeing 737-36N	bmi Baby (G-IGOO/G-SMDB)	
G-TOYG	Boeing 737-36N	bmi Baby (G-IGOJ)	
G-TOYH	Boeing 737-36N	bmi Baby (G-IGOY)	
G-TOYZ	Bell 206B JetRanger 3	Potter Aviation Ltd (G-RGER)	
G-TPSL	Cessna 182S	A. N. Purslow/Blackbushe	
G-TPWL	P & M Quik GT450	P. W. Lupton	
G-TRAC	Robinson R44	C. J. Sharples	
G-TRAM	Pegasus Quantum 15-912	I. W. Barlow	
G-TRAN	Beech 76 Duchess	Multiflight Ltd (G-NIFR)	
G-TRAT	Pilatus PC-12/45	D. J. Trathen	
G-TRAV	Cameron A-210 balloon	A. M. Holly	
G-TRAX	Cessna F.172M	Skytrax Aviation Ltd	
G-TRBO	Schleicher ASW-28-18E	C. J. Davison & A. Closkey	
G-TRCW	Robinson R44	Leus Aviation Ltd	
G-TRCY	Robinson R44	Sugarfree Air Ltd	
G-TREC	Cessna 421C	Sovereign Business Integration PLC (G-TLOL)	
G-TREE	Bell 206B JetRanger 3	Bush Woodlands	
G-TREK	Jodel D.18	R. H. Mole/Leicester	
G-TREX	Pioneer 300	R. K. King	
G-TRIB	Lindstrand HS-110 airship	J. Addison	
G-TRIC	DHC.1 Chipmunk 22 (18013:013)	A. A. Fernandez (G-AOSZ)	
G-TRIG	Cameron Z-90 balloon	Trigger Concepts Ltd	
G-TRIM	Monnett Moni	E. A. Brotherton-Ratcliffe	
G-TRIN	SOCATA TB20 Trinidad	Air Touring Ltd/Biggin Hill	
G-TRIO	Cessna 172M	C. M. B. Reid (G-BNXY)	
G-TRNT	Robinson R44 II	Charles Trent Ltd	
G-TROP	Cessna 310R II	D. E. Carpenter/Shoreham	
G-TROY	NA T-28A Fennec (51-7692)	S. G. Howell & S. Tilling	

G-TRUD – G-TYCN — BRITISH CIVIL REGISTRATIONS

Notes	Reg	Type	Owner or Operator
	G-TRUD	Enstrom 480	Sussex Aviation Ltd
	G-TRUE	MDH Hughes 369E	N. E. Bailey
	G-TRUK	Stoddard-Hamilton Glasair RG	M. P. Jackson
	G-TRUX	Colt 77A balloon	J. B. R. Elliot
	G-TRYK	Kiss 400-582 (1)	S. Elsbury & S. van Straten
	G-TRYX	Enstrom 480B	Atryx Aviation LLP
	G-TSDS	PA-32R-301 Saratoga SP	I. R. Jones (G-TRIP/G-HOSK)
	G-TSGJ	PA-28-181 Archer II	Golf Juliet Flying Club
	G-TSIX	AT-6C Harvard IIA (111836:JZ-6)	S. J. Davies
	G-TSKD	Raj Hamsa X'Air Jabiru J.2.2.	T. Sexton & K. B. Dupuy
	G-TSKY	Beagle B.121 Pup 2	R. G. Hayes (G-AWDY)
	G-TSLC	Schweizer 269C-1	TSL Contractors Ltd
	G-TSOB	Rans S.6-ES Coyote II	S. Luck
	G-TSOL	EAA Acrosport 1	A. G. Fowles (G-BPKI)
	G-TSUE	Shaw Europa	A. L. & S. Thorne
	G-TTDD	Zenair CH.701 STOL	D. B. Dainton & V. D. Asque
	G-TTHC	Robinson R22 Beta	Multiflight Ltd/Leeds-Bradford
	G-TTIA	Airbus A.321-231	GB Airways Ltd
	G-TTIB	Airbus A.321-231	GB Airways Ltd
	G-TTIC	Airbus A.321-231	GB Airways Ltd
	G-TTID	Airbus A.321-231	GB Airways Ltd
	G-TTIE	Airbus A.321-231	GB Airways Ltd
	G-TTMB	Bell 206B JetRanger 3	Sky Charter UK Ltd (G-RNME/G-CBDF)
	G-TTOA	Airbus A.320-232	GB Airways Ltd
	G-TTOB	Airbus A.320-232	GB Airways Ltd
	G-TTOC	Airbus A.320-232	GB Airways Ltd
	G-TTOD	Airbus A.320-232	GB Airways Ltd
	G-TTOE	Airbus A.320-232	GB Airways Ltd
	G-TTOF	Airbus A.320-232	GB Airways Ltd
	G-TTOG	Airbus A.320-232	GB Airways Ltd
	G-TTOH	Airbus A.320-232	GB Airways Ltd
	G-TTOI	Airbus A.320-232	GB Airways Ltd
	G-TTOJ	Airbus A.320-232	GB Airways Ltd
	G-TTOY	CFM Streak Shadow SA	J. Softley
	G-TUBB	Avtech Jabiru UL	A. H. Bower
	G-TUCK	Van's RV-8	M. A. Tuck
	G-TUDR	Cameron V-77 balloon	J. W. Soukup
	G-TUGG	PA-18 Super Cub 150	Ulster Gliding Club Ltd/Bellarena
	G-TUGS	PA-25-235 Pawnee D	J. A. Stephen (G-BFEW)
	G-TUGY	Robin DR.400/180	Buckminster Gliding Club/Saltby
	G-TULP	Lindstrand LBL Tulips SS balloon	Oxford Promotions (UK) Ltd
	G-TUNE	Robinson R22 Beta	HR Helicopters (G-OJVI)
	G-TURF	Cessna F.406	Atlantic Air Transport Ltd/Coventry
	G-TURN	Steen Skybolt	N. M. Forsberg
	G-TUSA	Pegasus Quantum 15-912	N. J. Holt
	G-TUTU	Cameron O-105 balloon	A. C. K. Rawson & J. J. Rudoni
	G-TVAM	MBB Bo105DBS-4	Bond Air Services Ltd (G-SPOL)
	G-TVBF	Lindstrand LBL-310A balloon	Virgin Balloons Flights
	G-TVCO	Gippsland GA-8 Airvan	Zyox Ltd
	G-TVEE	Hughes 369HS	M. Webb
	G-TVII	Hawker Hunter T.7 (XX467:86)	G-TVII Group/Exeter
	G-TVIJ	CCF Harvard IV (T-6J) (28521:TA-521)	R. W. Davies (G-BSBE)
	G-TVIP	Cessna 404	Capital Trading (Aviation) Ltd (G-KIWI/G-BHNI)
	G-TVTV	Cameron 90 TV SS balloon	J. Krebs/Germany
	G-TWEL	PA-28-181 Archer II	International Aerospace Engineering Ltd
	G-TWEY	Colt 69A balloon	N. Bland
	G-TWIN	PA-44-180 Seminole	Bonus Aviation Ltd/Cranfield
	G-TWIZ	Rockwell Commander 114	B. C. & P. M. Cox
	G-TWOC	Schempp-Hirth Ventus 2cT	D. Heslop
	G-TWOT	Schempp-Hirth Discus 2T	S. G. Lapworth
	G-TWSR	Silence Twister	J. A. Hallam
	G-TWST	Silence Twister	Zulu Glasstek Ltd
	G-TWTW	Denney Kitfox Mk.2	T. Willford
	G-TXSE	RAF 2000 GTX-SE gyroplane	A. Levitt
	G-TYAK	IDA Bacau Yakovlev Yak-52	S. J. Ducker
	G-TYCN	Agusta A109E Power	A. J. Walter (Aviation) Ltd (G-VMCO)

BRITISH CIVIL REGISTRATIONS G-TYER – G-UPFS

Reg	Type	Owner or Operator	Notes
G-TYER	Robin DR.400/500	Chartfleet Ltd	
G-TYGA	AA-5B Tiger	D. H. & R. J. Carman (G-BHNZ)	
G-TYGR	Best Off Skyranger 912S (1)	M. J. Poole	
G-TYKE	Avtech Jabiru UL-450	J. Rochead & R. Rhodes	
G-TYNE	SOCATA TB20 Trinidad	N. V. Price	
G-TYRE	Cessna F.172M	S. C. Moss	
G-TZEE	SOCATA TB10 Tobago	Zytech Ltd	
G-TZII	Thorp T.211B	AD Aviation Ltd/Barton	
G-UACA	Skyranger R.100	R. G. Openshaw	
G-UAKE	NA P-51D-5-NA Mustang	P. S. Warner	
G-UANO	DHC.1 Chipmunk 20	Gooney Bird Group (G-BYYW)	
G-UANT	PA-28 Cherokee 140	Air Navigation & Trading Co Ltd/Blackpool	
G-UAPA	Robin DR.400/140B	Carlos Saraive Lda/Portugal	
G-UAPO	Ruschmeyer R.90-230RG	P. Randall	
G-UAVA	PA-30 Twin Comanche	Small World Aviation Ltd	
G-UCCC	Cameron 90 Sign SS balloon	B. Conway	
G-UDGE	Thruster T.600N	G-UDGE Syndicate (G-BYPI)	
G-UDOG	SA Bulldog Srs 120/121 (XX518:S)	Gamit Ltd	
G-UFAW	Raj Hamsa X'Air 582 (5)	P. Batchelor	
G-UFCB	Cessna 172S	The Cambridge Aero Club Ltd	
G-UFCC	Cessna 172S	Oxford Aviation Services Ltd	
G-UFCD	Cessna 172S	Iolar Ltd/Kidlington (G-OYZK)	
G-UFCG	Cessna 172S	Ulster Flying Club (1961) Ltd	
G-UFCH	Cessna 172S	Ulster Flying Club (1961) Ltd	
G-UFLY	Cessna F.150H	Westair Flying Services Ltd/Blackpool (G-AVVY)	
G-UGLY	SE.313B Alouette II	Helicopter Services (G-BSFN)	
G-UHIH	Bell UH-1H Iroquois (21509)	MSS Holdings Ltd	
G-UILD	Grob G.109B	M. H. Player	
G-UILE	Lancair 320	R. J. Martin	
G-UILT	Cessna T.303	Rock Seat Ltd (G-EDRY)	
G-UINN	Stolp SA.300 Starduster Too	J. D. H. Gordon	
G-UIST	BAe Jetstream 3102	Highland Airways Ltd	
G-UJAB	Avtech Jabiru UL	C. A. Thomas	
G-UJGK	Avtech Jabiru UL	W. G. Upton & J. G. Kosak	
G-UKAT	Aero AT-3	G-UKAT Group	
G-UKOZ	Avtech Jabiru SK	D. J. Burnett	
G-UKRB	Colt 105A balloon	Virgin Airship & Balloon Co Ltd	
G-UKUK	Head Ax8-105 balloon	P. A. George	
G-ULAS	DHC.1 Chipmunk 22 (WK517)	ULAS Flying Club Ltd/Denham	
G-ULES	AS.355F2 Twin Squirrel	Select Plant Hire Company Ltd (G-OBHL/G-HARO/G-DAFT/G-BNNN)	
G-ULHI	SA Bulldog Srs.100/101	Power Aerobatics Ltd (G-OPOD/G-AZMS)	
G-ULIA	Cameron V-77 balloon	J. M. Dean	
G-ULLY	Thruster T600N VW	The Swallow 2 Group (G-CCRP)	
G-ULPS	Everett Srs 1 gyroplane	C. J. Watkinson (G-BMNY)	
G-ULSY	Ikarus C.42 FB 80	Ikarus 1 Flying Group	
G-ULTR	Cameron A-105 balloon	P. Glydon	
G-UMBO	Thunder Ax7-77A balloon	Virgin Airship & Balloon Co Ltd	
G-UMMI	PA-31-310 Turbo Navajo	Messrs Rees of Poynston West (G-BGSO)	
G-UMMY	Best Off Skyranger J2.2(2)	A. R. Williams	
G-UNDD	PA-23 Aztec 250E	G. J. & D. P. Deadman (G-BATX)	
G-UNER	Lindstrand LBL-90A balloon	St. Dunstans	
G-UNGE	Lindstrand LBL-90A balloon	Silver Ghost Balloon Club (G-BVPJ)	
G-UNGO	Pietenpol Air Camper	A. R. Wyatt	
G-UNIV	Montgomerie-Parsons 2-seat gyroplane	University of Glasgow (G-BWTP)	
G-UNIX	VPM M16 Tandem Trainer	A. P. Wilkinson	
G-UNRL	Lindstrand LBL-21A balloon	Virgin Balloon & Airship Co Ltd	
G-UNYT	Robinson R22 Beta	D. I. Pointon (G-BWZV/G-LIAN)	
G-UORO	Shaw Europa	D. Dufton	
G-UPFS	Waco UPS-7	D. N. Peters & N. R. Finlayson	

G-UPHI – G-VCIO | BRITISH CIVIL REGISTRATIONS

Notes	Reg	Type	Owner or Operator
	G-UPHI	Best Off Skyranger Swift 912S(1)	Flylight Airsports Ltd
	G-UPHL	Cameron 80 Concept SS balloon	Uphill Motor Co
	G-UPPP	Colt 77A balloon	D. Michel/France
	G-UPPY	Cameron DP-80 HA Airship	J. W. Soukup
	G-UPTA	Skyranger 912S (1)	P. E. Tait
	G-UPUP	Cameron V-77 balloon	S. F. Burden/Netherlands
	G-UPUZ	Lindstrand LBL-120A balloon	C.J. Sanger-Davies
	G-UROP	Beech 95-B55 Baron	Pooler International Ltd/Sleap
	G-URRR	Air Command 582 Sport	L. Armes
	G-URUH	Robinson R44	Heli Air Ltd/Wellesbourne
	G-URUS	Maule MX7-180B Super Rocket	Broomco Ltd
	G-USAM	Cameron Uncle Sam SS balloon	Corn Palace Balloon Club Ltd
	G-USIL	Thunder Ax7-77 balloon	Window On The World Ltd
	G-USKE	Aviat A-1B Husky	Aviat Aircraft (UK) Ltd
	G-USKY	Aviat A-1B Husky	B. Walker and Co (Dursley) Ltd
	G-USMC	Cameron Chestie-90 balloon	J. W. Soukup
	G-USRV	Van's RV-6	D. S. Watt
	G-USSI	Stoddard-Hamilton Glasair III	Lord Rotherwick
	G-USSR	Cameron 90 Doll SS balloon	Corn Palace Balloon Club Ltd
	G-USSY	PA-28-181 Archer II	Western Air (Thruxton) Ltd
	G-USTB	Agusta A109A	Newton Aviation Ltd
	G-USTH	Agusta A109A-II	Cheqair Ltd
	G-USTS	Agusta A109A-II	MB Air Ltd (G-MKSF)
	G-USTY	FRED Srs 2	R. G. Hallam
	G-UTSI	Rand-Robinson KR-2	K. B. Gutridge/Thruxton
	G-UTSY	PA-28R-201 Arrow III	Arrow Aviation Ltd
	G-UTTS	Robinson R44	Heli Hire Ltd (G-ROAP)
	G-UTZI	Robinson R44 II	S. K. Miles/Spain
	G-UURO	Aerotechnik EV-97 Eurostar	E. M. Middleton
	G-UVBF	Lindstrand LBL-400A balloon	Virgin Balloon Flights
	G-UVIP	Cessna 421C	Capital Trading Aviation/Filton (G-BSKH)
	G-UVNR	BAC.167 Strikemaster Mk 87	Global Aviation Services Ltd (G-BXFS)
	G-UZEL	Aérospatiale SA.341G Gazelle 1	Fairalls of Godstone Ltd (G-BRNH)
	G-UZLE	Colt 77A balloon	Flying Pictures Ltd
	G-UZUP	Aerotechnik EV-97A Eurostar	S. A. Woodhams
	G-UZZL	Van's RV-7	P. Chaplin
	G-UZZY	Enstrom 480	Shoreham Helicopters (G-BWMD)
	G-VAIR	Airbus A.340-313	Virgin Atlantic Airways Ltd *Maiden Tokyo*
	G-VALS	Pietenpol Air Camper	J. R. D. Bygraves
	G-VALV	Robinson R44	Valve Train Components
	G-VALY	SOCATA TB21 Trinidad GT Turbo	R. J. Thwaites and Westflight Aviation Ltd
	G-VALZ	Cameron N-120 balloon	D. Ling
	G-VANA	Gippsland GA-8 Airvan	P. Marsden
	G-VANC	Gippsland GA-8 Airvan	IAE Ltd
	G-VANN	Van's RV-7A	D. N. & J. A. Carnegie
	G-VANS	Van's RV-4	M. Swanborough & D. Jones
	G-VANZ	Van's RV-6A	S. J. Baxter
	G-VARG	Varga 2150A Kachina	J. Denton
	G-VART	Rotorway Executive 90	I. R. Brown & K. E. Parker (G-BSUR)
	G-VASA	PA-34-200	H. Hafez
	G-VAST	Boeing 747-41R	Virgin Atlantic Airways Ltd *Ladybird*
	G-VATL	Airbus A.340-642	Virgin Atlantic Airways Ltd *Miss Kitty*
	G-VBFA	Ultramagic N-250 balloon	Virgin Balloon Flights
	G-VBFB	Ultramagic N-355 balloon	Virgin Balloon Flights
	G-VBFC	Ultramagic N-250 balloon	Virgin Balloon Flights
	G-VBFD	Ultramagic N-250 balloon	Virgin Balloon Flights
	G-VBFE	Ultramagic N-255 balloon	Virgin Balloon Flights
	G-VBFF	Lindstrand LBL-360A balloon	Virgin Balloon Flights
	G-VBIG	Boeing 747-4Q8	Virgin Atlantic Airways Ltd *Tinker Belle*
	G-VBLU	Airbus A.340-642	Virgin Atlantic Airways Ltd *Soul Sister*
	G-VBUG	Airbus A.340-642	Virgin Atlantic Airways Ltd
	G-VBUS	Airbus A.340-311	Virgin Atlantic Airways Ltd *Lady in Red*
	G-VCED	Airbus A.320-231	MyTravel Airways
	G-VCIO	EAA Acro Sport II	V. Millard & A. Barlow

BRITISH CIVIL REGISTRATIONS — G-VCML – G-VILA

Reg	Type	Owner or Operator	Notes
G-VCML	Beech 58 Baron	St. Angelo Aviation Ltd	
G-VCXT	Schempp-Hirth Ventus 2cT	R. F. Aldous/Germany	
G-VDIR	Cessna T.310R	J. Driver	
G-VDOG	Cessna 305C Bird Dog	J. W. Salter & E. P. Morrow	
G-VECD	Robin R.1180T	B. Lee	
G-VECE	Robin R.2120U	Mistral Aviation Ltd	
G-VECG	Robin R.2160	Mistral Aviation Ltd	
G-VEGA	Slingsby T.65A Vega	R. A. Rice (G-BFZN)	
G-VEIL	Airbus A.340-642	Virgin Atlantic Airways Ltd *Queen of the Skies*	
G-VEIT	Robinson R44 II	Field Marshall Helicopters Ltd	
G-VELA	SIAI-Marchetti S.205-22R	Broadland Flyers Ltd	
G-VELD	Airbus A.340-313	Virgin Atlantic Airways Ltd *African Queen*	
G-VENI	DH.112 Venom FB.50 (VV612)	Lindsay Wood Promotions Ltd/Bournemouth	
G-VENM	DH.112 Venom FB.50 (WK436)	Kennet Aviation (stored)/Yeovilton (G-BLIE)	
G-VENT	Schempp-Hirth Ventus 2CM	S. G. Jones	
G-VERA	Gardan GY-201 Minicab	D. K. Shipton	
G-VERN	PA-32R-300 Cherokee Lance	D. J. Whitcombe (G-BVBG)	
G-VETA	Hawker Hunter T7	Skyblue Aviation Ltd (G-BVWN)	/WARRINGTON
G-VETS	Enstrom 280C-UK Shark	A. J. Warburton/Barton (G-FSDC/G-BKTG)	
G-VEYE	Robinson R22	RK Transport Services Ltd (G-BPTP)	
G-VEZE	Rutan Vari-Eze	S. D. Brown & ptnrs	
G-VFAB	Boeing 747-4Q8	Virgin Atlantic Airways Ltd *Lady Penelope*	
G-VFAR	Airbus A.340-313	Virgin Atlantic Airways Ltd *Diana*	
G-VFIT	Airbus A.340-642	Virgin Atlantic Airways Ltd *Dancing Queen*	
G-VFIZ	Airbus A.340-642	Virgin Atlantic Airways Ltd *Bubbles*	
G-VFOX	Airbus A.340-642	Virgin Atlantic Airways Ltd *Silver Lady*	
G-VGAG	Cirrus SR20 GTS	Alfred Graham Ltd	
G-VGAL	Boeing 747-443	Virgin Atlantic Airways Ltd *Jersey Girl*	
G-VGAS	Airbus A.340-542	Virgin Atlantic Airways Ltd *Varga Girl*	
G-VGMC	Eurocopter AS.355N Twin Squirrel	Eassda Aviation (G-HEMH)	
G-VGOA	Airbus A.340-642	Virgin Atlantic Airways Ltd *Indian Princess*	
G-VHOL	Airbus A.340-311	Virgin Atlantic Airways Ltd *Jetstreamer*	
G-VHOT	Boeing 747-4Q8	Virgin Atlantic Airways Ltd *Tubular Belle*	
G-VIBA	Cameron DP-80 HA Airship	J. W. Soukup	
G-VICC	PA-28-161 Warrior II	Charlie Charlie Syndicate (G-JFHL)	
G-VICE	MDH Hughes 369E	M. W. A. Dunn	
G-VICI	DH.112 Venom FB.50 (J-1573)	Lindsay Wood Promotions Ltd/Bournemouth	
G-VICM	Beech F33C Bonanza	Velocity Engineering Ltd	
G-VICS	Commander 114B	Millennium Aviation Ltd	
G-VICT	PA-31-310 Turbo Navajo	Direct Air Ltd (G-BBZI)	
G-VIEW	Vinten-Wallis WA-116/100	K. H. Wallis	
G-VIIA	Boeing 777-236	British Airways	
G-VIIB	Boeing 777-236	British Airways	
G-VIIC	Boeing 777-236	British Airways	
G-VIID	Boeing 777-236	British Airways	
G-VIIE	Boeing 777-236	British Airways	
G-VIIF	Boeing 777-236	British Airways	
G-VIIG	Boeing 777-236	British Airways	
G-VIIH	Boeing 777-236	British Airways	
G-VIIJ	Boeing 777-236	British Airways	
G-VIIK	Boeing 777-236	British Airways	
G-VIIL	Boeing 777-236	British Airways	
G-VIIM	Boeing 777-236	British Airways	
G-VIIN	Boeing 777-236	British Airways	
G-VIIO	Boeing 777-236	British Airways	
G-VIIP	Boeing 777-236	British Airways	
G-VIIR	Boeing 777-236	British Airways	
G-VIIS	Boeing 777-236	British Airways	
G-VIIT	Boeing 777-236	British Airways	
G-VIIU	Boeing 777-236	British Airways	
G-VIIV	Boeing 777-236	British Airways	
G-VIIW	Boeing 777-236	British Airways	
G-VIIX	Boeing 777-236	British Airways	
G-VIIY	Boeing 777-236	British Airways	
G-VIKE	Bellanca 1730A Viking	W. G. Prout	
G-VIKY	Cameron A-120 balloon	P. J. Stanley	
G-VILA	Avtech Jabiru UL	R. W. Sage & T. R. Villa (G-BYIF)	

G-VILL – G-VPSI — BRITISH CIVIL REGISTRATIONS

Notes	Reg	Type	Owner or Operator
	G-VILL	Lazer Z.200 (modified)	J. Owczarek (G-BOYZ)
	G-VINH	Flight Design CTSW	Aardbus Ltd
	G-VINO	Sky 90-24 balloon	Fivedata Ltd
	G-VIPA	Cessna 182S	Stallingborough Aviation Ltd
	G-VIPH	Agusta A109C	Cheqair Ltd (G-BVNH/G-LAXO)
	G-VIPI	BAe 125 Srs 800B	Yeates of Leicester Ltd
	G-VIPP	PA-31-350 Navajo Chieftain	Capital Trading Aviation/Filton (G-OGRV/G-BMPX)
	G-VIPR	Eurocopter EC 120B Colibri	Amey Aviation LLP
	G-VIPY	PA-31-350 Navajo Chieftain	Capital Trading Aviation/Filton (G-POLO)
	G-VIPZ	Sikorsky S-61N	Veritair Ltd (G-DAWS/G-LAWS/G-BHOF)
	G-VITE	Robin R.1180T	G-VITE Flying Group
	G-VITL	Lindstrand LBL-105A balloon	Vital Resources
	G-VIVA	Thunder Ax7-65 balloon	R. J. Mitchener
	G-VIVI	Taylor JT.2 Titch	D. G. Tucker
	G-VIVM	P.84 Jet Provost T.5	The Skys The Ltd/North Weald (G-BVWF)
	G-VIVO	Nicollier HN700 Menestrel II	D. G. Tucker
	G-VIVS	PA-28-151 Cherokee Warrior	S. J. Harrison & V. A. Donnelly
	G-VIXN	DH.110 Sea Vixen FAW.2 (XS587) ★	P. G. Vallance Ltd/Charlwood
	G-VIZA	LBL-260A balloon	A. Nimmo
	G-VIZZ	Sportavia RS.180 Sportsman	Exeter Fournier Group
	G-VJAB	Avtech Jabiru UL	A. S. R. Milner
	G-VJET	Avro 698 Vulcan B.2 (XL426) ★	Vulcan Restoration Trust/Southend
	G-VJIM	Colt 77 Jumbo Jim SS balloon	Magical Adventures Ltd/USA
	G-VKIT	Shaw Europa	T. H. Crow
	G-VKNA	Boeing 757-2Y0ER	XL Airways UK Ltd (G-OOOU)
	G-VKND	Boeing 757-225	XL Airways UK Ltd (G-OOOM)
	G-VKNG	Boeing 767-3Z9ER	XL Airways UK Ltd
	G-VKNH	Boeing 767-3YOER	XL Airways UK Ltd
	G-VKNI	Boeing 767-383ER	XL Airways UK Ltd
	G-VKUP	Cameron Z-90 balloon	Global Brands Ltd
	G-VKVK	Eurocopter AS.350B3 Ecureuil	GBL Aviation LLP (G-XMEN/G-ZWRC)
	G-VLCN	Avro 698 Vulcan B.2 (XH558) ★	Vulcan to the Sky Trust/Bruntingthorpe
CLARE FROM AMERICA	G-VLIP	Boeing 747-443	Virgin Atlantic Airways Ltd *Hot Lips*
	G-VMCG	PA-38-112 Tomahawk	D. F. Brenchley (G-BSVX)
	G-VMDE	Cessna P210N	P. L. Goldberg
	G-VMEG	Airbus A.340-642	Virgin Atlantic Airways Ltd *Mystic Maiden*
	G-VMFC	Piper PA-32R-301	The Van Meeuwen Flying Club Ltd
	G-VMJM	SOCATA TB10 Tobago	S. C. Brown (G-BTOK)
	G-VMSL	Robinson R22A	L. L. F. Smith (G-KILY)
	G-VNOM	DH.112 Venom FB.50 (J-1632) ★	de Havilland Heritage Museum/London Colney
	G-VNON	Escapade Jabiru (3)	P. A. Vernon
	G-VNUS	Hughes 269C	Enable international Ltd (G-BATT)
	G-VOAR	PA-28-181 Archer III	Solent Flight Ltd
	G-VODA	Cameron N-77 balloon	Racal Telecom PLC
	G-VOGE	Airbus A.340-642	Virgin Atlantic Airways Ltd *Cover Maiden*
	G-VOID	PA-28RT-201 Arrow IV	B. R. Green
	G-VOIP	Westland SA.341G Gazelle	Q. Milne (G-HOBZ/G-CBSJ)
	G-VOLO	Alpi Pioneer 300	J. Buglass
	G-VONA	Sikorsky S-76A	Von Essen Aviation Ltd (G-BUXB)
	G-VONB	Sikorsky S-76B	Von Essen Aviation Ltd (G-POAH)
	G-VONC	Sikorsky S-76B	Von Essen Aviation Ltd
	G-VOND	Bell 222	Von Essen Aviation Ltd (G-OWCG/G-VERT/G-JLBZ/G-BNGB)
	G-VONE	Eurocopter AS355N Twin Squirrel	Von Essen Aviation Ltd (G-LCON)
	G-VONF	AS.355F1 Twin Squirrel	Von Essen Aviation Ltd (G-TMMC/G-JLCO/G-BXBT)
	G-VONG	AS.355F1 Twin Squirrel	Von Essen Aviation Ltd (G-OILX/G-RMGN/G-BMCY)
	G-VONH	AS.355F1 Twin Squirrel	Von Essen Aviation Ltd (G-BKUL/G-FFHI/G-GWHH)
	G-VONJ	Raytheon 390 Premier 1	Von Essen Aviation Ltd
	G-VONK	AS.355F1 Squirrel	Von Essen Aviation Ltd (G-BLRI/G-NUTZ)
	G-VONS	PA-32R-301T Saratoga IITC	W. S. Stanley
	G-VOOM	Pitts S-1S Special	P. G. Roberts
	G-VPAT	Evans VP-1 Srs 2	A. P. Twort
	G-VPSI	Cameron Z-1600 balloon	JK (England) Ltd

BRITISH CIVIL REGISTRATIONS

G-VPSJ – G-WAIR

Reg	Type	Owner or Operator	Notes
G-VPSJ	Shaw Europa	J. D. Bean	
G-VRED	Airbus A.340-642	Virgin Atlantic Airways Ltd *Scarlet Lady*	
G-VROC	Boeing 747-41R	Virgin Atlantic Airways Ltd *Mustang Sally*	
G-VROD	Aeroprakt A.22 Foxbat	C. S. Bourne & G. P. Wiley	
G-VROE	Avro 652A Anson T.21 (WD413)	Air Atlantique Ltd/Coventry (G-BFIR)	
G-VROM	Boeing 747-443	Virgin Atlantic Airways Ltd *Barbarella*	
G-VROS	Boeing 747-443	Virgin Atlantic Airways Ltd *English Rose*	
G-VROY	Boeing 747-443	Virgin Atlantic Airways Ltd *Pretty Woman*	
G-VRST	PA-46-350P Malibu Mirage	Avialec International Ltd	
G-VRTX	Enstrom 280FX	Bladerunner Aviation Ltd/Barton (G-CBNH)	
G-VRVI	Cameron O-90 balloon	SNT Property Ltd	
G-VSEA	Airbus A.340-311	Virgin Atlantic Airways Ltd *Plane Sailing*	
G-VSGE	Cameron O-105 balloon	G. Aimo (G-BSSD)	
G-VSHY	Airbus A.340-642	Virgin Atlantic Airways Ltd *Madam Butterfly*	
G-VSSH	Airbus A.340-642	Virgin Atlantic Airways Ltd *Sweet Dreamer*	
G-VSUN	Airbus A.340-313	Virgin Atlantic Airways Ltd *Rainbow Lady*	
G-VTAL	Beech V35 Bonanza	R. Chamberlain	
G-VTII	DH.115 Vampire T.11 (XX507:74)	Vampire Preservation Group, Bournemouth	
G-VTOL	Hawker Siddeley Harrier T.52 ★	Brooklands Museum of Aviation/Weybridge	
G-VTOP	Boeing 747-4Q8	Virgin Atlantic Airways Ltd *Virginia Plain*	
G-VTWO	Schempp-Hirth Ventus 2c	F. & B. Birlison	
G-VUEA	Cessna 550 Citation II	AD Aviation Ltd (G-BWOM)	
G-VUEM	Cessna 501 Citation I	Frandley Aviation Partnership LLP (G-FLVU)	
G-VUEZ	Cessna 550 Citation II	AD Aviation Ltd	
G-VULC	Avro 698 Vulcan B.2A (XM655) ★	Radarmoor Ltd/Wellesbourne	
G-VVBF	Colt 315A balloon	Virgin Balloon Flights	
G-VVBK	PA-34-200T Seneca II	Ravenair Aircraft Ltd/Liverpool (G-BSBS/G-BDRI)	
G-VVIP	Cessna 421C	My Sky Air Charter Ltd (G-BMWB)	
G-VVTV	Diamond DA42 Twin Star	A. D. R. Northeast & S. A. Cook	
G-VVVV	Skyranger 912 (2)	J. Thomas	
G-VVWW	Enstrom 280C Shark	P. J. Odendaal	
G-VWEB	Airbus A.340-642	Virgin Atlantic Airways Ltd *Surfer Girl*	
G-VWIN	Airbus A.340-642	Virgin Atlantic Airways Ltd *Lady Luck*	
G-VWKD	Airbus A.340-642	Virgin Atlantic Airways Ltd *Miss Behavin'*	
G-VWOW	Boeing 747-41R	Virgin Atlantic Airways Ltd *Cosmic Girl*	
G-VXLG	Boeing 747-41R	Virgin Atlantic Airways Ltd *Ruby Tuesday*	
G-VYGR	Colt 120A balloon	A. van Wyk	
G-VYOU	Airbus A.340-642	Virgin Atlantic Airways Ltd *Emmeline Heaney*	
G-WAAC	Cameron N-56 balloon	N. P. Hemsley	
G-WAAN	MBB Bö.105DB	PLM Dollar Group Ltd (G-AZOR)	
G-WAAS	MBB Bö.105DBS-4	Bond Air Services Ltd (G-ESAM/G-BUIB/G-BDYZ)	
G-WABH	Cessna 172S Skyhawk	Blackhawk Aviation Ltd	
G-WACB	Cessna F.152 II	Wycombe Air Centre Ltd	
G-WACE	Cessna F.152 II	Wycombe Air Centre Ltd	
G-WACF	Cessna 152 II	Wycombe Air Centre Ltd	
G-WACG	Cessna 152 II	Wycombe Air Centre Ltd	
G-WACH	Cessna FA.152 II	Wycombe Air Centre Ltd	
G-WACI	Beech 76 Duchess	Wycombe Air Centre Ltd	
G-WACJ	Beech 76 Duchess	Wycombe Air Centre Ltd	
G-WACL	Cessna F.172N	A. G. Arthur (G-BHGG)	
G-WACO	Waco UPF-7	R. F. L. Cuypers/Belgium	
G-WACT	Cessna F.152 II	L. A. Flisher (G-BKFT)	
G-WACU	Cessna FA.152	Wycombe Air Centre Ltd (G-BJZU)	
G-WACW	Cessna 172P	The Exeter Flying Club Ltd	
G-WACY	Cessna F.172P	Wycombe Air Centre Ltd	
G-WADI	PA-46-350P Malibu Mirage	Air Malibu AG/Liechtenstein	
G-WADS	Robinson R22 Beta	Whizzard Helicopters (G-NICO)	
G-WAFU	Robinson R44	Midland Crane Hire	
G-WAGG	Robinson R22 Beta II	N. J. Wagstaff Leasing	
G-WAGN	Stinson 108-3 Voyager	S. E. H. Ellcome	
G-WAGS	Robinson R44 II	Wagstaff Homes Ltd	
G-WAHL	QAC Quickie	A. A. A. Wahlberg	
G-WAIN	Cessna 550 Citation Bravo	Ferron Trading Ltd	
G-WAIR	PA-32-301 Saratoga	Finningley Aviation	

G-WAIT – G-WGHB — BRITISH CIVIL REGISTRATIONS

Notes	Reg	Type	Owner or Operator
	G-WAIT	Cameron V-77 balloon	C. P. Brown
	G-WAKE	Mainair Blade 912	B. W. Webster
	G-WAKY	Cyclone AX2000	Cyclone Airsports Ltd
	G-WALI	Robinson R44 II	Casdron Enterprises Ltd
	G-WALY	Maule MX-7-180	A. J. West
	G-WAMS	PA-28R-201 Arrow	Stapleford Flying Club Ltd
	G-WARA	PA-28-161 Warrior III	Aviation Rentals
	G-WARB	PA-28-161 Warrior III	Muller Aircraft Leasing Ltd
	G-WARD	Taylor JT.1 Monoplane	R. P. J. Hunter
	G-WARE	PA-28-161 Warrior II	W. B. Ware/Filton
	G-WARH	PA-28-161 Warrior III	Central Aircraft Leasing Ltd
	G-WARK	Schweizer 269C	AB Erection Ltd
	G-WARO	PA-28-161 Warrior III	Aviation Rentals
	G-WARP	Cessna 182F Sylane	R. D. Fowden (G-ASHB)
	G-WARR	PA-28-161 Warrior II	T. J. & G. M. Laundy
	G-WARS	PA-28-161 Warrior III	Blaneby Ltd
	G-WARU	PA-28-161 Warrior III	Aviation Rentals
	G-WARV	PA-28-161 Warrior III	Plane Talking Ltd/Elstree
	G-WARW	PA-28-161 Warrior III	Lomac Aviators Ltd
	G-WARX	PA-28-161 Warrior III	C. M. A. Clark
	G-WARY	PA-28-161 Warrior III	Transport Command Ltd
	G-WARZ	PA-28-161 Warrior III	Aviation Rentals/Bournemouth
	G-WATR	Christen A1 Husky	S. N. Gregory
	G-WATV	Robinson R44 II	Heli Air Ltd
	G-WAVA	Robin HR.200/120B	Wellesbourne Aviation
	G-WAVE	Grob G.109B	C. G. Wray
	G-WAVI	Robin HR.200/120B	Wellesbourne Flyers Ltd (G-BZDG)
	G-WAVN	Robin HR.200/120B	Wellesbourne Flyers Ltd (G-VECA)
	G-WAVS	PA-28-161 Warrior III	Wellesbourne Flyers Ltd (G-WARC)
	G-WAVT	Robin R.2160i	Wellesbourne Flyers Ltd (G-CBLG)
	G-WAVV	Robon HR200/120B	Wellesbourne Flyers Ltd (G-GORF)
	G-WAVY	Grob G.109B	G-WAVY Group
	G-WAZP	Skyranger 912 (2)	L. V. McClune
	G-WAZZ	Pitts S-1S Special	D. T. Knight (G-BRRP)
	G-WBAT	Wombat gyroplane	M. R. Harrisson (G-BSID)
	G-WBEV	Cameron N-77 balloon	T. J. & M. Turner (G-PVCU)
	G-WBLY	Mainair Pegasus Quik	A. J. Lindsey
	G-WBMG	Cameron N Ele-90 SS balloon	P. H. E. van Overwalle/Belgium (G-BUYV)
	G-WBTS	Falconar F-11	W. C. Brown (G-BDPL)
	G-WBVS	Diamond DA.4D Star	G. W. Beavis
	G-WCAO	Eurocopter EC 135T2	Avon & Somerset Constabulary & Gloucestershire Constabulary
	G-WCAT	Colt Flying Mitt SS balloon	Balloon Preservation Flying Group
	G-WCCP	Beech B200 Super King Air	William Cook Aviation Ltd
	G-WCEI	MS.894E Rallye 220GT	R. A. L. Lucas (G-BAOC)
	G-WCIN	Cessna 560XL Citation Excel	TAG aviation (UK) Ltd
	G-WCRD	Aérospatiale SA.341G Gazelle	Wickford Development Co Ltd
	G-WCUB	PA-18 Super Cub 150	P. A. Walley
	G-WDEB	Thunder Ax-7-77 balloon	A. Heginbottom
	G-WDEV	Westland SA.341G Gazelle 1	Mentorvale Construction Ltd/Ireland (G-IZEL/G-BBHW)
	G-WEBS	American Champion 7ECA Citabria Aurora	P. J. Webb
	G-WEEK	Skyranger 912(2)	D. J. Prothero
	G-WEGO	Robinson R44 II	A and E Fire Equipment Ltd
	G-WELI	Cameron N-77 balloon	M. A. Shannon
	G-WELL	Beech E90 King Air	Colt Group Ltd
	G-WELS	Cameron N-65 balloon	K. J. Vickery
	G-WENA	AS.355F2 Twin Squirrel	Kensington & Chelsea Aviation Ltd (G-CORR/G-MUFF/G-MOBI)
	G-WEND	PA-28RT-201 Arrow IV	Tayside Aviation Ltd/Dundee
	G-WERY	SOCATA TB20 Trinidad	WERY Flying Group
	G-WESX	CFM Streak Shadow	M. Catania
	G-WFFW	PA-28-161 Warrior II	S. Letheren & D. Jelly
	G-WFLY	Mainair Pegasus Quik	D. E. Lord
	G-WFOX	Robinson R22 Beta II	J. W. Clutton
	G-WGCS	PA-18 Super Cub 95	S. C. Thompson
	G-WGHB	Canadair T-33AN Silver Star 3	Parkhouse Aviation

BRITISH CIVIL REGISTRATIONS — G-WGSC – G-WOOF

Reg	Type	Owner or Operator	Notes
G-WGSC	Pilatus PC-6/B2-H4 Turbo Porter	D. M. Penny	
G-WHAL	QAC Quickie	A. A. M. Wahiberg	
G-WHAM	AS.350B3 Ecureuil	Horizon Helicopter Hire Ltd/Kidlington	
G-WHAT	Colt 77A balloon	M. A. Scholes	
G-WHEE	Pegasus Quantum 15-912	Airways Airsports Ltd	
G-WHEN	Tecnam P92-EM Echo	E. Windle	
G-WHIM	Colt 77A balloon	D. L. Morgan	
G-WHIN	Eurocopter EC 135T2	McAlpine Helicopters Ltd	
G-WHOG	CFM Streak Shadow	B. R. Cannell	
G-WHOO	Rotorway Executive 162F	C. A. Saul	
G-WHOT	Ultramagic T-210 balloon	M. A. Scholes	
G-WHRL	Schweizer 269C	M. Gardiner	
G-WHST	AS.350B2 Ecureuil	Hawkrise Ltd (G-BWYA)	
G-WIBB	Jodel D.18	M. N. Martin	
G-WIBS	CASA 1-131E Jungmann 2000	C. Willoughby	
G-WIDZ	Staaken Z-21 Flitzer	T. F. Crossman	
G-WIFE	Cessna R.182 RG II	Wife Group (G-BGVT)	
G-WIFI	Cameron Z-90 balloon	Trigger Concepts Ltd	
G-WIIZ	Augusta-Bell 206B JetRanger 2	Helicopters R Go (G-DBHH/G-AWVO)	
G-WILD	Pitts S-1T Special	N. J. Wakefield	
G-WILG	PZL-104 Wilga 35	M. H. Bletsoe-Brown (G-AZYJ)	
G-WILT	Ikarus C.42 FB 100	M. G. Wiltshire	
G-WIMP	Colt 56A balloon	T. & B. Chamberlain	
G-WINA	Cessna 560XL Citation XL	Ability Air Ltd	
G-WINE	Thunder Ax7-77Z balloon ★	Balloon Preservation Group/Lancing	
G-WINI	SA Bulldog Srs.120/121 (XX546:03)	A. Bole (G-CBCO)	
G-WINK	AA-5B Tiger	B. St. J. Cooke	
G-WINS	PA-32 Cherokee Six 300	Cheyenne Ltd	
G-WIRE	AS.355F1 Twin Squirrel	National Grid Co PLC (G-CEGB/G-BLJL)	
G-WIRL	Robinson R22 Beta	Rivermead Aviation Ltd/Switzerland	
G-WISH	Lindstrand LBL Cake SS balloon	Oxford Promotions (UK) Ltd/USA	
G-WIXI	Avions Mudry CAP-10B	P. A. Willmington	
G-WIZA	Robinson R22 Beta	Patriot Aviation Ltd/Cranfield (G-PERL)	
G-WIZD	Lindstrand LBL-180A balloon	Wizard Balloons Cambridge Ltd	
G-WIZI	Enstrom 280FX	D. I. Wadsworth	
G-WIZO	PA-34-220T Seneca III	B. J. Booty	
G-WIZR	Robinson R22 Beta II	Longmint Properties Ltd	
G-WIZS	Mainair Pegasus Quik	G. R. Barker	
G-WIZY	Robinson R22 Beta	Fancy Plates Ltd/Wellesbourne (G-BMWX)	
G-WIZZ	Agusta-Bell 206B JetRanger 2	Rivermead Aviation Ltd	
G-WJAC	Cameron TR-70 balloon	S. J. & J. A. Bellaby	
G-WJCJ	Eurocopter EC 155B1	Starspeed Ltd	
G-WKRD	AS.350B2 Ecureuil	Eassda Aviation (G-BUJG/G-HEAR)	
G-WLAC	PA-18 Super Cub 150	White Waltham Airfield Ltd (G-HAHA/G-BSWE)	
G-WLDN	Robinson R44 Raven	Fly Executive Ltd	
G-WLMS	Mainair Blade 912	I. D. Smart & C. J. Coggins	
G-WLSN	Best Off Skyranger 912S (1)	A. Wilson & ptnrs	
G-WLVE	Cameron Buddy-90 SS balloon	Escuela de Aeronautas de Aerodifusion SL	
G-WMAO	Eurocopter EC 135P2	McAlpine Helicopters Ltd	
G-WMAS	Eurocopter EC 135T1	Bond Air Services Ltd/Aberdeen	
G-WMBT	Robinson R44 II	P. Winslow	
G-WMID	MDH MD-900 Explorer	West Midlands Police Authority/Birmingham	
G-WMLT	Cessna 182Q	G. Wimlett (G-BOPG)	
G-WMPA	AS.355F2 Twin Squirrel	Police Aviation Services Ltd	
G-WMTM	AA-5B Tiger	Falcon Flying Group	
G-WMWM	Robinson R44	MMAir Ltd	
G-WNAA	Agusta A109E Power	Sloane Helicopters Ltd (G-TVAC)	
G-WNGS	Cameron N-105 balloon	R. M. Horn	
G-WNTR	PA-28-161 Warrior II	Fleetlands Flying Association Ltd (G-BFNJ)	
G-WOCO	Waco YMF-5C	P. A. Good	
G-WOFM	Agusta A109E Power	Quinnasette Ltd (G-NWRR)	
G-WOLF	PA-28 Cherokee 140	The Yak Group	
G-WOLV	Ikarus C42 FB100	Aerosport Ltd	
G-WOOD	Beech 95-B55A Baron	M. A. Rooney (G-AYID)	
G-WOOF	Enstrom 480	Netcopter.co.uk Ltd & Curvature Ltd	

G-WOOL – G-XIIX — BRITISH CIVIL REGISTRATIONS

Notes	Reg	Type	Owner or Operator
	G-WOOL	Colt 77A balloon	Whacko Balloon Group
	G-WORM	Thruster T.600N	S. & M. Rickett
	G-WOSY	MBB Bö.105DBS/4	Redwood Aviation Ltd (G-PASD/G-BNRS)
	G-WOWA	DHC.8-311 Dash Eight	Air Southwest Ltd/Plymouth (G-BRYS)
	G-WOWB	DHC.8-311 Dash Eight	Air Southwest Ltd/Plymouth (G-BRYT)
	G-WOWC	DHC.8-311 Dash Eight	Air Southwest Ltd/Plymouth (G-BRYO)
	G-WOWD	DHC.8-311 Dash Eight	Air Southwest Ltd/Plymouth
	G-WOWE	DHC.8-311 Dash Eight.	Air Southwest Ltd/Plymouth (G-BRYI)
	G-WPAS	MDH MD-900 Explorer	Police Aviation Services Ltd
	G-WREN	Pitts S-2A Special	Northamptonshire School of Flying Ltd/Sywell
	G-WRFM	Enstrom 280C-UK Shark	A. J. Clark (G-CTSI/G-BKIO)
	G-WRIT	Thunder Ax7-77A balloon	G. Pusey
	G-WRLY	Robinson R22 Beta	Burman Aviation Ltd/Cranfield (G-OFJS/G-BNXJ)
	G-WRSY	Enstrom 480B	Pietas Ltd
	G-WRWR	Robinson R22 Beta II	Longmint Aviation Ltd
	G-WSEC	Enstrom F-28C	G. Tracey (G-BONF)
	G-WSKY	Enstrom 280C-UK-2 Shark	M. I. Edwards Engineers (G-BEEK)
	G-WSSX	Ikarus C42 FB100	Haimoss Ltd
	G-WUFF	Shaw Europa	M. A. Barker
	G-WULF	WAR Focke-Wulf Fw.190 (8+)	A. Howe
	G-WUSH	Eurocopter EC 120B	Innovation Helicopters LLP
	G-WVBF	Lindstrand LBL-210A balloon	Virgin Balloon Flights Ltd
	G-WVIP	Beech B.200 Super King Air	Capital Trading (Aviation) Ltd
	G-WWAL	PA-28R Cherokee Arrow 180	White Waltham Airfield Ltd (G-AZSH)
	G-WWAY	Piper PA-28-181 Archer II	R. A. Witchell
	G-WWBB	Airbus A.330-243	bmi british midland
	G-WWBC	Airbus A.330-243	bmi british midland
	G-WWBD	Airbus A.330-243	bmi british midland
	G-WWBM	Airbus A.330-243	bmi british midland
	G-WWIZ	Beech 95-58 Baron	Scenestage Ltd/Bournemouth (G-GAMA/G-BBSD)
	G-WYAT	CFM Streak Shadow Srs SA	M. G. Whyatt
	G-WYCH	Cameron 90 Witch SS balloon	Corn Palace Balloon Club Ltd
	G-WYLE	Rans S.6-ES Coyote II	A. & R. W. Osborne
	G-WYND	Wittman W.8 Tailwind	Forge Group
	G-WYNE	BAe 125 Srs 800B	Mercury Air Ltd (G-CJAA/G-HCFR/G-SHEA/G-BUWC)
	G-WYNT	Cameron N-56 balloon	S. L. G. Williams
	G-WYPA	MBB Bö.105DBS/4	Police Aviation Services Ltd/Gloucestershire
	G-WYSP	Robinson R44	C. G. Robinson Ltd
	G-WYVN	DG Flugzeugbau DG-1000S	Army Gliding Association
	G-WZOL	RL.5B LWS Sherwood Ranger	S. J. Spavins (G-MZOL)
	G-WZRD	Eurocopter EC 120B Colibri	McAlpine Helicopters Ltd
	G-XALT	PA-38-112 Tomahawk	D. Shew
	G-XARV	ARV Super 2	D. J. Burton (G-OPIG/G-BMSJ)
	G-XATS	Aerotek Pitts S-2A Special	Air Training Services Ltd/Booker
	G-XAVI	PA-28-161 Warrior II	J. R. Santamaria (G-SACZ)
	G-XAXA	BN-A-26 Islander	Blue Island Air (G-LOTO/G-BDWG)
	G-XAYR	Raj Hamsa X'Air 582 (6)	D. L. Connolly & R. V. Barber
	G-XBCI	Bell 206B JetRanger 3	BCI Helicopter Charters Ltd
	G-XBOX	Bell 206B JetRanger 3	Mainstream Digital Ltd (G-OOHO/G-OCHC/G-KLEE/G-SIZL/G-BOSW)
	G-XCCC	Extra EA.300/L	P. T. Fellows
	G-XCIT	Pioneer 300	A. Thomas
	G-XCUB	PA-18 Super Cub 150	M. C. Barraclough
	G-XELA	Robinson R44 II	A. Yew
	G-XENA	PA-28-161 Warrior II	P. Brewer
	G-XFLY	Lambert Mission M212-100	Lambert Aircraft Engineering BVBA
	G-XHOT	Cameron Z-105 balloon	S. F. Burden
	G-XIII	Van's RV-7	G-XIII Group
	G-XIIX	Robinson R22 Beta ★	(Static exhibit)/Blackbushe

BRITISH CIVIL REGISTRATIONS

G-XINE – G-YAKA

Reg	Type	Owner or Operator	Notes
G-XINE	PA-28-161 Warrior II	P. Tee (G-BPAC)	
G-XIOO	Raj Hamsa X'Air 133 (1)	J. Campbell	
G-XKEN	PA-34-200T Seneca III	Choicecircle Ltd	
G-XLAA	Boeing 737-8Q8	XL Airways UK Ltd (G-OKDN)	
G-XLAB	Boeing 737-8Q8	XL Airways UK Ltd (G-OJSW)	
G-XLAC	Boeing 737-81Q	XL Airways UK Ltd (G-LFJB)	
G-XLAD	Boeing 737-81Q	XL Airways UK Ltd (G-ODMW)	
G-XLAF	Boeing 737-86N	XL Airways UK Ltd	
G-XLAG	Boeing 737-86N	XL Airways UK Ltd	
G-XLAI	Boeing 737-8Q8	XL Airways UK Ltd	
G-XLAJ	Boeing 737-8Q8	XL Airways UK Ltd	
G-XLAK	Boeing 737-8FH	XL Airways UK Ltd	
G-XLAL	Boeing 737-8FH	XL Airways UK Ltd	
G-XLAM	Best Off Skyranger 912S	X-LAM Skyranger Syndicate	
G-XLIV	Robinson R44	Rotorcraft Ltd	
G-XLKF	Cessna 310Q	Excel Aviation Ltd (G-BMMC)	
G-XLLL	AS.355F1 Twin Squirrel	Sharpness Dock Ltd (G-PASF/G-SCHU)	
G-XLMB	Cessna 560XL Citation Excel	Aviation Beauport Ltd	
G-XLNT	Zenair CH.601XL	Zenair G-XLNT Group	
G-XLTG	Cessna 182S	D. H. Morgan	
G-XLXL	Robin DR.400/160	L. R. Marchant/Biggin Hill (G-BAUD)	
G-XMGO	Aeromot AMT-200S Super Ximango	G. McLean & R. P. Beck	
G-XMII	Eurocopter EC 135T1	Merseyside Police Authority/Woodvale	
G-XOIL	AS.355N Twin Squirrel	Firstearl Marine and Aviation Ltd (G-LOUN)	
G-XOXO	Extra EA.300/L	Skyhigh Aerobatics Ltd	
G-XPBI	Letov LK-2M Sluka	K. Harness	
G-XPII	Cessna R.172K	R. J. Harris (G-DIVA)	
G-XPSS	Short SD3-60 Variant 100	BAC Group Ltd (G-OBOH/G-BNDJ)	
G-XPXP	Aero Designs Pulsar XP	B. J. Edwards	
G-XRAF	Raj Hamsa X'Air 582 (2)	S. Marathe	
G-XRAY	Rand-Robinson KR-2	R. S. Smith	
G-XRED	Pitts S-1C Special	J. E. Rands (G-SWUN/G-BSXH)	
G-XRLD	Cameron A-250 balloon	J. A. B. Gray	
G-XRVX	Van's RV-10	N. K. Lamping	
G-XRXR	Raj Hamsa X'Air 582 (1)	R. J. Philpotts	
G-XSAM	Van's RV-9A	D. G. Lucas	
G-XSDJ	Shaw Europa XS	D. N. Joyce	
G-XSEA	Van's RV-8	Skyview Systems Ltd	
G-XSFT	PA-23 Aztec 250F	T. L. B. Dykes/Goodwood (G-CPPC/G-BGBH)	
G-XSKY	Cameron N-77 balloon	T. D. Gibbs	
G-XTEE	Airborne XT912-B/Streak III	Airborne Australia UK	
G-XTEK	Robinson R44	Leavesley Aviation Ltd	
G-XTNI	AirBorne XT912-B/Streak	D. Carnichael	
G-XTNR	Edge XT912-B/Streak III-B	N. Rose	
G-XTOR	BN-2A Mk III-2 Trislander	Aurigny Air Services Ltd (G-BAXD)	
G-XTRA	Extra EA.230	Xtra Aerobatics Ltd	
G-XTUN	Westland-Bell 47G-3B1 (XT223)	Hields Aviation (G-BGZK)	
G-XVBF	Lindstrand LBL-330A balloon	Virgin Balloon Flights	
G-XVOM	Van's RV-6	A. Baker-Munton	
G-XWEB	Best Off Skyranger 912 (2)	K. B. Woods	
G-XXEA	Sikorsky S-76C	Director of Royal Travel/Blackbushe	
G-XXIV	Agusta-Bell 206B JetRanger 3	Bart Fifty Nine Ltd	
G-XXRS	Bombardier BD-700 Global Express	TAG Aviation (UK) Ltd	
G-XXTR	Extra EA.300/L	Airpark Flight Centre Ltd (G-ECCC)	
G-XXVI	Sukhoi Su-26M	A. N. Onn/Headcorn	
G-XYAK	IDA Bacau Yakovlev Yak-52 (69 blue)	NRG Technology Ltd	
G-XYJY	Best Off Skyranger 912 (2)	A. V. Francis	
G-YAAK	Yakovlev Yak-50	R. J. Luke (G-BWJT)	
G-YACB	Robinson R22 Beta	Property Network (G-VOSL)	
G-YAKA	Yakovlev Yak-50	M. Chapman	

G-YAKB – G-YORK — BRITISH CIVIL REGISTRATIONS

Notes	Reg	Type	Owner or Operator
	G-YAKB	Aerostar Yakovlev Yak-52	Kemble Air Services Ltd
	G-YAKC	Yakovlev Yak-52	T. J. Wilson
	G-YAKH	IDA Bacau Yakovlev Yak-52	Plus 7 minus 5 Ltd
	G-YAKI	IDA Bacau Yakovlev Yak-52 (100 blue)	Yak One Ltd/White Waltham
	G-YAKK	Yakovlev Yak-50	K. J. Pilling/North Weald
	G-YAKM	IDA Bacau Yakovlev Yak-50 (61 red)	Airborne Services Ltd
	G-YAKN	IDA Bacau Yakovlev Yak-52 (66 red)	Airborne Services Ltd
	G-YAKO	IDA Bacau Yakovlev Yak-52	M. K. Shaw
	G-YAKR	IDA Bacau Yakovlev Yak-52 (03 white)	A. S. Nottage & R. A. Alexander
	G-YAKT	IDA Bacau Yakovlev Yak-52	G-YAKT Group
	G-YAKU	IDA Bacau Yakovlev Yak-50 (49 red)	D. J. Hopkinson (G-BXND)
	G-YAKV	IDA Bacau Yakovlev Yak-52 (31 grey)	P. D. Scandrett
	G-YAKX	IDA Bacau Yakovlev Yak-52 (27 red)	The X-Flyers Ltd
	G-YAKY	Aerostar Yakovlev Yak-52	W. T. Marriott
	G-YAKZ	IDA Bacau Yakovlev Yak-50 (33 red)	P. D. Scandrett
	G-YANK	PA-28-181 Archer II	G-YANK Flying Group
	G-YARR	Mainair Rapier	D. Yarr
	G-YARV	ARV Super 2	P. R. Snowden (G-BMDO)
	G-YAWW	PA-28RT-201T Turbo Arrow IV	Barton Aviation Ltd
	G-YBAA	Cessna FR.172J	A. Evans
	G-YCII	LET Yakovlev C-11 (11 yellow)	R. W. Davies
	G-YCUB	PA-18 Super Cub 150	F. W. Rogers Garage (Saltash) Ltd
	G-YEAH	Robinson R44 II	Turboprop Leasing LLP
	G-YELL	Murphy Rebel	A. D. Keen
	G-YEOM	PA-31-350 Navajo Chieftain	Foster Yeoman Ltd/Exeter
	G-YEWS	Rotorway Executive 152	R. Turrell & P. Mason
	G-YFLY	VPM M-16 Tandem Trainer	A. J. Unwin (G-BWGI)
	G-YFUT	Yakovlev Yak-52	R. Oliver
	G-YFZT	Cessna 172S	AB Integro
	G-YHPV	Cessna E310N	V. E Young & P. O. Hayes/Ireland (G-AWTA)
	G-YIAN	Embraer EMB-135BJ Legacy	Yianis Air Ltd
	G-YIII	Cessna F.150L	Sherburn Aero Club Ltd
	G-YIIK	Robinson R44	South West Air Charter Ltd
	G-YIPI	Cessan FR.172K	A. J. G. Davis
	G-YJET	Montgomerie-Bensen B.8MR	A. Shuttleworth (G-BMUH)
	G-YKCT	Aerostar Yakovlev Yak-52	N. Gooderham
	G-YKSO	Yakovlev Yak-50	Classic Displays Ltd
	G-YKSS	Yakovlev Yak-55	I. D. Trask
	G-YKSZ	Aerostar Yakovlev Yak-52 (01 yellow)	Tzarina Group
	G-YKYK	Aerostar Yakovlev Yak-52	K. J. Pilling/North Weald
	G-YLYB	Cameron N-105 balloon	ABC Flights Ltd
	G-YMBO	Robinson R22M Mariner	J. Robinson
	G-YMFC	Waco YMF	S. J. Brenchley
	G-YMMA	Boeing 777-236ER	British Airways
	G-YMMB	Boeing 777-236ER	British Airways
	G-YMMC	Boeing 777-236ER	British Airways
	G-YMMD	Boeing 777-236ER	British Airways
	G-YMME	Boeing 777-236ER	British Airways
	G-YMMF	Boeing 777-236ER	British Airways
	G-YMMG	Boeing 777-236ER	British Airways
	G-YMMH	Boeing 777-236ER	British Airways
	G-YMMI	Boeing 777-236ER	British Airways
	G-YMMJ	Boeing 777-236ER	British Airways
	G-YMMK	Boeing 777-236ER	British Airways
	G-YMML	Boeing 777-236ER	British Airways
	G-YMMM	Boeing 777-236ER	British Airways
	G-YMMN	Boeing 777-236ER	British Airways
	G-YMMO	Boeing 777-236ER	British Airways
	G-YMMP	Boeing 777-236ER	British Airways
	G-YNOT	D.62B Condor	T. Littlefair (G-AYFH)
	G-YNYS	Cessna 172S Skyhawk	T. V. Hughes
	G-YOGI	Robin DR.400/140B	M. M. Pepper (G-BDME)
	G-YORK	Cessna F.172M	H. Waetjen

BRITISH CIVIL REGISTRATIONS

G-YOTS – G-ZEPI

Reg	Type	Owner or Operator	Notes
G-YOTS	IDA Bacau Yakovlev Yak-52	YOTS Group	
G-YOXI	Zenair 601UL Zodiac	B. & K. Yoxall	
G-YOYO	Pitts S-1E Special	J. D. L. Richardson (G-OTSW/G-BLHE)	
G-YPOL	MDH MD-900 Explorer	West Yorkshire Police Authority	
G-YPSY	Andreasson BA-4B	D. J. Howell	
G-YRAF	RAF 2000 GTX-SE gyroplane	J. R. Cooper	
G-YRIL	Luscombe 8E Silvaire	C. Potter	
G-YROI	Air Command 532 Elite	W. B. Lumb	
G-YROJ	RAF 2000 GTX-SE gyroplane	J. R. Mercer	
G-YROO	RAF 2000 GTX-SE gyroplane	K. D. Rhodes & C. S. Oakes	
G-YROS	Montgomerie-Bensen B.8M	Flight Academy (Gyrocopters) Ltd	
G-YROW	VPM M-16 Tandem Trainer	B. Jones	
G-YROX	Rotorsport UK MT-03	Surplus Art	
G-YROY	Montgomerie-Bensen B.8MR	S. Brennan	
G-YRUS	Jodel D.140E	W. E. Massam (G-YRNS)	
G-YSMO	Mainair Pegasus Quik	W. J. Byrd & I. G. Harban	
G-YSPY	Cessna 172Q	J. Henderson	
G-YSTT	PA-32R-301 Saratoga II HP	A. W. Kendrick	
G-YUGO	HS.125 Srs 1B/R-522 ★	Fire Section/Dunsfold (G-ATWH)	
G-YULL	PA-28 Cherokee 180E	G. Watkinson-Yull (G-BEAJ)	
G-YUMM	Cameron N-90 balloon	Wunderbar Ltd	
G-YUPI	Cameron N-90 balloon	MCVH SA/Belgium	
G-YURO	Shaw Europa ★	Yorkshire Air Museum/Elvington	
G-YVBF	Lindstrand LBL-317S balloon	Virgin Balloon Flights	
G-YVES	Alpi Pioneer 300	M. C. Birchall	
G-YVET	Cameron V-90 balloon	J. A. Hibberd	
G-YYAK	Aerostar SA Yak-52	J. Armstrong & D. W. Lamb	
G-YYYY	MH.1521C-1 Broussard	Aerosuperbatics Ltd/Rendcomb	
G-YZYZ	Mainair Blade 912	P. G. Eastlake	
G-ZAAZ	Van's RV-8	P. A. Soper	
G-ZABC	Sky 90-24 balloon	P. Donnelly	
G-ZACE	Cessna 172S	M. C. Tonsbeek	
G-ZACH	Robin DR.400/100	A. P. Wellings/Sandown (G-FTIO)	
G-ZADA	Best Off Skyranger 912S(1)	D. F. Hughes	
G-ZADY	Eurocopter EC 120B	Cambridge Aviation Ltd	
G-ZAHN	Cessna 172S Skyhawk	Carpe D Aviation Ltd	
G-ZAIR	Zenair CH 601HD	J. R. Standring	
G-ZANG	PA-28 Cherokee 140	I. D. Gale	
G-ZANY	Diamond DA40D Star	Altair Aviation Ltd	
G-ZAPH	Bell 206B JetRanger 4	Northern Flights Ltd/Stansted (G-DBMW)	
G-ZAPK	BAe 146-200QC	Titan Airways Ltd/Stansted (G-BTIA/G-PRIN)	
G-ZAPM	Boeing 737-33A	Titan Airways Ltd/Stansted	
G-ZAPN	BAe 146-200QC	Titan Airways Ltd/Stansted (G-BPBT)	
G-ZAPO	BAe 146-200QC	Titan Airways Ltd/Stansted (G-BWLG/G-PRCS)	
G-ZAPR	BAe 146-200F	Titan Airways Ltd/Stansted (G-BOXE)	
G-ZAPU	Boeing 757-2Y0	Titan Airways Ltd/Stansted	
G-ZAPV	Boeing 737-3Y0	Titan Airways Ltd/Royal Mail/Stansted (G-IGOC)	
G-ZAPW	Boeing 737-3L9	Titan Airways Ltd/Stansted (G-BOZB/G-IGOX)	
G-ZAPX	Boeing 757-256	Titan Airways Ltd/Stansted	
G-ZAPY	Robinson R22 Beta	Heli Air Ltd/Wellesbourne (G-INGB)	
G-ZAPZ	Boeing 737-33A	Titan Airways Ltd/Stansted	
G-ZARI	AA-5B Tiger	ZARI Aviation Ltd (G-BHVY)	
G-ZARV	ARV Super 2	P. R. Snowden	
G-ZAVI	Ikarus C42 FB100	G-ZAVI Group	
G-ZAZA	PA-18 Super Cub 95	Airborne Taxi Services Ltd	
G-ZBED	Robinson R22 Beta	P. D. Spinks	
G-ZBLT	Cessna 182S Skylane	Cessna 182S Group/Ireland	
G-ZEBO	Thunder Ax8-105 S2 balloon	S. M. Waterton	
G-ZEBY	PA-28 Cherokee 140	G. Gee (G-BFBF)	
G-ZEIN	Slingsby T.67M Firefly 260	R. C. P. Brookhouse	
G-ZELE	Westland Gazelle HT.Mk.2	London Helicopter Centres Ltd (G-CBSA)	
G-ZENA	Zenair CH.701UL	A. N. Aston	
G-ZENI	Zenair CH.601HD Zodiac	P. P. Plumley	
G-ZENN	Schempp-Hirth Ventus 2cT	Z. Marczynski	
G-ZEPI	Colt GA-42 gas airship	P. A. Lindstrand (G-ISPY/G-BPRB)	

G-ZERO – G-ZZZG — BRITISH CIVIL REGISTRATIONS

Notes	Reg	Type	Owner or Operator
	G-ZERO	AA-5B Tiger	N. F. Duke
	G-ZETA	Lindstrand LBL-105A balloon	S. Travaglia/Italy
	G-ZEXL	Extra EA.300/L	2 Excel Aviation Ltd
	G-ZFLY	Robinson R22 Beta	Ground Effect Ltd
	G-ZHKF	Escapade 912(1)	C. D. & C. M. Wills
	G-ZHWH	Rotorway Executive 162F	B. Alexander
	G-ZIGI	Robin DR.400/180	D. C. R. Writer
	G-ZIGY	Europa XS	K. D. Weston
	G-ZIII	Pitts S-2B	J. W. Sullivan (G-CDBH)
	G-ZINT	Cameron Z-77 balloon	Film Production Consultants SRL
	G-ZIPA	Rockwell Commander 114A	A. C. Lees (G-BHRA)
	G-ZIPI	Robin DR.400/180	H. U. & D. C. Stahlberg/Headcorn
	G-ZIPY	Wittman W.8 Tailwind	K. J. Nurcombe
	G-ZITZ	AS.355F2 Twin Squirrel	Heli Aviation Ltd
	G-ZIZI	Cessna 525 CitationJet	Ortac Air Ltd
	G-ZLIN	Z.526 Trener Master	N. J. Arthur (G-BBCR)
	G-ZLLE	Aérospatiale SA.341G Gazelle	MW Helicopters Ltd
	G-ZLOJ	Beech A36 Bonanza	W. D. Gray
	G-ZMAM	PA-28-181 Archer II	Z. Mahmood (G-BNPN)
	G-ZODI	Zenair CH.601UL Zodiac	B. McFadden
	G-ZODY	Zenair CH.601UL Zodiac	Sarum AX2000 Group
	G-ZOOL	Cessna FA.152	G. G. Hammond (G-BGXZ)
	G-ZORO	Shaw Europa	N. T. Read
	G-ZOSA	Champion 7GCAA	R. McQueen
	G-ZSKD	Cameron Z-90 balloon	M. J. Gunston
	G-ZTED	Shaw Europa	J. J. Kennedy & E. W. Gladstone
	G-ZUMI	Van's RV-8	P. M. Wells
	G-ZUMO	Pilatus PC-12/47	Breckenridge Ltd
	G-ZVBF	Cameron A-400 balloon	Virgin Balloon Flights
	G-ZVKO	Edge 360	C. Butler
	G-ZWAR	Eurocopter EC 120B	Hedgeton Trading Ltd
	G-ZXCL	Extra EA.300/L	2 Excel Aviation Ltd
	G-ZXEL	Extra EA.300/L	2 Excel Aviation Ltd
	G-ZXZX	Learjet 45	Gama Aviation Ltd
	G-ZYAK	IDA Bacau Yakovlev YAK-52	K. A. Boost
	G-ZZAJ	Schleicher ASH-26E	A.T. Johnstone
	G-ZZAP	Champion 8KCAB	L. Maikowski & ptnrs
	G-ZZDG	Cirrus SR20 G2	D. M. Green
	G-ZZEL	Westland Gazelle AH.1	Tregenna Castle Hotel Ltd
	G-ZZLE	Westland Gazelle AH.2	Estates (UK) Management Ltd (G-CBSE)
	G-ZZOE	Eurocopter EC 120B	J. F. H. James
	G-ZZOW	Medway Eclipse	P. J. Croney
	G-ZZSA	Eurocopter EC.225LP Super Puma	Bristow Helicopters Ltd
	G-ZZSB	Eurocopter EC.225LP Super Puma	Bristow Helicopters Ltd
	G-ZZSC	Eurocopter EC.225LP Super Puma	Bristow Helicopters Ltd
	G-ZZSD	Eurocopter EC.225LP Super Puma	Bristow Helicopters Ltd
	G-ZZXX	P & M Quik GT450	Nature First Ltd
	G-ZZZA	Boeing 777-236	British Airways
	G-ZZZB	Boeing 777-236	British Airways
	G-ZZZC	Boeing 777-236	British Airways
	G-ZZZG	Alpi Pioneer 300	C. K. Parsons

Originally imported in 1959 Tri-Pacer G-APUR is one of the oldest of the many US light aircraft flying in the UK today. *DP*

Although retaining its UK registration Chipmunk G-AKDN is based in Saskatoon, Canada. *Dick Barrett*

Pietenpol Air Camper G-OFFA is one of several examples of this classic pre-war US homebuilt design. *DP*

Aerotechnik EV-97 Eurostar G-LYNI is one of many assembled from kits produced in the Czech Republic. *DP*

Hughes 369D G-HKHM was imported from Hong Kong as its registration suggests. *DP*

DA40D Diamond Star G-CCXU has a diesel engine and is manufactured in Austria. *DP*

Now preserved, Cameron special shape balloons G-DERV and G-BUUU still receive an occasional airing. *DP*

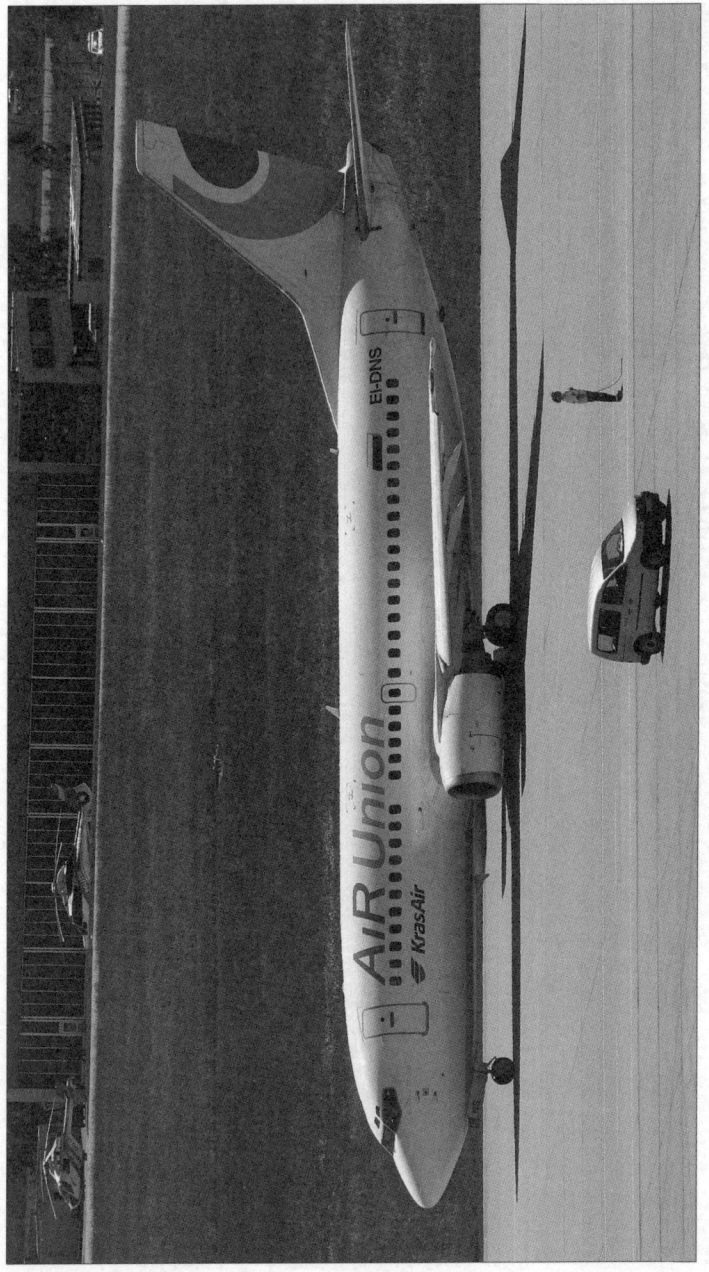

Owned by an Irish leasing company, AiRUnion Boeing 737 EI-DNS is one of the many Irish-registered airliners that rarely see the Emerald Isle. *DP*

Military to Civil Cross-Reference

Serial carried	Civil identity	Serial carried	Civil identity
001	G-BYPY	1164:64 (USAAC)	G-BKGL
1	G-BPVE	1180 (USN)	G-BRSK
6G-ED (Luftwaffe)	G-BZOB	1211(North Korean AF)	G-MIGG
9 (Soviet AF)	G-OYAK	1342 (Soviet AF)	G-BTZD
09 (DOSAAF)	G-BVMU	1363 (Portuguese AF)	G-DHPM
10 (DOSAAF)	G-BTZB	1377 (Portuguese AF)	G-BARS
10 (DOSAAF)	G-CBMD	1747 (Portuguese AF)	G-BGPB
11 (Soviet AF)	G-YCII	2345 (RFC)	G-ATVP
26 (USAAC)	G-BAVO	3066	G-AETA
26 (DOSAAF)	G-BVXK	3072:72 (USN)	G-TEXN
27 (Soviet AF)	G-YAKX	3349 (RCAF)	G-BYNF
27 (USN)	G-BRVG	3397:174 (USN)	G-OBEE
27 (USAAC)	G-AGYY	4034 (Luftwaffe)	G-CDTI
27 (Soviet AF)	G-YAKX	4406:12 (USN)	G-ONAF
42 (Soviet AF)	G-CBRU	4513:1 (French AF)	G-BFYO
43:SC (USAF)	G-AZSC	5429 (RCAF)	G-KAMM
44 (DOSAAF)	G-BXAK	5964 (RFC)	G-BFVH
49 (USAAF)	G-KITT	6136:205 (USN)	G-BRUJ
48 (DOSAAF)	G-CBSN	7198/18 (Luftwaffe)	G-AANJ
50 (DOSAAF)	G-CBPM	7797 (USAAF)	G-BFAF
50 (DOSAAF)	G-CBRW	8110 (Croatian AF)	G-AGFT
50 (DOSAAF)	G-EYAK	8178:FU-178 (USAF)	G-SABR
52 (DOSAAF)	G-BWVR	8449M (RAF)	G-ASWJ
55 (DOSAAF)	G-BVOK	9917	G-EBKY
62 (DOSAAF)	G-LAOK	01420 (Polish AF but in Korean colours)	G-BMZF
67 (DOSAAF)	G-CBSL	14863 (USAAF)	G-BGOR
68 (Chinese AF)	G-BVVG	16693:693 (RCAF)	G-BLPG
69 (Russian AF)	G-XYAK	18013:013 (RCAF)	G-TRIC
78 (French Army)	G-BIZK	18393:393 (RCAF)	G-BCYK
82:8 (French AF)	G-CCVH	18671:671 (RCAF)	G-BNZC
85 (USAAF)	G-BTBI	20310:310 (RCAF)	G-BSBG
93 (DOSAAF)	G-JYAK	21261:261 (RCAF)	G-TBRD
100 (DOSAAF)	G-YAKI	21509 (US Army)	G-UHIH
112 (USAAC)	G-BSWC	28521:TA-521 (USAF)	G-TVIJ
118 (USAAC)	G-BSDS	30140 (Yugoslav Army)	G-RADA
124 (French Army)	G-BOSJ	30146 (Yugoslav Army)	G-BSXD
139 (DOSAAF)	G-BWOD	30149 (Yugoslav Army)	G-SOKO
143 (French AF)	G-MSAL	31145:G-26 (USAAF)	G-BBLH
152/17 (Luftwaffe)	G-ATJM	3-1923 (USAAF)	G-BRHP
156 (French AF)	G-NIFE	31952 (USAAF)	G-BRPR
157 (French AF)	G-AVEB	39624:D-39 (USAAF)	G-BVMH
161 (Irish Air Corps)	G-CCCA	40467:19 (USN)	G-BTCC
168 (RFC)	G-BFDE	56321:U-AB (Royal Norwegian AF)	G-BKPY
174 (Royal Netherlands Navy)	G-BEPV	80425:WT-4 (USN)	G-RUMT
177 (Irish Air Corps)	G-BLIW	89542:LTA-542 (USAF)	G-BRLV
185 (French AF)	G-BWLR	111836:JZ-6 (USN)	G-TSIX
311 (Singapore AF)	G-SARK	115042:TA-042 (USAF)	G-BGHU
379 (USAAC)	G-ILLE	115227 (USN)	G-BKRA
394 (French AF)	G-BIMO	115302:TP (USMC)	G-BJTP
408 (Royal Jordanian AF)	G-BDIN	115684 (USAAF)	G-BKVM
422/15 (Luftwaffe)	G-AVJO	121714:201-B (USN)	G-RUMM
423 / 427 (Royal Norwegian AF)	G-AMRK	124485:DF-A (USAAF)	G-BEDF
425 (Oman AF)	G-SOAF	126922:402-AK (USN)	G-RADR
441 (USN)	G-BTFG	150225:123 (USMC)	G-AWOX
450/17 (Luftwaffe)	G-BVGZ	18-2001 (USAAF)	G-BIZV
503 (Hungarian AF)	G-BRAM	18-5395:CDG (French Army)	G-CUBJ
540 (USAAF)	G-BCNX	212540:RF-40 (USN)	G-BBHK
669 (USAAC)	G-CCXA	217786:25 (USAAF)	G-BRTK
699 (USAAC)	G-CCXB	238410:A-44 (USAAF)	G-BHPK
781-32 (Spanish AF)	G-BPDM	314887 (USAAF)	G-AJPI
854 (USAAC)	G-BTBH	315509:W7-S (USAAF)	G-BHUB
897:E (USN)	G-BJEV	329405:A-23 (USAAF)	G-BCOB
99+26 (Luftwaffe)	G-BZGL	329417 (USAAF)	G-BDHK
99+32 (Luftwaffe)	G-BZGK	329471:F-44 (USAAF)	G-BGXA
1018 (Polish AF)	G-ISKA	329601:D-44 (USAAF)	G-AXHR
1102:102 (USN)	G-AZLE	329854:R-44 (USAAF)	G-BMKC
1104 (Royal Saudi AF)	G-SMAS	329934:B-72 (USAAF)	G-BCPH
1130 (Royal Saudi AF)	G-CDHB	330238:A-24 (USAAF)	G-LIVH

MILITARY/CIVIL CROSS-REFERENCE

Serial carried	Civil identity	Serial carried	Civil identity
330485:C-44 (USAAF)	G-AJES	F5447:N	G-BKER
343251:27 (USAAC)	G-NZSS	F5459:Y	G-INNY
414419:LH-F (USAAF)	G-MSTG	F8010:Z	G-BDWJ
463864:HL-W (USAAF)	G-CBNM	F8614	G-AWAU
433915 (USAAF)	G-PBYA	G-48-1 (Class B)	G-ALSX
436021 (USAAF)	G-BWEZ	H5199	G-ADEV
44-1307: 87-H (USAAF)	G-BTCD	J-1573 (Swiss AF)	G-VICI
454467:J-44 (USAAF)	G-BILI	J-1605 (Swiss AF)	G-BLID
454537:J-04 (USAAF)	G-BFDL	J-1632 (Swiss AF)	G-VNOM
461748:Y (USAF)	G-BHDK	J-1758 (Swiss AF)	G-BLSD
472035 (USAAF)	G-SIJJ	J-4021 (Swiss AF)	G-HHAC
472216:HO-M (USAAF)	G-BIXL	J-4031 (Swiss AF)	G-BWFR
472218:WZ-I (USAAF)	G-HAEC	J-4081 (Swiss AF)	G-HHAF
472773:QP-M (USAAF)	G-CDHI	J-4083 (Swiss AF)	G-EGHH
479744:M-49 (USAAF)	G-BGPD	J-4090 (Swiss AF)	G-SIAL
479766:D-63 (USAAF)	G-BKHG	J7326	G-EBQP
480015:M-44 (USAAF)	G-AKIB	J9941:57	G-ABMR
480133:B-44 (USAAF)	G-BDCD	K1786	G-AFTA
480173:57-H (USAAF)	G-RRSR	K1930	G-BKBB
480321:H-44 (USAAF)	G-FRAN	K2048	G-BZNW
480480:E-44 (USAAF)	G-BECN	K2050	G-ASCM
480636:A-58 (USAAF)	G-AXHP	K2059	G-PFAR
480723:E5-J (USAAF)	G-BFZB	K2075	G-BEER
480752:E-39 (USAAF)	G-BCXJ	K2227	G-ABBB
493209 (US ANG)	G-DDMV	K2567	G-MOTH
542447 (USAF)	G-SCUB	K2572	G-AOZH
2632019 (Chinese AF)	G-BXZB	K2585	G-ANKT
41-33275:CE (USAAF)	G-BICE	K2587	G-BJAP
42-58678:IY (USAAF)	G-BRIY	K3241	G-AHSA
42-78044 (USAAF)	G-BRXL	K3661	G-BURZ
42-84555:EP-H (USAAF)	G-ELMH	K3731	G-RODI
44-79609:44-S (USAAF)	G-BHXY	K4259:71	G-ANMO
44-80594 (USAAF)	G-BEDJ	K5054	G-BRDV
44-83184 (USAAF)	G-RGUS	K5414:XV	G-AENP
51-7692 (French AF)	G-TROY	K5600	G-BVVI
51-11701A:AF258 (USAF)	G-BSZC	K5673	G-BZAS
54-2445 (USAF)	G-OTAN	K5674	G-CBZP
A-10 (Swiss AF)	G-BECW	K8203	G-BTVE
A16-199:SF-R (RAAF)	G-BEOX	K8303:D	G-BWWN
A17-48 (RAAF)	G-BPHR	L2301	G-AIZG
A-57 (Swiss AF)	G-BECT	L6906	G-AKKY
A-125 (Swiss AF)	G-BLKZ	N500	G-BWRA
A-806 (Swiss AF)	G-BTLL	N1854	G-AIBE
A8226	G-BIDW	N1977:8 (French AF)	G-BWMJ
B595:W	G-BUOD	N3788	G-AKPF
B1807	G-EAVX	N4877:MK-V	G-AMDA
B2458:R	G-BPOB	N5182	G-APUP
B6401	G-AWYY	N5195	G-ABOX
C1904:Z	G-PFAP	N5199	G-BZND
C3009	G-BFWD	N5719	G-CBHO
C3011:S	G-SWOT	N5903:H	G-GLAD
C4918	G-BWJM	N6-766 (Royal Australian Navy)	G-SPDR
C4994	G-BLWM	N6290	G-BOCK
C5430	G-CCXG	N6452	G-BIAU
C9533:M	G-BUWE	N6466	G-ANKZ
D-692	G-BVAW	N6473	G-AOBO
D5397/17 (Luftwaffe)	G-BFXL	N6537	G-AOHY
D7889	G-AANM	N6720:VX	G-BYTN
D8084	G-ACAA	N6797	G-ANEH
D8096:D	G-AEPH	N6847	G-APAL
E-15 (Royal Netherlands AF)	G-BIYU	N6965:FL-J	G-AJTW
E3B-143 (Spanish AF)	G-JUNG	N9191	G-ALND
E3B-153:781-75 (Spanish AF)	G-BPTS	N9192:RCO-N	G-DHZF
E3B-350:05-97 (Spanish AF)	G-BHPL	N9389	G-ANJA
E449	G-EBJE	P2902:DX-X	G-ROBT
E8894	G-CDLI	P6382:C	G-AJRS
F141:G	G-SEVA	P9374	G-MKIA
F235:B	G-BMDB	R-151 (RNethAF)	G-BIYR
F904	G-EBIA	R-163 (RNethAF)	G-BIRH
F938	G-EBIC	R-167 (RNethAF)	G-LION
F943	G-BIHF	R1914	G-AHUJ
F943	G-BKDT	R3821:UX-N	G-BPIV

MILITARY/CIVIL CROSS-REFERENCE

Serial carried	Civil identity	Serial carried	Civil identity
R4118:UP-W	G-HUPW	FB226:MT-A	G-BDWM
R4922	G-APAO	FE695:94	G-BTXI
R4959:59	G-ARAZ	FE788	G-CTKL
R5136	G-APAP	FJ777 (RCAF)	G-BIXN
R5172:FIJ-E	G-AOIS	FR886	G-BDMS
R5250	G-AODT	FS628	G-AIZE
S1287	G-BEYB	FT391	G-AZBN
S1579:571	G-BBVO	FX301:FD-NQ	G-JUDI
S1581:573	G-BWWK	FZ626:YS-DH	G-AMPO
T5672	G-ALRI	HB275	G-BKGM
T5854	G-ANKK	HB751	G-BCBL
T5879:RUC-W	G-AXBW	HD-75 (R Belgian AF)	G-AFDX
T6313	G-AHVU	HG691	G-AIYR
T6562	G-ANTE	HM580	G-ACUU
T6953	G-ANNI	JF343:JW-P	G-CCZP
T7230	G-AFVE	JG891:T-B	G-LFVC
T7281	G-ARTL	JV579:F	G-RUMW
T7328	G-APPN	KB889:NA-I	G-LANC
T7793	G-ANKV	KD345:130-A	G-FGID
T7842	G-AMTF	KF584:RAI-X	G-RAIX
T7909	G-ANON	KF729	G-BJST
T8191	G-BWMK	KG651	G-AMHJ
T9707	G-AKKR	KK116	G-AMPY
T9738	G-AKAT	KN353	G-AMYJ
U-0247 (Class B identity)	G-AGOY	LB264	G-AIXA
U-80 (Swiss AF)	G-BUKK	LB294	G-AHWJ
U-95 (Swiss AF)	G-BVGP	LB312	G-AHXE
U-99 (Swiss AF)	G-AXMT	LB323	G-AHSD
U-108 (Swiss AF)	G-BJAX	LB367	G-AHGZ
U-110 (Swiss AF)	G-PTWO	LB375	G-AHGW
V-54 (Swiss AF)	G-BVSD	LF858	G-BLUZ
V3388	G-AHTW	LZ766	G-ALCK
V7497	G-HRLI	MH434:ZD-B	G-ASJV
V9312	G-CCOM	MJ627:9G-P	G-BMSB
V9367:MA-B	G-AZWT	ML407:OU-V	G-LFIX
V9673:MA-J	G-LIZY	MP425	G-AITB
W2718	G-RNLI	MS824 (French AF)	G-AWBU
W5856:A2A	G-BMGC	MT197	G-ANHS
W9385:YG-L	G-ADND	MT438	G-AREI
X4276	G-CDGU	MT928:ZX-M	G-BKMI
X7688	G-DINT	MV268:JE-J	G-SPIT
Z2033:N/275	G-ASTL	MW401	G-PEST
Z5140:HA-C	G-HURI	MW763:HF-A	G-TEMT
Z5207	G-BYDL	NJ633	G-AKXP
Z5252:GO-B	G-BWHA	NJ673	G-AOCR
Z7015:7-L	G-BKTH	NJ695	G-AJXV
Z7197	G-AKZN	NJ719	G-ANFU
Z7288	G-AHGD	NL750	G-AOBH
AP506	G-ACWM	NL985	G-BWIK
AP507:KX-P	G-ACWP	NM181	G-AZGZ
AR213:PR-D	G-AIST	NX534	G-BUDL
AR501:NN-A	G-AWII	NX611:LE-C/DX-C	G-ASXX
BB697	G-ADGT	PL965:R	G-MKXI
BB807	G-ADWO	PL983	G-PRXI
BE417:LK-A	G-HURR	PS853:C	G-RRGN
BI-005 (RNethAF)	G-BUVN	PT462:SW-A	G-CTIX
BM597:JH-C	G-MKVB	PT879	G-BYDE
CW-BG (Luftwaffe)	G-BXBD	RG333	G-AIEK
DE208	G-AGYU	RG333	G-AKEZ
DE470	G-ANMY	RH377	G-ALAH
DE623	G-ANFI	RL962	G-AHED
DE673	G-ADNZ	RM221	G-ANXR
DE992	G-AXXV	RN218:N	G-BBJI
DF112	G-ANRM	RR232	G-BRSF
DF128:RCO-U	G-AOJJ	RT486:PF-A	G-AJGJ
DF155	G-ANFV	RT520	G-ALYB
DF198	G-BBRB	RT610	G-AKWS
DG590	G-ADMW	RW386:NG-D	G-BXVI
EM720	G-AXAN	RX168	G-BWEM
EN224	G-FXII	SM845:GZ-J	G-BUOS
EP120:AE-A	G-LFVB	SM969:D-A	G-BRAF
ES.1-4 (Spanish AF)	G-BUTX	SX336:105-VL	G-KASX

MILITARY/CIVIL CROSS-REFERENCE

Serial carried	Civil identity	Serial carried	Civil identity
TA634:8K-K	G-AWJV	WD413	G-VROE
TA719:6T	G-ASKC	WE569	G-ASAJ
TA805:FX-M	G-PMNF	WE724:062	G-BUCM
TD248:CR-S	G-OXVI	WF118	G-DACA
TE184:D	G-MXVI	WF877	G-BPOA
TJ534	G-AKSY	WG308:8	G-BYHL
TJ569	G-AKOW	WG316	G-BCAH
TJ652	G-AMVD	WG321:G	G-DHCC
TJ672:TS-D	G-ANIJ	WG348	G-BBMV
TJ704:JA	G-ASCD	WG350	G-BPAL
TS798	G-AGNV	WG407:67	G-BWMX
TW439	G-ANRP	WG422:16	G-BFAX
TW467	G-ANIE	WG465	G-BCEY
TW511	G-APAF	WG469:72	G-BWJY
TW536:TS-V	G-BNGE	WG472	G-AOTY
TW591:N	G-ARIH	WG719	G-BRMA
TW641	G-ATDN	WJ358	G-ARYD
TX213	G-AWRS	WJ368	G-ASZX
VF512:PF-M	G-ARRX	WJ945:21	G-BEDV
VF516	G-ASMZ	WK163	G-BVWC
VF526:T	G-ARXU	WK436	G-VENM
VF581	G-ARSL	WK512:A	G-BXIM
VL348	G-AVVO	WK514	G-BBMO
VL349	G-AWSA	WK517	G-ULAS
VM360	G-APHV	WK522	G-BCOU
VN799	G-CDSX	WK549	G-BTWF
VP955	G-DVON	WK577	G-BCYM
VP981	G-DHDV	WK585	G-BZGA
VR192	G-APIT	WK586:V	G-BXGX
VR249:FA-EL	G-APIY	WK590:69	G-BWVZ
VR259:M	G-APJB	WK609:93	G-BXDN
VS356	G-AOLU	WK611	G-ARWB
VS610:K-L	G-AOKL	WK624	G-BWHI
VS623	G-AOKZ	WK628	G-BBMW
VT871	G-DHXX	WK630	G-BXDG
VV612	G-VENI	WK633:A	G-BXEC
VX113	G-ARNO	WK640:C	G-BWUV
VX118	G-ASNB	WK642:94	G-BXDP
VX147	G-AVIL	WL505	G-MKVI
VX927	G-ASYG	WL626:P	G-BHDD
VZ638:HF	G-JETM	WM167	G-LOSM
VZ728	G-AGOS	WP308:572CU	G-GACA
WA576	G-ALSS	WP321	G-BRFC
WA577	G-ALST	WP788	G-BCHL
WA591:W	G-BWMF	WP790:T	G-BBNC
WB188 (green)	G-BZPB	WP795:901	G-BVZZ
WB188 (red)	G-BZPC	WP800:2	G-BCXN
WB565:X	G-PVET	WP803	G-HAPY
WB569:R	G-BYSJ	WP805:D	G-MAJR
WB571:34	G-AOSF	WP808	G-BDEU
WB585:M	G-AOSY	WP809:78 RN	G-BVTX
WB588:D	G-AOTD	WP840:9	G-BXDM
WB615:E	G-BXIA	WP844:85	G-BWOX
WB652:V	G-CHPY	WP857:24	G-BDRJ
WB654:U	G-BXGO	WP859:E	G-BXCP
WB671:910	G-BWTG	WP860:6	G-BXDA
WB697:95	G-BXCT	WP896	G-BWVY
WB702	G-AOFE	WP901:B	G-BWNT
WB703	G-ARMC	WP903	G-BCGC
WB711	G-APPM	WP925:C	G-BXHA
WB726:E	G-AOSK	WP928:D	G-BXGM
WB763:14	G-BBMR	WP929:F	G-BXCV
WD286	G-BBND	WP930:J	G-BXHF
WD292	G-BCRX	WP970:12	G-BCOI
WD305	G-ARGG	WP971	G-ATHD
WD310:B	G-BWUN	WP983:B	G-BXNN
WD331:J	G-BXDH	WP984:H	G-BWTO
WD347	G-BBRV	WR360:K	G-DHSS
WD363:5	G-BCIH	WR410:N	G-BLKA
WD373:12	G-BXDI	WR410	G-DHUU
WD379:K	G-APLO	WR421	G-DHTT
WD390:68	G-BWNK	WR470	G-DHVM

MILITARY/CIVIL CROSS-REFERENCE

Serial carried	Civil identity	Serial carried	Civil identity
WT333	G-BVXC	XM223:J	G-BWWC
WT722:878/VL	G-BWGN	XM370:10	G-BVSP
WT723:866/VL	G-PRII	XM376	G-BWDR
WT933	G-ALSW	XM424	G-BWDS
WV198:K	G-BJWY	XM478:33	G-BXDL
WV318	G-FFOX	XM479:54	G-BVEZ
WV322:Y	G-BZSE	XM553	G-AWSV
WV372:R	G-BXFI	XM575	G-BLMC
WV493:29	G-BDYG	XM655	G-VULC
WV740	G-BNPH	XM685:513/PO	G-AYZJ
WV783	G-ALSP	XM819	G-APXW
WW453:W-S	G-TMKI	XN351	G-BKSC
WZ507:74	G-VTII	XN437	G-AXWA
WZ589	G-DHZZ	XN441	G-BGKT
WZ662	G-BKVK	XN459:N	G-BWOT
WZ711	G-AVHT	XN498	G-BWSH
WZ847:F	G-CPMK	XN510:40	G-BXBI
WZ868:H	G-ARMF	XN629	G-KNOT
WZ872:E	G-BZGB	XN637:03	G-BKOU
WZ879	G-BWUT	XP242	G-BUCI
WZ882:K	G-BXGP	XP254	G-ASCC
XA880	G-BVXR	XP279	G-BWKK
XD693:Z-Q	G-AOBU	XP282	G-BGTC
XE489	G-JETH	XP355	G-BEBC
XE601	G-ETPS	XP672:03	G-RAFI
XE665:876/VL	G-BWGM	XP907	G-SROE
XE685:861/VL	G-GAII	XR240	G-BDFH
XE689:864/VL	G-BWGK	XR241	G-AXRR
XE856	G-DUSK	XR246	G-AZBU
XE897	G-DHVV	XR486	G-RWWW
XE956	G-OBLN	XR502:Z	G-CCUP
XF114	G-SWIF	XR537:T	G-NATY
XF303:105-A	G-BWOU	XR538:01	G-RORI
XF515:R	G-KAXF	XR595:M	G-BWHU
XF597:AH	G-BKFW	XR673:L	G-BXLO
XF603	G-KAPW	XR724	G-BTSY
XF690	G-MOOS	XR944	G-ATTB
XF785	G-ALBN	XR991	G-MOUR
XF836:J-G	G-AWRY	XR993	G-BVPP
XF877:JX	G-AWVF	XS104	G-FRCE
XF995:K	G-BZSF	XS111	G-TIMM
XG160:U	G-BWAF	XS165:37	G-ASAZ
XG452	G-BRMB	XS235	G-CPDA
XG547:S-T	G-HAPR	XS587	G-VIXN
XG775	G-DHWW	XS765	G-BSET
XH134	G-OMHD	XS770	G-HRHI
XH558	G-VLCN	XT223	G-XTUN
XJ389	G-AJJP	XT420:606	G-CBUI
XJ398	G-BDBZ	XT435:430	G-RIMM
XJ615	G-BWGL	XT634	G-BYRX
XJ729	G-BVGE	XT671	G-BYRC
XJ771	G-HELV	XT787	G-KAXT
XK416	G-AYUA	XT788:316	G-BMIR
XK417	G-AVXY	XT793:456	G-BZPP
XK895:19/CU	G-SDEV	XV130:R	G-BWJW
XK896	G-RNAS	XV134:P	G-BWLX
XK940:911	G-AYXT	XV137	G-CRUM
XL426	G-VJET	XV268	G-BVER
XL500	G-KAEW	XW289:73	G-JPVA
XL502	G-BMYP	XW293:Z	G-BWCS
XL571:V	G-HNTR	XW310	G-BWGS
XL573	G-BVGH	XW324:K	G-BWSG
XL577:V	G-BXKF	XW325:E	G-BWGF
XL587	G-HPUX	XW333:79	G-BVTC
XL602	G-BWFT	XW354	G-JPTV
XL621	G-BNCX	XW422:3	G-BWEB
XL714	G-AOGR	XW423:14	G-BWUW
XL716	G-AOIL	XW433	G-JPRO
XL809	G-BLIX	XW635	G-AWSW
XL812	G-SARO	XW784:VL	G-BBRN
XL929	G-BNPU	XW854:46/CU	G-CBSD
XL954	G-BXES	XW858:C	G-DMSS

MILITARY/CIVIL CROSS-REFERENCE

Serial carried	Civil identity	Serial carried	Civil identity
XW866:E	G-BXTH	XX693:07	G-BZML
XW898:G	G-CBXT	XX694:E	G-CBBS
XX406:P	G-CBSH	XX695:3	G-CBBT
XX432	G-CDNO	XX698:9	G-BZME
XX467:86	G-TVII	XX699:F	G-CBCV
XX469	G-BNCL	XX700:17	G-CBEK
XX513:10	G-CCMI	XX702:II	G-CBCR
XX514	G-BWIB	XX704	G-BCUV
XX515:4	G-CBBC	XX707:4	G-CBDS
XX518:S	G-UDOG	XX711:X	G-CBBU
XX521:H	G-CBEH	XX713:2	G-CBJK
XX522:06	G-DAWG	XX885	G-HHAA
XX524:04	G-DDOG	XZ934:U	G-CBSI
XX525:8	G-CBJJ	XZ937:Y	G-CBKA
XX528:D	G-BZON	XZ940:O	G-CBBV
XX534:B	G-EDAV	ZA250	G-VTOL
XX537:C	G-CBCB	ZA634:C	G-BUHA
XX538:O	G-TDOG	ZA652	G-BUDC
XX543:F	G-CBAB	ZB500	G-LYNX
XX546:03	G-WINI	ZB627:A	G-CBSK
XX549:6	G-CBID	ZB646:59/CU	G-CBGZ
XX550:Z	G-CBBL	2+1:7334 Luftwaffe)	G-SYFW
XX551:E	G-BZDP	3+ (Luftwaffe)	G-BAYV
XX554	G-BZMD	4+ (Luftwaffe)	G-BSLX
XX561:7	G-BZEP	4-97/MM52801 (Italian)	G-BBII
XX611:7	G-CBDK	07 (Russian AF)	G-BMJY
XX612:A, 03	G-BZXC	8+ (Luftwaffe)	G-WULF
XX614:V	G-GGRR	F+IS (Luftwaffe)	G-BIRW
XX619:T	G-CBBW	BU+CC (Luftwaffe)	G-BUCC
XX621:H	G-CBEF	BU+CK (Luftwaffe)	G-BUCK
XX622:B	G-CBGZ	CC+43 (Luftwaffe)	G-CJCI
XX624:E	G-KDOG	CF+HF (Luftwaffe)	EI-AUY
XX625:01, N	G-CBBR	DM+BK (Luftwaffe)	G-BPHZ
XX626:02, W	G-CDVV	LG+01 (Luftwaffe)	G-AYSJ
XX628:9	G-CBFU	LG+03 (Luftwaffe)	G-AEZX
XX629:V	G-BZXZ	KG+EM (Luftwaffe)	G-ETME
XX630:5	G-SIJW	NJ+C11 (Luftwaffe)	G-ATBG
XX631:W	G-BZXS	S4+A07 (Luftwaffe)	G-BWHP
XX636:Y	G-CBFP	S5-B06 (Luftwaffe)	G-BSFB
XX638	G-DOGG	6J+PR (Luftwaffe)	G-AWHB
XX658:07	G-BZPS	57-H (USAAC)	G-AKAZ
XX667:16	G-BZFN	97+04 (Luftwaffe)	G-APVF
XX668:1	G-CBAN	+14 (Luftwaffe)	G-BSMD
XX692:A	G-BZMH	146-11083 (5)	G-BNAI

Popham-based Nieuport Scout replica G-BWMJ now has a dispensation to fly in WW1 French Air Force colours. *DP*

Republic of Ireland Civil Registrations

Notes	Reg	Type	Owner or Operator
	EI-ABI	DH.84 Dragon	Aer Lingus Iolar (EI-AFK)
	EI-ADV	PA-12 Super Cruiser	R. E. Levis
	EI-AFE	Piper J3C-65 Cub	J. Conlan
	EI-AFF	B.A. Swallow 2	J. J. Sullivan & ptnrs
	EI-AGD	Taylorcraft Plus D	B. & K. O'Sullivan
	EI-AGJ	Auster J/1 Autocrat	T. G. Rafter
	EI-AHI	DH.82A Tiger Moth	High Fidelity Flyers
	EI-AKM	Piper J-3C-65 Cub	Setanta Flying Group
	EI-ALH	Taylorcraft Plus D	N. Reilly
	EI-ALP	Avro 643 Cadet	J.C. O'Loughlin *(stored)*
	EI-AMK	Auster J/1 Autocrat	J. J. Sullivan
	EI-AMY	Auster J/1N Alpha	T. Lennon
	EI-ANT	Champion 7ECA Citabria	T. Croke & ptnrs
	EI-ANY	PA-18 Super Cub 95	Bogavia Group
	EI-AOB	PA-28 Cherokee 140	Knock Flying Group
	EI-AOS	Cessna 310B	Southair
	EI-APS	Schleicher ASK.14	E. Shiel & ptnrs
	EI-ARH	Currie Wot/S.E.5 Replica	L. Garrison
	EI-ARM	Currie Wot/S.E.5 Replica	L. Garrison
	EI-ARW	Jodel D.R.1050	J. Davy
	EI-ASR	McCandless Gyroplane Mk 4	J. J. Fasenfeld
	EI-AST	Cessna F.150H	Ormond Flying Club
	EI-ATJ	B.121 Pup Srs 2	L. O'Leary
	EI-ATK	PA-28 Cherokee 140	Mayo Flying Club
	EI-ATL	Aeronca 7AC Champion	Kildare Flying Club
	EI-ATP	Luton LA-4A Minor	Hanging in the Terminal of Miami International
	EI-ATS	MS.880B Rallye Club	ATS Group
	EI-AUE	MS.880B Rallye Club	Kilkenny Flying Club
	EI-AUG	MS.894 Rallye Minerva 220	K. O'Leary
	EI-AUM	Auster J/1 Autocrat	T. G. Rafter
	EI-AUO	Cessna FA.150K Aerobat	S. Burke & L. Bagnell
	EI-AUS	Auster J/5F Aiglet Trainer	T. Stevens & ptnrs
	EI-AUT	Forney F-1A Aircoupe	Southair
	EI-AUY	Morane-Saulnier MS.502 (CF+HF)	Historical Aircraft Preservation Group
	EI-AVB	Aeronca 7AC Champion	T. Brett
	EI-AVM	Cessna F.150L	Tojo Air Leasing
	EI-AWD	PA-22 Tri-Pacer 160	J. P. Montcalm
	EI-AWH	Cessna 210J	Rathcoole Flying Club
	EI-AWP	DH.82A Tiger Moth	A. P. Bruton
	EI-AWR	Malmö MFI-9 Junior	A. Szorfy
	EI-AWU	MS.880B Rallye Club	Longford Aviation
	EI-AYA	MS.880B Rallye Club	Limerick Flying Club (Coonagh)
	EI-AYB	GY-80 Horizon 180	J. B. Smith
	EI-AYD	AA-5 Traveler	V. O'Rourke & ptnrs
	EI-AYF	Cessna FRA.150L	S. Bruton
	EI-AYI	MS.880B Rallye Club	J. McNamara
	EI-AYK	Cessna F.172M	D. Gallagher
	EI-AYN	BN-2A-8 Islander	Aer Arann
	EI-AYR	Schleicher ASK-16	B. O'Broin & ptnrs
	EI-AYT	MS.894A Rallye Minerva	K. A. O'Connor
	EI-AYV	MS.892A Rallye Commodore 150	P. Murtagh
	EI-AYY	Evans VP-1	R. Dowd & P. O'Rourke
	EI-BAJ	Stampe SV.4C	Dublin Tiger Group
	EI-BAR	Thunder Ax8-105 balloon	J. Burke & ptnrs
	EI-BAT	Cessna F.150M	K. A. O'Connor
	EI-BAV	PA-22 Colt 108	E. Finnamore & J. Deegan
	EI-BBC	PA-28 Cherokee 180C	Vero Beach
	EI-BBD	Evans VP-1	Volksplane Group
	EI-BBE	Champion 7FC Tri-Traveler (tailwheel)	R. McNally & C. Carey
	EI-BBG	MS.880B Rallye Club ★	Weston Ltd *(stored)*
	EI-BBI	MS.892 Rallye Commodore	Ossory Flying & Gliding Club
	EI-BBJ	MS.880B Rallye Club	Weston Ltd
	EI-BBO	MS.893E Rallye 180GT	G. P. Moorhead
	EI-BBV	Piper J-3C-65 Cub	F. Cronin
	EI-BCE	BN-2A-26 Islander	Aer Arann
	EI-BCF	Bensen B.8M	P. Flanagan
	EI-BCJ	Aeromere F.8L Falco 1 Srs 3	M. P. McLoughlin
	EI-BCK	Cessna F.172N II	K. A. O'Connor
	EI-BCL	Cessna 182P	L. Burke

EI-BCM – EI-BMH   REPUBLIC OF IRELAND

Notes	Reg	Type	Owner or Operator
	EI-BCM	Piper J-3C-65 Cub	Kilmoon Flying Group
	EI-BCN	Piper J-3C-65 Cub	H. Diver
	EI-BCO	Piper J-3C-65 Cub	J. Molloy
	EI-BCP	D.62B Condor	T. Delaney
	EI-BCS	MS.880B Rallye Club	Organic Fruit & Vegetables of Kilmeadan
	EI-BCU	MS.880B Rallye Club	Weston Ltd
	EI-BCW	MS.880B Rallye Club	Kilkenny Flying Club
	EI-BDH	MS.880B Rallye Club	Munster Wings
	EI-BDK	MS.880B Rallye Club	Limerick Flying Club (Coonagh)
	EI-BDL	Evans VP-2	P. Buggle
	EI-BDM	PA-23 Aztec 250D	G. A. Costello
	EI-BDR	PA-28 Cherokee 180	Cherokee Group
	EI-BEA	MS.880B Rallye 100ST	Weston Ltd *(stored)*
	EI-BEN	Piper J-3C-65 Cub	Capt. J. J. Sullivan
	EI-BEP	MS.892A Rallye 150	H. Lynch & J. O'Leary
	EI-BFE	Cessna F.150G	Southair
	EI-BFF	Beech A.23 Musketeer	J. Lankfer
	EI-BFI	MS.880B Rallye 100ST	J. O'Neill
	EI-BFO	Piper J-3C-90 Cub	D. Gordon
	EI-BFP	MS.800B Rallye 100ST	Limerick Flying Club (Coonagh)
	EI-BFR	MS.880B Rallye 100ST	Wexford Flying Group
	EI-BGA	SOCATA Rallye 100ST	J. J. Frew
	EI-BGB	MS.880B Rallye Club	Limerick Flying Club (Coonagh)
	EI-BGC	MS.880B Rallye Club	P. Moran
	EI-BGD	MS.880B Rallye Club	N. Kavanagh
	EI-BGF	PA-28R Cherokee 180	Arrow Group
	EI-BGJ	Cessna F.152 II	Sligo Aero Club
	EI-BGS	MS.893E Rallye	M. Farrelly
	EI-BGT	Colt 77A balloon	M. J. Mills
	EI-BGU	MS.880B Rallye Club	M. F. Neary
	EI-BHC	Cessna F.177RG	L. Gavin
	EI-BHF	MS.892A Rallye Commodore 150	B. Mullen
	EI-BHI	Bell 206B JetRanger 2	G. Tracey
	EI-BHM	Cessna F.337E	City of Dublin VE College
	EI-BHN	MS.893A Rallye Commodore 180T	T. Garvan
	EI-BHP	MS.893A Rallye Commodore 180T	Spanish Point Flying Club
	EI-BHT	Beech 77 Skipper	Waterford Aero Club
	EI-BHV	Champion 7EC Traveler	P. O'Donnell & ptnrs
	FI-BHW	Cessna F.150F	R. Sharpe
	EI-BHY	SOCATA Rallye 150ST	Limerick Flying Club (Coonagh)
	EI-BIB	Cessna F.152	Galway Flying Club
	EI-BID	PA-18 Super Cub 95	S. Coghlan & P. Ryan
	EI-BIG	Zlin 526	P. von Lonkhuyzen
	EI-BIJ	AB-206B JetRanger 2	Medeva Properties
	EI-BIK	PA-18 Super Cub 180	Dublin Gliding Club
	EI-BIM	MS.880B Rallye Club	D. Millar
	EI-BIO	Piper J-3C-65 Cub	H. Duggan
	EI-BIR	Cessna F.172M	T. Bradford & ptnrs
	EI-BIS	Robin R.1180TD	Robin Aiglon Group
	EI-BIT	MS.887 Rallye 125	Spanish Point Flying Club
	EI-BIV	Bellanca 8KCAB	AEROCRAT PILOTS LTD
	EI-BIW	MS.880B Rallye Club	E. J. Barr
	EI-BJB	Aeronca 7AC Champion	A. W. Kennedy
	EI-BJC	Aeronca 7AC Champion	A. E. Griffin
	EI-BJI	Cessna FR.172E	Irish Parachute Club
	EI-BJJ	Aeronca 15AC Sedan	O. Bruton
	EI-BJK	MS.880B Rallye 110ST	M. Keenen
	EI-BJM	Cessna A.152	K. A. O'Connor
	EI-BJO	Cessna R.172K	Merlin Mfg (Galway) Ltd
	EI-BJT	PA-38-112 Tomahawk	S. Corrigan & W. Lennon
	EI-BKC	Aeronca 15AC Sedan	G. Hendrick & M. Farrell
	EI-BKF	Cessna F.172H	D. Darby
	EI-BKK	Taylor JT.1 Monoplane	J. J. Sullivan
	EI-BKN	MS.880B Rallye 100ST	Weston Ltd
	EI-BKU	MS.892A Rallye Commodore 150	Limerick Flying Club (Coonagh)
	EI-BLB	SNCAN Stampe SV.4C	J. Hutchinson & R. A. Stafford
	EI-BLD	Bolkow Bö.105DB	Irish Helicopters
	EI-BLE	Eipper Quicksilver Microlight	R. Smith & P. St. George
	EI-BLN	Eipper Quicksilver MX	O. J. Conway & ptnrs
	EI-BMA	MS.880B Rallye Club	W. Rankin & M. Kelleher
	EI-BMB	MS.880B Rallye 100T	Glyde Court Developments
	EI-BMF	Laverda F.8L Falco srs IV	M. Slazenger
	EI-BMH	MS.880B Rallye Club	N. S. Bracken

REPUBLIC OF IRELAND   EI-BMI – EI-CAC

Reg	Type	Owner or Operator	Notes
EI-BMI	SOCATA TB9 Tampico	D. Pratt	
EI-BMJ	MS.880B Rallye 100T	Limerick Flying Club (Coonagh)	
EI-BMM	Cessna F.152 II	P. Redmond	
EI-BMN	Cessna F.152 II	K. A. O'Connor	
EI-BMU	Monnet Sonerai IIL	A. Fenton	
EI-BMV	Grumman AA-5 Traveler	E. Tierney & K. A. Harold	
EI-BMW	Vulcan Air Trike	L. Maddock & ptnrs	
EI-BNF	Eurowing Goldwing Canard	T. Morelli	
EI-BNH	Hiway Skytrike	M. Martin	
EI-BNJ	Evans VP-2	G. Cashman	
EI-BNK	Cessna U.206F	Irish Parachute Club	
EI-BNL	Rand-Robinson KR-2	K. Hayes	
EI-BNP	Rotorway 133	R. L. Renfroe	
EI-BNT	Cvjetkovic CA-65	B. Tobin & ptnrs	
EI-BNU	MS.880B Rallye Club	P. A. Doyle	
EI-BOA	Pterodactyl Ptraveller	A. Murphy	
EI-BOE	SOCATA TB10 Tobago	Tobago Group	
EI-BOH	Eipper Quicksilver	J. Leech	
EI-BOV	Rand-Robinson KR-2	G. O'Hara & G. Callan	
EI-BOX	Jordan Duet	Dr. K. Riccius	
EI-BPE	Viking Dragonfly	G. G. Bracken	
EI-BPL	Cessna F.172K	Phoenix Flying	
EI-BPN	Flexiform Striker	P. H. Collins	
EI-BPO	Southdown Sailwings Lightning DS	A. Channing	
EI-BPP	Quicksilver MX	J. A. Smith	
EI-BPT	Skyhook Sabre	T. McGrath	
EI-BPU	Hiway Demon	A. Channing	
EI-BRK	Flexiform Trike	L. Maddock & ptnrs	
EI-BRS	Cessna P.172D	P. Mathews	
EI-BRU	Evans VP-1	Home Bru Flying Group	
EI-BRV	Hiway Demon	M. Garvey & C. Tully	
EI-BRW	Hovey Deltabird	A & E Aerosport	
EI-BSB	Wassmer Jodel D.112	Estartit Ltd	
EI-BSC	Cessna F.172N	S. Phelan	
EI-BSG	Bensen B.80	J. Todd	
EI-BSK	SOCATA TB9 Tampico	T. Drury	
EI-BSL	PA-34-220T Seneca III	P. Sreenan	
EI-BSN	Cameron O-65 balloon	C. O'Neill & T. Hooper	
EI-BSO	PA-28 Cherokee 140B	H. N. Hanley	
EI-BSV	SOCATA TB20 Trinidad	J. Condron	
EI-BSW	Solar Wings Pegasus XL-R	E. Fitzgerald	
EI-BSX	Piper J-3C-65 Cub	J. & T. O'Dwyer	
EI-BTX	McD Douglas MD-83	Airplanes Holdings/Aeromexico	
EI-BTY	McD Douglas MD-82	Airplanes Holdings/Aeromexico	
EI-BUA	Cessna 172M	K. A. O'Connor	
EI-BUC	Jodel D.9 Bébé	B. Lyons & M. Blake	
EI-BUF	Cessna 210N	210 Group	
EI-BUG	SOCATA ST.10 Diplomate	J. Cooke	
EI-BUH	Lake LA.4-200 Buccaneer	P. Redden	
EI-BUJ	MS.892A Rallye Commodore 150	T. Cunniffe	
EI-BUL	Whittaker MW5 Sorcerer	J. Culleton	
EI-BUN	Beech 76 Duchess	K. A. O'Connor	
EI-BUT	MS.893A Commodore 180	T. Keating	
EI-BVB	Whittaker MW6 Merlin	R. England	
EI-BVJ	AMF Chevvron 232	A. Dunn	
EI-BVK	PA-38-112 Tomahawk	M. Martin	
EI-BVT	Evans VP-2	P. Morrison	
EI-BVY	Zenith 200AA-RW	J. Matthews & M. Skelly	
EI-BWH	Partenavia P.68C	K. Buckley	
EI-BXL	Polaris F1B-OK350	M. McKeon	
EI-BXO	Fouga CM.170 Magister	G. Connolly	
EI-BXT	D.62B Condor	The Condor Group	
EI-BYA	Thruster TST Mk 1	E. Fagan	
EI-BYF	Cessna 150M	High Kings Flying Group	
EI-BYG	SOCATA TB9 Tampico	M. McGinn	
EI-BYJ	Bell 206B JetRanger	Medeva Properties	
EI-BYL	Zenith CH.250	M. McLoughlin	
EI-BYO	Aérospatiale ATR-42-310	Aer Arann	
EI-BYR	Bell 206L-3 LongRanger 3	R. Mockler & L. Cullen	
EI-BYX	Champion 7GCAA	P. J. Gallagher	
EI-BYY	Piper J-3C-85 Cub	The Cub Club	
EI-CAC	Grob G.115A	G. Tracey	

301

EI-CAD – EI-CIJ   REPUBLIC OF IRELAND

Notes	Reg	Type	Owner or Operator
	EI-CAD	Grob G.115A	Flightwise Training Ltd
	EI-CAE	Grob G.115A	K. A. O'Connor
	EI-CAN	Aerotech MW5 Sorcerer	V. A. Vaughan
	EI-CAP	Cessna R.182RG	M. J. Hanlon
	EI-CAU	AMF Chevvron 232	J. Tarrant
	EI-CAW	Bell 206B JetRanger	Celtic Helicopters
	EI-CAX	Cessna P.210N	K. A. O'Connor
	EI-CAY	Mooney M.20C	Ranger Flights Ltd
	EI-CBK	Aérospatiale ATR-42-310	Aer Arann
	EI-CBR	McD Douglas MD-83	Airplanes 111/Avianca
	EI-CBS	McD Douglas MD-83	GECAS Technical Services/Avianca
	EI-CBY	McD Douglas MD-83	GECAS Technical Services/Avianca
	EI-CBZ	McD Douglas MD-83	GECAS Technical Services/Avianca
	EI-CCC	McD Douglas MD-83	Airplanes 111/Avianca
	EI-CCD	Grob G.115A	Kal Aviation
	EI-CCE	McD Douglas MD-83	GECAS Technical Services/Avianca
	EI-CCF	Aeronca 11AC Chief	G. McGuinness & R. Whalley
	EI-CCJ	Cessna 152 II	P. Cahill
	EI-CCK	Cessna 152 II	P. Cahill
	EI-CCL	Cessna 152 II	P. Cahill
	EI-CCM	Cessna 152 II	E. Hopkins
	EI-CCV	Cessna R.172K-XP	Kerry Aero Club
	EI-CDD	Boeing 737-548	Castle 2003-2 Ireland/Pulkovo Airlines
	EI-CDE	Boeing 737-548	Castle 2003-2 Ireland/Pulkovo Airlines
	EI-CDF	Boeing 737-548	Jetscope Aviation Ireland/Pulkovo Airlines
	EI-CDG	Boeing 737-548	Jetscope Aviation Ireland/Pulkovo Airlines
	EI-CDH	Boeing 737-548	Jetscope Aviation Ireland/Pulkovo Airlines
	EI-CDP	Cessna 182L	Irish Parachute Club
	EI-CDV	Cessna 150G	K. A. O'Connor
	EI-CDX	Cessna 210K	Falcon Aviation
	EI-CDY	McD Douglas MD-83	GECAS Technical Services/Avianca
	EI-CEG	MS.893A Rallye 180GT	M. Farrelly
	EI-CEN	Thruster T.300	P. A. J. Murphy
	EI-CEP	McD Douglas MD-83	GECAS Technical Services/Avianca
	EI-CEQ	McD Douglas MD-83	GECAS Technical Services/Avianca
	EI-CER	McD Douglas MD-83	Airplanes 111/Avianca
	EI-CES	Taylorcraft BC-65	B. J. Douglas
	EI-CEY	Boeing 757-2Y0	Pergola/Avianca
	EI-CEZ	Boeing 757-2Y0	Airplanes Holdings/Avianca
	EI-CFE	Hobinson R22 Beta	Millicent Golf & Country Club
	EI-CFF	PA-12 Super Cruiser	J. & T. O'Dwyer
	EI-CFG	CP.301B Emeraude	F. Doyle
	EI-CFH	PA-12 Super Cruiser	G. Treacy
	EI-CFN	Cessna 172P	B. Fitzmaurice & G. O'Connell
	EI-CFO	Piper J-3C-65 Cub	J. Matthews & ptnrs
	EI-CFP	Cessna 172P (floatplane)	K. A. O'Connor
	EI-CFX	Robinson R22 Beta	Brian O'Sullivan
	EI-CFY	Cessna 172N	K. A. O'Connor
	EI-CFZ	McD Douglas MD-83	Airplanes 111/Avianca
	EI-CGB	TEAM mini-MAX	M. Garvey
	EI-CGC	Stinson 108-3	A. D. Weldon & L. Shoebridge
	EI-CGD	Cessna 172M	J. Murray
	EI-CGF	Luton LA-5 Major	J. Duggan
	EI-CGG	Erco Ercoupe 415C	Irish Ercoupe Group
	EI-CGH	Cessna 210N	J. Smith
	EI-CGJ	Solar Wings Pegasus XL-R	A. P. Hearty
	EI-CGM	Solar Wings Pegasus XL-R	Microflight Ltd
	EI-CGN	Solar Wings Pegasus XL-R	V. Power
	EI-CGP	PA-28 Cherokee 140C	G. Cashman
	EI-CGQ	AS.350B Ecureuil	Blue Star Helicopters
	EI-CGT	Cessna 152 II	J. Rafter
	EI-CGV	Piper J-5A Cub Cruiser	J5 Group
	EI-CHH	Boeing 737-317	Airplanes Finance/KLD – KD-Avia
	EI-CHK	Piper J-3C-65 Cub	N. Higgins
	EI-CHM	Cessna 150M	K. A. O'Connor
	EI-CHR	CFM Shadow Srs BD	B. Kelly
	EI-CHS	Cessna 172M	B. A. Mills
	EI-CHT	Solar Wings Pegasus XL-R	J. Grattan
	EI-CHV	Agusta A109A-II	Celtic Helicopters
	EI-CIA	MS.880B Rallye Club	G. Hackett & C. Mason
	EI-CIF	PA-28 Cherokee 180C	AA Flying Group
	EI-CIG	PA-18 Super Cub 150	K. A. O'Connor
	EI-CIJ	Cessna 340	Airlink Airways

REPUBLIC OF IRELAND

EI-CIM – EI-CRE

Reg	Type	Owner or Operator	Notes
EI-CIM	Avid Flyer Mk IV	P. Swan	
EI-CIN	Cessna 150K	K. A. O'Connor	
EI-CIR	Cessna 551 Citation II	Aircraft International Renting	
EI-CIV	PA-28 Cherokee 140	G. Cashman & E. Callanan	
EI-CIW	McD Douglas MD-83	East Dover/Meridiana	
EI-CIZ	Steen Skybolt	J. Keane	
EI-CJR	SNCAN Stampe SV.4A	P. McKenna	
EI-CJS	Jodel D.120A	A. Flood	
EI-CJT	Slingsby Motor Cadet III	J. Tarrant	
EI-CJV	Moskito 2	M. Peril & ptnrs	
EI-CJZ	Whittaker MW6 Merlin	M. McCarthy	
EI-CKG	Avon Hunt Weightlift	B. Kenny	
EI-CKH	PA-18 Super Cub 95	G. Brady	
EI-CKI	Thruster TST Mk 1	N. Furlong	
EI-CKJ	Cameron N-77 balloon	A. F. Meldon	
EI-CKM	McD Douglas MD-83	Airplanes Finance/Meridiana	
EI-CKN	Whittaker MW6-S Fatboy Flyer	F. Byrne & M. O.'Carroll	
EI-CKT	Mainair Gemini/Flash	A. C. Burke	
EI-CKU	Solar Wings Pegasus SLR	M. O'Regan	
EI-CKZ	Jodel D.18	J. O'Brien	
EI-CLA	HOAC Katana DV.20	Weston Ltd	
EI-CLL	Whittaker MW6-S Fat Boy Flyer	F. Stack	
EI-CLQ	Cessna F.172N	Just Having Fun 172 Group	
EI-CLW	Boeing 737-3Y0	Airplanes Finance/Kras Air/AirUnion	
EI-CLZ	Boeing 737-3Y0	Airplanes Finance/Kras Air/AirUnion	
EI-CMB	PA-28 Cherokee 140	Dublin Flyers	
EI-CMK	Goldwing ST	M. Gavigan	
EI-CML	Cessna 150M	K. A. O'Connor	
EI-CMN	PA-12 Super Cruiser	A. McNamee & ptnrs	
EI-CMR	Rutan LongEz	F. & C. O'Caoimh	
EI-CMS	BAe 146-200	CityJet/Air France Express	
EI-CMT	PA-34-200T Seneca II	Atlantic Flight Training	
EI-CMU	Mainair Mercury	L. Langan & L. Laffan	
EI-CMV	Cessna 150L	K. A. O'Connor	
EI-CMW	Rotorway Executive	B. McNamee	
EI-CMY	BAe 146-200	CityJet/Air France Express	
EI-CNA	Letov LK-2M Sluka	G. Doody	
EI-CNB	BAe 146-200	CityJet	
EI-CNC	TEAM mini-MAX	A. M. S. Allen	
EI-CNG	Air & Space 18A gyroplane	P. Joyce	
EI-CNJ	Avro 146 RJ 85	Peregrine Aviation Leasing Co *(stored)*	
EI-CNL	Sikorsky S-61N	CHC Ireland	
FI-CNQ	BAe 146-200	CityJet	
EI-CNU	Pegasus Quantum 15-912	M. Ffrench	
EI-COE	Shaw Europa	F. Flynn	
EI-COG	Gyroscopic Rotorcraft gyroplane	R. C. Fidler & D. Bracken	
EI-COH	Boeing 737-430	ACS Acft Lsg/Air One	
EI-COI	Boeing 737-430	Challey Ltd/Air One	
EI-COJ	Boeing 737-430	Challey Ltd/Air One	
EI-COK	Boeing 737-430	Constitution Acft Lsg/Air One	
EI-COM	Whittaker MW6-S Fatboy Flyer	M. Watson	
EI-COO	Carlson Sparrow II	D. Logue	
EI-COQ	Avro 146 RJ 70	Peregrine Aviation Leasing Co/Transwede/SAS	
EI-COT	Cessna F.172N	Tojo Air Leasing	
EI-COY	Piper J-3C-65 Cub	D. Bruton & W. Flood	
EI-COZ	PA-28 Cherokee 140C	G. Cashman	
EI-CPC	Airbus A.321-211	Aer Lingus *St Fergus*	
EI-CPD	Airbus A.321-211	Aer Lingus *St Davnet*	
EI-CPE	Airbus A.321-211	Aer Lingus *St Enda*	
EI-CPF	Airbus A.321-211	Aer Lingus *St Ide*	
EI-CPG	Airbus A.321-211	Aer Lingus *St Aidan*	
EI-CPH	Airbus A.321-211	Aer Lingus *St Dervilla*	
EI-CPI	Rutan LongEz	D. J. Ryan	
EI-CPJ	Avro 146 RJ 70	Peregrine Aviation Leasing Co *(stored)*	
EI-CPK	Avro 146 RJ 70	Peregrine Aviation Leasing Co *(stored)*	
EI-CPN	Auster J/4	E. Fagan	
EI-CPO	Robinson R22 Beta 2	D. O'Gorman & D. Lowe	
EI-CPP	Piper J-3C-65 Cub	E. Fitzgerald	
EI-CPT	Aérospatiale ATR-42-320	Aer Arann	
EI-CPX	I.I.I. Sky Arrow 650T	M. McCarthy	
EI-CRB	Lindstrand LBL-90A balloon	J. & C. Concannon	
EI-CRD	Boeing 767-31BER	ILFC Ireland/Alitalia	
EI-CRE	McD Douglas MD-83	AAR Ireland/Meridiana	

303

EI-CRF – EI-CWC REPUBLIC OF IRELAND

Notes	Reg	Type	Owner or Operator
	EI-CRF	Boeing 767-31BER	ILFC Ireland/Alitalia
	EI-CRG	Robin DR.400/180R	D. & B. Lodge
	EI-CRH	McD Douglas MD-83	Airplanes 111/Meridiana
	EI-CRJ	McD Douglas MD-83	C. A. Aviation/Meridiana
	EI-CRK	Airbus A.330-301	Aer Lingus *St Brigid*
	EI-CRL	Boeing 767-343ER	Aircraft Finance Trust Ireland/Alitalia
	EI-CRM	Boeing 767-343ER	GECAS Technical Services/Alitalia
	EI-CRO	Boeing 767-3Q8ER	ILFC Ireland/Alitalia
	EI-CRR	Aeronca 11AC Chief	L. Maddock & ptnrs
	EI-CRU	Cessna 152	W. Reilly
	EI-CRV	Hoffman H-36 Dimona	The Dimona Group
	EI-CRW	McD Douglas MD-83	Airplanes IAL/Meridiana
	EI-CRX	SOCATA TB-9 Tampico	Hotel Bravo Flying Club
	EI-CRY	Medway Eclipser	G. A. Murphy
	EI-CRZ	Boeing 737-36E	ILFC Ireland/Air One
	EI-CSA	Boeing 737-8AS	Ryanair
	EI-CSB	Boeing 737-8AS	Ryanair
	EI-CSC	Boeing 737-8AS	Ryanair
	EI-CSD	Boeing 737-8AS	Ryanair
	EI-CSE	Boeing 737-8AS	Ryanair
	EI-CSF	Boeing 737-8AS	Ryanair
	EI-CSG	Boeing 737-8AS	Ryanair
	EI-CSH	Boeing 737-8AS	Ryanair
	EI-CSI	Boeing 737-8AS	Ryanair
	EI-CSJ	Boeing 737-8AS	Ryanair
	EI-CSK	BAe 146-200	CityJet/Air France Express
	EI-CSL	BAe 146-200	CityJet/Air France Express
	EI-CSM	Boeing 737-8AS	Ryanair
	EI-CSN	Boeing 737-8AS	Ryanair
	EI-CSO	Boeing 737-8AS	Ryanair
	EI-CSP	Boeing 737-8AS	Ryanair
	EI-CSQ	Boeing 737-8AS	Ryanair
	EI-CSR	Boeing 737-8AS	Ryanair
	EI-CSS	Boeing 737-8AS	Ryanair
	EI-CST	Boeing 737-8AS	Ryanair
	EI-CSU	Boeing 737-36E	ILFC Ireland/Air One
	EI-CSV	Boeing 737-8AS	Ryanair
	EI-CSW	Boeing 737-8AS	Ryanair
	EI-CSX	Boeing 737-8AS	Ryanair
	EI-CSY	Boeing 737-8AS	Ryanair
	EI-CSZ	Boeing 737-8AS	Ryanair
	EI-CTA	Boeing 737-8AS	Ryanair
	EI-CTB	Boeing 737-8AS	Ryanair
	EI-CTC	Medway Eclipser	P. A. McMahon
	EI-CTG	Stoddard-Hamilton Glasair RG	K. Higgins
	EI-CTI	Cessna FRA.150L	J. Logan & T. Bradford
	EI-CTL	Aerotech MW-5B Sorcerer	M. Wade
	EI-CTT	PA-28-161 Warrior II	Conair Group
	EI-CUA	Boeing 737-4K5	Aerco Ireland/Blue Panorama
	EI-CUD	Boeing 737-4Q8	Castle 2003-2 Ireland/Blue Panorama
	EI-CUE	Cameron N-105 balloon	Eircom
	EI-CUG	Bell 206B Jet Ranger	Avatar Aviation
	EI-CUJ	Cessna 172N	M. Nally
	EI-CUM	Airbus A.320-232	ILFC Ireland/Wind Jet
	EI-CUN	Boeing 737-4K5	Aerco Ireland/Blue Panorama
	EI-CUP	Cessna 335	J. Greany
	EI-CUS	AB-206B JetRanger 3	Doherty Quarries and Waste Management
	EI-CUT	Maule MX-7-180A	Cosair
	EI-CUW	BN-2B-20 Islander	Aer Arann
	EI-CVA	Airbus A.320-214	Aer Lingus *St Schira*
	EI-CVB	Airbus A.320-214	Aer Lingus *St Mobhi*
	EI-CVC	Airbus A.320-214	Aer Lingus *St Kealin*
	EI-CVD	Airbus A.320-214	Aer Lingus *St Kevin*
	EI-CVL	Ercoupe 415CD	B. Lyons & J. Hackett
	EI-CVM	Schweizer S.269C	B. Moloney
	EI-CVO	Boeing 737-4S3	Aerco Ireland/Philippine Airlines
	EI-CVR	Aérospatiale ATR-42-300	Aer Arann
	EI-CVS	Aérospatiale ATR-42-300	Aer Arann
	EI-CVW	Bensen B.8M	F. Kavanagh
	EI-CVY	Brock KB-2 Gyro	G. Smyth
	EI-CWA	BAe 146-200	CityJet/Air France Express
	EI-CWB	BAe 146-200	CityJet/Air France Express
	EI-CWC	BAe 146-200	CityJet/Air France Express

REPUBLIC OF IRELAND — EI-CWD – EI-DCE

Reg	Type	Owner or Operator	Notes
EI-CWD	BAe 146-200	CityJet/Air France Express	
EI-CWE	Boeing 737-42C	Rockshaw/Air One	
EI-CWF	Boeing 737-42C	Rockshaw/Air One	
EI-CWH	Agusta A109E	Lochbrea Aircraft	
EI-CWL	Robinson R22 Beta	J. McLoughlin	
EI-CWR	Robinson R22 Beta	Eirecopter Helicopters	
EI-CWW	Boeing 737-4Y0	Airplanes Holdings/Air One	
EI-CWX	Boeing 737-4Y0	Airplanes Holdings/Air One	
EI-CXC	Raj Hamsa X'Air 502T	T. McDevitt	
EI-CXI	Boeing 737-46Q	Bellevue Aircraft Leasing/Air One	
EI-CXJ	Boeing 737-4Q8	Castle 2003-1 Ireland/Air One	
EI-CXK	Boeing 737-4S3	Bravo Aircraft Management/Transaero	
EI-CXL	Boeing 737-46N	Monroe Aircraft Ireland/Air One	
EI-CXM	Boeing 737-4Q8	ILFC Ireland/Air One	
EI-CXN	Boeing 737-329	Embarcadero Aircraft Ireland/Transaero	
EI-CXO	Boeing 767-3G5ER	ILFC Ireland/Blue Panorama	
EI-CXR	Boeing 737-329	Embarcadero Aircraft Ireland/Transaero	
EI-CXV	Boeing 737-8CX	Jackson Leasing Ireland/MIAT Mongolian Airlines	
EI-CXY	Evektor EV-97 Eurostar	G. Doody & ptnrs	
EI-CXZ	Boeing 767-216ER	Embarcadero Aircraft Ireland/Transaero	
EI-CZA	ATEC Zephyr 2000	P. Whitehouse-Tedd	
EI-CZC	CFM Streak Shadow Srs II	M. Culhane & D. Burrows	
EI-CZD	Boeing 767-216ER	ILFC Ireland/Transaero	
EI-CZG	Boeing 737-4Q8	ILFC Ireland/Air One	
EI-CZH	Boeing 767-3G5ER	ILTU Ireland/Blue Panorama	
EI-CZK	Boeing 737-4Y0	East Dover/Transaero	
EI-CZM	Robinson R44	Wellingford Construction	
EI-CZN	Sikorsky S-61N	CHC Ireland	
EI-CZO	BAe 146-200	CityJet/Air France Express	
EI-CZP	Schweizer 269C-1	T. Ng Kam	
EI-DAA	Airbus A.330-202	Aer Lingus *St Keeva*	
EI-DAC	Boeing 737-8AS	Ryanair	
EI-DAD	Boeing 737-8AS	Ryanair	
EI-DAE	Boeing 737-8AS	Ryanair	
EI-DAF	Boeing 737-8AS	Ryanair	
EI-DAG	Boeing 737-8AS	Ryanair	
EI-DAH	Boeing 737-8AS	Ryanair	
EI-DAI	Boeing 737-8AS	Ryanair	
EI-DAJ	Boeing 737-8AS	Ryanair	
EI-DAK	Boeing 737-8AS	Ryanair	
EI-DAL	Boeing 737-8AS	Ryanair	
EI-DAM	Boeing 737-8AS	Ryanair	
EI-DAN	Boeing 737-8AS	Ryanair	
EI-DAO	Boeing 737-8AS	Ryanair	
EI-DAP	Boeing 737-8AS	Ryanair	
EI-DAR	Boeing 737-8AS	Ryanair	
EI-DAS	Boeing 737-8AS	Ryanair	
EI-DAT	Boeing 737-8AS	Ryanair	
EI-DAV	Boeing 737-8AS	Ryanair	
EI-DAW	Boeing 737-8AS	Ryanair	
EI-DAX	Boeing 737-8AS	Ryanair	
EI-DAY	Boeing 737-8AS	Ryanair	
EI-DAZ	Boeing 737-8AS	Ryanair	
EI-DBF	Boeing 767-3Q8ER	ACG Acquisition Ireland/Transaero	
EI-DBG	Boeing 767-3Q8ER	Charlie Aircraft Management/Transaero	
EI-DBH	CFM Streak Shadow SA-11	M. O'Mahony	
EI-DBI	Raj Hamsa X'Air Mk.2 Falcon	E. Hamilton	
EI-DBJ	Huntwing Pegasus XL Classic	P. A. McMahon	
EI-DBK	Boeing 777-243ER	GECAS Technical Services/Alitalia	
EI-DBL	Boeing 777-243ER	GECAS Technical Services/Alitalia	
EI-DBM	Boeing 777-243ER	GECAS Technical Services/Alitalia	
EI-DBN	Bell 407	AV-8 Helicopters	
EI-DBO	Air Creation Kiss 400	E. Spain	
EI-DBP	Boeing 767-35H	CIT Aerospace International/Alitalia	
EI-DBU	Boeing 767-37EER	Pegasus Aviation Ireland/Transaero	
EI-DBV	Rand Kar X' Air 602T	S. Scanlon	
EI-DBW	Boeing 767-201	BA Finance (Ireland)/Transaero	
EI-DBX	Magni M.18 Spartan	M. Concannon	
EI-DCA	Raj Hamsa X'Air	S. Cahill	
EI-DCB	Boeing 737-8AS	Ryanair	
EI-DCC	Boeing 737-8AS	Ryanair	
EI-DCD	Boeing 737-8AS	Ryanair	
EI-DCE	Boeing 737-8AS	Ryanair	

EI-DCF – EI-DFW   REPUBLIC OF IRELAND

Notes	Reg	Type	Owner or Operator
	EI-DCF	Boeing 737-8AS	Ryanair
	EI-DCG	Boeing 737-8AS	Ryanair
	EI-DCH	Boeing 737-8AS	Ryanair
	EI-DCI	Boeing 737-8AS	Ryanair
	EI-DCJ	Boeing 737-8AS	Ryanair
	EI-DCK	Boeing 737-8AS	Ryanair
	EI-DCL	Boeing 737-8AS	Ryanair
	EI-DCM	Boeing 737-8AS	Ryanair
	EI-DCN	Boeing 737-8AS	Ryanair
	EI-DCO	Boeing 737-8AS	Ryanair
	EI-DCP	Boeing 737-8AS	Ryanair
	EI-DCR	Boeing 737-8AS	Ryanair
	EI-DCS	Boeing 737-8AS	Ryanair
	EI-DCT	Boeing 737-8AS	Ryanair
	EI-DCV	Boeing 737-8AS	Ryanair
	EI-DCW	Boeing 737-8AS	Ryanair
	EI-DCX	Boeing 737-8AS	Ryanair
	EI-DCY	Boeing 737-8AS	Ryanair
	EI-DCZ	Boeing 737-8AS	Ryanair
	EI-DDA	Robinson R44 II	J. O'R Security
	EI-DDB	Eurocopter EC 120B	J. Cuddy
	EI-DDC	Cessna F.172M	Trim Flying Club
	EI-DDD	Aeronca 7AC	J. Sullivan & M. Quinn
	EI-DDE	BAe 146-200	CityJet/Air France Express
	EI-DDH	Boeing 777-243ER	GECAS Technical Services/Alitalia
	EI-DDI	Schweizer S.269C-1	B. Hade
	EI-DDJ	Raj Hamsa X'Air 582	J. P. McHugh
	EI-DDK	Boeing 737-4S3	Boeing Capital Leasing/Transaero
	EI-DDN	CFM Metal Fax Shadow Srs CD	F. Lynch
	EI-DDO	Montgomerie Merlin	C. Condell
	EI-DDP	Southdown International microlight	P. O'Reilly
	EI-DDR	Bensen B.8V	P. MacCabe & K. Renolds
	EI-DDW	Boeing 767-3S1ER	Pegasus Aviation Ireland/Alitalia
	EI-DDX	Cessna 172S	Atlantic Flight Training
	EI-DDY	Boeing 737-4Y0	Aerco Ireland/Transaero
	EI-DDZ	Piper PA-28-181 Archer II	Ardnari Ltd
	EI-DEA	Airbus A.320-214	Aer Lingus *St Fidelma*
	EI-DEB	Airbus A.320-214	Aer Lingus *St Nathy*
	EI-DEC	Airbus A.320-214	Aer Lingus *St Fergal*
	EI-DEE	Airbus A.320-214	Aer Lingus *St Fintan*
	EI-DEF	Airbus A.320-214	Aer Lingus *St Declan*
	EI-DEG	Airbus A.320-214	Aer Lingus *St Fachtna*
	EI-DEH	Airbus A.320-214	Aer Lingus *St Malachy*
	EI-DEI	Airbus A.320-214	Aer Lingus *St Kilian*
	EI-DEJ	Airbus A.320-214	Aer Lingus *St Oliver Plunkett*
	EI-DEK	Airbus A.320-214	Aer Lingus *St Eunan*
	EI-DEL	Airbus A.320-214	Aer Lingus *St Ibar*
	EI-DEM	Airbus A.320-214	Aer Lingus *St Canice*
	EI-DEN	Airbus A.320-214	Aer Lingus *St Kieran*
	EI-DEO	Airbus A.320-214	Aer Lingus *St Senan*
	EI-DEP	Airbus A.320-214	Aer Lingus *St Eugene*
	EI-DER	Airbus A.320-214	Aer Lingus *St Mel*
	EI-DES	Airbus A.320-214	Aer Lingus *St Pappin*
	EI-DET	Airbus A.320-214	Aer Lingus *St Brendan*
	EI-DEW	BAe 146-300	CityJet/Air France Express
	EI-DEX	BAe 146-300	CityJet/Air France Express
	EI-DEY	Airbus A.319-112	Permeke Aircraft Leasing/Meridiana
	EI-DEZ	Airbus A.319-112	Permeke Aircraft Leasing/Meridiana
	EI-DFA	Airbus A.319-112	Permeke Aircraft Leasing/Meridiana
	EI-DFD	Boeing 737-4S3	Orix Aircraft Management/Air One
	EI-DFE	Boeing 737-4S3	Orix Aircraft Management/Air One
	EI-DFF	Boeing 737-4S3	Orix Aircraft Management/Air One
	EI-DFG	Embraer ERJ-170-100LR	GECAS Technical Services/Alitalia Express
	EI-DFH	Embraer ERJ-170-100LR	GECAS Technical Services/Alitalia Express
	EI-DFI	Embraer ERJ-170-100LR	GECAS Technical Services/Alitalia Express
	EI-DFJ	Embraer ERJ-170-100LR	GECAS Technical Services/Alitalia Express
	EI-DFK	Embraer ERJ-170-100LR	GECAS Technical Services/Alitalia Express
	EI-DFL	Embraer ERJ-170-100LR	GECAS Technical Services/Alitalia Express
	EI-DFM	Evektor EV-97 Eurostar	G. Doody
	EI-DFO	Airbus A.320-211	Triton Aviation Ireland/Wind Jet
	EI-DFP	Airbus A.319-112	Delvaux Aircraft Leasing/Meridiana
	EI-DFS	Boeing 767-33AER	Jeritt Ltd/Transaero
	EI-DFW	Robinson R44	Blue Star Helicopters

REPUBLIC OF IRELAND

EI-DFX – EI-DKT

Reg	Type	Owner or Operator	Notes
EI-DFX	Air Creation Kiss 400	L. Daly	
EI-DFY	Raj Hamsa R100 (2)	P. McGirr & R Gillespie	
EI-DGA	Urban Air UFM-11UK Lambada	Dr. P. & D. Durkin	
EI-DGD	Boeing 737-430	Challey Ltd/Air One	
EI-DGG	Raj Hamsa X'Air 582	N. Geh	
EI-DGH	Raj Hamsa X'Air 582	M. Garvey & T. McGowan	
EI-DGI	MXP-740 Savannah	N. Farrell	
EI-DGJ	Raj Hamsa X'Air 582	R. Morelli	
EI-DGK	Raj Hamsa X'Air 133	B. Chambers	
EI-DGL	Boeing 737-46J	AAR-GS737 Classic Acft Lsg/Air One	
EI-DGN	Boeing 737-4C9	Lux Aircraft Leasing/Blue Panorama	
EI-DGP	Urban Air UFM-11 Lambada	M. Tormey	
EI-DGR	Urban Air UFM-11UK Lambada	M. Tormey	
EI-DGS	ATEC Zephyr 2000	K. Higgins	
EI-DGT	Urban Air UFM-11UK Lambada	A. & P. Aviation	
EI-DGV	ATEC Zephyr 2000	A. Higgins	
EI-DGW	Cameron Z-90 balloon	J. Leahy	
EI-DGX	Cessna 152 II	K. A. O'Connor	
EI-DGY	Urban Air UFM-11 Lambada	J. Keena	
EI-DGZ	Boeing 737-86N	Celestial Avn Trading/Futura International	
EI-DHA	Boeing 737-8AS	Ryanair	
EI-DHB	Boeing 737-8AS	Ryanair	
EI-DHC	Boeing 737-8AS	Ryanair	
EI-DHD	Boeing 737-8AS	Ryanair	
EI-DHE	Boeing 737-8AS	Ryanair	
EI-DHF	Boeing 737-8AS	Ryanair	
EI-DHG	Boeing 737-8AS	Ryanair	
EI-DHH	Boeing 737-8AS	Ryanair	
EI-DHI	Boeing 737-8AS	Ryanair	
EI-DHJ	Boeing 737-8AS	Ryanair	
EI-DHK	Boeing 737-8AS	Ryanair	
EI-DHM	Boeing 737-8AS	Ryanair	
EI-DHN	Boeing 737-8AS	Ryanair	
EI-DHO	Boeing 737-8AS	Ryanair	
EI-DHP	Boeing 737-8AS	Ryanair	
EI-DHR	Boeing 737-8AS	Ryanair	
EI-DHS	Boeing 737-8AS	Ryanair	
EI-DHT	Boeing 737-8AS	Ryanair	
EI-DHV	Boeing 737-8AS	Ryanair	
EI-DHW	Boeing 737-8AS	Ryanair	
EI-DHX	Boeing 737-8AS	Ryanair	
EI-DHY	Boeing 737-8AS	Ryanair	
EI-DHZ	Boeing 737-8AS	Ryanair	
EI-DIA	Solar Wings Pegasus XL-Q	P. Byrne	
EI-DIB	Air Creation Kiss 400	E. Redmond	
EI-DIF	PA-31-350 Navajo Chieftain	Visionair Ltd	
EI-DIY	Van's RV-4	J. A. Kent	
EI-DIZ	Robinson R22 Beta	Blue Star Helicopters	
EI-DJH	Airbus A.320-212	ILFC Ireland/MyAir	
EI-DJI	Airbus A.320-214	ILFC Ireland/MyAir	
EI-DJJ	BAe 146-200	CityJet (stored)	
EI-DJK	Boeing 737-382	Triton Aviation Ireland/KLD – KD-Avia	
EI-DJM	PA-28-161 Warrior II	Waterford Aero Club	
EI-DJO	Agusta A109E	Tandrelle Ltd	
EI-DJR	Boeing 737-3YO	Larrett/KLD – KD-Avia	
EI-DJS	Boeing 737-3YO	Wodell/KLD – KD-Avia	
EI-DJT	Boeing 737-86N	Lift Ireland Leasing/Futura International	
EI-DJU	Boeing 737-86N	Celestial Avn Trading/Futura International	
EI-DJW	Robinson R44	Horizon Helicopters	
EI-DJX	Farrington Twinstarr	F. Kavanagh	
EI-DJY	Grob G.115	Atlantic Flight Training	
EI-DJZ	Lindstrand LBL-31A Cloudhopper	M. E. White	
EI-DKB	MXP-740 Savannah	B. Gurnett & partners	
EI-DKC	Solar Wings Quasar	K. Daly	
EI-DKD	Boeing 737-86N	OH Aircraft (Ireland)/Futura International	
EI-DKE	Air Creation Kiss 450-582	J. Bennett	
EI-DKI	Robinson R22 Beta	Goldcrest Aviation	
EI-DKJ	Thruster T.600N	C. Brogan	
EI-DKK	Raj Hamsa X'Air Jabiru	M. Tolan	
EI-DKL	Boeing 757-231	Pegasus Palls 99/Blue Panorama	
EI-DKM	AB-206B JetRanger	Stelbury Ltd	
EI-DKN	ELA Aviacion ELA-07 gyrocopter	S. Brennan	
EI-DKT	Raj Hamsa X'Air 582 (11)	I. Brereton	

EI-DKU – EI-DOO REPUBLIC OF IRELAND

Notes	Reg	Type	Owner or Operator
	EI-DKU	Air Creation Kiss 450-582 (1)	J. Doran
	EI-DKV	Boeing 737-505	Brookdell/Avolar
	EI-DKW	Evektor EV-97 Eurostar	Ormand Flying Club
	EI-DKY	Raj Hamsa X'Air 582	D. Minnock
	EI-DKZ	Reality Aircraft Escapade 912 (1)	J. Deegan
	EI-DLB	Boeing 737-8AS	Ryanair
	EI-DLC	Boeing 737-8AS	Ryanair
	EI-DLD	Boeing 737-8AS	Ryanair
	EI-DLE	Boeing 737-8AS	Ryanair
	EI-DLF	Boeing 737-8AS	Ryanair
	EI-DLG	Boeing 737-8AS	Ryanair
	EI-DLH	Boeing 737-8AS	Ryanair
	EI-DLI	Boeing 737-8AS	Ryanair
	EI-DLJ	Boeing 737-8AS	Ryanair
	EI-DLK	Boeing 737-8AS	Ryanair
	EI-DLM	Boeing 737-8AS	Ryanair
	EI-DLN	Boeing 737-8AS	Ryanair
	EI-DLO	Boeing 737-8AS	Ryanair
	EI-DLR	Boeing 737-8AS	Ryanair
	EI-DLS	Boeing 737-8AS	Ryanair
	EI-DLT	Boeing 737-8AS	Ryanair
	EI-DLV	Boeing 737-8AS	Ryanair
	EI-DLW	Boeing 737-8AS	Ryanair
	EI-DLX	Boeing 737-8AS	Ryanair
	EI-DLY	Boeing 737-8AS	Ryanair
	EI-DLZ	Boeing 737-8AS	Ryanair
	EI-DMA	MS.892E Rallye 150	Kerry Aero Club
	EI-DMB	Best Off Skyranger 912S (1)	Fun 2 Fly Ltd
	EI-DMC	Schweizer 269C-1	B. Hade
	EI-DMG	Cessna 441	Dawn Meats Group
	EI-DMH	Boeing 767-260	Woodrow Leasing/Kras Air/AiRUnion
	EI-DMJ	Boeing 767-306ER	ILFC Ireland/Neos
	EI-DMK	BAe 146-200	CityJet/Air France Express
	EI-DML	Bell 206B JetRanger	Morrissey Fencing
	EI-DMM	Boeing 737-33A	Wodell Ltd/KLD – KD-Avia
	EI-DMN	Boeing 737-3K2	Pegasus Palls/KLD – KD-Avia
	EI-DMP	Boeing 767-2Q8	ILFC Ireland/Kras Air/AiRUnion
	EI-DMR	Boeing 737-436	Dillondell Ltd/Air One
	EI-DMS	Robinson R22 Beta	Tarmacadam Paving Services Ltd
	EI-DMT	Agusta A109C	Dasbar Ltd
	EI-DMU	Whittaker MW6S Merlin	G. W. Maher
	EI-DMX	Boeing 737-752	Mexican Aircraft Leasing/Aeromexico
	EI-DMY	Boeing 737-752	Mexican Aircraft Leasing/Aeromexico
	EI-DMZ	Boeing 737-8FH	RBS Aerospace/Futura International
	EI-DNA	Boeing 757-231	Rockshaw Ltd/Blue Panorama
	EI-DNB	Boeing 737-752	Mexican Aircraft Leasing/Aeromexico
	EI-DNC	Boeing 737-752	Mexican Aircraft Leasing/Aeromexico
	EI-DND	Boeing 737-86N	Celestial Aviation Trading/Futura International
	EI-DNH	Boeing 737-3Y5	Boeing Capital Leasing/Kras Air/AiRUnion
	EI-DNJ	BAe 146-200	CityJet/Air France Express
	EI-DNL	Bensen B-8M	J. Henry & H. O'Driscoll
	EI-DNM	Boeing 737-4S3	Boeing Capital Leasing/Transaero
	EI-DNP	Airbus A.320-212	Ovenstone Ltd/Wind Jet
	EI-DNR	Raj Hamsa X'Air 582 (5)	N. Furlong & J. Grattan
	EI-DNS	Boeing 737-329	Embarcadero Acft Securitization/Kras Air/AiRUnion
	EI-DNT	Boeing 737-329	Embarcadero Acft Securitization/Kras Air/AiRUnion
	EI-DNU	Schweizer 269C-1	T. Ng Kam
	EI-DNV	Urban Air UFM-11UK Lambada	F. Maughan
	EI-DNW	Skyranger J2.2 (1)	M. Kerrison
	EI-DNX	Boeing 737-31S	Challey Ltd/Air One
	EI-DNY	Boeing 737-3T0	BCI Aircraft Leasing/Avolar
	EI-DNZ	Boeing 737-3T0	BCI Aircraft Leasing/Avolar
	EI-DOD	Airbus A.320-231	Hanover Aircraft Leasing/MyAir
	EI-DOE	Airbus A.320-211	ALS Irish Aircraft Leasing/Wind Jet
	EI-DOF	Boeing 767-306ER	ILFC Ireland/Neos
	EI-DOH	Boeing 737-31S	Challey Ltd/Air One
	EI-DOI	Evektor EV-97 Eurostar	E. McEvoy & G. Doody
	EI-DOJ	Schweizer 269C-1	J. O'R Security
	EI-DOM	Boeing 737-3G7	CIT Capital Finance/KLD – KD-Avia
	EI-DON	Boeing 737-3Y0	CIT Capital Finance/KLD – KD-Avia
	EI-DOO	Boeing 737-35B	CIT Capital Finance/KLD – KD-Avia

REPUBLIC OF IRELAND
EI-DOP – EI-DUY

Reg	Type	Owner or Operator	Notes
EI-DOP	Airbus A.320-232	ILFC Ireland/Wind Jet	
EI-DOR	Boeing 737-4Y0	Airplanes Finance/Futura International	
EI-DOS	Boeing 737-49R	Celestial Avn Trading/Air One	
EI-DOT	Bombardier CL-600-2D24	Challey Ltd/Air One	
EI-DOU	Bombardier CL-600-2D24	Challey Ltd/Air One	
EI-DOV	Boeing 737-48E	ILFC Ireland/Air One	
EI-DOW	Mainair Blade 912	G. D. Fortune	
EI-DOX	Solar Wings XL-R	T. Noonan	
EI-DOY	PZL Koliber 150A	Limerick Flying Club	
EI-DPA	Boeing 737-8AS	Ryanair	
EI-DPB	Boeing 737-8AS	Ryanair	
EI-DPC	Boeing 737-8AS	Ryanair	
EI-DPD	Boeing 737-8AS	Ryanair	
EI-DPE	Boeing 737-8AS	Ryanair	
EI-DPF	Boeing 737-8AS	Ryanair	
EI-DPG	Boeing 737-8AS	Ryanair	
EI-DPH	Boeing 737-8AS	Ryanair	
EI-DPI	Boeing 737-8AS	Ryanair	
EI-DPJ	Boeing 737-8AS	Ryanair	
EI-DPK	Boeing 737-8AS	Ryanair	
EI-DPL	Boeing 737-8AS	Ryanair	
EI-DPM	Boeing 737-8AS	Ryanair	
EI-DPN	Boeing 737-8AS	Ryanair	
EI-DPO	Boeing 737-8AS	Ryanair	
EI-DPP	Boeing 737-8AS	Ryanair	
EI-DPR	Boeing 737-8AS	Ryanair	
EI-DPS	Boeing 737-8AS	Ryanair	
EI-DPT	Boeing 737-8AS	Ryanair	
EI-DPV	Boeing 737-8AS	Ryanair	
EI-DRA	Boeing 737-852	Mexican Aircraft Leasing/Aeromexico	
EI-DRB	Boeing 737-852	Mexican Aircraft Leasing/Aeromexico	
EI-DRC	Boeing 737-852	Mexican Aircraft Leasing/Aeromexico	
EI-DRD	Boeing 737-852	Mexican Aircraft Leasing/Aeromexico	
EI-DRE	Boeing 737-752	Mexican Aircraft Leasing/Aeromexico	
EI-DRG	Airbus A.321-231	Malc Lease One (Dublin)/MyAir	
EI-DRH	Mainair Blade	J. McErlain	
EI-DRI	Bombardier CL-600-2D24	Challey Ltd/Air One	
EI-DRJ	Bombardier CL-600-2D24	Challey Ltd/Air One	
EI-DRK	Bombardier CL-600-2D24	Challey Ltd/Air One	
EI-DRL	Raj Hamsa X'Air Jabiru	C. Kiernan	
EI-DRM	Urban Air UFM-10 Samba	M. Tormey	
EI-DRN	Robinson R44	Blue Star Helicopters	
EI-DRO	Tecnam P2002-JF	Ossory Flying & Gliding Club	
EI-DRR	Boeing 737-347	BCI Aircraft Leasing/Avolar	
EI-DRT	Air Creation Tanarg 912	L. Daly	
EI-DRU	Tecnam P92/EM Echo	P. Gallogly	
EI-DRW	Evektor EV-97R Eurostar	Eurostar Flying Club	
EI-DRX	Raj Hamsa X'Air 582 (5)	M. Sheelan & D. McShane	
EI-DRZ	Boeing 737-36N	Lift Ireland Leasing/Hainan Airlines	
EI-DSA	Airbus A.320-216	Aircraft Purchase Company/Air One	
EI-DSB	Airbus A.320-216	Aircraft Purchase Company/Air One	
EI-DSC	Airbus A.320-216	Aircraft Purchase Company/Air One	
EI-DTP	Boeing 737-347	BCI Aircraft Leasing/Avolar	
EI-DTR	Robinson R44	Loughoran Properties	
EI-DTS	PA-18 Super Cub	J. Dolan	
EI-DTT	ELA-07 R-100 Gyrocopter	N. Steele	
EI-DTU	Boeing 737-5Y0	Celestial Aviation Trading/Transaero	
EI-DTV	Boeing 737-5Y0	Airplanes Holdings/Transaero	
EI-DTW	Boeing 737-5Y0	Airplanes Finance/Transaero	
EI-DTX	Boeing 737-5Q8	ILFC Ireland/Transaero	
EI-DTY	Boeing 737-3M8	Celestial Aviation Trading/KLD – KD-Avia	
EI-DUA	Boeing 757-256	ILFC Ireland/Kras Air/AiRUnion	
EI-DUB	Airbus A.330-301	Aer Lingus *St Patrick*	
EI-DUC	Boeing 757-256	ILFC Ireland/Kras Air/AiRUnion	
EI-DUD	Boeing 757-256	ILFC Ireland/Kras Air/AiRUnion	
EI-DUH	Scintex CP.1310C3 Emeraude	W. Kennedy	
EI-DUK	Bombardier CL-600-2D24	Challey Ltd/Air One	
EI-DUM	Bombardier CL-600-2D24	MyAir	
EI-DUN	Agusta A109E	Barkisland (Developments)	
EI-DUS	Boeing 737-32B	Mistral Air	
EI-DUU	Bombardier CL-600-2D24	MyAir	
EI-DUX	Bombardier CL-600-2D24	MyAir	
EI-DUY	Bombardier CL-600-2D24	MyAir	

EI-DVB – EI-JWM   REPUBLIC OF IRELAND

Notes	Reg	Type	Owner or Operator
	EI-DVB	Airbus A.330-322	Bella Aircraft Leasing (stored)
	EI-EBJ	Robinson R44	Donville Heli's Ltd
	EI-ECA	Agusta A109A-II	Blue Star Helicopters
	EI-EDR	PA-28R Cherokee Arrow 200	Dublin Flyers
	EI-EGG	Robinson R44 Raven	In-Flight Aviation
	EI-EGR	Robinson R44 II	J. C. Southern Helicopters
	EI-EHB	Robinson R22 Beta	Blue Star Helicopters
	EI-EHC	Robinson R22 Beta	Nocnaggud Ltd
	EI-EHD	Robinson R22 Beta 2	South Coast Helicopters
	EI-EHE	Robinson R22 Beta	Blue Star Helicopters
	EI-EHG	Robinson R22 Beta	G. Jordan
	EI-EJR	Robinson R44	Gerair Ltd
	EI-ELL	Medway Eclipser	Microflex Ltd
	EI-EMG	Robinson R22 Beta	M. Brennan
	EI-EUR	Eurocopter EC 120B	Atlantic Helicopters
	EI-EWR	Airbus A.330-202	Aer Lingus *Lawrence O' Toole*
	EI-EXC	Robinson R44	S. Geany
	EI-EXG	Robinson R22 Beta	21st Century Aviation
	EI-FAR	Robinson R44 II	Fardolan Ltd
	EI-FBG	Cessna F.182Q	J. Paxton
	EI-FXA	Aérospatiale ATR-42-300	Air Contractors (Ireland)
	EI-FXB	Aérospatiale ATR-42-300	Air Contractors (Ireland)
	EI-FXC	Aérospatiale ATR-42-300	Air Contractors (Ireland)
	EI-FXD	Aérospatiale ATR-42-300	Air Contractors (Ireland)
	EI-FXE	Aérospatiale ATR-42-300	Air Contractors (Ireland)
	EI-FXF	Aérospatiale ATR-42-300	Air Contractors (Ireland)
	EI-FXG	Aérospatiale ATR-72-202	Air Contractors (Ireland)
	EI-FXH	Aérospatiale ATR-72-202	Air Contractors (Ireland)
	EI-FXI	Aérospatiale ATR-72-202	Air Contractors (Ireland)
	EI-GAA	Boeing 767-266ER	Arbor Finance/Kras Air/AiRUnion
	EI-GAN	Bell 407	Robswall Property
	EI-GAV	Robinson R22 Beta	Western Davinci Services
	EI-GBA	Boeing 767-266ER	Arbor Finance/Kras Air/AiRUnion
	EI-GDL	Gulfstream GV-SP (G550)	Westair Aviation
	EI-GER	Maule MX7-180A	R. Lanigan & J.Patrick
	EI-GFC	SOCATA TB9 Tampico	B. McGrath & ptnrs
	EI-GHT	Bell 206B JetRanger	Duncan High Reach Equipment
	EI-GKL	Robinson R22 Beta	Gerry Keyes Ltd
	EI-GPT	Robinson R22 Beta	Treaty Plant & Tool (Hire & Sales)
	EI-GPZ	Robinson R44 II	G & P Transport
	EI-GSE	Cessna F.172M	K. A. O'Connor
	EI-GSM	Cessna 182S	Westpoint Flying Group
	EI-GTY	Robinson R22 Beta	Lockson Investments
	EI-GWT	Agusta-Bell 206B JetRanger	G. Tracey
	EI-GWY	Cessna 172R	Atlantic Flight Training
	EI-HAM	Light Aero Avid Flyer	H. Goulding
	EI-HAZ	Robinson R44	Forestbrook Developments Ltd
	EI-HCS	Grob G.109B	H. Sydner
	EI-HER	Bell 206B JetRanger 3	S. Lanigan Ryan
	EI-HHH	Agusta A109E	F. Gormley & G. Coughlan
	EI-HOK	Eurocopter EC.130B4	Heli Leasing Partnership
	EI-HXM	Bell 206B JetRanger	Premier Star Equipment
	EI-IAN	Pilatus PC-6/B2-H4	Irish Parachute Club
	EI-IAW	Learjet 60	Voltage Plus Ltd
	EI-IGA	Boeing 757-230	GAIF Ireland/Air Italy
	EI-IGB	Boeing 757-230	GAIF Ireland/Air Italy
	EI-IGC	Boeing 757-230	GAIF Ireland/Air Italy
	EI-IHL	Aérospatiale AS.350B1	Irish Helicopters
	EI-ING	Cessna F.172P	21st Century Flyers
	EI-IPC	BN-2A-26 Islander	Irish Parachute Club
	EI-IRE	Canadair CL.600-2B16	Starair (Ireland)
	EI-IRV	AS.350B Ecureuil	Harrcops Ltd
	EI-JAC	Bell 206B JetRanger	Aerial Explorations
	EI-JAL	Robinson R44 II	D. Doherty
	EI-JAR	Robinson R44	J. Coleman
	EI-JBC	Agusta A109A	Medeva Properties
	EI-JFC	Agusta A109S	John J. Fleming Construction Company
	EI-JFD	Robinson R44	New World Plant Ltd
	EI-JFK	Airbus A.330-301	Aer Lingus *St Colmcille*
	EI-JIM	Urban Air Samba XLA	Jim Smith
	EI-JIV	L.382G-44K-30 Hercules	Air Contractors (Ireland)
	EI-JON	Agusta A109E	Castlelands Construction
	EI-JWM	Robinson R22 Beta	C. Shiel

REPUBLIC OF IRELAND
EI-KDH – EI-RHM

Reg	Type	Owner or Operator	Notes
EI-KDH	Piper PA-28-181 Archer II	K. O'Driscoll & D. Harris	
EI-KEV	Raj Hamsa R133 (1)	K. Glynn	
EI-KEY	Robinson R44	Gerry Keyes Ltd	
EI-KHL	Robinson R44 II	B. Kavanagh	
EI-KHR	Robinson R22 Beta	Billy Jet Ltd	
EI-KJC	Hawker 850XP	Airlink Airways	
EI-LAF	Bell 206B JetRanger	Shamrock Helicopters	
EI-LAJ	Robinson R44 II	Heliwest Ltd	
EI-LAL	Agusta A109E	Lalco Development Company	
EI-LAX	Airbus A.330-202	Aer Lingus *St Mella*	
EI-LIT	MBB Bö.105CBS	Irish Helicopters	
EI-LKS	Eurocopter EC-130B4	Wigaf Leasing Company	
EI-LNX	Eurocopter EC-130B4	Wigaf Leasing Company	
EI-LOC	Robinson R44	Donville Heli's Ltd	
EI-LTA	Boeing 757-23N	City Leasing/VIM Airlines	
EI-LTO	Boeing 757-23N	Fastway Leasing/Air Bashkortostan	
EI-LTU	Boeing 757-23N	Fastway Leasing/VIM Airlines	
EI-LTY	Boeing 757-23N	City Leasing/VIM Airlines	
EI-MAG	Robinson R22 Beta 2	Jarlath Smyth & Sons Ltd	
EI-MAX	Learjet 31A	Airlink Airways	
EI-MCC	Robinson R44 II	Coates Aviation Ltd	
EI-MCF	Cessna 172R	Galway Flying Club	
EI-MCP	Agusta A109C	Quarry & Mining Equipment	
EI-MEJ	Bell 206B JetRanger	Gaelic Helicopters	
EI-MEL	Agusta A109C	Kildare Aviation	
EI-MEN	Agusta A109S	Men-Entirl Ltd	
EI-MER	Bell 206B JetRanger III	Gaelic Helicopters	
EI-MES	Sikorsky S-61N	CHC Ireland	
EI-MIK	Eurocopter EC 120B	Milltown Engineering	
EI-MIP	SA.365N Dauphin 2	CHC Ireland	
EI-MIT	Agusta A109E	Mercury Engineering	
EI-MJR	Robinson R44	M. Melville	
EI-MLN	Agusta A109E	Earthquake (Ireland) Ltd	
EI-MOR	Robinson R44	Blue Star Helicopters	
EI-MPW	Robinson R44	Connacht Helicopters	
EI-MUL	Robinson R44	Cotton Box Design Group	
EI-MVK	Robinson R44 II	Ashleypark International	
EI-NBD	Robinson R44	N. B. Property Developments	
EI-NFW	Cessna 172S	Galway Flying Club	
EI-NPG	Agusta A109E	A. Logue & W. Moffett	
EI-NVL	Jora spol S. R. O. Jora	N. Van Lonkhuyzen	
EI-NZO	Eurocopter EC 120B	Billy Jet Ltd	
EI-OBJ	Robinson R22 Beta	Loughbeigh Properties	
EI-ODD	Bell 206B JetRanger	Zero Altitude Ltd	
EI-OFM	Cessna F.172N	21st Century Flyers	
EI-ORD	Airbus A.330-301	Aer Lingus *St Maeve*	
EI-OZA	Airbus A.300B4-103F	Air Contractors (Ireland)	
EI-OZB	Airbus A.300B4-103F	Air Contractors (Ireland)	
EI-OZC	Airbus A.300B4-103F	Air Contractors (Ireland)	
EI-PAT	BAe 146-200	CityJet/Air France Express	
EI-PCI	Bell 206B JetRanger	Malcove Ltd	
EI-PEC	Robinson R44 II	P. Sexton	
EI-PEL	Agusta A109E	P. Elliott & Co Ltd	
EI-PJD	AS.350B2 Twin Squirrel	New World Plant	
EI-PJW	Eurocopter EC 120B	P. White	
EI-PKS	Bell 206B JetRanger	Bellisle Properties	
EI-PMI	Agusta-Bell 206B JetRanger III	Ping Golf Equipment	
EI-POD	Cessna 177B	Trim Flying Club	
EI-POP	Cameron Z-90 balloon	The Travel Department	
EI-PRI	Bell 206B JetRanger	Brentwood Properties	
EI-RAV	Robinson R44	Executive Helicopters Maintenance	
EI-RCG	Sikorsky S-61N	CHC Ireland	
EI-REA	Aérospatiale ATR-72-202	Aer Arann	
EI-REB	Aérospatiale ATR-72-202	Aer Arann	
EI-RED	Aérospatiale ATR-72-202	Aer Arann	
EI-REE	Aérospatiale ATR-72-202	Aer Arann	
EI-REF	Aérospatiale ATR-72-202	Aer Arann	
EI-REG	Aérospatiale ATR-72-202	Aer Arann	
EI-REH	Aérospatiale ATR-72-201	Aer Arann	
EI-REI	Aérospatiale ATR-72-201	Aer Arann	
EI-REJ	Aérospatiale ATR-72-201	Aer Arann	
EI-REX	Learjet 60	Airlink Airways	
EI-RHM	Bell 407	Eurojet Ireland	

EI-RJD – EI-YLG   REPUBLIC OF IRELAND

Notes	Reg	Type	Owner or Operator
	EI-RJD	Avro RJ85	Cityjet
	EI-RJE	Avro RJ85	Cityjet
	EI-RJI	Avro RJ85	Cityjet
	EI-RJN	Avro RJ85	Cityjet
	EI-RJO	Avro RJ85	Cityjet
	EI-RJP	Avro RJ85	Cityjet *Clare Island*
	EI-RJR	Avro RJ85	Cityjet
	EI-RJU	Avro RJ85	Cityjet
	EI-RMC	Bell 206B JetRanger	Westair Aviation
	EI-ROB	Robin R.1180TD	Extras Ltd
	EI-RON	Robinson R44	Atlantic Distributors
	EI-SAC	Cessna 172P	Sligo Aero Club
	EI-SAM	Extra EA.300/200	D. Bruton
	EI-SAR	Sikorsky S-61N	CHC Ireland
	EI-SAT	Steen Skybolt	Capt. B. O'Sullivan
	EI-SBM	Agusta A109E	Ballymore Management Services
	EI-SBP	Cessna T.206H	P. Morrissey
	EI-SEA	SeaRey	J. Brennan
	EI-SGF	Robinson R44	M. Reilly & S. Filan
	EI-SGN	Robinson R44	M. Reilly & S. Filan
	EI-SKP	Cessna F.172P	Shemburn Ltd
	EI-SKR	PA-44-180 Seminole	Shemburn Ltd
	EI-SKS	Robin R.2160	Shemburn Ltd
	EI-SKT	PA-44-180 Seminole	Shemburn Ltd
	EI-SKU	PA-28RT-201 Arrow IV	Shemburn Ltd
	EI-SKV	Robin R.2160	Shemburn Ltd
	EI-SKW	PA-28-161 Warrior II	Shemburn Ltd
	EI-SLA	Aérospatiale ATR-42-310	Air Contractors (Ireland)
	EI-SLB	Aérospatiale ATR-42-310	Air Contractors (Ireland)
	EI-SLC	Aérospatiale ATR-42-310	Air Contractors (Ireland)
	EI-SLD	Aérospatiale ATR-42-310	Air Contractors (Ireland)
	EI-SLE	Aérospatiale ATR-42-310	Air Contractors (Ireland)
	EI-SLF	Aérospatiale ATR-72-201	Air Contractors (Ireland)
	EI-SLG	Aérospatiale ATR-72-202	Air Contractors (Ireland)
	EI-SLH	Aérospatiale ATR-72-202	Air Contractors (Ireland)
	EI-SMB	Short SD3-60 Variant 100	Air Contractors (Ireland)
	EI-SMK	Zenair CH701	S. King
	EI-SNJ	Bell 407	Morlam Ltd
	EI-SQG	Agusta A109E	Quinn Group
	EI-STR	Bell 407	G & H Homes
	EI-STT	Cessna 172M	Trim Flying Club
	EI-SUB	Robinson R44	EI-SUB Ltd
	EI-SWD	Robinson R44	New World Plant Ltd
	EI-TAB	Airbus A.320-233	CIT Aerospace International/TACA/Cubana
	EI-TAC	Airbus A.320-233	CIT Aerospace International/TACA/Cubana
	EI-TAD	Airbus A.320-233	Alvi Leasing/TACA/Cubana
	EI-TAF	Airbus A.320-233	Alix Leasing/TACA/Cubana
	EI-TAG	Airbus A.320-233	CIT Aerospace International/TACA
	EI-TBM	SOCATA TBM-700	Folens Management Services
	EI-TGF	Robinson R22 Beta	Skyexpress Ltd
	EI-TIP	Bell 430	Starair (Ireland)
	EI-TKI	Robinson R22 Beta	J. McDaid
	EI-TMH	Robinson R44	T. Maybury
	EI-TON	M. B. Cooke 582 (5)	T. Merrigan
	EI-TOY	Robinson R44	Metroheli
	EI-TWO	Agusta A109E	Alburn Transport
	EI-UFO	PA-22 Tri-Pacer 150 (tailwheel)	W. Treacy
	EI-UNI	Robinson R44 II	Unipipe (Irl) Ltd
	EI-UPA	McD Douglas MD-11F	Pegasus Aviation/Alitalia
	EI-UPE	McD Douglas MD-11F	Pegasus Aviation/Alitalia
	EI-UPI	McD Douglas MD-11F	Pegasus Aviation/Alitalia
	EI-UPO	McD Douglas MD-11F	Pegasus Aviation/Alitalia
	EI-UPU	McD Douglas MD-11F	Pegasus Aviation/Alitalia
	EI-WAC	PA-23 Aztec 250E	Westair Aviation
	EI-WAV	Bell 430	Westair Aviation
	EI-WJN	HS.125 Srs 700A	Westair Aviation
	EI-WMN	PA-23 Aztec 250F	Westair Aviation
	EI-WOW	Eurocopter EC.130B4	Skyheli Ltd
	EI-WRN	PA-28-151 Warrior	Waterford Aero Club
	EI-XLA	Urban Air Samba XLA	M. Tormey
	EI-YBZ	Robinson R44	ILH Enterprises
	EI-YLG	Robin HR.200/120B	Leinster Aero Club

Overseas Airliner Registrations

Aircraft included in this section are those most likely to be seen at UK and nearby European airports or overflying UK airspace.

Reg	Type	Owner or Operator	Notes

A4O (Oman)

A4O-KA	Airbus A.330-243 (501)	Gulf Air	
A4O-KB	Airbus A.330-243 (502)	Gulf Air	
A4O-KC	Airbus A.330-243 (503)	Gulf Air	
A4O-KD	Airbus A.330-243 (504)	Gulf Air	
A4O-KE	Airbus A.330-243 (505)	Gulf Air	
A4O-KF	Airbus A.330-243 (506)	Gulf Air *Aldafra*	
A4O-LB	Airbus A.340-312 (402)	Gulf Air *Al Fateh*	
A4O-LC	Airbus A.340-312 (403)	Gulf Air *Doha*	
A4O-LD	Airbus A.340-312 (404)	Gulf Air *Abu Dhabi*	
A4O-LE	Airbus A.340-312 (405)	Gulf Air	
A4O-LF	Airbus A.340-312 (406)	Gulf Air	
A4O-LG	Airbus A.340-313X (407)	Gulf Air	
A4O-LH	Airbus A.340-313X (408)	Gulf Air	
A4O-LI	Airbus A.340-313X (409)	Gulf Air	
A4O-LJ	Airbus A.340-313X (410)	Gulf Air	
A4O-OMN	Boeing 747-430	Oman Royal Flight	
A4O-SO	Boeing 747SP-27	Oman Royal Flight	

A6 (Arab Emirates)

A6-EAA	Airbus A.330-243	Emirates Airlines	
A6-EAB	Airbus A.330-243	Emirates Airlines	
A6-EAC	Airbus A.330-243	Emirates Airlines	
A6-EAD	Airbus A.330-243	Emirates Airlines	
A6-EAE	Airbus A.330-243	Emirates Airlines	
A6-EAF	Airbus A.330-243	Emirates Airlines	
A6-EAG	Airbus A.330-243	Emirates Airlines	
A6-EAH	Airbus A.330-243	Emirates Airlines	
A6-EAI	Airbus A.330-243	Emirates Airlines	
A6-EAJ	Airbus A.330-243	Emirates Airlines	
A6-EAK	Airbus A.330-243	Emirates Airlines	
A6-EAL	Airbus A.330-243	Emirates Airlines	
A6-EAM	Airbus A.330-243	Emirates Airlines	
A6-EAN	Airbus A.330-243	Emirates Airlines	
A6-EAO	Airbus A.330-243	Emirates Airlines	
A6-EAP	Airbus A.330-243	Emirates Airlines	
A6-EAQ	Airbus A.330-243	Emirates Airlines	
A6-EAR	Airbus A.330-243	Emirates Airlines	
A6-EAS	Airbus A.330-243	Emirates Airlines	
A6-EBA	Boeing 777-31HER	Emirates Airlines	
A6-EBB	Boeing 777-36NER	Emirates Airlines	
A6-EBC	Boeing 777-36NER	Emirates Airlines	
A6-EBD	Boeing 777-31HER	Emirates Airlines	
A6-EBE	Boeing 777-36NER	Emirates Airlines	
A6-EBF	Boeing 777-31HER	Emirates Airlines	
A6-EBG	Boeing 777-36NER	Emirates Airlines	
A6-EBH	Boeing 777-31HER	Emirates Airlines	
A6-EBI	Boeing 777-36NER	Emirates Airlines	
A6-EBJ	Boeing 777-36NER	Emirates Airlines	
A6-EBK	Boeing 777-31HER	Emirates Airlines	
A6-EBL	Boeing 777-31HER	Emirates Airlines	
A6-EBM	Boeing 777-31HER	Emirates Airlines	
A6-EBN	Boeing 777-36NER	Emirates Airlines	
A6-EBO	Boeing 777-36NER	Emirates Airlines	
A6-EBP	Boeing 777-31HER	Emirates Airlines	
A6-EBQ	Boeing 777-36NER	Emirates Airlines	
A6-EBR	Boeing 777-31HER	Emirates Airlines	
A6-EBS	Boeing 777-31HER	Emirates Airlines	
A6-EBT	Boeing 777-31HER	Emirates Airlines	
A6-EBU	Boeing 777-31HER	Emirates Airlines	
A6-EBV	Boeing 777-31HER	Emirates Airlines	
A6-EBW	Boeing 777-36NER	Emirates Airlines	

OVERSEAS AIRLINERS

Reg	Type	Owner or Operator
A6-EBX	Boeing 777-31HER	Emirates Airlines
A6-EBY	Boeing 777-36NER	Emirates Airlines
A6-EBZ	Boeing 777-31HER	Emirates Airlines
A6-ECA	Boeing 777-36NER	Emirates Airlines
A6-ECB	Boeing 777-31HER	Emirates Airlines
A6-ECC	Boeing 777-36NER	Emirates Airlines
A6-ECD	Boeing 777-36NER	Emirates Airlines
A6-EHA	Airbus A.340-541	Etihad Airways
A6-EHB	Airbus A.340-541	Etihad Airways
A6-EHC	Airbus A.340-541	Etihad Airways
A6-EHD	Airbus A.340-541	Etihad Airways
A6-EKQ	Airbus A.330-243	Emirates Airlines
A6-EKR	Airbus A.330-243	Emirates Airlines
A6-EKS	Airbus A.330-243	Emirates Airlines
A6-EKT	Airbus A.330-243	Emirates Airlines
A6-EKU	Airbus A.330-243	Emirates Airlines
A6-EKV	Airbus A.330-243	Emirates Airlines
A6-EKW	Airbus A.330-243	Emirates Airlines
A6-EKX	Airbus A.330-243	Emirates Airlines
A6-EKY	Airbus A.330-243	Emirates Airlines
A6-EKZ	Airbus A.330-243	Emirates Airlines
A6-EMD	Boeing 777-21H	Emirates Airlines
A6-EME	Boeing 777-21H	Emirates Airlines
A6-EMF	Boeing 777-21H	Emirates Airlines
A6-EMG	Boeing 777-21HER	Emirates Airlines
A6-EMH	Boeing 777-21HER	Emirates Airlines
A6-EMI	Boeing 777-21HER	Emirates Airlines
A6-EMJ	Boeing 777-21HER	Emirates Airlines
A6-EMK	Boeing 777-21HER	Emirates Airlines
A6-EML	Boeing 777-21HER	Emirates Airlines
A6-EMM	Boeing 777-31H	Emirates Airlines
A6-EMN	Boeing 777-31H	Emirates Airlines
A6-EMO	Boeing 777-31H	Emirates Airlines
A6-EMP	Boeing 777-31H	Emirates Airlines
A6-EMQ	Boeing 777-31H	Emirates Airlines
A6-EMR	Boeing 777-31H	Emirates Airlines
A6-EMS	Boeing 777-31H	Emirates Airlines
A6-EMT	Boeing 777-31H	Emirates Airlines
A6-EMU	Boeing 777-31H	Emirates Airlines
A6-EMV	Boeing 777-31H	Emirates Airlines
A6-EMW	Boeing 777-31H	Emirates Airlines
A6-EMX	Boeing 777-31H	Emirates Airlines
A6-ERA	Airbus A.340-541	Emirates Airlines
A6-ERB	Airbus A.340-541	Emirates Airlines
A6-ERC	Airbus A.340-541	Emirates Airlines
A6-ERD	Airbus A.340-541	Emirates Airlines
A6-ERE	Airbus A.340-541	Emirates Airlines
A6-ERF	Airbus A.340-541	Emirates Airlines
A6-ERG	Airbus A.340-541	Emirates Airlines
A6-ERH	Airbus A.340-541	Emirates Airlines
A6-ERI	Airbus A.340-541	Emirates Airlines
A6-ERJ	Airbus A.340-541	Emirates Airlines
A6-ERM	Airbus A.340-313X	Emirates Airlines
A6-ERN	Airbus A.340-313X	Emirates Airlines
A6-ERO	Airbus A.340-313X	Emirates Airlines
A6-ERP	Airbus A.340-313X	Emirates Airlines
A6-ERQ	Airbus A.340-313X	Emirates Airlines
A6-ERR	Airbus A.340-313X	Emirates Airlines
A6-ERS	Airbus A.340-313X	Emirates Airlines
A6-ERT	Airbus A.340-313X	Emirates Airlines
A6-ETA	Boeing 777-3FXER	Etihad Airways
A6-ETB	Boeing 777-3FXER	Etihad Airways
A6-ETC	Boeing 777-3FXER	Etihad Airways
A6-ETD	Boeing 777-3FXER	Etihad Airways
A6-ETE	Boeing 777-3FXER	Etihad Airways
A6-EYC	Airbus A.340-313X	Etihad Airways
A6-EYD	Airbus A.330-243	Etihad Airways
A6-EYE	Airbus A.330-243	Etihad Airways
A6-EYF	Airbus A.330-243	Etihad Airways
A6-EYG	Airbus A.330-243	Etihad Airways
A6-EYH	Airbus A.330-243	Etihad Airways
A6-EYI	Airbus A.330-243	Etihad Airways
A6-EYK	Airbus A.330-243	Etihad Airways

OVERSEAS AIRLINERS

A6/A7/AP

Reg	Type	Owner or Operator	Notes
A6-EYL	Airbus A.330-243	Etihad Airways	
A6-EYM	Airbus A.330-243	Etihad Airways	
A6-EYN	Airbus A.330-243	Etihad Airways	
A6-EYO	Airbus A.330-243	Etihad Airways	
A6-EYP	Airbus A.330-243	Etihad Airways	
A6-EYQ	Airbus A.330-243	Etihad Airways	
A6-EYV	Airbus A.330-202	Etihad Airways	
A6-EYW	Airbus A.330-202	Etihad Airways	
A6-GDP	Boeing 747-2B4BF	Dubai Government	
A6-HRM	Boeing 747-422	Dubai Government	
A6-MMM	Boeing 747-422	Dubai Government	
A6-SMR	Boeing 747SP-31	United Arab Emirates	
A6-UAE	Boeing 747-48E	United Arab Emirates	
A6-YAS	Boeing 747-4F6	United Arab Emirates	
A6-ZSN	Boeing 747SP-Z5	United Arab Emirates	

Note: United Arab Emirates also operates An-124 UR-ZYD. Emirates SkyCargo operates B.747Fs N408MC, N415MC, N497MC and N498MC.

A7 (Qatar)

A7-AAF	Airbus A.310-304	Qatar Government	
A7-AAG	Airbus A.320-232	Qatar Government	
A7-ACA	Airbus A.330-202	Qatar Airways *Alwajba*	
A7-ACB	Airbus A.330-202	Qatar Airways *Al Majida*	
A7-ACC	Airbus A.330-202	Qatar Airways *Al Shahaniya*	
A7-ACD	Airbus A.330-202	Qatar Airways *Al Wusell*	
A7-ACE	Airbus A.330-202	Qatar Airways *Al Dhakira*	
A7-ACF	Airbus A.330-202	Qatar Airways *Al Kara'anah*	
A7-ACG	Airbus A.330-202	Qatar Airways	
A7-ACH	Airbus A.330-202	Qatar Airways *Al Mafjar*	
A7-ACI	Airbus A.330-202	Qatar Airways	
A7-ACJ	Airbus A.330-202	Qatar Airways	
A7-ACK	Airbus A.330-202	Qatar Airways	
A7-ACL	Airbus A.330-202	Qatar Airways	
A7-ACM	Airbus A.330-202	Qatar Airways	
A7-AEA	Airbus A.330-302	Qatar Airways *Al Muntazah*	
A7-AEB	Airbus A.330-302	Qatar Airways*Al Sayliyah*	
A7-AEC	Airbus A.330-302	Qatar Airways	
A7-AED	Airbus A.330-302	Qatar Airways	
A7-AEE	Airbus A.330-302	Qatar Airways	
A7-AEF	Airbus A.330-302	Qatar Airways	
A7-AEG	Airbus A.330-302	Qatar Airways	
A7-AEH	Airbus A.330-302	Qatar Airways	
A7-AEI	Airbus A.330-302	Qatar Airways	
A7-AFL	Airbus A.330-202	Qatar Airways*Al Messilah*	
A7-AFM	Airbus A.330-202	Qatar Airways*Al Udaid*	
A7-AFN	Airbus A.330-202	Qatar Airways*Al Wakra*	
A7-AFO	Airbus A.330-202	Qatar Airways*Al Ghariyah*	
A7-AFP	Airbus A.330-202	Qatar Airways	
A7-AFW	Airbus A.330-202	Qatar Airways	
A7-AGA	Airbus A.340-642	Qatar Airways	
A7-AGB	Airbus A.340-642	Qatar Airways	
A7-AGC	Airbus A.340-642	Qatar Airways	
A7-AGD	Airbus A.340-642	Qatar Airways	
A7-HHH	Airbus A.340-541	Qatar Government	
A7-HHK	Airbus A.340-211	Qatar Government	
A7-HHM	Airbus A.330-203	Qatar Government	
A7-HJJ	Airbus A.330-203	Qatar Government	

AP (Pakistan)

AP-BAK	Boeing 747-240B (SCD)	Pakistan International Airlines	
AP-BAT	Boeing 747-240B (SCD)	Pakistan International Airlines	
AP-BDZ	Airbus A.310-308	Pakistan International Airlines	
AP-BEB	Airbus A.310-308	Pakistan International Airlines	
AP-BEC	Airbus A.310-308	Pakistan International Airlines	
AP-BEG	Airbus A.310-308	Pakistan International Airlines	
AP-BEQ	Airbus A.310-308	Pakistan International Airlines	

AP/B · OVERSEAS AIRLINERS

Notes	Reg	Type	Owner or Operator
	AP-BEU	Airbus A.310-308	Pakistan International Airlines
	AP-BFU	Boeing 747-367	Pakistan International Airlines
	AP-BFV	Boeing 747-367	Pakistan International Airlines
	AP-BFW	Boeing 747-367	Pakistan International Airlines
	AP-BFX	Boeing 747-367	Pakistan International Airlines
	AP-BFY	Boeing 747-367	Pakistan International Airlines
	AP-BGG	Boeing 747-367	Pakistan International Airlines
	AP-BGJ	Boeing 777-240ER	Pakistan International Airlines
	AP-BGK	Boeing 777-240ER	Pakistan International Airlines
	AP-BGL	Boeing 777-240ER	Pakistan International Airlines
	AP-BGN	Airbus A.310-324	Pakistan International Airlines
	AP-BGO	Airbus A.310-324	Pakistan International Airlines
	AP-BGP	Airbus A.310-324	Pakistan International Airlines
	AP-BGQ	Airbus A.310-324	Pakistan International Airlines
	AP-BGR	Airbus A.310-324	Pakistan International Airlines
	AP-BGS	Airbus A.310-324	Pakistan International Airlines
	AP-BGY	Boeing 777-240LR	Pakistan International Airlines
	AP-BGZ	Boeing 777-240LR	Pakistan International Airlines
	AP-BHV	Boeing 777-340ER	Pakistan International Airlines
	AP-BHW	Boeing 777-340ER	Pakistan International Airlines
	AP-BHX	Boeing 777-240ER	Pakistan International Airlines

B (China/Taiwan/Hong Kong)

Reg	Type	Owner or Operator
B-HIH	Boeing 747-267F (SCD)	Cathay Pacific Airways
B-HKD	Boeing 747-412	Cathay Pacific Airways
B-HKE	Boeing 747-412	Cathay Pacific Airways
B-HKF	Boeing 747-412	Cathay Pacific Airways
B-HKH	Boeing 747-412BCF	Cathay Pacific Airways
B-HKT	Boeing 747-412BCF	Cathay Pacific Airways
B-HMD	Boeing 747-2L5F (SCD)	Cathay Pacific Airways
B-HME	Boeing 747-2L5F (SCD)	Cathay Pacific Airways
B-HMF	Boeing 747-2L5F (SCD)	Cathay Pacific Airways
B-HOO	Boeing 747-467	Cathay Pacific Airways
B-HOP	Boeing 747-467	Cathay Pacific Airways
B-HOR	Boeing 747-467	Cathay Pacific Airways
B-HOS	Boeing 747-467	Cathay Pacific Airways
B-HOT	Boeing 747-467	Cathay Pacific Airways
B-HOU	Boeing 747-467BCF	Cathay Pacific Airways
B-HOV	Boeing 747-467	Cathay Pacific Airways
B-HOW	Boeing 747-467	Cathay Pacific Airways
B-HOX	Boeing 747-467	Cathay Pacific Airways
B-HOY	Boeing 747-467	Cathay Pacific Airways
B-HOZ	Boeing 747-467	Cathay Pacific Airways
B-HUA	Boeing 747-467	Cathay Pacific Airways
B-HUB	Boeing 747-467	Cathay Pacific Airways
B-HUD	Boeing 747-467	Cathay Pacific Airways
B-HUE	Boeing 747-467	Cathay Pacific Airways
B-HUF	Boeing 747-467	Cathay Pacific Airways
B-HUG	Boeing 747-467	Cathay Pacific Airways
B-HUH	Boeing 747-467F (SCD)	Cathay Pacific Airways
B-HUI	Boeing 747-467	Cathay Pacific Airways
B-HUJ	Boeing 747-467	Cathay Pacific Airways
B-HUK	Boeing 747-467F (SCD)	Cathay Pacific Airways
B-HUL	Boeing 747-467F (SCD)	Cathay Pacific Airways
B-HUO	Boeing 747-467F (SCD)	Cathay Pacific Airways
B-HUP	Boeing 747-467F (SCD)	Cathay Pacific Airways
B-HUQ	Boeing 747-467F (SCD)	Cathay Pacific Airways
B-HUR	Boeing 747-444BCF	Cathay Pacific Airways
B-HUS	Boeing 747-444BCF	Cathay Pacific Airways
B-HVX	Boeing 747-267F (SCD)	Cathay Pacific Airways
B-HVY	Boeing 747-236F (SCD)	Cathay Pacific Airways
B-HVZ	Boeing 747-267F (SCD)	Cathay Pacific Airways
B-HQA	Airbus A.340-642	Cathay Pacific Airways
B-HQB	Airbus A.340-642	Cathay Pacific Airways
B-HQC	Airbus A.340-642	Cathay Pacific Airways
B-HXA	Airbus A.340-313X	Cathay Pacific Airways
B-HXB	Airbus A.340-313X	Cathay Pacific Airways
B-HXC	Airbus A.340-313X	Cathay Pacific Airways
B-HXD	Airbus A.340-313X	Cathay Pacific Airways
B-HXE	Airbus A.340-313X	Cathay Pacific Airways

OVERSEAS AIRLINERS

B

Reg	Type	Owner or Operator	Notes
B-HXF	Airbus A.340-313X	Cathay Pacific Airways	
B-HXG	Airbus A.340-313X	Cathay Pacific Airways	
B-HXH	Airbus A.340-313X	Cathay Pacific Airways	
B-HXI	Airbus A.340-313X	Cathay Pacific Airways	
B-HXJ	Airbus A.340-313X	Cathay Pacific Airways	
B-HXK	Airbus A.340-313X	Cathay Pacific Airways	
B-HXL	Airbus A.340-313X	Cathay Pacific Airways	
B-HXM	Airbus A.340-313X	Cathay Pacific Airways	
B-HXN	Airbus A.340-313X	Cathay Pacific Airways	
B-HXO	Airbus A.340-313X	Cathay Pacific Airways	
B-KAA	Boeing 747-312F (SCD)	Dragonair Cargo	
B-KAB	Boeing 747-312F (SCD)	Dragonair Cargo	
B-KAC	Boeing 747-3H6F (SCD)	Dragonair Cargo	
B-KAD	Boeing 747-209F (SCD)	Dragonair Cargo	
B-KAE	Boeing 747-412BCF	Dragonair Cargo	
B-LFA	Boeing 747-412	Oasis Hong Kong Airlines	
B-LFB	Boeing 747-412	Oasis Hong Kong Airlines	
B-2380	Airbus A.340-313X	China Eastern Airlines	
B-2381	Airbus A.340-313X	China Eastern Airlines	
B-2382	Airbus A.340-313X	China Eastern Airlines	
B-2383	Airbus A.340-313X	China Eastern Airlines	
B-2384	Airbus A.340-313X	China Eastern Airlines	
B-2385	Airbus A.340-313X	Air China	
B-2386	Airbus A.340-313X	Air China	
B-2387	Airbus A.340-313X	Air China	
B-2409	Boeing 747-412F (SCD)	Air China Cargo	
B-2425	Boeing 747-4B0ERF	China Cargo Airlines	
B-2443	Boeing 747-4J6	Air China	
B-2445	Boeing 747-4J6	Air China	
B-2446	Boeing 747-2J6B (SF)	Air China Cargo	
B-2447	Boeing 747-4J6	Air China	
B-2448	Boeing 747-2J6B (SF)	Air China Cargo	
B-2450	Boeing 747-2J6B (SF)	Air China Cargo	
B-2456	Boeing 747-4J6	Air China	
B-2458	Boeing 747-4J6	Air China	
B-2460	Boeing 747-4J6	Air China	
B-2462	Boeing 747-2J6F (SCD)	Air China Cargo	
B-2467	Boeing 747-4J6	Air China	
B-2468	Boeing 747-4J6	Air China	
B-2469	Boeing 747-4J6	Air China	
B-2470	Boeing 747-4J6	Air China	
B-2471	Boeing 747-4J6	Air China	
B-2472	Boeing 747-4J6	Air China	
B-2475	Boeing 747-4FTF (SCD)	Air China Cargo	
B-2476	Boeing 747-4FTF (SCD)	Air China Cargo	
B-2477	Boeing 747-433SF	Air China Cargo	
B-2478	Boeing 747-433SF	Air China Cargo	
B-6050	Airbus A.340-642	China Eastern Airlines	
B-6051	Airbus A.340-642	China Eastern Airlines	
B-6052	Airbus A.340-642	China Eastern Airlines	
B-6053	Airbus A.340-642	China Eastern Airlines	
B-6055	Airbus A.340-642	China Eastern Airlines	
B-16101	McD Douglas MD-11F	EVA Air Cargo	
B-16102	McD Douglas MD-11F	EVA Air Cargo	
B-16106	McD Douglas MD-11F	EVA Air Cargo	
B-16107	McD Douglas MD-11F	EVA Air Cargo	
B-16108	McD Douglas MD-11F	EVA Air Cargo	
B-16109	McD Douglas MD-11F	EVA Air Cargo	
B-16110	McD Douglas MD-11F	EVA Air Cargo	
B-16111	McD Douglas MD-11F	EVA Air Cargo	
B-16112	McD Douglas MD-11F	EVA Air Cargo	
B-16113	McD Douglas MD-11F	EVA Air Cargo	
B-16401	Boeing 747-45E	EVA Airways	
B-16402	Boeing 747-45E	EVA Airways	
B-16403	Boeing 747-45E	EVA Airways	
B-16405	Boeing 747-45E	EVA Airways	
B-16406	Boeing 747-45E	EVA Airways	
B-16407	Boeing 747-45E	EVA Airways	
B-16408	Boeing 747-45E	EVA Airways	
B-16409	Boeing 747-45E	EVA Airways	
B-16410	Boeing 747-45E	EVA Airways	
B-16411	Boeing 747-45E	EVA Airways	
B-16412	Boeing 747-45E	EVA Airways	

B/C OVERSEAS AIRLINERS

Notes	Reg	Type	Owner or Operator
	B-16461	Boeing 747-45E (SCD)	EVA Airways
	B-16462	Boeing 747-45E (SCD)	EVA Airways
	B-16463	Boeing 747-45E (SCD)	EVA Airways
	B-16465	Boeing 747-45E (SCD)	EVA Airways
	B-16481	Boeing 747-45EF (SCD)	EVA Air Cargo
	B-16482	Boeing 747-45EF (SCD)	EVA Air Cargo
	B-16483	Boeing 747-45EF (SCD)	EVA Air Cargo
	B-16701	Boeing 777-35EER	EVA Airways
	B-16702	Boeing 777-35EER	EVA Airways
	B-16703	Boeing 777-35EER	EVA Airways
	B-16705	Boeing 777-35EER	EVA Airways
	B-16706	Boeing 777-35EER	EVA Airways
	B-16707	Boeing 777-35EER	EVA Airways
	B-16708	Boeing 777-35EER	EVA Airways
	B-16709	Boeing 777-35EER	EVA Airways
	B-18701	Boeing 747-409F (SCD)	China Airlines
	B-18702	Boeing 747-409F (SCD)	China Airlines
	B-18703	Boeing 747-409F (SCD)	China Airlines
	B-18705	Boeing 747-409F (SCD)	China Airlines
	B-18706	Boeing 747-409F (SCD)	China Airlines
	B-18707	Boeing 747-409F (SCD)	China Airlines
	B-18708	Boeing 747-409F (SCD)	China Airlines
	B-18709	Boeing 747-409F (SCD)	China Airlines
	B-18710	Boeing 747-409F (SCD)	China Airlines
	B-18711	Boeing 747-409F (SCD)	China Airlines
	B-18712	Boeing 747-409F (SCD)	China Airlines
	B-18715	Boeing 747-409F (SCD)	China Airlines
	B-18716	Boeing 747-409F (SCD)	China Airlines
	B-18717	Boeing 747-409F (SCD)	China Airlines
	B-18718	Boeing 747-409F (SCD)	China Airlines
	B-18719	Boeing 747-409F (SCD)	China Airlines
	B-18720	Boeing 747-409F (SCD)	China Airlines
	B-18721	Boeing 747-409F (SCD)	China Airlines
	B-18722	Boeing 747-409F (SCD)	China Airlines
	B-18723	Boeing 747-409F (SCD)	China Airlines
	B-18725	Boeing 747-409F (SCD)	China Airlines

Note: EVA Air Cargo also operates MD-11F N105EV.

C (Canada)

Reg	Type	Owner or Operator
C-FBEF	Boeing 767-233ER (617)	Air Canada
C-FBEG	Boeing 767-233ER (618)	Air Canada
C-FBEM	Boeing 767-233ER (619)	Air Canada
C-FCAB	Boeing 767-375ER (681)	Air Canada
C-FCAE	Boeing 767-375ER (682)	Air Canada
C-FCAF	Boeing 767-375ER (683)	Air Canada
C-FCAG	Boeing 767-375ER (684)	Air Canada
C-FDAT	Airbus A.310-308 (305)	Air Transat
C-FDRO	Airbus A.340-312 (983)	Air Canada
C-FMWP	Boeing 767-333ER (631)	Air Canada
C-FMWQ	Boeing 767-333ER (632)	Air Canada
C-FMWU	Boeing 767-333ER (633)	Air Canada
C-FMWV	Boeing 767-333ER (634)	Air Canada
C-FMWY	Boeing 767-333ER (635)	Air Canada
C-FMXC	Boeing 767-333ER (636)	Air Canada
C-FOCA	Boeing 767-375ER (640)	Air Canada
C-FPCA	Boeing 767-375ER (637)	Air Canada
C-FTCA	Boeing 767-375ER (638)	Air Canada
C-FTNQ	Airbus A.340-313 (981)	Air Canada
C-FVNM	Boeing 767-209ER (621)	Air Canada
C-FXCA	Boeing 767-375ER (639)	Air Canada
C-FYKX	Airbus A.340-313X (901)	Air Canada
C-FYKZ	Airbus A.340-313X (902)	Air Canada
C-FYLC	Airbus A.340-313X (903)	Air Canada
C-FYLD	Airbus A.340-313X (904)	Air Canada
C-FYLG	Airbus A.340-313X (905)	Air Canada
C-FYLU	Airbus A.340-313X (906)	Air Canada
C-GBZR	Boeing 767-38EER (645)	Air Canada
C-GDSP	Boeing 767-233ER (613)	Air Canada
C-GDSS	Boeing 767-233ER (614)	Air Canada

OVERSEAS AIRLINERS

C/CC/CN

Reg	Type	Owner or Operator	Notes
C-GDSU	Boeing 767-233ER (615)	Air Canada	
C-GDSY	Boeing 767-233ER (616)	Air Canada	
C-GDUZ	Boeing 767-38EER (646)	Air Canada	
C-GDVW	Airbus A.340-313X (909)	Air Canada	
C-GDVZ	Airbus A.340-313X (910)	Air Canada	
C-GEOQ	Boeing 767-375ER (647)	Air Canada	
C-GEOU	Boeing 767-375ER (648)	Air Canada	
C-GFAF	Airbus A.330-343X (931)	Air Canada	
C-GFAH	Airbus A.330-343X (932)	Air Canada	
C-GFAJ	Airbus A.330-343X (933)	Air Canada	
C-GFAT	Airbus A.310-304 (301)	Air Transat	
C-GFUR	Airbus A.330-343X (934)	Air Canada	
C-GGFJ	Boeing 767-3Y0ER (652)	Air Canada	
C-GGMX	Boeing 767-3Y0ER (653)	Air Canada	
C-GGTS	Airbus A.330-243 (101)	Air Transat	
C-GHKR	Airbus A.330-343X (935)	Air Canada	
C-GHKW	Airbus A.330-343X (936)	Air Canada	
C-GHKX	Airbus A.330-343X (937)	Air Canada	
C-GHLA	Boeing 767-35HER (656)	Air Canada	
C-GHLK	Boeing 767-35HER (657)	Air Canada	
C-GHLM	Airbus A.330-343X (938)	Air Canada	
C-GHLQ	Boeing 767-333ER (658)	Air Canada	
C-GHLT	Boeing 767-333ER (659)	Air Canada	
C-GHLU	Boeing 767-333ER (660)	Air Canada	
C-GHLV	Boeing 767-333ER (661)	Air Canada	
C-GHOZ	Boeing 767-375ER (685)	Air Canada	
C-GHPA	Boeing 767-3Y0ER (686)	Air Canada	
C-GHPD	Boeing 767-3Y0ER (687)	Air Canada	
C-GHPF	Boeing 767-3Y0ER (689)	Air Canada	
C-GHPH	Boeing 767-3Y0ER (690)	Air Canada	
C-GITS	Airbus A.330-243 (102)	Air Transat	
C-GKOL	Airbus A.340-541 (951)	Air Canada	
C-GKOM	Airbus A.340-541 (952)	Air Canada	
C-GKTS	Airbus A.330-342 (100)	Air Transat	
C-GLAT	Airbus A.310-308 (302)	Air Transat	
C-GLCA	Boeing 767-375ER (641)	Air Canada	
C-GPAT	Airbus A.310-308 (303)	Air Transat	
C-GPTS	Airbus A.330-243 (103)	Air Transat	
C-GSAT	Airbus A.310-308 (304)	Air Transat	
C-GSCA	Boeing 767-375ER (642)	Air Canada	
C-GTSD	Airbus A.310-304 (341)	Air Transat	
C-GTSF	Airbus A.310-304 (345)	Air Transat	
C-GTSH	Airbus A.310-304 (343)	Air Transat	
C-GTSI	Airbus A.310-304 (342)	Air Transat	
C-GTSX	Airbus A.310-304	Air Transat	
C-GTSY	Airbus A.310-304 (361)	Air Transat	
C-GVAT	Airbus A.310-304 (321)	Air Transat	
C-GVKI	Airbus A.330-343X	Skyservice Airlines	
C-GZMM	Boeing 767-328ER (102)	Zoom Airlines *City of Halifax*	
C-GZNA	Boeing 767-306ER (103)	Zoom Airlines *City of Toronto*	
C-GZNC	Boeing 767-306ER (104)	Zoom Airlines *City of Vancouver*	
C-GZUM	Boeing 767-328ER (101)	Zoom Airlines *City of Ottawa*	

Note: Airline fleet number when carried on aircraft is shown in parentheses.
Air Canada Cargo uses World Airways MD-11Fs and Gemini Air Cargo DC-10Fs.
Air Canada intends to use A.319s on its St. John's-Heathrow service from April 2007.

CC (Chile)

CC-CZY	Boeing 767-316F	LAN Airlines	
CC-CZZ	Boeing 767-38EF	LAN Airlines	

Note: LAN Airlines also operates B.767-316Fs N312LA and N418LA.

CN (Morocco)

CN-RGA	Boeing 747-428	Royal Air Maroc	
CN-RMF	Boeing 737-4B6	Atlas Blue	
CN-RMG	Boeing 737-4B6	Atlas Blue	

CN/CS — OVERSEAS AIRLINERS

Notes	Reg	Type	Owner or Operator
	CN-RMM	Boeing 737-2B6C	Royal Air Maroc
	CN-RMN	Boeing 737-2B6C	Royal Air Maroc
	CN-RMT	Boeing 757-2B6	Royal Air Maroc
	CN-RMV	Boeing 737-5B6	Royal Air Maroc
	CN-RMW	Boeing 737-5B6	Royal Air Maroc
	CN-RMX	Boeing 737-4B6	Atlas Blue
	CN-RMY	Boeing 737-5B6	Royal Air Maroc
	CN-RMZ	Boeing 757-2B6	Royal Air Maroc
	CN-RNA	Boeing 737-4B6	Atlas Blue
	CN-RNB	Boeing 737-5B6	Royal Air Maroc
	CN-RNC	Boeing 737-4B6	Atlas Blue
	CN-RND	Boeing 737-4B6	Atlas Blue
	CN-RNG	Boeing 737-5B6	Royal Air Maroc
	CN-RNH	Boeing 737-5B6	Royal Air Maroc
	CN-RNJ	Boeing 737-8B6	Royal Air Maroc
	CN-RNK	Boeing 737-8B6	Royal Air Maroc
	CN-RNL	Boeing 737-7B6	Royal Air Maroc
	CN-RNM	Boeing 737-7B6	Royal Air Maroc
	CN-RNP	Boeing 737-8B6	Royal Air Maroc
	CN-RNQ	Boeing 737-7B6	Royal Air Maroc
	CN-RNR	Boeing 737-7B6	Royal Air Maroc
	CN-RNS	Boeing 767-3B6ER	Royal Air Maroc
	CN-RNT	Boeing 767-3B6ER	Royal Air Maroc
	CN-RNU	Boeing 737-8B6	Royal Air Maroc
	CN-RNV	Boeing 737-7B6	Royal Air Maroc
	CN-RNW	Boeing 737-8B6	Royal Air Maroc
	CN-RNX	Airbus A.321-211	Royal Air Maroc
	CN-RNY	Airbus A.321-211	Royal Air Maroc
	CN-RNZ	Boeing 737-8B6	Royal Air Maroc
	CN-ROA	Boeing 737-8B6	Royal Air Maroc
	CN-ROB	Boeing 737-8B6	Royal Air Maroc
	CN-ROC	Boeing 737-8B6	Royal Air Maroc
	CN-ROD	Boeing 737-8B6	Royal Air Maroc
	CN-ROE	Boeing 737-8B6	Royal Air Maroc
	CN-ROF	Airbus A.321-211	Atlas Blue
	CN-ROG	Boeing 767-328ER	Royal Air Maroc
	CN-ROH	Boeing 737-8B6	Royal Air Maroc
	CN-ROJ	Boeing 737-8B6	Atlas Blue

CS (Portugal)

Notes	Reg	Type	Owner or Operator
	CS-TDI	Airbus A.310-308	TAP Portugal *Padre Antonio Vieira*
	CS-TEB	L.1011-385 TriStar 500	Euro Atlantic Airways *Naughton Simao*
	CS-TEH	Airbus A.310-304	TAP Portugal *Bartolomeu Dias*
	CS-TEI	Airbus A.310-304	TAP Portugal *Fernao de Magalhaes*
	CS-TEJ	Airbus A.310-304	TAP Portugal *Pedro Nunes*
	CS-TEW	Airbus A.310-304	TAP Portugal *Vasco da Gama*
	CS-TEX	Airbus A.310-304	TAP Portugal *Joao XXI*
	CS-TGU	Airbus A.310-304	SATA International *Terceira*
	CS-TJE	Airbus A.321-211	TAP Portugal *Pero Vaz de Caminha*
	CS-TJF	Airbus A.321-211	TAP Portugal *Luis Vaz de Camoes*
	CS-TJG	Airbus A.321-211	TAP Portugal *Amelia Rodrigues*
	CS-TKJ	Airbus A.320-212	SATA International *Pico*
	CS-TKK	Airbus A.320-214	SATA International *Corvo*
	CS-TKL	Airbus A.320-214	SATA International *S Jorge*
	CS-TKM	Airbus A.310-304	SATA International *Autonomia*
	CS-TLO	Boeing 767-383ER	Euro Atlantic Airways
	CS-TLQ	Boeing 767-3Y0ER	Euro Atlantic Airways
	CS-TLX	Boeing 757-2G5	Euro Atlantic Airways
	CS-TMW	Airbus A.320-214	TAP Portugal *Luisa Todi*
	CS-TNA	Airbus A.320-211	TAP Portugal *Grao Vasco*
	CS-TNB	Airbus A.320-211	TAP Portugal *Sophia de Mello Breyner*
	CS-TNE	Airbus A.320-212	TAP Portugal *Sa de Miranda*
	CS-TNG	Airbus A.320-214	TAP Portugal *Mouzinho da Silveira*
	CS-TNH	Airbus A.320-214	TAP Portugal *Almada Negreiros*
	CS-TNI	Airbus A.320-214	TAP Portugal *Aquilino Ribiera*
	CS-TNJ	Airbus A.320-214	TAP Portugal *Florbela Espanca*
	CS-TNK	Airbus A.320-214	TAP Portugal *Teofilo Braga*
	CS-TNL	Airbus A.320-214	TAP Portugal *Vitorino Nermesio*
	CS-TNM	Airbus A.320-214	TAP Portugal *Natalia Correia*
	CS-TNN	Airbus A.320-214	TAP Portugal *Gil Vicente*

OVERSEAS AIRLINERS

CS/CU/D

Reg	Type	Owner or Operator	Notes
CS-TNO	Airbus A.320-211	TAP Portugal *Luis de Freitas Branco*	
CS-TNP	Airbus A.320-214	TAP Portugal *Alexandre O'Neill*	
CS-TOA	Airbus A.340-312	TAP Portugal *Fernao Mendes Pinto*	
CS-TOB	Airbus A.340-312	TAP Portugal *D Joao de Castro*	
CS-TOC	Airbus A.340-312	TAP Portugal *Wenceslau de Moraes*	
CS-TOD	Airbus A.340-312	TAP Portugal *D Francisco de Almeida*	
CS-TOE	Airbus A.330-223	TAP Portugal *Pedro Alvares Cabal*	
CS-TOF	Airbus A.330-223	TAP Portugal *Infante D Henrique*	
CS-TOG	Airbus A.330-223	TAP Portugal *Bartolomeu de Gusmão*	
CS-TQD	Airbus A.320-214	TAP Portugal *Eugenio de Andrade*	
CS-TTA	Airbus A.319-111	TAP Portugal *Vieira da Silva*	
CS-TTB	Airbus A.319-111	TAP Portugal *Gago Coutinho*	
CS-TTC	Airbus A.319-111	TAP Portugal *Fernando Pessoa*	
CS-TTD	Airbus A.319-111	TAP Portugal *Amadeo de Souza-Cardoso*	
CS-TTE	Airbus A.319-111	TAP Portugal *Francisco d'Ollanda*	
CS-TTF	Airbus A.319-111	TAP Portugal *Calouste Gulbenkian*	
CS-TTG	Airbus A.319-111	TAP Portugal *Humberto Delgado*	
CS-TTH	Airbus A.319-111	TAP Portugal *Antonio Sergio*	
CS-TTI	Airbus A.319-111	TAP Portugal *Eca de Queiros*	
CS-TTJ	Airbus A.319-111	TAP Portugal *Eusebio*	
CS-TTK	Airbus A.319-111	TAP Portugal *Miguel Torga*	
CS-TTL	Airbus A.319-111	TAP Portugal *Almeida Garrett*	
CS-TTM	Airbus A.319-111	TAP Portugal *Alexandre Herculano*	
CS-TTN	Airbus A.319-111	TAP Portugal *Camilo Castelo Branco*	
CS-TTO	Airbus A.319-111	TAP Portugal *Antero de Quental*	
CS-TTP	Airbus A.319-111	TAP Portugal *Josefa d'Obidos*	
CS-TTQ	Airbus A.319-112	TAP Portugal *Agostinho da Silva*	

CU (Cuba)

Note: Cubana flights to London-Gatwick are currently operated by Boeing 767s of Air Europa.

D (Germany)

Reg	Type	Owner or Operator	Notes
D-ABAA	Boeing 737-76Q	Air Berlin	
D-ABAB	Boeing 737-76Q	Air Berlin	
D-ABAC	Boeing 737-86J	Air Berlin	
D-ABAD	Boeing 737-86J	Air Berlin	
D-ABAE	Boeing 737-86J	Air Berlin	
D-ABAF	Boeing 737-86J	Air Berlin	
D-ABAG	Boeing 737-86J	Air Berlin	
D-ABAN	Boeing 737-86J	Air Berlin	
D-ABAO	Boeing 737-86J	Air Berlin	
D-ABAP	Boeing 737-86J	Air Berlin	
D-ABAQ	Boeing 737-86J	Air Berlin	
D-ABAR	Boeing 737-86J	Air Berlin	
D-ABAS	Boeing 737-86J	Air Berlin	
D-ABAT	Boeing 737-86J	Air Berlin	
D-ABAU	Boeing 737-86J	Air Berlin	
D-ABAV	Boeing 737-86J	Air Berlin	
D-ABAW	Boeing 737-86J	Air Berlin	
D-ABAX	Boeing 737-86J	Air Berlin	
D-ABAY	Boeing 737-86J	Air Berlin	
D-ABAZ	Boeing 737-86J	Air Berlin	
D-ABBA	Boeing 737-86J	Air Berlin	
D-ABBB	Boeing 737-86J	Air Berlin	
D-ABBC	Boeing 737-86J	Air Berlin	
D-ABBD	Boeing 737-86J	Air Berlin	
D-ABBE	Boeing 737-86J	Air Berlin	
D-ABBF	Boeing 737-86J	Air Berlin	
D-ABBG	Boeing 737-86J	Air Berlin	
D-ABBH	Boeing 737-86J	Air Berlin	
D-ABBI	Boeing 737-86J	Air Berlin	
D-ABBJ	Boeing 737-86Q	Air Berlin	
D-ABBK	Boeing 737-8BK	Air Berlin	
D-ABBL	Boeing 737-85F	Air Berlin	
D-ABBM	Boeing 737-85F	Air Berlin	
D-ABBN	Boeing 737-76Q	Air Berlin	
D-ABBO	Boeing 737-86J	Air Berlin	

OVERSEAS AIRLINERS

Notes	Reg	Type	Owner or Operator
	D-ABBP	Boeing 737-86J	Air Berlin
	D-ABBQ	Boeing 737-86N	Air Berlin
	D-ABBR	Boeing 737-85F	Air Berlin
	D-ABBS	Boeing 737-76N	Air Berlin
	D-ABBT	Boeing 737-76N	Air Berlin
	D-ABDA	Airbus A.320-214	Air Berlin
	D-ABDB	Airbus A.320-214	Air Berlin
	D-ABDC	Airbus A.320-214	Air Berlin
	D-ABDD	Airbus A.320-214	Air Berlin
	D-ABDE	Airbus A.320-214	Air Berlin
	D-ABDF	Airbus A.320-214	Air Berlin
	D-ABDG	Airbus A.320-214	Air Berlin
	D-ABDH	Airbus A.320-214	Air Berlin
	D-ABDI	Airbus A.320-214	Air Berlin
	D-ABDJ	Airbus A.320-214	Air Berlin
	D-ABDK	Airbus A.320-214	Air Berlin
	D-ABDL	Airbus A.320-214	Air Berlin
	D-ABDM	Airbus A.320-214	Air Berlin
	D-ABDN	Airbus A.320-214	Air Berlin
	D-ABEA	Boeing 737-330	Lufthansa *Saarbrücken*
	D-ABEB	Boeing 737-330	Lufthansa *Xanten*
	D-ABEC	Boeing 737-330	Lufthansa *Karlsruhe*
	D-ABED	Boeing 737-330	Lufthansa *Hagen*
	D-ABEE	Boeing 737-330	Lufthansa *Ulm*
	D-ABEF	Boeing 737-330	Lufthansa *Weiden i.d.Obf.*
	D-ABEH	Boeing 737-330	Lufthansa *Bad Kissingen*
	D-ABEI	Boeing 737-330	Lufthansa *Bamberg*
	D-ABEK	Boeing 737-330	Lufthansa *Wuppertal*
	D-ABEL	Boeing 737-330	Lufthansa *Pforzheim*
	D-ABEM	Boeing 737-330	Lufthansa *Eberswalde*
	D-ABEN	Boeing 737-330	Lufthansa *Neubrandenburg*
	D-ABEO	Boeing 737-330	Lufthansa *Plauen*
	D-ABEP	Boeing 737-330	Lufthansa *Naumburg (Saale)*
	D-ABER	Boeing 737-330	Lufthansa *Merseburg*
	D-ABES	Boeing 737-330	Lufthansa *Koethen/Anhalt*
	D-ABET	Boeing 737-330	Lufthansa *Gelsenkirchen*
	D-ABEU	Boeing 737-330	Lufthansa *Goslar*
	D-ABEW	Boeing 737-330	Lufthansa *Detmold*
	D-ABGA	Airbus A.319-132	Air Berlin
	D-ABGB	Airbus A.319-132	Air Berlin
	D-ABGC	Airbus A.319-132	Air Berlin
	D-ABGD	Airbus A.319-132	Air Berlin
	D-ABIA	Boeing 737-530	Lufthansa *Greifswald*
	D-ABIB	Boeing 737-530	Lufthansa *Esslingen*
	D-ABIC	Boeing 737-530	Lufthansa *Krefeld*
	D-ABID	Boeing 737-530	Lufthansa *Aachen*
	D-ABIE	Boeing 737-530	Lufthansa *Hildesheim*
	D-ABIF	Boeing 737-530	Lufthansa *Landau*
	D-ABIH	Boeing 737-530	Lufthansa *Bruchsal*
	D-ABII	Boeing 737-530	Lufthansa *Lörrach*
	D-ABIK	Boeing 737-530	Lufthansa *Rastatt*
	D-ABIL	Boeing 737-530	Lufthansa *Memmingen*
	D-ABIM	Boeing 737-530	Lufthansa *Salzgitter*
	D-ABIN	Boeing 737-530	Lufthansa *Langenhagen*
	D-ABIO	Boeing 737-530	Lufthansa *Wesel*
	D-ABIP	Boeing 737-530	Lufthansa *Oberhausen*
	D-ABIR	Boeing 737-530	Lufthansa *Anklam*
	D-ABIS	Boeing 737-530	Lufthansa *Rendsburg*
	D-ABIT	Boeing 737-530	Lufthansa *Neumünster*
	D-ABIU	Boeing 737-530	Lufthansa *Limburg a.d. Lahn*
	D-ABIW	Boeing 737-530	Lufthansa *Bad Nauheim*
	D-ABIX	Boeing 737-530	Lufthansa *Iserlohn*
	D-ABIY	Boeing 737-530	Lufthansa *Lingen*
	D-ABIZ	Boeing 737-530	Lufthansa *Kirchheim unter Teck*
	D-ABJA	Boeing 737-530	Lufthansa *Bad Segeberg*
	D-ABJB	Boeing 737-530	Lufthansa *Rheine*
	D-ABJC	Boeing 737-530	Lufthansa *Erding*
	D-ABJD	Boeing 737-530	Lufthansa *Freising*
	D-ABJE	Boeing 737-530	Lufthansa *Ingelheim am Rhein*
	D-ABJF	Boeing 737-530	Lufthansa *Aalen*
	D-ABJH	Boeing 737-530	Lufthansa *Heppenheim/Bergstrasse*
	D-ABJI	Boeing 737-530	Lufthansa *Siegburg*
	D-ABOA	Boeing 757-330	Condor

OVERSEAS AIRLINERS

Reg	Type	Owner or Operator	Notes
D-ABOB	Boeing 757-330	Condor	
D-ABOC	Boeing 757-330	Condor	
D-ABOE	Boeing 757-330	Condor	
D-ABOF	Boeing 757-330	Condor	
D-ABOG	Boeing 757-330	Condor	
D-ABOH	Boeing 757-330	Condor	
D-ABOI	Boeing 757-330	Condor	
D-ABOJ	Boeing 757-330	Condor	
D-ABOK	Boeing 757-330	Condor	
D-ABOL	Boeing 757-330	Condor	
D-ABOM	Boeing 757-330	Condor	
D-ABON	Boeing 757-330	Condor	
D-ABTA	Boeing 747-430 (SCD)	Lufthansa *Sachsen*	
D-ABTB	Boeing 747-430 (SCD)	Lufthansa *Brandenburg*	
D-ABTC	Boeing 747-430 (SCD)	Lufthansa *Mecklenburg-Vorpommern*	
D-ABTD	Boeing 747-430 (SCD)	Lufthansa *Hamburg*	
D-ABTE	Boeing 747-430 (SCD)	Lufthansa *Sachsen-Anhalt*	
D-ABTF	Boeing 747-430 (SCD)	Lufthansa *Thüringen*	
D-ABTH	Boeing 747-430 (SCD)	Lufthansa *Duisburg*	
D-ABTK	Boeing 747-430 (SCD)	Lufthansa *Kiel*	
D-ABTL	Boeing 747-430 (SCD)	Lufthansa	
D-ABUA	Boeing 767-330ER	Condor	
D-ABUB	Boeing 767-330ER	Condor	
D-ABUC	Boeing 767-330ER	Condor	
D-ABUD	Boeing 767-330ER	Condor	
D-ABUE	Boeing 767-330ER	Condor	
D-ABUF	Boeing 767-330ER	Condor	
D-ABUH	Boeing 767-330ER	Condor	
D-ABUI	Boeing 767-330ER	Condor	
D-ABUZ	Boeing 767-330ER	Condor	
D-ABVA	Boeing 747-430	Lufthansa *Berlin*	
D-ABVB	Boeing 747-430	Lufthansa *Bonn*	
D-ABVC	Boeing 747-430	Lufthansa *Baden-Württemberg*	
D-ABVD	Boeing 747-430	Lufthansa *Bochum*	
D-ABVE	Boeing 747-430	Lufthansa *Potsdam*	
D-ABVF	Boeing 747-430	Lufthansa *Frankfurt am Main*	
D-ABVH	Boeing 747-430	Lufthansa *Düsseldorf*	
D-ABVK	Boeing 747-430	Lufthansa *Hannover*	
D-ABVL	Boeing 747-430	Lufthansa *Muenchen*	
D-ABVM	Boeing 747-430	Lufthansa *Hessen*	
D-ABVN	Boeing 747-430	Lufthansa *Dortmund*	
D-ABVO	Boeing 747-430	Lufthansa *Mulheim a.d.Ruhr*	
D-ABVP	Boeing 747-430	Lufthansa *Bremen*	
D-ABVR	Boeing 747-430	Lufthansa *Koln*	
D-ABVS	Boeing 747-430	Lufthansa *Saarland*	
D-ABVT	Boeing 747-430	Lufthansa *Rheinland Pfalz*	
D-ABVU	Boeing 747-430	Lufthansa *Bayern*	
D-ABVW	Boeing 747-430	Lufthansa *Wolfsburg*	
D-ABVX	Boeing 747-430	Lufthansa *Schleswig-Holstein*	
D-ABVY	Boeing 747-430	Lufthansa *Nordrhein Westfalen*	
D-ABVZ	Boeing 747-430	Lufthansa *Niedersachsen*	
D-ABWH	Boeing 737-330	Lufthansa *Rothenburg o. d. Taube*	
D-ABXL	Boeing 737-330	Lufthansa *Neuss*	
D-ABXM	Boeing 737-330	Lufthansa *Herford*	
D-ABXN	Boeing 737-330	Lufthansa *Böblingen*	
D-ABXO	Boeing 737-330	Lufthansa *Schwäbisch-Gmünd*	
D-ABXP	Boeing 737-330	Lufthansa *Fulda*	
D-ABXR	Boeing 737-330	Lufthansa *Celle*	
D-ABXS	Boeing 737-330	Lufthansa *Sindelfingen*	
D-ABXT	Boeing 737-330	Lufthansa *Reutlingen*	
D-ABXU	Boeing 737-330	Lufthansa *Seeheim-Jugenheim*	
D-ABXW	Boeing 737-330	Lufthansa *Hanau*	
D-ABXX	Boeing 737-330	Lufthansa *Bad Homburg v.d. Höhe*	
D-ABXZ	Boeing 737-330	Lufthansa *Bad Mergentheim*	
D-ACFA	BAe 146-200	Lufthansa Regional	
D-ACHA	Canadair CL.600-2B19 RJ	Lufthansa Regional *Murrhardt*	
D-ACHB	Canadair CL.600-2B19 RJ	Lufthansa Regional *Meersburg*	
D-ACHC	Canadair CL.600-2B19 RJ	Lufthansa Regional *Füssen*	
D-ACHD	Canadair CL.600-2B19 RJ	Lufthansa Regional *Lutherstadt Eisleben*	
D-ACHE	Canadair CL.600-2B19 RJ	Lufthansa Regional *Meissen*	
D-ACHF	Canadair CL.600-2B19 RJ	Lufthansa Regional *Montabaur*	
D-ACHG	Canadair CL.600-2B19 RJ	Lufthansa Regional *Weil am Rhein*	
D-ACHH	Canadair CL.600-2B19 RJ	Lufthansa Regional *Kronach*	

D — OVERSEAS AIRLINERS

Notes	Reg	Type	Owner or Operator
	D-ACHI	Canadair CL.600-2B19 RJ	Lufthansa Regional *Deidesheim*
	D-ACHK	Canadair CL.600-2B19 RJ	Lufthansa Regional *Schkeuditz*
	D-ACIA	Embraer RJ145LU	Cirrus Airlines
	D-ACIN	Boeing 737-53C	Cirrus Airlines
	D-ACIR	Embraer RJ145MP	Cirrus Airlines *Saarbrücken*
	D-ACJA	Canadair CL.600-2B19 RJ	Lufthansa Regional
	D-ACJB	Canadair CL.600-2B19 RJ	Lufthansa Regional
	D-ACJC	Canadair CL.600-2B19 RJ	Lufthansa Regional
	D-ACJD	Canadair CL.600-2B19 RJ	Lufthansa Regional
	D-ACJE	Canadair CL.600-2B19 RJ	Lufthansa Regional
	D-ACJF	Canadair CL.600-2B19 RJ	Lufthansa Regional
	D-ACJG	Canadair CL.600-2B19 RJ	Lufthansa Regional
	D-ACJH	Canadair CL.600-2B19 RJ	Lufthansa Regional
	D-ACJI	Canadair CL.600-2B19 RJ	Lufthansa Regional
	D-ACJJ	Canadair CL.600-2B19 RJ	Lufthansa Regional
	D-ACKA	Canadair CL.600-2D24 RJ	Lufthansa Regional
	D-ACKB	Canadair CL.600-2D24 RJ	Lufthansa Regional
	D-ACKC	Canadair CL.600-2D24 RJ	Lufthansa Regional
	D-ACKD	Canadair CL.600-2D24 RJ	Lufthansa Regional
	D-ACKE	Canadair CL.600-2D24 RJ	Lufthansa Regional
	D-ACKF	Canadair CL.600-2D24 RJ	Lufthansa Regional
	D-ACKG	Canadair CL.600-2D24 RJ	Lufthansa Regional
	D-ACKH	Canadair CL.600-2D24 RJ	Lufthansa Regional
	D-ACKI	Canadair CL.600-2D24 RJ	Lufthansa Regional
	D-ACKJ	Canadair CL.600-2D24 RJ	Lufthansa Regional
	D-ACKK	Canadair CL.600-2D24 RJ	Lufthansa Regional
	D-ACKL	Canadair CL.600-2D24 RJ	Lufthansa Regional
	D-ACLB	Canadair CL.600-2B19 RJ	Lufthansa Regional
	D-ACLP	Canadair CL.600-2B19 RJ	Lufthansa Regional
	D-ACLQ	Canadair CL.600-2B19 RJ	Lufthansa Regional
	D-ACLR	Canadair CL.600-2B19 RJ	Lufthansa Regional
	D-ACLS	Canadair CL.600-2B19 RJ	Lufthansa Regional
	D-ACLT	Canadair CL.600-2B19 RJ	Lufthansa Regional
	D-ACLU	Canadair CL.600-2B19 RJ	Lufthansa Regional
	D-ACLW	Canadair CL.600-2B19 RJ	Lufthansa Regional
	D-ACLY	Canadair CL.600-2B19 RJ	Lufthansa Regional
	D-ACLZ	Canadair CL.600-2B19 RJ	Lufthansa Regional
	D-ACPA	Canadair CL.600-2C10 RJ	Lufthansa Regional *Westerland/Sylt*
	D-ACPB	Canadair CL.600-2C10 RJ	Lufthansa Regional *Rudesheim a. Rhein*
	D-ACPC	Canadair CL.600-2C10 RJ	Lufthansa Regional *Espelkamp*
	D-ACPD	Canadair CL.600-2C10 RJ	Lufthansa Regional *Vilshofen*
	D-ACPE	Canadair CL.600-2C10 RJ	Lufthansa Regional *Belzig*
	D-ACPF	Canadair CL.600-2C10 RJ	Lufthansa Regional *Uhingen*
	D-ACPG	Canadair CL.600-2C10 RJ	Lufthansa Regional *Leinfelden-Echterdingen*
	D-ACPH	Canadair CL.600-2C10 RJ	Lufthansa Regional *Eschwege*
	D-ACPI	Canadair CL.600-2C10 RJ	Lufthansa Regional *Viernheim*
	D-ACPJ	Canadair CL.600-2C10 RJ	Lufthansa Regional *Neumarkt i. d. Oberfalz*
	D-ACPK	Canadair CL.600-2C10 RJ	Lufthansa Regional *Besigheim*
	D-ACPL	Canadair CL.600-2C10 RJ	Lufthansa Regional *Halberstadt*
	D-ACPM	Canadair CL.600-2C10 RJ	Lufthansa Regional *Heidenheim an der Brenz*
	D-ACPN	Canadair CL.600-2C10 RJ	Lufthansa Regional *Quedlinburg*
	D-ACPO	Canadair CL.600-2C10 RJ	Lufthansa Regional *Spaichingen*
	D-ACPP	Canadair CL.600-2C10 RJ	Lufthansa Regional *Torgau*
	D-ACPQ	Canadair CL.600-3C10 RJ	Lufthansa Regional *Lübbecke*
	D-ACPR	Canadair CL.600-3C10 RJ	Lufthansa Regional *Weinheim an der Bergstrasse*
	D-ACPS	Canadair CL.600-3C10 RJ	Lufthansa Regional *Berchtesgarten*
	D-ACPT	Canadair CL.600-3C10 RJ	Lufthansa Regional *Altötting*
	D-ACRA	Canadair CL.600-2B19 RJ	Lufthansa Regional
	D-ACRB	Canadair CL.600-2B19 RJ	Lufthansa Regional
	D-ACRC	Canadair CL.600-2B19 RJ	Lufthansa Regional
	D-ACRD	Canadair CL.600-2B19 RJ	Lufthansa Regional
	D-ACRE	Canadair CL.600-2B19 RJ	Lufthansa Regional
	D-ACRF	Canadair CL.600-2B19 RJ	Lufthansa Regional
	D-ACRG	Canadair CL.600-2B19 RJ	Lufthansa Regional
	D-ACRH	Canadair CL.600-2B19 RJ	Lufthansa Regional
	D-ACRI	Canadair CL.600-2B19 RJ	Lufthansa Regional
	D-ACRJ	Canadair CL.600-2B19 RJ	Lufthansa Regional
	D-ACRK	Canadair CL.600-2B19 RJ	Lufthansa Regional
	D-ACRL	Canadair CL.600-2B19 RJ	Lufthansa Regional
	D-ACRM	Canadair CL.600-2B19 RJ	Lufthansa Regional
	D-ACRN	Canadair CL.600-2B19 RJ	Lufthansa Regional
	D-ACRO	Canadair CL.600-2B19 RJ	Lufthansa Regional
	D-ACRP	Canadair CL.600-2B19 RJ	Lufthansa Regional

OVERSEAS AIRLINERS

Reg	Type	Owner or Operator	Notes
D-ACRQ	Canadair CL.600-2B19 RJ	Lufthansa Regional	
D-AERK	Airbus A.330-322	LTU	
D-AERQ	Airbus A.330-322	LTU	
D-AERS	Airbus A.330-322	LTU	
D-AEWA	BAe 146-300	Lufthansa Regional	
D-AEWB	BAe 146-300	Lufthansa Regional	
D-AEWD	BAe 146-200	Lufthansa Regional	
D-AEWE	BAe 146-200	Lufthansa Regional	
D-AEWL	BAe 146-300	Lufthansa Regional	
D-AEWM	BAe 146-300	Lufthansa Regional	
D-AEWN	BAe 146-300	Lufthansa Regional	
D-AEWO	BAe 146-300	Lufthansa Regional	
D-AEWP	BAe 146-300	Lufthansa Regional	
D-AEWQ	BAe 146-300	Lufthansa Regional	
D-AGEL	Boeing 737-75B	Hapag-Lloyd Express	
D-AGEN	Boeing 737-75B	Hapag-Lloyd Express	
D-AGEP	Boeing 737-75B	Hapag-Lloyd Express	
D-AGEQ	Boeing 737-75B	Hapag-Lloyd Express	
D-AGER	Boeing 737-75B	Hapag-Lloyd Express	
D-AGES	Boeing 737-75B	Hapag-Lloyd Express	
D-AGET	Boeing 737-75B	Hapag-Lloyd Express	
D-AGEU	Boeing 737-75B	Hapag-Lloyd Express	
D-AGPA	Fokker 100	Air Berlin	
D-AGPB	Fokker 100	Air Berlin	
D-AGPC	Fokker 100	Air Berlin	
D-AGPD	Fokker 100	Air Berlin	
D-AGPE	Fokker 100	Air Berlin	
D-AGPF	Fokker 100	DBA	
D-AGPG	Fokker 100	Air Berlin	
D-AGPH	Fokker 100	Air Berlin	
D-AGPI	Fokker 100	DBA	
D-AGPJ	Fokker 100	Air Berlin	
D-AGPK	Fokker 100	Air Berlin	
D-AGPL	Fokker 100	Air Berlin	
D-AGPM	Fokker 100	DBA	
D-AGPO	Fokker 100	Air Berlin	
D-AGPQ	Fokker 100	Air Berlin	
D-AGPR	Fokker 100	Air Berlin	
D-AGPS	Fokker 100	Air Berlin	
D-AGWA	Airbus A.319-132	Germanwings	
D-AGWB	Airbus A.319-132	Germanwings	
D-AGWC	Airbus A.319-132	Germanwings	
D-AGWD	Airbus A.319-132	Germanwings	
D-AHFA	Boeing 737-8K5	Hapag-Lloyd	
D-AHFB	Boeing 737-8K5	Hapag-Lloyd	
D-AHFC	Boeing 737-8K5	Hapag-Lloyd	
D-AHFD	Boeing 737-8K5	TUIfly	
D-AHFE	Boeing 737-8K5	Hapag-Lloyd	
D-AHFF	Boeing 737-8K5	Hapag-Lloyd	
D-AHFG	Boeing 737-8K5	Hapag-Lloyd	
D-AHFH	Boeing 737-8K5	Hapag-Lloyd	
D-AHFI	Boeing 737-8K5	TUIfly	
D-AHFJ	Boeing 737-8K5	Hapag-Lloyd	
D-AHFK	Boeing 737-8K5	Hapag-Lloyd	
D-AHFL	Boeing 737-8K5	Hapag-Lloyd	
D-AHFM	Boeing 737-8K5	Hapag-Lloyd	
D-AHFN	Boeing 737-8K5	Hapag-Lloyd	
D-AHFO	Boeing 737-8K5	Hapag-Lloyd Express	
D-AHFP	Boeing 737-8K5	Hapag-Lloyd	
D-AHFQ	Boeing 737-8K5	Hapag-Lloyd	
D-AHFR	Boeing 737-8K5	TUIfly	
D-AHFS	Boeing 737-86N	Hapag-Lloyd Express	
D-AHFT	Boeing 737-8K5	Hapag-Lloyd	
D-AHFU	Boeing 737-8K5	TUIfly	
D-AHFV	Boeing 737-8K5	Hapag-Lloyd	
D-AHFW	Boeing 737-8K5	Hapag-Lloyd	
D-AHFX	Boeing 737-8K5	Hapag-Lloyd Express	
D-AHFY	Boeing 737-8K5	Hapag-Lloyd	
D-AHFZ	Boeing 737-8K5	Hapag-Lloyd	
D-AHIA	Boeing 737-73S	Hamburg International Airlines	
D-AHIB	Boeing 737-73S	Hamburg International Airlines	
D-AHIC	Boeing 737-7BK	Hamburg International Airlines	
D-AHID	Boeing 737-73S	Hamburg International Airlines	

OVERSEAS AIRLINERS

Notes	Reg	Type	Owner or Operator
	D-AHIE	Boeing 737-73S	Hamburg International Airlines
	D-AHIF	Boeing 737-73S	Hamburg International Airlines
	D-AHIG	Boeing 737-33A	Hamburg International Airlines
	D-AHLD	Boeing 737-5K5	Germania/Hapag-Lloyd Express
	D-AHLF	Boeing 737-5K5	Germania/Hapag-Lloyd Express
	D-AHLG	Boeing 737-5K5	Germania/Hapag-Lloyd Express
	D-AHLI	Boeing 737-5K5	Germania/Hapag-Lloyd Express
	D-AHLN	Boeing 737-5K5	Germania/Hapag-Lloyd Express
	D-AHLP	Boeing 737-8K5	Hapag-Lloyd
	D-AHLQ	Boeing 737-8K5	TUIfly
	D-AHLR	Boeing 737-8K5	Hapag-Lloyd
	D-AHOI	BAe 146-300	Lufthansa Regional
	D-AHXC	Boeing 737-7K5	Hapag-Lloyd Express
	D-AIAH	Airbus A.300B4-603	Lufthansa *Lindau/Bodensee*
	D-AIAI	Airbus A.300B4-603	Lufthansa *Erbach/Odenwald*
	D-AIAK	Airbus A.300B4-603	Lufthansa *Kronberg/Taunus*
	D-AIAL	Airbus A.300B4-603	Lufthansa *Stade*
	D-AIAM	Airbus A.300B4-603	Lufthansa *Rosenheim*
	D-AIAN	Airbus A.300B4-603	Lufthansa *Nördlingen*
	D-AIAP	Airbus A.300B4-603	Lufthansa *Donauwörth*
	D-AIAR	Airbus A.300B4-603	Lufthansa *Bingen am Rhein*
	D-AIAS	Airbus A.300B4-603	Lufthansa *Mönchengladbach*
	D-AIAT	Airbus A.300B4-603	Lufthansa *Bottrop*
	D-AIAU	Airbus A.300B4-603	Lufthansa *Bocholt*
	D-AIAX	Airbus A.300B4-605R	Lufthansa/Hapag-Lloyd
	D-AIAY	Airbus A.300B4-605R	Lufthansa
	D-AIAZ	Airbus A.300B4-605R	Lufthansa
	D-AICA	Airbus A.320-212	Condor
	D-AICB	Airbus A.320-212	Condor
	D-AICC	Airbus A.320-212	Condor
	D-AICD	Airbus A.320-212	Condor
	D-AICE	Airbus A.320-212	Condor
	D-AICF	Airbus A.320-212	Condor
	D-AICG	Airbus A.320-212	Condor
	D-AICH	Airbus A.320-212	Condor
	D-AICI	Airbus A.320-212	Condor
	D-AICJ	Airbus A.320-212	Condor
	D-AICK	Airbus A.320-212	Condor
	D-AICL	Airbus A.320-212	Condor
	D-AICM	Airbus A.320-214	Condor
	D-AICN	Airbus A.320-214	Condor
	D-AIFA	Airbus A.340-313X	Lufthansa *Dorsten*
	D-AIFB	Airbus A.340-313X	Lufthansa *Gummersbach*
	D-AIFC	Airbus A.340-313X	Lufthansa *Gander/Halifax*
	D-AIFD	Airbus A.340-313X	Lufthansa *Giessen*
	D-AIFE	Airbus A.340-313X	Lufthansa *Passau*
	D-AIFF	Airbus A.340-313X	Lufthansa *Delmenhorst*
	D-AIGA	Airbus A.340-311	Lufthansa *Oldenburg*
	D-AIGB	Airbus A.340-311	Lufthansa *Recklinghausen*
	D-AIGC	Airbus A.340-311	Lufthansa *Wilhelmshaven*
	D-AIGD	Airbus A.340-311	Lufthansa *Remscheid*
	D-AIGF	Airbus A.340-311	Lufthansa *Gottingen*
	D-AIGH	Airbus A.340-311	Lufthansa *Koblenz*
	D-AIGI	Airbus A.340-311	Lufthansa *Worms*
	D-AIGK	Airbus A.340-311	Lufthansa *Bayreuth*
	D-AIGL	Airbus A.340-313X	Lufthansa *Herne*
	D-AIGM	Airbus A.340-313X	Lufthansa *Görlitz*
	D-AIGN	Airbus A.340-313X	Lufthansa *Solingen*
	D-AIGO	Airbus A.340-313X	Lufthansa *Offenbach*
	D-AIGP	Airbus A.340-313X	Lufthansa *Paderborn*
	D-AIGR	Airbus A.340-313X	Lufthansa *Leipzig*
	D-AIGS	Airbus A.340-313X	Lufthansa *Bergisch-Gladbach*
	D-AIGT	Airbus A.340-313X	Lufthansa *Viersen*
	D-AIGU	Airbus A.340-313X	Lufthansa *Castrop-Rauxei*
	D-AIGV	Airbus A.340-313X	Lufthansa *Dinslaken*
	D-AIGW	Airbus A.340-313X	Lufthansa *Gladbeck*
	D-AIGX	Airbus A.340-313X	Lufthansa *Duren*
	D-AIGY	Airbus A.340-313X	Lufthansa *Lünen*
	D-AIGZ	Airbus A.340-313X	Lufthansa *Villingen-Schwenningen*
	D-AIHA	Airbus A.340-642	Lufthansa *Nurnberg*
	D-AIHB	Airbus A.340-642	Lufthansa *Bremerhaven*
	D-AIHC	Airbus A.340-642	Lufthansa *Essen*
	D-AIHD	Airbus A.340-642	Lufthansa *Stuttgart*

OVERSEAS AIRLINERS

D

Reg	Type	Owner or Operator	Notes
D-AIHE	Airbus A.340-642	Lufthansa *Leverkusen*	
D-AIHF	Airbus A.340-642	Lufthansa *Lübeck*	
D-AIHH	Airbus A.340-642	Lufthansa	
D-AIHI	Airbus A.340-642	Lufthansa	
D-AIHK	Airbus A.340-642	Lufthansa	
D-AIHL	Airbus A.340-642	Lufthansa	
D-AIHM	Airbus A.340-642	Lufthansa	
D-AIHN	Airbus A.340-642	Lufthansa	
D-AIHO	Airbus A.340-642	Lufthansa	
D-AIHP	Airbus A.340-642	Lufthansa	
D-AIHQ	Airbus A.340-642	Lufthansa	
D-AIHR	Airbus A.340-642	Lufthansa	
D-AIKA	Airbus A.330-343X	Lufthansa *Minden*	
D-AIKB	Airbus A.330-343X	Lufthansa *Cuxhaven*	
D-AIKC	Airbus A.330-343X	Lufthansa *Hamm*	
D-AIKD	Airbus A.330-343X	Lufthansa *Siegen*	
D-AIKE	Airbus A.330-343X	Lufthansa *Landshut*	
D-AIKF	Airbus A.330-343X	Lufthansa *Witten*	
D-AIKG	Airbus A.330-343X	Lufthansa *Ludwigsburg*	
D-AIKH	Airbus A.330-343X	Lufthansa	
D-AIKI	Airbus A.330-343X	Lufthansa	
D-AIKJ	Airbus A.330-343X	Lufthansa	
D-AILA	Airbus A.319-114	Lufthansa *Frankfurt (Oder)*	
D-AILB	Airbus A.319-114	Lufthansa *Lutherstadt Wittenburg*	
D-AILC	Airbus A.319-114	Lufthansa *Russelsheim*	
D-AILD	Airbus A.319-114	Lufthansa *Dinkelsbühl*	
D-AILE	Airbus A.319-114	Lufthansa *Kelsterbach*	
D-AILF	Airbus A.319-114	Lufthansa *Trier*	
D-AILH	Airbus A.319-114	Lufthansa *Norderstedt*	
D-AILI	Airbus A.319-114	Lufthansa *Ingolstadt*	
D-AILK	Airbus A.319-114	Germanwings	
D-AILL	Airbus A.319-114	Lufthansa *Marburg*	
D-AILM	Airbus A.319-114	Lufthansa *Friedrichshafen*	
D-AILN	Airbus A.319-114	Germanwings	
D-AILP	Airbus A.319-114	Lufthansa *Tubingen*	
D-AILR	Airbus A.319-114	Lufthansa *Tegernsee*	
D-AILS	Airbus A.319-114	Lufthansa *Heide*	
D-AILT	Airbus A.319-114	Lufthansa *Straubing*	
D-AILU	Airbus A.319-114	Lufthansa *Verden*	
D-AILW	Airbus A.319-114	Lufthansa *Donaueschingen*	
D-AILX	Airbus A.319-114	Lufthansa *Feilbach*	
D-AILY	Airbus A.319-114	Lufthansa *Schweinfurt*	
D-AIPA	Airbus A.320-211	Lufthansa *Buxtehude*	
D-AIPB	Airbus A.320-211	Lufthansa *Heidelberg*	
D-AIPC	Airbus A.320-211	Lufthansa *Braunschweig*	
D-AIPD	Airbus A.320-211	Lufthansa *Freiburg*	
D-AIPE	Airbus A.320-211	Lufthansa *Kassel*	
D-AIPF	Airbus A.320-211	Lufthansa *Deggendorf*	
D-AIPH	Airbus A.320-211	Lufthansa *Munster*	
D-AIPK	Airbus A.320-211	Lufthansa *Wiesbaden*	
D-AIPL	Airbus A.320-211	Lufthansa *Ludwigshafen am Rhein*	
D-AIPM	Airbus A.320-211	Lufthansa *Troisdorf*	
D-AIPP	Airbus A.320-211	Lufthansa *Starnberg*	
D-AIPR	Airbus A.320-211	Lufthansa *Kaufbeuren*	
D-AIPS	Airbus A.320-211	Lufthansa *Augsburg*	
D-AIPT	Airbus A.320-211	Lufthansa *Cottbus*	
D-AIPU	Airbus A.320-211	Lufthansa *Dresden*	
D-AIPW	Airbus A.320-211	Lufthansa *Schwerin*	
D-AIPX	Airbus A.320-211	Lufthansa *Mannheim*	
D-AIPY	Airbus A.320-211	Lufthansa *Magdeburg*	
D-AIPZ	Airbus A.320-211	Lufthansa *Erfurt*	
D-AIQA	Airbus A.320-211	Lufthansa *Mainz*	
D-AIQB	Airbus A.320-211	Lufthansa *Bielefeld*	
D-AIQC	Airbus A.320-211	Lufthansa *Zwickau*	
D-AIQD	Airbus A.320-211	Lufthansa *Jena*	
D-AIQE	Airbus A.320-211	Lufthansa *Gera*	
D-AIQF	Airbus A.320-211	Lufthansa *Halle (Saale)*	
D-AIQH	Airbus A.320-211	Lufthansa *Dessau*	
D-AIQK	Airbus A.320-211	Lufthansa *Rostock*	
D-AIQL	Airbus A.320-211	Lufthansa *Stralsund*	
D-AIQM	Airbus A.320-211	Lufthansa *Nordenham*	
D-AIQN	Airbus A.320-211	Lufthansa *Laupheim*	
D-AIQP	Airbus A.320-211	Lufthansa *Suhl*	

D
OVERSEAS AIRLINERS

Notes	Reg	Type	Owner or Operator
	D-AIQR	Airbus A.320-211	Lufthansa *Lahr/Schwarzwald*
	D-AIQS	Airbus A.320-211	Lufthansa *Eisenach*
	D-AIQT	Airbus A.320-211	Lufthansa *Gotha*
	D-AIQU	Airbus A.320-211	Lufthansa *Backnang*
	D-AIQW	Airbus A.320-211	Lufthansa *Kleve*
	D-AIRA	Airbus A.321-131	Lufthansa *Finkenwerder*
	D-AIRB	Airbus A.321-131	Lufthansa *Baden-Baden*
	D-AIRC	Airbus A.321-131	Lufthansa *Erlangen*
	D-AIRD	Airbus A.321-131	Lufthansa *Coburg*
	D-AIRE	Airbus A.321-131	Lufthansa *Osnabrueck*
	D-AIRF	Airbus A.321-131	Lufthansa *Kempten*
	D-AIRH	Airbus A.321-131	Lufthansa *Garmisch-Partenkirchen*
	D-AIRK	Airbus A.321-131	Lufthansa *Freudenstadt/Schwarzwald*
	D-AIRL	Airbus A.321-131	Lufthansa *Kulmbach*
	D-AIRM	Airbus A.321-131	Lufthansa *Darmstadt*
	D-AIRN	Airbus A.321-131	Lufthansa *Kaiserslautern*
	D-AIRO	Airbus A.321-131	Lufthansa *Konstanz*
	D-AIRP	Airbus A.321-131	Lufthansa *Lüneburg*
	D-AIRR	Airbus A.321-131	Lufthansa *Wismar*
	D-AIRS	Airbus A.321-131	Lufthansa *Husum*
	D-AIRT	Airbus A.321-131	Lufthansa *Regensburg*
	D-AIRU	Airbus A.321-131	Lufthansa *Würzburg*
	D-AIRW	Airbus A.321-131	Lufthansa *Heilbronn*
	D-AIRX	Airbus A.321-131	Lufthansa *Weimar*
	D-AIRY	Airbus A.321-131	Lufthansa *Flensburg*
	D-AISB	Airbus A.321-231	Lufthansa *Hameln*
	D-AISC	Airbus A.321-231	Lufthansa *Speyer*
	D-AISD	Airbus A.321-231	Lufthansa *Chemnitz*
	D-AISE	Airbus A.321-231	Lufthansa *Neustadt an der Weinstrasse*
	D-AISF	Airbus A.321-231	Lufthansa *Lippstadt*
	D-AISG	Airbus A.321-231	Lufthansa *Dormagen*
	D-AJET	BAe 146-200	Lufthansa Regional
	D-AKNF	Airbus A.319-112	Germanwings
	D-AKNG	Airbus A.319-112	Germanwings
	D-AKNH	Airbus A.319-112	Germanwings
	D-AKNI	Airbus A.319-112	Germanwings
	D-AKNJ	Airbus A.319-112	Germanwings *City of Athens*
	D-AKNK	Airbus A.319-112	Germanwings
	D-AKNL	Airbus A.319-112	Germanwings
	D-AKNM	Airbus A.319-112	Germanwings
	D-AKNN	Airbus A.319-112	Germanwings
	D-AKNO	Airbus A.319-112	Germanwings
	D-AKNP	Airbus A.319-112	Germanwings
	D-AKNQ	Airbus A.319-112	Germanwings
	D-AKNR	Airbus A.319-112	Germanwings *Spirit of T-Com*
	D-AKNS	Airbus A.319-112	Germanwings *Spirit of T Mobile*
	D-AKNT	Airbus A.319-112	Germanwings *City of Hamburg*
	D-AKNU	Airbus A.319-112	Germanwings
	D-AKNV	Airbus A.319-112	Germanwings
	D-AKNX	Airbus A.320-232	Germanwings
	D-AKNY	Airbus A.320-212	Germanwings
	D-AKNZ	Airbus A.320-212	Germanwings
	D-ALCA	McD Douglas MD-11F	Lufthansa Cargo
	D-ALCB	McD Douglas MD-11F	Lufthansa Cargo
	D-ALCC	McD Douglas MD-11F	Lufthansa Cargo
	D-ALCD	McD Douglas MD-11F	Lufthansa Cargo
	D-ALCE	McD Douglas MD-11F	Lufthansa Cargo
	D-ALCF	McD Douglas MD-11F	Lufthansa Cargo
	D-ALCG	McD Douglas MD-11F	Lufthansa Cargo
	D-ALCH	McD Douglas MD-11F	Lufthansa Cargo
	D-ALCI	McD Douglas MD-11F	Lufthansa Cargo
	D-ALCJ	McD Douglas MD-11F	Lufthansa Cargo
	D-ALCK	McD Douglas MD-11F	Lufthansa Cargo
	D-ALCL	McD Douglas MD-11F	Lufthansa Cargo
	D-ALCM	McD Douglas MD-11F	Lufthansa Cargo
	D-ALCN	McD Douglas MD-11F	Lufthansa Cargo
	D-ALCO	McD Douglas MD-11F	Lufthansa Cargo
	D-ALCP	McD Douglas MD-11F	Lufthansa Cargo
	D-ALCQ	McD Douglas MD-11F	Lufthansa Cargo
	D-ALCR	McD Douglas MD-11F	Lufthansa Cargo
	D-ALCS	McD Douglas MD-11F	Lufthansa Cargo
	D-ALIA	Embraer RJ170-100LR	Cirrus Airlines
	D-ALIE	Embraer RJ170-100LR	Cirrus Airlines

OVERSEAS AIRLINERS

D

Reg	Type	Owner or Operator	Notes
D-ALPA	Airbus A.330-223	LTU	
D-ALPB	Airbus A.330-223	LTU	
D-ALPC	Airbus A.330-223	LTU	
D-ALPD	Airbus A.330-223	LTU	
D-ALPE	Airbus A.330-223	LTU	
D-ALPF	Airbus A.330-223	LTU	
D-ALPG	Airbus A.330-223	LTU	
D-ALPH	Airbus A.330-223	LTU	
D-ALSA	Airbus A.321-211	LTU	
D-ALSB	Airbus A.321-211	LTU	
D-ALSC	Airbus A.321-211	LTU	
D-ALSD	Airbus A.321-211	LTU	
D-ALTB	Airbus A.320-214	LTU	
D-ALTC	Airbus A.320-214	LTU	
D-ALTD	Airbus A.320-214	LTU	
D-ALTF	Airbus A.320-214	LTU	
D-ALTG	Airbus A.320-214	LTU	
D-ALTH	Airbus A.320-214	LTU	
D-ALTI	Airbus A.320-214	LTU	
D-ALTJ	Airbus A.320-214	LTU	
D-ALTK	Airbus A.320-214	LTU	
D-ALTL	Airbus A.320-214	LTU	
D-ANNB	Airbus A.320-232	Blue Wings	
D-ANNC	Airbus A.320-232	Blue Wings	
D-ANND	Airbus A.320-232	Blue Wings/Air Berlin	
D-ANNE	Airbus A.320-232	Blue Wings	
D-ANNF	Airbus A.320-232	Blue Wings/Air Berlin	
D-AOLA	SAAB 2000	OLT	
D-AOLB	SAAB 2000	OLT	
D-AOLT	SAAB 2000	OLT *Emden*	
D-APAA	Airbus A.319-132	PrivatAir/Airbus	
D-APAB	Airbus A.319-132	PrivatAir/Airbus	
D-APAC	Airbus A.319-132LR	PrivatAir/Lufthansa	
D-APAD	Airbus A.319-132LR	PrivatAir/Lufthansa	
D-AQUA	BAe 146-300	Lufthansa Regional	
D-AQUI	Junkers Ju.52/3m	Lufthansa Traditionsflug	
D-ATUA	Boeing 737-8K5	Hapag-Lloyd	
D-ATUB	Boeing 737-8K5	Hapag-Lloyd	
D-ATUC	Boeing 737-8K5	Hapag-Lloyd	
D-ATUD	Boeing 737-8K5	Hapag-Lloyd	
D-ATUE	Boeing 737-8K5	Hapag-Lloyd	
D-ATUF	Boeing 737-8K5	Hapag-Lloyd	
D-ATUG	Boeing 737-8K5	Hapag-Lloyd	
D-ATUH	Boeing 737-8K5	Hapag-Lloyd	
D-ATUI	Boeing 737-8K5	Hapag-Lloyd	
D-AVRA	Avro RJ85	Lufthansa Regional	
D-AVRB	Avro RJ85	Lufthansa Regional	
D-AVRC	Avro RJ85	Lufthansa Regional	
D-AVRD	Avro RJ85	Lufthansa Regional	
D-AVRE	Avro RJ85	Lufthansa Regional	
D-AVRF	Avro RJ85	Lufthansa Regional	
D-AVRG	Avro RJ85	Lufthansa Regional	
D-AVRH	Avro RJ85	Lufthansa Regional	
D-AVRI	Avro RJ85	Lufthansa Regional	
D-AVRJ	Avro RJ85	Lufthansa Regional	
D-AVRK	Avro RJ85	Lufthansa Regional	
D-AVRL	Avro RJ85	Lufthansa Regional	
D-AVRM	Avro RJ85	Lufthansa Regional	
D-AVRN	Avro RJ85	Lufthansa Regional	
D-AVRO	Avro RJ85	Lufthansa Regional	
D-AVRP	Avro RJ85	Lufthansa Regional	
D-AVRQ	Avro RJ85	Lufthansa Regional	
D-AVRR	Avro RJ85	Lufthansa Regional	
D-AXLA	Airbus A.320-232	XL Airways Germany	
D-AXLB	Airbus A.320-214	XL Airways Germany	
D-AXLC	Airbus A.320-214	XL Airways Germany	
D-BEBA	DHC.8Q-314 Dash Eight	Lufthansa Regional	
D-BGAL	Dornier 328JET	Cirrus Airlines	
D-BGAQ	Dornier 328JET	Cirrus Airlines	
D-BHOQ	DHC.8Q-314 Dash Eight	Lufthansa Regional	
D-BMMM	Aérospatiale ATR-42-512	Lufthansa Regional	
D-BNNN	Aérospatiale ATR-42-512	Lufthansa Regional	
D-BOOO	Aérospatiale ATR-42-512	Lufthansa Regional	

D/EC

OVERSEAS AIRLINERS

Notes	Reg	Type	Owner or Operator
	D-BPAD	DHC.8Q-314 Dash Eight	Lufthansa Regional
	D-BPPP	Aérospatiale ATR-42-512	Lufthansa Regional
	D-BQQQ	Aérospatiale ATR-42-512	Lufthansa Regional
	D-BSSS	Aérospatiale ATR-42-512	Lufthansa Regional
	D-BTTT	Aérospatiale ATR-42-512	Lufthansa Regional
	D-CAAM	Dornier 228-212	Arcus Air
	D-CASB	SAAB SF.340B	OLT *Birdie*
	D-CBIN	Swearingen SA227AT Expediter IVC	Binair
	D-CCCC	Swearingen SA227AT Expediter IVC	Binair
	D-CCIR	Dornier 328-130	Cirrus Airlines
	D-CIRA	Dornier 328-120	Cirrus Airlines
	D-CIRB	Dornier 328-110	Cirrus Airlines
	D-CIRC	Dornier 328-110	Cirrus Airlines
	D-CIRD	Dornier 328-110	Cirrus Airlines
	D-COLE	SAAB SF.340A	OLT *Bremen*
	D-COSA	Dornier 328-110	Cirrus Airlines
	D-CPRP	Dornier 328-110	Cirrus Airlines
	D-CUTT	Dornier 228-212	Arcus Air
	D-IBIN	Swearingen SA226TC Metro II	Binair
	D-ICRK	Swearingen SA226TC Metro II	Binair

Note: Many livery changes will occur during 2007 as Air Berlin has acquired DBA while Hapag-Lloyd and Hapag-Lloyd Express are to merge as TUIfly. Lufthansa also operates B.737 HB-IIQ.

EC (Spain)

Reg	Type	Owner or Operator
EC-ELT	BAe 146-200QT	Pan Air/TNT Airways
EC-EMD	Douglas DC-8-62F	Cygnus Air
EC-EMX	Douglas DC-8-62F	Cygnus Air
EC-EXF	McD Douglas MD-87	Iberia *Ciudad de Pamplona*
EC-EXG	McD Douglas MD-87	Iberia *Ciudad de Almeria*
EC-EXM	McD Douglas MD-87	Iberia *Ciudad de Zaragoza*
EC-EXN	McD Douglas MD-87	Iberia *Ciudad de Badajoz*
EC-EXR	McD Douglas MD-87	Iberia *Ciudad de Oviedo*
EC-EXT	McD Douglas MD-87	Iberia *Ciudad de Albacete*
EC-EYB	McD Douglas MD-87	Iberia *Cangas de Onis*
EC-EYX	McD Douglas MD-87	Iberia *Ciudad de Caceres*
EC-EYY	McD Douglas MD-87	Iberia *Ciudad de Barcelona*
EC-EYZ	McD Douglas MD-87	Iberia *Ciudad de Las Palmas*
EC-EZA	McD Douglas MD-87	Iberia *Ciudad de Segovia*
EC-EZS	McD Douglas MD-87	Iberia *Ciudad de Mahon*
EC-FCB	Airbus A.320-211	Iberia *Montana de Covadonga*
EC-FDA	Airbus A.320-211	Iberia *Lagunas de Ruidera*
EC-FDB	Airbus A.320-211	Iberia *Lago de Sanabria*
EC-FEY	McD Douglas MD-87	Iberia *Ciudad de Jaen*
EC-FEZ	McD Douglas MD-87	Iberia *Ciudad de Malaga*
EC-FFA	McD Douglas MD-87	Iberia *Ciudad de Avila*
EC-FFH	McD Douglas MD-87	Iberia *Ciudad de Logrono*
EC-FFI	McD Douglas MD-87	Iberia *Ciudad de Cuenca*
EC-FGH	Airbus A.320-211	Iberia *Caldera de Taburiente*
EC-FGM	McD Douglas MD-88	Iberia *Torre de Hercules*
EC-FGR	Airbus A.320-211	Iberia *Dehesa de Moncayo*
EC-FGV	Airbus A.320-211	Iberia *Monfrague*
EC-FHD	McD Douglas MD-87	Iberia *Ciudad de Leon*
EC-FHG	McD Douglas MD-87	Iberia *La Almudiana*
EC-FHK	McD Douglas MD-87	Iberia *Ciudad de Tarragona*
EC-FIG	McD Douglas MD-88	Iberia *Penon de Ifach*
EC-FIH	McD Douglas MD-88	Iberia *Albaicin*
EC-FJE	McD Douglas MD-88	Iberia *Gibralfaro*
EC-FLK	McD Douglas MD-88	Iberia *Palacio de la Magdalena*
EC-FLN	McD Douglas MD-88	Iberia *Puerta de Tierra*
EC-FLP	Airbus A.320-211	Iberia *Torcal de Antequera*
EC-FLQ	Airbus A.320-211	Iberia *Dunas de Liencres*
EC-FND	McD Douglas MD-88	Iberia *Playa de la Concha*
EC-FNR	Airbus A.320-211	Iberia *Monte el Valle*
EC-FOF	McD Douglas MD-88	Iberia *Puerta de Alcala*
EC-FOG	McD Douglas MD-88	Iberia *La Giralda*
EC-FOZ	McD Douglas MD-88	Iberia *Montjuic*
EC-FPD	McD Douglas MD-88	Iberia *Lagos de Coradonga*
EC-FPJ	McD Douglas MD-88	Iberia *Ria de Vigo*
EC-FQY	Airbus A.320-211	Iberia *Joan Miro*

OVERSEAS AIRLINERS

EC

Reg	Type	Owner or Operator	Notes
EC-FTS	McD Douglas MD-83	Spanair *Sunbird*	
EC-FVY	BAe 146-200QT	Pan Air/TNT Airways	
EC-FXA	McD Douglas MD-83	Spanair *Sunstar*	
EC-FZE	BAe 146-200QT	Pan Air/TNT Airways	
EC-GAT	McD Douglas MD-83	Spanair *Sunmyth*	
EC-GBA	McD Douglas MD-83	Spanair *Sungod*	
EC-GCV	McD Douglas MD-82	Spanair *Sunburst*	
EC-GGS	Airbus A.340-313	Iberia *Concha Espina*	
EC-GGV	McD Douglas MD-83	Spanair *Sunbow*	
EC-GHE	McD Douglas MD-83	Spanair *Sunset*	
EC-GHH	McD Douglas MD-83	Spanair *Sundance*	
EC-GHX	Airbus A.340-313	Iberia *Rosalia de Castro*	
EC-GJT	Airbus A.340-313	Iberia *Rosa Chacel*	
EC-GLE	Airbus A.340-313	Iberia *Concepcion Arenal*	
EC-GMU	Airbus A.310-324	Air Plus Comet	
EC-GNY	McD Douglas MD-83	Spanair *Sunflash*	
EC-GNZ	Boeing 737-4Y0	Futura International Airways	
EC-GOM	McD Douglas MD-83	Spanair *Sunlight*	
EC-GOT	Airbus A.310-324	Air Plus Comet	
EC-GOU	McD Douglas MD-83	Spanair *Sunlover*	
EC-GPB	Airbus A.340-313X	Iberia *Teresa de Avila*	
EC-GQG	McD Douglas MD-83	Spanair *Sunrise*	
EC-GQK	Airbus A.340-313X	Iberia *Emilia Pardo Bazan*	
EC-GQO	BAe 146-200QT	Pan Air/TNT Airways	
EC-GRE	Airbus A.320-211	Clickair	
EC-GRF	Airbus A.320-211	Clickair	
EC-GRG	Airbus A.320-211	Iberia *Timanfaya*	
EC-GRH	Airbus A.320-211	Clickair	
EC-GRI	Airbus A.320-211	Iberia *Delta del Ebro*	
EC-GRJ	Airbus A.320-211	Iberia *Canon del Rio Lobos*	
EC-GRK	McD Douglas MD-87	Iberia *Ciudad de Savilla*	
EC-GRL	McD Douglas MD-87	Spanair	
EC-GRM	McD Douglas MD-87	Iberia *Ciudad de Burgos*	
EC-GRN	McD Douglas MD-87	Spanair	
EC-GRO	McD Douglas MD-87	Spanair	
EC-GTO	McD Douglas MD-82	Spanair *Sunjet*	
EC-GUP	Airbus A.340-313X	Iberia *Agustina De Aragon*	
EC-GUQ	Airbus A.340-313X	Iberia *Beatriz Galindo*	
EC-GVE	Swearingen SA227AC Metro III	Aeronova	
EC-GVI	McD Douglas MD-83	Spanair *Sunup*	
EC-GVO	McD Douglas MD-83	Spanair *Sunspot*	
EC-GXU	McD Douglas MD-83	Spanair *Sunray*	
EC-HAF	Airbus A.320-214	Iberia *Santiago de Compostela*	
EC-HAG	Airbus A.320-214	Iberia *Senorio de Bertiz*	
EC-HBL	Boeing 737-85P	Air Europa *Travelplan*	
EC-HBM	Boeing 737-85P	Air Europa *La Gaceta*	
EC-HBN	Boeing 737-85P	Air Europa *Llucmajor*	
EC-HCH	Swearingen SA227AC Metro III	Aeronova	
EC-HDH	BAe 146-200QT	Pan Air/TNT Airways	
EC-HDK	Airbus A.320-214	Iberia *Mar Ortigola*	
EC-HDN	Airbus A.320-214	Iberia *Parque National de Omiedo*	
EC-HDO	Airbus A.320-214	Iberia *Formentera*	
EC-HDP	Airbus A.320-214	Iberia *Parque de Cabarceno*	
EC-HDQ	Airbus A.340-313X	Iberia *Sor Juana Ines de la Cruz*	
EC-HDR	Boeing 757-256	Iberia *Pont Aeri Madrid-Barcelona*	
EC-HDS	Boeing 757-256	Iberia *Paraguay*	
EC-HDT	Airbus A.320-214	Iberia *Museo Guggenheim Bilbao*	
EC-HDU	Boeing 757-256	Iberia *Uruguay*	
EC-HDV	Boeing 757-256	Iberia *Nicaragua*	
EC-HFP	McD Douglas MD-83	Spanair *Sunbreeze*	
EC-HFS	McD Douglas MD-82	Spanair *Sunbeach*	
EC-HFT	McD Douglas MD-82	Spanair *Sunspirit*	
EC-HGA	McD Douglas MD-83	Spanair *Sunisland*	
EC-HGJ	McD Douglas MD-82	Spanair *Sunworld*	
EC-HGO	Boeing 737-85P	Air Europa	
EC-HGP	Boeing 737-85P	Air Europa *Marbella*	
EC-HGQ	Boeing 737-85P	Air Europa *El Mundo-El Dia de Baleares*	
EC-HGR	Airbus A.319-111	Iberia *Ribeira Sacra*	
EC-HGS	Airbus A.319-111	Iberia *Bardenas Reales*	
EC-HGT	Airbus A.319-111	Iberia *Icnitas de Enciso*	
EC-HGU	Airbus A.340-313X	Iberia *Maria de Molina*	
EC-HGV	Airbus A.340-313X	Iberia *Maria Guerrero*	
EC-HGX	Airbus A.340-313X	Iberia *Maria Pita*	

EC OVERSEAS AIRLINERS

Notes	Reg	Type	Owner or Operator
	EC-HGY	Airbus A.320-214	Iberia *Albarracin*
	EC-HGZ	Airbus A.320-214	Iberia *Boi Taull*
	EC-HHA	Airbus A.320-214	Iberia *Serrania de Ronda*
	EC-HHF	McD Douglas MD-82	Spanair *Sunward*
	EC-HHP	McD Douglas MD-82	Spanair *Sunshiny*
	EC-HIT	Boeing 757-256	Iberia *Guatemala*
	EC-HIV	Boeing 757-256	Iberia *Villa de Bilbao*
	EC-HIX	Boeing 757-256	Iberia *Cuba*
	EC-HJB	McD Douglas MD-82	Spanair *Suntrek*
	EC-HJH	BAe 146-200QT	Pan Air/TNT Airways
	EC-HJP	Boeing 737-85P	Air Europa
	EC-HJQ	Boeing 737-85P	Air Europa
	EC-HKO	Airbus A.319-111	Iberia *Gorbia*
	EC-HKP	McD Douglas MD-83	Spanair *Suntrail*
	EC-HKQ	Boeing 737-85P	Air Europa *San Pedro Alcantara*
	EC-HKR	Boeing 737-85P	Air Europa
	EC-HKS	Boeing 767-3Q8ER	Air Europa
	EC-HLA	Airbus A.310-324	Air Plus Comet
	EC-HMS	Convair 580	Swiftair/DHL
	EC-HNC	McD Douglas MD-83	Spanair *Sunplace*
	EC-HOV	McD Douglas MD-82	Spanair *Sunspeed*
	EC-HPM	Airbus A.321-231	Spanair *Camillo José Cela*
	EC-HPU	Boeing 767-3Q8ER	Air Europa
	EC-HQF	Airbus A.340-313X	Iberia *Maria de Zayas y Sotomayor*
	EC-HQG	Airbus A.320-214	Iberia *Las Hurdes*
	EC-HQH	Airbus A.340-313X	Iberia *Mariana de Silva*
	EC-HQI	Airbus A.320-214	Iberia *La Albufera*
	EC-HQJ	Airbus A.320-214	Iberia *Bosque de Muniellos*
	EC-HQK	Airbus A.320-214	Iberia *Macarella*
	EC-HQL	Airbus A.320-214	Iberia *Liebana*
	EC-HQM	Airbus A.320-214	Iberia *Rio Jucar*
	EC-HQN	Airbus A.340-313X	Iberia *Luisa Carvajal y Mendoza*
	EC-HQT	Airbus A.300B4-103F	Pan Air/TNT Airways
	EC-HQZ	Airbus A.321-231	Spanair
	EC-HRG	Airbus A.321-231	Spanair *Placido Domingo*
	EC-HRP	Airbus A.320-232	Spanair *Juan de Avalos*
	EC-HSF	Airbus A.320-214	Iberia *Mar Menor*
	EC-HSV	Boeing 767-3Q8ER	Air Europa
	EC-HTA	Airbus A.320-214	Iberia *Cadaques*
	EC-HTB	Airbus A.320-214	Iberia *Playa de las Americas*
	EC-HTC	Airbus A.320-214	Iberia *Alpujarra*
	EC-HTD	Airbus A.320-214	Iberia *Calblanque*
	EC-HUH	Airbus A.321-211	Iberia *Benidorm*
	EC-HUI	Airbus A.321-211	Iberia *Comunidad Autonoma de la Rioja*
	EC-HUJ	Airbus A.320-214	Iberia *Getaria*
	EC-HUK	Airbus A.320-214	Iberia *Laguna Negra*
	EC-HUL	Airbus A.320-214	Iberia *Monasterio de Rueda*
	EC-HVZ	Airbus A.300B4-203F	Pan Air/TNT Airways
	EC-HXA	Airbus A.320-232	Spanair
	EC-HYC	Airbus A.320-214	Iberia *Cuidad de Ceuta*
	EC-HYD	Airbus A.320-214	Iberia *Maspalomas*
	EC-HZH	Swearingen SA227AC Metro III	Aeronova
	EC-HZS	Boeing 737-86Q	Air Europa
	EC-HZU	Airbus A.320-214	Iberworld
	EC-IAZ	Airbus A.320-232	Spanair
	EC-ICD	Boeing 737-81Q	Air Europa
	EC-ICF	Airbus A.340-313X	Iberia *Maria Zambrano*
	EC-ICL	Airbus A.320-232	Spanair
	EC-ICQ	Airbus A.320-211	Iberia *Sierra Espuna*
	EC-ICR	Airbus A.320-211	Clickair
	EC-ICS	Airbus A.320-211	Clickair
	EC-ICT	Airbus A.320-211	Clickair
	EC-ICU	Airbus A.320-211	Iberia *Hayedo de Tejera Negra*
	EC-ICV	Airbus A.320-211	Clickair
	EC-IDA	Boeing 737-86Q	Air Europa
	EC-IDB	Airbus A.330-243	Iberworld *Sabine Thienemann*
	EC-IDF	Airbus A.340-313X	Iberia *Mariana Pineda*
	EC-IDT	Boeing 737-86Q	Air Europa
	EC-IEF	Airbus A.320-214	Iberia *Castillo de Loarre*
	EC-IEG	Airbus A.320-214	Iberia *Costa Brava*
	EC-IEI	Airbus A.320-214	Iberia *Monasterio de Valldigna*
	EC-IEJ	Airbus A.320-232	Spanair
	EC-IGK	Airbus A.321-211	Iberia *Costa Calida*

OVERSEAS AIRLINERS

EC

Reg	Type	Owner or Operator	Notes
EC-IGZ	Douglas DC-8-73F	Cygnus Air	
EC-IIG	Airbus A.321-211	Iberia *Ciudad de Siguenza*	
EC-IIH	Airbus A.340-313X	Iberia *Maria Barbara de Braganza*	
EC-III	Boeing 737-86Q	Air Europa	
EC-IIZ	Airbus A.320-232	Spanair	
EC-IJH	Airbus A.330-322	Iberworld *Gloria Fluxa*	
EC-IJN	Airbus A.321-211	Iberia *Merida*	
EC-IJU	Airbus A.321-231	Spanair	
EC-ILH	Airbus A.320-232	Spanair	
EC-ILO	Airbus A.321-211	Iberia *Cueva de Nerja*	
EC-ILP	Airbus A.321-211	Iberia *Peniscola*	
EC-ILQ	Airbus A.320-214	Iberia *La Pedrera*	
EC-ILR	Airbus A.320-214	Iberia *San Juan de la Pena*	
EC-ILS	Airbus A.320-214	Iberia *Sierra de Cameros*	
EC-IMB	Airbus A.320-232	Spanair	
EC-IMU	Airbus A.320-214	Iberworld	
EC-INB	Airbus A.321-231	Spanair	
EC-INM	Airbus A.320-232	Spanair	
EC-INO	Airbus A.340-642	Iberia *Gaudi*	
EC-INQ	Boeing 737-4Q8	Futura International Airways/Binter Canarias	
EC-INZ	Airbus A.320-214	Iberworld	
EC-IOB	Airbus A.340-642	Iberia *Julio Romanes de Torres*	
EC-IOH	Airbus A.320-232	Spanair	
EC-IOO	Boeing 747-341	Air Pullmantur *Illusions*	
EC-IOR	Boeing 737-33A	Hola Airlines	
EC-IPI	Airbus A.320-232	Spanair	
EC-IPT	Airbus A.310-325ET	Air Plus Comet	
EC-IPV	Fokker 100	GirJet	
EC-IQR	Airbus A.340-642	Iberia *Salvador Dali*	
EC-ISE	Boeing 737-86Q	Air Europa	
EC-ISI	Airbus A.320-214	LTE/Nas Air	
EC-ISN	Boeing 737-86Q	Air Europa	
EC-ISY	Boeing 757-256	Hola Airlines *Privilege*	
EC-ITN	Airbus A.321-211	Iberia *Empuries*	
EC-IVG	Airbus A.320-232	Spanair	
EC-IVO	Fokker 100	GirJet	
EC-IVR	Boeing 737-408	Futura International Airways	
EC-IVV	Boeing 737-883	Air Europa *Camino de Santiago*	
EC-IXD	Airbus A.321-211	Iberia *Vall d'Aran*	
EC-IXE	Boeing 737-883	Air Europa *Disneyland Resort Paris*	
EC-IXO	Boeing 737-883	Air Europa	
EC-IYG	Airbus A.320-232	Spanair	
EC-IYI	Boeing 737-883	Air Europa *Disneyland Resort Paris*	
EC-IYS	Boeing 737-4Y0	Futura International Airways	
EC-IZG	Boeing 737-46J	Futura International Airways	
EC-IZH	Airbus A.320-214	Iberia *San Pere de Roda*	
EC-IZK	Airbus A.320-232	Spanair	
EC-IZL	Boeing 747-287B	Air Plus Comet	
EC-IZR	Airbus A.320-214	Iberia *Urkiola*	
EC-IZX	Airbus A.340-642	Iberia *Mariano Benlliure*	
EC-IZY	Airbus A.340-642	Iberia *I. Zuloaga*	
EC-JAB	Airbus A.320-214	Vueling *Born to be Vueling*	
EC-JAP	Boeing 737-85P	Air Europa	
EC-JAZ	Airbus A.319-111	Iberia *Las Medulas*	
EC-JBA	Airbus A.340-642	Iberia *Joaquin Rodrigo*	
EC-JBJ	Boeing 737-85P	Air Europa	
EC-JBK	Boeing 737-85P	Air Europa	
EC-JBL	Boeing 737-85P	Air Europa	
EC-JCU	Swearingen SA227AC Metro III	Aeronova	
EC-JCY	Airbus A.340-642	Iberia *Andrés Segovia*	
EC-JCZ	Airbus A.340-642	Iberia *Vicente Aleixandre*	
EC-JDH	Boeing 747-287B	Air Plus Comet	
EC-JDK	Airbus A.320-214	Vueling *Vueling the sky*	
EC-JDL	Airbus A.319-111	Iberia *Los Llanos de Aridane*	
EC-JDM	Airbus A.321-211	Iberia *Cantabria*	
EC-JDO	Airbus A.320-214	Vueling *Vini, vidi, vueling*	
EC-JDU	Boeing 737-86N	Futura International Airways	
EC-JEI	Airbus A.319-111	Iberia *Xàtiva*	
EC-JEJ	Airbus A.321-211	Iberia *Río Frío*	
EC-JEX	Boeing 737-86N	Air Europa	
EC-JFB	Boeing 737-86N	Futura International Airways	
EC-JFF	Airbus A.320-214	Vueling *Vueling the world*	
EC-JFG	Airbus A.320-214	Iberia *Valle de Ricote*	

EC OVERSEAS AIRLINERS

Reg	Type	Owner or Operator
EC-JFH	Airbus A.320-214	Iberia *Trujillo*
EC-JFN	Airbus A.320-214	Iberia *Sirrea de las Nieves*
EC-JFR	Boeing 747-228B	Air Pullmantur
EC-JFX	Airbus A.340-642	Iberia *Jacinto Benavente*
EC-JGM	Airbus A.320-214	Vueling *The joy of vueling*
EC-JGS	Airbus A.321-211	Iberia *Guadelupe*
EC-JGU	Airbus A.340-211	Air Europa *Pedro Duque*/ConViasa
EC-JHD	Boeing 747-228B (SCD)	Air Pullmantur
EC-JHK	Boeing 737-85P	Air Europa
EC-JHL	Boeing 737-85P	Air Europa
EC-JHP	Airbus A.330-343X	Iberworld
EC-JHV	Boeing 737-8FH	Futura International Airways/Arkefly
EC-JIB	Airbus A.320-232	LTE
EC-JJD	Airbus A.320-232	Spanair
EC-JJG	Boeing 747-287B	Air Plus Comet
EC-JJJ	Boeing 767-328ER	Air Europa
EC-JKZ	Boeing 737-86N	Air Europa
EC-JLE	Airbus A.340-642	Iberia *Santiago Ramon y Cajal*
EC-JLI	Airbus A.321-211	Iberia *Delta del Llobregrat*
EC-JMB	Airbus A.320-214	Vueling *Eloy Fructuoso*
EC-JMR	Airbus A.321-211	Iberia *Aranjuez*
EC-JNA	Airbus A.320-214	Vueling *La vita e vueling*
EC-JNC	Airbus A.320-214	Spanair *Juan Antonio Samaranch*
EC-JNF	Boeing 737-85P	Air Europa
EC-JNI	Airbus A.321-211	Iberia *Palmeral de Eiche*
EC-JNQ	Airbus A.340-642	Iberia *Antonio Machado*
EC-JNT	Airbus A.320-214	Vueling *Quien no corre Vueling*
EC-JNU	Boeing 737-4Q8	Futura International Airways
EC-JOH	Airbus A.340-642	Iberia *Miguel de Unamuno*
EC-JOI	McD Douglas MD-88	Air Plus Comet
EC-JOZ	Boeing 767-219ER	LAC Bravo Airlines
EC-JPF	Airbus A.330-202	Air Europa
EC-JPL	Airbus A.320-214	Vueling *Vueldone*
EC-JPU	Airbus A.340-642	Iberia *Pio Baroja*
EC-JQG	Airbus A.330-202	Air Europa *Estepona – Costa del Sol*
EC-JQP	Airbus A.320-214	Iberworld
EC-JQQ	Airbus A.330-202	Air Europa
EC-JQX	Boeing 737-329	Hola Airlines/Olympic
EC-JQZ	Airbus A.321-211	Iberia *Generalife*
EC-JRC	Airbus A.320-212	LTE
EC-JRE	Airbus A.321-211	Iberia *Villa de Uncastillo*
EC-JRI	Airbus A.320-214	Vueling *Vueling voy, Vueling vengo*
EC-JRL	Boeing 737-85F	Futura International Airways/Arkefly
EC-JRR	McD Douglas MD-87	Spanair
EC-JRU	Airbus A.320-214	Iberworld
EC-JRX	Airbus A.320-232	LTE
EC-JSB	Airbus A.320-214	Iberia *Benalmadena*
EC-JSJ	Boeing 737-4K5	Futura International Airways
EC-JSK	Airbus A.320-214	Iberia *Ciudad Encantada*
EC-JSS	Boeing 737-4K5	Futura International Airways
EC-JSU	McD Douglas MD-87	Spanair
EC-JTA	Airbus A.320-212	LTE
EC-JTK	McD Douglas MD-87	Spanair
EC-JTQ	Airbus A.320-214	Vueling *Vueling, que es gerundio*
EC-JTR	Airbus A.320-214	Vueling *No Vueling no party*
EC-JTV	Boeing 737-33A	Hola Airlines/Olympic
EC-JVE	Airbus A.319-111	Iberia *Puerto de la Cruz*
EC-JVV	McD Douglas MD-82	Air Plus Comet
EC-JXA	Airbus A.319-111	Iberia *Ciudad de Ubeda*
EC-JXD	Boeing 737-33A	Futura International Airways
EC-JXJ	Airbus A.319-111	Iberia *Ciudad de Baeza*
EC-JXV	Airbus A.319-111	Iberia *Concejo de Cabrales*
EC-JXZ	Canadair CL.600-2D24 RJ	Air Nostrum
EC-JYA	Canadair CL.600-2D24 RJ	Air Nostrum
EC-JYD	McD Douglas MD-87	Spanair
EC-JYX	Airbus A.320-214	Vueling *Elisenda Masana*
EC-JZI	Airbus A.320-214	Vueling *Vueling in love*
EC-JZM	Airbus A.321-211	Iberia *Águila Imperial Ibérica*
EC-JZQ	Airbus A.320-214	Clickair

Note: Futura also operates 737s EI-DGZ, EI-DJT, EI-DJU, EI-DKD, EI-DMZ, EI-DND and EI-DOR.
Hola also operates 737 OK-TVR.
MyAir also operates A.321 EI-DRG and A.320s EI-DJH, EI-DJI, EI-DOD and HB-IJZ.

OVERSEAS AIRLINERS

EP/ES/ET/EW/EZ

Reg	Type	Owner or Operator	Notes

EP (Iran)

EP-IAB	Boeing 747SP-86	Iran Air *Khorasan*
EP-IAD	Boeing 747SP-86	Iran Air
EP-IAG	Boeing 747-286B (SCD)	Iran Air *Azarabadegan*
EP-IAH	Boeing 747-286B (SCD)	Iran Air *Khuzestan*
EP-IAM	Boeing 747-186B	Iran Air
EP-IBA	Airbus A.300B4-605R	Iran Air
EP-IBB	Airbus A.300B4-605R	Iran Air
EP-IBC	Airbus A.300B4-605R	Iran Air
EP-IBD	Airbus A.300B4-605R	Iran Air
EP-MHJ	Airbus A.320-232	Mahan Air
EP-MHK	Airbus A.320-232	Mahan Air

Note: Mahan Air also operates A.310s F-OJHH and F-OJHI.

ES (Estonia)

ES-ABC	Boeing 737-5Q8	Estonian Air *Koit*
ES-ABD	Boeing 737-5Q8	Estonian Air *Hamarik*
ES-ABH	Boeing 737-53S	Estonian Air *Sinilind*
ES-ABJ	Boeing 737-33R	Estonian Air
ES-ABK	Boeing 737-36N	Estonian Air

ET (Ethiopia)

ET-AIF	Boeing 767-260ER	Ethiopian Airlines
ET-AJS	Boeing 757-260PF	Ethiopian Airlines
ET-AJX	Boeing 757-260F	Ethiopian Airlines
ET-AKC	Boeing 757-260	Ethiopian Airlines
ET-AKE	Boeing 757-260	Ethiopian Airlines
ET-AKF	Boeing 757-260	Ethiopian Airlines
ET-ALC	Boeing 767-33AER	Ethiopian Airlines
ET-ALH	Boeing 767-3BGER	Ethiopian Airlines
ET-ALJ	Boeing 767-360ER	Ethiopian Airlines
ET-ALL	Boeing 767-3BGER	Ethiopian Airlines
ET-ALO	Boeing 767-360ER	Ethiopian Airlines
ET-ALP	Boeing 767-360ER	Ethiopian Airlines
ET-ALY	Boeing 757-231	Ethiopian Airlines
ET-ALZ	Boeing 757-231	Ethiopian Airlines
ET-AME	Boeing 767-306ER	Ethiopian Airlines

EW (Belarus)

EW-250PA	Boeing 737-524	Belavia
EW-251PA	Boeing 737-5Q8	Belavia
EW-85703	Tu-154M	Belavia
EW-85706	Tu-154M	Belavia
EW-85741	Tu-154M	Belavia
EW-85748	Tu-154M	Belavia
EW-85815	Tu-154M	Belarus Government

EZ (Turkmenistan)

EZ-A010	Boeing 757-23A	Turkmenistan Airlines
EZ-A011	Boeing 757-22K	Turkmenistan Airlines
EZ-A012	Boeing 757-22K	Turkmenistan Airlines
EZ-A014	Boeing 757-22K	Turkmenistan Airlines
EZ-A700	Boeing 767-32KER	Turkmenistan Airlines

F (France)

Reg	Type	Owner or Operator
F-BTDG	Boeing 747-2B3B (SCD)	Air France
F-BTDH	Boeing 747-2B3B (SCD)	Air France
F-GCBD	Boeing 747-228B (SF)	Air France
F-GCBF	Boeing 747-228B (SCD)	Air France Cargo
F-GCBG	Boeing 747-228F (SCD)	Air France Cargo
F-GCBH	Boeing 747-228F (SCD)	Air France Cargo
F-GCBK	Boeing 747-228F (SCD)	Air France Cargo
F-GCBL	Boeing 747-228F (SCD)	Air France Cargo
F-GCBM	Boeing 747-228F	Air France Cargo
F-GEMO	Airbus A.310-304	Eagle Aviation
F-GEXA	Boeing 747-4B3	Air France
F-GEXB	Boeing 747-4B3	Air France
F-GFKA	Airbus A.320-111	Air France *Ville de Paris*
F-GFKB	Airbus A.320-111	Air France *Ville de Rome*
F-GFKD	Airbus A.320-111	Air France *Ville de Londres*
F-GFKE	Airbus A.320-111	Air France *Ville de Bonn*
F-GFKF	Airbus A.320-111	Air France *Ville de Madrid*
F-GFKG	Airbus A.320-111	Air France *Ville d'Amsterdam*
F-GFKH	Airbus A.320-211	Air France *Ville de Bruxelles*
F-GFKI	Airbus A.320-211	Air France *Ville de Lisbonne*
F-GFKJ	Airbus A.320-211	Air France *Ville de Copenhague*
F-GFKK	Airbus A.320-211	Air France *Ville d'Athenes*
F-GFKL	Airbus A.320-211	Air France *Ville de Dublin*
F-GFKM	Airbus A.320-211	Air France *Ville de Luxembourg*
F-GFKN	Airbus A.320-211	Air France *Ville de Strasbourg*
F-GFKO	Airbus A.320-211	Air France *Ville de Milan*
F-GFKP	Airbus A.320-211	Air France *Ville de Nice*
F-GFKQ	Airbus A.320-111	Air France *Ville de Berlin*
F-GFKR	Airbus A.320-211	Air France *Ville de Barceloune*
F-GFKS	Airbus A.320-211	Air France *Ville de Marseilles*
F-GFKT	Airbus A.320-211	Air France *Ville de Lyon*
F-GFKU	Airbus A.320-211	Air France *Ville de Manchester*
F-GFKV	Airbus A.320-211	Air France *Ville de Bordeaux*
F-GFKX	Airbus A.320-211	Air France *Ville de Francfort*
F-GFKY	Airbus A.320-211	Air France *Ville de Toulouse*
F-GFKZ	Airbus A.320-211	Air France *Ville de Turin*
F-GGEA	Airbus A.320-111	Air France
F-GGEB	Airbus A.320-111	Air France
F-GGEC	Airbus A.320-111	Air France
F-GGEE	Airbus A.320-111	Air France
F-GGEF	Airbus A.320-111	Air France
F-GGEG	Airbus A.320-111	Air France
F-GHQA	Airbus A.320-211	Air France
F-GHQB	Airbus A.320-211	Air France
F-GHQC	Airbus A.320-211	Air France
F-GHQD	Airbus A.320-211	Air France
F-GHQE	Airbus A.320-211	Air France
F-GHQF	Airbus A.320-211	Air France
F-GHQG	Airbus A.320-211	Air France
F-GHQH	Airbus A.320-211	Air France
F-GHQI	Airbus A.320-211	Air France
F-GHQJ	Airbus A.320-211	Air France
F-GHQK	Airbus A.320-211	Air France
F-GHQL	Airbus A.320-211	Air France
F-GHQM	Airbus A.320-211	Air France
F-GHQO	Airbus A.320-211	Air France
F-GHQP	Airbus A.320-211	Air France
F-GHQQ	Airbus A.320-211	Air France
F-GHQR	Airbus A.320-211	Air France
F-GHXM	Boeing 737-53A	Air France
F-GIDK	Douglas DC-3C	Dakota Air Legend
F-GIOG	Fokker 100	Regional Airlines *L'Esprit Liberte*
F-GISA	Boeing 747-428 (SCD)	Air France
F-GISB	Boeing 747-428 (SCD)	Air France
F-GISC	Boeing 747-428 (SCD)	Air France
F-GISD	Boeing 747-428 (SCD)	Air France
F-GISE	Boeing 747-428 (SCD)	Air France
F-GITA	Boeing 747-428	Air France
F-GITB	Boeing 747-428	Air France
F-GITC	Boeing 747-428	Air France

OVERSEAS AIRLINERS   F

Reg	Type	Owner or Operator	Notes
F-GITD	Boeing 747-428	Air France	
F-GITE	Boeing 747-428	Air France	
F-GITF	Boeing 747-428	Air France	
F-GITH	Boeing 747-428	Air France	
F-GITI	Boeing 747-428	Air France	
F-GITJ	Boeing 747-428	Air France	
F-GIUA	Boeing 747-428ERF (SCD)	Air France Cargo	
F-GIUB	Boeing 747-428ERF (SCD)	Air France Cargo	
F-GIUC	Boeing 747-428ERF (SCD)	Air France Cargo	
F-GIUD	Boeing 747-428ERF (SCD)	Air France Cargo	
F-GIUE	Boeing 747-428ERF (SCD)	Air France Cargo	
F-GIUF	Boeing 747-406ERF (SCD)	Air France Cargo	
F-GIXG	Boeing 737-382QC	Axis Airways	
F-GIXH	Boeing 737-3S3QC	Axis Airways	
F-GIXM	Boeing 737-36EQC	Axis Airways	
F-GJNC	Boeing 737-528	Air France	
F-GJND	Boeing 737-528	Air France	
F-GJNE	Boeing 737-528	Air France	
F-GJNF	Boeing 737-528	Air France	
F-GJNG	Boeing 737-528	Air France	
F-GJNH	Boeing 737-528	Air France	
F-GJNM	Boeing 737-528	Air France	
F-GJVA	Airbus A.320-211	Air France	
F-GJVB	Airbus A.320-211	Air France	
F-GJVF	Airbus A.320-211	Aigle Azur	
F-GJVG	Airbus A.320-211	Air France	
F-GJVW	Airbus A.320-211	Air France	
F-GKXA	Airbus A.320-211	Air France	
F-GKXB	Airbus A.320-212	Air France	
F-GKXD	Airbus A.320-214	Air France	
F-GKXE	Airbus A.320-214	Air France	
F-GKXF	Airbus A.320-214	Air France	
F-GKXG	Airbus A.320-214	Air France	
F-GKXH	Airbus A.320-214	Air France	
F-GKXI	Airbus A.320-214	Air France	
F-GKXJ	Airbus A.320-214	Air France	
F-GKXK	Airbus A.320-214	Air France	
F-GKXL	Airbus A.320-214	Air France	
F-GKXM	Airbus A.320-214	Air France	
F-GKXN	Airbus A.320-214	Air France	
F-GLGG	Airbus A.320-212	Air France	
F-GLGH	Airbus A.320-212	Air France	
F-GLGM	Airbus A.320-212	Air France	
F-GLIR	Fokker 100	Regional Airlines/Air France	
F-GLIS	Fokker 70	Regional Airlines/Air France	
F-GLIT	Fokker 70	Regional Airlines/Air France	
F-GLIU	Fokker 70	Regional Airlines/Air France	
F-GLIV	Fokker 70	Regional Airlines	
F-GLIX	Fokker 70	Regional Airlines/Air France	
F-GLXQ	Boeing 737-4Y0	Axis Airways	
F-GLZA	Airbus A.340-312	Air France	
F-GLZC	Airbus A.340-312	Air France	
F-GLZG	Airbus A.340-312	Air France	
F-GLZH	Airbus A.340-312	Air France	
F-GLZI	Airbus A.340-312	Air France	
F-GLZJ	Airbus A.340-313X	Air France	
F-GLZK	Airbus A.340-313X	Air France	
F-GLZL	Airbus A.340-313X	Air France	
F-GLZM	Airbus A.340-313X	Air France	
F-GLZN	Airbus A.340-313X	Air France	
F-GLZO	Airbus A.340-313X	Air France	
F-GLZP	Airbus A.340-313X	Air France	
F-GLZR	Airbus A.340-313X	Air France	
F-GLZS	Airbus A.340-313X	Air France	
F-GLZT	Airbus A.340-313X	Air France	
F-GLZU	Airbus A.340-313X	Air France	
F-GMLI	McD Douglas MD-83	Blue Line	
F-GMLK	McD Douglas MD-83	Blue Line	
F-GMZA	Airbus A.321-111	Air France	
F-GMZB	Airbus A.321-111	Air France	
F-GMZC	Airbus A.321-111	Air France	
F-GMZD	Airbus A.321-111	Air France	
F-GMZE	Airbus A.321-111	Air France	

F — **OVERSEAS AIRLINERS**

Notes	Reg	Type	Owner or Operator
	F-GNIF	Airbus A.340-313X	Air France
	F-GNIG	Airbus A.340-313X	Air France
	F-GNIH	Airbus A.340-313X	Air France
	F-GNII	Airbus A.340-313X	Air France
	F-GNLG	Fokker 100	Blue Line
	F-GNLH	Fokker 100	Blue Line
	F-GNLI	Fokker 100	Regional Airlines/Air France
	F-GNLJ	Fokker 100	Regional Airlines/Air France
	F-GNLK	Fokker 100	Regional Airlines/Air France
	F-GOAF	Boeing 737-242C	Air Mediterranée
	F-GOHA	Embraer RJ135ER	Regional Airlines/Air France
	F-GOHB	Embraer RJ135ER	Regional Airlines/Air France
	F-GOHC	Embraer RJ135ER	Regional Airlines/Air France
	F-GOHD	Embraer RJ135ER	Regional Airlines/Air France
	F-GOHE	Embraer RJ135ER	Regional Airlines/Air France
	F-GOHF	Embraer RJ135ER	Regional Airlines/Air France
	F-GOMA	BAe 146-200QC	Axis Airways
	F-GPAN	Boeing 747-2B3F (SCD)	Air France Cargo
	F-GPMA	Airbus A.319-113	Air France
	F-GPMB	Airbus A.319-113	Air France
	F-GPMC	Airbus A.319-113	Air France
	F-GPMD	Airbus A.319-113	Air France
	F-GPME	Airbus A.319-113	Air France
	F-GPMF	Airbus A.319-113	Air France
	F-GPMG	Airbus A.319-113	Air France
	F-GPMH	Airbus A.319-113	Air France
	F-GPMI	Airbus A.319-113	Air France
	F-GPNK	Fokker 100	Regional Airlines/Air France
	F-GPNL	Fokker 100	Regional Airlines/Air France
	F-GPPP	Airbus A.320-232	Eagle Aviation
	F-GPXA	Fokker 100	Brit Air/Air France
	F-GPXB	Fokker 100	Brit Air/Air France
	F-GPXC	Fokker 100	Brit Air/Air France
	F-GPXD	Fokker 100	Brit Air/Air France
	F-GPXE	Fokker 100	Brit Air/Air France
	F-GPXF	Fokker 100	Brit Air/Air France
	F-GPXG	Fokker 100	Brit Air/Air France
	F-GPXH	Fokker 100	Brit Air/Air France
	F-GPXJ	Fokker 100	Brit Air/Air France
	F-GPXK	Fokker 100	Brit Air/Air France
	F-GPXL	Fokker 100	Brit Air/Air France
	F-GPXM	Fokker 100	Brit Air/Air France
	F-GRGA	Embraer RJ145EU	Regional Airlines/Air France
	F-GRGB	Embraer RJ145EU	Regional Airlines/Air France
	F-GRGC	Embraer RJ145EU	Regional Airlines/Air France
	F-GRGD	Embraer RJ145EU	Regional Airlines/Air France
	F-GRGE	Embraer RJ145EU	Regional Airlines/Air France
	F-GRGF	Embraer RJ145EU	Regional Airlines/Air France
	F-GRGG	Embraer RJ145EU	Regional Airlines/Air France
	F-GRGH	Embraer RJ145EU	Regional Airlines/Air France
	F-GRGI	Embraer RJ145EU	Regional Airlines/Air France
	F-GRGJ	Embraer RJ145EU	Regional Airlines/Air France
	F-GRGK	Embraer RJ145EU	Regional Airlines/Air France
	F-GRGL	Embraer RJ145EU	Regional Airlines/Air France
	F-GRGM	Embraer RJ145EU	Regional Airlines/Air France
	F-GRGP	Embraer RJ135ER	Regional Airlines/Air France
	F-GRGQ	Embraer RJ135ER	Regional Airlines/Air France
	F-GRGR	Embraer RJ135ER	Regional Airlines/Air France
	F-GRHA	Airbus A.319-111	Air France
	F-GRHB	Airbus A.319-111	Air France
	F-GRHC	Airbus A.319-111	Air France
	F-GRHD	Airbus A.319-111	Air France
	F-GRHE	Airbus A.319-111	Air France
	F-GRHF	Airbus A.319-111	Air France
	F-GRHG	Airbus A.319-111	Air France
	F-GRHH	Airbus A.319-111	Air France
	F-GRHI	Airbus A.319-111	Air France
	F-GRHJ	Airbus A.319-111	Air France
	F-GRHK	Airbus A.319-111	Air France
	F-GRHL	Airbus A.319-111	Air France
	F-GRHM	Airbus A.319-111	Air France
	F-GRHN	Airbus A.319-111	Air France
	F-GRHO	Airbus A.319-111	Air France

OVERSEAS AIRLINERS   F

Reg	Type	Owner or Operator	Notes
F-GRHP	Airbus A.319-111	Air France	
F-GRHQ	Airbus A.319-111	Air France	
F-GRHR	Airbus A.319-111	Air France	
F-GRHS	Airbus A.319-111	Air France	
F-GRHT	Airbus A.319-111	Air France	
F-GRHU	Airbus A.319-111	Air France	
F-GRHV	Airbus A.319-111	Air France	
F-GRHX	Airbus A.319-111	Air France	
F-GRHY	Airbus A.319-111	Air France	
F-GRHZ	Airbus A.319-111	Air France	
F-GRJA	Canadair CL.600-2B19 RJ	Brit Air/Air France	
F-GRJB	Canadair CL.600-2B19 RJ	Brit Air/Air France	
F-GRJC	Canadair CL.600-2B19 RJ	Brit Air/Air France	
F-GRJD	Canadair CL.600-2B19 RJ	Brit Air/Air France	
F-GRJE	Canadair CL.600-2B19 RJ	Brit Air/Air France	
F-GRJF	Canadair CL.600-2B19 RJ	Brit Air/Air France	
F-GRJG	Canadair CL.600-2B19 RJ	Brit Air/Air France	
F-GRJH	Canadair CL.600-2B19 RJ	Brit Air/Air France	
F-GRJI	Canadair CL.600-2B19 RJ	Brit Air/Air France	
F-GRJJ	Canadair CL.600-2B19 RJ	Brit Air/Air France	
F-GRJK	Canadair CL.600-2B19 RJ	Brit Air/Air France	
F-GRJL	Canadair CL.600-2B19 RJ	Brit Air/Air France	
F-GRJM	Canadair CL.600-2B19 RJ	Brit Air/Air France	
F-GRJN	Canadair CL.600-2B19 RJ	Brit Air/Air France	
F-GRJO	Canadair CL.600-2B19 RJ	Brit Air/Air France	
F-GRJP	Canadair CL.600-2B19 RJ	Brit Air/Air France	
F-GRJQ	Canadair CL.600-2B19 RJ	Brit Air/Air France	
F-GRJR	Canadair CL.600-2B19 RJ	Brit Air/Air France	
F-GRJT	Canadair CL.600-2B19 RJ	Brit Air/Air France	
F-GRSD	Airbus A.320-214	XL Airways France	
F-GRSE	Airbus A.320-214	XL Airways France	
F-GRSI	Airbus A.320-214	XL Airways France	
F-GRSQ	Airbus A.330-243	XL Airways France	
F-GRXA	Airbus A.319-111	Air France	
F-GRXB	Airbus A.319-111	Air France	
F-GRXC	Airbus A.319-111	Air France	
F-GRXD	Airbus A.319-111	Air France	
F-GRXE	Airbus A.319-111	Air France	
F-GRXF	Airbus A.319-111	Air France	
F-GRXG	Airbus A.319-115LR	Air France Dedicate	
F-GRXH	Airbus A.319-115LR	Air France Dedicate	
F-GRXI	Airbus A.319-115LR	Air France Dedicate	
F-GRXJ	Airbus A.319-115LR	Air France Dedicate	
F-GRXK	Airbus A.319-115LR	Air France Dedicate	
F-GRXL	Airbus A.319-112	Air France	
F-GRXM	Airbus A.319-112	Air France	
F-GRZA	Canadair CL.600-2C10 RJ	Brit Air/Air France Express	
F-GRZB	Canadair CL.600-2C10 RJ	Brit Air/Air France Express	
F-GRZC	Canadair CL.600-2C10 RJ	Brit Air/Air France Express	
F-GRZD	Canadair CL.600-2C10 RJ	Brit Air/Air France Express	
F-GRZE	Canadair CL.600-2C10 RJ	Brit Air/Air France Express	
F-GRZF	Canadair CL.600-2C10 RJ	Brit Air/Air France Express	
F-GRZG	Canadair CL.600-2C10 RJ	Brit Air/Air France Express	
F-GRZH	Canadair CL.600-2C10 RJ	Brit Air/Air France Express	
F-GRZI	Canadair CL.600-2C10 RJ	Brit Air/Air France Express	
F-GRZJ	Canadair CL.600-2C10 RJ	Brit Air/Air France Express	
F-GRZK	Canadair CL.600-2C10 RJ	Brit Air/Air France Express	
F-GRZL	Canadair CL.600-2C10 RJ	Brit Air/Air France Express	
F-GSEU	Airbus A.330-243	XL Airways France	
F-GSKY	Boeing 747-312	Corsair	
F-GSPA	Boeing 777-228ER	Air France	
F-GSPB	Boeing 777-228ER	Air France	
F-GSPC	Boeing 777-228ER	Air France	
F-GSPD	Boeing 777-228ER	Air France	
F-GSPE	Boeing 777-228ER	Air France	
F-GSPF	Boeing 777-228ER	Air France	
F-GSPG	Boeing 777-228ER	Air France	
F-GSPH	Boeing 777-228ER	Air France	
F-GSPI	Boeing 777-228ER	Air France	
F-GSPJ	Boeing 777-228ER	Air France	
F-GSPK	Boeing 777-228ER	Air France	
F-GSPL	Boeing 777-228ER	Air France	
F-GSPM	Boeing 777-228ER	Air France	

F   **OVERSEAS AIRLINERS**

Notes	Reg	Type	Owner or Operator
	F-GSPN	Boeing 777-228ER	Air France
	F-GSPO	Boeing 777-228ER	Air France
	F-GSPP	Boeing 777-228ER	Air France
	F-GSPQ	Boeing 777-228ER	Air France
	F-GSPR	Boeing 777-228ER	Air France
	F-GSPS	Boeing 777-228ER	Air France
	F-GSPT	Boeing 777-228ER	Air France
	F-GSPU	Boeing 777-228ER	Air France
	F-GSPV	Boeing 777-228ER	Air France
	F-GSPX	Boeing 777-228ER	Air France
	F-GSPY	Boeing 777-228ER	Air France
	F-GSPZ	Boeing 777-228ER	Air France
	F-GSQA	Boeing 777-328ER	Air France
	F-GSQB	Boeing 777-328ER	Air France
	F-GSQC	Boeing 777-328ER	Air France
	F-GSQD	Boeing 777-328ER	Air France
	F-GSQE	Boeing 777-328ER	Air France
	F-GSQF	Boeing 777-328ER	Air France
	F-GSQG	Boeing 777-328ER	Air France
	F-GSQH	Boeing 777-328ER	Air France
	F-GSQI	Boeing 777-328ER	Air France
	F-GSQJ	Boeing 777-328ER	Air France
	F-GSQK	Boeing 777-328ER	Air France
	F-GSQL	Boeing 777-328ER	Air France
	F-GSQM	Boeing 777-328ER	Air France
	F-GSQN	Boeing 777-328ER	Air France
	F-GSQO	Boeing 777-328ER	Air France
	F-GSQP	Boeing 777-328ER	Air France
	F-GSQQ	Boeing 777-328ER	Air France
	F-GSQR	Boeing 777-328ER	Air France
	F-GSQS	Boeing 777-328ER	Air France
	F-GSQT	Boeing 777-328ER	Air France
	F-GSTA	Airbus A.300-608ST Beluga (1)	Airbus Transport International
	F-GSTB	Airbus A.300-608ST Beluga (2)	Airbus Transport International
	F-GSTC	Airbus A.300-608ST Beluga (3)	Airbus Transport International
	F-GSTD	Airbus A.300-608ST Beluga (4)	Airbus Transport International
	F-GSTF	Airbus A.300-608ST Beluga (5)	Airbus Transport International
	F-GTAD	Airbus A.321-211	Air France
	F-GTAE	Airbus A.321-211	Air France
	F-GTAF	Airbus A.321-211	Air France/Royal Jordanian
	F-GTAH	Airbus A.321-211	Air France
	F-GTAI	Airbus A.321-211	Air France
	F-GTAJ	Airbus A.321-211	Air France
	F-GTAK	Airbus A.321-211	Air France
	F-GTAL	Airbus A.321-211	Air France
	F-GTAM	Airbus A.321-211	Air France
	F-GTUI	Boeing 747-422	Corsair
	F-GUAA	Airbus A.321-211	Air Méditerranée
	F-GUAM	Embraer RJ145MP	Regional Airlines/Air France
	F-GUBA	Embraer RJ145MP	Regional Airlines/Air France
	F-GUBB	Embraer RJ145MP	Regional Airlines/Air France
	F-GUBC	Embraer RJ145MP	Regional Airlines/Air France
	F-GUBD	Embraer RJ145MP	Regional Airlines/Air France
	F-GUBE	Embraer RJ145MP	Regional Airlines/Air France
	F-GUBF	Embraer RJ145MP	Regional Airlines/Air France
	F-GUBG	Embraer RJ145MP	Regional Airlines/Air France
	F-GUEA	Embraer RJ145MP	Regional Airlines/Air France
	F-GUFD	Embraer RJ145EU	Regional Airlines/Air France
	F-GUGA	Airbus A.318-111	Air France
	F-GUGB	Airbus A.318-111	Air France
	F-GUGC	Airbus A.318-111	Air France
	F-GUGD	Airbus A.318-111	Air France
	F-GUGE	Airbus A.318-111	Air France
	F-GUGF	Airbus A.318-111	Air France
	F-GUGG	Airbus A.318-111	Air France
	F-GUGH	Airbus A.318-111	Air France
	F-GUGI	Airbus A.318-111	Air France
	F-GUGJ	Airbus A.318-111	Air France
	F-GUGK	Airbus A.318-111	Air France
	F-GUGL	Airbus A.318-111	Air France
	F-GUGM	Airbus A.318-111	Air France
	F-GUGN	Airbus A.318-111	Air France
	F-GUGO	Airbus A.318-111	Air France

OVERSEAS AIRLINERS

Reg	Type	Owner or Operator	Notes
F-GUGP	Airbus A.318-111	Air France	
F-GUGQ	Airbus A.318-111	Air France	
F-GUGR	Airbus A.318-111	Air France	
F-GUJA	Embraer RJ145MP	Regional Airlines/Air France	
F-GUMA	Embraer RJ145MP	Regional Airlines/Air France	
F-GUPT	Embraer RJ145MP	Regional Airlines/Air France	
F-GUYH	Boeing 737-329	Aigle Azur	
F-GVGS	Embraer RJ145MP	Regional Airlines/Air France	
F-GVHD	Embraer RJ145EU	Regional Airlines/Air France	
F-GXAG	Airbus A.319-132	Aigle Azur	
F-GXAH	Airbus A.319-132	Aigle Azur	
F-GYAI	Airbus A.320-211	Air Mediterranée	
F-GYAJ	Airbus A.321-111	Air Mediterranée	
F-GYAN	Airbus A.321-111	Air Mediterranée	
F-GYAO	Airbus A.321-111	Air Mediterranée	
F-GYAP	Airbus A.321-111	Air Mediterranée	
F-GYAQ	Airbus A.321-211	Air Mediterranée	
F-GYAR	Airbus A.321-211	Air Mediterranée	
F-GYAS	Airbus A.319-115LR	Aero Services Executive/Air France	
F-GYAZ	Airbus A.321-111	Air Mediterranée	
F-GZCA	Airbus A.330-203	Air France	
F-GZCB	Airbus A.330-203	Air France	
F-GZCC	Airbus A.330-203	Air France	
F-GZCD	Airbus A.330-203	Air France	
F-GZCE	Airbus A.330-203	Air France	
F-GZCF	Airbus A.330-203	Air France	
F-GZCG	Airbus A.330-203	Air France	
F-GZCH	Airbus A.330-203	Air France	
F-GZCI	Airbus A.330-203	Air France	
F-GZCJ	Airbus A.330-203	Air France	
F-GZCK	Airbus A.330-203	Air France	
F-GZCL	Airbus A.330-203	Air France	
F-GZCM	Airbus A.330-203	Air France	
F-GZCN	Airbus A.330-203	Air France	
F-GZCO	Airbus A.330-203	Air France	
F-GZCP	Airbus A.330-203	Air France	
F-HAVN	Boeing 757-230	L'Avion	
F-HAXY	Boeing 757-2K2	Axis Airways	
F-HBAB	Airbus A.321-211	Aigle Azur	
F-HBAC	Airbus A.320-214	Aigle Azur	
F-HBAD	Airbus A.320-233	Aigle Azur	
F-HBAE	Airbus A.320-233	Aigle Azur	
F-HBAF	Airbus A.321-211	Aigle Azur	
F-HBIL	Airbus A.330-243	Corsair	
F-HBLA	Embraer RJ190	Regional Airlines/Air France	
F-HCAT	Airbus A.330-243	Corsair	
F-HDDD	Airbus A.300B4-622R	Eagle Aviation	
F-HEEE	Airbus A.300B4-622R	Eagle Aviation	
F-HJAC	Boeing 747-312	Corsair	
F-HKIS	Boeing 747-422	Corsair	
F-HLOV	Boeing 747-422	Corsair	
F-HSEA	Boeing 747-422	Corsair	
F-HSEX	Boeing 747-422	Corsair	
F-HSUN	Boeing 747-422	Corsair	
F-ODVF	Airbus A.310-304F	Royal Jordanian Cargo	
F-ODVG	Airbus A.310-304F	Royal Jordanian Cargo	
F-OGYO	Airbus A.310-324ET	Yemenia	
F-OHGU	Airbus A.321-211	Royal Jordanian	
F-OHGV	Airbus A.320-232	Royal Jordanian *Irbid*	
F-OHGX	Airbus A.320-232	Royal Jordanian *Madaba*	
F-OHLP	Airbus A.340-211	Royal Jordanian	
F-OHLQ	Airbus A.340-211	Royal Jordanian	
F-OHPR	Airbus A.310-325	Yemenia	
F-OHPS	Airbus A.310-325	Yemenia	
F-OJGF	Airbus A.340-313X	Air Tahiti Nui *Mangareva*	
F-OJHH	Airbus A.310-304ET	Mahan Air	
F-OJHI	Airbus A.310-304ET	Mahan Air	
F-OJTN	Airbus A.340-313X	Air Tahiti Nui *Bora Bora*	
F-OLOV	Airbus A.340-313E	Air Tahiti Nui *Nuku Hiva*	
F-OMAY	Boeing 777-2Q8ER	Air Austral	
F-OMEA	Airbus A.330-243	Middle East Airlines	
F-OMEB	Airbus A.330-243	Middle East Airlines	
F-OMEC	Airbus A.330-243	Middle East Airlines	

F/HA — OVERSEAS AIRLINERS

Notes	Reg	Type	Owner or Operator
	F-OPAR	Boeing 777-2Q8ER	Air Austral
	F-OPTP	Airbus A.330-223	Air Caraibes
	F-ORLY	Airbus A.330-223	Air Caraibes
	F-ORME	Airbus A.321-231	Middle East Airlines
	F-ORMF	Airbus A.321-231	Middle East Airlines
	F-ORMG	Airbus A.321-231	Middle East Airlines
	F-ORMH	Airbus A.321-231	Middle East Airlines
	F-ORMI	Airbus A.321-231	Middle East Airlines
	F-ORMJ	Airbus A.321-231	Middle East Airlines
	F-ORUN	Boeing 777-2Q8ER	Air Austral
	F-OSEA	Airbus A.340-313X	Air Tahiti Nui *Rangiroa*
	F-OSUN	Airbus A.340-313X	Air Tahiti Nui *Moorea*

Note: Air Mediterranée also operates B.757 TF-FII.

HA (Hungary)

Reg	Type	Owner or Operator
HA-FAB	F.27 Friendship Mk 500	Farnair Europe
HA-FAC	F.27 Friendship Mk 500	Farnair Europe
HA-FAD	F.27 Friendship Mk 500	Farnair Europe
HA-FAE	F.27 Friendship Mk 500	Farnair Europe
HA-FAF	F.27 Friendship Mk 500	Farnair Europe
HA-FAH	F.27 Friendship Mk 500	Farnair Europe
HA-LHA	Boeing 767-27GER	Malev *Szent-Györgyi Albert*
HA-LHB	Boeing 767-27GER	Malev
HA-	Boeing 767-306ER	Malev
HA-LKB	Boeing 737-86Q	Travel Service Airlines
HA-LKU	Boeing 737-33V	SkyEurope Hungary
HA-LKV	Boeing 737-33V	SkyEurope Hungary
HA-LMA	Fokker 70	Malev
HA-LMB	Fokker 70	Malev
HA-LMC	Fokker 70	Malev
HA-LME	Fokker 70	Malev
HA-LMF	Fokker 70	Malev
HA-LOA	Boeing 737-7Q8	Malev
HA-LOB	Boeing 737-7Q8	Malev
HA-LOC	Boeing 737-8Q8	Malev
HA-LOD	Boeing 737-6Q8	Malev
HA-LOE	Boeing 737-6Q8	Malev
HA-LOF	Boeing 737-6Q8	Malev
HA-LOG	Boeing 737-6Q8	Malev
HA-LOH	Boeing 737-6Q8	Malev
HA-LOI	Boeing 737-7Q8	Malev
HA-LOJ	Boeing 737-6Q8	Malev
HA-LOK	Boeing 737-6Q8	Malev
HA-LOL	Boeing 737-7Q8	Malev
HA-LOM	Boeing 737-8Q8	Malev
HA-LON	Boeing 737-6Q8	Malev
HA-LOP	Boeing 737-7Q8	Malev
HA-LOR	Boeing 737-7Q8	Malev
HA-LOS	Boeing 737-7Q8	Malev
HA-LOU	Boeing 737-8Q8	Malev
HA-LPA	Airbus A.320-233	Wizz Air
HA-LPB	Airbus A.320-233	Wizz Air
HA-LPC	Airbus A.320-233	Wizz Air
HA-LPD	Airbus A.320-233	Wizz Air
HA-LPE	Airbus A.320-233	Wizz Air
HA-LPF	Airbus A.320-233	Wizz Air
HA-LPH	Airbus A.320-233	Wizz Air
HA-LPI	Airbus A.320-233	Wizz Air
HA-TCN	Antonov An-26B	Cityline Hungary
HA-TCP	Antonov An-26B	Cityline Hungary
HA-TCX	Antonov An-26B	Budapest Aircraft Service
HA-TCY	Antonov An-26B	Budapest Aircraft Service
HA-YFG	Let L410UVP-E5	Manx2

Note: Wizz Air also operates A.320 LZ-WZA.

OVERSEAS AIRLINERS — HB

Reg	Type	Owner or Operator	Notes

HB (Switzerland)

Reg	Type	Owner or Operator
HB-AFC	Aerospatiale ATR-42-320	Farnair Europe
HB-AFD	Aerospatiale ATR-42-320	Farnair Europe
HB-AFF	Aerospatiale ATR-42-320	Farnair Europe
HB-IEE	Boeing 757-23A	PrivatAir
HB-IHR	Boeing 757-2G5	Belair *Solemar*
HB-IHS	Boeing 757-2G5	Belair *Horizonte*
HB-IHX	Airbus A.320-214	Edelweiss Air *Calvaro*
HB-IHY	Airbus A.320-214	Edelweiss Air *Upali*
HB-IHZ	Airbus A.320-214	Edelweiss Air *Viktoria*
HB-IIO	Boeing 737-7AK	PrivatAir
HB-IIQ	Boeing 737-7CN	PrivatAir/Lufthansa
HB-IIR	Boeing 737-86Q	PrivatAir/Swiss International
HB-IJB	Airbus A.320-214	Swiss International *Embrach*
HB-IJI	Airbus A.320-214	Swiss International *Basodino*
HB-IJJ	Airbus A.320-214	Swiss International *Les Diablerets*
HB-IJK	Airbus A.320-214	Swiss International *Wissigstock*
HB-IJL	Airbus A.320-214	Swiss International *Pizol*
HB-IJM	Airbus A.320-214	Swiss International *Schilthorn*
HB-IJN	Airbus A.320-214	Swiss International *Vanil Noir*
HB-IJO	Airbus A.320-214	Swiss International *Lissengrat*
HB-IJP	Airbus A.320-214	Swiss International *Nollen*
HB-IJQ	Airbus A.320-214	Swiss International *Agassizhorn*
HB-IJR	Airbus A.320-214	Swiss International *Dammastock*
HB-IJS	Airbus A.320-214	Swiss International *Creux du Van*
HB-IJU	Airbus A.320-214	Swiss International *Bietschhorn*
HB-IJV	Airbus A.320-214	Swiss International *Wildspitz*
HB-IJW	Airbus A.320-214	Swiss International *Bachtel*
HB-IJZ	Airbus A.320-211	MyAir
HB-IOC	Airbus A.321-111	Swiss International *Eiger*
HB-IOH	Airbus A.321-111	Swiss International *Piz Palu*
HB-IOK	Airbus A.321-111	Swiss International *Biefertenstock*
HB-IOL	Airbus A.321-111	Swiss International *Kaiseregg*
HB-IPR	Airbus A.319-112	Swiss International *Commune de Champagne*
HB-IPS	Airbus A.319-112	Swiss International *Weiach*
HB-IPT	Airbus A.319-112	Swiss International *Stadel*
HB-IPU	Airbus A.319-112	Swiss International *Hochfelden*
HB-IPV	Airbus A.319-112	Swiss International *Rumlang*
HB-IPX	Airbus A.319-112	Swiss International *Steinmaur*
HB-IPY	Airbus A.319-112	Swiss International *Hori*
HB-IQA	Airbus A.330-223	Swiss International *Lauteraarhorn*
HB-IQC	Airbus A.330-223	Swiss International *Breithorn*
HB-IQG	Airbus A.330-223	Swiss International *Jungfrau*
HB-IQH	Airbus A.330-223	Swiss International *Allalinhorn*
HB-IQI	Airbus A.330-223	Swiss International *Piz Bernina*
HB-IQJ	Airbus A.330-223	Swiss International *Aletschorn*
HB-IQK	Airbus A.330-223	Swiss International *Strahlhorn*
HB-IQO	Airbus A.330-223	Swiss International *Weissmies*
HB-IQP	Airbus A.330-223	Swiss International *Monch*
HB-IQQ	Airbus A.330-223	Swiss International *Bern*
HB-IQR	Airbus A.330-223	Swiss International
HB-IQZ	Airbus A.330-243	Edelweiss Air *Bahari*
HB-ISE	Boeing 767-3Q8ER	Belair *RondoMondo*
HB-IXF	Avro RJ85	Swiss International *Karpf 2794m*
HB-IXG	Avro RJ85	Swiss International *Lindenberg 878m*
HB-IXH	Avro RJ85	Swiss International *Montchaibeux 627m*
HB-IXK	Avro RJ85	Swiss International *Piz Julier 3380m*
HB-IXN	Avro RJ100	Swiss International *Balmhorn 3699m*
HB-IXO	Avro RJ100	Swiss International *Brisen 2404m*
HB-IXP	Avro RJ100	Swiss International *Chestenberg 647m*
HB-IXQ	Avro RJ100	Swiss International *Corno Gries 2969m*
HB-IXR	Avro RJ100	Swiss International *Hoho Winde 1204m*
HB-IXS	Avro RJ100	Swiss International *Mont Velan 3731m*
HB-IXT	Avro RJ100	Swiss International *Ottenberg 681m*
HB-IXU	Avro RJ100	Swiss International *Pfannenstiel 853m*
HB-IXV	Avro RJ100	Swiss International *Saxer First 2151m*
HB-IXW	Avro RJ100	Swiss International *Shafarnisch 2107m*
HB-IXX	Avro RJ100	Swiss International *Silberen 2319m*
HB-IYQ	Avro RJ100	Swiss International *Piz Buin 3312m*
HB-IYR	Avro RJ100	Swiss International *Vrenelisgärtli 2904m*
HB-IYS	Avro RJ100	Swiss International *Churfirsten 2306m*

HB/HL　　　　　　　　　　　　　　　　　　　　　　　　OVERSEAS AIRLINERS

Notes	Reg	Type	Owner or Operator
	HB-IYT	Avro RJ100	Swiss International *Bluemlisalp 3663m*
	HB-IYU	Avro RJ100	Swiss International *Rot Turm 2002m*
	HB-IYV	Avro RJ100	Swiss International *Pizzo Barone 2864m*
	HB-IYW	Avro RJ100	Swiss International *Spitzmeilen 2501m*
	HB-IYY	Avro RJ100	Swiss International *Titlis 3238m*
	HB-IYZ	Avro RJ100	Swiss International *Tour d'Ai 2331m*
	HB-IZG	SAAB 2000	Darwin Airline
	HB-IZH	SAAB 2000	Darwin Airline
	HB-IZJ	SAAB 2000	Darwin Airline
	HB-IZZ	SAAB 2000	Darwin Airline
	HB-JIA	McD Douglas MD-90-30	Hello
	HB-JIB	McD Douglas MD-90-30	Hello/BritishJet
	HB-JIC	McD Douglas MD-90-30	Hello/Iceland Express
	HB-JID	McD Douglas MD-90-30	Hello/Iceland Express
	HB-JIE	McD Douglas MD-90-30	Hello
	HB-JIF	McD Douglas MD-90-30	Hello/Iceland Express
	HB-JJA	Boeing 737-7AK	PrivatAir/KLM
	HB-JJG	Boeing 767-306ER	PrivatAir/KLM
	HB-JMA	Airbus A.340-313X	Swiss International *Matterhorn*
	HB-JMB	Airbus A.340-313X	Swiss International *Dufourspitze*
	HB-JMC	Airbus A.340-313X	Swiss International *Zumsteinspitze*
	HB-JMD	Airbus A.340-313X	Swiss International *Signalkuppe*
	HB-JME	Airbus A.340-313X	Swiss International *Dom*
	HB-JMF	Airbus A.340-313X	Swiss International *Liskamm*
	HB-JMG	Airbus A.340-313X	Swiss International *Weisshorn*
	HB-JMH	Airbus A.340-313X	Swiss International *Parrotspitze*
	HB-JMI	Airbus A.340-313X	Swiss International *Dent Blanche*
	HB-JVC	Fokker 100	Helvetic Airways
	HB-JVE	Fokker 100	Helvetic Airways
	HB-JVF	Fokker 100	Helvetic Airways
	HB-JVG	Fokker 100	Helvetic Airways
	HB-JZF	Airbus A.319-111	easyJet Switzerland
	HB-JZG	Airbus A.319-111	easyJet Switzerland
	HB-JZH	Airbus A.319-111	easyJet Switzerland
	HB-JZI	Airbus A.319-111	easyJet Switzerland
	HB-JZJ	Airbus A.319-111	easyJet Switzerland
	HB-JZK	Airbus A.319-111	easyJet Switzerland
	HB-JZL	Airbus A.319-111	easyJet Switzerland
	HB-JZM	Airbus A.319-111	easyJet Switzerland
	HB-JZN	Airbus A.319-111	easyJet Switzerland
	HB-JZO	Airbus A.319-111	easyJet Switzerland
	HB-JZP	Airbus A.319-111	easyJet Switzerland

HL (Korea)

Reg	Type	Owner or Operator
HL7400	Boeing 747-4B5F	Korean Air Cargo
HL7402	Boeing 747-4B5	Korean Air
HL7403	Boeing 747-4B5F	Korean Air Cargo
HL7404	Boeing 747-4B5	Korean Air
HL7412	Boeing 747-4B5	Korean Air
HL7413	Boeing 747-48E	Asiana Airlines
HL7414	Boeing 747-48E	Asiana Airlines
HL7415	Boeing 747-48E	Asiana Airlines
HL7417	Boeing 747-48E	Asiana Airlines
HL7418	Boeing 747-48E	Asiana Airlines
HL7419	Boeing 747-48EF (SCD)	Asiana Airlines
HL7420	Boeing 747-48EF (SCD)	Asiana Airlines
HL7421	Boeing 747-48E	Asiana Airlines
HL7423	Boeing 747-48E	Asiana Airlines
HL7426	Boeing 747-48EF (SCD)	Asiana Airlines
HL7428	Boeing 747-48E	Asiana Airlines
HL7434	Boeing 747-4B5F	Korean Air Cargo
HL7436	Boeing 747-48EF (SCD)	Asiana Airlines
HL7437	Boeing 747-4B5F	Korean Air Cargo
HL7438	Boeing 747-4B5ERF	Korean Air Cargo
HL7439	Boeing 747-4B5ERF	Korean Air Cargo
HL7448	Boeing 747-4B5F (SCD)	Korean Air Cargo
HL7449	Boeing 747-4B5F (SCD)	Korean Air Cargo
HL7460	Boeing 747-4B5	Korean Air
HL7461	Boeing 747-4B5	Korean Air
HL7462	Boeing 747-4B5F	Korean Air Cargo

OVERSEAS AIRLINERS

HL/HS

Reg	Type	Owner or Operator	Notes
HL7465	Boeing 747-4B5	Korean Air	
HL7466	Boeing 747-4B5F	Korean Air Cargo	
HL7467	Boeing 747-4B5F	Korean Air Cargo	
HL7472	Boeing 747-4B5	Korean Air	
HL7473	Boeing 747-4B5	Korean Air	
HL7480	Boeing 747-4B5 (SCD)	Korean Air	
HL7482	Boeing 747-4B5	Korean Air	
HL7483	Boeing 747-4B5	Korean Air	
HL7484	Boeing 747-4B5	Korean Air	
HL7485	Boeing 747-4B5	Korean Air	
HL7486	Boeing 747-4B5	Korean Air	
HL7487	Boeing 747-4B5	Korean Air	
HL7488	Boeing 747-4B5	Korean Air	
HL7489	Boeing 747-4B5	Korean Air	
HL7490	Boeing 747-4B5	Korean Air	
HL7491	Boeing 747-4B5	Korean Air	
HL7492	Boeing 747-4B5	Korean Air	
HL7493	Boeing 747-4B5	Korean Air	
HL7494	Boeing 747-4B5	Korean Air	
HL7495	Boeing 747-4B5	Korean Air	
HL7497	Boeing 747-4B5F	Korean Air Cargo	
HL7498	Boeing 747-4B5	Korean Air	
HL7499	Boeing 747-4B5ERF	Korean Air Cargo	
HL7500	Boeing 777-28EER	Asiana Airlines	
HL7526	Boeing 777-2B5ER	Korean Air	
HL7530	Boeing 777-2B5ER	Korean Air	
HL7531	Boeing 777-2B5ER	Korean Air	
HL7532	Boeing 777-3B5	Korean Air	
HL7533	Boeing 777-3B5	Korean Air	
HL7534	Boeing 777-3B5	Korean Air	
HL7573	Boeing 777-3B5	Korean Air	
HL7574	Boeing 777-2B5ER	Korean Air	
HL7575	Boeing 777-2B5ER	Korean Air	
HL7596	Boeing 777-28EER	Asiana Airlines	
HL7597	Boeing 777-28EER	Asiana Airlines	
HL7598	Boeing 777-2B5ER	Korean Air	
HL7600	Boeing 747-4B5ERF	Korean Air Cargo	
HL7601	Boeing 747-4B5ERF	Korean Air Cargo	
HL7602	Boeing 747-4B5ERF	Korean Air Cargo	
HL7603	Boeing 747-4B5ERF	Korean Air Cargo	
HL7604	Boeing 747-48EF (SCD)	Asiana Airlines	
HL7605	Boeing 747-4B5ERF	Korean Air Cargo	
HL7606	Boeing 747-4B5BCF	Korean Air Cargo	
HL7607	Boeing 747-4B5	Korean Air	
HL7700	Boeing 777-28EER	Asiana Airlines	
HL7714	Boeing 777-2B5ER	Korean Air	
HL7715	Boeing 777-2B5ER	Korean Air	
HL7721	Boeing 777-2B5ER	Korean Air	
HL7732	Boeing 777-28EER	Asiana Airlines	
HL7733	Boeing 777-2B5ER	Korean Air	
HL7734	Boeing 777-2B5ER	Korean Air	
HL7739	Boeing 777-28EER	Asiana Airlines	
HL7742	Boeing 777-28EER	Asiana Airlines	
HL7743	Boeing 777-2B5ER	Korean Air	

HS (Thailand)

Reg	Type	Owner or Operator
HS-TGA	Boeing 747-4D7	Thai Airways International *Srisuriyothai*
HS-TGB	Boeing 747-4D7	Thai Airways International *Si Satchanulai*
HS-TGD	Boeing 747-3D7	Thai Airways International *Suchada*
HS-TGE	Boeing 747-3D7	Thai Airways International *Chutamat*
HS-TGF	Boeing 747-4D7	Thai Airways International *Sri Ubon*
HS-TGG	Boeing 747-4D7	Thai Airways International *Pathoomawadi*
HS-TGH	Boeing 747-4D7	Thai Airways International *Chaiprakarn*
HS-TGJ	Boeing 747-4D7	Thai Airways International *Hariphunchai*
HS-TGK	Boeing 747-4D7	Thai Airways International *Alongkorn*
HS-TGL	Boeing 747-4D7	Thai Airways International *Theparat*
HS-TGM	Boeing 747-4D7	Thai Airways International *Chao Phraya*
HS-TGN	Boeing 747-4D7	Thai Airways International *Simongkhon*
HS-TGO	Boeing 747-4D7	Thai Airways International *Bowonrangsi*
HS-TGP	Boeing 747-4D7	Thai Airways International *Thepprasit*

HS/HZ/I
OVERSEAS AIRLINERS

Notes	Reg	Type	Owner or Operator
	HS-TGR	Boeing 747-4D7	Thai Airways International *Siriwatthana*
	HS-TGT	Boeing 747-4D7	Thai Airways International *Watthanothai*
	HS-TGW	Boeing 747-4D7	Thai Airways International *Visuthakasatriya*
	HS-TGX	Boeing 747-4D7	Thai Airways International *Sirisobhakya*
	HS-TGY	Boeing 747-4D7	Thai Airways International *Dararasmi*
	HS-TGZ	Boeing 747-4D7	Thai Airways International *Phimara*
	HS-TLA	Airbus A.340-541	Thai Airways International *Chiang Kham*
	HS-TLB	Airbus A.340-541	Thai Airways International *Uttaradit*
	HS-TLC	Airbus A.340-541	Thai Airways International *Phitsanulok*

HZ (Saudi Arabia)

Reg	Type	Owner or Operator
HZ-AIF	Boeing 747SP-68	Saudi Arabian Airlines
HZ-AIJ	Boeing 747SP-68	Saudi Royal Flight
HZ-AIU	Boeing 747-268F	Saudi Arabian Airlines
HZ-AIV	Boeing 747-468	Saudi Arabian Airlines
HZ-AIW	Boeing 747-468	Saudi Arabian Airlines
HZ-AIX	Boeing 747-468	Saudi Arabian Airlines
HZ-AIY	Boeing 747-468	Saudi Arabian Airlines
HZ-AKA	Boeing 777-268ER	Saudi Arabian Airlines
HZ-AKB	Boeing 777-268ER	Saudi Arabian Airlines
HZ-AKC	Boeing 777-268ER	Saudi Arabian Airlines
HZ-AKD	Boeing 777-268ER	Saudi Arabian Airlines
HZ-AKE	Boeing 777-268ER	Saudi Arabian Airlines
HZ-AKF	Boeing 777-268ER	Saudi Arabian Airlines
HZ-AKG	Boeing 777-268ER	Saudi Arabian Airlines
HZ-AKH	Boeing 777-268ER	Saudi Arabian Airlines
HZ-AKI	Boeing 777-268ER	Saudi Arabian Airlines
HZ-AKJ	Boeing 777-268ER	Saudi Arabian Airlines
HZ-AKK	Boeing 777-268ER	Saudi Arabian Airlines
HZ-AKL	Boeing 777-268ER	Saudi Arabian Airlines
HZ-AKM	Boeing 777-268ER	Saudi Arabian Airlines
HZ-AKN	Boeing 777-268ER	Saudi Arabian Airlines
HZ-AKO	Boeing 777-268ER	Saudi Arabian Airlines
HZ-AKP	Boeing 777-268ER	Saudi Arabian Airlines
HZ-AKQ	Boeing 777-268ER	Saudi Arabian Airlines
HZ-AKR	Boeing 777-268ER	Saudi Arabian Airlines
HZ-AKS	Boeing 777-268ER	Saudi Arabian Airlines
HZ-AKT	Boeing 777-268ER	Saudi Arabian Airlines
HZ-AKU	Boeing 777-268ER	Saudi Arabian Airlines
HZ-AKV	Boeing 777-268ER	Saudi Arabian Airlines
HZ-AKW	Boeing 777-268ER	Saudi Arabian Airlines
HZ-ANA	McD Douglas MD-11F	Saudi Arabian Airlines
HZ-ANB	McD Douglas MD-11F	Saudi Arabian Airlines
HZ-ANC	McD Douglas MD-11F	Saudi Arabian Airlines
HZ-AND	McD Douglas MD-11F	Saudi Arabian Airlines
HZ-HM1	Boeing 747-468	Saudi Arabian Airlines
HZ-HM1A	Boeing 747-3G1	Saudi Royal Flight
HZ-HM1B	Boeing 747SP-68	Saudi Royal Flight
HZ-HM5	L.1011-385 TriStar 500	Saudi Royal Flight
HZ-HM6	L.1011-385 TriStar 500	Saudi Royal Flight
HZ-HM7	McD Douglas MD-11	Saudi Royal Flight

I (Italy)

Reg	Type	Owner or Operator
I-AIGA	Boeing 757-230	Air Italy
I-AIGG	Boeing 767-204ER	Air Italy
I-BIKA	Airbus A.320-214	Alitalia *Johann Sebastian Bach*
I-BIKB	Airbus A.320-214	Alitalia *Wolfgang Amadeus Mozart*
I-BIKC	Airbus A.320-214	Alitalia *Zefiro*
I-BIKD	Airbus A.320-214	Alitalia *Maestrale*
I-BIKE	Airbus A.320-214	Alitalia *Franz Liszt*
I-BIKF	Airbus A.320-214	Alitalia *Grecale*
I-BIKG	Airbus A.320-214	Alitalia *Scirocco*
I-BIKI	Airbus A.320-214	Alitalia *Girolamo Frescobaldi*
I-BIKL	Airbus A.320-214	Alitalia *Libeccio*
I-BIKO	Airbus A.320-214	Alitalia *George Bizet*
I-BIKU	Airbus A.320-214	Alitalia *Frederyk Chopin*
I-BIMA	Airbus A.319-112	Alitalia *Isola d'Elba*

OVERSEAS AIRLINERS

Reg	Type	Owner or Operator	Notes
I-BIMB	Airbus A.319-112	Alitalia *Isola del Giglio*	
I-BIMC	Airbus A.319-112	Alitalia *Isola di Lipari*	
I-BIMD	Airbus A.319-112	Alitalia *Isola di Capri*	
I-BIME	Airbus A.319-112	Alitalia *Isola di Panarea*	
I-BIMF	Airbus A.319-112	Alitalia *Isola Tremiti*	
I-BIMG	Airbus A.319-112	Alitalia *Isola di Pantelleria*	
I-BIMH	Airbus A.319-112	Alitalia *Isola di Ventotene*	
I-BIMI	Airbus A.319-112	Alitalia *Isola di Ponza*	
I-BIMJ	Airbus A.319-112	Alitalia *Isola di Caprera*	
I-BIML	Airbus A.319-112	Alitalia *Isola La Maddalena*	
I-BIMO	Airbus A.319-112	Alitalia *Isola d'Ischia*	
I-BIXA	Airbus A.321-112	Alitalia *Piazza del Duomo Milano*	
I-BIXB	Airbus A.321-112	Alitalia *Piazza Castello Torino*	
I-BIXC	Airbus A.321-112	Alitalia *Piazza del Campo Siena*	
I-BIXD	Airbus A.321-112	Alitalia *Piazza Pretoria Palermo*	
I-BIXE	Airbus A.321-112	Alitalia *Piazza di Spagna Roma*	
I-BIXF	Airbus A.321-112	Alitalia *Piazza Maggiore Bologna*	
I-BIXG	Airbus A.321-112	Alitalia *Piazza dei Miracoli Pisa*	
I-BIXH	Airbus A.321-112	Alitalia *Piazza della Signoria*	
I-BIXI	Airbus A.321-112	Alitalia *Piazza San Marco-Venezia*	
I-BIXJ	Airbus A.321-112	Alitalia *Piazza del Municipio-Noto*	
I-BIXK	Airbus A.321-112	Alitalia *Piazza Ducale Vigevano*	
I-BIXL	Airbus A.321-112	Alitalia *Piazza del Duomo Lecce*	
I-BIXM	Airbus A.321-112	Alitalia *Piazza di San Franceso Assisi*	
I-BIXN	Airbus A.321-112	Alitalia *Piazza del Duomo Catania*	
I-BIXO	Airbus A.321-112	Alitalia *Piazza Plebiscito Napoli*	
I-BIXP	Airbus A.321-112	Alitalia *Carlo Morelli*	
I-BIXQ	Airbus A.321-112	Alitalia *Domenico Colapietro*	
I-BIXR	Airbus A.321-112	Alitalia *Piazza dell Campidoglio-Roma*	
I-BIXS	Airbus A.321-112	Alitalia *Piazza San Martino-Lucca*	
I-BIXT	Airbus A.321-112	Alitalia *Piazza dei Miracoli Pisa*	
I-BIXU	Airbus A.321-112	Alitalia *Piazza dell Signori Firenze*	
I-BIXV	Airbus A.321-112	Alitalia *Piazza dell Rinaccimento-Urbino*	
I-BIXZ	Airbus A.321-112	Alitalia *Piazza del Duomo Orvieto*	
I-CGIA	Douglas DC-10-30	Cargoitalia	
I-DACM	McD Douglas MD-82	Alitalia *La Spezia*	
I-DACN	McD Douglas MD-82	Alitalia *Rieti*	
I-DACP	McD Douglas MD-82	Alitalia *Padova*	
I-DACQ	McD Douglas MD-82	Alitalia *Taranto*	
I-DACR	McD Douglas MD-82	Alitalia *Carrara*	
I-DACS	McD Douglas MD-82	Alitalia *Maratea*	
I-DACT	McD Douglas MD-82	Alitalia *Valtellina*	
I-DACU	McD Douglas MD-82	Alitalia *Fabriano*	
I-DACV	McD Douglas MD-82	Alitalia *Riccione*	
I-DACW	McD Douglas MD-82	Alitalia *Vieste*	
I-DACX	McD Douglas MD-82	Alitalia *Piacenza*	
I-DACY	McD Douglas MD-82	Alitalia *Novara*	
I-DACZ	McD Douglas MD-82	Alitalia *Castelfidardo*	
I-DAND	McD Douglas MD-82	Alitalia *Bolzano*	
I-DANF	McD Douglas MD-82	Alitalia *Vicenza*	
I-DANG	McD Douglas MD-82	Alitalia *Benevento*	
I-DANH	McD Douglas MD-82	Alitalia *Messina*	
I-DANL	McD Douglas MD-82	Alitalia *Cosenza*	
I-DANM	McD Douglas MD-82	Alitalia *Vicenza*	
I-DANP	McD Douglas MD-82	Alitalia *Fabriano*	
I-DANQ	McD Douglas MD-82	Alitalia *Lecce*	
I-DANR	McD Douglas MD-82	Alitalia *Matera*	
I-DANU	McD Douglas MD-82	Alitalia *Trapani*	
I-DANV	McD Douglas MD-82	Alitalia *Forte dei Marmi*	
I-DANW	McD Douglas MD-82	Alitalia *Siena*	
I-DATA	McD Douglas MD-82	Alitalia *Gubbio*	
I-DATB	McD Douglas MD-82	Alitalia *Bergamo*	
I-DATC	McD Douglas MD-82	Alitalia *Foggia*	
I-DATD	McD Douglas MD-82	Alitalia *Savona*	
I-DATE	McD Douglas MD-82	Alitalia *Grosseto*	
I-DATF	McD Douglas MD-82	Alitalia *Vittorio Veneto*	
I-DATG	McD Douglas MD-82	Alitalia *Arezzo*	
I-DATH	McD Douglas MD-82	Alitalia *Pescara*	
I-DATI	McD Douglas MD-82	Alitalia *Siracusa*	
I-DATJ	McD Douglas MD-82	Alitalia *Lunigiana*	
I-DATK	McD Douglas MD-82	Alitalia *Ravenna*	
I-DATL	McD Douglas MD-82	Alitalia *Alghero*	
I-DATM	McD Douglas MD-82	Alitalia *Cividale del Friuli*	

OVERSEAS AIRLINERS

Notes	Reg	Type	Owner or Operator
	I-DATO	McD Douglas MD-82	Alitalia *Reggio Emilia*
	I-DATQ	McD Douglas MD-82	Alitalia *Modena*
	I-DATR	McD Douglas MD-82	Alitalia *Livorno*
	I-DATS	McD Douglas MD-82	Alitalia *Foligno*
	I-DATU	McD Douglas MD-82	Alitalia *Verona*
	I-DAVB	McD Douglas MD-82	Alitalia *Ferrara*
	I-DAVJ	McD Douglas MD-82	Alitalia *Parma*
	I-DAVM	McD Douglas MD-82	Alitalia *Caserta*
	I-DAVP	McD Douglas MD-82	Alitalia *Gorizia*
	I-DAVR	McD Douglas MD-82	Alitalia *Pisa*
	I-DAVS	McD Douglas MD-82	Alitalia *Catania*
	I-DAVT	McD Douglas MD-82	Alitalia *Como*
	I-DAVU	McD Douglas MD-82	Alitalia *Udine*
	I-DAVV	McD Douglas MD-82	Alitalia *Pavia*
	I-DAVW	McD Douglas MD-82	Alitalia *Camerino*
	I-DAVX	McD Douglas MD-82	Alitalia *Asti*
	I-DAVZ	McD Douglas MD-82	Alitalia *Brescia*
	I-DAWA	McD Douglas MD-82	Alitalia *Roma*
	I-DAWB	McD Douglas MD-82	Alitalia *Cagliari*
	I-DAWC	McD Douglas MD-82	Alitalia *Campobasso*
	I-DAWD	McD Douglas MD-82	Alitalia *Catanzaro*
	I-DAWE	McD Douglas MD-82	Alitalia *Milano*
	I-DAWF	McD Douglas MD-82	Alitalia *Firenze*
	I-DAWG	McD Douglas MD-82	Alitalia *L'Aquila*
	I-DAWH	McD Douglas MD-82	Alitalia *Palermo*
	I-DAWI	McD Douglas MD-82	Alitalia *Ancona*
	I-DAWJ	McD Douglas MD-82	Alitalia *Genova*
	I-DAWL	McD Douglas MD-82	Alitalia *Perugia*
	I-DAWM	McD Douglas MD-82	Alitalia *Potenza*
	I-DAWO	McD Douglas MD-82	Alitalia *Bari*
	I-DAWP	McD Douglas MD-82	Alitalia *Torino*
	I-DAWQ	McD Douglas MD-82	Alitalia *Trieste*
	I-DAWR	McD Douglas MD-82	Alitalia *Venezia*
	I-DAWS	McD Douglas MD-82	Alitalia *Aosta*
	I-DAWT	McD Douglas MD-82	Alitalia *Napoli*
	I-DAWU	McD Douglas MD-82	Alitalia *Bologna*
	I-DAWV	McD Douglas MD-82	Alitalia *Trento*
	I-DEIB	Boeing 767-33AER	Alitalia *Pier Paolo Racchetti*
	I-DEIC	Boeing 767-33AER	Alitalia *Alberto Nassetti*
	I-DEID	Boeing 767-33AER	Alitalia *Marco Polo*
	I-DEIF	Boeing 767-33AER	Alitalia *Cristoforo Colombo*
	I-DEIG	Boeing 767-33AER	Alitalia *Francesco Agello*
	I-DEIL	Boeing 767-33AER	Alitalia *Arturo Ferrarin*
	I-DISA	Boeing 777-243ER	Alitalia *Taromina*
	I-DISB	Boeing 777-243ER	Alitalia *Portor Rotondo*
	I-DISD	Boeing 777-243ER	Alitalia *Cortina d'Ampezzo*
	I-DISE	Boeing 777-243ER	Alitalia *Portofino*
	I-DISO	Boeing 777-243ER	Alitalia *Positano*
	I-DISU	Boeing 777-243ER	Alitalia *Madonna di Campiglio*
	I-ECJA	Airbus A.319-115LR	Eurofly
	I-EEZA	Airbus A.330-223	Eurofly
	I-EEZB	Airbus A.330-223	Eurofly
	I-EEZC	Airbus A.320-214	Eurofly
	I-EEZD	Airbus A.320-214	Eurofly
	I-EEZE	Airbus A.320-214	Eurofly
	I-EEZF	Airbus A.320-214	Eurofly
	I-EEZG	Airbus A.320-214	Eurofly
	I-EEZH	Airbus A.320-214	Eurofly
	I-EEZI	Airbus A.320-214	Eurofly
	I-EEZJ	Airbus A.330-223	Eurofly
	I-EEZK	Airbus A.320-214	Eurofly
	I-EEZL	Airbus A.330-223	Eurofly
	I-EXMA	Embraer RJ145LR	Alitalia Express *Giosue Carducci*
	I-EXMB	Embraer RJ145LR	Alitalia Express *Salvatori Quasidomo*
	I-EXMC	Embraer RJ145LR	Alitalia Express *Emilio Gino Segre*
	I-EXMD	Embraer RJ145LR	Alitalia Express *Eugenio Montale*
	I-EXME	Embraer RJ145LR	Alitalia Express *Guglielmo Marconi*
	I-EXMF	Embraer RJ145LR	Alitalia Express *Guilio Nattai*
	I-EXMG	Embraer RJ145LR	Alitalia Express *Daniel Bovetea*
	I-EXMH	Embraer RJ145LR	Alitalia Express *Camillo Golgi*
	I-EXMI	Embraer RJ145LR	Alitalia Express *Grazia Deledda*
	I-EXML	Embraer RJ145LR	Alitalia Express *Ernesto Teodoro Moneta*
	I-EXMM	Embraer RJ145LR	Alitalia Express *Anna Magnani*

OVERSEAS AIRLINERS

I/JA

Reg	Type	Owner or Operator	Notes
I-EXMN	Embraer RJ145LR	Alitalia Express *Vittorio de Sica*	
I-EXMO	Embraer RJ145LR	Alitalia Express *Luigi Pirandello*	
I-EXMU	Embraer RJ145LR	Alitalia Express *Enrico Fermi*	
I-LIVA	Airbus A.321-231	Livingston *Capt Aldo Giannelli*	
I-LIVB	Airbus A.321-231	Livingston *Jacaranda*	
I-LIVD	Airbus A.321-231	Livingston *Boavista*	
I-LIVL	Airbus A.330-243	Livingston *Andilana*	
I-LIVM	Airbus A.330-243	Livingston *Playa Maroma*	
I-LIVN	Airbus A.330-243	Livingston *Gran Dominicus*	
I-LLAG	Boeing 767-330ER	Blue Panorama	
I-MSAA	BAe 146-200QT	Mistral Air/TNT Airways	
I-NEOS	Boeing 737-86N	Neos	
I-NEOT	Boeing 737-86N	Neos	
I-NEOU	Boeing 737-86N	Neos	
I-NEOX	Boeing 737-86N	Neos	
I-OCEA	Boeing 747-230F (SCD)	Ocean Airlines	
I-OCEU	Boeing 747-230F (SCD)	Ocean Airlines	
I-SIXA	F.27 Friendship Mk 500RF	SixCargo	
I-SMEB	McD Douglas MD-82	Meridiana	
I-SMEC	McD Douglas MD-83	Meridiana	
I-SMED	McD Douglas MD-83	Meridiana	
I-SMEL	McD Douglas MD-82	Meridiana	
I-SMEM	McD Douglas MD-82	Meridiana	
I-SMEP	McD Douglas MD-82	Meridiana	
I-SMER	McD Douglas MD-82	Meridiana	
I-SMES	McD Douglas MD-82	Meridiana	
I-SMET	McD Douglas MD-82	Meridiana	
I-SMEV	McD Douglas MD-82	Meridiana	
I-SMEZ	McD Douglas MD-83	Meridiana	
I-TNTC	BAe 146-200QT	Mistral Air/TNT Airways	
I-VIMQ	Boeing 767-352ER	Air Europe *Citta di Gallarate*	

Note: Meridiana also operates A.319s EI-DEY, EI-DEZ, EI-DFA and EI-DFP; plus MD-83s EI-CIW, EI-CKM, EI-CRE, EI-CRH, EI-CRJ and EI-CRW.
Alitalia operates B.767s EI-CRD, EI-CRF, EI-CRL, EI-CRM, EI-CRO, EI-DBP and EI-DDW; MD-11Fs EI-UPA, EI-UPE, EI-UPI, EI-UPO and EI-UPU plus B.777s EI-DBK, EI-DBL, EI-DBM and EI-DDH.
Alitalia Express operates ERJ-170s EI-DFG, EI-DFH, EI-DFI, EI-DFJ, EI-DFK and EI-DFL.
Blue Panorama operates B.737s EI-CUA, EI-CUD, EI-CUN and EI-DGN; B.757s EI-DKL and EI-DNA; plus B.767s EI-CXO and EI-CZH.
Neos operates B.767s EI-DMJ and EI-DOF. Air Italy operates B.757s EI-IGA, EI-IGB and EI-IGC.

JA (Japan)

JA01KZ	Boeing 747-481F	Nippon Cargo Airlines	
JA02KZ	Boeing 747-481F	Nippon Cargo Airlines	
JA03KZ	Boeing 747-4KZF	Nippon Cargo Airlines	
JA04KZ	Boeing 747-4KZF	Nippon Cargo Airlines	
JA401J	Boeing 747-446F	Japan Airlines	
JA402J	Boeing 747-446F	Japan Airlines	
JA403A	Boeing 747-481	All Nippon Airways	
JA404A	Boeing 747-481	All Nippon Airways	
JA405A	Boeing 747-481	All Nippon Airways	
JA704J	Boeing 777-246ER	Japan Airlines	
JA705J	Boeing 777-246ER	Japan Airlines	
JA706J	Boeing 777-246ER	Japan Airlines	
JA707J	Boeing 777-246ER	Japan Airlines	
JA708J	Boeing 777-246ER	Japan Airlines	
JA709J	Boeing 777-246ER	Japan Airlines	
JA710J	Boeing 777-246ER	Japan Airlines	
JA711J	Boeing 777-246ER	Japan Airlines	
JA731A	Boeing 777-381ER	All Nippon Airways	
JA731J	Boeing 777-346ER	Japan Airlines	
JA732A	Boeing 777-381ER	All Nippon Airways	
JA732J	Boeing 777-346ER	Japan Airlines	
JA733A	Boeing 777-381ER	All Nippon Airways	
JA733J	Boeing 777-346ER	Japan Airlines	
JA734A	Boeing 777-381ER	All Nippon Airways	
JA734J	Boeing 777-346ER	Japan Airlines	
JA735A	Boeing 777-381ER	All Nippon Airways	
JA735J	Boeing 777-346ER	Japan Airlines	
JA736A	Boeing 777-381ER	All Nippon Airways	

JA/JY

OVERSEAS AIRLINERS

Notes	Reg	Type	Owner or Operator
	JA736J	Boeing 777-346ER	Japan Airlines
	JA777A	Boeing 777-381ER	All Nippon Airways
	JA778A	Boeing 777-381ER	All Nippon Airways
	JA811J	Boeing 747-246F	Japan Airlines
	JA8071	Boeing 747-446	Japan Airlines
	JA8072	Boeing 747-446	Japan Airlines
	JA8073	Boeing 747-446	Japan Airlines
	JA8074	Boeing 747-446	Japan Airlines
	JA8075	Boeing 747-446	Japan Airlines
	JA8076	Boeing 747-446	Japan Airlines
	JA8077	Boeing 747-446	Japan Airlines
	JA8078	Boeing 747-446	Japan Airlines
	JA8079	Boeing 747-446	Japan Airlines
	JA8080	Boeing 747-446	Japan Airlines
	JA8081	Boeing 747-446	Japan Airlines
	JA8082	Boeing 747-446	Japan Airlines
	JA8085	Boeing 747-446	Japan Airlines
	JA8086	Boeing 747-446	Japan Airlines
	JA8087	Boeing 747-446	Japan Airlines
	JA8088	Boeing 747-446	Japan Airlines
	JA8089	Boeing 747-446	Japan Airlines
	JA8094	Boeing 747-481	All Nippon Airways
	JA8095	Boeing 747-481	All Nippon Airways
	JA8096	Boeing 747-481	All Nippon Airways
	JA8097	Boeing 747-481	All Nippon Airways
	JA8098	Boeing 747-481	All Nippon Airways
	JA8160	Boeing 747-221F (SCD)	Japan Airlines
	JA8161	Boeing 747-246B (SF)	Japan Airlines
	JA8165	Boeing 747-221F (SCD)	Japan Airlines
	JA8167	Boeing 747-281F (SCD)	Nippon Cargo Airlines
	JA8169	Boeing 747-246B (SF)	Japan Airlines
	JA8171	Boeing 747-246F (SCD)	Japan Airlines
	JA8172	Boeing 747-281F (SCD)	Nippon Cargo Airlines
	JA8180	Boeing 747-246F (SCD)	Japan Airlines
	JA8181	Boeing 747-281B (SF)	Nippon Cargo Airlines
	JA8182	Boeing 747-281B (SF)	Nippon Cargo Airlines
	JA8188	Boeing 747-281F (SCD)	Nippon Cargo Airlines
	JA8190	Boeing 747-281B (SF)	Nippon Cargo Airlines
	JA8191	Boeing 747-281F (SCD)	Nippon Cargo Airlines
	JA8192	Boeing 747-2D3F (SCD)	Nippon Cargo Airlines
	JA8193	Boeing 747-212F (SCD)	Japan Airlines
	JA8194	Boeing 747-281F (SCD)	Nippon Cargo Airlines
	JA8901	Boeing 747-446	Japan Airlines
	JA8902	Boeing 747-446BCF	Japan Airlines
	JA8906	Boeing 747-446BCF	Japan Airlines
	JA8909	Boeing 747-446BCF	Japan Airlines
	JA8910	Boeing 747-446	Japan Airlines
	JA8911	Boeing 747-446	Japan Airlines
	JA8912	Boeing 747-446	Japan Airlines
	JA8913	Boeing 747-446	Japan Airlines
	JA8914	Boeing 747-446	Japan Airlines
	JA8915	Boeing 747-446	Japan Airlines
	JA8916	Boeing 747-446	Japan Airlines
	JA8917	Boeing 747-446	Japan Airlines
	JA8918	Boeing 747-446	Japan Airlines
	JA8919	Boeing 747-446	Japan Airlines
	JA8920	Boeing 747-446	Japan Airlines
	JA8921	Boeing 747-446	Japan Airlines
	JA8922	Boeing 747-446	Japan Airlines
	JA8937	Boeing 747-246F	Japan Airlines
	JA8958	Boeing 747-481	All Nippon Airways
	JA8962	Boeing 747-481	All Nippon Airways

JY (Jordan)

Notes	Reg	Type	Owner or Operator
	JY-ABH	Airbus A.340-211	Kingdom of Jordan
	JY-AGM	Airbus A.310-304	Royal Jordanian *Prince Hamzeh*
	JY-AGN	Airbus A.310-304	Royal Jordanian *Princess Haya*
	JY-AGP	Airbus A.310-304	Royal Jordanian
	JY-AGV	Airbus A.310-203	Libyan Arab Airlines
	JY-AIA	Airbus A.340-211	Royal Jordanian *Hussein Bin Abdullah*

OVERSEAS AIRLINERS

JY/LN

Reg	Type	Owner or Operator	Notes
JY-AIB	Airbus A.340-211	Royal Jordanian *Princess Iman Bint Abdullah*	
JY-AYD	Airbus A.320-232	Royal Jordanian *Amman*	
JY-AYF	Airbus A.320-232	Royal Jordanian *Aqaba*	
JY-AYG	Airbus A.320-232	Royal Jordanian *As-Salt*	
JY-AYH	Airbus A.320-232	Royal Jordanian	
JY-JAH	Airbus A.310-304	Jordan Aviation	
JY-JAV	Airbus A.310-222	Jordan Aviation	

Note: Royal Jordanian also operates A.310s registered F-ODVF and F-ODVG, A.320s F-OHGV and F-OHGX, A.321s F-GTAF and F-OHGU and A.340s F-OHLP and F-OHLQ.

LN (Norway)

Reg	Type	Owner or Operator
LN-BRD	Boeing 737-505	SAS-Braathens *Harald Gille*
LN-BRE	Boeing 737-405	SAS-Braathens *Haakon V Magnusson*
LN-BRH	Boeing 737-505	SAS-Braathens *Haakon den Gode*
LN-BRI	Boeing 737-405	SAS-Braathens *Harald Haarfagre*
LN-BRK	Boeing 737-505	SAS-Braathens *Olav Tryggvason*
LN-BRM	Boeing 737-505	SAS-Braathens *Olav den Hellige*
LN-BRO	Boeing 737-505	SAS-Braathens *Magnus Haraldsson*
LN-BRQ	Boeing 737-405	SAS-Braathens *Harald Graafell*
LN-BRR	Boeing 737-505	SAS-Braathens *Halvdan Svarte*
LN-BRS	Boeing 737-505	SAS-Braathens *Olav Kyrre*
LN-BRV	Boeing 737-505	SAS-Braathens *Haakon Sverresson*
LN-BRX	Boeing 737-505	SAS-Braathens *Sigurd Munn*
LN-BUC	Boeing 737-505	SAS-Braathens *Magnus Erlingsson*
LN-BUD	Boeing 737-505	SAS-Braathens *Inge Krokrygg*
LN-BUE	Boeing 737-505	SAS-Braathens *Erling Skjalgsson*
LN-BUF	Boeing 737-405	SAS-Braathens *Magnus den Gode*
LN-BUG	Boeing 737-505	SAS-Braathens *Oystein Haraldsson*
LN-FAC	BAe Jetstream 3200	Coast Air *Skien*
LN-FAJ	BAe Jetstream 3100	Coast Air *Bokn*
LN-FAM	BAe Jetstream 3100	Coast Air *Feöy*
LN-FAN	BAe Jetstream 3200	Coast Air *Utsira*
LN-FAO	Aerospatiale ATR-42-300	Coast Air *Karmöy*
LN-FAP	Aerospatiale ATR-42-300	Coast Air *Florö*
LN-FAR	Aerospatiale ATR-42-300	Coast Air
LN-FAQ	BAe Jetstream 3200	Coast Air
LN-FAV	BAe Jetstream 3100	Coast Air *Bomlo*
LN-FAZ	BAe Jetstream 3100	Coast Air *Rovaer*
LN-KKA	Boeing 737-33A	Norwegian Air Shuttle
LN-KKB	Boeing 737-33A	Norwegian Air Shuttle
LN-KKC	Boeing 737-3Y5	Norwegian Air Shuttle
LN-KKF	Boeing 737-3K2	Norwegian Air Shuttle *Fridtjof Nansen*
LN-KKG	Boeing 737-3K2	Norwegian Air Shuttle *Gidsken Jakobse*
LN-KKH	Boeing 737-3K2	Norwegian Air Shuttle *Otto Sverdrup*
LN-KKI	Boeing 737-3K2	Norwegian Air Shuttle *Helge Ingstad*
LN-KKJ	Boeing 737-36N	Norwegian Air Shuttle *Sonja Henie*
LN-KKL	Boeing 737-36N	Norwegian Air Shuttle *Roald Amundsen*
LN-KKM	Boeing 737-3Y0	Norwegian Air Shuttle *Thor Heyerdahl*
LN-KKN	Boeing 737-3Y0	Norwegian Air Shuttle *Sigrid Undset*
LN-KKO	Boeing 737-3Y0	Norwegian Air Shuttle *Henrik Ibsen*
LN-KKP	Boeing 737-3MQ	Norwegian Air Shuttle *Kirsten Flagstad*
LN-KKQ	Boeing 737-36Q	Norwegian Air Shuttle *Alf Proysen*
LN-KKR	Boeing 737-3Y0	Norwegian Air Shuttle
LN-KKS	Boeing 737-33A	Norwegian Air Shuttle *Eduard Munch*
LN-KKT	Boeing 737-3L9	Norwegian Air Shuttle
LN-KKU	Boeing 737-3L9	Norwegian Air Shuttle
LN-KKV	Boeing 737-3Y5	Norwegian Air Shuttle *Niels Henrik Abel*
LN-KKW	Boeing 737-3K9	Norwegian Air Shuttle
LN-KKX	Boeing 737-33S	Norwegian Air Shuttle
LN-KKY	Boeing 737-33S	Norwegian Air Shuttle
LN-KKZ	Boeing 737-33A	Norwegian Air Shuttle *Silver*
LN-RCN	Boeing 737-883	SAS-Braathens *Hedrun Viking*
LN-RCT	Boeing 737-683	SAS-Braathens *Fridlev Viking*
LN-RCU	Boeing 737-683	SAS *Sigfrid Viking*
LN-RCW	Boeing 737-683	SAS-Braathens *Yngvar Viking*
LN-RCX	Boeing 737-883	SAS-Braathens *Hottur Viking*
LN-RCY	Boeing 737-883	SAS-Braathens *Eylime Viking*
LN-RCZ	Boeing 737-883	SAS-Braathens *Glitne Viking*
LN-RDA	DHC.8Q-402 Dash Eight	SAS Commuter *Frej Viking*

LN OVERSEAS AIRLINERS

Notes	Reg	Type	Owner or Operator
	LN-RDB	DHC.8Q-402 Dash Eight	SAS Commuter *Kari Viking*
	LN-RDC	DHC.8Q-402 Dash Eight	SAS Commuter *Hader Viking*
	LN-RDD	DHC.8Q-402 Dash Eight	SAS Commuter *Loge Viking*
	LN-RDE	DHC.8Q-402 Dash Eight	SAS Commuter *Dore Viking*
	LN-RDF	DHC.8Q-402 Dash Eight	SAS Commuter *Fenja Viking*
	LN-RDG	DHC.8Q-402 Dash Eight	SAS Commuter *Greip Viking*
	LN-RDH	DHC.8Q-402 Dash Eight	SAS Commuter *Gloe Viking*
	LN-RDI	DHC.8Q-402 Dash Eight	SAS Commuter *Asta Viking*
	LN-RDJ	DHC.8Q-402 Dash Eight	SAS Commuter *Toke Viking*
	LN-RDK	DHC.8Q-402 Dash Eight	SAS Commuter *Ingrid Viking*
	LN-RDL	DHC.8Q-402 Dash Eight	SAS Commuter *Ulv Viking*
	LN-RDM	DHC.8Q-402 Dash Eight	SAS Commuter *Banke Viking*
	LN-RDN	DHC.8Q-402 Dash Eight	SAS Commuter *Gnupa Viking*
	LN-RDO	DHC.8Q-402 Dash Eight	SAS Commuter *Frid Viking*
	LN-RDP	DHC.8Q-402 Dash Eight	SAS Commuter *Huge Viking*
	LN-RDQ	DHC.8Q-402 Dash Eight	SAS Commuter *Herta Viking*
	LN-RDR	DHC.8Q-402 Dash Eight	SAS Commuter *Terje Viking*
	LN-RDS	DHC.8Q-402 Dash Eight	SAS Commuter *Gote Viking*
	LN-RDT	DHC.8Q-402 Dash Eight	SAS Commuter *Kile Viking*
	LN-RKF	Airbus A.340-313X	SAS *Godfred Viking*
	LN-RKG	Airbus A.340-313X	SAS *Gudrod Viking*
	LN-RKH	Airbus A.330-343X	SAS *Emund Viking*
	LN-RKI	Airbus A.321-231	SAS *Gunnhild Viking*
	LN-RKK	Airbus A.321-231	SAS *Viger Viking*
	LN-RLE	McD Douglas MD-82	SAS *Ketiil Viking*
	LN-RLF	McD Douglas MD-82	SAS *Finn Viking*
	LN-RLG	McD Douglas MD-82	SAS *Trond Viking*
	LN-RLR	McD Douglas MD-82	SAS *Vegard Viking*
	LN-RMG	McD Douglas MD-87	SAS *Snorre Viking*
	LN-RML	McD Douglas MD-82	SAS *Aud Viking*
	LN-RMM	McD Douglas MD-82	SAS *Blenda Viking*
	LN-RMO	McD Douglas MD-82	SAS *Bergljot Viking*
	LN-RMP	McD Douglas MD-87	SAS *Reidun Viking*
	LN-RMR	McD Douglas MD-81	SAS *Olav Viking*
	LN-RMS	McD Douglas MD-81	SAS *Nial Viking*
	LN-RMT	McD Douglas MD-81	SAS *Jarl Viking*
	LN-RMU	McD Douglas MD-87	SAS *Grim Viking*
	LN-RNN	Boeing 737-783	SAS-Braathens *Borgny Viking*
	LN-RNO	Boeing 737-783	SAS-Braathens *Gjuke Viking*
	LN-ROM	McD Douglas MD-81	SAS *Albin Viking*
	LN-RON	McD Douglas MD-81	SAS *Holmfrid Viking*
	LN-ROO	McD Douglas MD-81	SAS *Kristin Viking*
	LN-ROP	McD Douglas MD-82	SAS *Bjoern Viking*
	LN-ROR	McD Douglas MD-82	SAS *Assur Viking*
	LN-ROS	McD Douglas MD-82	SAS *Isulv Viking*
	LN-ROT	McD Douglas MD-82	SAS *Ingjaid Viking*
	LN-ROU	McD Douglas MD-82	SAS *Ring Viking*
	LN-ROW	McD Douglas MD-82	SAS *Ottar Viking*
	LN-ROX	McD Douglas MD-82	SAS *Ulvrik Viking*
	LN-ROY	McD Douglas MD-82	SAS *Spjute Viking*
	LN-ROZ	McD Douglas MD-87	SAS *Slagfinn Viking*
	LN-RPA	Boeing 737-683	SAS *Arnljot Viking*
	LN-RPB	Boeing 737-683	SAS *Bure Viking*
	LN-RPE	Boeing 737-683	SAS-Braathens
	LN-RPF	Boeing 737-683	SAS-Braathens *Frede Viking*
	LN-RPG	Boeing 737-683	SAS-Braathens *Geirmund Viking*
	LN-RPH	Boeing 737-683	SAS-Braathens *Hamder Viking*
	LN-RPJ	Boeing 737-783	SAS-Braathens *Grimhild Viking*
	LN-RPK	Boeing 737-683	SAS-Braathens *Heimer Viking*
	LN-RPL	Boeing 737-883	SAS-Braathens *Svanevit Viking*
	LN-RPM	Boeing 737-883	SAS-Braathens *Frigg Viking*
	LN-RPN	Boeing 737-883	SAS *Bergfora Viking*
	LN-RPS	Boeing 737-683	SAS *Gautrek Viking*
	LN-RPT	Boeing 737-683	SAS *Ellida Viking*
	LN-RPU	Boeing 737-683	SAS-Braathens *Ragna Viking*
	LN-RPW	Boeing 737-683	SAS *Alvid Viking*
	LN-RPX	Boeing 737-683	SAS-Braathens *Nanna Viking*
	LN-RPY	Boeing 737-683	SAS *Olof Viking*
	LN-RPZ	Boeing 737-683	SAS-Braathens *Bera Viking*
	LN-RRK	Boeing 737-883	SAS *Gerud Viking*
	LN-RRL	Boeing 737-883	SAS-Braathens *Jarlabanke Viking*
	LN-RRM	Boeing 737-783	SAS-Braathens *Erland Viking*
	LN-RRN	Boeing 737-783	SAS-Braathens *Solveig Viking*

OVERSEAS AIRLINERS

LN/LV/LX

Reg	Type	Owner or Operator	Notes
LN-RRO	Boeing 737-683	SAS *Bernt Viking*	
LN-RRP	Boeing 737-683	SAS *Vilborg Viking*	
LN-RRR	Boeing 737-683	SAS *Torbjorn Viking*	
LN-RRS	Boeing 737-883	SAS *Ymir Viking*	
LN-RRT	Boeing 737-883	SAS-Braathens *Lodyn Viking*	
LN-RRU	Boeing 737-883	SAS-Braathens *Vingolf Viking*	
LN-RRW	Boeing 737-883	SAS *Saga Viking*	
LN-RRX	Boeing 737-683	SAS *Ragnfast Viking*	
LN-RRY	Boeing 737-683	SAS *Signe Viking*	
LN-RRZ	Boeing 737-683	SAS *Gisla Viking*	
LN-SVZ	BAe Jetstream 3102	Sun-Air	
LN-TUA	Boeing 737-705	SAS-Braathens *Ingeborg Eriksdatter*	
LN-TUD	Boeing 737-705	SAS-Braathens *Margrete Skulesdatter*	
LN-TUF	Boeing 737-705	SAS-Braathens *Tyra Haraldsdatter*	
LN-TUH	Boeing 737-705	SAS-Braathens *Margrete Ingesdatter*	
LN-TUI	Boeing 737-705	SAS-Braathens *Kristin Knudsdatter*	
LN-TUJ	Boeing 737-705	SAS-Braathens *Eirik Blodoks*	
LN-TUK	Boeing 737-705	SAS-Braathens *Inge Bardsson*	
LN-TUL	Boeing 737-705	SAS-Braathens *Haakon IV Haakonson*	
LN-TUM	Boeing 737-705	SAS-Braathens *Oystein Magnusson*	
LN-VIP	BAe Jetstream 3200	Coast Air	
LN-WDA	DHC.8Q-402 Dash Eight	Wideroe's Flyveselskap	
LN-WDB	DHC.8Q-402 Dash Eight	Wideroe's Flyveselskap *Stavanger*	
LN-WDC	DHC.8Q-402 Dash Eight	Wideroe's Flyveselskap *Trondheim*	
LN-WDD	DHC.8Q-402 Dash Eight	Wideroe's Flyveselskap	
LN-WFA	DHC.8-311 Dash Eight	Wideroe's Flyveselskap	
LN-WFB	DHC.8-311 Dash Eight	Wideroe's Flyveselskap	
LN-WFC	DHC.8-311 Dash Eight	Wideroe's Flyveselskap	
LN-WFE	DHC.8Q-311 Dash Eight	Wideroe's Flyveselskap *Sandefjord*	
LN-WFH	DHC.8-311 Dash Eight	Wideroe's Flyveselskap	
LN-WFO	DHC.8Q-311 Dash Eight	Wideroe's Flyveselskap	
LN-WFP	DHC.8Q-311 Dash Eight	Wideroe's Flyveselskap	
LN-WFS	DHC.8Q-311 Dash Eight	Wideroe's Flyveselskap	
LN-WFT	DHC.8Q-311 Dash Eight	Wideroe's Flyveselskap	

LV (Argentina)

LV-BBN	Boeing 737-5H6	Aerolineas Argentinas	

Note: Aerolineas Argentinas serves London-Gatwick with a connecting service from Madrid, operated by the above or an Air Plus Comet B.737 or MD-88.

LX (Luxembourg)

Reg	Type	Owner or Operator	Notes
LX-FCV	Boeing 747-4R7F (SCD)	Cargolux *City of Luxembourg*	
LX-GCV	Boeing 747-4R7F (SCD)	Cargolux *City of Esch/Alzette*	
LX-ICV	Boeing 747-428F (SCD)	Cargolux *City of Ettelbruck*	
LX-KCV	Boeing 747-4R7F (SCD)	Cargolux *City of Dudelange*	
LX-LCV	Boeing 747-4R7F (SCD)	Cargolux *City of Grevenmacher*	
LX-LGI	Embraer RJ145LU	Luxair	
LX-LGJ	Embraer RJ145LU	Luxair	
LX-LGK	Embraer RJ135LR	Luxair	
LX-LGL	Embraer RJ135LR	Luxair	
LX-LGP	Boeing 737-5C9	Luxair *Chateau de Bourglinster*	
LX-LGQ	Boeing 737-7C9	Luxair *Chateau de Burg*	
LX-LGR	Boeing 737-7C9	Luxair *Chateau de Fischbach*	
LX-LGS	Boeing 737-7C9	Luxair *Chateau de Senningen*	
LX-LGU	Embraer RJ145EP	Luxair *Prince Sebastian*	
LX-LGV	Embraer RJ145LU	Luxair	
LX-LGW	Embraer RJ145LU	Luxair	
LX-LGX	Embraer RJ145LU	Luxair	
LX-LGY	Embraer RJ145LU	Luxair	
LX-LGZ	Embraer RJ145LU	Luxair	
LX-MCV	Boeing 747-4R7F (SCD)	Cargolux *City of Echternach*	
LX-NCV	Boeing 747-4R7F (SCD)	Cargolux *City of Vianden*	
LX-OCV	Boeing 747-4R7F (SCD)	Cargolux *City of Differdange*	
LX-PCV	Boeing 747-4R7F (SCD)	Cargolux *City of Diekirch*	
LX-RCV	Boeing 747-4R7F (SCD)	Cargolux *City of Schengen*	
LX-SCV	Boeing 747-4R7F (SCD)	Cargolux *City of Niederanven*	

LX/LY/LZ/N

OVERSEAS AIRLINERS

Notes	Reg	Type	Owner or Operator
	LX-TCV	Boeing 747-4R7F (SCD)	Cargolux *City of Sandweiler*
	LX-UCV	Boeing 747-4R7F (SCD)	Cargolux *City of Bertragne*
	LX-VCV	Boeing 747-4R7F (SCD)	Cargolux *City of Walferdange*

Note: Cargolux also operates B.747s TF-AMI and TF-AMO.

LY (Lithuania)

LY-AGQ	Boeing 737-524	Lithuanian Airlines
LY-AGZ	Boeing 737-524	Lithuanian Airlines
LY-APK	Antonov An-26B	Aviavilsa
LY-APN	Antonov An-26B	Aviavilsa
LY-AZW	Boeing 737-5Q8	Lithuanian Airlines
LY-AZX	Boeing 737-5Q8	Lithuanian Airlines
LY-AZY	Boeing 737-548	Lithuanian Airlines

LZ (Bulgaria)

LZ-BHB	Airbus A.320-212	Balkan Holidays
LZ-BHC	Airbus A.320-212	Balkan Holidays
LZ-BHD	Airbus A.320-212	Balkan Holidays
LZ-BHE	Airbus A.320-211	Balkan Holidays
LZ-BOI	Boeing 737-530	Bulgaria Air
LZ-BOJ	Boeing 737-3L9	Bulgaria Air
LZ-BOM	Boeing 737-31S	Bulgaria Air
LZ-BON	Boeing 737-31S	Bulgaria Air
LZ-BOO	Boeing 737-341	Bulgaria Air
LZ-BOP	Boeing 737-522	Bulgaria Air
LZ-BOQ	Boeing 737-522	Bulgaria Air
LZ-BOR	Boeing 737-548	Bulgaria Air
LZ-BOT	Boeing 737-322	Bulgaria Air
LZ-BOU	Boeing 737-3L9	Bulgaria Air
LZ-BOV	Boeing 737-330	Bulgaria Air
LZ-BOW	Boeing 737-330	Bulgaria Air
LZ-HBA	BAe 146-200	Hemus Air
LZ-HBB	BAe 146-200	Hemus Air
LZ-HBD	BAe 146-300	Hemus Air
LZ-HBE	BAe 146-300	Hemus Air
LZ-HBF	BAe 146-300	Hemus Air
LZ-HBG	BAe 146-300	Hemus Air
LZ-HMI	Tupolev Tu-154M	Balkan Holidays
LZ-HMQ	Tupolev Tu-154M	Balkan Holidays
LZ-HMW	Tupolev Tu-154M	Balkan Holidays
LZ-HVA	Boeing 737-4Y0	Hemus Air
LZ-HVB	Boeing 737-3S1	Hemus Air
LZ-LDA	McD Douglas MD-83	Bulgarian Air Charter
LZ-LDC	McD Douglas MD-82	Bulgarian Air Charter
LZ-LDD	McD Douglas MD-82	Bulgarian Air Charter
LZ-LDF	McD Douglas MD-82	Bulgarian Air Charter
LZ-LDG	McD Douglas MD-83	Bulgarian Air Charter
LZ-LDK	McD Douglas MD-82	Bulgarian Air Charter/Albanian Airlines
LZ-LDL	McD Douglas MD-82	Bulgarian Air Charter
LZ-LDR	McD Douglas MD-82	Bulgarian Air Charter
LZ-LDV	McD Douglas MD-83	Bulgarian Air Charter
LZ-LDX	McD Douglas MD-83	Bulgarian Air Charter
LZ-LDY	McD Douglas MD-82	Bulgarian Air Charter
LZ-LDZ	McD Douglas MD-83	Bulgarian Air Charter
LZ-WZA	Airbus A.320-233	Wizz Air Bulgaria

N (USA)

N104UA	Boeing 747-422	United Airlines
N105EV	McD Douglas MD-11F	EVA Air Cargo
N105UA	Boeing 747-451	United Airlines
N107UA	Boeing 747-422	United Airlines *William A Patterson*
N116UA	Boeing 747-422	United Airlines
N117UA	Boeing 747-422	United Airlines

OVERSEAS AIRLINERS

Reg	Type	Owner or Operator	Notes
N118UA	Boeing 747-422	United Airlines	
N119UA	Boeing 747-422	United Airlines	
N120UA	Boeing 747-422	United Airlines	
N121UA	Boeing 747-422	United Airlines	
N122UA	Boeing 747-422	United Airlines	
N127UA	Boeing 747-422	United Airlines	
N128UA	Boeing 747-422	United Airlines	
N152DL	Boeing 767-3P6ER	Delta Air Lines	
N153DL	Boeing 767-3P6ER	Delta Air Lines	
N154DL	Boeing 767-3P6ER	Delta Air Lines	
N155DL	Boeing 767-3P6ER	Delta Air Lines	
N156DL	Boeing 767-3P6ER	Delta Air Lines	
N161AT	L.1011-385 TriStar 500	ATA Airlines	
N162AT	L.1011-385 TriStar 500	ATA Airlines	
N163AT	L.1011-385 TriStar 500	ATA Airlines	
N164AT	L.1011-385 TriStar 500	ATA Airlines	
N169DZ	Boeing 767-332ER	Delta Air Lines	
N171DN	Boeing 767-332ER	Delta Air Lines	
N171DZ	Boeing 767-332ER	Delta Air Lines	
N171UA	Boeing 747-422	United Airlines *Spirit of Seattle II*	
N172DN	Boeing 767-332ER	Delta Air Lines	
N172DZ	Boeing 767-332ER	Delta Air Lines	
N173DN	Boeing 767-332ER	Delta Air Lines	
N173DZ	Boeing 767-332ER	Delta Air Lines	
N173UA	Boeing 747-422	United Airlines	
N174DN	Boeing 767-332ER	Delta Air Lines	
N174DZ	Boeing 767-332ER	Delta Air Lines	
N174UA	Boeing 747-422	United Airlines	
N175DN	Boeing 767-332ER	Delta Air Lines	
N175DZ	Boeing 767-332ER	Delta Air Lines	
N175UA	Boeing 747-422	United Airlines	
N176DN	Boeing 767-332ER	Delta Air Lines	
N176DZ	Boeing 767-332ER	Delta Air Lines	
N177DN	Boeing 767-332ER	Delta Air Lines	
N177DZ	Boeing 767-332ER	Delta Air Lines	
N177UA	Boeing 747-422	United Airlines	
N178DN	Boeing 767-332ER	Delta Air Lines	
N178DZ	Boeing 767-332ER	Delta Air Lines	
N178UA	Boeing 747-422	United Airlines	
N179DN	Boeing 767-332ER	Delta Air Lines	
N179DZ	Boeing 767-332ER	Delta Air Lines	
N179UA	Boeing 747-422	United Airlines	
N180DN	Boeing 767-332ER	Delta Air Lines	
N180UA	Boeing 747-422	United Airlines	
N181DN	Boeing 767-332ER	Delta Air Lines	
N181UA	Boeing 747-422	United Airlines	
N182DN	Boeing 767-332ER	Delta Air Lines	
N182UA	Boeing 747-422	United Airlines	
N183AN	Boeing 757-223ET	American Airlines	
N183DN	Boeing 767-332ER	Delta Air Lines	
N184AN	Boeing 757-223ET	American Airlines	
N184DN	Boeing 767-332ER	Delta Air Lines	
N185AN	Boeing 757-223ET	American Airlines	
N185DN	Boeing 767-332ER	Delta Air Lines	
N186AN	Boeing 757-223ET	American Airlines	
N186DN	Boeing 767-332ER	Delta Air Lines	
N187AN	Boeing 757-223ET	American Airlines	
N187DN	Boeing 767-332ER	Delta Air Lines	
N187UA	Boeing 747-422	United Airlines	
N188AN	Boeing 757-223ET	American Airlines	
N188DN	Boeing 767-332ER	Delta Air Lines	
N189AN	Boeing 757-223ET	American Airlines	
N189DN	Boeing 767-332ER	Delta Air Lines	
N190AA	Boeing 757-223ET	American Airlines	
N190DN	Boeing 767-332ER	Delta Air Lines	
N191AN	Boeing 757-223ET	American Airlines	
N191DN	Boeing 767-332ER	Delta Air Lines	
N192AN	Boeing 757-223ET	American Airlines	
N192DN	Boeing 767-332ER	Delta Air Lines	
N193AN	Boeing 757-223ET	American Airlines	
N193DN	Boeing 767-332ER	Delta Air Lines	
N193UA	Boeing 747-422	United Airlines	
N194AA	Boeing 757-223ET	American Airlines	

N — OVERSEAS AIRLINERS

Notes	Reg	Type	Owner or Operator
	N194DN	Boeing 767-332ER	Delta Air Lines
	N194UA	Boeing 747-422	United Airlines
	N195DN	Boeing 767-332ER	Delta Air Lines
	N195UA	Boeing 747-422	United Airlines
	N196DN	Boeing 767-332ER	Delta Air Lines
	N196UA	Boeing 747-422	United Airlines
	N197DN	Boeing 767-332ER	Delta Air Lines
	N197UA	Boeing 747-422	United Airlines
	N198DN	Boeing 767-332ER	Delta Air Lines
	N198UA	Boeing 747-422	United Airlines
	N199DN	Boeing 767-332ER	Delta Air Lines
	N199UA	Boeing 747-422	United Airlines
	N204UA	Boeing 777-222ER	United Airlines
	N206UA	Boeing 777-222ER	United Airlines
	N207UA	Boeing 777-222ER	United Airlines
	N208UA	Boeing 777-222ER	United Airlines
	N209UA	Boeing 777-222ER	United Airlines
	N216UA	Boeing 777-222ER	United Airlines
	N217UA	Boeing 777-222ER	United Airlines
	N218UA	Boeing 777-222ER	United Airlines
	N219UA	Boeing 777-222ER	United Airlines
	N220UA	Boeing 777-222ER	United Airlines
	N221UA	Boeing 777-222ER	United Airlines
	N222UA	Boeing 777-222ER	United Airlines
	N223UA	Boeing 777-222ER	United Airlines
	N224UA	Boeing 777-222ER	United Airlines
	N225UA	Boeing 777-222ER	United Airlines
	N226UA	Boeing 777-222ER	United Airlines
	N227UA	Boeing 777-222ER	United Airlines
	N228UA	Boeing 777-222ER	United Airlines
	N229UA	Boeing 777-222ER	United Airlines
	N245AY	Boeing 767-201ER	US Airways
	N246AY	Boeing 767-201ER	US Airways
	N248AY	Boeing 767-201ER	US Airways
	N249AU	Boeing 767-201ER	US Airways
	N250AY	Boeing 767-201ER	US Airways
	N250MY	Boeing 767-238ER	Maxjet Airways
	N250UP	McD Douglas MD-11F	United Parcel Service
	N251AY	Boeing 767-2B7ER	US Airways
	N251MY	Boeing 767-269ER	Maxjet Airways
	N251UP	McD Douglas MD-11F	United Parcel Service
	N252AU	Boeing 767-2B7ER	US Airways
	N252UP	McD Douglas MD-11F	United Parcel Service
	N253AY	Boeing 767-2B7ER	US Airways
	N253UP	McD Douglas MD-11F	United Parcel Service
	N254UP	McD Douglas MD-11F	United Parcel Service
	N255AY	Boeing 767-2B7ER	US Airways
	N255UP	McD Douglas MD-11F	United Parcel Service
	N256AY	Boeing 767-2B7ER	US Airways
	N256UP	McD Douglas MD-11F	United Parcel Service
	N257UP	McD Douglas MD-11F	United Parcel Service
	N258UP	McD Douglas MD-11F	United Parcel Service
	N259UP	McD Douglas MD-11F	United Parcel Service
	N260MY	Boeing 767-205	Maxjet Airways
	N260UP	McD Douglas MD-11F	United Parcel Service
	N270AX	Douglas DC-10-30	Omni Air International
	N270AY	Airbus A.330-323X	US Airways
	N270UP	McD Douglas MD-11F	United Parcel Service
	N271AY	Airbus A.330-323X	US Airways
	N271UP	McD Douglas MD-11F	United Parcel Service
	N271WA	McD Douglas MD-11 (271)	World Airways
	N272AY	Airbus A.330-323X	US Airways
	N272UP	McD Douglas MD-11F	United Parcel Service
	N272WA	McD Douglas MD-11 (272)	World Airways
	N273AY	Airbus A.330-323X	US Airways
	N273UP	McD Douglas MD-11F	United Parcel Service
	N273WA	McD Douglas MD-11 (273)	World Airways
	N274AY	Airbus A.330-323X	US Airways
	N274UP	McD Douglas MD-11F	United Parcel Service
	N274WA	McD Douglas MD-11F (274)	World Airways
	N275AY	Airbus A.330-323X	US Airways
	N275UP	McD Douglas MD-11F	United Parcel Service
	N275WA	McD Douglas MD-11CF (275)	World Airways

OVERSEAS AIRLINERS

Reg	Type	Owner or Operator	Notes
N276AY	Airbus A.330-323X	US Airways	
N276UP	McD Douglas MD-11F	United Parcel Service	
N276WA	McD Douglas MD-11CF (276)	World Airways	
N277AY	Airbus A.330-323X	US Airways	
N277UP	McD Douglas MD-11F	United Parcel Service	
N277WA	McD Douglas MD-11 (277)	World Airways	
N278AY	Airbus A.330-323X	US Airways	
N278UP	McD Douglas MD-11F	United Parcel Service	
N278WA	McD Douglas MD-11F (278)	World Airways/Sonair	
N279AX	Douglas DC-10-30F	Centurion Air Cargo *Wings of Miami*	
N279UP	McD Douglas MD-11F	United Parcel Service	
N279WA	McD Douglas MD-11 (279)	World Airways	
N280UP	McD Douglas MD-11F	United Parcel Service	
N281UP	McD Douglas MD-11F	United Parcel Service	
N282UP	McD Douglas MD-11F	United Parcel Service	
N283UP	McD Douglas MD-11F	United Parcel Service	
N284UP	McD Douglas MD-11F	United Parcel Service	
N285UP	McD Douglas MD-11F	United Parcel Service	
N286UP	McD Douglas MD-11F	United Parcel Service	
N291UP	McD Douglas MD-11F	United Parcel Service	
N292UP	McD Douglas MD-11F	United Parcel Service	
N293UP	McD Douglas MD-11F	United Parcel Service	
N301UP	Boeing 767-34AFER	United Parcel Service	
N302FV	Douglas DC-10-30F	Centurion Air Cargo	
N302UP	Boeing 767-34AFER	United Parcel Service	
N303UP	Boeing 767-34AFER	United Parcel Service	
N303WL	Douglas DC-10-30F (303)	World Airways	
N304UP	Boeing 767-34AFER	United Parcel Service	
N304WL	Douglas DC-10-30F (304)	World Airways	
N305UP	Boeing 767-34AFER	United Parcel Service	
N306FV	Douglas DC-10-30CF	Centurion Air Cargo	
N306UP	Boeing 767-34AFER	United Parcel Service	
N307UP	Boeing 767-34AFER	United Parcel Service	
N308UP	Boeing 767-34AFER	United Parcel Service	
N309UP	Boeing 767-34AFER	United Parcel Service	
N310UP	Boeing 767-34AFER	United Parcel Service	
N311UP	Boeing 767-34AFER	United Parcel Service	
N312LA	Boeing 767-316F	LAN Airlines	
N312UP	Boeing 767-34AFER	United Parcel Service	
N313UP	Boeing 767-34AFER	United Parcel Service	
N314UP	Boeing 767-34AFER	United Parcel Service	
N315UP	Boeing 767-34AFER	United Parcel Service	
N316UP	Boeing 767-34AFER	United Parcel Service	
N317UP	Boeing 767-34AFER	United Parcel Service	
N318UP	Boeing 767-34AFER	United Parcel Service	
N319UP	Boeing 767-34AFER	United Parcel Service	
N320UP	Boeing 767-34AFER	United Parcel Service	
N322UP	Boeing 767-34AFER	United Parcel Service	
N323UP	Boeing 767-34AFER	United Parcel Service	
N324UP	Boeing 767-34AFER	United Parcel Service	
N325UP	Boeing 767-34AFER	United Parcel Service	
N326UP	Boeing 767-34AFER	United Parcel Service	
N327UP	Boeing 767-34AFER	United Parcel Service	
N328UP	Boeing 767-34AFER	United Parcel Service	
N329UP	Boeing 767-34AER	United Parcel Service	
N330UP	Boeing 767-34AER	United Parcel Service	
N331UP	Boeing 767-34AER	United Parcel Service	
N332UP	Boeing 767-34AER	United Parcel Service	
N334UP	Boeing 767-34AER	United Parcel Service	
N342AN	Boeing 767-223ER	American Airlines	
N343AN	Boeing 767-223ER	American Airlines	
N344AN	Boeing 767-223ER	American Airlines	
N345AN	Boeing 767-223ER	American Airlines	
N346AN	Boeing 767-223ER	American Airlines	
N347AN	Boeing 767-223ER	American Airlines	
N348AN	Boeing 767-223ER	American Airlines	
N349AN	Boeing 767-223ER	American Airlines	
N350AN	Boeing 767-223ER	American Airlines	
N351AA	Boeing 767-323ER	American Airlines	
N352AA	Boeing 767-323ER	American Airlines	
N353AA	Boeing 767-323ER	American Airlines	
N353WL	Douglas DC-10-30	World Airways	
N354AA	Boeing 767-323ER	American Airlines	

OVERSEAS AIRLINERS

Notes	Reg	Type	Owner or Operator
	N355AA	Boeing 767-323ER	American Airlines
	N355MC	Boeing 747-341F	Polar Air Cargo
	N357AA	Boeing 767-323ER	American Airlines
	N358AA	Boeing 767-323ER	American Airlines
	N359AA	Boeing 767-323ER	American Airlines
	N360AA	Boeing 767-323ER	American Airlines
	N361AA	Boeing 767-323ER	American Airlines
	N362AA	Boeing 767-323ER	American Airlines
	N363AA	Boeing 767-323ER	American Airlines
	N366AA	Boeing 767-323ER	American Airlines
	N368AA	Boeing 767-323ER	American Airlines
	N369AA	Boeing 767-323ER	American Airlines
	N369AX	Boeing 757-28A	Omni Air International
	N370AA	Boeing 767-323ER	American Airlines
	N371AA	Boeing 767-323ER	American Airlines
	N372AA	Boeing 767-323ER	American Airlines
	N373AA	Boeing 767-323ER	American Airlines
	N374AA	Boeing 767-323ER	American Airlines
	N376AN	Boeing 767-323ER	American Airlines
	N377AN	Boeing 767-323ER	American Airlines
	N378AN	Boeing 767-323ER	American Airlines
	N379AA	Boeing 767-323ER	American Airlines
	N380AN	Boeing 767-323ER	American Airlines
	N380WA	McD Douglas MD-11F (380)	World Airways
	N381AN	Boeing 767-323ER	American Airlines
	N381WA	McD Douglas MD-11F (381)	World Airways
	N382AN	Boeing 767-323ER	American Airlines
	N383AN	Boeing 767-323ER	American Airlines
	N384AA	Boeing 767-323ER	American Airlines
	N385AM	Boeing 767-323ER	American Airlines
	N386AA	Boeing 767-323ER	American Airlines
	N387AM	Boeing 767-323ER	American Airlines
	N388AA	Boeing 767-323ER	American Airlines
	N389AA	Boeing 767-323ER	American Airlines
	N390AA	Boeing 767-323ER	American Airlines
	N391AA	Boeing 767-323ER	American Airlines
	N392AN	Boeing 767-323ER	American Airlines
	N393AN	Boeing 767-323ER	American Airlines
	N394AN	Boeing 767-323ER	American Airlines
	N394DL	Boeing 767-324ER	Delta Air Lines
	N395AN	Boeing 767-323ER	American Airlines
	N396AN	Boeing 767-323ER	American Airlines
	N397AN	Boeing 767-323ER	American Airlines
	N398AN	Boeing 767-323ER	American Airlines
	N399AN	Boeing 767-323ER	American Airlines
	N401JS	Boeing 757-2Q8	EOS Airlines
	N403JS	Boeing 757-2Q8	EOS Airlines
	N408MC	Boeing 747-47UF	Atlas Air/Emirates SkyCargo
	N409MC	Boeing 747-47UF	Atlas Air
	N412MC	Boeing 747-47UF	Atlas Air
	N415MC	Boeing 747-47UF	Atlas Air/Emirates SkyCargo
	N416MC	Boeing 747-47UF	Atlas Air
	N418LA	Boeing 767-316F	LAN Airlines
	N418MC	Boeing 747-47UF	Atlas Air
	N420LA	Boeing 767-316F	LAN Airlines
	N450PA	Boeing 747-46NF	Polar Air Cargo
	N451PA	Boeing 747-46NF	Polar Air Cargo
	N452PA	Boeing 747-46NF	Polar Air Cargo
	N453PA	Boeing 747-46NF	Polar Air Cargo
	N454PA	Boeing 747-46NF	Polar Air Cargo
	N459AX	Boeing 757-2Q8	Omni Air International
	N470EV	Boeing 747-273C Supertanker	Evergreen International Airlines
	N471EV	Boeing 747-273C	Evergreen International Airlines
	N478EV	Boeing 747SR-46 (SCD)	Evergreen International Airlines
	N479EV	Boeing 747-132 (SCD)	Evergreen International Airlines
	N480EV	Boeing 747-121F	Evergreen International Airlines
	N481EV	Boeing 747-132 (SCD)	Evergreen International Airlines
	N482EV	Boeing 747-212B (SCD)	Evergreen International Airlines
	N485EV	Boeing 747-212B (SCD)	Evergreen International Airlines
	N486EV	Boeing 747-212B (SCD)	Evergreen International Airlines
	N487EV	Boeing 747-230B (SF)	Evergreen International Airlines
	N488EV	Boeing 747-230B (SF)	Evergreen International Airlines
	N489EV	Boeing 747-230B (SF)	Evergreen International Airlines

OVERSEAS AIRLINERS

Reg	Type	Owner or Operator	Notes
N492MC	Boeing 747-47UF	Atlas Air *Spirit of Panalpina*	
N493MC	Boeing 747-47UF	Atlas Air	
N496MC	Boeing 747-47UF	Polar Air Cargo	
N497MC	Boeing 747-47UF	Atlas Air/Emirates SkyCargo	
N498MC	Boeing 747-47UF	Atlas Air/Emirates SkyCargo	
N499MC	Boeing 747-47UF	Atlas Air	
N505MC	Boeing 747-2D3B (SCD)	Atlas Air	
N506MC	Boeing 747-2D3B (SCD)	Atlas Air	
N508MC	Boeing 747-230B (SCD)	Atlas Air/Tradewinds	
N509MC	Boeing 747-230B (SCD)	Southern Air	
N512MC	Boeing 747-230B (SCD)	Atlas Air	
N514AT	Boeing 757-23N	ATA Airlines	
N516MC	Boeing 747-243F (SCD)	Atlas Air	
N517AT	Boeing 757-23N	ATA Airlines	
N517MC	Boeing 747-243F (SCD)	Atlas Air	
N518AT	Boeing 767-23N	ATA Airlines	
N518MC	Boeing 747-243F (SCD)	Atlas Air	
N519AT	Boeing 757-23N	ATA Airlines	
N520AT	Boeing 757-23N	ATA Airlines	
N521FE	McD Douglas MD-11F	Federal Express	
N522AT	Boeing 757-23N	ATA Airlines	
N522AX	Douglas DC-10-30	Omni Air International	
N522FE	McD Douglas MD-11F	Federal Express	
N523FE	McD Douglas MD-11F	Federal Express	
N523MC	Boeing 747-2D7B (SF)	Atlas Air	
N524FE	McD Douglas MD-11F	Federal Express	
N524MC	Boeing 747-2D7BF	Atlas Air	
N525FE	McD Douglas MD-11F	Federal Express	
N526FE	McD Douglas MD-11F	Federal Express	
N526MC	Boeing 747-2D7BF	Atlas Air	
N527FE	McD Douglas MD-11F	Federal Express	
N527MC	Boeing 747-2D7BF	Atlas Air	
N528FE	McD Douglas MD-11F	Federal Express	
N528MC	Boeing 747-2D7BF	Atlas Air	
N529FE	McD Douglas MD-11F	Federal Express	
N531AX	Douglas DC-10-30	Omni Air International	
N534MC	Boeing 747-2F6B	Southern Air	
N535US	Boeing 757-251	Northwest Airlines	
N536MC	Boeing 747-228F	Atlas Air	
N536US	Boeing 757-251	Northwest Airlines	
N537MC	Boeing 747-271C (SCD)	Atlas Air	
N538US	Boeing 757-251	Northwest Airlines	
N540AX	Douglas DC-10-30	Omni Air International	
N540MC	Boeing 747-243B (SCD)	Atlas Air	
N549AX	Boeing 757-23A	Omni Air International	
N550TZ	Boeing 757-33N	ATA Airlines	
N552TZ	Boeing 757-33N	ATA Airlines	
N560TZ	Boeing 757-33N	ATA Airlines	
N561TZ	Boeing 757-33N	ATA Airlines	
N574FE	McD Douglas MD-11F	Federal Express	
N575FE	McD Douglas MD-11F	Federal Express	
N576FE	McD Douglas MD-11F	Federal Express	
N578FE	McD Douglas MD-11F	Federal Express *Stephen*	
N579FE	McD Douglas MD-11F	Federal Express *Nash*	
N580FE	McD Douglas MD-11F	Federal Express *Ashton*	
N582FE	McD Douglas MD-11F	Federal Express *Jamie*	
N583FE	McD Douglas MD-11F	Federal Express *Nancy*	
N584FE	McD Douglas MD-11F	Federal Express *Jeffrey Wellington*	
N585FE	McD Douglas MD-11F	Federal Express *Katherine*	
N586FE	McD Douglas MD-11F	Federal Express *Dylan*	
N587FE	McD Douglas MD-11F	Federal Express *Jeanna*	
N588FE	McD Douglas MD-11F	Federal Express *Kendra*	
N589FE	McD Douglas MD-11F	Federal Express *Shaun*	
N590FE	McD Douglas MD-11F	Federal Express	
N591FE	McD Douglas MD-11F	Federal Express *Giovanni*	
N592FE	McD Douglas MD-11F	Federal Express *Joshua*	
N593FE	McD Douglas MD-11F	Federal Express *Harrison*	
N594FE	McD Douglas MD-11F	Federal Express	
N595FE	McD Douglas MD-11F	Federal Express *Avery*	
N596FE	McD Douglas MD-11F	Federal Express	
N597FE	McD Douglas MD-11F	Federal Express	
N598FE	McD Douglas MD-11F	Federal Express	
N599FE	McD Douglas MD-11F	Federal Express *Mariana*	

OVERSEAS AIRLINERS

Notes	Reg	Type	Owner or Operator
	N600GC	Douglas DC-10-30F	Gemini Air Cargo
	N601FE	McD Douglas MD-11F	Federal Express *Jim Riedmeyer*
	N601GC	Douglas DC-10-30F	Gemini Air Cargo
	N602AL	Douglas DC-8-73CF	Air Transport International
	N602FE	McD Douglas MD-11F	Federal Express *Malcolm Baldridge 1990*
	N602GC	Douglas DC-10-30F	Gemini Air Cargo
	N603AL	Douglas DC-8-73AF	Air Transport International
	N603AX	Douglas DC-10-30	Omni Air International
	N603FE	McD Douglas MD-11F	Federal Express *Elizabeth*
	N604BX	Douglas DC-8-73CF	Air Transport International
	N604FE	McD Douglas MD-11F	Federal Express *Hollis*
	N604GC	Douglas DC-10-30F	Gemini Air Cargo
	N605AL	Douglas DC-8-73CF	Air Transport International
	N605FE	McD Douglas MD-11F	Federal Express *April Star*
	N605GC	Douglas DC-10-30F	Gemini Air Cargo
	N606AL	Douglas DC-8-73AF	Air Transport International
	N606FE	McD Douglas MD-11F	Federal Express *Charles & Theresa*
	N606GC	Douglas DC-10-30F	Gemini Air Cargo
	N607FE	McD Douglas MD-11F	Federal Express *Christina*
	N607GC	Douglas DC-10-30F	Gemini Air Cargo
	N608AA	Boeing 757-223ET	American Airlines
	N608FE	McD Douglas MD-11F	Federal Express *Karen*
	N609AA	Boeing 757-223ET	American Airlines
	N609FE	McD Douglas MD-11F	Federal Express *Scott*
	N610FE	McD Douglas MD-11F	Federal Express *Marisa*
	N612AX	Douglas DC-10-30	Omni Air International
	N612FE	McD Douglas MD-11F	Federal Express *Alyssa*
	N612GC	Douglas DC-10-30F	Centurion Air Cargo *Jessica*
	N613FE	McD Douglas MD-11F	Federal Express *Krista*
	N614FE	McD Douglas MD-11F	Federal Express *Christy Allison*
	N615FE	McD Douglas MD-11F	Federal Express *Max*
	N616FE	McD Douglas MD-11F	Federal Express *Shanita*
	N616US	Boeing 747-251F (SCD)	Northwest Airlines
	N617FE	McD Douglas MD-11F	Federal Express *Travis*
	N617US	Boeing 747-251F (SCD)	Northwest Airlines
	N618FE	McD Douglas MD-11F	Federal Express *Justin*
	N618US	Boeing 747-251F (SCD)	Northwest Airlines
	N619FE	McD Douglas MD-11F	Federal Express *Lyndon*
	N619US	Boeing 747-251F (SCD)	Northwest Airlines
	N620FE	McD Douglas MD-11F	Federal Express
	N621FE	McD Douglas MD-11F	Federal Express *Connor*
	N623FE	McD Douglas MD-11F	Federal Express *Meghan*
	N623US	Boeing 747-251B	Northwest Airlines
	N624US	Boeing 747-251B	Northwest Airlines
	N628FE	McD Douglas MD-11F	Federal Express
	N629US	Boeing 747-251F (SCD)	Northwest Airlines
	N630AX	Douglas DC-10-30	Omni Air International
	N630US	Boeing 747-2J9F (SCD)	Northwest Airlines
	N631NW	Boeing 747-251F (SCD)	Northwest Airlines
	N632NW	Boeing 747-251F (SCD)	Northwest Airlines
	N636FE	Boeing 747-245F (SCD)	Federal Express
	N637US	Boeing 747-251B	Northwest Airlines
	N638US	Boeing 747-251B	Northwest Airlines
	N639AX	Boeing 757-28A	Omni Air International
	N639FE	Boeing 747-2R7F (SCD)	Federal Express
	N639US	Boeing 747-251F (SCD)	Northwest Airlines
	N640US	Boeing 747-251F (SCD)	Northwest Airlines
	N641UA	Boeing 767-322ER	United Airlines
	N642UA	Boeing 767-322ER	United Airlines
	N642UW	Boeing 757-23N	US Airways
	N643NW	Boeing 747-249F (SCD)	Northwest Airlines
	N643UA	Boeing 767-322ER	United Airlines
	N643UW	Boeing 757-23N	US Airways
	N644NW	Boeing 747-212F (SCD)	Northwest Airlines
	N644UA	Boeing 767-322ER	United Airlines
	N644UW	Boeing 757-23N	US Airways
	N645NW	Boeing 747-222SF	Northwest Airlines
	N646NW	Boeing 747-222SF	Northwest Airlines
	N646UA	Boeing 767-322ER	United Airlines
	N647UA	Boeing 767-322ER	United Airlines
	N648UA	Boeing 767-322ER	United Airlines
	N649UA	Boeing 767-322ER	United Airlines
	N651UA	Boeing 767-322ER	United Airlines

OVERSEAS AIRLINERS

Reg	Type	Owner or Operator	Notes
N652UA	Boeing 767-322ER	United Airlines	
N653UA	Boeing 767-322ER	United Airlines	
N654UA	Boeing 767-322ER	United Airlines	
N655UA	Boeing 767-322ER	United Airlines	
N656UA	Boeing 767-322ER	United Airlines	
N657UA	Boeing 767-322ER	United Airlines	
N658UA	Boeing 767-322ER	United Airlines	
N659UA	Boeing 767-322ER	United Airlines	
N660UA	Boeing 767-322ER	United Airlines	
N661UA	Boeing 767-322ER	United Airlines	
N661US	Boeing 747-451	Northwest Airlines	
N662UA	Boeing 767-322ER	United Airlines	
N662US	Boeing 747-451	Northwest Airlines	
N663UA	Boeing 767-322ER	United Airlines	
N663US	Boeing 747-451	Northwest Airlines	
N664US	Boeing 747-451	Northwest Airlines *The Spirit of Beijing*	
N665US	Boeing 747-451	Northwest Airlines	
N666US	Boeing 747-451	Northwest Airlines	
N667US	Boeing 747-451	Northwest Airlines	
N668US	Boeing 747-451	Northwest Airlines	
N669US	Boeing 747-451	Northwest Airlines	
N670US	Boeing 747-451	Northwest Airlines *The Alliance-Spirit*	
N671US	Boeing 747-451	Northwest Airlines *City of Detroit*	
N672US	Boeing 747-451	Northwest Airlines *Spirit of Asia*	
N673US	Boeing 747-451	Northwest Airlines *Spirit of Tokyo*	
N674US	Boeing 747-451	Northwest Airlines *City of Shanghai*	
N675NW	Boeing 747-451	Northwest Airlines *Spirit of the Northwest People*	
N676NW	Boeing 747-451	Northwest Airlines	
N687AA	Boeing 757-223ET	American Airlines	
N688AA	Boeing 757-223ET	American Airlines	
N689AA	Boeing 757-223ET	American Airlines	
N690AA	Boeing 757-223ET	American Airlines	
N691AA	Boeing 757-223ET	American Airlines	
N692AA	Boeing 757-223ET	American Airlines	
N701CK	Boeing 747-259B (SF)	Kalitta Air	
N701GC	McD Douglas MD-11F	Gemini Air Cargo	
N702CK	Boeing 747-146 (SF)	Kalitta Air	
N702GC	McD Douglas MD-11F	Gemini Air Cargo	
N703GC	McD Douglas MD-11F	Gemini Air Cargo	
N703CK	Boeing 747-212B (SF)	Kalitta Air	
N704CK	Boeing 747-209F (SCD)	Kalitta Air	
N705CK	Boeing 747-246F (SCD)	Kalitta Air	
N705GC	McD Douglas MD-11F	Gemini Air Cargo	
N706CK	Boeing 747-249F (SCD)	Kalitta Air	
N707CK	Boeing 747-246F (SCD)	Kalitta Air	
N709CK	Boeing 747-132 (SF)	Kalitta Air	
N710CK	Boeing 747-2B4B (SF)	Kalitta Air	
N712CK	Boeing 747-122 (SF)	Kalitta Air	
N713CK	Boeing 747-2B4B (SF)	Kalitta Air	
N714CK	Boeing 747-209B (SF)	Kalitta Air	
N715CK	Boeing 747-209B (SF)	Kalitta Air	
N716CK	Boeing 747-122 (SF)	Kalitta Air	
N717CK	Boeing 747-123 (SF)	Kalitta Air	
N719CK	Boeing 747SR-46F (SF)	Kalitta Air	
N720AX	Douglas DC-10-30	Omni Air International	
N727CK	Boeing 747-246B	Kalitta Air	
N740CK	Boeing 747-246B	Kalitta Air	
N742CK	Boeing 747-246B	Kalitta Air	
N743CK	Boeing 747-246B	Kalitta Air	
N745AM	Boeing 777-2Q8ER	Aeromexico	
N746AM	Boeing 777-2Q8ER	Aeromexico	
N748SA	Boeing 747-206F (SCD)	Southern Air	
N750AN	Boeing 777-223ER	American Airlines	
N750NA	Boeing 757-28A	North American Airlines	
N751AN	Boeing 777-223ER	American Airlines	
N752AN	Boeing 777-223ER	American Airlines	
N752NA	Boeing 757-28A	North American Airlines *Alisa Ferrera*	
N753AN	Boeing 777-223ER	American Airlines	
N753SA	Boeing 747-228F	Southern Air	
N754AN	Boeing 777-223ER	American Airlines	
N754NA	Boeing 757-28A	North American Airlines	
N755AN	Boeing 777-223ER	American Airlines	
N755NA	Boeing 757-28A	North American Airlines *John Plueger*	

OVERSEAS AIRLINERS

Notes	Reg	Type	Owner or Operator
	N756AM	Boeing 777-223ER	American Airlines
	N756NA	Boeing 757-28A	North American Airlines *Claudette Abrahams*
	N757AN	Boeing 777-223ER	American Airlines
	N758AN	Boeing 777-223ER	American Airlines
	N759AN	Boeing 777-223ER	American Airlines
	N760AN	Boeing 777-223ER	American Airlines
	N760NA	Boeing 767-39HER	North American Airlines *Tom Cygan*
	N761AJ	Boeing 777-223ER	American Airlines
	N762AN	Boeing 777-223ER	American Airlines
	N765AN	Boeing 777-223ER	American Airlines
	N765NA	Boeing 767-306ER	North American Airlines
	N766AN	Boeing 777-223ER	American Airlines
	N767AJ	Boeing 777-223ER	American Airlines
	N767NA	Boeing 767-324ER	North American Airlines *Janice M.*
	N767UA	Boeing 777-222	United Airlines
	N768AA	Boeing 777-223ER	American Airlines
	N768NA	Boeing 767-36NER	North American Airlines *Lisa Caroline*
	N768UA	Boeing 777-222	United Airlines
	N769NA	Boeing 767-304ER	North American Airlines
	N769UA	Boeing 777-222	United Airlines
	N770AN	Boeing 777-223ER	American Airlines
	N770UA	Boeing 777-222	United Airlines
	N771AN	Boeing 777-223ER	American Airlines
	N771UA	Boeing 777-222	United Airlines
	N772AN	Boeing 777-223ER	American Airlines
	N772UA	Boeing 777-222	United Airlines
	N773AN	Boeing 777-223ER	American Airlines
	N773UA	Boeing 777-222	United Airlines
	N774AM	Boeing 777-2Q8ER	Aeromexico
	N774AN	Boeing 777-223ER	American Airlines
	N774UA	Boeing 777-222	United Airlines
	N775AN	Boeing 777-223ER	American Airlines
	N775UA	Boeing 777-222	United Airlines
	N776AN	Boeing 777-223ER	American Airlines
	N776UA	Boeing 777-222	United Airlines
	N777AN	Boeing 777-223ER	American Airlines
	N777UA	Boeing 777-222	United Airlines
	N778AN	Boeing 777-223ER	American Airlines
	N778UA	Boeing 777-222	United Airlines
	N779AN	Boeing 777-223ER	American Airlines
	N779UA	Boeing 777-222	United Airlines
	N780AN	Boeing 777-223ER	American Airlines/Boeing
	N780UA	Boeing 777-222	United Airlines
	N781AN	Boeing 777-223ER	American Airlines
	N781UA	Boeing 777-222	United Airlines
	N782AN	Boeing 777-223ER	American Airlines
	N782UA	Boeing 777-222ER	United Airlines
	N783AN	Boeing 777-223ER	American Airlines
	N783UA	Boeing 777-222ER	United Airlines
	N784AN	Boeing 777-223ER	American Airlines
	N784UA	Boeing 777-222ER	United Airlines
	N785AN	Boeing 777-223ER	American Airlines
	N785UA	Boeing 777-222ER	United Airlines
	N786AN	Boeing 777-223ER	American Airlines
	N786UA	Boeing 777-222ER	United Airlines
	N787AL	Boeing 777-223ER	American Airlines
	N787UA	Boeing 777-222ER	United Airlines
	N788AN	Boeing 777-223ER	American Airlines
	N788UA	Boeing 777-222ER	United Airlines
	N789AN	Boeing 777-223ER	American Airlines
	N790AN	Boeing 777-223ER	American Airlines
	N791AN	Boeing 777-223ER	American Airlines
	N791UA	Boeing 777-222ER	United Airlines
	N792AN	Boeing 777-223ER	American Airlines
	N792UA	Boeing 777-222ER	United Airlines
	N793AN	Boeing 777-223ER	American Airlines
	N793UA	Boeing 777-222ER	United Airlines
	N794AN	Boeing 777-223ER	American Airlines
	N794UA	Boeing 777-222ER	United Airlines
	N795AN	Boeing 777-223ER	American Airlines
	N795UA	Boeing 777-222ER	United Airlines
	N796AN	Boeing 777-223ER	American Airlines
	N796UA	Boeing 777-222ER	United Airlines

OVERSEAS AIRLINERS

Reg	Type	Owner or Operator	Notes
N797AN	Boeing 777-223ER	American Airlines	
N797UA	Boeing 777-222ER	United Airlines	
N798AN	Boeing 777-223ER	American Airlines	
N798UA	Boeing 777-222ER	United Airlines	
N799AN	Boeing 777-223ER	American Airlines	
N799UA	Boeing 777-222ER	United Airlines	
N801DE	McD Douglas MD-11 (801)	World Airways	
N801DH	Douglas DC-8-73AF	DHL Air Cargo	
N801NW	Airbus A.330-323X	Northwest Airlines	
N802DH	Douglas DC-8-73AF	DHL Air Cargo	
N802NW	Airbus A.330-323X	Northwest Airlines	
N803DE	McD Douglas MD-11 (803)	World Airways	
N803DH	Douglas DC-8-73AF	DHL Air Cargo	
N803NW	Airbus A.330-323X	Northwest Airlines	
N804DE	McD Douglas MD-11 (804)	World Airways	
N804DH	Douglas DC-8-73AF	DHL Air Cargo	
N804NW	Airbus A.330-323X	Northwest Airlines	
N805DH	Douglas DC-8-73AF	DHL Air Cargo	
N805NW	Airbus A.330-323X	Northwest Airlines	
N806DH	Douglas DC-8-73AF	DHL Air Cargo	
N806NW	Airbus A.330-323X	Northwest Airlines	
N807DH	Douglas DC-8-73AF	DHL Air Cargo	
N807NW	Airbus A.330-323X	Northwest Airlines	
N808NW	Airbus A.330-323X	Northwest Airlines	
N809MC	Boeing 747-228F (SCD)	Atlas Air	
N809NW	Airbus A.330-323E	Northwest Airlines	
N810AX	Douglas DC-10-30	Omni Air International	
N810NW	Airbus A.330-323E	Northwest Airlines	
N811NW	Airbus A.330-323E	Northwest Airlines	
N812NW	Airbus A.330-323E	Northwest Airlines	
N813NW	Airbus A.330-323E	Northwest Airlines	
N814NW	Airbus A.330-323E	Northwest Airlines	
N815NW	Airbus A.330-323E	Northwest Airlines	
N816NW	Airbus A.330-323E	Northwest Airlines	
N825MH	Boeing 767-432ER (1801)	Delta Air Lines	
N826MH	Boeing 767-432ER (1802)	Delta Air Lines	
N827MH	Boeing 767-432ER (1803)	Delta Air Lines	
N828MH	Boeing 767-432ER (1804)	Delta Air Lines	
N829MH	Boeing 767-432ER (1805)	Delta Air Lines	
N830MH	Boeing 767-432ER (1806)	Delta Air Lines	
N831MH	Boeing 767-432ER (1807)	Delta Air Lines	
N832MH	Boeing 767-432ER (1808)	Delta Air Lines	
N833MH	Boeing 767-432ER (1809)	Delta Air Lines	
N834MH	Boeing 767-432ER (1810)	Delta Air Lines	
N835MH	Boeing 767-432ER (1811)	Delta Air Lines	
N836MH	Boeing 767-432ER (1812)	Delta Air Lines	
N837MH	Boeing 767-432ER (1813)	Delta Air Lines	
N838MH	Boeing 767-432ER (1814)	Delta Air Lines	
N839MH	Boeing 767-432ER (1815)	Delta Air Lines	
N840MH	Boeing 767-432ER (1816)	Delta Air Lines	
N841MH	Boeing 767-432ER (1817)	Delta Air Lines	
N842MH	Boeing 767-432ER (1818	Delta Air Lines	
N843MH	Boeing 767-432ER (1819)	Delta Air Lines	
N844MH	Boeing 767-432ER (1820)	Delta Air Lines	
N845MH	Boeing 767-432ER (1821)	Delta Air Lines	
N851NW	Airbus A.330-223	Northwest Airlines	
N852NW	Airbus A.330-223	Northwest Airlines	
N853NW	Airbus A.330-223	Northwest Airlines	
N854NW	Airbus A.330-223	Northwest Airlines	
N855NW	Airbus A.330-223	Northwest Airlines	
N856NW	Airbus A.330-223	Northwest Airlines	
N857NW	Airbus A.330-223	Northwest Airlines	
N858NW	Airbus A.330-223	Northwest Airlines	
N859NW	Airbus A.330-223	Northwest Airlines	
N860DA	Boeing 777-232ER (7001)	Delta Air Lines	
N860NW	Airbus A.330-223	Northwest Airlines	
N861DA	Boeing 777-232ER (7002)	Delta Air Lines	
N861NW	Airbus A.330-223	Northwest Airlines	
N862DA	Boeing 777-232ER (7003)	Delta Air Lines	
N863DA	Boeing 777-232ER (7004)	Delta Air Lines	
N864DA	Boeing 777-232ER (7005)	Delta Air Lines	
N865DA	Boeing 777-232ER (7006)	Delta Air Lines	
N866DA	Boeing 777-232ER (7007)	Delta Air Lines	

N
OVERSEAS AIRLINERS

Notes	Reg	Type	Owner or Operator
	N867DA	Boeing 777-232ER (7008)	Delta Air Lines
	N922FT	Boeing 747-2U3BF	Tradewinds Cargo
	N923FT	Boeing 747-2U3BF	Tradewinds Cargo
	N926JS	Boeing 757-2Q8	EOS Airlines
	N929RD	Boeing 757-2G5	Ryan International
	N930RD	Boeing 757-225	Ryan International
	N1200K	Boeing 767-332ER (200)	Delta Air Lines
	N1201P	Boeing 767-332ER (201)	Delta Air Lines
	N1501P	Boeing 767-3P6ER (1501)	Delta Air Lines
	N1602	Boeing 767-332ER (1602)	Delta Air Lines
	N1603	Boeing 767-332ER (1603)	Delta Air Lines
	N1604R	Boeing 767-332ER (1604)	Delta Air Lines
	N1605	Boeing 767-332ER (1605)	Delta Air Lines
	N1606P	Boeing 767-332ER (1606)	Delta Air Lines
	N1607B	Boeing 767-332ER (1607)	Delta Air Lines
	N1608B	Boeing 767-332ER (1608)	Delta Air Lines
	N1609B	Boeing 767-332ER (1609)	Delta Air Lines
	N1610D	Boeing 767-332ER (1610)	Delta Air Lines
	N1611B	Boeing 767-332ER (1611)	Delta Air Lines
	N1612T	Boeing 767-332ER (1612)	Delta Air Lines
	N1613B	Boeing 767-332ER (1613)	Delta Air Lines
	N7375A	Boeing 767-323ER	American Airlines
	N12109	Boeing 757-224 (109)	Continental Airlines
	N12114	Boeing 757-224 (114)	Continental Airlines
	N12116	Boeing 757-224 (116)	Continental Airlines
	N12125	Boeing 757-224 (125)	Continental Airlines
	N13110	Boeing 757-224 (110)	Continental Airlines
	N13113	Boeing 757-224 (113)	Continental Airlines
	N13118	Boeing 757-224 (118)	Continental Airlines
	N14075	Douglas DC-10-30 (351)	World Airways
	N14102	Boeing 757-224 (102)	Continental Airlines
	N14106	Boeing 757-224 (106)	Continental Airlines
	N14107	Boeing 757-224 (107)	Continental Airlines
	N14115	Boeing 757-224 (115)	Continental Airlines
	N14118	Boeing 757-224 (118)	Continental Airlines
	N14120	Boeing 757-224 (120)	Continental Airlines
	N14121	Boeing 757-224 (121)	Continental Airlines
	N16065	Boeing 767-332ER	Delta Air Lines
	N16078	Boeing 767-332ER	Delta Air Lines
	N17085	Douglas DC-10-30	Omni Air International
	N17104	Boeing 757-224 (104)	Continental Airlines
	N17105	Boeing 757-224 (105)	Continental Airlines
	N17122	Boeing 757-224 (122)	Continental Airlines
	N17126	Boeing 757-224 (126)	Continental Airlines
	N17128	Boeing 757-224 (128)	Continental Airlines
	N17133	Boeing 757-224 (133)	Continental Airlines
	N17139	Boeing 757-224 (139)	Continental Airlines
	N18112	Boeing 757-224 (112)	Continental Airlines
	N18119	Boeing 757-224 (119)	Continental Airlines
	N19117	Boeing 757-224 (117)	Continental Airlines
	N19130	Boeing 757-224 (130)	Continental Airlines
	N19136	Boeing 757-224 (136)	Continental Airlines
	N19141	Boeing 757-224 (141)	Continental Airlines
	N21108	Boeing 757-224 (108)	Continental Airlines
	N26123	Boeing 757-224 (123)	Continental Airlines
	N27015	Boeing 777-224ER (015)	Continental Airlines
	N29124	Boeing 757-224 (124)	Continental Airlines
	N29129	Boeing 757-224 (129)	Continental Airlines
	N33103	Boeing 757-224 (103)	Continental Airlines
	N33132	Boeing 757-224 (132)	Continental Airlines
	N34131	Boeing 757-224 (131)	Continental Airlines
	N34137	Boeing 757-224 (13)	Continental Airlines
	N37018	Boeing 777-224ER (018)	Continental Airlines
	N39356	Boeing 767-323ER	American Airlines
	N39364	Boeing 767-323ER	American Airlines
	N39365	Boeing 767-323ER	American Airlines
	N39367	Boeing 767-323ER	American Airlines
	N41135	Boeing 757-224 (135)	Continental Airlines
	N41140	Boeing 757-224 (140)	Continental Airlines
	N47888	Douglas DC-10-30F	Centurion Air Cargo *Captain Mike*
	N48127	Boeing 757-224 (127)	Continental Airlines
	N48277	Douglas DC-10-30F	Centurion Air Cargo
	N49082	Douglas DC-10-30	Omni Air International

OVERSEAS AIRLINERS N/OD/OE

Reg	Type	Owner or Operator	Notes
N57016	Boeing 777-224ER (016)	Continental Airlines	
N57111	Boeing 757-224 (111)	Continental Airlines	
N58101	Boeing 757-224 (101)	Continental Airlines	
N59053	Boeing 767-424ER (053)	Continental Airlines	
N59083	Douglas DC-10-30	Omni Air International	
N66051	Boeing 767-424ER (051)	Continental Airlines	
N66056	Boeing 767-424ER (056)	Continental Airlines	
N66057	Boeing 767-424ER (057)	Continental Airlines	
N67052	Boeing 767-424ER (052)	Continental Airlines	
N67058	Boeing 767-424ER (058)	Continental Airlines	
N67134	Boeing 757-224 (134)	Continental Airlines	
N67157	Boeing 767-224ER (157)	Continental Airlines	
N67158	Boeing 767-224ER (158)	Continental Airlines	
N68061	Boeing 767-424ER (061)	Continental Airlines	
N68155	Boeing 767-224ER (155)	Continental Airlines	
N68159	Boeing 767-224ER (159)	Continental Airlines	
N68160	Boeing 767-224ER (160)	Continental Airlines	
N69059	Boeing 767-424ER (059)	Continental Airlines	
N69063	Boeing 767-424ER (063)	Continental Airlines	
N69154	Boeing 767-224ER (154)	Continental Airlines	
N73152	Boeing 767-224ER (152)	Continental Airlines	
N74007	Boeing 777-224ER (007)	Continental Airlines	
N76010	Boeing 777-224ER (010)	Continental Airlines	
N76054	Boeing 767-424ER (054)	Continental Airlines	
N76055	Boeing 767-424ER (055)	Continental Airlines	
N76062	Boeing 767-424ER (062)	Continental Airlines	
N76064	Boeing 767-424ER (064)	Continental Airlines	
N76065	Boeing 767-424ER (065)	Continental Airlines	
N76066	Boeing 767-424ER (066)	Continental Airlines	
N76151	Boeing 767-224ER (151)	Continental Airlines	
N76153	Boeing 767-224ER (153)	Continental Airlines	
N76156	Boeing 767-224ER (156)	Continental Airlines	
N77006	Boeing 777-224ER (006)	Continental Airlines	
N77012	Boeing 777-224ER (012)	Continental Airlines	
N77014	Boeing 777-224ER (014)	Continental Airlines	
N77019	Boeing 777-224ER (019)	Continental Airlines	
N78001	Boeing 777-224ER (001)	Continental Airlines	
N78002	Boeing 777-224ER (002)	Continental Airlines	
N78003	Boeing 777-224ER (003)	Continental Airlines	
N78004	Boeing 777-224ER (004)	Continental Airlines	
N78005	Boeing 777-224ER (005)	Continental Airlines	
N78008	Boeing 777-224ER (008)	Continental Airlines	
N78009	Boeing 777-224ER (009)	Continental Airlines	
N78013	Boeing 777-224ER (013)	Continental Airlines	
N78017	Boeing 777-224ER (017)	Continental Airlines	
N78060	Boeing 767-424ER (060)	Continental Airlines	
N79011	Boeing 777-224ER (011)	Continental Airlines	

OD (Lebanon)

Middle East Airlines operates Airbus A.321s F-ORME to F-ORMJ together with Airbus A.330s F-OMEA, F-OMEB and F-OMEC.

OE (Austria)

OE-HBB	DHC.8-201 Dash Eight	Euromanx Airways
OE-HBC	DHC.8-311 Dash Eight	Euromanx Airways
OE-LAE	Boeing 767-3Z9ER	Austrian Airlines *Malaysia*
OE-LAK	Airbus A.340-313X	Austrian Airlines *Afrika*
OE-LAL	Airbus A.340-313X	Austrian Airlines *America*
OE-LAM	Airbus A.330-223	Austrian Airlines *Daschstein*
OE-LAN	Airbus A.330-223	Austrian Airlines *Arlberg*
OE-LAO	Airbus A.330-223	Austrian Airlines *Grossglockner*
OE-LAP	Airbus A.330-223	Austrian Airlines *Semmering*
OE-LAT	Boeing 767-31AER	Lauda Air
OE-LAW	Boeing 767-3Z9ER	Austrian Airlines *China*
OE-LAX	Boeing 767-3Z9ER	Lauda Air
OE-LAY	Boeing 767-3Z9ER	Austrian Airlines *Japan*
OE-LAZ	Boeing 767-3Z9ER	Austrian Airlines

OE — OVERSEAS AIRLINERS

Notes	Reg	Type	Owner or Operator
	OE-LBA	Airbus A.321-111	Austrian Airlines *Salzkammergut*
	OE-LBB	Airbus A.321-111	Austrian Airlines *Pinzgau*
	OE-LBC	Airbus A.321-111	Austrian Airlines *Sudtirol*
	OE-LBD	Airbus A.321-111	Austrian Airlines *Steirisches Weinland*
	OE-LBE	Airbus A.321-111	Austrian Airlines *Wachau*
	OE-LBF	Airbus A.321-111	Austrian Airlines *Wien*
	OE-LBN	Airbus A.320-214	Austrian Airlines *Osttirol*
	OE-LBO	Airbus A.320-214	Austrian Airlines *Pyhrn-Eisenwurzen*
	OE-LBP	Airbus A.320-214	Austrian Airlines *Neusiedler See*
	OE-LBQ	Airbus A.320-214	Lauda Air *Wienerwald*
	OE-LBR	Airbus A.320-214	Lauda Air *Frida Kahle*
	OE-LBS	Airbus A.320-214	Austrian Airlines *Waldviertel*
	OE-LBT	Airbus A.320-214	Austrian Airlines *Worthersee*
	OE-LBU	Airbus A.320-214	Austrian Airlines *Muhlviertel*
	OE-LCF	Canadair CL.600-2B19 RJ	Austrian Arrows *Dusseldorf*
	OE-LCG	Canadair CL.600-2B19 RJ	Tyrolean Airways *Köln*
	OE-LCH	Canadair CL.600-2B19 RJ	Austrian Arrows *Amsterdam*
	OE-LCI	Canadair CL.600-2B19 RJ	Austrian Arrows *Zürich*
	OE-LCJ	Canadair CL.600-2B19 RJ	Austrian Arrows *Hannover*
	OE-LCK	Canadair CL.600-2B19 RJ	Tyrolean Airways *Brussel*
	OE-LCL	Canadair CL.600-2B19 RJ	Austrian Arrows *Oslo*
	OE-LCM	Canadair CL.600-2B19 RJ	Austrian Arrows *Bologna*
	OE-LCN	Canadair CL.600-2B19 RJ	Austrian Arrows *Bremen*
	OE-LCO	Canadair CL.600-2B19 RJ	Austrian Arrows *Göteborg*
	OE-LCP	Canadair CL.600-2B19 RJ	Austrian Arrows *Hamburg*
	OE-LCQ	Canadair CL.600-2B19 RJ	Tyrolean Airways *Strassburg*
	OE-LCR	Canadair CL.600-2B19 RJ	Austrian Arrows *Baden*
	OE-LDA	Airbus A.319-112	Austrian Airlines *Sofia*
	OE-LDB	Airbus A.319-112	Austrian Airlines *Bucharest*
	OE-LDC	Airbus A.319-112	Austrian Airlines *Kiev*
	OE-LDD	Airbus A.319-112	Austrian Airlines *Moscow*
	OE-LDE	Airbus A.319-112	Austrian Airlines *Baku*
	OE-LDF	Airbus A.319-112	Austrian Airlines *Sarajevo*
	OE-LDG	Airbus A.319-112	Austrian Airlines *Tbilisi*
	OE-LEA	Airbus A.320-214	Niki *Rock 'n Roll*
	OE-LEE	Airbus A.320-214	Niki
	OE-LEO	Airbus A.320-214	Niki *Soul*
	OE-LEU	Airbus A.320-214	Niki
	OE-LEX	Airbus A.320-214	Niki
	OE-LFG	Fokker 70	Austrian Arrows *Innsbruck*
	OE-LFH	Fokker 70	Austrian Arrows *Salzburg*
	OE-LFI	Fokker 70	Austrian Arrows *Klagenfurt*
	OE-LFJ	Fokker 70	Austrian Arrows *Graz*
	OE-LFK	Fokker 70	Austrian Arrows *Wien*
	OE-LFL	Fokker 70	Austrian Arrows *Linz*
	OE-LFP	Fokker 70	Austrian Airlines *Wels*
	OE-LFQ	Fokker 70	Austrian Airlines *Dornbirn*
	OE-LFR	Fokker 70	Austrian Airlines *Steyr*
	OE-LGA	DHC.8Q-402 Dash Eight	Austrian Arrows *Karnten*
	OE-LGB	DHC.8Q-402 Dash Eight	Austrian Arrows *Tirol*
	OE-LGC	DHC.8Q-402 Dash Eight	Austrian Arrows *Salzburg*
	OE-LGD	DHC.8Q-402 Dash Eight	Austrian Arrows *Steiermark*
	OE-LGE	DHC.8Q-402 Dash Eight	Tyrolean Airways *Oberosterreich*
	OE-LGF	DHC.8Q-402 Dash Eight	Tyrolean Airways *Niederosterreich*
	OE-LGG	DHC.8Q-402 Dash Eight	Austrian Arrows *Budapest*
	OE-LGH	DHC.8Q-402 Dash Eight	Austrian Arrows *Vorarlberg*
	OE-LGI	DHC.8Q-402 Dash Eight	Austrian Arrows *Eisenstadt*
	OE-LGJ	DHC.8Q-402 Dash Eight	Austrian Arrows *St Pölten*
	OE-LNJ	Boeing 737-8Z9	Lauda Air *Falco*
	OE-LNK	Boeing 737-8Z9	Lauda Air *Freddie Mercury*
	OE-LNM	Boeing 737-6Z9	Lauda Air *Innsbruck*
	OE-LNN	Boeing 737-7Z9	Lauda Air *Maria Callas*
	OE-LNO	Boeing 737-7Z9	Lauda Air *Greta Garbo*
	OE-LNP	Boeing 737-8Z9	Lauda Air *George Harrison*
	OE-LNQ	Boeing 737-8Z9	Lauda Air *Gregory Peck*
	OE-LNR	Boeing 737-8Z9	Lauda Air
	OE-LNS	Boeing 737-8Z9	Lauda Air *Miles Davis*
	OE-LNT	Boeing 737-8Z9	Austrian Airlines *Kurt Cobain*
	OE-LOG	McD Douglas MD-87	MAP Jet/Centralwings
	OE-LOS	Airbus A.321-231	Niki *Kurt Hofmeister*
	OE-LPA	Boeing 777-2Z9	Austrian Airlines *Melbourne*
	OE-LPB	Boeing 777-2Z9	Austrian Airlines *Sydney*
	OE-LPC	Boeing 777-2Z9ER	Austrian Airlines *Donald Bradman*

OVERSEAS AIRLINERS
OE/OH

Reg	Type	Owner or Operator	Notes
OE-LPD	Boeing 777-2B8ER	Austrian Airlines *America*	
OE-LRH	Canadair CL.600-2B19 RJ	Austrian Arrows *Berlin*	
OE-LTD	DHC.8-314 Dash Eight	Austrian Arrows *Villach*	
OE-LTF	DHC.8-314 Dash Eight	Austrian Arrows *Zillertal*	
OE-LTG	DHC.8-314 Dash Eight	Austrian Arrows *Hall in Tirol*	
OE-LTH	DHC.8-314 Dash Eight	Austrian Arrows *Kitzbuhel*	
OE-LTI	DHC.8-314 Dash Eight	Austrian Arrows *Bregenz*	
OE-LTJ	DHC.8-314 Dash Eight	Austrian Arrows *Seefeld*	
OE-LTK	DHC.8-314 Dash Eight	Austrian Arrows *Oetztal*	
OE-LTL	DHC.8-314 Dash Eight	Austrian Arrows *Stubaital*	
OE-LTM	DHC.8-314 Dash Eight	Austrian Arrows *Achensee*	
OE-LTN	DHC.8-314 Dash Eight	Austrian Arrows *St Anton*	
OE-LTO	DHC.8-314 Dash Eight	Austrian Arrows *Kufstein*	
OE-LTP	DHC.8-314 Dash Eight	Austrian Arrows *Lienz*	
OE-LVA	Fokker 100	Austrian Arrows *Riga*	
OE-LVB	Fokker 100	Austrian Arrows *Vilnius*	
OE-LVC	Fokker 100	Austrian Arrows *Tirana*	
OE-LVD	Fokker 100	Austrian Arrows *Belgrade*	
OE-LVE	Fokker 100	Austrian Arrows *Zagreb*	
OE-LVF	Fokker 100	Austrian Arrows *Yerevan*	
OE-LVG	Fokker 100	Austrian Arrows *Krakow*	
OE-LVH	Fokker 100	Austrian Arrows *Minsk*	
OE-LVI	Fokker 100	Austrian Arrows *Prague*	
OE-LVJ	Fokker 100	Austrian Arrows *Bratislava*	
OE-LVK	Fokker 100	Austrian Arrows *Timisoara*	
OE-LVL	Fokker 100	Austrian Arrows	

OH (Finland)

Reg	Type	Owner or Operator	Notes
OH-AFI	Boeing 757-2K2	Air Finland	
OH-AFJ	Boeing 757-2Q8	Air Finland	
OH-AFK	Boeing 757-28A	Air Finland	
OH-BLC	McD Douglas MD-90-30	Blue 1	
OH-BLD	McD Douglas MD-90-30	Blue 1 *Kallavesi*	
OH-BLU	McD Douglas MD-90-30	Blue 1	
OH-LBO	Boeing 757-2Q8	Finnair	
OH-LBR	Boeing 757-2Q8	Finnair	
OH-LBS	Boeing 757-2Q8	Finnair	
OH-LBT	Boeing 757-2Q8	Finnair	
OH-LBU	Boeing 757-2Q8	Finnair	
OH-LBV	Boeing 757-2Q8	Finnair	
OH-LBX	Boeing 757-2Q8	Finnair	
OH-LEE	Embraer RJ170 100LR	Finnair	
OH-LEF	Embraer RJ170 100LR	Finnair	
OH-LEG	Embraer RJ170 100LR	Finnair	
OH-LEH	Embraer RJ170 100LR	Finnair	
OH-LEI	Embraer RJ170 100LR	Finnair	
OH-LEK	Embraer RJ170 100LR	Finnair	
OH-LEL	Embraer RJ170 100LR	Finnair	
OH-LEM	Embraer RJ170 100LR	Finnair	
OH-LEN	Embraer RJ170 100LR	Finnair	
OH-LEO	Embraer RJ170 100LR	Finnair	
OH-LGA	McD Douglas MD-11	Finnair	
OH-LGB	McD Douglas MD-11	Finnair	
OH-LGC	McD Douglas MD-11	Finnair	
OH-LGD	McD Douglas MD-11	Finnair	
OH-LGE	McD Douglas MD-11	Finnair	
OH-LGF	McD Douglas MD-11	Finnair	
OH-LGG	McD Douglas MD-11	Finnair	
OH-LKE	Embraer RJ190 100LR	Finnair	
OH-LKF	Embraer RJ190 100LR	Finnair	
OH-LKG	Embraer RJ190 100LR	Finnair	
OH-LKH	Embraer RJ190 100LR	Finnair	
OH-LKI	Embraer RJ190 100LR	Finnair	
OH-LKK	Embraer RJ190 100LR	Finnair	
OH-LQA	Airbus A.340-311	Finnair	
OH-LVA	Airbus A.319-112	Finnair	
OH-LVB	Airbus A.319-112	Finnair	
OH-LVC	Airbus A.319-112	Finnair	
OH-LVD	Airbus A.319-112	Finnair	
OH-LVE	Airbus A.319-112	Finnair	

OH/OK
OVERSEAS AIRLINERS

Notes	Reg	Type	Owner or Operator
	OH-LVF	Airbus A.319-112	Finnair
	OH-LVG	Airbus A.319-112	Finnair
	OH-LVH	Airbus A.319-112	Finnair
	OH-LVI	Airbus A.319-112	Finnair
	OH-LVK	Airbus A.319-112	Finnair
	OH-LVL	Airbus A.319-112	Finnair
	OH-LXA	Airbus A.320-214	Finnair
	OH-LXB	Airbus A.320-214	Finnair
	OH-LXC	Airbus A.320-214	Finnair
	OH-LXD	Airbus A.320-214	Finnair
	OH-LXE	Airbus A.320-214	Finnair
	OH-LXF	Airbus A.320-214	Finnair
	OH-LXG	Airbus A.320-214	Finnair
	OH-LXH	Airbus A.320-214	Finnair
	OH-LXI	Airbus A.320-214	Finnair
	OH-LXK	Airbus A.320-214	Finnair
	OH-LXL	Airbus A.320-214	Finnair
	OH-LXM	Airbus A.320-214	Finnair
	OH-LZA	Airbus A.321-211	Finnair
	OH-LZB	Airbus A.321-211	Finnair
	OH-LZC	Airbus A.321-211	Finnair
	OH-LZD	Airbus A.321-211	Finnair
	OH-LZE	Airbus A.321-211	Finnair
	OH-LZF	Airbus A.321-211	Finnair
	OH-SAH	Avro RJ85	Blue1
	OH-SAI	Avro RJ85	Blue1
	OH-SAJ	Avro RJ85	Blue1
	OH-SAK	Avro RJ85	Blue1
	OH-SAL	Avro RJ85	Blue1
	OH-SAM	Avro RJ100	Blue1
	OH-SAN	Avro RJ100	Blue1
	OH-SAO	Avro RJ85	Blue1
	OH-SAP	Avro RJ85	Blue1

OK (Czech Republic)

Reg	Type	Owner or Operator
OK-CEC	Airbus A.321-211	CSA Czech Airlines *Nove Mesto nad Metuji*
OK-CED	Airbus A.321-211	CSA Czech Airlines *Havlikuv Brod*
OK-CGH	Boeing 737-55S	CSA Czech Airlines *Usti n. Labem*
OK-CGI	Boeing 737-49R	CSA Czech Airlines *Prostejov*
OK-CGJ	Boeing 737-55S	CSA Czech Airlines *Hradec Kralove*
OK-CGK	Boeing 737-55S	CSA Czech Airlines *Pardubice*
OK-CGT	Boeing 737-46M	CSA Czech Airlines *Pisek*
OK-DGB	Boeing 737-5L9	CSA Czech Airlines *Beroun*
OK-DGC	Boeing 737-5L9	CSA Czech Airlines *Cesky Brod*
OK-DGL	Boeing 737-55S	CSA Czech Airlines *Tabor*
OK-DGM	Boeing 737-45S	CSA Czech Airlines *Trebon*
OK-DGN	Boeing 737-45S	CSA Czech Airlines *Trebic*
OK-EGO	Boeing 737-55S	CSA Czech Airlines *Jindrichuv Hradec*
OK-EGP	Boeing 737-45S	CSA Czech Airlines *Kladno*
OK-FGR	Boeing 737-45S	CSA Czech Airlines *Ostrava*
OK-FGS	Boeing 737-45S	CSA Czech Airlines *Brno*
OK-GEA	Airbus A.320-214	CSA Czech Airlines *Roznovpod Radhostem*
OK-GEB	Airbus A.320-214	CSA Czech Airlines *Strakonice*
OK-LEE	Airbus A.320-214	CSA Czech Airlines
OK-LEF	Airbus A.320-214	CSA Czech Airlines
OK-LEG	Airbus A.320-214	CSA Czech Airlines
OK-LEH	Airbus A.320-214	CSA Czech Airlines
OK-RDA	Let L410UVP-E5	Manx2
OK-SWU	Boeing 737-522	Smart Wings
OK-SWV	Boeing 737-522	Smart Wings
OK-TVA	Boeing 737-86N	Travel Service Airlines
OK-TVC	Boeing 737-86Q	Travel Service Airlines
OK-TVD	Boeing 737-86N	Travel Service Airlines
OK-TVF	Boeing 737-8FH	Travel Service Airlines
OK-TVR	Boeing 737-4Y0	Travel Service Airlines/Hola Airlines
OK-TVQ	Boeing 737-86N	Travel Service Airlines
OK-TVS	Boeing 737-4Y0	Travel Service Airlines
OK-UBA	Let L410UVP-E16	Manx2
OK-VGZ	Boeing 737-4K5	CSA Czech Airlines *Policka*
OK-WAA	Airbus A.310-304	CSA Czech Airlines *Praha*

OVERSEAS AIRLINERS

OK/OM/OO

Reg	Type	Owner or Operator	Notes
OK-WAB	Airbus A.310-304	CSA Czech Airlines *Bratislava*	
OK-WGD	Boeing 737-59D	CSA Czech Airlines *Pizen*	
OK-WGX	Boeing 737-436	CSA Czech Airlines *Unicov*	
OK-WGY	Boeing 737-436	CSA Czech Airlines *Roudnice*	
OK-XGA	Boeing 737-55S	CSA Czech Airlines *Plzen*	
OK-XGB	Boeing 737-55S	CSA Czech Airlines *Olomouc*	
OK-XGC	Boeing 737-55S	CSA Czech Airlines *Ceske Budejovice*	
OK-XGD	Boeing 737-55S	CSA Czech Airlines *Poprad*	
OK-XGE	Boeing 737-55S	CSA Czech Airlines *Kosice*	
OK-XGV	Boeing 737-5H6	CSA Czech Airlines *Frantisovky lazne*	
OK-XGW	Boeing 737-5H6	CSA Czech Airlines *Marianske lazne*	
OK-YAC	Airbus A.310-325ET	CSA Czech Airlines *Zlin*	
OK-YAD	Airbus A.310-325ET	CSA Czech Airlines *Frydek-Mistek*	
OK-YGA	Boeing 737-4Q8	CSA Czech Airlines *Bechyne*	
OK-YGU	Boeing 737-4Q8	CSA Czech Airlines *Melnik*	

OM (Slovakia)

Reg	Type	Owner or Operator
OM-ASA	Boeing 757-236	Air Slovakia
OM-ASB	Boeing 757-236	Air Slovakia
OM-BYO	Tupolev Tu-154M	Slovak Government.
OM-BYR	Tupolev Tu-154M	Slovak Government
OM-NGA	Boeing 737-76N	SkyEurope Airlines
OM-NGB	Boeing 737-76N	SkyEurope Airlines
OM-NGC	Boeing 737-76N	SkyEurope Airlines
OM-NGD	Boeing 737-76N	SkyEurope Airlines
OM-NGE	Boeing 737-76N	SkyEurope Airlines
OM-NGF	Boeing 737-76N	SkyEurope Airlines
OM-NGG	Boeing 737-76N	SkyEurope Airlines
OM-NGH	Boeing 737-76N	SkyEurope Airlines
OM-RAN	Boeing 737-230	Air Slovakia
OM-SEC	Boeing 737-5Y0	SkyEurope Airlines
OM-SEE	Boeing 737-53C	SkyEurope Airlines
OM-SEG	Boeing 737-5Y0	SkyEurope Airlines

OO (Belgium)

Reg	Type	Owner or Operator
OO-DJE	BAe 146-200	Brussels Airlines
OO-DJF	BAe 146-200	Brussels Airlines
OO-DJG	BAe 146-200	Brussels Airlines
OO-DJH	BAe 146-200	Brussels Airlines
OO-DJJ	BAe 146-200	Brussels Airlines
OO-DJK	Avro RJ85	Brussels Airlines
OO-DJL	Avro RJ85	Brussels Airlines
OO-DJN	Avro RJ85	Brussels Airlines
OO-DJO	Avro RJ85	Brussels Airlines
OO-DJP	Avro RJ85	Brussels Airlines
OO-DJQ	Avro RJ85	Brussels Airlines
OO-DJR	Avro RJ85	Brussels Airlines
OO-DJS	Avro RJ85	Brussels Airlines
OO-DJT	Avro RJ85	Brussels Airlines
OO-DJV	Avro RJ85	Brussels Airlines
OO-DJW	Avro RJ85	Brussels Airlines
OO-DJX	Avro RJ85	Brussels Airlines
OO-DJY	Avro RJ85	Brussels Airlines
OO-DJZ	Avro RJ85	Brussels Airlines
OO-DIB	Airbus A.300B4-203F	European Air Transport (DHL)
OO-DIC	Airbus A.300B4-203F	European Air Transport (DHL)
OO-DLC	Airbus A.300B4-203F	European Air Transport (DHL)
OO-DLD	Airbus A.300B4-203F	European Air Transport (DHL)
OO-DLE	Airbus A.300B4-203F	European Air Transport (DHL)
OO-DLG	Airbus A.300B4-203F	European Air Transport (DHL)
OO-DLI	Airbus A.300B4-203F	European Air Transport (DHL)
OO-DLJ	Boeing 757-23APF	European Air Transport (DHL)
OO-DLN	Boeing 757-236F	European Air Transport (DHL)
OO-DLP	Boeing 757-236F	European Air Transport (DHL)
OO-DLQ	Boeing 757-236F	European Air Transport (DHL)
OO-DLR	Airbus A.300B4-203F	European Air Transport (DHL)

OO — OVERSEAS AIRLINERS

Notes	Reg	Type	Owner or Operator
	OO-DLT	Airbus A.300B4-203F	European Air Transport (DHL)
	OO-DLU	Airbus A.300B4-203F	European Air Transport (DHL)
	OO-DLV	Airbus A.300B4-203F	European Air Transport (DHL)
	OO-DLW	Airbus A.300B4-203F	European Air Transport (DHL)
	OO-DLY	Airbus A.300B4-203F	European Air Transport (DHL)
	OO-DLZ	Airbus A.300B4-203F	European Air Transport (DHL)
	OO-DPB	Boeing 757-236F	European Air Transport (DHL)
	OO-DPF	Boeing 757-236F	European Air Transport (DHL)
	OO-DPI	Boeing 757-236F	European Air Transport (DHL)
	OO-DPJ	Boeing 757-236F	European Air Transport (DHL)
	OO-DPK	Boeing 757-236F	European Air Transport (DHL)
	OO-DPL	Boeing 757-236F	European Air Transport (DHL)
	OO-DPM	Boeing 757-236F	European Air Transport (DHL)
	OO-DPN	Boeing 757-236F	European Air Transport (DHL)
	OO-DPO	Boeing 757-236F	European Air Transport (DHL)
	OO-DWA	Avro RJ100	Brussels Airlines
	OO-DWB	Avro RJ100	Brussels Airlines
	OO-DWC	Avro RJ100	Brussels Airlines
	OO-DWD	Avro RJ100	Brussels Airlines
	OO-DWE	Avro RJ100	Brussels Airlines
	OO-DWF	Avro RJ100	Brussels Airlines
	OO-DWG	Avro RJ100	Brussels Airlines
	OO-DWH	Avro RJ100	Brussels Airlines
	OO-DWI	Avro RJ100	Brussels Airlines
	OO-DWJ	Avro RJ100	Brussels Airlines
	OO-DWK	Avro RJ100	Brussels Airlines
	OO-DWL	Avro RJ100	Brussels Airlines
	OO-LTM	Boeing 737-3M8	Brussels Airlines
	OO-MJE	BAe 146-200	Brussels Airlines
	OO-SFM	Airbus A.330-301	Brussels Airlines
	OO-SFN	Airbus A.330-301	Brussels Airlines
	OO-SFO	Airbus A.330-301	Brussels Airlines
	OO-SSG	Airbus A.319-112	Brussels Airlines
	OO-SSK	Airbus A.319-112	Brussels Airlines
	OO-SSM	Airbus A.319-112	Brussels Airlines
	OO-TAA	BAe 146-300QT	TNT Airways
	OO-TAD	BAe 146-300QT	TNT Airways
	OO-TAE	BAe 146-300QT	TNT Airways
	OO-TAF	BAe 146-300QT	TNT Airways
	OO-TAH	BAe 146-300QT	TNT Airways
	OO-TAJ	BAe 146-300QT	TNT Airways
	OO-TAK	BAe 146-300QT	TNT Airways
	OO-TAR	BAe 146-200QT	TNT Airways
	OO-TAS	BAe 146-300QT	TNT Airways
	OO-TAU	BAe 146-200QT	TNT Airways
	OO-TAW	BAe 146-200QT	TNT Airways
	OO-TAY	BAe 146-200QT	TNT Airways
	OO-TAZ	BAe 146-200QC	TNT Airways
	OO-TCI	Airbus A.320-214	Thomas Cook Airlines Belgium *relax*
	OO-TCJ	Airbus A.320-214	Thomas Cook Airlines Belgium *inspire*
	OO-TCK	Airbus A.320-212	Thomas Cook Airlines Belgium *enjoy*
	OO-TCL	Airbus A.320-212	Thomas Cook Airlines Belgium *discover*
	OO-TCM	Airbus A.320-211	Thomas Cook Airlines Belgium *explore*
	OO-TCN	Airbus A.320-212	Thomas Cook Airlines Belgium *dream*
	OO-THA	Boeing 747-4HAERF	TNT Airways
	OO-THB	Boeing 747-4HAERF	TNT Airways
	OO-TNA	Boeing 737-3T0F	TNT Airways
	OO-TNB	Boeing 737-3T0F	TNT Airways
	OO-TNC	Boeing 737-3T0F	TNT Airways
	OO-TNE	Boeing 737-3Q8	TNT Airways
	OO-TNF	Boeing 737-3Q8F	TNT Airways
	OO-TNG	Boeing 737-3Y0QC	TNT Airways
	OO-TNH	Boeing 737-301F	TNT Airways
	OO-TNI	Boeing 737-301F	TNT Airways
	OO-TNJ	Boeing 737-301F	TNT Airways
	OO-TUA	Boeing 737-4K5	Jetair *Passion*
	OO-TUB	Boeing 737-4K5	Jetair *Devotion*
	OO-TUC	Boeing 767-341ER	Jetair *Discover*
	OO-TUF	Fokker 100	Jetair *Distinction*
	OO-TUI	Boeing 737-4K5	Jetair *Innovation*
	OO-TUM	Boeing 737-4B3	Jetair/Jet4you
	OO-TZA	Airbus A.300B4-203F	TNT Airways
	OO-TZB	Airbus A.300B4-203F	TNT Airways

OVERSEAS AIRLINERS

OO/OY

Reg	Type	Owner or Operator	Notes
OO-TZC	Airbus A.300B4-203F	TNT Airways	
OO-TZD	Airbus A.300B4-203F	TNT Airways	
OO-VAC	Boeing 737-8BK	Jetair *Rising Sun*	
OO-VAS	Boeing 737-86Q	Jetair *Welcome*	
OO-VBR	Boeing 737-4Y0	Brussels Airlines	
OO-VEG	Boeing 737-36N	Brussels Airlines	
OO-VEH	Boeing 737-36N	Brussels Airlines	
OO-VEJ	Boeing 737-405	Brussels Airlines	
OO-VEK	Boeing 737-405	Brussels Airlines	
OO-VEN	Boeing 737-36N	Brussels Airlines	
OO-VEP	Boeing 737-43Q	Brussels Airlines	
OO-VES	Boeing 737-43Q	Brussels Airlines	
OO-VEX	Boeing 737-36N	Brussels Airlines	
OO-VLE	Fokker 50	VLM Airlines	
OO-VLI	Fokker 50	VLM Airlines	
OO-VLJ	Fokker 50	VLM Airlines	
OO-VLK	Fokker 50	VLM Airlines	
OO-VLL	Fokker 50	VLM Airlines	
OO-VLM	Fokker 50	VLM Airlines	
OO-VLN	Fokker 50	VLM Airlines	
OO-VLO	Fokker 50	VLM Airlines	
OO-VLQ	Fokker 50	VLM Airlines	
OO-VLR	Fokker 50	VLM Airlines	
OO-VLS	Fokker 50	VLM Airlines	
OO-VLV	Fokker 50	VLM Airlines	
OO-VLX	Fokker 50	VLM Airlines	
OO-VLY	Fokker 50	VLM Airlines	
OO-VLZ	Fokker 50	VLM Airlines	

Note: DHL Air also operates a number of Boeing 757s which retain their UK registrations. TNT operates parcel services throughout Europe, aircraft in their livery are also registered in Spain, Italy, Egypt and Iceland. VLM aircraft are named, but the names change too frequently to be listed here.

OY (Denmark)

Reg	Type	Owner or Operator	Notes
OY-APB	Boeing 737-5L9	Sterling Airlines	
OY-APH	Boeing 737-5L9	Sterling Airlines	
OY-API	Boeing 737-5L9	Sterling Airlines	
OY-APK	Boeing 737-5L9	Sterling Airlines	
OY-APL	Boeing 737-5L9	Sterling Airlines/DBA	
OY-BJP	Swearingen SA.227AC Metro III	Benair	
OY-CIR	Aérospatiale ATR-42-310	Danish Air Transport	
OY-CIU	Aérospatiale ATR-42-320	Danish Air Transport	
OY-FJE	Avro RJ100	Atlantic Airways	
OY-JRI	Beech 1900C-1	Danish Air Transport	
OY-JRJ	Aérospatiale ATR-42-320	Danish Air Transport	
OY-JRV	Beech 1900D	Danish Air Transport	
OY-JRY	Aérospatiale ATR-42-320	Danish Air Transport	
OY-KBA	Airbus A.340-313X	SAS *Adalstein Viking*	
OY-KBB	Airbus A.321-231	SAS *Hjorulf Viking*	
OY-KBC	Airbus A.340-313X	SAS *Fredis Viking*	
OY-KBD	Airbus A.340-313X	SAS *Toste Viking*	
OY-KBE	Airbus A.321-231	SAS *Emma Viking*	
OY-KBF	Airbus A.321-231	SAS *Skapti Viking*	
OY-KBH	Airbus A.321-231	SAS *Sulke Viking*	
OY-KBI	Airbus A.340-313X	SAS *Rurik Viking*	
OY-KBK	Airbus A.321-231	SAS *Arne Viking*	
OY-KBL	Airbus A.321-231	SAS *Gynnbjorn Viking*	
OY-KBM	Airbus A.340-313X	SAS *Astrid Viking*	
OY-KBN	Airbus A.330-343X	SAS *Eystein Viking*	
OY-KBO	Airbus A.319-131	SAS *Christian Valdemar Viking*	
OY-KBP	Airbus A.319-131	SAS *Viger Viking*	
OY-KCD	DHC.8Q-402 Dash Eight	SAS Commuter *Bjarke Viking*	
OY-KCE	DHC.8Q-402 Dash Eight	SAS Commuter *Alf Viking*	
OY-KCF	DHC.8Q-402 Dash Eight	SAS Commuter *Asa Viking*	
OY-KCG	DHC.8Q-402 Dash Eight	SAS Commuter *Sote Viking*	
OY-KGT	McD Douglas MD-82	SAS *Hake Viking*	
OY-KGY	McD Douglas MD-81	SAS *Rollo Viking*	
OY-KGZ	McD Douglas MD-81	SAS *Hagbard Viking*	
OY-KHC	McD Douglas MD-82	SAS *Faste Viking*	
OY-KHE	McD Douglas MD-82	SAS *Saxo Viking*	

OY — OVERSEAS AIRLINERS

Notes	Reg	Type	Owner or Operator
	OY-KHF	McD Douglas MD-87	SAS *Ragnar Viking*
	OY-KHG	McD Douglas MD-82	SAS *Alle Viking*
	OY-KHI	McD Douglas MD-87	SAS *Torkel Viking*/Spanair
	OY-KHM	McD Douglas MD-82	SAS *Mette Viking*
	OY-KHN	McD Douglas MD-81	SAS *Dan Viking*
	OY-KHP	McD Douglas MD-81	SAS *Harild Viking*
	OY-KHR	McD Douglas MD-81	SAS *Torkild Viking*
	OY-KHU	McD Douglas MD-87	SAS *Ravn Viking*
	OY-KKG	Boeing 737-683	SAS *Sindre Viking*
	OY-KKH	Boeing 737-683	SAS *Embla Viking*
	OY-KKS	Boeing 737-683	SAS *Ramveig Viking*
	OY-MAA	Boeing 737-5L9	Sterling Airlines/Jettime
	OY-MAE	Boeing 737-5L9	Sterling Airlines/Jettime
	OY-MAV	Canadair CL.600-2B19 RJ	Cimber Air
	OY-MBI	Canadair CL.600-2B19 RJ	Cimber Air
	OY-MBJ	Canadair CL.600-2B19 RJ	Cimber Air/SAS
	OY-MBT	Canadair CL.600-2B19 RJ	Cimber Air/SAS
	OY-MBU	Canadair CL.600-2B19 RJ	Cimber Air/SAS
	OY-MLW	Boeing 737-73S	Sterling Airlines
	OY-MRC	Boeing 737-7L9	Sterling Airlines
	OY-MRD	Boeing 737-7L9	Sterling Airlines
	OY-MRE	Boeing 737-7L9	Sterling Airlines
	OY-MRF	Boeing 737-7L9	Sterling Airlines
	OY-MRG	Boeing 737-7L9	Sterling Airlines
	OY-MRH	Boeing 737-7L9	Sterling Airlines
	OY-MRI	Boeing 737-7L9	Sterling Airlines
	OY-MRJ	Boeing 737-7L9	Sterling Airlines
	OY-MUE	BAe Jetstream 3100	Sun-Air/British Airways
	OY-NCA	Dornier 328-100	Sun-Air/British Airways
	OY-NCC	Dornier 328-100	Sun-Air/British Airways
	OY-NCD	Dornier 328-100	Sun-Air/British Airways
	OY-NCE	Dornier 328-100	Sun-Air/British Airways
	OY-NCG	Dornier 328-100	Sun-Air/British Airways
	OY-NCK	Dornier 328-100	Sun-Air/British Airways
	OY-NCM	Dornier 328-300 JET	Sun-Air
	OY-NCO	Dornier 328-300 JET	Sun-Air
	OY-NCP	Dornier 328-300 JET	Sun-Air
	OY-NCS	Dornier 328-100	Sun-Air/British Airways
	OY-PBH	Let L410UVP-E20	Benair
	OY-PBI	Let L410UVP-E20	Benair
	OY-RCA	BAe 146-200	Atlantic Airways
	OY-RCB	BAe 146-200	Atlantic Airways
	OY-RCC	Avro RJ100	Atlantic Airways
	OY-RCW	BAe 146-200	Atlantic Airways
	OY-RCZ	BAe 146-200	Atlantic Airways
	OY-RJA	Canadair CL.600-2B19 RJ	Cimber Air
	OY-RJB	Canadair CL.600-2B19 RJ	Cimber Air
	OY-RJC	Canadair CL.600-2B19 RJ	Cimber Air
	OY-RJD	Canadair CL.600-2B19 RJ	Cimber Air
	OY-RTD	Aérospatiale ATR-72-202	Cimber Air
	OY-RUB	Aérospatiale ATR-72-202	Danish Air Transport
	OY-SEB	Boeing 737-8Q8	Sterling Airlines
	OY-SEC	Boeing 737-8Q8	Sterling Airlines
	OY-SED	Boeing 737-8Q8	Sterling Airlines
	OY-SEH	Boeing 737-85H	Sterling Airlines
	OY-SEI	Boeing 737-85H	Sterling Airlines
	OY-SEJ	Boeing 737-85H	Sterling Airlines
	OY-SEK	Boeing 737-86Q	Sterling Airlines
	OY-SEL	Boeing 737-8BK	Sterling Airlines
	OY-SEM	Boeing 737-8BK	Sterling Airlines
	OY-SRF	Boeing 767-219 (SF)	Star Air
	OY-SRG	Boeing 767-219 (SF)	Star Air
	OY-SRH	Boeing 767-204 (SF)	Star Air
	OY-SRI	Boeing 767-25E (SF)	Star Air
	OY-SRJ	Boeing 767-25E (SF)	Star Air
	OY-SRK	Boeing 767-204 (SF)	Star Air
	OY-SRL	Boeing 767-232 (SF)	Star Air
	OY-SRM	Boeing 767-25E (SF)	Star Air
	OY-SRN	Boeing 767-219 (SF)	Star Air
	OY-SRO	Boeing 767-25E (SF)	Star Air
	OY-SRP	Boeing 767-232 (SF)	Star Air
	OY-SRN	Boeing 767-219 (SF)	Star Air
	OY-SVB	BAe Jetstream 3202	Sun-Air/British Airways

OVERSEAS AIRLINERS

OY/P4/PH

Reg	Type	Owner or Operator	Notes
OY-SVF	BAe Jetstream 3102	Sun-Air/British Airways	
OY-SVJ	BAe Jetstream 3102	Sun-Air/British Airways	
OY-SVR	BAe Jetstream 3202	Sun-Air/British Airways	
OY-SVY	BAe Jetstream 3202	Sun-Air/British Airways	
OY-VKA	Airbus A.321-211	MyTravel Airways	
OY-VKB	Airbus A.321-211	MyTravel Airways	
OY-VKC	Airbus A.321-211	MyTravel Airways	
OY-VKD	Airbus A.321-211	MyTravel Airways	
OY-VKE	Airbus A.321-211	MyTravel Airways	
OY-VKF	Airbus A.330-243	MyTravel Airways	
OY-VKG	Airbus A.330-343X	MyTravel Airways	
OY-VKH	Airbus A.330-343X	MyTravel Airways	
OY-VKI	Airbus A.330-343X	MyTravel Airways	
OY-VKM	Airbus A.320-214	MyTravel Airways	
OY-VKS	Airbus A.320-214	MyTravel Airways	

P4 (Aruba)

Reg	Type	Owner or Operator	Notes
P4-EAS	Boeing 757-2G5	Air Astana	
P4-FAS	Boeing 757-2G5	Air Astana	
P4-GAS	Boeing 757-2G5	Air Astana	
P4-MAS	Boeing 757-28A	Air Astana	

PH (Netherlands)

Reg	Type	Owner or Operator	Notes
PH-AHQ	Boeing 767-383ER	Arkefly	
PH-AHX	Boeing 767-383ER	Arkefly	
PH-AHY	Boeing 767-383ER	Arkefly	
PH-AOA	Airbus A.330-203	KLM *Dam – Amsterdam*	
PH-AOB	Airbus A.330-203	KLM *Potsdamer Platz – Berlin*	
PH-AOC	Airbus A.330-203	KLM *Place de la Concorde – Paris*	
PH-AOD	Airbus A.330-203	KLM *Plazza del Duomo – Milano*	
PH-AOE	Airbus A.330-203	KLM *Parliament Square – Edinburgh*	
PH-AOF	Airbus A.330-203	KLM *Federation Square – Melbourne*	
PH-AOH	Airbus A.330-203	KLM	
PH-AOI	Airbus A.330-203	KLM	
PH-AOK	Airbus A.330-203	KLM	
PH-BDA	Boeing 737-306	KLM *Willem Barentsz*	
PH-BDC	Boeing 737-306	KLM *Cornelis De Houteman*	
PH-BDD	Boeing 737-306	KLM *Anthony van Diemen*	
PH-BDE	Boeing 737-306	KLM *Abel J. Tasman*	
PH-BDG	Boeing 737-306	KLM *Michiel A. de Ruyter*	
PH-BDI	Boeing 737-306	KLM *Maarten H. Tromp*	
PH-BDK	Boeing 737-306	KLM *Jan H. van Linschoten*	
PH-BDN	Boeing 737-306	KLM *Willem van Ruysbroeck*	
PH-BDO	Boeing 737-306	KLM *Jacob van Heemskerck*	
PH-BDP	Boeing 737-306	KLM *Jacob Roggeveen*	
PH-BDR	Boeing 737-406	KLM *Willem C. Schouten*	
PH-BDS	Boeing 737-406	KLM *Jorris van Spilbergen*	
PH-BDT	Boeing 737-406	KLM *Gerrit de Veer*	
PH-BDU	Boeing 737-406	KLM *Marco Polo*	
PH-BDW	Boeing 737-406	KLM *Leifur Eiriksson*	
PH-BDY	Boeing 737-406	KLM *Vasco da Gama*	
PH-BDZ	Boeing 737-406	KLM *Christophorus Columbus*	
PH-BFA	Boeing 747-406	KLM *City of Atlanta*	
PH-BFB	Boeing 747-406	KLM *City of Bangkok*	
PH-BFC	Boeing 747-406 (SCD)	KLM *City of Calgary*	
PH-BFD	Boeing 747-406 (SCD)	KLM *City of Dubai*	
PH-BFE	Boeing 747-406 (SCD)	KLM *City of Melbourne*	
PH-BFF	Boeing 747-406 (SCD)	KLM *City of Freetown*	
PH-BFG	Boeing 747-406	KLM *City of Guayaquil*	
PH-BFH	Boeing 747-406 (SCD)	KLM *City of Hong Kong*	
PH-BFI	Boeing 747-406 (SCD)	KLM *City of Jakarta*	
PH-BFK	Boeing 747-406 (SCD)	KLM *City of Karachi*	
PH-BFL	Boeing 747-406	KLM *City of Lima*	
PH-BFM	Boeing 747-406 (SCD)	KLM *City of Mexico*	
PH-BFN	Boeing 747-406	KLM *City of Nairobi*	
PH-BFO	Boeing 747-406 (SCD)	KLM *City of Orlando*	
PH-BFP	Boeing 747-406 (SCD)	KLM *City of Paramaribo*	

PH — OVERSEAS AIRLINERS

Notes	Reg	Type	Owner or Operator
	PH-BFR	Boeing 747-406 (SCD)	KLM *City of Rio de Janeiro*
	PH-BFS	Boeing 747-406 (SCD)	KLM *City of Seoul*
	PH-BFT	Boeing 747-406 (SCD)	KLM *City of Tokyo*
	PH-BFU	Boeing 747-406 (SCD)	KLM *City of Beijing*
	PH-BFV	Boeing 747-406	KLM *City of Vancouver*
	PH-BFW	Boeing 747-406	KLM *City of Shanghai*
	PH-BFY	Boeing 747-406	KLM *City of Johannesburg*
	PH-BPB	Boeing 737-4Y0	KLM *Jan Tinbergen*
	PH-BPC	Boeing 737-4Y0	KLM *Ernest Hemingway*
	PH-BQA	Boeing 777-206ER	KLM *Albert Plesman*
	PH-BQB	Boeing 777-206ER	KLM *Borobudur*
	PH-BQC	Boeing 777-206ER	KLM *Chichen-Itza*
	PH-BQD	Boeing 777-206ER	KLM *Darjeeling Highway*
	PH-BQE	Boeing 777-206ER	KLM *Epidaurus*
	PH-BQF	Boeing 777-206ER	KLM *Ferrara City*
	PH-BQG	Boeing 777-206ER	KLM *Galapagos Islands*
	PH-BQH	Boeing 777-206ER	KLM *Hadrian's Wall*
	PH-BQI	Boeing 777-206ER	KLM *Iguazu Falls*
	PH-BQK	Boeing 777-206ER	KLM *Mount Kilimanjaro*
	PH-BQL	Boeing 777-206ER	KLM *Litomysl Castle*
	PH-BQM	Boeing 777-206ER	KLM *Macchu Picchu*
	PH-BQN	Boeing 777-206ER	KLM *Nahanni National Park*
	PH-BQO	Boeing 777-206ER	KLM *Old Rauma*
	PH-BTA	Boeing 737-406	KLM *Fernao Magalhaes*
	PH-BTB	Boeing 737-406	KLM *Henry Hudson*
	PH-BTD	Boeing 737-306	KLM *James Cook*
	PH-BTE	Boeing 737-306	KLM *Roald Amundsen*
	PH-BTF	Boeing 737-406	KLM *Alexander von Humboldt*
	PH-BTG	Boeing 737-406	KLM *Henry Morton Stanley*
	PH-BTH	Boeing 737-306	KLM *Heike Kamerlingh-Onnes*
	PH-BTI	Boeing 737-306	KLM *Niels Bohr*
	PH-BXA	Boeing 737-8K2	KLM *Zwaan/Swan*
	PH-BXB	Boeing 737-8K2	KLM *Valk/Falcon*
	PH-BXC	Boeing 737-8K2	KLM *Korhoen/Grouse*
	PH-BXD	Boeing 737-8K2	KLM *Arend/Eagle*
	PH-BXE	Boeing 737-8K2	KLM *Harvik/Hawk*
	PH-BXF	Boeing 737-8K2	KLM *Zwallou/Swallow*
	PH-BXG	Boeing 737-8K2	KLM *Kraanvogel/Crane*
	PH-BXH	Boeing 737-8K2	KLM *Gans/Goose*
	PH-BXI	Boeing 737-8K2	KLM *Zilvermeeuw*
	PH-BXK	Boeing 737-8K2	KLM *Gierzwallou/Swift*
	PH-BXL	Boeing 737-8K2	KLM *Sperwer/Sparrow*
	PH-BXM	Boeing 737-8K2	KLM *Kluut/Avocet*
	PH-BXN	Boeing 737-8K2	KLM *Merel/Blackbird*
	PH-BXO	Boeing 737-9K2	KLM *Plevier/Plover*
	PH-BXP	Boeing 737-9K2	KLM *Meerkoet/Crested Coot*
	PH-BXR	Boeing 737-9K2	KLM *Nachtegaal/Nightingale*
	PH-BXS	Boeing 737-9K2	KLM *Buizerd/Buzzard*
	PH-BXT	Boeing 737-9K2	KLM *Zeestern/Sea Tern*
	PH-BXU	Boeing 737-8BK	KLM *Albatros/Albatross*
	PH-BXV	Boeing 737-8K2	KLM
	PH-CKA	Boeing 747-406ERF	KLM Cargo *Eendracht*
	PH-CKB	Boeing 747-406ERF	KLM Cargo *Leeuwin*
	PH-CKC	Boeing 747-406ERF	KLM Cargo *Oranje*
	PH-DDZ	Douglas DC-3	Dutch Dakota Association
	PH-DMS	Fokker 50	Denim Air/VLM
	PH-DMT	Fokker 50	Denim Air/VLM
	PH-FHF	F.27 Friendship Mk 100	F.27 Friendship Association
	PH-FZG	Fokker 50	Denim Air/VLM
	PH-HZA	Boeing 737-8K2	Transavia
	PH-HZB	Boeing 737-8K2	Transavia
	PH-HZC	Boeing 737-8K2	Transavia
	PH-HZD	Boeing 737-8K2	Transavia
	PH-HZE	Boeing 737-8K2	Transavia *City of Rhodos*
	PH-HZF	Boeing 737-8K2	Transavia
	PH-HZG	Boeing 737-8K2	Transavia
	PH-HZI	Boeing 737-8K2	Transavia
	PH-HZJ	Boeing 737-8K2	Transavia
	PH-HZK	Boeing 737-8K2	Transavia/KLM
	PH-HZL	Boeing 737-8K2	Transavia
	PH-HZM	Boeing 737-8K2	Transavia/KLM
	PH-HZN	Boeing 737-8K2	Transavia
	PH-HZR	Boeing 737-86N	Transavia/Spicejet

OVERSEAS AIRLINERS

PH

Reg	Type	Owner or Operator	Notes
PH-HZV	Boeing 737-8K2	Transavia	
PH-HZW	Boeing 737-8K2	Transavia	
PH-HZX	Boeing 737-8K2	Transavia	
PH-HZY	Boeing 737-8K2	Transavia	
PH-JCE	Fokker 50	Denim Air	
PH-JCH	Fokker 70	KLM CityHopper	
PH-JCT	Fokker 70	KLM CityHopper	
PH-JXJ	Fokker 50	Denim Air	
PH-JXK	Fokker 50	Denim Air	
PH-JXM	Fokker 50	Denim Air	
PH-JXN	Fokker 50	Denim Air	
PH-KBX	Fokker 70	Netherlands Government	
PH-KCA	McD Douglas MD-11	KLM *Amy Johnson*	
PH-KCB	McD Douglas MD-11	KLM *Maria Montessori*	
PH-KCC	McD Douglas MD-11	KLM *Marie Curie*	
PH-KCD	McD Douglas MD-11	KLM *Florence Nightingale*	
PH-KCE	McD Douglas MD-11	KLM *Audrey Hepburn*	
PH-KCF	McD Douglas MD-11	KLM *Annie Romein*	
PH-KCG	McD Douglas MD-11	KLM *Maria Callas*	
PH-KCH	McD Douglas MD-11	KLM *Anna Pavlova*	
PH-KCI	McD Douglas MD-11	KLM *Ingrid Bergman*	
PH-KCK	McD Douglas MD-11	KLM *Marie Servaes*	
PH-KLD	Fokker 100	KLM CityHopper	
PH-KLE	Fokker 100	KLM CityHopper	
PH-KLG	Fokker 100	KLM CityHopper	
PH-KLI	Fokker 100	KLM CityHopper	
PH-KVC	Fokker 50	KLM CityHopper *Stavanger*	
PH-KVD	Fokker 50	KLM CityHopper *Dusseldorf*	
PH-KVE	Fokker 50	KLM CityHopper *Amsterdam*	
PH-KVF	Fokker 50	KLM CityHopper *Paris/Paris*	
PH-KVG	Fokker 50	KLM CityHopper *Stuttgart*	
PH-KVH	Fokker 50	KLM CityHopper *Hannover*	
PH-KVI	Fokker 50	KLM CityHopper *Bordeaux*	
PH-KVK	Fokker 50	KLM CityHopper *London*	
PH-KXH	Fokker 50	KLM CityHopper *City of Bradford*	
PH-KXM	Fokker 50	Denim Air	
PH-KZA	Fokker 70	KLM CityHopper	
PH-KZB	Fokker 70	KLM CityHopper	
PH-KZC	Fokker 70	KLM CityHopper	
PH-KZD	Fokker 70	KLM CityHopper	
PH-KZE	Fokker 70	KLM CityHopper	
PH-KZF	Fokker 70	KLM CityHopper	
PH-KZG	Fokker 70	KLM CityHopper	
PH-KZH	Fokker 70	KLM CityHopper	
PH-KZI	Fokker 70	KLM CityHopper	
PH-KZK	Fokker 70	KLM CityHopper	
PH-KZL	Fokker 70	KLM CityHopper	
PH-KZM	Fokker 70	KLM CityHopper	
PH-KZN	Fokker 70	KLM CityHopper	
PH-KZO	Fokker 70	KLM CityHopper	
PH-KZP	Fokker 70	KLM CityHopper	
PH-KZR	Fokker 70	KLM CityHopper	
PH-LXJ	Fokker 50	KLM CityHopper *City of Hull*	
PH-LXK	Fokker 50	KLM CityHopper *City of York*	
PH-LXP	Fokker 50	KLM CityHopper *City of Durham*	
PH-LXR	Fokker 50	KLM CityHopper *City of Amsterdam*	
PH-LXT	Fokker 50	KLM CityHopper *City of Stavanger*	
PH-MCE	Boeing 747-21AC (SCD)	Martinair *Prins van Oranje*	
PH-MCF	Boeing 747-21AC (SCD)	Martinair *Prins Claus*	
PH-MCG	Boeing 767-31AER	Martinair *Prins Johan Friso*	
PH-MCH	Boeing 767-31AER	Martinair *Prins Constantijn*	
PH-MCI	Boeing 767-31AER	Martinair *Prins Pieter-Christiaan*	
PH-MCJ	Boeing 767-33AER	Martinair	
PH-MCL	Boeing 767-31AER	Martinair *Koningin Beatrix*	
PH-MCM	Boeing 767-31AER	Martinair *Prins Floris*	
PH-MCN	Boeing 747-228F	Martinair Cargo *Prins Bernhard Junior*	
PH-MCP	McD Douglas MD-11CF	Martinair Cargo	
PH-MCR	McD Douglas MD-11CF	Martinair Cargo	
PH-MCS	McD Douglas MD-11CF	Martinair Cargo	
PH-MCT	McD Douglas MD-11CF	Martinair Cargo	
PH-MCU	McD Douglas MD-11F	Martinair Cargo *Prinses Maxima*	
PH-MCV	Boeing 767-31AER	Arkefly/bmi	
PH-MCW	McD Douglas MD-11CF	Martinair Cargo	

PH/PP/PR/PT/PZ/RA — OVERSEAS AIRLINERS

Reg	Type	Owner or Operator
PH-MCY	McD Douglas MD-11F	Martinair Cargo
PH-MPD	Airbus A.320-232	Martinair
PH-MPE	Airbus A.320-232	Martinair
PH-MPF	Airbus A.320-232	Martinair
PH-MPP	Boeing 747-412BCF	Martinair Cargo
PH-OFA	Fokker 100	KLM CityHopper
PH-OFB	Fokker 100	KLM CityHopper
PH-OFC	Fokker 100	KLM CityHopper
PH-OFD	Fokker 100	KLM CityHopper
PH-OFE	Fokker 100	KLM CityHopper
PH-OFF	Fokker 100	KLM CityHopper
PH-OFG	Fokker 100	KLM CityHopper
PH-OFH	Fokker 100	KLM CityHopper
PH-OFI	Fokker 100	KLM CityHopper
PH-OFJ	Fokker 100	KLM CityHopper
PH-OFK	Fokker 100	KLM CityHopper
PH-OFL	Fokker 100	KLM CityHopper
PH-OFM	Fokker 100	KLM CityHopper
PH-OFN	Fokker 100	KLM CityHopper
PH-PBA	Douglas DC-3C	Dutch Dakota Association
PH-PRJ	Fokker 50	Denim Air
PH-RXB	Embraer RJ145MP	City Airline
PH-WXA	Fokker 70	KLM CityHopper
PH-WXC	Fokker 70	KLM CityHopper
PH-WXD	Fokker 70	KLM CityHopper
PH-XRA	Boeing 737-7K2	Transavia *Leontien van Moorsel*
PH-XRB	Boeing 737-7K2	Transavia
PH-XRC	Boeing 737-7K2	Transavia
PH-XRD	Boeing 737-7K2	Transavia
PH-XRE	Boeing 737-7K2	Transavia
PH-XRV	Boeing 737-7K2	Transavia
PH-XRW	Boeing 737-7K2	Transavia
PH-XRX	Boeing 737-7K2	Transavia
PH-XRY	Boeing 737-7K2	Transavia
PH-XRZ	Boeing 737-7K2	Transavia

Note: KLM also operates B.737 HB-JJA and B.767 HB-JJG.

PP/PR/PT (Brazil)

Reg	Type	Owner or Operator
PP-VMT	Douglas DC-10-30F	VARIG Log
PP-VMU	Douglas DC-10-30F	VARIG Log
PP-VQY	Douglas DC-10-30F	VARIG Log
PR-LGD	McD Douglas MD-11F	VARIG Log
PR-LGE	McD Douglas MD-11F	VARIG Log
PT-MSH	McD Douglas MD-11	TAM Linhas aereas
PT-MVA	Airbus A.330-223	TAM Linhas aereas
PT-MVB	Airbus A.330-223	TAM Linhas aereas
PT-MVC	Airbus A.330-223	TAM Linhas aereas *The Magic Red Carpet*
PT-MVD	Airbus A.330-223	TAM Linhas aereas
PT-MVE	Airbus A.330-223	TAM Linhas aereas
PT-MVF	Airbus A.330-223	TAM Linhas aereas
PT-MVG	Airbus A.330-203	TAM Linhas aereas
PT-MVH	Airbus A.330-203	TAM Linhas aereas
PT-MVK	Airbus A.330-203	TAM Linhas aereas
PT-MVL	Airbus A.330-203	TAM Linhas aereas

PZ (Surinam)

Reg	Type	Owner or Operator
PZ-TCM	Boeing 747-306 (SCD)	Surinam Airways *Ronald Elwin Kappel*

RA (Russia)

Reg	Type	Owner or Operator
RA-76950	Ilyushin IL-76TD-90VD	Volga-Dnepr *Vladimir Kokkinaki*
RA-82010	An-124	Polet
RA-82014	An-124	Polet
RA-82024	An-124	Polet

OVERSEAS AIRLINERS

RA/S2

Reg	Type	Owner or Operator	Notes
RA-82026	An-124	Polet	
RA-82042	An-124	Volga-Dnepr	
RA-82043	An-124	Volga-Dnepr	
RA-82044	An-124	Volga-Dnepr	
RA-82045	An-124	Volga-Dnepr	
RA-82046	An-124	Volga-Dnepr	
RA-82047	An-124	Volga-Dnepr	
RA-82068	An-124	Polet	
RA-82074	An-124	Volga-Dnepr	
RA-82075	An-124	Polet	
RA-82077	An-124	Polet	
RA-82078	An-124	Volga-Dnepr	
RA-82079	An-124	Volga-Dnepr	
RA-82080	An-124	Polet	
RA-82081	An-124	Volga-Dnepr	
RA-85171	Tu-154M	Pulkovo Aviation	
RA-85185	Tu-154M	Pulkovo Aviation	
RA-85187	Tu-154M	Pulkovo Aviation	
RA-85204	Tu-154M	Pulkovo Aviation	
RA-85658	Tu-154M	Pulkovo Aviation	
RA-85695	Tu-154M	Pulkovo Aviation	
RA-85739	Tu-154M	Pulkovo Aviation	
RA-85753	Tu-154M	Pulkovo Aviation	
RA-85767	Tu-154M	Pulkovo Aviation	
RA-85769	Tu-154M	Pulkovo Aviation	
RA-85770	Tu-154M	Pulkovo Aviation	
RA-85771	Tu-154M	Pulkovo Aviation	
RA-85779	Tu-154M	Pulkovo Aviation	
RA-85785	Tu-154M	Pulkovo Aviation	
RA-85800	Tu-154M	Pulkovo Aviation	
RA-85832	Tu-154M	Pulkovo Aviation	
RA-85834	Tu-154M	Pulkovo Aviation	
RA-85835	Tu-154M	Pulkovo Aviation	
RA-85836	Tu-154M	Pulkovo Aviation	
RA-86466	IL-62M	Russia State Transport	
RA-86467	IL-62M	Russia State Transport	
RA-86468	IL-62M	Russia State Transport	
RA-86536	IL-62M	Russia State Transport	
RA-86537	IL-62M	Russia State Transport	
RA-86540	IL-62M	Russia State Transport	
RA-86559	IL-62M	Russia State Transport	
RA-86561	IL-62M	Russia State Transport	
RA-86710	IL-62M	Russia State Transport	
RA-86712	IL-62M	Russia State Transport	
RA-96012	IL-96	Russia State Transport	

Note: Aeroflot Russian International also operates Airbus A.319s VP-BDM, VP-BDN, VP-BDO, VP-BWA, VP-BWG, VP-BWJ, VP-BWK and VP-BWL; A.320s VP-BDK, VP-BQP, VP-BQV, VP-BQW, VP-BWD, VP-BWE, VP-BWF, VP-BWH, VP-BWI and VP-BWM; A.321s VP-BQR, VP-BQS, VP-BQT, VP-BQX, VP-BWN, VP-BWO and VP-BWP; plus B.767s VP-BAV, VP-BAX, VP-BAY, VP-BAZ, VP-BDI, VP-BWQ, VP-BWT, VP-BWU, VP-BWV, VP-BWW and VP-BWX.

Transaero employs Boeing 737s EI-CXK, EI-CXN, EI-CXR, EI-CZK, EI-DDK, EI-DDY, EI-DNM, EI-DTU, EI-DTV and EI-DTW plus Boeing 767s EI-CXZ, EI-CZD, EI-DBF, EI-DBG, EI-DBU, EI-DBW and EI-DFS. Pulkovo Aviation also operates B.737s EI-CDD, EI-CDE, EI-CDF, EI-CDG and EI-CDH.

S2 (Bangladesh)

S2-ACO	Douglas DC-10-30	Bangladesh Biman *City of Shah Makhdum (R.A.)*	
S2-ACP	Douglas DC-10-30	Bangladesh Biman *The City of Dhaka*	
S2-ACQ	Douglas DC-10-30	Bangladesh Biman *The City of Hazarat-Shah Jalal (R.A.)*	
S2-ACR	Douglas DC-10-30F	Bangladesh Biman *The New Era*	
S2-ACS	Douglas DC-10-30	Bangladesh Biman	
S2-ADE	Airbus A.310-325	Bangladesh Biman *City of Hazrat Khan Jahan Ali (R.A.)*	
S2-ADF	Airbus A.310-325	Bangladesh Biman *City of Chittagong*	
S2-ADH	Airbus A.310-324	Bangladesh Biman	
S2-ADK	Airbus A.310-324	Bangladesh Biman	
S2-ADN	Douglas DC-10-30	Bangladesh Biman	

Reg	Type	Owner or Operator

S5 (Slovenia)

Reg	Type	Owner or Operator
S5-AAA	Airbus A.320-231	Adria Airways
S5-AAB	Airbus A.320-231	Adria Airways/Afriquiyah Airways
S5-AAC	Airbus A.320-231	Adria Airways
S5-AAD	Canadair CL.600-2B19 RJ	Adria Airways
S5-AAE	Canadair CL.600-2B19 RJ	Adria Airways
S5-AAF	Canadair CL.600-2B19 RJ	Adria Airways
S5-AAG	Canadair CL.600-2B19 RJ	Adria Airways
S5-AAH	Canadair CL.600-2B19 RJ	Adria Airways
S5-AAI	Canadair CL.600-2B19 RJ	Adria Airways
S5-AAJ	Canadair CL.600-2B19 RJ	Adria Airways

Note: Adria Airways also operates B.737 UR-GAS.

S7 (Seychelles)

Reg	Type	Owner or Operator
S7-AHM	Boeing 767-37DER	Air Seychelles *Vallee de Mai*
S7-ASY	Boeing 767-3Q8ER	Air Seychelles *Aldabra*

SE (Sweden)

Reg	Type	Owner or Operator
SE-DIC	McD Douglas MD-87	SAS *Grane Viking*
SE-DIF	McD Douglas MD-87	SAS *Hjorulf Viking*
SE-DIK	McD Douglas MD-82	SAS *Stenkil Viking*
SE-DIL	McD Douglas MD-82	SAS *Tord Viking*
SE-DIN	McD Douglas MD-82	SAS *Eskil Viking*
SE-DIP	McD Douglas MD-87	SAS *Margret Viking*
SE-DIR	McD Douglas MD-81	SAS *Nora Viking*
SE-DIS	McD Douglas MD-81	SAS *Sigmund Viking*
SE-DIU	McD Douglas MD-87	SAS *Torsten Viking*
SE-DJX	Avro RJ70	Transwede Airways/Air One
SE-DJY	Avro RJ70	Transwede Airways/Air One
SE-DJZ	Avro RJ70	Transwede Airways/Air One
SE-DMB	McD Douglas MD-81	SAS *Bjarne Viking*
SE-DMF	McD Douglas MD-90-30	Nordic Leisure
SE-DMH	McD Douglas MD-90-30	Nordic Leisure
SE-DMT	McD Douglas MD-81	Nordic Leisure
SE-DTH	Boeing 737-683	SAS *Vile Viking*
SE-DUO	Boeing 757-236	TUIfly Nordic
SE-DUP	Boeing 757-236	TUIfly Nordic
SE-DZB	Embraer RJ145EP	Skyways Express
SE-DZK	Boeing 737-804	TUIfly Nordic
SE-DZN	Boeing 737-804	TUIfly Nordic
SE-DZV	Boeing 737-804	TUIfly Nordic
SE-KXP	BAe ATP	West Air Europe
SE-LGU	BAe ATP	West Air Europe
SE-LGV	BAe ATP	West Air Europe
SE-LGX	BAe ATP	West Air Europe
SE-LGY	BAe ATP	West Air Europe
SE-LGZ	BAe ATP	West Air Europe
SE-LNX	BAe ATP	West Air Europe
SE-LNY	BAe ATP	West Air Europe
SE-LPR	BAe ATP	West Air Europe
SE-LPS	BAe ATP	West Air Europe
SE-LPV	BAe ATP	West Air Europe
SE-LPX	BAe ATP	West Air Europe
SE-MAJ	BAe ATP	West Air Europe
SE-MAP	BAe ATP	West Air Europe
SE-RAA	Embraer RJ135ER	City Airline *City of Gothenburg*
SE-RAB	Embraer RJ135LR	City Airline *City of Linkoping*
SE-RAC	Embraer RJ145LR	City Airline
SE-RBA	McD Douglas MD-87	Nordic Leisure
SE-RBF	Airbus A.330-223	Novair Airlines
SE-RBG	Airbus A.330-223	Novair Airlines
SE-RCO	Boeing 737-33A	FlyMe
SE-RCP	Boeing 737-33A	FlyMe
SE-RCR	Boeing 737-33A	FlyMe

OVERSEAS AIRLINERS

SE/SP

Reg	Type	Owner or Operator	Notes
SE-RCS	Boeing 737-3Q8	FlyMe	
SE-RDE	McD Douglas MD-83	Viking Airlines	
SE-RDF	McD Douglas MD-83	Viking Airlines	
SE-RDG	McD Douglas MD-83	Viking Airlines	
SE-RDI	McD Douglas MD-83	Viking Airlines	
SE-RDM	McD Douglas MD-83	Nordic Leisure	
SE-RDN	Airbus A.321-231	Novair Airlines	
SE-RDO	Airbus A.321-231	Novair Airlines	
SE-RDP	Airbus A.321-231	Novair Airlines	
SE-REE	Airbus A.330-343X	SAS *Sigrid Viking*	
SE-REF	Airbus A.330-343X	SAS *Erik Viking*	
SE-RGP	McD Douglas MD-83	Nordic Leisure	

Note: City Airline also operates ERJ145 PH-RXB.

SP (Poland)

Reg	Type	Owner or Operator
SP-FDO	An-26B	Exin Air
SP-FDP	An-26B	Exin Air/DHL
SP-FDR	An-26B	Exin Air/DHL
SP-FDS	An-26B	Exin Air
SP-FDT	An-26B	Exin Air
SP-LDA	Embraer RJ170 100ST	LOT
SP-LDB	Embraer RJ170 100ST	LOT
SP-LDC	Embraer RJ170 100ST	LOT
SP-LDD	Embraer RJ170 100ST	LOT
SP-LDE	Embraer RJ170 100LR	LOT
SP-LDF	Embraer RJ170 100LR	LOT
SP-LDG	Embraer RJ170 100LR	LOT
SP-LDH	Embraer RJ170 100LR	LOT
SP-LDI	Embraer RJ170 100LR	LOT
SP-LDK	Embraer RJ170 100LR	LOT
SP-LGD	Embraer RJ145EP	LOT
SP-LGE	Embraer RJ145LR	LOT
SP-LGF	Embraer RJ145MP	LOT
SP-LGG	Embraer RJ145MP	LOT
SP-LGH	Embraer RJ145MP	LOT
SP-LGL	Embraer RJ145MP	LOT
SP-LGM	Embraer RJ145MP	LOT
SP-LGN	Embraer RJ145MP	LOT
SP-LGO	Embraer RJ145MP	LOT
SP-LIA	Embraer RJ175ST	LOT
SP-LIB	Embraer RJ175ST	LOT
SP-LIC	Embraer RJ175ST	LOT
SP-LID	Embraer RJ175ST	LOT
SP-LKA	Boeing 737-55D	LOT
SP-LKB	Boeing 737-55D	LOT
SP-LKC	Boeing 737-55D	LOT
SP-LKD	Boeing 737-55D	LOT
SP-LKE	Boeing 737-55D	LOT
SP-LKF	Boeing 737-55D	LOT
SP-LLA	Boeing 737-45D	LOT
SP-LLB	Boeing 737-45D	LOT
SP-LLC	Boeing 737-45D	LOT
SP-LLD	Boeing 737-45D	Centralwings
SP-LLE	Boeing 737-45D	Centralwings
SP-LLF	Boeing 737-45D	Centralwings
SP-LLG	Boeing 737-45D	Centralwings
SP-LLI	Boeing 737-4Q8	Centralwings
SP-LMC	Boeing 737-36N	Centralwings
SP-LMD	Boeing 737-36N	Centralwings
SP-LME	Boeing 737-36N	Centralwings
SP-LOA	Boeing 767-25DER	LOT *Gniezno*
SP-LOB	Boeing 767-25DER	LOT *Krakow*
SP-LPA	Boeing 767-35DER	LOT *Warszawa*
SP-LPB	Boeing 767-35DER	LOT *Gdansk*
SP-LPC	Boeing 767-35DER	LOT *Poznan*
SP-LPE	Boeing 767-341ER	LOT
SP-LPF	Boeing 767-319ER	LOT

Note: Centralwings also operates MD-87 OE-LOG.

ST/SU/SX — OVERSEAS AIRLINERS

Notes	Reg	Type	Owner or Operator

ST (Sudan)

Reg	Type	Owner or Operator
ST-AST	Airbus A.310-322	Sudan Airways
ST-ATA	Airbus A.300B4-622R	Sudan Airways
ST-ATB	Airbus A.300B4-622R	Sudan Airways *Elburag*

SU (Egypt)

Reg	Type	Owner or Operator
SU-BDG	Airbus A.300B4-203F	EgyptAir Cargo *Toshki*
SU-EAG	Tupolev Tu-204-120S	Cairo Aviation/TNT Airways
SU-EAJ	Tupolev Tu-204-120S	Cairo Aviation/TNT Airways
SU-GAC	Airbus A.300B4-203F	EgyptAir Cargo *New Valley*
SU-GAS	Airbus A.300F4-622RF	EgyptAir Cargo *Cheops*
SU-GAY	Airbus A.300B4-622RF	EgyptAir Cargo *Seti I*
SU-GBA	Airbus A.320-231	EgyptAir *Aswan*
SU-GBB	Airbus A.320-231	EgyptAir *Luxor*
SU-GBC	Airbus A.320-231	EgyptAir *Hurghada*
SU-GBD	Airbus A.320-231	EgyptAir *Taba*
SU-GBE	Airbus A.320-231	EgyptAir *El Alamein*
SU-GBF	Airbus A.320-231	EgyptAir *Sharm El Sheikh*
SU-GBG	Airbus A.320-231	EgyptAir *Saint Catherine*
SU-GBM	Airbus A.340-212	EgyptAir *Osirus Express*
SU-GBN	Airbus A.340-212	EgyptAir *Cleo Express*
SU-GBO	Airbus A.340-212	EgyptAir *Hathor Express*
SU-GBP	Boeing 777-266ER	EgyptAir *Nefertiti*
SU-GBR	Boeing 777-266ER	EgyptAir *Nefertari*
SU-GBS	Boeing 777-266ER	EgyptAir *Tyie*
SU-GBT	Airbus A.321-231	EgyptAir *Red Sea*
SU-GBU	Airbus A.321-231	EgyptAir *Sinai*
SU-GBV	Airbus A.321-231	EgyptAir/Air Cairo
SU-GBW	Airbus A.321-231	EgyptAir *The Nile*
SU-GBX	Boeing 777-266ER	EgyptAir *Neit*
SU-GBY	Boeing 777-266ER	EgyptAir *Titi*
SU-GBZ	Airbus A.320-232	EgyptAir
SU-GCA	Airbus A.320-232	EgyptAir
SU-GCB	Airbus A.320-232	EgyptAir
SU-GCC	Airbus A.320-232	EgyptAir
SU-GCD	Airbus A.320-232	EgyptAir
SU-GCE	Airbus A.330-243	EgyptAir
SU-GCF	Airbus A.330-243	EgyptAir
SU-GCG	Airbus A.330-243	EgyptAir
SU-GCH	Airbus A.330-243	EgyptAir
SU-GCI	Airbus A.330-243	EgyptAir
SU-GCJ	Airbus A.330-243	EgyptAir
SU-GCK	Airbus A.330-243	EgyptAir

SX (Greece)

Reg	Type	Owner or Operator
SX-BBU	Boeing 737-33A	Aegean Airlines *Joanna*
SX-BEM	Airbus A.300B4-605R	Olympic Airlines *Creta*
SX-BGH	Boeing 737-4Y0	Aegean Airlines *Iniochos*
SX-BGI	Boeing 737-3L9	Aegean Airlines
SX-BGJ	Boeing 737-4S3	Aegean Airlines
SX-BGK	Boeing 737-3Y0	Aegean Airlines *Thessaloniki*
SX-BGQ	Boeing 737-4Y0	Aegean Airlines
SX-BGR	Boeing 737-4Q8	Aegean Airlines
SX-BGS	Boeing 737-4Q8	Aegean Airlines
SX-BGV	Boeing 737-4Q8	Aegean Airlines
SX-BGW	Boeing 737-31S	Aegean Airlines
SX-BGX	Boeing 737-46B	Aegean Airlines
SX-BGY	Boeing 737-31S	Aegean Airlines
SX-BGZ	Boeing 737-31S	Aegean Airlines
SX-BKA	Boeing 737-484	Olympic Airlines *Vergina*
SX-BKB	Boeing 737-484	Olympic Airlines *Olynthos*
SX-BKC	Boeing 737-484	Olympic Airlines *Philipoli*
SX-BKD	Boeing 737-484	Olympic Airlines *Amphipoli*

OVERSEAS AIRLINERS

SX/TC

Reg	Type	Owner or Operator	Notes
SX-BKE	Boeing 737-484	Olympic Airlines *Stagira*	
SX-BKF	Boeing 737-484	Olympic Airlines *Dion*	
SX-BKG	Boeing 737-484	Olympic Airlines *Pella*	
SX-BKH	Boeing 737-4Q8	Olympic Airlines	
SX-BKI	Boeing 737-4Q8	Olympic Airlines	
SX-BKL	Boeing 737-4Y0	Olympic Airlines	
SX-BKM	Boeing 737-4Q8	Olympic Airlines	
SX-BKN	Boeing 737-4Q8	Olympic Airlines	
SX-BLC	Boeing 737-3Q8	Olympic Airlines	
SX-BLM	Boeing 737-42C	Aegean Airlines	
SX-BLX	Airbus A.320-211	Greece Airways	
SX-BMC	Boeing 737-42J	Olympic Airlines *City of Alexandroupoli*	
SX-BMP	McD Douglas MD-82	Alexandair	
SX-BSW	McD Douglas MD-83	Skywings Airlines/UK Jet	
SX-BTN	Boeing 737-43Q	Aegean Airlines	
SX-BTO	Boeing 737-33A	Aegean Airlines	
SX-DFA	Airbus A.340-313X	Olympic Airlines *Olympia*	
SX-DFB	Airbus A.340-313X	Olympic Airlines *Delphi*	
SX-DFC	Airbus A.340-313X	Olympic Airlines *Marathon*	
SX-DFD	Airbus A.340-313X	Olympic Airlines *Epidaurus*	
SX-DVG	Airbus A.320-232	Aegean Airlines	

TC (Turkey)

Reg	Type	Owner or Operator	Notes
TC-AAB	Boeing 737-86N	Pegasus Airlines	
TC-AAP	Boeing 737-86N	Pegasus Airlines	
TC-ABK	Airbus A.300B4-203F	Kuzu Cargo *Siirt 1*	
TC-ACB	Airbus A.300B4-203F	ACT Cargo	
TC-ACT	Airbus A.300B4-203F	ACT Cargo *Mersin*	
TC-ACU	Airbus A.300B4-203F	ACT Cargo	
TC-ACZ	Airbus A.300B4-103F	ACT Cargo	
TC-AGK	Airbus A.300B4-203F	Kuzu Cargo *Siirt 5*	
TC-APD	Boeing 737-42R	Pegasus Airlines/Atlas Jet	
TC-APF	Boeing 737-86N	Pegasus Airlines	
TC-APH	Boeing 737-8S3	Pegasus Airlines/Air Algerie	
TC-API	Boeing 737-86N	Pegasus Airlines	
TC-APJ	Boeing 737-86N	Pegasus Airlines	
TC-APM	Boeing 737-809	Pegasus Airlines	
TC-APN	Boeing 737-86N	Pegasus Airlines/Fly Air	
TC-APU	Boeing 737-82R	Pegasus Airlines	
TC-APY	Boeing 737-86N	Pegasus Airlines	
TC-APZ	Boeing 737-809	Pegasus Airlines	
TC-FBE	Airbus A.320-212	Freebird Airlines	
TC-FBF	Airbus A.320-212	Freebird Airlines	
TC-FBG	Airbus A.321-131	Freebird Airlines	
TC-FBT	Airbus A.321-131	Freebird Airlines	
TC-FBY	Airbus A.320-211	Freebird Airlines	
TC-JCO	Airbus A.310-203	Turkish Airlines *Lerkosa*	
TC-JCT	Airbus A.310-304F	Turkish Airlines *Samsun*	
TC-JCV	Airbus A.310-304	Turkish Airlines *Aras*	
TC-JCY	Airbus A.310-304	Turkish Airlines *Coruh*	
TC-JCZ	Airbus A.310-304	Turkish Airlines *Ergene*	
TC-JDA	Airbus A.310-304	Turkish Airlines *Aksu*	
TC-JDB	Airbus A.310-304	Turkish Airlines *Gˆksu*	
TC-JDF	Boeing 737-4Y0	Turkish Airlines *Ayvalik*	
TC-JDG	Boeing 737-4Y0	Turkish Airlines *Marmaris*	
TC-JDH	Boeing 737-4Y0	Turkish Airlines *Amasra*	
TC-JDJ	Airbus A.340-311	Turkish Airlines *Istanbul*	
TC-JDK	Airbus A.340-311	Turkish Airlines *Diyarbakir*	
TC-JDL	Airbus A.340-311	Turkish Airlines *Ankara*	
TC-JDM	Airbus A.340-311	Turkish Airlines *Izmir*	
TC-JDN	Airbus A.340-313	Turkish Airlines *Adana*	
TC-JDT	Boeing 737-4Y0	Turkish Airlines *Alanya*	
TC-JDY	Boeing 737-4Y0	Turkish Airlines *Antalya*	
TC-JEN	Boeing 737-4Q8	Turkish Airlines *Gelibolu*	
TC-JEO	Boeing 737-4Q8	Turkish Airlines *Anadolu*	
TC-JER	Boeing 737-4Y0	Turkish Airlines *Mugla*	
TC-JET	Boeing 737-4Y0	Turkish Airlines *Canakkale*	
TC-JEU	Boeing 737-4Y0	Turkish Airlines *Kayseri*	
TC-JEV	Boeing 737-4Y0	Turkish Airlines *Efes*	

TC OVERSEAS AIRLINERS

Notes	Reg	Type	Owner or Operator
	TC-JEY	Boeing 737-4Y0	Turkish Airlines *Side*
	TC-JEZ	Boeing 737-4Y0	Turkish Airlines *Bergama*
	TC-JFC	Boeing 737-8F2	Turkish Airlines *Diyarbakir*
	TC-JFD	Boeing 737-8F2	Turkish Airlines *Rize*
	TC-JFE	Boeing 737-8F2	Turkish Airlines *Hatay*
	TC-JFF	Boeing 737-8F2	Turkish Airlines *Afyon*
	TC-JFG	Boeing 737-8F2	Turkish Airlines *Mardi*
	TC-JFH	Boeing 737-8F2	Turkish Airlines *Igdir*
	TC-JFI	Boeing 737-8F2	Turkish Airlines *Sivas*
	TC-JFJ	Boeing 737-8F2	Turkish Airlines *Agri*
	TC-JFK	Boeing 737-8F2	Turkish Airlines *Zonguldak*
	TC-JFL	Boeing 737-8F2	Turkish Airlines *Ordu*
	TC-JFM	Boeing 737-8F2	Turkish Airlines *Nigde*
	TC-JFN	Boeing 737-8F2	Turkish Airlines *Bitlis*
	TC-JFO	Boeing 737-8F2	Turkish Airlines *Batman*
	TC-JFP	Boeing 737-8F2	Turkish Airlines *Amasya*
	TC-JFR	Boeing 737-8Y0	Turkish Airlines *Giresun*
	TC-JFT	Boeing 737-8F2	Turkish Airlines *Kastamonu*
	TC-JFU	Boeing 737-8F2	Turkish Airlines *Elazig*
	TC-JFV	Boeing 737-8F2	Turkish Airlines *Tunceli*
	TC-JFY	Boeing 737-8F2	Turkish Airlines *Manisa*
	TC-JFZ	Boeing 737-8F2	Turkish Airlines *Bolu*
	TC-JGA	Boeing 737-8F2	Turkish Airlines *Malatya*
	TC-JGB	Boeing 737-8F2	Turkish Airlines *Eskisehir*
	TC-JGC	Boeing 737-8F2	Turkish Airlines *Kocaeli*
	TC-JGD	Boeing 737-8F2	Turkish Airlines *Nevsehir*
	TC-JGE	Boeing 737-8F2	Turkish Airlines *Tekirdag*
	TC-JGF	Boeing 737-8F2	Turkish Airlines *Ardahan*
	TC-JGG	Boeing 737-8F2	Turkish Airlines *Erzincan*
	TC-JGH	Boeing 737-8F2	Turkish Airlines *Tokat*
	TC-JGI	Boeing 737-8F2	Turkish Airlines *Siirt*
	TC-JGJ	Boeing 737-8F2	Turkish Airlines *Ayidn*
	TC-JGK	Boeing 737-8F2	Turkish Airlines *Kirsehir*
	TC-JGL	Boeing 737-8F2	Turkish Airlines *Karaman*
	TC-JGM	Boeing 737-8F2	Turkish Airlines *Hakkari*
	TC-JGN	Boeing 737-8F2	Turkish Airlines *Bilecik*
	TC-JGO	Boeing 737-8F2	Turkish Airlines *Kilis*
	TC-JGP	Boeing 737-8F2	Turkish Airlines *Bartin*
	TC-JGR	Boeing 737-8F2	Turkish Airlines *Usak*
	TC-JGS	Boeing 737-8F2	Turkish Airlines
	TC-JGT	Boeing 737-8F2	Turkish Airlines *Avanos*
	TC-JGU	Boeing 737-8F2	Turkish Airlines *Bodrum*
	TC-JGV	Boeing 737-8F2	Turkish Airlines *Cesme*
	TC-JIH	Airbus A.340-313X	Turkish Airlines *Kocaeli*
	TC-JII	Airbus A.340-313X	Turkish Airlines *Aydin*
	TC-JLB	Airbus A.320-214	Turkish Airlines *Balikesir*
	TC-JLD	Airbus A.320-214	Turkish Airlines *Trabzon*
	TC-JLF	Airbus A.320-214	Turkish Airlines *Sakarya*
	TC-JLG	Airbus A.320-214	Turkish Airlines *Adiyman*
	TC-JLH	Airbus A.320-214	Turkish Airlines *Corum*
	TC-JLI	Airbus A.320-214	Turkish Airlines *Batman*
	TC-JLJ	Airbus A.320-232	Turkish Airlines *Sirnak*
	TC-JLK	Airbus A.320-232	Turkish Airlines *Kirklareli*
	TC-JLL	Airbus A.320-232	Turkish Airlines *Duzce*
	TC-JMA	Airbus A.321-111	Turkish Airlines *Yozgat*
	TC-JMB	Airbus A.321-111	Turkish Airlines *Osmaniye*
	TC-JMC	Airbus A.321-231	Turkish Airlines *Aksaray*
	TC-JMD	Airbus A.321-231	Turkish Airlines *Cankiri*
	TC-JME	Airbus A.321-211	Turkish Airlines *Burdur*
	TC-JMF	Airbus A.321-211	Turkish Airlines *Bingol*
	TC-JMG	Airbus A.321-211	Turkish Airlines *Kirikkale*
	TC-JNA	Airbus A.330-203	Turkish Airlines *Gaziantep*
	TC-JNB	Airbus A.330-203	Turkish Airlines *Konya*
	TC-JNC	Airbus A.330-203	Turkish Airlines *Bursa*
	TC-JND	Airbus A.330-203	Turkish Airlines *Antalya*
	TC-JNE	Airbus A.330-203	Turkish Airlines *Kayseri*
	TC-JPA	Airbus A.320-232	Turkish Airlines *Mus*
	TC-JPB	Airbus A.320-232	Turkish Airlines *Rize*
	TC-JPC	Airbus A.320-232	Turkish Airlines *Erzurum*
	TC-JPD	Airbus A.320-232	Turkish Airlines *Isparta*
	TC-JPE	Airbus A.320-232	Turkish Airlines *Gumushane*
	TC-JPF	Airbus A.320-232	Turkish Airlines *Yozgat*

OVERSEAS AIRLINERS

TC

Reg	Type	Owner or Operator	Notes
TC-JPG	Airbus A.320-232	Turkish Airlines *Osmaniye*	
TC-JRA	Airbus A.321-231	Turkish Airlines *Kutayha*	
TC-JRB	Airbus A.321-231	Turkish Airlines *Sanliurfa*	
TC-JRC	Airbus A.321-231	Turkish Airlines *Sakarya*	
TC-JRD	Airbus A.321-231	Turkish Airlines	
TC-KTC	Airbus A.321-211	Kibris Turkish Airlines *Girne*	
TC-KTD	Airbus A.321-211	Kibris Turkish Airlines *Iskele*	
TC-KTY	Airbus A.321-211	Kibris Turkish Airlines *Lefke*	
TC-KZU	Airbus A.300B4-203F	Kuzu Cargo *Siirt 2*	
TC-KZV	Airbus A.300B4-103F	Kuzu Cargo *Siirt 4*	
TC-KZY	Airbus A.300B4-103F	Kuzu Cargo *Siirt 3*	
TC-MAO	Boeing 737-86N	Kibris Turkish Airlines *Karpaz*	
TC-MBE	F.27 Friendship Mk 500F	MNG Kargo	
TC-MBF	F.27 Friendship Mk 500F	MNG Kargo	
TC-MBG	F.27 Friendship Mk 500F	MNG Kargo	
TC-MBH	F.27 Friendship Mk 500F	MNG Kargo	
TC-MNA	Airbus A.300B4-203F	MNG Cargo	
TC-MNB	Airbus A.300B4-203F	MNG Cargo	
TC-MNC	Airbus A.300B4-203F	MNG Cargo	
TC-MND	Airbus A.300B4-203F	MNG Cargo	
TC-MNJ	Airbus A.300B4-203F	MNG Cargo	
TC-MNN	Airbus A.300B4-203F	MNG Cargo	
TC-MSO	Boeing 737-8S3	Kibris Turkish Airlines *Magusa*	
TC-MZZ	Boeing 737-8S3	Kibris Turkish Airlines *Guzelyurt*	
TC-OAA	Airbus A.300B4-605R	Onur Air	
TC-OAB	Airbus A.300B4-605R	Onur Air	
TC-OAC	Airbus A.320-212	Onur Air	
TC-OAD	Airbus A.320-212	Onur Air	
TC-OAE	Airbus A.321-231	Onur Air	
TC-OAF	Airbus A.321-231	Onur Air	
TC-OAG	Airbus A.300B4-605R	Onur Air	
TC-OAH	Airbus A.300B4-605R	Onur Air	
TC-OAI	Airbus A.321-231	Onur Air	
TC-OAK	Airbus A.321-231	Onur Air	
TC-OAL	Airbus A.321-231	Onur Air	
TC-OAN	Airbus A.321-231	Onur Air	
TC-OAO	Airbus A.300B4-605R	Onur Air	
TC-OAY	Airbus A.300B4-622R	Onur Air	
TC-OGE	Airbus A.320-214	Atlasjet	
TC-OGF	Airbus A.320-214	Atlasjet	
TC-OGG	Boeing 757-2G5	Atlasjet	
TC-OGI	Airbus A.320-232	Atlasjet	
TC-OGJ	Airbus A.320-232	Atlasjet	
TC-OGK	Airbus A.320-232	Atlasjet	
TC-OGL	Airbus A.320-232	Atlasjet	
TC-OGO	Airbus A.320-232	Atlasjet	
TC-OGP	Airbus A.320-232	Atlasjet	
TC-OGR	Airbus A.320-232	Atlasjet	
TC-OGS	Boeing 757-256	Atlasjet	
TC-ONK	Airbus A.300B4-103	Onur Air *Pinar*	
TC-ONM	McD Douglas MD-88	Onur Air *Yasemin*	
TC-ONN	McD Douglas MD-88	Onur Air *Ece*	
TC-ONO	McD Douglas MD-88	Onur Air *Yonca*	
TC-ONP	McD Douglas MD-88	Onur Air *Esra*	
TC-ONR	McD Douglas MD-88	Onur Air *Evren*	
TC-ONT	Airbus A.300B4-203	Onur Air *B. Basar*	
TC-ONU	Airbus A.300B4-203	Onur Air	
TC-ONY	Airbus A.300B2K-3C	Onur Air	
TC-SNA	Boeing 757-2Q8	SunExpress	
TC-SUG	Boeing 737-8CX	SunExpress	
TC-SUH	Boeing 737-8CX	SunExpress	
TC-SUI	Boeing 737-8CX	SunExpress	
TC-SUJ	Boeing 737-8CX	SunExpress	
TC-SUL	Boeing 737-85F	SunExpress	
TC-SUM	Boeing 737-85F	SunExpress	
TC-SUO	Boeing 737-86Q	SunExpress	
TC-SUU	Boeing 737-86Q	SunExpress	
TC-TJA	Boeing 737-3Q8	Corendon Airlines	
TC-TJB	Boeing 737-3Q8	Corendon Airlines	
TC-TJC	Boeing 737-4Q8	Corendon Airlines	
TC-TJD	Boeing 737-4Q8	Corendon Airlines	
TC-TUB	Airbus A.321-131	Alajnihah Airways	

TF/TS — OVERSEAS AIRLINERS

Notes	Reg	Type	Owner or Operator

TF (Iceland)

Reg	Type	Owner or Operator
TF-AMC	Boeing 747-2B3F (SCD)	Air Atlanta Icelandic/Saudi Arabian Airlines
TF-AME	Boeing 747-312	Air Atlanta Icelandic/Travelcitydirect
TF-AMI	Boeing 747-412BCF	Air Atlanta Icelandic/Cargolux
TF-AMJ	Boeing 747-312	Air Atlanta Icelandic
TF-AMK	Boeing 747-312	Air Atlanta Icelandic
TF-AMO	Boeing 747-48E (SCD)	Air Atlanta Icelandic/Cargolux
TF-ARH	Boeing 747-230B (SF)	Air Atlanta Cargo
TF-ARJ	Boeing 747-236B (M)	Air Atlanta Cargo
TF-ARL	Boeing 747-230BF (SCD)	Air Atlanta Cargo
TF-ARM	Boeing 747-230BF (SCD)	Air Atlanta Icelandic/MAS Kargo
TF-ARN	Boeing 747-2F6B (SCD)	Air Atlanta Icelandic/MAS Kargo
TF-ARP	Boeing 747-230F (SCD)	Air Atlanta Cargo
TF-ARS	Boeing 747-357	Air Atlanta Europe/Saudi Arabian Airlines
TF-ARU	Boeing 747-344	Air Atlanta Icelandic
TF-ARV	Boeing 747-230F (SCD)	Air Atlanta Cargo
TF-ARW	Boeing 747-256B (SF)	Air Atlanta Icelandic/MAS Kargo
TF-ATI	Boeing 747-341	Air Atlanta Icelandic/Saudi Arabian Airlines
TF-ATJ	Boeing 747-341	Air Atlanta Icelandic/Saudi Arabian Airlines
TF-ATX	Boeing 747-236B (SF)	Air Atlanta Icelandic/MAS Kargo
TF-ATZ	Boeing 747-236B (SF)	Air Atlanta Icelandic/MAS Kargo
TF-BBA.	Boeing 737-46JF	Bluebird Cargo
TF-BBB	Boeing 737-46JF	Bluebird Cargo
TF-BBC	Boeing 737-3Q4F	Bluebird Cargo
TF-BBD	Boeing 737-3Y0F	Bluebird Cargo
TF-BBE	Boeing 737-36EF	Bluebird Cargo
TF-BBF	Boeing 737-36EF	Bluebird Cargo
TF-BBG	Boeing 737-36EF	Bluebird Cargo
TF-CIB	Boeing 757-204F	Icelandair Cargo
TF-CSA	Dornier 328-110	City Star Airlines
TF-CSB	Dornier 328-110	City Star Airlines
TF-CSC	Dornier 328-110	City Star Airlines
TF-ELR	Airbus A.310-324	Air Atlanta Icelandic
TF-ELW	Airbus A.300C4-605RF	Islandsflug Cargo
TF-FIB	Boeing 767-383ER	Icelandair/Santa Barbara Airlines
TF-FIC	Boeing 767-383ER	Icelandair/Israir
TF-FID	Boeing 757-23APF	Icelandair Cargo/TNT
TF-FIE	Boeing 757-23APF	Icelandair Cargo
TF-FIG	Boeing 757-23APF	Icelandair Cargo
TF-FIH	Boeing 757-208PCF	Icelandair Cargo
TF-FII	Boeing 757-208	Icelandair/Air Mediterranée
TF-FIJ	Boeing 757-208	Icelandair *Svandis*
TF-FIK	Boeing 757-28A	Icelandair *Soldis*
TF-FIN	Boeing 757-208	Icelandair *Bryndis*
TF-FIO	Boeing 757-208	Icelandair *Valdis*
TF-FIP	Boeing 757-208	Icelandair *Leifur Eiriksson*
TF-FIR	Boeing 757-256	Icelandair
TF-FIS	Boeing 757-256	Loftleidir Icelandic
TF-FIT	Boeing 757-256	Loftleidir Icelandic
TF-FIU	Boeing 757-256	Icelandair
TF-FIV	Boeing 757-208	Icelandair *Gudridur Porbjarnardottir*
TF-FIW	Boeing 757-27B	Loftleidir Icelandic
TF-FIX	Boeing 757-308	Icelandair *Snorri Porfinnsson*
TF-LLA	Boeing 767-366ER	Icelandair/Ghana International
TF-LLZ	Boeing 757-225	Loftleidir Icelandic
TF-JXA	McD Douglas MD-82	JetX/Sterling Airlines
TF-JXB	McD Douglas MD-82	JetX/Sterling Airlines
TF-JXC	McD Douglas MD-83	JetX/Blue Line
TF-MIL	Dornier 328-300 JET	Icejet
TF-MIO	Dornier 328-300 JET	Icejet
TF-NPA	Dornier 328-310 JET	City Star Airlines

Note: Air Atlanta and Islandsflug aircraft are frequently leased to other airlines on a short-term basis. Iceland Express operates MD-90s HB-JIC, HB-JID and HB-JIF.

TS (Tunisia)

Reg	Type	Owner or Operator
TS-IEC	Boeing 737-33A	Karthago Airlines
TS-IED	Boeing 737-33A	Karthago Airlines

OVERSEAS AIRLINERS

TS/UK/UN/UR

Reg	Type	Owner or Operator	Notes
TS-IEE	Boeing 737-33A	Karthago Airlines	
TS-IEF	Boeing 737-3Q8	Karthago Airlines	
TS-IEG	Boeing 737-31S	Karthago Airlines	
TS-IEJ	Boeing 737-322	Karthago Airlines	
TS-IMB	Airbus A.320-211	Tunis Air *Fahrat Hached*	
TS-IMC	Airbus A.320-211	Tunis Air *7 Novembre*	
TS-IMD	Airbus A.320-211	Tunis Air *Khereddine*	
TS-IME	Airbus A.320-211	Tunis Air *Tabarka*	
TS-IMF	Airbus A.320-211	Tunis Air *Djerba*	
TS-IMG	Airbus A.320-211	Tunis Air *Abou el Kacem Chebbi*	
TS-IMH	Airbus A.320-211	Tunis Air *Ali Belhaouane*	
TS-IMI	Airbus A.320-211	Tunis Air *Jughurta*	
TS-IMJ	Airbus A.319-114	Tunis Air *El Kantaoui*	
TS-IMK	Airbus A.319-114	Tunis Air *Kerkenah*	
TS-IML	Airbus A.320-211	Tunis Air *Gafsa el Ksar*	
TS-IMM	Airbus A.320-211	Tunis Air *Le Bardo*	
TS-IMN	Airbus A.320-211	Tunis Air *Ibn Khaldoun*	
TS-IMO	Airbus A.319-114	Tunis Air *Hannibal*	
TS-IMP	Airbus A.320-211	Tunis Air *La Galite*	
TS-INA	Airbus A.320-214	Nouvelair	
TS-INB	Airbus A.320-214	Nouvelair	
TS-INC	Airbus A.320-214	Nouvelair *Youssef*	
TS-IND	Airbus A.320-212	Nouvelair	
TS-INE	Airbus A.320-212	Nouvelair	
TS-INF	Airbus A.320-212	Nouvelair	
TS-INH	Airbus A.320-211	Nouvelair/Afriquiyah Airways	
TS-INI	Airbus A.320-212	Nouvelair	
TS-INK	Airbus A.320-211	Nouvelair	
TS-INL	Airbus A.320-212	Nouvelair	
TS-IOG	Boeing 737-5H3	Tunis Air *Sfax*	
TS-IOH	Boeing 737-5H3	Tunis Air *Hammamet*	
TS-IOI	Boeing 737-5H3	Tunis Air *Mahida*	
TS-IOJ	Boeing 737-5H3	Tunis Air *Monastir*	
TS-IOK	Boeing 737-6H3	Tunis Air *Kairouan*	
TS-IOL	Boeing 737-6H3	Tunis Air *Tozeur-Nefta*	
TS-IOM	Boeing 737-6H3	Tunis Air *Carthage*	
TS-ION	Boeing 737-6H3	Tunis Air *Utique*	
TS-IOP	Boeing 737-6H3	Tunis Air *El Jem*	
TS-IOQ	Boeing 737-6H3	Tunis Air *Bizerte*	
TS-IOR	Boeing 737-6H3	Tunis Air *Tahar Haddad*	
TS-IPA	Airbus A.300B4-605R	Tunis Air *Sidi Bou Said*	
TS-IPB	Airbus A.300B4-605R	Tunis Air *Tunis*	
TS-IPC	Airbus A.300B4-605R	Tunis Air *Amilcar*	
TS-IQA	Airbus A.321-211	Nouvelair	
TS-IQB	Airbus A.321-211	Nouvelair	

UK (Uzbekistan)

UK-31001	Airbus A.310-324	Uzbekistan Airways *Tashkent*	
UK-31002	Airbus A.310-324	Uzbekistan Airways *Fergana*	
UK-31003	Airbus A.310-324	Uzbekistan Airways *Bukhara*	
UK-75700	Boeing 757-23P	Uzbekistan Airways	

Note: Uzbekistan Airways also operates B.767s VP-BUA, VP-BUE, VP-BUF and VP-BUZ; plus 757s VP-BUB, VP-BUD, VP-BUH, VP-BUI and VP-BUJ.

UN (Kazakhstan)

Note: Air Astana operates Boeing 757s P4-EAS, P4-FAS and P4-GAS.

UR (Ukraine)

UR-BWM	Antonov An-12BK	Volare Airlines	
UR-GAH	Boeing 737-32Q	Ukraine International *Mayrni*	
UR-GAJ	Boeing 737-5Y0	Ukraine International	
UR-GAK	Boeing 737-5Y0	Ukraine International	
UR-GAL	Boeing 737-341	Ukraine International	

UR/V5/V8/VH OVERSEAS AIRLINERS

Notes	Reg	Type	Owner or Operator
	UR-GAM	Boeing 737-4Y0	Ukraine International
	UR-GAN	Boeing 737-36N	Ukraine International
	UR-GAO	Boeing 737-4Z9	Ukraine International
	UR-GAP	Boeing 737-4Z9	Ukraine International
	UR-GAQ	Boeing 737-33R	Ukraine International
	UR-GAR	Boeing 737-4Y0	Ukraine International
	UR-GAS	Boeing 737-528	Ukraine International/Adria Airways
	UR-GAT	Boeing 737-528	Ukraine International
	UR-GAU	Boeing 737-5Y0	Ukraine International
	UR-GAV	Boeing 737-4C9	Ukraine International
	UR-LAI	Antonov An-12BP	Volare Airlines
	UR-LMI	Antonov An-12BK	Volare Airlines
	UR-LTG	Antonov An-12BP	Volare Airlines
	UR-SMA	Antonov An-12BK	Volare Airlines
	UR-SVG	Antonov An-12BP	Volare Airlines
	UR-VVA	Boeing 737-3Q8	Aerosvit Airlines
	UR-VVB	Boeing 737-529	Aerosvit Airlines
	UR-VVD	Boeing 737-529	Aerosvit Airlines
	UR-VVE	Boeing 737-448	Aerosvit Airlines
	UR-VVF	Boeing 767-383ER	Aerosvit Airlines
	UR-VVG	Boeing 767-383ER	Aerosvit Airlines
	UR-VVI	Boeing 737-33A	Aerosvit Airlines
	UR-VVJ	Boeing 737-448	Aerosvit Airlines
	UR-VVK	Boeing 737-4Q8	Aerosvit Airlines
	UR-VVL	Boeing 737-448	Aerosvit Airlines
	UR-VVM	Boeing 737-448	Aerosvit Airlines
	UR-VVN	Boeing 737-4Y0	Aerosvit Airlines
	UR-ZYD	Antonov An-124	United Arab Emirates
	UR-09307	Antonov An-22A	Antonov Airlines
	UR-82007	Antonov An-124	Antonov Airlines
	UR-82008	Antonov An-124	Antonov Airlines
	UR-82009	Antonov An-124	Antonov Airlines
	UR-82027	Antonov An-124	Antonov Airlines
	UR-82029	Antonov An-124	Antonov Airlines
	UR-82060	Antonov An-225	Antonov Airlines
	UR-82072	Antonov An-124	Antonov Airlines
	UR-82073	Antonov An-124	Antonov Airlines

V5 (Namibia)

V5-NMF	Airbus A.340-311	Air Namibia

V8 (Brunei)

V8-ALI	Boeing 747-430	Brunei Sultan's Flight
V8-BKH	Airbus A.340-212	Brunei Sultan's Flight
V8-MHB	Boeing 767-27GER	Brunei Sultan's Flight
V8-RBF	Boeing 767-33AER	Royal Brunei Airlines
V8-RBG	Boeing 767-33AER	Royal Brunei Airlines
V8-RBH	Boeing 767-33AER	Royal Brunei Airlines
V8-RBJ	Boeing 767-33AER	Royal Brunei Airlines
V8-RBK	Boeing 767-33AER	Royal Brunei Airlines
V8-RBL	Boeing 767-33AER	Royal Brunei Airlines

VH (Australia)

VH-OEB	Boeing 747-48E	QANTAS *Phillip Island*
VH-OEC	Boeing 747-4H6	QANTAS *King Island*
VH-OED	Boeing 747-4H6	QANTAS *Kangaroo Island*
VH-OEE	Boeing 747-438ER	QANTAS
VH-OEF	Boeing 747-438ER	QANTAS
VH-OEG	Boeing 747-438ER	QANTAS
VH-OEH	Boeing 747-438ER	QANTAS
VH-OEI	Boeing 747-438ER	QANTAS
VH-OEJ	Boeing 747-438ER	QANTAS

OVERSEAS AIRLINERS

VH/VN/VP-B

Reg	Type	Owner or Operator	Notes
VH-OJA	Boeing 747-438	QANTAS *City of Canberra*	
VH-OJB	Boeing 747-438	QANTAS *City of Sydney*	
VH-OJC	Boeing 747-438	QANTAS *City of Melbourne*	
VH-OJD	Boeing 747-438	QANTAS *City of Brisbane*	
VH-OJE	Boeing 747-438	QANTAS *City of Adelaide*	
VH-OJF	Boeing 747-438	QANTAS *City of Perth*	
VH-OJG	Boeing 747-438	QANTAS *City of Hobart*	
VH-OJH	Boeing 747-438	QANTAS *City of Darwin*	
VH-OJI	Boeing 747-438	QANTAS *Longreach*	
VH-OJJ	Boeing 747-438	QANTAS *Winton*	
VH-OJK	Boeing 747-438	QANTAS *City of Newcastle*	
VH-OJL	Boeing 747-438	QANTAS *City of Ballaarat*	
VH-OJM	Boeing 747-438	QANTAS *City of Gosford*	
VH-OJN	Boeing 747-438	QANTAS *City of Dubbo*	
VH-OJO	Boeing 747-438	QANTAS *City of Toowoomba*	
VH-OJP	Boeing 747-438	QANTAS *City of Albury*	
VH-OJQ	Boeing 747-438	QANTAS *City of Mandurah*	
VH-OJR	Boeing 747-438	QANTAS *City of Bathurst*	
VH-OJS	Boeing 747-438	QANTAS	
VH-OJT	Boeing 747-438	QANTAS	
VH-OJU	Boeing 747-438	QANTAS	

VN (Vietnam)

Reg	Type	Owner or Operator	Notes
VN-A141	Boeing 777-2Q8ER	Vietnam Airlines	
VN-A142	Boeing 777-2Q8ER	Vietnam Airlines	
VN-A143	Boeing 777-26KER	Vietnam Airlines	
VN-A144	Boeing 777-26KER	Vietnam Airlines	
VN-A145	Boeing 777-26KER	Vietnam Airlines	
VN-A146	Boeing 777-26KER	Vietnam Airlines	
VN-A147	Boeing 777-2Q8ER	Vietnam Airlines	
VN-A149	Boeing 777-2Q8ER	Vietnam Airlines	
VN-A150	Boeing 777-2Q8ER	Vietnam Airlines	
VN-A151	Boeing 777-2Q8ER	Vietnam Airlines	

VP-B (Bermuda)

Reg	Type	Owner or Operator	Notes
VP-BAT	Boeing 747SP-21	Worldwide Aviation	
VP-BAV	Boeing 767-36NER	Aeroflot Russian International *L.Tolstoy*	
VP-BAX	Boeing 767-36NER	Aeroflot Russian International *F. Dostoevsky*	
VP-BAY	Boeing 767-36NER	Aeroflot Russian International *I.Turgenev*	
VP-BAZ	Boeing 767-36NER	Aeroflot Russian International *N. Nekrasov*	
VP-BBR	Boeing 757-22L	Azerbaijan Airlines *Garabagh*	
VP-BBS	Boeing 757-22L	Azerbaijan Airlines	
VP-BDI	Boeing 767-38AER	Aeroflot Russian International *A. Pushkin*	
VP-BDK	Airbus A.320-214	Aeroflot Russian International *G. Sviridov*	
VP-BDM	Airbus A.319-111	Aeroflot Russian International *A. Borodin*	
VP-BDN	Airbus A.319-111	Aeroflot Russian International *A. Dargomyzhsky*	
VP-BDO	Airbus A.319-111	Aeroflot Russian International *I. Stravinsky*	
VP-BQP	Airbus A.320-214	Aeroflot Russian International *A. Rublev*	
VP-BQR	Airbus A.321-211	Aeroflot Russian International *I. Repin*	
VP-BQS	Airbus A.321-211	Aeroflot Russian International *I. Kramskoi*	
VP-BQT	Airbus A.321-211	Aeroflot Russian International *I. Shishkin*	
VP-BQV	Airbus A.320-214	Aeroflot Russian International *V. Vasnetsov*	
VP-BQW	Airbus A.320-214	Aeroflot Russian International *V. Vereshchagin*	
VP-BQX	Airbus A.321-211	Aeroflot Russian International *I. Ayvazovsky*	
VP-BUA	Boeing 767-33PER	Uzbekistan Airways *Samarkand*	
VP-BUB	Boeing 757-23P	Uzbekistan Airways *Urgench*	
VP-BUD	Boeing 757-23P	Uzbekistan Airways *Shahrisabz*	
VP-BUE	Boeing 767-3CBER	Uzbekistan Airways	
VP-BUF	Boeing 767-33PER	Uzbekistan Airways	
VP-BUH	Boeing 757-231	Uzbekistan Airways	
VP-BUI	Boeing 757-231	Uzbekistan Airways	
VP-BUJ	Boeing 757-231	Uzbekistan Airways	
VP-BUZ	Boeing 767-33PER	Uzbekistan Airways *Khiva*	
VP-BWA	Airbus A.319-111	Aeroflot Russian International *S. Prokofiev*	
VP-BWD	Airbus A.320-214	Aeroflot Russian International *A. Aliabiev*	
VP-BWE	Airbus A.320-214	Aeroflot Russian International *H.Rimsky-Korsakov*	
VP-BWF	Airbus A.320-214	Aeroflot Russian International *D. Shostakovich*	

VP-B/VT/XA/YK — OVERSEAS AIRLINERS

Notes	Reg	Type	Owner or Operator
	VP-BWG	Airbus A.319-111	Aeroflot Russian International *A. Aleksandrov*
	VP-BWH	Airbus A.320-214	Aeroflot Russian International *M. Balakirev*
	VP-BWI	Airbus A.320-214	Aeroflot Russian International *A. Glazunov*
	VP-BWJ	Airbus A.319-111	Aeroflot Russian International *A. Shnitke*
	VP-BWK	Airbus A.319-111	Aeroflot Russian International *S. Taneyev*
	VP-BWL	Airbus A.319-111	Aeroflot Russian International *A. Grechaninov*
	VP-BWM	Airbus A.320-214	Aeroflot Russian International *S. Rakhmaninov*
	VP-BWN	Airbus A.321-211	Aeroflot Russian International *A. Skriabin*
	VP-BWO	Airbus A.321-211	Aeroflot Russian International *P. Chaikovsky*
	VP-BWP	Airbus A.321-211	Aeroflot Russian International *M. Musorgsky*
	VP-BWQ	Boeing 767-341ER	Aeroflot Russian International *M. Lermontov*
	VP-BWT	Boeing 767-38AER	Aeroflot Russian International *A. Chekhov*
	VP-BWU	Boeing 767-3T7ER	Aeroflot Russian International *I. Bunin*
	VP-BWV	Boeing 767-3T7ER	Aeroflot Russian International *A. Kuprin*
	VP-BWW	Boeing 767-306ER	Aeroflot Russian International *S. Esenin*
	VP-BWX	Boeing 767-306ER	Aeroflot Russian International *A. Blok*

VT (India)

Reg	Type	Owner or Operator
VT-AID	Boeing 747-4B5	Air-India *Kaziranga*
VT-AIE	Boeing 747-412	Air-India *Mamallapuram*
VT-AIF	Boeing 747-412	Air-India *Ellora*
VT-AIJ	Boeing 777-222ER	Air-India *Neelambam*
VT-AIK	Boeing 777-222ER	Air-India *Megh Malhaar*
VT-AIL	Boeing 777-222ER	Air-India *Kalyani*
VT-AIM	Boeing 747-433	Air-India *Sunderbans*
VT-AIQ	Boeing 747-412	Air-India *Elephanta*
VT-AIR	Boeing 777-222ER	Air-India *Hamsadhwani*
VT-ALA	Boeing 777-237LR	Air-India *State of Andhra Pradesh*
VT-ALB	Boeing 777-237LR	Air-India
VT-ALC	Boeing 777-237LR	Air-India
VT-EDU	Boeing 747-237B	Air-India *Akbar*
VT-EGA	Boeing 747-237B	Air-India *Samudra Gupta*
VT-EGB	Boeing 747-237B	Air-India *Mahendra Varman*
VT-EGC	Boeing 747-237B	Air-India *Harsha Vardhana*
VT-EPW	Boeing 747-337 (SCD)	Air-India *Shivaji*
VT-EPX	Boeing 747-337 (SCD)	Air-India *Narasimha Varman*
VT-ESM	Boeing 747-437	Air-India *Konark*
VT-ESN	Boeing 747-437	Air-India *Tanjore*
VT-ESO	Boeing 747-437	Air-India *Khajuraho*
VT-ESP	Boeing 747-437	Air-India *Ajanta*
VT-EVA	Boeing 747-437	Air-India *Agra*
VT-EVB	Boeing 747-437	Air-India *Velha Goa*
VT-JWA	Airbus A.340-313E	Jet Airways
VT-JWB	Airbus A.340-313E	Jet Airways
VT-JWC	Airbus A.340-313E	Jet Airways
VT-JWD	Airbus A.330-243	Jet Airways
VT-JWE	Airbus A.330-243	Jet Airways
VT-JWF	Airbus A.330-243	Jet Airways

Note: Air-India also operates B.767 G-CDPT.

XA (Mexico)

Reg	Type	Owner or Operator
XA-APB	Boeing 767-3Q8ER	Aeromexico
XA-JBC	Boeing 767-284ER	Aeromexico
XA-OAM	Boeing 767-2B1ER	Aeromexico
XA-RVZ	Boeing 767-284ER	Aeromexico
XA-TOJ	Boeing 767-283ER	Aeromexico

Note: Aeromexico also operates B.777s N745AM, N746AM and N774AM.

YK (Syria)

Reg	Type	Owner or Operator
YK-AHA	Boeing 747SP-94	Syrianair *November 16*
YK-AHB	Boeing 747SP-94	Syrianair *Arab Solidarity*
YK-AKA	Airbus A.320-232	Syrianair *Ugarit*

OVERSEAS AIRLINERS

YK/YL/YR/YU/YV/Z

Reg	Type	Owner or Operator	Notes
YK-AKB	Airbus A.320-232	Syrianair *Ebla*	
YK-AKC	Airbus A.320-232	Syrianair *Afamia*	
YK-AKD	Airbus A.320-232	Syrianair *Mari*	
YK-AKE	Airbus A.320-232	Syrianair *Bosra*	
YK-AKF	Airbus A.320-232	Syrianair *Amrit*	

YL (Latvia)

Reg	Type	Owner or Operator
YL-BBA	Boeing 737-505	Air Baltic
YL-BBB	Boeing 737-505	Air Baltic
YL-BBD	Boeing 737-53S	Air Baltic
YL-BBE	Boeing 737-53S	Air Baltic
YL-BBF	Boeing 737-548	Air Baltic
YL-BBG	Boeing 737-548	Air Baltic
YL-BBH	Boeing 737-548	Air Baltic
YL-BBK	Boeing 737-33V	Air Baltic
YL-BBL	Boeing 737-33V	Air Baltic
YL-KSA	Antonov An-74-200	KS-Avia
YL-KSB	Antonov An-74	KS-Avia
YL-RAA	Antonov An-26	RAF-Avia
YL-RAB	Antonov An-26	RAF-Avia
YL-RAC	Antonov An-26B	RAF-Avia
YL-RAD	Antonov An-26B	RAF-Avia
YL-RAE	Antonov An-26	RAF-Avia
YL-RAF	Antonov An-74TK-100	RAF-Avia
YL-RAG	Saab SF340A Cargo	RAF-Avia

YR (Romania)

Reg	Type	Owner or Operator
YR-BGA	Boeing 737-38J	Tarom *Alba Iulia*
YR-BGB	Boeing 737-38J	Tarom *Bucuresti*
YR-BGC	Boeing 737-38J	Tarom *Constanta*
YR-BGD	Boeing 737-38J	Tarom *Deva*
YR-BGE	Boeing 737-38J	Tarom *Timisoara*
YR-BGF	Boeing 737-78J	Tarom *Braila*
YR-BGG	Boeing 737-78J	Tarom *Craiova*
YR-BGH	Boeing 737-78J	Tarom *Hunedoara*
YR-BGI	Boeing 737-78J	Tarom *Iasi*

YU (Serbia and Montenegro)

Reg	Type	Owner or Operator
YU-AND	Boeing 737-3H9	JAT Airways *City of Krusevac*
YU-ANF	Boeing 737-3H9	JAT Airways
YU-ANH	Boeing 737-3H9	JAT Airways
YU-ANI	Boeing 737-3H9	JAT Airways
YU-ANJ	Boeing 737-3H9	JAT Airways
YU-ANK	Boeing 737-3H9	JAT Airways
YU-ANL	Boeing 737-3H9	JAT Airways
YU-ANV	Boeing 737-3H9	JAT Airways
YU-ANW	Boeing 737-3H9	JAT Airways
YU-AON	Boeing 737-3Q4	JAT Airways
YU-AOR	Boeing 737-4B7	JAT Airways
YU-AOS	Boeing 737-4B7	JAT Airways

YV (Venezuela)

Note: ConViasa intends to operate A.340s to London during 2007.

Z (Zimbabwe)

Reg	Type	Owner or Operator
Z-AVT	Douglas DC-10-30F	Avient Aviation
Z-WPE	Boeing 767-2N0ER	Air Zimbabwe *Victoria Falls*
Z-WPF	Boeing 767-2N0ER	Air Zimbabwe *Chimanimani*

ZA/ZK/ZS/3B　　　　　　　　　　　　　　　OVERSEAS AIRLINERS

Notes	Reg	Type	Owner or Operator

ZA (Albania)

ZA-MAK	BAe 146-100	Albanian Airlines
ZA-MAL	BAe 146-200	Albanian Airlines
ZA-MEV	BAe 146-300	Albanian Airlines

ZK (New Zealand)

ZK-NBS	Boeing 747-419	Air New Zealand *Bay of Islands*
ZK-NBT	Boeing 747-419	Air New Zealand *Kaikoura*
ZK-NBU	Boeing 747-419	Air New Zealand *Rotorua*
ZK-NBV	Boeing 747-419	Air New Zealand *Christchurch*
ZK-NBW	Boeing 747-419	Air New Zealand *Wellington*
ZK-OKA	Boeing 777-219ER	Air New Zealand
ZK-OKB	Boeing 777-219ER	Air New Zealand
ZK-OKC	Boeing 777-219ER	Air New Zealand
ZK-OKD	Boeing 777-219ER	Air New Zealand
ZK-OKE	Boeing 777-219ER	Air New Zealand
ZK-OKF	Boeing 777-219ER	Air New Zealand
ZK-OKG	Boeing 777-219ER	Air New Zealand
ZK-OKH	Boeing 777-219ER	Air New Zealand
ZK-SUH	Boeing 747-475	Air New Zealand *Dunedin*
ZK-SUI	Boeing 747-441	Air New Zealand *Queenstown*
ZK-SUJ	Boeing 747-4F6	Air New Zealand *Auckland*

ZS (South Africa)

ZS-OSI	Douglas DC-8-62F	African International Airways
ZS-OZV	Douglas DC-8-62F	African International Airways
ZS-PBI	Boeing 767-3Y0ER	Nationwide Airlines
ZS-POL	Douglas DC-8-62F	African International Airways
ZS-SAK	Boeing 747-444	South African Airways *Ibhayi*
ZS-SAV	Boeing 747-444	South African Airways *Durban*
ZS-SAX	Boeing 747-444	South African Airways *Kempton Park*
ZS-SAY	Boeing 747-444	South African Airways *Vulindlela*
ZS-SAZ	Boeing 747-444	South African Airways *Imonti*
ZS-SBK	Boeing 747-4F6	South African Airways *The Great North*
ZS-SBS	Boeing 747-4F6	South African Airways
ZS-SLA	Airbus A.340-211	South African Airways
ZS-SLB	Airbus A.340-211	South African Airways
ZS-SLC	Airbus A.340-211	South African Airways
ZS-SLD	Airbus A.340-211	South African Airways
ZS-SLE	Airbus A.340-211	South African Airways
ZS-SLF	Airbus A.340-211	South African Airways
ZS-SNA	Airbus A.340-642	South African Airways
ZS-SNB	Airbus A.340-642	South African Airways
ZS-SNC	Airbus A.340-642	South African Airways
ZS-SND	Airbus A.340-642	South African Airways
ZS-SNE	Airbus A.340-642	South African Airways
ZS-SNF	Airbus A.340-642	South African Airways
ZS-SNG	Airbus A.340-642	South African Airways
ZS-SNH	Airbus A.340-642	South African Airways
ZS-SNI	Airbus A.340-642	South African Airways
ZS-SXA	Airbus A.340-313E	South African Airways
ZS-SXB	Airbus A.340-313E	South African Airways
ZS-SXC	Airbus A.340-313E	South African Airways

3B (Mauritius)

3B-NAU	Airbus A.340-312	Air Mauritius *Pink Pigeon*
3B-NAV	Airbus A.340-312	Air Mauritius *Kestrel*
3B-NAY	Airbus A.340-313X	Air Mauritius *Cardinal*
3B-NBD	Airbus A.340-313X	Air Mauritius *Parakeet*
3B-NBE	Airbus A.340-313X	Air Mauritius *Paille en Queue*
3B-NBI	Airbus A.340-313E	Air Mauritius *Le Flamboyant*
3B-NBJ	Airbus A.340-313E	Air Mauritius *Le Chamarel*

OVERSEAS AIRLINERS — 3D/4K/4R/4X

Reg	Type	Owner or Operator	Notes

3D (Swaziland)

3D-AFR	Douglas DC-8-54F	African International Airways

Note: Other African International Airways aircraft are registered in South Africa.

4K (Azerbaijan)

4K-AZ01	Airbus A.319-115X	Azerbaijan Airlines
4K-AZ03	Airbus A.319-111	Azerbaijan Airlines
4K-AZ04	Airbus A.319-111	Azerbaijan Airlines
4K-AZ05	Airbus A.319-111	Azerbaijan Airlines
4K-AZ38	Boeing 757-256	Azerbaijan Airlines
4K-AZ43	Boeing 757-2M6	Azerbaijan Airlines

Note: Azerbaijan Airlines also operates Boeing 757s VP-BBR and VP-BBS.

4R (Sri Lanka)

4R-ADA	Airbus A.340-311	SriLankan Airlines
4R-ADB	Airbus A.340-311	SriLankan Airlines
4R-ADC	Airbus A.340-311	SriLankan Airlines
4R-ADE	Airbus A.340-313X	SriLankan Airlines
4R-ADF	Airbus A.340-313X	SriLankan Airlines

4X (Israel)

4X-AXF	Boeing 747-258C	El Al Cargo
4X-AXK	Boeing 747-245F (SCD)	El Al Cargo
4X-AXL	Boeing 747-245F (SCD)	El Al Cargo
4X-AXM	Boeing 747-2B5BF	El Al Cargo
4X-AXQ	Boeing 747-238B	El Al
4X-BAU	Boeing 757-3E7	Arkia
4X-BAW	Boeing 757-3E7	Arkia
4X-BAZ	Boeing 757-236	Arkia
4X-EAA	Boeing 767-258ER	El Al
4X-EAB	Boeing 767-258ER	El Al
4X-EAC	Boeing 767-258ER	El Al
4X-EAD	Boeing 767-258ER	El Al
4X-EAE	Boeing 767-27EER	El Al
4X-EAF	Boeing 767-27EER	El Al
4X-EAJ	Boeing 767-330ER	El Al
4X-EAP	Boeing 767-3Y0ER	El Al
4X-EAR	Boeing 767-352ER	El Al
4X-EBI	Boeing 757-258	Israir
4X-EBM	Boeing 757-258	Israir
4X-EBO	Boeing 757-258	El Al/Sun d'Or
4X-EBS	Boeing 757-258	El Al
4X-EBT	Boeing 757-258	El Al
4X-EBU	Boeing 757-258	El Al
4X-EBV	Boeing 757-258	El Al
4X-EBY	Boeing 757-27B	El Al/Sun d'Or
4X-ECA	Boeing 777-258ER	El Al *Galilee*
4X-ECB	Boeing 777-258ER	El Al *Negev*
4X-ECC	Boeing 777-258ER	El Al *Hasharon*
4X-ECD	Boeing 777-258ER	El Al *Carmel*
4X-EKA	Boeing 737-858	El Al *Tiberias*
4X-EKB	Boeing 737-858	El Al *Eilat*
4X-EKC	Boeing 737-858	El Al *Beit Shean*
4X-EKD	Boeing 737-758	El Al *Ashkelon*
4X-EKE	Boeing 737-758	El Al *Nazareth*
4X-EKI	Boeing 737-86N	El Al
4X-EKO	Boeing 737-86Q	El Al
4X-EKP	Boeing 737-8Q8	El Al
4X-ELA	Boeing 747-458	El Al *Tel Aviv-Jaffa*
4X-ELB	Boeing 747-458	El Al *Haifa*

4X/5A/5B/5N/5R/5X/5Y — OVERSEAS AIRLINERS

Notes	Reg	Type	Owner or Operator
	4X-ELC	Boeing 747-458	El Al *Beer Sheva*
	4X-ELD	Boeing 747-458	El Al *Jerusalem*
	4X-ICL	Boeing 747-271C (SCD)	Cargo Airlines
	4X-ICM	Boeing 747-271C (SCD)	Cargo Airlines

Note: Israir also operates B.767 TF-FIC.

5A (Libya)

5A-DKL	Antonov An-124	Libyan Arab Air Cargo
5A-DKN	Antonov An-124	Libyan Arab Air Cargo
5A-DLZ	Airbus A.300B4-622R	Libyan Arab Airlines

Note: Libyan Arab Airlines also operates Airbus A.320s of Nouvelair and Air Malta.
Afriquiyah Airways operates Airbus A.320s S5-AAB and TS-INH plus A.300 TS-IAY.
Alajnihah Airways operates Airbus A.321 TC-TUB.

5B (Cyprus)

5B-DAU	Airbus A.320-231	Cyprus Airways *Evelthon*
5B-DAV	Airbus A.320-231	Cyprus Airways *Kinyras*
5B-DAW	Airbus A.320-231	Cyprus Airways *Agapinor*
5B-DBA	Airbus A.320-231	Cyprus Airways *Evagoras*
5B-DBB	Airbus A.320-231	Cyprus Airways *Akamas*
5B-DBC	Airbus A.320-231	Cyprus Airways *Tefkros*
5B-DBD	Airbus A.320-231	Cyprus Airways *Onisillos*
5B-DBO	Airbus A.319-132	Cyprus Airways *Nikoklis*
5B-DBP	Airbus A.319-132	Cyprus Airways *Chalkanor*
5B-DBS	Airbus A.330-223	Cyprus Airways *Ammochostos*
5B-DBT	Airbus A.330-223	Cyprus Airways *Keryneia*
5B-DBU	Boeing 737-8Q8	Eurocypria Airlines *Zephyros*
5B-DBV	Boeing 737-8Q8	Eurocypria Airlines *Levantes*
5B-DBW	Boeing 737-8Q8	Eurocypria Airlines *Maistros*
5B-DBZ	Boeing 737-8BK	Eurocypria Airlines *Notoí*

5N (Nigeria)

5N-BGG	Boeing 767-241ER	Bellview Airlines
5N-BGH	Boeing 767-241ER	Bellview Airlines *Charity*

Note: Virgin Nigeria operates A.340s G-VBUS and G-VSUN on its Lagos-Gatwick service.

5R (Madagascar)

5R-MFF	Boeing 767-3S1ER	Air Madagascar
5R-MFG	Boeing 767-383ER	Air Madagascar

5X (Uganda)

5X-BON	Douglas DC-10-30F	DAS Air Cargo
5X-DAS	Douglas DC-10-30F	DAS Air Cargo
5X-JOE	Douglas DC-10-30F	DAS Air Cargo
5X-ROY	Douglas DC-10-30F	DAS Air Cargo

5Y (Kenya)

5Y-KQP	Boeing 767-38EER	Kenya Airways
5Y-KQQ	Boeing 767-33AER	Kenya Airways
5Y-KQR	Boeing 767-3P6ER	Kenya Airways
5Y-KQS	Boeing 777-2U8ER	Kenya Airways
5Y-KQT	Boeing 777-2U8ER	Kenya Airways

OVERSEAS AIRLINERS

5Y/6Y/7O/7T/9A

Reg	Type	Owner or Operator	Notes
5Y-KQU	Boeing 777-2U8ER	Kenya Airways	
5Y-KQX	Boeing 767-36NER	Kenya Airways	
5Y-KQY	Boeing 767-36NER	Kenya Airways	
5Y-KQZ	Boeing 767-36NER	Kenya Airways	
5Y-KYZ	Boeing 777-2U8ER	Kenya Airways	
5Y-VIP	Airbus A.310-308	African Safari Airways	

6Y (Jamaica)

6Y-JMM	Airbus A.340-313X	Air Jamaica *Spirit of Jamaica – Atlantic Limousine*	
6Y-JMP	Airbus A.340-313X	Air Jamaica *Spirit of Jamaica – Atlantic Limousine II*	

7O (Yemen)

7O-ADJ	Airbus A.310-324	Yemenia	
7O-ADP	Airbus A.330-243	Yemenia *Sana'a*	
7O-ADT	Airbus A.330-243	Yemenia *Aden*	
7O-YMN	Boeing 747SP-27	Yemenia	

Note: Yemenia also operates Airbus A.310s registered F-OGYO, F-OHPR and F-OHPS.

7T (Algeria)

7T-VJG	Boeing 767-3D6ER	Air Algerie	
7T-VJH	Boeing 767-3D6ER	Air Algerie	
7T-VJI	Boeing 767-3D6ER	Air Algerie	
7T-VJJ	Boeing 737-8D6	Air Algerie *Jugurtha*	
7T-VJK	Boeing 737-8D6	Air Algerie *Mansourah*	
7T-VJL	Boeing 737-8D6	Air Algerie *Allizi*	
7T-VJM	Boeing 737-8D6	Air Algerie	
7T-VJN	Boeing 737-8D6	Air Algerie	
7T-VJO	Boeing 737-8D6	Air Algerie	
7T-VJP	Boeing 737-8D6	Air Algerie	
7T-VJQ	Boeing 737-6D6	Air Algerie	
7T-VJR	Boeing 737-6D6	Air Algerie	
7T-VJS	Boeing 737-6D6	Air Algerie	
7T-VJT	Boeing 737-6D6	Air Algerie	
7T-VJU	Boeing 737-6D6	Air Algerie	
7T-VJV	Airbus A.330-202	Air Algerie *Tinhinan*	
7T-VJW	Airbus A.330-202	Air Algerie *Lalla Setti*	
7T-VJX	Airbus A.330-202	Air Algerie *Mers el Kebir*	
7T-VJY	Airbus A.330-202	Air Algerie *Monts des Beni Chougrane*	
7T-VJZ	Airbus A.330-202	Air Algerie	
7T-VKA	Boeing 737-8D6	Air Algerie	
7T-VKB	Boeing 737-8D6	Air Algerie	
7T-VKC	Boeing 737-8D6	Air Algerie	

9A (Croatia)

9A-CBC	McD Douglas MD-82	Air Adriatic *My Dream*	
9A-CBF	McD Douglas MD-82	Air Adriatic/MyAir *I'm the winner*	
9A-CBG	McD Douglas MD-82	Air Adriatic/MyAir *No guts, no glory*	
9A-CBH	McD Douglas MD-82	Air Adriatic *Happy you happy !*	
9A-CBJ	McD Douglas MD-83	Air Adriatic *Lucky Number 7*	
9A-CDA	McD Douglas MD-83	Dubrovnik Airline *Revelin*	
9A-CDB	McD Douglas MD-83	Dubrovnik Airline *Lovrijenac*	
9A-CDC	McD Douglas MD-83	Dubrovnik Airline *Minceta*	
9A-CDD	McD Douglas MD-82	Dubrovnik Airline *Bckar*	
9A-CDE	McD Douglas MD-82	Dubrovnik Airline	
9A-CTF	Airbus A.320-211	Croatia Airlines *Rijeka*	
9A-CTG	Airbus A.319-112	Croatia Airlines *Zadar*	
9A-CTH	Airbus A.319-112	Croatia Airlines *Zagreb*	
9A-CTI	Airbus A.319-112	Croatia Airlines *Vukovar*	
9A-CTJ	Airbus A.320-214	Croatia Airlines *Dubrovnik*	

9A/9G/9H/9K/9L/9M — OVERSEAS AIRLINERS

Notes	Reg	Type	Owner or Operator
	9A-CTK	Airbus A.320-214	Croatia Airlines *Split*
	9A-CTL	Airbus A.319-112	Croatia Airlines *Pula*
	9A-CTM	Airbus A.320-212	Croatia Airlines *Sibenik*

9G (Ghana)

9G-MKG	Douglas DC-8-62AF	MK Airlines/stored Filton
9G-MKH	Douglas DC-8-62AF	MK Airlines/stored Filton
9G-MKK	Douglas DC-8-62AF	MK Airlines
9G-MKL	Boeing 747-2R7F	MK Airlines
9G-MKM	Boeing 747-2B5F	MK Airlines
9G-MKP	Boeing 747-245F	MK Airlines
9G-MKR	Boeing 747-2B5F	MK Airlines
9G-MKS	Boeing 747-2B5F	MK Airlines
9G-MKU	Boeing 747-249F	MK Airlines

Note: Ghana International Airways' services are operated by B.767 TF-LLA.

9H (Malta)

9H-AEF	Airbus A.320-214	Air Malta/Excel Airways
9H-AEG	Airbus A.319-111	Air Malta *Mdina*
9H-AEH	Airbus A.319-111	Air Malta *Floriana*
9H-AEI	Airbus A.320-214	Air Malta *Rabat – Citta Vittoria*
9H-AEJ	Airbus A.319-111	Air Malta *San Pawl il-Bahar*
9H-AEK	Airbus A.320-214	Air Malta *San Giljan*
9H-AEL	Airbus A.319-111	Air Malta *Marsaxlokk*
9H-AEM	Airbus A.319-111	Air Malta *Birgu*
9H-AEN	Airbus A.320-214	Air Malta/Excel Airways
9H-AEO	Airbus A.320-214	Air Malta

9K (Kuwait)

9K-ADE	Boeing 747-469 (SCD)	Kuwait Airways *Al-Jabariya*
9K-ALA	Airbus A.310-308	Kuwait Airways *Al-Jahra*
9K-ALB	Airbus A.310-308	Kuwait Airways *Gharnada*
9K-ALC	Airbus A.310-308	Kuwait Airways *Kazma*
9K-ALD	Airbus A.310-308	State of Kuwait *Al-Sabahiya*
9K-AMA	Airbus A.300B4-605R	Kuwait Airways *Failaka*
9K-AMB	Airbus A.300B4-605R	Kuwait Airways *Burghan*
9K-AMC	Airbus A.300B4-605R	Kuwait Airways *Wafra*
9K-AMD	Airbus A.300B4-605R	Kuwait Airways *Wara*
9K-AME	Airbus A.300B4-605R	Kuwait Airways *Al-Rawdhatain*
9K-ANA	Airbus A.340-313	Kuwait Airways *Warba*
9K-ANB	Airbus A.340-313	Kuwait Airways *Bayan*
9K-ANC	Airbus A.340-313	Kuwait Airways *Meskan*
9K-AND	Airbus A.340-313	Kuwait Airways *Al-Riggah*
9K-AOA	Boeing 777-269ER	Kuwait Airways *Al-Grain*
9K-AOB	Boeing 777-269ER	Kuwait Airways *Garouh*

9L (Sierra Leone)

Note: Bellview Airlines operates a Freetown-London service with B.767s 5N-BGG and 5N-BGH.

9M (Malaysia)

9M-MPA	Boeing 747-4H6	Malaysian Airlines *Ipoh*
9M-MPB	Boeing 747-4H6	Malaysian Airlines *Shah Alam*
9M-MPC	Boeing 747-4H6	Malaysian Airlines *Kuantan*
9M-MPD	Boeing 747-4H6	Malaysian Airlines *Serembam*
9M-MPE	Boeing 747-4H6	Malaysian Airlines *Kangar*
9M-MPF	Boeing 747-4H6	Malaysian Airlines *Kota Bharu*
9M-MPG	Boeing 747-4H6	Malaysian Airlines *Kuala Terengganu*

OVERSEAS AIRLINERS

9M/9V

Reg	Type	Owner or Operator	Notes
9M-MPH	Boeing 747-4H6	Malaysian Airlines *Langkawi*	
9M-MPI	Boeing 747-4H6	Malaysian Airlines *Tioman*	
9M-MPJ	Boeing 747-4H6	Malaysian Airlines *Labuan*	
9M-MPK	Boeing 747-4H6	Malaysian Airlines *Johor Bahru*	
9M-MPL	Boeing 747-4H6	Malaysian Airlines *Penang*	
9M-MPM	Boeing 747-4H6	Malaysian Airlines *Melaka*	
9M-MPN	Boeing 747-4H6	Malaysian Airlines *Pangkor*	
9M-MPO	Boeing 747-4H6	Malaysian Airlines *Alor Setar*	
9M-MPP	Boeing 747-4H6	Malaysian Airlines *Putrajaya*	
9M-MPQ	Boeing 747-4H6	Malaysian Airlines *Kuala Lumpur*	
9M-MPR	Boeing 747-4H6F	Malaysian Airlines	
9M-MPS	Boeing 747-4H6F	Malaysian Airlines	
9M-MRA	Boeing 777-2H6ER	Malaysian Airlines	
9M-MRB	Boeing 777-2H6ER	Malaysian Airlines	
9M-MRC	Boeing 777-2H6ER	Malaysian Airlines	
9M-MRD	Boeing 777-2H6ER	Malaysian Airlines	
9M-MRE	Boeing 777-2H6ER	Malaysian Airlines	
9M-MRF	Boeing 777-2H6ER	Malaysian Airlines	
9M-MRG	Boeing 777-2H6ER	Malaysian Airlines	
9M-MRH	Boeing 777-2H6ER	Malaysian Airlines	
9M-MRI	Boeing 777-2H6ER	Malaysian Airlines	
9M-MRJ	Boeing 777-2H6ER	Malaysian Airlines	
9M-MRK	Boeing 777-2H6ER	Malaysian Airlines	
9M-MRL	Boeing 777-2H6ER	Malaysian Airlines	
9M-MRM	Boeing 777-2H6ER	Malaysian Airlines	
9M-MRN	Boeing 777-2H6ER	Malaysian Airlines	
9M-MRO	Boeing 777-2H6ER	Malaysian Airlines	
9M-MRP	Boeing 777-2H6ER	Malaysian Airlines	
9M-MRQ	Boeing 777-2H6ER	Malaysian Airlines	

Note: MAS Kargo operates B.747Fs leased from Air Atlanta Icelandic.

9V (Singapore)

Reg	Type	Owner or Operator
9V-SFA	Boeing 747-412F	Singapore Airlines Cargo
9V-SFB	Boeing 747-412F	Singapore Airlines Cargo
9V-SFD	Boeing 747-412F	Singapore Airlines Cargo
9V-SFE	Boeing 747-412F	Singapore Airlines Cargo
9V-SFF	Boeing 747-412F	Singapore Airlines Cargo
9V-SFG	Boeing 747-412F	Singapore Airlines Cargo
9V-SFH	Boeing 747-412F	Singapore Airlines Cargo
9V-SFI	Boeing 747-412F	Singapore Airlines Cargo
9V-SFJ	Boeing 747-412F	Singapore Airlines Cargo
9V-SFK	Boeing 747-412F	Singapore Airlines Cargo
9V-SFL	Boeing 747-412F	Singapore Airlines Cargo
9V-SFM	Boeing 747-412F	Singapore Airlines Cargo
9V-SFN	Boeing 747-412F	Singapore Airlines Cargo
9V-SFO	Boeing 747-412F	Singapore Airlines Cargo
9V-SFP	Boeing 747-412F	Singapore Airlines Cargo
9V-SFQ	Boeing 747-412F	Singapore Airlines Cargo
9V-SGA	Airbus A.340-541	Singapore Airlines
9V-SGB	Airbus A.340-541	Singapore Airlines
9V-SGC	Airbus A.340-541	Singapore Airlines
9V-SGD	Airbus A.340-541	Singapore Airlines
9V-SGE	Airbus A.340-541	Singapore Airlines
9V-SMM	Boeing 747-412	Singapore Airlines
9V-SMP	Boeing 747-412	Singapore Airlines
9V-SMR	Boeing 747-412	Singapore Airlines
9V-SMS	Boeing 747-412	Singapore Airlines
9V-SMU	Boeing 747-412	Singapore Airlines
9V-SMV	Boeing 747-412	Singapore Airlines
9V-SMW	Boeing 747-412	Singapore Airlines
9V-SMY	Boeing 747-412	Singapore Airlines
9V-SMZ	Boeing 747-412	Singapore Airlines
9V-SPA	Boeing 747-412	Singapore Airlines
9V-SPB	Boeing 747-412	Singapore Airlines
9V-SPC	Boeing 747-412	Singapore Airlines
9V-SPD	Boeing 747-412	Singapore Airlines
9V-SPE	Boeing 747-412	Singapore Airlines
9V-SPF	Boeing 747-412	Singapore Airlines
9V-SPG	Boeing 747-412	Singapore Airlines

9V/9Y OVERSEAS AIRLINERS

Notes	Reg	Type	Owner or Operator
	9V-SPH	Boeing 747-412	Singapore Airlines
	9V-SPI	Boeing 747-412	Singapore Airlines
	9V-SPJ	Boeing 747-412	Singapore Airlines
	9V-SPL	Boeing 747-412	Singapore Airlines
	9V-SPM	Boeing 747-412	Singapore Airlines
	9V-SPN	Boeing 747-412	Singapore Airlines
	9V-SPO	Boeing 747-412	Singapore Airlines
	9V-SPP	Boeing 747-412	Singapore Airlines
	9V-SPQ	Boeing 747-412	Singapore Airlines
	9V-SVA	Boeing 777-212ER	Singapore Airlines
	9V-SVB	Boeing 777-212ER	Singapore Airlines
	9V-SVC	Boeing 777-212ER	Singapore Airlines
	9V-SVD	Boeing 777-212ER	Singapore Airlines
	9V-SVE	Boeing 777-212ER	Singapore Airlines
	9V-SVG	Boeing 777-212ER	Singapore Airlines
	9V-SVH	Boeing 777-212ER	Singapore Airlines
	9V-SVI	Boeing 777-212ER	Singapore Airlines
	9V-SVJ	Boeing 777-212ER	Singapore Airlines
	9V-SVK	Boeing 777-212ER	Singapore Airlines
	9V-SVL	Boeing 777-212ER	Singapore Airlines
	9V-SVM	Boeing 777-212ER	Singapore Airlines
	9V-SVN	Boeing 777-212ER	Singapore Airlines
	9V-SVO	Boeing 777-212ER	Singapore Airlines
	9V-SWA	Boeing 777-312ER	Singapore Airlines
	9V-SWB	Boeing 777-312ER	Singapore Airlines
	9V-SWD	Boeing 777-312ER	Singapore Airlines
	9V-SWE	Boeing 777-312ER	Singapore Airlines
	9V-SWF	Boeing 777-312ER	Singapore Airlines
	9V-SWG	Boeing 777-312ER	Singapore Airlines

9Y (Trinidad and Tobago)

Note: Caribbean Airlines' services to London-Gatwick are operated under a code-share agreement by British Airways B.777s.

Air Canada Boeing 767 C-FBEG sports the carrier's attractive new livery. *GM*

Swiss Avro RJ100 HB-IXW was one of the last airliners to be built in the United Kingdom. *DP*

Wingletted Continental Boeing 757 N13110 is one of their large fleet employed on transatlantic services to a number of UK airports. *GM*

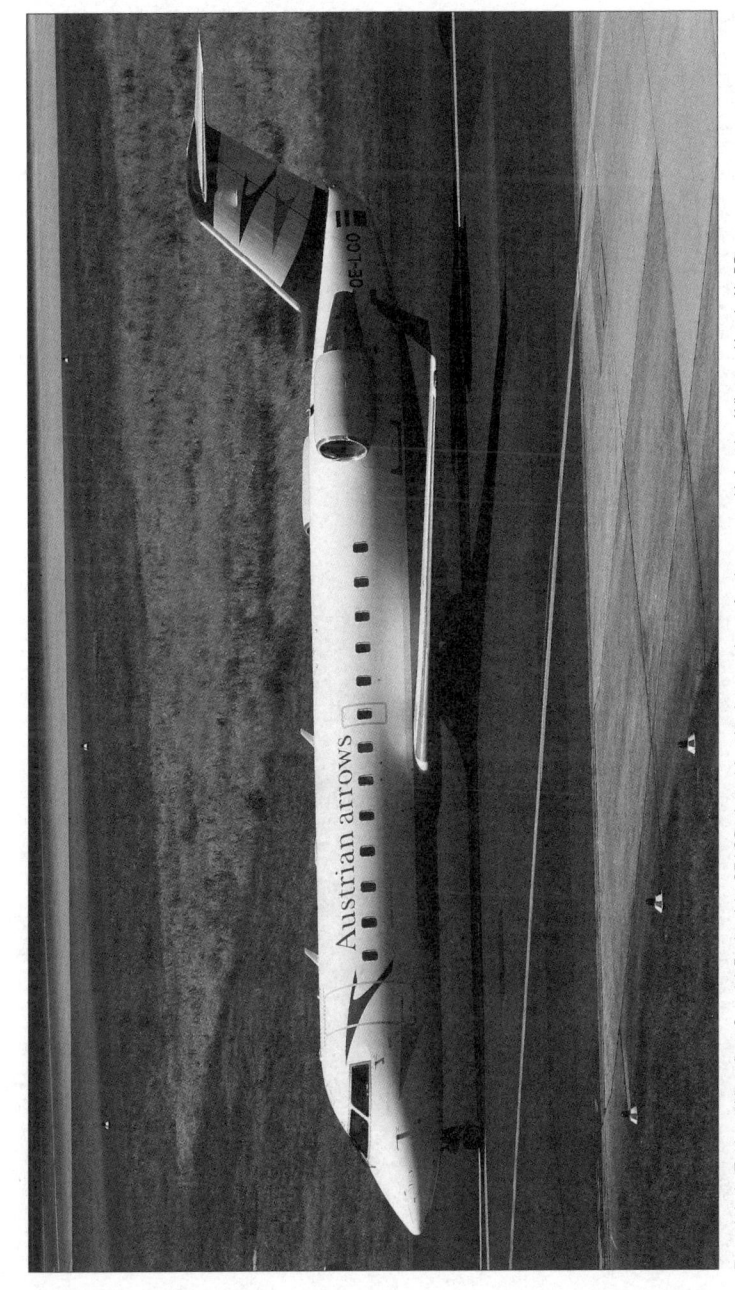

Formerly in the Tyrolean Airlines fleet, Canadair Regional Jet OE-LCO adopted Austrian Arrows colours after the merger with Austrian Airlines and Lauda Air. *DP*

LOT Polish Airlines ERJ175 SP-LDB is an example of the mid-sized variant in that airline's expanding Embraer fleet. *DP*

Uzbekistan Airways Boeing 757 VP-BUH is registered in Bermuda by the leasing company that owns it. *DP*

Radio Frequencies

The frequencies used by the larger airfields/airports are listed below. Abbreviations used: TWR – Tower, APP – Approach, A/G – Air-Ground advisory. It is possible that changes will be made from time to time with the frequencies allocated, all of which are quoted in Megahertz (MHz).

Airfield	TWR	APP	A/G
Aberdeen	118.1	119.05	
Alderney	125.35	128.65	
Andrewsfield			130.55
Barton			120.25
Barrow			123.2
Beccles			120.375
Belfast International	118.3	128.5	
Belfast City	122.825	130.85	
Bembridge	123.25		
Biggin Hill	134.8	129.4	
Birmingham	118.3	118.05	
Blackbushe			122.3
Blackpool	118.4	119.95	
Bodmin			122.7
Bourn			124.35
Bournemouth	125.6	119.475	
Breighton		129.80	
Bristol/Filton	132.35	122.725	
Bristol/Lulsgate	133.85	125.65	
Bruntingthorpe			122.825
Caernarfon			122.25
Cambridge	122.2	123.6	
Cardiff	125.0	126.625	
Carlisle	123.6		
Clacton			118.15
Compton Abbas			122.7
Conington			129.725
Cosford	128.65	135.875	
Coventry	124.8	119.25	
Cranfield	134.925	122.85	
Denham			130.725
Doncaster RHA	128.775	126.225	
Dundee	122.9		
Dunkeswell			123.475
Durham Tees Valley	119.8	118.85	
Duxford			122.075
Earls Colne			122.425
Edinburgh	118.7	121.2	
Elstree			122.4
Exeter	119.8	128.975	
Fairoaks			123.425
Farnborough	122.5	134.35	
Fenland			122.925
Fowlmere			135.7
Gamston			130.475
Gatwick	124.225	126.825	
Glasgow	118.8	119.1	
Gloucester/Staverton	122.9	128.55	
Goodwood			122.45
Guernsey	119.95	128.65	
Haverfordwest			122.2
Hawarden	124.95	123.35	
Headcorn			122.0
Heathrow	118.7	119.725	
	118.5	134.975	
Hethel			122.35
Hucknall			130.8
Humberside	124.9	119.125	
Inverness	122.6		

Airfield	TWR	APP	A/G
Jersey	119.45	120.3	
Kemble			118.9
Land's End	120.25		
Leeds Bradford	120.3	123.75	
Leicester			122.125
Liverpool	126.35	119.85	
London City	118.075	132.7	
Luton	132.55	129.55	
Lydd			120.7
Manchester	118.625	135.0	
Manston	119.925	126.35	
Netherthorpe			123.275
Newcastle	119.7	124.375	
Newquay	123.4		
North Denes	123.4		
North Weald			123.525
Norwich	124.25	119.35	
Nottingham EMA	124.0	134.175	
Old Warden			123.05
Oxford	121.95	125.325	
Penzance			118.1
Perth			119.8
Plymouth	118.15	133.55	
Popham			129.8
Prestwick	118.15	120.55	
Redhill	119.6		
Rochester			122.25
Ronaldsway IOM	118.9	120.85	
Sandown			123.5
Sandtoft			130.425
Scilly Isles			123.825
Seething			122.6
Sheffield City			128.525
Sherburn			122.6
Shipdham			132.25
Shobdon			123.5
Shoreham	125.4	123.15	
Sibson			122.3
Sleap			122.45
Southampton	118.2	128.85	
Southend	127.725	130.775	
Stansted	123.8	126.95	
Stapleford			122.8
Sumburgh	118.25	131.3	
Swansea			119.7
Sywell			122.7
Tatenhill			124.075
Thruxton			130.45
Tollerton			134.875
Wellesbourne			124.025
Welshpool			128.0
White Waltham			122.6
Wick	119.7		
Wickenby			122.45
Wolverhampton			123.0
Woodford	120.7	130.75	
Woodvale	119.75	121.0	
Wycombe Air Park			126.55
Yeovil	125.4	130.85	

Airline Flight Codes

Those listed below identify the UK and Overseas carriers most likely to appear in or over the UK.

Code	Airline		Code	Airline		Code	Airline	
AAF	Aigle Azur	F	BMI	bmi Baby	G	FHY	Freebird Airlines	TC
AAG	Atlantic Air Transport	G	BMM	Atlas Blue	CN	FIF	Air Finland	OH
AAL	American Airlines	N	BPA	Blue Panorama	I	FIN	Finnair	OH
AAR	Asiana Airlines	HL	BRT	BA Citiexpress	G	FJE	Fly Jet	G
AAW	Afriqiyah Airways	5A	BRU	Belavia	EW	FLI	Atlantic Airways	OY
ABD	Air Atlanta Icelandic	TF	BTI	Air Baltic	YL	FLT	Flightline	G
ABR	Air Contractors	EI	BUC	Bulgarian Air Charter	LZ	FLY	FlyMe	SE
ACA	Air Canada	C	BZH	Brit Air	F	FUA	Futura International A/W	EC
ADB	Antonov Airlines	UR	CAJ	Air Caraibes	F-O	GAO	Golden Air	SE
ADH	Air One	I	CAL	China Airlines	B	GBL	GB Airways	G
ADR	Adria Airways	S5	CCA	Air China	B	GCO	Gemini Air Cargo	N
AEA	Air Europa	EC	CES	China Eastern	B	GEC	Lufthansa Cargo	D
AEE	Aegean Airlines	SX	CFG	Condor	D	GFA	Gulf Air	A4O
AEU	Astraeus	G	CIM	Cimber Air	OY	GHA	Ghana Airways	9G
AEW	Aerosvit Airlines	UR	CKS	Kalitta Air	N	GIA	Garuda	PK
AEY	Air Italy	I	CLH	Lufthansa CityLine	D	GJJ	GirJet	EC
AFL	Aeroflot	RA	CLI	Clickair	EC	GMI	Germania	D
AFR	Air France	F	CLW	Centralwings	SP	GRE	Greece Airways	SX
AHR	Air Adriatic	9A	CLX	Cargolux	LX	GSM	Flyglobespan	G
AHY	Azerbaijan Airlines	4K	CNO	SAS-Braathens	LN	GTI	Atlas Air	N
AIC	Air-India	VT	COA	Continental Airlines	N	GWI	Germanwings	D
AIN	African International A/W	3D	CPA	Cathay Pacific	B	HDA	Dragonair	B
AIZ	Arkia	4X	CRL	Corsair	F	HHI	Hamburg International A/L	D
AJM	Air Jamaica	6Y	CSA	CSA Czech Airlines	OK	HLF	Hapag-Lloyd	D
AKL	Air Kilroe	G	CTN	Croatia Airlines	9A	HLX	Hapag-Lloyd Express	D
ALK	SriLankan Airlines	4R	CUB	Cubana	CU	HMS	Hemus Air	LZ
AMC	Air Malta	9H	CWC	Centurion Air Cargo	N	HOA	Hola Airlines	EC
AMT	ATA Airlines	N	CYP	Cyprus Airways	5B	HSK	SkyEurope Hungary	HA
AMV	AMC Airlines	SU	DAH	Air Algerie	7T	HVN	Vietnam Airlines	VN
AMX	Aeromexico	XA	DAL	Delta Air Lines	N	HWY	Highland Airways	G
ANA	All Nippon Airways	JA	DAN	Maersk Air	OY	IBE	Iberia	EC
ANZ	Air New Zealand	ZK	DAT	SN Brussels Airlines	OO	ICB	Islandsflug	TF
ARG	Aerolineas Argentinas	LV	DBK	Dubrovnik Airline	9A	ICE	Icelandair	TF
ATN	Air Transport International	N	DHL	DHL Express	N/OO	ICL	Cargo Airlines	4X
AUA	Austrian Airlines	OE	DLH	Lufthansa	D	IOS	Isles of Scilly Skybus	G
AUI	Ukraine International	UR	DNM	Denim Air	PH	IRA	Iran Air	EP
AUR	Aurigny A/S	G	DSR	DAS Air Cargo	5X	IRM	Mahan Air	EP
AWC	Titan Airways	G	DTR	Danish Air Transport	OY	ISL	City Star Airlines	TF
AXN	Alexandair	SX	DWT	Darwin Airline	HB	ISS	Meridiana	I
AXY	Axis Airways	F	EAF	European Air Charter	G	IWD	Iberworld	EC
AZA	Alitalia	I	ECA	Eurocypria Airlines	5B	IYE	Yemenia	7O
AZE	Arcus Air	D	EDW	Edelweiss Air	HB	JAI	Jet Airways	VT
AZW	Air Zimbabwe	Z	EEZ	Eurofly	I	JAL	Japan Airlines	JA
BAG	Deutsche BA	D	EIA	Evergreen International	N	JAT	JAT Airways	YU
BAW	British Airways	G	EIN	Aer Lingus	EI	JET	Wind Jet	I
BBC	Bangladesh Biman	S2	ELL	Estonian Air	ES	JKK	Spanair	EC
BBD	Bluebird Cargo	TF	ELY	El Al	4X	JXX	Iceland Express	TF
BCS	European A/T	OO	EMX	Euromanx	G	KAC	Kuwait Airways	9K
BCY	CityJet	EI	ESK	SkyEurope	OM	KAJ	Karthago Airlines	TS
BDI	BenAir A/S	OY	ESS	EOS Airlines	N	KAL	Korean Air	HL
BEE	Flybe	G	ETD	Etihad Airways	A6	KLC	KLM CityHopper	PH
BER	Air Berlin	D	ETH	Ethiopian Airlines	ET	KLM	KLM	PH
BGA	Airbus Tpt International	F	EUK	Air Atlanta Europe	TF	KQA	Kenya Airways	5Y
BGH	Balkan Holidays	LZ	EVA	EVA Airways	B	KSA	KS-Avia	YL
BHP	Belair	HB	EWG	Eurowings	D	KYV	Kibris Turkish Airlines	TC
BID	Binair	D	EXS	Channel Express/Jet2	G	KZR	Air Astana	UN
BIE	Air Mediterranée	F	EZE	Eastern Airways	G	KZU	Kuzu Airlines Cargo	TC
BIH	CHC Scotia	G	EZS	easyJet Switzerland	HB	LAA	Libyan Arab Airlines	5A
BLC	TAM Linhas Aereas	PT	EZY	easyJet	G	LAJ	BMed	G
BLE	Blue Line	F	FCA	First Choice Airways	G	LAN	LAN Airlines	CC
BLF	Blue 1	OH	FDX	Federal Express	N	LBC	Albanian Airlines	CC
BMA	bmi british midland	G	FHE	Hello	HB	LBT	Nouvelair	TS

AIRLINE FLIGHT CODES

Code	Airline		Code	Airline		Code	Airline	
LCO	LAN Cargo Airlines	CC	OHY	Onur Air	TC	SUD	Sudan Airways	ST
LDA	Lauda Air	OE	OLT	OLT	D	SUS	Sun-Air	OY
LGL	Luxair	LX	OOM	Zoom Airlines	C	SVA	Saudi Arabian Airlines	HZ
LIL	Lithuanian Airlines	LY	OVA	Aeronova	EC	SVK	Air Slovakia	OM
LOG	Loganair	G	PAC	Polar Air Cargo	N	SWE	Swedair	SE
LOT	Polish Airlines (LOT)	SP	PGT	Pegasus Airlines	TC	SWN	West Air Sweden	SE
LTE	Volar	EC	PIA	Pakistan International A/L	AP	SWR	Swiss	HB
LTU	LTU	D	PLK	Pulkovo Aviation	RA	SXS	SunExpress	TC
LVG	Livingston	I	PLM	Air Pullmantur	EC	SYR	Syrianair	YK
LXR	Air Luxor	CS	POT	Polet	RA	TAP	TAP Portugal	CS
LZB	Bulgaria Air	LZ	PTG	PrivatAir	D	TAR	Tunis Air	TS
MAH	Malev	HA	PTI	PrivatAir	HB	TAY	TNT Airways	OO
MAS	Malaysian Airlines	9M	QFA	QANTAS	VH	TCW	Thomas Cook Belgium	OO
MAU	Air Mauritius	3B	QSC	African Safari Airways	5Y	TCX	Thomas Cook Airlines	G
MEA	Middle East Airlines	OD	QTR	Qatar Airways	A7	TFL	Arkefly	PH
MKA	MK Airlines	9G	RAE	Regional Airlines	F	THA	Thai Airways International	HS
MMZ	Euro Atlantic Airways	CS	RAM	Royal Air Maroc	CN	THT	Air Tahiti Nui	F-O
MNB	MNG Airlines	TC	RBA	Royal Brunei Airlines	V8	THY	Turkish Airlines	TC
MON	Monarch Airlines	G	REA	Aer Arann	EI	TOM	Thomsonfly	G
MPD	Air Plus Comet	EC	REU	Air Austral	F-O	TRA	Transavia	PH
MPH	Martinair	PH	RJA	Royal Jordanian	JY	TSC	Air Transat	C
MSR	EgyptAir	SU	ROT	Tarom	YR	TSO	Transaero	RA
MTL	RAF-Avia	YL	RPX	BAC Express Airlines	G	TUA	Turkmenistan Airlines	EZ
MXJ	Maxjet Airways	N	RUS	Cirrus Airlines	D	TUB	TUI Airlines Belgium	OO
MYT	MyTravel Airways	G	RYN	Ryan International	N	TVS	Travel Service/Smart Wings	OK
MYW	MyAir	I	RYR	Ryanair	EI	TYR	Tyrolean Airways	OE
NAO	North American Airlines	N	RZO	SATA International	CS	UAE	Emirates Airlines	A6
NAX	Norwegian Air Shuttle	LN	SAA	South African Airways	ZS	UAL	United Airlines	N
NCA	Nippon Cargo Airlines	JA	SAS	SAS	SE/ OY/ LN	UPS	United Parcel Service	N
NEX	Northern Executive	G	SAY	Scot Airways	G	USA	US Airways	N
NLY	Niki	OE	SCW	Malmo Aviation	SE	UYC	Cameroon Airlines	TJ
NMB	Air Namibia	V5	SDR	City Airline	SE	UZB	Uzbekistan Airways	UK
NOS	Neos	I	SEU	Star Airlines	F	VDA	Volga-Dnepr	RA
NPT	Atlantic Airlines	G	SEY	Air Seychelles	S7	VIR	Virgin Atlantic	G
NTW	Nationwide Airlines	ZS	SHD	Air Sahara	VT	VLG	Vueling	EC
NVR	Novair Airlines	SE	SIA	Singapore Airlines	9V	VLM	VLM	OO
NWA	Northwest Airlines	N	SLL	Slovak Airlines	OM	VLO	VarigLog	PP/PR
OAE	Omni Air International	N	SLM	Surinam Airways	PZ	WIF	Wideroe's	LN
OAL	Olympic Airlines	SX	SNB	Sterling Airlines	OY	WOA	World Airways	N
OAW	Helvetic Airways	HB	SQC	Singapore Airlines Cargo	9V	WZZ	Wizz Air	HA/LZ
OGE	Atlasjet	TC	SRR	Starair	OY	XLA	Excel Airways	G

Although based in the Isle of Man, Dash 8 OE-HBC retains its Austrian registration. *GM*

British Aircraft Preservation Council Register

The British Aircraft Preservation Council was formed in 1967 to co-ordinate the works of all bodies involved in the preservation, restoration and display of historical aircraft. Membership covers the whole spectrum of national, Service, commercial and voluntary groups, and meetings are held regularly at the bases of member organisations. The Council is able to provide a means of communication, helping to resolve any misunderstandings or duplication of effort. Every effort is taken to encourage the raising of standards of both organisation and technical capacity amongst the member groups to the benefit of everyone interested in aviation. To assist historians, the B.A.P.C. register has been set up and provides an identity for those aircraft which do not qualify for a Service serial or inclusion in the UK Civil Register. Aircraft on the current B.A.P.C. Register are as follows:

Notes	Reg	Type	Owner or Operator
	1	Roe Triplane Type 4 (replica)	Shuttleworth Collection as G-ARSG (not carried)
	2	Bristol Boxkite (replica)	Shuttleworth Collection as G-ASPP (not carried)
	6	Roe Triplane Type IV (replica)	Manchester Museum of Science & Industry
	7	Southampton University MPA	Solent Sky, Southampton
	8	Dixon ornithopter	The Shuttleworth Collection
	9	Humber Monoplane (replica)	Midland Air Museum/Coventry
	10	Hafner R.II Revoplane	Museum of Army Flying/Middle Wallop
	12	Mignet HM.14	Museum of Flight/East Fortune
	13	Mignet HM.14	Brimpex Metal Treatments
	14	Addyman Standard Training Glider	A. Lindsay & N. H. Ponsford
	15	Addyman Standard Training Glider	The Aeroplane Collection
	16	Addyman ultra-light aircraft	N. H. Ponsford
	17	Woodhams Sprite	BB Aviation/Canterbury
	18	Killick MP Gyroplane	A. Lindsay & N. H. Ponsford
	20	Lee-Richards annular biplane (replica)	Visitor Centre Shoreham Airport
	21	Thruxton Jackaroo	M. J. Brett
	22	Mignet HM.14 (G-AEOF)	Aviodome/Netherlands
	23	SE-5A Scale Model	Newark Air Museum
	24	Currie Wot (replica)	Newark Air Museum
	25	Nyborg TGN-III glider	Midland Air Museum
	26	Auster AOP6 (fuselage frame)	Remains scrapped
	27	Mignet HM.14	M. J. Abbey
	28	Wright Flyer (replica)	Corn Exchange/Leeds
	29	Mignet HM.14 (replica) (G-ADRY)	Brooklands Museum of Aviation/Weybridge
	32	Crossley Tom Thumb	Midland Air Museum
	33	DFS.108-49 Grunau Baby IIb	–
	34	DFS.108-49 Grunau Baby IIb	D. Elsdon
	35	EoN primary glider	–
	36	Fieseler Fi 103 (V-1) (replica)	Kent Battle of Britain Museum/Hawkinge
	37	Blake Bluetit (G-BXIY)	The Shuttleworth Collection/Old Warden
	38	Bristol Scout replica (A1742)	K. Williams & M. Thorn
	39	Addyman Zephyr sailplane	A. Lindsay & N. H. Ponsford
	40	Bristol Boxkite (replica)	Bristol City Museum
	41	B.E.2C (replica) (6232)	Yorkshire Air Museum/Elvington
	42	Avro 504 (replica) (H1968)	Yorkshire Air Museum/Elvington
	43	Mignet HM.14	Newark Air Museum/Winthorpe
	44	Miles Magister (L6906)	Museum of Berkshire Aviation (G-AKKY)/Woodley
	45	Pilcher Hawk (replica)	Stanford Hall Museum
	46	Mignet HM.14	Stored
	47	Watkins Monoplane	National Museum of Wales
	48	Pilcher Hawk (replica)	Glasgow Museum of Transport
	49	Pilcher Hawk	Royal Scottish Museum/East Fortune
	50	Roe Triplane Type 1	Science Museum/South Kensington
	51	Vickers Vimy IV	Science Museum/South Kensington
	52	Lilienthal glider	Science Museum Store/Hayes
	53	Wright Flyer (replica)	Science Museum/South Kensington
	54	JAP-Harding monoplane	Science Museum/South Kensington
	55	Levavasseur Antoinette VII	Science Museum/South Kensington
	56	Fokker E.III (210/16)	Science Museum/South Kensington
	57	Pilcher Hawk (replica)	Science Museum/South Kensington
	58	Yokosuka MXY7 Ohka II (15-1585)	F.A.A. Museum/Yeovilton
	59	Sopwith Camel (replica) (D3419)	Aerospace Museum/Cosford
	60	Murray M.1 helicopter	The Aeroplane Collection Ltd
	61	Stewart man-powered ornithopter	Lincolnshire Aviation Museum
	62	Cody Biplane (304)	Science Museum/South Kensington
	63	Hurricane (replica) (P3208)	Kent Battle of Britain Museum/Hawkinge

BRITISH AIRCRAFT PRESERVATION

Notes	Reg	Type	Owner or Operator
	64	Hurricane (replica) (P3059)	Kent Battle of Britain Museum/Hawkinge
	65	Spitfire (replica) (N3289)	Kent Battle of Britain Museum/Hawkinge
	66	Bf 109 (replica) (1480)	Kent Battle of Britain Museum/Hawkinge
	67	Bf 109 (replica) (14)	Kent Battle of Britain Museum/Hawkinge
	68	Hurricane (replica) (H3426)	Midland Air Museum
	69	Spitfire (replica) (N3313)	Kent Battle of Britain Museum/Hawkinge
	70	Auster AOP5 (TJ398)	Museum of Flight/East Fortune
	71	Spitfire (replica) (P8140)	Norfolk & Suffolk Aviation Museum
	72	Hurricane (model) (V6779)	Gloucestershire Aviation Collection
	73	Hurricane (replica)	—
	74	Bf 109 (replica) (6357)	Kent Battle of Britain Museum/Hawkinge
	75	Mignet HM.14 (G-AEFG)	N. H. Ponsford
	76	Mignet HM.14 (G-AFFI)	Yorkshire Air Museum/Elvington
	77	Mignet HM.14 (replica) (G-ADRG)	Lower Stondon Transport Museum
	78	Hawker Hind (K5414) (G-AENP)	The Shuttleworth Collection/Old Warden
	79	Fiat G.46-4B (MM53211)	British Air Reserve/France
	80	Airspeed Horsa (KJ351)	Museum of Army Flying/Middle Wallop
	81	Hawkridge Dagling	Russavia Collection
	82	Hawker Hind (Afghan)	RAF Museum/Hendon
	83	Kawasaki Ki-100-1b (24)	Aerospace Museum/Cosford
	84	Nakajima Ki-46 (Dinah III)(5439)	Aerospace Museum/Cosford
	85	Weir W-2 autogyro	Museum of Flight/East Fortune
	86	de Havilland Tiger Moth (replica)	Yorkshire Aircraft Preservation Society
	87	Bristol Babe (replica) (G-EASQ)	Bristol Aero Collection/Kemble
	88	Fokker Dr 1 (replica) (102/17)	F.A.A. Museum/Yeovilton
	89	Cayley glider (replica)	Manchester Museum of Science & Industry
	90	Colditz Cock (replica)	Imperial War Museum/Duxford
	91	Fieseler Fi 103 (V-1)	Lashenden Air Warfare Museum
	92	Fieseler Fi 103 (V-1)	RAF Museum/Hendon
	93	Fieseler Fi 103 (V-1)	Imperial War Museum/Duxford
	94	Fieseler Fi 103 (V-1)	Aerospace Museum/Cosford
	95	Gizmer autogyro	F. Fewsdale
	96	Brown helicopter	North East Aircraft Museum
	97	Luton L.A.4A Minor	North East Aircraft Museum
	98	Yokosuka MXY7 Ohka II (997)	Manchester Museum of Science & Industry
	99	Yokosuka MXY7 Ohka II (8486M)	Aerospace Museum/Cosford
	100	Clarke Chanute biplane gliderr	RAF Museum/Hendon
	101	Mignet HM.14	Newark Air Museum/Winthorpe
	102	Mignet HM.14	Not completed
	103	Hulton hang glider (replica)	Personal Plane Services Ltd
	104	Blériot XI	Sold in France
	105	Blériot XI (replica)	Arango Collection/Los Angeles
	106	Blériot XI (164)	RAF Museum/Hendon
	107	Blériot XXVII	RAF Museum/Hendon
	108	Fairey Swordfish IV (HS503)	RAF Restoration Centre/Wyton
	109	Slingsby Kirby Cadet TX.1	RAF Museum/Henlow store
	110	Fokker D.VII replica (static) (5125)	Stored
	111	Sopwith Triplane replica (static) (N5492)	F.A.A. Museum/Yeovilton
	112	DH.2 replica (static) (5964)	Museum of Army Flying/Middle Wallop
	113	S.E.5A replica (static) (B4863)	Stored
	114	Vickers Type 60 Viking (static) (G-EBED)	Brooklands Museum of Aviation/Weybridge
	115	Mignet HM.14	Norfolk & Suffolk Aviation Museum/Flixton
	116	Santos-Dumont Demoiselle (replica)	Cornwall Aero Park/Helston
	117	B.E.2C (replica)(1701)	Stored Hawkinge
	118	Albatros D.V (replica) (C19/18)	North Weald Aircraft Restoration Flight
	119	Bensen B.7	North East Aircraft Museum
	120	Mignet HM.14 (G-AEJZ)	South Yorkshire Aviation Museum/Doncaster
	121	Mignet HM.14 (G-AEKR)	South Yorkshire Aviation Society
	122	Avro 504 (replica) (1881)	Stored
	123	Vickers FB.5 Gunbus (replica)	A. Topen (stored)/Cranfield
	124	Lilienthal Glider Type XI (replica)	Science Museum/South Kensington
	125	Clay Cherub	ground trainer/Coventry
	126	D.31 Turbulent (static)	Midland Air Museum/Coventry
	127	Halton Jupiter MPA	The Shuttleworth Collection
	128	Watkinson Cyclogyroplane Mk IV	IHM/Weston-super-Mare
	129	Blackburn 1911 Monoplane (replica)	Cornwall Aero Park/Helston store
	130	Blackburn 1912 Monoplane (replica)	Yorkshire Air Museum
	131	Pilcher Hawk (replica)	C. Paton
	132	Blériot XI (G-BLXI)	Stored
	133	Fokker Dr 1 (replica) (425/17)	Kent Battle of Britain Museum/Hawkinge
	134	Pitts S-2A static (G-CARS)	Toyota Ltd/Sywell
	135	Bristol M.1C (replica) (C4912)	Stored

BRITISH AIRCRAFT PRESERVATION

Reg	Type	Owner or Operator	Notes
136	Deperdussin Seaplane (replica)	National Air Race Museum/USA	
137	Sopwith Baby Floatplane (replica) (8151)	Stored	
138	Hansa Brandenburg W.29 Floatplane (replica) (2292)	Stored	
139	Fokker Dr 1 (replica) 150/17	Stored	
140	Curtiss 42A (replica)	Stored	
141	Macchi M39 (replica)	Switzerland	
142	SE-5A (replica) (F5459)	Stored	
143	Paxton MPA	R. A. Paxton/Gloucestershire	
144	Weybridge Mercury MPA	Cranwell Gliding Club	
145	Oliver MPA	Stored	
146	Pedal Aeronauts Toucan MPA	Stored	
147	Bensen B.7	Norfolk & Suffolk Aviation Museum/Flixton	
148	Hawker Fury II (replica) (K7271)	High Ercall Aviation Museum	
149	Short S.27 (replica)	F.A.A. Museum (stored)/Yeovilton	
150	SEPECAT Jaguar GR.1 (replica) (XX728)	RAF M & R Unit/St. Athan RAF Marketing & Recruitment Unit/St. Athan	
151	SEPECAT Jaguar GR.1 (replica) (XZ363)	RAF M & R Unit/St. Athan	
152	BAe Hawk T.1 (replica) (XX226)	RAF M & R Unit/St. Athan	
153	Westland WG.33	IHM/Weston-super-Mare	
154	D.31 Turbulent	Lincolnshire Aviation Museum/E. Kirkby	
155	Panavia Tornado GR.1 (model) (ZA556)	RAF M & R Unit/St. Athan	
156	Supermarine S-6B (replica)	National Air Race Museum/USA	
157	Waco CG-4A (237123)	Yorkshire Air Museum/Elvington	
158	Fieseler Fi 103 (V-1)	Defence Ordnance Disposal School/Chattenden	
159	Yokosuka MXY7 Ohka II	Defence Ordnance Disposal School/Chattenden	
160	Chargus 18/50 hang glider	Museum of Flight/East Fortune	
161	Stewart Ornithopter Coppelia	Bomber County Museum	
162	Goodhart MPA	Science Museum/Wroughton	
163	AFEE 10/42 Rotabuggy (replica)	Museum of Army Flying/Middle Wallop	
164	Wight Quadruplane Type 1 (replica)	Solent Sky, Southampton	
165	Bristol F.2b (E2466)	RAF Museum/Hendon	
166	Bristol F.2b (D7889)	Stored	
167	Bristol SE-5A	Stored	
168	DH.60G Moth (static replica)	Stored Hawkinge (G-AAAH)	
169	BAC/Sepecat Jaguar GR.1 (XX110)	RAF Training School/Cosford	
170	Pilcher Hawk (replica)	A. Gourlay/Strathallan	
171	BAe Hawk T.1 (model) (XX253)	RAF Marketing & Recruitment Unit/St. Athan	
172	Chargus Midas Super 8 hang glider	Science Museum/Wroughton	
173	Birdman Promotions Grasshopper	Science Museum/Wroughton	
174	Bensen B.7	Science Museum/Wroughton	
175	Volmer VJ-23 Swingwing	Manchester Museum of Science & Industry	
176	SE-5A (replica) (A4850)	South Yorks Aviation Society/Firbeck	
177	Avro 504K (replica) (G-AACA)	Brooklands Museum of Aviation/Weybridge	
178	Avro 504K (replica) (E373)	Bygone Times Antique Warehouse/Eccleston, Lancs	
179	Sopwith Pup (replica) (A7317)	Midland Air Museum/Coventry	
180	McCurdy Silver Dart (replica)	Reynolds Pioneer Museum/Canada	
181	RAF B.E.2b (replica) (687)	RAF Museum/Hendon	
182	Wood Ornithopter	Manchester Museum of Science & Industry	
183	Zurowski ZP.1 helicopter	Newark Air Museum/Winthorpe	
184	Spitfire IX (replica) (EN398)	Fighter Wing Display Team/North Weald	
185	Waco CG-4A (243809)	Museum of Army Flying/Middle Wallop	
186	DH.82B Queen Bee (LF789)	de Havilland Heritage Museum	
187	Roe Type 1 biplane (replica)	Brooklands Museum of Aviation/Weybridge	
188	McBroom Cobra 88	Science Museum/Wroughton	
189	Bleriot XI (replica)	Stored	
190	Spitfire (replica) (K5054)	P. Smith/Hawkinge	
191	BAe Harrier GR.7 (model) (ZH139)	RAF M & R Unit/St. Athan	
192	Weedhopper JC-24	The Aeroplane Collection	
193	Hovey WD-11 Whing Ding	The Aeroplane Collection	
194	Santos Dumont Demoiselle (replica)	RAF Museum Store/RAF Stafford	
195	Moonraker 77 hang glider	Museum of Flight/East Fortune	
196	Sigma 2M hang glider	Museum of Flight/East Fortune	
197	Scotkites Cirrus III hang glider	Museum of Flight/East Fortune	
198	Fieseler Fi 103 (V-1)	Imperial War Museum/Lambeth	
199	Fieseler Fi 103 (V-1)	Science Museum/South Kensington	
200	Bensen B.7	K. Fern Collection/Stoke	
201	Mignet HM.14	Caernarfon Air Museum	
202	Spitfire V (model) (MAV467)	Maes Artro Craft Centre	

BRITISH AIRCRAFT PRESERVATION

Notes	Reg	Type	Owner or Operator
	203	Chrislea LC.1 Airguard (G-AFIN)	The Aeroplane Collection
	204	McBroom hang glider	Newark Air Museum
	205	Hurricane (replica) (BE421)	RAF Museum/Hendon
	206	Spitfire (replica) (MH486)	RAF Museum/Hendon
	207	Austin Whippet (replica) (K.158)	South Yorkshire Aviation Museum/Doncaster
	208	SE-5A (replica) (D276)	Prince's Mead Shopping Precinct/Farnborough
	209	Spitfire IX (replica) (MJ751)	Museum of D-Day Aviation/Shoreham
	210	Avro 504J (replica) (C4451)	Solent Sky, Southampton
	211	Mignet HM.14 (replica) (G-ADVU)	North East Aircraft Museum
	212	Bensen B.8	IHM/Weston-super-Mare
	213	Vertigo MPA	IHM/Weston-super-Mare
	214	Spitfire prototype (replica) (K5054)	Tangmere Military Aviation Museum
	215	Airwave hang-glider prototype	Solent Sky, Southampton
	216	DH.88 Comet (replica) (G-ACSS)	de Havilland Heritage Museum/London Colney
	217	Spitfire (replica) (K9926)	RAF Museum/Bentley Priory
	218	Hurricane (replica) (P3386)	RAF Museum/Bentley Priory
	219	Hurricane (replica) (L1710)	RAF Memorial Chapel/Biggin Hill
	220	Spitfire 1 (replica) (N3194)	RAF Memorial Chapel/Biggin Hill
	221	Spitfire LF.IX (replica) (MH777)	RAF Museum/Northolt
	222	Spitfire IX (replica) (BR600)	RAF Museum/Uxbridge
	223	Hurricane 1 (replica) (V7467)	RAF Museum/Coltishall
	224	Spitfire V (replica) (BR600)	Ambassador Hotel/Norwich
	225	Spitfire IX (replica) (P8448)	RAF Museum/Cranwell
	226	Spitfire XI (replica) (EN343)	RAF Museum/Benson
	227	Spitfire 1A (replica) (L1070)	RAF Museum/Turnhouse
	228	Olympus hang-glider	North East Aircraft Museum/Usworth
	229	Spitfire IX (replica) (MJ832)	RAF Museum/Digby
	230	Spitfire (replica) (AA550)	Eden Camp/Malton
	231	Mignet HM.14 (G-ADRX)	South Copeland Aviation Group
	232	AS.58 Horsa I/II	de Havilland Heritage Museum/London Colney
	233	Broburn Wanderlust sailplane	Museum of Berkshire Aviation/Woodley
	234	Vickers FB.5 Gunbus (replica)	RAF Manston Museum
	235	Fieseler Fi 103 (V-1) (replica)	Eden Camp Wartime Museum
	236	Hurricane (replica) (P2793)	Eden Camp Wartime Museum
	237	Fieseler Fi 103 (V-1)	RAF Museum Store/RAF Stafford
	238	Waxflatter ornithopter	Personal Plane Services Ltd
	239	Fokker D.VIII 5/8 scale replica	Norfolk & Suffolk Aviation Museum/Flixton
	240	Messerschmitt Bf.109G (replica)	Yorkshire Air Museum/Elvington
	241	Hurricane 1 (replica) (L1679)	Tangmere Military Aviation Museum
	242	Spitfire Vb (replica) (BL924)	Tangmere Military Aviation Museum
	243	Mignet HM.14 (replica) (G-ADYV)	P. Ward
	244	Solar Wings Typhoon	Museum of Flight/East Fortune
	245	Electraflyer Floater hang glider	Museum of Flight/East Fortune
	246	Hiway Cloudbase hang glider	Museum of Flight/East Fortune
	247	Albatross ASG.21 hang glider	Museum of Flight/East Fortune
	248	McBroom hang glider	Museum of Berkshire Aviation/Woodley
	249	Hawker Fury 1 (replica) (K5673)	Brooklands Museum of Aviation/Weybridge
	250	RAF SE-5A (replica) (F5475)	Brooklands Museum of Aviation/Weybridge
	251	Hiway Spectrum hang glider (replica)	Manchester Museum of Science & Industry
	252	Flexiform Wing hang glider	Manchester Museum of Science & Industry
	253	Mignet HM.14 (G-ADZW)	H. Shore/Sandown
	254	Hawker Hurricane (P3873)	Yorkshire Air Museum/Elvington
	255	NA P-51D Mustang (replica) (463209)	American Air Museum/Duxford
	256	Santos Dumont Type 20 (replica)	Brooklands Museum of Aviation/Weybridge
	257	DH.88 Comet (G-ACSS)	The Galleria/Hatfield
	258	Adams balloon	British Balloon Museum
	259	Gloster Gamecock (replica)	Jet Age Museum Gloucestershire
	260	Mignet HM280	–
	261	GAL Hotspur (replica)	Museum of Army Flying/ Middle Wallop
	262	Catto CP-16	Museum of Flight/East Fortune
	263	Chargus Cyclone	Ulster Aviation Heritage/Langford Lodge
	264	Bensen B.8M	IHM/Weston-super-Mare
	265	Spitfire 1 (P3873)	Yorkshire Air Museum/Elvington
	266	Rogallo hang glider	Ulster Aviation Heritage
	267	Hurricane (model)	Duxford
	268	Spifire (model)	–
	269	Spitfire (model) USAF	Lakenheath
	270	DH.60 Moth (model)	Yorkshire Air Museum
	271	Messerschmitt Me 163B	Shuttleworth Collection/Old Warden
	272	Hurricane (model)	Kent Battle of Britain Museum/Hawkinge
	273	Hurricane (model)	Kent Battle of Britain Museum/Hawkinge
	274	Boulton & Paul P.6 (model)	Boulton & Paul Aircraft Heritage Project
	275	Bensen B.7 gyroglider	Doncaster Museum

BRITISH AIRCRAFT PRESERVATION

Reg	Type	Owner or Operator	Notes
276	Hartman Ornithcopter	Science Museum/Wroughton	
277	Mignet HM.14	Visitor Centre Shoreham Airport	
278	Hurricane (model)	Kent Battle of Britain Museum/Hawkinge	
279	Airspeed Horsa	Shawbury	
280	DH.89A Dragon Rapide (model)	–	
281	Boulton & Paul Defian (model)	–	
282	Manx Elder Duck	Isle of Man Airport Terminal	
283	Spitfire (model	Jurby, Isle of Man	
284	Gloster E.28/39 (model)	Lutterworth Leics	
285	Gloster E.28/39 (model)	Farnborough	
286	Mignet HM.14	Caernarfon Air Museum	
287	Blackburn F.2 Lincock (model)	Street Life Museum/Hull	
288	Hurricane (model)	Wonderland Pleasure Park, Mansfield	
289	Gyro Boat	IHM Weston-super-Mare	
290	Fieseler Fi 103 (V1) (model)	Dover Museum	
291	Hurricane (model)	National Battle of Britain Memorial, Capel-le-Ferne, Kent	
292	Eurofighter Typhoon (model)	RAF Museum/Hendon	
293	Spitfire (model)	RAF Museum/Hendon	
294	Fairchild Argus (model)	Visitor Centre, Thorpe Camp, Woodhall Spa	
295	Da Vinci hang glider (replica)	Skysport Engineering	
296	Army Balloon Factory NuIII (replica)	RAF Museum, Hendon	
297	Spitfire (replica)	Kent Battle of Britain Museum/Hawkinge	
298	Spitfire IX (Model)	Kent Battle of Britain Museum/ Hawkinge	
299	Spitfire 1 (model).	National Battle of Britain Memorial, Capel-le-Ferne, Kent	
300	Hummingbird (replica)	Shoreham Airport Historical Association	

Note: Registrations/Serials carried are mostly false identities.
MPA = Man Powered Aircraft, IHM = International Helicopter Museum. The aircraft, listed as 'models' are generally intended for exhibition purposes and are not airworthy although they are full scale replicas. However, in a few cases the machines have the ability to taxi when used for film work.

T-6G G-DDMV is painted in the bright yellow colours of the California Air National Guard. *DP*

Future Allocations Log

The grid provides the facility to record future registrations as they are issued or seen. To trace a particular code, refer to the left hand column which contains the three letters following the G prefix. The final letter can be found by reading across the columns headed A to Z. For example, the box for G-CENT is located 6 rows down (CEB) and then 19 across to the T column.

G-	A	B	C	D	E	F	G	H	I	J	K	L	M	N	O	P	R	S	T	U	V	W	X	Y	Z
CEI																									
CEJ																									
CEK																									
CEL																									
CEM																									
CEN																									
CEO																									
CEP																									
CER																									
CES																									
CET																									
CEU																									
CEV																									
CEW																									
CEX																									
CEY																									
CEZ																									
CFA																									
CFB																									
CFC																									
CFD																									
CFE																									
CFF																									
CFG																									
CFH																									
CFI																									
CFJ																									
CFK																									
CFL																									
CFM																									
CFN																									
CFO																									
CFP																									
CFR																									
	A	B	C	D	E	F	G	H	I	J	K	L	M	N	O	P	R	S	T	U	V	W	X	Y	Z

Credit: Wal Gandy

Future Allocation Groups

This grid can be used to record registrations as they are issued or seen. The first column is provided for the ranges prefixed with G-C, ie from G-CFxx to G-CZxx. The remaining columns cover the sequences from G-Dxxx to G-Zxxx and in this case it is necessary to insert the last three letters in the appropriate section.

G-C	G-D	G-F	G-H	G-J	G-L	G-N	G-O	G-P	G-S	G-U
										G-V
	G-E	G-G			G-M	G-O				
				G-K						
										G-W
			G-I							
								G-R		
									G-T	
										G-X
G-D	G-F			G-L	G-N					
										G-Y
										G-Z

Overseas Airliners Registration Log

This grid may be used to record airliner registrations not included in the main section.

Reg	Type	Owner or Operator

Air-Berlin Airbus A.319 D-ABGB is one of their large and growing fleet offering low-cost services from a number of UK airports. *DP*

Addenda

Notes	Reg	Type	Owner or Operator
	Additions		

The Brooklands Flying Club at Sywell is the first UK flying school to adopt the Polish-designed Aero AT-3. *DP*

AIR International

AIR International features:

- News – Military, civil and contemporary aviation technology
- Informed coverage of military aircraft
- In-depth analysis of commercial operators and aircraft types
- Exclusive cutaway drawings and three-view illustrations
- Flight bag – Detailed reviews of aviation books, art and more
- Talkback – reader's letters and photographs

DON'T MISS OUT – SUBSCRIBE and SAVE on the news-stand cost!

AIR International has established an unrivalled reputation for authoritative reporting and coverage of aviation subjects.

The magazine regularly features reviews of air arms and exercises. The major airshows are covered to keep readers abreast of military, commercial and industry news.

Some of the most renowned writers in the aerospace world provide technical assessments, which include specifications and unique detailed cutaway illustrations.

AIR International provides informed coverage of military air arms, civil airliners, aerospace companies and future trends.

Visit www.airinternational.com or call +44 (0) 1780 480 404 for details of our latest subscription deal!